04

D1609004

Dictionary of Literary Biography

1 *The American Renaissance in New England,* edited by Joel Myerson (1978)

2 *American Novelists Since World War II,* edited by Jeffrey Helterman and Richard Layman (1978)

3 *Antebellum Writers in New York and the South,* edited by Joel Myerson (1979)

4 *American Writers in Paris, 1920–1939,* edited by Karen Lane Rood (1980)

5 *American Poets Since World War II,* 2 parts, edited by Donald J. Greiner (1980)

6 *American Novelists Since World War II, Second Series,* edited by James E. Kibler Jr. (1980)

7 *Twentieth-Century American Dramatists,* 2 parts, edited by John MacNicholas (1981)

8 *Twentieth-Century American Science-Fiction Writers,* 2 parts, edited by David Cowart and Thomas L. Wymer (1981)

9 *American Novelists, 1910–1945,* 3 parts, edited by James J. Martine (1981)

10 *Modern British Dramatists, 1900–1945,* 2 parts, edited by Stanley Weintraub (1982)

11 *American Humorists, 1800–1950,* 2 parts, edited by Stanley Trachtenberg (1982)

12 *American Realists and Naturalists,* edited by Donald Pizer and Earl N. Harbert (1982)

13 *British Dramatists Since World War II,* 2 parts, edited by Stanley Weintraub (1982)

14 *British Novelists Since 1960,* 2 parts, edited by Jay L. Halio (1983)

15 *British Novelists, 1930–1959,* 2 parts, edited by Bernard Oldsey (1983)

16 *The Beats: Literary Bohemians in Postwar America,* 2 parts, edited by Ann Charters (1983)

17 *Twentieth-Century American Historians,* edited by Clyde N. Wilson (1983)

18 *Victorian Novelists After 1885,* edited by Ira B. Nadel and William E. Fredeman (1983)

19 *British Poets, 1880–1914,* edited by Donald E. Stanford (1983)

20 *British Poets, 1914–1945,* edited by Donald E. Stanford (1983)

21 *Victorian Novelists Before 1885,* edited by Ira B. Nadel and William E. Fredeman (1983)

22 *American Writers for Children, 1900–1960,* edited by John Cech (1983)

23 *American Newspaper Journalists, 1873–1900,* edited by Perry J. Ashley (1983)

24 *American Colonial Writers, 1606–1734,* edited by Emory Elliott (1984)

25 *American Newspaper Journalists, 1901–1925,* edited by Perry J. Ashley (1984)

26 *American Screenwriters,* edited by Robert E. Morsberger, Stephen O. Lesser, and Randall Clark (1984)

27 *Poets of Great Britain and Ireland, 1945–1960,* edited by Vincent B. Sherry Jr. (1984)

28 *Twentieth-Century American-Jewish Fiction Writers,* edited by Daniel Walden (1984)

29 *American Newspaper Journalists, 1926–1950,* edited by Perry J. Ashley (1984)

30 *American Historians, 1607–1865,* edited by Clyde N. Wilson (1984)

31 *American Colonial Writers, 1735–1781,* edited by Emory Elliott (1984)

32 *Victorian Poets Before 1850,* edited by William E. Fredeman and Ira B. Nadel (1984)

33 *Afro-American Fiction Writers After 1955,* edited by Thadious M. Davis and Trudier Harris (1984)

34 *British Novelists, 1890–1929: Traditionalists,* edited by Thomas F. Staley (1985)

35 *Victorian Poets After 1850,* edited by William E. Fredeman and Ira B. Nadel (1985)

36 *British Novelists, 1890–1929: Modernists,* edited by Thomas F. Staley (1985)

37 *American Writers of the Early Republic,* edited by Emory Elliott (1985)

38 *Afro-American Writers After 1955: Dramatists and Prose Writers,* edited by Thadious M. Davis and Trudier Harris (1985)

39 *British Novelists, 1660–1800,* 2 parts, edited by Martin C. Battestin (1985)

40 *Poets of Great Britain and Ireland Since 1960,* 2 parts, edited by Vincent B. Sherry Jr. (1985)

41 *Afro-American Poets Since 1955,* edited by Trudier Harris and Thadious M. Davis (1985)

42 *American Writers for Children Before 1900,* edited by Glenn E. Estes (1985)

43 *American Newspaper Journalists, 1690–1872,* edited by Perry J. Ashley (1986)

44 *American Screenwriters, Second Series,* edited by Randall Clark, Robert E. Morsberger, and Stephen O. Lesser (1986)

45 *American Poets, 1880–1945, First Series,* edited by Peter Quartermain (1986)

46 *American Literary Publishing Houses, 1900–1980: Trade and Paperback,* edited by Peter Dzwonkoski (1986)

47 *American Historians, 1866–1912,* edited by Clyde N. Wilson (1986)

48 *American Poets, 1880–1945, Second Series,* edited by Peter Quartermain (1986)

49 *American Literary Publishing Houses, 1638–1899,* 2 parts, edited by Peter Dzwonkoski (1986)

50 *Afro-American Writers Before the Harlem Renaissance,* edited by Trudier Harris (1986)

51 *Afro-American Writers from the Harlem Renaissance to 1940,* edited by Trudier Harris (1987)

52 *American Writers for Children Since 1960: Fiction,* edited by Glenn E. Estes (1986)

53 *Canadian Writers Since 1960, First Series,* edited by W. H. New (1986)

54 *American Poets, 1880–1945, Third Series,* 2 parts, edited by Peter Quartermain (1987)

55 *Victorian Prose Writers Before 1867,* edited by William B. Thesing (1987)

56 *German Fiction Writers, 1914–1945,* edited by James Hardin (1987)

57 *Victorian Prose Writers After 1867,* edited by William B. Thesing (1987)

58 *Jacobean and Caroline Dramatists,* edited by Fredson Bowers (1987)

59 *American Literary Critics and Scholars, 1800–1850,* edited by John W. Rathbun and Monica M. Grecu (1987)

60 *Canadian Writers Since 1960, Second Series,* edited by W. H. New (1987)

61 *American Writers for Children Since 1960: Poets, Illustrators, and Nonfiction Authors,* edited by Glenn E. Estes (1987)

62 *Elizabethan Dramatists,* edited by Fredson Bowers (1987)

63 *Modern American Critics, 1920–1955,* edited by Gregory S. Jay (1988)

64 *American Literary Critics and Scholars, 1850–1880,* edited by John W. Rathbun and Monica M. Grecu (1988)

65 *French Novelists, 1900–1930,* edited by Catharine Savage Brosman (1988)

66 *German Fiction Writers, 1885–1913,* 2 parts, edited by James Hardin (1988)

67 *Modern American Critics Since 1955,* edited by Gregory S. Jay (1988)

68 *Canadian Writers, 1920–1959, First Series,* edited by W. H. New (1988)

69 *Contemporary German Fiction Writers, First Series,* edited by Wolfgang D. Elfe and James Hardin (1988)

70 *British Mystery Writers, 1860–1919,* edited by Bernard Benstock and Thomas F. Staley (1988)

71 *American Literary Critics and Scholars, 1880–1900,* edited by John W. Rathbun and Monica M. Grecu (1988)

72 *French Novelists, 1930–1960,* edited by Catharine Savage Brosman (1988)

73 *American Magazine Journalists, 1741–1850,* edited by Sam G. Riley (1988)

74 *American Short-Story Writers Before 1880,* edited by Bobby Ellen Kimbel, with the assistance of William E. Grant (1988)

75 *Contemporary German Fiction Writers, Second Series,* edited by Wolfgang D. Elfe and James Hardin (1988)

76 *Afro-American Writers, 1940–1955,* edited by Trudier Harris (1988)

77 *British Mystery Writers, 1920–1939*, edited by Bernard Benstock and Thomas F. Staley (1988)

78 *American Short-Story Writers, 1880–1910*, edited by Bobby Ellen Kimbel, with the assistance of William E. Grant (1988)

79 *American Magazine Journalists, 1850–1900*, edited by Sam G. Riley (1988)

80 *Restoration and Eighteenth-Century Dramatists, First Series*, edited by Paula R. Backscheider (1989)

81 *Austrian Fiction Writers, 1875–1913*, edited by James Hardin and Donald G. Daviau (1989)

82 *Chicano Writers, First Series*, edited by Francisco A. Lomelí and Carl R. Shirley (1989)

83 *French Novelists Since 1960*, edited by Catharine Savage Brosman (1989)

84 *Restoration and Eighteenth-Century Dramatists, Second Series*, edited by Paula R. Backscheider (1989)

85 *Austrian Fiction Writers After 1914*, edited by James Hardin and Donald G. Daviau (1989)

86 *American Short-Story Writers, 1910–1945, First Series*, edited by Bobby Ellen Kimbel (1989)

87 *British Mystery and Thriller Writers Since 1940, First Series*, edited by Bernard Benstock and Thomas F. Staley (1989)

88 *Canadian Writers, 1920–1959, Second Series*, edited by W. H. New (1989)

89 *Restoration and Eighteenth-Century Dramatists, Third Series*, edited by Paula R. Backscheider (1989)

90 *German Writers in the Age of Goethe, 1789–1832*, edited by James Hardin and Christoph E. Schweitzer (1989)

91 *American Magazine Journalists, 1900–1960, First Series*, edited by Sam G. Riley (1990)

92 *Canadian Writers, 1890–1920*, edited by W. H. New (1990)

93 *British Romantic Poets, 1789–1832, First Series*, edited by John R. Greenfield (1990)

94 *German Writers in the Age of Goethe: Sturm und Drang to Classicism*, edited by James Hardin and Christoph E. Schweitzer (1990)

95 *Eighteenth-Century British Poets, First Series*, edited by John Sitter (1990)

96 *British Romantic Poets, 1789–1832, Second Series*, edited by John R. Greenfield (1990)

97 *German Writers from the Enlightenment to Sturm und Drang, 1720–1764*, edited by James Hardin and Christoph E. Schweitzer (1990)

98 *Modern British Essayists, First Series*, edited by Robert Beum (1990)

99 *Canadian Writers Before 1890*, edited by W. H. New (1990)

100 *Modern British Essayists, Second Series*, edited by Robert Beum (1990)

101 *British Prose Writers, 1660–1800, First Series*, edited by Donald T. Siebert (1991)

102 *American Short-Story Writers, 1910–1945, Second Series*, edited by Bobby Ellen Kimbel (1991)

103 *American Literary Biographers, First Series*, edited by Steven Serafin (1991)

104 *British Prose Writers, 1660–1800, Second Series*, edited by Donald T. Siebert (1991)

105 *American Poets Since World War II, Second Series*, edited by R. S. Gwynn (1991)

106 *British Literary Publishing Houses, 1820–1880*, edited by Patricia J. Anderson and Jonathan Rose (1991)

107 *British Romantic Prose Writers, 1789–1832, First Series*, edited by John R. Greenfield (1991)

108 *Twentieth-Century Spanish Poets, First Series*, edited by Michael L. Perna (1991)

109 *Eighteenth-Century British Poets, Second Series*, edited by John Sitter (1991)

110 *British Romantic Prose Writers, 1789–1832, Second Series*, edited by John R. Greenfield (1991)

111 *American Literary Biographers, Second Series*, edited by Steven Serafin (1991)

112 *British Literary Publishing Houses, 1881–1965*, edited by Jonathan Rose and Patricia J. Anderson (1991)

113 *Modern Latin-American Fiction Writers, First Series*, edited by William Luis (1992)

114 *Twentieth-Century Italian Poets, First Series*, edited by Giovanna Wedel De Stasio, Glauco Cambon, and Antonio Illiano (1992)

115 *Medieval Philosophers*, edited by Jeremiah Hackett (1992)

116 *British Romantic Novelists, 1789–1832*, edited by Bradford K. Mudge (1992)

117 *Twentieth-Century Caribbean and Black African Writers, First Series*, edited by Bernth Lindfors and Reinhard Sander (1992)

118 *Twentieth-Century German Dramatists, 1889–1918*, edited by Wolfgang D. Elfe and James Hardin (1992)

119 *Nineteenth-Century French Fiction Writers: Romanticism and Realism, 1800–1860*, edited by Catharine Savage Brosman (1992)

120 *American Poets Since World War II, Third Series*, edited by R. S. Gwynn (1992)

121 *Seventeenth-Century British Nondramatic Poets, First Series*, edited by M. Thomas Hester (1992)

122 *Chicano Writers, Second Series*, edited by Francisco A. Lomelí and Carl R. Shirley (1992)

123 *Nineteenth-Century French Fiction Writers: Naturalism and Beyond, 1860–1900*, edited by Catharine Savage Brosman (1992)

124 *Twentieth-Century German Dramatists, 1919–1992*, edited by Wolfgang D. Elfe and James Hardin (1992)

125 *Twentieth-Century Caribbean and Black African Writers, Second Series*, edited by Bernth Lindfors and Reinhard Sander (1993)

126 *Seventeenth-Century British Nondramatic Poets, Second Series*, edited by M. Thomas Hester (1993)

127 *American Newspaper Publishers, 1950–1990*, edited by Perry J. Ashley (1993)

128 *Twentieth-Century Italian Poets, Second Series*, edited by Giovanna Wedel De Stasio, Glauco Cambon, and Antonio Illiano (1993)

129 *Nineteenth-Century German Writers, 1841–1900*, edited by James Hardin and Siegfried Mews (1993)

130 *American Short-Story Writers Since World War II*, edited by Patrick Meanor (1993)

131 *Seventeenth-Century British Nondramatic Poets, Third Series*, edited by M. Thomas Hester (1993)

132 *Sixteenth-Century British Nondramatic Writers, First Series*, edited by David A. Richardson (1993)

133 *Nineteenth-Century German Writers to 1840*, edited by James Hardin and Siegfried Mews (1993)

134 *Twentieth-Century Spanish Poets, Second Series*, edited by Jerry Phillips Winfield (1994)

135 *British Short-Fiction Writers, 1880–1914: The Realist Tradition*, edited by William B. Thesing (1994)

136 *Sixteenth-Century British Nondramatic Writers, Second Series*, edited by David A. Richardson (1994)

137 *American Magazine Journalists, 1900–1960, Second Series*, edited by Sam G. Riley (1994)

138 *German Writers and Works of the High Middle Ages: 1170–1280*, edited by James Hardin and Will Hasty (1994)

139 *British Short-Fiction Writers, 1945–1980*, edited by Dean Baldwin (1994)

140 *American Book-Collectors and Bibliographers, First Series*, edited by Joseph Rosenblum (1994)

141 *British Children's Writers, 1880–1914*, edited by Laura M. Zaidman (1994)

142 *Eighteenth-Century British Literary Biographers*, edited by Steven Serafin (1994)

143 *American Novelists Since World War II, Third Series*, edited by James R. Giles and Wanda H. Giles (1994)

144 *Nineteenth-Century British Literary Biographers*, edited by Steven Serafin (1994)

145 *Modern Latin-American Fiction Writers, Second Series*, edited by William Luis and Ann González (1994)

146 *Old and Middle English Literature*, edited by Jeffrey Helterman and Jerome Mitchell (1994)

147 *South Slavic Writers Before World War II*, edited by Vasa D. Mihailovich (1994)

148 *German Writers and Works of the Early Middle Ages: 800–1170*, edited by Will Hasty and James Hardin (1994)

149 *Late Nineteenth- and Early Twentieth-Century British Literary Biographers*, edited by Steven Serafin (1995)

150 *Early Modern Russian Writers, Late Seventeenth and Eighteenth Centuries*, edited by Marcus C. Levitt (1995)

151 *British Prose Writers of the Early Seventeenth Century*, edited by Clayton D. Lein (1995)

152 *American Novelists Since World War II, Fourth Series*, edited by James R. Giles and Wanda H. Giles (1995)

153 *Late-Victorian and Edwardian British Novelists, First Series,* edited by George M. Johnson (1995)

154 *The British Literary Book Trade, 1700–1820,* edited by James K. Bracken and Joel Silver (1995)

155 *Twentieth-Century British Literary Biographers,* edited by Steven Serafin (1995)

156 *British Short-Fiction Writers, 1880–1914: The Romantic Tradition,* edited by William F. Naufftus (1995)

157 *Twentieth-Century Caribbean and Black African Writers, Third Series,* edited by Bernth Lindfors and Reinhard Sander (1995)

158 *British Reform Writers, 1789–1832,* edited by Gary Kelly and Edd Applegate (1995)

159 *British Short-Fiction Writers, 1800–1880,* edited by John R. Greenfield (1996)

160 *British Children's Writers, 1914–1960,* edited by Donald R. Hettinga and Gary D. Schmidt (1996)

161 *British Children's Writers Since 1960, First Series,* edited by Caroline Hunt (1996)

162 *British Short-Fiction Writers, 1915–1945,* edited by John H. Rogers (1996)

163 *British Children's Writers, 1800–1880,* edited by Meena Khorana (1996)

164 *German Baroque Writers, 1580–1660,* edited by James Hardin (1996)

165 *American Poets Since World War II, Fourth Series,* edited by Joseph Conte (1996)

166 *British Travel Writers, 1837–1875,* edited by Barbara Brothers and Julia Gergits (1996)

167 *Sixteenth-Century British Nondramatic Writers, Third Series,* edited by David A. Richardson (1996)

168 *German Baroque Writers, 1661–1730,* edited by James Hardin (1996)

169 *American Poets Since World War II, Fifth Series,* edited by Joseph Conte (1996)

170 *The British Literary Book Trade, 1475–1700,* edited by James K. Bracken and Joel Silver (1996)

171 *Twentieth-Century American Sportswriters,* edited by Richard Orodenker (1996)

172 *Sixteenth-Century British Nondramatic Writers, Fourth Series,* edited by David A. Richardson (1996)

173 *American Novelists Since World War II, Fifth Series,* edited by James R. Giles and Wanda H. Giles (1996)

174 *British Travel Writers, 1876–1909,* edited by Barbara Brothers and Julia Gergits (1997)

175 *Native American Writers of the United States,* edited by Kenneth M. Roemer (1997)

176 *Ancient Greek Authors,* edited by Ward W. Briggs (1997)

177 *Italian Novelists Since World War II, 1945–1965,* edited by Augustus Pallotta (1997)

178 *British Fantasy and Science-Fiction Writers Before World War I,* edited by Darren Harris-Fain (1997)

179 *German Writers of the Renaissance and Reformation, 1280–1580,* edited by James Hardin and Max Reinhart (1997)

180 *Japanese Fiction Writers, 1868–1945,* edited by Van C. Gessel (1997)

181 *South Slavic Writers Since World War II,* edited by Vasa D. Mihailovich (1997)

182 *Japanese Fiction Writers Since World War II,* edited by Van C. Gessel (1997)

183 *American Travel Writers, 1776–1864,* edited by James J. Schramer and Donald Ross (1997)

184 *Nineteenth-Century British Book-Collectors and Bibliographers,* edited by William Baker and Kenneth Womack (1997)

185 *American Literary Journalists, 1945–1995, First Series,* edited by Arthur J. Kaul (1998)

186 *Nineteenth-Century American Western Writers,* edited by Robert L. Gale (1998)

187 *American Book Collectors and Bibliographers, Second Series,* edited by Joseph Rosenblum (1998)

188 *American Book and Magazine Illustrators to 1920,* edited by Steven E. Smith, Catherine A. Hastedt, and Donald H. Dyal (1998)

189 *American Travel Writers, 1850–1915,* edited by Donald Ross and James J. Schramer (1998)

190 *British Reform Writers, 1832–1914,* edited by Gary Kelly and Edd Applegate (1998)

191 *British Novelists Between the Wars,* edited by George M. Johnson (1998)

192 *French Dramatists, 1789–1914,* edited by Barbara T. Cooper (1998)

193 *American Poets Since World War II, Sixth Series,* edited by Joseph Conte (1998)

194 *British Novelists Since 1960, Second Series,* edited by Merritt Moseley (1998)

195 *British Travel Writers, 1910–1939,* edited by Barbara Brothers and Julia Gergits (1998)

196 *Italian Novelists Since World War II, 1965–1995,* edited by Augustus Pallotta (1999)

197 *Late-Victorian and Edwardian British Novelists, Second Series,* edited by George M. Johnson (1999)

198 *Russian Literature in the Age of Pushkin and Gogol: Prose,* edited by Christine A. Rydel (1999)

199 *Victorian Women Poets,* edited by William B. Thesing (1999)

200 *American Women Prose Writers to 1820,* edited by Carla J. Mulford, with Angela Vietto and Amy E. Winans (1999)

201 *Twentieth-Century British Book Collectors and Bibliographers,* edited by William Baker and Kenneth Womack (1999)

202 *Nineteenth-Century American Fiction Writers,* edited by Kent P. Ljungquist (1999)

203 *Medieval Japanese Writers,* edited by Steven D. Carter (1999)

204 *British Travel Writers, 1940–1997,* edited by Barbara Brothers and Julia M. Gergits (1999)

205 *Russian Literature in the Age of Pushkin and Gogol: Poetry and Drama,* edited by Christine A. Rydel (1999)

206 *Twentieth-Century American Western Writers, First Series,* edited by Richard H. Cracroft (1999)

207 *British Novelists Since 1960, Third Series,* edited by Merritt Moseley (1999)

208 *Literature of the French and Occitan Middle Ages: Eleventh to Fifteenth Centuries,* edited by Deborah Sinnreich-Levi and Ian S. Laurie (1999)

209 *Chicano Writers, Third Series,* edited by Francisco A. Lomelí and Carl R. Shirley (1999)

210 *Ernest Hemingway: A Documentary Volume,* edited by Robert W. Trogdon (1999)

211 *Ancient Roman Writers,* edited by Ward W. Briggs (1999)

212 *Twentieth-Century American Western Writers, Second Series,* edited by Richard H. Cracroft (1999)

213 *Pre-Nineteenth-Century British Book Collectors and Bibliographers,* edited by William Baker and Kenneth Womack (1999)

214 *Twentieth-Century Danish Writers,* edited by Marianne Stecher-Hansen (1999)

215 *Twentieth-Century Eastern European Writers, First Series,* edited by Steven Serafin (1999)

216 *British Poets of the Great War: Brooke, Rosenberg, Thomas. A Documentary Volume,* edited by Patrick Quinn (2000)

217 *Nineteenth-Century French Poets,* edited by Robert Beum (2000)

218 *American Short-Story Writers Since World War II, Second Series,* edited by Patrick Meanor and Gwen Crane (2000)

219 *F. Scott Fitzgerald's* The Great Gatsby: *A Documentary Volume,* edited by Matthew J. Bruccoli (2000)

220 *Twentieth-Century Eastern European Writers, Second Series,* edited by Steven Serafin (2000)

221 *American Women Prose Writers, 1870–1920,* edited by Sharon M. Harris, with the assistance of Heidi L. M. Jacobs and Jennifer Putzi (2000)

222 *H. L. Mencken: A Documentary Volume,* edited by Richard J. Schrader (2000)

223 *The American Renaissance in New England, Second Series,* edited by Wesley T. Mott (2000)

224 *Walt Whitman: A Documentary Volume,* edited by Joel Myerson (2000)

225 *South African Writers,* edited by Paul A. Scanlon (2000)

226 *American Hard-Boiled Crime Writers,* edited by George Parker Anderson and Julie B. Anderson (2000)

227 *American Novelists Since World War II, Sixth Series,* edited by James R. Giles and Wanda H. Giles (2000)

228 *Twentieth-Century American Dramatists, Second Series,* edited by Christopher J. Wheatley (2000)

229 *Thomas Wolfe: A Documentary Volume,* edited by Ted Mitchell (2001)

230 *Australian Literature, 1788–1914,* edited by Selina Samuels (2001)

231 *British Novelists Since 1960, Fourth Series,* edited by Merritt Moseley (2001)

232 *Twentieth-Century Eastern European Writers, Third Series,* edited by Steven Serafin (2001)

233 *British and Irish Dramatists Since World War II, Second Series,* edited by John Bull (2001)

234 *American Short-Story Writers Since World War II, Third Series*, edited by Patrick Meanor and Richard E. Lee (2001)

235 *The American Renaissance in New England, Third Series*, edited by Wesley T. Mott (2001)

236 *British Rhetoricians and Logicians, 1500–1660*, edited by Edward A. Malone (2001)

237 *The Beats: A Documentary Volume*, edited by Matt Theado (2001)

238 *Russian Novelists in the Age of Tolstoy and Dostoevsky*, edited by J. Alexander Ogden and Judith E. Kalb (2001)

239 *American Women Prose Writers: 1820–1870*, edited by Amy E. Hudock and Katharine Rodier (2001)

240 *Late Nineteenth- and Early Twentieth-Century British Women Poets*, edited by William B. Thesing (2001)

241 *American Sportswriters and Writers on Sport*, edited by Richard Orodenker (2001)

242 *Twentieth-Century European Cultural Theorists, First Series*, edited by Paul Hansom (2001)

243 *The American Renaissance in New England, Fourth Series*, edited by Wesley T. Mott (2001)

244 *American Short-Story Writers Since World War II, Fourth Series*, edited by Patrick Meanor and Joseph McNicholas (2001)

245 *British and Irish Dramatists Since World War II, Third Series*, edited by John Bull (2001)

246 *Twentieth-Century American Cultural Theorists*, edited by Paul Hansom (2001)

247 *James Joyce: A Documentary Volume*, edited by A. Nicholas Fargnoli (2001)

248 *Antebellum Writers in the South, Second Series*, edited by Kent Ljungquist (2001)

249 *Twentieth-Century American Dramatists, Third Series*, edited by Christopher Wheatley (2002)

250 *Antebellum Writers in New York, Second Series*, edited by Kent Ljungquist (2002)

251 *Canadian Fantasy and Science-Fiction Writers*, edited by Douglas Ivison (2002)

252 *British Philosophers, 1500–1799*, edited by Philip B. Dematteis and Peter S. Fosl (2002)

253 *Raymond Chandler: A Documentary Volume*, edited by Robert Moss (2002)

254 *The House of Putnam, 1837–1872: A Documentary Volume*, edited by Ezra Greenspan (2002)

255 *British Fantasy and Science-Fiction Writers, 1918–1960*, edited by Darren Harris-Fain (2002)

256 *Twentieth-Century American Western Writers, Third Series*, edited by Richard H. Cracroft (2002)

257 *Twentieth-Century Swedish Writers After World War II*, edited by Ann-Charlotte Gavel Adams (2002)

258 *Modern French Poets*, edited by Jean-François Leroux (2002)

259 *Twentieth-Century Swedish Writers Before World War II*, edited by Ann-Charlotte Gavel Adams (2002)

260 *Australian Writers, 1915–1950*, edited by Selina Samuels (2002)

261 *British Fantasy and Science-Fiction Writers Since 1960*, edited by Darren Harris-Fain (2002)

262 *British Philosophers, 1800–2000*, edited by Peter S. Fosl and Leemon B. McHenry (2002)

263 *William Shakespeare: A Documentary Volume*, edited by Catherine Loomis (2002)

264 *Italian Prose Writers, 1900–1945*, edited by Luca Somigli and Rocco Capozzi (2002)

265 *American Song Lyricists, 1920–1960*, edited by Philip Furia (2002)

266 *Twentieth-Century American Dramatists, Fourth Series*, edited by Christopher J. Wheatley (2002)

267 *Twenty-First-Century British and Irish Novelists*, edited by Michael R. Molino (2002)

268 *Seventeenth-Century French Writers*, edited by Françoise Jaouën (2002)

269 *Nathaniel Hawthorne: A Documentary Volume*, edited by Benjamin Franklin V (2002)

270 *American Philosophers Before 1950*, edited by Philip B. Dematteis and Leemon B. McHenry (2002)

271 *British and Irish Novelists Since 1960*, edited by Merritt Moseley (2002)

272 *Russian Prose Writers Between the World Wars*, edited by Christine Rydel (2003)

273 *F. Scott Fitzgerald's Tender Is the Night: A Documentary Volume*, edited by Matthew J. Bruccoli and George Parker Anderson (2003)

274 *John Dos Passos's U.S.A.: A Documentary Volume*, edited by Donald Pizer (2003)

275 *Twentieth-Century American Nature Writers: Prose*, edited by Roger Thompson and J. Scott Bryson (2003)

276 *British Mystery and Thriller Writers Since 1960*, edited by Gina Macdonald (2003)

277 *Russian Literature in the Age of Realism*, edited by Alyssa Dinega Gillespie (2003)

278 *American Novelists Since World War II, Seventh Series*, edited by James R. Giles and Wanda H. Giles (2003)

279 *American Philosophers, 1950–2000*, edited by Philip B. Dematteis and Leemon B. McHenry (2003)

280 *Dashiell Hammett's The Maltese Falcon: A Documentary Volume*, edited by Richard Layman (2003)

281 *British Rhetoricians and Logicians, 1500–1660, Second Series*, edited by Edward A. Malone (2003)

282 *New Formalist Poets*, edited by Jonathan N. Barron and Bruce Meyer (2003)

283 *Modern Spanish American Poets, First Series*, edited by María A. Salgado (2003)

284 *The House of Holt, 1866–1946: A Documentary Volume*, edited by Ellen D. Gilbert (2003)

285 *Russian Writers Since 1980*, edited by Marina Balina and Mark Lipovetsky (2003)

Dictionary of Literary Biography Documentary Series

1 *Sherwood Anderson, Willa Cather, John Dos Passos, Theodore Dreiser, F. Scott Fitzgerald, Ernest Hemingway, Sinclair Lewis*, edited by Margaret A. Van Antwerp (1982)

2 *James Gould Cozzens, James T. Farrell, William Faulkner, John O'Hara, John Steinbeck, Thomas Wolfe, Richard Wright*, edited by Margaret A. Van Antwerp (1982)

3 *Saul Bellow, Jack Kerouac, Norman Mailer, Vladimir Nabokov, John Updike, Kurt Vonnegut*, edited by Mary Bruccoli (1983)

4 *Tennessee Williams*, edited by Margaret A. Van Antwerp and Sally Johns (1984)

5 *American Transcendentalists*, edited by Joel Myerson (1988)

6 *Hardboiled Mystery Writers: Raymond Chandler, Dashiell Hammett, Ross Macdonald*, edited by Matthew J. Bruccoli and Richard Layman (1989)

7 *Modern American Poets: James Dickey, Robert Frost, Marianne Moore*, edited by Karen L. Rood (1989)

8 *The Black Aesthetic Movement*, edited by Jeffrey Louis Decker (1991)

9 *American Writers of the Vietnam War: W. D. Ehrhart, Larry Heinemann, Tim O'Brien, Walter McDonald, John M. Del Vecchio*, edited by Ronald Baughman (1991)

10 *The Bloomsbury Group*, edited by Edward L. Bishop (1992)

11 *American Proletarian Culture: The Twenties and The Thirties*, edited by Jon Christian Suggs (1993)

12 *Southern Women Writers: Flannery O'Connor, Katherine Anne Porter, Eudora Welty*, edited by Mary Ann Wimsatt and Karen L. Rood (1994)

13 *The House of Scribner, 1846–1904*, edited by John Delaney (1996)

14 *Four Women Writers for Children, 1868–1918*, edited by Caroline C. Hunt (1996)

15 *American Expatriate Writers: Paris in the Twenties*, edited by Matthew J. Bruccoli and Robert W. Trogdon (1997)

16 *The House of Scribner, 1905–1930*, edited by John Delaney (1997)

17 *The House of Scribner, 1931–1984*, edited by John Delaney (1998)

18 *British Poets of The Great War: Sassoon, Graves, Owen*, edited by Patrick Quinn (1999)

19 *James Dickey*, edited by Judith S. Baughman (1999)

See also DLB 210, 216, 219, 222, 224, 229, 237, 247, 253, 254, 263, 269, 273, 274, 280, 284

Dictionary of Literary Biography Yearbooks

1980 edited by Karen L. Rood, Jean W. Ross, and Richard Ziegfeld (1981)

1981 edited by Karen L. Rood, Jean W. Ross, and Richard Ziegfeld (1982)

1982 edited by Richard Ziegfeld; associate editors: Jean W. Ross and Lynne C. Zeigler (1983)

1983 edited by Mary Bruccoli and Jean W. Ross; associate editor Richard Ziegfeld (1984)

1984 edited by Jean W. Ross (1985)

1985 edited by Jean W. Ross (1986)

1986 edited by J. M. Brook (1987)

1987 edited by J. M. Brook (1988)

1988 edited by J. M. Brook (1989)

1989 edited by J. M. Brook (1990)

1990 edited by James W. Hipp (1991)

1991 edited by James W. Hipp (1992)

1992 edited by James W. Hipp (1993)

1993 edited by James W. Hipp, contributing editor George Garrett (1994)

1994 edited by James W. Hipp, contributing editor George Garrett (1995)

1995 edited by James W. Hipp, contributing editor George Garrett (1996)

1996 edited by Samuel W. Bruce and L. Kay Webster, contributing editor George Garrett (1997)

1997 edited by Matthew J. Bruccoli and George Garrett, with the assistance of L. Kay Webster (1998)

1998 edited by Matthew J. Bruccoli, contributing editor George Garrett, with the assistance of D. W. Thomas (1999)

1999 edited by Matthew J. Bruccoli, contributing editor George Garrett, with the assistance of D. W. Thomas (2000)

2000 edited by Matthew J. Bruccoli, contributing editor George Garrett, with the assistance of George Parker Anderson (2001)

2001 edited by Matthew J. Bruccoli, contributing editor George Garrett, with the assistance of George Parker Anderson (2002)

2002 edited by Matthew J. Bruccoli and George Garrett; George Parker Anderson, Assistant Editor (2003)

Concise Series

Concise Dictionary of American Literary Biography, 7 volumes (1988–1999): *The New Consciousness, 1941–1968; Colonization to the American Renaissance, 1640–1865; Realism, Naturalism, and Local Color, 1865–1917; The Twenties, 1917–1929; The Age of Maturity, 1929–1941; Broadening Views, 1968–1988; Supplement: Modern Writers, 1900–1998.*

Concise Dictionary of British Literary Biography, 8 volumes (1991–1992): *Writers of the Middle Ages and Renaissance Before 1660; Writers of the Restoration and Eighteenth Century, 1660–1789; Writers of the Romantic Period, 1789–1832; Victorian Writers, 1832–1890; Late-Victorian and Edwardian Writers, 1890–1914; Modern Writers, 1914–1945; Writers After World War II, 1945–1960; Contemporary Writers, 1960 to Present.*

Concise Dictionary of World Literary Biography, 4 volumes (1999–2000): *Ancient Greek and Roman Writers; German Writers; African, Caribbean, and Latin American Writers; South Slavic and Eastern European Writers.*

Russian Writers
Since 1980

Dictionary of Literary Biography® • Volume Two Hundred Eighty-Five

Russian Writers
Since 1980

Edited by
Marina Balina
Illinois Wesleyan University
and
Mark Lipovetsky
University of Colorado at Boulder

A Bruccoli Clark Layman Book

GALE®

TM

Detroit • New York • San Diego • San Francisco • Cleveland • New Haven, Conn. • Waterville, Maine • London • Munich

Dictionary of Literary Biography
Volume 285: Russian Writers Since 1980
Marina Balina
Mark Lipovetsky

Advisory Board
John Baker
William Cagle
Patrick O'Connor
George Garrett
Trudier Harris
Alvin Kernan
Kenny J. Williams

Editorial Directors
Matthew J. Bruccoli and Richard Layman

LIBRARY OF CONGRESS CATALOGING-IN-PUBLICATION DATA

Russian writers since 1980 / edited by Marina Balina and Mark Lipovetsky.
    p. cm. — (Dictionary of literary biography ; v. 285)
"A Bruccoli Clark Layman book."
Includes bibliographical references and index.
        ISBN 0-7876-6822-2 (hardcover)
        1. Russian literature—20th century—Bio-bibliography.
        I. Balina, Marina. II. Lipoveëtiskiæi, M. N. III. Series.

Z2500.R85 2003
[PG2991.4]
891.709'0044—dc21   2003014684

Printed in the United States of America
10 9 8 7 6 5 4 3 2 1

To Daniel and Dima

Contents

Plan of the Series xv
Introduction xvii

Boris Akunin (Grigorii Shalvovich Chkhartishvili)
(1956–) 3
Konstantine Klioutchkine

Petr Markovich Aleshkovsky (1957–) 11
Valentina G. Brougher

Joseph Brodsky (Iosif Aleksandrovich Brodsky)
(1940–1996). 17
Alyssa Dinega Gillespie

Andrei Viktorovich Dmitriev
(1956–) 40
Tatiana Spektor

Sergei Donatovich Dovlatov
(1941–1990). 48
Jekaterina Young

Mikhail Naumovich Epshtein (Mikhail Epstein)
(1950–). 61
Thomas Epstein

Venedikt Vasil'evich Erofeev
(1938–1990). 69
Anindita Banerjee

Viktor Vladimirovich Erofeev
(1947–) 82
Larissa Rudova and Tatiana Spektor

Sergei Markovich Gandlevsky
(1952–). 89
Dmitrii Bak

Boris Efimovich Groys (1947–) 101
Alexander Prokhorov and Elena Prokhorova

Igor' Mironovich Guberman
(1936–) 108
Greta N. Slobin

Bakhyt Shkurullaevich Kenzheev
(1950–) 115
Marina Kanevskaya

Evgenii Vladimirovich Kharitonov
(1941–1981) 122
Evgenii Bershtein

Mark Sergeevich Kharitonov
(1937–) 129
Nina Kolesnikoff

Timur Iur'evich Kibirov (Timur
Iur'evich Zapoev) (1955–) 137
Andrei Nemzer and Mark Lipovetsky

Anatolii Andreevich Kim (1939–) 149
Nadya L. Peterson

Viktor Borisovich Krivulin
(1944–2001) 156
Alexandra Smith

Mikhail Nikolaevich Kuraev
(1939–) 165
Valentina G. Brougher

Vladimir Semenovich Makanin
(1937–) 172
Byron Lindsey

Aleksandra Marinina (Marina Anatol'evna
Alekseeva) (1957–) 184
Eliot Borenstein

Valeriia Spartakovna Narbikova
(1958–) 189
Larissa Rudova

Marina Anatol'evna Palei
(1955–) 196
Alexander Prokhorov

Aleksei Maksimovich Parshchikov (Raiderman)
(1954–) 202
Alexandra Smith

Viktor Olegovich Pelevin
(1962–) 208
Gerald McCausland

Ludmila Petrushevskaya
(1938–) 220
Helena Goscilo

Contents

Evgenii Anatol'evich Popov (1946–) 230
   Robert Porter

Dmitrii Aleksandrovich Prigov (1940–) 239
   Evgeny Dobrenko

Dina Il'inichna Rubina (1953–) 248
   Marina Adamovitch

Lev Semenovich Rubinshtein
   (1947–) 254
   Mark Lipovetsky

Nina Nikolaevna Sadur
   (1950–) 268
   Birgit Beumers

Vladimir Aleksandrovich Sharov
   (1952–) 277
   Thomas Epstein

Galina Nikolaevna Shcherbakova
   (1932–) 284
   Maria Litovskaia

Sasha Sokolov (Aleksandr Vsevolodovich
   Sokolov) (1943–) 291
   Anna Brodsky

Vladimir Georgievich Sorokin
   (1955–) 301
   Konstantin V. Kustanovich

Tatyana Tolstaya (1951–) 316
   Helena Goscilo

Lyudmila Ulitskaya (1943–) 329
   Maria Litovskaia

Petr L'vovich Vail' (1949–) and Aleksandr
   Aleksandrovich Genis (1953–) 336
   Ivan Tolstoi

Svetlana Vladimirovna Vasilenko
   (1956–) 350
   Elena Prokhorova

Mikhail Mikhailovich Zhvanetsky (1934–) 357
   Seth Graham

Books for Further Reading 365

Contributors 371

Cumulative Index 375

Plan of the Series

. . . Almost the most prodigious asset of a country, and perhaps its most precious possession, is its native literary product—when that product is fine and noble and enduring.

Mark Twain*

The advisory board, the editors, and the publisher of the *Dictionary of Literary Biography* are joined in endorsing Mark Twain's declaration. The literature of a nation provides an inexhaustible resource of permanent worth. Our purpose is to make literature and its creators better understood and more accessible to students and the reading public, while satisfying the needs of teachers and researchers.

To meet these requirements, *literary biography* has been construed in terms of the author's achievement. The most important thing about a writer is his writing. Accordingly, the entries in *DLB* are career biographies, tracing the development of the author's canon and the evolution of his reputation.

The purpose of *DLB* is not only to provide reliable information in a usable format but also to place the figures in the larger perspective of literary history and to offer appraisals of their accomplishments by qualified scholars.

The publication plan for *DLB* resulted from two years of preparation. The project was proposed to Bruccoli Clark by Frederick G. Ruffner, president of the Gale Research Company, in November 1975. After specimen entries were prepared and typeset, an advisory board was formed to refine the entry format and develop the series rationale. In meetings held during 1976, the publisher, series editors, and advisory board approved the scheme for a comprehensive biographical dictionary of persons who contributed to literature. Editorial work on the first volume began in January 1977, and it was published in 1978. In order to make *DLB* more than a dictionary and to compile volumes that individually have claim to status as literary history, it was decided to organize volumes by topic, period, or

From an unpublished section of Mark Twain's autobiography, copyright by the Mark Twain Company

genre. Each of these freestanding volumes provides a biographical-bibliographical guide and overview for a particular area of literature. We are convinced that this organization—as opposed to a single alphabet method—constitutes a valuable innovation in the presentation of reference material. The volume plan necessarily requires many decisions for the placement and treatment of authors. Certain figures will be included in separate volumes, but with different entries emphasizing the aspect of his career appropriate to each volume. Ernest Hemingway, for example, is represented in *American Writers in Paris, 1920–1939* by an entry focusing on his expatriate apprenticeship; he is also in *American Novelists, 1910–1945* with an entry surveying his entire career, as well as in *American Short-Story Writers, 1910–1945, Second Series* with an entry concentrating on his short fiction. Each volume includes a cumulative index of the subject authors and articles.

Since 1981 the series has been further augmented by the *DLB Yearbooks,* which update published entries, add new entries to keep the *DLB* current with contemporary activity, and provide articles on literary history. There have also been nineteen *DLB Documentary Series* volumes, which provide illustrations, facsimiles, and biographical and critical source materials for figures, works, or groups judged to have particular interest for students. In 1999 the *Documentary Series* was incorporated into the *DLB* volume numbering system beginning with *DLB 210: Ernest Hemingway.*

We define literature as the *intellectual commerce of a nation:* not merely as belles lettres but as that ample and complex process by which ideas are generated, shaped, and transmitted. *DLB* entries are not limited to "creative writers" but extend to other figures who in their time and in their way influenced the mind of a people. Thus the series encompasses historians, journalists, publishers, book collectors, and screenwriters. By this means readers of *DLB* may be aided to perceive literature not as cult scripture in the keeping of intellectual high priests but firmly positioned at the center of a nation's life.

DLB includes the major writers appropriate to each volume and those standing in the ranks behind them. Scholarly and critical counsel has been sought in deciding which minor figures to include and how full their entries should be. Wherever possible, useful references are made to figures who do not warrant separate entries.

Each *DLB* volume has an expert volume editor responsible for planning the volume, selecting the figures for inclusion, and assigning the entries. Volume editors are also responsible for preparing, where appropriate, appendices surveying the major periodicals and literary and intellectual movements for their volumes, as well as lists of further readings. Work on the series as a whole is coordinated at the Bruccoli Clark Layman editorial center in Columbia, South Carolina, where the editorial staff is responsible for accuracy and utility of the published volumes.

One feature that distinguishes *DLB* is the illustration policy—its concern with the iconography of literature. Just as an author is influenced by his surroundings, so is the reader's understanding of the author enhanced by a knowledge of his environment. Therefore *DLB* volumes include not only drawings, paintings, and photographs of authors, often depicting them at various stages in their careers, but also illustrations of their families and places where they lived. Title pages are regularly reproduced in facsimile along with dust jackets for modern authors. The dust jackets are a special feature of *DLB* because they often document better than anything else the way in which an author's work was perceived in its own time. Specimens of the writers' manuscripts and letters are included when feasible.

Samuel Johnson rightly decreed that "The chief glory of every people arises from its authors." The purpose of the *Dictionary of Literary Biography* is to compile literary history in the surest way available to us—by accurate and comprehensive treatment of the lives and work of those who contributed to it.

The *DLB* Advisory Board

Introduction

The literary and cultural life in Russia during the last twenty years of the past century can be characterized as highly diverse and controversial. The multitude of changes in Russia between 1980 and 2000 reached gigantic proportions. The major shifts on the political scene influenced Russian literature of these past two decades. The period from 1980 to 2002 may be compared in its intensity (with regard to political and cultural life) with the first two decades of the twentieth century. In both cases, the exhausted empires—the Russian Empire at the beginning of the twentieth century and the Soviet Empire at the end of it—were going through a rapid decline and collapse. The new cultural and political order was constructed from the chaos of social and political shifts. In both instances the initial enthusiasm of the intelligentsia, those traditional movers and shakers of drastic social changes, was replaced soon with the disappointment caused by unforeseen results of the very changes it had brought on. Literature managed to find in the political and historical turbulence of this period a source of powerful artistic insight. Writers managed to transform social catastrophes into nonclassical poetics such as modernism, avant-gardism, expressionism, and various hybrids of these trends with sentimentalism, romanticism, and realism. Often different, sometimes mutually exclusive, these discourses and literary practices formed peculiar combinations that surprised contemporaries by their disturbing novelty.

Three major periods within the constantly changing portrait of this epoch may be identified: 1980 to 1987, 1987 to 1991, and, finally, 1991 to the present. The divisions between these periods are vague and conditional, since many events overlap or find their reflection in literary and cultural life after the fact. Each one of these periods may be placed into certain sociocultural frameworks that, in many instances, served as a trigger point for the majority of those changes.

The cultural and political atmosphere in the first half of the 1980s was depressing indeed. The crisis of the Soviet political and economic system became quite evident. Shortages of virtually everything, from food items to medical supplies, especially outside of Moscow, made the start of black markets an inevitable direction of the economy in the first socialist state. The corrup-tion of the *nomenklatura* (members of the full-time staff of paid party officials) in all spheres of the state bureaucracy was shameless, and the senility of state and party leaders was obvious to everyone inside and outside the Soviet Union. The authorities' suspicion of any innovative thought became customary. The persecution of those who dared to be active, especially in the field of culture—coupled with official, yet concealed, anti-Semitism, xenophobia, and religious intolerance—became increasingly common. In return, the general population responded with bitter cynicism toward any manifestation of government-sponsored activities. Life within the system of "double standards" was accepted as a behavioral mode not only among the intelligentsia but also among the apparatchiks (party machine operatives). Reading samizdat (self-published literature banned for publication in the U.S.S.R.) and *tamizdat* (émigré editions smuggled from abroad) became a fashionable part of the lives of both of these groups; yet, only the representatives of the intelligentsia seriously risked their well-being by keeping this officially forbidden literature at home. All these and various other trends corrupted more than one generation of Soviets during the Stagnation period (1968–1986). By the 1980s, literary existence based on double standards became a hopeless way of life that seemed to last forever.

The literary scene in the Soviet Union became the subject of equally restrained policies. In 1979 a group of both established and novice writers attempted to produce an independent literary almanac. Titled *Metropol': Literaturnyi al'manakh* (Metropolis: A Literary Almanac, 1979), this collection of works by twenty-three writers of prose and poetry was the first public attempt, since the 1960s, to break through the dominant literature of socialist realism. The organizers of the project were Vasilii Pavlovich Aksenov, Fazil Abdulovich Iskander, Viktor Vladimirovich Erofeev, and Evgenii Anatol'evich Popov. The first public presentation of the almanac was performed without official approval in a Moscow café. Since the publication of *Metropol'* was not feasible, the volume was sent abroad and published in the United States, both in Russian and in English translation. The reaction of the Soviet Writers' Union, backed by the Komitet gosudarstvennoi bezopasnosti

(KGB, State Security Committee) and officials of the Communist Party, was predictable yet disproportionally aggressive. With no exception, all participants of *Metropol'*–even celebrated writers such as Iskander, Andrei Georgievich Bitov, Bella Akhatovna Akhmadulina, Genrikh Veniaminovich Sapgir, Semen Izraelevich Lipkin, and Inna L'vovna Lisnianskaia–were banned from publishing for several years. Aksenov, who was abroad at the time of this decision, was stripped of his Soviet citizenship and was not able to return to Russia. Younger authors, such as Viktor Erofeev and Popov, were expelled from the Soviet Writers' Union, effectively signaling the end of their writing careers. In protest against this persecution by the government, Lipkin and Lisnianskaia refused to remain members of the union and turned in their membership cards to union officials by mail. This scandal was the largest literary-political confrontation between the government and the creative community since the trial of Joseph Brodsky in 1964, the arrest and trial of Andrei Donatovich Siniavsky and Iulii Markovich Daniel in 1965, and the expulsion of Aleksandr Isaevich Solzhenitsyn from the Soviet Union in 1974.

The profound difference between these trials and the case of *Metropol',* however, was that the texts published in the almanac did not have any political overtones. They represented aesthetic, rather than ideological, dissent, but the Soviet system proved to be so rigid and sclerotic that even *Metropol',* an example of experimentation outside the socialist realist canon, caused an aggressive reaction. This response was an obvious sign that the romance between literature and power, fueled by the de-Stalinization of the 1960s, had ended. An equal contributor was the exhaustion of the liberal sectors of the literati, who had made all possible attempts to cope with, or at least to find a niche within, "developed socialism." That the beginning of the 1980s was marked with the voluntary (in some instances, even forced) exodus of the so-called creative intelligentsia from the Soviet Union is no wonder: Iuz (Iosif Efimovich) Aleshkovsky emigrated in 1979, Vladimir Nikolaevich Voinovich and Fridrikh Naumovich Gorenshtein in 1980, Andrei Arsen'evich Tarkovsky in 1982, Georgii Nikolaevich Vladimov in 1983, and Iurii Petrovich Liubimov in 1984. The sudden deaths of relatively young writers also occured during this period. In the summer of 1980 the renowned poet and singer Vladimir Semenovich Vysotsky died. In many ways his songs embodied the spirit of freedom that, nevertheless, had survived throughout the political freeze of the Stagnation period. In 1981 Evgenii Vladimirovich Kharitonov, a gay poet and prose writer as well as a playwright and one of the most influential figures in the Moscow literary underground, died of a heart attack on

a Moscow street. Even Soviet official literature started to demonstrate small, but nevertheless visible, shifts within its seemingly monolithic structure. Several years later these changes became dominant in post-Soviet literary development.

The aging political leadership of the country also influenced the perception of the age of Soviet culture in general. The average age of a "young" writer publishing his or her first book in the Soviet Union was around forty years. A group that generated one of the few literary discussions of the period was called "the generation of the forty-year-olds" and was identified as such because of their age rather than their literary merit. To this group belonged, for example, Anatolii Andreevich Kim, Ruslan Timofeevich Kireev, Anatolii Nikolaevich Kurchatkin, and Vladimir Semenovich Makanin. They discovered an existential hopelessness in a comforting, yet almost immobile, lifestyle during the 1980s. The authors presented this hopelessness as a drama of the individual whose existence is virtually erased by the impersonality of this lifestyle. Their works were not banned from publication in the Soviet press since their narratives touched on quite private areas of human experience. In regard to the writings of these authors Deming Brown states in *The Last Years of Soviet Literature: Prose Fiction, 1975–1991* (1993) that ". . . there is an absence of dogmatism, an ideological tentativeness, and lack of doctrinal certainty. They do not fear ambiguity and ambivalence, and in some cases they in fact cultivate such attitudes. To a great extent they seem to feel that as artists their task is investigative and cognitive, not didactic." The "forty-year-olds" did not escape harsh criticism for their Chekhovian aesthetics. The proponents of socialist realism accused them for their "absence of a definite authorial position," which was viewed as lacking in optimism and promoting a "narrow-minded" focus on everyday matters *(byt),* rather than on critically engaging, socially significant events. The liberal critics of the "Thaw" generation–those who were inspired by the short period of liberalization during Nikita Sergeevich Khrushchev's governance (1954–1964)–voiced their disagreement with the lack of sociopolitical criticism of the Soviet system. They accused the writers of committing the same "sin" as their conservative counterparts. In their interpretation "absence of a definite authorial position" appeared as a sign of conformism. The fact remains that the mere act of publishing these works led to the first cracks in the monolithic socialist realist canon.

During the 1980s, in their attempt to save the collapsing colossus, the defenders of socialist realism began to reshape this outdated monster, declaring it an "open system." They tried to downplay the "formalist" label that, since the 1930s, had been used against any literary innovation stretching beyond realistic verisimilitude. Thus, the ban on formal experiments was lifted, and Soviet writers were allowed to play with "innovative" forms. Soviet literature of the 1980s was marked with an increasing interest in the grotesque, fantasy, mythologism, and parable. These literary devices became incredibly popular, even fashionable, in the works of Russian authors, ranging from the officially promoted "minority" writer Chingiz Torekulovich Aitmatov, to the intelligentsia sweetheart Iskander, to the émigré postmodernist Sasha Sokolov. The experimentation with style and form demonstrated by these and other writers earned the 1980s the label of "fantastic decade."

The younger generation, those who were born in the 1950s, also made significant contributions to the destruction of socialist realism. Between 1982 and 1984 *Literaturnaia gazeta* (The Literary Gazette) and, later, *Literaturnaia ucheba* (Literary Education), two of the most influential periodicals on literature, started a discussion on so-called complex poetry—actually the modernist and postmodernist poetry of the younger generation, though never labeled as such. The discussion elicited the participation of many young poets. Only one of them, Ivan Fedorovich Zhdanov, had published a book of verse, *Portret* (The Portrait), by some unexplainable fluke, in 1982. The discussion of the works by poets of this generation—Aleksander Viktorovich Eremenko, Nina Iur'evna Iskrenko, and Aleksei Maksimovich Parshchikov, among others—was based either on a few minor publications or on unpublished material. Yet, the precise fact that critical discussion of this poetry took place in the official press enabled the process of its "legitimization." This literary discussion opened doors to journals and publishing houses for these poets and provided them with an opportunity for public readings of their works. It marked the largest influx into Soviet literature of new, and openly nonconformist, works since the liberal period of the Thaw in the 1960s.

The reaction of these young literati to the attention given to their creative work was quite different from the way their predecessors had responded. These newly published writers did not openly pay any attention to whether they gained recognition from the Soviet authorities. Many of them deliberately rejected any type of active participation in the life of the Soviet literary establishment. The hippie movement reached Soviet youth by 1980. Around this same time Western rock music, which had been totally prohibited by Soviet officials, became the favorite music of millions of Soviet youngsters. Boris Grebenshchikov, rock poet and one of the most popular singers of this generation (whose own performances were limited to underground concerts), identified his peers as a "pokolenie dvornikov i storozhei" (generation of janitors and night guards). In fact, these two professions—along with that of firefighting—became the most popular affiliations for young and frequently brilliantly (self-)educated intellectuals. Writers, artists, and musicians of this new generation did not want to compromise their creativity as well as human integrity in exchange for accepting the Soviet artistic establishment and membership in its various party-controlled unions. Those nonconformists and their mentors, who earlier in the 1960s had chosen similar paths of nonparticipation in the official cultural life of the country, contributed to the formation of underground Soviet culture.

In his novel *Andegraund, ili Geroi nashego vremeni* (The Underground, Or A Hero of Our Time), published in 1998, Makanin commented on the nature of underground culture: ". . . The social subconscious. And the underground attitude is focused somehow. Somehow it does matter. Carries weight. All the more if it never (even accidentally, through a slip of the tongue) ascends into daylight." The literary taste of this cultural underground was formed in direct contrast to the Soviet socialist realist canon. Underground publications and underground artistic activities became a sort of laboratory, where interrupted development of Russian modernism was continued and where Russian postmodernism was conceived.

In the early 1980s there were at least two major underground circles, in Moscow and in Leningrad. The underground literary scene in Leningrad was strongly affected by the influence of two major literary figures—first, in the 1960s, by the poet Anna Andreevna Akhmatova and, later, by Brodsky, who had been forced to leave the Soviet Union in 1972. In his Nobel address, delivered in December 1987, Brodsky reflected on the role of this literary circle and defined its major contribution:

> Looking back, I can say again that we were beginning in an empty—indeed, a terrifyingly wasted—place, and that, intuitively rather than consciously, we aspired precisely to the re-creation of the culture's continuity, to the reconstruction of its forms, and tropes, and filling its few surviving, and often totally compromised, forms, with our new, or appearing to us as new, contemporary content.

In the 1980s this circle continued to preserve its orientation toward a highly sophisticated development of modernist traditions, especially those resembling the neoclassic acmeist circle and the absurdist group Ob"edinenie real'nogo iskusstva (OBERIU, Association for Real Art). Among the most prominent representatives of the Leningrad underground modernist movement of the late 1970s to the early 1980s were Arkadii Trofimovich Dragomoshchenko, Viktor Borisovich Krivulin, and Elena Andreevna Shvarts. Members of the "Circle of Mikhail Krasil'nikov," another innovative literary group, included poets such as Mikhail Fedorovich Eremin, Lev Vladimirovich Losev, and Vladimir Iosifivich Ufliand. Accomplished poets such as Gleb Iakovlevich Gorbovsky and Nonna Mendelevna Slepakova participated in Gleb Sergeevich Semenov's LITO, short for Literaturnoe ob"edinenie (Literary Union). Other important creative groups included Verpa (to which the poets Aleksei Khvostenko and Anri Girshovich Volokhonsky belonged); Konstantin Konstantinovich Kus'minsky's circle of poets; and the poetic group Helenukty (which included Vladimir Ibragimovich Erl'). The group Gorozhane (City Dwellers) united prose writers such as Sergei Donatovich Dovlatov, Igor' Markovich Efimov, Vladimir Andreevich Gubin, Vladimir Rafailovich Maramzin, and Boris Borisovich Vakhtin. The Leningrad literary underground became known in the 1980s for its samizdat journals—for example, *Severnaia pochta* (The Northern Post), *37* (published by Krivulin), *Mitin zhurnal* (Mitia's Journal, started by Dmitrii Volchek), *Obvodnoi kanal* (Bypass Canal), *Chasy* (The Hours), and *Beseda* (Colloquy).

In his Nobel speech Brodsky described another alternative direction of underground literature:

> There existed, presumably, another path: the path of further deformation, poetics of ruins and debris, of minimalism, of choked breath. . . . We rejected it, because in reality the choice wasn't ours, but, in fact, culture's own—and this choice, again, was aesthetic, rather than moral.

Here the poet is referring to the conceptualist circle, which was at the core of Moscow underground culture and included artists (Erik Vladimirovich Bulatov, Francisco Infante, Il'ia Iosifovich Kabakov, Vitalii Anatol'evich Komar and Aleksandr Danilovich Melamid, and Oskar Rabin), writers (Popov, Igor' Sergeevich Kholin, Vsevolod Nikolaevich Nekrasov, Dmitrii Aleksandrovich Prigov, Lev Semenovich Rubinshtein, and, later, Timur Iur'evich Kibirov, and Vladimir Georgievich Sorokin), and theoreticians (Boris Efimovich Groys and, later, Mikhail Naumovich Epshtein [Epstein]). By the mid 1970s the conceptualists had formed an original artistic ideology and strategy, inspired primarily by visual art. Many of the artists, such as Prigov, combined an interest and ability to create both visual art and literature. Others, like Kabakov, brought extremely strong verbal components into their visual imagery. At the basis of this creative philosophy was the idea that visual imagery is at the heart of the consistent deconstruction of totalitarian language and

power. This effect was achieved by the exaggeration of its ritualistic, myth-forming nature and the production of absurd and parodic mythological images (such as many of Prigov's poetic cycles on the Soviet Militiaman or Komar and Melamid's portrait "Stalin and the Muses," a work in oil on canvas dating to 1981–1982). The works of artists Bulatov and Kabakov used a different device: they revealed present reality as empty or ruined and hid it under the cover of ideological simulacra. In actuality, postmodernism provided the aesthetic foundation for this group, but the term per se was not applied to characterize their works until the 1990s.

Underground literature in Moscow, however, was not limited to conceptualist writings. Its most profound figures included Venedikt Vasil'evich Erofeev, author of the legendary novel *Moskva-Petushki* (completed in 1970 and first published in 1977; translated as *Moscow to the End of the Line,* 1980), which was published abroad and later circulated in thousands of samizdat copies throughout the Soviet Union. Evgenii Kharitonov was the founding father of underground gay culture and had his own group of followers. There were also poetic associations such as Gruppa Chertkova (Chertkov's Group), centered on poet Leonid Natanovich Chertkov. Well-known in underground culture were the poets of the Lianosovo Circle, whose works preceded conceptualist experiments; this group was responsible for further fostering postmodern culture. Sokolov belonged for a short period to the poetic underground circle Samoe molodoe obshchetvo geniev (SMOG, The Youngest Society of Geniuses). The group Moskovskoe vremia (Moscow Time) was, among other participants, represented by Sergei Markovich Gandlevsky, Bakhyt Shkurullaevich Kenzheev, Aleksandr Aleksandrovich Soprovsky, and Aleksei Petrovich Tsvetkov. Among many unpublished but renowned poets, prose writers, and essayists of the Moscow literary and artistic underground were Genadii Nikolevich Aigi, Igor' Mironovich Guberman, Mark Sergeevich Kharitonov, Ol'ga Aleksandrovna Sedakova, and Ludmila Petrushevskaya.

Several private poetic salons, both in Moscow and Leningrad, as well as in some provincial centers, signified another possible form of literary existence. No matter how different these groups were in their articulation of their aesthetics, for the time being they represented a unified field of underground literature. Although opposition to the socialist realist canon constituted an important part of the modernist stance in the Soviet Union from the 1970s to the 1980s, Russian "belated modernists" were more concerned with the "re-creation of the culture's continuity," in Brodsky's words, than with political confrontation with the existing regime. In the 1990s the different platforms of these groups became the engines for harsh literary polemics.

The obvious split within Soviet literature was one of the many indicators of instability in the entire system. The Soviet Union faced a series of crises abroad; for example, in the eyes of the West, the Soviet military invasion of Afghanistan cast a blemish upon the political image of the U.S.S.R. A stagnated economy, heavy drinking, and rising crime rates contributed to general feelings of inevitable catastrophe. Even official Soviet literature reflected the inevitability of coming cataclysms, as evidenced by Valintin Grigor'evich Rasputin's novel *Pozhar* (Fire, 1985) and Aitmatov's novels *I dol'she veka dlitsia den'* (The Day Lasts More than a Hundred Years, 1980) and *Plakha* (The Execution Block, 1986). The disaster at the nuclear power plant in Chernobyl, in northern Ukraine, on 26 April 1986 materialized apocalyptic sentiment. The Soviet authorities took several weeks to break the boundaries of secrecy and admit to the huge impact of the catastrophe on the Soviet population. In his chapter on the "Gorbachev 'revolution'" in *A Vision Unfulfilled: Russia and the Soviet Union in the Twentieth Century* (1996), John Thompson identifies the Chernobyl tragedy as a major stimulus to glasnost—the policy of openness and criticism (of the Soviet system and its failures) introduced by Mikhail Sergeevich Gorbachev. The open discussion of this disaster in the Soviet press during the summer of 1986 revealed a shocking level of incompetence within the Soviet economic and ideological apparatus. The Soviet system, however, agonized for another five years, and this agony was labeled perestroika (ostensibly, reconstruction—though sometimes defined as deconstruction).

Gorbachev came to power on 11 March 1985. His perestroika was initiated as an attempt to modernize Soviet society, but his reforms steadily revealed the irreparableness of the regime. His official "announcement" of the politics of glasnost at the Twenty-Seventh Congress of the Communist Party of the Soviet Union (which, in fact, became the last congress) opened the floodgates of criticism for the past and present Soviet economic, political, and ideological systems. This critical approach and the reevaluation of society in Soviet history surpassed the "liberalism" of the Thaw period. The outburst of critical material broke the silence of the 1980s. Archival materials that were revealed to the public called into question the very legitimacy of the Soviet system and its leaders. These unbridled political revelations almost stopped with the steady control and introduction of political repression. Several attempts were made to engage this highly proven political tool during the era of perestroika. Acts of violence were witnessed in Vilnius, Tbilisi, Sumgait, and Nagorny Karabakh.

The "coup" organized by the highest officials of Gorbachev's government took place in 1991. None of these and other attempts was consistent enough to stop the collapse of the Soviet political system and ensure the victory of anticommunist forces.

The "coup" of 1991, despite the intentions of its leaders, turned into the final historical act of the Soviet Union, the Communist Party in the Soviet Union, and the communist utopia and marked the beginning of the post-Soviet era. On 23 August 1991, after the failed "coup" attempt of the members of the Politburo to reinstate the Soviet system, Boris Nikolaevich Yeltsin signed a decree discontinuing all activities of the Communist Party of the Russian Federation. Four months later, on 26 December 1991, the Union of the Soviet Socialist Republics ceased to exist. A multiparty system was established almost immediately, and pluralism became an officially accepted political and ideological enterprise.

A high level of euphoria marked the cultural atmosphere during the years of glasnost, and there were good reasons for such elevated feelings. The ideas and theories that, not long ago, were punishable by imprisonment suddenly filled the pages of newspapers and literary journals. Criticism of the government, of the repressive politics of the totalitarian past, of dissident movements, of underground culture—topics that were traditionally reserved for private "kitchen talk" in the apartments of the intelligentsia—were spouted from the podium of the Soviet parliament. The works of underground, as well as émigré, writers found their way to the most popular literary journals, which were sold during this time in record amounts—from one to three million copies! The main reason for the popularity of the journals was associated with the so-called *vozvrashennaia literatura* (returned literature), referring to the works of Russian modernist classics banned or partially restricted for various political reasons from publication during the Soviet period. Authors of *vozvrashennaia literatura* included Akhmatova, Mikhail Afanas'evich Bulgakov, Nikolai Ivanovich Gumilev, Osip Emil'evich Mandel'shtam, Vladimir Vladimirovich Nabokov, Andrei Platonovich Platonov, and Evgenii Ivanovich Zamiatin. The newly available works of these authors simultaneously began the process of introducing the public to the new names of underground and émigré literature.

These first published literary works of *vozvrashennaia literatura* were "politically incorrect" from the Soviet viewpoint, but aesthetically they were close to the socialist realism ideal, or to the realist tradition in general. To this group of texts belonged the novels *Deti Arbata* (1987; translated as *Children of the Arbat,* 1988) by Anatolii Naumovich Rybakov; *Zhizn' i sud'ba* (first published in the U.S.S.R., 1988; translated as *Life and Fate,* 1985) by Vasily Semenovich Grossman; *Belye odezhdy*

(The White Robes, 1988) by Vladimir Dmitrievich Dudintsev; *Fakul'tet nenuzhnykh veshchei* (The Department of Unnecessary Things, 1989) by Iurii Osipovich Dombrovsky; *Zhizn' i neobyknovennye prikliucheniia soldata Ivana Chonkina* (first published in the U.S.S.R., 1990; translated as *The Life and Extraordinary Adventures of Private Ivan Chonkin,* 1977) by Vladimir Nikolaevich Voinovich; and the play *Dal'she! Dal'she! Dal'she!* (Further! Further! Further!, 1989) by Mikhail Filippovich Shatrov. These publications sparked heated political discussions and defined the major power spheres of the so-called battle of the journals: a confrontation between the liberal and conservative (typically procommunist, anti-Semitic, and chauvinist) periodicals in Russia.

A criticism of Soviet totalitarianism and its ideology, an orientation toward the West, and a liberalism that emphasized human rights unified periodicals such as *Literaturnaia gazeta, Ogonek* (The Flame), *Izvestiia* (The News), *Znamia* (The Banner), *Novyi mir* (New World), *Iunost'* (Youth), *Oktiabr'* (October), *Knizhnoe obozrenie* (The Book Review), *Daugava* (Riga), *Ural,* and *Volga.* Opposing such an approach were journals and newspapers such as *Nash sovremennik* (Our Contemporary), *Molodaia gvardiia* (The Young Guard), *Literaturnaia Rossiia* (Literary Russia), *Moskva* (Moscow), and *Pravda* (Truth), as well as several regional journals. The authors who were frequently published in these periodicals relied heavily on concepts that included the Russian nation and enemies of the nation (that is, "minor nations" and Jews). These writers created a cult out of Russia's prerevolutionary past and inspired the struggle against "Russophobia" and "rootless cosmopolitanism" by attacking the Western liberalism of the intelligentsia. Once again, the age-old polemics between Slavophiles and Westernizers were resurrected, but this time they gained revitalized impetus through new institutional forms supported by the opportunities that glasnost had created. If the liberal wing of the literati revitalized in many respects the ideals of the Thaw generation of the 1960s, the "patriotic" camp produced a new merger of the most conservative dogmas of communist ideology (exemplified, for instance, by *Molodaia gvardiia*) with anti-Soviet nationalism (endorsed by *Nash sovremennik*). This peculiar combination provided the theoretical basis for newly born political organizations with clearly profascist and anti-Semitic—as well as anti-Western—orientations, which included *Pamiat'* (Memory) and *Russkoe Natsional'noe Edinstvo* (Russian National Unity).

The struggle between these literary-ideological camps reached its climax by the end of 1989. The event that triggered this climax was the appearance that year of Grossman's novel *Vse Techet . . .* (Everything Is in Flux) and a small fragment of Siniavsky's *Progulki s Pushkinym* (A Stroll with Pushkin), both in the literary journal

Oktiabr'. These publications were immediately labeled by the conservative press as "Russophobic." The scandal went so far that the Secretariat of the Union of Writers of the Russian Federation, controlled by nationalist writers, tried to remove Anatoly Andreevich Anan'ev from his position as editor in chief of the journal *Oktiabr'.* This attempt failed, but the confrontation between liberal and conservative forces eventually led to the breakup of the writers' union into two independent organizations: the Union of Russian Writers (liberal) and the Union of Writers of the Russian Federation (nationalist). These battles of the journals actually stopped after 1991, their end coinciding with the dissolution of the Communist Party and the subsequent end of the Soviet Empire. All the aforementioned periodicals remained rooted in their ideological positions; they ceased to react to their opponents, however, and confined their views to the pages of their own publications.

The events of Yeltsin's decade (1991–2000) and the beginning of Vladimir Vladimirovich Putin's reign (since 2000) present an extremely controversial image of the political and cultural changes in Russia. They are marked by the Communist coup of 1993 and its elimination by military force, the collapse of the Russian economic system in 1998, and two Chechen wars (1994–1996 and 1999 to the present). During this period Russia witnessed the abolition of any censorship, something that it had never before experienced—except for the short period between the February Revolution and the October Revolution, both of 1917. The "pauperization" of the general population, and especially of the intelligentsia, was at its highest point since the dissolution of the Soviet Empire, as was the intensity of the struggle between different political parties. This period is also characterized by an increase in local and ethnic conflicts. The intensity of Russian fascism; the criminalization of the economy and the leadership of the country; and the political and economic domination of the "oligarchs" and their ensuing expulsion (in 2000–2001) were strangely combined in post-Soviet life with strong feelings of nostalgia for the Soviet Empire and the growth of anti-American sentiment, especially after the bombing in the Balkans by the North American Treaty Organization (NATO). While the restoration of the Soviet national anthem in 2001 was an obvious step back into the totalitarian past, growing cooperation with NATO (especially by 2002) and radical economic reforms promised some kind of different future. The persecution of independent media groups and the simultaneous existence of the free book market sent contradicting messages. Stunned and horrified by the terrorist explosions in Moscow apartment buildings in 1999, Russian citizens looked forward to a period of political stabilization under the leadership of Putin, a former KGB colonel.

The first steps of radical economic reform almost totally destroyed the production system of books and periodicals that had existed during Soviet times. Many regular publications could not cope with the rising costs of production; after a brief period of struggle, they simply ceased to exist. Among the most successful publishing houses that survived between 1992 and 1995 were newly started enterprises such as Vagrius, Ad Marginem Press, and Limbus Press, as well as publishing concerns based at journals, including *Novoe literaturnoe obozrenie* (The New Literary Review).

Since the nineteenth century, literary periodicals—especially the so-called *tolstye zhurnaly* (thick journals, which, because of their size, looked more like books than periodicals)—played a distinctive role in Russian culture. They served as major sources for organizing the literary process by assuring its stable structure. This structure included the publication of new works of poetry and prose, of critical reviews, and of archival and bibliographical information. These periodicals provided space for discussions (albeit ideologically controlled) of literary works by leading critics. After the failure of state institutions in the 1990s and the abolishment of many of these periodicals, a newly established format for the support of literature and the literati took their place—literary prizes. The importance of literary prizes goes beyond financial support, for they provide a unifying factor for the literary community in Russia today. Discussions about prize candidates forced the representatives of different aesthetics to seek a dialogue with their opponents and help them provide structural unity for the expanding universe of post-Soviet literature.

One of the first, and initially the most influential, awards was the Booker Russian Novel Prize (since 1999 known as the Smirnoff/Booker Prize). This program was launched in 1992 under the supervision of the British Council in Moscow. The Anti-Booker Prize, established by *Nezavisimaia gazeta* (The Independent Gazette) and financed by one of the most notorious Russian "oligarchs," Boris Abramovich Berezovsky, was subsequently established. The aim behind the Anti-Booker was to counterbalance the Booker in several categories, including poetry, drama, and criticism; the Booker is given only for novels. There were some cases, however, when the same works were nominated for both the Booker and the Anti-Booker. The Pushkin Award was established by the German Fund of Alfred Toffler. The prize "Triumph," also financed by Berezovsky, largely reflects the values of the generation of the 1960s. The Solzhenitsyn Prize, established in 1997 and awarded by the committee, which Solzhenitsyn himself chaired, recognizes writers whose creativity

appeals to traditional values. The most respected literary prize, offering the most lucrative honorarium, was named after the nineteenth-century poet and literary critic Apollon Aleksandrovich Grigor'ev; the Academy of Contemporary Russian Writers, which united the most active contemporary literary critics of the era, established this award. Among the prizes of a smaller scale are those that focus on particular genres. The literary journal *Novyi mir* annually awards the Iurii Kazakov Prize for the best short story. Another literary journal, *Znamia,* created a prize for the best Russian novella, or *povest',* and named the award after Ivan Petrovich Belkin, a title character in one of Aleksandr Sergeevich Pushkin's novellas.

The most remarkable phenomenon in the development of Russian literature in the 1990s is the restoration of its unity for the first time since the Silver Age (1890s to 1917). The political cataclysms at the beginning of the twentieth century divided Russian literature into almost totally noncommunicating realms. These realms included official (or at least tolerated) Soviet literature, underground literature with its internal division of the political-ideological and aesthetic underground, and the literature of emigration. During the last two decades of the century—but especially during the period that began with Gorbachev's perestroika and continued with the anticommunist revolution of 1991—a formal reunification of Russian literature as well as the restitution of full communication between all three realms took place.

The present panorama of literary life in Russia is complete and diverse. The works of former underground writers have become contemporary classics, and the books of émigré authors are published, reviewed, and sold in Russia along with the works of former Soviet writers. Close interaction between these groups remains an ongoing process. Yet, far from idyllic, this process is full of conflicts and dramatic tensions. The conflict between the official and nonofficial literature of the Stagnation period has now transformed into a reunited Russian literature that is at the same time split by ideological and aesthetic confrontations. This situation resembles the literary struggles of the prerevolutionary period between 1900 and 1910, as well as the early days of postrevolutionary Russia of the 1920s, when representatives of different literary platforms were competing over possible cultural dominance.

Perestroika opened the doors of journals and publishing houses for the vast majority of the so-called delayed and truly young authors, who represented a wide variety of aesthetics, from naturalism (*chernukha,* or dark and shocking discourse) to extreme forms of avant-garde and postmodernism. Hidden previously in the shadow of ideological polemics, aesthetic problems were now at the forefront of literary discussions. Thus, the early 1990s started with a debate on Russian postmodernism and neorealism.

The explosion of postmodernism in the 1990s is rooted in underground culture, especially within Moscow conceptualism and the experiments of writers such as Venedikt Erofeev. The responsibility for the emergence of underground postmodernism is grounded in the general crisis of the grand narratives of the communist utopia genre. These crises began in the 1960s and defined the cultural atmosphere of the 1970s to 1980s. Russian postmodernism was born out of an irony toward any ideology and a deep disappointment in any kind of utopian thinking that was enhanced by the failure to modernize socialism during the Thaw period. The interest in experimenting with alternative forms of artistic expression began in the late 1960s as a form of resistance to official ideology and aesthetics. The term "postmodernism" was not used in Russia until the late 1980s, because "postmodernist" was also used to define the explosion of "new wave" literature in the 1990s. The works of at least three generations (born in the 1940s, 1950s, and 1960s) of Russian postmodernists appeared in the 1990s as a powerful aesthetic blast. Such writers included Epshtein, Venedikt Erofeev, Viktor Erofeev, Groys, Kibirov, Parshchikov, Popov, Prigov, Rubinshtein, Sorokin, Aleksandr Viktorovich Eremenko, Aleksandr Aleksandrovich Genis, Valeriia Spartakovna Narbikova, Viktor Olegovich Pelevin, Nina Sadur, Vladimir Aleksandrovich Sharov, Tatyana Tolstaya, and Petr L'vovich Vail. These generations were united by the dominant features of their creative works, which became trademarks of Russian postmodern writing. The defining characteristics of these writers' works encompassed a mockery of sacred discourses of Soviet and prerevolutionary Russian culture alike; shocking effects and an "irresponsible" playfulness; montages of various literary styles and the lack of an original, individual style; the deconstruction of subjectivity; and abundant sexual themes and obscenities. All of these features invariably caused fury and disgust among traditionalists.

The literary trend that finally received the name of Russian postmodernism was, in fact, a merger of at least two juxtaposed tendencies. The first developed conceptualist methods shaped within underground culture. The leading representatives of the Moscow conceptualist circle, Prigov and Rubinshtein, acquired the status of living classicists in Russian culture of the 1990s. Yet, both of these authors continued to seek innovative forms, experimenting with different genres of prose, performances, journalism, and memoirs. The poetry of Kibirov and Sorokin presented further developments in conceptualism. Kibirov combines the radi-

cal deconstruction of authoritative language structures with a song-like lyricism, thus creating popular versions of conceptualism. Sorokin, on the contrary, shocked Russian readers with his experimental prose, in which he exposes and destroys the totalitarian power of any cultural tradition or canon—Russian classics notwithstanding. His work is realized through different forms of transgression. A direct materialization of his discursive power is expressed in his writings through obscenities, horrors, gore, violence, and sadistic rituals.

Unlike Western postmodernism, Russian postmodernism is not opposed to the modernist tradition. As a rule it emerges from an attempt to regenerate modernism, as defined in works of Russian postmodernist classicists such as Venedikt Erofeev and Sokolov. Foremost, the works of Tolstaya and Pelevin, along with those by Viktor Erofeev, Krivulin, Narbikova, Parshchikov, Popov, Sharov, Sadur, and Shvarts, represent another alternative to a conceptualist mode of postmodernist writing. Their texts combine modernist aestheticism with postmodernist mischievousness. They simultaneously reproduce and undermine modernist myths of art and the individual. Their theatricality of style defines the elusiveness of the depicted world. The Russian postmodernists' ornamental language forms the poetics of metamorphoses and multiplication, coupled with constant wordplay that produces bifurcating personalities and realities. All these features resemble the baroque tradition and may be linked with the similar neobaroque phenomenon as it is represented by European and American writers such as Nabokov, Jorge Luis Borges, Italo Calvino, Julio Cortázar, Umberto Eco, Milorad Pavić, and John Barth.

Even the most ardent defenders of traditionalist values have to admit that realism in Russia underwent drastic changes during the last two decades. In the 1970s, and especially in the 1980s and 1990s, writers of different backgrounds—including the émigré writers Dovlatov and Gorenshtein; underground writers or writers limited in their ability to publish, such as Petrushevskaya, Kharitonov, Mikhail Nikolaevich Kuraev, Anatolii Genrichovich Naiman, Asar Eppel', and Andrei Sergeev; and officially "accepted" writers such as Iurii Valentinovich Trifonov and Bulat Shalvovich Okudzhava—consistently expanded the limits of realist poetics by fusing it with modernist philosophy and aesthetic devices. The first traces of these experiments are found in the prose of the "forty-year-olds" with their shift toward private issues, their detailed dissection of moral dilemmas and compromises, and their attention to the psychological motivation behind human actions. The writers of the younger generation who followed this path, such as Petr Markovich Aleshkovsky, Dmitrii L'vovich Bykov, Andrei Viktorovich Dmitriev, Oleg

Nikolaevich Ermakov, Igor' Iur'evich Klekh, Yuri Iosifovich Maletsky, Marina Anatol'evna Palei, Irina Nikolaevna Polianskaia, Dina Il'inichna Rubina, Lyudmila Ulitskaya, Svetlana Vladimirovna Vasilenko, Aleksei Slapovsky, and Marina Arturovna Vishnevetskaya continue to add postmodern elements to their style, which is based on the combination of realism and modernism. Makanin and Petrushevskaya, writers of the previous generation, successfully employed a wide spectrum of postmodernist devices in their later works.

Unlike postmodernists, who perceive reality as a total simulacrum and a fictitious nonentity, Russian neorealists continue to believe in the substantial character of reality and human relations. At the same time, they admit and accept the chaotic nature of changes and shifts within societies. These writers perceive the notion of any pregiven, universal or "total" order of reality as being false, but in their opinion the individual has the responsibility to deal with, and adjust to, this chaos. The psychological tradition of Russian realism in their works is applied to the analysis of ruptures and fragmentation of the world around, and within, an individual. The world manifests mostly desperate and tragic attempts by the authors and their characters to construct meaning in their lives within a world that has posited nothing but its chaotic essence. To some extent, these characteristics are also applicable to the poetry of Gandlevsky, Kenzheev, Losev, Mikhail Natanovich Aisenberg, Vladimir Arkad'evich Gandel'sman, as well as Larisa Emel'ianovna Miller, among others. This current trend in contemporary Russian literature resembles the works of Western authors such as Joseph Heller, Raymond Carver, Donald Barthelme, Margaret Atwood, Don DeLillo, Toni Morrison, Milan Kundera, or J. M. Coetzee. As Alan Wilde stated in his book *Middle Grounds: Studies in Contemporary American Fiction* (1987), this writing trend is precisely "the kind of fiction that rejects equally the oppositional extremities of realism on the one hand and a world-denying reflexivity on the other, and that invites to perceive the moral, as well as epistemological, perplexities of inhabiting and coming to terms with a world that is itself ontologically contingent and problematic."

Women's prose in Russian literature also has developed within the neorealist tradition, though somewhat independently. The earliest works are represented by Petrushevskaya's short stories and date back to the 1970s and early 1980s. The virtual explosion of women's writing occurred in the late 1980s to early 1990s. It was connected with the success of Petrushevskaya's best works and the emergence of new names in literature, such as Vasilenko, Palei, Ulitskaya, and Rubina. Russian women's prose attracted intense critical attention both at home and abroad. Within the neorealist trend, Russian women's prose is distinguished through a daring and sometimes shocking naturalism that focuses on the body and sexuality. Every conflict is brought to the level of a neomythological parable in which the female personality confronts the cruel, frequently misogynistic, world around her.

A drastic change in the disposition of literary forces on the Russian literary scene took place in the late 1990s. The confrontation between postmodernism and neorealism was overshadowed by the closure of the gap between highbrow and popular literature. Despite denial by the critics of the Soviet era to recognize this fact, popular literature certainly existed in Russia during the Soviet period. It was represented by the detective stories of the Vainer brothers, as well as family sagas by Anatolii Stepanovich Ivanov and Petr Lukich Proskurin that mix wild sex and violence with ideologically correct quasi historicism. Historical rumors in novels by Valentin Savvich Pikul'; spy novels by Iulian Semenovich Semenov; and sci-fi allegories by Arkadii Natanovich and Boris Natanovich Strugatsky are typical though scarce examples of Soviet popular literature. The situation changed radically in the late 1980s immediately after the loosening of Soviet censorship. Vast amounts of pulp fiction—both original and translated (usually badly)—filled booksellers' shelves, along with hard-core pornography, translations of various mystical and occult books, as well as reprints of the Bible, the Bhagavad Gita, and *The Protocols of the Elders of Zion* (a well-known anti-Semitic forgery published in Russian in 1897, supposedly compiled by Sergei Nilus). In the early 1990s many professional writers turned to mass literature and, for obvious commercial reasons, started to produce cheap pulp fiction (frequently under pseudonyms). Writing only works categorized as "high" culture no longer made for a viable living.

An "injection" of quality literary works into popular culture is evidenced by the successes of Mikhail Mikhailovich Zhvanetsky and Guberman. In the 1980s the popularity of these writers was restricted to circles of the liberal Soviet intelligentsia. The distribution of their texts was limited to samizdat and *magnitofonizdat* (circulation via tape recordings). In the post-Soviet period both writers entered the sphere of popular culture and managed to reinvent their popularity as pop figures, performers, and commentators. Galina Nikolaevna Shcherbakova, being faithful to the neosentimental style of her works, which brought her popularity in the early 1980s, continues to produce popular versions of women's prose.

Two extremely successful writers, Aleksandra Marinina and Boris Akunin, whose works are oriented toward atypical readers' groups, represent the genre of the mystery novel in post-Soviet culture. To convey their stories, both of these authors invented special personae that completely replaced the writer's personality. Marinina is the pseudonym of Marina Anatol'evna Alekseeva, a detective for the Moscow police. Writing as Marinina, Alekseeva produced a series of best-sellers that displayed a concealed, but detectable, anti-intelligentsia sentiment. Akunin is the pen name of a professional translator of Japanese and English, as well as a literary scholar, Grigorii Shalvovich Chkhartishvili. In the late 1990s, as Akunin, he published a series of stylized detective novels in which he resurrected the world of nineteenth-century Russia—when, as written on the back covers of his novels about Erast Fandorin, "literature was great, trust of progress was endless, and crimes were performed and solved with grace and taste." Akunin's skillful and entertaining postmodernist fun with motifs of Russian nineteenth-century literature, as well as with current political themes, was highly successful among the post-Soviet intelligentsia and among the younger, depoliticized generation of intellectuals.

Wide popularity and commercial success recently came to Pelevin, whose works were relatively unknown until 1998. His novel *Generation "P"* (1999; translated in the United Kingdom as *Babylon,* 1999; republished in the United States as *Homo Zapiens,* 2002) sold millions of copies. Such esoteric writers as Sorokin—beginning with his *Goluboe salo* (Blue Lard, 1999)—and Tolstaya (her 2001 novel *Kys'* sold fifty thousand copies) also enjoy growing popularity. In the late 1990s the book market in Russia finally became stable and even started to flourish. The changing literary and commercial environment led to the establishment of new tendencies in post-Soviet literature. The desire of postmodernist writers to reach out to a wider audience caused visible simplifications in literary discourse and increased the use of, rather than traditional deconstruction of, populist mythologies. Among these discourses are nationalism (bordering on chauvinism), anti-Western sentiment, conspiracy theories, Russian messianism, nostalgia for a "strong hand," and the promise of the restoration of former national pride. The dangerous aspects of these discourses became obvious in 2002 when the postmodernist publishing house Ad Marginem published and promoted the profascist novel *Gospodin Geksogen* (Mister Hexogen) by Aleksandr Andreevich Prokhanov. Prokhanov is editor in chief of the newspaper *Zavtra* (Tomorrow), notorious for its aggressive anti-Semitism. A widespread public-relations campaign for the promotion of his novel was organized by a group of young and seemingly liberal critics. The novel was awarded the National Bestseller Prize in 2002, and this decision caused a new dramatic split in the literary world, to a certain extent similar to the period of the "journal wars," among post-Soviet generations of writers and critics.

In spite of the similarities between the beginning and the end of the twentieth century, the understanding of the meanings and of the results of these periods in Russian culture are quite different. The myth of the revolution that was central to the beginning of the century was, in keeping with the modernist and avant-garde zeitgeist, the myth of the new. The myth that is dominant up to the end of the century is the myth of *return*. This return is one that interrupted the modernist tradition. It signifies a return to the "Russia that we've lost" (also the title of a popular documentary from the early 1990s). It is also a return to Western civilization, from which Russia was isolated for more than seventy years.

These two opposing myths create the framework for the entire twentieth century in Russia. According to Iurii Mikhailovich Lotman and Boris Andreevich Uspensky in their treatise "Binary Models in the Dynamics of Russian Culture," published in *The Semiotics of Russian Culture* (1985), the culture of Russia moves from one extreme to another, constantly skipping the neutral axiological zone: "Duality and the absence of a neutral axiological sphere led to a conception of the new not as continuation but as a total eschatological change." These scholars argue that the repetition of this pattern at various stages in Russian history, concentrating either on the future or on the past, doubled in quantity upon an obliteration of the present, leading to the pendulum-like character of Russian cultural dynamics.

Did Russian literature of the last two decades in the twentieth century manage to solve this cultural problem, or did it carve, at least, a path for future transitions with its "*posts-*" (as in *post*modernism)? The answer to this question is negative: binary opposition remains an acute issue for the literary struggle in both the late-Soviet as well as the post-Soviet periods. This fact, however, is not a pessimistic view of the future of Russian literature. Despite the attempts of various authors (Akunin, Pelevin, Ulitskaya, and Zhvanetsky, to name a few) to construct such middle ground, Russian literature of the 1980s to 2000s failed to build a foundation of valid cultural opposition to its traditional binary model of cultural reasoning. The development of Russian literature in the post-Soviet period externalized the concealed conflicts of the Soviet period and added new confrontations to existing ones. As a result, contemporary Russian writing remains explosive and conflictual, filled with passion and antagonism. Russian writing is anything but unconventional—which paradoxically may serve as the best proof of the persistence and the indestructibility of traditions that have secured the originality and the greatness of Russian literature since Pushkin.

—Mark Lipovetsky
and Marina Balina

Acknowledgments

This book was produced by Bruccoli Clark Layman, Inc. Patricia Hswe was the in-house editor.

Production manager is Philip B. Dematteis.

Administrative support was provided by Ann M. Cheschi and Carol A. Cheschi.

Accountant is Ann-Marie Holland.

Copyediting supervisor is Sally R. Evans. The copyediting staff includes Phyllis A. Avant, Caryl Brown, Leah M. Cutsinger, Melissa D. Hinton, Philip I. Jones, Rebecca Mayo, and Nancy E. Smith.

Editorial associates are Amelia B. Lacey, Michael S. Martin, Catherine M. Polit, and William Mathes Straney.

In-house prevetting is by Nicole A. La Rocque.

Permissions editor and database manager is Amber L. Coker.

Layout and graphics supervisor is Janet E. Hill. The graphics staff includes Zoe R. Cook and Sydney E. Hammock.

Office manager is Kathy Lawler Merlette.

Photography supervisor is Paul Talbot. Photography editor is Scott Nemzek.

Digital photographic copy work was performed by Joseph M. Bruccoli.

Systems manager is Donald Kevin Starling.

Typesetting supervisor is Kathleen M. Flanagan. The typesetting staff includes Patricia Marie Flanagan, Mark J. McEwan, and Pamela D. Norton. Freelance typesetter is Rebecca Mayo.

Walter W. Ross did library research. He was assisted by Jo Cottingham and the following librarians at the Thomas Cooper Library of the University of South Carolina: circulation department head Tucker Taylor; reference department head Virginia W. Weathers; reference department staff Brette Barron, Marilee Birchfield, Paul Cammarata, Gary Geer, Michael Macan, Tom Marcil, Rose Marshall, and Sharon Verba; interlibrary loan department head John Brunswick; and interlibrary loan staff Robert Arndt, Hayden Battle, Alex Byrne, Bill Fetty, Marna Hostetler, and Nelson Rivera.

Dictionary of Literary Biography® • Volume Two Hundred Eighty-Five

Russian Writers
Since 1980

Dictionary of Literary Biography

Boris Akunin
(Grigorii Shalvovich Chkhartishvili)
(20 May 1956 –   )

Konstantine Klioutchkine
Pomona College

BOOKS: *Azazel'* (Moscow: Zakharov, 1998; enlarged, 2000); translated by Andrew Bromfield as *The Winter Queen* (London: Weidenfeld & Nicolson, 2003; New York: Random House, 2003);

Turetskii gambit (Moscow: Zakharov, 1998; enlarged, 2000);

Leviafan (Moscow: Zakharov, 1998);

Smert' Akhillesa (Moscow: Zakharov, 1998);

Osobye porucheniia (Moscow: Zakharov, 1999);

Statskii sovetnik (Moscow: Zakharov, 1999);

Pisatel' i samoubiistvo, as Grigorii Chkhartishvili (Moscow: Novoe literaturnoe obozrenie, 1999);

Koronatsiia, ili, Poslednii iz romanov (Moscow: Zakharov, 2000);

Pelagiia i belyi bul'dog (Moscow: Zakharov, 2000);

Altyn-tolobas (St. Petersburg: Neva / Moscow: OLMA, 2000);

Skazki dlia idiotov (St. Petersburg: Neva / Moscow: OLMA, 2000);

Chaika: Komediia i ee prodolzhenie (Jerusalem: Gesharim / Moscow: Mosty kul'tury, 2000);

Liubovnik smerti (Moscow: Zakharov, 2001);

Liubovnitsa smerti (Moscow: Zakharov, 2001);

Pelagiia i chernyi monakh (Moskva: AST, Astrel', 2001);

Vneklassnoe chtenie, 2 volumes (Moscow: OLMA, 2002).

PLAY PRODUCTIONS: *Chaika,* Moscow, Shkola sovremennoi p'esy, 26 April 2001;

Erast Fandorin, Moscow, Rossiiskii akademicheskii molodezhnyi teatr, 2 June 2002.

Boris Akunin (Grigorii Shalvovich Chkhartishvili)
(photograph © Eberhard Schorr)

PRODUCED SCRIPT: *Azazel'*, television, ORT, 10 March 2002.

TRANSLATIONS: *Doroga k zamku: Sovremennaia iaponskaia novella* (Moscow: Izvestiia, 1987);

Seiichi Morimura, *Ispytanie zveria* (Moscow: Raduga, 1989);

Ubiitsvo na Rozovoi ville: Sovremennyi iaponskii detektiv (Moscow: Raduga, 1990);

Yukio Mishima, *Izbrannoe,* compiled and translated, with an introduction, by Chkhartishvili (Moscow: Terra, 1996);

Tikamatsu Mondzaemon and others, *Iaponskii teatr,* translated, with an introduction and commentary, by Chkhartishvili (St. Petersburg: Severo-Zapad, 1997);

Iaponskie dzuikhitsu (St. Petersburg: Severo-Zapad, 1998);

Mishima, *Ispoved' maski* (St. Petersburg: Simpozium, 2000);

Mishima, *Markiz de Sad* (St. Petersburg: Azbuka, 2000);

Mishima, *Zolotoi khram* (St.Petersburg: Simpozium, 2000).

SELECTED PERIODICAL PUBLICATIONS–UNCOLLECTED: Malcolm Bradbury, *Professor Kriminale,* translated by Grigorii Chkhartishvili, V. Kuz'minsky, and N. Stavrovskaia, *Izvestina,* 1 (1995): 5–187;

Peter Ustinov, *Starik i mister Smit,* translated by Chkhartishvili, *Inostrannaia literatura,* 7 (1996): 65–145;

"Gamlet. Versiia: Tragediia v dvukh aktakh," *Novyi mir,* 6 (2002).

The name Boris Akunin arrived on the Russian literary scene in 1998 with a force little precedented in the post-Soviet history of the country. After publishing more than ten full-length books in the next three years, Akunin was established as one of the most widely read writers in Russia. Critics have attributed his success to the opening of a new territory in contemporary Russian letters; during the first years after the collapse of the Soviet Union, Russian writing became polarized between sophisticated prose for highbrow readers and "sex-and-violence" pulp for the mass audience. Largely on his own, Akunin created a middle ground by writing novels widely described as "pulp for the intellectuals." In a country where reading has often been associated with cultural distinction–yet where few have the time and sensibility to tackle demanding texts–the marriage of entertainment and intellectualism received a broad welcome. The success of Akunin's project has far-reaching implications not only for literature and culture but also for Russian politics and national identity. His works compel a contemporary recognition of Russian literary classics and at the same time fashion popular material for the reevaluation of Russian history. They prompt a rediscovery of political programs that were available in the past and model moral dilemmas facing its citizens in a new national environment.

The fascinating detective plots of Akunin's novels unfold in the last third of the nineteenth century and draw on classical works of Russian literature. Akunin's main characters combine the traits of detective characters from European Victorian fiction, from Edgar Allan Poe's Auguste Dupin to Sir Arthur Conan Doyle's Sherlock Holmes, with those of Russian literary characters, from Mikhail Iur'evich Lermontov's Grigorii Pechorin to Fyodor Dostoevsky's Prince Myshkin. His protagonists encounter complex puzzles of crime and face profound ethical dilemmas in a world populated by historical figures occupying important government positions; by fictional ideologues eloquently articulating views on Russian politics and national identity; and by a score of less notable, but always lively, figures.

Akunin's work has occasioned spirited discussion in newspapers and journals and on the Internet. Such debates will likely continue, as the publication dates for Akunin's new works, as well as for the motion-picture versions of his novels, are announced. On the strength of his growing popularity, in 2000 he was short-listed for the Smirnoff/Booker Prize (formerly the Booker Russian Novel Prize), the most prestigious literary award in the country. Failing to receive this award, however, he was given the Anti-Booker Prize (established in 1995 in response to the creation of the elite Booker Russian Novel Prize) in 2000 as the best fiction writer of the year. The Association of Russian Journalists also named Akunin writer of the year in 2000. He has garnered international acclaim, and his novels have been translated into European languages and Japanese.

Akunin was born Grigorii Shalvovich Chkhartishvili in Tbilisi, Georgia, on 20 May 1956. Within a year of his birth, his family moved to Moscow, and–by Akunin's own later admission–he lost all connection with his birthplace, adopting the Russian capital in lieu of his motherland, Georgia. As a child, Chkhartishvili was fascinated by Kabuki theater and developed an interest in Japanese culture. In the early 1970s he entered the Institute of Asia and Africa at the University of Moscow and, after graduating, worked as a translator of scientific literature. Little creative work was possible in the cultural climate of the Soviet Union in the 1970s and early 1980s, a period that, in retrospect, Akunin subsequently described as profoundly boring more than anything else. Chkhartishvili did, however, publish scholarly essays on Japanese literature and found diversion translating Japanese- and English-language fiction, including the works of Yukio

Mishima, Kobo Abe, Malcolm Bradbury, and Peter Ustinov. His literary translations could not be published until the political situation changed drastically during the era of Mikhail Sergeevich Gorbachev.

In the much more permissive atmosphere of glasnost, Chkhartishvili's scholarly and translation work began to receive public recognition. Shortly after joining *Inostrannaia literatura* (Foreign Literature), a major literary journal, he assumed the highly prestigious position of deputy editor in charge of oriental literature there. An important periodical of the Soviet era, *Inostrannaia literatura* served as the main channel for information about world culture. The ethos of enlightenment at the journal—conceived in the traditional spirit of the Russian intelligentsia—was shared by Chkhartishvili and remains an emphatic aspect of his work.

Toward the second half of the 1990s Chkhartishvili—as he later admitted—found himself in an existential crisis. Its fruit was the book *Pisatel' i samoubiistvo* (The Writer and Suicide), released in 1999 by Novoe literaturnoe obozrenie, a well-regarded publisher of works in the humanities. While devoted to a problem of much personal significance to Chkhartishvili, *Pisatel' i samoubiistvo* is also aimed at a popular audience. The book summarizes various theories on the social affliction of suicide, collects basic data on the topic, and offers brief biographies of literary suicides. The intention of this popular essay is not to generate profound or original philosophical insight but, rather, to amass valuable information, on the basis of which readers can make their own ethical choices. The salient feature of the book is the exceedingly tactful, albeit firm, way in which Chkhartishvili espouses his views—a manner of presentation indicative of his own ideology. An agnostic, Chkhartishvili believes that each individual has the right to make any decision whatsoever on the matter of suicide, provided that he does not impose his views on others. The restrained delivery, the firm division between private and public spheres, and the emphasis on individual values—while nothing out of the ordinary in Western culture—make the book distinctive in the Russian context. It is, in the vein of Aleksandr Isaevich Solzhenitsyn, more resonant with forceful articulations of personal ideologies intended for universal public acceptance. *Pisatel' i samoubiistvo* ultimately constitutes a moderate enlightenment project reminiscent of the work of Nikolai Mikhailovich Karamzin, the late-eighteenth- to early-nineteenth-century Russian writer whose name is mentioned early in the text.

Chkhartishvili's book about suicide proved difficult, and for amusement, before *Pisatel' i samoubiistvo* was published, he decided to write a detective novel. From an early age he was fond of composing stories, and

writing a novel came easily. Some two or three months after embarking on the novel, Chkhartishvili offered the manuscript for *Azazel'* (1998; translated as *The Winter Queen*, 2003) to an up-and-coming publisher, Igor' Valentinovich Zakharov, who himself has since achieved controversial success by straddling the boundary between high literature and mass fare. The novel, the first that Chkhartishvili wrote and published as Akunin, was sufficiently successful to warrant the writing of a sequel, whose publication brought Akunin further exposure. With every sequel Akunin's popularity grew exponentially, each installment requiring additional printings. The ultimate marker of Akunin's success was the appearance of *Altyn-tolobas* (Altyn-tolobas) in 2000; OLMA-Press, a major Russian commercial publishing house, produced a print run of 250,000 copies—a surprisingly high number for a book of fiction in Russia—that turned out to be insufficient, and the novel quickly went into new printings.

All of Chkhartishvili's fictional works have been published under the pseudonym Akunin; the ostensible purpose of the pen name was to deflect potential reprimands from academic peers. Yet, the implications of Chkhartishvili's recourse to the pseudonym went much further than a mere attempt at anonymity. The mystery surrounding the author of these detective novels (until he made public his real name) had contributed to their success. More important, in adopting a suggestive pseudonym, Chkhartishvili commenced the cultural project of creating an author of a new type in Russian literature. The initial and surname "B. Akunin" is richly symbolic: read as a single word, it spells the name of the well-known nineteenth-century Russian (as well as European) rebel Mikhail Aleksandrovich Bakunin. From a classical Marxist perspective, Bakunin—who participated in the French revolutions of 1848 and 1870—was a bourgeois revolutionary. Chkhartishvili's project was thus conceived as a kind of bourgeois revolution in literature benefiting readers in middle-class professions. Another implication of the pen name relates to its meaning in Japanese. Defined as "evil person," the pseudonym "Akunin" is consonant with the violence that the author renders in his fiction by reinterpreting events from Russian cultural, political, and social history. These reinterpretations are especially insidious in Akunin's case because the high entertainment value of his texts conceals the author's manipulation of the Russian past from his readers.

Akunin's first novel, *Azazel'*, published when he was forty-two, encompasses many of the ingredients of his later work. The story begins in Moscow in May 1876, the month when Anna Karenina—in Leo Tolstoy's eponymous novel (1875–1877)—commits suicide just outside the city. The first chapter of *Azazel'* draws

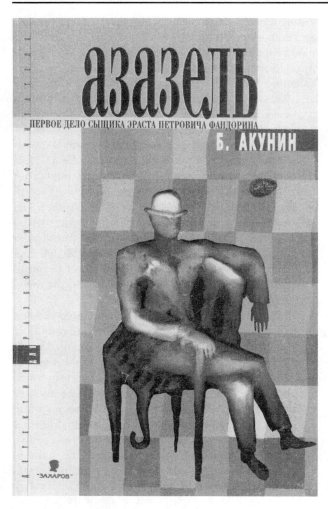

Paperback cover for Akunin's Azazel' *(1998; translated as* The Winter Queen, *2003), the first of his detective novels, featuring Erast Petrovich Fandorin as the crime-solving protagonist (Duke University Library)*

refreshing naiveté in dealing with central existential issues is reminiscent of Prince Myshkin in Dostoevsky's *Idiot* (1868); and Fandorin's looks, sense of style, and touch of the demonic hark back to Pechorin in Lermontov's *Geroi nashego vremeni* (A Hero of Our Time, 1840).

At the beginning of the book, Fandorin is employed as a minor clerk in a police department and busily writes official correspondence on behalf of a superior officer. He quickly overcomes, however, the stigma of the little man in Russian literature—along the lines of Akakakii Akakievich Bashmachkin from Nikolai Vasil'evich Gogol's short story "Shinel" (The Overcoat, 1842) or Makar Devushkin from Dostoevsky's novella *Bednye liudi* (Poor Folk, 1846)—and begins to show initiative and determination. These qualities quickly place Fandorin in a broader world, in which he deals with international political developments; universal, moral, and philosophical problems; and issues of Russian national identity.

In *Azazel'*, Fandorin uncovers an international conspiracy. Its mastermind, Lady Ester, directs an orphanage from which, by virtue of her educational prowess, she turns out highly trained members for a secret society that penetrates world governments in order to put into practice a humanitarian program. The road to this goal, however, is paved with the bodies of innocent victims. Fandorin's destruction of this conspiracy comes at a human price—the children for whom the society cared are left to beg on the street. Owing to Akunin's mastery of the detective genre, the treatment of this moral conundrum of Dostoevskian proportions is never oppressive or tedious in the novel. Akunin's skills appear through a precise and clear style, as well as through an artful balance between the development of a complex, compelling plot and brief digressions that heighten the feeling of suspense by retarding the pace of the narrative. In addition, Akunin avoids the seriousness inappropriate to the genre by tactfully reining in the scope of his character's goals. Rather than striving to arrive at universal solutions, Fandorin focuses only on his personal choices in the face of overbearing moral dilemmas. His superior intellect is tested not only by the perplexities of the detective case but also by the complexity of human problems, in which Fandorin's goal is to preserve personal ethical integrity.

With *Turetskii Gambit* (The Turkish Gambit, 1998), the Fandorin series moves to the theater of the war between Russia and Turkey in 1877. This novel comes closer to dealing with actual events in the history of Russia. While solving a case of wartime espionage, Fandorin finds himself at an important juncture in Russian history and begins to meet real historical figures, the identities of whom are veiled only slightly, since their pseudonyms are rather transparent. The novel

on the opening pages of Mikhail Afanas'evich Bulgakov's *Master i Margarita* (written, 1928–1940; published, 1966–1967): a typical everyday scene in a Moscow park, despite all its quietude, bears the premonition that something extraordinary is about to occur. The novelistic world of *Azazel'* continues building on reconstructions of an historical context mixed with allusions to Russian and European literary and cultural history. The richness of this mixture prompted critics to call Akunin "the Russian Umberto Eco." Erast Petrovich Fandorin, the main character of the novel, exemplifies this trend in combining the qualities of Sherlock Holmes with features reminiscent of Russian literary characters; Fandorin's deductive reasoning and investigative intuition in particular parallel those of Holmes. His determination and focus also recall Prince Andrei in Tolstoy's *Voina i mir* (War and Peace, 1868–1869); his

inaugurates the theme of responsibility for national disasters, a responsibility that lies largely with a tsarist government dominated by individuals who place personal agendas above national interests. Powerful government figures are juxtaposed with honest and hardworking civil servants reminiscent of Tolstoy's modest Captain Tushin from *Voina i mir*. Such characters, with their straightforward selflessness, fare badly in the world of large-scale corruption and intrigue.

In the next installment, titled *Leviafan* (Leviathan, 1998), Fandorin flees the disagreeable Russian milieu to assume a post at the Russian embassy in Japan. The title of the novel is derived from the name of the steamship on which Fandorin solves a murder case. With *Leviafan,* Akunin fulfills the promise (made when publishing the first of his novels) that the Fandorin series was to feature all variations of the detective genre. *Azazel'* was an example of the "conspiratorial" story, while *Turetskii Gambit* represented the "espionage" version. *Leviafan* exemplifies the "hermetic" subgenre, in which action is limited to a particular space—that is, the ship; in this sense, the novel appropriates the model best represented by Agatha Christie's *Murder on the Orient Express* (1934). On a philosophical level the title invokes Thomas Hobbes's *Leviathan, or, The Matter, Forme, & Power of a Common-Wealth Ecclesiasticall and Civill* (1651), although Akunin's novel exhibits little in the way of a theory of government. Instead, in bringing together characters from France, England, Japan, and Russia—characters who stand for the national identities of their countries—the novel addresses the national characteristics that determine personal self-government. *Leviafan* is more about the conduct of one's life rather than the conduct of state affairs.

The next novel, *Smert' Akhillesa* (The Death of Achilles, 1998), corresponds to the "murder-for-hire" subgenre and jumps four years ahead to 1882, when Fandorin returns to Moscow on the day of the assassination of General Sobolev, who first appeared in *Turetskii Gambit;* the historical prototype for Sobolev is the distinguished General Mikhail Dmitrievich Skobelev, who had leading roles in the Russian conquest of Turkistan and in the Russo-Turkish War (waged from 1877 to 1878). The novel features other famous historical personalities (whose identities in the novel are hidden behind pseudonyms that are similar to their actual names): Grand Duke Vladimir Aleksandrovich (brother of Tsar Aleksandr III); the governor of Moscow, Prince Vladimir Andreevich Dolgorukov; and the chief of the Moscow Gendarmerie, Sergei Vasil'evich Zubatov. While the novel questions the role of the ruling class in Russian history, the plethora of historical detail available for identification by the reader

also turns *Smert' Akhillesa* into a kind of board game for Akunin's more knowledgeable readership.

Smert' Akhillesa was followed by *Osobye porucheniia* (Special Assignments, 1999), which comprises two stories—*Pikovyi valet* (The Jack of Spades) and *Dekorator* (The Decorator). These two narratives employ, respectively, the "embezzlement" and "psychopath" subgenres (in the latter story Akunin has Jack the Ripper end his career in Moscow). The stories of *Osobye porucheniia* inaugurate the metafictional trend typical of Akunin's shorter pieces by way of an indirect commentary on the nature of his art. The descriptions of the villains in these stories hint at Akunin's methods of writing. The embezzler in *Pikovyi valet* displays a lively imagination in creating sophisticated scams and in this way resembles Akunin in his creation of complex plots. The murderer in *Dekorator* is obsessed with cutting up and reorganizing the bodies of his victims, just as Akunin dissects and recomposes canonical texts of Russian literature.

Another significant new element in these stories is the greater attention given to the characterization of the villains, who—in their criminal activities—change identities and switch between simulated personalities. The resulting complexity has important parallels in Akunin's work as a whole. Like his criminal characters, Akunin's postmodern writing is never quite equal to itself as it incessantly simulates a variety of literary models. For the sophisticated reader, Akunin's fiction is not about plots and characters but about the process of conjuring up a complex network of citations from Russian cultural history. The ultimate goal of this process is not to pass new judgment on historical events but to revive them in the cultural memory by turning them into material for a literary game. Another important implication lies in the assumption of different identities by the villains; occupying various positions in the Russian social spectrum, the criminals are able to articulate different perspectives on the meaning of Russian history. Akunin's work as a whole is similarly remarkable for articulating various opinions on the Russian past without giving clear priority to any one view. In this sense his writing approximates Dostoevsky's ideological novels. Yet, he significantly departs from Dostoevsky in his ultimate message transmitted via his main character. Fandorin believes that in a complex and disorganized world, the central task of an individual is the attempt to make one's own life as orderly and harmonious as possible.

After the metafictional digression of *Osobye porucheniia,* Akunin returned to an investigation of key themes in Russian history in his next two novels. *Statskii sovetnik* (Council to the State, 1999), a story about a political crime, concerns the struggle between terrorists and the

Russian police. The resolute and unyielding terrorist hero, reminiscent of the superman Rakhmetov from Nikolai Gavrilovich Chernyshevsky's *Chto delat'?* (What Is to Be Done?, 1863), is juxtaposed with the intellectually refined but profoundly corrupt state agents. In confronting the crimes, Fandorin is caught fighting on two fronts. At the end he has to make a difficult personal choice as he comes under pressure to assume the position of the chief of Moscow police at the price of complicitous participation in government intrigues. He chooses to resign from service and becomes a private investigator in the style of Sherlock Holmes. *Statskii sovetnik* is perhaps the most anachronistic of all of Akunin's novels. The action is set in 1893, by which time terrorist activity, rampant in the 1870s and early 1880s, has been crushed. Whereas the novel met with criticism that questioned its historical accuracy, its anachronism served to convey an important point: Akunin's writing is not a history but a collection of tales on the cultural myths of Russia's past.

The ostensibly fictional status of Akunin's work is again apparent in *Koronatsiia, ili, Poslednii iz romanov* (The Coronation, or, The Last of the Novels, 2000). Featuring a high-society crime and returning the Fandorin series to the topics of Russian identity and Russian history, this novel offers an intensely fictional description of the events that triggered the Khodynka tragedy, when scores of people died in a stampede during the coronation of Nicholas II. The thematic focus of the novel is the historical role of the tsarist family, whose members are easily recognizable in the fictional characters. The helpless and innocent victim closely resembles Nicholas's hemophiliac son, Alexis, while the uncles of the tsar are patterned after the Grand Dukes Sergei Aleksandrovich and Aleksandr Mikhailovich. The portrait of the family is highly unflattering: while the tsar utterly fails to overcome the weakness of his character, one of his uncles incessantly strives for power and the other pursues a life of dissipation. Despite these personal differences, the family as a whole is more concerned about its public image than about the fate of its members or that of the Russian people. The novel suggests that the blame for the disastrous events lies squarely with the government and the royal family, who had the power but not the will to take Russia along a different historical course. Yet, the link between the end of the imperial period and the conclusion of the Fandorin series points at the affection of the author for what was the most prosperous time, both economically and culturally, in the history of Russia.

After devoting himself exclusively for two years to the "Adventures of Erast Fandorin," the series name for Akunin's detective novels, Akunin introduced two new series of novels. One series opened with *Pelagiia i*

belyi bul'dog (Pelagiia and the White Bulldog, 2000), which reconfigured some familiar ingredients: the detective is a nun reminiscent of Christie's Miss Marple and G. K. Chesterton's Father Brown. While the historical period is the same as the Fandorin series, the setting is a distant Russian province beyond the Volga River; *Pelegiia i belyi bul'dog* thus belongs to the "provincial story" subgenre of detective novels, like the works of Christie and Doyle. Continuing to draw on actual, major historical characters, Akunin relies even more heavily on the Russian literary tradition with an ethnographic tone borrowed from Nikolai Semenovich Leskov that came to dominate a range of nineteenth-century Russian styles. In addition, Akunin derives less from Doyle and more from Wilkie Collins and Christie; in fact, Collins's gothic aura exerts a substantial influence over the novel. The plot develops more slowly than in the earlier novels—on the one hand, imitating the more sedate pace of provincial life and, on the other, allowing for more extended digressions into matters of Russian national identity. The views and behavior of a major positive character, Bishop Mitrofanius (inspired by Leskov's accounts of Russian monastic life, as in his novel *Sobriane* [Cathedral Folk, 1872]), constitute a program of national development, applicable to the present day. This program, seemingly shared by the author, envisions gradual social evolution on the basis of a compromise between Russian national specificity and the achievements of Western European civilization.

The second novel in the Pelagiia series, titled *Pelagiia i chernyi monakh* (Pelagiia and the Black Monk, 2001), departs in a significant compositional way from Akunin's earlier work yet continues to include new aspects of stock historical and literary themes established in Akunin's previous writing. The new aspect of the novel is the much greater freedom with which Akunin approaches his material. The novel is set on monastery lands that closely resemble the famous Valaam Island in northern Russia. The monks are in the process of building a utopian society confined within the borders of a single island, to paraphrase Stalin's dictum about the construction of "socialism within one country." This male utopia realizes the misogynist implications of early Soviet ideology. The key differences, however, are the capitalist methods used in the construction of the new society. This curious mix of the monastic context, Bolshevik ideology, and capitalist economics would have appeared outlandish had it not drawn on the real aspirations of Russian culture at the beginning of the twentieth century.

A similarly unexpected concatenation of elements embraces the literary allusions of the novel. The text is populated with grotesque shadows of actual literary characters who live in a psychiatric asylum that rents land from the monastery. The asylum is ruled by a physician named Korovin, who sets in motion the themes of Bulgakov's *Master i Margarita*. Korovin's progressive institution allows its patients a sense of complete freedom. These patients include Lev Nikolaevich, who resembles not only Tolstoy (in first name and patronymic especially) but also Prince Myshkin from Dostoevsky's *Idiot;* a mad physicist whose appearance reminds the reader of the character of the Devil from Bulgakov's novel; and a femme fatale inspired by Dostoevsky's Nastas'ia Filippovna Barashkova, also from *Idiot*. In addition, there are two Stavrogins from Dostoevsky's *Besy* (The Possessed, 1872), and further parallels can be drawn between Akunin's characters and the Karamazov brothers (from Dostoevsky's *Brat'ia Karamazovy* [The Brothers Karamazov], 1879–1880). The lives of this motley collection of characters are haunted by the mysterious presence of the black monk, a phantom figure that Akunin borrowed from Anton Pavlovich Chekhov's story of the same name "Chernyi monakh" (The Black Monk, 1893). By bringing these literary figures into his novel, Akunin exposes the principles upon which his writing has always relied. Although this move conclusively undermines any claims to the historicity of the novel, it also enables Akunin to recast pivotal themes from the history of Russian culture in new and more pointed ways. Structurally, his most impressive feat lies in his ability to construct a consistent detective narrative within this cultural mayhem. As always, the highly suspenseful story involves several subplots as well as a series of false denouements, unexpectedly exposing the ultimate villain only in the last pages.

Before writing the sequel to the first Pelagiia novel, Akunin began another new series with *Altyn-tolobas*. Although it extends greatly the scope of Akunin's engagement with Russian history, a main thread of his detective series, *Altyn-tolobas* nonetheless diverges significantly from his earlier works. It features parallel adventure narratives, one set in pre-Petrine Russia and the other in the Russian Federation of the turn of the twenty-first century. Downplaying the detective aspect of the novel, Akunin places the action and adventure elements of the plot in the foreground. Critics unanimously observed that in *Altyn-tolobas* Akunin jettisoned the intellectual aspirations of earlier works to target his skills at the broadest possible audience. One of the more striking characteristics of the novel is the sense that whereas pre-Petrine Russia was badly in need of a civilizing Western influence, post-Soviet Russia (that is, Russia today) is not as gloomy as the majority of the population seems to believe. Indeed, the optimism of the book is quite distinctive in contemporary Russian

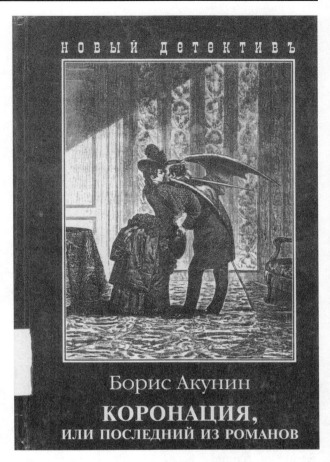

Front cover for Akunin's Koronatsiia, ili, Poslednii iz romanov *(The Coronation, or, The Last of the Novels, 2000), in which Fandorin takes on a high-profile criminal case involving the tsar's family (Jean and Alexander Heard Library, Vanderbilt University)*

literature, which is dominated by a despondent, if not altogether apocalyptic, mood.

Along with these novels, Akunin has also published many shorter pieces in magazines and on the Internet. A series of such pieces was collected in the book *Skazki dlia idiotov* (Tales for Idiots, 2000). While these stories are remarkable for their lively satirical treatment of the contemporary realities of Russian political life, they also provide the reader with an indirect commentary on how Akunin's earlier texts were created. The same function is served by Akunin's continuation of Chekhov's four-act play *Chaika* (The Seagull, 1896), to which Akunin added two new acts. In Akunin's version, however, the suicide at the end of Chekhov's play turns into murder, and in the additional acts each character gradually is proven guilty of the crime. The playful rewriting of Chekhov's drama is a showcase of Akunin's narrative devices and his literary skill.

The positive critical reception of Akunin's writings—and their popularity with readers in Russia—contributed greatly to his success. Subsequently, however, this enthusiastic response gave way to controversies concerning the ideology, historical accuracy, pecuniary implications, and other richly problematic aspects of his writing. These controversies have made the author even more popular.

Perhaps the most notable critique of Akunin's work has come from Roman Arbitman, who warned about what he saw as the dangerous ideological implications of a new brand of entertainment. In the review "Bumazhnyi oplot prianichnoi derzhavy" (A Paper Foundation of the Honey-Cake State), published in the journal *Znamia* (The Banner) in 1999, Arbitman argues that the detective facade of Akunin's novels conceals a Russophile ideology residing in the cultural myth that the smooth operation of the monarchic government was the reason for national achievement during the imperial period in Russia. He writes that Akunin's fiction juxtaposes the good Russia, personified to a large extent by Fandorin, with the evil outside influences represented by criminals of foreign extraction. This critique came out after Akunin's first four novels—before the evil forces that Fandorin encounters within Russia and its government force him to abandon the service of the state. Although Arbitman's conclusions suffer from exaggeration, his observations do reflect an important feature of Akunin's fictional world, in which social change, ideas, and narrative development usually come from the top of the social hierarchy, while the broad masses at the bottom are powerless, if not always mute.

Arbitman's critique brings out another distinctive feature of Akunin's fictional universe. Whereas the critic envisions a dual world, which breaks down along the binary opposition of pro- and anti-Russian attitudes, Akunin's world adheres rather to a tripartite model, which allows for a middle ground between the ideological extremes. Ideological extremes are less important in his novels than the behavior of the central characters, who must make personal decisions that fail to satisfy a rigorous moral scrutiny. His most interesting characters, which include mainly detectives, gravitate toward the center of the social spectrum and have no choice but to live with compromise.

Like many aspects of Akunin's novels, this tripartite approach to life has an identifiable point of reference. In *Pelagüa i chernyi monakh* Bishop Mitrofanius attempts to escape a dual view of the world by discussing the differences between Catholicism and Orthodoxy. Unlike Orthodoxy, which imagines the afterlife as divided between the spheres of heaven and hell, "Catholicism also envisions Purgatory because there

are very few people who are entirely good or bad." While the bishop's view finds certain correspondences with Western Christianity in early-twentieth-century Russia, Akunin's reference is rather to the landmark article "Rol' dual'nykh modelei v russkoi kul'ture" (Binary Models in Russian Culture, 1977), published in *Uchenye zapiski Tartuskogo universiteta* by Iurii Mikhailovich Lotman and Boris Andreevich Uspensky. Lotman and Uspensky drew on the same opposition between the Western and Eastern Churches to suggest that the calamitous paths of Russian history stemmed from the lack of a middle ground in Russian culture. Chkhartishvili's cultural project in writing novels as Akunin can be seen as an attempt to construct such middle ground, beginning with Russian literature.

In the early years of the twenty-first century the popularity of Boris Akunin's name rests on the major literary achievements of and cultural discoveries by Grigorii Chkhartishvili. With their precise style, well-balanced composition, and an acute awareness of readers' expectations, the novels that Chkartishvili has written as Akunin set a precedent for professionalism in Russian literature, the renown of which originates largely in the irreverent attitudes that Russian writers exhibit toward formal and professional concerns. While Akunin's multidimensional texts are designed to entertain diverse readers, his literary project goes a long way toward his stated goal of enlightenment—that of creating a social category of middle-class professionals who are also readers. To the members of this class, Akunin brings the history of European and Russian prerevolutionary culture in a respectable and entertaining literary form. This cultural project has been quite successful, as the new middle-class professionals have appreciated Akunin's fiction. Yet, the final critical evaluation of Akunin's work will likely depend on whether other writers come to occupy the cultural space he founded and whether the success of his project affects the course of Russian literature. Regardless of the outcome, however, there is little doubt that Akunin has achieved a permanent place in the annals of Russian culture.

Interviews:

[Interviews with Akunin] <http://www.fandorin.ru/akunin/interviews.html> [accessed 10 June 2003].

References:

The Boris Akunin Page <www.akunin.ru> [accessed 10 June 2003];

The Erast Fandorin Page <http://www.fandorin.ru> [accessed 10 June 2003];

Georgii Tsiplakov, "Zlo, voznikaiushchee v doroge, i dao Érasta," *Novyi mir,* 11 (2001).

Petr Markovich Aleshkovsky

(22 September 1957 –   )

Valentina G. Brougher
Georgetown University

BOOKS: *Kak novgorodtsy na Iugru khodili: Rasskaz o novgorodtsakh – otvazhnykh moreplavateliakh XII v.,* with drawings by G. Iudin (Moscow: Malysh, 1988);

Stargorod. Golosa iz khora (Moscow: Sabashnikovy, 1995);

Arlekin. Istoricheskii roman (Moscow: Radiks, 1995);

Vladimir Chigrintsev (Moscow: Vagrius, 1997);

Sed'moi chemodanchik. Povesti i rasskazy (Moscow: Vagrius, 1999)—comprises "Sed'moi chemodanchik," *Zhizneopisanie khor'ka,* "O pol'ze sotovykh telefonov," "Taksist i Zolushka," and "Istoria o Prekrasnoi Zinaide."

Edition: *Arlekin* (Moscow: ARMADA, 1996).

Edition in English: *Skunk: A Life,* translated by Arch Tait (Moscow: Glas, 1997).

OTHER: [Autobiography], in *Pisateli Rossii: Avtobiografii sovremennikov,* edited by M. V. Voronov (Moscow: Glasnost', 1998), pp. 25–27.

SELECTED PERIODICAL PUBLICATIONS– UNCOLLECTED: "Chaiki," *Druzhba narodov,* 4 (1992): 9–83;

"Raz kartoshka, dva kartoshka," *Oktiabr',* 1 (1999): 160–175.

Petr Markovich Aleshkovsky (from the cover for Sed'moi chemodanchik, *1999; Collection of Valentina G. Brougher)*

Petr Aleshkovsky's interest in human psychology and his ability to craft an engaging tale and endow his writing with both a philosophical depth and a strong moral dimension follow in the tradition of Russian classical writing. His incorporation of folk beliefs and the mystical and irrational into his narratives, as well as his attention to history, are in concert with the literary dynamics and thematic preoccupations of the post-perestroika period. Although Aleshkovsky (a nephew of the writer Iosif Efimovich Aleshkovsky, also known as Iuz Aleshkovsky) began to be published only in the 1990s, he is already recognized as one of the most promising writers of the younger generation. His *povest',* or novella, *Zhizneopisanie khor'ka* (first published in the journal *Druzhba narodov* [The People's Friend-

ship], 1993; collected in book form, 1999; translated as *Skunk: A Life,* 1997) was short-listed for the Booker Russian Novel Prize in 1994, and his novel *Vladimir Chigrintsev* (first published in *Druzhba narodov,* 1995; collected in book form, 1997) was short-listed for the same prize in 1996.

Petr Markovich Aleshkovsky was born in Moscow on 22 September 1957. In his autobiographical piece published in *Pisateli Rossii: Avtobiografii sovremennikov* (The Writers of Russia: Autobiographies of Contemporaries, 1998), Aleshkovsky writes that he grew up in a Moscow apartment without a television, surrounded by the family's huge collection of books. His mother, Natal'ia Nedoshivina (Germonovna) Aleshkovskaia, worked in the State Museum of History and began to take him on archaeological expeditions when he was in the fifth grade. His father, Mark Khaimovich Aleshkovsky, was also an archaeologist, which influenced his son's decision to study history at Moscow State University. In his 1998 autobiography Aleshkovsky claims that he covered "half of Russia" by participating in various historical expeditions. After five years (1974–1979) at the university, he went to work in the restoration studios of the Andronikov Monastery in Moscow. He left after six years, concluding, again in his autobiography, that he did not want to "devote his life to restoring one or two churches." According to Aleshkovsky, fate and family connections brought him into contact with the publishing world. He credits his father-in-law, Natan Iakovlevich Eidel'man, a well-known scholar of nineteenth-century Russian history, with introducing him to editors and putting him on the road to becoming a writer. In 1982 Aleshkovsky married Tamara Natanovna Eidel'man, with whom he has two children.

Aleshkovsky's first published work, the novella "Chaiki" (Seagulls), which appeared in *Druzhba nardodov* in 1992, is set in a mythical old provincial town, Stargorod (literally, Old Town). As is true of the work of many Russian writers in the 1990s, Aleshkovsky seeds the biographies of his characters with details that serve as reminders of Soviet history and ideology. Several characters have spent time in labor camps. The experiences of two characters, Serezha and Pavel Ivanovich, at a Moscow art institute illuminate the ideological constraints placed on the arts in Soviet times and bring the question of artistic creativity and freedom to the forefront of the thematics of the novella. From his earliest years the main character, Serezha, has been unusual. He does not speak like other two-year-olds but chirps like the seagulls, who become his friends; he even claims to understand the seagulls' "simple, artless language." Aleshkovsky intensifies this image of a human being who stands apart from his peers when he depicts Serezha studying art in Moscow. Serezha believes that a sensitivity to nature, appreciated with all the senses, and freedom of the imagination are prerequisites for meaningful art; this attitude puts him at odds with his teachers, who insist on rules and conformity.

The other central character, Pavel Ivanovich, an artist who leaves Moscow for Stargorod to escape the ideological demands placed on his work, is Serezha's kindred spirit. A skilled restorer of icons, he plays old Russian music on the *gusli* (a zither-like instrument)—a

talent the authorities do not appreciate. He also fervently supports Serezha's desire for artistic freedom. Aleshkovsky's portrait of Pavel Ivanovich is resonant with the author's own experiences studying history at Moscow State University and working as a restorer of churches, as seen especially through the detailed descriptions of icons and restoration work in the novella. Various misunderstandings and coincidences involving icons intertwine the lives of various characters, at times informing "Chaiki" with elements of an eighteenth-century comedy of errors. Two local thieves steal icons from a monastery church; Serezha dreams of selling his mother's icons in Moscow to pay his debts; and Nadezhda, Serezha's girlfriend and mother of his child, shows quick thinking to save Serezha from falling victim to accusations that he has stolen church icons.

In addition, nature plays a prominent role in "Chaiki." Because of Aleshkovsky's talent for capturing the contours, colors, and sounds of the setting, the reader receives a vivid sense of the landscape through which Aleshkovsky's characters move. He uses nature to add a mystical, occultist coloring to the novella. For example, the death of the old man Aleksei Platonovich is depicted as a blending of his body and spirit with an old linden tree that had been his favorite. Nadezhda's desire to escape this world is captured in the image of her flying like a seagull above her home. A need to place his own angle on human reality and existence by drawing on Russian folklore and world mythology marks Aleshkovsky's other works as well.

The collection *Stargorod. Golosa iz khora* (Old Town. Voices from a Chorus, 1995) is actually a cycle of thirty narratives set in the same mythical provincial town as "Chaiki" and offers brief stories and vignettes about colorful, sometimes eccentric, characters. An old woman lives in an animal hole filled with money; a beggar who spent time in a Siberian prison is killed in an accident, and his icon begins to work miracles for the local populace; and a woman with a reputation for being a witch attributes her pregnancy to the devil, but the townspeople reject her claim although it is in keeping with her reputation. Aleshkovsky's portrayals of such townsfolk allow for different levels of reality, with superstitions and folk beliefs constituting a vital dimension of their lives. In populating Stargorod with a variety of personages and imbuing it with gossip, stories, and legends to give it a sense of identity and character, Aleshkovsky experiments with various narrative strategies and points of view. The most striking quality of his narratives in *Stargorod,* however, is their style and tone, which is generally chatty, friendly, and intimate. It reflects the lexicon, rhythm, and flavor typical of the conversational speech of people living in a small, provincial town. In his evaluation (published in the journal *Novyi mir* [New

Front cover for Vladimir Chigrintsev *(1997), a novel about several generations of the Derbetev family, from the era of Catherine the Great to the postperestroika years of 1990s Russia (Collection of Valentina G. Brougher)*

World], 1996) of Aleshkovsky's prose, the critic Vladimir Ivanovich Slavetsky singles out the writer's talent for stylized speech, arguing that it captures a vital dimension of the Russian national character.

The novella *Zhizneopisanie khor'ka,* as Aleksandr Arkhangel'sky points out in his review for the journal *Ural* in 1994, brought Aleshkovsky renown almost overnight. Its hero, whom Arkhangel'sky describes as someone who constantly changes his physical as well as inner space, is yet another strong, eccentric personality. Danny has earned the nickname "Skunk" from other children because of his appearance. The label is strangely appropriate. Early in life Skunk exhibits a wild animal's traits and instincts, which help him survive in the town of Stargorod (by now quite familiar to Aleshkovsky's readers). He is also a glutton, a loner, and a misfit who engages in unconscionable behavior. At one point in the novel, Skunk as a teenager takes vengeance on a local gang member by pushing him off

a roof to his death. Significantly, he feels no pangs of guilt. Aleshkovsky takes his hero through several stages of development, involving him in various escapades and adventures. After spending some time picking people's pockets and living on the outskirts of town like an animal, Skunk settles in an empty dacha deep in the forest. Here he is in his element, sharing his physical space only with the birds and animals who seemingly accept him as one of their own. When his isolation becomes a burden, a hunter comes along whose presence in the hut and eventual death on the horns of a gigantic elk bring Skunk out of his spiritual slumber. He stalks and kills the elk, and for the first time experiences feelings of both fear and guilt.

In the next stage of Skunk's physical and spiritual journey he is again in Stargorod, where he is forced to confront the impact of his past actions on others in the context of Russian Orthodox beliefs. He is brought to a trance-like state by the discoveries of a local legend about a rock on which St. Andronicus is said to have sailed from Rome to Stargorod; of church icons depicting the sufferings of sinners in hell; and of talk of the Second Coming and the Antichrist. In his mind's eye he escapes demons by seeking refuge on the St. Andronicus rock, which is venerated by the local people. After confessing his sins, he stays with Father Boris, who engages him in discourse on Orthodoxy and Catholicism and the role of pagan traditions, magic, and miracle in religious belief. Of some interest is the argument that Father Boris makes: that the Fourth Kingdom, as described in the Book of Daniel and the Book of Revelation, has already arrived—with Joseph Stalin, Adolf Hitler, the gulag, the atom bomb, and AIDS as concrete manifestations. Whether Aleshkovsky truly believes this argument, or is simply adding an apocalyptic dimension to his tale in accordance with a 1990s trend to do so, is difficult to say.

The last stage in Skunk's development finds him once more in the wilderness and brings him in touch with Father Innokentyi. The latter's life has a natural appeal for Skunk: the monk had retreated from the world of bureaucrats and the privileged to worship the beauty of nature as God's work and to serve a handful of worshipers. When the monk disappears, Skunk returns to town, this time to experience a kind of epiphany: lying cold and feverish on St. Andronicus's rock, he feels incomprehensible, mystical forces surging through him. By the time of the epilogue in Aleshkovsky's short novel, Skunk is living somewhere in the distant north of Russia—no longer atypical but, rather, closely resembling those around him. Yet, there is part of the old Skunk left in him still, for he continues to experience complete fulfillment only in the forest. Here, Aleshkovsky opts for a realistic ending. He suggests that the benefits of a spiritual journey are limited, and a person is ultimately unable to change his nature completely.

Aleshkovsky worked on *Arlekin* (Harlequin, first published in *Soglasie* [Consent], 1993–1994) from 1984 to 1988 and considered it the history dissertation that he never got to write, since he did not pursue graduate studies; the novel appeared in book form only in 1995. *Arlekin* tells the story of the poet Vasilii Kirillovich Trediakovsky (1703–1769), from his difficult, poor life in Astrakhan, where the Volga River empties into the Caspian Sea, to his position as official translator and poet in the Academy of Sciences and at the tsar's court in the 1730s. The last thirty years of Trediakovsky's life are covered briefly in an epilogue. The title of the novel, *Arlekin,* fits the poet's life quite well. It comes from the name of an Italian comedy in which the main character suffers a slap in the face but is forced to smile and pretend that nothing has happened. In the late

1730s Trediakovsky was brutally beaten by Cabinet Minister Artemii Petrovich Volynsky, yet was forced to come to court and read an ode that he had written for a special day of entertainment for Empress Anna. In the last decades of his life Trediakovsky did indeed become a "harlequin" of Russian letters, a man who suffered various humiliations and insults but nevertheless persisted in his work.

In his afterword to *Arlekin* Aleshkovsky discloses that he focused on available archival documents for guidance and inspiration, while his imagination filled in the details and brought people of the era to life. In fact, he intersperses the documents that he consulted throughout his narrative, including excerpts from state edicts, speeches, eulogies, newspaper reports, and letters, as well as translations and theoretical writings by Trediakovsky and other literary figures. According to Aleshkovsky, for example, Peter the Great and fate—or Fortuna—played key roles in Trediakovsky's departure from Astrakhan to study in Moscow. Trediakovsky's attendance at the Slavic-Greek-Latin Academy is given extensive attention in the text, as Aleshkovsky depicts in great detail the curriculum, discipline, school intrigues, and student life. At the academy Trediakovsky's ear, accustomed in Astrakhan to psalms and folk songs, becomes awakened to the rhythmic and melodic potential of language.

As Aleshkovsky shows, Trediakovsky also begins to develop an understanding of the complex and tangled relationship between politics and religion in eighteenth-century Russia, with Jesuits, Catholics, and Lutherans vying to change the religion of the country. Aleshkovsky provides a comprehensive portrait of the social atmosphere and political-religious dynamics in the European cities to which fate, apparently, sends the young Trediakovsky—cities such as The Hague, Hamburg, and Paris. Paying little attention to the costume, dress, or interiors of palaces and houses, which are often the staple of historical novels, Aleshkovsky is, rather, interested in the life of the heart and mind. He employs an omniscient narrator to capture Trediakovsky's intellectual and spiritual development and to keep the focus of the storytelling on the poet's inner life. This approach enables the reader to learn of Trediakovsky's reactions to friends, teachers, and famous men of letters; his thoughts on the literary polemics of the day, especially in France; his perceptions of academic, political, and religious intrigues; and the role he is frequently forced to play in order to survive. Although some dialogue figures into the narrative, it plays a relatively minor role.

Ultimately, Aleshkovsky depicts Trediakovsky as a tragic figure whose major flaw is his inability to allow that other men, such as Mikhail Vasil'evich Lomonosov, might be more perceptive and innovative than he in the development of Russian versification. Aleshkovsky nonetheless cannot bring himself to condemn Trediakovsky. Notes of admiration can be felt in Aleshkovsky's characterization of the poet as a talented individual who struggles with poverty his whole life but continues the work in which he so fervently believes. Consequently, in his lengthy review of *Arlekin,* Igor' Nikolaevich Kuznetsov charged that Aleshkovsky had "partly whitewashed" his subject.

Aleshkovsky's next book, *Vladimir Chigrintsev,* is a thematically rich novel, in which the lives of several generations of one family are placed in the context of Russian history. Through his use of folk beliefs and the occult, Aleshkovsky weaves a symbolic text for the reader to unravel. *Vladimir Chigrintsev* also features elements of the Gothic novel–such as vampires, a family curse, an old mansion, and hidden treasure–that add a dimension of suspense and intrigue to the plot. The action of the novel takes place both in Moscow and its countryside. The time span includes several centuries, from the second half of the eighteenth century to the post-perestroika period of the 1990s. Aleshkovsky relies on a system of symbols, allusions, and associations to comment on the essence of Russian life in the twentieth century.

Vladimir Chigrintsev depicts the life of the Derbetev family in different periods of Russian political and social history to suggest both continuity and change. In the eighteenth century, during the rule of Catherine the Great, Prince Derbetev fights against the peasant rebels led by Emel'ian Pugachev and comes to be associated with a legend about stolen treasure and a werewolf. After the Bolshevik Revolution, a descendant of the prince is forced to give up the family estate to the Soviets but stays on as its watchman, only to die in mysterious circumstances. In the 1990s, before Professor Derbetev dies of cancer, he gives his daughters some antique family jewelry (part of the old treasure?) and bemoans the "werewolf century" in which he lived. Finally, young Volia Chigrintsev, a relation of the professor who has studied history and now illustrates books, visits the old ruined Derbetev estate, where he has an unusual, troubling dream. The symbolism of Volia's dream identifies Stalin as the werewolf and vampire of the twentieth century. The dream also has an admonitory aspect: it suggests that Stalin is still a force propelling others and needs to be exorcised, like an unclean spirit, from Russian life–an exorcism that must be performed by historians, who now have the documents and archives for study.

Of some interest is the view of the United States, referred to as America, that Aleshkovsky presents in the novel. One of the professor's daughters, who calls

Front cover for Aleshkovsky's 1999 book, Sed'moi chemodanchik (The Seventh Little Suitcase), in which the title essay is an autobiographical narrative (Collection of Valentina G. Brougher)

Russia a swamp, has an idealistic view of America. But Aleshkovsky suggests that she and other members of her generation may have replaced the fairy tales of the old generation (Stalin as the Great Father and the Soviet Union as a land of equality and happiness for all, for example) with a fairy tale of their own. Perhaps the view that Larry, an American character in the story, has of Russia is meant to encapsulate its true history and character. Larry, who frequently travels to Russia on research and is a close friend of Volia and the Derbetev family, loves Russia. Yet, he feels sorry for it: he calls it a land of suffering and compassion.

Aleshkovsky's most recent book, *Sed'moi chemodanchik* (The Seventh Little Suitcase, 1999), which consists of one previously published novella, a new autobiographical narrative, and several short stories, reveals a writer who is able to structure his stories on the synergy between the past and the present and shows a talent for irony and satire. In the autobiographical narrative "Sed'moi chemodanchik," which gives the collection its name, Aleshkovsky offers an intimate look at his daily life, particularly his role as a reader as well as a creator of literature. He discusses world writers who have influenced him to look to the past—in the form of photos, postcards, documents, and family stories—and to bring the past to life through word and imagination. He "resurrects" ancestors and family members by organizing his memories into memorable portraits, rewrites an old legend his father used to tell him and gives it new significance, and makes himself a character in several realistic as well as surrealistic episodes. In the story "Raz kartoshka, dva kartoshka" (One Potato, Two Potatoes), for example, Aleshkovsky describes a trip to the Kola Peninsula, sharing his impressions of contemporary life in the towns and cities of the North. Other short stories in the volume blend characteristics of the fairy tale with details from contemporary Russian life. "O pol'ze sotovykh telefonov" (On the Use of Cell Phones) is a particularly humorous story about the devil and his adventures in 1990s Moscow and immediately brings to mind Mikhail Afanas'evich Bulgakov's novel *Master i Margarita* (The Master and Margarita, written during 1928–1940, published in 1966–1967), which depicts what happens when the devil visits Moscow in the 1930s.

Petr Markovich Aleshkovsky's interest in the history and literary heritage of Russia inspired his first book, the life story of Trediakovsky. This dual interest is also strongly present in his novel, *Vladimir Chi-grintsev,* which poses questions about the course of Russian history and the life of the intelligentsia under Soviet rule. Aleshkovsky is also a postmodern writer; exploring different levels of reality in *Zhizneopisanie khor'ka,* he skillfully centers the novella on a deeply alienated individual, the antithesis of the positive hero of Soviet times. Aleshkovsky's prose forms an important part of the literature being published in the new Russia, and critics voice disappointment when a year goes by without new work from him. This kind of attention suggests that Aleshkovsky has the potential for becoming a major writer.

References:

Aleksandr Arkhangel'sky, "Mtsyri enskogo uezda," *Ural,* 2–3 (1994): 241–242;

Pavel Basinsky, "Aleshkovsky Petr Mikhailovich," *Russkie pisateli 20 veka: Biograficheskii slovar',* edited by Petr Alekseevich Nikolaev (Moscow: Bol'shaia Rossiiskaia Entsiklopediia, 2000), pp. 22–23;

Basinsky, "Drugoi Aleshkovsky," *Novyi mir,* 3 (1994), pp. 241–242;

Valentina G. Brougher, "Werewolves and Vampires, Historical Questions and Symbolic Answers, in Petr Aleshkovsky's *Vladimir Chigrintsev,*" *Slavic and East European Journal,* 45, no. 3 (2001): 491–505;

Marya Setiukova, "Skromnoe oboianie realizma," *Literaturnaia gazeta,* 16 March 1994, p. 4;

Vladimir Ivanovich Slavetsky, "Restavratsia vedetsia," *Novyi mir,* 4 (1996): 224–228;

M. V. Voronov, ed., *Pisateli Rossii: Avtobiografii sovremennikov* (Moscow: Glasnost', 1998), pp. 23–27.

Joseph Brodsky
(Iosif Aleksandrovich Brodsky)
(24 May 1940 – 28 January 1996)

Alyssa Dinega Gillespie
University of Notre Dame

See also the Brodsky entry in *DLB Yearbook: 1987*.

BOOKS: *Stikhotvoreniia i poemy* (Washington, D.C. & New York: Inter-Language Literary Associates, 1965)–includes "Bol'shaia elegiia Dzhonu Donnu," "Evreiskoe kladbishche," "Glagoly," "Ia obnial eti plechi . . . ," "Isaak i Avraam," "Kholmy," "Oboz," "Piligrimy," "Stansy," "Vorotish'sia na rodinu . . . ," and "Vot ia vnov' posetil . . .";

Ostanovka v pustyne (New York: Izdatel'stvo imeni Chekhova, 1970; revised, Ann Arbor, Mich.: Ardis, 1989)–includes "Bol'shaia elegiia Dzhonu Donnu," "Derev'ia v moem okne . . . ," "Dlia shkol'nogo vozrasta," "Einem Alten Architekten in Rom," "Enei i Didona," "Glagoly," "Gorbunov i Gorchakov," "Ia obnial eti plechi . . . ," "Isaak i Abraam," "Kholmy," "K Likomedu, na Skiros," "Lomtik medovogo mesiatsa," "Novye stansy k Avguste," "Oboz," "Ot okrainy k tsentru," "Pis'mo v butylke," "Sonet," "Stikhi na smert' T. S. Eliota," "Strofy," "Prorochestvo," "Ty vyporkhnesh', malinovka . . . ," and "Vorotish' sia rodinu . . .";

Chast' rechi: Stikhotvoreniia 1972–76 (Ann Arbor, Mich.: Ardis, 1977)–includes "1972 god," "Odissei–Telemaku," "Sreten'e," and "Tors";

Konets prekrasnoi epokhi: Stikhotvoreniia 1964–71 (Ann Arbor, Mich.: Ardis, 1977)–includes "Natiurmort," "Post Aetatem Nostram," "Rech' o prolitom moloke," and "Vremia goda–zima . . .";

V Anglii (Ann Arbor, Mich.: Ardis, 1977);

A Part of Speech (New York: Farrar, Straus & Giroux, 1980)–includes "1972," "Nunc Dimittis," "Odysseus to Telemachus," "Six Years Later," and "Torso";

Rimskie elegii (New York: Russica, 1982);

Novye stansy k Avguste: Stikhi k M.B., 1962–1982 (Ann Arbor, Mich.: Ardis, 1983);

Mramor (Ann Arbor, Mich.: Ardis, 1984); translated by Alan Myers with Brodsky as *Marbles: A Play in*

Joseph Brodsky (photograph by Sergey Bermenyev; from the dust jacket for So Forth, *1996; Richland County Public Library)*

Three Acts (New York: Farrar, Straus & Giroux, 1989);

Less Than One: Selected Essays (New York: Farrar, Straus & Giroux, 1986)–includes "Flight from Byzantium," "A Guide to a Renamed City," "In a Room and a Half," and "Less Than One"; Russian version published as *Men'she edinitsy: Izbrannye esse* (Moscow: Nezavisimaia gazeta, 1999);

Uraniia (Ann Arbor, Mich.: Ardis, 1987)–includes "Biust Tiberiia," "Ia vkhodil vmesto dikogo zveria . . . ," and "Osennii krik iastreba";

To Urania (New York: Farrar, Straus & Giroux, 1988)–includes "The Bust of Tiberius," "Gorbunov and Gorchakov," "The Hawk's Cry in Autumn," and "May 24, 1980";

Fondamenta degli Incurabili, translated by Gilberto Forti (Venice: Consorzio Venezia nuova, 1989); English version published as *Watermark* (New York: Farrar, Straus & Giroux, 1992);

Primechaniia paporotnika (Bromma, Sweden: Hylaea, 1990);

Ballada o malen'kom buksire (Leningrad: Detskaia literatura, 1991);

Naberezhnaia neistselimykh. Trinadtsat' essei (Moscow: Slovo, 1992)–includes "Naberezhnaia neistselimykh" [incomplete version]; complete version in *Venetsianskie tetradi: Iosif Brodskii i drugie,* by Brodsky and others, compiled by Ekaterina Margolis (Moscow: Ob"edinennoe gumanitarnoe izdatel'stvo, 2002);

Sochineniia, 4 volumes, edited by Gennadii F. Komarov (St. Petersburg: Pushkinskii fond / Paris, Moscow & New York: Tret'ia volna, 1992–1995; enlarged edition, 8 volumes, St. Petersburg: Pushkinskii fond, 1998–);

Vspominaia Akhmatovu, by Brodsky and Solomon Volkov (Moscow: Nezavisimaia gazeta, 1992);

Kappadokiia (St. Petersburg, 1993);

Persian Arrow/Persidskaia strela, with etchings by Edik Steinberg (Verona: Edizione d'Arte Gibralfaro & ECM, 1994);

On Grief and Reason: Essays (New York: Farrar, Straus & Giroux, 1995)–includes "An Immodest Proposal";

V okrestnostiakh Atlantidy: Novye stikhotvoreniia (St. Petersburg: Pushkinskii fond, 1995);

Peizazh s navodneniem, compiled by Aleksandr Sumerkin (Dana Point, Cal.: Ardis, 1996)–includes "Dedal v Sitsilii," "Fin de Siècle," "Menia uprekali vo vsem . . . ," and "Peizazh s navodneniem";

So Forth: Poems (New York: Farrar, Straus & Giroux, 1996)–includes "Daedalus in Sicily," "Taps," "To My Daughter," "Fin de Siècle," and "View with a Flood";

Discovery, illustrated by Vladimir Radunsky (New York: Farrar, Straus & Giroux, 1999);

Collected Poems in English, 1972–1999, edited by Ann Kjellberg (New York: Farrar, Straus & Giroux, 2000);

Vtoroi vek posle nashei ery: Dramaturgiia Iosifa Brodskogo (St. Petersburg: Zvezda, 2001)–includes *Rosenkrants i Gil'denstern mertvy,* by Tom Stoppard, translated by Brodsky.

Editions and Collections: *Nazidanie: Stikhi 1962–1989,* compiled by Vladimir I. Ufliand (Leningrad: Smart, 1990);

Chast' rechi: Izbrannye stikhi 1962–1989 (Moscow: Khudozhestvennaia literatura, 1990);

Osennii krik iastreba: Stikhotvoreniia 1962–1989 (Leningrad: KTP LO IMA Press, 1990);

Kholmy: Bol'shie stikhotvoreniia i poemy, compiled by Iakov Gordin (St. Petersburg: LP VTPO "Kinotsentr," 1991);

Stikhotvoreniia, compiled by Gordin (Tallinn: Eesti Raamat, 1991);

Rozhdestvenskie stikhi (Moscow: Nezavisimaia gazeta, 1992; revised, 1996); translated by Melissa Green and others as *Nativity Poems* (New York: Farrar, Straus & Giroux, 2001);

Forma vremeni: Stikhotvoreniia, esse, p'esy, 2 volumes, compiled by Vladimir I. Ufliand (Minsk: Eridan, 1992);

Peresechennaia mestnost': Puteshestviia s kommentariiami, edited by Petr L'vovich Vail' (Moscow: Nezavisimaia gazeta, 1995);

Brodskii o Tsvetaevoi (Moscow: Nezavisimaia gazeta, 1997);

Pis'mo Goratsiiu (Moscow: Nash dom, 1998);

Gorbunov i Gorchakov (St. Petersburg: Pushkinskii fond, 1999);

Ostanovka v pustyne (St. Petersburg: Pushkinskii fond, 2000);

Chast' rechi (St. Petersburg: Pushkinskii fond, 2000);

Konets prekrasnoi epokhi (St. Petersburg: Pushkinskii fond, 2000);

Novye stansy k Avguste (St. Petersburg: Pushkinskii fond, 2000);

Uraniia (St. Petersburg: Pushkinskii fond, 2000);

Peizazh s navodneniem (St. Petersburg: Pushkinskii fond, 2000);

Novaia Odisseia: Pamiati Iosifa Brodskogo (Moscow: Staroe literaturnoe obozrenie, 2001);

Peremena imperii: Stikhotvoreniia 1960–1996 (Moscow: Nezavisimaia gazeta, 2001).

Editions in English: *Elegy for John Donne and Other Poems,* translated by Nicholas William Bethell (London: Longmans, 1967)–includes "Farewell . . . ," "A Jewish Cemetery by Leningrad," "You've finally come home . . . ," "Pilgrims," "I can visit, once more . . . ," "I kissed those shoulders . . . ," "Hills," and "Elegy to John Donne";

The Living Mirror: Five Young Poets from Leningrad, with contributions by Brodsky, edited by Suzanne Massie, translated by Massie, Max Hayward, and

George Kline (Garden City, N.Y.: Doubleday, 1972);

Selected Poems, translated by Kline (Harmondsworth, U. K.: Penguin, 1973; New York: Harper & Row, 1973)—includes "Aeneas and Dido," "After Our Era," "Einem Alten Architekten in Rom," "Elegy to John Donne," "A Letter in a Bottle," "New Stanzas to Augusta," "Nunc Dimittis," "Odysseus to Telemachus," "A Prophecy," "A Slice of Honeymoon," "Stanzas," "Still Life," "To Lycomedes on Scyros," "The trees in my window, in my wooden-framed window . . . ," "You're coming home again. What does that mean?" "You'll flutter, robin redbreast, from those three . . . ," "Verses on the Death of T. S. Eliot," "Wagon Train," and "When I embraced these shoulders, I beheld";

Poems and Translations (Keele: University of Keele, 1977).

RECORDINGS: *Joseph Brodsky Reading His Poems in Russian,* read by Brodsky and John Francis, Washington, D.C., Archive of Recorded Poetry and Literature (Library of Congress), 1979;

Joseph Brodsky, read by Brodsky and Mark Strand, New York, Academy of American Poets, 1980;

Joseph Brodsky Reading His Poems, read by Brodsky and Anthony Hecht, Washington, D.C., Gertrude Clarke Whittall Poetry and Literature Fund, 1984;

Winter, read by Brodsky, Watershed Media, 1987;

Joseph Brodsky Reads His Poetry, New York, Caedmon, 1988;

Joseph Brodsky Reading His Poetry, Washington, D.C., Gertrude Clarke Whittall Poetry and Literature Fund, 1992;

Rannie stikhotvoreniia, read by Brodsky, Moscow, Sintez, 1995;

A Maddening Space, read by Brodsky, New York, Mystic Fire, 1996.

OTHER: Vladislav Felitsianovich Khodasevich, *Izbrannaia proza,* 2 volumes, edited by Brodsky (New York: Serebriannyi vek, 1972);

Andrei Platonovich Platonov, *Kotlovan,* afterword by Brodsky (Ann Arbor, Mich.: Ardis, 1973);

Modern Russian Poets on Poetry, edited by Brodsky and Carl Proffer, introduction by Brodsky (Ann Arbor, Mich.: Ardis, 1976);

Osip Emil'evich Mandel'shtam, *Fifty Poems,* translated by Bernard Meares, introduction by Brodsky (New York: Persea Books, 1977); introduction republished as "The Child of Civilization," in Brodsky's *Less Than One* (New York: Farrar, Straus & Giroux, 1986);

Marina Ivanovna Tsvetaeva, *Stikhotvoreniia i poemy,* 5 volumes, edited by Alexander Sumerkin, foreword by Brodsky (New York: Russica, 1980–1990); foreword translated by Barry Rubin as "Footnote to a Poem," in his *Less Than One* (New York: Farrar, Straus & Giroux, 1986);

Anna Andreevna Akhmatova, *Poems of Akhmatova,* translated by Lyn Coffin, introduction by Brodsky (New York & London: Norton, 1983); introduction republished as "The Keening Muse," in Brodsky's *Less Than One* (New York: Farrar, Straus & Giroux, 1986);

Derek Walcott, *The Caribbean Poetry of Derek Walcott & the Art of Romare Bearden,* with an introduction by Brodsky (New York: Limited Editions Club, 1983); introduction republished as "The Sound of the Tide," in Brodsky's *Less Than One* (New York: Farrar, Straus & Giroux, 1986);

Irina Ratushinskaia, *No, I'm Not Afraid,* translated by David McDuff, introduction by Brodsky (Newcastle upon Tyne: Bloodaxe, 1986);

An Age Ago: A Selection of Nineteenth-Century Russian Poetry, foreword by Brodsky, translated by Alan Myers (New York: Farrar, Straus & Giroux, 1988);

"Puteshestvie v Stambul," in *Iosif Brodskii razmerom podlinnika,* compiled by Gennadii F. Komarov (Leningrad & Tallinn: LO SP SSSR, 1990);

Lev Poliakov, *Russia: A Portrait,* introduction by Brodsky (New York: Farrar, Straus & Giroux, 1991);

Evgenii Rein, *Protiv chasovoi strelki: Izbrannye stikhi,* preface by Brodsky (Tenafly, N.J.: Ermitazh, 1991);

Aleksandr Kushner, *Apollo in the Snow: Selected Poems,* translated by Paul Graves and Carol Ueland, introduction by Brodsky (New York: Farrar, Straus & Giroux, 1991);

Alexander Liberman, *Campidoglio; Michelangelo's Roman Capitol,* with an essay by Brodsky, photographs by Liberman (New York: Random House, 1994); essay republished as "Homage to Marcus Aurelius," in Brodsky's *On Grief and Reason* (New York: Farrar, Straus & Giroux, 1995);

Peter Viereck, *Tide and Continuities: Last and First Poems, 1995–1938,* foreword by Brodsky (Fayetteville: University of Arkansas Press, 1995);

Thomas Hardy, *The Essential Hardy,* selected, with an introduction, by Brodsky (Hopewell, N.J.: Ecco Press, 1995); introduction republished as "Wooing the Inanimate," in Brodsky's *On Grief and Reason* (New York: Farrar, Straus & Giroux, 1995);

Siobhan Dowd, *This Prison Where I Live: The Penn Anthology of Imprisoned Writers,* foreword by Brodsky (New York: Cassell Academic Press, 1996); foreword republished as "On Grief and Reason," in *On Grief and Reason* (New York: Farrar, Straus &

Giroux, 1995); republished in *Homage to Robert Frost*, by Brodsky, Seamus Heaney, and Walcott (New York: Farrar, Straus & Giroux, 1996);

Tomas Venclova, *Winter Dialogue*, translated by Diana Senechal, foreword by Brodsky (Evanston, Ill.: Hydra Books, 1999);

Streaked with Light and Shadow: Portraits of Former Soviet Jews in Utah, with an essay by Brodsky, text and interviews by Leslie G. Kelen, photographs by Kent M. Miles and Stacie Ann Smith (Salt Lake City: Oral History Institute, 2000);

V ozhidanii varvarov: Mirovaia poeziia v perevodakh Iosifa Brodskogo, translated by Brodsky, compiled by A. A. Purin (St. Petersburg: Zvezda, 2001).

SELECTED PERIODICAL PUBLICATIONS—UNCOLLECTED:

"Says poet Brodsky: 'A writer is a lonely traveler and no one is his helper,'" *New York Times Magazine* (1 October 1972): 11, 78–79, 82–85;

"Reflections on a Spawn of Hell," *New York Times Magazine* (4 March 1973): 10, 66–70;

"Beyond Consolation," *New York Review of Books* (7 February 1974): 13–16;

"Presentation of Czeslaw Milosz to the Jury," *World Literature Today* (Summer 1978): 364;

"Why the Peace Movement Is Wrong," *TLS: The Times Literary Supplement* (24 August 1984): 942–943;

"Literature and War—A Symposium," *TLS: The Times Literary Supplement* (17 May 1985): 543–544;

"The Meaning of Meaning," *New Republic* (20 January 1986): 32–35;

"History of the Twentieth Century: A Roadshow," *Partisan Review*, 53 (1986): 327–343;

"The Acceleration of the Poet," *Poetry Review*, 78, no. 1 (1988): 4–5;

"Demokratiia!" *Kontinent*, 62 (1990): 14–42; translated as "Democracy!" (Act I) in *Granta*, 30 (Winter 1990): 199–233; and "Democracy!" (Act II) in *Partisan Review* (Spring 1993): 184–194, 260–288;

"Poeziia kak forma soprotivleniia real'nosti," *Russkaia mysl'*, 3829 (25 May 1990); translated by Alexander Sumerkin and Jamey Gambrell as "Poetry as a Form of Resistance to Reality," *PMLA*, 107 (March 1992): 220–225.

Joseph Brodsky came of age in the Soviet Union during the "Thaw" period (late 1950s to early 1960s), and he has been widely recognized as the most gifted Russian poet of his generation. He is the direct successor to an illustrious quartet of modernist Russian poets who reached maturity during the pre-Soviet era and later suffered severely under Soviet rule: Marina Ivanovna Tsvetaeva, Osip Emil'evich Mandel'shtam, Anna Andreevna Akhmatova, and Boris Leonidovich Pasternak. The works and lives of these poets, among others, strongly influenced Brodsky's poetics and conditioned his fidelity to the Russian bardic tradition—of which he was, perhaps, the last true practitioner. Throughout his years living in emigration in the United States, Brodsky measured his own poetic merit against the reflections of fellow Soviet émigré poets who also distanced themselves from the overbearing Soviet state machine. At the same time he drew upon the Anglo-American poetic tradition to propel Russian verse well beyond the frontier of the hackneyed into new realms of form and meaning.

Brodsky's literary legacy is enormous and varied. It consists of multiple volumes of poetry, most written originally in Russian but some written in English; Brodsky's own translations of his poems, sometimes undertaken jointly with professional Anglophone translators and poets; two plays that exist in divergent Russian and English variants; two hefty volumes of collected essays written in English, Brodsky's adopted tongue; a prose reminiscence of Venice; several poems for children; and scores of book reviews, introductions, tributes to fellow poets, articles, and formal addresses published in a variety of books and periodicals. Many interviews with Brodsky have also been published in both English and Russian, although in some cases these pieces have been edited heavily and their reliability is uncertain. In the English-speaking world, Brodsky's reputation is primarily as an essayist and a quixotic, modern-day oracle; in the context of Russian letters, he is revered most of all for his masterful poetry.

Brodsky was born Iosif Aleksandrovich Brodsky on 24 May 1940 in Leningrad, just one year before Nazi Germany invaded the Soviet Union and Leningrad came under siege, an event that inflicted widespread death from starvation and disease. The young Brodsky, together with his mother, survived the Siege of Leningrad intact; his father, meanwhile, was serving in the Soviet Navy on the Finnish front. Apart from the fact that his mother taught him to read at the age of four, little is known about Brodsky's early childhood. He was the only child of Mariia Moiseevna Vol'pert and Aleksandr Ivanovich Brodsky. Mariia Moiseevna, the daughter of a Singer sewing-machine salesman, spent her childhood years in Latvia; Aleksandr Ivanovich, the son of a St. Petersburg printshop owner, earned degrees in geography from the University of Leningrad and in journalism from the School of Red Journalists. Both were Jews, a circumstance that played no small role in their own—and, later, their son's—fates in the context of the official anti-Semitic hype that exploded in the Soviet Union in the postwar years.

In 1950, in response to a Politburo ruling that Jews should not hold high military rank, Aleksandr Ivanovich was dismissed from the navy. He eventually found a job as a freelance photojournalist, but the family's finances remained tight, and both of Brodsky's parents began to experience problems with their health. During the campaign against "rootless cosmopolites" of the early 1950s that led to the 1953 "Doctors' Plot" (a fabricated conspiracy in which nine doctors, most of them Jewish, were accused of plotting to murder top Soviet officials), Mariia Moiseevna and Aleksandr Ivanovich made preparations for the mass deportations of Jews to the Russian Far East that Stalin was rumored to be planning. However, Joseph Stalin's death in 1953 obviated this move.

Brodsky spent his childhood and adolescent years in a small communal apartment located in an elaborate, six-story building on the corner of Pestel' (Panteleimonovskaia) and Liteinyi Streets, an area that boasted a rich literary history. His parents filled their living quarters with heavy wooden furniture, dating to the turn of the century, which seemed to Brodsky too large and whimsical for the cramped space. As he grew older, he barricaded off a small section of the family's forty-square-meter room with thick curtains and heavy chests and shelves heaped to the ceiling with suitcases. This cavernous hideout eventually become his private lair, which he stocked with piles of forbidden books—including the novels of Charles Dickens, James Joyce, John Dos Passos, and Ernest Hemingway and the poetry of Robert Frost, Boris Abramovich Slutsky, John Donne, Konstanty Gałczyński, Tsvetaeva, and Mandel'shtam. Here the young Brodsky listened to his beloved phonograph records—an eclectic mix of Dixieland jazz, Henry Purcell, and Joseph Haydn—and experienced his first romantic encounters; here, too, he kept his first typewriter and pounded out his first poems.

Brodsky was a wholly self-educated man. As a child, he attended several different public schools. Enamored of his father's navy uniform, he applied at age fourteen for admission to a submarine academy. Although he easily passed the admission examinations, he nonetheless was rejected because he was Jewish. A year later, at age fifteen, Brodsky stood up one day during class at Middle School No. 196 on Mokhovaia Street and walked out the door, never to return. He later recalled this spontaneous moment as his first free act—an instinctive protest against the conformity and half-lies that the Soviet educational system inculcated in the youth of the nation. He rationalized his decision by the need to alleviate his family's dire financial situation, and, indeed, he soon went to work as a milling-machine operator at the arsenal factory, which produced not military hardware but agricultural machinery and air com-

Brodsky at twenty-one, in the small Leningrad apartment—later dubbed a "room-and-a-half" in his book Less Than One: Selected Essays *(1986)—that he shared with his parents (from the journal* Chast' rechi: Al'manakh literatury i iskusstva, *no. 1 [1980])*

pressors. This job was Brodsky's first contact with the true proletariat, and he relished the fresh range of linguistic expression to which it gave exposure. A year later, however, nurturing a fleeting dream of becoming a neurosurgeon, he quit his factory job and went to work at the hospital morgue located next door to the arsenal. He did not stay long at this gruesome post. From 1957 onward he enlisted as a physical laborer in a series of geological expeditions that allowed him to travel all over the territory of the Soviet Union, from the White Sea in the north to the Tien Shan Mountains of Central Asia, and from Iakutsk in northeastern Siberia to Kazakhstan in the south. Between 1956 and 1962 he changed jobs no fewer than thirteen times.

While he was in Iakutsk in 1957, Brodsky stumbled upon a volume of verse by the early-nineteenth-century philosophical poet Evgenii Abramovich Baratynsky. The intellectual acuity of Baratynsky's poetry greatly attracted Brodsky, and he later claimed that he realized at this moment that poetry was his calling–the only thing he understood in life. Brodsky's own earliest poems date from 1957 and 1958. These years were a tumultuous period in Soviet history. The Hungarian uprising of 1956, crushed by the Soviet Army, had shocked the youth of Brodsky's generation into adulthood. Meanwhile, the Congress of Soviet Writers had been reconvened after a hiatus of twenty years, and Akhmatova was reinstated as a member; the unmasking of Stalin's cult of personality was in full swing; literary societies sprang up throughout Leningrad; and poetry, disseminated in samizdat (self-published) copies, displaced other forms of spiritual expression such as religion or philosophy. The unofficial literature of the late 1950s was devoted to bearing witness to evils of the past.

By the end of the decade, however, some of the younger authors took a turn away from social responsibility toward aestheticism. For Brodsky, the work of the older poet Slutsky served as a kind of bridge between the two tendencies, moving as it did from bureaucratese and concrete historicism toward pure existentialism. Evgenii Borisovich Rein, a poet of Brodsky's own generation, was also influential; Brodsky and Rein, together with the young poets Anatolii Genrikhovich Naiman and Dmitrii Vasil'evich Bobyshev, first met at Leningrad poetry readings in 1959 and soon became close friends and associates. Brodsky's own public appearances at such evenings began in 1958, and in March 1959 his declamation of his poem "Evreiskoe kladbishche" (1965; translated as "A Jewish Cemetery by Leningrad," 1967) at a poetry competition held at the Gor'ky House of Books in Leningrad was a scandalous success.

Brodsky's earliest works are characterized by metrical experimentation, musicality, and the presence of historical, mythological, and religious imagery. The poems are prone to overstatement, and at times their meanings do not quite match the force of the formal contortions to which the poet subjects his verse. This poetry, for the most part, is apolitical. In fact, the combination of the poet's studied social nonconformism with the location of his poems "on the border between song and . . . sacral hymns" has prompted the critic Viktor Sergeevich Kulle, in "Iosif Brodskii: Novaia Odisseia" (Joseph Brodsky: A New Odyssey, published in Brodsky's Sochineniia [Works], 1998), to dub Brodsky's juvenilia his "Romantic" period. Common themes in the earliest poems include the cityscapes of Leningrad, the poet's alienation from surrounding Soviet society and the bombastic idiom it fosters, and an ironic

recognition of the insistent materialism of the world in which the poet finds himself. This last theme is prominent in "Evreiskoe kladbishche": "Beyond the crooked fence lie close together / lawyers, merchants, musicians, revolutionaries. / For themselves they sang. / For themselves they saved. / For others they died. / But first they paid taxes, respected the police, / and in this inescapably material world, / they interpreted the Talmud, remaining idealists."

In another poem of 1958, "Piligrimy" (1965; translated as "Pilgrims," 1967), Brodsky charts a path out of this world and away from the false comforts it offers, including religious faith: "And this means, there is no point / In having faith in oneself or in God. / And this means that all that remains / Are Illusion and the Road." These examples illustrate why the authorities at the time found Brodsky's apolitical poetry to be so much more pernicious than works of overtly political dissent by other young writers such as the poet Evgenii Aleksandrovich Evtushenko. As David MacFadyen shows in his study *Joseph Brodsky and the Soviet Muse* (2000), Brodsky subverts Soviet sloganeering from within, thereby transcending the narrow political jargon that encapsulates Soviet reality, to speak instead in the expansive language of existential quest. At the same time, Brodsky signals, through biting irony and linguistic play, that he does not lose sight of the confining facts of his life. He goes outside the rules of the political game being played, in the unofficial literature of the time as well as in the sanctioned, official literature; he dispenses with the rules entirely and simply talks about life, the soul, and longing. This psychological liberation from the mental grip of the system could not fail for long to attract the attention of the Komitet gosudarstvennoi bezopasnosti (KGB, State Security Committee).

Brodsky's first arrest came soon after the appearance of Aleksandr Ginzburg's samizdat publication *Sintaksis* (Syntax), a typewritten poetry journal put out in Moscow in the spring of 1960, which included both "Evreiskoe kladbishche" and "Piligrimy." Other poems by Brodsky had also been circulating in handwritten copies, and some were even being set to music. Brodsky was picked up by the KGB and taken for interrogation to the famous Kresty (Crosses) prison in Leningrad, which was located next to the hospital where just a few years previously he had been employed in the morgue. He was kept in solitary confinement under the most austere conditions and was interrogated for twelve-hour stretches. No formal charges were filed, however, and he was soon released. A year or two later, a second arrest followed when Brodsky was implicated in the so-called Umansky affair, in which he was accused of planning to hijack a plane to Kabul, Afghanistan, and thereby escape the Soviet Union. Once again, he was released when no clear evidence was found against him.

The next several years were packed full of momentous events in Brodsky's life. In August 1961 Rein took Brodsky to meet Akhmatova at her dacha (summer cottage) in Komarovo. Together with Naiman and Bobyshev, the four young poets began frequenting Akhmatova's home; their relationship to her was one of spiritual, more than literary, discipleship, while she herself dubbed the four the "magic chorus" and welcomed their company. Brodsky's poetic sensibilities were quite distant from Akhmatova's; indeed, he felt a direct poetic debt not to Akhmatova but to Tsvetaeva, whose fierce individualism and unflinching quest to go beyond all frontiers were much closer to Brodsky's own metaphysical drive than was Akhmatova's dignified restraint. Yet, Akhmatova was a powerful moral influence on the young Brodsky. Their friendship and mutual admiration—in 1963, Akhmatova autographed a copy of her latest book "To Iosif Brodsky, whose verses seem magical to me"—was immensely meaningful to Brodsky, in that it seemed to sanction his position as the heir to the great poetic tradition of the Silver Age. At the same time Brodsky absorbed from Akhmatova a reverence for the poet as an interpreter of Christian culture (his first reading of an underground copy of the Old and New Testaments in 1963 affected him profoundly); he also learned the power of concrete detail and precise psychological motivations from her poetry.

A different kind of meeting with another woman who was to play a fateful role in Brodsky's life occurred in February 1962, when the poet's friends introduced him to Marina Pavlovna Basmanova, a Leningrad artist and illustrator of children's books two years his senior. She was tall, slender, with dark hair cut in a bob, green eyes, a keen wit, and a deceptively reserved manner that masked the ardor of her personality. Acquaintances recall that she was an aficionado of film and classical music; that it was difficult to get close to her; and that she apparently had little appreciation for the magnitude of Brodsky's poetic talent. According to the bohemian mores of the period, the romance between Brodsky and Basmanova developed almost overnight. There was a strong physical attraction between the couple; yet, Basmanova was unwilling to commit to marriage (Brodsky's precarious political status, along with the fact that all he had to his name was his little corner of his parents' communal apartment, may have had something to do with her reluctance), while Brodsky insistently demanded her full and undying dedication to him. The result of this emotional mismatch was to be a long-lived, extremely painful love-hate relationship punctu-

ated by alternating fights, separations, and passionate reunions.

The poems that Brodsky wrote beginning in the early 1960s show him moving away from the sometimes clumsy experimentation and concrete settings of his juvenilia into a mature poetics, in which a metaphysical bent is already apparent. In the 1960 poem "Glagoly" (Verbs, 1965), for instance, verbs become things with their own independent existence that seem to take the place of humans and, in so doing, satirize the automatization of Soviet life: "Verbs, which live in cellars, / speak—in cellars, are born—in cellars / beneath several stories / of general optimism. // Every morning they go to work, / mix chemicals and haul stones, / but, in erecting a city, they erect not a city, / but a monument to their own loneliness." These verbs, as a stand-in for the poet, eventually are sacrificed to societal regimentation and "ascend Golgotha." The rhythmic driving-in of nails becomes the suffering, liberating rhythm of poetry, which will never desist in any of the three tenses of the verb—past, present, or future—and which ushers in the freedom of poetic imagination at the end of the poem: "The land of hyperboles lies beneath them, / as the heaven of metaphors soars above us!" No matter how brutally the state persecutes verbs (that is, poets and poetry), Brodsky seems to be saying, their subversive power will only increase with time.

In other poems of this period Brodsky abandons his earlier Romantic stance of protest against the insufficiencies of life toward a cool alienation from human society and companionship. Not only metaphysical imaginings but also, strangely, his relationships to inanimate things and places begin to play a central role in his developing poetics. An example of this tendency can be found in the poem "Ia obnial eti plechi . . ." (1965; translated as "I kissed those shoulders . . . ," 1967), in which the poet, in bidding farewell to his lover, does not see or think of her at all (beyond the fragmented shoulders he embraces) but meditates instead on "what turned out to be behind her back": a table, a wall, a bright lamp, assorted shabby furniture, and a circling moth—all of which convey, tacitly, the poet's emotional detachment from the scene in which he himself participates. In "Vorotish'sia na rodinu . . ." (1965; translated as "You've finally come home . . . ," 1967) the poet, arriving home after a long absence, unfalteringly assesses the extent of his own aloneness—which is, in fact, absolute: "How good it is that there is no one to blame, / how good it is that you are not tied to anyone, / how good it is that no one in the world / is obliged to love you until death." This proud declaration that "there is no one to blame" for the vicissitudes of his fate was later to mature into an insistent eschewal of victimhood, a key ingredient of Brodsky's poetic self-definition.

Brodsky during his exile in Norinskaia, 1964 (from the journal
Chast' rechi: Al'manakh literatury i iskusstva,
no. 1 [1980])

In his poem "Ot okrainy k tsentru" (From the Suburbs toward the Center; published as "Vot ia vnov' posetil . . ." in 1965 in *Stikhotvoreniia i poemy;* translated as "I can visit, once more . . . ," 1967), Brodsky renders his alienation from the homeland in the form of a farewell jaunt through the suburbs of Leningrad in the company of his own "bednaia iunost'" (poor youth), which replaces any real human company to function as a kind of substitute muse: "The jazz of outskirts greets us, / you hear the pipes of outskirts, / a golden dixieland / handsome, charming in black caps, / neither soul nor flesh— / someone's shade above the native gramophone, / like your dress suddenly dropped upwards by the saxophone." As in "Ia obnial eti plechi . . . ," the poet's attention here is captured by the dilapidated objects that compose his physical surroundings—the bridges, industrial complexes, tramcars, cranes, silent hordes of storefronts, and black smoke that characterize the outskirts of contemporary Leningrad. These objects, rather than

an emotional relationship to any other human being, propel him into a contemplation of soul, death, hell, heaven, and the uncertainty of life eternal. The statement of alienation from life that ends this poem is Brodsky's most potent to date: "Thank God, I'm an alien. / I don't blame anyone here. / There's nothing to learn. / I walk, hurry, overtake. / How easy it is for me now / since I have not parted with anyone. / Thank God that I am left on the earth without a fatherland." From then on, all the poet's efforts were directed toward chasing and "overtaking" his own potential, without regard for the proscriptions of the Soviet literary establishment.

In 1962 Brodsky discovered the work of the English metaphysical poets, primarily Donne. Donne's poetry—full of wit, coolly passionate, philosophically detached, highly intellectual, exquisitely crafted with intricate conceits and geometric figures—galvanized Brodsky. Both in its themes and in its foreignness to the dominant Russian poetic tradition, Donne's work corresponded perfectly to the feelings of alienation that Brodsky had already discovered in himself. At the same time Brodsky saw an equivalence between the English cultural vantage—an islander's perspective on the European continent—and his own Leningrad perch on the edge of the Soviet Empire. He located his feelings of cultural estrangement in the urban geography of Leningrad that had formed him as a child: the cold, mists, bridges, white nights and cruel winters, fantastic architectural styles, and endless, gray expanses of water—the element he always associated with the idea of freedom. These surroundings prompted him to believe more in the truth of the poetic word than in the inescapability of the daily grind, the necessity of political servitude, or the rectitude of conventional morality. Years later, he ended his essay "A Guide to a Renamed City" (written 1979; published 1986) with the following tribute to the city of his birth: "Any dream will be inferior to this reality. Where a man doesn't cast a shadow, like water."

In 1962 and 1963, under the influence of Donne as well as of Tsvetaeva, whose powerful *poemy* (long narrative poems) he had recently discovered, Brodsky composed his own first *poemy*. This genre, distanced from the intimacy of the short lyric form, held the potential for the creation of a kind of "lyrico-philosophical" epic that remained attractive to Brodsky throughout the remainder of his creative life, becoming the hallmark of his poetic legacy. The characteristics of Brodsky's works in this genre are rhythmic and stanzaic inventiveness, extended complex metaphors, the mingling of wildly different linguistic registers, paradoxical thought patterns, a tight weaving together of intricate compositional and metaphysical strands, and an acidic sense of humor. Brodsky's earliest *poemy* all participated in the preservative or "neoclassical" mission of his verse with respect to the Russian poetic culture and language of previous ages; included among these works are the masterpieces "Kholmy" (1965; translated as "Hills," 1967), "Bol'shaia elegiia Dzhonu Donnu" (1965; translated as "Elegy to John Donne," 1967), and "Isaak i Avraam" (Isaac and Abraham, 1965)–inspired, respectively, by Tsvetaeva, Donne, and the Old Testament.

On 4 May 1961 a decree announcing a struggle against so-called *tuneiadstvo* (social parasitism) was passed in the Soviet Union. Just two years later, on 29 November 1963, a lengthy lampoon appeared in the newspaper *Vechernii Leningrad* (Evening Leningrad) under the heading "Okololiteraturnyi truten'" (A Semi-Literary Drone), signed by A. Ionin, M. Medvedev, and Iakov Lerner, a retired KGB agent. Lerner did not stop at denouncing Brodsky to his former employer but also took the trouble to convince Aleksandr Andreevich Prokof'ev, the secretary of the Leningrad Writers' Union, to have a unanimous resolution drafted that stated that Brodsky was "incapable of contributing anything to literature" and that his works were "anti-Soviet and pornographic" and to recommend that Brodsky be expelled from Leningrad. Lerner's lampoon accused the poet of harboring plans to "betray the homeland" and dubbed Brodsky a "pigmy, self-assuredly clambering onto Parnassus." The article concluded with a call to the authorities to protect Leningrad and Leningraders from Brodsky's threat: "It's clear that we must cease coddling such semi-literary parasites . . . Not only Brodsky, but also all those who surround him, are walking along the same dangerous path . . . May semi-literary idlers like Joseph Brodsky receive the sternest rebuff. Let us teach them not to muddy the water!" During 1963 Brodsky had composed more than two thousand lines of poetry; he had also been translating the work of Cuban, Yugoslav, and Polish poets, among others.

Lerner's lampoon portended trouble for Brodsky. In December 1963, at the urging of his friends, the poet fled Leningrad for Moscow. He voluntarily checked himself into the Kashchenko psychiatric hospital in Moscow, hoping to escape the authorities' notice there. Accounts of what followed are somewhat confused. Brodsky apparently soon learned that Basmanova had greeted the New Year in the company of his friend and fellow poet Bobyshev at a dacha belonging to mutual friends in Zelenogorsk (outside Leningrad); Basmanova supposedly betrayed Brodsky with Bobyshev and then set the curtains of the house on fire, coolly commenting how beautiful the flames were. Brodsky, tormented by jealousy and anger, checked out of the psychiatric hospital on 5 January and returned to Leningrad in haste to sort matters out with Basmanova. During January and the first part of February he stayed constantly on the move, sleeping at various friends'

dachas on the outskirts of the city. He seems to have spent some time with friends in the town of Tarusa, a writers' colony near Moscow, as well. In his 1967 poem "K Likomedu, na Skiros" (To Lycomedes on Scyros, 1970), he reminisces obliquely about this chain of events when he identifies himself with Theseus, who escapes from the Minotaur (a stand-in for the KGB) and his hostile labyrinth (Leningrad) only to discover that Ariadne has taken up with Bacchus.

On the evening of 13 February 1964 Brodsky was unexpectedly arrested for the third time as he walked down a Leningrad street. He was brought to a closed trial on a charge of *tuneiadstvo* on 18 February at 36 Vosstaniia (Uprising) Street in the Dzerzhinskii district of Leningrad. The presiding judge, Savel'eva, ruled that Brodsky be sent for mandatory forensic psychiatric testing to determine whether he was suffering from any disorder that precluded a sentence of hard physical labor. On 19 February, accordingly, Brodsky was sent for three weeks to the Priazhka psychiatric hospital. His *poema* "Gorbunov i Gorchakov" (Gorbunov and Gorchakov, written between 1965 and 1968, published in 1970), written in the form of an extended philosophical dialogue between two hospital inmates–who discuss their dreams, their meals, the view outside their window, and their musings about the soul and immortality–chronicles his experiences there. Brodsky was the only inmate in the hospital not allowed to have visits from his family. He claimed to find the violation of proportions in the ward's design (low ceilings, small windows that always remained locked, and large beds) maddening, and to prefer solitary confinement in prison–his favorite formula for which was, as he wrote in his essay "Less Than One" (1986), "a lack of space counterbalanced by a surplus of time"–to this psychiatric torture. During his incarceration in the Priazhka hospital he was routinely injected with various substances and subjected to other invasive "treatments" such as the "wrap," which consisted of being wrapped tightly in sheets and submerged in a tub of cold water and then left to dry, still confined in the wet linens. Ultimately, Brodsky was declared psychologically healthy and fit for work and was released.

Brodsky's second, open trial was held on 13 March 1964 in the club building of the fifteenth *remstroikontora* (renovation and construction agency) at 22 Naberezhnaia Fontanki. At the trial Brodsky was defended by respected members of the Leningrad Writers' Union: among them, journalist and literary critic Frida Abramovna Vigdorova, editor Natal'ia Grudinina, and Herzen Institute professors Efim Grigor'evich Etkind and Vladimir Grigorevich Admoni, all of whom testified to Brodsky's immense talent as both a poet and a translator of poetry. Akhmatova also solicited the support of three Lenin Prize laureates in Brodsky's defense: composer Dmitrii Dmitrievich Shostakovich and writers Samuil Iakovlevich Marshak and Kornei Ivanovich Chukovsky addressed appeals for Brodsky's release to the Writers' Union, the Leningrad Party Committee, and Nikita Sergeevich Khrushchev himself. All these attempts proved ineffectual in the face of testimony by other witnesses, such as one worker who claimed that Brodsky's poetry was having a bad influence on his son, inciting him not to work. Throughout the trial Brodsky impressed his friends by his calm, unruffled mien; he claimed later that this ordeal was less important to him at the time than the recent catastrophe in his relationship with Basmanova, which had already sapped all his emotional energy.

Vigdorova made a stenographic record of a portion of the trial proceedings until she was forbidden by the judge to continue. She circulated these notes in samizdat, and they soon found their way abroad, where they were published in English translation in *The New Leader* and *Encounter* in August and September 1964, and in Russian in the émigré almanac *Vozdushnye puti* (Airy Paths) in 1965. This was the first time the internal workings of the Soviet legal system had been revealed to the outside world, and the transcript created an international sensation. Radio Free Europe made much of the story, and the British Broadcasting Corporation even produced a dramatization of the trial on radio. In the West, Brodsky's confused responses to Judge Savel'eva's relentless questions about his lack of professional qualifications to be a writer ("I didn't think—I didn't think this was a matter of education . . . I think that it is . . . from God") came to symbolize the clash between the evil Soviet bureaucracy and human truth and goodness, between unbridled state power and individual rights.

As a result of the publication of the court proceedings Brodsky, who previously had been known only to a narrow circle of Leningrad writers and poets, became an international cause célèbre. Akhmatova even quipped wryly, "What a biography they are making for our redhead. You'd think he had hired them on purpose!" (quoted in Solomon Volkov's *Conversations with Joseph Brodsky: A Poet's Journey through the Twentieth Century*, 1998). Brodsky himself interpreted his trial as his necessary initiation into the grand tradition of Russian poets at odds with the state. Although in later years he usually refrained from discussing these painful events, he did maintain a sense of humor about them and once offered the following commentary on the reasons for his persecution: "I combined in myself the most attractive features, in that I wrote poems and was a Jew" (from Etkind's 1988 biographical notes on Brodsky). He also noted with macabre irony that, in contrast to the punishments meted out to other dissenting literary figures in the decade that followed, by Soviet standards his own treatment was "something absolutely homeopathic" (quoted in *The Economist* in its 1996 obituary on Brodsky).

Despite the efforts of numerous cultural figures on Brodsky's behalf, he was nevertheless sentenced to five years of hard labor; the court explained that "Brodsky systematically fails to fulfill the obligation of a Soviet man with respect to material values and personal well-being as is evident from his frequent changes of jobs." Brodsky himself viewed the trial as something surreal, like a scene out of a Franz Kafka work, and he distanced himself emotionally from what was happening. He was again imprisoned in the Kresty prison, and on 22 March he was shipped out on a prison train with other convicts (who, unlike Brodsky, had committed actual criminal acts) to the Konosha district in the region of Arkhangel'sk, in the far north of Russia; he settled in the village of Norinskaia, which consisted of just fourteen peasant families. The village was twenty miles from the nearest railroad station, surrounded by swampy northern forests. At first he was put up by a dairy farmer, Anisiia Pestereva; later he rented a tiny room in the hut of an old peasant couple, Konstantin and Afanasiia Pesterev, furnished only with a table and sofa. He paid for the room with the small salary he earned for his work, which was seasonal and consisted variously of chopping wood, carting manure, shoveling grain stores, and laboring in the fields of the local state farm. His landlady later remembered him fondly and claimed that the villagers often took pity on him and assigned him comparatively easier tasks, such as pasturing the cows. On 14 August 1965 the village newspaper *Prizyv* (The Summons) published Brodsky's poem "Traktory na rassvete" (Tractors at Dawn, appears in full in MacFadyen's *Joseph Brodsky and the Soviet Muse*), and on 4 September 1965 it published his poem "Oboz" (Wagon Train), for which he was paid two rubles and some change.

His grim surroundings and the hardships of daily life in Norinskaia notwithstanding, Brodsky was to remember this period happily: "That was one of the best periods in my life. There have been no worse, but I don't think there have been better" (quoted in Volkov's *Conversations with Joseph Brodsky*). Vigdorova sent him her typewriter; Lidiia Korneevna Chukovskaia sent him the Modern Library Edition of Donne's works as a birthday gift; other friends sent him books, letters, and tins of instant coffee. When he returned to Leningrad after his release, he brought more than one hundred kilograms of books back with him. Because the farm work in the village was seasonal, Brodsky had long stretches of free time; because for the most part he spent his time in isolation, there were few distractions from his intellectual pursuits. During this period he perfected his knowledge of English, continued his translating work, read Donne from cover to cover, and discovered to his great excitement the work of the American poets T. S. Eliot and W. H. Auden. His own poetry was nourished by this reading and for the first time departed entirely from the Romantic idiom of his juvenilia and the pathetic idiom of official Soviet discourse. He achieved new spiritual and metaphysical heights in his writing that were, however, conditioned by a wry Romantic irony that remained characteristic of Brodsky's poetics and even of his conversational style for the remainder of his life. In his Norinskaia poems Brodsky makes use of the compositional possibilities of the baroque—the juxtaposition of the grotesque and the serious, the ephemeral and the eternal, the coarse and the eloquent—while at the same time distancing himself from pure lyricism and adopting, instead, a profoundly intellectual worldview. His language becomes saturated with subtextual references, sometimes preservative and sometimes parodic in function.

Exemplary of all these developments in Brodsky's poetics is his poignant elegy "Stikhi na smert' T. S. Eliota" (Verses on the Death of T. S. Eliot, 1970), written upon Eliot's death on 4 January 1965. In this poem Eliot's magi (from his poem "The Journey of the Magi," 1927) are replaced by the androgynous figures of two mythic maidens, England and America, the two nations where Eliot made his home. Time is an overwhelming presence, and in fact time itself—not death or God—claims the poet's life: "The young tribe of giant waves / will bear the burden of his flight until / it strikes the far edge of its flowering fringe, / to bid a slow farewell, breaking against / the limit of the earth. Exuberant / in strength, it laughs, a January gulf / in that dry land of days where we remain." As Eliot departs the temporal world, "latching his door with a chain of years," Poetry, though orphaned by his death, still "breeds within the glass / of lonely days, each echoing each." Poetry, as Brodsky often wrote, is time reconfigured: "in the rhyme / of years the voice of poetry stands plain." Through the strength of his poetry Eliot has inscribed his being on the physical world. The living will remember him intimately through his poems "as the body holds in mind / the lost caress of lips and arms." Poetic language is the vessel of memory; Brodsky's own poetic signature is now developed to the point at which he, too, etches himself into the consciousness of his physical surroundings—he knows now his own poetic strength. Even the remote village of Norinskaia will be immortalized in his works. As Brodsky wrote in a letter to I. N. Tomashevskaia on 19 January 1965 (quoted by

Paperback cover for Brodsky's Chast' rechi (A Part of Speech, 1977), the first collection that he published in exile (Thomas Cooper Library, University of South Carolina)

A. N. Krivomazov in his on-line biography of Brodsky): "I have accelerated too far now, and I will never stop until death itself. Everything somehow shimmers in the background, but that's not the main thing. Inside me is some sort of unheard-of infinity and indifference, and I will gather more and more speed all the time."

Many of Brodsky's best works were written during his exile in Norinskaia, including more than seventy lyric poems and the following *poemy* (all first published in book form in *Ostanovka v pustyne* [A Halt in the Desert, 1970]): "Pis'mo v butylke" (Letter in a Bottle, 1965), "Einem Alten Architekten in Rom" (To an Old Architect in Rome, 1964), and "Novye stansy k Avguste" (New Stanzas to Augusta, 1964). This last work is dedicated to Basmanova (or M.B., as Brodsky inscribed such poems), who later visited him during his exile for a period of several months. He gladly welcomed other visitors as well—Rein and Naiman came, bringing an encouraging letter from Akhmatova on the occasion of Brodsky's twenty-fifth birthday—but the period he spent with Basmanova was the highlight of his exile, the happiest time in his long relationship with her. In "Novye stansy k Avguste" the absent Basmanova, like Augusta, the sister of George Gordon, Lord Byron, plays muse to Brodsky's exiled poet. Brodsky's loneliness takes on existential proportions, as the northern cold becomes a metaphor for spiritual paralysis: "Here on the hills, among empty skies, / among roads that only lead into the forest, / life steps away from itself / and gazes in surprise at the forms / that rustle all around. And roots / catch at one's boots, sniffling, / and all the lights in the village go out. / And so here I wander over a no-man's-land / and beg a lease on Nonexistence." In addition to this poem, Brodsky dedicated many others to Basmanova during his time in Norinskaia, including "Ty vyporkhnesh', malinovka . . ." (You'll flutter, robin redbreast, from these three, 1964), "Dlia shkol'nogo vozrasta" (For School Age, 1964, translated in David M. Bethea's *Joseph Brodsky and the Creation of Exile* [1994]), "Lomtik medovogo mesiatsa" (A Slice of Honeymoon, 1963), "Derev'ia v moem okne . . ." (The trees in my window, in my wooden-framed window . . . , 1964), and "Prorochestvo" (A Prophecy, 1965), all of which were first published in book form in *Ostanovka v pustyne*. Brodsky later collected his love poems to Basmanova, in the volume *Novye stansy k Avguste* (New Stanzas to Augusta, 1983).

The furor that Brodsky's trial had raised abroad did not dissipate but rather escalated after his exile to Norinskaia. A collection of his works, titled *Stikhotvoreniia i poemy* (Lyric and Narrative Poems), compiled by Gleb Petrovich Struve and Boris Andreevich Filippov, and financed by the Central Intelligence Agency, was published in New York in 1965. During the next few years, translations into English, German, French, Hebrew, Polish, and Czech followed. By contrast, only a handful of Brodsky's poems had been published by this time in Soviet periodicals—the first of these, "Proshchai . . ." (translated as "Farewell . . . ," 1967), in 1957. The authorities eventually bowed to international pressure and commuted Brodsky's sentence to one year and five months, and he was released in September 1965. Now world-renowned, he was allowed to return to his native Leningrad and to earn a living as a translator; he translated Donne and Andrew Marvell into Russian and focused especially on the works of the Polish poets Cyprian Norwid, Zbigniew Herbert, Czesław Miłosz, and Konstanty Gałczyński, from whom he learned to approach a serious subject indirectly, with a degree of jest, without losing sight of its deeper implications. He traveled freely, often visiting Lithuania and wintering in writers' colonies in the Crimea. He spent time in Moscow as well, where his friends Naiman and

Rein had moved after the breakdown of their friendship with Bobyshev and Brodsky's subsequent exile. When Akhmatova died on 5 March 1966, Brodsky was a pallbearer at her funeral; this sad occasion was the last time that the four young poets (the "magic chorus") gathered together. Brodsky's poem "Sreten'e" (Candlemas Day, 1977; translated as "Nunc Dimittis" in *A Part of Speech*, 1980), written on the sixth anniversary of Akhmatova's death, envisions the elder poet as a composite of the Virgin Mary (representing Akhmatova's sufferings as the mother of a son who fell victim to Stalin's Great Terror) and the prophetess Anna (representing Akhmatova in venerable old age).

For two or three years after Brodsky's return to Leningrad, his relationship with Basmanova continued in fits and starts, and in 1968 she gave birth to his son Andrei, whom, despite Brodsky's resistance, she registered under the maternal surname Basmanov. As before, she had no intention of marrying Brodsky, who was barely managing to make ends meet with the small income that his translations brought in, and who still lived in an alcove in his parents' share of the communal apartment on Liteinyi Street. By the time of Andrei's birth, Brodsky's relationship with Basmanova was decidedly over, although he continued wistfully addressing love poems to her during the next two decades of his life. Several passages in his 1967 *poema* "Rech' o prolitom moloke" (A Speech about Spilled Milk, 1977) gesture at the disintegration of his romantic hopes, as when he complains: "Knowing my status, my fiancée / for the fifth year hasn't budged to get married; / and where she is now, I have no idea: / the devil himself couldn't pry the truth out of her." This work is a self-deprecatory rant against Brodsky's disappointments in life—and, in particular, against the depraved political ideology that contaminates the society in which he lives. He voices his determination to continue his rebellion against the system and to fight for "democracy in the full sense of the word," claiming that "evil exists to be fought with, / and not to be hung like a yoke on one's shoulders." His motto, contrary to Marxist wisdom, is not solidarity with the masses but the realization of individual potential: "For me the trees are dearer than the forest. / I don't have any interest in the general good. / But the speed of my internal progress / is greater than the world's speed." Brodsky's disillusionment with Basmanova is overlaid, throughout this poem, upon his disgust at the maxims that regulate Soviet society ("Like a bachelor I weep for marriage. / . . . But spouses are the only type of property owners / who possess what they create in joy"), and his emotional loneliness becomes a calque for his deep sense of cultural alienation.

In several poems written in the late 1960s and first published in book form in *Ostanovka v pustyne*, Brod-

Brodsky at Columbia University, 1978 (photograph © by Marianna Volkova)

sky sadly, or bitterly, bids good-bye to his affair with Basmanova. In "Sonet" (A Sonnet; translated as "Postscriptum" in *Selected Poems,* 1973), he begins, "What a pity that what your existence has come to mean for me, my existence did not come to mean for you." In "Strofy" (Stanzas, 1968) he muses, "But my world will not end if / in future we share / only those jagged edges / where we've broken apart." In "Enei i Didona" (Aeneas and Dido, 1969) Dido has a premonition of Carthage crumbling to ash and looks on stoically as her lover sails away to found a new empire; her despair is Aeneas's liberation: "just at the instant / of despair does a favorable wind / begin to blow." In "Shest' let spustia" (Six Years Later, 1968) Brodsky memorializes his frustrated love for Basmanova in a poignant sequence of metaphors that ends with a conceit distinctly reminiscent, in its elaborateness and its sad wit, of Donne's poetics: "She and I lived so long together, / that we made from our own shadows / a door for ourselves— whether we worked or slept, / the shutters did not swing apart, / and we, apparently, passed right through / and went out into the future through the back way." In the wake of his breakup with Basmanova, Brodsky had several short-lived relationships with various women, among them both Soviets and foreign Slavicists who came to meet him while traveling in the Soviet Union, but none of these connections ultimately endured.

After his release from northern exile in 1965, Brodsky's political troubles were far from ended. Khrushchev had been forced from power in late 1964, and Leonid Il'ich Brezhnev took over, becoming the new General Secretary of the Communist Party in 1966. The decade of the Thaw was coming to a close, and there began a wave of arrests and deportations of important writers and scholars, including in 1974 Etkind, who had defended Brodsky at his 1964 trial, and the writer Vladimir Rafailovich Maramzin, who was in the process of compiling a samizdat collection of Brodsky's poetry. The availability today of much of Brodsky's early work results from Maramzin's efforts at collecting and organizing the poet's writings, given Brodsky's own carelessness with his archive, particularly in his youth. The literary critic Mikhail Kheifets, who had written an introduction to Maramzin's volume titled "Iosif Brodskii i nashe pokolenie" (Joseph Brodsky and Our Generation), was sentenced to four years in a labor camp and two years in exile.

Brodsky himself was one of the first casualties of the new cultural repression. Although immediately after his return to Leningrad he was offered the opportunity of publishing a selection of his poems in the journal *Iunost'* (Youth), the publication was canceled when Brodsky refused to acquiesce to Evtushenko's choice of his works, saying the selection made him emerge "looking like a shorn sheep" (cited in Volkov's *Conversations with Joseph Brodsky*). Several of Brodsky's poems were, however, published in Soviet periodicals and almanacs in 1966 and 1967. In addition, in 1966 he prepared a collection titled "Zimniaia pochta" (Winter Mail) for printing by the Leningrad branch of the publishing house Sovetskii pisatel' (Soviet Writer), but these plans fell through when Brodsky was advised that the book would be published only if he agreed to become an informant for the KGB. In 1969 Robert Lowell invited Brodsky to take part in an international poetry festival in London; the same year, he was also asked to appear at the Festival of Two Worlds in Spoleto. He was refused a visa to attend either one; the bizarre response of the Soviet authorities to the latter invitation was that "There is no such poet. True, there was a Brodsky sent to prison a few years ago." Permission for Brodsky to attend a poetry festival in Czechoslovakia was also denied.

Events came to a head on the morning of 10 May 1972. Brodsky was at home in his parents' apartment when the telephone rang. Afraid it was the military commissariat trying to draft him into service, he nervously took the receiver, only to discover that the caller was in fact from the Office of Visas and Registrations (OVIR), whence he was urgently summoned. Once there, after dodging a measure of inane small talk about the weather, he was asked point-blank whether he had received an invitation to Israel. Brodsky replied that he had received two such invitations, although he had no idea who had sent them, and that he hadn't used them because, in the first place, he had not expected to be allowed to go and, in the second place, he had no interest in leaving home permanently. The official responded by setting before Brodsky a visa application accompanied by an invitation from a certain "Evrei Iakov" (Jacob the Jew), whom Brodsky was told to identify as his grandnephew; he was also assured that if he did not fill out the forms on the spot, he would be in for a "very hot time." Weary of his struggles and recognizing the inescapability of the situation, Brodsky complied. The following Monday he was ordered to turn in his passport, and he was given two weeks to leave the country. Brodsky told Volkov that he suspected that Evtushenko had been instrumental in urging this turn of events. Whatever the case, a bold open letter that Brodsky wrote to Brezhnev himself, asserting that "even if my nation does not need my body, my soul will come in handy," expressing his certainty that he would return some day to his native land "in the flesh or on paper," and urging Brezhnev to allow him at least to publish in the Soviet Union, had no effect. This outcome is hardly surprising, given not only the external circumstances but also the morally elevated tone of Brodsky's address to the Soviet leader (quoted in Iakov Arkad'evich Gordin's "Delo Brodskogo," 1989):

> We are all condemned to one and the same end: to death. I who write these lines will die, as will you who read them. Only our deeds will remain, but they too will succumb to destruction. Therefore no one should prevent anyone from doing his own thing. The conditions of existence are too grim to allow for further complication.

Brodsky at last was beyond the reach of the strong grasp of the state, and so he managed to have the final word. In this answer of the poet to the tyrant, reminiscent of Percy Bysshe Shelley's portrait of the fallen Ozymandias, the balance of power is suddenly shifted: the empire is deflated by the individual's word of truth, and poetry is victorious.

The theme of Empire—exemplified by Rome—is a common one in Brodsky's writings, beginning in the late 1960s. Earlier, the idea of Empire had naively signified for Brodsky the conflict between poet and society; in his mature poems, however, the disintegration of the Roman Empire became his way of describing the particular atmosphere of stagnation that was inaugurated under Brezhnev. For example, in Brodsky's poem "Vremia goda—zima . . ." (The time of year is winter . . . , 1977, translated in Bethea's *Joseph Brodsky and the Creation of Exile*), written between 1967 and 1970, the poet dwells on the edge of the empire, at the end of an era, and speaks through a state of stifling half-slumber about his feeling of entrapment: "On the borders all is calm. Dreams / are overfilled with something marital, like thick jam." Caught like a fish on a hook, the poet attempts in vain to escape by exercising the powers of his magical language, which is a priori older than any state, and contents himself by observing stoically that "If we can't get the better of the evil power, then at least we can get the better of ourselves." In his 1981 poem "Biust Tiberiia" (The Bust of Tiberius, 1987), Brodsky equates Rome with "everything lower than one's chin," the expanse of a headless body: "A bust / is like the symbol of the brain's independence / from the life of the body. One's own and / the Empire's." The result of Tiberius's destructive cruelty—defined by Brodsky as "the acceleration of the shared / fate of material things"—is much the same as the result of the poet's creative endeavor: "As concerns what I have said, / what I have said no one needs—not only in the future, but already now. / Isn't that also the acceleration / of history?" In several poems by Brodsky, indeed, thought and feeling undergo a transformation into dead matter and then into nothingness. Brodsky's poetics is infected by the decay of the Empire, which both gave rise to him and later attempted to edge him out of existence.

Thus, in poems such as the 1973 "Tors" (Torso, 1977) he sardonically admits the dangerous allure of any empire's promise of oblivion: "If you suddenly find yourself wandering on petrified grass, / looking better in its marbled form than in nature, / or you notice a faun who's given himself over to flirtation / with a nymph, and both of them are happier in bronze than in dreams, / you may drop your staff from your weary hands: / you're in the Empire, friend… // This is the end of matter, this is a mirror / at the end of the road, an entrance." Empire, according to Brodsky, is the conquest of space; yet, space represents bare "thingness," whereas speech (and therefore the poet) is an attribute of time. As Brodsky wrote in his essay "Flight from Byzantium" (1986), which is a significantly revised version of his Russian essay "Puteshestvie v Stambul" (Journey to Istanbul, 1990): "Space to me is, indeed, both lesser and less dear than time. Not because it is lesser but because it is a thing, while time is an idea about a thing. In choosing between a thing and an idea, the latter is always to be preferred." Or, as Brodsky expresses this thought in poetic terms in his 1971 "Natiurmort" (Still Life, 1977; translated as "Nature Morte" in *Selected Poems*): "A thing / itself, as a rule, does not try // to conquer dust, / does not furrow its brow. / Since dust is the flesh / of time: the flesh and blood." Space, for Brodsky, is connected with the Eastern world, with autocracy, with mute obedient masses, with evil, and with Russia; whereas time is connected with the West, democracy, and individualism. Yet, he later makes clear in his 1975 *poema* "Kolybel'naia Treskovogo mysa" (Lullaby of Cape Cod) that he is at core a scion of the East after all, that there is no escape, and that his move to America is just a move to yet another Empire: "Just as the omnipotent Sheikh can deceive the numberless wives / of his harem only with another harem, / so I have switched empires."

On 4 June 1972 Brodsky arrived in Vienna—ostensibly en route to Israel—where he was met by his friend Carl Proffer, founder of the American publishing house Ardis. Proffer soon led Brodsky to a meeting with Auden at that poet's summer residence, a farmhouse in the Austrian countryside, where he spent the next three weeks. In June and July, Brodsky and Auden appeared together at poetry readings in London and Oxford. Soon afterward, Brodsky accepted Proffer's invitation to the post of poet-in-residence with professorial status at the University of Michigan in Ann Arbor. Brodsky's way in the West had been paved by the appearance in New York in 1970 of his first authorized collection, *Ostanovka v pustyne*. This book encompassed a selection of his best lyrics written up to that point, along with several important *poemy*, including "Gorbunov i Gorchakov," and translations into Russian of four of

Donne's poems. After the publication of the book, Brodsky was elected a member of the Bavarian Academy of Fine Art. Anglophone readers were also able to become acquainted with his poetry through his first English-language collections *Elegy for John Donne and Other Poems* (1967) and *Selected Poems* (1973). The latter volume consisted of translations by George Kline that were overseen by Brodsky himself, and the book included a glowing preface written by Auden.

The history of Brodsky's life in emigration is far less eventful than that of his early years in the Soviet Union. Always a private man, he became more so as he grew older and settled into his hybrid identity as an American professor and man of letters and a Russian émigré poet. Brodsky remained at the University of Michigan for the next nine years. In 1981 he accepted a permanent position as Andrew Mellon Professor of Literature at Mount Holyoke College in South Hadley, Massachusetts. Over the years he also appeared as a guest lecturer and visiting professor at many other universities in both the United States and Britain, including Amherst College, Columbia University, New York University, Queens College, Smith College, and Cambridge University. During his early years in the United States, Brodsky confided in friends his fear of losing the pulse of Russian poetry and becoming alienated from the expressive possibilities of his native language even as he had already been squeezed out from his native country. These fears proved, however, to be in vain; with time, the Russian language became the vessel for Brodsky's identity, the only defining reality in his life, and indeed the exact substance of sanctity and human meaning. "The holiest thing we have," Brodsky said in a 1983 interview with Natal'ia Gorbanevskaia (quoted in Valentina Polukhina's 2000 compilation), "is, perhaps, not our icons, not even our history—it is our language."

In Brodsky's haunting cycle "Chast' rechi" (A Part of Speech), published in *Chast' rechi: Stikhotvoreniia 1972–76* (A Part of Speech: Poems 1972–76, 1977), his language is jumbled and fragmented but does not lose its potency. When the opening poem lurches through neologisms, grammatical impossibilities, and pure nonsense, for example, the result is a surprisingly eloquent statement of loneliness and alienation: "From nowhere with love, the umpteenth of Martober, / dear respected mister sweetie, but it doesn't even matter / who, since the features of the face, speaking / frankly, I can no longer remember, neither yours, nor / anyone's either true friend I greet you from one / of the five continents, which is propped up by cowboys; / I loved you more than the angels or god himself, / and therefore I'm farther from you now, than from them both." As the title of this cycle indicates, the poet himself is pared down,

Dust jacket for Brodsky's 1988 collection of poetry, his second authorized collection in English
(Richland County Public Library)

along with his utterances, to the elementary unit of meaning—the part of speech—and just as the splitting of the atom releases enormous stores of hidden energy, so too this fragmentation of linguistic matter gives rise to a corresponding intensification of meaning: "Of the entire person left to you is only a part / of speech. A part of speech in general. A part of speech." Not only did Brodsky's experience of exile not deprive him of his command of the Russian tongue but, indeed, he came to feel that (as he told Giovanni Buttafava in a 1987 interview, collected in Polukhina's 2000 compilation) "perhaps exile is the natural condition of a poet's existence, in contrast to the novelist, who must exist within the structures of the society he describes."

Exile became the source of Brodsky's mature metaphysics in poems such as the 1975 "Osennii krik iastreba" (The Hawk's Cry in Autumn, 1987), prompting him to formulate in his works a law of subtraction by which the process of living consists of the gradual shedding of every extraneous emotion, connection, and possession until the essential core of being is revealed

through poetic truths, the primary instrument of which is rhyme. Bethea has traced this development in his *Joseph Brodsky and the Creation of Exile*. Perhaps the best illustration of the process is found in Brodsky's biting "1972 god" (1972), published in 1977, a wry self-portrait in verse written shortly after his emigration, where unorthodox rhymes such as "trusosti / trudnosti / trupnosti" (cowardice / difficulty / corpseness) and "doverii / materii / poteri i" (trust / material / loss and) convey the inevitable, gradual decay of physical existence and of the poet's own body in particular. Brodsky's sense of humor, in this poem and throughout his poetry, was a saving power. His lifelong aversion to the stance of victimhood resulted, in his later years, in a trenchant command of language and its expressive possibilities that amounted to a prophetic bent almost searing in its singsong, self-confident precision. Brodsky likewise practiced a stoic gaze backward on all his losses. His stoicism is voiced most eloquently in his 1980 poem "Ia vkhodil vmesto dikogo zveria . . ." (1987, I entered in place of a wild beast . . . ; translated as "May 24, 1980,"

1988), which ends with these well-known lines: "What should I say about life? / That it turned out to be long. / I feel solidarity with grief alone. / But as long as they haven't stuffed my mouth with clay, / only gratefulness will gush from it."

The immense strength of Brodsky's poetic voice and vision is demonstrated again and again in the hundreds of poems published in his major collections of the American years: *Chast' rechi, Konets prekrasnoi epokhi* (End of the Belle Epoque, 1977), *Novye stansy k Avguste* (New Stanzas to Augusta, 1983), *Uraniia* (Urania, 1987), *Primechaniia paporotnika* (Notes of a Fern, 1990), and *Peizazh s navodneniem* (View with a Flood, 1996). Brodsky's stoic refusal to relinquish either his command of the Russian language or his rightful position in the Russian poetic pantheon was not, however, the only factor that guaranteed the potency of his poetic survival in emigration. His adoption of the English language as his second mother tongue and of the United States as his second homeland undoubtedly played an important role in ensuring that he did not fade into nonexistence as the Soviet authorities had hoped. Instead, Brodsky remained an imposing literary presence. He gratefully received his U.S. citizenship in 1977 (some sources give the date as 1980); his posthumous children's book *Discovery* (1999) pays tribute to his love for his adoptive country. Brodsky's knowledge of the English language and love of English and American poetry prior to his emigration facilitated this turn of events. His love affair with English only deepened after he took up residency in the United States, and he often stressed his feeling of obligation toward the English language, as he observed in his essay "The Writer Is a Lonely Traveler" (*The New York Times Magazine,* 1972): "The measure of a writer's patriotism is how he writes in the language of the people among whom he lives." Despite the privacy of Brodsky's habits, his outsider's gaze upon his host culture, and his often critical view of American society, he remained always passionately engaged in dialogue with his adoptive country, and isolationism of the type practiced by another involuntary Russian exile, Aleksandr Isaevich Solzhenitsyn, was unimaginable for him.

Brodsky's first poem in English was "Elegy," dedicated to his mentor Auden. In 1972 Brodsky finally met the American poet Lowell, with whom he felt more comfortable than with Auden; in 1977 he wrote "Elegy: For Robert Lowell" in English and included it with the translations of his Russian lyrics in his 1980 collection *A Part of Speech.* This English collection was followed in 1988 by *To Urania* and, in 1996, by the posthumous collection *So Forth.* With each progressive collection in English, there is a visible acceleration of Brodsky's authorial control over the English versions of his poetry, demonstrating his increasing feeling of ease in the English language and his increasing desire to exist as a full poetic presence in the Anglophone literary space. In *So Forth* translations are not even marked as such, so that distinguishing between poems that exist in Russian-language versions and poems that do not is impossible at first glance. On many occasions Brodsky's authorized versions of works previously published in Russian depart significantly from the original versions, as he alters the semantic content of his lines to preserve a rhyme or metrical pattern or attempts to harness the different idiomatic potential of the English language, with varying degrees of success. Indeed, critical opinion on Brodsky's English-language poetry is strongly divided. Some commentators discern the same linguistic and philosophical brilliance in his English poems that marks his Russian works and find the oddities of his English appealing, revealing, even poetic. Other scholars contend that Brodsky never managed to develop a true understanding of the unique qualities of English verse or even a good grasp of English grammar, and that his English poems and translations suffer badly from his attempts to graft his extremely Russian sensibilities regarding rhyme, meter, and diction onto an unaccommodating medium; the unfortunate result, they claim, is often humor or vulgarity where, clearly, only a scintillating, keen irony is intended.

Critical opinion on Brodsky's English-language prose, however, is essentially unanimous; in this genre, freed of the structural requirements of verse, Brodsky's expressive genius truly shines. His first collection of essays in English, *Less Than One,* was published in 1986, followed by *On Grief and Reason* in 1995; many of these essays first appeared as introductions to poetry collections. In addition, he published several articles and editorials in Anglophone periodicals over the years, including *The New York Times Magazine, TLS: The Times Literary Supplement, The New Yorker, The New York Review of Books, Newsweek, Vogue,* and *Mademoiselle.* Through these appearances in the mainstream press, he attained a powerful voice in the pressing intellectual debates of his time. The essays included in *Less Than One* and *On Grief and Reason* serve as a continuation of Brodsky's poetry and a kind of supplemental poetic autobiography, characterized by the same trenchant intellect and the same linguistic and metaphoric density that mark his poems. *Less Than One* mostly looks backward–to Brodsky's parentage and childhood, which he chronicles in the two essays that frame the collection, as well as to his cultural inheritance in his native city of Leningrad and in the Russian poetic tradition championed by his predecessors Akhmatova, Tsvetaeva, and Mandel'shtam. In other essays in this volume Brodsky ruminates engagingly on various topics, including the state of contemporary Russian prose, the nature of political tyranny, the legacy of poets such as Eugenio Montale and Constantine Cavafy, and the pernicious encroachment, in his view, of Eastern despotism on Russian cultural forms (including Christian Orthodoxy). Brodsky broaches this last topic in his essay "Flight from Byzantium." In the essays that make up *On Grief and Reason* Brodsky mostly turns aside from his Russian background to address the works of American and European poets such as Frost, Thomas Hardy, and Rainer Maria Rilke, as well as his perceptions of the contemporary American society in which he lives.

Brodsky's prolific writings brought him many honors, and in the years following his emigration his literary success was staggering. In 1978 he was awarded an honorary degree of Doctor of Letters by Yale University; in 1979 an Italian translation of his works received both the Feltrinelli Prize for Poetry and the Mondello Literary Prize; on 23 May 1979 he was elected to the American Academy and Institute of Arts and Letters (in 1987 he resigned his membership in protest against the induction of Evtushenko as a foreign member of the Institute); in 1981 he was granted a "genius" award by the John D. and Catherine T. MacArthur Foundation; he received the National Book Critics Circle Award for criticism for his collection *Less Than One* in 1986; in 1987 he was awarded the Nobel Prize in literature; in 1991 he was granted an honorary degree by Oxford University; also in 1991 he was chosen by the Library of Congress to serve as the Poet Laureate of the United States. Brodsky was frequently invited to give readings of his poetry, and he became famous for his powerful, sing-song declamatory style and his sardonic, witty, penetrating monologues in response to his audience's questions. He was also fortunate to be able to cultivate friendships with other leading contemporary poets, including Lowell, Miłosz, Richard Wilbur, Mark Strand, Derek Walcott, Seamus Heaney, and Tomas Venclova, as well as with Western and Russian intellectuals such as Susan Sontag, Lev Vladimirovich Losev, and Aleksandr Sumerkin. Brodsky often traveled to England, and he made a habit of visiting Venice—the watery city that reminded him of his native Leningrad—almost every year during his winter break from teaching. These Venetian odysseys are memorialized in his book-length meditative essay *Watermark* (1992), published first in Italian translation as *Fondamenta degli Incurabili* (Fundamentals of the Incurable) in 1989, and translated into Russian as "Naberezhnaia neistselimykh" (Shores of the Incurable).

Brodsky was grateful for his relative good fortune; he once said, "I'm the happiest combination you can think of. I'm a Russian poet, an English essayist, and an American citizen!" (quoted in Cissie Dore Hill's "Remembering Joseph Brodsky," 2000). However,

despite his professional successes in emigration, his life during these years was largely a solitary one, and his vocation as a university professor never became a true avocation. In addition to the keen feeling of cultural and linguistic alienation that was the norm of his new existence and shaped his writing so distinctively, he had another, more particular sorrow to bear: his parents were repeatedly denied permission by the Soviet authorities to visit their son even for a short time, despite their ceaseless attempts over the years. Brodsky paid tribute to them in his essay "In a Room and a Half" (included in *Less Than One*), hoping that by writing about them in the English language he would somehow manage to free them from their unwitting mental servitude to the Soviet regime, which had swallowed them alive: "I want English verbs of motion to describe their movements. This won't resurrect them, but English grammar may at least prove to be a better escape route from the chimneys of the state crematorium than the Russian." Brodsky's mother, ill with cancer, died in 1983, while his father passed away from a heart attack the following year. From the day in 1972 when he boarded an airplane for the West, Brodsky never saw them again. Over the years Brodsky's own health suffered. He had inherited his father's heart condition, and the emotional strain of his political persecution in the Soviet Union and the physical strain of his eighteen months of hard labor in the far north had worsened matters. Moreover, heedless of doctors' orders, Brodsky all his life was an inveterate hard drinker and chain smoker; during the last two decades of his life he underwent three separate heart bypass operations.

Still, Brodsky's last years were eventful, busy, and largely peaceful. In South Hadley, Massachusetts, where he lived each spring, he owned a house built in the eighteenth century, the rustic decor and rough maple floors of which reminded him of his parents' room in the communal apartment of his youth. Brodsky was famous for his poetry courses at Mount Holyoke College, in which he required his students to memorize hundreds of lines of poetry during the course of the semester. He spent his autumns and winters in the bohemian environment of Greenwich Village in New York City, where he lived in an apartment on Morton Street with his cat. In New York, Brodsky had a wide circle of acquaintances within the Soviet émigré community, in particular the dancer Mikhail Nikolaevich Baryshnikov and the writer, translator, and dance aficionado Gennadii Smakov, a close friend of Brodsky's youth from Leningrad who died of AIDS in New York in 1988.

While continuing to write poetry and essays in both English and Russian, in 1984 Brodsky completed

*Dust jacket for Brodsky's 1995 collection of prose writings, which includes essays on Thomas Hardy
and Robert Frost, as well as an open letter to Václav Havel and the text
of Brodsky's Nobel lecture (Richland County Public Library)*

a drama, which he had begun in the Soviet Union in the 1960s, titled *Mramor* (Marbles). This play premiered on the New York stage with Wallace Shawn and Alex Gregory in the roles of Publius and Tullius, respectively, in 1986 and was subsequently performed in various locations in Europe and North America. The play, like "Gorbunov i Gorchakov," was inspired by Brodsky's nightmarish experience in Soviet psychiatric hospitals, and it continues the dialogue that shapes the earlier *poema;* at the same time the play develops the picture of a post-Christian empire that Brodsky first put forth in his 1970 *poema* "Post Aetatem Nostram" (After Our Era, 1977). In *Mramor* Brodsky heightens both the terror and the humor of his poetic treatment of the subject, going beyond absurdism to portray a hilarious, horrible dystopia two hundred years in the future. A resurrected Roman Empire has established statistical norms for imprisonment, according to which three percent of the population, irrespective of any crimes committed, is shut up for life in a mile-high steel tower in the heart of the new Rome. The two characters of the play, Publius and

Tullius, are unlikely cell mates in the prison tower, doomed to each other's company. Escape is unthinkable; when Tullius succeeds in an ingenious plan to exit briefly into the outside world, he nevertheless returns voluntarily to confinement, opting for the oblivion of sleeping pills over the liberation of real existence.

Brodsky's 1987 Nobel Prize address was an eloquent testament to his own refusal to submit to such oblivion; he declared the complete independence of the poet from any social or political norm, claimed that the only dictator to whom the poet must submit is language itself, and celebrated the continuity of culture according to aesthetic intuition—the source, according to Brodsky, of morality, rather than the other way around: "For a man with taste, particularly with literary taste, is less susceptible to the refrains and the rhythmical incantations peculiar to any version of political demagogy. The point is not so much that virtue does not constitute a guarantee for producing a masterpiece as that evil, especially political evil, is always a bad stylist." After Brodsky received the Nobel Prize, his fame soared, and he was often distracted from his writing by the inevitable parade of journalists, letters from aspiring young poets, and other public obligations.

His commitment to his compatriots did not wane, either; in 1979 he had been instrumental in the defection to the United States of the Bol'shoi Theater ballet star Aleksandr Godunov, and in later years he was active in assisting many Russian émigrés to the United States with letters of recommendation and well-placed telephone calls. He concerned himself fervently with the state of American literary culture as well. In his October 1991 address to the Library of Congress as Poet Laureate he made what he termed, parodying Jonathan Swift, "An Immodest Proposal" (1995) that called for the dissemination of poetry in public places such as hotels and supermarkets in order to counteract what he saw as the degenerative effects of American popular culture. Ludicrous as the proposal might have sounded, it piqued the interest of Andrew Carroll, a young Columbia University graduate, and in 1993 they founded together the American Poetry and Literacy Project, a not-for-profit organization which, in the words of Brodsky's address, was devoted to making poetry a part of American culture "as ubiquitous as gas stations, if not as cars themselves," since poetry "is the only insurance available against the vulgarity of the human heart. Therefore, it should be available to everyone in this country and at a low cost." Carroll continued this project after Brodsky's death, and hundreds of thousands of free books of poetry were given away in hotel rooms and grocery stores, at truck stops and post offices.

Beginning in the early 1990s, Brodsky at last ceased addressing poems to the elusive "M.B." He was an intensely private person, and the few published accounts of events in his personal life are often of doubtful accuracy. What is clear, though, is that in his last years the poet's life changed dramatically. Reportedly, after an epistolary romance with a beautiful young translator named Maria Sozzani and several joint sojourns with her in his beloved Venice, the couple were married in Stockholm in September 1990. Maria Sozzani Brodsky was thirty years Brodsky's junior, the daughter of an Italian father and Russian mother. According to the reminiscences of Brodsky's friends, she was completely different from Basmanova and some of the poet's earlier romantic interests; modest and generous, with not a hint of affectation or manipulativeness, she was devoted to her husband. Some of Brodsky's friends observed that he was changed, softened, and seemed happy as never before. The couple's decision to leave his high-profile residence in Greenwich Village for the comparative tranquility of Brooklyn Heights also contributed significantly to his feeling of contentment. At the time of his marriage Brodsky attributed an air of fatedness to the union when he joked, "I'm Joseph, she's Mary, let's see who'll be born!" (quoted by Andrei Gamalov in his 2000 article). In June 1993 Sozzani Brodsky gave birth to the couple's only child, their daughter Anna Alexandra Maria. Brodsky explained that he had chosen the name "Anna" in honor of Anna Akhmatova; "Alexandra" in honor of his father, Aleksandr Ivanovich; and "Maria" in honor of his mother, Mariia Moiseevna. Brodsky loved his daughter dearly. He felt that she was the embodiment of the feminine ideal that he and his poetic companions had so longed for in their youth.

Brodsky's poems of the 1990s occasionally hint at the poet's emotional transformation when, at rare intervals, his tone of stoic forbearance and the landscape of psychic desolation give way to unprecedented intonations of wonder, meekness, and tenderness. A poignant example of this development is the 1994 poem "To My Daughter" (1996), written in English, in which Brodsky wistfully and a trifle ironically attempts to foresee himself reincarnated after his death—which, he rightly senses, is impending—as an item of "furniture in the corner." He thus tries to imagine away the impossibility of maintaining contact with the daughter whom he will never see grown: "Yet partly because no century from now on will ever manage / without caffeine or jazz, I'll sustain this damage, / and through my cracks and pores, varnish and dust all over, / observe you, in twenty years, in your full flower." Ultimately, the metaphor of the stoic poet transformed into a chair is realized at the end of the poem in Brodsky's resorting to "somewhat wooden lines in our common language"; he intuits, sadly, that his feeble attempt to leave a poetic "message in a bottle" for his child is sure to fail. This intuition may have been prompted by Brodsky's disappointment after a long-awaited reunion with his son, Andrei Basmanov. In 1972 Brodsky had addressed his tender poem "Odissei–Telemaku" (Odysseus to Telemachus, 1977) to the four-year-old Andrei as the poet faced expulsion from the Soviet Union. Yet, the meeting between father and son in the mid 1990s was a failure, as they discovered how little they had in common beyond their extreme physical similarity to each other.

With the advent of perestroika, Brodsky's reputation in his homeland began to change. For the first time since his exile, in 1987–1988 Brodsky's poems were published in the journals *Novyi mir* (New World) and *Neva;* the first Soviet editions of his collected works appeared in 1990, followed by many more such publications in Russia over the next several years. In March 1995 Brodsky went to the Waldorf Astoria Hotel in New York to meet with Anatolii Aleksandrovich Sobchak, the mayor of St. Petersburg, who issued a warm invitation to him to visit his native city the following summer. Brodsky accepted the invitation; however, on 8 April he sent a letter to Sobchak, thanking him for his kindness but explaining that his plans had changed; he had neither the emotional nor the physical resources available to weather such a public journey, although he planned a private one at some future date.

For the most part, the poems of Brodsky's final decade are dark, emotionally blank, intellectually acute, acridly humorous, and frankly self-deprecatory. He foresaw his own death clearly and linked it with the demise of his century, while taking stock of the achievements and failures of both. Such is the case, for example, in his 1989 poem "Fin de Siècle" (Turn of the Century, 1996), which begins with the keen prediction that "The century soon will end, but I'll end sooner. / This is, I fear, not a matter of intuition. / Rather—the influence of nonbeing // on being: of the hunter, so to speak, on his prey, / whether it be the heart's muscle or a brick." The poet continues his meditation, claiming that the century was "not so bad" except for its surplus of dead—but, then again, the living are also in surplus and could just as well (with the exception of the author himself!) be pickled or whipped into a cheese. In his 1993 poem "Dedal v Sitsilii" (Daedalus in Sicily, 1996), Brodsky's portrait of the ancient inventor in old age is also a trenchant self-portrait: "An old man sits, who is able to travel / through air, if it's impossible to go by sea or dry land. / All his life he was building something, inventing something. / All his life from these structures, from these inventions / he had to flee." At the end of the poem Daedalus/Brodsky, as Ariadne once did, ties a thread to his ankle and sets off for the kingdom of the dead; he will journey backward through the labyrinth that he himself has spent his life creating. Brodsky looks forward to his death in poem after poem in a matter-of-fact way, without a trace of sentimentality and often with a quiet, wry humor. Such is the case, too, in the untitled 1994 poem "Menia uprekali vo vsem . . ." (I've been reproached for everything . . . , 1996) with which he ends his collection So Forth (translated as "Taps" in Brodsky's translated version that begins: "I've been reproached for everything save the weather, / and in turn my own neck was seeking a scimitar. / But soon, I'm told, I'll lose my epaulets altogether / and dwindle into a little star"). So resigned to death is Brodsky in poems like these that there is a sense that he has come to the end of his road and is ready—almost impatient—to die. He is tired of life and secure in the knowledge that he has imprinted himself as indelibly as possible on human letters. As in his 1993 poem "Peizazh s navodneniem" (View with a Flood, 1996), the flood of time rises to obliterate him, and he "wants to say something, sputtering with excitement, / but out of the multitude of words only one remains: *was*."

Brodsky died of massive heart failure on the night of 28 January 1996 at the age of fifty-five. Shortly afterward, his longtime friend Rein flew in from Moscow to speak at a memorial service in the Morse Auditorium of Boston University, where Brodsky had given his last public reading on 9 April 1995; friends and family remembered Brodsky at a service held at the Cathedral of St. John the Divine in New York City on 8 March 1996. Following a temporary interment at the cathedral, Brodsky's body was moved to its final resting place in the Cimitero di San Michele in Venice, where he had spent many of his happiest days.

Since his death, Brodsky's life and career have been commemorated many times, and two instances in particular stand out. The first occurred on what would have been his fifty-sixth birthday, 24 May 1996. A massive granite slab, inscribed "In this house from 1955 until 1972 lived the poet Iosif Aleksandrovich Brodsky," was unveiled outside the poet's childhood residence at 24 Liteinyi Street in St. Petersburg. Plans are currently underway for the establishment of a Brodsky literary museum to be housed in the same building. The other commemorative act was the creation, by the poet's widow, Sozzani Brodsky, of the Joseph Brodsky Memorial Fellowship Fund, which enables Russian writers, artists, and scholars to live and work in Italy. The idea for the fellowship had come from Brodsky himself. Shortly before he died, he had appealed to the mayor of Rome for the establishment of a Russian academy in that city. As Brodsky wrote to the mayor, "Italy was a revelation to the Russians; now it can become the source of their renaissance." The fund selected its first recipients, three Russian poets and scholars, in the spring of 2000 and awarded each a three-month fellowship at the American Academy or the French Academy in Rome.

Although the significance and worth of Joseph Brodsky's creative opus continues to be debated to this day, the fact that he challenged many preconceived political, aesthetic, and philosophical sensibilities of his time—in both his poetry and his prose works, in both English and Russian—is indisputable; indeed, precisely for this reason his writings still raise some hackles. Aware of his poetic calling at an early age, he firmly upheld the ideal of free poetic expression throughout his life, seemingly impervious to the potential damage of social pressure, political persecution, and cultural isolation. In his distinctive position as a citizen of two worlds, a master of two literary languages, and an inheritor of two poetic traditions, Brodsky devoted his talent to the creation of a hybrid poetry in which multiple literary tendencies were grafted together: baroque and avant-garde, ancient and metaphysical, English free verse and Russian metered and rhymed verse. The result was the literary rehabilitation of both languages in which Brodsky worked. He freed Russian from the trite phrases of Soviet propaganda and the sentimentality of Russian émigré culture, injecting the language with intellectual heft, jolting rhythms, and disquieting—sometimes even crude—thematic content that was previously unthinkable. At the same time he attempted to release contemporary American belles lettres from the trend he perceived toward amorphousness and irrelevance, and, by reintroducing the English language to the forgotten discipline of aesthetic form, to reconnect Anglophone poetry with its roots in Western high culture. Whether Brodsky will be judged by posterity to have been entirely successful in these endeavors still remains to be seen. What can be said with certainty, however, is that, thanks to his mastery of the art of detachment, Brodsky modeled an eloquent literary protest to both state-sponsored tyranny and the stifling banality of conformism that will not soon be forgotten.

Interviews:

Marianna Volkova and Solomon Volkov, *Iosif Brodskii v N'iu-Iorke: Fotoportrety i besedy s poetom* (New York: Slovo, 1990);

Solomon Volkov, *Razgovory s Iosifom Brodskim* (New York: Slovo, 1997);

Volkov, *Conversations with Joseph Brodsky: A Poet's Journey through the Twentieth Century,* translated by Marian Schwartz (New York & London: Free Press, 1998); Russian version published as *Dialogi s Iosifom Brodskim* (Moscow: Nezavisimaia gazeta, 1998);

Valentina Polukhina, ed., *Bol'shaia kniga inter'viu* (Moscow: Zakharov, 1998; revised and enlarged, 2000);

"Form in Poetry: Joseph Brodsky and Derek Walcott in a Conversation with Bengt Jangfeldt," *Kenyon Review,* 23 (Spring 2001): 185–202;

Peter Vail, "A Conversation with Joseph Brodsky," in *Nativity Poems* (New York: Farrar, Straus & Giroux, 2001), pp. 103–112;

Cynthia L. Haven, *Joseph Brodsky: Conversations* (Jackson: University Press of Mississippi, 2003).

Bibliographies:

Valentina Polukhina, "Bibliography of Russian Poets Talking and Writing about Brodsky," in *Russian Writers on Russian Writers,* edited by Faith Wigzell (Oxford: Berg, 1994), pp. 153–159;

[Bibliografiia perevodov Iosifa Brodskogo], compiled by Viktor Kulle, *Russian, Croatian and Serbian, Czech and Slovak, Polish Literature,* 37, nos. 2–3 (1995): 427–440;

A. Ia. Lapidus and K. M. Azadovsky, *Iosif Brodskii: Ukazatel' literatury na russkom iazyke za 1962–1995 gg.* (St. Petersburg: Rossiiskaia natsional'naia biblioteka, 1997; enlarged, 1999);

Polukhina, "Bibliografiia interv'iu Iosifa Brodskogo," in *Iosif Brodskii: Bol'shaia kniga interv'iu* (Moscow: Zakharov, 1998; revised and enlarged, 2000), pp. 686–701;

Polukhina and Thomas Bigelow, "Selected Bibliography of Brodsky's Essays, Introductions, Reviews and Letters (in English and Russian Only)," *Russian, Croatian and Serbian, Czech and Slovak, Polish Literature,* 47, nos. 3–4 (2000): 409–416;

Inez Ramsey, "Joseph Brodsky: Bibliography" <http://falcon.jmu.edu/~ramseyil/brodskybib.htm>;

Viktor Sergeevich Kulle, "Bibliografiia Iosifa Brodskogo" <http://www.liter.net/=/Kulle/brodsky-bibiograf. htm> [accessed 5 June 2003].

Biographies:

Anna Tavis, "A Journey from Petersburg to Stockholm: Preliminary Biography of Joseph Brodsky," *Slavic Review,* 47 (Fall 1988): 499–501;

Efim Grigor'evich Etkind, *Protsess Iosifa Brodskogo* (London: Overseas Publications Interchange, 1988);

Iakov Arkad'evich Gordin, "Delo Brodskogo," *Neva,* 2 (1989): 165–166;

Iosif Brodskii: Tvorchestvo, lichnost', sud'ba (Itogi trekh konferentsii), compiled by Gordin (St. Petersburg: Zvezda, 1998);

Viktor Sergeevich Kulle, "Iosif Brodskii: Novaia Odisseia," in Brodsky's *Sochineniia,* 8 volumes (St. Petersburg: Pushkinskii fond, 1998), I: 283–297;

A. N. Krivomazov, "Biografiia Iosifa Brodskogo" <http://br00.narod.ru> [accessed 25 July 2003];

Lev Losev and Petr Vail', comps., *Iosif Brodskii: Trudy i dni* (Moscow: Nezavisimaia gazeta, 1998);

Aleksandr Genis, "Brodskii v N'iu-Iorke," in his *Dovlatov i okrestnosti* (Moscow: Vagrius, 1999), pp. 237–258;

Liudmila Shtern, *Brodskii: Osia, Iosif, Joseph* (Moscow: Nezavisimaia gazeta, 2001).

References:

David M. Bethea, *Joseph Brodsky and the Creation of Exile* (Princeton: Princeton University Press, 1994);

Sven Birkerts, "The Art of Poetry XXVII: Joseph Brodsky," *Paris Review,* 83 (Spring 1982): 83–126;

Chast' rechi: Al'manakh literatury i iskusstva, special Brodsky issue, no. 1 (1980);

Piotr Fast, "(Pseudo)-Autobiography in Brodsky's Lyrical Poetry," *Auto-Biography Studies,* 11 (Fall 1996): 125–139;

Andrei Gamalov, "Poka ty byla so mnoiu, ia znal, chto ia sushchestvuiu," *Kar'era,* 12 (December 2000);

Iakov Arkad'evich Gordin, *Pereklichka vo mrake: Iosif Brodskii i ego sobesedniki* (St. Petersburg: Pushkinskii fond, 2000);

Cissie Dore Hill, "Remembering Joseph Brodsky," *Hoover Digest,* 4 (2000);

Evgenii Kelebai, *Poet v dome rebenka: Prolegomeny k filosofii tvorchestva Iosifa Brodskogo* (Moscow: Universitet, 2000);

Gennadii F. Komarov, comp., *Iosif Brodskii razmerom podlinnika (Sbornik statei posviashchennyi 50-letiiu I. Brodskogo)* (Leningrad & Tallinn: LO SP SSSR, 1990);

Mikhail Kreps, *O poezii Iosifa Brodskogo* (Ann Arbor, Mich.: Ardis, 1984);

D. L. Lakerbai, *Rannii Brodskii: Poetika i sud'ba* (Ivanovo: Ivanovskii gosudarstvennyi universitet, 2000);

R. C. Lamont, "Joseph Brodsky: A Poet's Classroom," *Massachusetts Review,* 15 (1974): 553–577;

Lev Losev, ed., *Poetika Brodskogo: Sbornik statei* (Tenafly, N.J.: Ermitazh, 1986);

Losev and Valentina Polukhina, eds., *Brodsky's Poetics and Aesthetics* (New York: St. Martin's Press, 1990);

Losev and Polukhina, eds., *Joseph Brodsky: The Art of a Poem* (New York: St. Martin's Press, 1998);

Losev and Polukhina, eds., *Kak rabotaet stikhotvorenie Brodskogo: Iz issledovanii slavistov na Zapade* (Moscow: Novoe literaturnoe obozrenie, 2002);

David MacFadyen, *Joseph Brodsky and the Baroque* (Montreal: McGill-Queen's University Press, 1998);

MacFadyen, *Joseph Brodsky and the Soviet Muse* (Montreal: McGill-Queen's University Press, 2000);

Polukhina, *Brodsky through the Eyes of His Contemporaries* (New York: St. Martin's Press, 1992); republished in Russian as *Brodskii glazami sovremennikov* (St. Petersburg: Zvezda, 1997);

Polukhina, "Brodsky's Self-Portrait," in *Russian Literature Since 1917: New Directions,* edited by S. Grahem (London: Macmilan, 1992), pp. 122–135;

Polukhina, *Joseph Brodsky: A Poet for Our Time* (Cambridge & New York: Cambridge University Press, 1989);

Polukhina, "Landshaft liricheskoi lichnosti v poezii Brodskogo," in *Literary Tradition and Practice in Russian Culture: Papers from an International Conference on the Occasion of the Seventieth Birthday of Yury Mikhailovich Lotman,* edited by Polukhina, Joe Andrew, and Robert Reid (Amsterdam & Atlanta: Rodopi, 1993), pp. 229–245;

Polukhina, "The Myth of the Poet and the Poet of the Myth: Russian Poets on Brodsky," in *Russian Writers on Russian Writers,* edited by Faith Wigzell (Oxford: Berg, 1994), pp. 139–153;

Polukhina, "Poeticheskii avtoportret Brodskogo," *Russian, Croatian and Serbian, Czech and Slovak, Polish Literature,* 31 (1992): 375–392;

Polukhina, "The Prose of Joseph Brodsky: A Continuation of Poetry by Other Means," *Russian, Croatian and Serbian, Czech and Slovak, Polish Literature,* 41 (1997): 223–240;

Evgenii Rein, "Brodskii–poslednii real'nyi novator," *Knizhnoe obozrenie,* 18 May 1990;

David Rigsbee, *Styles of Ruin: Joseph Brodsky and the Postmodernist Elegy,* Contributions to the Study of World Literature, no. 93 (Westport, Conn.: Greenwood Press, 1999);

Russian, Croatian and Serbian, Czech and Slovak, Polish Literature, special Brodsky issues, 37, nos. 2–3 (1995); 47, nos. 3–4 (2000);

Natal'ia Strizhevskaia, *Pis'mena, perspektivy: O poezii Iosifa Brodskogo* (Moscow: Graal', 1997).

Papers:

Joseph Brodsky's papers, representing all of his work up to the time he went into exile (June 1972), are located in the Russian National Library (RNB) in St. Petersburg. His papers from the émigré period are held in New York City by his widow, Maria Sozzani Brodsky, and the Brodsky Estate.

Andrei Viktorovich Dmitriev

(7 May 1956 -)

Tatiana Spektor
Holy Trinity Seminary

BOOKS: *Povorot reki* (Moscow: Vagrius, 1998)–comprises "Shtil'," "Shagi," *Voskoboev i Elizaveta, Povest' o poteriannom, Povorot reki, Golubev,* and *Proletarii Elistratov;*

Zakrytaia kniga. Roman i povesti (Moscow: Vagrius, 2000)–includes *Zakrytaia kniga;*

Doroga obratno. Roman i povesti (Moscow: Vagrius, 2003)–comprises *Voskoboev i Elizaveta, Povorot reki, Zakrytaia kniga,* and *Doroga obratno.*

PRODUCED SCRIPTS: *Radosti srednego vozrasta,* motion picture, by Dmitriev and Ilia Kulik, Estonia-Film, 1987;

Alisa i bukinist, motion picture, Estonia-Film, 1992;

Chernaia vual', motion picture, by Dmitriev and Stanislav Govorukhin, Mosfilm, 1995;

Revizor, motion picture, by Dmitriev and Sergei Gazarov, Most Group and Nikita & Petr Film Company, 1996;

Proshchai, XX vek (Natsism i totalitarism), television, Kul'tura, TV-6, 1999–2001.

SELECTED PERIODICAL PUBLICATIONS–UNCOLLECTED: "'Idi, kuda vlechet tebia svobodnyi um . . . ,'" by Dmitriev and others, *Znamia,* 6 (1999): 172–175;

"O proze real'noi i virtualnoi," by Dmitriev and others, *Druzhba narodov,* 11 (1999): 181–198;

"Segodnia, zavtra, dalee–vezde," by Dmitriev and others, *Novyi mir,* 4 (2000): 223–230;

"Po etu storonu teleekrana," by Dmitriev and others, *Znamia,* 4 (2000): 197–209;

"Odnazhdy v *Znameni,*" by Dmitriev and others, *Znamia,* 1 (2001): 193–215;

"Rossiia 1991–2001: Pobedy i porazheniia," by Dmitriev and others, *Znamia,* 8 (2001): 155–171;

"Govoriat finalisty premii Ivana Petrovicha Belkina," by Dmitriev and others, *Znamia,* 6 (2002): 164–178;

Prizrak teatr, Znamia, 6 (2003).

Andrei Viktorovich Dmitriev (photograph by Mark Lipovetsky)

In the atmosphere of scandal and provocation that has pervaded Russian literature in the last two decades, Andrei Dmitriev occupies an isolated position; not concerned with glory, he works in solitude and deep concentration, publishing rarely. Dmitriev's writings address above all the category of the sublime–a value completely obliterated in contemporary Russian culture–which he persistently reveals as inherent in the most prosaic events of everyday life. The sublime in his work is expressed only through the subtle and dramatically fragile shifts in communication between the human psyche, nature, and cultural tradition. Dmitriev's task is to present these fluctuations. He has developed an individual style that fuses sentimentalist and Romantic motifs with the art of psychological analysis, as inherited from the tradition of Russian realism. His work also draws on emphatically modernist elements such as estrangement, intertextuality, an amalgamation of diverse discursive layers, and mythologism.

Dmitriev was born on 7 May 1956 in Leningrad to Viktor Andreevich Dmitriev and his Lithuanian wife Niele Apollonia Martino (Patkaustkaite), then students at Leningrad State University. Soon after Dmitriev's birth and the couple's graduation, the family moved to Pskov, an old city of the Russian North on the border between Latvia, Estonia, and Belorussia. The distinctive image of Pskov, shaped by proximity to the Pskov Monastery of the Caves and to the Pushkin National Museum, made a deep impression on the writer. Nearly all of Dmitriev's fiction is permeated by the atmosphere of the Russian North.

When Dmitriev was thirteen, his father, a literary scholar, received a position at the Agentsvo Pechati Novosti (State News Agency) and the family moved to Moscow. At Moscow State University, where Dmitriev studied Old Russian literature in the mid 1970s, he made friends with the future literary theorists and critics Andrei Zorin, Oleg Proskurin, Vera Mil'china, Andrei Nemzer, Alexander Stroev, and Boris Berman. These critics and literary scholars became influential figures in the post-Soviet culture of the 1990s. In 1977 Dmitriev withdrew from Moscow State to enroll in the State Institute of Cinematography. He had already been writing fiction by the time of his 1982 graduation from the institute, and his first story, "Shtil'" (Still Weather), was published at approximately the same time, in April 1983 in the journal *Novyi mir* (New World). Besides fiction, in the early 1980s he was also writing screenplays as school projects at the Institute of Cinematography. One of them became the 1987 motion picture *Radosti srednego vozrasta* (The Joys of Middle Age). After graduating from the institute, Dmitriev spent about a year at Mos'film as a screenwriter. From 1984 to 1986 he worked as an editor at the Central Screenplay Office of the State Cinema of the U.S.S.R. He has been writing full-time since 1986. In January 2000 Dmitriev married Ol'ga Iur'evna Bogomolova, daughter of Iurii Aleksandrovich Bogomolov, the well-known movie critic and journalist for *Izvestiia* (The News). An art critic and scholar, Ol'ga works as a senior researcher at the Moscow Institute of the Arts. Dmitriev and his wife have a son, Artem (Tioma), who was born on 28 December 2000.

Although critics had noticed Dmitriev's talents upon the publication of "Shtil'," he did not garner well-deserved acclaim until much later. His novella *Povorot reki* (A Bend in the River, collected in 1998) first appeared in *Znamia* in 1995 and was short-listed for the Russian Booker Prize in 1996. He also received the annual Pushkin stipend in 1995, and in 1997 he was accepted as a mentor to the Russian PEN Center. Dmitriev achieved genuine fame in 2001 upon the publication in *Znamia* of his novella *Doroga obratno* (The Way Back Home). It was short-listed for two prominent national literary prizes: the Ivan Petrovich Belkin Prize, founded by *Znamia* and the publishing house EKSMO, and the Apollon Grigor'ev Literary Prize, established by the Akademiia sovremennoi rossiskoi slovesnosti (Academy of Contemporary Russian Letters). Because of his growing renown, Dmitriev was invited by various institutions and organizations to visit the United States in 2001 and 2002.

Povorot reki is Dmitriev's first book, a collection of prose fiction that includes three stories and four novellas, all of which—except the novella *Golubev*—were published previously by influential literary magazines such as *Znamia, Novyi mir,* and *Druzhba narodov* (The People's Friendship). In "Shtil'," which opens the collection, Dmitriev provides a sentimental view of Soviet life in the early 1980s. Like the idylls of the writer Nikolai Mikhailovich Karamzin—who lived from 1766 to 1826—that discuss edenic harmony before the Fall, Dmitriev's story actualizes the archetype of the Garden of Eden. It begins and ends with a description of a garden in two phases—with and without its tree, which at once represents the "tree of life" and the "tree of knowledge"—before and after the Fall.

The three main characters—Tamara, Nastia, and Vladimir—spend their summer vacation by the sea. Living together in rented housing, with a garden on the property, they talk about various compelling subjects, including modern man's function in the Garden of Eden. Vladimir asserts that the Garden of Eden either does not exist or is tiny in size because of the small number of virtuous people, whom he regards as not exactly human but "something in between a bacterium and fantasy." The women disagree, and Tamara claims that Nastia is a genuinely virtuous person. Thus, according to Dmitriev, modern man's existence "in between" is the result of his conscious rejection of the divine. Through the character of Nastia, Dmitriev suggests that the restoration of virtue will lead humanity out of this helpless situation. He contradicts Karamzin's skeptical views and supports Ivan Sergeevich Turgenev's belief in the spiritual strength of Russian women, like Parasha in Turgenev's 1847 poem named for her, Lisa in *Dvorianskoe gnezdo* (Home of the Gentry, 1859), Elena in *Nakanune* (On the Eve, 1860), and many others in Turgenev's prose and poetry.

Nevertheless, the finale of Dmitriev's story is pessimistic: the protagonists have been "banished"

Dust jacket for Dmitriev's first book, Povorot reki *(A Bend in the River, 1998), a collection of stories and novellas that was short-listed for the Booker Russian Novel Prize (Collection of Mark Lipovetsky)*

from the garden, because its new owners—grandchildren of the previous landlord—have found that renting the house is unprofitable. In a further link with the exile of Adam and Eve from Eden, the owners cut down the tree in the garden, a development that renders the situation hopeless for the protagonists.

The exile of modern man from the Garden of Eden is interpreted by Dmitriev in accordance with Anton Pavlovich Chekhov's *Vishnevyi sad* (The Cherry Orchard, 1904), in which Chekhov shows the displacement of a declining gentry by crass parvenu merchants in the 1900s. The symbol of the cherry orchard points to the landowners' highly developed sense of cultural heritage and love of beauty, as well as to the merchants' greed and vulgarity. The merchant Lopakhin, who purchases the orchard in the play, has little feeling for the beautiful though unproductive trees that he orders to be removed. In Dmitriev's story, as in Chekhov's play, intellectual paradise has been destroyed by a new generation that prefers practical values to ideals. Banished from the garden, Tamara, Nastia, and Vladimir stay in a nearby resort and either spend hours in silence or

mull over everyday petty problems. The lofty meaning of their relationship has been lost.

The short stories "Shagi" (Steps, 1998) and "Proletarii Elistratov," both included in the collection *Povorot reki,* represent the next stage in the development of Dmitriev's style. The contrast between a sentimentalist idyllic plot and a sorrowful finale develops to the point of catastrophe. In both stories an endless chain of mundane events is interrupted by a sudden emotional outburst—the reaction of an individual to the pressure of the collective. This theme depicts the stage in the protagonist's life when he finally loses all hope for a better existence. In "Shagi" a shy and weak construction worker, Ivan Korolev, attempts to "vindicate" the community of the city of Pytavino, which is hostile to him, by robbing one of its inhabitants. On his way home from a local bar, Korolev jumps through the window of an old man's house and fills his pockets with odd items such as pills, nails, and old bills. His infantile "crime" leads to a real tragedy. At the end of the story Korolev is sentenced to jail, and his mother is certain that, as he is weak and sickly, he has no chance of surviving the

Page from the manuscript for Dmitriev's story "Shagi" (Steps), written in the 1980s and collected in Povorot reki *(courtesy of the author)*

sentence. "Shagi"–like "Shtil'"–has a circular composition. The story begins and ends in the same place, a train station. At the beginning of the story Korolev hurries to the station after work to meet his mother and walk her home (she sells frozen fish in an underground passage by the station). On his way he challenges the approaching train by walking on the rails. The story ends with his mother listening to the "irrepressible and free iron roar" of the train while selling frozen fish in the tunnel after the trial.

The triumph of the irrepressible and senseless power over the protagonist's weak, yet sensitive, psyche constitutes the central conflict in the story. This conflict is described as a person's striving for self-expression and the fundamental dehumanization of Soviet/Russian society. The shy and weak Korolev challenges the blind will of the collective in every social situation, even though he is aware that its power inevitably crushes everyone who does not conform. His mother, who tries to create a warm shelter of unconditional mutual love within an alienating societal atmosphere, provides the only support for his efforts. The finale of the story is thus utterly pessimistic. Not only Korolev's life but also the entire nucleus of love has been destroyed by the collective will.

The subconscious battle between the individual and the collective is further explored in "Proletarii Elistratov." The plot of the story is similar to that of "Shagi." Like Korolev, Evgeny Elistratov commits a senseless "crime" against a stranger during an emotional crisis caused by his conflict with society. Other details connecting "Shagi" and "Proletarii Elistratov," as in a diptych, include the city of Pytavino as a major setting and the character of Elistratov. Although similar in many aspects, these two texts differ in their representation of the conflict between the individual and the collective. While in "Shagi" Dmitriev explores this conflict in a totalitarian context, in "Proletarii Elistratov" he places the problem in the new cultural situation of the early post-Soviet period.

Elistratov moves with his wife and two sons to Moscow, while his father stays in Pytavino, where he has been constantly harassed by a group of criminals. The Pytavino police are unable and unwilling to protect the old man, and Elistratov cannot take his father to Moscow because of the housing shortage there; Elistratov and his family live in a workers' (militia) dormitory. In a deep emotional crisis caused by insomnia and helplessness, Elistratov attacks a stranger in a fast-food restaurant and beats him senseless. Whether Elistratov will be punished for his crime is not certain, but as his assault on the stranger makes evident, his life has arrived at a point of total hopelessness. Looking out of the window of his dormitory room at the end of the narrative, Elistratov suffers from an acute feeling of estrangement awakened in him by the brightness of the "alien" windows around–the same feeling that made Korolev in "Shagi" jump through such a window. Thus, in the diptych encompassed by these two stories that explore the relationship between the individual and faceless societal forces during Soviet and post-Soviet times, Dmitriev arrives at the conclusion that the recent changes in the political structure of Russia have not improved society itself. Repression and fear have remained its ruling forces.

Two novellas, *Voskoboev i Elizaveta* (Voskoboev and Elizabeth, 1992) and *Povorot reki,* which together also compose a diptych, conclude Dmitriev's first book. These two texts are connected by the same setting, the Russian Northwest, and the same event, a duel between the military pilot Trutko and his wife's lover. The novellas are also united by their characters' perennial search for solace from the cruelty and chaos of everyday life, as well as from the historical and political turmoil of the 1990s. In *Voskoboev i Elizaveta* Dmitriev makes direct references to Karamzin's *Bednaia Liza* (Poor Liza, 1792) and Henry David Thoreau's *Walden; Or, Life in the Woods* (1854). Dmitriev demonstrates how the idealistic beliefs of the Russian sentimentalist Karamzin and of American transcendentalist writers such as Thoreau; the beneficial influence of nature on humanity; and the ability of human beings to build their own lives are crushed when met with modern reality. In *Voskoboev i Elizaveta* ferocious death and chaos reign in both the world of nature and the world of humans. Barred from flying because of causing an aircraft explosion that killed his fellow pilot and destroyed a large part of a national nature reserve, the military pilot Voskoboev withdraws from a happy family life and spends his days and nights hunting in this same reserve. In a rage and armed with explosives he finally detonates himself by the door to his apartment, which has been locked by his pregnant wife Elizaveta, who is inside.

Even literature brings death and destruction in *Voskoboev i Elizaveta.* Trutko, another military pilot, kills himself to confirm the "laws" of literature as he understands them. He tries to construct his personal life according to the universal principles that he has found in great works of literature, such as *Bednaia Liza.* Trutko abandons his wife but discovers that, unlike Liza in Karamzin's narrative, Trutko's wife becomes happy with someone else. Although disappointed, he does not give up and engages in another literary thematic convention when he challenges his rival to a duel in which each man will shoot himself. The rival understands the challenge as "military humor" and jokingly accepts it, but Trutko is not joking and kills himself.

Death reigns at the end of the novella on a larger scale, too. On 31 December 1979 the entire military regiment is sent to a remote "southern" area to participate in "real actions" (the Afghan war, the reader assumes), which means that the surviving male characters are assigned to die together with a hundred thousand victims of ideological manipulation. This mass destruction, considered a legitimate contribution to a political dialogue, is similar to Trutko's beliefs in the universal principles of life as he perceives them in literature.

While in *Voskoboev i Elizaveta* Dmitriev is mostly concerned with exploring the correlation between humans and nature and between life and literature, in *Povorot reki* he examines the relationship between the earthly and the divine. In the latter novella two of the four main characters—the boy Smirnov and a nameless woman—find refuge from contemporary reality in the realm of the divine. Two other characters—the doctor Snetkov and Smirnov's father—are faced with the tragedy of the boy's death, which destroys the illusory worlds they have been creating.

The reader meets the doctor and Smirnov's father at the point of their rivalry over the boy, a patient in a mountain resort for tubercular children. The father, a character who appeared as Trutko's rival in *Voskoboev i Elizaveta* and is now unhappily married to the pilot's widow, wants to take the boy home to stop his mother from leaving him. The doctor, aware that Smirnov's health is deteriorating during his visits home, makes the boy hide. Smirnov obeys and spends quite a cold day in a crevice above a bend in a river, where his condition worsens, and he dies.

While in the crevice, the boy dreams that he jumps from the mountain and runs on the water out of a strong desire to pass over the bend in the river. When he reaches the bend, he enters a sea and runs toward fishermen, smiling at him humbly from a sailboat. Then he hears an almost inaudible yet familiar voice calling him from a sunlit distance, and hesitantly he walks toward it. When the boy hears a trumpet, he continues walking in the same direction, confidently and joyfully. The dream is full of Christian symbolism alluding to resurrection; in particular, two references to the Gospels—Christ walking on the water and the last trumpet sound—render Smirnov's journey toward the light a metaphor for resurrection.

While dreaming, the boy overhears a conversation of a man and a woman sitting by the crevice. Although they arrived at the resort on the same bus, the man and woman do not know one another, nor do they learn one another's names. The woman has come to the mountain to visit a former Orthodox convent, presently a resort, where she hopes to witness her own resurrection to a "new, true life." Her decision to join a

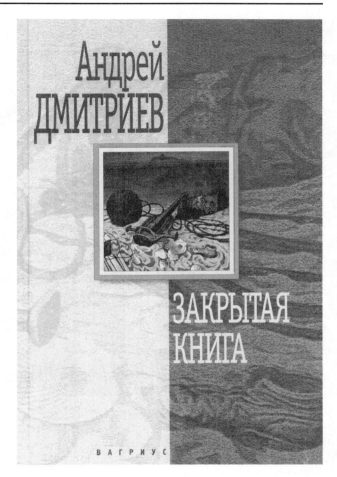

Cover for Dmitriev's 2000 collection Zakrytaia kniga (The Closed Book), which includes his novel with the same title (Collection of Mark Lipovetsky)

monastic community results from her spiritual suffering after an abortion and a wish to "hear" God's responses to her prayers. She wants to view this place—its deserted garden and an abandoned church with medieval frescoes. Yet, the man, uninvited, follows the woman everywhere in her wanderings on the mountain. He offers her wine, sexual pleasures, and an overseas trip. He recounts for her the story of Christ as a modern version of the Nietzschean "God is dead!"; all the while, the boy overhears this story while dreaming of the resurrection. The man's role in the novella is to challenge the woman's faith through temptations of flesh and spirit. She confronts the challenge effortlessly—in response to his "You will never hear from Him, darling," she describes a new garden that she will plant on the site of a destroyed one.

Once again, Dmitriev employs the symbol of a garden in the tradition of Chekhov—as representing a new stage in national, cultural development. In *Povorot reki* the restoration of a monastic garden brings hope in

Dmitriev with his wife, Ol'ga Iur'evna Bogomolova, in Moscow, June 2003
(photograph by Mark Lipovetsky)

spite of the tragic finale to the novella. The boy enters a heavenly world upon his death, and the nameless woman intuitively finds faith and remains steadfast in spite of temptation.

Dmitriev's second collection, *Zakrytaia kniga. Roman i povesti* (The Closed Book. Novel and Novellas, 2000), includes his largest novel to date, *Zakrytaia kniga,* and garnered considerable critical acclaim. Reporting on modern man's encounters with history and eternity, the novel *Zakrytaia kniga* is presented as a family chronicle spanning almost a century, from the early 1900s to the 1990s. Here, Dmitriev continues his examination of the relationship between humanity and nature and between the individual and the collective subconscious. Critics have differed widely in their opinions of the novel; some, such as Nemzer and Aleksandr Arkhangelsky, considered *Zakrytaia kniga* as one of the best novels of 2000, while others, such as Maria Remizova, regarded it as a failure, and still others, such as Evegnii Ermolin, doubted whether the work was even a novel.

Beginning in 1963 and ending in 1993, *Zakrytaia kniga* has flashbacks to World War I, the October Revolution of 1917, World War II, the Thaw (1953–1968), and the Stagnation (1968–1987). At the same time the novel does not resemble a journalistic report on the major events of the century but, rather, presents a fantastic medley of historical facts and cultural myths. Under slightly disguised names, real historical personages such as the prose writer Veniamin Aleksandrovich (Zil'ber) Kaverin, two Russian formalists, Yurii Nikolaevich Tynianov and Viktor Borisovich Shklovsky, and the microbiologist Lev Aleksandrovich Zil'ber exist in the world of Dmitriev's novel along with completely fictional characters. Although such features remind the reader of a derisive postmodernist play mixed with national history and mythology, the subtext in *Zakrytaia kniga* is patterned after a biblical parable. The stories of the lives of a father, his son, and his grandson are told through the circular pattern of a myth—the birth, youth, marriage, and death of an older man are followed by the birth, childhood, marriage, and death of a younger one. Moreover, these twentieth-century biographies are symbolically connected to the eternal stories of Adam, Moses, Jonah, and Christ.

The father, introduced to the reader only by his initials, V.V., is a geography teacher highly respected by the entire population of a northern provincial city. His love for nature is symbolized by the presence of the Garden of Eden in his life: he abandons a paradise of primitive existence in a Northern tribe in the 1910s, grows a beautiful garden by his house in the 1930s, and builds a nature reserve as the city museum dedicated to Northern wildlife in the 1940s. This love of nature saves him from the dangers of dark Soviet history, although he voluntarily left the primordial paradise of a Scandinavian tribe after the October Revolution. The life of V.V.'s son, Seraphim, reminds one of a saint's vita (life). In this character Dmitriev emphasizes features especially valued by the Russian Orthodox Church, such as humility, wandering, and holy foolishness. Seraphim leads a humble life in the shadow of his famous father. He is a devout hiker but claims to be insane. He eventually becomes the holy fool of the village. The life of Seraphim's son, Jonah, alludes to another biblical character and story. Jonah lives on a barge and justifies his choice of such a bizarre abode in biblical terms: "Water is more reliable in today's Russia than 'firmness'." In 1993 Jonah is bankrupt and hides from both state officials and criminal partners. His father, Seraphim, however, leads hired killers to believe that he is Jonah and is shot on the barge.

Dmitriev's most recent work, the novella *Doroga obratno* (The Way Back Home), published in 2001 in *Znamia,* pays tribute to his childhood in Pskov, of which he has acute and vivid memories. In the novella Dmitriev continues the exploration of his favorite theme of the individual versus the collective in the context of national history. The protagonist Maria, based on Dmitriev's nanny of the same name, is a victim of both World War II and Soviet postwar internal policy. Maria's unassuming acceptance of humiliation and suffering is utterly different, not only from a Soviet citizen's combative attitude toward life but also from a similarly aggressive Protestant spirit represented by another nanny in Dmitriev's family. *Doroga obratno* won Dmitriev the Apollon Grigor'ev Prize of the Academy of Contemporary Russian Writers for the best literary work of 2001.

Compared to his prose, Andrei Viktorovich Dmitriev's scripts for Russian and Estonian cinema are about far less serious topics and demonstrate a great sense of humor and playfulness. While his prose fiction focuses more on contemplation than action, Dmitriev's movies combine vivid dialogue with action. At the same time his screen scenarios address the same existential problem that can be found in his fiction—the individual struggle against the cruelty and senselessness of collective existence in the modern world. Nonetheless, in both his fiction and screenplays Dmitriev mixes meta-

physical insights into the national and individual psyche with sound social criticism. His sensitivity to the life of the spirit and his alarm over the fate of the natural world make his vision one of the most memorably artistic in post-Soviet literature and cinema.

Interview:

Maria Setiukova, "Dmitriev, Andrei. Mifologiia svobodnogo poleta," *Literaturnia gazeta,* 8 June 1994, p. 5.

References:

Nikolai Aleksandrov, "Diagnoz—entropia (Sovetskaia i post-sovetskaia russkaia literatura)," *Druzhba narodov,* 11 (1996): 160–176; republished as "Diagnosis-Entropy: Soviet and Post-Soviet Russian Literature," *Russian Studies in Literature,* 34 (1998): 80–96;

Aleksandr Arkhangelsky, "Koshach'i shagi komandora," *Izvestiia,* 8 May 2003, p. 5;

Arkhangelsky, "Pepel ostyvshikh polemik—russkie pisateli vtoroi poloviny 90-kh," *Novyi mir,* 1 (1996): 215–217;

Pavel Basinsky, "Sumerki realizma," *Literaturnaia gazeta,* 27 September 1995, p. 4;

Evgenii Ermolin, "Zakladka," *Novyi mir,* 9 (1999): 206–212;

Alla Marchenko, "Otchego tak legko zarydat': Andrei Dmitriev. Povorot reki," *Novyi mir,* 1 (1999): 194–198;

Andrei Nemzer, "Chem otkrovennee, tem zagadochnee. O proze Andreia Dmitrieva," *Druzhba narodov,* 10 (1996): 157–170;

Nemzer, "Posle shtilia i bur'," in *Povorot reki,* by Dmitriev (Moscow: Vagrius, 1998), pp. 5–17;

Nemzer, "Vse eto Khnov" and "Ty zavtra ochneshsia ot spiachki," in his *Literaturnoe segodnia. O russkoi proze. 90-e* (Moscow: Novoe literaturnoe obozrenie, 1998), pp. 144–147;

Nemzer, "Zamechatel'noe desiatiletie," *Novyi mir,* 1 (2000): 199–219;

Evgenii Shklovsky, "Razgovory skvoz' vatu: O povesti Andreiia Dmitrieva 'Povorot reki'," *Obshchaia gazeta,* 37 (1995).

Papers:

Some of Andrei Viktorovich Dmitriev's papers have been collected by the Museum of Pskov High School No. 8 in Pskov, Russia.

Sergei Donatovich Dovlatov

(3 September 1941– 24 August 1990)

Jekaterina Young
University of Manchester

BOOKS: *Nevidimaia kniga* (Ann Arbor, Mich.: Ardis, 1977); translated by Katherine O'Connor and Diana Burgin as *The Invisible Book* (Ann Arbor, Mich.: Ardis, 1979);

Solo na undervude: Zapisnye knizhki (Paris & New York: Tret'ia volna, 1980);

Kompromiss (New York: Serebrianyi vek, 1981); translated by Anne Frydman as *The Compromise* (London: Chatto & Windus, 1983; New York: Knopf, 1983);

Zona. Zapiski nadziratelia (Ann Arbor, Mich.: Ermitazh, 1982); translated by Frydman as *The Zone: A Prison Camp Guard's Story* (New York: Knopf, 1985);

Literatura prodolzhaetsia. Esse (Paris: Sintaksis, 1982);

Zapovednik (Ann Arbor, Mich.: Ardis, 1983);

Marsh odinokikh (Holyoke, Mass.: New England Publishing, 1983); translated by Roman Sonynn as *The March of the Lonely* (Holyoke, Mass.: New England Publishing, 1983);

Nashi (Ann Arbor, Mich.: Ardis, 1983); translated by Frydman as *Ours: A Russian Family Album* (New York: Weidenfeld & Nicolson, 1989);

Demarsh entuziastov, by Dovlatov, Vagrich Bakhchanian, and Naum Sagalovsky (Paris: Sintaksis, 1985);

Remeslo: Povest' v dvukh chastiakh (Ann Arbor, Mich.: Ardis, 1985);

Inostranka (New York: Russica, 1986); translated by Antonina W. Bouis as *A Foreign Woman* (New York: Grove Weidenfeld, 1991);

Chemodan (Tenafly, N.J.: Ermitazh, 1986; Moscow: Moskovskii rabochii, 1991); translated by Bouis as *The Suitcase* (New York: Grove Weidenfeld, 1991);

Predstavlenie i drugie rasskazy (New York: Russica, 1987);

Filial. Zapiski vedushchego (New York: Russica, 1989);

Ne tol'ko Brodskii: Russkaia kul'tura v portretakh i anekdotakh, with photographs by Marianna Volkova (New York: Slovo, 1990); translated by Brian Baer as *Not Just Brodsky: Russian Culture in Portraits and Anecdotes* (New York: Slovo, 1988);

Sergei Donatovich Dovlatov (photograph by Jerry Bauer; from the dust jacket for Ours: A Russian Family Album, *1989; Richland County Public Library)*

Zapisnye knizhki (New York: Slovo, 1990);

Filial (New York: Slovo, 1990);

TSDL: Tsentral'nyi dom literatorov, by Lev Khalif and Dovlatov (Ekaterinburg: U-Faktoriia, 2001).

Editions and Collections: *Solo na undervude* (Holyoke, Mass.: New England Publishing, 1983);

Chemodan. Povesti, foreword by Iurii Arpishkin (Moscow: Moskovskii rabochii, 1991);

Rasskazy (Moscow: Renaissance, 1991);

Zona; Kompromiss; Zapovednik (Moscow: PIK, 1991);

Remeslo; Nashi (Leningrad & Tallinn: Zvezda, 1991);

Sobranie prozy, 3 volumes (St. Petersburg: Limbus, 1993);

Maloizvestnyi Dovlatov (St. Petersburg: Zvezda, 1995);

Chekhov, Il'f, Dovlatov: Iz zapisnykh knizhek (New York: Alexandria, 1999);

Sobranie sochinenii, 4 volumes (St. Petersburg: Azbuka, 2000);

Posledniaia kniga (St. Petersburg: Azbuka-klassika, 2001).

OTHER: "Kak izdavat'sia na Zapade," in *The Third Wave: Russian Literature in Emigration,* edited by Olga Matich, with Michael Heim (Ann Arbor, Mich.: Ardis, 1984), pp. 53–62.

SELECTED PERIODICAL PUBLICATION–UNCOLLECTED: Po sobstvennomu zhelaniu, *Neva,* 5 (1973): 8–19;

"Interv'iu," *Iunost',* 6 (1974): 41–51.

Barely published and known only to limited circles in Russia, Sergei Dovlatov began to receive recognition only after his immigration to the United States in 1978. In the years after his death in 1990 he was recognized in Russia as one of the most significant writers of his generation. He published many books and during his lifetime his works were translated not only into English but also several other languages, including French, German, Swedish, Finnish, Japanese, Danish, and Hungarian. Dovlatov enjoyed considerable critical acclaim in the United States, receiving hundreds of positive reviews for his books in English translation. He won the American PEN club prize for the best short story written in 1986, and he was one of the Russian writers whose work appeared in the prestigious magazine *The New Yorker.* What preoccupied him was language, and for this reason recognition in Russia was paramount to him. Once his works were published in Russia, beginning in 1989, his popularity reached almost cult status.

Sergei Donatovich Dovlatov was born on 3 September 1941 in Ufa into a theatrical family. His father, Donat Isaakovich Mechik, was a theater director, and his mother, Nora Sergeevna Dovlatova, was of Armenian descent and an actress. In 1944 the family moved back to Leningrad, where Dovlatov spent most of his life until immigration to the United States in the late 1970s. Donat Mechik and Dovlatova divorced shortly after moving to Leningrad; Dovlatov's father married for a second time in the 1950s and had a daughter, Ksenia Mechik (who later published as Ksenia Mechik-Blank). In 1959 Dovlatov entered Leningrad State University to study Finnish but did not complete his courses. As a consequence, he entered the army, serving from 1962 to 1965 in the troops of the Ministry of Internal Affairs as a guard in the Glavnoe upravlenie ispravitel'no-trudovykh lagerei (GULAG, labor camp).

First stationed in Syktyvkar, the capital of the Komi autonomous republic and a port on the river Sysola, he was then dispatched to Ust'vymlag.

Dovlatov's first attempts at writing began in the 1960s, and in the army he concentrated on it in earnest, as letters to his father testify. The bulk of these letters consists of poems that Dovlatov wrote during his years of service; in this correspondence he also discusses the process of writing poetry, seeking out his father's opinion on the poems he has written and offering his own criticism of them. The poems describe everyday life in the camp. "I sincerely don't consider myself a poet," wrote Dovlatov in a letter to his father, "it is simply at the moment poetry helps me out and besides, the boys like the poems very much." One of the poems, "Leningradtsy v Komi" (Leningraders in Komi, published in Zvezda [The Star], 1998), which, according to Dovlatov in his correspondence, provoked a howl when read to the other soldiers, has the following lines: "I only want to get out of here alive / I only want to survive, I only want not to betray myself under the blow of a knife." Attacks (particularly knife attacks) on armed camp guards and military personnel were commonplace. In Dovlatov's 1982 novel, *Zona. Zapiski nadziratelia* (translated as *The Zone: A Prison Camp Guard's Story,* 1985), one of the camp guards tells the story of how some prisoners wanted to behead him with a chainsaw. As Dovlatov's sister, now known as Ksenia Mechik-Blank, writes in her introduction to "Armeiskie pis'ma k ottsu" (Army Letters to Father, published in the journal *Zvezda,* 1998), featuring Dovlatov's correspondence with Donat Mechik, Dovlatov employed this recurring theme–that life "on both sides of the barbed wire was similar"–in his early poems. In practically all of these poems, one or another of his early stories can be recognized.

After about a year in Ust'vymlag, Dovlatov spent the remaining years of his military service not far from Leningrad. He returned from the army in 1965 with a collection of short stories, some of which were included in the novel *Zona.* One of Dovlatov's first readers in the late 1960s was the writer Izrail' Moiseevich Metter, who was an unofficial mentor of young authors. In the introduction to his recently published correspondence with Dovlatov, which can be found in Metter's *Izbrannoe* (Selections, 1999), he recalls his first impressions of reading Dovlatov's early stories:

> When I read the stories what struck me was not merely and not particularly the extraordinary ugliness depicted in them, the nightmare of human existence, although that certainly gave me quite a shock–I was astounded by Dovlatov's literary skill, his mature talent, and the originality of his authorial position.

After the army, Dovlatov again enrolled at Leningrad State University, this time to study journalism. While he failed to finish this degree as well, he became a journalist nevertheless. He worked on the newspapers of the Marine Technological Institute and of the Institute of the Optical and Mechanical Association. In the Soviet Union, Dovlatov published one story in the journal *Neva* in 1967, and one story commissioned by *Iunost'* (Youth), which was published in 1974; their republication has been prohibited in accordance with Dovlatov's will. During 1975 to 1976 he worked at the children's magazine *Koster* (The Campfire). Though working as a journalist, Dovlatov continued to write and tried to get his short stories published, but they proved unacceptable to Soviet publishers and began circulating in samizdat. According to Lev Vladimirovich Losev, these stories in samizdat won Dovlatov not only great popularity but also the wrath of the authorities. In order to avoid being charged with "social parasitism" in the late 1960s, he became the literary secretary to Vera Fedorovna Panova, a prominent writer in post–World War II Soviet literature.

Dovlatov was a member of the short-lived literary association of Leningrad writers who called themselves the *gorozhane* (city dwellers)–as opposed to the *derevenshchiki* (village writers). Founded by Boris Borisovich Vakhtin, the *gorozhane* included the writers Igor' Markovich Efimov, Vladimir Rafailovich Maramzin, and Vladimir Andreevich Gubin. More than anything else, the independent position of these writers attracted Dovlatov to this group: irony, parody, and the absurd, combined with literary allusions and a precision of language, are the features common to all of these writers.

For the majority of young writers in the Soviet Union at this time, any possibility of self-realization within the framework of official culture was out of the question. Many intellectuals left Leningrad in the stifling atmosphere of the mid 1970s, and two favorite destinations were Tallinn and Tartu, both in Estonia, where the intellectual atmosphere appears to have been more relaxed than in the rest of the Soviet Union. For this reason Dovlatov worked for a time (from 1972 to 1975) in Tallinn for the newspaper *Sovetskaia Estoniia* (Soviet Estonia). Since he was not a member of the Communist Party, he was employed to write columns with such titles as "People and Professions," "Tallinn's Guests," "Humoresque," "Reportage," "Talk Back," and "Morality Issues." Dovlatov also wrote theater, concert, and book reviews, material that was typically found toward the back of the newspaper. Apart from using his real name, he often signed his contributions as S. Ader, S. Sergeev, and occasionally R. Must. According to Mikhail Roginsky, who was a fellow journalist at *Sovetskaia Estoniia*–and the prototype for

the character Mikhail Shablinsky in Dovlatov's novel *Kompromiss* (1981; translated as *The Compromise*, 1983)–everyone was encouraged to use different names to sign their articles, in order to give the appearance that many contributors of different nationalities were writing for the paper.

For Dovlatov the chances of being published in Estonia were much greater than in Leningrad or Moscow, because censorship in the Baltic republic was not so strict. The small circle of Russian intellectuals to which Dovlatov belonged found conditions more liberal in Estonia than elsewhere. For example, his manuscript "Piat' uglov" was accepted for publication and even reached the page-proof stage. The Komitet gosudarstvennoi bezopasnosti (KGB, State Security Committee) had a last-minute change of mind, however, and the manuscript was banned from publication. (Although never published as "Piat' uglov," the stories comprising the manuscript later formed the bulk of *Zona*.) Evidently, Dovlatov's book fell afoul of directives from Moscow, which had instructed that more attention be paid to the education of the masses. The situation left Dovlatov quite distressed, and shortly afterward he returned to Leningrad.

Dovlatov's *Nevidimaia kniga* (1977; translated as *The Invisible Book,* 1979), written in Leningrad in 1975 to 1976 and smuggled to the West for publication, is based on his experiences trying to publish a book in the Soviet Union; it originally formed the last chapter of his unfinished novel "Odin na ringe" (Alone in the Ring). In *Nevidimaia kniga* Dovlatov includes–as he does in other works–"documents" to enhance the effect of the story. Here, he reproduces letters, declarations, and official papers to emphasize the absurdity of the events.

By this time Dovlatov was married and had a family. His wife, Elena, and their daughter, Katia, had immigrated to the United States by 1978, and Dovlatov's position grew extremely difficult. He could not get any work; he was arrested and then released; he was beaten up, threatened, and eventually "advised" by the KGB to leave the country. That year he departed for Vienna with his mother and his dog, Glasha. He spent a few months in Austria and during this time managed to publish some stories in Russian-language émigré periodicals such as *Kontinent* (The Continent), *Ekho* (The Echo), and *Vremia i my* (Time and Us).

In 1980, shortly after his immigration to the United States, Dovlatov cofounded and began editing *Novyi amerikanets* (The New American), to which he also contributed a weekly editorial, titled "Kolonka redaktora" (The Editor's Column); Dovlatov served as editor of *Novyi amerikanets* from 1980 to 1983, after which the paper ceased to exist. He later published in book form a selection of the pieces he wrote for "Kolonka

Postcard that Dovlatov wrote to his sister, Ksenia Mechik (addressed here by her nickname, Ksanka), while he was serving in the military during the 1960s (courtesy of Elena Dovlatova)

redaktora." *Marsh odinokikh* (1983; translated as *The March of the Lonely,* 1983) gives an example of Dovlatov's journalistic style. Touching upon a wide variety of topics, the editorials discuss everything from the nature of patriotism and democracy to details of service in the supermarket or the relationship with the first and second waves of Soviet émigrés. (The first wave of Russian emigration began after the 1917 Revolution; nearly 10 million people left the country. The second wave, consisting mainly of displaced persons, occurred after World War II. The third wave of emigration, to which Dovlatov belonged, started in the 1970s and ended in 1985.) It charts the hopes and disappointments that the paper went through during its existence. Dovlatov writes about his expectations of America and his gradually changing attitude: "I became convinced that America was not a branch of paradise on earth." In summing up, he considers why the attempt was not successful and concludes that the attempt to publish such a paper was premature. He decides that in working as a journalist one comes under some sort of ideological pressure—wherever one is. This perspective is played out in a later work, *Filial. Zapiski vedushchego* (A Branch Office. Notes of a Presenter, 1989), when the narrator is briefed about working at a radio station known as "The Third Wave":

> "Don't write about the Kremlin's frenzied sabre-rattling and don't say that the Kremlin gerontocracy are holding their sclerotic fingers . . ."
> I interrupted him: "On the trigger of war?"
> "How do you know?"
> "I have been writing about it in Soviet papers for ten years."
> "About the Kremlin gerontocracy?"
> "No, about the hawks from the Pentagon."

Depicting Russian culture in emigration, *Marsh odinokikh* is a fascinating collection of the ideas and thoughts—the spiritual baggage and ethical principles—that third-wave émigrés brought with them from the U.S.S.R. to the West.

In May 1981 several Russian writers, all recent émigrés from the Soviet Union who were living in various parts of the United States and Europe, were invited to the conference "Russian Literature in Emigration: The Third Wave" at the University of Southern California in Los Angeles (USC). Dovlatov attended this gathering on two counts: as a writer (and thus a subject) and as a journalist to cover the event for Radio Liberty. A great many participants were at the conference—among them Vasilii Pavlovich Aksenov, Iuz (Iosif Efimovich) Aleshkovsky, Dmitrii Vasil'evich Bobyshev, Anatolii Kuz'mich Gladilin, Naum (Emmanuil Moiseevich) Korzhavin, Eduard Limonov, Viktor Pla-

tonovich Nekrasov, Sasha Sokolov, Andrei Donatovich Siniavsky, and Vladimir Nikolaevich Voinovich, as well as several Western Slavicists. Dovlatov participated in two round-table discussions—"Two Literatures or One?" and "The Russian Emigré Press"—and gave a paper, titled "Kak izdavat'sia na Zapade?" (How to Publish in the West?). The proceedings of this conference were published by Ardis in 1984, and Dovlatov's paper appeared in his four-volume *Sobranie sochinenii* (Collected Works, 2000).

The conference at USC also inspired him to write *Filial.* In the book the narrator's first wife, Tasia—whom he has not seen for twenty years—turns up unexpectedly at a conference that he is attending. Dovlatov alternates ironic sketches of the conference events with the narrator's reminiscences about his first meeting with Tasia during his student days at Leningrad University. As many critics (including Andrei Iur'evich Ar'ev and Viktor Segeevich Kulle) have noted, *Filial* is Dovlatov's tribute to an idol of the 1960s, Ernest Hemingway. Dovlatov's early prose was greatly influenced by American fiction and, as Ar'ev asserts in his introduction to *Sobranie prozy* (Collected Prose, 1993), its traces can be found in later works as well, such as in *Filial*:

> This last of Dovlatov's stories ends with a passage, which is as effective as it is familiar: "I lit a cigarette and went out of the hotel into the rain." Anybody who has read Hemingway will immediately recall (and with justification) the ending of *A Farewell to Arms* (1929): "After a while I went out and left the hospital and walked back to the hotel in the rain."

In his article "Bessmertnyi variant prostogo cheloveka" (The Eternal Variant of an Ordinary Person, published in *Zvezda,* 1994) Kulle remarks that "The echo of these last words is very significant. *Filial* is Dovlatov's most 'Hemingway-like' work and at the same time it is a farewell to the master, an establishment of his own way." In "Papa i bludnye deti," a short review of Raisa Orlova's book *Kheminguei v Rossii* (Hemingway in Russia, 1985), he expresses the sentiments of his generation: "Hemingway was our idol. He was not only loved as a writer, but many of us tried to emulate him in life. Our disappointment in him was particularly acutely felt, because a person is able truly to despise and hate only his own weaknesses and sins." In *Filial* Dovlatov's narrator also muses over his immature behavior in his relationship with his first wife—the same bewilderment he is experiencing about the conference of writers, at which the fate of Russia and the election of a president in exile are being discussed. After long and heated debates between the Slavophiles and the Westerners, Tasia ("the most Hemingwayan heroine," as Kulle calls her) is elected president.

When Dovlatov left the Soviet Union in 1978, he had the draft of what became his 1981 novel, *Kompromiss,* with him, as he wrote in a letter to Liudmila Shtern: "I have a semidocumentary manuscript about journalism." Most of the stories in the novel were written between 1973 and 1980—with the exception of the Tenth Compromise, "Lishnii" (Superfluous), which was written in 1984. *Kompromiss* is a collection of stories that reflect Dovlatov's experiences as a journalist for the Tallinn newspaper, *Sovetskaia Estoniia.* It consists of twelve chapters, titled "First Compromise," "Second Compromise," "Third Compromise," and so on. Each story can stand on its own, and, as with several of Dovlatov's works, many were published in *The New Yorker* and in émigré journals such as *Grani* (Facets), *Vremia i my,* and *Kontinent.* As in Dovlatov's earlier work, the first-person storyteller unifies the novel. Unlike in *Zona,* in which Dovlatov uses a fictitious name for the author-narrator, in *Kompromiss* the real name Dovlatov is used.

In his interview with John Glad, Dovlatov discusses the significance of the "true story element" in fiction:

> It is most often not novels that become best-sellers, but books built on some factual basis—local interest books or an account of some political event that forms the basis of the book, and so on. I take advantage of this and try to give my stories a documentary feel but in essence, it's fiction, made-up stories, disguised as real events.

This technique is precisely what Dovlatov employs in *Kompromiss.* The work consists of stories about the writing of newspaper articles, and in order to give the story a "true" documentary flavor, he quotes such articles within the body of the text. Each story is in two parts: the first is in the form of a quoted newspaper article, some of which Dovlatov himself wrote and published in *Sovetskaia Estoniia.* The majority of them have not been traced, however, to published sources, and—though attributed to particular newspapers such as *Vechernii Tallinn* (Tallinn Evening News) and *Molodezh Estonii* (The Youth of Estonia)—they appear to have been invented for the purposes of the story. This real, or ostensible, newspaper article is differentiated by italics from the rest of the text, in which the events underlying the article are described by Dovlatov as the first-person narrator.

In *Kompromiss* Dovlatov utilizes a fusion between real-life experience and its aesthetic interpretation to create what Lidiia Yakovlevna Ginzburg describes in her book *O psikhologicheskoi proze* (1971; translated as *On Psychological Prose,* 1991) as a "second reality":

Fiction, in its departure from actual experience, creates a "second reality," while documentary literature provides the reader with a dual cognition and a two-fold emotion. This is because his experience of the authenticity of the real life event remains unmediated by any art at all. A few lines of newsprint affect us differently than does the greatest novel.

Moreover, besides the stylistic differences between the newspaper articles and the language of the "fictional" stories, important contrasts are drawn between the image of Soviet reality purveyed in the press and the experienced reality recounted in the stories. In the Soviet Union in the 1970s the role of the press—together with that of other mass media (and literature)—was viewed as significant in the ideological struggle: the press functioned not merely to provide "news"; it also served to guide and educate the population in the spirit of socialism and mobilize it for the task of "building communism."

One year after *Kompromiss* appeared, *Zona*—Dovlatov's novel based on his experiences as a gulag guard—was published. Prison-camp narrative generally pivots on one of two basic moral reference points: either the convict is a victim and, correspondingly, the regime is the negative force, or the convict is evil and the punitive forces are positive. *Zona* demonstrates that Dovlatov asserts the existence of a third moral reference point: the victims and the oppressors, sharing many commonalities, are almost indistinguishable from each other:

> The high security prisoners and the camp guards are incredibly similar. Their language, way of thinking, folklore, aesthetic canons, moral attitudes are the same. It's the consequence of mutual influence. There is an indivisible, cruel world on both sides of the barbed wire.

This idea of similarity is arguably a hallmark of Dovlatov's narrative writing. His *Zona* deliberately gets over the barbed wire that divides Russia and makes prison experience everyone's property, for according to Dovlatov, everyone is an accomplice to history.

The action in *Zona* takes place in Chin'ia-Voryk camp within a fairly short time span. Each of the fourteen stories is preceded by a letter written to an American publisher. The use of such letters is a structural device that enables the author to put into contemporary perspective stories that were written in the 1960s. He also employs the letters as a way of explaining the apparent fragmentation of the narrative. Filled with comments, explanations, and biographical notes, the letters are dated approximately seventeen years later than the writing of the stories and shed some light on

Dust jacket for the first English-language edition (1983) of Dovlatov's novel Kompromiss *(1981) based on his experiences working as a journalist in Tallinn, Estonia, during the 1970s (Richland County Public Library)*

Dovlatov's feelings and the transformation that he has experienced in the meantime:

> I was overwhelmed by the depth and diversity of life. I understood how low man could fall. And how high he is able to fly. I understood for the first time the nature of freedom, cruelty and violence. I saw freedom behind bars. I saw cruelty that was as senseless as poetry. Violence that was as ordinary as dampness. I observed man reduced to an animal state. I understood what a small thing could bring him joy. And it seems to me that my eyes were opened.

Dovlatov establishes the distance between the author (himself) and the narrator in the fictional part of the book, Boris Alikhanov. Presented in the third person at the beginning of the book, Alikhanov later appears only as a first-person narrator, and by the last chapter he is virtually indistinguishable from the author.

In spite of the seemingly chaotic nature of *Zona,* an overall plot can be discerned—one addressing the moral and intellectual development of the narrator—although each individual story can stand as an entity. *Zona* is held together primarily by narrative voice, and Dovlatov alternates narrative viewpoint as a means of expressing an unstable emotional state. He aims to express the atrocities that he has experienced in neutral tones and thereby render the impact even more powerful. Yet, for Dovlatov there remains beneath the narrative much that is left unsaid. He does not make any overt attempt to elicit compassion, and the effect on the reader is all the stronger because of such reticence. This quality is particularly noticeable when suffering is described. In *Zona,* Dovlatov does not portray the horrors of the prison camps in the manner that prevailed at the time, as seen in Aleksandr Isaevich Solzhenitsyn's *Arkhipelag GULAG, 1918–1956: Opyt khudozhestvennogo issledovaniia* (1973–1975; translated as *The Gulag Archipelago, 1918–1956: An Experiment in Literary Investigation,* 1974) or in Varlaam Tikhonovich Shalamov's *Kolymskie rasskazy* (1978; translated as *Kolyma Tales,* 1980). Nevertheless, however low-key the depiction of evil, the pessimistic message that it is inherent in human nature demands a psychological counterweight, which for Dovlatov-Alikhanov is creativity–mainly, the writing of poetry. As Dovlatov confided to his father in one letter, "You noticed that we talk calmly and even merrily about various horrendous things. I am glad you noticed this. It is very typical for us." The most that Dovlatov's narrator says after going through an extremely ghastly experience–when a gang of prisoners attack him with a knife–is, "For a second I felt a nauseating chill in the pit of the stomach."

The writing of Dovlatov's next novel, *Zapovednik* (The Sanctuary, 1983), was begun in Leningrad the year before he emigrated (from 1977 to 1978). Its story is based loosely upon Dovlatov's own experiences during a period (from 1976 to 1977) spent working in the Pushkinskie Gory (Pushkin Hills) Museum at Mikhailovskoe. Work as a museum guide was not unusual for members of the Moscow and Leningrad intelligentsia; when Dovlatov's life in Estonia became unbearable and he could neither find employment in Leningrad nor persuade publishers there to accept his work, he took the job in Mikhailovskoe in order to earn a living. He finished the book in 1982, and it was published in the United States the next year.

Zapovednik is framed by the journeys of the narrator (also called Boris Alikhanov, as in *Zona*), from Leningrad to Pushkinskie Gory at the beginning and then back again at the end, some two or three months later. Boris's arrival and departure are marked by bouts of heavy drinking. The museum is known as "Pushkinskii zapovednik," a name that, on the one hand, connotes a nature reserve or a bird sanctuary–a place for the preservation of rare and exotic species–and, on the other, is akin to the modern English "theme park." It is a kind of "Pushkinland." That is, Dovlatov presents it not merely as a museum–a legitimate preservation in present time of something valuable from time past–but as a fictionalized past, a willfully manipulated version of the past designed to fulfill a specific function in the present.

Apart from Boris Alikhanov's arrivals at and departures from "Pushkinskii zapovednik," there is little in the narrative that can be called action. The story is essentially plotless, since, as Iurii Mikhailovich Lotman argues in *O russkoi literature* (On Russian Literature, 1997), the movement of the protagonist within defined boundaries cannot be seen as event or action. In *Zapovednik* the focus of interest lies in the development–largely through dialogue–of various themes, all of which are concerned, in one way or another, with literature. Foremost among these is the exploitation of Aleksandr Sergeevich Pushkin's biography, as revealed in conversations with various guides and administrators.

In the Soviet Union the reading and studying of the works and life of Pushkin in mainly hagiographical terms was encouraged by the authorities, who had a particular aim in mind. Pushkin was used to manipulate society–deflecting its interest from the real issues–but, at the same time, to allow some safe topics for public discussion. No diversion from ready-made clichés about Pushkin was possible, and this fact informs Dovlatov's novel *Zapovednik* in large measure. Dovlatov was by no means alone at this time in reevaluating his attitude toward Pushkin. From the late 1960s onward the Soviet intelligentsia began to approach Pushkin with light-hearted irreverence and to establish distance from official writing on Pushkin. Siniavsky's *Progulki s Pushkinym* (1975; translated as *Strolls with Pushkin,* 1993), written in the early 1970s, is perhaps the most famous example.

Dovlatov's prose style is somewhat reminiscent of Pushkin's own. As the scholar Abram Gavrilovich Lezhnev notes about the poet's style in *Proza Pushkina. Opyt stilevogo issledovaniia* (Pushkin's Prose. An Investigation of Style, 1937), "He uses short, firm, swift phrases, and prefers to avoid subordinate clauses." Just such an alternation of short, energetic phrases creates the swift pace of Dovlatov's style, a deliberate restraint that became another hallmark of his prose. He consciously continues many aspects of Pushkin's style, such as the sparing use of epithets in combination with a great wealth and variety of verbs. Lezhnev observes that an overabundance of epithets slows a phrase down and makes it static, while the use of verbs, on the other hand, adds liveliness and intensity. The absolute limit that Pushkin is aiming for, according to Lezhnev, is described as "noun plus verb, the naked phrase without adornments." Like Pushkin, Dovlatov reduces his sentences to a bare expressive minimum, using "noun plus verb" constructions: "Ia *peresek* derevniu, *vernulsia*. *Pomedlil* vozle odnogo iz domov. *Khlopnula* dver'" (I *walked* across the village, then *returned*. I *lingered* by one of the houses. A door *banged*).

The breakthrough that Pushkin made in adapting the Russian language–by combining its different layers into a single literary language–is well documented. His particular achievement, however, was the creation of lively dialogues and the conversational intonation of much of his prose. Similarly, Dovlatov's stories are written in an everyday language. Their ordinariness is such that many perceive his writing as made up of direct quotes or verbatim renderings of actual conversations. But just like Pushkin's dialogue, Dovlatov's has a descriptive function as well as a function in the plot. This parallel, too, is brought out clearly in *Zapovednik*.

Three of Dovlatov's books came out in 1983–*Zapovednik, Marsh odinokikh,* and *Nashi* (1983; translated

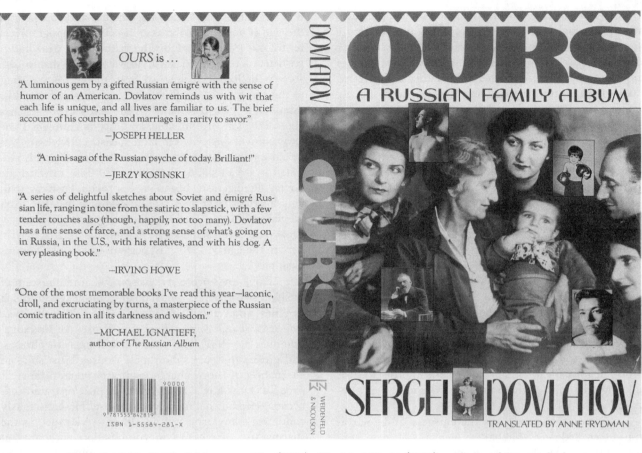

Dust jacket for the first English-language edition (1989) of Dovlatov's Nashi *(1983), a collection of character sketches spanning four generations of a Soviet family (Richland County Public Library)*

OURS is ...

"A luminous gem by a gifted Russian émigré with the sense of humor of an American. Dovlatov reminds us with wit that each life is unique, and all lives are familiar to us. The brief account of his courtship and marriage is a rarity to savor."

–JOSEPH HELLER

"A mini-saga of the Russian psyche of today. Brilliant!"

–JERZY KOSINSKI

"A series of delightful sketches about Soviet and émigré Russian life, ranging in tone from the satiric to slapstick, with a few tender touches also (though, happily, not too many). Dovlatov has a fine sense of farce, and a strong sense of what's going on in Russia, in the U.S., with his relatives, and with his dog. A very pleasing book."

–IRVING HOWE

"One of the most memorable books I've read this year—laconic, droll, and excruciating by turns, a masterpiece of the Russian comic tradition in all its darkness and wisdom."

–MICHAEL IGNATIEFF,
author of *The Russian Album*

ISBN 1-55584-281-X

as *Ours: A Russian Family Album,* 1989), an autobiographical collection of character sketches. An engaging glimpse of four generations of a Soviet family, *Nashi* at first consisted of twelve chapters written in the early 1980s as separate stories and published individually in various journals. The thirteenth chapter was specially added for the book edition and is about Dovlatov's son, Nicholas, who was born in the United States in 1982—the first native-born American in the family. Most of the stories were translated into English, and of the ten stories Dovlatov published in *The New Yorker* between 1980 and 1989, five originated in *Nashi.*

Dovlatov depicts in *Nashi* an array of family members: his parents and grandparents; his aunt and her husband, Aron; his uncles; his cousin Boria; himself and his wife, their daughter, Katya, and their family dog, Glafira. Each chapter tells the reader about family gossip, sayings, or legends surrounding one of the author's relatives. Dovlatov's grandfather, Isaak, is described in folk-epic style: he was notable for his height (he stood about seven feet tall), strength (during

the war with Japan the tsar personally chose him to serve in the artillery), his voracious appetite, and for the fact that he had three sons. This good-humored story suddenly veers into horror when the grandfather is shot in the late 1930s; he is condemned as a foreign spy, only because his émigré son's friend comes to visit him from Belgium. As it happens, however, the Belgian is a great admirer of Joseph Stalin. Dovlatov's parents' generation—at least the members that made a career under Stalin—suffer doubts later on. Aunt Mara acknowledges the bitter truth (many of her literary friends were informers), and this acknowledgment comes only on her deathbed; even then she has difficulty facing it. Her husband, Aron, falls ill and likewise abandons his faith in the ideology; he begs his nephew (the author) to smother him. Yet, as soon as he recovers, his faith in the system returns.

Similar to other works by Dovlatov, *Nashi* has a narrative technique that is relatively straightforward and simple. The narrator is a participant (except in the earlier chapters) in the events that he relates. In her *Con-*

temporary Russian Satire: A Genre Study (1995) Karen Ryan-Hayes writes: "Even when he was not a direct participant, Dovlatov's use of the conventions of the family chronicle allow him to report events as if he participated in them or witnessed them because they constitute family lore. This should not obscure the tension, which is nonetheless present, between the realm of the author and the literary realm of his text."

In the mid 1980s Dovlatov revised the text of *Nevidimaia kniga* extensively (apart from stylistic changes, he also changed some of the names of the characters), and in this new form it was published as *Remeslo: Povest' v dvukh chastiakh* (The Craft: A Novella in Two Parts, 1985). Besides the revised version of *Nevidimaia kniga*, *Remeslo* also consists of *Nevidimaia gazeta* (The Invisible Newspaper). Written in 1984 to 1985, *Nevidimaia gazeta* reflects Dovlatov's experiences as a journalist and editor at the Russian-language newspaper *Novyi amerikanets*. The fate of the protagonist—that is, the author—unites both parts of *Remeslo*. The first part (the new *Nevidimaia kniga*) describes the life of nonconformist writers, painters, musicians, and others in 1970s Leningrad. The description is good-humored, as Dovlatov himself says: "Perhaps, I could have remembered something nasty about these people. However, I don't want to do that. I don't want to be objective. I love my friends. . . ." The protagonists of the second part, *Nevidimaia gazeta,* are third-wave émigrés. They brought with them Soviet attitudes and habits, and Dovlatov laments the fact that one of the most difficult things for an émigré is to overcome his own mentality, as he writes in this part of *Remeslo:* "We have other enemies apart from the decayed Communist doctrine. It is our own stupidity and godlessness. Our selfishness and sanctimoniousness. Our intolerance and lying. Self-interest and mercenariness. . . ."

Dovlatov's next book, after *Remeslo,* was *Inostranka* (1986; translated as *A Foreign Woman,* 1991), which he wrote in New York in 1985. The novel carries the dedication "To lonely Russian women in America with love, sadness, and hope." About Russian émigré life in Forest Hills, New York, *Inostranka* depicts a community of former dissidents, bibliophiles, and lawyers, who grapple with having to begin their lives again—and thus at the bottom. The narrative centers on Marusia Tatarovich, the spoiled daughter of party functionaries. Marusia emigrated not for political reasons but because she imagined life outside the Soviet Union as a fairy tale. She has been married more than once: first to a general's son and then to a famous singer named Razudalov (and the father of her son, Liova); her third marriage was one of convenience to a Jew, Tsekhnovitser, so that she could emigrate. In Austria, however, they part—Tsekhnovitser flies to Israel (Marusia, out of con-

cern for him, says, "How are you going to survive in Israel? It's full of Jews!"), while Marusia departs for the United States. She attends a jewelry workshop in an attempt to gain some qualifications, an experience that echoes Dovlatov's own at the beginning of his émigré life; according to his wife, Elena, Dovlatov himself attended a jewelry workshop in the United States. In the Soviet Union, Marusia never did real work; her party functionary parents provided everything for her. After an unsuccessful attempt to return to the Soviet Union, Marusia takes up with a middle-aged Hispanic man, Rafael, who has a parrot, Lolo. The novel is a kaleidoscope of portraits of third-wave émigrés, and Dovlatov shows that their lives and hopes barely differ from what they were in the Soviet Union. As in *Zona,* which shows that camp guards and prisoners have more in common than one may think, life for a Soviet émigré is the same on both sides of the Atlantic.

The stories included in Dovlatov's next book, *Chemodan* (1986; translated as *The Suitcase,* 1991), were written in the 1980s in New York. The novel takes its name from a battered old suitcase that the narrator, an émigré, brought with him upon leaving the Soviet Union. He comes across the dust-covered object in his closet, and rummaging through its contents provides him with the inspiration for the eight stories that make up the novel. Each of the items found in the suitcase serves as the basis for a story about a bizarre event connected with the acquisition of the item. "Finskie krepovye noski" (The Finnish Crepe Socks) describes Dovlatov's attempt to become a black marketeer while still a university student. In "Prilichnyi dvubortnyi kostium" (Decent Double-Breasted Suit) Dovlatov is working as a journalist in Tallinn and is approached by the KGB to spy on a Swede. "Poplinovaia rubashka" (A Poplin Shirt) examines the narrator's troubled relationship with his wife and her decision to leave the Soviet Union. In her article "O nazvaniiakh dovlatovskikh knizhek" (On the Titles of Dovlatov's Books), found in the book *Sergei Dovlatov: Tvorchestvo, lichnost', sud'ba* (Sergei Dovlatov: Creation, Personality, Fate, 1999), Mechik-Blank considers that the title *Chemodan* is a symbol for all of Dovlatov's wanderings. A last paragraph was added to the novel, which Dovlatov prepared for publication immediately prior to his death:

> The journey doesn't end. And when my turn comes I will come to some other gates. And I will hold in my hand a cheap American suitcase. And I will hear:
>
> What did you bring to us?
>
> Here, I will reply, look.
>
> And I will also add:
>
> Not without reason—any, even the least serious book, has the shape of a suitcase.

Caricature of Dovlatov drawn by poet Joseph Brodsky during a writers' conference in Lisbon, Portugal, May 1988 (from Maloizvestnyi Dovlatov, *1995; University of Massachusetts, Amherst Libraries)*

All through his career Dovlatov wrote frequently on literary topics. Some of his articles were published in *Sovetskaia Estoniia,* and these pieces include "Ia khochu vam rasskazat' . . ." (I would like to tell you . . .) and "Ia znaiu silu slov . . ." (I know the power of words . . .), but he did not consider them sufficiently important for revision. Most of his criticism collected in *Sobranie sochinenii* was written when he was already in emigration, between 1978 and 1990. This edition also includes radio stories and interviews. According to Ar'ev, Dovlatov was a wonderful storyteller, although Ar'ev notes that all Dovlatov's so-called improvisations were carefully thought through and repeated in front of different listeners many times—a process similar to the writing of a majority of his texts. Dovlatov wanted to have an immediate impact on the reader in the same way that a jazz player can affect a listener. Petr L'vovich Vail' recalls in his contribution to *Sergei Dovlatov* that "Dovlatov liked to say that if he weren't a writer, he would have loved to be a jazz player, who raises the trumpet and as the first sound comes out, everybody's heart stands still. Dovlatov achieved this effect with his prose: it's effective and soluble without a residue, like instant coffee."

During this period Ar'ev and some other friends of Dovlatov who visited him in his New York apartment were struck by a sealed envelope with the inscription, "To be opened after my death," which dangled on a string to the right of his desk. This envelope was not just an affectation. The narrator in *Kompromiss* remarks that each time he buys a pair of new shoes lately, he wonders if he is going to be buried in them. In another of the stories from *Kompromiss,* when the narrator is delegated from the newspaper to make a speech at the funeral of a party functionary, he suddenly realizes that he is at the same time dead and making a speech at his own funeral. In a more jocular mode Dovlatov suggested in his diary that it would be interesting to hear the deceased saying that such and such people and deeds drove him to his grave. The last line of Dovlatov's *Zapisnye knizhki* (Notebooks, 1990) questions, "What is there after death? After death history begins."

Sergei Donatovich Dovlatov died on 24 August 1990 in New York. His death coincided with radical changes in Russian literary culture. Dovlatov lived to see some of his work published in the Soviet Union in the late 1980s, and in the last years of his life he became the subject of critical acclaim. His posthumous reputation has only grown apace. He is the subject of two books, Mikhail Iosifovich Veller's *Nozhik Serezhi Dovlatova* (Serezha Dovlatov's Pen-Knife, 2000) and Aleksandr Aleksandrovich Genis's "philological novel" *Dovlatov i okrestnosti* (Dovlatov and His Environs, 1999). Beginning in 1996, many of Dovlatov's letters have been published in literary journals and popular magazines. Reminiscences and eulogies by his friends and relatives have proliferated since 1990. As soon as his works appeared in Russia, his popularity reached almost cult status. A literary prize (awarded for the best short story published in Russia) was established in St. Petersburg in 1993 and named after Sergei Dovlatov. So appreciated are his works and so strong is his reputation that aspiring authors in present-day Russia try to write "à la Dovlatov."

Letters:

Elena Skul'skaia, *Zapiski k N . . . Perekrestnaia rifma* (Tallinn: Antek-Koostöö, 1996);

Ksenia Mechik-Blank, "Armeiskie pis'ma k ottsu," *Zvezda,* 5 (1998): 108–142;

Izrail' Moiseevich Metter, *Izbrannoe* (St. Petersburg, 1999), pp. 252–252;

Sergei Dovlatov, "Deviat' pisem Tamare Urzhumovoi," *Zvezda,* 8 (2000): 137–147;

Dovlatov and Igor' Efimov, *Epistoliarnyi roman s Igorem Efimovym* (Moscow: Zakharov, 2001);

Dovlatov, *Skvoz' dzhungli bezumnoi zhizni: Pis'ma k rodnym druz'iam* (St. Petersburg: Zvezda, 2003).

Interview:

John Glad, "Pisat' ob absurde iz liubvi k garmonii," *Vremia i my,* 110 (1990): 158–173.

References:

Zara Abdulaeva, "Mezhdu zonoi i ostrovom. O proze Sergeia Dovlatova," *Druzhba narodov,* 7 (1996): 153–166;

Nikolai Anastas'ev, "'Slova—moia professiia'. O proze Sergeia Dovlatova," *Voprosy literatury,* 1 (1995): 3–22;

Andrei Iur'evich Ar'ev, "Obzor," *Neva,* 1 (1990);

Ar'ev, "Sergei Dovlatov," in *Russkie pisateli XX veka: Biograficheskii slovar',* edited by Petr Alekseevich Nikolaev (Moscow: Bol'shaia Rossiiskaia Entsiklopediia, 2000), pp. 236–238;

Ar'ev, "Sergei Dovlatov," *Russkie pisateli: XX vek: Bibliobiograficheskii slovar',* 2 volumes, edited by Nikolai Nikolaevich Skatov (Moscow: Prosveshchenie, 1998), I: 438–442;

Ar'ev, "Teatralizovannyi realizm. O povesti Sergeia Dovlatova *Filial,*" *Zvezda,* 10 (1989): 19–20;

Ar'ev, ed., *Sergei Dovlatov: Tvorchestvo, lichnost', sud'ba* (St. Petersburg: Zvezda, 1999);

Dmitrii Bobyshev, "Poniat' Dovlatova trudno . . . ," *Nezavisimaia gazeta,* 16 March 1996, p. 8;

Vladimir Bondarenko, "Plebeiskaia proza Sergeia Dovlatova," *Nash sovremennik,* 12 (1997): 257–271;

Maria V. Bourlatskaia, "Soviet Prison-camp Literature: The Structure of Confinement" (Varlam Shalamov, Georgi Vladimov), dissertation, University of Pennsylvania, 1999;

Joseph Brodsky, "O Serezhe Dovlatove," in Brodsky's *Sobranie prozy,* 3 volumes (St. Petersburg: Limbus, 1993, 1995), III: 355–363;

Elena Dovlatova, comp., *O Dovlatove: Stat'i, retsenzii, vospominaniia* (Tver: Drugie berega, 2001), pp. 64–72;

Nikita Eliseev, "Chelovecheskii golos," *Novyi mir,* 11 (1994): 212–225;

David James Galloway, "The Prison Camp Theme in Russian Literature as Reworked by Lev Razgon and Sergei Dovlatov," dissertation, Cornell University, 1999;

Aleksandr Aleksandrovich Genis, *Dovlatov i okrestnosti* (Moscow: Vagrius, 1999);

Genis, "Korova bez vymeni, ili metafizika oshibki," *Literaturnaia gazeta,* 24 December 1997, p. 11;

Genis, "Peterburgskie shkol'niki o Sergee Dovlatove," *Zvezda,* 5 (1998): 217–222;

Genis, "Sad kamnei. Sergei Dovlatov," *Zvezda,* 7 (1997): 235–238;

Lidiia Yakovlevna Ginzburg, *O psikhologicheskoi proze* (Leningrad: Sovetskii pisatel', Leningradskoe otdelenie, 1971); translated by Judson Rosengrant as *On Psychological Prose* (Princeton: Princeton University Press, 1991);

Viktor Kamianov, "Svoboden ot postoia," *Novyi mir,* 2 (1992): 242–244;

Iurii Karabchievsky, "Pamiati Sergeia Dovlatova," *Literaturnaia gazeta,* 29 August 1990, p. 7;

Viktor Sergeevich Kulle, "Bessmertnyi variant prostogo cheloveka," *Zvezda,* 3 (1994);

Viacheslav Kuritsyn, "Vesti iz Filiala, ili duratskaia retsenziia na prozu Sergeia Dovlatova," *Literaturnoe obozrenie,* 12 (1990): 41–42;

Boris Lanin, "The Image of Women in the Prose of Sergei Dovlatov," in *Women and Russian Culture,* edited by Rosalind Marsh (New York & Oxford: Berghan Books, 1998), pp. 252–259;

Alexandra Leontieva, "Some Trends in Contemporary Russian Prose in the Light of Bakhtin's Genre Theory," in *Dialogue and Rhetoric,* edited by Ingunn Lunde (Bergen: University of Bergen Press, 1999), pp. 132–146;

Abram Gavrilovich Lezhnev, *Proza Pushkina. Opyt stilevogo issledovaniia* (Moscow: Khudozhestvennaia literatura, 1937);

Mark Lipovetsky, "Uchites', tvari, kak zhit': Paranoia, zona i literaturnyi kontekst," *Znamia,* 5 (1997): 199–212;

Lev Vladimirovich Losev, "Russkii pisatel' Sergei Dovlatov," *Russkaia mysl',* 31 August 1990, p. 3;

Iurii Mikhailovich Lotman, *O russkoi literature* (St. Petersburg: Iskusstvo-SPB, 1997);

Andrei Mal'gin, "Ia vstretilsia s pisatelem Sergeem Dovlatovym v New Yorke," *Nedelia,* 3 (1990), pp. 4–8;

Alla Marchenko, ". . . Obratitsia v pechal'noe . . . ," *Literaturnaia gazeta,* 16 May 1990, p. 4;

K. C. Mason, "The Family Chronicle and Modern America," dissertation, University of Nebraska-Lincoln, 1981;

Olga Matich and Michael Heim, eds., *The Third Wave: Russian Literature in Emigration* (Ann Arbor, Mich.: Ardis, 1984);

Donat Mechik, *Vesnushki: Iz zapisnykh knizhek; Naedine s synom: Otryvki iz vospominanii* (St. Petersburg: [Mechik], 1993);

Iunna Morits, "Predislovie k publikatsii rasskazov iz *Chemodana,*" *Oktiabr',* 7 (1989), p. 67;

Mikhail Nekhoroshev, "Veller i Dovlatov: Bitva geroev i prizrakov," *Neva,* 8 (1996): 183–191;

Asia Pekurovskaia, "Dovlatov bez mifa," *Vremia i my,* 139 (1998): 202–275;

Pekurovskaia, *Kogda sluchilos' pet' S. D. i mne* (St. Petersburg: Symposium, 2001);

Peterburgskii literator, special Dovlatov issue, 30 December 1992;

Petropol', special Dovlatov issue, 5 (1994);

Valerii Popov, "Pobeda neudachnika Dovlatova," *Literaturnaia gazeta,* 22 October 1997, p. 12;

V. Radzishevsky, "Triumf bez tragedii: tri dnia na druzheskoi noge s Sergeem Dovlatovym," *Literaturnaia gazeta,* 13 May 1998, p. 6;

Evgenii Rein, *Mne skuchno bez Dovlatova. Novye stseny iz zhizni moskovskoi bogemy* (St. Petersburg: Limbus, 1997);

Karen Ryan-Hayes, "The Family Chronicle Revisited: Dovlatov's *Ours,*" in her *Contemporary Russian Satire: A Genre Study* (Cambridge: Cambridge University Press, 1995), pp. 150–193;

Ryan-Hayes, "Narrative Strategies in the Works of Sergei Dovlatov," *Russian Literature Journal,* 45, no. 153 (1992): 155–178;

Laura Salmon, "Naimenee sovetskii gorod Rossii: khronotop dovlatovskikh rasskazov," *Zvezda,* 8 (2000): 151–155;

Salmon, "Neobychnoe v obydennom," *Vestnik MGU,* 4 (1999): 59–75;

A. Semenenko, "Linda Peips kak zerkalo sovetskoi deistvitel'nosti ili o metode Sergeia Dovlatova," *Russkaia filologia,* 9 (1998): 137–142;

Il'ia Serman, "Teatr Sergeia Dovlatova," *Grani,* 136 (1985): 138–163;

Andrei Donatovich Siniavsky, *Progulki s Pushkinym* (London: Overseas Publication Interchange, 1975); translated by Catherine Theimer Nepomnyashchy as *Strolls with Pushkin* (New Haven: Yale University Press, 1993);

Slovo/Word, special Dovlatov issue, 9 (1991);

Igor Smirnov, "O smysle kratkosti (Pamiati Sergeia Dovlatova)," in *Russkaia novella. Problemy teorii i istorii,* edited by V. M. Markovich and V. Schmidt (St. Petersburg: Izdatel'stvo Sankt-Peterburgskogo universiteta, 1993), pp. 5–13;

Nadia Sokolova, "Snova o lagernoi teme: *Zona* Sergeia Dovlatova," *Australian Slavonic and East European Studies,* 10 (1996): 157–164;

Vladimir Solov'ev and Elena Klepikova, *Dovlatov vverkh nogami: tragediia veselogo cheloveka* (Moscow: Sovershenno sekretno, 2001);

Igor' Sukhikh, *Sergei Dovlatov: Vremia, mesto, sud'ba* (St. Petersburg: Kul'tInform Press, 1996);

Tatiana V. Tsiv'ian, "Veshchi iz *Chemodana* Sergeia Dovlatova i byvshaia (?) sovetskaia model' mira," *Russian Literature,* 37 (1995): 647–658;

Elena Tudorovskaia, "Na ozere Gennisaretskom," *Grani,* 140 (1986): 138–149;

Tudorovskaia, "Russkii pisatel' v Amerike," *Grani,* 140 (1986);

Petr L'vovich Vail', "Brodskii o Dovlatove," *Zvezda,* 8 (2000): 148–150;

Vail' and Genis, "Iskusstvo avtoportreta," *Literaturnaia gazeta,* 4 September 1991, p. 11;

Vail' and Genis, "Literaturnye mechtaniia. Ocherk russkoi prozy s kartinkami," *Chast' rechi, Al'manakh,* 1 (1980): 204–233;

O. V. Vasil'eva, "Evoliutsiia lagernoi temy i ee vliianie na russkuiu literaturu 50-80x godov," *Vestnik Sankt-Peterburgskogo universiteta,* 23 (1996): 54–63;

Jekaterina Young, "Dovlatov's *Compromise:* Journalism, Fiction, Documentary," *Slavonica,* 6 (2000): 44–68;

Young, "Dovlatov's Reception of Salinger," *Forum for Modern Language Studies,* 36 (2000): 412–425;

Young, "Dovlatov's *Sanctuary* and Pushkin," *Slavica,* 30 (2000): 133–151;

Aleksei Zverev, "Zapiski sluchaianogo postoial'tsa," *Literaturnoe obozrenie,* 4 (1991): 65–73;

Zvezda, special Dovlatov issue, 3 (1994).

Papers:

The papers of Sergei Donatovich Dovlatov are kept by his widow, Elena Dovlatova.

Mikhail Naumovich Epshtein
(Mikhail Epstein)
(21 April 1950 –   )

Thomas Epstein
Boston College

BOOKS: *Novoe v klassike. Derzhavin, Pushkin, Blok v sovremennom vospriiatii* (Moscow: Znanie, 1982);

Paradoksy novizny. O literaturnom razvitii XIX–XX vekov (Moscow: Sovetskii pisatel', 1988);

"Priroda, mir, tainik vselennoi. . . ." Sistema peizazhnykh obrazov v russkoi poezii (Moscow: Vysshaia Shkola, 1990);

Relativistic Patterns in Totalitarian Thinking: An Inquiry into the Language of Soviet Ideology, Kennan Institute for Advanced Russian Studies, Occasional Paper, no. 243 (Washington: Woodrow Wilson International Center for Scholars, 1991);

Ottsovstvo: Esse (Tenafly, N.J.: Hermitage, 1992);

Novoe sektantstvo: Tipy religiozno-filosofskikh umonastroenii v Rossii, 1970-80-e gody (Holyoke, Mass.: New England Publishing, 1993); translated, with an introduction, by Eve Adler as *Cries in the New Wilderness: From the Files of the Moscow Institute of Atheism* (Philadelphia: Paul Dry Books, 2002);

Vera i obraz: Religioznoe bessoznatel'noe v russkoi kul'ture XX veka (Tenafly, N.J.: Hermitage, 1994);

Velikaia Sov'. Filosofsko-mifologicheskii ocherk (New York: Slovo, 1994);

After the Future: The Paradoxes of Postmodernism and Contemporary Russian Culture, translated, with an introduction, by Anesa Miller-Pogacar (Amherst: University of Massachusetts Press, 1995)–includes "The Origins and Meaning of Russian Postmodernism" and "New Currents in Russian Poetry: Conceptualism, Metarealism, and Presentism";

Na granitsakh kul'tur. Rossiiskoe–amerikanskoe–sovetskoe (New York: Slovo, 1995);

Bog detalei. Narodnaia dusha i chastnaia zhizn' v Rossii na iskhode imperii (New York: Slovo, 1997; revised and enlarged edition, Moscow: LIA Elinina, 1998);

Doubled Flowering from the Notebooks of Araki Yasusada, by Epshtein, Kent Johnson, and Jack Spicer (New York: Roof Books, 1997)–includes "Commentary and Hypotheses," pp. 134–147;

Russian Postmodernism: New Perspectives on Post-Soviet Culture, by Epshtein, Aleksander Aleksandrovich Genis, and Slobodanka Vladiv-Glover (New York & Oxford: Berghahn Books, 1999)–includes "An Essay on the Essay";

Transcultural Experiments: Russian and American Models of Creative Communication, by Epshtein and Ellen Berry (New York: St. Martin's Press, 1999);

Postmodern v Rossii: Literatura i teoriia (Moscow: R. Elinin, 2000);

Filosofiia vozmozhnogo, introduction by Grigorii Tul'chinsky (St. Petersburg: Aleteia, 2001).

OTHER: "Daniil Andreev and the Mysticism of Femininity," in *The Occult in Russian and Soviet Culture,* edited by Bernice Glatzer Rosenthal (Ithaca, N.Y. & London: Cornell University Press, 1997), pp. 325–355;

"Ot Interneta k InteLnetu," in *Rossiiskii internet: Nakanune bol'shikh peremen* (Moscow: IREX, 2000), pp. 196–204;

"Postmodernism, Communism, and Sots-Art," in *Endquote: Sots-Art Literature and Soviet Grand Style,* edited by Marina Balina, Nancy Condee, and Evgeny Dobrenko (Evanston, Ill.: Northwestern University Press, 2000), pp. 3–31;

"Main Trends of Contemporary Russian Thought," in *Intercultural Philosophy,* Proceedings of the Twentieth World Congress of Philosophy, volume 12, edited by Stephen Dawson and Tomoko Iwasawa (Bowling Green, Ohio: Philosophy Documentation Center, Bowling Green State University, 2001), pp. 131–146.

SELECTED PERIODICAL PUBLICATIONS–UNCOLLECTED: "Esse ob esse," *Opyty. Zhurnal Esseistiki, Publikatsii, Retsenzii, Khroniki,* 1 (1994): 23–26;

Mikhail Naumovich Epshtein, 2002 (courtesy of the author)

"*Symposion* and Russian *Filosofiia,*" *Symposion. A Journal of Russian Thought,* 1 (1996): 3–7;

"The Phoenix of Philosophy: On the Meaning and Significance of Contemporary Russian Thought," *Symposion. A Journal of Russian Thought,* 1 (1996): 35–74;

"Letter to Tosa Motokiyu," *Denver Quarterly,* 31 (Spring 1997): 100–105;

"Some Speculations on the Mystery of Araki Yasusada," *Witz,* 5 (Summer 1997): 4–13;

"Nabroski k ekologii teksta," *Kommentarii,* 13 (1997): 3–41;

"On Hyperauthorship: Hypotheses on Potential Identities of Araki Yasusada," *Sycamore Review,* 10 (Winter/Spring 1998): 71–81;

"Internet kak slovesnost'," *Pushkin,* 1 (1 May 1998): 44–46;

"Iz totalitarnoi epokhi – v virtual'nuiu: Vvedenie v Knigi knig," *Kontinent,* 102 (1999): 355–366;

"Kniga, zhdushchaia avtorov," *Inostrannaia literatura,* 5 (1999): 217–228;

"Russkaia kul'tura na rasput'ie. Sekuliarizatsiia i perekhod ot dvoichnoi modeli k troichnoi," *Zvezda,* 1 (1999): 202–220; 2 (1999): 155–176;

"The Teachings of Iakov Abramov As Interpreted by His Disciples. Compiled, edited and commented by Mikhail Epstein," translated by Anesa Miller-Pogacar, *Symposion. A Journal of Russian Thought,* 3 (1999): 29–66;

"Khasid i Talmudist. Sravnitel'nyi opyt o Pasternake i Mandel'shtame," *Zvezda,* 4 (2000): 82–96;

"Khronotsid. Prolog k voskresheniiu vremeni," *Oktiabr',* 7 (2000): 157–171;

"Odnoslovie kak literaturnyj zhanr," *Kontinent,* 104 (2000): 279–313;

"Slovo kak proizvedenie: O zhanre odnosloviia," *Novyi mir,* 9 (2000): 204–215;

"Amerossiia. Dvukul'turie i svoboda. Rech' pri poluchenii premii *Liberty,*" *Zvezda,* 7 (2001): 221–227;

"Ateizm kak dukhovnoe prizvanie. Iz arkhivov Prof. R. O. Gibaidulinoi," *Zvezda,* 4 (2001): 159–174;

"Début de siecle, ili Ot Post- k Proto-. Manifest novogo veka," *Znamia,* 5 (2001);

"Mistika upakovki, ili Vvedenie v tegimenologiiu," *Kommentarii,* 20 (2001): 249–261;

"The Role of the Humanities in Global Culture: Questions and Hypotheses," *Rhizomes: Cultural Studies in Emerging Knowledge,* 2 (2001) <http://www.rhizomes.net/CurrentIssue/epstein/epstein.html>.

Mikhail Epshtein, also known as Mikhail Epstein, is one of the leading cultural theorists of the past quarter century, as well as one of the most complex. He has written on subjects as diverse as the American fascination with dinosaurs and the role of apophatic theology (negative theology which describes God by what he is not) in Russian culture; on the meaning of waiting in line in Soviet culture and the "trauma" of the information explosion; on the "mystery" of (former) Soviet hockey invincibility and the sophiological (having to do with the science of divine wisdom, or Sophia) speculations of Daniil Leonidovich Andreev. He has been both a central analyst and publicist for Russian postmodernism as well as its pathologist, having declared it dead in the mid 1990s. He has written both under his own name and under a variety of pseudonyms, such as the sexual theorist Ivan Solovyov, the spiritual teacher Iakov Vasil'evich Abramov, and the Communist sociologist of religion Raisa Omarovna Gibaydulina. While inspired by Vladimir Sergeevich Solovyov's philosophy of *vseedinstvo* (total-unity), Epshtein insists on the necessity of diversity and the importance—even sacredness—of the smallest object, even the detritus of society (for example, the used candy wrapper, a central object in his imagined Lyrical Museum and its related science of things, termed "realogy" by Epshtein). A Russian intellectual to the core, he has made the Bakhtinian "crossing of borders" (both intellectual and geographic) the center of his culturological project. While completely serious about his aims, he employs play, fantasy, and humor as fundamental analytic-creative tools. Perhaps the best way to summarize the overarching spirit of his various investigations is to invoke the title of his 2001 book, *Filosofiia vozmozhnogo* (The Philosophy of the Possible), which is a study and transformation of modal analysis.

Mikhail Naumovich Epshtein was born in Moscow on 21 April 1950 to Naum Moiseevich Epshtein, an accountant, and Mariia Samuilovna Lifshits, an employee at Transport Publishing House. Epshtein was their only child. He graduated from the Department of Philology at Moscow State University in 1972 and then worked for five years in the Department of Theory at the Institute of World Literature. During this period at the institute he assimilated some of the methodology developed by the eminent culturologist Grigorii Dmitrievich Gachev and mastered the structuralism of Iurii Mikhailovich Lotman. While engaged in this academic work, Epshtein struck out in two related directions: he became involved in the underground poetry and art scene in Moscow, establishing particularly close ties with the conceptualists (especially Il'ia Iosifovich Kabakov) and metarealists (a neologism of Epshtein's) such as Ol'ga Aleksandrovna Sedakova, and he participated in the creation of a new type of cultural interaction and its institutions—a virtual "laboratory" for what he calls "transculture."

The encounter with conceptualism was crucial in two ways; Epshtein became one of its chief theorists and champions, even as the "ideational" approach of conceptualism to culture and language resonated with,

and influenced, his own thinking. In 1982, attempting to expand interdisciplinary pursuits and the crossing of intellectual borders (which remains a central concern for him), Epshtein founded the Essayists' Club. Later, during the era of glasnost, he started the association known as Image and Thought (from 1986 to the present), under whose aegis the Bank of New Ideas and Terms and the Laboratory of Contemporary Culture were formed (in Moscow). At the same time the openness associated with glasnost brought with it a resurgence of anti-Semitism. The reactionary group Pamyat' (Memory) made Epshtein an object of their threats and intimidation, and he was compelled to emigrate to the United States in 1990. The painful experience of leaving his home country did not mean—as it has for many Soviet émigrés—creative stagnation or irrelevancy in America. Throughout the 1990s he not only continued to be a close observer of the Russian scene but wrote extensively about his American experience; joined the faculty of Emory University (where he is the Samuel Candler Dobbs Professor of Cultural Theory and Russian Literature); engaged in a variety of cross-cultural projects—including an American version of Image and Thought; collaborated with the American cultural theorist Ellen Berry; and has been active in a variety of Russian-American organizations. Perhaps the most significant aspect of Epshtein's American period has been his intense involvement with the World Wide Web, culminating in his creation of the InteLnet, or the Intellectual Network (which includes the Bank of Interdisciplinary Ideas in the Humanities).

Although his greatest legacy may be as a culturologist, to date Epshtein is best known as a theorist of Russian postmodernism. His extensive study of the subject has produced three primary areas of inquiry: its historical origins and prospects, its meaning and significance, and its practitioners' achievements.

The question of the historical origins of Russian postmodernism is a thorny one. As was the case with Soviet Communism, Russia seems to lack the theoretically necessary conditions for the development of the phenomenon in question, since the country was subject neither to the "cultural logic of late capitalism," in the words of Fredric Jameson, nor to the tyranny of the image, as described by Jean Baudrillard in his *Simulacra et Simulation* (1981; translated as *Simulacra and Simulation*, 1994). Moreover, the repression of modernism in Russia, and its consequent incompleteness, tends to negate the possibility of an emerging *post*modern culture.

Epshtein has answers for both Jameson and Baudrillard. While embracing the latter's concepts of hyperreality and simulation, he replaces image with idea: ideology replaces videology, producing the same logic as described both by Jameson and Baudrillard. At the same time, arguing for the deep historical roots of Russian postmodernism, Epshtein emphasizes the simulative nature of Russian culture as a whole. Beginning with St. Vladimir's "imitative" conversion of himself and his nation to Christianity in 988 (described in *Povest' vremennykh let* [The Russian Chronicle, compiled in 1113] as brought about in part by Vladimir's desire to be like his neighbors), continuing with Peter the Great's forced, simulated westernization of Russia, and perhaps culminating in Soviet Marxism, where the ideology of materialism replaced matter itself, Russia is depicted as a postmodern nation par excellence and *avant la lettre* (that is, before the term for, and period of, postmodernism existed). For this reason, Epshtein can argue that not only is postmodernism not alien to Russian culture, but it is indeed profoundly native. Most radically (and in contrast to Boris Groys), Epshtein contends that socialist realism is itself a stage in the development of historical postmodernism (in this sense, Russia for once anticipates rather than follows a Western development). In his essay "Istoki i smysl russkogo postmodernizma" (The Origins and Meaning of Russian Postmodernism, 1995), Epshtein identifies seven ways in which socialist-realist practice coincides with postmodernism. First, it creates a hyperreality that is "neither truthful nor false but consists of ideas that become reality for millions of people." Second, it describes modernism as an obsolete mode of "aesthetic individualism and linguistic purism." Third, it abandons a specifically Marxist discourse to become a pastiche of several ideologies and philosophies, even combining materialism and idealism. Fourth, it abjures any specific artistic style, aspiring instead to a new, "metadiscursive" level of culture that combines classicist, Romantic, realist, and futurist models. Fifth, it rejects what it calls "subjectivist" and naive discursive strategies, replacing them with quotation marks as a mode of hyperauthorship and hyperpersonality. Sixth, it negates the opposition between elitist and mass culture. Finally, it attempts to "construct a posthistorical space where all great discourses of the past should find their ultimate resolution."

All that is lacking in this first phase of postmodernism is the irony and playfulness that mark so-called mature postmodernism. These qualities are supplied in full measure by the Russian artists and writers of the conceptualist school of the 1970s and 1980s—in particular Kabakov, Erik Vladimirovich Bulatov, Dmitrii Aleksandrovich Prigov, Lev Semenovich Rubinshtein, and Vladimir Georgievich Sorokin.

No less original is Epshtein's injection of spirituality into the Russian postmodern paradigm. Discussing spirituality in his study of conceptualism, he equates its unveiling of the emptiness (the absence of the signified) at the heart of (Soviet) discourse with the Byzantine apophatic tradition as expressed in Russian theology and society. For Epshtein, Russia is caught in the middle, both geographically and historically: it is neither wholly Western nor wholly Eastern. It sees reality neither in Western terms of empiricism and self-creation nor in the Eastern way, as "a product interwoven of the many-colored veil of Maya, which must be cast off to reveal Absolute Nothingess," as he says in "Istoki i smysl russkogo postmodernizma." The "solution" for Russia lies with Christian Orthodoxy, the implicit motto of which is, as described by Anesa Miller-Pogacar in her introduction to Epshtein's *After the Future: The Paradoxes of Postmodernism and Contemporary Russian Culture* (1995), that

> it is necessary to begin but impossible to finish: such is the intermediate stance of the free Russian spirit, which is as alien to the Eastern contemplative practice of world-negation as it is to the energetic Western ethos of world-organization.
>
> Indeed, even our cities and buildings, those that manage to arise from the heaps of garbage, from the muddy grave prepared for them in advance appear to be dilapidated and decrepit. Brand-new structures can scarcely survive: in a matter of days, they will be broken down, plastered with leaflets, and splashed with slops, as they return willy-nilly to a state of being under construction.

Such a condition, Epshtein argues, is the visible form of apophatic spirituality, first articulated by the Pseudo-Dionysius. Russian postmodernism thus aspires neither to nihilism nor to "mere" negation of metanarratives but to apophatic, or negative, seeing. In this form of spirituality, God is approached not positively, through what "he is," but negatively, by sloughing off the conceptual schema that claim to make defining God possible. Apophaticism—and conceptualism—enact their own inadequacy to name; yet, paradoxically, in this neutralization of the ability of humanity (poetry) to encompass God (things) with positive concepts, God (the real) is approached indirectly, though immediately, in Divine Silence and Invisibility. For Epshtein, this negative form of spirituality is precisely what marks Russian conceptualism: its "play," self-irony, and neutralization create an opening to "elsewhereness."

He identifies this apophatic tendency—this compulsive confession of human inadequacy—not only with Russian culture but also with the roots of Russian civilization. The apophatic tendency also strongly marks contemporary spirituality itself, which he dubs the kingdom of "minimal, or poor, religion." Analogous to both Italian "arte povera" and Jerzy Grotowski's "poor theater," Epshtein's poor religion as a way of life marks an entire postaesthetic generation: lacking a visible church, this generation finds God only at the borders of the religiously intelligible.

The third service that Epshtein does for Russian postmodernism is to identify its leading practitioners and to analyze their methods and contributions. Along with the aforementioned conceptualists, to whom he devotes the majority of his energy, Epshtein, in his essay "New Currents in Russian Poetry: Conceptualism, Metarealism, and Presentism" (1995), also discusses and in fact devises names for two other leading Russian postmodern tendencies in poetry: metarealism and presentism. According to Epshtein, metarealism is the use of complex metaphorical figures in order to return semantic fullness to the word (and thus is at the opposite pole from the conceptualists' destructive strategies), and presentism is the attempt to avoid the excesses of both metarealism and conceptualism by turning to visible, tangible surfaces and treating them as the ultimate depth. By identifying the conceptualists as the successors to futurism, the metarealists (who include Ivan Fedorovich Zhdanov, Sedakova, Elena Andreevna Shvarts, Aleksandr Viktorovich Eremenko, and Viktor Borisovich Krivulin) successors to the symbolists, and the presentists (Aleksei Maksimovich Parshchikov, Il'ia Kutik, Aleksei Korolev) to acmeists, Epshtein creates a new canon—one that has in fact held fast. Moreover, while acknowledging the fundamental differences between metarealism and conceptualism, he also identifies their unity, or their shared treatment of phenomena, "not so much as physical data or emotional conditions, but rather as a system of culturally established significations." This insistence on simultaneous difference and similarity marks much of Epshtein's theorizing, both literary and cultural.

Simultaneously, with this work of analysis, advocacy, and explication, Epshtein contributes to postmodernist "creativity" through his essay and treatise writing. This crossing of borders, from critic to creator and back again, is an organic part of his method, and the essay form has proven to be one of the most productive vehicles for this activity. Part of the purpose behind his creation and direction of the Essayists' Club in Moscow in the early 1980s was to explore and inspire the growth of a genre that he considered the most appropriate to postmodern culture; most appropriate because the genre of essay is "legitimated by its existence outside of any genre," existing by its nature on the margins of all genres, as Epshtein asserts in his "Essay on the Essay" (1999). Capable of marshaling the heart and the head, the lyric and the epic, the scientific and the poetic, the essay is mythmaking without authority, mighty in its weakness:

Essayism is a mythology based on *authorship*. The self-consciousness of a single individual tests the limits of its freedom and plays with all possible conceptual connections in the unity of the world. In an essay, individual freedom is not negated in the name of a myth, with its tendency for depersonalization but flourishes in the right to the individual myth. This authorial, mythopoetic freedom, which includes freedom from the logic of myth itself, constitutes the foundation of the genre. The essay thus constantly vacillates between myth and non-myth, between unity and difference. Consequently, the particular coincides with the universal, image with concept, being with meaning. However, these correspondences are not complete, edges protrude, creating uneven surfaces, disruptions and discrepancies. This is the only way in which the contemporary perception of the world can come to realization: aiming for totality, it at the same time does not claim to overcome difference in its constituent parts.

Epshtein's own version of essayism is impressively enacted in *Bog detalei. Narodnaia dusha i chastnaia zhizn' v Rossii na iskhode imperii* (The Deity of Details. The People's Soul and Private Life in Russia at the End of the Empire, 1997) and *Na granitsakh kul'tur. Rossiiskoe—amerikanskoe—sovetskoe* (On the Border of Cultures. Russian–American–Soviet, 1995), the second of which takes up the encounter between Russia and America (self and other, on the level of national myths) from the point of view of a new immigrant, Epshtein himself.

Essayism as postmodern myth is further explored in two mock treatises, *Velikaia Sov'. Filosofsko-mifologicheskii ocherk* (The Great Owl Land. A Philosophical-Mythological Study, 1994) and *Novoe sektantstvo: Tipy religiozno-filosofskikh umonastroenii v Rossii, 1970-80-e gody* (1993; translated as *Cries in the New Wilderness: From the Files of the Moscow Institute of Atheism*, 2002). *Velikaia Sov'*, in spirit reminiscent of the satirical method of Jonathan Swift, purports to be an anthropological study of an obscure "Northern people" who believed the Great Owl to be their holy ancestor and so became "owlish" in their souls: what results is a picture of the "deep structure" of the Soviet mentality. *Novoe sektantstvo* takes the form of a "scientific inquiry" into contemporary Russian sectarianism, carried out by the Institute of Atheism. Here, myth and its bearer, language, prove to be truer than reality itself: although none of the sectarian groups described in the book are in fact real, the fantasy that they portray captures the deeper reality of overdetermined ideological consciousness—of both investigator and investigated—in Russia.

After his immigration to the United States, though continuing to follow closely and to comment on events in the former Soviet Union, Epshtein turned some of his attention and energy toward matters of

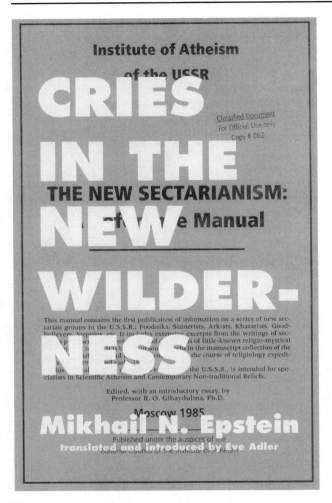

Institute of Atheism
of the USSR

CRIES IN THE NEW WILDER-NESS

THE NEW SECTARIANISM: e Manual

*Classified Document
For Official Use only
Copy # 062*

This manual contains the first publication of information on a series of new sectarian groups in the U.S.S.R.: Foodniks, Sinnerists, Arkists, Khazarists, Goodbelievers, Steppies, etc. It includes extensive excerpts from the writings of sec... of little-known religio-mystical ... in the manuscript collection of the ... the course of religiology expedi... the U.S.S.R., is intended for specialists in Scientific Atheism and Contemporary Non-traditional Beliefs.

Edited, with an introductory essay, by
Professor R. O. Gibaydulina, Ph.D.

Moscow 1985

Mikhail N. Epstein

Published under the auspices of the
Editorial Council of the Institute of Atheism
translated and introduced by Eve Adler

*Dust jacket for the first English-language edition (2002) of Epshtein's
Novoe sektanstvo: Tipy religiozno-filosofskikh
umonastroenii v Rossii, 1970-80-e gody
(1993, Richland County Public Library)*

interest to the American academy (in particular, cultural studies and the future of the humanities) and to the World Wide Web. These interests proved, however, to have significant coherence with his earlier activities and tended to demonstrate that his postmodernism was subsumed by his culturology.

Culturology, Epshtein explains in *Transcultural Experiments: Russian and American Models of Creative Communication* (1999), which he co-authored with cultural theorist Berry, is a Russian discipline, although its approach can be traced back to the German intellectual tradition, especially to Johann Wolfgang von Goethe, Johann Gottfried Herder, Wilhelm Windelband, Georg Simmel, and Osvald Spengler, all of whom treated culture as an integral organism. In Russia the culturological approach begins with the nineteenth-century Slavophile thinker Nikolai Iakovlevich Danilevsky and continues in the twentieth century with figures as diverse as the

theologian Pavel Aleksandrovich Florensky, the philosophers Mikhail Mikhailovich Bakhtin and Aleksei Fedorovich Losev, the semioticians Iurii Mikhailovich Lotman and Vladimir Solomonovich Bibler, and the philosopher-culturologists Sergei Sergeevich Averintsev and Georgii Dmitrievich Gachev. The fundamental aim of this discipline is, in Epshtein's view, to be the self-consciousness of culture, to explore those borders between various isolated cultures (scientific, artistic, and professional cultures, for example) in an attempt to locate their unity and to widen the possibilities of all culture and cultures.

In order to carry this out, Epshtein uses the concept and methods of "transculture," the crossing of borders into a zone of no culture, where identity and difference intersect. In *Transcultural Experiments,* Epshtein contrasts transculture with deconstruction and multiculturalism, "two principle aspects of postmodern theory that are increasingly found to be in fundamental disagreement." Deconstruction is, at least in part, a critique of essentialism (the philosophical idea whereby the essence of something evident to the senses is made real or endowed with a defining reality) and the entire Western tradition of the metaphysics of presence and origin. Finding no moment in time or physical event in which to locate the origin of the being of beings, deconstruction sees language as a bearer of mere "traces," which are themselves at best the origin of the origin—the myth of presence. Everything (what *is* or what exists) exhibits differences from itself, such that everything is the play of these differences.

By contrast, multiculturalism tends to posit an essentialism in which "cultural production" is the expression of a definable origin, one that is often "hidden" by and from its producer and that the field of cultural studies purports to uncover. Rather than a free play of differences, or signifiers attached to no signified (the world of internal difference), multiculturalist theorists trace the sources of culture to various material origins, whether gender, race, class, or age, for instance (the world of external difference). The goal of multiculturalism is to validate and ensure respect for these differences, to posit "each culture" as self-sufficient and equal to itself.

Epshtein's transculture sees and rejects the one-sidedness of both of these positions. Like multiculturalism, transculture accepts that cultures "do have origins and are indeed sustained and determined by these origins." For Epshtein, however, this insight is only the point of departure for culture (that is, culture begins in nature); but the goal of culture is to liberate the individual from nature, in order to increase human possibility and freedom. This idea is where the liberating potential of deconstruction enters. By historicizing deconstruction—by accepting the notion of real origins—"we can posit the goal of dis-organization, the flight from origins as an historical possibility," as Epshtein suggests in *Transcultural Experiments*. The result is transculture, which is the acknowledgment by each individual of his state of inadequacy: each needs to cross over into the other. Epshtein calls this notion positive deconstruction, or positive otherness: the multiplication of possible worlds as opposed to the negation (or affirmation) of a single presence. The subjunctive is the mode—and the mood—of positive deconstruction.

This insight has been the guiding principle of Epshtein's activities in the later 1990s, which include the rebirth of his laboratory model of transcultural activity on American soil (improvisational sessions at Bowling Green State University and Emory University in 1996 and 1998); the publication of the book *Transcultural Experiments;* the crucial invention of InteLnet (http://comm.cudenver.edu/~inteLnet), for which he was awarded the Social Innovations Award in 1995 from the Institute for Social Inventions in London; a stream of articles in which his culturological approach is employed on a variety of topics; and the 2001 publication of his study of modal philosophy, *Filosofiia vozmozhnogo*.

The InteLnet is in many ways the most perfect realization of Epshtein's culturological aspirations. As he himself said, again in *Transcultural Experiments:*

> For me, the InteLnet is analogous to the human mind, with its infinite conceptual links and associations. Now, retrospectively, I can interpret our attempts at collective improvisations in Moscow (1982 to 1989) as a search for cyberspace within the more traditional space of a room and a roundtable. The idea of the InteLnet, an electronic community of creative minds, though in essence as old as the world, or at least as old as Plato's Academia, comes from my experience in that late-Soviet intellectual milieu. Together we tried to create integrated, "polyphonic" descriptions of certain cultural phenomena and to work out patterns of "translation" for different professional languages. Our improvisational community was a sort of pre-electronic InteLnet, which can now develop in a technologically more mature, global form.

The purpose of InteLnet is as simple as it is all-encompassing: to link everything to everything else. A certain conceptualist intention is evident here, a hint of self-parody that both undercuts and sustains the utopianism of this project. The InteLnet currently consists of five subheadings: the Bank of New Ideas, Aphorisms, Thinklinks, Intelnetics, and The Book of Books. Each has its own liberating aim: to advance new ideas, investigate connections between concepts, elaborate a methodology of a new humanistic metadiscipline, and create new intertextual bodies.

This growing emphasis on possible worlds and on virtuality has stimulated Epshtein to a reassessment of both the meaning of Russian postmodernism and the general prospects of Russian culture. His reassessment of Russian postmodernism began with his observation of its end, the catalyst for which he saw in the gradual overcoming of total irony (the "new sincerity," as he termed it). But how, Epshtein asked in *After the Future,* could there be an *end* to a movement that proclaimed itself "the last receptacle of everything that ever unfolded and took shape within history"? Such an assumption—like all other utopian illusions, including socialist realism—would seem to close off the indeterminacy of the future, of the possible. Perhaps more adequately understood, true postmodernism—a world of true possibility and a real future—is the entry into a broader period of culture (tentatively called the postmodern, as opposed to the postmodernist), which is better designated with the prefix "proto," or incipient. In his welcome to the new century, "Début de siecle, ili Ot Post- k Proto-. Manifest novogo veka," published in *Znamia* (The Banner, 2001), he in fact playfully describes the *début de siècle* (beginning of the century) as an "archaic" deposit of some future culture.

This process of "opening up" the postmodern has led Epshtein to various attempts at articulating a new overall paradigm for Russian—and perhaps world—culture. Among them (as seen in "Russkaia kul'tura na rasput'ie. Sekuliarizatsiia i perekhod ot dvoichnoi modeli k troichnoi" [Russian Culture at a Crossroads: Secularism and the Transition from a Binary to a Ternary Model], published in *Zvezda* [The Star], 1999) is one that he terms *troichnyi* (ternary). At its base is a culturological critique of Hegelian dialectical thinking, Aristotelian "median" thinking, and the project of "total unity" (ultimately Hegelian in outlook) that seduced—and continues to seduce—the Russian spirit. The dialectical path to unity, through the synthesis of thesis and antithesis, is, for Epshtein, limiting and ultimately destructive: it adds one thing to another and calls their sum one instead of three, which Epshtein sees as the totalitarian approach to plurality. The Aristotelian solution—that of the "golden mean," the creation of a "neutral zone" of nonvalue, or pure secularization—leads, in his opinion, to the spiritual mediocrity that marks contemporary Western life. His ternary model (itself modeled on the Holy Trinity) is another form of positive deconstruction: it strives neither to negate all identity nor to subsume identity within a single idea (the curse of all the metahistorical modernist discourses, whether Marxist, Freudian, or Nietzschean, for example). His culturology instead attempts to maximize all forms of possibility, virtuality, imagination, and openness: it allows for as many constellations of meanings as human culture can invent.

Epshtein's contributions to contemporary cultural discourse are many. As an intellectual figure he is in several ways the paradigmatic embodiment of the ideals of the nineteenth-century Russian intelligentsia: a specialist of the universal. As distinguished from his forebears, however, such as Nikolai Aleksandrovich Berdiaev and Dmitrii Sergeevich Merezhkovsky, he is opposed to any and all total solutions. The unity he proclaims is a unity ever in the making and unmaking. On the other hand, from a Western point of view his postmodernism may be seen as too totalizing, too utopian and religious, and too apolitical. It seems to give away too much. But this testing of ideas, of exploring their limits, is quite at the heart of his experimental method. Moreover, in recent years Epshtein has distanced himself from postmodernism in general, making the possible—what he calls "possibilism"—the measure of the new millenium.

Mikhail Naumovich Epshtein's stance as a theorist is also ambivalent and complex. While learned and intellectually rigorous, Epshtein sees science itself as a form of play, and play requires both fantasy and unexpectedness. His crossing of borders between theory, imagination, and science is as organic for him as it is unsettling for the reader who seeks a single privileged stance. In addition, in his *Vera i obraz* (Faith and Image, 1994), Epshtein freely asserts that literary theory should not so much aim for a *poznanie istiny* (cognition of truth) but is, rather, a method for "widening our readerly and human experience." To this goal, all his endeavors aspire.

Interviews:

Sally Laird, "Life after Utopia: New Poets in Moscow," *Index on Censorship* (January 1988): 12–14;

Ellen Berry, Kent Johnson, and Anesa Miller-Pogacar, "Postcommunist Postmodernism," *Common Knowledge,* 2 (1993): 103–118;

Evgeny Shklovsky, "From Internet to InteLnet: Electronic Media and Intellectual Creativity," *ART-MARGINS: Contemporary Central and East European Visual Culture* (August 1999) <http://www.artmargins.com/content/interview/epshtein.html>.

References:

Lev Aleksandrovich Anninsky, "Sovki Minervy," *Svobodnaia mysl'*, 9 (1995): 97–107;

Jean Baudrillard, *Simulacra and Simulation,* translated by Sheila Faria Glaser (Ann Arbor: University of Michigan Press, 1994);

Caryl Emerson, *The First Hundred Years of Mikhail Bakhtin* (Princeton: Princeton University Press, 1997), pp. 12–17, 147–148, 194;

Fredric Jameson, *Postmodernism, or, The Cultural Logic of Late Capitalism* (Durham, N.C.: Duke University Press, 1991);

Viacheslav Kuritsyn, *Russkii literaturnyi postmodernism* (Moscow: OGI, 2000), pp. 157–159, 194–196, 221–225;

Ilya Kutik, "After the Future," in *Hieroglyphs of Another World: On Poetry, Swedenborg and Other Matters,* edited by Andrew Wachtel (Evanston, Ill.: Northwestern University Press, 2000), pp. 31–35;

Dale Peterson, Edith W. Clowes, Anesa Miller-Pogacar, and Epshtein, "Russian Critical Theory and Postmodernism: The Theoretical Writings of Mikhail Epstein," *Slavic and East European Journal,* 39 (Fall 1995): 329–366;

Donatella Possamai, "Michail Epstejn," in his *Che cos'è il postmodernismo russo? Cinque percorsi interpretativi* (Padua: Il Poligrafo, 2000), pp. 38–47;

Victor Terras, "Sweet Moments of Recognition: Epshtein on Postmodernism," *Slavic and East European Journal,* 41 (Fall 1997): 477–481.

Venedikt Vasil'evich Erofeev

(26 October 1938 – 11 May 1990)

Anindita Banerjee
University of Oregon

BOOKS: *Moskva-Petushki* (Paris: YMCA Press, 1977; revised, 1981); translated by H. William Tjalsma as *Moscow to the End of the Line,* with an introduction by Vera Dunham (New York: Taplinger, 1980);

Glazami ektsentrika (New York: Serebriannyi vek, 1982)—translated as "Through the Eyes of an Eccentric," in *The Penguin Book of New Russian Writing: Russia's Fleurs Du Mal,* edited by Victor Erofeyev and Andrew Reynolds (London: Penguin, 1995), pp. 126–145;

"Byt' russkim – legkaia provinnost'": Shtrikhi k portretu. Zapisnye knizhki, edited by Irina Tosunian (St. Petersburg: Izdatel'stvo fonda russkoi poezii, 1999);

Zapiski psikhopata, with an introduction by Vladimir Murav'ev (Moscow: Vagrius, 2000);

Val'purgieva noch' (Moscow: Vagrius, 2001);

Bespoleznoe iskopaemoe: Iz zapisnykh knizhek (Moscow: Vagrius, 2001).

Editions and Collections: *Moskva-Petushki i pr.,* with an introduction by Vladimir S. Murav'ev (Moscow: Prometei, 1989);

Ostav'te moiu dushu v pokoe—includes "Sasha Chernyi i drugie," with an introduction by Mikhail Naumovich Epshtein (Moscow: Kh.G.S., 1995);

Moskva-Petushki, edited by Eduard Vlasov, with a foreward by Evgenii Anatol'evich Popov (Moscow: Vagrius, 2000);

Sobranie sochinenii, 2 volumes (Moscow: Vagrius, 2001).

Editions in English: *Moscow Circles,* translated by J. R. Dorrell (London: Writers and Readers Publishing Cooperative, 1981);

Moscow Stations: A Poem, translated by Stephen Mulrine (London: Faber & Faber in association with Brian Bolly, 1997).

PLAY PRODUCTION: *Val'purgieva noch', ili shagi komandora,* Moscow, Teatr na Maloi Bronnoi, 1989.

Venedikt Vasil'evich Erofeev (from the paperback cover for Glazami ektsentrika, *1982; Jean and Alexander Heard Library, Vanderbilt University)*

69

RECORDING: *Moskva-Petushki,* read by Erofeev, Vagrius, 2000.

OTHER: *Vest',* edited by Veniamin Aleksandrovich Kaverin, with a contribution by Erofeev (Moscow: Knizhnaia palata, 1989), pp. 418–506;
"Val'purgieva noch', ili shagi komandora," in *Vosem' nekhoroshikh p'es,* edited by Z. K. Abdullaeva and A. D. Mikhaleva, with an introduction by Iurii Aichenvald (Moscow: Soiuzteatr, 1990), pp. 5–74.

SELECTED PERIODICAL PUBLICATION–UNCOLLECTED: "Poslednyi dnevnik (October 1989–March 1990)," edited by Igor Avdiev, *Novoe literaturnoe obozrenie,* no. 18 (1996): 161–209.

The *elektrichka,* or suburban slow train, is the most vilified form of transport in Russia. It stops frequently at both idyllic-looking villages and towns laid to waste by industry. It also provides a space in which one can encounter the entire spectrum of society in motion. Mendicants, alcoholics, and crippled soldiers, whom both Soviet society and its new capitalist incarnation prefer to forget, roam its compartments and corridors. Venedikt Erofeev became a cult figure of contemporary Russian literature by telling the story of exactly such a marginal character—an alcoholic—traveling on the *elektrichka* from Moscow to Petushki, an obscure station some three hours away from the capital.

Moskva-Petushki (1977; translated as *Moscow to the End of the Line,* 1980), the work that brought Erofeev renown in Soviet underground literature in 1970, was subversive in its essence. Each and every element opposed the officially mandated standards of socialist realism. Its narrator-protagonist is neither positive nor filled with revolutionary fervor to advance his country into the golden age of communism—in fact, he comes across as a decidedly antiproductive element of society. His name is Venichka, a diminutive form of the author's name, which lends a dangerous degree of individual subjectivity to what he has to say. His narrative is not "realistic" at all but rather a compendium of impressions and images culled from a consciousness that is not only nonconformist but also deluded by alcohol.

Neither this original character nor his story lacked for an audience. *Moskva-Petushki* was circulated illegally and eventually developed a following both inside and outside the Soviet Union. Irreverent and boisterous yet hauntingly tragic and lyrical, the work possessed a rebellious appeal that transcended cultural boundaries and resonated with Erofeev's contemporary generation in both Russia and the West; the celebrated American prose writer John Updike titled his *New Yorker* (7 June 1982)

review of the book "How the Other Half Lives." The fictional character of Venichka—a derelict dissolute imbued with painful sensitivity and penetrating intellect—became indistinguishable from its creator in the reader's mind. Although Erofeev's life and circumstances remained largely obscure to his audience, his work made him an iconic representative of disillusionment and dissent flowing under the monumental edifice of Soviet life.

Homelessness, hardship, and hunger were an inalienable part of Erofeev's life from the beginning and remained its defining element almost until the end. Venedikt Vasil'evich Erofeev was born on 26 October 1938 in the town of Chupa in the region of Karelia. His parents originally hailed from the Ulianovsk region on the Volga, a famine-prone area from which his father had immigrated to the far North and obtained employment as a railway stationmaster in the Murmansk region bordering Finland. The family lived in considerable poverty. Erofeev was the youngest of six children born to his parents, of which five survived. He was especially close to his brother Boris, with whom he shared clothes and even a school satchel. He possessed a prodigious memory that became family lore even in his childhood. His sister Nina Vasil'evna Frolova writes, in her contribution to a 1991 biography of Erofeev published in *Teatr* (The Theater), that Erofeev learned to read at the age of two. There were not many books in the house, so he directed his fierce memorizing powers toward the calendar hanging on the wall. His siblings entertained and amazed visitors by having their little brother demonstrate that he could recall instantly the day of the week, sunrise and sunset hours, tide levels, festivals and holidays—all the information found in the calendar—for any given date.

The family's meager pleasures, among which was an annual trip to Erofeev's parents' ancestral village on his father's free railway pass, came to an abrupt end with the outbreak of the World War II. Railway stations, particularly on the sensitive border with German-occupied Finland, were especially vulnerable to attack. His father stayed back while his mother, along with the children, was evacuated to Kirovsk, a city on the Kol'skii peninsula. Another catastrophe struck the family soon after the war ended: in 1946 Erofeev's father was incarcerated under the notorious Article 58, a statute condemning the dissemination of anti-Soviet propaganda. The actual reasons for the arrest are controversial. While Erofeev said in interviews that his father was either accused of colluding with the Germans or mocking the Stalinist regime in the company of his friends, his sister maintained that their father's habit of telling potentially subversive anecdotes might have triggered a denunciation. Regardless of cause, the arrest had drastic material consequences for the family. Unable to obtain sufficient rations as the wife of an enemy of the people, Erofeev's mother, Anna Andreevna, secretly left for Moscow and pretended to abandon her children to the state. The eight-year-old Erofeev and his brother Boris were taken to an orphanage, where they remained until their father's release. Thus, Erofeev grew up and attended school, until the eighth grade, in a state institution in Kirovsk.

Institutional life, by all accounts, was grim in the lean postwar years. As an introspective and physically delicate boy, Erofeev was bullied brutally. Later, the writer vividly recalled rumors that the orphanage served black-market meat in which human fingernails were found. His father was released only in 1954. Two years after the family was reunited, Erofeev won a gold medal for scholastic excellence and was admitted directly into the Philology Department of Moscow State University. Not yet eighteen, he crossed the Arctic Circle for the first time in his life and arrived in the capital city that subsequently attained much mythic significance in *Moskva-Petushki.*

Erofeev benefited greatly from the formal education that he received in Moscow. Only as a university student did he encounter the full spectrum of Russian literature. His upbringing in the provinces had offered him few books to read beyond "edifying" socialist realist novels such as Nikolai Alekseevich Ostrovsky's *Kak zakalialas' stal'* (1932, 1934; translated as *How the Steel was Tempered,* 1952). At the university Erofeev also befriended Vladimir S. Murav'ev, who rapidly became, and remained, an intellectual interlocutor, mentor, and confidant throughout his life. Murav'ev witnessed and shared the growth of Erofeev's ardent, if nonacademic and intuitive, engagement with literature and later edited several editions of his works. His accounts of their days at the university indicate that the preferences Erofeev developed early in life exerted a decisive influence on his literary development.

Erofeev voraciously read works of literature, history, and philosophy. He began to study Latin and German. He was acutely aware of the complex dynamics between history and literature in twentieth-century Russia. He knew and admired many poets of the Silver Age, the period at the turn of the century that had generated a spate of modernist movements and genres. As a young student of philology, he devoured and eventually memorized many poems from this turbulent period of creativity in Russian arts. He read the works of Russian decadent and symbolist poets Feodor Kuz'mich Sologub, Konstantin Dmitrievich Bal'mont, Valerii Iakovlevich Briusov, Aleksander Aleksandrovich Blok, and Andrei Bely (Boris Nikolaevich Bugaev); the acmeists Osip Emil'evich Mandel'shtam and Anna Andreevna Akhmatova; and the futurists Igor' Severianin (pseudonym of Igor' Vasil'evich Lotarev) and Vladimir Vladimirovich

Mayakovsky. Erofeev attempted to put together an anthology, to be called "Russkie poety" (Russian Poets), by simply reproducing from memory the works of the many poets who had fallen into disfavor in Joseph Stalin's time and therefore remained unpublished in the 1940s and 1950s.

As friend and fellow poet Ol'ga Aleksandrovna Sedakova characterized him in her reminiscences, published in 1991 in the journal *Stolitsa* (The Capital), Erofeev from the beginning "loved ugly ducklings." Canonization transformed a literary persona into a cultural edifice, and such an edifice, by definition, contradicted Erofeev's intensely personal appreciation of literature. He believed that critical acclaim transformed writers into veritable institutions of correctness. In contrast, literary imagination that celebrated the absurd side of reality and remained elusive to academic evaluation welcomed the reader to participate in its creative processes. His own literary models were writers who rejected conventional "realistic" ways of viewing life and eschewed the clarity associated with rational thought. They cultivated genres such as satire and the picaresque. Their preferred methods were fantastic realism—especially through the employment of psychologically aberrant discourse—and the absurd. Erofeev's idols included Henry Fielding, author of the eighteenth-century picaresque novel *The History of Tom Jones, A Foundling* (1749), and the nineteenth-century Russian satirist Mikhail Evgrafovich Saltykov. Nikolai Vasil'evich Gogol and Fyodor Dostoevsky, founders of the Russian tradition of fantastic realism, became his favorites. Both had experimented with first-person narratives of the delusive and neuropathologically ill and perhaps inspired Erofeev's original way of representing the world through eyes crippled with alcoholism and existential angst. But above all, the young scholar came to appreciate playfulness, mockery, and subversion of literary canons.

Erofeev reveled in exposing the humorous underside of so-called socially conscious nineteenth-century literature that was deified in Soviet Russia. He planned to write papers on absurd elements in Leo Tolstoy's didactic writings; investigated comedic moments in the works of Nikolai Gavrilovich Chernyshevsky, philosopher and author of the socialist utopia *Chto delat'?* (1863; translated as *What Is to Be Done?* 1961); and sought to connect the thoughts of Nikolai Aleksandrovich Dobroliubov, nineteenth-century Social Democrat and influential literary critic, with his sordid love life. The literary avant-garde of early-twentieth-century Russia, in contrast, piqued Erofeev's interest. He developed a particular affinity toward those poets who were known for their lexical and semantic experiments for creating a nonrational, or, according to the futurists, "trans-rational," lan-

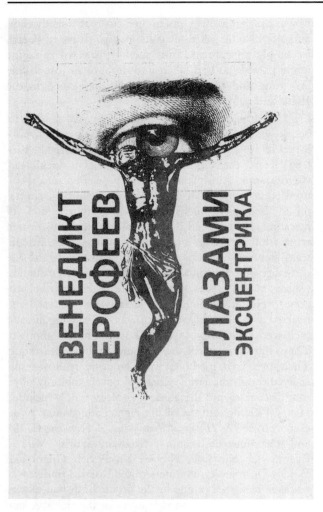

Paperback cover for Erofeev's Glazami ektsentrika, *an essay*
inspired by nineteenth-century Russian writer and philosopher
Vasilii Vasil'evich Rozanov (Jean and Alexander
Heard Library, Vanderbilt University)

guage. Among this latter group, Erofeev's favorite was Igor' Severianin: according to Murav'ev, Erofeev composed parodies on current events, particularly the belligerent politics of the Cold War, modeled after Severianin's poetry. Like the futurists, who declared that all preexistent literature should be thrown out of the ship of modernity, Erofeev dreamed of re-creating the Russian language, whose present form "bored him to death."

Literary innovators who defied categorization, such as the absurdist poet and children's writer Sasha Chernyi (pseudonym of Aleksandr Mikhailovich Glikberg), attracted him. Erofeev subsequently titled his only essay on modern Russian literature, which he wrote in 1982; "Sasha Chernyi i drugie" (Sasha Chernyi and Others, published in *Kontinent* [The Continent], 1991; collected, 1995), subsuming all famous names under "others." Chernyi was close to him because one "could

get away with anything in his company." Erofeev developed a particular attachment to poets of the literary group Ob"edinenoe real'noe iskusstvo (Association for Real Art), also known by its acronym, OBERIU; these poets in the 1930s continued to celebrate the absurd and play with the instability of meaning even as socialist realism was ominously becoming the only form of representation permitted by the state. He made his acquaintance with the exuberant, irreverent prose of François Rabelais through the rendition of Nikolai Alekseevich Zabolotsky, a member of OBERIU. Soon after his arrival in Moscow, Erofeev began a collection of banned authors and developed a discriminating taste for émigré writing: he advised his sister Nina to read Vladimir Nabokov, who was practically unknown among Soviet intellectuals at that time.

Erofeev's time at Moscow State University was cut short because of his contrary attitude toward all forms of indoctrination, whether in the form of classroom lectures or mandatory military training. Like most other events in his life, exactly why he was expelled after three semesters is shrouded in mystery. While Erofeev maintained that he just lost faith in the process of learning and stopped attending classes, commentators and critics have offered various interpretations. Murav'ev suggests that he was thrown out after he refused to attend mandatory military training classes, ostensibly supervised by a Hermann Göering–like major; other critics have also traced the reason for his ignominious exit to participation in an unauthorized students' play. In any event, Erofeev's uneasy relationship with structured education continued while he joined and left several academic institutions in succession, chiefly in an effort to preserve his residential status as a student in Moscow. He finally wound up at the Vladimir Pedagogical Institute, where he met a group of like-minded young intellectuals who remained his closest friends and admirers. Analogous to Venia and Venichka, the protagonists and narrators of many of Erofeev's writings, these friends later were fictionalized and mythologized as myriad characters in his literary creations.

The unusual life and views of these moderate dissidents evidently nurtured Erofeev's distinctive way of seeing and representing his contemporary reality. His companions perceived themselves as people existing on the margin, outside the norms and codes of mainstream society. Such self-perception can be identified with the countercultural attitudes of the generation known as the *shestidesiatniki,* or "people of the 1960s." The characteristics attributed to this generation include spiritual and epistemological restlessness, its accompanying skepticism toward all forms of ideology, and creative protest against institutionalized life and art. Conscious cultivation of behavior that was considered aberrant by existing standards was an integral part of such a personality, and its artistic expression often included a strong element of performance. In the ossifying conservatism of the era aptly called *zastoi* (stagnation), such performance could manifest itself in active repudiation of all state-sponsored institutions, alcoholism, or sexual libertarianism and was embodied in art through the profanity, parody, travesty, and satire of the many truisms upon which the giant illusion of Soviet life had been constructed and sustained. Vladimir Semenovich Vysotsky, an iconic figure of the age, sang ballads with incendiary subtexts to a captivated audience while getting steadily drunk on stage.

The performative aspect of nonconformism, however, was rather subdued in Erofeev's personality. Reminiscences of his friends from the Vladimir Pedagogical Institute repeatedly stress that although alcohol—to which he was seriously initiated in their circle—became a leitmotiv of his life and art, his quiet introspective personality underwent no change even at the most intense moments of intoxication. Despite his friend Igor Avdiev's later postulation that Erofeev began to perceive alcoholism as a vocation and a way of life, his other friends note that they had never in the course of their long acquaintance seen him get loud or aggressive when drunk.

Erofeev's lingering and visible poverty, which seemed extreme even to his equally impoverished friends at the institute, also provides a strong counterpoint to the perception that his life had become a carnival, or bacchanalia. Clad in threadbare clothes, he "migrated" from dormitories to the homes of friends who provided him with both physical and emotional sustenance. Erofeev's manners—astonishingly refined for a person so obviously in need—usually became most apparent at the difficult moments when he received a share of the meager resources his friends themselves could barely afford. Far from rambunctiously devouring food and drink, the deprived Erofeev carefully spaced each bite of a simple meal of scrambled eggs, drew out a shared bottle of cheap wine, and slept on a bed made up on the floor in a crowded communal apartment. Apparently, his early life had forged such deliberate reticence in the face of extreme physical hardship: his sister Frolova recalls how in the war years he divided up and ate a single piece of rationed bread with infinite patience and delicacy. In stark contrast to the verbal freedom that he exercised with his friends, in whose company he parodied officialese and liberally spiced his speech with obscenities, he was physically modest and rather conservative in dress. Buttonless shirts did not deter him from keeping his jacket on even in hot weather.

Erofeev's many contradictory faces, some of them masked in colorful myths, manifest themselves fully only in literary practice. The multiple personae of penetrating intellectual and helpless drunk; trenchant philosopher and dissolute lowlife; silent introspective observer and verbose commentator; and jester of contemporary morals and seeker of beauty in the stultifying grimness of the so-called socialist utopia are all present in his first significant work. *Zapiski psikhopata* (Notes of a Psychopath, 2000) was begun soon after his arrival in Moscow and completed in 1958 toward the end of his sojourn at the pedagogical institute. It remained unpublished for more than forty years, partly because of Erofeev's dismissive attitude. However immature the work may have seemed, it nevertheless carries the seeds of many cardinal elements that made both *Moskva-Petushki* a cult novel and its author a major cultural myth of his time. Murav'ev, who was entrusted with the manuscript, describes this first work as Erofeev's rehearsal, or creative warm-up, in preparation for the discovery of his true voice.

Zapiski psikhopata displays all the ambiguity of theme, structure, lexicon, syntax, and meaning that eventually became the hallmark of Erofeev's prose. It is a quasi-fictive, lyrical diary of a seventeen- or eighteen-year-old youth who is a doppelgänger, or double, of the author himself. The narrator and protagonist is variously known as "Venia," "Venichka," or "Erofeichik," which are intimate diminutive forms of Erofeev's own name and became well known later because of *Moskva-Petushki*.

Thematically and structurally, *Zapiski psikhopata* bears some resemblance to Gogol's novella *Zapiski sumashedshego* (Diary of a Madman, 1835) and Dostoevsky's shorter fictional works, *Dvoinik* (The Double, 1846) and *Zapiski iz podpol'ia* (Notes from the Underground, 1864). The text centers on a sociopathic individual whose subjectivity is jeopardized in a world completely devoid of convictions: there is no truth but, rather, a plethora of half-truths behind which lurks an abyss of chaos. Both physically and epistemologically, the subject of the diaries is condemned to wandering and homelessness. His circumstances—penniless and living in a communal dormitory in postwar Moscow—evoke the dismal times and places in which Gogol and Dostoevsky had situated their heroes. Delusion, induced in part by alcohol, only throws a thin veil over a reality that functions upon the principle of collective conformity, leaving no room for the individual. The protagonist attempts to create a material and spiritual sanctuary in his humble room but is finally forced to abandon it.

At the same time, Erofeev's work departs radically from his literary predecessors in significant ways. Autobiography and fiction are interwoven throughout the text: not only is the protagonist the author's namesake, but his circumstances and even the characters involved in his fictive life intermittently refer to actual events and people. *Zapiski psikhopata* generates two contrary perceptions of the relationship between Erofeev the author and Venichka his fictive narrator that continue to freight evaluations of the famous *Moskva-Petushki* and his life and work as a whole. The first perception is that Erofeev used the fictional medium to construct a multitude of myths around himself and, through this gesture, attempted to transcend his real persona through art. Indeed, a lingering motif of his first work is Venichka's existential search for a definition of his own identity. The conclusions of this search are presented in long passages of propositional statements, each of which contradicts the other—for example, "Amazing man. Untalented oaf. Genius . . . Anarchist. Poet. Eccentric." In these contradictions lies the futility of Venichka's agony, and, moreover, his words and actions confirm all these definitions and yet negate them. Like all other phenomena in his world, he finally proves to be a mirage, a no one, both in his own eyes and those of the readers'. Therefore, Erofeev's essential motivation for creating a fictional alter ego may also be interpreted in a second way: as a conscious effort to abnegate all conceptions of the self. In other words, the birth of Venichka, who does not know whether, why, or how he exists, is tantamount to the death of his creator. In this connection, Murav'ev cites Erofeev's habit of signing his name as "V. Er.," which, when transliterated into German, is *Wer* (Who), as proof of his constant attempts to challenge his own authority as writer and subject.

The form of the notebook, which Erofeev adopted for his first work, further complicates the issue. Although the device of first-person narrative in diaries is well established in literature, in Erofeev's context it acquires a particular significance. An inveterate note-taker in real life, he began maintaining elaborate notebooks since his university days; few of these writings have survived or even been published. Such jottings, which he religiously continued throughout his life, were a mishmash of quotes, paraphrases, parodies, aphoristic summaries of events—mostly of a sardonic nature—as well as terse philosophical and emotional statements. The fictional Venichka's diary reproduces many features of Erofeev's own notebooks. Were a biographer to seek a cogent account of the author's life and times in his archives, he would be utterly frustrated: Erofeev's diaries do not narrate events but rather roam over personal and place names, quotations, numbers, observations, exclamations, puns, jokes, and mathematical theorems. They defy causality and mock memory. An alleged quote from Catherine the Great could be sandwiched between verses from the Scriptures, the current price of vodka, irreverent anecdotes about Karl Marx and Friedrich Engels, and a pun he had just thought up.

The closing passage of *Zapiski psikhopata* represents an attempt to resolve the sharply contradicting registers of the entries, or notes, through a rather curious device—sentimentality. Venichka summarizes his life as a failed endeavor of hanging violet curtains in a meager room. Asserting that red, the color of aggression, disturbs and agitates him, he selects the subdued violet tone for symbolizing the one metaphysical category that has sustained itself through disillusionment—beauty in all its humble, unobtrusive incarnations.

Erofeev's abiding receptivity toward beauty and the intense lyricism with which he perceived and represented nature remained an enigma to those who witnessed his harsh circumstances and rebellious outlook. Combined with refined manners and an attractive appearance, however, his sensitivity made him extraordinarily successful in matters of the heart. The tall young man with dark hair and blue eyes reportedly had several female admirers at the Vladimir Pedagogical Institute. Among them was his first wife, Valentina Zimakova. Zimakova hailed from Myshlino, a village near Petushki, where she moved after graduation and gave birth to Erofeev's son. The child was named after his father, who was fond of calling him the twice-blessed one because of his name, Venedikt Venediktovich, or, literally, Benediction of the Blessed One.

Neither marriage nor the birth of his child, however, exorcised the lingering specters of homelessness and hardship from Erofeev's life. He was a particularly tragic victim of the system by which demographics were coordinated in the Soviet Union. Residency was regulated by a strict system of internal passports and the notorious *propiska,* a permit to live, study, or work in a particular region. In Moscow, for example, a person who was not born there had to prove his affiliation to an educational or professional institution. Anyone without this document was barred from fundamental rights and privileges, which included housing, medical care, and other services controlled and administered by the state. After Erofeev was expelled from the pedagogical institute—either for composing satirical poems or for carrying a Bible—finding a fixed place of residence and work was almost impossible for him. By extension, his identity was essentially denied by a system in which a people were valued if they were productive in service to the state. Erofeev gradually grew estranged from his wife and child in Myshlino as he quit his studies and began to look for employment.

With the dubious idyll of student life behind him, Erofeev now faced the true horror of surviving as an unskilled worker without identification papers. From March of 1957 through the 1960s and 1970s, he migrated from job to job in various provinces. Most of them were menial and some rather bizarre. He worked intermittently as a deliveryman, glassware inspector, stoker, night watchman, librarian, fitter, laborer in highway and construction projects, and layer of telephone cables. Throughout this period his family and friends kept in touch with him, providing him with accommodation and financial support on his visits and between jobs.

They attempted to help him resolve the problem of his residential status, sometimes at great cost to themselves. His sister Nina, for example, once sold her personal effects to secure him a place in an expedition to Uzbekistan so that he could apply for identification papers as a bona fide scientific researcher.

Among the myriad professions that Erofeev tried, the one that he held for the longest duration–and of which he retained the most vivid memories–was repairman of telephone cables running along railway lines. From 1969 to 1974 he traveled back and forth between Moscow and its suburbs as a laborer and, later, as a foreman of communications maintenance crews. The Moscow-Petushki route was one of his beats on the job.

The novel that instantly made Erofeev renowned and controversial, *Moskva-Petushki,* was written in the drafty wagons of the maintenance train. His recollection of the circumstances under which it was composed show nothing redeeming. At the end of a grueling workday, in a railway compartment that also served as the communal dormitory, he lay on his upper bunk and wrote, while fellow laborers jeered him for his intellectualism and tried to lure him away for a drink and a game of cards. The damning self-perception that he did not belong either to their world or to that of the Moscow intelligentsia–that he was nothing but a loser with pretensions–assaulted him almost constantly. In an interview with Igor Bolychev published in 1989, Erofeev recalled that he was repairing a punctured sewage line once when a young woman passing by admonished her child to study well or he would end up like that respectable-looking man face down in the dirt.

Such materially and psychologically harrowing, yet creatively exhilarating, moments comprise the background against which *Moskva-Petushki* was created. By Erofeev's own accounts, again in the interview with Bolychev, it was written at a frenzied pace between 19 January and 6 March 1970. His friend Avdiev, who often sought out the writer in his lonely suburban commissions, recalls that the work was originally composed to entertain mutual friends from their days at Vladimir Pedagogical Institute. Erofeev believed that they would recognize themselves in the various characters and events. Whatever the author's initial motivation might have been, his friends certainly played a crucial role in the survival and distribution of a work that was never accepted for "official" publication in the Soviet press.

Moskva-Petushki, originally produced in a single typewritten manuscript, is one of the best-known beneficiaries of a strong underground literary subculture distinctive to Soviet Russia. In the underground the works of authors who were banned or deemed potentially subversive were copied manually on typewriters and circulated informally–the more controversial the work, the

greater the number of copies created. Alongside this system of samizdat, or self-publication, a parallel process known as *tamizdat'* (publication over there) had developed, whereby manuscripts were smuggled out beyond the Iron Curtain.

Samizdat and *tamizdat'* played a crucial role in the initial propagation and subsequent worldwide reception of Erofeev's work. Shortly after his friends first saw the manuscript of *Moskva-Petushki,* it disappeared briefly–Erofeev and his friends were apparently attempting to trade it for vodka–but resurfaced again and began to be distributed in hundreds of copies. In two years it had breached the border and was first published in 1973 in an Israeli émigré periodical, *AMI.* Four years later the original Russian text was published in Paris by YMCA Press. By this time, too, the book had appeared in both French and German translation.

Moskva-Petushki was not published in the Soviet Union until the advent of glasnost in the late 1980s–and then only in a severely abbreviated, distorted form in the journal *Trezvost' i kul'tura* (Sobriety and Culture), where it was presented, of all things, as a didactic treatise against alcoholism. Following a fairly complete edition in 1989 from the independent publisher Vest', the first "authentic version" of the work, according to Murav'ev, came out in the same year from the Moscow publishing house Prometei. All these editions–except the initial *tamizdat'* publication–preserve an enigmatic modification that the author allegedly made in the second edition of his work. In a preface he claims to have expurgated all but the first line "I nemedlenno vypil" (And I drank immediately) from one chapter that consisted entirely of obscenities. With characteristic irreverence for authorial protocol, Erofeev informs readers that the disclaimer in the first edition about profane language did not prevent them–especially women–from going straight to the offensive passage. He has apparently decided to throw out the list of potentially incendiary words not only to restore the dignity of his readers but also to make sure that they follow the order in which the book was originally meant to be read.

Moskva-Petushki recounts a journey between the two railway stations, Moscow and Petushki, by *elektrichka,* the plebeian slow suburban train. The trip is narrated from the point of view of the protagonist, alternatively called Venia, Venichka, or Erofeichik. The defining feature of this character is his inveterate alcoholism. At the start of the story Venichka wakes up in Moscow in the haze of a hangover in front of a stranger's doorway, a suitcase at his side and full of treats for his infant son living in Petushki. The story continues in time with Venichka's growing inebriation. Disorientation, however, is the principal element of his universe. Even before he launches into the tale, he veers into a digression about the meaninglessness of space and time. The Kremlin—the symbolic heart of Moscow and its traditional center of history and power—is a landmark that he has never been able to find in spite of many trips undertaken especially to see it. Instead, he winds up each time at the Kursk railway station from which the Moscow-Gor'kovskaia suburban train leaves; Petushki is a station on this line.

This opening passage serves well to prepare the reader for accompanying Venichka on his journey. The implied reader is engaged as a traveling companion and interlocutor from the beginning: "And you, of course, will ask: and then, Venichka, and then—what did you drink?" In the course of the journey, however, this question is perhaps the only one answered with any degree of consistency. The rest of the narrative is constructed upon the obverse logic that arises from alcoholic delusion, disintegrating illusions, and free association, ultimately dissolving into complete and irredeemable chaos. Chaos—or, rather, a deliberate attempt to reverse and obfuscate order—functions as the governing principle of both the formal coordinates and the contents of Erofeev's work. *Moskva-Petushki* is divided into chapters corresponding to, and named after, the geographical points traversed by the protagonist. The opening passage, titled "Moscow: On the Way to Kursk Station," is followed by "Moscow: The Station Square," "Moscow: In the Station Restaurant," and "Moscow: Toward the Train by Way of the Liquor Store." As the train begins to move, Moscow is left behind and replaced by station names, each chapter marking the route between two of them—"Moskva-Serp i Molot" (Moscow-Hammer and Sickle) and "Serp i Molot-Karacharovo" (Hammer and Sickle-Karacharovo), for example—until Venichka's destination, Petushki, appears. Thereafter, the chapter headings evolve into a Möbius strip of space, in which the destination of the journey starts to fold back into its origin and becomes indistinguishable from it. Moscow landmarks from the chapters at the beginning are suspiciously superimposed upon what the protagonist thinks is Petushki. Following "Petushki: The Platform" comes "Petushki: The Station Square" and "Petushki: The Garden Ring," the road that circumvents central Moscow. Venichka's progression toward the city center ultimately leads him to the long-awaited and impossibly inaccessible symbol of Russian identity, "Petushki: The Kremlin." The Kremlin, however, is of little use to Venichka at the end of the road. In the "Unknown Doorway," the final chapter, titled after the place from which he emerged out of oblivion at the beginning of the narrative to embark on his peregrinations, four anonymous assassins armed with an awl send him brutally back to eternal rest.

Moskva-Petushki is conventionally referred to as a novel, although the work constantly defies categorization by genre. Its space and time frames do not adhere to linear progression. Monologue, dialogue, and reflective passages are liberally interspersed with discourses that are not traditionally associated with narrative genres—such as Venichka's graphs of drinking habits, cocktail recipes, lists of obscenities, or even long gaps signifying oblivion. In addition, Erofeev subtitled it a "poema," or narrative poem. Many scholars, including Mark Altshuller, Monika Majewska, and Elena A. Smirnova, identify *Moskva-Petushki* with Gogol's monumental *Pokhozhdeniia Chichikova, ili Mertvye dushi. Poema* (The Adventures of Chichikov, Or Dead Souls. A Narrative Poem, 1842, 1855; translated as *Dead Souls,* 1948), also known as *Mertvye dushi*—a prose narrative, bearing the same subtitle, whose characters, motivation, and tone resonate with those of Erofeev's text. The protagonists of both works are dissolute antiheroes and wanderers across the Russian countryside. Just as Venichka's adventures span biblical times and the era of Leonid Il'ich Brezhnev, *Mertvye dushi* was meant to offer a sweeping revelation of the essence of mid-nineteenth-century Russia beyond the constraints of realistic representation and contemporaneity. Both works are rendered in a combination of intensely lyrical and scathingly satirical passages in which the trivial is poeticized, and monumental issues are presented as hilarious parody.

A rich scholarly tradition has sprung up around *Moskva-Petushki* since the early 1980s. For example, critics such as Karen L. Ryan-Hayes and Laura Beraha have analyzed the work, with its overarching theme of wandering and its many plotlines, both as a picaresque novel and as a distinctive inversion of the picaresque form. Some scholars label the internal dynamics of *Moskva-Petushki*—its juxtaposition of the comic and the tragic and its tendency to create a travesty of the elevated—"carnivalization," which the critic Mikhail Mikhailovich Bakhtin associated with the birth of the novel; others assert that Erofeev's work, on the contrary, stands for the devolution of the modern novel. The rich matrix of literary and cultural allusions and extreme heterogeneity of style, voice, register, and discourse in the narrative have prompted a few scholars to examine *Moskva-Petushki* in interpretive frameworks that span many centuries. Erofeev's obvious familiarity with the Bible has generated studies on the spiritual motivation and content of his work. Irina Paperno and Boris Gasparov postulate that Venichka's biography is an inverted allegory on the vita of Christ by citing the liberal use of scriptural allusions, biblical discourse, and the theme of resurrection. In differing approaches, Mikhail Naumovich Epshtein and Mark Lipovetsky identify the synthesis and interchangeability of sacred and profane elements in the narrator's persona with the discourse of the *iurodivyi,* or holy fool, in Orthodox Christian tradition.

Furthermore, various elements of Erofeev's work, including—but not limited to—satire, parody, colloquialization, folkloric motifs, and semantic inversion have also been traced back to a large spectrum of sources. Ekaterina Orlova associates the juxtaposition and mixture of literary and colloquial aspects in *Moskva-Petushki* not only with the use of language found in the works of Rabelais and William Shakespeare, but also with the stylized *skaz* (approximation of oral narration in written discourse) used by Russian satirists, including Nikolai Semenovich Leskov and Mikhail Mikhailovich Zoshchenko. Scholars such as Eduard Vlasov and Katerine Moskver find precedents of the underlying motif of travel in Erofeev's work among the landmark texts of Russian Enlightenment thinkers Nikolai Mikhailovich Karamzin and Aleksandr Nikolaevich Radishchev. Iurii Zav'ialov-Leving compares Erofeev's use of folkloric imagery and discourse with that of Aleksandr Sergeevich Pushkin, while Iurii Levin examines the surreal atmosphere and grotesque characters of *Moskva-Petushki* against the world of the schizophrenic and delusive in Dostoevsky's works.

Despite the many scholarly approaches to his magnum opus, Erofeev enjoyed none of the fruits of critical recognition during his lifetime. His estrangement from his first wife and child during the creation of *Moskva-Petushki* accelerated into a complete loss of contact with them. Although this single work made him a commonly recognized name among the intelligentsia, its large readership did not assuage his crisis of not having an official place of residence or legitimate professional status as writer. His condition improved somewhat after he met his future second wife, Galina, in 1974, who began to provide him with a home and some material assistance; he continued to be an itinerant worker until he settled down with her in the late 1970s, marrying her in 1979.

Erofeev produced a few more works after *Moskva-Petushki,* almost all of which were published posthumously. In 1972 he began a novel tentatively titled "Dmitrii Shostakovich," the manuscript of which was mostly lost in constant transition. From the small fragment that was preserved and eventually published in *Ostav'te moiu dushu v pokoe* (Leave My Soul in Peace) 1995, its eponymous hero seems to be not the renowned composer but a glassware inspector of the same name—another "double" culled from Erofeev's motley work experience. A creative essay from 1973 was published without a title in the underground émigré journal *Veche* (the term for popular assembly in a medieval Russian town) in 1978. This work was subsequently included in anthologies under the title "Vasily Rozanov glazami ektsentrika" (Vasilii Rozanov in the Eyes of an Eccentric) and published in a separate edition as *Glazami ektsentrika* (Through the Eyes of An Eccentric, 1982). It was translated into English as "Through the Eyes of an Eccentric"

Front cover for the 2000 edition of Erofeev's Moskva-Petushki *(1977; translated as* Moscow to the End of the Line, *1980), about an alcoholic's railway journey (Jean and Alexander Heard Library, Vanderbilt University)*

in *The Penguin Book of New Russian Writing* only in 1995. It also displays Erofeev's inimitable penchant for parodying so-called great works or great people and applying their message to the existential crises of his own context. The essay highlights the affinities between the spiritual, epistemological, and aesthetic crises of the last fin de siècle and that of the late twentieth century. Venichka returns as the narrator, dying of alcoholism and a desperate weltschmerz. Unable to commit suicide by any decent means, he accidentally encounters the works of Vasilii Vasil'evich Rozanov, a controversial thinker from the turn of the twentieth century. Rozanov's highly original views on religion and sexuality find instant resonance with the protagonist, who is beleaguered by the horrors and hypocrisy of his own age. Venichka engages in a discourse with the philosopher's double, applying random quotations from Rozanov's works to comment on the great cataclysms of the late twentieth century: Nazism, the Holocaust, the world wars, the Vietnam War, the

Cold War, and the constant shift and migration of people. Another work consisting almost exclusively of quotations, called "Moia malen'kaia leniniana" (My Little Leninisms), first appeared in the émigré journal *Kontinent* (The Continent) in 1988. In this hilarious essay, in which the author strategically places excerpts from Vladimir Lenin's correspondence among his own satirical comments on history according to Bolshevism, Erofeev exposes the mechanisms by which the epic of the Soviet Empire was composed out of words abstracted from their context.

Neither the wide readership of *Moskva-Petushki* nor Erofeev's growing audience in the West significantly changed his dire financial situation. According to his wife Galina's reminiscences published in *Stolitsa* (The Capital) in 1991, royalties could not be transferred to the Soviet Union from abroad. The writer harbored some bitterness over the issue that his publishers in England, France, and the United States made no concerted effort to alleviate his hardship. Even after the publication of *Moskva-Petushki* in Erofeev's home country, the lingering deadwood of Soviet bureaucracy continued to prevent him from crossing the border. In 1986, for instance, when he became gravely ill with throat cancer, his petition for permission to travel to Paris for treatment was rejected on the grounds that there was a gap in his employment records for the greater part of 1968.

Toward the end of his life, as he struggled with the cumbersome apparatus that later substituted for his voice, Erofeev began experimenting with a new genre—drama. He started work on a projected trilogy of plays, to be titled after the three nights that are traditionally associated with the supernatural, animistic ritual, and Satanism: The Night of Ivan Kupala, a Slavic pre-Christian festival that provided the title for one of Gogol's early fantastic stories, "Vecher nakanune Ivana Kupala" (published in *Vechera na khutore bliz Dikan'ki* [Evenings on a Farm near Dikanka], 1831–1832); Walpurgis Night; and The Night Before Christmas. He was able to complete and witness the staging of only the second part. *Val'purgieva noch, ili shagi komandora* (Walpurgis Night, or the Commander's Steps, 1990), subtitled "a tragedy in five acts," was written in 1985 and staged in 1989 in the Teatr na Maloi Bronnoi (Malaia Bronnaia Theater) in Moscow, but Erofeev, who was not particularly fond of the theater, reportedly disapproved of the production.

Val'pugieva noch' is set in a psychiatric ward, one of many institutions of the Soviet state that acquired a distinctly mythic character in popular lore and literature. Subversive thinkers and political dissidents were reportedly held alongside bona fide patients under nightmarish conditions in these "wards" for the mentally ill. The only forms of treatment administered indiscriminately to both groups consisted of shock therapy and sedative injections. Physical and emotional abuse by doctors and nursing staff were rife, since the government invested little in patients who only represented an aberration from the heroic, healthy ideal of citizens in a perfect social system.

The title of the play is particularly significant in the context of the protagonist's relation to, and his fate in, the chaos that reigns around him. Walpurgis Night is celebrated on the night of 30 April and continues through 1 May. The festival originated in Scandinavia among the Vikings and is still celebrated in Sweden and northern Russia (where Erofeev grew up) as a pre-Christian fertility rite celebrating the arrival of spring. Its rituals include the building of a Maypole, a phallic symbol penetrating Mother Earth, and a bonfire over which young couples jump. In stark contrast to the mystery, carnival atmosphere, and eroticism of the midnight rituals—or perhaps in a daytime mirror image of it—the first day of May was also the biggest festival in postpagan, post-Christian Bolshevik Russia. The president and Politburo members, demigods of the nation, appeared on the balcony of the Kremlin to cheering crowds and a most impressive display of Soviet military might. Through the machismo and charisma displayed in May Day parades, which were broadcast live on all television and radio channels, the most potent myths about the State and its leaders were indelibly etched into public memory.

The mental hospital provides the perfect allegory for the abysmally depressing, yet profoundly absurd, atmosphere of Erofeev's contemporary Russia. Lev Isaakovich Gurevich, hero of the play, arrives in the living hell of such an institution from which there is only one way out: on a stretcher bound for the morgue. He is forcibly admitted on the basis of the denunciation that his breath does not condense even on the frostiest mornings. This physical characteristic, which seems Satanic from the Christian point of view, is only the most superficial of Gurevich's many "dangerous" psychological qualities that are anathema in the eyes of the government. Not only is his father a Jew, but Gurevich also loved him; he does not believe in empirical notions of time and space, thus violating the basic tenets of scientific materialism; he is an inveterate wanderer and ruthlessly criticizes obfuscations of meaning, the stock-in-trade of official rhetoric in his milieu. He declares that the only drawbacks in his motherland are "a ban on wandering and flagrant disregard for the Word." Gurevich shares many qualities with his literary predecessor Venichka; unlike the hero of *Moskva-Petushki,* however, his rebellion is not purely self-destructive.

The biblical phrase, "Arise and go," which serves as the leitmotiv of Venichka's futile journey toward resurrection in *Moskva-Petushki,* reappears in the first scene of *Val'purgieva noch'* as Gurevich's existential credo. But whereas Erofeev's alter ego in *Moskva-Petushki* could not garner the spiritual strength to carry out this command, Gurevich has a precise definition for the state he is striving to overcome: *nebytie,* or nonexistence. He grasps at once that institutionalized brainwashing, which epitomizes the nonexistence of the individual psyche, is the enemy that should be vanquished first and foremost; passivity is not a choice. He watches in horror as his companions retreat into their illusory worlds and pays particular attention to an old peasant, Vova, whose dream life centers on a utopian bucolic village similar to Venichka's imaginary Petushki. Gurevich decides early upon a course of action. He rallies his ward mates, particularly a senior internee, Prokhorov, to aid and abet a plot for exploding the entire complex. In a replay of the sexual carnival that takes place on Walpurgis Night, Gurevich seduces the night nurse, Natalie, on the night of 30 April and manages to appropriate her keys to the storeroom. But the dawn of May Day reveals that the plan has somehow failed, and all the inmates are still incarcerated in their communal cell. Even as they discuss how their celebration of the great holiday is more profound, more "normal," than the kitsch that represents "official" rituals of the day, a mysterious affliction transforms their song and dance into a *danse macabre* (dance of death). The so-called fools and reactionaries, who could dream and think better than the petty bureaucrats who controlled them, die in the midst of a final carnival, discussing until their last breath the joys of Gustav Mahler's music and the pristine beauty of the village from which Vova had been transported against his will. Although he goes blind and is dragged ignominiously by a warden shouting anti-Semitic abuse, Gurevich goes down fighting and unrepentant of his views.

In the late 1980s Erofeev, whom *Moskva-Petushki* had transformed into a cultural myth even before its formal publication in Russia, became something of a media icon in the first jubilant years of glasnost. Several interviews with him were published in both Russian and émigré journals in which he obligingly reiterated the dramatic story of his life and commented on his elusive and original aesthetic. In each account he subtly changed or reinterpreted the details, betraying his ironic attitude toward so-called objective facts and his original perception of the chronological and geographical framework of a curriculum vitae.

The interviews also reveal Erofeev's unusual approach to the issue of self-mythologization. Knowing that his biography was now inextricably bound with that of his fictional doppelgänger and antihero, Venichka, the author liked to shock his audience with a device that Epshtein, in his 1995 essay, names "demythologization." Just as Venichka exposes the emptiness behind the grandiloquent rhetoric of socialist realism and Soviet propaganda, Erofeev liked to deflate conceptions about himself as a dissident writer in a totalitarian state starving and drinking to death. He strenuously disassociated himself from his contemporary authors, and with a characteristic lack of self-aggrandizement he refused to believe that he had exerted any decisive influence on either individual writers or literature as a whole.

Four years after his cancer diagnosis, Erofeev succumbed to the disease and died in Moscow on 11 May 1990. While his antihero and his unusual language, narrative devices, and discourse mark a radical departure from dominant norms and conventions, Erofeev's contribution to Russian literary culture is not limited to aesthetic sensationalism. His extensive and ongoing influence is apparent in the works of successive generations of writers. Many of them, including Evgenii Anatol'evich Popov, Viktor Vladimirovich Erofeev, and the postmodern art collective *Mit'ki,* experiment with fragmented subjectivity and multiple narrative voices. Their fictional heroes often bear their own names and wildly contradicting characters. Intertextuality and parody made Erofeev's work resonate particularly well with the memories and perceptions of his contemporaries. These hallmark devices, moreover, have evolved into basic mechanisms for the post-Soviet literary imagination continually engaged in reexamination of past values, cults, and convictions.

Venedikt Vasil'evich Erofeev and his double, Venichka, continue to thrive in contemporary Russian life; two different editions of his works appeared in 2000 alone. Venichka's ongoing dialogue with his audience of multiple generations, whose youngest members have scarcely any memory of Soviet reality, vindicates Erofeev's prophetic statement that his fictional personalities will ensure the survival and immortality of his creation. In a diary entry from his hardest days in the early 1970s he declared: "What saves me is that each of them is one and I am many."

Letters:

"Pis'ma k sestre," *Teatr,* 9 (1992): 122–144;

"I ia ostaius' v zhivykh," *Stolitsa,* 32 (1992): 58–63;

Anatolii Nabatov, *Perepiska Venichki Erofeeva i Abrama Proletarskogo* (Moscow: Strakhovoe reviu, 1999).

Interviews:

Igor Bolychev, "Umru, no nikogda ne poimu . . . ," *Moskovskie novosti,* 10 December 1989, p. 13;

V. Lomazov, "Nechto vrode besedy s Venediktom Erofeevym," *Teatr,* 4 (1989): 33–34;

Irina Tosunian, "Ot Moskvy do samykh Petushkov," *Literaturnaia gazeta,* 3 January 1990, p. 5;

L. Prudovsky, "Zhit' v Rossii s umom i talantom: Beseda s V. Erofeevym. 7 Marta 1989 g.," *Aprel'* (1991): 236–250.

Bibliographies:

Sergei P. Bavin, "*Samovozrastaiushchii logos*": *Venedikt Erofeev: bibliograficheskii ocherk* (Moscow: Rossiiskaia gosudarstvennaia biblioteka, 1995);

Karen L. Ryan-Hayes, [Bibliography], in *Venedikt Erofeev's* Moscow-Petushki: *Critical Perspectives,* edited by Ryan-Hayes (New York: Peter Lang, 1995).

Biographies:

I. Maryniak, "A Hero of Our Time: Filming Venedikt Erofeev," *Index on Censorship,* 20, no. 2 (1991): 8–9;

Nina Vasil'evna Frolova and others, "Neskol'ko monologov o Venedikte Erofeeve," *Teatr,* 9 (1991): 74–122;

Ol'ga Aleksandrovna Sedakova, "Neskazannaia rech' na vechere Venedikta Erofeeva," *Druzhba narodov,* 12 (1991): 264–265;

Galina Erofeeva, "I priroda cheshet v zatylke," *Stolitsa,* 30 (1991): 62–63;

Lidiia Liubchikova, "Krasiv, beden, i schastliv v liubvi," *Stolitsa,* 30 (1991): 63;

Vladimir S. Murav'ev, "My zhili veselo," *Stolitsa,* 30 (1991): 62;

Sedakova, "Gadkikh utiat liubil, ot lebedei – toshnilo," *Stolitsa,* 30 (1991): 63;

Natalya Smelkova, "Vremeni net . . . ," *Literaturnoe obozrenie,* 2 (1992): 39–45;

Elena Ignatova, "Venedikt," *Dom,* 1 (1993): 66–95;

Ignatova, "Venedikt," *Panorama,* 3–9 February 1993, pp. 22–23;

Anatolii Ivanov, "Kak steklyshko: Venedikt Erofeev vblizi i izdaleche," *Znamia,* 9 (1998): 170–177;

Vladimir Bondarenko, "Podlinnyi Venichka," *Nash sovremennik,* 7 (1999): 177–185.

References:

Valentina Baslyk, "Venedikt Erofeev's *Moskva-Petushki:* The Subversive Samizdat' Text," dissertation, University of Toronto, 1995;

Baslyk, "Venichka's Divided Self: The Sacred and the Monstrous," in *Venedikt Erofeev's* Moskva-Petushki: *Critical Perspectives,* edited by Karen L. Ryan-Hayes (New York: Peter Lang, 1997), pp. 53–78;

Ziva Bencic, "Obraz Venichki Erofeeva," *Russian Literature,* 51–3 (April 2002): 243–260;

Laura Beraha, "Out of and into the Void: Picaresque Absences and Annihilation," in *Venedikt Erofeev's* Moscow-Petushki: *Critical Perspectives,* edited by Ryan-Hayes (New York: Peter Lang, 1995), pp. 19–52;

David M. Bethea, *The Shape of Apocalypse in Modern Russian Fiction* (Princeton: Princeton University Press, 1989);

Nikolai A. Bogomolov, "Blokovskii plast' v Moskve-Petushkakh," *Novoe literaturnoe obozrenie,* no. 4 (2000): 126–135;

Deming Brown, *The Last Years of Soviet Russian Literature: Prose Fiction, 1975–1991* (Cambridge: Cambridge University Press, 1993);

Marietta Chudakova, "Put' k sebe: Literaturnaia situatsiia – 89," *Literaturnoe obozrenie,* no. 1 (1990): 33–38;

Edith Clowes, *Russian Experimental Fiction: Resisting Ideology after Utopia* (Princeton: Princeton University Press, 1993);

L. V. Fast, "Osobennosti rechevogo standarta v iazyke sovremennoi dramaturgii," *Russkii iazyk za rubezhom,* nos. 5–6 (1992): 73–76;

Igor' Fomenko, ed., *Analiz odnogo proizvedeniia: "Moskva-Petushki" Ven. Erofeeva: Sbornik naychnykh trudov* (Tver': Tverskoi gosudarstvennyi universitet, 2000);

Svetlana Geisser-Schnittman, *Venedikt Erofeev "Moskva-Petushki" ili "The Rest Is Silence"* (Bern: Peter Lang, 1989);

Mikhail Heller, "Voyage vers le Bonheur dont parlent les Journaux," in Erofeev's *Moscou-Sur-Vodka (Moscou-Petouchki),* translated by Annie Sabatier and Antoine Pingaud (Paris: Michel, 1976), pp. 193–204;

Petra Hesse, "K funktsii 'probela' v neofitsial'noi literature 60-ikh godov: Moskva-Petushki Venedikta Erofeeva," *Russian Literature,* no. 2 (1998): 221–243;

Guy Houk, "Erofeev and Evtushenko," in *Venedikt Erofeev's* Moscow-Petushki: *Critical Perspectives,* edited by Ryan-Hayes (New York: Peter Lang, 1995), pp. 179–196;

Maia Kaganskaia, "Shutovskoi khorovod," *Sintaksis,* no. 13 (1984): 139–190;

Viacheslav Kuritsyn, "My poedem s toboiu na 'a' i na 'iu'," *Novoe literaturnoe obozrenie,* no. 1 (1992): 296–304;

Konstantin Kustanovich, "Venichka Erofeev's Grief and Solitude: Existentialist Motifs in the Poema," in *Venedikt Erofeev's* Moscow-Petushki: *Critical Perspectives,* edited by Ryan-Hayes (New York: Peter Lang, 1995), pp. 123–152;

Iurii Levin, "Klassicheskie traditsii v drugoi literature: Venedikt Erofeev i Feodor Dostoevskii," *Literaturnoe obozrenie,* no. 2 (1992): 45–50;

Levin, *Kommentarii k poeme "Moskva-Petushki" V. Erofeeva* (Gratz: Grazer Gesellschaft zur Forderung slawischer Kulturstudien, 1996);

Mark Lipovetsky, "Apofeoz chastis, ili dialog s khaosom: Zametki o klassike, Venedikte Erofeeve, poeme 'Moskva-Petushki' i russkom postmodernizme," *Znamia*, no. 8 (1989): 214–224;

Lipovetsky, "S potustoronnei tochki zreniia: postmodernistskaia versiia dialogizma," in *Venedikt Erofeev's* Moscow-Petushki: *Critical Perspectives,* edited by Ryan-Hayes (New York: Peter Lang, 1995), pp. 79–100;

Lipovetsky, "Svobody chernaia rabota: ob artisticheskoi proze novogo pokoleniia," *Voprosy literatury,* no. 9 (1989): 3–44;

Monika Majewska, "Venedikt Erofeev's 'Moskva-Petushki': An Insight into Russia's Spirits and Spirituality," in *East-Central European Traumas and a Millenial Condition,* edited by Zbigniew Bialas and Wieslaw Krajka (Boulder, Colo.: East European Monographs, 1999), pp. 125–148;

Iurii Mal'tsev, *Vol'naia Russkaia Literatura* (Frankfurt: Possev, 1976);

Marie R. Martin, "From *Byt* to *Bytie:* The Game of Parody in the Poetics of Venedikt Erofeev," dissertation, University of Chicago, 1995;

Martin, "The Story of Russian," in *Venedikt Erofeev's* Moscow-Petushki: *Critical Perspectives,* edited by Ryan-Hayes (New York: Peter Lang, 1995), pp. 153–178;

Arnold McMillin, "Russian Prose in the 1970s: From Erofeev to Edichka," *Journal of Russian Studies,* 45 (1983): 25–33;

Katerine Moskver, "Back on the Road: Erofeev's Moskva-Petushki and Traditions of Russian Literature," *Russian, Croatian and Serbian, Czech and Slovak, Polish Literature,* 8, no. 2 (2000): 195–204;

Ekaterina Orlova, "Posle skaza: Mikhail Zoshchenko–Venedikt Erofeev–Abram Terts," *Filologicheskie nauki,* 6 (1996): 13–22;

Irina Paperno and Boris Gasparov, "'Vstan' i idi'," *Slavica Hierosolymitana,* 5–6 (1981): 387–400;

Robert Porter, "Venedikt Erofeev–a Short Journey to Eternity," in his *Russia's Alternative Prose* (Oxford: Berg, 1994), pp. 72–87;

Ryan-Hayes, "Beyond Picaresque: Erofeev's *Moscow-Petushki*," in her *Contemporary Russian Satire: A Genre Study* (Cambridge: Cambridge University Press, 1995), pp. 58–100;

Ryan-Hayes, "Erofeev's Grief: Inconsolable and Otherwise," in *Venedikt Erofeev's* Moscow-Petushki: *Criti-*

cal Perspectives, edited by Ryan-Hayes (New York: Peter Lang, 1995), pp. 101–122;

Ryan-Hayes, ed., *Venedikt Erofeev's* Moscow-Petushki: *Critical Perspectives* (New York: Peter Lang, 1995);

Cynthia Simmons, "An Alcoholic Narrative as 'Time out' and The Double in *Moskva-Petushki*," *Canadian-American Slavic Studies,* 24 (Summer 1990): 155–168;

Simmons, *Their Father's Voice: Vassily Aksyonov, Venedikt Erofeev, Eduard Limonov, and Sasha Sokolov* (New York: Peter Lang, 1993);

Elena A. Smirnova, "Mifologema stradaiushchego boga i strasti Venichki Erofeeva," *Sintaksis,* 33 (1992): 96–107;

Smirnova, "Venedikt Erofeev glazami gogoloveda," *Russkaia literatura,* no. 3 (1990): 58–66;

Neil Stewart, *"Vstan' I vspominaj": Auferstehung als Collage in Venedikt Erofeev* Moskva-Petushki (Frankfurt & New York: Peter Lang, 1999);

Vladimir Tumanov, "The End in V. Erofeev's Moskva-Petushki," *Russian Literature,* 1 (1996): 95–114;

Erzhebet Vari, "'Moi antiiazyk ot antizhizni': Mesto poemy Venedikta Erofeeva 'Moskva-Petushki' v sovremennoi russkoi literature," *Studia Slavica Academiae Scientiarum Hungaricae,* 1–2 (1999): 153–190;

A. Velichansky, "Fenomen Erofeeva," foreword to *Moskva-Petushki i pr.* (Moscow: Prometei, 1989);

Eduard Vlasov, "Bessmertnaia poema Venedikta Erofeeva 'Moskva-Petushki'. Sputnik pisatelia," in *Moskva Petushki* (Moscow: Vagrius, 2000), pp. 121–559;

Vlasov, "Zagranitsa glazami ektsentrika: k analizu 'zagranichnykh glav'," in *Venedikt Erofeev's* Moscow-Petushki: *Critical Perspectives,* edited by Ryan-Hayes (New York: Peter Lang, 1995), pp. 197–220;

Iurii Zav'ialov-Leving, "Shilo i spitsa: Moskva-Petushki i Zolotoi petushok," *Wiener Slavistischer Almanach,* 42 (1998): 175–187;

Natal'ia V. Zhivopulova, "Palomnichestvo v Petushki, ili problema metafizicheskogo bunta v ispovedi Venichki Erofeeva," *Chelovek,* 1 (1992): 78–91;

Andrei Zorin, "Opoznavatel'nyi znak," *Teatr,* 9 (1991): 119–122;

Zorin, "Venichka: Opoznavatel'nyi znak," *Stolitsa,* 30 (1991): 58–63;

Livia Zvonnikova, "'Moskva-Petushki i pr.': Popytka interpretatsii," *Znamia,* 8 (1996): 214–220.

Viktor Vladimirovich Erofeev

(19 September 1947 –   )

Larissa Rudova
Pomona College

and

Tatiana Spektor
Holy Trinity Seminary

BOOKS: *Telo Anny, ili konets russkogo avangarda* (Moscow: Moskovskii rabochii, 1989)–includes "Pis'mo k materi," "Belyi kastrirovannyi kot s glazami krasavitsy," "Kak my zarezali frantsuza," "Devushka i smert'," "Telo Anny, ili konets russkogo avangarda," "Govnososka," and "Popugaichik";

Russkaia krasavitsa (Moscow: Vsia Moskva, 1989; Moscow: Moskovskii rabochii, 1990);

V labirinte prokliatykh vorposov (Moscow: Sovetskii pisatel', 1990);

Naiti v cheloveke cheloveka. Dostoevsky i ekzistentsializm (Benson, Vt.: Chalidze Press, 1991);

Zhizn' s idiotom (Moscow: Interbuk, 1991)–includes "Zhizn' s idiotom," "Podrugi," and "Berdiaev";

Popugaichik. Rasskazy (Moscow: Pravda, 1991);

Izbrannoe, ili, Karmannyi apokalipsis. Povesti i rasskazy (Moscow & Paris: Tret'ia volna, 1993);

Strashnyi sud (Moscow: Soiuz fotokhudozhnikov Rossii, 1996);

Muzhchiny (Moscow: Podkova, 1997);

Piat' rek zhizni. Roman-reka (Moscow: Podkova, 1998);

Entsiklopediia russkoi dushi (Moscow: Podkova, 1999);

Piat' rek zhizni. Zaria novogo otkroveniia (Moscow: Podkova, 2000);

Labirint dva (Moscow: EKSMO, 2002);

Pupok: Rasskazy krasnogo cherviaka (Moscow: ZebraE, 2002).

Collections: *Sobranie sochinenii*, 3 volumes (Moscow: Molodaia gvardiia, 1994–1996);

V labirinte prokliatykh vorposov (Moscow: Soiuz fotokhudozhnikov Rossii, 1996);

Russkaia krasavitsa: Roman, rasskazy (Moscow: Astreia, 1997);

Sobranie sochinenii, 3 volumes (Moscow: Podkova, 1998);

Zhizn' s idiotom: Rasskazy molodogo cheloveka (Moscow: ZebraE, 2001);

Viktor Vladimirovich Erofeev (from the dust jacket for Russian Beauty, *1993; Richland County Public Library)*

Bog X: Rasskazy o liubvi (Moscow: ZebraE, 2001);

Strashnyi sud (Moscow: ZebraE, 2001).

Editions in English: "Humping Hannah," "A Fin de Siècle Orgasm," and "A Creation in Three Chapters," translated by Martin Horwitz in *Metropol: A*

Literary Almanac, with an introduction by Kevin Klose (Toronto: George J. McLeod, 1982; New York: Norton, 1982), pp. 457–526;

"The Parakeet" and "Anna's Body, or The End of the Russian Avant-garde," translated by Leonard J. Stanton in *Glasnost': An Anthology of Russian Literature under Gorbachev,* edited by Helena Goscilo and Byron Lindsey (Ann Arbor, Mich.: Ardis, 1990), pp. 367–377, 379–382;

"De Profundis" and "Cheekbones, a Nose, and a Gully," translated by Andrew Bromfield, in *Glas: New Russian Writing,* no. 2 (Moscow: Russlit, 1991);

"Sludge-sucker," translated by Cathy Porter, in *Dissonant Voices: The New Russian Fiction,* edited by Oleg Chukhontsev (London: Harvill, 1991), pp. 268–274;

Russian Beauty, translated by Andrew Reynolds (London: Hamilton, 1992; New York: Viking, 1993).

OTHER: *Metropol'. Literaturnyi almanakh,* edited, with contributions, by Erofeev, Vasily Pavlovich Aksenov, Andrei Georgievich Bitov, Evgenii Anatol'evich Popov, and Fazil Abdulovich Iskander (Ann Arbor, Mich.: Ardis, 1979; Moscow: Tekst, 1991)–includes "Iadrena Fenia," "Prispushchennyi orgazm stolet'ia," and "Trekhglavoe detishche";

Vladimir Nabokov, *Sobranie sochinenii,* 4 volumes, compiled by Erofeev (Moscow: Pravda, 1990);

Frantsuzskaia literatura, 1945–1990, with contributions by Erofeev, L. G. Andreev, Z. I. Kirnoze, and others (Moscow: Nasledie, 1995);

"Russia's Fleurs du Mal," in *The Penguin Book of New Russian Writing: Russia's Fleurs Du Mal,* compiled and translated by Andrew Reynolds (New York: Penguin, 1995); Russian version published as "Russkie tsvety zla," in *Russkie tsvety zla. Rodnaia proza kontsa XX veka,* compiled by Erofeev (Moscow: Podkova, 1997);

"Deti Pushkina," in *Shinel' Pushkina: Sbornik k 200-letnemu iubileiiu Pushkina,* edited by Mikhail Berg (Moscow: Pentagraphic, 2000);

Vremia rozhat', edited by Erofeev (Moscow: Podkova, 2001);

EPS, with contributions by Erofeev, Dmitrii Prigov, and Vladimir Sorokin (Moscow: ZebraE, 2002);

Sof'ia Kupriashina, *Schast'e: Rasskazy,* with a foreword by Erofeev (Moscow: ZebraE, 2002);

"Sila lobnogo mesta," in *Viktor Pelevin. Viktor Erofeev. Vladimir Sorokin: Sbornik,* by Erofeev, Viktor Olegovich Pelevin, and Vladimir Georgievich Sorokin (Moscow: ZebraE/EKSMO, 2003).

SELECTED PERIODICAL PUBLICATIONS: "Metamorfoza odnoi literturnoi reputatsii. Markiz de Sad, sadism i XX vek," *Voprosy literatury,* 17 (1973): 135–168;

"Ostaetsia odno–proizvol: Filosofiia odinochestva i literaturnoe kredo L. Shestova," *Voprosy literatury,* 10 (1975): 153–188;

"Pominki po sovetskoi literature," *Literaturnaia gazeta,* 27 (1990): 8; translated by Andrew Meier as "Soviet Literature: In Memoriam," in *Re-entering the Sign: Articulating New Russian Culture,* edited by Ellen Berry and Anesa Miller-Pogacar (Ann Arbor: University of Michigan Press, 1995), pp. 147–154;

"Irina's Miracle," translated by Andrew Reynolds, *Grand Street,* 11, no. 3 (1992): 102–132;

"Russkie tsvety zla," *Moskovskie novosti,* 27 June 1993, p. 4;

"The Good Stalin: Wine, Caviar, and a Life of Politburo Privilege," translated by Peter Carson, *New Yorker* (28 December 1998–4 January 1999): 44–47;

"A Murder in Moscow: A Cold War Family Story," translated by Carson, *New Yorker* (27 December 1999–3 January 2000): 48–50, 52–59.

Viktor Erofeev is one of the most prominent figures in Russian literature in the period of transition from Soviet to post-Soviet times. In his critical ideas and fictional writing Erofeev is indebted to the tradition of Western and Russian modernism and to his association with unofficial Soviet culture. His critical contributions to Russian literature are examples of his deep conviction that realism in its nineteenth-century forms and socialist realism had failed to answer fundamental questions of existence; according to Erofeev, a new kind of literature had to replace realism in order to describe the omnipotent evil of Soviet society. Practicing in his own fiction what he preaches in his criticism, Erofeev has written on the taboo topics of Soviet literature. His works are saturated with graphic descriptions of bodily functions, sex, sadistic violence against innocent victims (including children), and death. The intentional superabundance of these phenomena in his works suggests the diseased moral consciousness of Soviet society in which lofty principles and ideas are used to conceal the living hell of its subjects. With piercing postmodern irony, Erofeev deconstructs socialist realist values and presents them as detestable, grotesque, and perverse.

The new literature *(novaia literatura),* or alternative literature, *(drugging literatura),* to which Erofeev's writing belongs emerged in the mid 1980s during the years of Mikhail Sergeevich Gorbachev–the eras of glasnost and perestroika, when the liberal, cultural-political climate became conducive to innovative artistic expression. Alternative writers, who since the mid 1990s have been more commonly referred to as postmodernists, emphasized the idea that literature can exist for its own sake rather than for the purpose of serving the state. They insisted on the fictional construction of reality and used linguistic experimentation and provocative subject matter to portray it. The alternative writers who became prominent during the late Soviet and early post-Soviet period include figures such as Valery Georgievich Popov, Tatyana Tolstaya, Dmitrii Aleksandrovich Prigov, Vladimir Georgievich Sorokin, Igor Iarkevich, and Valeria Spartakovna Narbikova.

Like many other alternative writers, Erofeev embarked on a literary career during the years of Leonid Il'ich Brezhnev–the period known as the Stagnation–and thus found himself in opposition to the repressive cultural establishment. His biography reflects the spirit of the nonconformist intellectuals and writers of his generation. Viktor Vladimirovich Erofeev was born in Moscow on 19 September 1947 to the family of a high-ranking career diplomat. Erofeev enjoyed a privileged childhood, spending part of it in Paris when his father was appointed an adviser to the Soviet embassy in France. He read ardently in his youth and, because of his privileged position, had access to Russian and Western avant-garde and philosophical literature, which was either blacklisted or in limited circulation in the Soviet Union at that time. The authors whose works affected Erofeev's later views on literature include Vasily Vasil'evich Rozanov, Lev Shestov, Konstantin Nikolaevich Leont'ev, Viacheslav Ivanovich Ivanov, Mikhail Gershenzon, Vladimir Nabokov, and the Marquis de Sade.

In 1970 Erofeev graduated from Moscow University with a major in philology. In 1973 he completed his graduate work at the Institute of World Literature, and in 1975 he received a doctoral degree for his dissertation, "Dostoevsky and French Existentialism." Erofeev had already established himself as a provocative literary critic when his scholarly article "Metamorfoza odnoi literaturnoi reputatsii. Markiz de Sad, sadism i XX vek" (Metamorphosis of a Literary Reputation: The Marquis de Sade, Sadism, and the Twentieth Century) appeared in 1973 in the journal *Voprosy literatury* (Questions of Literature). The article addresses de Sade's rebellion against the destruction of the natural order of things by social and religious norms. Through his interpretation of de Sade, Erofeev implicitly states that societal norms should be ignored in order to allow individuals to explore the limits of the "natural" principle of pleasure. Although the destruction of social and religious norms will inevitably unleash vice, human beings should not be afraid of it since violence, like

pleasure, is a fundamental principle of human existence. Erofeev hails de Sade for his contribution to the elucidation of the complexities of human nature.

Despite the predominantly interpretative nature of this article, its subject matter and the manner of its treatment were highly provocative for the puritanical literary establishment. Erofeev's daring discussion of sex and sexual violence in particular caused a scandal in the official press, but he did not fall from grace, and his other controversial criticism in well-established official journals continued to be tolerated. At this time he also began formulating his vision of a new literature. His 1975 article "Ostaetsia odno–proizvol" ("One Thing Is Left–Arbitrary Rule"), also published in *Voprosy literatury,* pointed out the direction in which he believed new literature would develop. The article focused on the writings of the philosopher and critic Shestov, who rejected the tradition of rational humanism in Russia. Shestov, like many intellectuals of his generation, was influenced by Friedrich Nietzsche's philosophy and believed that evil–not good–would lead people to salvation. Identifying for the most part with Shestov's views, Erofeev voices in the article his hostility toward the traditional Russian ideas of collectivist salvation through good deeds. Like Shestov, Erofeev also believes that people are confined to an existential "underground" where evil reigns.

By the late 1970s Erofeev had become quite successful in his scholarly and literary career. He was a prolific critic of Russian and European literature and received admission to the Union of Soviet Writers in 1978. At the same time he was deeply dissatisfied with the state of Soviet literature and had begun associating with nonconformist literary circles. Although socialist realism remained the only official method of representing reality in the Soviet Union, nonconformist–or unofficial–culture had started to emerge, especially in its cultural centers, Moscow and Leningrad. Despite harassment by the authorities, unofficial art exhibits and samizdat publications were rapidly contributing to the creation of an alternative culture. In this atmosphere Erofeev gained fame and notoriety by organizing, with a group of well-established literary figures, the publication of *Metropol'. Literaturnyi al'manakh* (1979; translated as *Metropol: A Literary Almanac,* 1982), which consisted of writings by official (social realist) and unofficial (nonconformist) authors.

After several attempts to publish *Metropol'* through official Soviet channels failed, it was sent abroad. The almanac, edited by Erofeev, Vasilii Pavlovich Aksenov, Andrei Georgievich Bitov, Evgenii Anatol'evich Popov, and Fazil Abdulovich Iskander, eventually appeared in the West in 1979–first in Russian and then in translation in English and French, although samizdat copies were also available in the Soviet Union. The publication of *Metropol'* created a scandal and was viciously attacked by the Soviet press and the Komitet gosudarstvennoi bezopasnosti (KGB, State Security Committee). As a result of the official outrage, Erofeev and Popov were excluded from the Union of Soviet Writers, despite the protest of distinguished Soviet and Western literary figures. Aksenov was advised by the KGB to go abroad, and in 1981 he was stripped of his Soviet citizenship.

The incident involving *Metropol'* not only aligned Erofeev firmly with nonconformist culture but also established him as an author in his own right: the almanac featured his first published fiction—two short stories, "Iadrena Fenia" (Humping Hannah) and "Prispushchennyi orgazm stolet'ia" (A Fin de Siécle Orgasm), and the novella "Trekhglavoe detishche" (A Creation in Three Chapters). Unmistakably indebted to the avant-garde tradition in literature, Erofeev's literary debut addressed the ideas of sex, violence, and death—the mainstay themes of his future works—and indulged his penchant for rich intertextuality, parody, the grotesque, and the absurd.

Gorbachev's period of liberalization brought significant changes to Erofeev's career: he was reinstated in the Union of Soviet Writers in 1988, visited America for the first time the same year, and in 1989 published his novel *Russkaia krasavitsa* (translated as *Russian Beauty*, 1992), which brought him international recognition.

In the early 1990s Erofeev wrote two important critical essays, "Pominki po sovetskoi literature" (1990, translated as "Soviet Literature: In Memoriam," 1995) and "Russkie tsvety zla" (1993; translated as "Russia's Fleurs Du Mal," 1995), that have become indispensable reading for any student of late-twentieth-century Russian literature. In these essays he expresses his views on the past, present, and future of Russian literature. While the goal of the earlier essay is to clear the space for new, or alternative, literature, the latter articulates its philosophical and aesthetic principles. These two essays, in a sense, constitute Erofeev's artistic manifesto.

In "Pominki po sovetskoi literature," originally published in a large state newspaper, *Literaturnaia gazeta* (The Literary Gazette), Erofeev denounces Soviet literature as a cultural embodiment of totalitarianism, the ugly result of an attempt to create a socialist utopia. He accuses the regime not only of physically destroying many outstanding literary figures but also of corrupting a great many Soviet writers through a system of privileges in exchange for their loyalty to the party and to socialist realism.

Erofeev distinguishes and analyzes three major trends in Soviet literature—official style, village prose,

Dust jacket for the 1993 English-language edition of Erofeev's 1989 novel, Russkaia krasavitsa, *an exploration of sex, violence, and ideology in the context of 1980s Russian culture and society (Richland County Public Library)*

and liberal writing. He blames official style, or literature, for neglecting artistic innovation and for creating the myth of the happy Soviet society, which manipulated the Russian national consciousness. In contrast to official literature, Soviet *derevenshchiki* (village writers) earn Erofeev's praise for their unbending moral integrity, truthful portrayal of life in the countryside, and representation of authentic Russian characters—homegrown philosophers, village fools, and the heralds of national wisdom. At the same time the Slavophile beliefs of the village prose writers put them in opposition to the new, pro-Western, liberal ferment in Russia and made them embrace nationalism. In addition to exercising an ideological conservatism, the *derevenshchiki* approached language in an equally traditionalist manner that led them to reject any stylistic innovation. In his article Erofeev ultimately perceives village prose as a hostile force that preaches the spiritual and religious heritage of Russia as the answer to its future while rejecting progressive political and artistic developments. For him, liberal literature is also withering away; its main purpose—to expose lies about the Soviet regime—has been undermined by glasnost. All three models have been nourished by the Soviet system and share its view of the spiritual and moral nature of human beings. What Russia needs now, however, is a new kind of literature, radically different from its Soviet predecessor and continuing the aesthetic tradition of modernism. Erofeev concludes his essay by reaffirming the existence of such new, or alternative, literature, free from the fetters of social demand (*sotsial'nyi zakaz*) and exploring new means of self-expression.

"Pominki po sovetskoi literature" triggered a mass of critical responses. Although none of the critics rejected Erofeev's point that socialist realist literature played a significant role in falsifying history, his "burial" of Soviet literature struck many as premature. What some critics sensed correctly was that in his essay Erofeev targeted not only Soviet literature but also its predecessor—nineteenth-century realism, with which socialist realism shared certain aesthetic methods of representation, messianic and prophetic tendencies, and a belief in the spiritual nature of human beings. Erofeev unambiguously rejects not only the moral messianism of Russian literature but also its poetics; he advocates its replacement by the poetics of Russian modernism and the avant-garde as the new basis for the emerging alternative literature.

In the other essay, "Russkie tsvety zla," Erofeev reiterates his point about the "dead humanism" of the realist tradition and explores the sources of inspiration for alternative literature. He lists authors who, in his opinion, inspire the new literature, such as de Sade, Nabokov, Nikolai Vasil'evich Gogol, Andrei Platonovich Platonov, Ezra Pound, and Jorge Luis Borges. According to Erofeev, realism inevitably yields to alternative literature that emphasizes existential and biological evil and is stylistically challenging and inventive. Through an examination of the dark moments in Russian history, alternative prose writers have lost their belief in the traditional values of the Russian intelligentsia: love, children, faith, church, culture, beauty, dignity, motherhood, the peoples' wisdom, and even the West. To these writers all aspects of human life seem permeated by evil. The traditional value of beauty has lost its significance in new literature and been replaced by the poetics of the ugly. The aesthetics of negativity and the desire to shock constitute the poetics of this new literature.

New literature describes the rot and the stench of everyday life and destroys the distinction between positive and negative characters. Any character can unexpectedly become an instrument of destruction or a victim of unmotivated and unmitigated violence. In new literature the world is an ugly and brutal place, where scandal, violence, humiliation, and repression are common. The language of new literature overcomes the limitations of the dead official discourse and becomes a character in its own right. In conclusion, however, Erofeev admits that the current literary market is saturated with this literature of evil; yet, what will take its place is not clear.

In his major work, the novel *Russkaia krasavitsa*, Erofeev applies his poetics of evil and continues to explore the themes of sex, violence, and ideology. *Russkaia krasavitsa* shocked the public with its erotic content and was labeled as pornographic by some critics. Erofeev himself, however, viewed his novel as an examination of Russian culture and society in the 1980s. His protagonist is a young bisexual beauty, Irina Tarakanova. She arrives in Moscow from a provincial town and becomes a high-class prostitute for the elite. She eventually meets an older man who promises to marry her, but he dies unexpectedly during one of their sadomasochistic love acts. Following her lover's death, Irina is in danger of being arrested by the KGB. To help her avoid arrest, her loyal friend Ksenia sends Irina's nude pictures to a popular sex magazine abroad. Upon their publication, Irina becomes an international celebrity and receives protection and support from American politicians, intellectuals, and beauty queens.

But Irina is unhappy. Her realization of the injustices of the Soviet system leads her to dissident groups. To help them save Russia from suffering, she offers to sacrifice herself to the evil spirit possessing the country. Although nothing remarkable happens at the place of sacrifice, Irina becomes pregnant by her dead lover upon her return to Moscow. His ghost comes for a visit and rapes her. Terrified, Irina runs to a church and asks God to free her from the dreaded visits. Her wish is fulfilled, but as soon as she realizes that she is pregnant, Irina begs a witch to reunite her with her lover. The novel ends with Irina's apparent suicide: in a delirium, she both suffocates in her dead lover's arms and looks at her own pregnant body hanging in the bathroom.

Since Erofeev's novel addresses many issues of Soviet life and Russian cultural tradition, it resists a single interpretation. According to Andrew Reynolds, for example, Irina's existential drama in *Russkaia krasavitsa* mirrors that of Russia: all attempts to "save" it—following either the Slavophiles' or Westernizers' or Bolsheviks' or dissidents' ways—ended in failure. Erofeev's novel thus becomes a polemic against the intelligentsia's messianic visions of Russian history.

After *Russkaia krasavitsa* Erofeev's fiction is increasingly provocative and shocking. Sexual perversions of every kind flood his writing. His fictional world manifests itself as an ominous and sadistic place in which insatiable evil incessantly demands new victims. Among Erofeev's works of this period are "Telo Anny, ili konets russkogo avangarda" (1989; translated as "Anna's Body, or The End of the Russian Avant-garde" 1990), "Devushka i smert'" (Death and the Maiden, 1989), "Zhizn' s idiotom" (Life with an Idiot, 1991), "Popugaichik" (1989; translated as "The Parakeet," 1990), *Izbrannoe, ili, Karmannyi apokalipsis* (Selected Works: A Portable Apocalypse, 1993), and "Belyi kastrirovannyi kot s glazami krasavitsy" (A White Castrated Cat with the Eyes of a Beauty, 1989). These works unmistakably point to Erofeev's disappointment with humanism and its fundamental principles of equality and brotherly love as the basis of socialist society, which he persistently rejects. In contrast to the official assertion that the creation of the new socialist man leads to the triumph of good, Erofeev's characters unleash a reign of evil. Contrary to the popular conviction that the new society strengthens the spirit of community and brotherly love, it encourages alienation and aggression.

In the story "Devushka i smert'," for instance, Erofeev reverses the central idea–"love triumphs over death"–of Maksim Gor'ky's poem of the same title (written in the 1890s and published in 1917) to show that in a "rational" society based on Communism, love and death acquire different meanings. In Gorky's poem, death–impressed by the maiden's power of love for her beloved–spares the maiden's life. In Erofeev's variation on Gorky's theme, a maniacal character tortures, mutilates, and brutally murders a beautiful woman friend to take control over her life. Erofeev's character explains his murder as a triumph of the human mind over the metaphysical forces ruling the "blind chance" of life. He is a product of a society based on the principles of rational humanism and acts according to them.

A triumph of evil is also portrayed in the short story "Popugaichik," a disturbing representation of contemporary Russian life. The narrator is an interrogator-executioner of an innocent child. The boy is severely humiliated in the style of medieval tortures–sodomized, mutilated, and forced to jump down from a church bell tower–for trying to "resurrect" a dead parakeet by throwing it up in the air. These tortures are described with astonishing precision by the leading executioner in a letter to the boy's father. The torturer explains that his highly professional work was inspired by his duty to protect the moral and ideological fundamentals of Russian society against violations.

The narrator's rich language is a mixture of different layers of Russian: elements of folklore poetics and contemporary criminal jargon coexist with a terminology of torture and Soviet ideological clichés. Erofeev's use of this stylized vocabulary reveals in the narrator a Russian nationalist, a "deep-rooted Slavophile," in his own words. In this multidimensional narrative Erofeev presents the metahistorical discourses of the Russian mentality, which remain constant in time and ensure continuity. "Popugaichik" constitutes Erofeev's argument against the Slavophiles' idealization of the moral and spiritual qualities of the Russian people.

Erofeev's frustration at the failure of humanism reaches its peak in "Zhizn' s idiotom." Not only does he negate the socialist ideas of rational humanism by imparting the features of a Bolshevik leader to an idiot, but he also, once again, undercuts the Slavophile idealization of the Russian national character. Each of the qualities of the authentic Russian character receives a horrifying interpretation in the story. "Zhizn' s idiotom" symbolizes Erofeev's final categorical break with the humanist tradition in the cultural heritage of Russia.

Erofeev's major publications of the mid-to-late 1990s include the novels *Strashnyi sud* (The Last Judgment, 1996) and *Piat' rek zhizni. Roman-reka* (Five Rivers of Life. A Novel-River, 1998); two collections of essays, *Muzhchiny* (Men, 1997) and *Entsiklopediia russkoi dushi* (An Encyclopedia of the Russian Soul, 1999); and a collection of new Russian fiction, *Vremia rozhat'* (Time to Give Birth, 2001), which he edited. In his essays Erofeev continues to attack the Russian national character. A three-volume collection of his writings, published by Molodaia gvardiia, appeared beginning in 1994.

Viktor Vladimirovich Erofeev continues to live in Moscow; he is married and has a son. Since the era of perestroika, Erofeev has kept a high profile in Russian literature and cultural life by publishing fiction, criticism, and scholarly articles, as well as lecturing regularly in Russia and abroad. He started out as one of the most ardent and consistent propagandists and practitioners of Russian postmodernism. At a time of great transition (from the late Soviet to the early post-Soviet years), he provided a provocative critique of the humanist tradition in Russian literature and proclaimed its ideals false and misleading. To him, the poetics of evil at that time of painful transition was the only possible answer to the bankrupt humanist rhetoric of the past. Yet, in a 1996 interview with *Ogonek* (The Flame), Erofeev strikes a new chord. He declares that the creative drive of his generation of writers to describe evil has been fulfilled and that his own novel *Strashnyi sud* writes the last tribute to the poetics of evil. In a prophetic manner Erofeev proclaims the future emergence of "optimistic prose," a compromise between socialist realism and the idealism of the 1960s. This new prose will celebrate the joy of life and the aspiration of Russia to reach prosperity. Time will tell whether Erofeev's hopeful conjecture comes true.

Interviews:

Georgii Elin, "Nakanune 'Strashnogo suda,'" *Literaturnaia gazeta,* 1 February 1995, p. 6;

Elizabeth Rich and Charles Rougle, "Viktor Erofeyev," *South Central Bulletin,* 12 (Fall–Winter 1995): 70–83;

"My vybili pochvu iz-pod nog molodogo pokoleniia," *Ogonek,* 4 (January 1996): 75.

References:

Vadim Balduev, "Viktor Erofeev v labirinte prokliatykh voprosov," *Druzhba narodov,* 2 (1996): 180–184;

Pavel Basinsky, "Sumerki realizma," *Literaturnaia gazeta,* 27 September 1995, p. 4;

Deming Brown, "'Tough' and 'Cruel' Prose," in his *The Last Years of Soviet Russian Literature: Prose Fiction 1975–1991* (Cambridge & New York: Cambridge University Press, 1993), pp. 147–170;

Oleg Dark, "Mir mozhet byt' liuboi: Razmyshleniia o 'novoi' proze," *Druzhba narodov,* 6 (1990): 223–235.

Mikhail Epstein, "Iskusstvo avangarda i religioznoe soznanie," *Novyi mir,* 12 (1989): 222–235;

Evgenii Ermolin, "Russkii Sad, ili Viktor Erofeev bez alibi," *Novyi mir,* 12 (1996): 227–231;

Petra Hesse, "Pri-otsustvie sub'ekta: 'Zhizn' s idiotom' Viktora Erofeeva," *Russian Literature,* 51–53 (April 2002): 261–272;

Ruslan Kireev, "Panikhida s knutikom," *Literaturnaia gazeta,* 8 August 1990, p. 5;

Naum Leiderman and Mark Lipovetsky, "Mezhdu khaosom. i kosmosom: Rasskaz v kontekste vremeni," *Novyi mir,* 7 (July 1991): 240–257;

Lipovetsky, "Izzhivanie smerti. Spetsifika russkogo postmodernizma," *Znamia,* 8 (August 1995): 194–205;

Lipovetsky, "Mir kak tekst," *Literaturnoe obozrenie,* 6 (1990): 63–65;

Lipovetsky, *Russian Postmodernist Fiction: Dialogue with Chaos,* edited by Eliot Borenstein (Armonk, N.Y.: M. E. Sharpe, 1999);

Robert Porter, *Russia's Alternative Prose* (Oxford: Berg, 1994);

Vladimir Potapov, "Na vykhode iz 'andegraunda,'" *Novyi mir,* 10 (1989): 251–257;

Sergei Reingold, "Russkaia literatura i postmodernism: Nesluchainye itogi novatsii 90-kh godov," *Znamia,* 9 (1998): 209–220;

Elizabeth Rich, "Lolita Grows Up," *Nation* (21 June 1993): 875–878;

Serafima Roll, *Postmodernisty o postkul'ture* (Moscow: R. Elinin, 1996);

Roll, "Re-Surfacing: The Shades of Violence in Viktor Yerofeev's Short Stories," *Australian Slavonic and East European Studies,* 9, no. 2 (1995): 27–46;

Barry Scherr, "After Perestroika: The Era of Rasstroika," *South Central Bulletin,* 12 (Fall–Winter 1995): 153–167;

Ulrich Schmid, "Flowers of Evil: The Poetics of Monstrosity in Contemporary Russian Literature: Erofeev, Mamleev, Sokolov, Sorokin," *Russian Literature,* 48 (August 2000): 205–222;

Gleb Shil'piakov, "Skazka pro serogo bychka. Viktor Erofeev poslednii pisatel' zemli russkoi," *ExLibris,* 7 (24 February 2000);

Boris Sokolov, "Russkii bog," *Druzhba narodov,* 2 (1996): 184–188;

Elena Tikhomirova, "Eros iz podpolia: Seks-bestsellery 90-kh i russkaia literaturnaia traditsia," *Znamia,* 6 (1992): 220–228; translated as "Eros from the Underground: Sex Bestsellers of the 1990s and the Russian Literary Tradition," *Russian Studies in Literature,* 30, no. 3 (1994): 43–57;

The Viktor Erofeev Page <www.erofeev.ru> [accessed 28 July 2003];

Aleksandr Zholkovsky, "V minus pervom i minus vtorom zerkale: Tatiana Tolstaia, Viktor Erofeev–akhmatoviana i arkhetipy," *Literaturnoe obozrenie,* 6 (1995): 25–41.

Sergei Markovich Gandlevsky

(21 December 1952 –   )

Dmitrii Bak
Russian University for the Humanities (Moscow)

(Translated by Gary Cox)

BOOKS: *Rasskaz: Kniga stikhotvorenii* (Moscow: Moskovskii rabochii, 1989);

Prazdnik (St. Petersburg: Pushkinskii fond, 1995);

Trepanatsiia cherepa: Istoriia bolezni (St. Petersburg: Pushkinskii fond, 1996);

Stikhi Sergei Gandlevskii, Vechera v muzee Vadima Sidura, no. 31 (Moscow: Moskovskii gosudarstvennyi muzei Vadima Sidura, 1997);

Poeticheskaia kukhnia (St. Petersburg: Pushkinskii fond, 1998);

Konspekt (St. Petersburg: Pushkinskii fond, 1999);

Poriadok slov (Ekaterinburg: U-Faktoriia, 2000);

Dvavtsad' deviat' stikhotvorenii (Novosibirsk: Naprasnyi trud, 2001);

<NRZB>: Roman (Moscow: Inostranka, 2002).

Editions in English: "An Attempt at a Manifesto," "There's still some time before I'll be a patriarch," "A Lynch law of unexpected maturity," "To Dmitri Prigov," "To Aleksey Magarik," "To Aleksandr Soprovsky," "Ah yes, the lilac this May. Bulging clusters," and "The dawn came late. The blanket slid," translated by Andrew Wachtel, in *Third Wave: The New Russian Poetry,* edited by Kent Johnson and Stephen M. Ashby (Ann Arbor: University of Michigan Press, 1992), pp. 117–128;

"There's our street," "Dear God, allow me," "It is time," and "Oh, how the lilacs are," translated by Philip Metres, in *In the Grip of Strange Thoughts: Russian Poetry in a New Era,* compiled and edited by J. Kates (Brookline, Mass.: Zephyr, 1999), pp. 327–342;

"Pillars of Salt: An Essay and Poems by Sergey Gandlevsky," translated, with an introduction, by Metres, *Mid-American Review,* 22 (2001): 51–72.

OTHER: *Ponedel'nik,* with contributions by Gandlevsky and others, compiled by Dmitrii Aleksandrovich Prigov (Moscow: Prometei, 1990).

Sergei Markovich Gandlevsky (from the paperback cover for Poriadok slov, *2000; Collection of Mark Lipovetsky)*

SELECTED PERIODICAL PUBLICATIONS–UNCOLLECTED: [Poems of the group "Moskovskoe vremia"], *Neue Russische Literatur: Almanach,* 2–3 (1980): 1–27;

"Stikhi," *Kontinent,* 2 (1981): 16–18;

"Chetyre stikhotvoreniia," *Kontinent,* 1 (1984): 7–13;

"Chtenie: Odnoaktnaia p'esa," *Zvezda,* 5 (1999);

"Podvig," *Ezhenedel'nyi zhurnal,* 21 (5 June 2002): 2.

Poet, prose-fiction writer, essayist, and playwright, Sergei Gandlevsky was one of the key figures of literary life in the Soviet Union and Russia during the 1980s and 1990s. His path as a poet is highly characteristic for this pivotal epoch in the history of the new Russian literature, when in the course of ten to fifteen years the barriers that earlier had been insurmountable were destroyed—such as the boundary between "underground" poetry and the poetry submitted to the censors for publication in legitimate periodicals or as Soviet-sanctioned books; the boundary between poets of the "Metropol'" group and those of the "Russian emigration"; and, finally, the boundary between the poets of the 1960s, who used to give readings in stadiums during the years of the "Thaw," initiated by Nikita Sergeevich Khrushchev, and the younger lyric poets who belonged to the "lost generation" of the 1970s.

Gandlevsky's literary fate is unusual. He was able to avoid the unhealthy decline experienced by poets of the underground—who preserved their reputations only in a narrow circle of admirers—and poets who, in just a short while, rose to heights of popularity, stimulated by the immediate slogans of perestroika. Eschewing a prolific output and creating—just as in his youth—no more than two or three poems a year, Gandlevsky acquired a stable reputation as one of the most significant contemporary poets in Russia. Many readers and critics see in him a distinctive halfway point between traditional and underground poetry, a lyrical "archaist" who nonetheless responds penetratingly to all the new currents in Russian poetry.

Sergei Markovich Gandlevsky was born on 21 December 1952 to a Moscow intelligentsia family. By his own acknowledgment he began to write poetry at about the age of ten, often skipping school and sneaking back home without telling his parents, in order to "give himself over to versification." In one of his interviews, Gandlevsky says his poetic urge took shape fairly early as a conscious desire to take up literature seriously: "One day I was coming back from my English teacher's house, it was autumn, I was in the ninth grade, and I just decided, apropos of nothing, that I'd become a writer." His parents were opposed to their son's desire to devote himself to literature. Rather, they saw him as a future biologist and convinced Gandlevsky that "humanities in a totalitarian social structure must deform the soul."

Gandlevsky's youth came during the time of the first perestroika—when Khrushchev led the country, and the fundamentals of life were shaken for a whole generation of people who had grown up during the height of Stalinism. To many contemporaries of the Twentieth Party Congress, at which Joseph Stalin's "cult of personality" was publicly dethroned,

the 1960s brought long-awaited freedom to the Soviet Union. More than a few people experienced a sharp disappointment, however—the bitter feeling of a life lived in vain because of the false ideals of Stalinism.

Gandlevsky's earliest impressions of childhood—family, school, and everyday life—compose an extremely important background for the themes and problems of his lyric poetry. A laconic concreteness of details and an acknowledged precision of names and titles are integral features of his verses, as seen in the poem "Chikilikan'e galok v osennem dvore" (The chirp of jackdaws in the courtyard in autumn . . . , 1981):

Chikilikan'e galok v osennem dvore,
I trezvon peremeny v trinadtsatoi shkole,
Roscherk TU–104 na chistoi zare,
I keimo na skam'e: "Khabibulin + Olia."

(The chirping of jackdaws in the courtyard in autumn;
The class-change bell in school No. 13;
The streak of a TU–104 on the clean sky at sunset;
And "Khabidulin and Olya" carved on a bench).

In the 1980 poem "Vot nasha ulitsa, dopustim . . ." (Here's our street, let's say . . .) Gandlevsky defines with aphoristic precision the contours of his "cultural habitat": "Takaia vot Ioknopatofa" (That's Ioknopatofa for you). ("Ioknopatofa" refers to Yoknapatawpha, the county that serves as the setting for most of William Faulkner's novels about the American South.) Inhabiting a joyless world of Moscow suburbs, the young hero of Gandlevsky's poems feels most like himself among a multitude of people, who represent the various phases of the Soviet era. Gandlevsky sketches a postwar Soviet variant of a "portrait of the artist as a young man" in surroundings that match the spirit of the time.

Like the composer Bashilov in Vladimir Semenovich Makanin's novella, *Gde skhodilos' nebo s kholmami* (Where the Sky Meets the Hills, 1984), Gandlevsky's lyric hero first discovers the harmonic rhythms of his creativity, not in a burst of inspiration, but simply by hearing the stammered "song of the streetcorner with its throaty refrain." Precisely these criminalized "melodramatic love songs" arouse the singer of a Stalin-era slum to poetry, as seen in "Evreiskim bliudom ugoshchala" (She served some Jewish food . . . , 1994): "I choked on my first shot of vodka, / For the first time stuttered my way into rhyme. . . ." All of the villagers of Gandlevsky's Ioknopatofa are from the intelligentsia; they quietly curse the party and the Komitet gosudarstvennoi bezopasnosti (KGB, State Security Committee) in

*Manuscript for Skripit? . . . (Is it squeaking? . . .), a poem published in 1993
(Jean and Alexander Heard Library, Vanderbilt University)*

the kitchen—right down to the street-corner drunks and gang bosses, who are united by a feeling of a common past, as shown by these lines from "Vot nasha ulitsa, dopustim . . .":

> No znala chertova dyra
> Rodstvo sirotstvo—my otsiuda.
> Tak po rodimomu piatnu
> Detei iskali v starinu.

> (But that damned hole knew
> The kinship of orphanhood—that's where we're from.
> That's how, by a birthmark
> People used to look for their children).

In 1970 Gandlevsky matriculated in the Department of Russian Philology at Moscow State University. That same year, by his own acknowledgment, he began to write poetry seriously, largely under the influence of his poet friends Aleksandr Aleksandrovich Soprovsky, Aleksei Petrovich Tsvetkov, Bakhyt Shkurullaevich Kenzheev, and Aleksandr Kazintsev. He attended the Moscow University literary studio, "Luch sveta" (Ray of Light), which had been founded by Igor' Leonidovich Volgin, now a well-known literary critic and author of many books on Fyodor Dostoevsky.

During the early 1970s, along with the officially organized university literary studio, Gandlevsky joined the poetry group "Moskovskoe vremia" (Moscow Time), which was just then being formed. In his opinion "Moskovskoe vremia" existed from 1972 to 1974 in its most complete form, when the collective samizdat books of verse were being done by Tsvetkov, Kenzheev, Soprovsky, Gandlevsky, Tatiana Poletaeva, Kazintsev, and other participants of the group. In 1974 Tsvetkov emigrated, and a few years later Kenzheev also left Russia. In addition, Kazintsev became more closely allied with literary figures of the Neo-Slavophile, "fundamentalist" orientation and was finally named deputy chief editor of the journal *Nash sovremennik* (Our Contemporary).

A few contemporary critics spread stories about "Moskovskoe vremia" in the 1980s and even the 1990s. Thus, Mikhail Natanovich Aizenberg names Grigorii Mikhailovich Dashevsky, Dmitrii Iur'evich Vedeniapin, and Viktor Genrikhovich Sanchuk as the representatives of the younger generation in the group. Nonetheless, there is no doubt that during the 1970s the group was under the leadership of Tsvetkov, Gandlevsky, Kenzheev, and Soprovsky and that it rendered its most important service in defining a national school of uncensored poetry after the Golden and Silver Ages of Russian literature.

Gandlevsky considers the most important achievement of "Moskovskoe vremia" its departure from the creative and personal principles of the Russian symbolist poets of the early twentieth century: "The 'shamanistic' stance in its pure, symbolist, form was never welcomed. . . . Rather, acmeism seemed to us then to be the clear victor and the arena of our strivings," he wrote later. The tradition of acmeist poetics may serve as an explanation for Gandlevsky's drive toward absolute precision, toward the monosemic character of the poetic word, and toward the absence in his poetry of any prophetic glossolalia or obscurity of meaning. Every possibility of symbolic or symbolist profundity (á la the poetry of Aleksandr Aleksandrovich Blok) and "ambiguity" leads right away to irony. As his poem "Rastroganno prislushivat'sia k laiu . . ." (Listen to the howling with emotion . . . , 1986) demonstrates, Gandlevsky's everyday descriptions are absolutely concrete, devoid of any mysterious spiritual subtext:

> Smotret', stiraia robu, kak voda
> Namatyvvaet vodorosl' na svaiu,
> Po otmeli rasseivaet staiu
> Mal'kov i razduvaet nevoda.

> (To watch, wiping off your overalls, how water
> Winds water plants around a bridge piling;
> Along the sandbar it scatters a school
> Of minnows, and blows away whatever isn't water).

In many ways, under the influence of Gandlevsky's stylistic experiments in "Moskovskoe vremia" during the 1970s, there was a "reworking of the dominant style, (a reworking) of verse norms, many years in the making" as Aizenberg describes; in other words, an "Acmeist crystallization" was achieved. In his 1999 book *Poeziia kak fakt* (Poetry as Fact) Vladislav Kulakov makes even more voluminous generalizations, basing his judgment on the creative work of underground Leningrad poets during the 1960s as well: "Poets of the 'Moskovskoe vremia' group continued the work of the neo-Acmeists ('Akhmatovites') of the 1960s, in their creation of a 'firm style,' and in their reestablishment of an interrupted tradition of lyric poetry." The poetics of the "Moskovskoe vremia" group largely shaped the ethics of its members' literary behavior as well. Their verse compositions were deprived of a prophetic aura, and increasingly they turned into a calculated gesture of cultural escapism. The attitude of poetic professionalism on the margins of society, as worked out by the "Moskovskoe vremia" poets, stood in marked contrast to the lifestyle of the "Soviet writer." Later, in the novella *Trepanatsiia cherepa: Istoriia bolezni* (The Trepanation of the Skull: The Story of a Disease, 1996), Gandlevsky wrote, "I have the honor to belong . . . to a circle of writers who have banished from their minds once and for all the desire to get into print. In the Soviet press, at least. In our circle you could be a bore or the life of the party, a coward or a daredevil, a skinflint or a pauper, a drunk or a teetotaler, a debauchee or an anchorite, a skirt-chaser or a 'one-woman-man,' but to go knocking on the doors of publishers–that was out!"

Voluntary marginality was a matter not only of personal creative behavior but also of citizenship. In contrast to many of the representatives of the engagé generation of the 1960s, the writers of the 1970s–the young people of Venedikt Vasil'evich Erofeev's generation–were for the most part apolitical. "When Soviet troops invaded Czechoslovakia, we were riding bikes," wrote Gandlevsky in *Trepanatsiia cherepa*. The ideal of socially active behavior that settled upon the Soviet period was often replaced by an idiosyncratic alcoholic metaphysics that defined the wellsprings of life for the epic heroes of Erofeev's *Moskva-Petushki* (1977; translated as *Moscow to the End of the Line,* 1980). Such "alcoholic discourse" abounds in Gandlevsky's poetry, too; certain lines of his verse have acquired the status of, and are perceived as, aphorisms: "Kogda volnuetsia zhelteiushchee pivo . . ." (When the yellow beer is waving . . .) paraphrases a well-known verse by Mikhail Iur'evich Lermontov, "Kogda volnuetsia zhelteiushchaia niva" (When the yellow field of crops is waving), for example.

After graduation from Moscow State University in the mid 1970s, an extended period of bohemian existence began for Gandlevsky; he took many adventurous trips to exotic corners of the Soviet Union and occasionally held a job, experiences that he describes in "Dai Bog pamiati vspomnit' raboty moi . . ." (God grant me the memory to recall my labors . . . , 1981). At this time, as another of his poems relates, Gandlevsky identified directly with the marginal hero of a rock ballad performed by the Leningrad band Aquarium, which was popular in the Soviet musical underground of the 1970s and 1980s. "A generation of janitors and night-watchmen" is what Boris Grebenshchikov, the lead singer of Aquarium, called these young men. In the poem "Mne tridtsat', a tebe semnadtsat' let . . ." (I'm thirty, and you're seventeen . . . , 1986) Gandlevsky declares, "I myself belong to the generation of night watchmen."

At the end of the 1970s and in the early 1980s Gandlevsky's poems began to appear in Russian émigré periodicals, including *Kontinent* (The Continent), *Russkaia mysl'* (Russian Thought), and *Strelets* (The Archer). He began to get recognition among those who valued uncensored Russian poetry, both in Russia and abroad. Everything changed radically in 1985, however, after Mikhail Sergeevich Gorbachev came to power. In the early years of Gorbachev's perestroika, fame

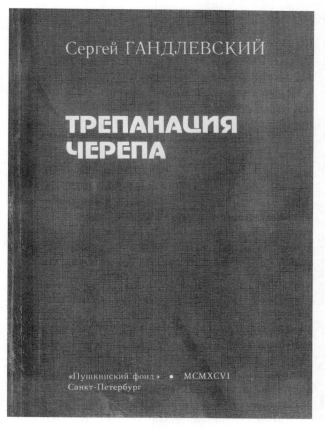

Front cover for Gandlevsky's Trepanatsiia cherepa *(The Trepanation of the Skull), an example of the postmodernist nonfiction genre known as "new documentalism" (Jean and Alexander Heard Library, Vanderbilt University)*

erupted for Gandlevsky, and his painstakingly preserved stance of "unpublished poet" was upset by his growing popularity. Events that normally occur during a poet's life span, or at least in the range of many years, took place in the course of only a few years for him. Readers became acquainted with Gandlevsky's first publications in the *tolstye* (thick) literary journals, such as *Novyi mir* (New World), *Iunost'* (Youth), *Znamia* (The Banner), *Oktiabr'* (October), and *Druzhba narodov* (The Peoples' Friendship). Along with these appearances in well-regarded periodicals, Gandlevsky's work was frequently selected for inclusion in respectable collections, which were starkly different from the amorphous, chaotically gathered anthologies–"fraternal graves," they used to be called–that had been routine venues for the work of the underground poets during the Soviet period. These collections were often organized conceptually, as several titles demonstrate: *Molodaia poeziia* (Young Poetry, 1989), *Zerkalo* (The Mirror, 1989), and *Grazhdane nochi* (Citizen of Night, 1990).

Finally, in 1989 the publishing house Moskovskii rabochii put out Gandlevsky's first book, *Rasskaz: Kniga stikhotvorenii* (Story: A Book of Poems). It comprised twenty-three poems, many of which were later considered programmatic and "of signal importance." These works included "Samosud neozhidannoi zrelosti . . ." (translated as "A lynch law of unexpected maturity," 1992); "Elegiia" (Elegy), which begins "Aprelia tsirkovaia muzyka . . . " (April's circus music . . .); and "Stansy" (Stanzas), the first line of which is "Govori. Chto ty khochesh' skazat'. Ne o tom li kak shla . . ." (Say it. What do you want to say? Isn't it about how . . .). The huge number of copies–ten thousand were printed– was still intended for a reading public based on Soviet marketing norms for publishing. Gandlevsky's collection came out at a moment of historical transition, for within just a couple of years such large publication runs for poetry books became senseless. In addition, all the essential institutions of Soviet publishing soon ceased to exist, including Moskovskii rabochii.

During these years another event of utmost importance took place. A decade after the golden age of "Moskovskoe vremia," in the second half of the 1980s, Gandlevsky and a circle of like-minded friends formed the club "Poeziia" (Poetry). Among his new colleagues in "Poeziia" were poets of various stylistic directions (such as Dmitrii Aleksandrovich Prigov and Lev Semenovich Rubinshtein), different generations (such as Aizenberg and Timur Iur'evich Kibirov), and different degrees of fame (such as Viktor Koval' and Denis Novikov). This "poets' collective" was quite varied, ranging, for example, from the poetic iconoclast and artist Prigov–one of the pillars of Moscow conceptualism–to the "neo-romantic" Kibirov. It created an atmosphere of mutual tolerance, as well as a variety of aesthetic tastes–a breadth of outlooks on contemporary poetry as a whole. Just as the 1980s were ending and the 1990s were beginning, many readers and critics in Russia found the chasm between traditional verse structure and avant-garde innovations growing wider. Gandlevsky's colleagues in "Poeziia" viewed the tremendous distance between traditional and avant-garde poetry, however, as a positive thing. For them, it was an occasion for fertile dialogue, rather than for routine squabbles or mutual reproaches regarding betrayed ideals of honesty.

The group's first joint project of note was the collective anthology *Ponedel'nik* (Monday), published in 1990 by the Moscow publisher Prometei, under the imprimatur of Ruslan Ellinin's literary publishing agency. The anthology carried the subheading "Sem' poetov samizdata" (Seven Samizdat Poets) and gave the poets' names: S. Gandlevsky, D. A. Prigov, M. Aizenberg, M. Sukhotin, V. Sanchuk, T. Kibirov, L. Rubinshtein. Aizenberg, who wrote the preface to the collection, sees precisely in Gandlevsky's verses the

clearest example of a "boundary-line" poetics; he states for the first time that Gandlevsky's "emergence from traditionalism may be termed 'biographical.'" The poet is at once both an artist and a model.

During those years the members of "Poeziia" felt that a public declaration of their aesthetic positions in completely unstandard ways was essential. Performance art, in the form of their show *Al'manakh* (Almanac), soon became a characteristic manifesto of the group. It was presented by Gandlevsky, Prigov, Rubinshtein, Koval', Aizenberg, Kibirov, Timur Novikov, and the singer A. Lipsky onstage at the Studios of the Union of Theatrical Personnel of the Soviet Union. In the aftermath of these poetry shows, which enjoyed an extraordinary popularity, the artistic-literary almanac *Lichnoe delo #__* (Personal Case No. __) appeared, signifying a milestone in the emergence of what had been uncensored poetry from the Soviet-era literary underground.

From the beginning, the almanac *Lichnoe delo #__* aspired to something much more significant than simply setting down on paper a successful collective performance of a group of poets. In putting together the published version, the well-known artist Aleksandr Iulikov included the work of several painters representing contemporary conceptualism and "sots-art" (art that shows socialist realism in decay) such as of Il'ia Iosifovich Kabakov, Vladimir Iankilevsky, and Erik Bulatov. This dialogue of visual and verbal codes of artistic language was accompanied by a combination of verse practice and the theoretical foundations behind it, a sort of self-definition reflecting a new sense of poetic collectivity. Included in the book right along with the poems were articles and essays by respected specialists on the new art, Andrei Zorin and Ekaterina Degot', as well as by Aizenberg, Rubinshtein, and Gandlevsky–that is, by the poets who took part in the *Almanakh* show. Although for Aizenberg the critical analysis of the developing trends of current Russian poetry over the course of many years had coincided with the writing of his own verses, the prose of Rubinshtein and Gandlevsky, on the other hand, began precisely with the essays published in *Lichnoe delo #__*.

The significance of Gandlevsky's manifesto, titled "Razreshenie ot skorbi" (Release from Grief) and included in the collection, goes far beyond the confines of the book and is not exhausted by the poet's traditional task of describing his (or her) personal creative credo. The concept of "critical sentimentalism" put forward by Gandlevsky has been understood by many readers as a key to describing the contemporary situation in Russian poetry. Not by accident was Gandlevsky's manifesto later republished (in 1998 and

2000) as "Kriticheskii sentimentalizm" (Critical Sentimentalism).

The thesis that provides Gandlevsky's starting point is extremely clear: "A poet's business is not to discover the mystery, but to reproduce it in purity and isolation, so that a person who partakes of that mystery may, with fear and rapture, discover it through your words." Only honest impressions draw one nearer to the mystery—strong, primal, usually child-like (reminiscent of the example of childhood found in the works of Vladimir Vladimirovich Nabokov, an author of no incidental significance for Gandlevsky). The childhood of the postwar generation coincided with times of deceit and violence, and nevertheless, exclaims Gandlevsky, "Although we know what we know, and rage as we rage—what are we to do with love, once it exists?"

Gandlevsky also addresses the opposition between avant-garde and "tradition" with insight, yet from a peripheral point of view. He makes his judgments as though "above the barriers"; for him, aesthetic problems turn out to be produced by different types of everyday behavior. Thus, there is a mystery concealed in the first impressions of a child's or a youth's existence under Soviet conditions. Precisely these impressions—negative but authentic—were fundamentally rethought and placed in doubt by many poets in the period when perestroika was unmasking everything so rapidly.

Gandlevsky outlines two possible reactions to this kind of change of orientations, calling them "willful" and "ironic," and each has its own poetic intonation. The willful reaction presupposes a search for a new kind of authenticity, a serious and considered rejection of all that has shown its dishonesty and falsehood in the post-Soviet age. According to Gandlevsky, "contemptuous judgments, combined with a style as fluid as an ode, are natural in this poetic." No doubt such stylistic combinations are nonorganic, whimsical, and short-lived. The ironic reaction seems to him even more limited and aesthetically unproductive: "The scope of ridicule is broad and keeps getting broader. Merriment grows stronger; its flame casts itself upon all ideals, upon all language, upon all authorities."

Gandlevsky also insists upon a third, intermediate path, which he even calls "critical sentimentalism." He views "belonging to the past, even if one is conscious of it . . . as something shameful. . . . It makes it impossible to have dialogue with one's times as though from on high, because that would be false." Consequently, Gandlevsky separates himself from "Symbolist" and "Petersburg" poetics in favor of a "post-Acmeist" clarity—in favor of restrained attention toward the features of a hateful past (which nonetheless belongs to him); toward the "dym otechestva" (smoke of the father-

Paperback cover for Gandlevsky's Poriadok slov *(Word Order, 2000), the fullest collection of his writings (Collection of Mark Lipovetsky)*

land), to use Aleksandr Sergeevich Griboedov's expression; and toward, in the words of Aleksandr Sergeevich Pushkin, the "rodnoe pepelishche" (home hearth).

The paradoxical blend of pathos and irony in Gandlevsky's poetic viewpoint gave his creative position extraordinary weight and authority. He formulated, after groping around for it, a personal creative output that was magisterial in its measured regularity on the path from "Moskovskoe vremia" to the club "Poeziia," from the 1970s to the 1990s. One way or another, all of the participants of the *Almanakh* show shared Gandlevsky's *profession de foi;* not by coincidence is the title of the collection *Lichnoe delo #__.* Along with its "archival" subtext, the title carries another meaning as well, later confirmed by Gandlevsky in *Trepanatsiia cherepa:* "Literature was for us a personal matter. Into the kitchen, into the pantry, into the furnace room, no abstract reader, no 'the people,' no 'the country,' found their way."

In 1991 Gandlevsky was accepted into the Writers' Union. Since 1992 he has been working as editor of the essays section at the journal *Inostrannaia literatura* (Foreign Literature). From 1992 to 1993 he was the scriptwriter for a prominent cycle of literary broadcasts called "Pokolenie" (Generation) on the radio station "Rossiia" (Rossiia). From 1995 to 1996 he taught a seminar on contemporary national poetry at the School of Contemporary Art (at the Russian State University for the Humanities).

In 1995 Gandlevsky arguably emerged once and for all from the underground with the appearance of a book of verses titled *Prazdnik* (Holiday), put out by "Pushkinskii fond," a St. Petersburg publisher. Enjoying great success, it received an award from *Nezavisimaia gazeta* (The Independent Gazette), a prize that has been called the "Anti-Booker Award," as the best poetry collection of the year. Yet, he promptly declined the award, owing to bureaucratic formalities inconsistent, in his opinion, with "proper literary behavior" for a poet. His refusal of the prize resonated broadly in the press nonetheless, and his poems remained the key subject of enlivened discussions at this time. Moreover, the appearance of *Prazdnik* made clear that Gandlevsky is a poet of one theme and thus the author of a single, never-ending book. This fact justifies his comparatively modest "productivity." Given the consistency of his theme and his faithfulness to his own stylistic principles, the conceptual weight of each newly composed verse increases many times over on the strength of all that he has written and published earlier. Gandlevsky's eternal and unchanging theme is simple: the relationship between the external biography and the authentic life of an individual, depicted with as much detail as possible.

Life, according to Gandlevsky, is always "being shaped"—one simply must have the power to see the forest for the trees and understand that in any segment of human existence, along with the circular motion of the second hand, beats the pulse of fate. Two peculiarities of Gandlevsky's poetics flow from this idea. First, the occasion for writing a poem is never, or almost never, an *ozarenie*—an epiphany—called forth by a transitional moment of growth, a beautiful landscape, or a book that one has just read. Poetry may come at any moment; it can be aroused by the most trifling everyday detail: "an occasion to compose verse is almost never linked with [poetic] intention for me," Gandlevsky underscores. Second, Gandlevsky's lyric tends toward narration, toward a story (the title of his first collection is *Rasskaz*) about something that has already taken place and needs only to be laid out coherently. His lyric is never born in the "here and now" or through the agency of a muse. The moment of everyday time, as measured in the course of the telling,

becomes commensurate with the scale of the eternal. Therefore, importantly, the summation often has nothing in common with the starting point of a reflection, as seen in "Skripit? . . ." (Is it squeaking? . . . , 1993):

Skripit? A ty loskut gazety
Slozhi v staratel'nyi kvadrat
I prisposob', chtob dvertsa eta
Ne otvorialas' nevpopad.
Porkhaet v kamennom proeme
Nevzrachnyi gorodskoi snezhok.
Vse, vrode by, no ostaetsia
Poslednii nebol'shoi dolzhok.
Eshche ostalos' cheloveku
Pripomnit' vse, chego on net . . . .

(Is it squeaking? Well, you take some scraps of newspaper
And stick them into the part that's acting so restless,
And fix it so this door won't
Open accidentally.
In the stone doorway flutter
Ordinary city snowflakes.
That's all, you'd think, but what remains
Is just the last little duty.
The one thing a person must still do
Is to remember everything he is not).

Gandlevsky suggests that the most important things in life may be pondered only in passing—while rolling up "scraps of newspaper" together or "Dorogoi, naprimer, v apteku" (On the way, for instance, to the drugstore). He implies that, consequently, there is nothing beautiful or excellent around people, and poems grow only out of trash and everyday banalities; they boil down to a physiological report that cannot take flight. Gandlevsky nudges the reader directly toward this conclusion in "Stansy" (Stanzas, 1987): "If you believe that speech must be set against the undertow of ideas / And an occasion in earnest—it means they've deceived you. . . ."

Nonetheless, this idea is not always true. Chaos takes over, as Gandlevsky's many aphorisms and well-honed verbal formulas (often imperative ones) reveal, and the unbearable disorder of everyday life acquires meaning, fixing the transition from biography to fate, as these lines show: "It is not pain that is hard—it is the monotony of pain" and "There's no doubt about it—memory is a torment, but even it / Dies. And to that one may become accustomed." For Gandlevsky, routine existence is transformed precisely in the process of telling about it—in the search for and the revelation of one's capacity to tell about what is passing, or about what usually slips along the sides of one's peripheral vision. In this regard, when traditional versification is emphasized, it gives a contrasting nuance to a paradoxical theme. Gandlevsky says, "Precise rhyming for me is just like brushing my teeth morning and evening–it's a reflex long conditioned by many years."

Thus, Gandlevsky's hero–whether he is a young man in love, a tramp going nowhere, a night watchman on the margins of society, or a spaced-out vacationer–is granted a poetic gift. Yet, the name one may assign to this gift is not inspiration, nor a special capacity for spiritual flight, but a simple facility for talk. Speech flows as though all on its own: "Talk. There's nothing to be done with this disaster." These words make up the last line of the programmatic poem "Stansy," which opens *Prazdnik,* dedicated to Gandlevsky's mother. The only thing distinguishing poetic speech from babbling that becomes bound up in trifles is the ability to explain it–if not to make life harmonious–and make it a bit more orderly. Gandlevsky shows that through verse, a story–loaded with aphorisms–can be rendered precisely, as implied in this line from "Budet vse. Okhalzhdennaia dolgim trudom" (Everything will be. Chilled by long-standing labor . . . , 1980): "the gibberish of my barbaric life / has achieved the simplicity of a symmetrical park."

In 1995 Gandlevsky's novella *Trepanatsiia cherepa* appeared in *Znamia* and was awarded its annual prize for a work "upholding liberal values." *Trepanatsiia cherepa* won a Little Booker Award in 1996, and that year the St. Petersburg publisher Pushkinskii fond brought it out as a separate book. The work appeared as the popularity of the "new documentalism" was heating up. This term was used for nonfiction that described actual events from the point of view of the people who took part in them; examples of the "new documentalism" are Andrei Sergeev's *Al'bom dlia marok* (Stamp Album), which was awarded the Booker Russian Novel Prize in 1996; Mikhail Bezrodnyi's *Konets tsitaty* (The Endquote, 1996); and Aleksandr Zholkovsky's partially memoiristic portraits.

All the heroes in Gandlevsky's novella are, more or less, well-known participants in the Muscovite literary and journalistic world of the last decades, neighbors, and people who run into each other coincidentally–these figures are brought into the story under their real names. Gandlevsky tells about things that actually happened; for example, an accidental injury makes complicated neurosurgery necessary for the hero (as it once did for the author himself). On the threshold of this inescapable event, the author-hero goes through a serious reconsideration of values: "Whether I was brushing my teeth, walking my dog, making jokes with my kids for all I was worth–everything I did had the flavor of possible death." After his recovery, this formerly marginal member of society experiences an enlightenment of the soul and heart and–above all–conceives a desire to write prose, for

which he expects to receive a fashionable literary prize: "The thought of the Booker Prize first occurred to me about twenty minutes after I, for the first time after the hospital, filled my Chinese pen with ink."

Such demonstrable interweaving of "literature" and "life" is a completely conscious strategy on Gandlevsky's part. He, in the capacity of his hero in *Trepanatsiia cherepa,* is drawn as an ironic fellow, betimes gloomy and inclined to extreme pessimism; yet, at all times and in all places he is trying to set life down on paper, to apply to it the keys given by art. There is a demonstrative parallel between the exposition of this novel and the first chapter of Nabokov's *Dar* (1952; translated as *The Gift,* 1963), in which Fedor Godunov-Cherdyntsev turns every single passing impression, reflection, and feeling that he has into a rhymed draft for a poem. Gandlevsky the character also rhymes things, almost mechanically (although he does vary the theme), such as a bunch of headlines from a scrap of newspaper, hurriedly torn in half, pinned on a bulletin board by the entrance of a resort: "In a word, the motherland–breadth and space: Papua-si, canoe lakes. Guten Tag, bonfire half the night! And of course it's our custom, to our shame. . . ."

The stylistic coordinates of Gandlevsky's prose emerge from presuppositions that are basic to the "critical sentimentalism" of his poetry. His mood of total skepticism after the operation, for example, gives way to a calm certainty that his personal existence is justified and sensible. Likewise, a prayerful rhetoric replaces the irony with which the novella began:

Lord, give me strength for the sake of God the all-holy! Give me strength for simple, everyday things, give me strength not to think eternally about one and the same thing, and to remember your deeds and your torments. Oh Lord the all-powerful, give me such strength that I may not grieve, that I may not wait upon life but live, that I may empower myself and know how to think with concentration about that which seems unnecessary to me, but which must seem necessary to others, and which in their opinion is necessary to me as well. Help me, help thou mine unbelief in life and in happiness, which are everywhere and always, only that I have not strength to notice them and feel their fullness in my breast. . . .

A fairly linear reading of the novella renders the conclusion that its chief worth lies in its absolutely confessional character–its bold attempt to expose oneself completely to public scrutiny, a feature that nonetheless concludes with the predictable "spiritual rebirth." This happy ending is set in motion from the start. Gandlevsky's acknowledgment that the tale is a documentary confession inevitably narrows its meaning; read in

Front cover for Gandlevsky's 2002 novel, whose title, <NRZB>, is the Russian editorial acronym for "illegible" (Jean and Alexander Heard Library, Vanderbilt University)

this way, the autobiographical details turn out to constitute the most important level—such as his ancestors and the grandparents of the author of *Trepanatsiia cherepa* and the endless romantic and alcoholic stories from the life of the literary circles of the capital. The attentive reader may discover substantive commentary on many of Gandlevsky's well-known poems and recognize the background of their creation, particularly the direct self-quotations (lines from Gandlevsky's verse). Finally, *Trepanatsiia cherepa* in no way fits into the narrow framework of creative auto-commentary. A remarkably reliable depiction of the actual events of his personal life, as well as an urge to view in everyday details the eternal laws of human existence as such, are present and on an equal footing in Gandlevsky's narrative.

In 1998 a collection of essays titled *Poeticheskaia kukhnia* (The Poet's Kitchen) was published by Pushkinskii fond. The texts included in this volume had been published earlier in *Znamia*, *Literaturnaia gazeta* (The Literary Gazette), *Kul'tura* (Culture), *Itogi* (Summing Up), *Novoe vremia* (New Times), and *Pushkin* (now the well-known Internet portal *The Russian Journal*). The texts collected in *Poeticheskaia kukhnia* are highly varied in theme and genre. Among them are "pure" essays (such as "From Behind the Back of the Authorities"); memoiristic sketches (about Soprovsky, Arsenii Aleksandrovich Tarkovsky, and Moscow in the 1960s and 1970s); fragments of correspondence (with Petr L'vovich Vail') and poetic manifestos ("Critical Sentimentalism" and "The Metaphysics of the Poet's Kitchen"); pieces on his poet friends (Tsvetkov, Aizenberg, and Lev Vladimirovich Losev); and essays about contemporaries and predecessors in poetry (from Evgenii Abramovich Baratynsky, Vladislav Felitsianovich Khodasevich, Nabokov, and Pushkin to Sergei Aleksandrovich Esenin and Aleksandr Arkad'evich Galich). *Poeticheskaia kukhnia* also features Gandlevsky's prefaces to books, clips from radio dialogues (with Aleksandr Aleksandrovich Genis on Radio Liberty), an interview (with Denis Novikov from the journal *Stas*), acceptance speeches for literary prizes, and, finally, reviews of books by other writers.

More than a few passages in *Poeticheskaia kukhnia* clarify Gandlevsky's specific position in the current polemic between "archaists and innovators"—that is, traditionalists and postmodernists. As he wrote in a letter to Vail', "For me postmodernism is neither a school nor a method but the contemporary mood and perception of the world, that is, it is a given, broader than a literary mode, or some other kind of mode, of perception. One may not approve or disapprove of the sea, the climate, and so forth." Gandlevsky relates to postmodernism in just this way in most of his writings, which is probably why his one-act play "Chtenie" (A Reading, 1999) has not enjoyed any particular success, since the concept of "laying bare the literary device" (an approach taken by the Russian formalists) was applied too directly in it. In the play several of the characters from *Trepanatsiia cherepa*—members of the intellectual demimonde in Moscow—carry on a few rather dejected dialogues, but the arbitrariness of their presentation is emphasized, and they have no intriguing similarities with known people.

From 1999 to 2002 several significant publications by Gandlevsky appeared—among them the almanac *Lichnoe delo #2* (Personal Case No. 2), published in 1999 by Novoe Literaturnoe Obozrenie and including works by the same group of authors as in the first issue. Gandlevsky's voluminous *Poriadok slov* (Word Order, 2000) was also published during this time. It includes the fullest collection to date of his poetry, fiction, dramaturgy, and essays.

Gandlevsky's novel <NRZB> (an editorial acronym for "illegible") appeared in the January 2002 issue of *Znamia;* a few months later it was published in book form. At first glance, this novel reproduces many of the motifs and situations of *Trepanatsiia cherepa,* which had brought Gandlevsky such great success, and, once again, the reader is presented with the customs and norms of unofficial literary Moscow (primarily during the 1970s). Lev Krivorotov, an unsuccessful writer now at the end of his fifth decade, recalls the wasted years of his young life. A quarter century before, he had fallen in love almost simultaneously with two women: Arina Vyshnevetskaia, a venerable activist of the quasi-literary "kitchen salons" of that time, whom he ended up marrying, and Anya, a young, captivating student who wrote derivative verse. Through Arina Krivorotova he then had a chance to become acquainted with Viktor Chigrashov, the acknowledged master of samizdat poetry, who later committed suicide.

The young Krivorotov did not know then that these three would remain the most important people in his whole life. The study of Chigrashov's archival legacy eventually became his "profession" during perestroika—the only way he could earn a living. Arina bore his son and subsequently left him to go overseas. Anya finally married Krivorotov's former friend Nikita; thirty years later she died of cancer without having a chance to realize all the power and distinction of Krivorotov's love: "that kind of Anya happens only once in millions of years."

The novel has garnered somewhat restrained praise; that the work displays a certain dissipation of plot and a great many reminiscences from former books is glaringly evident. Not one of the reviewers, however, has noticed in Gandlevsky's latest work its chief feature, the code that explains all of what seems to be the purposely emphasized "intersection of fates" in the novel: <NRZB> represents, in large measure, a sequence of events that concretize many of Gandlevsky's well-known poems.

For example, learning by accident of Anya's death, Krivorotov reflects in despair, "So it's come to that, she's died. She never cared for me in life, and now she's died all on her own—what madness, ennui, emptiness." These words echo certain lines from Gandlevsky's poem "Pamiati I.B." (In Memory of I.B., 1998): "I hadn't heard wrong—she's dead. My head went spinning. / She never loved me in her whole life, but at least she was alive." Telling Chigrashov about his romantic failures, Krivorotov makes reference to his acquaintance's lyric poetry: "No matter where you cast your gaze, everything is crossways, you could just shoot yourself—remember? 'bang-bang'—that's how it goes in one of your poems." The hero of the poem

"Neudachnik. Poliak i isterik . . ." (A loser. A hysterical Polish guy . . . , 1992) "is about to go bang-bang." The resonance of <NRZB> with several of Gandlevsky's lyrics makes the novel appear as if it were filling in the gaps between possible prototypical situations from poems quite different in style and tone.

On the boundary between the 1990s and the new millennium, Sergei Markovich Gandlevsky has experienced a period of creative searches that, of course, are not considered complete. The unfinalized nature of his work constantly provokes critics to a lively discussion, from which emerge important general statements that often go far beyond the boundaries of the analysis of concrete texts. Thus, in his 1997 contribution to the journal *Arion* Gleb Shul'piakov states that for Gandlevsky, "poetry . . . is its own kind of territory within the much larger space of life, and no linguistic means permits a crossing of the boundary between them. In other words, the picture outside the window is always bigger than what Gandlevsky writes about it." Mikhail Bezrodnyi, on the other hand, underscores not the metaphysical but the playful nature of Gandlevsky's poetics. In Bezrodnyi's opinion, "for variety and originality of devices that 'make classics out of play' . . . , Gandlevsky's poetic knows, it would seem, no equals." In his 1995 article for *Novyi mir* Sergei Kostyrko tries to identify other keys to Gandlevsky's creative manner, especially his prose, keys that lie within the sphere of post-Soviet literary *byt* (routine): "The number of sidelong glances at the institution of the Union of Soviet Writers, which supposedly did not exist at all for Gandlevsky's circle, is frankly irritating. Comments in passing, almost sparing and offhand, about certain prestigious attributes of their current life . . . force one . . . to come to the conclusion that a new literary establishment has arisen, or, to use the old terminology, a *nomenclatura,* with its characteristic way of life." One way or another, the discussion of Gandlevsky's work, the place of his poetry and prose in contemporary Russian letters, continues, and this discussion promises to be extremely substantial and fertile in the future as well.

Interviews:

A. Alekhin, *Arion,* 4 (1994);

Pavel Grushko, "Boius' tumana i sumiatitsy chuvstv na pis'me . . ." *Literaturnoe obozrenie,* 2 (1997);

"Chelovek s etiketki," *Stas,* 4 (1997);

Anastasiia Askochenskaia, "Vazhna tol'ko lichnost' . . ." *Literaturnoe obozrenie,* 2 (1998): 95–97;

Anastasiia Gosteva, "Konspekt," *Voprosy literatury* (September–October 2000): 264–285.

References:

Mikhail Natanovich Aizenberg, "Sergei Gandlevsky. *Konspekt*," *Itogi*, 7 (2000);

Dmitrii Bak, "Zakony zhanra," *Oktiabr'*, 9 (1996);

Vladimir Gandel'sman, "O stikhakh Sergeiia Gandlevskogo," *Novoe russkoe slovo*, 4 April 1997;

Aleksandr Aleksandrovich Genis, "Lestnitsa, pristavlennaia ne k toi stenke," in his *Ivan Petrovich umer: Stat'i i rassledovaniia* (Moscow: Novoe literaturnoe obozrenie, 1999), pp. 198–203;

E. Izvarina, "Chelovek srednikh let . . . ," *Ural*, 1 (2001);

Bakhyt Kenzheev, "Skazka lozh', da v nei namek," *Obshchaia gazeta*, 23 February 1995;

Leonid Kostiukov, "Svidetel'skie pokazaniia," *Druzhba narodov*, 7 (2001): 181–184;

Sergei Kostyrko, "Ot pervogo litsa: Tri profiliai na fone pokoleniia," *Novyi mir*, 6 (1995);

Vladislav Kulakov, "Posle katastrofy," in his *Poeziia kak fakt* (Moscow: Novoe literaturnoe obozrenie, 1999);

Viktor Kulle, "Nomenklatura," *Znamia*, 6 (1997);

Olga Kuznetsova, "Predstavlenie prodolzhaetsia," *Novyi mir*, 8 (1996): 218;

O. A. Lekmanov, "Propushchennoe zveno: Blok, (Brodsky), Gandlevsky," in his *Kniga ob akmeizme i drugie raboty* (Tomsk: Vodolei, 2000), pp. 350–361;

Lekmanov, "Rasskaz o Prazdnike: Zametki o poezii Sergeia Gandlevskogo," *Russkaia mysl'*, no. 4045 (1995);

Larisa Miller, "Iz 'kukhni' – v 'sad'," *Ex libris NG*, 5 August 1998;

Dmitrii Ol'shansky, "Zamyslovatyi konduit," *Segodnia*, 17 July 2000;

Lilia Pann, "Novosti Sergeia Gandlevskogo," *Literaturnaia gazeta*, 1–7 March 2000;

A. Panov, "Vot eto smert' i est'," *Nezavisimaia gazeta*, 22 March 1995;

Boris Paramonov, "Prekrasnyi gus' i parshivaia ovtsa, ili Sergei Gandlevsky kak zerkalo russkoi contrrevoliutsii," *Zvezda*, 2 (1998);

Maria Remizova, "Izvlechenie kamnia gluposti," *Literaturnaia gazeta*, 23 August 1995;

Remizova, "Ne naprasno," *Novyi mir*, 4 (2001);

Remizova, "Pisatel' fevralia," *Ogonek*, 5 (1995);

Lev Rubinshtein, "Poriadok dolzhen byt'," *Itogi*, 10 (2000);

Rubinshtein, "Razgovor o Velikom Avos'," *Kommersant - Daily*, no. 6, 23 January 1996;

S. Shapoval, "Poet sentimental'noi trezvosti," *Nezavisimaia gazeta*, 16 January 1996;

Ia. Shenkman, "Srednee mezhdu pravdoi i zhizn'iu," *Arion*, 1 (1999);

Evgenii Shklovsky, "Vremia i mesto," *Novyi mir*, 6 (1997);

Gleb Shul'piakov, "Siuzhet Pitera Breigelia," *Arion*, 3 (1997);

E. Skarlygina, "Popytka memuara, ili 'Andergraund' o sebe," in *Literatura rosyjska w nowych interpretacyjach*, edited by Haliny Mazurek-Wity (Katowice, Poland: Wyd. Uniwersytetu Ilåskiego, 1995);

E. Streshnev, "Knigi nedeli," *Nedelia*, 17 (1996).

Boris Efimovich Groys

(19 March 1947 –   )

Alexander Prokhorov
College of William & Mary

and

Elena Prokhorova
George Washington University

BOOKS: *Gesamtkunstwerk Stalin,* translated from the Russian by Gabriele Leupold (Munich: C. Hanser, 1988); translated by Charles Rougle as *The Total Art of Stalinism* (Princeton: Princeton University Press, 1992);

Dnevnik filosofa (Paris: Beseda-Sintaksis, 1989);

Zeitgenössische Kunst aus Moskau. Von der Neo-Avangarde zum Post-Stalinismus (Munich: Klinkhardt & Biermann, 1991);

Über das Neue. Versuch einer Kulturökonomie (Munich: C. Hanser, 1992);

Städte bauen, by Groys, Karl Markus Michel, and Tilman Spengler (Berlin: Rowohlt, 1993);

Utopiia i obmen. Stil' Stalin. O novom. Stat'i (Moscow: Znak, 1993)—includes *Stil' Stalin;*

Die Erfindung Russlands (Munich: C. Hanser, 1995);

Vizit (Moscow: Obscuri Viri, 1995);

Jeff Wall, by Groys, Thierry de Duve, and Arielle Pelenc (London: Phaidon, 1996);

Die Kunst der Installation, by Groys and Il'ia Iosifovich Kabakov (Munich: C. Hanser, 1996);

Kunst-Kommentare (Vienna: Passagen Verlag, 1997);

Logik der Sammlung: Am Ende des Musealen Zeitalters (Munich: C. Hanser, 1997);

Ilya Kabakov, by Groys, David A. Ross, and Iwona Blazwick (London: Phaidon, 1998);

Dialogi: 1990–1994. Il'ia Kabakov, Boris Grois, by Groys and Kabakov, with an introduction by Elena Vladimirovna Petrovskaia (Moscow: Ad Marginem, 1999);

Unter Verdacht: Eine Phänomenologie der Medien (Munich: C. Hanser, 2000);

Politik der Unsterblichkeit: Vier Gespräche mit Thomas Knoefel (Munich: C. Hanser, 2002).

Boris Efimovich Groys (from the Karlsruhe University website <http://solaris.hfg-karlsruhe.de/hfg/inhalt/de/Lehrende/1017>)

OTHER: "The Artist as Curator of Bad Art," in *L'Exposition imaginaire,* edited by Evelyn Beer and Riet de Leeuw (The Hague: Rijksdienst Beeldende Kunst, 1989), pp. 138–149;

"The Birth of Socialist Realism from the Spirit of the Russian Avant-Garde," in *The Culture of the Stalin Period,* edited by Hans Günther (New York: St. Martin's Press, 1990), pp. 122–148;

"The Struggle against the Museum, or the Display of Art in Totalitarian Space," in *Museum Culture: Histories, Discourses, Spectacles,* edited by Daniel J. Sherman and Irit Rogoff, Media & Society, no. 6 (Minneapolis: University of Minnesota Press, 1993), pp. 144–162;

Fluchtpunkt Moskau, edited by Groys (Ostfildern: Cantz, 1994);

Lev Shestov, *Tolstoi und Nietzsche,* translated by Nadja Strasser, with essays by Groys, Gustav A. Conradi, and Aleksei Remizov (Munich: Matthes & Seitz, 1994);

Tyrannei des Schönen: Architektur der Stalin-Zeit, edited by Peter Noever, with contributions by Groys and Il'ia Iosifovich Kabakov (Munich & New York: Prestel, 1994);

"The Speed of Art," in *Peter Fischli and David Weiss: In a Restless World* (Minneapolis: Walker Art Center, 1996), pp. 115–121;

Kierkegaard. Schriften. Diederichs, edited by Groys (Munich, 1996);

"The Archive of Ashes," translated by Matthew Partridge, in *The Colonies of Bees Undermining the Moles' Subversive Effort through Time,* by Rebecca Horn (Zurich & New York: Scalo, 2000);

"Text as a Ready-Made Object," in *Endquote: Sots-Art Literature and Soviet Grand Style,* edited by Marina Balina, Nancy Condee, and Evgenii Dobrenko (Evanston, Ill.: Northwestern University Press, 2000), pp. 32–45.

SELECTED PERIODICAL PUBLICATIONS–
UNCOLLECTED: "Dostoevsky i Kirkegor," *Vestnik RChD,* 123 (1977): 89–110;

"Moskovskii romanticheskii kontseptualizm," *A-Ia,* 1 (1979): 3–11;

"Poeziia, kul'tura i smert' v Moskve," *Kovcheg,* 5 (1981);

"O russkoi filosofii," *Sintaksis,* 11 (1983): 157–166;

"The Problem of Soviet Ideological Practice," *Studies in Soviet Thought,* 33 (1984): 191–208;

"Rossiia kak podsoznanie Zapada," *Wiener Slawistischer Almanach,* 23 (1989): 199–213;

"Russkii avangard po obe storony 'chernogo kvadrata'," *Voprosy filosofii,* 11 (1990): 67–73;

"Poisk russkoi natsional'noi identichnosti," *Voprosy filosofii,* 1 (1992): 52–60; translated as "Russia and the West: the Quest for Russian National Identity," in *Studies in Soviet Thought,* 43 (1992): 185–198;

"Russkii roman kak seriinyi ubiica, ili poetika biurokratii," in *Novoe literaturnoe obozrenie,* 27 (1997): 432–444; translated as "The Russian Novel as a Serial Murder of the Poetics of Bureaucracy," in *Subjectivity,* edited by Willem van Reijen and Willem G. Weststeijn (Amsterdam & Atlanta: Rodopi, 2000), pp. 235–254;

"Iskusstvo kak avangard ekonomiki," *Maksimka,* 4 (1999) <http://www.guelman.ru/maksimka/n4/kunst.htm> ;

"Die Verfilmung der Philosophie," *Schnitt,* 1 (2000) <http://www.schnitt.com/site/rubriken/thema/content/kolumne/groys_16.htm>.

Essayist, philosopher, art critic, and media theorist Boris Groys refers to himself as a *Kulturfilosof* (philosopher of culture). Groys's writing combines two seemingly incompatible traditions: French poststructuralism and Russian literary philosophizing about national and religious identity. He engages in dialogue with philosophers and practitioners of postmodernism such as Jean Baudrillard, Jacques Derrida, and Michel Foucault, while also continuing the Russian tradition of philosophical literature represented by the works of Fyodor Dostoevsky, Vasilii Vasil'evich Rozanov, and Andrei Donatovich Siniavsky.

In the late 1970s Groys coined the term "Moscow conceptualism" and introduced conceptualist poetry, prose, and art of the late Soviet period to the West. His *Gesamtkunstwerk Stalin* (1988; translated as *The Total Art of Stalinism,* 1992) and its subsequent translations into major European languages familiarized Western readers with Russian postmodernist writers, including Vladimir Georgievich Sorokin and Dmitrii Aleksandrovich Prigov. Soon after becoming a professor of aesthetics and media theory at the Zentrum für Kunst und Medientechnologie (ZKM) in Karlsruhe, Germany, Groys was elected provost of the Vienna Academy of Fine Arts. Despite his assertion that he prefers oral presentations to the printed word, his output is prodigious; in addition to producing several monographs, he has also edited collections of articles in Russian and German and written more than a hundred articles.

Boris Efimovich Groys was born on 19 March 1947 in Germany, where his engineer father was involved in rebuilding Berlin, which had been ruined by bombing from the Allied forces toward the end of World War II; not much else is known about Groys's parents or his youth. From 1965 to 1971 Groys studied philosophy and mathematics at Leningrad State University. For the next five years he worked at different science centers in Leningrad. From 1976 through 1981 he held a position as research fellow in the Department of Structural and Applied Linguistics (Artificial Intelligence Laboratory) at Moscow State University. Forbidden to teach because of his prominent role in unofficial literary and art circles, Groys nevertheless advised students with the tacit approval of the department head.

Soon after moving to Moscow in the mid 1970s, Groys (who had enjoyed active relations with Leningrad artists since the mid 1960s) became acquainted with a circle of unofficial Moscow poets, writers, and artists. His participation in private seminars and exhibits resulted in a series of articles in samizdat publications in the Soviet Union (such as the Leningrad journal *37*), as well as in émigré and Western editions. The most important of these articles, "Moskovskii romanticheskii kontseptualizm" (Moscow Romantic Conceptualism), appeared in the first issue of the Paris-based émigré journal *A-Ia* (1979). This essay introduced Groys as a writer who privileges paradoxes, *aporia* (irreconcilable contradictions), and oxymorons, as seen in his definition of Moscow unofficial art as "romanticheskii kontseptualizm." In effect, Groys contends that while Russian artists and poets from the 1970s and 1980s, including Lev Semenovich Rubinshtein, Ivan Semenovich Chuikov, and Francisco Infante, share some practices with Western conceptualist artists, they never abandon a belief in what Walter Benjamin called the aura of the artistic object. Russian art, in Groys's view, is still grounded in a quasi-religious perception of culture—hence Groys's oxymoronic name ("romanticheskii kontseptualizm") for this trend in late Soviet culture. Already these early works establish Groys as a writer who blurs traditional boundaries between visual and verbal art, art and politics, and criticism and philosophy. His novel *Vizit* (Visit, written in 1980; published in 1995) is similarly a synthesis of scholarly and fictional writing.

By the early 1980s ideological orthodoxy in the Soviet Union had retrenched, and in 1981 Groys immigrated to West Germany. Since then he has lived mostly in Cologne and taught philosophy at the University of Münster. His essays on Russian and Western literary and art theory have appeared in *A-Ia* and in the *Cahiers du musée national moderne* (Notebooks of the Modern National Museum) of the Centre Pompidou. During the late 1980s he contributed to the *Frankfurter Allgemeine Zeitung* (Frankfurter General Newspaper) and several European journals. He also regularly appears at lectures and performances sponsored by various conceptualist art exhibits.

Groys's best-known work to date, *Gesamtkunstwerk Stalin,* despite its time- and culture-specific title, is a broad examination of totalitarian forms of culture, among which Stalinism is but one. Groys avoids traditional historical periodization of twentieth-century Soviet culture, which is predicated on political landmarks. While the first two chapters of the book roughly correspond to the 1920s and 1930s, respectively (with New Economic Pol-

Paperback cover for Groys's Dnevnik filosofa *(A Philosopher's Diary, 1989), which explores the nature of avant-garde art and the idea of a modern Russian identity (Amherst College Library)*

icy, or NEP, as the period of transition), chapters 3 and 4 subsume the entire post-Stalin period under the term post-utopian art. Groys maintains that far from effecting a return to the "pure" avant-garde, Soviet art of the 1960s and 1970s is manifestly neotraditionalist and faithful to the socialist realist method. The major project of post-utopian art is not a subversion of the socialist realist tradition but, rather, an *obnazhenie* (laying bare) of the mythological structures that underlie it. Groys was the first to write about authors such as Sorokin and Prigov, who—with respect to Western literary criticism—have since become staple figures of Russian postmodernism. Groys's approach to their works, however, differs from Western approaches. In his view the paintings of Eric Vladimirovich Bulatov, and of Vitalii Anatol'evich Komar and Aleksandr Danilovich Melamid; Prigov's "Policeman" poems; and fiction by Sorokin and Sasha Sokolov each in their own way represent the "Soviet repressed": the urge to stop time and the impulse to dissolve individuality (including the artist's own) in the collective voice. Groys also points out that rather than speaking of "difference" and the "other," these works acknowledge the dissolution of the individual in the ideological text and rely on the narrative power of Marxism and other metanarratives.

In a recent interview conducted by Alexander Prokhorov and Elena Prokhorova in 2001 (but never published) Groys contends that his book was widely misread, especially by Anglophone scholars who focused primarily on the first two chapters and read his book as a cause-and-effect narrative. Pointing to the neglected discussion of post-utopian Soviet art, Groys argues that his work has a broader scope and examines strategies for articulating total narratives of culture, rather than just collapsing the opposition between the avant-garde and Stalinism. Indeed, polemicizing with traditional accounts of the Russian avant-garde as pure art and victim of the totalizing impulse of the Soviet state, he argues that the major reason for the demise of the avant-garde was its competition with the Party and the state in utopian life building. Similarly, in his discussion of socialist realist aesthetics he focuses on the concept of the "typical," which was interpreted both by the Russian avant-garde and theoreticians of socialist realism as the representation of a reality that is "coming into being." The urge to dissolve subjectivity in the collective will, according to Groys, underlies all of twentieth-century culture. Continuing the argument he initiated in "Moskovskii romanticheskii kontseptualizm," Groys contends, "Contemporary Russian artists or writers . . . integrate the myth of themselves as creators and demiurges into the inherited mythology. Fully aware of the universal mythicality of their personal utopias, they all build their own socialisms in one country."

The continuing controversy surrounding *Gesamtkunstwerk Stalin* and Groys's writing in general seems to originate in its reception as Western-style cultural criticism, while in fact his writing manifests the generic memory of Russian philosophical literature. A revealing example of such writing is Groys's *Dnevnik filosofa* (A Philosopher's Diary, 1989). It includes entries from February 1985 through October 1986 and engages a variety of philosophical and cultural issues, including the subject and nature of philosophy, theory, and ideology; the tension between the creative "I" and the social "we"; reality and subjectivity; and other, similar concerns. While the title of the work echoes Dostoevsky's *Dnevnik pisatelia* (A Writer's Diary, 1873–1874, 1876–1877, 1880–1881), the self-conscious and fragmented mode of Groys's philosophizing evokes such literary-philosophical projects as Rozanov's trilogy—*Uedinennoe* (Solitaria, 1912), *Opavshie list'ia I and II* (Fallen Leaves I and II, 1913–1915), and *Apokalipsis nashego vremeni* (Apocalypse of Our Time, 1917–1918)—and Siniavsky's

Golos iz khora (A Voice from the Chorus, 1973). Albeit necessarily disjointed, these entries include many issues that were developed in Groys's later works—for instance, the nature of avant-garde art, the production of a modern Russian identity, the relationship between tradition and innovation, and the function of modern museums.

Groys's reflections on the status of knowledge and on archives and museums as repositories of knowledge, as well as venues for the exchange and generation of knowledge, are not unlike Foucault's *l'archéologie du savoir* (archeology of knowledge). These themes are the primary focus of the next book that Groys wrote, *Über das Neue. Versuch einer Kulturökonomie* (On the New. A Study of Cultural Economics, 1992). He deliberately chooses an overtly nontrendy title: in the poststructuralist era, with its emphasis on the impossibility of innovation, Groys argues that innovative exchange, deriving from Friedrich Nietzsche's notions of value and reevaluation, constitutes the prime mechanism of cultural production. According to Groys, postmodernism does not suspend the possibility of cultural innovation but merely eliminates the spiritual aura enjoyed by the concept of the "new" in modernist culture. In this respect Groys follows the tradition of the Frankfurt School critics, such as Benjamin and Theodore Adorno, who linked the emergence of mass-media culture with the death of modernist utopianism. Postmodernist innovation is bereft of such utopianism, whether optimistic or apocalyptic, and instead expands into various zones of otherness, such as gender, sexuality, and race.

Groys develops his notion of cultural production as originating in the shifting border between the two zones of culturally valorized and culturally profane practices. For him, the major mode of innovation in contemporary art is the "ready-made," or the displaying of everyday objects as art, for it lays bare the innovative transition from the profane to the valorized zone. Every work of art contains within itself an immanent split between valorized and profane knowledge. In this respect all works of art and all discursive practices are inherently incoherent. Examining the dialectics of valorization and commercialization as cultural strategies, Groys contends that mass media and high-art production serve as two major venues for the circulation of cultural values.

Groys combines his scholarly projects with participation in art exhibitions, either as a commentator or a performer-critic. *Fluchtpunkt Moskau* (Vanishing Point Moscow, 1994) is a collection of articles, edited by Groys, that accompanied an exhibition of contemporary Russian art from Peter Ludwig's collection (undertaken in 1978) in Aachen. In his contribution to the edition, titled "Moscow Art between the Soviet Union and Russia," Groys refers to the art movements of the 1970s and 1980s in the Soviet Union as *aktuelle Kunst* (topical art) . Like the Russian avant-garde at the beginning of the twentieth century, conceptualism and its various forms, such as sots-art, an ironic recycling of Soviet iconography (as created by Komar, Melamid, Aleksandr Semenovich Kosolapov, and Grisha Davidovich Bruskin), or medical hermeneutics, a conceptualist art group interpreting and performing culture through its symptoms (as produced by Sergei Aleksandrovich Anufriev, Iurii Aleksandrovich Leiderman, and Pavel Viktorovich Peppershtein), adopted ideas and techniques from Western art movements, which Russian artists read as a critique of ideology. While Western art responded to commercial mass culture, Russian art had to confront bureaucratic texts. As a result, though employing techniques and strategies of Western art, Russo-Soviet conceptualist art had quite a different frame of reference.

Soviet art of the 1970s to the 1980s, Groys contends, has no direct political engagement. "Reflexive, analytical, and ironic," he writes in *Fluchtpunkt Moskau,* it is not anti-Soviet art but, rather, a form of parallel culture. It addresses the question of what it means to remain a Soviet artist when the artist distances himself from Soviet ideology and becomes ironic about the privileged status of art. In post-Soviet Russia, Groys remarks, art has to deal not with the state and a few devoted followers but with new, privately financed institutions and a new public. Within the new art market, conceptualism is marginalized because its contemplative mode evokes all too vividly the recent Soviet past on the one hand, and, on the other, because it is too removed from new consumer values.

In 1995 Groys published a collection of essays titled *Die Erfindung Russlands* (The Invention of Russia). Although most essays had appeared earlier in various periodicals and collections, here Groys rearranged them to address a new issue–the identity of Russia after the dissolution of the Soviet Union. The collection provides an overview of a century-long search for a cultural identity by Russian artists and philosophers. Groys begins by examining the late-nineteenth-century theory of Sophiology, Vladimir Sergeevich Solov'ev's study of the feminine hypostasis of divinity, and concludes with a glance at contemporary trends in Russian visual arts, such as medical hermeneutics. The merging of art and philosophy in these essays evokes the writings of Mikhail Naumovich Epshtein on Russian philosophy. Although Groys's views on Russian post-utopian discourses differ from those of Epshtein, both men trace the "concept of Russia" to a distinctive blend of art, literature, and philosophy.

Since the early 1990s Groys has explored the genre of cultural-philosophical dialogue, mainly in the form of conversations with the Russian conceptualist artist Il'ia Iosifovich Kabakov. Groys and Kabakov have performed their dialogues, which are open-ended and tend toward improvisation, on stage at various art exhibits around the world and have published these dialogues in German and Russian. In her introduction to their book *Dialogi: 1990–1994. Il'ia Kabakov, Boris Groys* (Dialogues: 1990–1994. Il'ia Kabakov, Boris Groys, 1999) Russian critic Elena Vladimirovna Petrovskaia considers the genre of a dialogue "the most adequate way to comment on contemporary art," and the large crowds that appear at the duo's performances suggest that the general public shares her opinion.

In 1996 Groys and Kabakov published the dialogue *Die Kunst der Installation* (The Art of Installation), in which they examine the role of art and the artist in contemporary Western culture. As a heuristic tool (that is, something that aids learning or discovery through experiment or a trial-and-error approach), the interlocutors, Groys and Kabakov, employ contrasting Russian and Western perspectives on art and artistic production. Like many Russian thinkers since the time of Nikolai Mikhailovich Karamzin and Petr Iakovlevich Chaadaev, who lived and wrote in nineteenth-century Russia, Groys and Kabakov do not limit their discussion to the sphere of artistic production but also interrogate the identity politics of Russia and the West. Both of them see a major difference in Russian and Western perceptions of an artistic project and its success. Groys argues that an individual in the West identifies himself as somebody capable of creating and successfully completing a project. Museum attendance in the West, therefore, always implies the viewing of projects that have proved successful. Russian artists, in contrast, often create projects that they do not plan to implement. Russian cultural history in this respect is often propelled by preprogrammed failures.

The interlocutors pay homage to Benjamin's distinguished 1936 essay, "The Work of Art in the Age of Mechanical Reproduction," when they discuss a model of representation and perception that deprives the artist's original product of its quasi-religious distinctiveness (its "aura"). Historically, the paradigm of maximum reproduction succeeds the paradigm of conserving the distinctive artistic object in a museum. For instance, displaying Marcel Duchamp's ready-mades is not unlike taking a picture of the object that may be reproduced ad infinitum. According to Groys and Kabakov, Pablo Picasso and Andy Warhol established a certain canon–or, to use the authors' idiom, a "currency standard"–for the artistic mode, which favors its reproducibility.

Paperback cover for Groys's Über das Neue. Versuch einer
Kulturökonomie *(On the New. A Study of Cultural
Economics, 1992), in which he reflects on the status
of knowledge (Young Research Library,
University of California, Los Angeles)*

The complex relationship between the modern museum and mass media is the subject of Groys's collection of essays titled *Logik der Sammlung: Am Ende des Musealen Zeitalters* (Logic of Collecting: The End of the Age of Museums, 1997). As Groys remarks in the introduction, "Das Museum im Zeitalter der Medien" (The Museum in the Age of the Media), the media displace museums as the distinctive space and context of art existence—a predicament that art is only too ready to follow. Groys examines museums both from the inside (through the totalizing view on the world as the potential new material for a collection) and from the outside (through the omnivorous search by the media for what is newsworthy). The focus of many essays is on the transition from the "new" to the "news."

According to Groys, ever since the emergence of modern museums, their function in culture was that of a secular substitute for a church or a monastery. Museums are places where things that have fulfilled some socially relevant function are "baptized" into art objects—the process exemplified by ready-mades. Inclusion in a museum separates "art" from "non-art" and "old" from "new." Museums are also a space where free subjectivity and pure creative originality manifest themselves: by being displayed in a museum, an object partakes of its aura and thus signifies individual genius.

Groys notes that the totalizing view on the world cast by museums has become a model replicated in other social phenomena structured similarly to a museum—from communism to fundamentalism—all of which claim total clarity of vision. Today, with media replacing the museum as the art context, art competes not with artistic tradition displayed in the museum but with everyday reality. The dynamic of art changes its direction: instead of a "museum look" from the inside to the outside in search of new and original things in reality, media look inside the museum in search of the news. For the media, the museum is a locus of the non-transparent, or the mysterious—the space of what Groys calls "the swindle of subjectivity"—which is both suspect and fascinating. Hence, while neither the concept of the museum nor art is dead, the age of mass media radically redefines the nature, dynamic, and social function of art and museums. Groys challenges the post-structuralist view of historicity and archive, above all Foucault's, and emphasizes the material nature of knowledge determined by a particular medium. In a 1998 interview with Sven Spieker, Groys contends: "For my part, I do not think that history is a narrative, whether it be factual or fictional. History occurs in a space between the archive and life, between the past that has been collected and reality, understood as everything that has not been collected."

In 1999 Groys and Kabakov published *Dialogi: 1990–1994,* a collection of conversations in Russian. While the second part of the collection is the translation of *Die Kunst der Installation,* the first part consists of nine dialogues and offers a pastiche of Soviet civilization: "Uzhas" (Horror), "Golosa" (Voices), "Personazhi" (Characters), "ZhEK" (Housing Office), "Zapad" (The West), "Kommunal'naia kvartira" (Communal Apartment), "Pustota" (Emptiness), "Musor" (Garbage), and "Begstvo" (Escape). Establishing Soviet communal space as a schema of perception, the dialogues examine the place of conceptualist art in this space and the mechanisms of artistic production in the postmodern era. While the dialogues constitute a reaction to the disintegration of the Soviet ideological horizon, they clearly belong to the tradition of Russian "philosophies of everyday life" as represented, for example, by Rozanov's writing.

The second dialogue, "Golosa," is of special importance because it provides a commentary on the dialogues themselves as cultural practice. Groys and Kabakov discuss post-utopian Soviet culture as robbed of the dream of an achievable paradise, both religious and communist, and, for that reason, as seeking cultural stability in a myth of infinite interpretation, a text that is unable to achieve closure. Groys acknowledges that such an approach to culture originates primarily in French poststructuralism, with one important reservation. Groys and Kabakov always try to anchor interpretation in the specific media of cultural production, be it such a down-to-earth phenomenon as garbage, or a more conventional one, such as mass media.

In the late 1990s Groys turned to cinema as an object of philosophical inquiry. In 1999 he participated in the conference "Inside the Matrix," organized by the ZKM. In his comments Groys referred to the 1999 motion picture *The Matrix* as the screen adaptation of philosophy after its death. This postphilosophy, however, celebrates not the disappearance of metaphysical thought but the new, commercially successful Enlightenment, which targets covert manipulations of consciousness. Groys claims that *The Matrix* and similar Hollywood movies of the last five years rescue the Enlightenment project by presenting it as entertainment.

The desire to penetrate the banality of the everyday is also at the center of Groys's monograph, *Unter Verdacht: Eine Phänomenologie der Medien* (Under Suspicion: A Phenomenology of the Media, 2000). In an interview with Geert Lovink, Groys notes that he uses the term "phenomenology" to emphasize "that every cultural product is an explanation of its own presence and multiplication in the first place." The title of the book, according to Groys, is supposed to remind the reader of crime fiction: "Our media always try to introduce an 'inside story,' to allow us to look behind the scenes." A media critic in this case becomes a detective uncovering valuable signs that belong to the archive of a specific culture. The first part of the book investigates the landscape behind the media; the second part focuses on the economy of suspicion—the mechanism by means of which things (rebaptized as signs) gain

access into the cultural archive. Groys views *Unter Verdacht* as a sequel to *Über das Neue*. While the latter describes the functioning of closed spaces—such as a museum, a library, or a university, where curiosity is directed to the outside—*Unter Verdacht* examines mechanisms of cultural production in open spaces, where suspicion is directed toward the hidden inside.

At times excessively abstract, generalizing, and paradoxical, the writings of Boris Efimovich Groys are nonetheless provocative and always original. By alternating ancient critical genres such as philosophical dialogue with rigorous academic writing and public performance, he creates insightful metacommentary and provides an example of contemporary mechanisms of cultural production. He transcends writerly traditions—above all the Russian tradition of "philosophizing reality"—and Western poststructuralist critiques of ideology. While his works have a clear affinity with post-structuralism, Groys is critical of its "infinite play of signifiers" in the void. Groys's writing and public performances are simultaneously radically innovative, inasmuch as they challenge conventional perspectives on cultural forms, and refreshingly cynical and pragmatic, insofar as they reclaim the primacy of the material, medium-bound existence of a work of art, cultural memory, and history itself.

Interviews:

Sven Spieker, "Interview: Boris Groys on the Logic of Collecting," *ArtMargins* (8 October 1998) <http://artmargins.com/content/interview/groys.html>;

Geert Lovink, "Interview with Boris Groys, Wednesday," *Nettime Archive* (4 October 2000) <http://www.nettime.org/nettime.23archive/200010/msg00036.html>.

References:

Mikhail Berg, "Utopicheskaia teoriia utopicheskogo postmodernizma," in *Literaturokratiia: problema prisvoeniia i pereraspredeleniia vlasti v literature* (Moscow: NLO, 2000), pp. 276–287;

Dragan Kujundžić, "Boris Groys and the Specters of Marx" <http://www.usc.edu/dept/comp-lit/tympanum/2/kujundzic.html> [accessed 12 May 2003];

Khol't Maier, "Institutsiia-institutio-institor," *Khudozhestvennyi zhurnal*, 23 (1999).

Igor' Mironovich Guberman

(7 July 1936 –   )

Greta N. Slobin
University of California, Santa Cruz

BOOKS: *Lokomotivy nastoiashchego i budushchego,* as Igor'
Mironovich Mironov (Moscow: Znanie, 1963);

Tretii triumvirat, as Mironov (Moscow: Detskaia literatura, 1965); as Guberman, enlarged edition
(Moscow: Detskaia literatura, 1974);

Chudesa i tragedii chernogo iashchika (Moscow: Detskaia literatura, 1969);

Pobezhdennoe vremia (Moscow: Politizdat, 1975);

Bekhterev: Stranitsy zhizni, as Mironov (Moscow: Znanie,
1977);

Evreiskie datszybao, as Igor' Garik (Jerusalem: Agasfer,
1978); as Guberman, republished as *Gariki:
Datszybao* (Jerusalem: Agasfer, 1988);

Bumerang, with drawings by David Miretsky (Ann
Arbor, Mich.: Ermitazh, 1982);

Progulki vokrug baraka (Tenafly, N.J.: Ermitazh, 1988);

Gariki na kazhdyi den', 2 volumes, with drawings by Aleksandr Okun' (Jerusalem: Agasfer, 1989);

Ierusalimskii dnevnik I (Jerusalem: Leksikon, 1991);

Kamernye gariki (Jerusalem: Leksikon, 1991);

Ierusalimskii dnevnik II (Jerusalem: Agasfer, 1993);

Ierusalimskie gariki (Moscow: Politekst, 1994);

Shtrikhi k portretu (Moscow: Molodaia gvardiia, 1994);

Ierusalimskii dnevnik III (Jerusalem: Agasfer, 1995);

Sobranie sochinenii, 4 volumes (Nizhnii Novgorod: DEKOM,
1996)—includes volume 4, *Pozhilye zapiski;*

Zakatnye gariki (Jerusalem: Agasfer, 1998);

Kniga stranstvii (Jerusalem: Agasfer, 2001);

Kazhdyi den' – prazdnik: Kniga-kalendar' (St. Petersburg:
Retro, 2001);

Kniga o vkusnoi i zdorovoi zhizni, by Guberman and Okun'
(St. Petersburg: Giperion, 2002).

Editions and Collections: *Evreiskie datszybao* (Ramat-
Gan, Israel: Moskva-Ierusalim, 1980);

Progulki vokrug barakha (Moscow: Glagol, 1993);

Gariki iz Erusalima I, II, III (Jerusalem: Agasfer, 1996);

Ierusalimskie gariki (Nizhnii Novgorod: DEKOM, 1997);

Sobranie sochinenii (Minsk: MET, 1999);

Sobranie sochinenii, 3 volumes (Ekaterinburg: U-faktoriia,
1999);

*Igor' Mironovich Guberman (from Igor' Guberman,
2001; University of Arizona Library)*

Shtrikhi k portretu. Gariki na kazhdyi den (Ekaterinburg:
U-faktoriia, 1999);

Pozhilye zapiski: Pozhilye zapiski, Zakatnye gariki (Ekaterinburg: U-faktoriia, 1999);

Igor Guberman, Antologiia satiry i iumora Rossii XX
veka, volume 17 (Smolensk: Rusich, 2001);

Gariki (Rostov-on-Don: Feniks, 2001);

Igor' Guberman (Moscow: EKSMO, 2002).

PRODUCED SCRIPT: *Dva chasa na sviatoi zemle: Uvle-katel'noe puteshestvie po Izrailiu s poétom Igorem Guber-manom,* video, LIL Productions, 1990.

Igor Guberman belongs to the generation of dissidents who came of age in the post-Stalinist Thaw of the late 1950s. He is well known for his satirical rhymed quatrains, later named *gariki,* whose compact form became a venue for a free-spirited voice that spoke of love, life, and its ironies. This voice expressed the passions and frustrations of Guberman's generation and acquired a great popularity among the contemporary intelligentsia through the underground distribution of the epigrammatic *gariki* often committed to memory, since they could not be published in the Soviet Union until the perestroika period in the late 1980s. Guberman has been called the Omar Khayyam (a twelfth-century Persian poet, widely popular in the West) of his time and compared to François Villon, the celebrated fourteenth-century French poet known for his prison verse. Many lines of Guberman's poems have become part of Russian folklore.

Igor' Mironovich Guberman was born in Moscow on 7 July 1936. In his memoir *Pozhilye zapiski* (Middle-Aged Notes, 1996) he lovingly remembers family stories about his maternal grandfather, Abram, a prominent merchant and a bon vivant in tsarist Russia, as well as his paternal grandmother, Liuba, whom he admired for her calm determination to protect the family in difficult times. He devotes a chapter to his wife's mother, Lidia Borisovna Libedinskaia, a theater actress and a great storyteller, who became a close friend. Guberman writes in the memoir of growing up in a poor but educated Jewish family, in which he learned to love music and reading from an early age. He also addresses his father's later worries about his son's precarious and dangerous existence as an underground poet and activist. Before immigrating to Israel in 1988, Guberman lived with his wife, Tata, and their two children, Tania (born in 1966) and Emil' (born in 1974), and worked in Moscow.

Guberman graduated from the Moscow Institute of Transportation Engineering in 1958 and worked as an electrical engineer for the next twenty years. In the 1960s he published books on psychology, brain research, and cybernetics and wrote articles for the popular-science magazine, *Znanie – sila* (Science is Knowledge), one of the most interesting journals of the day. He also worked as a ghostwriter for members of the Writers' Union, although he himself did not belong to it. Guberman was actively involved in dangerous dissident and samizdat activity, and around this time he began writing the quatrains upon which much of his fame is based.

As Guberman's quatrains targeted the increasing oppression of the Soviet state during the period of stagnation in the 1970s, also a period of intense Jewish activism and a wave of immigration to Israel, they became more politically explicit. He contributed to an underground dissident journal, *Evrei v Rossii* (Jews in Russia), and in 1978 he applied for an exit visa. In 1979 he was arrested on false charges and spent one and a half years in a Siberian labor camp in the Irkutsk region, followed by three and a half years of exile in the settlement of Borodino, located two hundred kilometers east of Krasnoiarsk, where his wife and children joined him. Soon after his arrest, an international campaign began in his defense, and he was made a member of the International PEN Club.

An early collection of Guberman's quatrains, titled *Bumerang,* a paranomastic transposition of the poet's name, was published in the United States in 1982 through the efforts of his friends and the Guberman Rescue Committee. The brief note on the back cover states that this collection is the first published under the author's name. It marks a shift in his status from a dissident to a published author. *Bumerang,* which features drawings by David Miretsky, opens with a brief preface by the author about writing poems and smuggling them out from the camp. The collection includes fragments from his "Tiuremnyi duevnik" (Prison Diary), "Stikhi razynkh let" (Poems of Different Years), and "Iz starykh stikhov" (From Old Verse). The poems in this early collection are rhymed quatrains, a form that became his trademark: a brilliantly compact poetic unit, with a witty punch line able to carry great semantic impact of philosophical and political significance. The poems are a sharp political satire of the repressive state and meditations on the dual identity of Russian Jews as a despised minority, both topics laced with sexual imagery.

The prison poems show that puns and wordplay are the mainspring of Guberman's verse: "Ia–v strane, a dusha–v moem tele–oba terpim ot vnutrennikh organov" (I–in the country, my soul–in my body–both suffer from internal organs). The double meaning of internal organs–its reference, that is, to the Komitet gosudarstvennosti bezopasnosti (KGB, State Security Committee)–will return in later quatrains. The opening line of another quatrain, "Umom Rossiiu ne spasti" (Russia cannot be saved by reason) paraphrases "Umom Rossiiu ne poniat'" (Russia cannot be understood by reason, 1866), a well-known first line from a lyric by nineteenth-century poet Fedor Ivanovich Tiutchev and reappears in another paraphrase in Guberman's later verse. "Poems of Different Years" suggests that Guberman's poetic diction in the early poems draws primarily on the classical tradition, and occasionally on unofficial lexicons and *mat* (obscenity).

Guberman with his father, Miron Davidovich Guberman, Moscow, 1973
(*from* Igor' Guberman, *2001; University of Arizona Library*)

The chapter title and the opening line of the first poem in "Poems of Different Years" parody an official state song, "Shiroka strana moia rodnaia" (Broad Is My Motherland), and are combined with strong expletives and swear words, "gde ne tknis', to suka, to mudak" (whatevever you bump into, there is a bitch or a motherfucker), resonating with transgression. In addition to political satire, the selection "From Old Verse" includes an early example of Yiddish-Russian pastiche, a mock-heroic parody of Russian folk songs about folk heroes, in which Sten'ka Razin (the leader of the seventeenth-century peasant rebellion) becomes "Sen'ka Raizman." The use of Yiddish names and jargon (or slang) here is also reminiscent of Isaac Emanuilovich Babel's *Odesskie rasskazy* (Odessa Stories, 1931) and the Jewish gangster Benia Krik, one of the heroes in these stories.

The Jewish theme is central in the earliest publication of Guberman's samizdat verse, collected in manuscript by various hands under the title *Evreiskie datszybao* (The Jewish Datszybao, 1978), for which Guberman used his pseudonym Igor' Garik. The collection was published for a third time in 1988, the year of Guberman's immigration, and bore his actual name as well as a new title, *Gariki: Datszybao*. The quatrains, now named *gariki* after the poet's childhood nickname given by his grandmother, are a verbal amalgam combining high poetic diction and quotations of classical Russian verse (from the works of Aleksandr Sergeevich Pushkin onward) with substandard prison slang and *mat,* sprinkled with Yiddish jargon. This strategy is doubly transgressive—the shocking proximity of "dirty" or "low" words, forbidden by Soviet standards, which were Victorian in nature, to the almost sacred classical lines that represent the national heritage, serves to undermine the ideological underpinnings of the system with epigrammatic wit and wordplay.

The subtitle *datszybao* is a reference to the "big character newspaper" in the early years of the Chinese Cultural Revolution. A public wall paper, on which any citizen was free to write in brush hand his opinion or criticism of a leader, the *datszybao* provided an uncensored venue that enabled people to have a voice; while it had Chairman Mao Tse-Tung's approval, the *datszybao* gradually became more controlled. Guberman's appropriation of the genre signaled his choice of an unofficial channel, or samizdat; using a variation of the *datszybao,* he could voice his independent opinion and criticism of the existing social order, for which there was no other venue at the time.

The titles of individual chapters of *gariki* here, as in subsequent collections, are rhymed aphoristic cou-

110

plets. The book opens with a cycle devoted to Russia, "Prichudlivee net na svete povesti, / Chem povest' o prichudakh russkoi sovesti" (There Is No Tale in the World More Capricious / Than the Tale of Caprices of the Russian Conscience). In this anticivic verse Russia appears as a mother who eats her own children and as a land of misbegotten ideas, where someone is always imprisoned—"some for spirituality, others for materialism." Guberman reiterates motives familiar from nineteenth-century literature, such as Fyodor Dostoevsky's Russian Devil *(russkii bes),* and the predilection of the country for oppression and excessive patriotism. He attacks the Soviet leaders Vladimir Lenin, "a dried up mummy, considered more alive than all the living," and Joseph Stalin, whose genius invented the prison regime and personality cult.

Gariki: Datszybao, Guberman's first extensive collection of *gariki,* is significant for the period of political repression during which it was written and conveys his double consciousness—that of a dissenter who is also a Jew. Along with political satire, the Jewish theme appears in the cycle with the ironic title "Gospod' likhuiu shutku uchinil, kogda siuzhet evreia sochinil" (God Made a Wild Joke, / When He Made Up the Story of the Jew), with poems that speak of the Jew as an outsider and an exile, "a scapegoat" whom "nobody loves and everyone loves to hate"—hence the source of Jewish laughter. Guberman predicts that Jews will pay a terrible price for their role in Russian history, especially their involvement in the *Russkii bunt* (Russian rebellion). The poems are at once a self-conscious comment on the Jewish minority and its status, as well on the less-than-glorious State, the source of its oppression.

The serious tone of the quatrains gathered in *Gariki: Datszybao* gives way to the spirited humor of the verbal pastiche in the second cycle, the title of which—"Obgusevshie lebedi" (Russified [or Goosed] Swans)—is a phonemic pun encompassing a stereotypical Jewish mispronunciation of a Russian *r,* which sounds like *g.* This single sound transforms the phrase "russianized swans" to a ridiculous "swans turned into geese," whose absurdity is a comment on "assimilation." This pun exemplifies the bilingual pastiche of Yiddish-Russian, whose economy of means has an immediate comic effect as the language of exile, or of a repressed minority in a great empire. Another favorite device is the appropriation of a classical poem, such as Mikhail Iur'evich Lermontov's well-known "Beleet parus odinokii" (The Lone Sail Whitens, 1832), which in this version, with Jewish names and puns, has a parodic, lowering effect.

Another source of humor is in mock-heroic Jewish travesties of popular folk songs and epics depicting glorious events in Russian history and their heroes.

Thus, Lermontov's renowned 1837 narrative poem, "Borodino," whose title refers to a decisive battle with Napoleon Bonaparte in the War of 1812, becomes "Borodino under Tel-Aviv." The Egyptian Port Said on the Suez Canal is punned as "Pots Aid" (Jewish Prick). Another mock-epic poem, titled "Montigomo, Neistrebimyi Kogan" (Montigomo, the Indestructible Kogan), is a brilliant pun on a well-known children's adventure tale by Thomas Mayne Reid, the title of which has been translated into Russian as "Montigomo, iastrebinyi kogot'" (Montigomo, a Hawk's Tylon). Guberman's poem describes a tribe of primitive Jews "on the banks of the Amazon" with hilarious names based on phonic puns or sound play: Aron Gutang (pun for Orangutang), for example, and Tamagavker, a pun on tomahawk. Another poem, with a title familiar from war poetry, "Pro tachanku" (About a Machine Gun Cart), is a parody of the civil war stories and, especially, of Babel's *Konarmiia* (1926; translated as *Red Cavalry,* 1929); the brave Cossacks of General Budennyi, a main character from *Konarmiia,* are replaced by Jewish fighters with stereotypical comic names, such as Srul' and Moishe.

After his release from exile in 1984, Guberman began work on a major prose project, a semi-autobiographical documentary novel (written at first "for the drawer"—that is, not necessarily for publication) about a search for the lost history of a remarkable man, Nikolai Aleksandrovich Bruni, a representative of the Russian cultural renaissance. A typical member of the intelligentsia, Bruni fell victim to the Stalinist purges and was shot in 1938. Through this effort to preserve the memory and history of the 1930s, Guberman sought to document the purges from the perspective of someone who went through a prison experience in the 1970s. In the afterword to the resulting book, *Shtrikhi k portretu* (Sketches for a Portrait, 1994), Guberman explains that he took down stories heard by *zeki* (fellow prisoners)—in other words, their eyewitness accounts.

In 1988 Guberman immigrated to Israel, working there on a Russian-language radio program and in the Russian press and giving public readings. That year his prison memoir in prose, *Progulki vokrug baraka* (Walks Around the Barracks), an understated, detailed eyewitness account of everyday prison existence, was also published in the United States. It did not appear in Russia until 1996. In a 1997 review in *Literaturnaia gazeta* Bulat Shalvovich Okudzhava called the book "a quiet confession."

A two-volume major collection of Guberman's verse, *Gariki na kazhdyi den'* (Gariki for Everyday), was published in Jerusalem in 1989. His introduction to this book of anti-authoritarian, philosophical verse is a tongue-in-cheek series of admonitions that makes fun of

*Guberman with his wife, Tata, and their children, Emil'
and Tania, Peredel'kino, Russia, in 1976 (from
Igor' Guberman, 2001; University
of Arizona Library)*

didactic Soviet advice to readers. Guberman suggests that "this book ought not to be read all at once and in order, but better a bit at a time and from different chapters as suits the mood," and that it ought not to be read "as a source of incontrovertible truth, since that does not exist in nature." The last page of the book, as of subsequent publications, is left blank, marked "for the reader's reflection." The two volumes, with ten chapters each, that constitute the collection are thematically organized and include chapters 5 and 6 from the second volume of the 1988 *Gariki* that are devoted to Russian and Jewish themes.

Guberman's satire of the Soviet system is rife with skepticism toward the received truths of Soviet ideology and includes a consistent philosophical critique of the belief in social and scientific progress. The quatrains are marked by a complex web of poetic reminiscences of nineteenth-century poetry—from Pushkin to Lermontov, Tiutchev, Nikolai Alekseevich Nekrasov, and Afanasii Afanas'evich Fet—but also of early-

twentieth-century poets such as Aleksandr Aleksandrovich Blok, Andrey Bely, Marina Ivanovna Tsvetaeva, and Osip Emil'evich Mandel'shtam. What is strikingly new in this collection, rendering the quatrains a truly original poetic genre, is the extensive use of substandard, unofficial lexicon of *mat* on a par with high poetic diction.

As with *Gariki,* chapter titles here are witty aphorisms in rhymed couplets, which announce the debunking of every sacred institution, the State and its prisons, Science, Family, and Matrimony: "It is simple to take away freedom from people: just simply entrust it to the people"; "Family is given to us by God, it is a substitute for happiness"; and "He who is tormented by spiritual thirst, must not await the love of his compatriots." The poems provide verbal equivalents of the toppling of official monuments after 1989. Poems reiterate the skepticism of the twentieth century, which revealed the "imperfection of human construction," thus postponing "hope for universal bliss." Chapter 5 in volume two of *Gariki na kazhdyi den'* presents meditations on the "peculiarities of Russian conscience," in which poems underscore the importance of freedom as moral "choice." Guberman uses a variety of verbal devices that telegraph subversive meaning: wordplay; phonemic punning, by which one sound can change the meaning of the phrase; parodic paraphrase of patriotic verse; and unofficial lexicon with strategically placed obscenity.

The penultimate chapter 9 uses obscene invective in a sarcastic, blatantly blasphemous condemnation of Mother Russia and its brutality and violence. Titled "Davno pora, ebena mat', / Umom Rossiiu ponimat'" (It's time, fucking mother / to understand Russia with a brain), it is to be read against Nekrasov's civic verse, familiar to every schoolchild, as well as the symbolist poetry of Blok, Bely, and Valerii Iakovlevich Briusov that is devoted to meditation on Russia after the 1905 Revolution. The title of the chapter is a variation of "Umom Rossiiu ne spasti," the poem from *Bumerang* that parodically paraphrases Tiutchev's "Umom Rossiiu ne poniat'," which mythologized the particularism of Russia. In Guberman's verse the tradition of mystical nationalism is ridicule, and reason—rather than emotion—is evoked. In this example of the economy of means in Guberman's approach, a triple transgression is accomplished in a single line. First, the line displays an unpatriotic, blasphemous swearing at Mother Russia; second, it constitutes a parodic paraphrase of a well-known high poetic line; and third, the ironic suggestion of the line implies that another body part is involved, whose unspoken identity is clear from the semantic context.

This poetic shorthand is one of the main devices in Guberman's linguistic revolution. The opening quatrain of the ninth chapter is justly famous. In a verbal counterpart of the sots-art (unofficial Soviet pop-art) of Vitalii Anatol'evich Komar and Aleksandr Danilovich Melamid, which debunks symbols of the omnipotent Soviet state, it represents a familiar statue of a bronze man of power–but with a difference, asserted by the words, "ogromnyi organ bezopasnosti" (under a small fig leaf hides an enormous organ of security). This line adds yet another semantic dimension to the term "organ." Elsewhere in this cycle, a distinct role is given to art, which can save the world with the trinity of image, harmony, and form; all but poetry will disappear after death without a trace.

In the early to mid 1990s Guberman published three consecutive books of diaries, which present a continued meditation on Jewish identity and history: *Ierusalimskii dnevnik I* (1991); *Ierusalimskii dnevnik II* (1993); and *Ierusalimskii dnevnik III* (1995). The entire series of the Jerusalem diaries appeared in a separate edition in 1996, as well as in the four-volume *Sobranie sochinenii* (Collected Works, 1996). A partial collection of verse, *Ierusalimskie gariki* (Jerusalem Gariki), which Guberman dedicated to his friend the artist Aleksandr Okun' (a drawing by Okun' serves as its cover), appeared in Moscow in 1994. Here Guberman writes of his double identity, of belonging to two nations. The poems present a continued meditation on Russia now seen from abroad, as in the title of the opening chapter, "Rossiiu uvidav na rasstoianii, / Grustit' perestaesh' o rasstavanii" (Seeing Russia at a Distance, / No Longer Sad About Parting). The poems also reiterate earlier motifs of Jewish identity and history, now tinged with postcommunist nostalgia for the "poisonous, stinking, and powerful breath of the immense empire." With characteristic irony, Guberman titles the second notebook with a rhymed aphorism, "Russia for the soul and the mind is like first love and like prison," noting that once the Jews left, "the empire immediately fell apart." Firmly ensconced in the historic Jewish homeland, Guberman remains a Russian.

His next major collection, *Zakatnye gariki* (The Sunset Gariki), a philosophical contemplation of maturity and the changes in perspective that it brings, came out in 1998. A video recording of his life and work in Jerusalem, titled *Igor Guberman s utra do vechera* (Igor Guberman, From Morning to Evening), was released in 2000. It features the poet in his apartment, filled with paintings of his favorite contemporary Russian artists, and accompanies him on walks around Jerusalem, which he calls "not a city, but a place, which is very well known to God," referring to the Jews as "not a nation, but a way of being." He speaks of himself as a man of Russian culture and Jewish soul.

Paperback cover for Guberman's Gariki: Datszybao *(1988), a collection of satirical rhymed quatrains* (gariki). Datszybao *refers to the oversized public signs on which Chinese citizens write their opinions of government leaders (Davis Library, University of North Carolina, Chapel Hill).*

The postcommunist 1990s brought fame and star status to Guberman as he became an international author and read his works in public to wide Russian audiences not only in Israel and the United States but also in the former Soviet Union, Canada, Australia, and Germany, as well as in other European countries. In *Pozhilye zapiski,* his prose memoir, Guberman remembers thinking to himself on the first flight back to Russia: "Where am I going? . . . Am I flying to my country or from it?" Guberman travels to Russia about twice a year and gives public readings in the capital and in provincial cities to enthusiastic audiences. He remains a best-selling author, with several editions of his work published in Moscow, Ekaterinburg, and Nizhnii Novgorod. M. Brenner has put Guberman's poems to music, with a compact disc released in Moscow in 1995. A video recording of Guberman reading his work was filmed in the Kremlin Concert Hall in Moscow on 18 March 1997. His astronomic rise in popularity in Russia and the former republics is referred to as the "Guberman phenomenon" in the media.

Guberman's *gariki,* his acutely witty epigrammatic rhymed quatrains, tap into vast reservoirs of collective cultural and historical memory, including the classical poetic tradition, anecdotes, folk songs, and popular Soviet songs of the postwar period. By combining the high poetic diction of Russian classical verse with substandard Soviet prison slang, unofficial *mat,* and Yiddish jargon, he creates a brilliant hybrid that at once lifts political, cultural, and sexual repression. In Guberman's verse the shock value of obscenity works to condemn the deformed Soviet social organism and repressive ideology. His writing recalls that of Ivan Semenovich Barkov, the eighteenth-century censored poet who used obscene sexual language in his works; Guberman considers Barkov an important part of the treasure-house of Russian literature. Mixing "unofficial" or censored language with substandard lexicon and slang, which includes forbidden and rarely used terms for body parts and sexual organs, Guberman effects a linguistic breach that is doubly transgressive: the blasphemous verse speaks directly to the reader or listener, even as it brings a release of repression—both political and sexual—and a recognition of something deeply familiar that has just been revealed.

Igor' Mironovich Guberman probes in his works the potential of laughter as a means of destabilizing power in the satirical tradition of the early Soviet writing of Mikhail Mikhailovich Zoshchenko, Evgenii Ivanovich Zamiatin, Il'ia Arnol'dovich Il'f, and Evgenii Petrovich Petrov. For Guberman, laughter has the capacity to break through the edifice erected by the omnipotent Soviet state and, with a word or phrase, to clear the space for free expression. In public performances registered on video recordings, one can observe listeners explode with laughter as Guberman delivers his lines with a straight face. His verse addresses the audience, whose memory of their painful past and the heavy legacy of repression is tinged with postcommunist nostalgia and anxiety about the future. The audience's laughter is not only cathartic; it is also therapeutic and enabling. By taking aim at repression and sexual anxieties, such laughter makes way for optimism, which, as Guberman notes, is missing among his compatriots. Guberman's poetic gift and brilliant verbal wit enable him to keep the pulse of the times for succeeding generations. His verse continues to touch the nerve of Russian Jews and Russians, as well as the people of the former Soviet Empire—wherever they may be.

Interviews:

L. Fomina, "Progulki vokrug granitsy," *Moskovskaia pravda,* 2 August 1994;

Sergei Shapran, "Igor Guberman: 'Tseniu v sebe bezpechnost'," *Belorusskaia Delovaia Gazeta,* 14 December 1998;

Marina Ovsova, "Kur'er kul'tury nezakatnyi Guberman zakatil v Moskvu," *Moskovskii komsomolets,* 15 December 1998;

Ekaterina Vasenina, "Igor Guberman: 367 prazdnichnykh dnei v godu. I po krainei mere odin prazdnik – obshchenie s avtorom," *Novaia gazeta,* 29 November 1999;

A. Chepalov, "Nezakatnye 'Gariki' Abrama Khaiama," *Kaleidoskop,* 19 April 2000.

Biography:

Vasilii M. Litvinov, "Igor Guberman," in *Russkie pisateli 20 veka. Biograficheskii slovar',* edited by Petr Alekseevich Nikolaev (Moscow: Bol'shaia Rossiiskaia Entsiklopediia, 2000), pp. 217–218.

References:

Alla Bossart, "Garik iz semeistva Atlantov," *Stolitsa,* 51 (1993);

I. Frolova, "Peterburgskie gariki Igoria Gubermana," *Smena,* 26 December 1995;

A. Kovaleva, "Ocharovatel'nyi bezdel'nik," *Moskovskii komsomolets,* 2 October 1996;

Bulat Shalvovich Okudzhava, "Tikhaia ispoved'," *Literaturnaia gazeta,* 12 March 1997;

Boris Zhutovsky, "Igor Guberman," *Stolitsa,* 41 (1992).

Bakhyt Shkurullaevich Kenzheev

(2 August 1950 –)

Marina Kanevskaya
University of Montana

BOOKS: *Izbrannaia lirika 1970–1981* (Ann Arbor, Mich.: Ardis, 1984)—includes "Ballada proshchaniia";

Osen' v Amerike. Stikhotvoreniia 1982–1987 (Tenafly, N.J.: Hermitage, 1988);

Stikhotvoreniia poslednikh let (Moscow, 1992);

Iz knigi "Amo ergo sum": Stikhotvoreniia (Moscow: Nezavisimaia gazeta, 1993);

Stikhotvoreniia Bakhyta Kenzheeva (Moscow: PAN, 1995);

Vozvrashchenie. Stikhi (Almaty: Zhibek Zholy, 1996);

Sochinitel' zvezd. Kniga novykh stikhotvorenii (St. Petersburg: Pushkinskii fond, 1997);

Sniashchaiasia pod utro: Kniga stikhotvorenii (Moscow: Klub Proekt OGI, 2000);

Iz semi knig, with an afterword by Sergei Sergeevich Averintsev (Moscow: Nezavisimaia gazeta, 2000);

Zoloto goblinov (Moscow: Nezavisimaia gazeta, 2000).

Editions in English: "Poets have often noticed . . . ," translated by Albert C. Todd, in *Twentieth Century Russian Poetry: Silver and Steel: An Anthology,* compiled by Yevgeny Yevtushenko, edited by Todd, Max Hayward, and Daniel Weissbort (New York: Doubleday, 1993);

Contemporary Russian Poetry. A Bilingual Anthology, translated and edited by Gerald S. Smith (Bloomington: Indiana University Press, 1993), pp. 168–174;

"You envied the flying birds," ". . . and a fool," and "Gone is the sound," translated by Nina Kossman, in *In the Grip of Strange Thoughts: Russian Poetry in a New Era,* compiled and edited by J. Kates (Brookline, Mass.: Zephyr, 1999), pp. 407–411.

OTHER: *Leninskie gory: Stikhi poetov MGU,* with contributions by Kenzheev, Irina Antonova, and others, compiled by Igor' Leonidovich Volgin (Moscow: Izdatel'stvo Moskovskogo universiteta, 1977).

TRANSLATIONS: C. S. Lewis, *Plemiannik charodeia* (Chicago: SGP, 1988);

Bakhyt Shkurullaevich Kenzheev (from the paperback cover for Stikhotvoreniia Bakhyta Kenzheeva, *1995; Paterno Library, Pennsylvania State University)*

Lewis, *Prints Kaspian, ili Puteshestvie v Narniiu* (Chicago: SGP, 1990);

Josh McDowell, *Neosporimye svidetel'stva: Istoricheskie svidetel'stva, fakty, dokumenty khristianstva* (Chicago: SGP, 1991).

SELECTED PERIODICAL PUBLICATIONS–UNCOLLECTED:

FICTION

Plato, Znamia, 3–4, 5 (1992): 5–78, 72–135;

Mladshii brat, Oktiabr', 7, 8, 9 (1992): 7–68, 22–80, 33–83;

Ivan Bezuglov: meshchanskii roman, Znamia, 1, 2 (1993): 62–102, 79–129;

Portret khudozhnika v iunosti, Oktiabr', 1 (1995): 3–102.

NONFICTION

"*Gorodskoi angel* Ally Golovinoi," *Kontinent,* 63 (1990): 331–336;

"O tekushchei poezii i ne tol'ko o nei," *Kontinent,* 63 (1990): 371–384;

"Antisovetchik Vladimir Sorokin," *Znamia,* 4 (1995): 202–205;

"Romans, ballada, pesnia," *Literaturnaia gazeta,* 9 August 1995, p. 4;

"Predskazaniia Evgeniia Reina," *Znamia,* 9 (1995): 220–222;

"Chastnyi chelovek Oleg Chukhontsev," *Arion,* 1 (1996): 31–36;

"Kliuch ippokreny," *Literaturnaia gazeta,* 26 June 1996, p. 4.

Among Russian poets of the twentieth and twenty-first centuries, Bakhyt Kenzheev enjoys a reputation as a traditionalist. Predominantly lyrical, his verse touches upon a wide range of modern phenomena. He is renowned for his ability to represent mundane life in an intensely Romantic style, creating a mystical dimension to human existence. Many critics acknowledge that his poetry incorporates the European and Central Asian mythological traditions as well as specifically Russian literary trends. Projecting traditional imagery on the minutiae of contemporary life, Kenzheev's poetry harks back to the Russian rhyming styles most brilliantly represented by figures such as Aleksandr Sergeevich Pushkin, Aleksandr Aleksandrovich Blok, and Osip Emil'evich Mandel'shtam. Poet and critic Efim Bershin in his review (*Literaturnaia gazeta* [The Literary Gazette], 1993) of Kenzheev's book *Stikhotvoreniia poslednikh let* (Poetry of Recent Years, 1992) confesses, "I like Kenzheev's poetry because it elevates you from mundane life and vanity; because there is nothing in it that is more important than love."

Bakhyt Shkurullaevich Kenzheev was born on 2 August 1950 in Chimkent (Kazakhstan). His father, Shkurulla Kenzheevich Kenzheev, a clergyman's son, worked as an English-language instructor. His mother, Elena Nikolaevna (Karaseva) Kenzheeva, graduated with a concentration in history from Moscow State University and worked as a museum guide and librarian. In 1953 the family moved to Moscow. In 1973 Kenzheev graduated with a degree in chemistry from Moscow State University. In the 1970s he belonged to an underground group of poets known as "Moskovskoe vremia" (Moscow Time), which included Sergei Markovich Gandlevsky, Aleksandr Soprovsky, Tatiana Poletaeva, and Aleksei Tsvetkov. The group circulated an almanac, in a typewritten copy, under the same title. In 1976 Kenzheev began to publish his poetry in the Soviet Union and abroad. In 1980 he married a Canadian scholar, Laura Beraha, and in 1982 immigrated to Canada. Currently a resident of Montreal, Kenzheev works as a translator for various international organizations, including the International Monetary Fund.

In 1984 Kenzheev published his first collection of poetry, titled *Izbrannaia lirika 1970–1981* (Selected Lyrics 1970–1981). In this collection he modeled himself after the great Russian poets of the nineteenth and twentieth centuries, such as Pushkin, Evgenii Abramovich Baratynsky, Mandel'shtam, Anna Andreevna Akhmatova, and Vladislav Felitsianovich Khodasevich. Russian critics and poets such as Dmitrii Bobyshev, Vasilii Betaki, Iurii Miloslavsky, and others have attributed Kenzheev to Pushkin's "school" of poetry. This attribution, however, fails to address the modernist significance of Kenzheev's verse. As poet and critic Betaki points out in his 1987 essay "Dve s lishnim vechnosti nazad" (Over Two Eternities Ago), Kenzheev's roots should be sought in the poetry of the turn of the century. His "Pushkinian" connection adheres to the tradition of acmeism (arguably the successor to Russian symbolism), with which Mandel'shtam and Akhmatova were prominently associated. Kenzheev's poetry invokes a harmony between the world of nature and the creation of art. He perceives the absence of this equanimity as the pivotal tragedy not only of human existence but also of his own life.

In his first collection Kenzheev follows the acmeist tradition. The poem "Proshlo, pomerklo, otgorelo" (Everything has come to an end, dimmed, died) is dedicated to Mandel'shtam's horrifying death in a Soviet labor camp. As Kenzheev admits in his essay "O tekushchei poezii i ne tol'ko o nei" (On the Current Poetry, Etc.), published in *Kontinent* (The Continent) in 1990, in his circle of poets this reference to Mandel'shtam signals that innermost issues are discussed. In other poems, such as "Lai sobachii, sukhaia trava" (Dog's barking and dry grass) or "Vsei gromadoi seroi, stal'noiu" (As a monolith of gray and steel), Mandel'shtam's and Akhmatova's voices and the imagery and intertextual allusions of these poets are made manifest. In accordance with acmeism, Kenzheev's poetry gives voice to the intimate feelings and sensations of the author, which merge with the impressions of both nature and culture that together form a microcosm in which his intellect and spirit abide.

If Kenzheev's verse rings with anti-Soviet sentiments, it does so not as a result of open subversiveness but, rather, because of his refusal to describe Soviet reality and because of his restraint regarding social issues. In the 1970s this mode of writing and thinking acquired the name "inner emigration," a term that in reality meant self-elimination from the public arena—a complete exclusion from official discourse. Inner-emigration artists paid for their privilege of creative freedom by losing other social, professional, and material privileges. This theme of alienation in his own land permeates Kenzheev's poem "Ballada proshchaniia" (The Ballad of Farewell) dated 1977–1981 and published in *Izbrannaia lirika 1970–1981*. Even before he left Russia, Kenzheev anticipated the pain of separation from his motherland. This pain later became the central leitmotiv of his poetry. The poem "Ballada vozvrashcheniia" (The Ballad of Return, 1984), written at the same time or even before "Ballada proshchaniia," bolsters the impression that the feeling of isolation in his own country has cultivated the soil for Kenzheev's nostalgia, which dominates the poetry of his emigration period.

Kenzheev's nostalgia for Russia and the Russian language sets him apart from the general Romantic tradition, which typically focuses on a poet's melancholy brought on by a lack of understanding and empathy from society. In the poems of 1979 the words "Russia" and "Russian" made their first appearance. For example, one of his poems begins with the line "V Rossii grustnaia pogoda" (There is sad weather in Russia, 1984). In another poem, "Khorosho, chto my odnazhdy" (Once upon a time, it was pleasant, 1984), he writes, "Khorosho v glukhoi Rossii slushat' zovy grozovye" (How pleasant it is to listen to the sounds of thunder in God-forsaken Russia). During the 1960s and 1970s the words "Russian" and "Russia" resounded with opposition to the officially accepted "Soviet." "Russian," although not by any means excluded from the official discourse, still retained connotations of something that had escaped "Sovietization" and, therefore, in spite of the oppressive regime, had its own appeal and was worth loving and longing for. This opposition between "Russian" and "Soviet" finds its representation in the poem "Kogda konchaetsia sezon" (When the season is over, 1984), written in 1979, in which Kenzheev, in a rare instance, makes a political commentary. In this poem "The Russian horizon pierced by numberless birds' wings" serves as a backdrop for the abandoned domes of the church. Because of the general negligence of the living environment in his country, this willfully forsaken sanctuary contrasts sharply with Lenin's granite monument, untidy and ugly despite its status as a venerated object. The silence of the church bells, in turn, clashes with the song of the "army boys" drinking beer at the railway station.

Kenzheev's second book, *Osen' v Amerike* (Autumn in America, 1988), which features poems written between 1982 and 1987, is a lamentation on losing the landscape, language, and culture of Russia and the Russian way of life in the broadest sense—including material shortages and pervasive drunkenness. In the first poem, "Dusha moia tianetsia k domu" (My soul longs for home), following the tradition of the nineteenth-century Slavophiles, Kenzheev equates Russia with the Holy Land and its soul with Christ crucified. In other poems of this collection,

such as "Nu chto molchish', raskaiavshiisia strannik?" (Why are you silent, a repenting wanderer?), the title poem "Osen' v Amerike," and "Mestnym zhiteliam vriad li zametno" (Local dwellers probably do not notice), Russia is presented as a land where even hardships themselves beget poetic inspiration rather than despair. In "Nu chto molchish', raskaiavshiisia strannik?" Kenzheev expresses his fear that an émigré poet loses his traditional status as a prophet and turns into a mere outcast. He expresses concern that upon the anticipated return to his motherland after years of wandering, his significance as a national poet will be reduced to a "rol' v groshovoi drame" (a role in a cheap drama). He fears that during the years of his relatively comfortable exile, other Russian poets will have earned their right for central positions on a Russian version of Mount Parnassus.

Gradually, Kenzheev's voice assimilated the tradition of another émigré poet, Khodasevich, who after the 1917 revolution lived and died in exile. To express his tremendous pain Kenzheev invokes Khodasevich's anesthetic detachment not only to survive but also to create poetry. As if trying to discern where this unbearable pain originates in himself, Kenzheev comes up with a peculiar distinction between the soul and the heart. Here, soul is equated with inspiration and creative ability, while heart represents something almost trivial, sensitive, and sensual—something that one may call human life itself. Thus, in comfortable but lonely exile the poet states that his soul thrives while his heart perishes.

This distinction is made most prominently in the poems "Mestnym zhiteliam vriad li zametno" and "Dobryi vecher ili utro?" (Good evening or good morning? 1988). In "Sniatsia li sny?" (Do dreams come to me? 1988) Kenzheev delves into the problem of why the motherland, which he has abandoned because of his disgust for its political and social life, now claims his heart so persistently. He dramatizes his own attempt to articulate the word "motherland" but interrupts himself on the second letter ("... Eto moia ro ... a dal'she – pustaia stranitsa" [This is my mo ... and the empty page–to follow]), because the word itself has been appropriated and contaminated with Soviet usage and meaning. An explanation of this paradoxical longing for the past appears in the poem "Otoshli osennie rasprodazhi" (The autumn sales are over, 1988), in which Kenzheev describes the impoverished, marginalized, and, at the same time, leisurely existence of "an unofficial" poet in Soviet Russia. In still another poem, "Otlaiali sobaki. Gasnut okna" (The dogs stopped barking; the windows grow dark, 1988), he lists the names of all his friends whom he expects to visit in order to share a bottle. He also names those who would skip his drinking party. The loss of friends serves as a reminder that the author has serious doubts about his present self-identity. In the last quatrain of this poem, he

Paperback cover for Kenzheev's Stikhotvoreniia Bakhyta Kenzheeva *(The Poetry of Bakhyt Kenzheev, 1995), in which
many of his poems appeared for the first time in book form (Paterno Library, Pennsylvania State University)*

questions his old self: "Gde ty teper', starinnyi moi tovarishch. . . . / Gde pishesh' ugriumye stikhi, ne ponimaia, / chto zhdet tebia? Pered tvoim oknom / uzhe togda zasnezhennoi tropinkoi / ia prokhodil, ne ostavliaia teni" (Where are you now, my old friend. . . . / Where do you write your gloomy poems, without the idea / about your own future? Down the path, snowy already, I have walked by your window, / not even casting a shadow). The poet admires his past life for its emotional intensity. He stresses that it was crowded with people close to him in interests and tastes—people who wrote poetry and created a feeling of belonging. In his poem "Vsiu zhizn' toropit'sia, tomit'sia, i vot . . ." (All my life I hastened, agonized, and now . . . , 1988) he sees his new existence in Canada as the epitome of stability and expresses the fear that his existence has come to a halt, at which point—as described by a popular Russian song—"nekuda bol'she speshit'" (one has nowhere to hasten).

Trying to find a way to survive, Kenzheev turns to the poetry of Vladimir Vladimirovich Nabokov, who presents a distinctive example of successful creativity in two languages (Russian and English) and two modes of existence (nostalgia for his Russian past and content in his American present). As a result he writes "Stikhi Nabokova. Amerika. Aprel'" (Nabokov's poetry; America; April, 1988). Yet, in the context of the second, present-affirming existence Nabokov's poetry fails to soothe Kenzheev's heart: "the heart keeps beating in the rhythm of sobs for its fatherland." In the same poem Kenzheev smiles sadly at scholarly discussions on Russian poetry. He finds these discussions not only shallow but also inherently alien to the spirit of Russian poetry. This stifling impression clashes with his memories of how his friends of the past intrinsically belonged to Russian literature in their creative work and way of thinking. He dramatizes his own dialogical involvement with Russian poetry through allusions to celebrated lines from Pushkin and Baratynsky. Suddenly he interrupts this intertextual play with an unfinished sentence similar to a sob, "Ia odinochestva takogo nikogda . . ." (Never in my life such loneliness . . .). For the poet and critic Betaki this undying ring of loneliness renders Kenzheev "a poet of solitude." In another poem, "Gorshe khiny liudskaia svoboda" (Human freedom is bitter as gall, 1988), Kenzheev depicts Moscow as Atlantis, recognizing that his nostalgia refers not so much to a realistic city but rather to a utopian idea. The collection *Osen' v Amerike* is arguably the most poignant expression of Kenzheev's longing for Russia. In his essay "Bakhyt Kenzheev. Remeslo nedobrogo roka" (Bakhyt Kenzheev. The Skill of an Unkind Fate, 1985) the critic Aleksandr Radashkevich maintains that the idealization of friends in Kenzheev's poetry connects it to the Russian elegiac tradition from Pushkin to Blok. Baratynsky's well-known poem "Osen'" (Autumn) is specifically dedicated to friendship of the past and no doubt inspired the title for Kenzheev's collection.

After the liberalization of the Russian press in the late 1980s, Kenzheev regularly published his poetry in literary periodicals. In 1991 a dozen poems from his "Poslaniia. Montreal', 1889" (Epistles. Montreal, 1889) appeared in the Saratov magazine *Volga* and marked his new interest in the stylization of the late-eighteenth-century genre of sentimentalism; all of these poems were subsequently published in book form in *Stikhotvoreniia poslednikh let*. The year 1889, however, points to the end of the nineteenth century, providing a link between two highly ornate styles: late-eighteenth-century rococo and the eclectic tenor of Art Nouveau. Kenzheev's irony shines through the discord between an exquisite and deliberately playful style, on the one hand, and a mundane and rather sad life, on the other. The old theme of nostalgia overgrows its national boundaries and merges with Romantic tenets of longing for the sublime and transcendental. This new ironic tone, however, allows him to address his melancholy with relative ease and evade the emotional lacerations characteristic of the poems in *Izbrannaia lirika* or *Osen' v Amerike*.

In 1991 Kenzheev published five poems in the journal *Novyi mir* (New World) under the title "Vremia deistviia" (Time of Action), which are permeated with heart-rending nostalgia. In "Vremia deistviia – osen'. Moskva" (The time of action is autumn and Moscow) Russia remains for him the eternal source of love and inspiration, while the "Free West," exemplified by the essentially wholesome Canada, still presents a ludicrous and alien object of observation. As he states in one of the poems, "Smotri, sgushchaetsia zima" (Look, the winter grows dense), "There are very few funny things here, to be precise, none at all."

In 1992 Kenzheev published his first book in Russia, *Stikhotvoreniia poslednikh let,* which incorporates both previously published poems and new verse. One of the most important lyrics, "Rasskazhi mne ob angelakh" (Tell me about angels), is dedicated to the late Venedikt Vasil'evich Erofeev, an archetypal underground Russian writer who rose to renown in the late Soviet period and author of the novel *Moskva-Petushki* (1977; translated as *Moscow to the End of the Line,* 1980), his best-known work. Kenzheev identifies closely with Erofeev, whom he calls "my frail invisible comrade who creates music for our sorrow."

In a short selection, "Iz novykh stikhov" (From the New Poems), published in *Novyi mir* in 1992, and the collection *Stikhotvoreniia Bakhyta Kenzheeva* (The Poetry of Bakhyt Kenzheev, 1995) Kenzheev turns to the tradition among Russian poets of conversing with the Muse. In one of the lyrics, "Net, ne bezumnaia tkachikha" (No, it was not a senseless weaver), the poet creates his own version of interacting with his "prostaia gost'ia" (simple lady guest), at the same time reminding the reader that this visitor had previously inspired geniuses such as Blok and Akhmatova.

Published in 1992 in the journal *Oktiabr'* (October), the poems under the title "Chem obrechennee, tem slashche" (The more doomed the sweeter) mark Kenzheev's growing interest in the dissimilarities between the language of nature and human speech. The poem "Zemli moei zhivoi gerbarii" (The living herbarium of my earth) enters into a dialogue of sorts with the next verse in the group, "Stalo molchanie zolotom" (The silence turned into gold). These two poems, which were also collected in *Stikhotvoreniia Bakhyta Kenzheeva,* are deeply embedded in the Russian tradition of philosophical discourse that reaches back to Fedor Ivanovich Tiutchev's "Silentium!" (1830) and continues through Mandel'shtam's poem of the same title, written in 1910. In the framework of this tradition the voice of nature is juxtaposed with the human utterance. While the former represents ineffable truth, the latter is rife with interpretation and, therefore, is doomed to deviate from the essential meaning. This theme is central for the whole selection. For example, in the poem "Drozhashchii nevedomym, dlinnoiu ryzhei nitkoi na rukave" (The trembling mysterious long red thread on my sleeve) the voice of the poet is transformed into the primordial sounds of nature, "obizhennyi shepot meteli stanut rech'iu tvoei, melkii gornyi ruchei v seredine aprelia" (bitter whisper of the blizzard and the bubbling of a mountain brook in the middle of April).

Throughout his literary career Kenzheev has also authored several prosaic works. His first novel, *Mladshii brat* (A Younger Brother, 1992), tells about a typical Soviet young man of the 1970s, Mark Solomin, who serves as an interpreter for a big tourist firm. Under circumstances beyond his control he breaches the tight constraints of the Soviet system and, against his wish, becomes a dissident. At the end of the novel Solomin dies in an attempt to cross the state border. In sharp contrast to his poetry, Kenzheev's prose belongs to the late social realist tradition. Though closely identifying himself with Solomin, Kenzheev does not cultivate his readers' sympathy for this character.

From 1993 to 2000 Kenzheev published six books of poetry, many of which featured verse that appeared first in journals and newspapers from the late 1980s to the 1990s. These volumes are *Iz knigi "Amo ergo sum"* (From the Book "Amo Ergo Sum," 1993), *Stikhotvoreniia Bakhyta Kenzheeva, Vozvrashchenie* (The Return, 1996), *Sochinitel' zvezd* (The Creator of Stars, 1997), *Sniashchaiasia pod utro* (She Who Arrives in Morning Dreams, 2000), and *Iz semi knig* (From Seven Books, 2000). *Stikhotvoreniia Bakhyta Kenzheeva* includes the most previously published verse. In his 1997 review of the volume for *Znamia* (The Banner) Oleg Rogov points out that the author's name becomes a part of the title, Kenzheev's playful allusion to Pushkin's title for his collection of poetry, *Stikhotvoreniia Aleksandra Pushkina* (1828). By invoking Pushkin's title Kenzheev seems to be responding to critics who traditionally compare his sonorous rhymes with those of the great poet. The book is illustrated with stylized "Gothic" prints by Aleksandr Smirnov.

In his 2000 book of poetry, *Sniashchaiasia pod utro*, Kenzheev's lyrical alter ego is a marginalized poet, "a hurt sparrow who survived winter and can hardly sing," from the poem "Kerosinka v dvornitskoi uglovoi" (Kerosene lamp in the janitor's corner room). In the same poem Kenzheev rethinks his love of God and admits that a human being has little in common with a saintly being. He asks whether the supreme force is nothing more than "God is sitting alone as an indifferent judge of the living and the dead." The moralistic dilemma of whether God appears to man as a benevolent or, on the contrary, harsh authority informs poems such as "Sushchestvuet li Bog v sinagoge?" (Does God Exist in Synagogue?) and "Organizatsiia Vselennoi byla neiasnoi nashim predkam" (The organization of the universe was unclear to our predecessors). Nostalgia remains a rich theme for Kenzheev, although at this time it seems to refer to his youth rather than to 1990s Russia, which has become accessible and at the same time disappointing for Kenzheev, as seen in the poems "Na tom kontse zemli, gde sniatsia sny" (On that side of the earth where dreams come to you) and "Syt po gorlo trevogoi i zlost'iu" (I am fed up with worries and anger).

Kenzheev's most prominent works of prose are four novels, the first of which serves as an introduction to the next three, which are considered a trilogy: *Plato* (Plato, 1992), *Ivan Bezuglov* (1993), *Portret khudozhnika v iunosti* (Portrait of an Artist as a Young Man, 1995), and,

finally, *Zoloto goblinov* (The Gold of the Goblins, 2000). The recurring characters in the last three novels are primarily what render it a trilogy. For example, a poet, Aleksei Tatarinov, is the protagonist of both *Portret khudozhnika v iunosti* and *Zoloto goblinov*. He is presented for the first time in the introductory *Plato,* which Kenzheev subtitles "Sochinenie Alekseia Tatarinova" (The Composition of Aleksei Tatarinov), as the fictitious author of this novel. Tatarinov in effect takes upon himself the traditional role of a narrator similar to Pushkin's Ivan Belkin, who explains in the introduction to *Povesti pokoinogo Ivana Petrovicha Belkina, izdannye A. P.* (The Tales of the late Ivan Petrovich Belkin, Published by A. P., 1831) that readers should not expect any particular order or continuity connecting his stories. Thus, the narrator assumes responsibility for the free association of the novels to follow. In *Plato* Kenzheev also sets the aura of stylization for the whole trilogy. Through its genre *Plato* simultaneously proposes utopia and anti-utopia and, as the critic Aleksandr Kursky observes, is reminiscent of the memoirs written by the representatives of the 1917 wave of Russian emigration.

The ensuing three novels represent three different tendencies in contemporary Russian prose: postmodernist conceptualism (*Ivan Bezuglov*), traditional realistic narrative (*Portret khudozhnika v iunosti*), and magic realism (*Zoloto goblinov*). The first and the third novels depict the world of the new Russian businessmen or the New Russians. In *Ivan Bezuglov* Kenzheev attempts to create the simulacrum of a pulp fiction by adhering to trite imagery and depersonalized language, following the path of the conceptualist writer Vladimir Georgievich Sorokin. An inherently lyrical author, Kenzheev fails to distance himself from his narrative, however, which would allow him to arrange his novel as an intertextual game à la conceptualist performance. Kenzheev encounters the same stylistic problem in his last novel, *Zoloto Goblinov*. Following the tenets of magic realism, he employs a realistic style to convey fantastic events. The novel tells about an émigré poet who collaborates with a gangster-controlled firm in order to support himself and also receive an opportunity to visit his home country, Russia. Finally, a crowd of deceived clients from the firm kills him. At the moment of his death, however, he stands tall above the crowd, clutching his lyre in his hands. Moralistic and Romantic passages of this kind destroy the conceptual design of the novel. An interview with Kenzheev follows the novel as an epilogue of sorts (it is titled "Posleslovie"). In it, the author explains that his novels should be perceived as a requiem for Russian spirituality and an impartial record of the new reality in which mass culture and material interest dominate human life.

In his concluding note to the collection *Iz semi knig* (2000) Sergei Sergeevich Averintsev defends Bakhyt

Shkurullaevich Kenzheev's adherence to the Russian classical poetic tradition. Indeed, Kenzheev's contribution to the contemporary literary process has helped develop a modernist cultural agenda of rethinking, reliving, and re-creating Russian, as well as a universal, cultural heritage.

Formally continuing to be a resident of Canada, Kenzheev, since the late 1990s, spends a significant part of his life in Russia, becoming an active and frequent figure in the Moscow cultural scene—one can see him at poetic readings, festivals, and conferences. His status in Russian literature of the last decade serves as living proof of the fallacy of such longstanding oppositions as the literature of emigration versus the literature of metropolia, or traditionalism versus experimentalism. Kenzheev successfully mediates between these formerly incompatible extremes. Kenzheev's ability to inscribe himself organically into the post-Soviet cultural context, across all the turmoil and shifts, proves once again the vitality of his poetic personality, based on the disregard for any categorization and restrictions, political or literary, as something opposite to freedom of self-expression.

Interviews:

Efim Bershin, "Chernogo kobelia ne otmoesh' do bela," *Literaturnaia gazeta,* 6 August 1997, p. 10;

"Poslanie: Neskol'ko voprosov Bakhytu Kenzheevu," *Oktiabr',* 12 (1998): 102–103.

Bibliography:

"Bakhyt Kenzheev," in *Slovar' poetov russkogo zarubezh'ia,* edited by Vadim Kreid (St. Petersburg: Russkii khristianskii gumanitarnyi institut, 1999), pp. 384–385.

References:

Tat'iana Aleksandrovna Bek, "I byl butonom kazhdyi atom . . . ," *Novyi mir,* 12 (1997);

Efim Bershin, "Bakhyt Kenzheev. *Stikhotvoreniia poslednikh let.* Izdatel'stvo 'P.S.,' 1992," *Literaturnaia gazeta,* 25 August 1993, pp. 4, 54–62;

Vasilii Betaki, "Dve s lishnim vechnosti nazad . . . ," in his *Russkaia poeziia za 30 let. 1956–1986* (Orange, Conn.: Antiquary, 1987), pp. 241–243;

Dmitrii Bobyshev, "Bakhyt Kenzheev i Prekrasnaia Dama," *Sintaksis,* 15 (1986): 200–204;

Vladimir Gubailovsky, "Dvor chudes," *Russkii zhurnal,* 27 June 2003;

Aleksandr Katsymov, "Gadanie po ogniu v antrakte i vo vremia filosofskogo seminara," *Znamia,* 11 (2000);

Kasymov, "Pis'ma, poluchennye po elektronnoi pochte, I rassuzhdeniia poluchatelia," *Voprosy literatury,* 6 (2001);

Aleksandr Kursky, "Bakhyt Kenzheev. *Zoloto goblinov // Oktiabr'.* 1998. No. 11–12," *Volga,* 3 (1999): 153–155;

Iurii Miloslavsky, "Khorosha, i legka, i nelepa . . . ," *Russkaia mysl'* (30 August 1985);

Aleksandr Radashkevich, "Bakhyt Kenzheev. Remeslo nedobrogo roka," *Strelets,* 12 (1985): 19–22;

Mariia Remizova, "Takoi priamoi aed: O romane Bakhyta Kenzheeva Portret khudozhnika v iunosti," *Literaturnaia gazeta,* 12 April 1995, p. 4;

Igor' Evgen'evich Vasil'ev, "Sopriazheniia (O poezii Bakhyta Kenzheeva)," *Ural,* 2 (2002);

Tat'iana Vol'tskaia, "Rozovatyi uzor zvukovoi," *Russkaia mysl',* 11 January 2001.

Evgenii Vladimirovich Kharitonov

(11 June 1941 – 29 June 1981)

Evgenii Bershtein
Reed College

BOOK: *Slezy na tsvetakh,* 2 volumes, edited, with an introduction, by Iaroslav Mogutin (Moscow: Glagol, 1993)–comprises volume 1, *Pod domashnim arestom;* and volume 2, *Dopolneniia i prilozheniia–* includes *Ocharovannyi ostrov.*

Editions in English: "Oven," translated by A. L. Tait, in *The Penguin Book of New Russian Writing: Russia's Fleurs du Mal,* edited by Victor Erofeev and Andrew Reynolds (London: Penguin, 1995), pp. 207–236;

"The Oven," "One Boy's Story: How I Got Like That," "Alyosha-Seryozha," and "The Leaflet," translated by Kevin Moss, in *Out of the Blue: Russia's Hidden Gay Literature: An Anthology,* edited by Moss (San Francisco: Gay Sunshine Press, 1996), pp. 197–225;

Under House Arrest, translated by Tait (London: Serpent's Tail, 1998)–includes "Alyosha Seryozha," "A., R., and I," "Teardrops on the Flowers," "Tears for the One Strangled and Dead," and "'How I Found Out': One Boy's Story";

Crossing Centuries: The New Generation in Russian Poetry, edited by John High and others, contributions by Kharitonov, translated by Sam Truitt, Vitaly Chernetsky, and Moss (Jersey City, N.J.: Talisman House, 2000), pp. 22–25, 340–348.

PLAY PRODUCTION: *Ocharovannyi ostrov,* Moscow, Theater of Mimicry and Gesture, 1972.

SELECTED PERIODICAL PUBLICATIONS– UNCOLLECTED: "Iz stikhov do 1969 goda," *Novoe literaturnoe obozrenie,* 3 (1993): 274–283;

"Pril'nu k slovam, v kotorykh–Bog . . . ," *Novaia russkaia kniga,* 6 (2000): 3–5.

Evgenii Vladimirovich Kharitonov (from Kharitonov's Slezy na tsvetakh, *1993; Amherst College Library)*

Evgenii Kharitonov's principal work is *Pod domashnim arestom* (Under House Arrest), a collection of prosaic and poetic texts written between 1969 and 1981 and published in book form only in 1993. While Kharitonov's work was a product of the 1970s, it was read only in the 1980s in emigration and, much more widely, in the 1990s in Russia. Kharitonov's prose influenced many contemporary writers and received an intense critical response when it was finally published in full in Russia in 1991 to 1993.

During his lifetime Kharitonov was known more as a man of the theater than as a writer. Evgenii Vladimirovich Kharitonov was born on 11 June 1941 in Novosibirsk and was brought up by his mother, Kseniia Ivanovna, who was a doctor. Kharitonov had great affection for her throughout his life, but he almost never showed his writings to her. In 1958 Kharitonov moved to Moscow to study acting at the All-Union State College of Cinematography, Vsesoiuznyi gosudarstvennyi institut kinematografii (VGIK), a leading Soviet film school. Following his graduation in 1964, he remained in the capital and embarked upon a modest career of teaching, acting, and stage directing. In the late 1960s and early 1970s Kharitonov taught courses on stage movement at VGIK, where he defended his doctoral thesis, "Pantomima v obuchenii kinoaktera" (Pantomime in the Instruction of Cinema Acting), in 1972. That same year he directed his pantomime play *Ocharovannyi ostrov* (Enchanted Island, published in *Slezy na tsvetakh* [Teardrops on the Flowers], 1993) for the Theater of Mimicry and Gesture, a company of deaf and mute actors. In the 1970s at Moscow State University, Kharitonov held a part-time position in the Department of Psychology, where he studied speech defects. He ran an amateur experimental theater, the School of Non-Traditional Stage Behavior, and from 1976 until the end of his life he choreographed the performances of the pop-music group Poslednii shans (Last Chance). While these and other semiofficial theatrical jobs and projects brought Kharitonov a certain renown in the Moscow theater world, he saw them as secondary to his true calling—writing.

Kharitonov could not publish in the Soviet Union. Toward the end of his life he made several unsuccessful attempts to reach readers outside of the narrow circles of those who had access to samizdat. In 1980 he participated in the independent writers' group "Klub belletristov" (The Fiction Writers' Club), which sought to publish experimental fiction without the approval of the authorities. A summons to the Komitet gosudarstvennoi bezopasnosti (KGB, State Security Committee) quickly followed, accompanied by police harassment. Such acts of intimidation, along with the threat of arrest, colored the last months of Kharitonov's life and possibly hastened its end. In order to publish *Pod domashnim arestom* abroad, he tried to enlist the assistance of the exiled writer Vasilii Pavlovich Aksenov, but the latter—disturbed by Kharitonov's subject matter—did not pursue the publication of the book. Kharitonov died on 29 June 1981. He was forty years old when he collapsed from a heart attack on Pushkin Street in Moscow. While *The New York Times* and some émigré periodicals marked his death with rather lengthy obituaries, his name meant nothing in the Soviet Union, even to the erudite reader of the time.

Being unpublished in their homeland was a natural condition for many Russian writers of Kharitonov's generation. Soviet censorship of the time, deeply suspicious of both literary experimentation and the slightest hints of political disloyalty, banned a majority of innovative writings from publication. There was a more fundamental reason, however, for Kharitonov's exclusion from the official literary world: his work treated as a theme relationships between men in the Moscow gay underground, the mere existence of which was denied by Soviet society. According to the official forensic line, homosexuality had disappeared in the Soviet Union along with the capitalist socio-economic conditions that had once produced it. Extremely rare cases of this "sexual disorder" could still be observed only as atavisms of the capitalist past. Under Article 121 of the Russian Criminal Code, male homosexuality was a crime punishable by imprisonment for up to five years. Not a single Soviet literary official in his right mind considered homosexual love a worthy subject for artistic exploration.

Kharitonov's professional milieu—the unofficial theatrical and literary scene in Moscow—was, not surprisingly, considerably more open-minded with regard to homosexuality than the Union of Soviet Writers or the Criminal Code. Still, even those writers who read and admired Kharitonov's work in samizdat form, and even admitted to being influenced by it, held their own reservations about his subject matter. In a 1981 samizdat review of *Pod domashnim arestom*, Kharitonov's good friend and fellow unpublished writer Evgenii Anatol'evich Popov expressed apprehension that Kharitonov's lyrical narrative could "scare off many readers" by its "deliberate shamelessness." Popov saw an element of reprehensible pride in Kharitonov's "physiological" description of gay love, as well as in his psychological analysis of, and metaphysical apology for, homosexuality. Suggesting that *Pod domashnim arestom* might benefit from the addition of a note of self-distancing irony, Popov noted, in reference to the West: "to, chto stalo tam [na Zapade] normoi, u nas normoi eshche dolgo ne stanet ili ne stanet nikogda. Ne tot klimat . . ." (That which has become the norm will not become the norm here for a long time if ever at all. The climate here is different . . .).

Popov's prediction turned out to be shortsighted. With censorship abandoned after 1991 and Article 121 dropped in 1993, Russian gay culture began rapidly to form its own institutions: there appeared gay-oriented literary journals, such as *Mitin zhurnal* (Mitia's Journal, based in St. Petersburg), which circulated in samizdat from 1985 to 1993 and has been in print officially since

Kharitonov with his mother, Kseniia Ivanovna, and his dog, Druzhok, in Novosibirsk, early 1950s
(*from* Slezy na tsvetakh, *1993; Amherst College Library*)

1993, and *Risk,* a Moscow-based periodical in circulation since 1995; gay-oriented publishing houses, such as Glagol; and websites that address gay life in Russia. Prominent writers and poets, including Aleksandr Shatalov, Iaroslav Mogutin, Dmitrii Volchek, and Aleksandr Il'ianen publicly identified themselves as gay men. Now the Russian Parliament even features a faction of flamboyantly gay deputies, who call themselves "The Generation of Freedom." The representatives of the emerging gay literary culture made a conscious and well-coordinated effort to establish a gay Russian literary canon. In the 1990s they not only collected, edited, and published Kharitonov's work but also affirmed his reputation as a classic gay Russian writer, second only to Mikhail Alekseevich Kuzmin, a poet who lived from 1872 to 1936.

That Kharitonov has been assigned the role of a gay icon in the Russia of today is both logical and surprising: logical, in that he has become widely respected as a writer of genius, one whose artistic identity integrated homosexuality as an all-important element; and surprising, because his vision of homosexuality could not be more at odds with the current, mainstream, Western-influenced ideology of gay equality. Kharitonov was following the development of this ideology in the West and, from what he knew of it, found it all too naive and disappointingly superficial. In "Listovka" (Leaflet, published in *Slezy na tsvetakh*), his gay manifesto, Kharitonov declares his understanding of "kosnaia moral' nashego Russkogo Sovetskogo Otechestva" (the stagnant morality of our Russian Soviet Fatherland). Paradoxically, he considers the refusal of the state to permit the visibility of gays to be a wise measure. In fact, he sees in it the state's admission of the utmost metaphysical danger of homosexuality—"chem my budem zametnee, tem blizhe Konets Sveta" (the more visible we are, the closer the End of the World). Rejecting the rationalist liberal interpretation of homosexuality as just another case of innocent human diversity, Kharitonov sees gay men as a secret apocalyptic sect of beauty worshipers who engage in an "ezhednevnye liubovnye poiski" (daily searches for love). Furthermore, he questions, "Zapadnyi zakon pozvoliaet nashim tsvetam otkrytye vstrechi, priamoi pokaz nas v khudozhestve, kluby, skhodki i zaiavleniia prav—no kakikh? i na chto?" (Western law allows our flowers open meetings, a direct showing of us in art, clubs, gatherings, and declarations of rights—but what rights? and rights to what?). For Kharitonov, gay desire is to incarnate absolute beauty, and therefore it is unfulfillable, tragic, and socially destructive; no political rights can free gay men from this existential burden. They are doomed to pain, contempt, and marginality in this world, but they will be redeemed by God in the next one, where "luchshikh iz nashikh iunykh pogibshikh sozdanii on posadit k sebe blizhe vsekh" (the best of our young perished creatures He will seat closest to Himself).

Kharitonov interprets the existential situation of a writer-poet as akin to that of a homosexual, and this makes his own homosexuality even more crucial to his artistic identity. As both writer and homosexual are led by an all-consuming drive to incarnate beauty and thus partake of the divine, they both are martyrs in the service of this impossible and holy task. While the resulting literary texts cannot reach this goal, they can chronicle every minute detail of the attempt to reach it. Kharitonov was deeply influenced by the Russian symbolist tradition, especially by Kuzmin and Vasilii Vasil'evich Rozanov, as well as by the theologian Pavel Aleksandrovich Florensky. Ideologically, the impact of these modernist writers on Kharitonov can be felt in his mystical and aesthete interpretation of homosexuality. In terms of poetics, he was particularly indebted to Rozanov's stylistic experimentation: following Rozanov, he employed the subgenre of the short prosaic note, both intensely personal and highly literary. Kharitonov compiled these notes into the cycles (all from *Pod domashnim arestom* and published in *Slezy na tsvetakh*) "Slezy na tsvetakh" (translated as "Teardrops on the Flowers," 1998), "V kholodnom vysshem smysle" (translated as "In the Cold Higher Sense," 1998), and "Slezy ob ubitom i zadushennom" (translated as "Tears for the One Strangled and Dead," 1998). Thematically, these notes focus on the main narrator's search for love and his labor in creating his own verbal "ornament," one that will be original and moving. Kharitonov's protagonist also shares with the reader shocking descriptions of his sexual experiences, his erotic daydreaming, and his fascination with the aesthetic grandeur of the Soviet Empire. He communicates minute humiliations and rejections, literary impressions, and thoughts about the metaphysical role of Jews in Russia (these thoughts have a strong, though stylized, anti-Semitic flavor; they seem at least in part to be a literary tribute to Rozanov's notorious Judeophobia). Employing first-person colloquial speech, Kharitonov experiments with various forms of *skaz,* a type of narrative that usually marks the speaking subject as distinctly different from the author. In Kharitonov's texts, narrators range from clearly fictional to lyrical, yet they all display an existentially and socially marginal consciousness. Besides the main autobiographic hero, a variety of young gay characters express themselves in his texts, often telling their lives in their own idiom (for instance, in "Rasskaz odnogo mal'chika – 'Kak ia stal takim,'" published in *Slezy na*

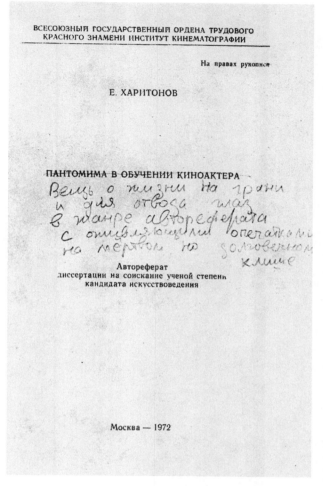

Title page for Kharitonov's dissertation abstract. He crossed out the title, "Pantomima v obuchenii kinoaktera" (Pantomime in the Instruction of Cinema Acting), and wrote: "A work about life on the edge, masked by the genre of a dissertation abstract, with animating typos on a dead but long-lasting cliché" (from Slezy na tsvetakh, 1993; Amherst College Library)

tsvetakh; translated as "'How I Found Out': One Boy's Story," 1998).

Kharitonov started writing poetry in the 1960s but found his own, deeply original voice only in 1969 with the short story "Dukhovka" (The Oven, published in *Slezy na tsvetakh*). Eleven years later he began *Pod domashnim arestom* with this text. "Dukhovka" tells the story of the narrator's infatuation and fleeting friendship with Misha, a handsome teenage boy whom he meets at a provincial summer resort. As the hero moves from a nearby city to the resort and from his own summer house to that of Misha's family—all in pursuit of the boy—his speech also circles around secret yet impractical plans for Misha's seduction or, at least, plans for becoming closer friends with him.

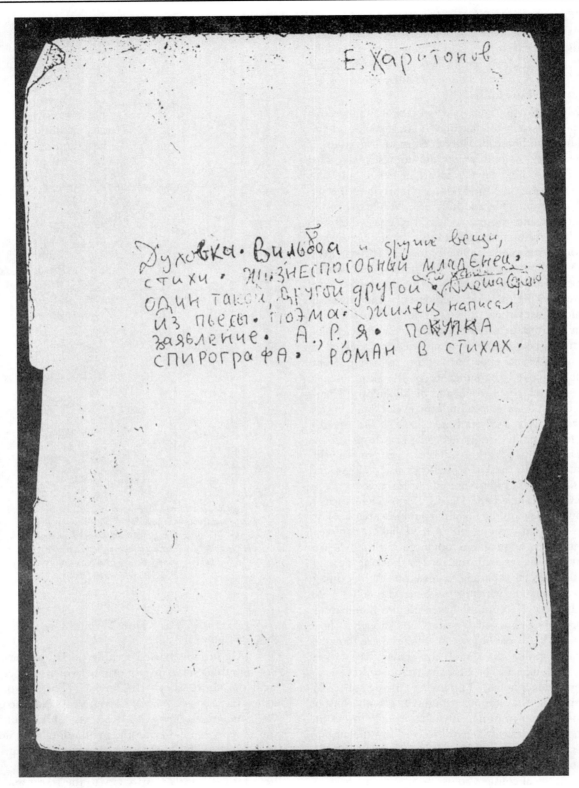

Title page of the manuscript for Kharitonov's principal work, Pod domashnim arestom *(Under House Arrest, 1993), a collection of prose and poetry written between 1969 and 1981 (from Slezy na tsvetakh, 1993; Amherst College Library)*

Either goal is utterly impossible, for the invisible wall that divides the narrator from Misha is not limited to the apparent incompatibility of their erotic inclinations. The hero, a Moscow intellectual in his late twenties, cannot penetrate the schoolboy's cultural and linguistic universe. He cannot make himself interesting at all to Misha, whose beauty is exceptional–he is "one in a hundred thousand."

"Dukhovka" elaborates upon an ancient theme of attraction: that of the developed mind for the perfect youthful body. Yet, the Platonic mutual gravitation of wisdom and beauty never takes place in Kharitonov's story. Embodied in Misha, beauty is self-contained, unknowing, and entirely inaccessible, while the narrator's intellect similarly bears little resemblance to Socratic wisdom. Incessantly immersed in cold reasoning and plotting, the protagonist never finds an adequate verbal outlet for his passion. Unable to let his love be known to Misha or any other new acquaintances, he is obsessed with endless calculations and analyses of his and Misha's actions; with how others perceive those actions; and with maintaining the secrecy of his own motives. Drawing more on Fyodor Dostoevsky's *Zapiski iz podpol'ia* (1864; translated as *Notes from the Underground,* 1913) than on Thomas Mann's *Der Tod in Venedig* (1912; translated as *Death in Venice,* 1925) or Vladimir Nabokov's *Lolita* (1955), "Dukhovka" presents an obsessive consciousness through obsessive forms of speech. Its haunted storytelling imitates the colloquial narration of events that have just happened. Such a narrative style lends an effect of breathlessness to the speaking subject. By portraying the narrator as someone who tells the story as if on the verge of suffocation, Kharitonov relays the constant presence of an inner wound in a hero who has become so accustomed to mental pain that it forms his normal, strangely enjoyable condition.

In two of his finest short stories, "Alesha Serezha" (published in *Slezy na tsvetakh;* translated as "Alyosha Seryozha," 1998) and "A., R., Ia" (also in *Slezy na tsvetakh;* translated as "A., R., and I," 1998), Kharitonov analyzes the psychological dynamic of love through an autobiographical narrator who is driven by the simultaneous desires to possess, dominate, and outwit his beloved. In search of endless love and unconditional submission, the hero of the stories stages and chronicles cruel psychological experiments that involve his lovers and friends. Seeking impossible love, he anatomizes his every actual love affair and puts extreme pressure upon them until he sees fracture. His pleasure is not in love but in "singing about love" like a singer does: "kogda ona poet o liubvi i vse vliubleny v nee za to kak poet, a liubit ona tol'ko pet'" (everyone is in love with her for her singing but she loves only to sing). In Kharitonov, an artistic act is an ideal substitute and metaphor for love.

While treating metaphysical questions, Kharitonov fills his texts with affectionate references to Soviet popular and material culture of the 1970s. He finds beauty in the facades of the seemingly eternal and unchangeable Empire, perceives wisdom in its laws, and detects harmony in its institutions. Destined to be an admiring outsider, he graphically marks the marginality of some of his texts by preserving his typewritten errors and corrections. In his 1995 essay "The Last Unprintable Writer," Shatalov pointed out the importance of "hand typing" to Kharitonov's project: "Kharitonov was a practitioner of artistic typing, if that makes sense: the alphabetical letters in his texts undulate or jump about at their author's behest; paragraphs are assembled into whimsical patterns; while the punctuation has a mind of its own and visits the text almost wantonly." Kharitonov's texts are hard to typeset, for they were never meant for print in both a literal and figurative sense. Rather, they were designed to become monuments to marginality, both social and artistic.

Some twelve years after his death, fame finally and momentously arrived for Evgenii Vladimirovich Kharitonov. Although when he was alive he saw his potential future audience as a small circle of the initiated, in the early 1990s his texts appeared in the mass-circulation media. Hungry for sensationalist material, Russian newspapers and magazines, including *Nezavisimaia gazeta* (The Independent Gazette), *Stolitsa* (The Capital), and even the extreme nationalist *Den'* (The Day), published Kharitonov's major texts, provoking loud critical controversy and public scandal. In 1993 Glagol released a two-volume edition of his texts, edited by Mogutin. From this edition Kharitonov's works have been translated into major European languages, studied by literary scholars, and anthologized both in Russia and in the West. Glagol has plans to publish a new critical edition of Kharitonov's complete works, prepared by Gleb Morev. Despite Kharitonov's many posthumous publications in the print media, however, the Internet has made him far more accessible to a wide, if self-selected, audience. To the displeasure of some mainstream critics, who admire his writing and wish to see him recognized within the national literary canon, Kharitonov has found his literary reputation and readership in Russian gay Web portals, where his work is posted and discussed under the category of "classic gay literature."

Bibliography:

Iaroslav Mogutin, "Bibliografiia Evgeniia Kharitonova," in Kharitonov's *Slezy na tsvetakh,* 2 volumes, edited by Mogutin (Moscow: Glagol, 1993), II: 205–206.

Biographies:

Aleksandr N. Shatalov, "Kharitonov Evgenii Vladimirovich," in *Russkie pisateli 20 veka: Biograficheskii slovar',* edited by Petr Alekseevich Nikolaev (Moscow: Bol'shaia Rossiiskaia Entsiklopediia, 2000), pp. 722–723;

Kevin Moss, "Kharitonov, Yevgeny," in *Who's Who in Contemporary Gay and Lesbian History: From World War II to the Present Day,* edited by Robert Aldrich and Garry Wotherspoon (London & New York: Routledge, 2001), pp. 225–226.

References:

Vasilii Pavlovich Aksenov, "Evgenii Kharitonov – podpol'nyi zhitel' Moskvy," in Kharitonov's *Slezy na tsvetakh,* 2 volumes, edited by Iaroslav Mogutin (Moscow: Glagol, 1993), II: 93–101;

Vitaly Chernetsky, "After the House Arrest: Russian Gay Poetry," in *Crossing Centuries: The New Generation in Russian Poetry,* edited by John High and others (Jersey City, N.J.: Talisman House, 2000), pp. 315–323;

Aleksandr Goldshtein, "Slezy na tsvetakh," *Novoe literaturnoe obozrenie,* 3 (1993): 259–264;

Nikolai Klimontovich, "Uedinennoe slovo," in Kharitonov's *Slezy na tsvetakh,* 2 volumes, edited by Mogutin (Moscow: Glagol, 1993), II: 108–115;

Evgenii Popov, "Kus ne po zubam: rassuzhdeniia o knige Evg. Kharitonova 'Pod domashnim arestom,' napisannye iskliuchitel'no v tseliakh lituicheby, no otniud' ne dlia rasprostraneniia," in Kharitonov's *Slezy na tsvetakh,* 2 volumes, edited by Mogutin (Moscow: Glagol, 1993), II: 102–105;

Kirill Rogov, "'Nevozmozhnoe slovo' i ideia stilia," *Novoe literaturnoe obozrenie,* 3 (1993): 265–273;

Serge Schmemann, "Yevgeny Kharitonov Dies at 40, Was Nonconformist Soviet Writer," *New York Times,* 6 July 1981, p. D7;

Aleksandr Shatalov, "The Last Unprintable Writer," *Index on Censorship,* 24 (January–February 1995): 54–57.

Mark Sergeevich Kharitonov

(31 August 1937 –   )

Nina Kolesnikoff
McMaster University

BOOKS: *Den' v fevrale* (Moscow: Sovetskii pisatel',
1988)–includes *Den' v fevrale;* "Muzei v Neche-
iske"; *Prokhor Men'shutin; Etiud o maskakh;* and *Dva
Ivana;*

Etiud o maskakh (Khar'kov: Folio, 1994);

Izbrannaia proza, 2 volumes (Moscow: Moskovskii rabochii, 1994)–comprises volume 1–includes *Golosa;
Linii sud'by, ili Sunduchok Milashevicha,* translated by
Helena Goscilo as *Lines of Fate,* with an introduction by Goscilo (New York: New Press, 1996);
and volume 2–includes *Storozh;* and "Agasfer,"
translated by Arch Tait as "Ahasuerus," in *Booker
Winners and Others II,* New Russian Writing, volume 10 (Moscow: GLAS, 1996), pp. 6–11;

Sposob sushchestvovaniia (Moscow: Novoe literaturnoe
obozrenie, 1998)–includes "Uchast'";

Vozvrashchenie niotkuda (Moscow: Vagrius, 1998)–
includes *Prokhor Men'shutin, Vozvrashchenie niotkuda,*
and *Provintsial'naia filosofiia;*

Amores novi, with drawings by Galina Edel'man (Moscow: Novoe literaturnoe obozrenie, 2000);

Stenografiia kontsa veka, with illustrations by Edel'man
(Moscow: Novoe literaturnoe obozrenie, 2002);

Uchitel' vran'ia (Moscow: Novoe literaturnoe obozrenie,
2003).

TRANSLATIONS: Hermann Hesse, "Palomnichestvo
Germana Gessa v stranu Vostoka," in *Vostok-
Zapad* (Moscow: Nauka, 1982);

Stefan Zweig, *Triumf i tragediia Erazma Rotterdamskogo*
(Moscow: Khudozhestvennaia literatura, 1984);

Pis'ma po krugu (Moscow: Progress, 1987);

Elias Canetti, "Peremigivanie," "Golosa Marrakesha,"
and "Massa i vlast'" (Moscow: Progress, 1990);

Thomas Mann, "Stradaia Germaniei: Dnevniki 1933–
1936 godov," *Inostrannaia literatura,* no. 1 (1992):
221–230;

Sigmund Freud, "Avtobiografiia," *Zigmund Freid: Po tu
storonu udovol'stviia* (Moscow: Progress, 1994);

Sobranie sochinenii, volumes 6, 8 (Moscow: Progress,
1995);

*Mark Sergeevich Kharitonov (photograph by Galina Edel'man;
courtesy of the author)*

Franz Kafka, "Pis'ma 1902–1924," in *Sochinenia,* volume
3 (Moscow: Progress, 1994);

Mann and Karl Kezényi, "Razgovor v pis'makh,"
Voprosy literatury, 5 (1999): 165–195.

SELECTED PERIODICAL PUBLICATIONS–
UNCOLLECTED: "Vremena zhizni," *Znamia,* 9
(1996): 56–92;

Priblizhenie, Druzhba narodov, 4 (1998): 6–76; 10 (1998);
"Konveer," *Druzhba narodov,* 11 (2000): 7–48;
"Glaz Khudozhnika," *Znamia,* 6 (2003).

In 1992 Mark Kharitonov was awarded the first Booker Russian Novel Prize for his novel, *Linii sud'by, ili Sunduchok Milashevicha* (1994; translated as *Lines of Fate,* 1996). He had made his literary debut many years earlier, in 1976, but subsequently was banned from print until 1988. Since the period of glasnost he has published several volumes of fiction and essays and established himself as one of the most important Russian writers of the late twentieth century. Translations of his selected works have appeared in the Czech Republic, France, Germany, Holland, Japan, Portugal, Sweden, and the United States.

Mark Sergeevich Kharitonov was born on 31 August 1937 in the Ukrainian town of Zhitomir, where his mother, Faina Lamberg–driven from Moscow in fear of the purges by Joseph Stalin–had moved to give birth. Both of Kharitonov's parents came from Jewish families who lived near the town of Vinnitsa in Ukraine. His father, Sergei, moved to Moscow in 1929, and following his service in the army in Ukraine, he returned to the capital with his new wife. He finished a program in the Forestry Technical School and worked his entire life in the lumber industry as a paper mill worker. Initially, Kharitonov's parents lived in a communal barrack near a paper mill on the outskirts of Moscow, but in 1938 they moved to a small house built overnight on a piece of property next to cement and enamel factories. Kharitonov remembers his childhood as a happy one, despite its bleak physical and cultural environment. He speaks with admiration about his family's old-fashioned values of hard work, honesty, and goodness, which were instilled in him and his two younger brothers, Leonid and Iuriis from a young age.

Kharitonov has vague memories of World War II. He recalls bomb shelters with their dim lights and a sensation of dust, as well as women carrying gas for barrage balloons. He remembers more vividly the sight of German prisoners of war and his feeling of pity toward them. Shortly after the war, Kharitonov's family moved to the Belorussian town of Dobrush, where his father was transferred. The family returned to Moscow in the late 1940s. As a boy and then a teenager, Kharitonov attended primary and secondary school in Moscow and, like his contemporaries, was subjected to intense ideological indoctrination.

Upon graduation from secondary school, Kharitonov attended Moscow Pedagogical Institute and majored in Russian language and literature. In his essay "Uchast'" (Fate), first published in *Sposob sushchestvovaniia* (A Mode of Existence) in 1998, Kharitonov comments on the fact that the institute was a safe place for many politically suspect professors and students. One of his professors was Aleksei Fedorovich Losev, a respected philosopher and scholar of ancient philology who had been demoted to teaching Latin to undergraduate students during the postwar purges of formalist academics. At the institute Kharitonov met several people who became some of his closest friends, including Il'ia Iankelevich Gabai, a dissident poet who committed suicide in 1973, to whom Kharitonov dedicated "Uchast'." In the essay, Kharitonov acknowledges the paramount importance of their friendship, which was for him a source of support and moral guidance during times of terribly difficult decisions.

Following graduation from the institute he worked as a secondary-school teacher and later as an executive secretary at the newspaper *Leninets* (The Leninist). Between the years 1960 and 1969 he worked as an editor at the publishing house Vysshaia shkola (Higher Education), which specialized in publishing textbooks and materials for university students. He quit this job in 1969 to devote himself to writing fiction and translating German literture into Russian. In 1964 Kharitonov married Galina Edel'man, a graphic artist and a mathematician who completed her graduate studies at Moscow Pedagogical Institute and was teaching math in high schools and colleges. Edel'man has also illustrated several of Kharitonov's books, including *Sposob sushchestvovaniia, Amores novi* (New Loves, 2000) and *Stenografiia kontsa veka* (Stenography at the End of the Century, 2002). The couple have three children, Aleksei (born in 1965), Tat'iana (born in 1969), and Elena (born in 1978).

Kharitonov's first literary work was a novella, *Prokhor Men'shutin,* written in 1971 but published in 1988 in his book *Den' v fevrale* (A Day in February). For his first fictional work Kharitonov chose as a protagonist the figure of an eccentric artist who dedicates his entire life to the theater. As the director of a cultural center in a small provincial town, Prokhor Men'shutin is not satisfied with the usual amateur activities. As a result, he undertakes a live production of the fairy tale *Cinderella,* staging it as a masquerade ball in the city park and involving all the townspeople in the various parts of the play; his adopted daughter, Zoia, assumes the title role. So obsessed is Men'shutin with his project that he marries a widow with two daughters, these three representing a perfect match for their roles as Cinderella's stepmother and stepsisters. While he succeeds in staging a live performance of *Cinderella,* this grand event turns into a tragedy when one of Zoia's suitors drowns, and Men'shutin himself dies. Despite its unhappy ending, the novella affirms the paramount importance of art and glorifies the figure of an artist

Paperback covers for volumes 1 and 2 of Kharitonov's Izbrannaia proza *(Selected Prose, 1994), in which many of his early works were published for the first time (Collection of Nina Kolesnikoff)*

totally dedicated to his vision. On a narrative level *Prokhor Men'shutin* exhibits many features that later became typical of Kharitonov's prose writing. The story is told by an external omniscient narrator who relies primarily on description to convey the plot and characters. It has little dialogue or reported speech, except for some crucial moments captured in the form of direct exchanges between characters. Stylistically, the narrative adheres to a sophisticated literary language characterized by a refined vocabulary and complex syntactic structures. Overall, the novella is written in the realistic tradition that influenced almost all of Kharitonov's fiction writing in his early period.

　　In 1972 Kharitonov wrote his second novella, *Etiud o maskakh* (Etude on Masks), also first published in *Den' v fevrale.* As in his first novella, Kharitonov places in the center of his narrative the figure of a creative personality. The protagonist of the novella, Gleb Skvortsov, is a writer known for his short miniatures and sketches, but he aspires to write a multilayered

book on the subject of masks. Short fragments of that book are inserted into the novella to demonstrate Skvortsov's ideas as well as to signal some mysterious connection between his work and the events taking place in his life. The novella is divided into two parts: part 1 depicts Skvortsov's childhood and his life as a writer, and part 2 focuses on his acquaintance with Tsezar Sleptsov, a mask maker from a nearby town. The first part is sustained in a realistic manner, whereas the second introduces elements of the fantastic in the mysterious figure of the mask maker, his unusual habitat, and a series of bizarre occurrences following his encounters with Gleb and his friends. Many of the thematic and stylistic features of the novella are reminiscent of Nikolai Vasil'evich Gogol, a writer whom Kharitonov greatly admired and who inspired him to write *Den' v fevrale.*

　　Kharitonov wrote his novella *Den' v fevrale* in 1974, and it appeared two years later in the prestigious Soviet journal *Novyi mir* (New World). Unlike his earlier fiction set in a contemporary period, *Den' v fevrale* is an historical novella and thus depicts events that take place in the past. Its plot is restricted to one February day in 1837, and it is set in the carnival streets of Paris. For his protagonist, Kharitonov chose the figure of Gogol, who was in Paris in February of 1837 and, while there, had learned about the death of Aleksandr Sergeevich Pushkin. Although he draws on biographical facts from Gogol's life, Kharitonov focuses his attention partly on the inner world of his protagonist, who suffers from hypochondria, insecurity, and, most of all, deeply felt trauma caused by the news of Pushkin's death. In addition to choosing Gogol as the main protagonist of the novella, Kharitonov incorporates several Gogolian devices in the narrative, including the fantastic, the imaginary, and the leitmotiv of the double. In the central two sections of the novella the narrative depicts Gogol in a restaurant conversing with an impostor who introduces himself as Gogol and later with the figure of a thin man who appears to be the double's double. The narrative does not draw a clear line between actual happenings and imaginary events, or between a sober perception of reality and a distorted view caused by intoxication. *Den' v fevrale* is distinguished by remarkable narrative diversity. Kharitonov juxtaposes long, descriptive passages with dialogue, reproducing the direct speech of the characters and the interior monologue of the protagonist. A pronounced stylistic diversity is also present, one that combines highly sophisticated language with colloquial speech, puns, and alliteration. So closely does *Den' v fevrale* imitate the stylistic peculiarities of Gogol's prose that it justifiably could be called a Gogolian stylization.

Den' v fevrale remains the only work by Kharitonov that appeared in print before glasnost. It appeared in book form in 1988. Faced with continuous rejection of his works by editors of literary journals and by publishers, Kharitonov persisted in writing for "the drawer," which in Soviet terminology meant writing for the sake of writing without any hope of seeing manuscripts published. He also turned his attention to literary translation and rendered into Russian the works of some twentieth-century German, Swiss, and Austrian writers, including Elias Canetti, Stefan Zweig, Thomas Mann, Hermann Hesse, and Franz Kafka.

In 1977 Kharitonov wrote a novella, *Provintsial'naia filosofiia* (A Provincial Philosophy), intended as the second part of a trilogy with the same title. The novella was not published until 1993, when it appeared in *Novyi mir*, one year after *Linii sud'by, ili Sunduchok Milashevicha*, which Kharitonov had designated as the concluding part of the trilogy. The three works are linked in terms of setting (it is the same for all of them) and character (some secondary characters reappear throughout the works). The central protagonist of *Provintsial'naia filosofiia* is Anton Lizavin, a young scholar with a Ph.D. in Russian literature who is conducting research on some minor writers from the Nechaisk area. The plot centers on some crucial moments in Lizavin's life: his accidental meeting with a wandering philosopher, Maks Sivers; the death of Lizavin's father; and his involvement with Zoia, the adopted daughter of Men'shutin. On a narrative level, Kharitonov continues to rely on the device of the omniscient narrator but combines this approach with the technique of a selected point of view—that of Lizavin. Though not an internal monologue per se, the narrative closely captures the protagonist's perception of reality and his evaluation of events and characters. It maintains the same description-oriented narrative and the same slow pace as the first part of the trilogy, which are perfectly fitting for works extolling the slow pace of provincial life.

In 1980 Kharitonov interrupted his work on the trilogy to write his second historical novella, *Dva Ivana* (Two Ivans), which was published in *Den' v fevrale*. The two Ivans of the title are Ivan Groznyi (Ivan the Terrible)—the infamous tsar—and Ivan Bespamiatnyi (Ivan the Forgetful), a wandering fool who does not know his name or the place of his origin. *Dva Ivana* depicts the most significant events from the lives of the two Ivans. In the case of Ivan Groznyi, these episodes include his staged departure from Moscow and his self-imposed exile in a monastery, followed by his return and his iron-fisted rule, aimed to crush any real or imaginary opposition. As for Ivan Bespamiatnyi, the novella portrays him first as a companion to the monk Makary, then as a member of a wandering group of minstrels, and finally as the monster Ivan Nagoi (Ivan the Naked), who dares to collect and bury the corpses of Ivan Groznyi's victims. Of the two story lines, the one that tells about Ivan Bespamiatnyi is clearly the centerpiece of the narrative, and thus the figure of a fool is the main character of the novella. By placing the story of a fairy-tale character at the center of the narrative, Kharitonov subverts the conventions of the historical novel, which is traditionally preoccupied with important historical figures or heroes. He follows the fairy-tale tradition in constructing the plot, which involves unexpected turns of events, mistaken identities, and a sudden confrontation of characters that leads to violent deaths. The narrative of *Dva Ivana* is distinguished by a fragmentary composition and a disregard for strict chronology and logic. The plot is constructed not on the basis of sequential events but rather on the free movement between different events and characters. Most of the narrative follows a descriptive mode with extremely little direct or reported speech. Conversely, some sections rely exclusively on dialogue, thus creating a sharp con-

Dust jacket for the English-language edition (1996) of Kharitonov's Linii sud'by, ili Sunduchok Milashevicha, *which appeared initially in the journal* Druzhba narodov *(The People's Friendship) in 1992 (Richland County Public Library)*

trast between the general narrative flow and the dramatic moments that drastically change the turn of events.

Between the years 1981 and 1985 Kharitonov worked on his novel, *Linii sud'by, ili Sunduchok Milashevicha,* which was first published in 1992 in the journal *Druzhba narodov* (The People's Friendship). In this concluding part of the trilogy, Kharitonov continues the story line of Anton Lizavin, introduced in *Provintsial'naia filosofiia,* but intertwines it with a second line, that of the forgotten writer Simeon Milashevich. Using the age-old device of a found manuscript–in this case, actually a series of notes and fragments written on the back of candy wrappers–Kharitonov constructs a complex narrative with several subplots as well as a wealth of secondary texts inserted into the novel, in the form of Milashevich's notes and passages from his texts, as well as memoirs and diaries of some secondary characters. The focus of this complex narrative is on the process of reconstruction undertaken by the researcher in order to capture the meaning of Milashevich's life and work and

ultimately of his provincial philosophy, which is defined not by geographic boundaries but by a spiritual realm and a way of life based on balance and harmony and a striving for a simple family happiness. The implications of Milashevich's philosophy are particularly striking in the context of 1920s Soviet reality and its emphasis on the inevitability of change and the need to renounce personal well-being for the benefit of society. The novel reaffirms the idea of a spiritual kinship and the preservation of spiritual values from one generation to another by portraying a strong affinity between Milashevich and his researcher, Lizavin. This affinity, however, presupposes a dialogical reinterpretation of some of Milashevich's ideas on the part of Lizavin, who has to find his own answers regarding the meaning of life and the role of art and creativity in that process.

With its multilevel structure and the themes of literary creativity and literary interpretation, *Linii sud'by, ili Sunduchok Milashevicha* is a perfect example of a metafictional text that centers on the process of fiction writing and displays the constructed nature of fictional

Front cover, illustrated by Kharitonov's wife, Galina Edel'man, for his Sposob sushchestvovaniia *(A Mode of Existence, 1998), a book of essays and reminiscences about his publishing difficulties in the 1970s and 1980s (courtesy of the author)*

texts. The narrative abounds with overt metafictional comments on the nature of fiction writing, the tenuous links between biography and fictional texts, and the challenges inherent in an act of literary interpretation. In terms of its overall narrative method, *Linii sud'by, ili Sunduchok Milashevicha* exhibits many characteristics of the realist tradition, including a detailed description of the setting of provincial Russia before and after the October Revolution. But the novel also departs from the realist tradition by dispensing with linear organization and logic and creating a circular composition based on repetitions and returns. Stylistically, Kharitonov continues to rely on description rather than on reported action or direct verbal exchanges. This technique is responsible for creating the slow narrative flow so characteristic of his fiction in general.

Winner of the first Booker Russian Novel Prize, *Linii sud'by, ili Sunduchok Milashevicha* brought Khari-

tonov well-deserved recognition in his country and abroad. Following the appearance of this novel, he was able to publish his earlier works in the two-volume *Izbrannaia proza* (Selected Prose, 1994), in which a later text, the cycle of short stories *Golosa* (Voices), also appeared. In addition, other novellas were published in periodicals, such as *Vozvrashchenie niotkuda* (Return from Nowhere), which appeared in *Znamia* (The Banner) in 1995; *Vremena zhizni* (Seasons of Life), published in 1996 also in *Znamia;* and *Priblizhenie* (Convergence), which came out in *Druzhba narodov* in 1998. All of Kharitonov's later works combine realism with the fantastic, producing a large measure of indeterminacy and ambiguity.

A combination of the realistic and the fantastic is evident in the novella *Storozh* (A Guard), written in 1988 and published in the 1994 edition of Kharitonov's *Izbrannaia proza. Storozh* begins in a realistic manner by depicting the circumstances surrounding the protagonist's return to his native town and his work at a secret research project, enigmatically named "The Site." The narrative introduces many realistic details related to the project, such as the flooding of the upper town and the emergence of a new town with its special status and privileges. It juxtaposes these realistic details, however, with things that are highly unusual or fantastic, such as the presence of a strange egg-shaped object immersed in water, its consumption of extraordinary amounts of energy, and an unknown substance produced by this same object and used as a miraculous cure for various ailments. In addition to these unusual phenomena, the narrative introduces hallucinations and dreams without marking transitions between these different narrative levels. One may read these sections as fictional texts created by a secondary character, Igor Chernobaev, who is introduced in the story as a researcher and an author of science fiction. This interpretation, however, does not remove the ambiguity of the shifting layers of reality and leaves one perplexed as to how to read and interpret the text.

Much ambiguity is also inherent in *Golosa* and *Vozvrashchenie niotkuda.* The ambiguity results from the subversion of a recognizable atmosphere of familiar places and routine activities by some inexplicable occurrences, as well as by the insertion of dreams and hallucinations into an otherwise realistic narrative. *Golosa* and *Vozvrashchenie niotkuda* mark a drastic departure from Kharitonov's earlier fiction in terms of their narrative techniques. Unlike his earlier works written from the point of view of an omniscient narrator, these later stories employ internal narrators who tell their tales in the first person singular. Besides their common technique of first-person narration oriented toward oral speech, the stories have several features in common.

First, they all assign the role of storyteller to highly unusual characters who bring with them some distinctive perspectives and new ways of seeing and interpreting events. Second, this distinctive perspective is linked with mental instability, ranging from retardation to a full-blown mental disorder. Many of the stories and large segments of *Vozvrashchenie niotkuda* depict the setting of a mental asylum, while others strongly suggest the possibility of considering the storytellers as mental patients. This unusual perspective is used by Kharitonov to portray some absurdities of Soviet and post-Soviet reality, including the work of the Komitet gosudarstvennoi bezopasnosti (KGB, State Security Committee). Whereas most of the stories in *Golosa* rely on a single narrative voice, *Vozvrashchenie niotkuda* captures the voices of several major characters. In addition to the predominant voice of the central narrator conveyed in the form of an extended internal monologue, *Vozvrashchenie niotkuda* incorporates the voices of other characters, most notably a psychiatrist who is treating the narrator, the narrator's parents, and some KGB officials. Significantly, all of these voices are filtered through the consciousness of the central narrator, who reports them as part of his real or imaginary conversations. The overall effect produced by these texts is that of bewilderment and uncertainty. Unable to distinguish clearly between the real and the imaginary—between actual happenings and hallucinations—the reader becomes unsure of how to interpret and respond to the events narrated in the texts.

The novella *Priblizhenie* places in the center of the narrative the figure of a fictional writer who explores metafictional issues concerning the relationship between fiction and reality, the author and his characters, and the writer and his readers. Outwardly, the novella follows the formula of a journey by depicting the protagonist undertaking a trip to an unknown destination to attend the funeral of a namesake who had earlier invited him to collaborate on a literary project. The trip turns into a series of nightmarish encounters that resemble the plot of an adventure novel, with sudden and unexpected turns of events, violent acts, and deaths. At the same time the narrative seems to emulate the principles of a computer game in which the protagonist tries to outsmart his adversaries in order to save his life. As in a computer game, the novella unfolds on several narrative levels, each presenting new obstacles that have to be overcome before the protagonist can proceed to the next level. The similarity between the narrative and a computer game is strengthened by the fact that most of the events, which have been framed initially in a realistic manner, turn out to be unreal and illusory. The narrative keeps the tension between the real and the virtual realms unresolved and leaves it up to the reader to decide how to understand the text.

Kharitonov's fictional texts since 2000 include his short-story collection *Amores novi* and a fairy tale, *Uchitel' vran'ia* (The Teacher of Lying, 2003). Inspired by Ovid's erotic tales, *Amores novi* comprises three stories on the subject of love. The first story depicts the innocent love of a young schoolgirl; the second one is a paradoxical attempt to understand love in terms of computer logic; and the third story captures the lifelong love of a married couple. *Uchitel' vran'ia* was written by Kharitonov some twenty years earlier for his own children but published only in 2003. Reminiscent of Lewis Carroll's *Alice in Wonderland* (1865), it depicts the adventures of two young children who, guided by their magician teacher, discover that the ordinary world around them is full of extraordinary and fantastic occurrences.

In addition to his fictional works, Kharitonov has published two volumes of essays and diaries. The first volume, *Sposob sushchestvovaniia,* includes essays and reminiscences depicting his difficulties in getting his work published during the 1970s and 1980s, whereas the second volume, *Stenografiia kontsa veka,* includes selected entries from his diaries written in encoded shorthand between 1975 and 1999. Recognizing the importance of his diaries in the way they capture significant historical events and his personal contacts with many Russian writers and artists, Kharitonov decided to decode his notes and publish them in book form. *Stenografiia kontsa veka* has a wealth of biographical information, which helps Kharitonov's readers understand his fiction writing, as well as general observations and comments on Soviet life and culture. He is particularly preoccupied with questions concerning the relationship between literature and ideology; the forced emigration of dissident writers; and the problem of Russian-Jewish identity for some Soviet writers, including himself.

Kharitonov's major literary achievement to date remains his trilogy, *Provintsial'naia filosofiia,* particularly its concluding part, the novel *Linii sud'by, ili Sunduchok Milashevicha.* The trilogy conveys a panoramic picture of Russian life over a period of more than fifty years, beginning with the decade before the October Revolution and ending with the 1970s. It has a distinct philosophical focus and portrays the major characters' search for the meaning and purpose of life. The overall narrative method employed by Kharitonov is that of realism, making the narrative fairly transparent in terms of its main ideas and its overall significance.

Whereas *Provintsial'naia filosofiia* exemplifies Mark Sergeevich Kharitonov's continuation of the realist tradition, many of his works written since the early 1990s rely on a diametrically different method of representation that involves the fantastic and the irrational. His

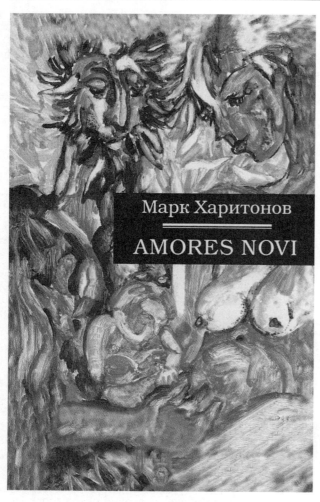

Paperback cover for Kharitonov's Amores novi *(New Loves, 2000), a collection of short stories inspired by the erotic tales of Ovid (courtesy of the author)*

cycle of short stories, *Golosa,* and his novellas, *Vozvra-shchenie niotkuda* and *Priblizhenie,* project a highly distorted vision of reality that combines the real and the fantastic, the probable and the imaginary, and the rational and the irrational. In these works Kharitonov exhibits a more questioning attitude toward simplistic accounts of realism and allows elements of the fantastic to enter a realistic narrative. As a result, these narratives are denser and less transparent and force the reader to engage in the texts more actively in order to create meaning.

Biography:

Evgenii Shklovsky, "Kharitonov Mark Sergeevich," in *Russkie pisateli 20 veka. Biograficheskii slovar',* edited by Petr Alekseevich Nikolaev (Moscow: Bol'shaia Rossiiskaia Entsiklopediia, 2000), pp. 723–724.

References:

Vera Chaikovskaia, "Linii sud'by v sovremennoi proze," *Voprosy literatury,* 4 (1993): 3–26;

Boris Khazanov, "Pokuda sam s soboi," *Znamia,* 10 (2002): 218–221;

Arthur Langeveld, "Mark Charitonov," *Raster,* 65 (1994): 33–38;

Alla Latynina, "Tvorets i kommentator," *Literaturnoe obozrenie,* 5–6 (1994): 34–35;

Naum Leiderman and Mark Lipovetsky, "Zhisn' posle smerti: Novye svedeniia o realizme," *Novyi mir,* 7 (1993): 246–248;

Mark Lipovetsky, "Dialogicheskoe voobrazhenie: O romane Marka Kharitonova *Linii sud'by, ili Sunduchok Milashevicha,*" *Russkii kur'er,* 2 (1993): 32–34;

Georges Nivat, "La réalisme magique de Kharitonov," in *Une journée en février* by Mark Kharitonov (Paris: Fayard, 1988): 7–15;

Grigorii Pomerants, "Chelovek bez maski na maskarade istorii," *Novyi mir,* 5 (1989): 259–262;

Andrei Ranchin, "Zybkii vozdukh povestvovaniia," *Novyi mir,* 12 (1992): 270–272;

Evgenii Shklovsky, "V granitsakh svoego ponimaniia," *Znamia,* 10 (1998): 224–227;

Norman Shneidman, *Russian Literature 1988–1994: The End of an Era* (Toronto: University of Toronto Press, 1995), pp. 142–145;

Valerii Surikov, "Sunduchok i stol: Spasenie i gibel' individual'nosti," *Literaturnoe obozrenie,* 2 (1995): 32–37;

Elena Tikhomirova, "Poetika pamiati v rossiiskoi proze: Pamiat' i sud'ba," in *Proza russkogo zarubezh'ia i Rossii v situatsii postmoderna* (Moscow: Narodnyi uchitel', 2002), pp. 123–136;

Marc Weinstein, "Mark Xaritonov: Un symboliste ironique," *Revue des Etudes Slaves,* 68 (1996): 37–54;

Miluše Zadražilova, "Carove, světci a básnici," in *Car a blázen, Lidovè noviny,* by Mark Charitonov (Prague: 1996): 247–266;

Zadražilova, "Tsari, sviatye i poety," *Druzhba narodov,* 8 (1997): 185–191.

Timur Iur'evich Kibirov
(Timur Iur'evich Zapoev)

(15 February 1955 –   )

Andrei Nemzer

Academy of Russian Contemporary Literature (Moscow)

and

Mark Lipovetsky

University of Colorado at Boulder

BOOKS: *Kalendar'* (Vladikavkaz: Ir, 1991);
Stikhi o liubvi (Moscow: Tsikady, 1993);
Santimenty: Vosem' knig, with a foreword by Sergei Markovich Gandlevsky (Belgorod: Risk, 1994)—includes "Tsikly: Liriko-didakticheskie poemy," "Rozhdestvenskaia pesn' kvartiranta," "Skvoz' proshchal'nye slezy," "Tri poslaniia," "Stikhi o liubvi," "Santimenty," "Poslanie Lenke," "Buran," and "Eleonora";
Kogda byl Lenin malen'kim (St. Petersburg: Ivan Limbakh, 1995);
Parafrazis (St. Petersburg: Pushkinskii fond, 1997);
Intimnaia lirika (St. Petersburg: Pushkinskii fond, 1998);
Pamiati Derzhavina: Stikhotvoreniia 1984–1994 (St. Petersburg: Iskusstvo, 1998);
Izbrannye poslaniia (St. Petersburg: Ivan Limbakh, 1998);
Notatsii (St. Petersburg: Pushkinskii fond, 1999);
Ulitsa Ostrovitianova (Moscow: Proekt OGI, 1999);
Iubilei liricheskogo geroia (Moscow: Proekt OGI, 2000);
Amour, exil . . . (St. Petersburg: Pushkinskii fond, 2000);
"Kto kuda, a ia–v Rossiiu . . ." (Moscow: Vremia, 2001).
Editions in English: "When Lenin Was Little" (excerpts), translated by Richard McKane in *The Poetry of Perestroika,* edited by Peter Mortimer and S. J. Litherland (London: Iron Press, 1991), pp. 56–60;
"Oh, How Strange It Is . . ." and "When Lenin Was Little," translated by McKane, and "A Song to Salami," translated by Oleg Atbashian, in *The Hungry Russian Winter: The Collection of Modern Russian Poetry in English Translations,* edited by Viktor Kulle (Moscow: N-Press, 1991), pp. 48–59;
"Banal Thoughts on the Purpose of Poetry and the Duty of the Poet," "When Lenin Was Young,"

Timur Iur'evich Kibirov (from the cover for Izbrannye poslaniia, *1998; Collection of Mark Lipovetsky)*

and "Christological Diptych," in *The Third Wave: The New Russian Poetry,* edited by Kent Johnson and Stephen M. Ashby (Ann Arbor: University of Michigan Press, 1992), pp. 223–234;
"To Serezha Gandlevsky: About Certain Aspects of the Present Sociocultural Sitiation," translated by

137

Kevin Platt in his *History in a Grotesque Key: Russian Literature and the Idea of Revolution* (Stanford: Stanford University Press, 1997), pp. 272–285.

OTHER: "Simvolicheskii obraz Kitaiia v tvorchestve V. G. Belinskogo," as Timur Iur'evich Zapoev, in *Dal'nii Vostok i Tsentral'naia Aziia* (Moscow: Nauka, 1985), pp. 148–155;

Zadushevnaia beseda [samizdat edition], with contributions by Kibirov, Dmitrii Aleksandrovich Prigov, and Lev Semenovich Rubinshtein (N.p., 1986)–includes "Zhizn' K. U. Chernenko," "Lesnaia shkola," and "Pesn' o Servelate";

Obshchie mesta, with contributions by Kibirov, A. Khabarov, V. Smyk, and A. Roskov (Moscow: Molodaia gvardiia, 1990).

SELECTED PERIODICAL PUBLICATIONS–UNCOLLECTED: "Utrachennye alluzii. Opyt avtorizovannogo kommentariia k poeme 'Lesnaia shkola'," by Kibirov and I. L. Fal'kovsky, *Philologica,* 4 (1997);

"Nishchaia nezhnost'," *Znamia,* 10 (2000);

"Po pervoi, ne chokaias' . . . ," *Znamia,* 1 (2002);

"Piroskaf," *Znamia,* 6 (2002).

Timur Kibirov earned recognition in the early years of perestroika for his carnivalizing, grotesque innovations in the Russian poetic tradition of lyrical commentary on acute social and political topics. He became known as one of the poets of Moscow conceptualism, along with Dmitrii Aleksandrovich Prigov and Lev Semenovich Rubinshtein. Kibirov's strategies, however, proved broader than the conceptualist (or postmodernist) deconstruction of authoritative cultural languages and traditions. He demonstratively combines the most canonical meters and diverse quotations with recognizable details of "public" life (ranging from public toilets to the army). Perhaps the most confessional poet in contemporary Russian literature, he invariably achieves an effect of striking sincerity. At the same time, many scholars have noted a link between Kibirov's poetics and the generic tradition of the song, specifically the Soviet song. Tat'iana Cherednichenko writes "In Kibirov's texts an amalgam of popular refrains and phrases that constituted either the thought material of the Soviet mentality or even forms of thought themselves, and which in any event pressed mass consciousness flat, becomes unexpectedly delicate lyrical matter." This combination of penetrating lyricism and deconstruction of mass-consciousness stereotypes, traditionality, and postmodern play is the likely reason for the amazing popularity of Kibirov's poetry. His verse won recognition not only among the Soviet academic intelligentsia; it became in many respects the voice of an entire generation.

Kibirov's real surname is Zapoev; the pseudonym Kibirov (taken from his mother's side of the family) appeared, beginning in 1980 (in one of his manuscripts), although at first in his early samizdat poems, he used the name Kirill Kibirov. Kibirov was born Timur Iur'evich Zapoev in Shepetovka (in the Khmel'nitsky region of Ukraine) on 15 February 1955 to Dzhemma Borisovna (Kibirova) Zapoeva and Iurii Kirillovich Zapoev. His father was a Soviet army officer (first in the artillery, later in political instruction), a profession that obligated the family to move often from one provincial garrison to the next. In 1998 Kibirov said in an interview with Viktor Kulle that he believes "the particular nature of the path I have taken is in part a result of the fact that I wasn't exactly a provincial but a super-provincial youth. I spent my childhood and adolescence in military towns. . . . The libraries were fantastic, and by age ten I had a borrower's card in all the libraries in this or that town." The first poet to make a deep impression on the young Zapoev was Aleksandr Aleksandrovich Blok. His love for Blok drew him not only to Silver Age poetry, which by his own admission he knew much better than he knew contemporary poetry and Soviet poetry in general, but also nudged him toward his own poetic creativity.

Zapoev's later school years, the time when he discovered the "poet" inside himself with all of the attendant, ultraromantic consequences (such as egocentrism, ostracism, struggles with God, and amoral aestheticism), surface frequently in the poetry he writes as Kibirov. In "Letnie razmyshleniia o sud'bakh iziashchnoi slovesnosti" (Summer Musings on the Fate of Elegant Literature), published in 1993 in *Druzhba narodov* (The People's Friendship), Kibirov exclaims: "It's been said that there is no such thing as an / immoral book, only a more or less talented one–so taught a gay Briton. / I understood this in the ninth grade! / But nowadays I don't get it. . . ." He is even harsher in "Solntsedar" (Solntsedar Wine, published in *Segodnia* [Today], 1994): "Having exhausted in political work the familiar arsenal of educational measures, / 'You read books, so tell me, do books really / teach that?'– father asked. // I was arrogantly silent. But it wasn't that / naïve a question actually. / These books do, father. Later / I barely grew into Pushkin."

Kibirov revealed in his interview with Kulle that for about a decade he showed no one his poems; all that time he was striving for perfection in form. He explains, "I didn't rest until I had learned to write in one try triolets and garlands of sonnets, until I had learned by heart Kviatkovsky's dictionary," which was a Soviet reference book on poetic form. His early poems, such as "Dlia togo, chtoby uznat' . . ." (To find out . . .), written in 1982 but published in his 1999 collection *Ulitsa Ostrovitianova* (Ostrovitianov Street), are essentially not that far removed from those unknown sonnets, "virelays, villanelles, sestinas, / and rondels and, Oh Lord, triolets, / and octaves, and ballads, and tercets" that comforted the inspired teenager in the early 1970s, which he wrote about in "Solntsedar" (A Gift of the Sun [the name of a lower-quality port]), published in *Parafrazis* (Paraphrase) in 1997. The long road of knowledge, which included high-school graduation, his initial college experiences, army service, and the return to civilian life, could not just drift away like smoke. The mature Kibirov has often come down hard on the "idiotic, drunk silver age," but in "Solntsedar" he felt obliged to make a basic proviso in a deliberately neutral manner, as if only for the sake of "historical objectivity": "I should note in passing that it was precisely / that cycle of old-fashioned reading / that poured icy loathing for Soviet power / into my soul."

Although he absorbed much of Russian poetry, from folkloric epics to the poems of Joseph Brodsky, Kibirov retained his gratitude toward Silver Age culture, as even his "anti-Blokian" poems attest. Reading such pieces, one understands that only a man who once discovered within himself a nascent bard of the "prekrasnaia dama" (beautiful lady)–from the title of Blok's first poetry volume, *Stikhi o prekrasnoi dame* (Poems about the Beautiful Lady, 1905)–would dare to write such verse. Of particular importance for Kibirov is Blok's strategy of the "lyrical novel," which allows a sequence of poetry collections to be perceived as a group of testimonials about the life and fate of the poet; amid rapid changes of circumstance in place, time, and action the familiar face is a constant presence.

In 1972 Zapoev finished high school in the military town of "Solnechnogorsk–7" near Moscow. He was accepted at Moscow Regional Pedagogical Institute, from which he was later expelled for academic failure. Soon after his expulsion he was drafted into the army. He served for two years (from 1974 to 1976) in Kazakhstan as part of an anti-aircraft division. Despite his familiarity with army life, service in the Soviet army could not but prove psychologically traumatic for a young man so taken with Blok. As Kibirov later explained to Kulle, "The break began in the army, when I encountered real, unmediated life. It wasn't that I was a mama's boy; I was a healthy kid with a streak of hooliganism, but still I knew nothing about real life. When I encountered that reality I understood that it required a different kind of language. I didn't imagine then what kind."

After the army Zapoev reenrolled at the Moscow Regional Pedagogical Institute, where he studied Rus-

sian philology from 1977 to 1982. During his years as a student a radical shift in his aesthetic tastes occurred. The frightening, grotesque image of reality that he had discovered during his army service first led to a definite disillusionment with symbolism, followed by an affinity for the poetry of Velemir Khlebnikov and the *oberiuty*, the Leningrad group of absurd poets that was active in the late 1920s to 1930s. At the same time he discovered banned contemporary literature–in particular Brodsky's poetry and Venedikt Vasil'evich Erofeev's *Moskva-Petushki* (1977; translated as *Moscow to the End of the Line,* 1980). The mixture of "outgrown" symbolism, Khlebnikov's experimentalism, *oberiuty* absurdism, Brodsky's tragic verse, and Erofeev's postmodernist grotesque formed the foundation of Kibirov's original poetic style. He himself refers to "U dorogi chibis" (A Lapwing by the Road)–which was first published in 1988 in the Vladikavkaz almanac *Literaturnaia Osetiia: Stikhi i proza molodykh* (Literary Osetia: The Poetry and Prose of Young Authors)–as the first poem "for which I am still prepared to answer."

After graduating from the pedagogical institute, Kibirov worked from 1981 to 1991 as a junior research associate at the Moscow Art Institute, and he even published (as Zapoev, however) the article "Simvolicheskii obraz Kitaiia v tvorchestve V. G. Belinskogo" (The Symbolic Image of China in the Work of V. G. Belinsky, 1985). In 1989 he married Elena Borisova, and in 1991 their daughter, Aleksandra (Sasha), was born. In the early 1980s he began to take part in underground poetry circles in Moscow. At first he was associated with Aleskei Didurov's circle and with poets who subsequently were called "ironists" (such as Viktor Korkiia, Vladimir Vishnevsky, and Viktor Stepantsov). Later he was part of the Moscow conceptualist circle, represented first and foremost by Prigov, Rubinshtein, and Vsevolod Nekrasov. Also close to this circle were the poets Mikhail Natanovich Aizenberg and Sergei Markovich Gandlevsky, who became Kibirov's close friends. Kibirov's original poetics were fully formed through his connection with the Moscow conceptualists. He said in his interview with Kulle that "meeting Rubinshtein and Prigov cured me forever of all literary conceits. . . . I knew that I could, like Prigov, reject lyricism, refuse to write in the first person, or on the contrary I could emphasize all of that, engage in the kind of sentimentalism that is so indecent in contemporary culture in order to demonstrate that I know it's indecent." Precisely the second option–sentimentality represented as a knowingly inappropriate, impossible, and indecent language–has defined Kibirov's poetic strategy. In 1986 the texts that brought him fame, "Zhizn' K. U. Chernenko" (The Life of K. U. Chernenko), "Lesnaia shkola" (Forest School), "Pesn' o Servelate" (Song of

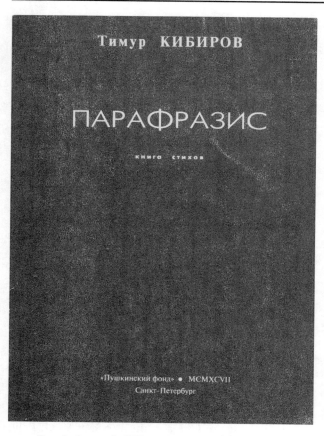

Paperback cover for Kibirov's Parafrazis *(Paraphrase), a collection of poetry written from 1992 to 1996 (Collection of Mark Lipovetsky)*

the Cervelat Salami), and a few others, were published in the samizdat collection *Zadushevnaia beseda* (An Intimate Chat) along with poems by Prigov and Rubinshtein.

There is almost nothing "personal" in the poems that first made Kibirov's name known outside narrow circles. They were published openly in the Soviet Union beginning in 1988—in the "framework of glasnost," as it was described at the time. The poems were striking for their complete rejection of the norms of poetic utterance as defined from "above." This dissonance was no secret to Kibirov, as suggested by his sarcastic adoption of the party formula "V ramkakh glasnosti" (In the Framework of Glasnost) as the title of one section of his manuscript collection "Rozhdestvenskaia pesn' kvartiranta" (The Lodger's Christmas Song), written in 1986 and published in 1994 in *Santimenty: Vosem' knig* (Sentimentality: Eight Books). He writes: "Believe me, I'll be the first to rise in defense! / I won't allow anyone to be executed! / I'll pray on my knees before the court, / so none of them [the communists] are killed! . . . Faster, faster, friends, / Organize a Nuremberg or / else we won't survive, I swear, we

won't! / For the sticky fear, for the immeasurable shame . . . / I swear I'll bring them packages in prison, the bastards."

The publication of such lines was possible in 1986 (although the state struck back at any writer who went too far), but even Kibirov's "typographical" breaches of 1988 to 1989 were seen as just that—breaches. When *Atmoda* (National Liberation), the newspaper of the Latvian People's Front, published sections of Kibirov's "Poslanie L. S. Rubinshteinu" (Epistle to L. S. Rubinshtein, 1989), he was denounced in *Pravda* itself. One year later, in 1990, the piece was published in full in the Leningrad newspaper *Chas pik* (Rush Hour), prompting a barrage of indignant letters from readers. Times were changing: the letters accused Kibirov not of anti-Soviet sentiments (of which there were plenty in the poem) but of obscenity. The threat of prosecution against the editor in chief of *Atmoda,* Aleksei Grigor'ev, for publishing the poem and the intervention of the renowned literary scholar Evgenii Abramovich Toddes in the capacity of literary expert (his opinion, published in the Riga journal *Rodnik* [The Creek], was one of the first works of criticism on Kibirov) only made Kibirov more famous, this time on a national scale. His name became known even outside the Soviet Union.

In those years Kibirov published little in Soviet journals—his work appeared in *Iunost'* (Youth), *Teatr* (The Theater), and *Teatral'naia zhizn'* (Theater Life)—but he was one of the favorite authors of the émigré journal *Sintaksis* (Syntax), published in Paris by Andrei Donatovich Siniavsky and Mariia Vasil'evna Rozanova, which printed four large selections of Kibirov's work between 1988 and 1990. For quite a long time Kibirov maintained the image of the "underground poet," for whom samizdat and foreign publishers were more natural "habitats" than Soviet periodicals. In addition to his pieces in *Sintaksis,* from 1988 to 1990 his work was published in the Paris journal *Kontinent* (The Continent), the Israeli journal *Vremia i my* (Time and Us), and in the samizdat publications *Tret'ia modernizatsiia* (Third Modernization) and *Mitin zhurnal* (Mitia's Journal). In the foreword to his first book, *Obshchie mesta* (Common Places, 1990)—akin to a communal apartment in that it includes the debuts of four poets at once, although the names of Kibirov's "neighbors" in this anthology virtually have been forgotten—Kibirov expresses apprehension: "I find it strange and a bit alarming to present my poems in print. Taken out of context, stripped of the aura of taboo, devoid of their social acuteness (an aesthetic as well as ethical quality) they are vulnerable to accusations of opportunism."

His central theme in the 1980s was entropy: the collapse of once stable, ossified structures that are not only ideological and historical but also existential. Addressing precisely this theme, the poem "Poslanie L. S. Rubinshteinu" depicts the signs of entropy, which is visible in everything. It is in the air–"Entropii svet postylyi / zalivaet vechera" (The repulsive light of entropy / inundates the evenings)–and in the permitted boldness of perestroika literature, which replaces the official texts of old: "Okh uzh mne literatura, entropiia, such'ia vosh', volch'e vymia, ryb'ia shkura, dereviannyi makintosh!" (Oh, I've had it with literature, entropy, goddamn louse, wolf's teat, fish skin, wooden mackintosh!). The political and ideological collapse of the Soviet system was but the most visible incarnation of the general tendency toward chaos and entropy: "Everything is passing. Everything is finished. / Malodorous smoke. The roar of wolves. / Fleeting like Chernenko / and nonsensical like Khrushchev, / barren like Il'ich, Leva, / and, like Krupskaia, terrible. / The foundations are collapsing, / shit is spreading everywhere." Despite his obvious disgust, however, Kibirov persistently engages in a dialogue with the entropic world, a dialogue that is painful and, as a rule, ruinous for a poet. Yet, he cannot, or, more accurately, will not, allow himself simply to turn away–to cast aside the portrait of collapse and go off into the sublime realms of poetic imagination. He grew up amid the daily nightmare, and his entire biography consists of "elements" of the collapse. For this reason, to stare into entropy is the only available form of self-knowledge–the only means by which to know destiny and Russia. To reject that dialogue arrogantly, according to Kibirov, is tantamount to cowardice and self-betrayal.

Kibirov creates an image of entropy by using traditional postmodernist means. He employs especially often a montage of quotations, a clash of diverse stylistic layers, and literalized poetic and ideological clichés. The "aesthetics of the base and worthless," as described by A. Hansen-Love in his 1997 article for *Novoe literaturnoe obozrenie,* so characteristic of early conceptualism, is also not unknown in his works. Yet, none of these devices separate his lyrical hero from the chaos surrounding him, nor do they transform his lyrical voice into a "mask," an image of Sovietized consciousness (as in the poetry of Prigov, for example). Kibirov unites the conceptualist devices with a powerful lyrical flow; the tragicomedy of entropy is simultaneously a self-portrait of the poet.

In *Postmodern v Rossii: Literatura i teoriia* (Postmodern in Russia: Literature and Theory, 2000) Mikhail Naumovich Epshtein, a preeminent scholar of Russian postmodernism, interprets the phenomenon of Kibirov's poetics as "soft conceptualism": "If 'hard' conceptualism (Prigov, Sorokin) exhibits a stereotyping of feelings, 'soft' conceptualism goes beyond the limits of conceptualism and consciously resurrects the emotional power and authenticity hidden within the stereotype." In Kibirov's poetry one can also see a distinctive kind of self-criticism toward conceptualism and postmodernism in general. Kibirov convinces the reader that the continuous destruction of simulacra and simulations leads not to the liberation of reality from the yoke of falsity but to emptiness. Simulation, like a malignant tumor, has eaten through reality to its foundations. Kibirov does not limit himself, however, to this discovery; he attempts to restore the real, existential meanings in the space gutted by simulation. His poems (like Rubinshtein's best work) reveal that the existential can be wrung out of the simulacra that absorbed it; this idea directly corresponds to Boris Leonidovich Pasternak's well-known metaphor in the poem "Vesna" (Spring, 1914): "Poetry! May you be a Greek sponge with suckers. . . . At night I will squeeze you out, poetry / To the health of the greedy paper." Kibirov plays with the most commonplace stereotypes of mass consciousness and is convinced that the simulacra "remember" the reality that they have swallowed up, and for that reason it is possible to restore that reality using a few details, signs, and feelings, though not by mechanically constructing a reality, but through organic resurrection.

Not by accident does Kibirov use the expression "common places" as the title of his first book. In it the "places of common usage" (from the cafeteria and the outhouse to the barracks and the university)–the *loci communes* (common places), or the common ideas available to all, which are secretly accepted by many, "overcome" by some, and in search of voices that will make them manifest–are tightly coupled. The belief that people need real "common places," and not deadly ideological equivalents, is characteristic of Kibirov from his earliest to his latest works. In the foreword to Kibirov's book *Santimenty,* Gandlevsky describes his friend's poetic position as consistently antiromantic: "Kibirov's poetic prowess lies in the fact that he was one of the first to sense that the pose of the outlaw poet had become ridiculous and vulgar, because the dream had come true. The poetic mutiny, altered to the point of unrecognizability, had long ago taken power. The 'universal drinking binge' had become an omnipresent way of life, and it turned out that it is no way to live."

In a paradoxical way "common places" became the foundation of individuality in Kibirov. Decomposing particles tastelessly intermingle and settle in personal memory and consciousness in obedience to the logic of the chaos that engendered them; they are capricious, unpredictable, and therefore absolutely individual. Here personal experience is distinctive because it is essentially disorderly and random. This paradox of world perception in Kibirov is presented especially clearly in his long poem "Sortiry" (Outhouses, first published in *Literaturnoe Obozrenie,* 1991), in which the hardly sympathetic image of "places of common usage" becomes a metaphor for poetry and a pretext for extremely personal reminiscences of childhood, first love, and army humiliations. At the same time, lyrical consciousness in Kibirov is not isolated in and of itself but open to dialogue with another consciousness that has absorbed the same products of entropy and is constituted from the same shards; it is only collected in a different, equally distinctive kaleidoscopic pattern (for this reason, Kibirov's favorite genre is the epistle to friends). His lyrical hero during this period—in "Lesnaia shkola," for example, he is a student at a Soviet "forest school" (for mentally handicapped children)—is doomed to be the same as its other inhabitants, but breaks free from its embrace: "We pray to the stumps, and the oaks, and the wolves, / we prostrate ourselves before the gnarled roots. / Let me go, I'm not yours, I'm gone . . . / I'll arrange planks into a cross, / I'll put it on a steep cliff. / I'll put the cross in those berry places, / those piney, primitive areas." As a rule the lyrical hero's attempts end in failure, for the pull of collapse and entropy is too great. Nothing can rid the mad hero of his complicity in, and responsibility for, the nightmare of "Lesnaia shkola"—not mischief, not curses, and not dashing off to nowhere. The poem continues, "Oh thank you, thank you, native land, / oh thank you, forest regions! / And in reply he heard: 'Don't mention it, brother, / you yourself after all are fully guilty.'" Only when one senses the lyrical hero's guilt does Kibirov make possible the preservation of hope for the hero's transformation (from a fool into a prince) and his forest world. In "Buran" (Snowstorm, first published in *Grazhdane Noche,* 1994) the "heavenly" dreams and the epistles to Rubinshtein are, of course, deceptive, but they cannot be reduced to lies. According to Kibirov, there is no Russia without Kitezh, the mythical village that defended itself from capture by the Tartars by submerging itself in a lake. In Russian culture Kitezh represents what might have been if authoritarian rule had not made its mark upon the country.

The acknowledgment of the individual's inseparability from the entropy of Soviet myth in Kibirov's poetry leads to a paradoxical conclusion: this repulsive world must be preserved in poetry, and its praises must be sung with love and tears. As he says in "Poslanie L. S. Rubinshteinu," "Lev Semenovich! Be a man! Don't shirk from tears!" By doing so, entropy and death are tricked into staying in poetry together with hateful, inseparable chaos, as seen in these lines from "Khudozhniku Semenu Faibisovichu" (To the Artist Semen Faibisovich, first published in *Novoe russkoe slovo,* 1995): "If only, Lord, this morbid light over the high-way could be engraved, / and the elder bush behind the wall of the kindergarten, / and the three winos over the chill of the river, / and the white brassiere, and the lipstick, / and that way defeat death!"

Immediately after his first publications Kibirov was noticed and made a standard-bearer by critics of the younger generation who, like the poet himself, were just starting out in literature. Aleksandr Nikolaevich Arkhangel'sky understands Kibirov's verse as poetic commentary on the impossibility of the prophetic word that is presupposed in the Russian tradition. He sees in Kibirov's poems the most profound and productive manifestation of the cultural crisis then plaguing Soviet communism. Placing Kibirov in the context of postmodernist culture, Andrei Leonidovich Zorin demonstrates in his article "Muza iazyka i semero poétov" (The Muse of Language and Seven Poets), published in 1990 in *Druzhba narodov* (The People's Friendship), that "Kibirov is faced with the question of whether one can speak in another language and still remain oneself. Kibirov answers this question in the affirmative with his poems." In his "malen'kaia dissertatsiia" (little dissertation) on Kibirov's "Poslanie L. S. Rubinshteinu," published in *Iunost'* in 1991, Mikhail Naftal'evich Zolotonosov writes: "Kibirov is searching intensively for the cultural firmament, for a means to create something from the shards. He uses a mosaic of quotations, and a new structure is built from the fragments. The resulting effect testifies to the complexity of the poem's internal structure. . . ." Zolotonosov believes that Kibirov has succeeded in transforming the entropy of cultural collapse described in the poem into an informational entropy that gives poetic expression an unpredictability and an indistinctness—that is, maximum freedom.

Kibirov's poetry has attracted the attention not only of journalists but also of scholars who typically show little interest in contemporary literature. In his 1990 article for *Rodnik,* Toddes detects in Kibirov's verse exchanges with quite a broad spectrum of phenomena in the Russian literary tradition, phenomena that are focused on a "strange" love-hate dynamic toward Russia: from Pushkin and Mikhail Iur'evich Lermontov to Sergei Donatovich Dovlatov and Brodsky. Mikhail Leonovich Gasparov devoted a special study to Kibirov's (and Rubinshtein's) poetic metrics. Nikolai Aleksandrovich Bogomolov wrote an article on the intertextual links between Kibirov and Aleksandr Arakd'evich Galich. Among others who have written about Kibirov are Marietta Omarovna Chudakova, the well-known Mikhial Afanas'evich Bulgakov specialist, and Roman Timenchuk, an expert on acmeism. Kibirov's poetry has also attracted the attention of Western scholars such as Willem Westensteijn and Kevin Platt.

At a moment when Kibirov's published poems unexpectedly coincided with the free thinking that was

* * *

С тёмным брюхом, с белым верхом
голубые облака.
Оказалось на поверку
жизнь легка и коротка.

Сосны рыжи и зелены,
волны сини иногда.
Нам, таким неприхотливым,
даже горе не беда.

Полудурки полустарцы
дела нету, смысла нет.
Пиво жёлто. Очи кары.
Разноцветен белый свет.

1998. о. Готланд.

Manuscript for Kibirov's poem "S temnym briukhom, s belym verkhom" (With a dark bottom and a white top), collected in his Notatsii *(Notations, 1999; Collection of Mark Lipovetsky)*

typical of semiofficial perestroika and also with the permissible mockery of Communist dogmas (a 1993 survey by the magazine *Ogonek* named Kibirov the most popular Russian poet), the newly fashionable author of "Lesnaia shkola," the epistles to Rubinshtein and the artist Faibisovich, and the poem "Skvoz' proshchal'nye slezy" (Through Tears of Farewell, 1994) executed a sudden change of course. Kibirov's "new" period began with a book bearing the demonstrative title *Stikhi o liubvi* (Poems about Love, 1993). It includes the even more demonstrative manifesto "Ot avtora" (From the Author): "In short— start perestroika with yourself. / And leave me in peace!" The "civic verse" is the domain of opportunists, next to whom it does not befit the poet to stand: "That your Lenin is scum—I already wrote that, / and now I'm completely free! / And if only you knew how much fun it is for me / and how carefree I've become!"

In these unquestionably sincere poems, however, there is a definite feeling of tension: the reader discovers that previously Kibirov was only political and did not write about love—as if he did not have enough inner freedom before and assembled his previous songs under duress, so to speak, "by command of civic duty." He writes in *Stikhi o liubvi,* "I feel drawn to change from Nekrasov's / mournful anapest to Nabokov's." In these lines one can divine a self-polemic with the last section of the long poem "Skvoz' proshchal'nye slezy": "And Nekrasov's mournful anapest / Stuffed my sinuses with tears." In Kibirov's verse "Nekrasov's mournful anapest" is inseparable from Nabokov's "Otviazhis', ia tebia umoliaiu" (Leave me alone, I beg you, 1939). Kibirov used that line from Nabokov's tragic poem, addressed to Russia, as an epigraph to "Rozhdestvenskaia allegoriia" (A Christmas Allegory, 1986), and even inserted it into his own text. In Kibirov's poem Russia is allegorically pictured as an unhappy, alcoholic woman, sober and dressed up, waiting for her New Year's guests. Yet, despite the repulsiveness of the portrait, the poet loves even this heroine, and in his love there are no boundaries between the "Nekrasovian" and "Nabokovian" elements and the "Blokian" metaphor of Russia as a wife that unites them.

Kibirov has never hidden this love however. His Freudian jokes about Blok's formula "Russ—wife" make Kibirov's subordination to that mythological motif even more apparent. He plays on his "being doomed to Blok" in one of his latest poems, "Bloku zhena. Isakovskomu mat' . . ." (A Wife to Blok, to Isakovsky a Mother, first published in *Iubilei liricheskogo geroia,* 2000). Comparing Russia not to a mother, a wife, or a grandmother but to a mother-in-law, Kibirov summarizes: "What is there for me in you? Nothing is good in you. Only, your daughter is pretty, / (. . .) She takes after Blok, most likely." All of Kibirov's books are essentially about love since they are either dedicated to the Beautiful Lady or portray her capti-

vating yet unattainable image. Kibirov is convinced that erotica without a "divine reflection" is no defense against entropy. Thus "Skvoz' proshchal'nye slezy" begins with an appeal to his beloved and ends with a prayer: "Lord, bless my Russia, / Save and protect my Russia, / Especially Mila and Shapiro. . . ." Kibirov has a single love—for a woman, for friends, for Russia, for the world.

Strictly speaking, there was no "depoliticization" of Kibirov's poetry at the end of the 1980s but, rather, simply a "laying bare" of what readers of his "political" poems did not notice, since those readers were politically oriented at the time. For this reason Kibirov's "severing gesture" with his "former self" was markedly ideological. First of all, his narrative poems of the 1980s—"Ballada o deve Belogo plesa" (Ballad of the Maiden of the White River), "Ballada ob Andriushe Petrove" (Ballad of Andriusha Petrov), and, to a certain extent, "Eleonora"—were read in a conceptualist key despite the author's will. Second, in his most confessional lyrical poems of the 1990s—the first of the "Romansy Cheremushkinskogo raiona" (Romances of the Cheremushki Region) and "Ballada o solnechnom livne" (Ballad of a Sunlit Downpour)—decidedly "political" clichés flare up. Third, soon after the demonstratively lyrical *Stikhi o liubvi* Kibirov later developed the verses in *Santimenty* with the poem "Epistola o stikhotvorstve" (Epistle on Writing Poetry, 1994), in which the rejection of "permitted civic spirit" once again affirms the unbreakable link between poetry, freedom, and human dignity and "Russkaia pesnia" (Russian song) and the apocalyptic "Voskresen'e" (Sunday).

The collections *Stikhi o liubvi* and *Santimenty* and the poem "Poslanie k Lenke . . ." (Epistle to Lenka . . . , first published in *Sintaksis,* 1990) prove that one cannot find protection from the scorching (or freezing) breath of contemporaneity in bright eros (as seen in "Romansy Cheremushkinskogo raiona"), in touching reminiscences, or in the cult of "domestic comfort" and anglicized privacy. The drama of the poet's entry into a new, unpredictable, and chaotic cultural environment required a different poetic language, which Kibirov by no means found immediately. Testifying to this change is the interval between "Poslanie k Lenke . . . " and *Parafrazis* (1997), the book comprising his works dating from 1992 to 1996. Never before or since has Kibirov turned out books so slowly. The effect of the early 1990s publishing crisis must be taken into account, but no less significant a factor is the author's comment to a single (yet not fully manifested) idea in *Parafrazis*—superficially one of Kibirov's most harmonious and happiest collections. The feeling of happiness (familial and domestic) is inseparable from his strengthened faith in himself as a poet.

The opening poem of *Parafrazis,* "Letnie razmyshleniia o sud'bakh iziashchnoi slovesnosti," is written in iambic hexameter, the nobly ceremonial "Russian

Alexandrine," with paired rhymes. Kibirov uses the "high style" to speak about lowly matters—specifically, a shortage of financial resources. Already in the opening lines the starkly physiological, seen in the expression "the sheepdog poops [*kakaet*]," closes ranks with the deliberately poetic, demonstrated by the line "A les kak by khrustal'nym siian'em napoen" (As if [*kak by*] the forest were impregnated with a crystalline radiance). The phonetic resonance between the "act" of the dog—*kakaet*—and the phrase *kak by* is a citation of Fedor Ivanovich Tiutchev: "Ves' den' stoit kak by Khrustal'nyi" (The whole day stands as if made of crystal), from his poem "Est' v oseni pervonachal'noi" (1857). The result is not dissonance, however, but a new harmony. The venerable meter, the bombastic style, and the easily recognizable quotations "dispel" the vain "reality." In such a light, that reality seems more funny than sinister. The author's "project"—to achieve glory and wealth by writing pulp fiction—is refuted in proportion to its own progress. The list of novels is so comical that it simply cannot become "reality." They encompass the same sort of fiction as the extinct "Soviet" literature. Laughter is stronger than fear, but the sense of being one of the poetically "chosen," confirmed by the intextextual links with many Russian poets, is stronger than fear: "They've repeated it for a century and a half—'peacefulness and will'— / Russian poets—'freedom and peacefulness'— / so I would betray them now? Behind the soul / there is a golden surplus, an unshakable cliff . . . // And in our cruel age it is not appropriate / to promise or to sulk. Let's go. The rocky path / is as bright as ever. . . ." "'Peacefulness and will'" allude to Pushkin, while "an unshakeable cliff" harks back to Osip Emil'evich Mandel'shtam, and "rocky path" recalls Lermontov.

"Parafrazis," the eponymous poem of the collection, begins with an intertextual reference to two equally important texts: the first verse of the first Psalm of David ("Blessed is the man that walketh not in the counsel of the ungodly . . .") and Horace's second epode ("Happy is the man who, far away from business cares . . . ," 13 B.C.). Russian poets, creating variations on these lofty models in different ways, have united the spiritual impulse of King David the psalmist with the ironic, thoroughly mundane wisdom of Horace. Kibirov continues the tradition by speaking about the human destiny to be free and happy. Repeating again and again the biblical "blessed," listing fears that have been overcome and joys still continuing, and wallowing in an almost divine life, he seems to be an enthusiastic simpleton until there is an explosion: "Radiant Thebes blazes from the sky. / Blessed is he who sees, hears, breathes, / happy is he who has visited that world! / A plague is coming. Prepare a feast." The penultimate line is an intertextual reference to Tiutchev's "Tsitseronu" (To Cicero, 1836), particularly when Tiutchev writes, "Happy is he who visited that world during its fateful moments. /

The almighty called him like a confidante to a feast." Kibirov's verse, however, connects happiness with the "fateful moments," which also recall Pushkin's "Pir vo vremia chumy" (Feast during the Time of the Plague, 1831) and Pasternak's "Vtoroe rozhdenie" (Second Birth, 1932). The intertextual links of the poem connect the capacity for happiness with a sober awareness of the impossibility of hiding from tragedy. A preparedness for death and recognition of the futility of trying to overcome chaos become a gift for finding happiness in the normal and the everyday—including emptiness, the direct result of the collapse: "That's what we'll write—the muted beauty / of the Voskresensky region is a joy to the eye, / as is its thick filth, its golden brocade, / and its emptiness to the end of time."

After the release of *Parafrazis* Kibirov's status as a contemporary classic was firmly established. The journal *Literaturnoe obozrenie* (The Literary Review) devoted a forty-five-page section to him in volume one, 1998, which included an interview, his long poem "Rozhdestvo" (Christmas, first published in *Darial*, 1992), poems dedicated to him, reminiscences of his writer friends, six critical articles, a survey of criticism about him, and a selected bibliography with 161 entries. This fact is noteworthy because previously such sections of the journal had been devoted mostly to deceased twentieth-century Russian writers, including Mandel'shtam, Nabokov, Brodsky, and Mikhail Afanase'vich Bulgakov. Until Kibirov the only living author that had been covered in *Literaturnoe obozrenie* was Gennadii Aigi.

Such recognition by experts was accompanied by literary prizes and awards. In 1993 Kibirov and Prigov shared the first Pushkin Prize, awarded by the Alfred Teopfer Foundation, based in Germany. In 1997 Kibirov received the St. Petersburg "Northern Palmira" Literary Prize. In 1998 he was awarded the Anti-Booker Prize, sponsored by *Nezavisimaia gazeta* (The Independent Gazette), in the poetry category. In 2000 he was one of the first to receive a Joseph Brodsky Memorial Fellowship. In the same period translations of his poetry appeared in Polish, Finnish, Hebrew, Italian, and English.

In Kibirov's next five collections, however, which range from *Intimnaia lirika* (Intimate Lyrics, 1998) to *Iubilei liricheskogo geroia* (A Lyric Hero's Jubilee, 2000), no trace of the idyll found in *Parafrazis* remains. The collections increasingly concern the motifs of solitude, restlessness, and irritation at the (mundane and especially intellectual) baseness that tirelessly alters appearances. With increasing clarity the distinctive face of the poet shows through—this poet who has started his fifth decade and suffered a difficult break with his family; the picture of the surrounding world becomes darker and darker; and the theme of self-dissatisfaction is heard ever more sharply. Alluding to lines from the verse of Vladimir Vladimirovich Mayakovsky in "Inventarizatsionnyi sonnet" (Inventorial Son-

Paperback cover for Kibirov's Iubilei liricheskogo geroia
(A Lyric Hero's Jubilee), considered a continuation of the
romance novel Amour, exil . . . *(Love, Exile . . .),*
published in the same year (Collection
of Mark Lipovetsky)

net), which opens *Notatsii* (Notations, 1999), Kibirov writes, "Vremia itozhit' to, chto prozhil, / i peretriakhivat' to, chto nazhil" (It is time to take stock of what I've lived through, / and revise what I've gained).

Critics immediately noticed the intonational shift that occurred during this period in Kibirov's poetry. In an article for *Druzhba narodov* (2000) on *Notatsii*, which Kibirov wrote in 1999 while living on Gotland Island in Sweden and serving as a fellow at the Baltic Center of Writers and Translators, Nikolai Aleksandrov notes the paradoxical combination of external simplicity—even oversimplification—with internal complexity and drama in the poems:

> Kibirov is pseudo-accessible. . . . Kibirov does not cross out the cultural tradition, but tries to free himself of the stamps and common places that have not only ceased to be discoveries but have transformed from fulcrums into

blinders. . . . The chief quality of his poetics is a declared bashfulness, tenderness, sensitivity, woundedness, almost a fear of words, in which there are so many dangers, which have been on so many lips and have become overgrown with so many meanings. It is better almost to speak. "Almost," since silence and mumbling, whispers and timid breathing are also part of culture. There remains a narrow path along which Kibirov walks, quietly and carefully, fearfully, shyly, squinting, complaining about the fruitless years, but also with a surprising adroitness.

In his 2001 article for *Znamia* (The Banner) Evgenii Ermolin proposes a somewhat different interpretation of the shift that occurred in Kibirov's poetry—one that is more sociological than poetic: "Kibirov's poetry is probably the most vivid marker of the catastrophe suffered by his generation. The spiritual crisis, the ruinous crackup that we went through in the 1990s is reflected in his poetry as in a mirror. . . ." Ermolin continues to assert that at the end of the 1980s "Kibirov represented the soul and voice of a generation inclined to radical spiritual renewal without looking back or compromising," while in the mid and late 1990s such "self-assurance disappeared. Suddenly there was a feeling of limitedness, triviality, even insignificance." Ermolin argues that now (particularly as suggested by the appearance of *Notatsii*) Kibirov "is cultivating within himself the qualities of a little poet and a little man. Minimalism in everything. In his position, his pose, his poetic means. Kibirov's new, self-inspired persona is that of a modest, private man with no global aspirations, no flights, and no arrogance."

Ermolin's stern diagnosis is only partly correct. Not by accident does "Inventarizatsionnyi sonnet," a poem consisting of a list of losses and expenditures, end unexpectedly: "Maybe I was careless and negligent— / but cared for and even tender." Tenderness in Kibirov remains even after nothing else remains. Two of his books convince one of this idea even more firmly—*Amour, exil . . .* (Love, Exile . . . , 2000) and *Iubilei liricheskogo geroia,* the fifth part of the romance novel that begins in *Amour, exil. . . .* Speaking with a staggering openness reminiscent of Mayakovsky, Kibirov "declassifies" the oppressive sadness of *Ulitsa Ostrovitianova* (the last attempt to hold onto the warm home in *Parafrazis*) and *Notatsii* with their thirst for the unattainable direct word. Everything has become clear: happiness nevertheless happened. Kibirov knew even earlier that happiness, in spite of Pushkin, does not always combine with "peace and will."

Kibirov's latest poems will give future commentators thoughtful pause. They emphasize not the reminiscences—which had appeared in his work even earlier—but the measure of specificity with which the "lyrical heroine" of *Amour, exil . . .* is described—a thoroughly "literary" specificity. Not only is she named Natal'ia (and her patronymic, it seems, is Nikolaevna–which echoes the name of Pushkin's wife Natal'ia Nikolaeva Goncharova); not only is she much younger than the "lyrical hero"; and not only does she not want to couple with her beloved (an allusion to Goncharova's refusal of the first matchmaking attempt with Pushkin and the "coldness" in their marriage that is traditionally attributed to her), but she is even cross-eyed! The "Goncharovian" code is also seasoned with "philology" in a slightly "anti-Pushkin" accent: the heroine busies herself with scholarly studies of the main friend and rival of the "first poet," as seen in *Amour, exil . . .* in the poem "Popytka shantazha" (Attempted Blackmail): "And Pushkin is mine, and Baratynsky is yours." Moreover, the final poems in *Amour, exil. . .* are addressed to N. N., which is reminiscent of both Lermontov's line about poets who appeal to "N. N., nevedomoi krase" (N. N., the unknown beauty) and Iurii Mikhailovich Lotman's concept of Pushkin's "secret love" (the mysterious lover did not have a prototype but was a "literary" figure). The suggestion arises that Kibirov also invented his N. N. in order to experiment with the theme of "new love, new life." The finale of Kibirov's poem "K N. N." (To N. N.) seems to confirm this hypothesis: "Hey, please! Where are you, my bright light? / But you're not here."

That view, however, despite being proffered by the poet, is off the mark; the essence of Kibirov's poetry is in the fact that he has always been able to recognize "eternal patterns" within the surrounding collapse. In an early draft of "Vnov' ia posetil . . ." (I've come again . . . , 1835) Pushkin recalls his years in internal exile: "But Holy Providence / secretly shielded me, / Poetry, like a comforting angel, / Saved me, and my soul was reborn." This confession is quite specific and intimate, and yet, at the same time, it stands as the credo of Pushkin's entire generation, which beginning with Vasilii Andrevich Zhukovsky firmly believed in the sanctity of poetry, its healing power, and might. Later this belief was constantly called into doubt, and hardly any of the works of the great Russian poets (from Tiutchev to Brodsky) have been free of that doubt.

The credo also hit Kibirov hard. He is convinced that poetry in and of itself cannot be a guarantee of success but can only fortify the soul, support one at the beginning of the "rocky path from the old song," as Osip Mandel'shtam says in his "Grifel'naia oda" (The Graphite Ode, 1923), and give promise of an encounter with the reader of posterity in order to remind one of the connections among love, freedom, and creative work–of the fact that life is a miracle not in spite of, but thanks to, the relativity and unpredictable mobility of the entropic universe. As Kibirov says in "Ladno uzh, moi milyi drug . . . " (It's OK, My Dear Friend, 2000), "There are of course pain and fear, / evil lust, mortal remains' dust, / in short, hooliganism. / Time and space, / alas and alack, are fragile. //

But that's not what the writing is about! / That dull shit / is not worth anger! / The crow cawed 'Nevermore!' / The hell with him–forever!"

In her analysis of Kibirov's stylistics the linguist Liudmila Zubova concludes in her article "Proshloe, nastoiashchee i budushchee v poetike Timura Kibrova" (The Past, Present, and Future in the Poetics of Timofei Kibirov, published in *Literaturnoe obozrenie,* 1998) that "Kibirov does not destroy; he records destruction, understands its inevitability and necessity but tries to save what is valuable (and this must be understood by the means of testing with irony and mockery). He builds new structures out of debris. . . . In this sense, perhaps, Kibirov's poetics are not so much 'deconstructive' as 'bricolage' as described by Levi-Strauss: the creation of mythological thought 'always comes down to a new arrangement of existing elements . . . in the uninterrupted reconstruction with the aid of those same materials the former goals play the role of means'. . . ." If this interpretation of Kibirov's poetics is valid (and it seems fairly accurate), then it suggests an impression of Kibirov as a kind of cultural mediator: bricolage, according to Claude Lévi-Strauss, after all, is the most important method of mediation between binary oppositions. Kibirov is the most traditional of the postmodernists and the most avant-garde of the traditionalists. He manages in his poetry organically to unite seemingly incompatible categories and qualities: lyrical self-expression and criticism of the subjectivity of impersonal discourses; openness and alienation; optimism and despair; childishness and cynicism; pathos and obscenity; edification and rejection of the authority of any kind of truth; sentimentality and deconstruction; romanticism and antiromanticism.

In Russian culture, which is traditionally dominated by the struggle between irreconcilable binaries, and in which compromise and mediation are rejected as unworthy–even base–the literary fate of artist-"mediators" as a rule has been highly dramatic. They typically either enjoy a short-lived recognition, which is quickly taken away by more radical figures, or a belated recognition (the best examples of which are Tiutchev, Khodasevich, and Bulgakov). Precisely the "mediators," however, take on the complicated task of maintaining the continuity of the cultural process, which is torn by historical ruptures and catastrophes. Thanks to these "mediators," the characteristic movement from one extreme to another does not become a closed circle. Timur Iur'evich Kibirov fulfills this difficult role well, combining in his poetry the tradition of Russian romanticism, the memory of late-Soviet totalitarian cynicism, and the experience of the postmoderist/postcommunist search for freedom as well as the disappointments that accompany that search.

Interviews:

S. Shapoval, "Traditsionnyi russkii poet," *Moskovskie novosti,* 45–46 (15 November 1992): 10;

N. L'vova, "Ia tsitiroval pesni i opisyval nravy kazarm," *Komsomol'skaia pravda,* 22 September 1994, p. 6;

E. Ukhova, "Esli poet stal zhit' khuzhe byvshego sekretaria obkoma, eto eshce ne oznachaet gibeli literatury," *Literaturnaia gazeta,* 13 July 1996, p. 5;

O. Natoloka, "Bez figovykh listochkov i vne tusovki," *Literaturnaia gazeta,* 48, 27 November 1996, p. 5;

Vladimir Tuchkov, "Mne otvratitel'na blatnaia kul'tura," *Kul'tura,* 21 December 1996, p. 7;

I. Kuznetsova, "Pravila igry," *Voprosy literatury,* 4 (1996): 214–225;

E. Seslavina, " . . . I spokoino zanimat'sia svoim delom," *Druzhba narodov,* 7 (1996): 167–174;

Viktor Kulle, "Ia ne veshchaiu–ia boltaiu . . . ," *Literaturnoe obozrenie,* 1 (1998): 10–16.

Bibliographies:

Viktor Kulle and Evgenii Natarov, "Timur Kibirov. Izbrannaia bibliografiia," *Literaturnoe Obozrenie,* 1 (1998): 40–43;

"Kibirov Timur," *Russkaia virtual'naia biblioteka* <http://www.rvb.ru/np/publication/02comm/41/02kibirov.htm> [accessed 2 June 2003].

References:

Mikhail Aizenberg, Viktor Koval', Dmitrii Aleksandrovich Prigov, and Lev Rubinshtein, "Zadushevnaia beseda, ili Diuzhinu let spustia," *Literaturnoe obozrenie,* 1 (1998): 8–9;

Nikolai Aleksandrov, "Robkii Kibirov, ili *Notatsii,*" *Druzhba narodov,* 2 (2000): 196–200;

Aleksandr Nikolaevich Arkhangel'sky, "'Byl vsesilen etot iazyk!': Pochti vse Timura Kibirova," *Literaturnaia gazeta,* 7 July 1992, p. 4;

Arkhangel'sky, "Griadushchim gunnam," *Literaturnaia gazeta,* 18 September 1990, p. 4;

Dmitrii Bavil'sky, "Avtonomiia nastoiashchego," *Arion,* 4 (1997);

Bavil'sky, "Zazaemlenie," *Literaturnoe obozrenie,* 1 (1998): 20–23;

Nikolai Aleksandrovich Bogomolov, "'Plast Galicha' v poézii Timura Kibirova," *Novoe Literaturnoe obozrenie,* 32 (April 1998): 90–111;

Mikhail Naumovich Epshtein, "Novaia sentimental'nost': Timur Kibirov i drugie," in his *Postmodern v Rossii: Literatura i teoriia* (Moscow: R. Elininin, 2000), pp. 274–282;

Evgenii Ermolin, "Slaboe serdtse," *Znamia,* 8 (2001): 200–211;

"The First Brodsky Fellowships," *New York Review of Books,* 9 March 2000, p. 54;

Mikhail Leonovich Gasparov, "Russkii stikh kak zerkalo postsovetskoi kul'tury," *Novoe Literaturnoe Obozrenie,* 32 (April 1998): 112–123;

Sofya Khagi, "Art as Aping: The Uses of Dialogism in Timur Kibirov's 'To Igor' Pomerantsev. Summer Reflections on the Fate of Belle Lettres,'" *Russian Review,* 61 (October 2002): 579–598;

Viacheslav Kuritsyn, "Tri debiuta Timura Kibirova v 1997 godu," *Literaturnoe obozrenie,* 1 (1998): 36–37;

Oleg Lekmanov, "Sasha vs. Masha. 20 sonetov Timura Kibirova i Iosifa Brodskogo," *Literaturnoe obozrenie,* 1 (1998): 35–36;

Evgenii Natarov, "Timur Kibirov. Obzor kritiki," *Literaturnoe obozrenie,* 1 (1998): 38–39;

Kevin Platt, "T. Kibirov's *About Certain Aspects of the Present Sociocultural Situation,*" in his *History in a Grotesque Key: Russian Literature and the Idea of Revolution* (Stanford: Stanford University Press, 1997), pp. 171–182;

"Poeziia Timura Kibirova," *Literaturnoe obozrenie,* 1 (1998): 4–43;

E. Solomenko, "Mrak da peretak," *Pravda,* 2 September 1989, p. 3;

Evgenii Abramovich Toddes, "'Entropii vopreki': Vokrug stikhov Timura Kibirova," *Rodnik,* 4 (1990): 67–71;

Willem Westensteijn, "Timur Kibirov," in *Neo-Formalist Papers: Contributions to the Silver Jubilee Conference to Mark 25 Years of the Neo-Formalist Circle, Held at Mansfield College, Oxford, 11–13 September, 1995,* edited by Joe Andrew and Robert Reid (Amsterdam & Atlanta: Rodopi, 1998), pp. 268–281;

Mikhail Naftal'evich Zolotonosov, "Logomakhiia: Znakomstvo s Timurom Kibirovym. Malen'kaia dissertatsiia," *Iunost',* 5 (1991): 78–81;

Andrei Leonidovich Zorin, "Muza iazyka i semero poétov," *Druzhba narodov,* 4 (1990): 240–249;

Liudmila Zubova, "Proshloe, nastoiashchee ibudushchee v poetike Timura Kibirova," *Literaturnoe obozrenie,* 1 (1998): 24–26.

Anatolii Andreevich Kim

(15 June 1939 –)

Nadya L. Peterson
Hunter College

BOOKS: *Goluboi ostrov* (Moscow: Sovetskii pisatel', 1976);

Chetyre ispovedi (Moscow: Sovetskii pisatel', 1978)–includes *Solov'inoe ekho,* translated by K. M. Cook as "The Nightingale Echo," in *The Nightingale Echo: New Soviet Stories* (Moscow: Raduga, 1983), and "Lukovoe Pole";

Solov'inoe ekho (Moscow: Sovetskii pisatel', 1980);

Nefritovyi poias (Moscow: Molodaia gvardiia, 1981)–includes *Utopiia Gurina,* and *Lotos;*

Belka (Moscow: Sovetskii pisatel', 1984);

Vkus terna na rassvete (Moscow: Molodaia gvardiia, 1985);

Otets-les: Roman-pritcha (Moscow: Sovetskii pisatel', 1989);

Budem krotkimi kak deti (Moscow: Sovetskaia Rossiia, 1991);

Poselok kentavrov: Mifologiia XX veka (Moscow: Kovcheg, 1993);

Sbor gribov pod muzyku Bakha (Moscow: Roman-gazeta, 1998);

Onliriia (Moscow: Tekst, 2000);

Ostrov Iony (Moscow: Tsentrpoligraf, 2002)–includes "Moe proshloe";

Sbor gribov pod muzykhu Bakha (Moscow: AST/Olimp, 2002)–includes *Bliznets.*

Editions and Collections: *Nevesta moria* (Moscow: Izvestiia, 1983);

Sobirateli trav (Moscow: Izvestiia, 1983);

Izbrannoe (Moscow: Sovetskii pisatel', 1988);

Sobranie sochinenii, 2 volumes (St. Petersburg: Kore Saram, 1997–);

Belka: Roman-Skazka (Moscow: Tsentrpoligraf, 2001);

Izbrannoe Anatolii Kim (Moscow: Terra, 2002).

PRODUCED SCRIPT: *Mest',* motion picture, Kazakhfil'm Studio, 1989.

OTHER: "Ot ottsa i materi," in *Skazochnik,* with an introduction by Kim (Moscow: Molodaia gvardiia, 1982);

Anatolii Andreevich Kim (from paperback cover for Goluboi ostrov, *1976; Doe Library, University of California, Berkeley)*

Tuda, gde konchaetsia solntse: Vospominaniia svidetel'stva, dokumenty, compiled by Kim, with an introduction by Ally Bossart (Moscow: Druzhba zhurnal, 2002).

SELECTED PERIODICAL PUBLICATIONS– UNCOLLECTED: "Proshlo dvesti let," *Sovremennaia dramaturgiia,* 4 (1984);

"Ostanovka v avguste," *Znamia,* 4 (1987);

"Kazak Davlet," *Novyi mir,* 2 (1994);

"Sobachonka Oori: Koreiskie baiki," *Druzhba narodov,* 11 (1999).

Anatolii Kim achieved almost immediate critical acclaim in Moscow literary circles after the publication of his short novel *Lotos* (Lotus) in the journal *Druzhba narodov* (The People's Friendship) in 1980; it appeared the following year in the collection *Nefritovyi poias* (The Jade Belt). The work, which *Druzhba narodov* awarded its annual literary prize in 1980, was palpably different from the transparently realistic writing of Soviet establishment authors and firmly placed Kim among the voices of the new generation. His mythological approach, whereby the East and the West are united in a single vision, was a novelty for literature of this period. Kim's flirtation with Buddhism—his startling ventures into the area of immortality and reincarnation—as well as his fascination with the irrational are all indicative of a dramatic shift in Soviet writing as well. When the book first appeared, bemused Soviet critics berated Kim for its naturalism, symbolism, and stylistic experimentation and for his preoccupation with death. Readers, on the other hand, clamored for more of his novels.

Of Korean heritage, Anatolii Andreevich Kim was born on 15 June 1939 in the village of Sergievka in southern Kazakhstan. His family was one of many that had been deported to the Central Asian republic from Sakhalin in the Stalinist 1930s. Published sources do not provide much detailed biographical information about Kim. What is known is that prior to his studies in Moscow at the Literary Institute, from which he graduated in 1971, Kim served in the army, took courses at a Moscow art school, and held a variety of jobs—including one as a carpenter at a furniture factory and another as a crane operator. He also worked as an appraiser at the U.S.S.R. Art Fund and taught fiction writing at the Gor'ky Literary Institute.

Kim's first stories, "Shipovnik Meiko" (Dog-Rose Meiko) and "Akvareli" (Water-Colors), submitted to the literary journal *Avrora* (Aurora) by the well-known Soviet actor Innokentii Smoktunovsky and published there in 1973, were generally overlooked by Soviet mainstream criticism. Yet, his early fiction betrays an intense interest in the themes and issues that became central in his more mature prose. The animalistic heritage of humans, the role of art in life, and the idea of death as a welcome transformation have remained the major areas of Kim's creative interest.

His first book, *Goluboi ostrov* (The Blue Island, 1976), a collection of short stories set in the Far East, fared better with the Soviet critical establishment and sparked its interest for the first time in this "exotic" writer. Critics conveniently linked the unorthodox locations and moods of *Goluboi ostrov* to Kim's ethnic background and to his family history. For this Russian Orthodox writer who writes in Russian and considers Russian his native tongue, Korean culture continues to serve as an inexhaustible resource for characters and ideas in his novels and stories. The message of universal synthesis found in his works undoubtedly has much to do with Kim's desire to accommodate the competing cultural influences of Russia and Korea upon his life.

More than twenty years after its initial publication, Kim's next significant work, *Lotos,* is one that now can be considered programmatic. Yet, at the time of its appearance it marked a radical departure from the typical Soviet novel. In *Lotos* Kim boldly experiments with point of view. Time and space change, or move, unpredictably; displacements in the narrative voice occur within a single utterance; and the prosaic shifts strangely to the poetic. All these tactics serve to unbalance the reader and to defamiliarize Kim's discourse. The narrative focuses on three main characters: Lokhov, a successful Soviet artist; his mother; and the collective spirit of the dead, called "My" (We). The interactions between the characters and the progression of events, however, are obfuscated by Kim's ingeniously kaleidoscopic style. Unfolded in a straight chronological line, the story of Lokhov is the story of a mother and her prodigal son. A woman whose links to the natural world and tradition are strong, Lokhov's mother survives unimaginable hardships while trying to save her infant son. As an adult Lokhov visits his mother before she dies and offers her an orange cut in the shape of a lotus. Many years later the artist himself dies after bringing another lotus-shaped orange to his mother's grave.

Characteristically, in this work Kim engages in an intertextual polemic that allows for the incorporation of, and interaction between, various literary trends. On the surface *Lotos* is reminiscent of several Soviet "village" novels, popular in the 1960s and 1970s, about prodigal sons and daughters who return to the country to ask their parents for understanding and forgiveness. By rediscovering their roots, these characters acknowledge their alienation from the city, the realization that takes place in a final encounter with the wise, saintly, and strong peasant woman—usually their mother. In *Lotos,* however, Kim grafts onto this basic model of the "village" novel the existential issue of the spiritual indebtedness of all children to their parents.

The complexity of Kim's philosophical design in *Lotos* is underscored by his innovative form. The portrayal of time and space is fluid. The point of narration shifts from the hero's youth to his childhood, to old age—long after the death of his mother—and then back to the time of his last visit. The narrative voice changes constantly—from the voice of the young woman to the voice of the son, to the stepfather of the hero, and then to the collective voice of the dead. Stream-of-consciousness technique, used for the mother's voice, alternates with highly poetic narration. Moreover, the linear progression of time in realism is replaced here by what can be called a "universal simultaneity." Kim is trying to embrace all of reality by condensing and expanding time and space into a single utterance. At times the text eludes the spatial and temporal ordering that any reading imparts to it, as if Kim wants to maneuver the reader into a position from which one is able to sense the powerful existential meaning hidden behind words.

Unpredictable shifts in the voice of narration, while keeping the reader in constant tension, also point to the basic idea of *Lotos:* there is no death, only a painful but necessary transition into something different. The idea of a transition from the prosaic to the elevated is supported by deliberate changes in voice and style of narration. An entire subchapter, written in six-foot iambic lines, marks such a transition—a transformation from the prosaic description of Lokhov's mother to the symbolic tale of Lokhov's encounter with the spirit of his mother. For Kim, art is also a transformation. The lotus, an artificial flower created of something no longer living (an orange), becomes newly alive as a symbol both of the connections between all things and of the moral responsibility of all people before their ancestors. Kim's hero bridges the gap between himself and his dying mother—his city life and his village roots—with a gift of art.

The chorus of the dead spirits "We," who actually mediate between the living and the dead, is a frequent character in Kim's work of the late 1970s and the 1980s. In "Lukovoe pole" (The Onion Field, 1978) Kim emphasizes the link of "We" to the natural cycle of regeneration and to the continuous transformation of death into life. Dead spirits make a brief appearance in the novella *Solov'inoe ekho* (1978; translated as "The Nightingale Echo," 1983), in which the narrator's voice commingles with the all-knowing "We." In his first full-length novel, *Belka* (The Squirrel, 1984), Kim is even more direct about attributing to the "We" the possibilities and the responsibility of immortality.

By the early 1980s Kim had established himself as a highly esteemed writer whose books enjoyed great popularity with the discerning Soviet reader. In 1991 he left Russia for an extended working visit to South Korea, where he stayed until 1995. Several of Kim's novels were published during his absence from Russia. In 1995 he returned to Moscow to serve as an assistant

Front cover for Kim's Belka *(The Squirrel, 1984), which he called a* roman-skazka *or fairy-tale novel (Doe Library, University of California, Berkeley)*

editor at the distinguished literary journal *Novyi mir* (New World).

Kim's experiments with representation and philosophical orientation were not isolated incidents in the Soviet literary landscape of the 1980s. From the mid 1970s until the collapse of the Soviet Union, Soviet literature exhibited a keen interest in alternative modes of thinking and writing. Fantastic motifs, plots, and devices permeated this literature on different levels and to different degrees. Kim's own innovations in writing belong resolutely to this "fantastic decade," from the 1970s to the 1980s, a prelude of sorts to the literature of glasnost that came on the heels of the dramatic social transformations of perestroika. During the "fantastic decade" many writers began to question the conventions of Soviet thinking and writing, using utopian motifs and gestures of fantasy to deal in an admissible format with the issues of social imagination and alternative social constructs, the limitations of the teleological view of history embedded in Marxism-Leninism, and the constraints on personal freedom that this vision of the world implied.

Some of the authors writing in this vein (such as Kim, Vladimir Semenovich Makanin, and Ruslan Kireev) were variously called "the forty-year-olds," representatives of the "Moscow school," or writers of "alternative literature." In contrast to the certainties of socialist realist writing, the world of this prose hovers on the border of reality and dream. Ideas, objects, and situations take on threatening forms and associations, and the precise notion about the possibility of full cognition is put to the test. Limits of human perception, a profound moral confusion stemming from the disintegration of former beliefs, and the propensity of the mind for mythmaking are important themes in this literature. Its pronounced utopian impulse is articulated through various allegorical representations of the desire for change—the fairy tale, romance, and science fiction. An aversion to the evils of the big industrialized city is common to most of these writers.

Kim's overarching preoccupation with existential concerns earned his writing yet another set of labels; his compositions were perceived as "ontological" and "ethical-philosophical prose." His skillful combination of realistic and fantastic plots in his works, as well as his reliance on myths, linked him in the minds of many critics to the Latin American trend of "magic realism."

The issues of ancestral debt and of alternative social scripts for the future of Russia play an important role in another of Kim's novels, *Utopiia Gurina* (Gurin's Utopia, 1981). Iurii Gurin, the main character of the novel, is an unsuccessful actor in a Moscow regional theater who leaves his unhappy marriage, work, and life in the city for a distant region somewhere in the northeast of Russia. After a brief stay with his friend, a construction engineer named Tianigin, Gurin understands that his attempt at simple living has not succeeded and leaves for Moscow. Before Gurin's departure the two friends witness a miracle—Gurin's unassisted flight through the air. Both men are transformed by the event.

Gurin's behavior challenges Tianigin's assumptions about life and helps transform him from a rational, narrow-minded, and sexually dependent man into a person who professes love for everyone and everything. Gurin, who was able to free himself from the demands of sexuality as well, proclaims his devotion to everything existing on the planet, including the spirits of people who formerly inhabited the earth. Death holds no power over Gurin because he does not believe in the complete obliteration of the human spirit. In Gurin's own literary work, "Utopia," death is a welcome act of fusion with nature, and the aged are

revered but given control over their own destiny. Kim's characters are more concerned with the catastrophic possibilities of the contemporary world than with their own personal mortality. The result of this concern is Gurin's "Utopia," written as a dialogue between the two protagonists. Tianigin's remarks on the margins of the work are a counterpoint to Gurin's assertions.

Gurin's perfect society is a Crystal Palace built by utopians in the harsh northern country; it is classless, ahistorical, and structureless and centers on moral questions—love, death, beauty, moral education, and relations between the old and the young. Education is individual, art is considered to be more important than science, and all utopians are vegetarians. Tianigin, however, objects to Gurin's neglect of technology and the "Prometheanism" of his utopian idea. Like many other works of the period, Kim's novel examines the dangers of unbridled technological experimentation. The conflict between civilization and native cultures—between technology and nature—is not easily resolved. For Gurin, urban life is the source of all evil, and the only way out of this modern dilemma can be found in natural beauty and art. Believing that the perfect society will be built by eccentrics and dreamers, he calls on benevolent scientists to reorganize nature and on artists to serve as its protectors.

In his next work, *Belka,* Kim attempts a full realization of the philosophical concepts partially articulated in his previous writings. Its subtitle, Roman-skazka (A Fairy-Tale Novel), and Kim's evocation of Aleksandr Sergeevich Pushkin's *Skaza o tsare Saltane* (Tale about Tsar Saltan) in the epigraph to the novel characterize certain preconceived notions about novelistic discourse as a problem. Temporal and spatial planes are fused; the reader is accosted by supernatural occurrences involving eccentric heroes; and the novel professes a profound concern with moral issues.

Belka describes four Moscow Art Institute students, one of whom calls himself the Squirrel. The life stories of three of the protagonists are sifted through the consciousness of the Squirrel, who is able to transform himself into any one of his friends. The Squirrel's voice constantly intrudes into the narrative, intermingling with the confessional voices of the three friends. This intentional complexity and innovative vigor of form makes the narrative quite dense, rendering it a coded text in need of deciphering. The Squirrel's "remarks on the margins"—a series of philosophical digressions concerning the state of his society and modern world—do not clarify but, rather, complicate the development of the various plots.

A recurrent idea runs through the inner monologues of the protagonists: the lives of true people are endangered by a conspiracy of man-beasts who are out to destroy the world. On a more realistic scale, the destinies of the four painters stand for temptations and pitfalls facing creative personalities in any modern society. Each of the four life stories in the novel is an illustration of this idea. One of the characters falls in love with an Australian millionairess, marries her, and leads a comfortable but dull life of leisure, which ends in the character's accidental death. Another tries the life of a village teacher, but this character's inactivity leads to depression, violence against his own mother, then to insanity and, eventually, to suicide. The third is murdered by a criminal but comes back to life, because his creative gift has not been exhausted and he, the true artist, cannot perish without completing his artistic work. The Squirrel's fate is no less gloomy. A writer, whose aim in life is to describe, record events, and warn the world of the conspiracy of the man-beasts, the Squirrel is also an animal, in that he was raised by a squirrel after the death of his biological mother. He becomes convinced that destroying the animalistic side of himself is necessary in order to be truly human; to carry out such destruction, he kills a squirrel, obliterates his identity, and turns into an ordinary man.

In its belief in the eventual immortality of people, its distaste for the animalistic (and sexual) instincts, and in its reverence for the sacredness of all matter, *Belka* is a logical summation of the ideas that populate Kim's earlier works. As before, the predominance of animalistic qualities in people is blamed for all their misfortunes. Yet, in a gesture of hope, Kim argues here for the possible emergence of a new human being, a Christ-like figure incapable of cruelty. There is, for Kim, a divine dimension in all people, one that can find its full realization in creativity and self-improvement. Finally, the direct authorial communications with the reader in *Belka,* the moralistic tone of the novel, and its sense of an approaching social catastrophe hang ominously over the characters. Yet, its basic storyline—the conspiracy of man-beasts against "real" people—is played out like a fairy tale, whose intricate magic plot and a pronounced hope for a happy resolution mitigate somewhat the apocalyptic flavor of Kim's philosophy.

In *Otets-les* (Father-Forest, 1989) Kim continues his exploration of the narrative and philosophical possibilities of his "synthetic" approach to the genre of the novel. Articulating his historic, social, ecological, and cosmological concerns against the background of densely forested Russia in the Meshchera region of Riazan province, this lengthy work centers on the story of several generations of the Turaevs. In *Otets-les,* as in other fiction by Kim, the unbreakable nature of the ties between the natural world and the world of men is emphasized. The kaleidoscopic, seemingly disjointed narrative flow—now familiar from Kim's previous

Paperback cover for Kim's 1989 novel, Otets-les, *about several generations of the Turaev family and the enduring bonds between nature and mankind (Memphis State University Library)*

work—is once more employed to serve his larger philosophical designs. Narrative shifts intensify; the point of view moves from an impersonal narrator to human characters, the spirits of the dead, Father-Forest, Jesus Christ, the Earth, and the Universe.

The conflation of Russian and non-Russian mythology, fantastic events, and occurrences is counterbalanced by the concrete, realistic details of the lives of the Turaev family. The members of this family share a genetic link with the life-giving Father-Forest, enabling them to survive the many hardships that fall their way. The destruction of this link is possibly the result of aggression against the life-sustaining force of nature, the fate against which Kim's novel sounds a clear warning. Because of the human resistance to the collective spirit of nature, the putative ecological end of the world described in the novel shows human history to be ruinous and suicidal.

Kim's novel *Poselok kentavrov: Mifologiia XX veka* (The Centaur Settlement: A Mythology of the Twentieth Century), published in 1993, employs Greek mythology to a specific end. This work plays out the idea, by now familiar from Kim's previous writings, that people can become human only when they have killed the animal in themselves. War, hunger, and sex are the main forces in the lives of Kim's characters— half-human centaurs—and, according to Kim, these lives will always be cruel and short if ungoverned by principles other than aggression and sexual desire.

Onliriia (written in the 1990s but published in 2000) is a further elaboration of the eschatological vision permeating *Belka* and *Otets-les*. Here, Kim portrays the destinies of his human and nonhuman characters before and after the Second Coming, which brings immortality to all people living on the earth at the time. The rule of the planet by the "demonarium," a group of angels who had rebelled against God and worked on exterminating the human race, is brought to a close. Angels, demons, Christ, historical figures, and ordinary people interact in the work to bring about the eventual victory of good over evil. Kim's style of "universal simultaneity" is once again employed to articulate the inseparability of humans from all-encompassing nature.

Kim's next major work, *Bliznets* (The Twin), written in 1999 and published in *Oktiabr'* (October) in 2000 in anticipation of the millennium celebration, reads like a brief compendium of his most cherished ideas and narrative devices. Its narrator is an artificially separated twin whose supernatural powers include transformation and immortality. Following his brother Vasily's writerly fantasies, the Twin is capable of transforming himself into any of the people or objects that populate Vasily's consciousness. The plot of the novel is a travelogue of transformations grafted onto a mystery—that of Vasily's murder. The Twin's travels through people, animals, objects, times, and spaces provide him with an opportunity to discourse on such varied topics as the nature of writing and the writer's responsibilities, contemporary post-Soviet society, the commercialization of literature, and the violence of birth. Kim is open here about his existential and ontological concerns, wondering about those who "think us into being" and then punish us for existing. His narrator is made capable of seeing, because of his "supernatural loneliness," the common cause of the people and their fate—the immortality of all that stems from a universal flame. According to the narrator, all humans possess a spiritual twin in this world—a twin who will not succumb to death because death is tied to the material, not the spiritual. The enigma of death and Kim's denial of its permanence and importance are again played out in *Bliznets*. The mystery of Vasily's murder, though solved at the end, is more of an afterthought than the core feature of Kim's plot.

Anatolii Andreevich Kim's contributions to Russian literature have been significant and manifold. He has taken issue with the existing social scripts and "establishment" modes of writing through the use of fantasy, multidimensional characters, and innovative stylistic techniques. Moreover, from his first works he offered the Russian middle-class reader a protagonist whose disaffection was recognizable and common, yet whose future was still in the making. The deep spirituality of Kim's vision nurtured his readers' need for existential meaning in a climate officially devoid of religious concerns. His eschatological outlook, with all of its claims to universality, was also a response to the immediate problems of ailing Soviet society. His latest works, including *Bliznets*, exemplify commentaries on the subsequent fate of his surroundings. Kim's fiction betrays a profound sense of disconnection, almost a grievance against the cataclysmic transformations that Soviet writers, with Kim among them, "thought into being."

Interviews:

"The Breath of a Legend: An Interview with Anatolii Kim," *Soviet Literature*, 4 (1982): 119–122;

Il'ia Tolstoy, "Mysli o chelovecheskom: Puteshestvie dushi," *Dialog*, 3 (1990): 119–122;

Elisabeth Rich, "Anatolii Kim," translated by Charles Rougle, *South Central Review*, 3–4 (1995): 127–134.

Biographies:

"Kim, Anatolii," in *Dictionary of Russian Literature since 1917*, by Wolfgang Kasack, translated by Maria Carlson and Jane T. Hedges (New York: Columbia University Press, 1988);

A. G. Kovalenko, "Kim Anatolii Andreevich," in *Russkie pisateli 20 veka. Biograficheskii slovar'*, edited by Petr Alekseevich Nikolaev (Moscow: Nauchnoe izdatel'svto "Bol'shaia Rossiiskaia Entsiklopediia." Izdatel'stvo "Randevu-AM," 2000), pp. 337–339.

References:

Galina Belaia, *Khudozhestvennyi mir sovremennoi prozy* (Moscow: Nauka, 1983);

Belaia, *Literatura v zerkale kritiki* (Moscow: Sovetskii pisatel', 1986);

Anatolii Bocharov, "Mchatsia mify, b'iutsia mify," *Oktiabr'*, 1 (1990): 181–191;

Bocharov, "Mify i prozreniia," *Oktiabr'*, 8 (1990): 160–173;

Bocharov, "Ternistye puti khudozhestvennoi pravdy," *Oktiabr'*, 8 (1979): 208–219;

Bocharov, "Vremia kristallizatsii," *Voprosy literatury,* 3 (1976): 29–57;

Vladimir Bondarenko, "Avtoportret pokoleniia," *Voprosy literatury,* 11 (1985): 79–114;

Deming Brown, *The Last Years of Soviet Russian Literature: Prose Fiction 1975–1991* (New York: Cambridge University Press, 1993);

Sally Dalton-Brown, "Centaurs, a Singing Squirrel, and a Lotus: Anatolii Kim's Portrait of the Evolving Human Animal," *Modern Language Review,* 4 (1995): 967–972;

L. Karashev, "O 'demonakh na dogovore,'" *Voprosy literatury,* 10 (1988): 3–27;

Zoia Kedrina, "Vremia tvorit'," *Druzhba narodov,* 5 (1983): 217–227;

A. Klitko, "Parenie dukha i zemnye materii," *Sibirskie ogni,* 6 (1983): 148–155;

Natasha Kolchevska, "Fathers, Sons and Trees: Myth and Reality in Anatolij Kim's *Otets-les,*" *Slavic and East European Journal,* 3 (1992): 339–352;

Leonid Kostiukov, "U vechnosti v plenu," *Literaturnaia gazeta,* 19 April 1995, p. 4;

Alla Latynina, *Znaki vremeni: Zametki o literaturnom protsesse 1970–80 godov* (Moscow: Sovetskii pisatel', 1987);

L. K. Maksimov, "Problema odinochestva v povesti A. Kima 'Lukovoe pole,'" in *Khudozhestvennoe tvorchestvo i literaturnyi protsess* (Tomsk: Izdatel'stvo Tomskogo universiteta, 1988), pp. 50–63;

Vladimir Novikov, "Pod sousom vechnosti?" *Literaturnaia gazeta,* 13 February 1985, p. 4;

Nadya L. Peterson, "Science Fiction and Fantasy: A Prelude to the Literature of Glasnost," *Slavic Review,* 2 (1989): 254–268;

Peterson, *Subversive Imaginations: Fantastic Prose and the End of Soviet Literature, 1970s–1990s* (Boulder, Colo.: Westview Press, 1997);

Svetlana Piskunova and Vladimir Piskunov, "V prostranstvakh novykh," *Literaturnoe obozrenie,* 11 (1986): 13–19;

Mariia Remizova, "Pisatel' prorochestvuet, chitatel' pozevyvaet," *Literaturnaia gazeta,* 19 April 1995, p. 4;

Elisabeth Rich, "Mortality, Immortality and Anatolii Kim's Father-Forest," *Soviet Literature,* 9 (1990): 176–186;

Peter Rollberg, "Man between Beast and God: Anatoly Kim's Apocalyptic Visions," *World Literature Today,* 67, no. 1 (1993): 100–106;

Charles Rougle, "On the 'Fantastic' Trend in Recent Soviet Prose," *Slavic and East European Journal,* 34 (1990): 308–321;

Iurii Seleznev, "Fantasticheskoe v sovremennoi proze," *Moskva,* 2 (1977): 198–206;

Valentin Semenov, "Neokonchennyi portret s lotosom," *Pod'em,* 5 (1982): 121–133;

Svetlana Semenova, *Preodolenie tragedii: Vechnye voprosy v literature* (Moscow: Sovetskii pisatel', 1989);

Semenova, "Voskhodiashchee dvizhenie," *Oktiabr',* 2 (1989): 181–191;

Evgenii Shklovsky, "Radostnaia taina bytiia," *Literaturnoe obozrenie,* 11 (1978): 53–54;

N. N. Shneidman, *Soviet Literature in the 1980s: Decade of Transition* (Toronto: University of Toronto Press, 1989);

Karen Stepanian, "Liudi bogi v svete ironii," *Nezavisimaia gazeta,* 11 September 1992, p. 4;

Stepanian, "Mozhno li zhit' buntom?" *Literaturnaia gazeta,* 4 October 1989, p. 4;

Viktor Surganov, "Energiia dobra," *Literaturnaia gazeta,* 13 February 1985, p. 4;

Pavel Ul'ashov, "I mif, i skaz, i pritcha," *Literaturnaia gazeta,* 8 March 1987, p. 5;

Dmitrii Urnov, "Bor'ba ili igra so zlom?" *Literaturnoe obozrenie,* 5 (1983): 43–45;

G. Viren, "Skazka-lozh'?" *Delovoi mir* (19 September 1992): 11;

Harry Walsh, "The Post-Soviet Apocalypse: Anatolii Kim's Quest for Universal Redemption," *Religion and Literature,* 3 (1999): 77–93;

Sergei Zalygin, "O novoi knige Anatoliia Kima," in Kim, *Nefritovyi poias* (Moscow: Molodaia gvardiia, 1981), pp. 392–398;

Aleksei Zverev, "Predchustvie epiki," *Novyi mir,* 9 (1980): 220–236.

Viktor Borisovich Krivulin

(4 July 1944 – 17 March 2001)

Alexandra Smith
University of Canterbury, New Zealand

BOOKS: *Voskresnye oblaka* (1972);

Stikhi (Paris: Ritm, 1981);

Stikhi, 2 volumes (Paris: Beseda, 1988);

Obrashchenie (Leningrad: Sovetskii pisatel', 1990);

Kontsert po zaiavkam (St. Petersburg: Fond russkoi poezii, 1993);

Predgranich'e: Teksty 1993–1994 (St. Petersburg: Borei Art, 1994);

Posledniaia kniga (Tallinn: Viimane raamat, 1996);

Kupanie v Iordani (St. Petersburg: Pushkinskii fond, 1998; revised <http: www.vavilon.ru/texts/krivulin2.html>);

Okhota na mamonta (St. Petersburg: BLITS, 1998);

Requiem: Tsikl stikhotvorenii (Moscow: Argo-Risk, 1998);

Kniga posle stikhov (St. Petersburg: BLITS, 2001);

Stikhi iubileinogo goda (Moscow: OGI, 2001);

Stikhi posle stikhov (St. Petersburg: BLITS, 2001).

Edition: *Kontsert po zaiavkam: Tri knigi stikhov* (St. Petersburg: Fond russkoi poezii, 2001).

Editions in English: "Into the Fluting of the Spinal Cord," "God Is Buried, God Is Risen!" "Komsomol Street," "All the Spring Walls Crumble Into Powder . . . , Don't Pin the Casual Passerby," and "Flight to Egypt," translated by Michael Molnar, in *Poetry World 1,* edited by Daniel Weissbort (London: Anvill Press, 1986), pp. 37–40;

[Poems by Krivulin], translated by Molnar, *Bomb,* 17 (Fall 1986): 74–75;

"It's Difficult" and "Deserted but Thirsty," translated by Richard McKane, in *The Poetry of Perestroika,* edited by Peter Mortimer and S. J. Litherland (Newcastle upon Tyne: Iron Press, 1990), p. 6;

"Maps and Calendars and Maps . . . ," "Some Few of All the Voices," "Lemony-Bitter Strip of Sunset," "News Gets Round," and "Flight to Egypt," translated by Molnar, in *Child of Europe: A New Anthology of East European Poetry,* edited by Michael March (Harmondsworth, U.K.: Penguin, 1990), pp. 219–223;

"Poetry in the Sunset of Empire, From the Cycle 'Poems on Maps,'" translated by Molnar, in *Third*

Viktor Borisovich Krivulin (from the paperback cover for Obrashchenie, *1990; University of Chicago Library)*

Wave: The New Russian Poetry, edited by Ken Johnson and Stephen M. Ashby (Ann Arbor: University of Michigan Press, 1991), pp. 235–242;

"The Idea of Russia," "Southwest," "And the Silver Age . . . ," "Two in a Room," and "Guard," translated by Anna Barker and Weissbort, in *Twentieth-Century Russian Poetry,* edited by John Glad and

Weissbort (Iowa City: University of Iowa Press, 1992), pp. 325–328;

"The Chinese Palace at Oranienbaum" and "Art. Fedotov," translated by Molnar, in *In the Grip of Strange Thoughts: Russian Poetry in a New Era,* compiled and edited by Jim Kates (Brookline, Mass.: Zephyr, 1999), pp. 243–250;

"According to Your World," "The Lynx," "Prodigal Son," "By the Window," "At the Blackboard," and "The Pool at Dusk," translated by Thomas Epstein in *Crossing Centuries: The New Generation in Russian Poetry,* edited by John High and others (Jersey City, N.J.: Talisman House, 2000), pp. 147–151.

OTHER: *The Blue Lagoon Anthology of Modern Russian Poetry,* 5 volumes, edited by Konstantin Konstantinovich Kuz'minsky, contributions by Krivulin (Newtonville, Mass.: Oriental Research Partners, 1980–1986) IVb: 179–181, 190–228; as Aleksandr Kalomirov; V: 460–465–includes *Stikhotvoreniia v istoricheskom rode* and *Voskresnye oblaka;*

Krug, edited by Boris Ivanov and Iurii V. Novikov, contributions by Krivulin (Leningrad: Sovetskii pisatel', 1985), pp. 72–77;

Irina Anokhina, *Vitrazhi dlia ptits,* foreword by Krivulin (Tallinn: Aleksandra, 1991);

Obe poloviny posylki, with a preface by Krivulin (Holyoke, Mass.: Korrida, 1994);

Iukka Malinen, *Novyi Valaam: Stikhi,* translated by Krivulin (St. Petersburg: Borei Art Gallery, 1994);

"Pisatel' posle istorii, ili Antigona-dva (K voprosu o roli pisatelia v situatsii postmoderna)," in *Modernism i Postmodernism v ruskoi literature i kul'ture,* Slavic Studies at the University of Helsinki / Russian Studies at the University of Helsinki and Tartu University (Helsinki: Helsinki University Press, 1996), V: 67–71;

"Zolotoi vek samizdasta," in *Samizdat veka,* compiled by Vladimir Solomonovich Bakhtin, N. G. Ordynsky, Genrikh Veniaminovich Sapgir, Anatolii Ivanovich Strelianyi (Minsk, Belarus & Moscow: Polifakt, 1997);

"Iz novykh khoreiambov" (1998–1999) <http://www.vavilon.ru/texts/prim/krivulin4.html>;

"Memuarnyi ocherk o Sergee Dovlatove," in *Maloizvestnyi Dovlatov: Sbornik* (St. Petersburg: AOZT "Zhurnal Zvezda," 1999), pp. 382–385;

"Peterburgskaia spiritual'naia lirika vchera i segodnia (K istorii neofitsial'noi poezii Leningrada 60-80-kh godov)," in *Istoriia leningradskoi nepodtsenzurnoi literatury: 1950-80-e gody* (St. Petersburg: Dean, 2000), pp. 99–109;

Anna Akhmatova–Poslednie gody, compiled by O. E. Rubinchik, contributions by Krivulin, Vladimir Sergeevich Murav'ev, and Tomas Venclova (St. Petersburg: Nevskii dialekt, 2001);

"Zolotoi vek samizdata," in *Samizdat veka: Neofitsial'noi poeziia,* edited by Genrikh Sapgir <http://www.rvb.ru/np/publication/00.htm> [1 July 2003].

SELECTED PERIODICAL PUBLICATIONS–UNCOLLECTED:
POETRY

"Stikhi anonimnogo poeta," *Grani,* 97 (1975): 137–142;

"Iz tsikla 'V poliakh Edema,'" *Kontinent,* 10, no. 4 (1976): 143–148;

"Peterburgskaia poeziia," *Grani,* 103 (1977): 106–108;

"Stikhi," *Grani,* 108 (1978): 120–123;

"Stikhi," *Kontinent,* 28, no. 2 (1981): 99–102;

[Poems by Krivulin], *Vestnik novoi literatury,* 1 (1990): 98–107; 2 (1990): 5–64; 4 (1992): 49–55;

"Pervaia babochka," *Oktiabr',* 7 (1990): 49–55;

"Stikhi leta 1993 goda," *Vestnik novoi literatury* (1993): 158–162;

"Iordan'," *Znamia,* 12 (1995);

"Teksty vremen chechenskoi kampanii," *Tsirk "Olimp,"* 15, no. 7 (1996): 8;

"Cherez poltora desiatiletiia: Dialog dvukh knig" ("Poslednee leto imperii" [1984] and "Novye khoreiamby" [1999]), *Volga,* 11 (1999);

"Stikhi posle stikhov," *Oktiabr',* 9 (2000): 52–57;

[Contributions by Krivulin], *Arion,* 4 (2000): 102–105;

"Mir bol'she ne budet buol'shim," *Stikhi 2000 goda* (2000) <http://www.vavilon.ru/texts/prim/krivulin5.html>;

"Iz stikhov poslednego goda," *Zvezda,* 5 (2001);

Izbrannoe 1970–2001 and "Background po-pionerski," *Novoe literaturnoe obozrenie,* 52 (2001): 253–270.

FICTION

"Shmon: Roman," *Vestnik novoi literatury,* 2 (1990): 5–64;

"Rodoslovnaia," *Kontinent,* 55, no. 1 (1998): 134–177.

NONFICTION

"U istokov nezavisimoi kul'tury," *Zvezda,* no.1 (1990): 184–205;

"O sebe," *Vavilon: Vestnik molodoi literatury, vypusk,* 2, no. 18 (1993) <http://www.vavilon.ru/metatext/vavilon2/krivulin-1.html>;

"Literaturnye portrety v esseistike Iosifa Brodskogo," *Vestnik novoi literatury,* 7 (1994): 241–249;

"Skromnoe obaianie poezii," *Tsirk "Olimp,"* 11, no. 5 (1996): 7;

"Vozrozhdenie ody kak preodolenie postmodernistskoi pauzy," *Novoe literaturnoe obozrenie,* no. 27 (1997);

"Zaveshchanie v zanaveshennom zerkale: K tret'ei godovshchine smerti Iosifa Brodskogo," *Russkii zhurnal* (1 February 1999) <http://www.russ.ru/journal/krug/99-02-01/krivul.htm>;

"Utka po-kitaiski i vizantiiskii orel," *Neprikosnovennyi zapas,* 2, no. 10 (2000);

"Golos i pauza Genrikha Sapgira," *Novoe literaturnoe obozrenie,* no. 41 (2000);

"Vlast' i Pisatel', Vlast' nad Pisatelem, Pisatel' nad Vlast'iu," *Neprikosnovennyi zapas,* 3, no. 11 (2000);

"Pobeda bessil'noi sily," *Neprikosnovennyi zapas,* 4, no. 12 (2000);

"Pokushenie na stellerovu korovu," *Novoe literaturnoe obozrenie,* no. 43 (2000);

"Mucheniki, strastoterptsy i voiteli," *Neprikosnovennyi zapas,* 6, no. 14 (2000).

Exemplifying an intrinsic bond between Russian modernism and postmodernism, the poetry of Viktor Krivulin presents him as an outstanding craftsman who easily combines different styles, meters, and images from Russian and European verse. His work as a poet, cultural critic, and political activist awaits reevaluation, particularly in the context of the history of Russian alternative culture in the 1970s and 1980s. Krivulin saw himself as a St. Petersburg poet and prophet in the style of Aleksandr Sergeevich Pushkin—as someone who could foresee the development of liberal ideas and civilized societal norms in Russia. Despite his premature passing in 2001, Krivulin's voice will be heard in his country for many years to come because of his writings, which call for a return of human values in postmodern times.

Viktor Borisovich Krivulin was born on 4 July 1944 in the village of Kadievka near Krasnodon, Ukraine, where his father served as an army officer; three years after Krivulin's birth the family moved to Leningrad. His father, Boris Afanas'evich Krivulin, was born in 1901 in Mogeliv into a Jewish family that eventually sent him to a Jewish religious school. In 1924 he moved to Leningrad, where he graduated from the Leningrad College of Communist Propaganda, where Communist officials and lecturers were trained. After serving as an officer in the army from 1930 to 1947, Boris Afanas'evich retired from service in the rank of major. Krivulin's mother, Evgeniia L'vovna (Beliatskaia) Krivulina, was born into a Polish aristocratic family and worked as a midwife.

In 1960 Krivulin met Anna Andreevna Akhmatova, whom he continued to visit throughout the early part of that decade. His philological studies at St. Petersburg University, from 1961 to 1967, in the departments of Italian, English, and Russian, enabled him to work as a translator, editor, and teacher. Special-

izing in Russian modernism, Krivulin graduated from St. Petersburg University in 1967; his master's thesis was on Innokentii Fedorovich Annensky. Just before graduation Krivulin left the university Komsomol organization for political reasons. In his autobiographical essay from *The Blue Lagoon Anthology of Modern Russian Poetry (1970–1986)* he presents himself as a St. Petersburg poet associated with the new Leningrad poetry, as exemplified by the work of Joseph Brodsky, Sergei Georgievich Stratanovsky, Elena Andreevna Shvarts, Aleksandr Nikolaevich Mironov, and Oleg Aleksandrovich Okhapkin. In Krivulin's view, as he writes in "O sebe" (About Myself) in *Vavilon' Vestnik molodoi literatury* (Babylon: The Messenger of New Literature, 1993), this group of poets had the ability "to hold a balance between irony and pathos; between absurdity and spiritual exaltation; between surreal and classical." At the same time, Krivulin began developing his own distinctive poetic voice, which became prominent in the 1970s and was deeply inspired by the verse of Evgenii Abramovich Baratynsky. Krivulin also acknowledged the influence of Moscow conceptualists on his worldview. His poetic voice experienced transformations over the course of twenty years, but his intonation stayed more or less intact. In "O sebe" he tells about his writing method: following structural principles that, in their conventions, are more musical and architectural than literary, he would write cycles, or blocks of poems; compile them into bigger units; and later publish them as books.

Krivulin's first poems of significance were produced in the early 1970s. His first collection of poetry, *Voskresnye oblaka* (Sunday Clouds), appeared in samizdat in 1972. His most important poem of this period, "P'iu vino arkhaismov . . ." (I drink the wine of archaisms . . .), written in 1973 but not published until its inclusion in *The Blue Moon Anthology,* states that poetic craft and divinity are entwined and compares poetic speech to the divine drink of life. In a postmodernist manner in this poem Krivulin both affirms his belief in the immortality of poetic speech and doubts it: "I would like to believe in the ashes at least, in the abysses, / that survive—as the trace / of the expired word that blazed inside me!" One of the most innovative devices of Krivulin's poetry is its array of unusual syntactical structures, which incorporate few, if any, established conventions. These loose syntactical forms allow his poetic voice to flow freely, in imitation of uninterrupted speech. Krivulin's interest in the oral aspect of verse results from his profound belief in the transformative power of poetry. In the view of postmodernist scholar Mikhail Naumovich Epshtein, Krivulin—together with Ol'ga Denisova, Ol'ga Sedakova, Ivan Fedorovich Zhdanov, and Shvarts—is a metarealist poet. Metarealist poetry strives to transcend reality and employs the universal images of the European cultural tradition, especially archetypal images—garden, wind, water, mirror, and book. Metarealist verse reinforces its links with the high culture and cult poetry of the past, ranging from biblical times to European modernism, and Krivulin's poetry of the early 1970s—replete with echoes from classical poets, an opposition to socialist realism, and variations on universal themes—indeed qualifies as metarealist.

In the 1970s Krivulin and his first wife, Tat'iana Goricheva, a feminist and philosopher whom he married in 1975 and divorced in 1980, were active members of the underground movement in Leningrad. Krivulin and Goricheva were widely known as the editors of the samizdat journal 37, which was in operation from 1975 to 1981. Krivulin's first essays appeared in this journal, which also included articles on Russian culture, literature, philosophy, and religion. In his short recollections of various poets and writers, Genrikh Veniaminovich Sapgir suggests that the title 37 is associated with the number of Krivulin's apartment. It also refers to the year 1937, the height of Joseph Stalin's terror, and alludes to the year of Pushkin's death, 1837. In Russian cultural memory, the monarchy was held responsible for the death of Pushkin, the national poet of Russia. Krivulin felt a strong affinity with Pushkin, who—in his opposition to censorship and totalitarian discourse—embodied free speech.

In spite of the metarealist nature of Krivulin's verse, modernism is a core element of Krivulin's poetics. In his poetic experiments Krivulin stands out as a self-conscious innovator. In 1978 he was awarded the Andrei Bely Prize for his nonconformist writings. From 1979 to 1980, together with Sergei Dediulin, Krivulin edited and published another samizdat journal, *Severnaia pochta* (The Northern Post). Now divorced from Goricheva, Krivulin married Ol'ga Borisovna Kushlina, a Leningrad poet, critic, and fiction writer, in 1980; that same year their son, Lev, was born. During this period Krivulin also organized unofficial seminars on Russian Silver Age culture and on the role of religion in the contemporary world. Krivulin's early poetry scrutinizes the traditional ways of conveying meaning as reflected in his use of syntax, and in many ways it transgresses all representational rules. Not to be overlooked, for example, is the way that Krivulin blends skillfully outmoded poetic forms—such as the sonnet, octave, tercet, and quatrain—with highly innovative metrical and rhyming patterns. This tendency is manifested already in Krivulin's early poems such as "Kogda pridiet pora meniat' nazvania . . ." (When the time comes to change names . . . , 1979), "Gobeleny" (Tapestries, 1981), and "Sonet k 'Kokteil' Molotoff"

Photograph of Krivulin (on which he drew a mustache), Leningrad, 1959 (from Anna Akhmatova—Poslednie gody *2001; Hayden Library, Arizona State University)*

(Sonnet to the Cocktail Molotov, 1982). Krivulin's poetic voice appears to be free from moral imperatives. It manifests somewhat therapeutic powers of poetry that could help readers to come to terms with Russia's past and present; to repent and to discover the inner self; and to engage in the divine discourse of life creation. Thus, Krivulin's poem "Gobeleny," first published in the Russian émigré journal *Kontinent* (The Continent) in 1981, considers memory an important element of personal renewal and transformation:

> Kak khorosho, chto mir ukhodit v pamiat',
> no vozvrashchaetsia vo sne
> preobrazhennym – s pobelevshimi gubami
> i golosom, podobnym tishine.
>
> (It's good to see the world disappearing into the memory,
> but it keeps coming back in sleep
> transformed—with the lips that became pale
> and with the voice, akin to the silence.)

Prior to 1986 Krivulin's work appeared only in samizdat and émigré journals. He also participated in the unofficial association "Klub-81," which published his poems in its 1986 anthology *Krug* (The Circle). In that same year Krivulin's cycle "Slabye stikhi" (Weak Poems) was included in the Leningrad samizdat journal *Chasy* (The Hours). From 1988 to 1989 Krivulin lived in Paris, where he made a five-hour documentary movie, commissioned by the Leningrad Television Company, about the life of the Russian émigré community. During this period he also produced various programs on Russian culture and life for the British Broadcasting Corporation (BBC) and Radio Liberty. In 1990 he joined the Union of Writers and was awarded a West German fellowship from the Alfred Topfer Foundation. Krivulin is also known in Germany for his contributions to the newspaper *Frankfurter Allgemeine Zeitung* (Frankfurt General Newspaper). In the 1990s he was a member of the editorial board at *Vestnik novoi literatury,* a journal that promoted new forms of writing in Russia. He also co-edited an anthology of Russian samizdat literature; served as a member of prize committees for Internet sites such as "Teneta"; and was vice president of the St. Petersburg branch of PEN from 1991 to 2006.

A key idea in Krivulin's philosophical meditations on life is his intimate bond with St. Petersburg, in both a physical sense (as a place in the Baltic) and a cultural sense (as a construct known as the "Petersburg text"). His poetry incorporates vivid images of St. Petersburg that are also conveyed in the work of Pushkin, Annensky, Bely, Brodsky, Aleksandr Aleksandrovich Blok, and Aleksandr Semenovich Kushner; an example of this combination of St. Petersburg imagery and tributes to poets of the past is "Aleksandr Blok edet v Strel'nu" (Alexander Blok Goes to Strelna), first published in *Kontsert po zaiavkam* (Concert on Demand, 1993). In his northern landscapes Krivulin also draws on the tradition of spiritual awakening through contact with nature, molding his own image of the hermit as conveyed in the poetry of Elena Genrikhovna Guro, Baratynsky, Akhmatova, and Brodsky. In his poem "Na doroge u kresta" (By the Cross on the Road, 1992), published in *Kontsert po zaiavkam,* Krivulin resurrects Guro's image of the Poor Knight, belonging to some unknown spiritual order, in order to inscribe into his post-Soviet verse the last vision of "the decisive and quiet conversation." Krivulin's own vision of the utopian transformation of the world is as persuasive and prophetic as Guro's visionary discourse. The poet-prophet, as Krivulin's text demonstrates, is pushed to the margins and to the borderlines in the modern metropolis. Krivulin's poetry presents strong intertextual links with Russian classical and modern poetry, exposing him as a perceptive reader of other poets. As his poem "Po techeniiu pesni" (With the Flow of Song, 1993–1994) illustrates, every

poet follows the flow of his or her song, floating "in Derzhavin's river of eternity." In his theoretical tract on lyric verse "Rassuzhdeniie o liricheskoi poezii ili ob ode" (A Meditation on Lyrical Poetry or Ode, 1811), the eighteenth-century poet Gavrila Romanovich Derzhavin suggests that an ode acts as a swift river, absorbing everything and overflowing its boundaries from time to time. Krivulin pays tribute to Derzhavin, the spiritual teacher of Pushkin, in an attempt to resurrect this important poet and free him from Soviet captivity, as many of Derzhavin's philosophical and religious poems were not published in the Soviet Union and were misappropriated to fit Marxist dogma.

Krivulin's most profound images of St. Petersburg can be found in his poem "Kladbishche pochtovykh furgonov" (The Cemetery of the Postal Carriages), published in *Predgranich'e: Teksty 1993–1994* (Before the Border: Texts 1993–1994, 1994), which laments the death of old technological modes of communication at the "cemetery of postal carriages" in the St. Petersburg suburb of Priazhka. He describes this location: "I was afraid of the embankment of Priazhka, where normal land ends." This area of St. Petersburg includes the famous asylum known as "the yellow house," immortalized in the poetry of Blok and Konstantin Konstantinovich Sluchevsky. Krivulin's poem creates another frightening image of urban phantasmagoria, whereby "the white dressing / . . . gowns fly and cry / mixed up with crows during the sunset"; in the night white carriages stand like ghosts, "following with their white eyes / and with frightening quiet whispers / a drunk postman. . . ." The fragmented state of the modern urban world, as portrayed in Krivulin's poem, frightens and lures him at the same time. His strong interest in the surreal and the mystical means that defining him only as a metarealist poet is difficult, if not incorrect. By implication, surrealism is antirational and antirealist, advocating the liberation of the mind from logic, and suggests that art should result from confrontation with the unconscious mind. The title *Predgranich'e* suggests that the poet uses dreams and hallucinating states of mind both as the inspiration and the subject matter for his poetry.

St. Petersburg, with its white nights in summer, provides Krivulin with the appropriate setting for his visionary experiences. Thus, in the poem "Na poroge" (At the Porch), published in *Predgranich'e,* the poetic persona indulges in a state of evasiveness during his walk one July evening through a field in the countryside: "where shall I go? . . . it does not matter to me / whether I embark on a journey into the 1910s / or to the hundredth kilometer zone in the open field / as long as it takes me far away / into the twilight to grow slowly, hard like honey." Once again the poet's future is not defined; he is happy to embark on a journey to the unknown, using a Russian poet from the Silver Age, Osip Emil'evich Mandel'shtam, as his spiritual guide. He evokes Mandel'shtam's presence by alluding to the poet's "Voz'mi na radost' iz moikh ladonei nemnogo solntsa i nemnogo meda" (Take from my hands for your enjoyment / A bit of the sun and a bit of honey . . ."), first published in the journal *Dom iskusstv* (House of Fine Arts) in 1921 and later collected in *O. Mandel'shtam, Stikhotvoreniia, Sovetskii, pisatel'* (1973), and its image of honey prepared by Persephone's bees. Through this subtle allusion Krivulin presents his own body as a slow stream of poetic speech, a mixture of honey and light. Krivulin's self-representation, pivoting on the image of a transcendental state that is compared to the fluidity of light and honey, might be seen as a powerful metaphor for Krivulin's philosophically charged writing, summoning readers to value poetry as the force that liberates imagination.

During the 1990s Krivulin also published several prose pieces. In one of them, "Pisatel' posle istorii, ili Antigona-dva (K voprosu o roli pisatelia v situatsii postmoderna" (The Author Beyond History, or Antigon-Two [Toward the Question of the Writer's Role in the Postmodern Situation]), which he presented at a conference in Finland in August 1995 and had published in *Modernism i postmodernism v ruskoi literature i kul'ture* (Modernism and Postmodernism in Russian Literature and Culture, 1996), Krivulin boldly voiced his concerns about the new role of the Russian poet in the 1990s. In 1995 he worked as a war journalist in Bosnia. In the mid 1990s he became politically active and passionately supported a prominent St. Petersburg liberal politician, Galina Nikolaevna Starovoitova, who was assassinated in November 1998. Krivulin's writings of this period display a preoccupation with human rights and political pluralism. In his introduction to the essay collection *Okhota na mamonta* (Hunting for Mammoths, 1998) Krivulin portrays himself as a person who belongs to the underground culture of the 1970s. He remembers the last decades of the Soviet era as a period when writing poetry was seen as an alternative lifestyle—when poets risked not only their health but also their lives. Krivulin crafts out of himself an image of the "last poet," suggesting that he wishes to be remembered as the last poet of his generation for whom literature signified a source of life.

In his book *Kupanie v Iordani* (Bathing in the River Jordan, 1998) Krivulin equates the river of life with the river of poetry, so that poetry becomes a source of life renewal. The book was written from 1995 to 1997 and thus partly during the first Chechen war (1994–1996). Its political overtones are juxtaposed with philosophical meditations on life and death, a combination evoking strong antiwar sentiments that are expressed through a wide range of poetic forms and unusual stanzas. In the poem "Voskresenie pod Narvoi" (Resurrection Near Narva) Krivulin denounces the images of masculinity represented by the OMON (*Otriad militsii osobogo naznacheniia*, special forces of the Russian police) soldiers engaged in the reproduction of spiritless matter: "you resurrect near Narva / to glorify new culinary delights / of fried eggs and bacon!" This poem is composed as an octave, which was used by Pushkin in "Domik v Kolomne" (Little House in Kolomna, 1830) to convey carnival playfulness. Given this fact, Krivulin perceives the resurrection of the OMON soldiers as false and wanting. Potent antiwar feelings are also felt in the poem "Legkie igry" (Easy Games), which was added to the Internet version of *Kupanie v Iordani* <http://www.vavilon.ru/texts/krivulin2.html>, through the use of an alienating effect on a structural level: the exclaimed word "nu!" (well!), for example, fills out the whole line. Krivulin depicts the Russian war games in a parodic manner, mimicking the style of Russian medieval texts. The epic-like qualities of the poem help the narrator to mold his voice in the guise of a traditional lyre singer who offers comments on contemporary historical events. Mocking the style of Soviet and post-Soviet history books, *Kupanie v Iordani* also inscribes Krivulin's lament over the death of Orpheus in the long narrative poem "Kontsert pamiati Sergeia Kurekhina" (Concert in Memory of Sergei Kurekhin). He talks of Russian contemporary history as a farce—"eto ved' igra" (after all, it's a play)—and calls for the preservation of ecologically clean landscapes and for the restoration of links with nature.

In the fourth part of *Kupanie v Iordani,* titled "Rekviem" (Requiem), Krivulin reenacts Mandel'shtam's words of farewell to Akhmatova, "ia k smerti gotov" (I am ready to die). This reenactment might be because in the last years of his life Krivulin was terminally ill with cancer. Notwithstanding his unassuming poetic voice, some of his pronouncements are not free from ironic social commentary. In the poem "Gde zhe nash novyi Tolstoi?" (Where Is at Long Last Our New Tolstoy?), first published in book form in *Stikhi iubileinogo goda* (Poems of the Jubilee Year, 2001)—from the cycle "Iz novykh khoreiambov" (From New Iambs and Trochees, 1998–1999), which first appeared online—Krivulin levels his criticism at the growing influence of the Russian military, which has failed to produce any writer in the mold of Leo Tolstoy: "it's strange that we already had had / two wars, and the third one is approaching / there is no sign of a Tolstoy whatsoever / neither in person nor in nature."

In 1997 Krivulin organized the Sankt-Peterburg-skii Teatr poezii (St. Peterburg Theater of Poetry). Dur-

Paperback cover for Krivulin's 1993 book, Kontsert po
zaiavkam *(Concert on Demand), which includes the
poem "Na doroge u kresta" (By the Cross on the
Road), about spiritual awakening and utopian
transformation (William T. Young Library,
University of Kentucky)*

course, 1998–1999), which is permeated with autobiographical elements:

> boius' ia: bart i derrida
> ne ponadelali b vreda
> oni sovsem ne v to igraiut
> chto mne diktuet moi background
>
> no mikhalkov-marshak-barto –
> vot nashe podlinnoe to
> otkuda lezut ruki-nogi
> kinogeroi polubogi
>
> (I am afraid that Barthes and Derrida
> might cause a trouble
> they play the games that
> are alien to my background
>
> but mikhalkov-marshak-barto–
> this is truly ours
> that shapes our arms-legs
> that makes our film heroes semi-gods).

The poem resembles Epshtein's view of Soviet
reality as being akin in its virtuality to the Western
postmodern world. Doubting the nature of postmodern
anxiety, Krivulin states playfully: "To conclude our
new Moscow mockery / is not a nail in the foreign coffin" but "a retarded boy, a holy fool / once beaten by
his father-admiral." Krivulin sees the amnesia present in
many postmodernist texts as a factor accompanying
any collapse of history and resulting from a collapse in
established social grammar. In the late 1990s Krivulin
was closely involved in the liberal-democratic movement in St. Petersburg. In November 1998 he took part
in local elections for the *Democraticheskaia Rossia* (Democratic Russia) in St. Petersburg, but he was not successful. His posters were subjected to anti-Semitic attacks.

Krivulin's 1999 review-article on Brodsky's writings, "Zaveshchanie v zanaveshennom zerkale: K ret'ei
godovshchine smerti Iosifa Brodskogo" (The Will in
the Veiled Mirror: On the Third Anniversary of Joseph
Brodsky's Death), first published in the Internet journal
Russkii zhurnal (Russian Journal), brings to the fore
Brodsky's ability to create a metaspace where he introduces other poets and cultural figures from the past
and, at the same time, exhibits himself. To Krivulin,
Brodsky's text centers on a dialogue with the past that
produces a discontinuous discourse. The image of the
mirror that opens the way to the museum-like other
world is an apt metaphor. "The modern poet's role is
reduced to the role of pretender," writes Krivulin, for
"he has to pretend that he is creating his own inner
space akin to a room of mirrors, which reflects the
whole world." In Krivulin's view Brodsky talks about
other poets as if he continues to write poetry for himself

ing the St. Petersburg Carnival, which took place in
June 1997, he and other performing poets organized a
show and a party to celebrate the opening of the new
Pushkin monument on 6 June 1997. The monument
was constructed only for the duration of carnival activities. Krivulin's theater produced more performances on
20 June 1997. His playful rediscovery of poetry as a
part of the mass carnival culture demonstrates his long-
standing commitment to the promotion of the freedom
of speech and creativity in Russia.

Krivulin's irony often aspires to eradicate several
phenomena: post-Soviet versions of masculinity, the
messianic idea of Russia, and the emerging new grand
narratives, including postmodernism. Krivulin's light-
hearted suspicion of new popular discourses can be
detected in his poem "Stolichnyi diskurs" (Capital Dis-

and for other authors—be they Russian or American. Krivulin asserts that poetry is a continuous dialogue with the past and with other cultural traditions. The article illustrates his growing belief in an impersonal and immortal divine voice that lives in every poet.

Krivulin's concerns with the preservation of cultural memory in postmodern times are comparable to the concerns of Mandel'shtam in the 1930s. Both poets expressed their awareness of a lost Russian heritage. Yet, Krivulin's poetry closes the gap between modernist and postmodernist modes of writing. The notion of cultural authority, as exemplified in Krivulin's opposition to various remnants of Soviet ideology in contemporary Russia, implies a sense of self-righteousness that nevertheless often turns into parody or journalism in his texts. An unusual mixture of parodic and nostalgic overtones can be found in his poem "Podsolnukhi" (Sunflowers, 2000), a highly skillful and sensitive rewriting of both Mandel'shtam's renowned poem "Bessonitsa. Gomer. Tugie parusa . . ." (Insomnia. Homer. The tense sails . . . , 1915) and of Vincent van Gogh's painting "Sunflowers." Mandel'shtam's iambic meter and intonation in Krivulin's rendering, "sunflowers van gogh again auction / I read up to the middle the list of lots," pays homage to Mandel'shtam. Krivulin's text illustrates at its best his method of weaving other poets' voices into his poetry, which is also framed here into the all-inclusive tradition of European culture, both verbal and visual. Krivulin uses van Gogh's image of dying sunflowers as an allegorical portrayal of the death of the poet in the post-Soviet culture of mass consumption:

no za stekliannoi dver'iu na balkon
eshche trudnei dyshat' – oni soorudili
industrial'nyi vid so vsekh storon
besplatnyi, vidimo, odnako obratimyi
v bumagi tsennye gde vnov' izobrazhien
vsie tot zhe izdykhaiushchii podsolnukh
za zhizn' tsepliaetsia, za vozdukh za gazon

(but behind the glass door in the balcony
it is even more suffocating—they created
an industrial landscape stretching everywhere
free, it seems, though convertible
into valuable papers where the image of the
same dying sunflower will be printed again
depicting it as struggling for life, clutching air and lawn).

The poem demonstrates Krivulin's chief preoccupation with the poet's place in contemporary society. Poetry, insists Krivulin, is an important source of spirituality that cannot be tailored to suit societal tastes and needs.

In another discourse on postmodernism—in the poem "Mir bol'she ne budet bol'shim" (This World Will Be Grand No More, 2000), published in the Internet collection *Stikhi 2000 goda* (Poems Written in 2000)–Krivulin states that "we could all gather one day / and decide that it [the world] exists no more." He writes, "Every person is an artist / who bleeds on the stage with cranberry blood." Notwithstanding his representation of the postmodern world as one of simulacra, Krivulin is suspicious of some ideological trends in the post-Soviet period. Thus, in his article "Mucheniki, strastoterptsy i voiteli" (Martyrs, Saints, and Fighters, 2000), first published in the journal *Neprikosnovennyi zapas* (The Iron Ration), he warns of an emergence of conservative tendencies (such as anti-Semitism, radical nationalism, and anti-Western propaganda) within the Russian Orthodox church. In one of his last poems, "Iz glubiny" (From the Depth, 2001), collected in *Stikhi iubileinogo goda,* Krivulin is critical of any postmodern outlook that opens a way to cynicism and reveals a lack of sensitivity toward the human dimension. The emerging grand narrative frightens Krivulin as a possible slide into fascist discourse, represented in this poem by an "obyvatel' gladkosherstnyi" (civilized-looking philistine) who is eager to beat up in his "institut ksenofobii" (xenophobic institution) any person from the Caucasus—the "other" in Russian political discourse. In his political views Krivulin stands close to Russian liberal politicians who persistently condemned nationalistic tendencies in Russian politics. Krivulin's strong opposition to Russian imperialist and military-oriented discourses is also expressed in his 2000 essay "Pobeda bessil'noi sily" (The Victory of Powerless Power), published in *Neprikosnovennyi zapas.* The essay is scornful of Vladimir Vladimirovich Putin and calls him a young teenager playing the role of Peter the Great. Krivulin also reveals his growing disillusionment with the policies of St. Petersburg governor Vladimir Iakovlev, who reinstated some forms of censorship in the local media in order to promote his own vision of patriotism.

Krivulin's late writings reinforce the idea of continuity as a prerequisite for the survival of poetry. Yet, in a postmodernist vein, he questions the ethics of representation. His poem "Iaponskii perevodchik" (Japanese Translator, 2001), also published in *Stikhi iubileinogo goda,* for example, presents him as a failed Japanese translator of Mandel'shtam's poetry, awaiting punishment for an attempt to copy another poet's intimate thoughts and emotions: "let them display my body all over the country / until I repent and prove that I am free from sin / as if I desired to get under his skin, into his soul. . . ." Krivulin's poem "Pushkin, tainaia svoboda" (Pushkin, the Secret Freedom, 2000) entwines images of Pushkin with those of freedom and suggests that a poet's life is a spiritual journey toward liberty and humanism. In his last essay, published on 21 February

2001 in the St. Petersburg newspaper *Chas PIK* (Rush Hour), Krivulin comments on the death of the freedom of speech in St. Petersburg media, an absence that makes his favorite city more detached from the image of the true European metropolis that he cherishes in his dreams.

Krivulin died on 17 March 2001. His last book, *Stikhi posle stikhov* (Poems After Poems), was published posthumously that same year. Before his death he had prepared a collection of poems, *Izbrannoe 1970–2001* (Selected [Poems] 1970–2001), originally published in June 2001 in *Novoe literaturnoe obozrenie* (The New Literary Review). In this collection, each year of Krivulin's creative life is represented by one poem, and the last poem, "Pis'mo kak telo" (Writing as Body, 2001), depicts the complete transformation of the poet's body into a space of discontinuous discourses.

In their memoirs Viktor Borisovich Krivulin's friends refer to him as a mythmaker, a mystic, a trembling figure of the Silver Age, and a collector of Russian culture. In spite of his sociable nature, Krivulin also had the distinctive personality of an eccentric lonely citizen of St. Petersburg, as if he were a creation of the most artificial city in the world. Encompassing a multitude of styles, Krivulin's poetry and essays bridged the gap between the high and low cultures that shaped the development of Russian contemporary verse. To a great extent he can be viewed as a major leader of the cultural revival in Leningrad that made possible the resurrection of the ideas of spiritual brotherhood and freedom in post-Soviet Russia. The most popular underground poet of the 1970s, Krivulin fought for the preservation of Russian language, poetic craftsmanship, and creative freedom in post-Soviet Russia. Exemplifying a great variety of styles, traditions, and epochs, Krivulin's poetry is full of allusions to Egyptian, Roman, biblical, medieval, and European texts that together, in a powerful gesture, subvert the Soviet legacy.

Interview:

Vladislav Kulakov, "Poeziia–eto razgovar samogo iazyka," *Novoe literaturnoe obozrenie* <http://www.ruthenia.ru:8085/60s/leningrad/krivulin/interview.htm> [accessed 30 June 2003].

References:

Irena Luksic, "Vremia nastupilo: *Shmon* Viktora Krivulina," *Russian Literature,* 51–53 (April 2002): 273–294;

Michael Molnar, "Viktor Borisovich Krivulin," in *Reference Guide to Russian Literature,* edited by Neil Cornwell (London & Chicago: Fitzroy Dearborn, 1998), pp. 467–468;

Ol'ga Aleksandrovna Sedakova, "Ocherk i drugoi poezii. Ocherk pervyi. Viktor Krivulin," *Druzhba narodov,* 10 (1991): 258–266;

Sedakova, "Pamiati Viktora Krivulina," *Novoe literaturnoe obozrenie,* 52, no. 6 (2001): 236–242;

I. [Mikhail Berg] Severin, "Novaia literatura 70–80kh," *Vestnik novoi literatury,* 1 (1990): 222–239;

Mikhail Sheinker, "Grivastaia krivaia Viktora Krivulina," *Novoe literaturnoe obozrenie,* 52, no. 6 (2001): 230–235;

Clint B. Walker, "The Spirit(s) of the Leningrad Underground: Viktor Krivulin's Communion with Russian Modernism," *Slavonic and East European Journal,* 43, no. 4 (Winter 1999): 674–698;

Sergei Zav'ialov, "Tishina i gospodstvo bessmertiia," *Novoe literaturnoe obozrenie,* 52, no. 6 (2001);

Liudmila Zubova, "Teoriia i praktika svobodnogo stikha Viktora Krivulina," *Novoe literaturnoe obozrenie,* 52, no. 6 (2001): 243–252.

Mikhail Nikolaevich Kuraev

(18 June 1939 –   )

Valentina G. Brougher
Georgetown University

BOOKS: *Kapitan Dikshtein: Fantasticheskoe povestvovanie* (Leningrad: Sovetskii pisatel', Leningradskoe otdelenie, 1988); translated as "Captain Dikshtein. A Fantastic Narrative," by Margareta O. Thompson, in *Glasnost: An Anthology of Russian Literature under Gorbachev,* edited by Helena Goscilo and Byron Lindsey (Ann Arbor, Mich.: Ardis, 1990);

Nochnoi dozor (Moscow: Sovremennik, 1990)—includes "Zhestokost': Iz semeinoi khroniki," "Nochnoi dozor," and "Sem' monologov v otkrytom more";

Malen'kaia semeinaia taina (Moscow: Slovo, 1992)—includes "Petia po doroge v tsarstvie nebesnoe" and "Malen'kaia semeinaia taina";

Zerkalo Montachki. Roman v stile kriminal'noi suity, v 23 chastiakh, s introduktsiei i teoremoi o prizrakakh (Moscow: Slovo, 1994);

Puteshestvie iz Leningrada v Sankt-Peterburg, with an introduction by A. Vel'tman (St. Petersburg: BLITS, 1996);

Zhrebii No. 241 (Moscow: Knizhnaia palata, 1996)—includes "Kak ia staralsia ne stat' pisatelem," "Druzhby nezhnoe volnen'e," "Vstrechaite Lenina," "Blok-ada," and "Zhrebii No. 241";

Piterskaia Atlantida (St. Petersburg: Lenizdat, 1999);

Zhizn' nezamechatel'nykh liudei (Kurgan: Zaural'e, 1999)—includes *Zerkalo Montachki,* "Blok-ada: Prazdnichnaia povest'," and "Puteshestvie iz Leningrada v Sankt-Peterburg";

Priiut tenei (Moscow: Tsentrpoligraf, 2001)—includes "Zolotukha po prozvishchu Odyshka" and "Smertnoe mgnovenie."

Edition: *Kapitan Dikshtein* (Moscow: Profizdat, 1990).

Edition in English: *Night Patrol and Other Stories,* translated by Margareta O. Thompson (Durham, N.C.: Duke University Press, 1994)—includes "Night Patrol" and "Petia on His Way to the Heavenly Kingdom."

Mikhail Nikolaevich Kuraev (from the cover for Zhizn' nezamechatel'nykh liudei, *1999; Collection of Valentina G. Brougher)*

PRODUCED SCRIPTS: *Piataia chetvert',* motion picture, Lenfil'm, 1969;

Strogaia muzhskaia zhizn', motion picture, Lenfil'm, 1974;

Progulka dostoinykh muzhchin, motion picture, Lenfil'm, 1984;

Ozhog, motion picture, Lenfil'm, 1988.

OTHER: *Okhota na svinei,* edited by Kuraev (St. Petersburg: BLITS, 1998).

SELECTED PERIODICAL PUBLICATIONS– UNCOLLECTED:

FICTION

"Malen'kaia domashniaia taina," *Novyi mir,* 3 (1990): 9–30;

"Kuranty b'iut," *Znamia,* 11 (1992): 24–37;

"Tikhie bezzlobnye pokhorony," *Znamia,* 9 (1998): 6–40.

NONFICTION

"O Rembrandte i o sebe," *Druzhba narodov,* 8 (1992): 85–101;

"Za kogo oni nas prinimaiut?" *Sintaksis,* 34 (1993): 164–196;

"Kto voidet v dom Chekhova?" *Druzhba narodov,* 1 (1993): 198–208;

"Pamiatnik Gogoliu," *Kontinent,* 83 (1995): 271–297;

"Chekhov poseredine Rossii," *Zvezda,* 3 (1997): 116–136;

"Aktual'nyi Chekhov," *Druzhba narodov,* 12 (1998): 168–179.

Mikhail Kuraev is a contemporary writer whose prose and articles have appeared in major journals since the late 1980s. His ability to craft a tale in which a broad historical canvas serves as the background for a focus on individual life, as well as on his modernist attitude toward time and space, has brought him recognition as a talented writer of Russian life in the post-Soviet years. Although his most recent work has not generated the same excitement as his first novellas, Kuraev's prose and essays continue to draw critical notice.

Mikhail Nikolaevich Kuraev was born in Leningrad on 18 June 1939 into a family of engineers. In February 1942 he was evacuated with his mother, Anna Petrovna Kuraeva, and older brother, Sergei, from Leningrad during its siege; his younger brother, Boris, had died shortly before. Kuraev returned to Leningrad in 1954 after living for some years in the polar regions (Zapoliar'e), where his father, Nikolai Nikolaevich Kuraev, worked as an engineer. Kuraev's father, awarded the Stalin Prize in 1949 for his work on an underground hydroelectric power station in Zapoliar'e, subsequently served as director of a design institute in Leningrad. Thanks to this position, Nikolai Nikolaevich was able to support his family relatively well. Kuraev remembers an apartment filled with books and music and a mother who made a concerted effort to expose her children to the rich cultural history and active cultural life of the city. In 1961 Kuraev graduated from the Leningrad Theater School, and from 1961 to 1988 he was employed as a scriptwriter for Lenfil'm Studio.

Kuraev's literary debut, the novella *Kapitan Dikshtein: Fantasticheskoe povestvovanie* (published in 1987 in the journal *Novyi mir* [New World]; translated as "Captain Dikshtein. A Fantastic Narrative," 1990), brought him immediate recognition. Although not all reviewers appreciated this "intense and rich work," as Margareta O. Thompson points out in her introduction to *Night Patrol and Other Stories* (1994), many admired Kuraev's courage for tackling what had been a taboo topic for decades: the uprising against Communist rule at the Kronstadt naval base in February and March of 1921. The novella captures the social and political dynamics of those turbulent times, the hunger and cold, the mood in a city of closing factories, dwindling population, and competing political voices. The rebellion at Kronstadt comes to dominate this canvas, and Kuraev's narrative effectively evokes the tragic dimensions of the insurrection.

The novella opens and closes with the death of Igor Ivanovich Dikshtein in the 1960s. He goes to turn in some empty bottles at a glass collection center, buys beer in a grocery store, and, on his way home, dies of a heart attack. (As Igor' Aleksandrovich Dedkov pointed out in his review of *Kapitan Dikshtein* for the journal *Znamia* [The Banner] in 1988, Kuraev's choice of such "a nobody" for his hero took readers by surprise; the public expected a grander figure as the hero of a literary work published during the glasnost period). The "fantastic" dimension to Dikshtein's life is that he is not who he pretends to be. When he worked aboard the ship *Sevastopol'* as a stoker, whom the narrator describes as a simple sailor "with a scalp lock," he assumed, through various coincidences and twists of fate, the identity of one Dikshtein, who at the time commanded the hold of a turret in the main battery of the ship. The real Dikshtein was eventually executed, but because the sailor takes on his identity, he continues to "live"; the title of "captain" is assigned to him later by friends.

Kuraev does not hide his authorial presence in the novella, often addressing his reader openly. In the tradition of the works of Nikolai Vasil'evich Gogol, whom Kuraev admires greatly, he frequently employs a satirical tone. He also anticipates events, introduces suspense to his tale, and engages the reader in a dialogue about the need for his "digressions"–which are many, for Kuraev is taken with the history and life of buildings, streets, towns, and even the clothing of his characters. Critics have described the structure of Kuraev's novella as a series of "meanderings," a "zigzagging" between different times, episodes, and topics. A strong or complicated plot is clearly not important to him.

Kuraev's second published work, "Nochnoi Dozor" (*Novyi mir,* 1988; translated as "Night Patrol," 1994), established him as a writer of note in the glasnost era. Written in a traditional realistic style, Kuraev's tale resonated with the readers of the day because of his choice of subject and theme. The narrative is structured on two alternating voices: that of the first-person narrator (and implied author) and of Comrade Polubolotov (literally, Comrade Half-Swamp). As in his first work, Kuraev shows a deep interest in the history of St. Petersburg and the legacy of its founder, Peter the Great. The narrator's view of history includes a critical look at the tyrannical ways of the rulers who followed Peter, their trust in the *knut* (knout) and in chambers of torture, and their staging of public executions to control the populace. Polubolotov, who serves as the second "voice" that commands the reader's attention, tells his story in a more personal, confessional mode. He served in the armed guard of the secret police for many years, and as he reminisces about that period in his life, he reveals who was arrested, how arrests were conducted, and how those arrested were treated and sentenced. The impression from his narrative is that–as in the time of Peter the Great–the individual is powerless to resist the Soviet government machine in operation; justice is absent; and individual life counts for nothing. Polubolotov is not totally without feeling or intellectual interest; he does talk of nightingales who "tear at your soul," and he admits to accumulating a vast amount of knowledge about science, medicine, and poetry from those whom he interrogated. He exhibits no sympathy, however, for his victims, and the reader can easily note his cold indifference to questions of right and wrong and his role in destroying human life.

The setting of Kuraev's third published work, "Petia po doroge v tsarstvie nebesnoe" (*Znamia*, 1991; translated as "Petia on His Way to the Heavenly Kingdom," 1994), immediately attracted the attention of critics. Rather than setting this novella in St. Petersburg, Kuraev shifts to the Kola Peninsula in the North. As was true of the structure of his previous works *Kapitan Dikshtein* and "Nochnoi Dozor," the narrative zigzags between the past, the distant past, and the present; Kuraev is particularly adept at giving the reader a feel for the landscape, weather, history, and human life in the distant North. Written in the realistic style that he favors, this work provides a detailed view of the life of various segments of the population: camp inmates and camp administration, people living in "internal exile," as well as those seduced by the promises of large bonuses for working in the polar regions. Much of the story is told by a first-person omniscient narrator who, the reader senses, represents Kuraev's alter ego. Since Kuraev lived in the polar regions as a child, the novella may have been inspired by his memories and family stories of the place.

The work opens with Petia's accidental death from machine-gun fire, an incident to which the title alludes. Kuraev uses the unusual character of Petia, a

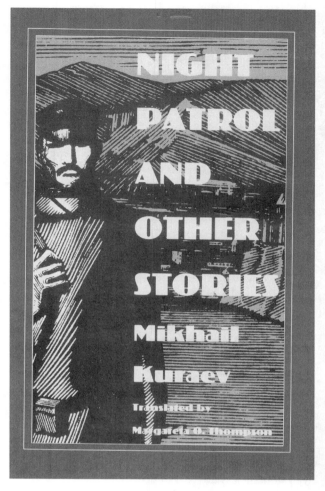

Paperback cover for 1994 collection of Kuraev's stories in English, which includes "Captain Dikshtein" and "Petia on His Way to the Heavenly Kingdom" (Richland County Public Library)

fellow with mental limitations who works as a traffic policeman, both to comment on labor-camp life that confronts him daily as well as to define the character of the people who witness the life in these camps. Several "triumphant" moments in Petia's life illustrate not only his limitations but, by extension, the limitations of the townspeople. One such "triumphant" moment is bound with the actor Nikolai Cherkasov, who was renowned for his portrayal of Alexander Nevsky in Sergei Eisenstein's movie of the same name. In the tones of irony and sarcasm that often color Kuraev's prose, the narrator captures the absurd limits of blind adoration. The same irony colors the narrator's attitude toward the first subterranean hydroelectric station in the world being built with slave labor to bring "socialism closer."

The narrator accuses people of "historical psychopathology"–of allowing themselves "to abstain" from developing their minds and souls. The plight of the overworked and maltreated camp workers, who can be shot at the whim of a guard, elicits no lamentation on their part. One of the many telling moments in the story concerns Joseph Stalin's death. Petia is horrified to note the happy eyes of the prisoners after Stalin's death, when he himself wants only to weep. For Petia, whose already limited mind was shaped by slogans and daily propaganda, Stalin represented truth, justice, and order. But what about the other people, Kuraev—a profoundly moral writer—asks, what is their excuse for totally closing their eyes to injustice and inhumanity?

Other stories written in the first half of the 1990s also confirm that Kuraev is deeply interested in Russian history and questions of morality. In "Malen'kaia domashniaia taina" (A Short Family Story, 1990) he explores the limits of human patience and suffering and the cumulative effect of affronts to human dignity. A Polish woman who survives exile and a harsh existence leaves her husband of one day, because his practicality blinds him to her craving need for one simple romantic gesture—a gift of flowers. In "Druzhby nezhnoe volnen'e" (The Tender Emotion of Friendship, published in *Novyi mir,* 1992) the thematics of the narrative center on the relationship between the ideals of honesty, honor, and real life. In "Kuranty b'iut" (Bells Ring, 1992), as in much of his prose, Kuraev shares Leo Tolstoy's view of history. In the story Kuraev draws attention to individuals whose lives will never figure into history books—such as the dedicated man who keeps the bells at the Peter and Paul Fortress chiming—but who nonetheless are part of history.

Kuraev's only full-length novel, *Zerkalo Montachki* (Montachka's Mirror), published in *Novyi mir* in 1993 and as a book in 1994, elicited starkly different reactions. Representing the minority view, critic Irina Bentsionovna Rodnianskaia opined that the novel was, "if not the best thing" she had read in 1993, "at least unquestionably excellent and in any event the most pleasant" work she had encountered that year. Other critics who took any note of the novel called it long and tedious.

Zerkalo Montachki is set in St. Petersburg, and much of the action takes place in an apartment house on Griboedov Canal (called Ekaterinskii until 1922), which forms an important part of the setting of Fedor Dostoevsky's *Prestuplenie i nakazanie* (Crime and Punishment, 1866) and on which lived such prominent literary figures as Anna Andreevna Akhmatova and Mikhail Mikhailovich Zoshchenk. Imbued with occultist shadings, the novel not unexpectedly focuses on questions of identity and of Russian history. The inhabitants of the apartment house wake up one day to discover that they have no reflection in the mirror—much like vampires, ghosts, and the dead in accordance with common folk beliefs. Incorporating various allusions,

Kuraev suggests that this loss of physical identity is mystically connected to the presence of an old general who, employed long ago in labor camps, resents the rehabilitation of camp victims, some of whom now are residents of the apartment house. Kuraev also implies that the apartment dwellers, suddenly having become "invisible," represent the latest stage in the phantom existence that has always characterized St. Petersburg life. That is, the many nameless workers and peasants who perished while building Peter the Great's capital in what was a swamp; the nineteenth-century political prisoners in the Peter and Paul Fortress who were deprived of their names and coded by ever-changing numbers; the people who disappeared during the purges; the artists and writers robbed of their identities because their works were never allowed to reach the public; and even the artists and intellectuals who left only shadow memories of themselves as they emigrated from the Soviet Union—all of these people represent, in a sense, the phantoms haunting the space that was and is St. Petersburg.

Kuraev's exploration of life in St. Petersburg and, by extension, in Russia and the Soviet Union is structured on intricate sets of connections between peoples' personal, family, and professional lives within the context of the history of the nation. His unique angle on St. Petersburg life and history, whereby he hones in on its "phantom" identity, places him in the company of writers such as Gogol and Andrei Bely, who also concentrate their vision on St. Petersburg and its special mystical character. In addition, *Zerkalo Montachki* includes a long essay on the history of mirrors, with particular attention to mirrors bought and sold in St. Petersburg, as well as a comprehensive survey of the magical qualities that people have ascribed to mirrors through the centuries. As in some of his previous works, Kuraev cannot refrain from digressing into areas that interest him but that sometimes interfere with the structural integrity of the novel.

"Blok-ada," which can be translated both as a "block of hell" as well as "blockade," appeared in 1994 with the subtitle "Prazdnichnaia povest'" (A Holiday Novella). The latter refers to the 1994 celebrations that marked the fiftieth anniversary of the end of the Leningrad blockade during World War II, on which Kuraev's story in fact ends. The work evokes images of the blockade, with which Russians are intensely familiar. As is true of the structure of his earlier work, in which the focus on individual lives is set within a much broader historical context, Kuraev does not restrict himself to memories of the blockade but makes references to the victims of Stalin's rule; the fate of those buried in various Russian cemeteries through the centuries; and Russian life in the post-Stalin decades. An extremely personal work, "Blok-ada" also constitutes a testimony to his family's resilience and decency amid the death, cold, and hunger that ruled a city constantly shelled by the Germans. Kuraev offers engaging portraits of various family members and relatives, but the most evocative, memorable one is that of his mother.

Although it has received little critical attention, Kuraev's prose of the mid 1990s is not without interest. The story "Vstrechaite Lenina" (Meet Lenin, published in *Novyi mir,* 1995) reads like a movie scenario that Kuraev might have wished to write in moments of bitterness while working at Lenfil'm studios and coping with censorship there. A Party worker dreams of staging a celebration in honor of the one hundredth anniversary of Vladimir Lenin's birth, an affair during which a specially commissioned bust of Lenin is to arrive at Finland station. Yet, the worker's plans are subjected to bureaucratic wrangling; "Lenin" never arrives at the celebration, and the ensuing chaos only underscores the ever-widening gulf between the older and younger generations. In "Zhrebii No. 241" (Lot No. 241, published in *Znamia,* 1995) Kuraev reproduces letters from his grandfather–a doctor in Siberia and Manchuria during the Russo-Japanese war (from 1904 to 1905)–to his future wife. Kuraev juxtaposes this correspondence with diary entries (of the same dates as the letters) by Tsar Nicholas II. Kuraev's voice is ever present in the commentary and interpretations that regularly punctuate this material, which is similar in style to a documentary script, and the vastly different personalities of his grandfather and the Tsar emerge. While his grandfather is a decent, caring individual, Nicholas II lacks intellectual depth, compassion, and humanity. He is reduced to a weak ruler, manipulated by his aides and wife, and exhibits no real interest in his country or his people. "Zhrebii No. 241" can be read as Kuraev's polemics with those today who idolize the fallen tsar and his family; the story also serves as a reminder to his countrymen that Russians should model their lives on deeply moral people such as his grandfather.

In the first half of the 1990s Kuraev wrote several interesting essays reflecting his interest in the history and development of Russia–pieces in which he passionately assumes the role of moralist and teacher. In "O Rembrandte i o sebe" (About Rembrandt and Myself), published in *Druzhba narodov* (The People's Friendship) in 1992, Kuraev reflects on the new freedoms in Russia as he ponders the various historical and religious forces that must have operated on Rembrandt's life. Kuraev makes the bold statement that Russia is even less prepared for the experiment in capitalism than it was prepared for the 1917 revolution. In "Za kogo oni nas prinimaiut" (What Do They Take Us For? 1993), he

explores the events surrounding the 1993 shelling of the Belyi dom (White House); in "Kto voidet v dom Chekhova?" (Who Will Enter Chekhov's House? 1993) he applies the social and moral dynamics of Anton Pavlovich Chekhov's play *Vishnevyi sad* (The Cherry Orchard, 1904) to what is happening in Russia in the 1990s. "Kak ia staralsia ne stat' pisatelem" (How I Tried Not to Become a Writer), which appeared in the journal *Zvezda* (The Star) in 1994, is a revealing look at the history of his first manuscript, which became *Kapitan Dikshtein,* and his attempt to "bring life to language [*slovo*] in its honesty and dignity." In "Pamiatnik Gogoliu" (A Monument to Gogol, 1995) Kuraev describes the different monuments to Gogol that have been erected and argues that just Gogol's fantastic feel for the Russian language will always constitute a grand monument to national culture in Russia.

Puteshestvie iz Leningrada v Sankt-Peterburg (A Trip from Leningrad to St. Petersburg, 1996) represents, in the form of seventeen short chapters, Kuraev's eloquent and passionate dialogue with his contemporaries about Russian political and intellectual history. He is particularly interested in the personality and accomplishments of Peter the Great and the founding tsar's subsequent influence on the course of Russian societal development–a subject that figured to some extent in Kuraev's earlier prose. Kuraev does not accept the prevailing mythology about Peter the Great as a key reformer who opened a "window" to the West. Rather, Kuraev views the tsar as a man of vast contradictions: interested in new knowledge and technical progress yet capable of despotic behavior, torture, and debauchery. In Kuraev's opinion, Peter the Great laid the foundations for despotism and autocracy because he ignored one vital dimension of life in foreign lands: respect for the law, for human life, and the rights of the individual.

Kuraev constantly finds analogies and associations between the rule of Peter the Great and that of Stalin: he notes the tsar's "paper snow-fall," or love of brutal *ukazy* (orders), and makes the observation that Stalin no doubt learned from them; he points to Peter the Great's use of denunciations and Stalin's continuation of that policy; and he makes connections between the tsar's belief in the *knut* as an instrument of power and Stalin's own immense abuse of power in the totalitarian state that he created. Kuraev also finds similarities between Peter the Great's goals and dreams and the building of socialism at any cost under the Soviets. He argues that the consequences of the "cult" of Peter the Great can be felt in contemporary Russian politics perhaps even more than the cult of Stalin.

Kuraev's excursion into history includes revelations about the Goodwill Games, comments about the changing nature of the Russian language in the 1990s

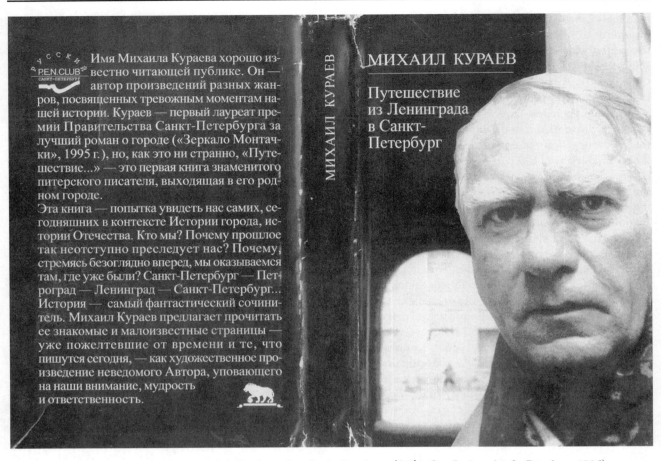

Dust jacket for Kuraev's Puteshestvie iz Leningrada v Sankt-Peterburg *(A Trip from Leningrad to St. Petersburg, 1996),*
in which he addresses topics in Russian political and intellectual history (Collection of Valentina G. Brougher)

and its effect on Russians, and questions about the popular image of President Boris Nikolaevich Yeltsin as a rebel. Noting the argument of some people that St. Petersburg is being reborn today (old names are being restored and churches reopened, for example), he wonders if perhaps the city is not dying away slowly and thus going, full circle, back to where it started. This point explains the title of the work. Nevertheless, the reader senses that Kuraev's love for the city—and the writers associated with it—is constant and ever present.

Kuraev's prose in the second half of the 1990s offers no surprises in his choice of topics or his approach to depicting reality. The long story "Zolotukha po prozvishchu Odyshka" (Zolotukha Nicknamed Odyshka, published in *Novyi mir,* 1997) tells about the "psychology" with which the minds of Soviet youth were inculcated during Stalin's rule. A fifth-grader named Odyshka dreams of joining the ranks of heroes; he lives in an era when great heroic deeds are touted and has heard that there is nothing more noble than to fight and die for Lenin and Stalin. When an ink bottle, passed by

many hands, is thrown against a classroom wall, Odyshka decides to take full blame as a demonstration of his heroism. Yet, this gesture is neither understood nor appreciated by his peers, and he is in fact accused by the principal of trying to shift the blame onto others. In a parallel and ironic illustration from the larger world of politics and ideology, Popkov—a Party member—tries to save his colleagues by saying that he alone was responsible for the "anti-Party path" that his group was accused of taking. All are shot anyway, including Popkov, on Stalin's orders.

"Tikhie bezzlobnye pokhorony" (A Quiet Amiable Funeral, 1998) centers on questions of literature, responsibility, and relevance. Kuraev offers the reader two perspectives: one from the world of writers who have come to a resort for a conference on "Survival and Development," and the other from the world of the guards who have been assigned to look after their safety. The writers spend their days arguing passionately and sometimes eloquently about Russian literature of the past; the guards watch television reports about unemployment, hunger, and violence in the new democratic state and argue in the crude, rough language of the street about what all this means for Russia.

Bridging these two worlds is Vasilii Berkutov, who works at the tourist base, is sensitive to the nature around him, and collects and reads books. His observations and eavesdropping often blend in with the narrator's perspective, strongly suggesting Kuraev's authorial presence. The story culminates in Berkutov witnessing the symbolic burial of three copies of a book by a fashionable poet who knows how to pander to public taste for the erotic and the mystical. This ritualistic "funeral" is amiable and without malice: the poet is invited to join in the drinking around the grave. Ultimately, Kuraev's message to his contemporaries is that writers should be more attuned to what is happening currently in Russia and more involved in the future of the country.

In the second half of the 1990s Kuraev produced several essays that have drawn attention to him as a moralist and teacher—a role that Russian writers have often assumed for themselves. "Chekhov poseredine Rossii" (Chekhov in the Middle of Russia, 1997) evaluates Chekhov's place in world culture and his role in depicting the Russian soul for the rest of the world. In exposing people's hypocrisy and philistinism in his prose, Chekhov represents Russian spirituality, which, Kuraev argues, complements European humanism. In another essay on Chekhov, "Aktual'nyi Chekhov" (Topical Chekhov, 1998), Kuraev argues that history is the sum of all human actions or deeds, a belief that is already evident in *Kapitan Dikshtein*. He praises Chekhov for uncovering greed, cynicism, hypocrisy, and baseness in his representation of Russian life and, at the same time, for believing in mankind and progress. In a time in Russia when power and money rule, and when crises are constant, Kuraev argues that Chekhov—and nineteenth-century classical literature as a whole—can offer valuable moral lessons. In "Smertnoe mgnovenie" (Deathly Moment, 1999) Kuraev describes his emotional journey to places connected with the life of Aleksandr Sergeevich Pushkin.

Given the nature and direction of Mikhail Nikolaevich Kuraev's writings, the St. Petersburg critic Viktor Toporov—in his brief look at Kuraev's literary biography, "Na polputi v neizvestnom napravlenii" (Half-Way in an Unknown Direction, 1998)—not surprisingly called Kuraev both a "demopatriot" and "patriodemocrat." But Toporov, who remembers the man whose first novella "agitated and enchanted" readers, also wonders what will become of the writer who cannot break free of repeating himself in his writing. Whatever path that Kuraev's writing takes, however, he will always be remembered for *Kapitan Dikshten,* a remarkable literary achievement and a publication that contributed significantly to the atmosphere of glasnost, or openness, under Mikhail Sergeevich Gorbachev.

Biographies:

Andrei Ar'ev, "Kuraev, Mikhail Nikolaevich," in *Russkie pisateli. XX vek. Biobibliograficheskii slovar',* edited by Nikolai Nikolaevich Skatov (Moscow: Prosveshchenie, 1998), pp. 719–721;

Ar'ev, "Kuraev, Mikhail Nikolaevich," in *Russkie pisateli 20 veka. Biograficheskii slovar',* edited by Petr Alekseevich Nikolaev (Moscow: Bol'shaia Rossiiskaia Entsiklopediia, 2000), pp. 395–396.

References:

Aleksandr Ageev, "Gosudarstvennyi sumasshedshii," *Literaturnoe obozrenie,* 8 (1989): 48–52;

Lev Anninsky, "Kak uderzhat' litso?" *Znamia,* 9 (1989): 218–221;

Igor' Aleksandrovich Dedkov, "Khozhdenie za pravdoi ili vzyskuiushchie novogo goda," *Znamia,* 2 (1988): 199–214;

Colin F. Dowsett, "Rewriting History and Reviving Modernism: Mikhail Kuraev's *Kapitan Dikshtein* and *Nochnoi dozor,*" *Canadian Slavonic Papers* (June 1991): 113–122;

Nikita Eliseev, "Ten' Amarkorda," *Novyi mir,* 4 (1995): 215–226;

Irina Bentsionovna Rodnianskaia, "Gipsovyi veter: O filosofskoi intoksikatsii v tekushchei slovesnosti," *Novyi mir,* 12 (1993): 215–231;

Viktor Toporov, "Na polputi v neizvestnom napravlenii," *Kul'tura,* no. 13 (April 1998): 11.

Vladimir Semenovich Makanin

(13 March 1937 –   )

Byron Lindsey
University of New Mexico

BOOKS: *Priamaia liniia* (Moscow: Sovetskii pisatel', 1967); translated by Robert Daglish as *The Straight Line, Soviet Literature,* nos. 2, 3 (1967), pp. 3–51, 34–135;

Bezotsovshchina (Moscow: Sovetskii pisatel', 1971);

Povest' o starom poselke (Moscow: Sovetskii pisatel', 1974)–includes "Poite im tikho";

Starye knigi (Moscow: Sovetskii pisatel', 1976);

Portret i vokrug (Moscow: Sovetskii pisatel', 1978);

Kliucharev i Alimushkin (Moscow: Molodaia gvardiia, 1979)–includes "Kliucharev i Alimushkin," translated by Byron Lindsey as "Kliucharev and Alimushkin," in *The Loss: Novella and Two Short Stories* (Evanston, Ill.: Northwestern University Press, 1998), pp. 87–116; "Reka s bystrym techeniem," translated by Mary Ann Szporluk as "Torrent River," *AGNI,* 48 (1998): 6–39;

V bol'shom gorode (Moscow: Sovremennik, 1980)–includes *Golosa,* excerpt translated by Michael Duncan as "Those Who Did Not Get into the Choir," in *Dissonant Voices: New Russian Fiction,* edited by Oleg Chukhontsev (London: Harvill, 1991);

Na zimnei doroge (Moscow: Sovetskii pisatel', 1980);

Predtecha (Moscow: Sovetskii pisatel', 1983);

Gde skhodilos' nebo s kholmami (Moscow: Sovremmenik, 1984)–includes "Gde skhodilos' nebo s kholmami" and "Grazhdanin ubegaiushchii";

Mesto pod solntsem (Moscow: Molodaia gvardiia, 1984)–includes "Chelovek svity" and "Antilider," translated by Jamey Gambrell as "Antileader," in *The New Soviet Fiction: Sixteen Short Stories,* edited by Sergei Zalygin (New York: Abbeville, 1989), pp. 163–203;

Otstavshii: Povesti i rasskazy (Moscow: Khudozhestvennaia literatura, 1988)–includes *Otstavshii,* translated by Nadezhda Peterson as "Left Behind," in *Glasnost: An Anthology of Literature under Gorbachev,* edited by Lindsey and Helena Goscilo (Ann Arbor, Mich.: Ardis, 1990), pp. 195–270;

Odin i Odna (Moscow: Sovremmenik, 1988);

Povesti, with an afterword by Inna Soloveva (Moscow: Knizhnaia palata, 1988)–includes *Utrata,* translated by Lindsey as "The Loss," in *The Loss* (Evanston, Ill.: Northwestern University Press, 1998), pp. 3–86;

Rasskazy (Moscow: Sovremennik, 1990);

Laz (St. Petersburg: Renessans, 1991)–includes *Dolog nash put';* *Laz* translated by Szporluk as *Escape Hatch* (Dana Point, Cal.: Ardis, 1996)–includes *The Long Road Ahead;*

Kavkazskii plennyi (Moscow: Panorama, 1997)–includes "Kavkazskii plennyi," translated by Lindsey as "The Prisoner from the Caucasus," in *The Loss* (Evanston, Ill.: Northwestern University Press, 1998), pp. 117–154;

Stol, pokryty suknom i s grafinom poseredine, translated by A. L. Tait as *Baize-Covered Table with Decanter* (Columbia, La.: Readers International, 1995);

Andegraund, ili Geroi nashego vremeni (Moscow: Vagrius, 1998);

Udavshiisia rasskaz o liubvi (Moscow: Vagrius, 2000)–includes *Bukva "A."*

Editions and Collections: *Golosa* (Moscow: Sovetskaia Rossiia, 1982);

Reka s bystrym techeniem: Povesti i rasskazy (Moscow: Moskovskii rabochii, 1983);

Izbrannoe (Moscow: Sovetskii pisatel', 1987);

Chelovek svity (Moscow: Moskovskii rabochii, 1988)–includes "Chelovek svity";

Utrata (Moscow: Molodaia gvardiia, 1989);

Odin i odna, foreward by Alla Marchenko (Moscow: Russkii Yazyk, 1991);

Sobranie sochinenii, 2 volumes (Moscow: Vagrius, 1998);

Na pervom dykhanii (Kurgan: Zaural'e, 1998);

Laz: Povesti i rasskazy (Moscow: Vagrius, 1998);

Liniia sud'by i liniia zhizni (Moscow: Tsentropoligraf, 2001);

Sobranie sochinenii, 4 volumes (Moscow: Materik, 2002–2003).

Vladimir Semenovich Makanin (courtesy of the author)

PRODUCED SCRIPT: *Priamaia Liniia,* motion picture, Gor'ky Studios, 1969.

SELECTED PERIODICAL PUBLICATIONS–
UNCOLLECTED: "Odnodnevnaia voina," *Novyi mir,*
    10 (2001);
"Ne adekvaten" and "Za kogo porogolosuet malen'kii
    chelovek," *Novyi mir,* 5 (2002).

On 12 June 2000 in St. George's Hall in the Kremlin, Vladimir Vladimirovich Putin, president of the Russian Federation, presented the State Prize in literature to Vladimir Makanin. For Makanin's longtime readers who managed to catch a glimpse of the ceremony on television, the moment was a joyful, if improbable, one in the history of contemporary Russian literature, undiminished by the irony in the lateness of the official recognition. Makanin's career as a writer began with his well-received first novel, *Priamaia liniia* (1967; translated as *The Straight Line,* 1967). As the period known as the Thaw, initiated by Nikita Sergeevich Khrushchev, which had permitted such success, came to a close, however, he endured some twenty years on the margins of Russian literature, only to be "rediscovered" in the late 1980s. The moment in the Kremlin in the summer of 2000 thus completed a

circle for Makanin–from his initial bright promise to the exclusion of his work from the central journals and his obscurity to critical acclaim and, finally, to his full embrace at the highest official level.

    The award essentially confirmed what readers and critics had known for at least two decades: Makanin is a fiercely independent writer who managed even during the darkest years of post-Stalinist censorship to write uncompromising, philosophically independent works of mainly short fiction. He endured all the psychological and material privations of being a widely published but (paradoxically) studiously ignored and barely rewarded writer in the politicized, byzantine world of Soviet literature. Rejection slips from the first tier of literary journals in Moscow and Leningrad, where writers' reputations were made, routinely followed his submissions. Instead, he published his works in books that, except within small literary circles, were lost in the vast sea of Soviet publications. In an unpublished 1995 interview with Byron Lindsey, Makanin calls that publishing venue "the fraternal grave" of writers deemed "secondary." Pressured to conform to the dogma of socialist realism and the perennial political campaigns of the party-controlled Union of Writers, Makanin not only survived with his personal reputation unblemished but managed to produce a body of work remarkable for its inner freedom and intellectual strength. His works have only recently been collected systematically, and the opus is somewhat smaller than the list of book titles suggests. While writing mainly short works but publishing them by necessity in book form, he added new stories to an alternating selection of older ones in order to produce new anthologies regularly. This method makes a chronological bibliography of Makanin's works especially complex, for he often has borrowed titles from previously published works as the name for a book that actually includes only a few new pieces, or occasionally even just one.

Vladimir Semenovich Makanin was born on 13 March 1937 in the town of Orsk in the foothills of the southern Urals, which border the great steppe of Kazakhstan. His father, Semen Stepanovich Makanin, came from a gentry family with an estate near Penza. Semen's own father fought on the side of the Whites in the Russian Civil War (1918–1920), was wounded and captured, then died in a Red Army hospital; his mother also died, and he was left to grow up in an orphanage. Educated as an engineer, Semen built one of several plants in Orsk during Joseph Stalin's rapid industrialization of the Urals. Makanin's mother, Anna Ivanovna Glushkova, born to a Cossack family, became a teacher of Russian language and literature. Makanin was the first of four sons born to the couple. During Stalin's renewed terror in the years immediately after World War II, Semen was falsely accused of being a saboteur of his own plant; he was arrested and held for more than a year in a local prison. This incident coincided with a famine, and the family fell upon especially hard times; the youngest son died. Finally, an uncle, himself a much decorated civil-war veteran, intervened, and Semen was released on the occasion of his son's funeral. Makanin gives an interesting account of his family background in Sally Laird's *Voices of Russian Literature: Interviews with Ten Contemporary Writers* (1999). The family's two different social origins—the gentry and the Cossack sides—provide the basis of his short story "Goluboie i Krasnoie" (Blue and Red), first published in book form in *Predtecha* (The Forerunner, 1983).

As a boy Makanin excelled at chess and by the sixth grade became the city champion. In 1954 he won entrance to the mathematics department of Moscow State University. His two younger brothers later followed him there. Philosophy became a strong interest for Makanin during his studies, but upon graduation in 1960 he started a career in applied mathematics and eventually became an instructor in the Military-Artillery Academy. His first publication was a monograph on the theory of linear programming.

Soon bored with teaching mathematics, he became attracted to the possibilities of literature as a vocation and began writing his first novel, *Priamaia liniia*. The Thaw was under way, and *molodaia proza* (youth prose), the exuberant new literary style exemplified by Vasilii Pavlovich Aksenov's prodigious novella *Zvezdnii bilet* (first published in *Iunost'* [Youth], 1961; translated as *A Starry Ticket*, 1962), was in full swing. The reins of censorship had loosened slightly, making editors unusually receptive to manuscripts from young writers. Starting with the prestigious Moscow-published *tolstye zhurnaly* (thick journals), Makanin submitted his manuscript to *Novyi mir* (New World), where the legendary editor Aleksandr Trifonovich Tvardovsky noticed the novel but felt it too "youthful" for his journal. He recommended it to the editors of the second-tier *Moskva* (Moscow). Probably by coincidence *Priamaia liniia* appeared there in 1965 in the same issue as Mikhail Afanas'evich Bulgakov's long-suppressed masterpiece, *Master i Margarita* (published in samizdat, 1966–1967; translated as *The Master and Margarita*, 1967). Encouraged both by Tvardovsky and the enthusiastic reception for his first novel, Makanin entered the All-Union Institute of Cinematography to study screenwriting. A fellow student there was Andrei Georgievich Bitov, whose career paralleled Makanin's, for Bitov, too, was an all but officially designated writer-outsider during the long regime of Leonid Il'ich Brezhnev; Bitov probably remains Makanin's closest contemporary among fellow writers. Makanin finished his degree, submitting a scenario of *Priamaia liniia* as a final project; in 1969 the scenario was made into a successful motion picture by Gor'ky Studios. Yet, he chose in the end not to pursue screenwriting as a career and devoted himself instead to writing works of fiction full-time.

Though presently overshadowed somewhat by the entirety of his opus, in retrospect Makanin's first novel, *Priamaia liniia,* is a fundamental work for understanding him. In fact, in an essay in *Golosa* (Voices, 1982) Makanin himself comments: "In the first book (of a writer) there is always novelty in the true sense of this worn word. . . . I would publish only authors' first books." Beyond its importance as Makanin's first work, *Priamaia liniia,* an excellent example of "youth prose," can stand alone on its own qualities. Makanin utilizes the first-person narrative style to maximum advantage, creating through the eyes of Volodia Belov—the naive, intelligent young man from the provinces—a relatively unfiltered but selectively realistic representation of Moscow and the military weapons lab that serves as the setting for much of the novel. Because he sees the large city as a strange place from his provincial point of view, Volodia serves in the narrative as an agent of *ostranenie,* or defamiliarization, through which the dehumanizing aspects of the urban environment become exposed and analyzed. As in other "youth prose" the narrator in *Priamaia liniia* seeks an apolitical orientation and exploits the opportunity to explore psychological moods and perceptions and to depict personal relationships as truly personal outside the political contexts of socialist realism. In addition, the narrative includes an informative "insider" point of view, which acts as a window on the restricted weapons lab during the Cuban Missile Crisis in 1962. The crisis creates an intense atmosphere within the lab and strains both professional and personal relations.

Perhaps the most crucial skill that Makanin demonstrates in this first novel is his ability to create full and convincing central characters, especially men. He is notably less successful at portrayals of women, who usually seem sketchy and stereotypical. Here, Volodia as the narrator and tragic hero is juxtaposed alongside Kostia Kniazhedgradsky in a binary country boy-city boy design, which enables the exploration of ethical choices to form the foundation of the novel. Although Volodia and Kostia are friends and coworkers, they are far from equals. Volodia, sensitive, curious, and unsure of the circuitous routes to success in the city and the world, relies on Kostia to be a guide, model, and teacher. Kostia—confident, bright, a streetwise Muscovite and poet—gives Volodia lessons in the art of achievement in mathematics and in life. Kostia's formula for all questions is to follow the mathematical "straight line," the metaphor that serves as the title of the novel. By applying this rule, he "gets the girl" and is promoted to work in a new "super-lab." But Volodia, open and vulnerable to the great unfamiliar world in which he finds himself, does not see the straight line. Driven by his emotions, he makes choices with devastating consequences, such as falling in love with a married woman and failing to hide this affection from coworkers. More damaging, however, is his blind admiration for Kostia, who must come first in all situations. Volodia allows himself to be a shadow of this dominant personality and neglects his own sense of self-worth—his amour propre.

The great social forces concentrated in Moscow—the laboratory, its staff, and the military structure itself—are aligned against Volodia. Kostia, pragmatic, savvy, and even ruthless in a genteel way, survives unscathed by the events that unfold in the novel. With these two counterparts as main characters Makanin creates a bipolar frame fraught with moral tension and seemingly ripe for discourse. This essential model of two men—one strong and the other weak—outwardly engaged in a form of friendship, yet psychologically and philosophically fighting a bitter struggle of values, is planted first in *Priamaia liniia* and becomes a continuing structural feature of Makanin's fiction. That he does not allow himself to engage in a discursive justification for the inevitable results of the struggle, neither to demean nec-

Front cover for Makanin's 1991 novel, Laz *(translated as* Escape Hatch, *1996), about a world where chaos reigns on the surface while expatriates lead a life of privilege and security underground (courtesy of the author)*

essarily the victor nor defend excessively the victim, tends to lend Makanin's writings the sense of an open invitation to debate rather than an announcement of a predetermined advocacy. He establishes his own voice as dispassionate, but it is not uncaring or immune to the presence of suffering in the world that he depicts.

A second novel, *Bezotsovshchina* (Orphanhood), a portrait of an idealistic foster father of orphaned boys in an increasingly materialistic social environment, was published in 1971, also in *Moskva,* but without notable response. By this time Makanin had married Irma Engvanovna Kim, a fellow mathematician, and their daughters, Ol'ga and Ekaterina, were soon born. In 1972 he suffered serious injuries in an automobile accident and underwent a long hospital confinement, an experience he has depicted in the poignant short story "Poite im tikho" (Sing to Them Softly), published in *Povest' o starom poselke* (The Old Town, 1974). Because his royalties from novels and the occasional collection of short stories and novellas were minimal and thus insufficient to support his family, Makanin took a job as a science editor at the publishing house Sovetskii pisatel', where he worked for several years during the 1970s. There he edited books about mathematicians and physicists.

With the publication of *Povest' o starom poselke*, Makanin's writing took on features that still constitute some of the prominent characteristics of his work. In such works the primary protagonist is a contemporary intellectual coping with compromises in his personal life. The setting is the urban milieu of Moscow and the daily life of its average citizens. Petty intrigues of the workplace and fleeting and unsatisfying extramarital romances provide the narrative dynamics. The displaced provincial man in the city idealizes and longs for the village of his childhood. When a trip back to his home village is eventually realized, it ends in a combination of disappointment (over the loss of the past) and acceptance (of the complex realities of the present). This spatial-cultural axis (formed at one end by the metropolis of Moscow and at the other by the small town in the Urals) constitutes an essential feature in such works, along with the transparently autobiographical material that Makanin transforms into fiction.

Povest' o starom poselke further establishes some of the fundamental features of Makanin's work. Here he introduces Viktor Kliucharev, a prototypical character depicted at various ages in four other important works—the stories "Kliucharev i Alimushkin" (first published in *Nash sovremennik* [Our Contemporary] in 1977; collected in 1979) and "Goluboe i krasnoe" and the novellas *Laz* (1991; translated as *Escape Hatch*, 1996) and *Stol, pokrytyi suknom i s grafinom poseredine* (first published in *Kavkazskii plennyi* [The Prisoner from the Caucasus] in 1997 and translated as *Baize-Covered Table with Decanter,* 1995). Both the narrative structure—its connective plotlines—and especially the stylistic tonal qualities are much simpler. The narrative is more purely linear: Kliucharev goes about his routine even as he dreams of visiting his boyhood home, Old Town, a little place far away from Moscow. A young scientist, likely on his way to a successful career, he is self-confident but cautious; lighthearted with a thoughtful, analytical side; and apparently rather pleased with himself. Moscow lacks the freedom and authentic color of Old Town, which Kliucharev tends to idealize and even mythicize as he remembers his upbringing in workers' barracks, the weekly collective visits to the communal steam bath, and a boisterous uncle's memorable antics. Moscow, by comparison, seems petty and calculating. In episode after episode throughout the narrative the reader is taken through the rounds of Kliucharev's life (home, family, job, and weekend social functions) and the people who populate it (his boss, his

secret former girlfriend who badgers him, and his friends). He is an Everyman—decent but with some flaws; responsible but not above betraying his wife on occasion; and intelligent but a little condescending. A light irony pervades many of his dialogues, even with his wife, who is essentially an appendage of Kliucharev.

Povest' o starom poselke is an upbeat, sunny picture of young family life, rendered in simple, unpretentious language. Perhaps even more than in *Priamaia liniia,* the spare details in *Povest' o starom poselke* seem chosen to convey a convincing, psychologically realistic, but slightly impressionistic, representation of the characters and their milieu—without ideological interpretation and almost neutral in tone. In fact, a more direct and unaffected portrait of daily life among the young Moscow scientific intelligentsia during the 1970s is hard to imagine. A swift reversal in fortune occurs, however, as a friend suddenly becomes an enemy. Beneath the smooth routine surface of ordinary life a dark layer of cunning manipulation and retribution is revealed.

Ethics is the crux of the matter. The best friend of Kliucharev's wife asks him as a favor to write a positive review of someone's research paper. Kliucharev finds the paper far below professional standards and impossible to recommend. The friend then banishes the Kliucharevs from her salon-like social gatherings, one of the couple's few genuine pleasures. She even manages to punish them financially by arranging through various remote connections to deny Kliucharev the chance to write occasional reviews for extra money—an income that the family relies on in order to supplement their tight budget. As if in cosmic compensation for this setback, a bit of luck at work sends Kliucharev on a business trip to his beloved Old Town. Before he departs, his parents—who no longer live in Old Town—ask that he visit the grave of his younger brother, and while Kliucharev finds the grave, nothing else remains of the cherished place of his childhood. The barracks are in ruins; the colorful uncle has long been in his own grave; and the scene in general is almost alien. Returning somberly to Moscow, Kliucharev reexamines his life there—its false starts and loose ends, its little deceptions and sinister pitfalls—with more detachment. Now he accepts his life in the city as something inevitably his own, as if he has been assigned a fate from which there is no retreat. The alternative of an escape to Old Town—to a country idyll away from the oppressive trivia and treachery of the city—no longer exists. A thoroughly congenial small work, the novella does not force the reader into any difficult discourse. The essential decency of Kliucharev and his wife makes the reader's identification with their problems and predicaments easy, creating sympathy for them at various times—as when the couple is brusquely excluded by the lady of the social salon, even as the spurious reason for their social exile underscores their innocence.

The short story "Kliucharev i Alimushkin," initially published three years after *Povest' o starom poselke*, emerges from the novella as if a slightly modified serial continuation. Critics frequently turn to the story as a condensed example of Makanin's prose in general and even as a key to the meanings of his fictional world. Some read it as a parable, at least in generic design. Actually, the ironic introduction to the story is rather more of a parody than a parable. One man notices that the luckier he gets in life, the more unlucky things go for a certain other man. Tongue in cheek, the lucky man starts a little conversation with God and in fact complains about the unfairness of this order of things. God tosses the whole argument off with a joke (about there not being enough of the blanket of happiness to cover everyone) and leaves without giving an answer. Here begins the actual narrative about the lucky Kliucharev and the unlucky Alimushkin, who loses his job and his wife (she leaves him), moves into a shabby apartment, falls ill, and finally dies. The original Kliucharev character is still intact; his situation both at home and at work seems little changed. Even as he avoids showing all signs of ambition, his career goes forward. Only his wife, who shows genuine concern for Alimushkin's misfortunes, worries: lucky streaks must alternate with unlucky ones—good alternates mechanistically with bad.

"Kliucharev i Alimushkin" was followed by a novel, *Portret i vokrug* (A Portrait in the Round, 1978). Centering on the efforts of a young writer to learn the truth about a senior professor of screenwriting—who is suspected of plagiarizing his students' scripts—the clunky "machinery" of the narrative slows its pace and diffuses its focus, to such an extent that a reader's interest eventually may wane. The design underscores Makanin's interest in the fictional portrait as a genre, as critics Svetlana Piskunova and Valery Maksimovich Piskunov have pointed out in their thorough study of Makanin, "Vse prochee – literatura" (All the Rest is Literature, published in 1988 in the journal *Voprosy literatury* [Questions of Literature]). The problem may be that, as Lev Anninsky describes in his 1986 contribution to *Znamia* (The Banner), "Makanin is more interested in the 'round' than in the portrait itself." The process of finding out the truth about the character (the epistemology, or the method of knowledge itself) undermines the total creative task—a problem in several of Makanin's works, including his later, much more ambitious novel *Andegraund, ili Geroi nashego vremeni* (The Underground, or A Hero of Our Time, 1998). He has doubts about grand narratives, a skepticism that gives

him strong affinities to existentialism and deconstructive literary theory yet surely hobbles him as a novelist.

Prominent on any map of Makanin's writings is *Golosa* (Voices), the sui generis composite of essays and short narratives published in 1980, immediately after *Portret i vokrug*. As a period marker it breaks with what Makanin has called in interviews his "movie style," an influence of his training in screenwriting—the traditional narrative style characteristic of his longer works in the 1960s and 1970s. *Golosa* also acts as an introduction to what is, by critical consensus, Makanin's richest period—the 1980s and early 1990s, when he published the novellas and short stories *Predtecha*, "Grazhdanin ubegaiushchii" (A Man on the Run, 1984), "Antilider" (Antileader, 1984), "Gde skhodilos' nebo s kholmami" (Where the Sky Meets the Hills, 1984), "Chelovek svity" (A Man of the Suite, 1984), *Utrata* (The Loss, 1988), *Otstavshii* (Left Behind, 1988), and *Laz*—works that probably best demonstrate Makanin's complex talent. In their seminal "Vse prochee – literatura" Piskunova and Piskunov write, "Both during the same period and after *Golosa* Makanin wrote novellas and short stories within which he opens for himself . . . basic new laws on the relationship between art and reality that in particular undercut the pretensions of the traditional genre in attempting essentially to form and complete an artistic whole."

Golosa is a compendium of short narratives and essays (which at times read like commentaries), and while the title itself may spring from Mikhail Mikhailovich Bakhtin's critical concepts of polyphony, Makanin does not develop the work along those lines. Instead he postulates his own concept of voice. Using Nikolai Vasil'evich Gogol's "Koliaska" (The Carriage, 1836) and "Shinel'" (The Overcoat, 1842) as examples, Makanin defines the term *golos* (voice) as the human quality in a character or a situation that captures the imagination of the writer. *Golos* is the opposite of a stereotype—whether in myth or literature—and by its individual vitality is preserved either through some oral tradition or through a writer; it then endures in the human imagination. Makanin's writer-persona says, "I don't know how I wrote that story, at first I didn't understand a thing myself, but then I suddenly heard a voice . . . It doesn't matter from above or below. I don't know. Only that this was a voice."

The strongest narrative in *Golosa* is the fragmented story about Kol'ka Mister, who through stoic courage in confronting his impending death—and yet believing in certain elusive spiritual secrets immanent in the nearby Yellow Hills—constitutes an iconographic and prototypical character for Makanin's works: the wise but fragile child who sees beyond the squalid adult world of material struggle and petty rivalries. Kol'ka's

*Makanin in the 1990s (photograph by Byron Lindsey;
from the cover for* Escape Hatch, *1996;
Richland County Public Library)*

who breaks out from the collective community and asserts himself in an endeavor with metaphorically spiritual implications that largely ends in failure. And fourth, Makanin typically employs in these works the motif of digging, or leading, an underground existence.

Makanin's own stylistic voice as a writer becomes markedly more confident and self-directed in the 1980s, beginning with *Predtecha,* the novella that suddenly boosted his career and belatedly brought him into the central circle of contemporary literature. First published in 1982 in the Karelian literary journal *Sever* (The North), *Predtecha* appeared in book form a year later in an edition of one hundred thousand copies, which sold out within a week. It is an intense, densely written tale about an elderly and eccentric folk healer whose messianic powers combine herbal concoctions with moralistic sermonizing: his ability to cure the dying mysteriously manifests itself and then just as strangely vanishes. Sergei Stepanovich Iakushkin, the self-possessed folk healer whose combination of holistic "prophecy" and homeopathic remedies offers hope for the hopelessly ill, perfectly represents Makanin's definition of "voice." Intuitively driven not just to save individuals but all humanity from an abusive, polluted environment, the healer Iakushkin embodies the perennial positive Russian folk hero, a hyperactive version of Leo Tolstoy's peasant hero Platon Karataev in *Voina i mir* (1868–1869; translated as *War and Peace,* 1886) or Aleksandr Isaevich Solzhenitsyn's Matrena in *Matrenin dvor* (Matrena's House, 1963) Iakushkin's difficult, obsessive life and ultimate death constitute a suggested parable on the dangers of modern life–its chemically polluted environment, self-destructive vices, and blind belief in scientific medicine.

In two masterful short stories, "Antilider" and "Grazhdanin ubegaiushchii," first published in 1983 and 1984, respectively, in the journal *Ural,* Makanin heightens his use of ambiguity in character portrayal. On the surface of the narrative the two works convey a negative version of his concept of voice, but techniques of chiaroscuro challenge the reader to understand the meanings of the portraits and decide whether they depict villains or saints, or criminals or victims.

In both stories the male protagonists are portrayed as antiheroes, strong negative characters obsessively driven to act against the norms of social behavior: in the first story Anatolii Kurenkov is the "antileader" because of his compulsion to pick a fight, and in the second story Pavel Alekseevich Kostiukov is the "citizen on the run," a roving Don Juan who spoils women's lives and moves on. Makanin's narrative distance ultimately gives both characters, especially Kurenkov, a complexity that a literal reading of the narrative does not immediately reveal. A "little man" in the

story is by far the most poignant of this collage, but others illustrate Makanin's interest in folk legends of the Urals, especially in their exceptional heroes who break both physical and social norms in their strength and willingness to take lonely risks. He uses them as a creative source for his own fictional counterparts. In *Golosa* Makanin also articulates an interest in Bakhtin's concept of "chronotope"–a special union of social space and historical time as a creative resource for fiction, and he illustrates it with the story of a would-be lovers' tryst of two couples in a borrowed apartment, a prototypical Russian situation in the recent past as he depicts it.

Four prominent features characterize Makanin's works from *Golosa* onward. First, narrative lines are broken up and point of view is experimented with, often seemingly even for its own sake, but the experimentation lends a formal basis to the ambiguities of the discourse. Second, *Golosa* and the works following it display a juxtaposition of myth–especially folklore from the Urals–with contemporary problems. Third, they frequently focus on an isolated, individualistic character

tradition of characters in the works of Pavlovich Gogol and Anton Chekhov, the plumber Kurenkov does not know how to stick up for himself, according to his workmates; moreover, he seems oblivious to the affair that his wife is having with a prominent movie critic. As if without reason, he takes an intense dislike to a new-comer in his circle of average citizens. He instigates a fight and is badly beaten, but this incident only seems to increase his rancor. He seeks out more fights and finally lands in prison, where his adversaries are hard-ened criminals. The inevitable trajectory is clear even if the ultimate fight is not depicted: he will be killed soon. Makanin depicts his character entirely from the side, or obliquely; there is never a definitive attempt at direct analysis. The reader gradually comes to see Kuren-kov's social environment as corrupt and his fights as a form of protest; they constitute a self-sacrificial struggle for fairness, equality, and even love, which in the end his wife truly offers him in an almost ritualized, poi-gnant meeting of farewell in his place of exile. "Anti-ider" is haunting in its understated depiction of psychological pain and cutting in its satire of both the intellectual movie critic's facile answers and the work-ing people's naive reactions to their friend's compul-sively aggressive behavior. Economical but inexorable in the dynamics of its narrative movement, the story is one of Makanin's most powerful artistic achievements.

A classical composer's relationship to his native roots and their folk music provides the discourse at the heart of the novella "Gde skhodilos' nebo s kholmami," Makanin's first publication in *Novyi mir,* where it appeared in 1984. Its lyrical narrative poses the ques-tion of whether the composer's work, inspired by folk songs and singing, paradoxically harms that same tradi-tion by creating an inhibiting echo effect. A bit reminis-cent of Kliucharev's troubling equation about his success growing in ratio to Alimushkin's decline, this time the issue formulates itself through the evidence of the fictional composer Georgii Bashilov's biographical narrative, which tracks his talent from childhood to world recognition at middle age. Eventually the cultural discourse tends to overwhelm the narrative and force it to become a mere illustration of its arguments. As Mikola Riabchuk notes in his review "Sindrom Bashilova" (*Literaturnoe obozrenie,* 1984), despite the validity of the premise and the importance of the ques-tion about the sources of a real decline in folk music, the problem is not solvable. Bashilov's only fault is "his partaking of life itself and participation in its unshake-able, indisputable laws."

Makanin successfully applies the new approaches begun in *Golosa* on a larger scale in *Utrata* and *Otstavshii,* two novellas published in the late 1980s at the height of Mikhail Sergeevich Gorbachev's glasnost. In their post-

modernist disruption of single narrative lines, their free mixing of story with essay, and their radical alternation of contextual time (in order to juxtapose myth) with contemporary characters, these two works make com-panion pieces, yet they are quite different in thematic conception. *Utrata* examines the meaning of life from an existential, ontological point of view, while *Otstavshii,* primarily historical and social in focus, revives peren-nial questions about the *lishnii chelovek* (superfluous man) in Russian literature.

In *Utrata* Makanin retells in contemporary lan-guage a legend about the digging of a tunnel under the Ural River and places the legend in the structural cen-ter of the novel. Then, in a mixture of narrative and essay, he attaches an account of a twentieth-century man's reconstruction of memory and meaning follow-ing a major injury. Pekalov, the master digger of the tunnel, stands as a model to the modern man in his dis-orientation and doubts. An ordinary man inspired by an extraordinary vision, he succeeds in digging through to the other shore of the river through a combination of sober-minded pragmatism, pernicious deceit, and self-sacrifice. The nameless contemporary protagonist, who finally refers to himself as the "man from the after-life," follows Pekalov's tough example in digging his way back to consciousness, responsibility, and purpose. The exercise in recapturing his own identity includes moral impulses that distinguish him from Pekalov—for example, his attempt to rescue a child in distress. Such efforts cause him to rediscover both the beauty of expe-rience (such as memories of his boyhood on the Ural River) and its finite dimensions. Rather than resolving doubts, the narrator bravely raises unresolvable ones, but from a healed, clearly reestablished consciousness. *Utrata* is not only one of Makanin's best works but also his most purely philosophical.

As exemplified by its title, meaning "left behind," *Otstavshii* intertwines three marginally connected narra-tives around the theme of exclusion. The matrix is a young writer's confessional account of a lost romance and the concurrent rejection of his stories by the journal *Novyi mir*. In a second related story his father has a recurring nightmare about being left behind, aban-doned and presumably unneeded, by his work crew. The third narrative is a parable-like retelling of a legend from the Urals. It tells of a boy's uncanny gift for divin-ing gold, a sixth sense that seems to depend on lagging behind the mining artel (a cooperative of workers or craftsmen, primarily in the U.S.S.R.) that is his surro-gate family. The miners perhaps even deliberately abandon and mistreat him in order to sharpen his abil-ity to find the gold. Myth, metaphor, and the realistic (if elliptical) satirical account of a misbegotten romance during the post-Stalinist years are lightly bound

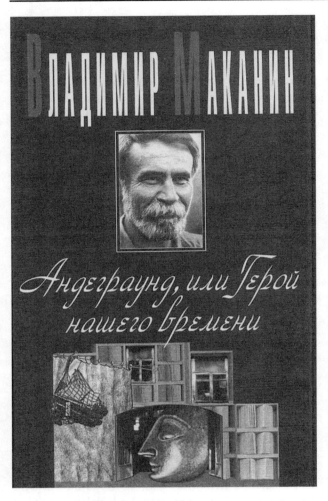

Front cover for Makanin's 1998 novel, Andegraund, ili Geroi nashego vremeni (The Underground, or A Hero of Our Time), about the difficult lives of two brothers (courtesy of the author)

together to constitute an implicit commentary on the talented individual's place in a collective society that lacks clarity and enduring values. Sufficiently ambiguous to lend itself to an historical discourse on the dogged persistence of the Russian artist in the face of antipathy, the interesting, commodious design of the novella leaves ample room for the reader's interpretation—a feature typical for Makanin but especially exemplary in this subtly provocative work.

An interval of four years, one of Makanin's longest gaps between works, separates his novellas of the late 1980s and a cluster of new works—*Laz, Dolog nash put'* (The Long Road Ahead), and *Siur v proletarskom raione* (Surreal in the Proletarian Neighborhood)—published in 1991 in *Novyi mir* and collected in 1997 in *Kavkazskii Plennyi*. Eclectic in their mixture of fantasy, realistic narration, satire, and philosophical discourse, these three compositions are written in an unrestrained, freely expressive style that sharply contrasts the laconic understatement so characteristic of Makanin's earlier writing. They reflect the virtual disappearance of censorship in 1991, the historic year of the end of the Soviet Union and of Communist rule in Russia. They also demonstrate Makanin's adaptation as a writer to the concurrently emerging fiction of Russian postmodernism—at least in *Laz,* the most original of the three and one of his best works. In *Laz* he uses his perennial character Kliucharev to explore a curiously split-level world. Chaos rules the surface, a place where, after some unnamed catastrophe, the populace stampedes and many are trampled in the panic that ensues as the necessities of life quickly disappear. The underground world to which Kliucharev has secret access (through an ever-narrowing crawl space) is a privileged enclave of concerned, but somewhat smug, expatriates, who live securely and rationally, with material abundance and an ingeniously devised system of artificial light. The sliding juxtaposition of the two spaces—surface and underground—provides the dynamics for the novella. Squeezing himself painfully between the levels, Kliucharev keenly observes, and tries intensely to analyze, their contrary qualities. The surface is home—family, the apartment, scattered friends, and the usual city neighborhood—transformed into an apocryphal nightmare. He begins digging a cave as a refuge for his family and uses his access to the well-supplied subterranean world to get the tools.

In his interview with Laird, Makanin compares the image of the narrow hole between the surface and underground to an hourglass. "It came to me as I pictured a man squeezing himself through a very narrow gap, like a grain of sand through the neck of a glass. The image has an obvious historical reference, to the idea of reversal, of things literally being turned upside-down: as they have been lately, and as happened most dramatically in 1917, when the top people went to the bottom, and what came to the top were the most ordinary, coarse elements of society." But in *Laz* the allusions are muted and ambiguous, and its structural plasticity produces a variety of readings, especially dystopian ones. The tight squeeze through this rough hourglass of earth is essentially another version of the escape hatch through which the trauma-ward patient in *Utrata* painfully crawled in order to help an endangered child, but if both the directions (in *Utrata* from the secure hospital to the outside, while in *Laz* from outside chaos to inside safety) and the reasons for the two crawls (the previous one to rescue an unknown child and the latter to save his own family) seem reversed, the intellectual protagonists' purpose remains the same: to travel at any cost between worlds arbitrarily severed from each other for the individual assertion of knowledge as access and action as moral responsibility. While the metaphors of digging, crawling, burrowing, and living underground lead the reader back to *Golosa, Utrata,* and *Otstavshii,* they also eventually lead forward chronologically to Makanin's novel *Andegraund, ili Geroi nashego vremeni.*

Makanin did not proceed, however, with the postmodernist trajectory commenced in the earlier works. Generic interplay, the use of fantasy, free formal design, and, to some extent, ambiguity as a poetic device disappear in his writing in the 1990s. In an unpublished essay, "Zametki o poetike V. Makanina," Piskunova draws a period marker from *Stol, pokrytyi suknom i s grafinom poseredine,* the novella that won the Booker Russian Novel Prize for Makanin in 1993, to the present, including *Andegraund, ili Geroi nashego vremeni* and the two novellas that immediately followed, *Udavshiisia rasskaz o liubvi* (A Successful Story about Love, 2000), and *Bukva "A"* (The Letter "A," 2000): "The new period . . . is slightly connected to his entire previous opus and at the same time significantly new, focused on a summing up of a life's experience within a context of Russian history." Piskunova sees *Stol, pokrytyi suknom i s grafinom poseredine* as an advance claim for the novel *Andegraund, ili Geroi nashego vremeni.* Taken together, the works of this period all postulate Makanin's vision of the gradual collapse of the collective life in Russia, often represented by barracks as a setting—a collectivism that undermines the individual and his creative initiatives but, at the same time, provides him warm shelter from the often fatal attacks of the "system."

Makanin's perennial protagonist, Kliucharev, is a character who—for all his intelligence, decency, and misgivings—compromised with the system. The comrades' court can be read as a metaphorical chronotype for that system depicted in *Stol, pokrytyi suknom i s grafinom poseredine.* The character himself collapses in a narrative gesture that clearly defines him as a victim of the ethos of presumed guilt, not innocence. In Makanin's view the system of justice has ancient roots that always favor the man of the masses over the individual person. Quite unlike his earlier works, the novella is striking in its open argumentation. As a string of individual yet stereotypical social portraits accompanied by Freudian analytic commentary, the jury of citizens fades in and out of Kliucharev's imagination on the eve of his hearing for unspecified violations. Awkward in composition, *Stol, pokrytyi suknom i s grafinom poseredine* is compelling mainly because of its grotesque gallery of broadly sketched anti-individual prototypes.

The work that stands out in this period, even beyond the large and bulky shadow cast by his novel *Andegraund, ili Geroi nashego vremeni,* is the short story "Kavkazskii plennyi" (1997; translated as "The Prisoner from the Caucasus," 1998). Makanin has charac-

terized the story as a "branch" that grew out of, and was pruned from, the novel. In external features, including generic ones, the two works could not be more dissimilar. The story is compact and tightly coiled in narrative mechanics. Much like his early, masterful "Kliucharev i Alimushkin," "Kavkazskii plennyi" conveys a powerful, ironic sense of inevitability that drives the story forward. It is set in the Caucasus in some periodic but fictitious war between Russia and a native people of the region. *Andegraund, ili Geroi nashego vremeni,* on the other hand, takes place entirely in Moscow. Loosely constructed and lumbering, it examines and reexamines points of view and potentially significant details as if suspicious of its own narrative. Yet, more crucially, the discourse in the two works is essentially the same. Upon the ruins of the failed commune-like system, which keeps the assertive individual on a short tether, Makanin advocates the establishment of a new kind of positive Russian hero: a modest, thoughtful, and even sensitive man of action who quickly defends himself in any threatening situation. Both Rubakhin, the good soldier of the short story and reminiscent of a hulking folk hero in *Golosa,* and Petrovich, the consummate underground intellectual of the novel, kill men from the Caucasus during sudden threats to their own lives.

With keen lyricism and compelling psychological characterization, "Kavkazskii plennyi" adroitly evokes the rich tradition of prisoners of the Caucasus in Russian literary classics by Aleksandr Aleksandrovich Bestuzhev (Marlinsky), Aleksandr Sergeevich Pushkin, Mikhail Iur'evich Lermontov, and Tolstoy. Turning this tradition on its head, however, Makanin's prisoner is the Russians' captive—an interesting twist as is the brief sexual attraction that develops between the Russian Rubakhin and the handsome young partisan. The partisan's representation as effeminate and possibly homosexual, however, raises questions of postcolonial stereotyping and cultural bias. Such a reading is furthered by Makanin's failure to lend any sense of legitimacy to the Caucasian people's war with the Russians. Even Rubakhin's fateful attraction to the beauty of the mountains may be read as evidence of a reinscribing of the Russian Empire's old claim to the Caucasus in this contemporary text.

Simply because it is a novel, *Andegraund, ili Geroi nashego vremeni* arguably dominates the landscape of Makanin's work since 1991. Announced long in advance and eagerly awaited, its critical reception has been mixed and muted, even slightly tinged with disappointment. Within a body of work characterized by difficulty of analytical access, *Andegraund, ili Geroi nashego vremeni* poses a special challenge to readers and critics. Rather typically for later works by Makanin, it is a sui generis example of the genre of the novel and essen-

Front cover for volume one of Makanin's 1998 Sobranie
sochinenii *(Collected Works), including his acclaimed*
Golosa *(Voices, 1980), short narratives, and
essays (courtesy of the author)*

tially constitutes several different varieties of the genre.
Yet, it does not use either postmodernism or any traditional literary license to mix its many narrative components.

Set in a wide sweep of time from the late
1950s to the present, the novel might be identified
as an historical-confessional detective story with strong
polemical positions on the trampling of the individual
by the combined machinery of the state and the impetus of its intimidated, disconnected society fleeing
responsibility. Told from the point of view of Petrovich, a contemporary underground man with some
affinities to Fyodor Dostoevsky's proud, irascible character in *Zapiski iz podpol'ia* (Notes from the Underground, 1864), the novel seeks to guide the reader
through a lightly metaphorical labyrinth of corridors
and subway routes reflecting the spiritual underground
to which he and his gifted brother Venia have been

condemned. Both brothers adapt or suffer through
their lives, and survival without compromise ultimately
becomes their moral victory over the darkness of history. Even if Venia's talent is shattered, his human dignity remains intact. A major stylistic problem in
Andegraund, ili Geroi nashego vremeni is that the narrative
fabric belongs exclusively to Petrovich, and not only
may monotony set in for the reader but also doubts
about his reliability as a witness. As a serious treatment
of the oppressive atmosphere of post-Stalinist Russia
and particularly its tool of pseudopsychiatry to control
or destroy its brightest minds, the novel deserves the
attention that it was awarded upon initial publication.
Only remotely autobiographical, *Andegraund, ili Geroi
nashego vremeni* is philosophically, nevertheless, a major
self-portrait of Makanin. In fact, Petrovich may be read
as a fictional alter ego: like Makanin, he is detached,
acutely conscious, analytical, curious, skilled in the
requirement for life underground, and self-assertively
free to draw his own conclusions about living—whether
above or below the surface.

Of course, these qualities also define Vladimir
Semenovich Makanin's voice throughout his career,
which came full circle when he received the State Prize
in literature. As a writer he is also innovative, elusive,
and scrupulously consistent in his concern for the individual and his disdain for the faceless throng and its
agencies. Unwilling to settle into a generic mold and
repeat even his most successful fictional modes, Makanin has explored his own talent at the same time that he
has pursued what remains uncaptured and unclassified
in his works—the complex, multitudinous, and ever
changing yet familiar Russian world that surrounds
him. His position as a major Russian writer is well
secured even as he continues to write, mainly at his
dacha near Moscow.

Interviews:

Peter Rollberg, "Interv'iu Petera Rolberga s
Vladimirom Makaninym," in *Odin i odna,* compiled by A. Marchenko (Moscow: Russkii Yazyk,
1991), pp. 259–277;

Valentina Polukhina, *A Video Interview with Vladimir
Makanin* (Keele: Media and Communications
Center, University of Keele, 1995);

Sally Laird, *Voices of Russian Literature: Interviews with Ten
Contemporary Writers,* edited by Laird (Oxford:
Oxford University Press, 1999), pp. 49–71.

Biography:

Tat'iana Sotnikova, "Makanin Vladimir Semenovich,"
in *Russkie pisateli 20 veka. Biograficheskii slovar',*
edited by Petr Alekseevich Nikolaev (Moscow:

Bol'shaia Rossiiskaia Entsiklopediia, 2000), pp. 435–437.

References:

Aleksandr Ageev, "Istina i svoboda. Vladimir Makanin: Vzgliad iz 1990," *Literaturnoe obozrenie,* 9 (1990): 25–33;

Lev Anninsky, "Struktura labrinta: Vladimir Makanin i literatura 'seredinnogo' cheloveka," *Znamia,* 12 (1986): 218–226;

Anatolii Bocharov, *Chem zhiva literatura? Sovremennost' i literaturnyj protsess* (Moscow: Sovetskii pisatel', 1986), pp. 209–233;

Vladimir Bondarenko, "Vremia nadezhd," *Zvezda,* 8 (1986): 184–194;

Sally Dalton-Brown, "Ineffectual Ideas, Violent Consequences: V. Makanin's Portrait of the Intelligentsia," *Slavonic and East European Review,* 70, no. 2 (1994): 220–232;

Igor' Dedkov, "Kogda rasseialsia liricheskii tuman," *Literaturnoe obozrenie,* 8 (1981): 21–32;

Andrei Viktorovich Dmitriev, "Voina i my: Razmyshleniia nad rasskazom V. Makanina 'Kavkazskii plennyi,'" *Znamia,* 4 (1996): 238–240;

Colin Dowsett, "Postmodernist Allegory in Contemporary Soviet Literature: Vladimir Makanin's *Utrata,*" *Australian Slavonic and East European Studies,* 4, nos. 1–2 (1990): 21–35;

Elena Gessen, "Vokrug Makanina, ili shtrikhi k portretu," *Grani,* 44, no. 161 (1991): 144–159;

Nataliia Ivanova, "Ochen' predvaritel'nye itogi," *Literaturnaia ucheba,* 1 (1981): 118–125;

Yurii N. Karaulov, *Slovar' Pushkina i evoliutsiia russkoi iazykovoi sposobnosti* (Moscow: Rossiiskaiia akademiia nauk, 1992);

Elena Aleksandrovna Krasnoshchekova, "Dva paradoksalista ('chelovek iz podpol'ia i cheloveka andegraunda')," *New Review/Novyi zhurnal,* 222 (2001): 176–186;

Mark Lipovetsky, "Protiv techeniia: Avtorskaia pozitsiia v proze V. Makanina," *Ural,* 12 (1985): 148–158;

Alla Marchenko, "Etimologiia shestidesiatykh: po povesti *Odin i Odna,*" *Soglasie,* 4 (1993): 179–192;

Andrei Nemzer, "Kogda? Gde? Kto? O romane V. Makanina *Andegraund:* opyt kratkogo putevoditelia," *Novyi mir,* 10 (1998): 183–195;

Svetlana Piskunova and Vladimir Piskunov, "Vse prochee–literatura," *Voprosy literatury,* 2 (1988): 39–77;

Irina Rodnianskaia, "Neznakomye znakomtsy: K sporam o geroiakh V. Makanina," *Novyi mir,* 8 (1986): 230–247;

Rodnianskaia, "Siuzhety trevogi: Makanin pod znakom 'novoi zhestokosti'," *Novyi mir,* 4 (1997): 200–212;

Peter Rollberg, "Invisible Transcendence: Vladimir Makanin's Outsiders," *Kennan Institute Occasional Papers,* 253 (1993);

Tatyana Tolstaya and Karen Stepanian, "Golos, letiashchii v kupol," *Voprosy literatury,* 2 (1988): 79–105.

Aleksandra Marinina
(Marina Anatol'evna Alekseeva)
(16 July 1957 –   )

Eliot Borenstein
New York University

BOOKS: *Shestikrylyi Serafim* (Moscow: Militsiia, 1992);
Stechenie obstoiatel'stv (Moscow: EKSMO, 1993);
Igra na chuzhom pole (Moscow: EKSMO, 1993);
Ukradennyi son (Moscow: EKSMO, 1994);
Ubiitsa ponevole (Moscow: EKSMO, 1995);
Smert' radi smerti (Moscow: EKSMO, 1995);
Shesterki umiraiut pervymi (Moscow: EKSMO, 1995);
Smert' i nemnogo liubvi (Moscow: EKSMO, 1995);
Chernyi spisok (Moscow: EKSMO, 1995);
Posmertnyi obraz (Moscow: EKSMO, 1995);
Za vse nado platit' (Moscow: EKSMO, 1995);
Chuzhaia maska (Moscow: EKSMO, 1996);
Ne meshaite palachu (Moscow: EKSMO, 1996);
Stilist (Moscow: EKSMO, 1996);
Illiuziia grekha (Moscow: EKSMO, 1996);
Svetlyi lik smerti (Moscow: EKSMO, 1996);
Imia poterpevshego—nikto (Moscow: EKSMO, 1996);
Muzhskie igry (Moscow: EKSMO, 1997);
Ia umer vchera (Moscow: EKSMO, 1997);
Rekviem (Moscow: EKSMO, 1998);
Prizrak muzyki (Moscow: EKSMO, 1998);
Sed'maia zhertva (Moscow: EKSMO, 1999);
Kogda bogi smeiutsia (Moscow: EKSMO, 2000);
Tot, kto znaet (Moscow: EKSMO, 2001);
Komedii (Moscow: EKSMO, 2001);
Nezapertaia dver' (Moscow: EKSMO, 2001);
Fantom pamiatii (Moscow: EKSMO, 2002);
Zakan trekh otritsanii (Moscow: EKSMO, 2003).

RECORDINGS: *Ne meshaite palachu,* read by Marinina, Moscow, TWIK-Lyrec, 2001;
Stilist, read by Marinina, Moscow, TWIK-Lyrec, 2002.

OTHER: *Priamye proizvodstvennye i nauchno-tekhnicheskie sviazi s zarubezhnymi partnerami v usloviiakh destviia zakona SSR "O gosudarstvennom predpriiatii (ob edinenii),"* edited by Alekseeva (Moscow: Upr. inform. TPP SSR, 1989);

Aleksandra Marinina (Marina Anatol'evna Alekseeva)

Voprosy sovershenstvovaniia pravookhranitel'noi deiatel'nosti organov vnutrennykh del, edited by Alekseeva (Moscow: MIUI, 1996);
Dolgosrochnyi prognoz razvitiia kriminal'noi situatsii v Rossiiskoi Federatsii, by Alekseeva, M. M. Babaev, N. Ia. Zablotskis, and others (Moscow: Akad. MVD RF, 1996).

In a post-Soviet publishing industry flooded with action novels, mysteries, sword-and-sorcery epic fantasies, and translations of the latest Western thrillers, Aleksandra Marinina was the undisputed champion of the Russian best-seller lists throughout the second half of the 1990s. Her mystery novels, most of which follow the exploits of the decidedly unadventurous Moscow police detective Anastasiia Pavlovna (Nastia) Kamenskaia, have a broad appeal among the Russian reading audience, largely transcending the categories of class, gender, and education. On its own, her popularity among the Russian reading public throughout the former Soviet Union would make Marinina's work significant for contemporary Russian literary culture, but the importance of her novels lies as much in their themes and preoccupations as in their marketplace success. Marinina's mysteries are often self-conscious reflections on the contemporary Russian literary market and the importance of professionalism and systematization, while the twists and turns of her plots betray a strong concern with the dangers of unchecked scientific progress and experimentation, the plight of the post-Soviet family, and the lives and careers of unconventional women.

Marinina's success in the Russian marketplace is a result of the features that make her stand out from her competitors: complex interwoven plot lines that, though often straining credibility, usually come together into a coherent narrative organized around a single, overarching idea; a set of easily recognizable and engaging protagonists; consistent attention to the psychology and motivations of her characters; a keen understanding of the nature, appeal, and limitations of serial narrative; frequent references to literary classics and high culture in general; and a readable individual prose style that, although subject to easy caricature, is far superior to that of the average Russian mystery or potboiler. Marinina no longer dominated the best-seller lists after 1999 to the same extent that she did in the 1990s, in part because the competition has become more fierce, and in part because she has not sustained the same breakneck writing pace that characterized her output in that decade (she now averages one book per year, as opposed to the eight new novels she published in 1995, the peak of her production). But the adaptation of her work into television movies (all of her novels either have been made into movies or are slated for production) ensures an ever-broadening audience for Marinina's stories.

Aleksandra Marinina is the pseudonym of Marina Anatol'evna Alekseeva, who was born in Leningrad on 16 July 1957, where she lived until moving to Moscow in 1971. Her father, Anatolii Alekseev, was a detective in the Leningrad militia, while her mother, Lidiia Alekseeva, is a professor of law and the first vice president of the Law Academy at the Russian Ministry of Justice. After a secondary education in special English and music schools, Alekseeva enrolled in the Department of Law at the prestigious Moscow State University. She graduated in 1979, whereupon she began her career in the Moscow Police

(militsiia). From the beginning, her police work was analytical rather than investigative. As a researcher with the rank of lieutenant, she specialized in profiling violent and mentally ill criminals. In 1986 Alekseeva defended her doctoral (kandidatskaia) dissertation, titled "Lichnost' osuzhdennogo za nasil'stvennye prestupleniia i preduprezhenii spetsial'nago retsidiva" (The Personality of the Convicted Violent Criminal and the Prevention of Special Recidivism). From 1987 to 1994 she continued her analytical work and was the author of more than thirty publications on crime prevention and forecasting; unfortunately, most of these articles cannot be identified.

Alekseeva began her literary career in 1991, when she and a colleague, Aleksandr Gorkin, drafted a short mystery novel called Shestikrylyi Serafim (Six-Winged Serafim), first published in the journal Militsiia in 1992. Though the product of a collaborative effort, this novel appeared under the sole name of Aleksandra Marinina, a pseudonym composed of the co-authors' first and last names, which they had previously used for occasional articles and humorous sketches in various professional and popular magazines. A story about the drug mafia's ties to law enforcement, Shestikrylyi Serafim is not part of Marinina's subsequent fictional world and is the only Marinina novel that had a co-author. Marinina has vowed that the book will never be reprinted.

From 1992 through 1998 Marinina combined her rapidly growing literary career with her police work. She wrote eighteen novels while still holding a full-time position at the Moscow Law Institute of the Russian Ministry of Internal Affairs. She finally retired with the rank of colonel in February 1998, in part because her fame was becoming an increasing distraction at work; readers who wanted legal and police advice from their favorite author were tying up the switchboard lines at the institute. She now devotes herself to her writing full-time. Marinina is married to Sergei Zatochnyi, a police detective who now teaches at the Academy of the Ministry of Internal Affairs.

All of Marinina's novels but one—Chernyi spisok (The Blacklist, 1995)—center on Nastia Kamenskaia, who is typically introduced to the reader as an exhausted, lazy woman in her thirties struggling to get out of bed. Kamenskaia's unwillingness to wake up in the morning, her daily rituals of conjugating foreign verbs while standing under a shower (of now hot, now cold water)—followed by the first of many cups of coffee that she will drink—become, in the course of the series, a touchstone that helps define and redefine the character and welcome the reader back into the detective's world. Unlike most of her colleagues in the Moscow Police Violent Crime Unit, Kamenskaia has a university education, relatively refined tastes, and a familiarity with five foreign languages (English, French, Italian, Portuguese, and Spanish). Her skills as a polyglot are of little help to her at work, but they do enable her to translate

Front cover for Marinina's Smert' radi smerti *(Death for the Sake of Death, 1995), in which a woman detective, Nastia Kamenskaia, finds out that a scientific experiment is causing people in a Moscow neighborhood to commit violent crimes (Skillman Library, Lafayette College)*

foreign mystery novels, thus supplementing her small police salary. Although journalists typically compare Marinina with Agatha Christie, a more accurate comparison would be between Kamenskaia and Nero Wolfe. Kamenskaia never carries a gun, wears a uniform only under duress, and does her best to avoid leaving her office. She prefers processing numbers and statistics and generating analytical reports for her supervisors to actual crime-solving. But she works for the maverick colonel Gordeev, and over the years he has painstakingly assembled a handpicked team of independent, professional police who are largely immune to the pressures of bribery and corruption that run rampant throughout the Interior Ministry. Besides Gordeev, the regular supporting cast includes Kamenskaia's fellow detectives; her husband, Alesha Chistiakov, a world-renowned professor of mathematics; Stasov, a former policeman who now provides private security; and Stasov's wife, Tat'iana Obraztsova, a police detective who writes murder mysteries under the pseudonym Tat'iana Tomilina.

Marinina distributes among her cast of characters a set of complementary talents and virtues that, while perhaps verging on caricature, are also evocative of the author's own preoccupation with professionalism and a systematic approach to one's life and work. Kamenskaia is, as the reader is told repeatedly, a walking computer, whose arcane system of graphs, charts, and databases allows her to solve the most convoluted mysteries. Her colleague Misha Dotsenko is unsurpassed at working with witnesses and getting them to recall details they thought long forgotten. Indeed, even the most minor characters in Marinina's novels—those with little or no connection to the business of solving crimes—display a thoroughness and concern for detail that at times seems incommensurate with the task at hand. Kamenskaia's sister-in-law Dasha indulges in lengthy monologues about the niceties of fine clothing and makeup (for which Kamenskaia herself has little patience). Irina, the young woman who runs the household for Obrastzova and Stasov, has a logical, systematic, and, above all, professional approach to shopping and cooking. One may argue that, given Kamenskaia's lack of interest in both traditional feminine pursuits and political feminism, characters such as Dasha and Irina are redeemed only through the professionalization of feminine virtues.

Marinina's concern with professionalism is so pervasive that it even characterizes her villains. In *Igra na chuzhom pole* (The Away Game, 1993) the plot hinges on the fact that even snuff films need classically trained, conscientious composers to write the movies' scores, and that a drug-addicted dwarf with a solid musical education can analyze the music and conclude that the film culminates in murder. On a metatexual level, Marinina's enthusiasm is understandable: not only is professionalism a quality that is arguably all too scarce throughout Russia today but it is also a sore point for both of the author's own chosen careers in law enforcement and popular entertainment. In her novels Marinina's narrator reserves particular warmth for those who exemplify professionalism in either endeavour, while violations of the codes and norms of professional behavior are often at the heart of her mysteries. That both Kamenskaia and Obraztsova—like their creator—combine police work with literary craft allows Marinina to create mysteries in which the ins and outs of each profession are explored in meticulous detail.

In *Ukradennyi son* (Stolen Dream, 1994) Kamenskaia's reading of works by a popular Russian émigré mystery writer solves the main dilemma. She discovers along the way that the author is not who he seems: he is a fictional construct used to group together the works of underpaid, unpublished Russian *graphomaniacs*. In *Stilist* (The Stylist, 1996) Kamenskaia's old lover and linguistic mentor, presented as the translator of wildly popular Japanese mystery novels, is tangentially connected to the main murder plot, but his presence allows the author to give a scathing insider's view of the world of contemporary publishing. Moreover, the murder mystery leads Kamenskaia to resolve a literary mystery: her former lover turns out to be the author, rather than translator, of these "Japanese" books. The plot of *Chuzhaia maska* (Someone Else's Mask, 1996) pivots on the murder of a male writer of best-selling romance novels. After his funeral his widow continues to peddle his last unpublished manuscripts, leading to speculation that she herself was the author or that her husband is not dead after all. Given the frequent (and evidently groundless) accusations that Marinina herself is nothing more than a name hiding several different ghost writers, the author's frequent investigations of the intricacies of authorship is understandable.

Marinina's concern with the business and politics of literature corresponds to a larger sociopolitical arena, that of the intelligentsia in post-Soviet society. Her own works are routinely reviled by highbrow critics as exemplifying the worst trends of a literary market that caters to the lowest common denominator, but her novels reveal a complex attitude toward the artistic and technical intelligentsia. In addition, Marinina's detective stories are a guilty pleasure, and many intellectuals who might otherwise think they are above crime fiction indulge in them. Part of Marinina's crossover appeal lies in her understanding of the cultural code: she herself is a product of the same cultural milieu that produced the intelligentsia in Russia. Though most of Marinina's characters are by no means intellectuals, the university-educated Kamenskaia and her immediate family have a perfect intelligentsia pedigree. Kamenskaia's familiarity with classical music, her taste in art, and her background in languages are a reassuring feature for educated readers, reminding them at regular intervals that they are in worthy company.

Despite the recurring references to the literary and artistic canon, the intelligentsia and high culture are not put on a pedestal. In *Igra na chuzhom pole* Kamenskaia engages in a spirited defense of Ed McBain's mysteries, which her new acquaintance, an elderly music teacher, considers devoid of artistic and intellectual value. To complicate matters even further, this same music teacher turns out to be a far less benign figure than she at first appears. Indeed, if Marinina's plots are at all predictable, her tendency to reveal unexpected motives and criminal actions on the part of cultured, intellectual, and highly pleasant people is the reason. In Marinina's world, the trail of corpses often leads to an overeducated, refined old lady who has every reason to turn to murder.

If the violent impulses of the artistic intelligentsia initially come as a surprise, they are no match for the cynicism and casual disregard for human life that Marinina so often attributes to members of the technical intelligentsia. By no means is the author making a blanket condemnation of an entire group. Just as Kamenskaia has one foot in

the world of humanities, her husband, Alyosha Chistiakov, is a world-renowned mathematician of impeccable virtue and good humor. More often than not, however, Marinina's doctors, technicians, and researchers turn out to be devoted more to blind ambition than to the alleviation of human suffering. *Smert' radi smerti* (Death for Death's Sake, 1995) establishes a mystery involving unusually high rates of violent crime in one particular Moscow neighborhood; Kamenskaia discovers that the rise in crime is the result of an antenna on a research institute that uses radio waves to experiment on the population. The bizarre murders that occur in *Chuzhaia maska* can be explained only by the revelation that a provincial doctor once ran a black-market baby ring, in which he used to deliver twins by cesarean section and tell the unwitting mothers that they were carrying singletons. Scientists and artist themselves become the victims of a cruel medical experiment in *Za vse nado platit'* (No Such Thing as a Free Lunch, 1995) when they voluntarily take a chemical compound meant to increase their intellectual and creative abilities; they have not been told that the treatment inevitably leads to death. The plot of *Illiuziia grekha* (The Illusion of Sin, 1996) centers on an obstetrician's attempts during the course of many years to create a new breed of superhumans by irradiating unsuspecting women whom he himself has impregnated. No doubt Marinina's mad science is convenient to the plot, allowing her to construct intricate stories that would otherwise be plausible only through recourse to the supernatural. Yet, by the same token, her manifest distrust of science gone wild reflects a marked trend in post-Soviet culture, recapitulating the relationship between the population of the former Soviet Union and the authorities: again and again, powerful people in Marinina's novels treat human lives as simply the raw materials on which they can perform both social and biological experiments.

Marinina's characteristically post-Soviet distrust for social experimentalism provides at least a partial explanation for her approach to gender in these novels. Her protagonist Kamenskaia is strong, brilliant, engaging, yet still deeply flawed; more important, she is virtually the only developed female character in contemporary Russian popular entertainment whose adventures and appeal do not lie in her sexual prowess. The world of action novels such as Mikhail Dotsenko's popular *Beshenyi* (Mad Dog) series is populated by attractive young women whose sole narrative purpose is to have sex with at least one of the men in the novel, while the female stars of other series, such as in Elena Kornilova's *Pantera* (The Panther, 1997) or Dmitrii Shcherbakov's *Nimfomanka* (The Nymphomaniac, 1998), tend to be aggressive, sex-crazed vixens. Kamenskaia has nothing in common with these heroines. Instead, the narrator repeatedly reminds her readers that Kamenskaia has only a passing interest in her appearance, but that when

Front cover for the 1998 edition of Marinina's novel Stilist *(The Stylist), in which the detective Kamenskaia investigates a murder that brings her in close touch with a former lover and mentor (University of Kansas Libraries)*

duty (or the occasional whim) demands, she can transform herself with the help of judiciously applied cosmetics and the designer clothes that her mother periodically brings back from Europe. This chameleon-like capacity, too, is presumably part of Kamenskaia's appeal: in Marinina's first few novels, Kamenskaia, like a superhero with a secret identity, frequently undergoes just such a transformation, from shy bookworm to femme fatale.

Throughout most of Marinina's books, Kamenskaia is quite satisfied with being the lone woman in a male-dominated profession, showing little interest in feminist politics or the question of equal rights. Only in the third novel, *Igra na chuzhom pole,* is Kamenskaia so offended by a police officer's refusal to take her seriously that she engages in an extended monologue about the outrages of sexual discrimination. Usually, any reflections on gender on the part of the narrator or Kamenskaia herself reinforce traditional assumptions of masculinity and femininity: over and over, Kamenskaia is shown to be the exception that proves the rule. While such a stance might not satisfy some of Marinina's Western readers, it does allow her Russian female audience to savor the adventures of an independent, powerful woman without having their worldview challenged.

Kamenskaia's appeal is intimately connected with the nature of open-ended serial fiction, itself a relatively rare phenomenon in Russian entertainment before the 1990s. Her legendary quirks give the returning reader a sense of familiarity, while the speed and frequency of Marinina's publication schedule allows the author to develop her character from book to book. Marinina has allowed Kamenskaia to age in real time. Readers watch her come to terms with the idea of marrying her longtime lover, Alesha, and their wedding provides the opportunity for yet another murder mystery (in *Smert' i nemnogo liubvi* [Death and a Little Love], 1995). She and Alesha drift apart over the years as Kamenskaia watches herself grow colder and less "human" with a vaguely dissatisfied detachment. Only when her own problems come to a head does she regain her enthusiasm for life and patch up her relationship with her husband (*Ia umer vchera* [Yesterday, I Died], 1997). Marinina rewards her longtime audience with plausible development of her leading characters.

This combination of stand-alone mysteries with up-to-the-minute serial fiction may ensure Aleksandra Marinina's historical significance, in that her novels are a fictionalized account of the daily life of post-Soviet Moscow. When pyramid schemes collapse, banks fail, or terrorists' bombs explode, such events are inevitably incorporated into the background of the novels. After the banking crisis of 1998, Kamenskaia and her husband lose all of their savings but still owe money for taxes (their insistence on paying every kopeck that the government demands of them is perhaps the greatest strain on the credibility of the novels). For the next several books, the couple count every ruble, living in an apartment that is halfway through a remodeling process that will probably never be completed. By developing her ingenious, impossible plots against the backdrop of an immediately recognizable post-Soviet urban life, Marinina has created a compromise between the fantastic and the mundane that holds a strong appeal for a weary Russian audience, hungry for magical entertainment that resonates with their everyday lives.

References:

"Feminist Pulp Fiction: Detecting Murder and Aleksandra Marinina," *Women East-West,* 50 (November 1997);

Helena Goscilo, "Big-Buck Books: Pulp Fiction in Post-Soviet Russia," *Harriman Review,* 12 (Winter 1999/2000): 6–24;

Catherine Theimer Nepomnyashchy, "Markets, Mirrors, and Mayhem: Aleksandra Marinina and the Rise of the New Russian *Detektiv,*" in *Consuming Russia,* edited by Adele Barker (Durham, N.C.: Duke University Press, 1999), pp. 161–191;

The Aleksandra Marinina Page <www.marinina.ru> [accessed 28 July 2003].

Valeriia Spartakovna Narbikova

(24 February 1958 –   )

Larissa Rudova
Pomona College

BOOKS: *Ravnovesie sveta dnevnykh i nochnykh zvezd* (Moscow: Stil', 1990); translated by Seth Graham as *Day Equals Night* (Dana Point, Cal.: Ardis, 1999);
Okolo ekolo (Moscow: Slovo, 1992); translated by Masha Gessen as *In the Here and There* (Dana Point, Cal.: Ardis, 1999);
Izbrannoe, ili Shepot shuma (Moscow, Paris & New York: Tret'ia volna, 1994)—includes *Shepot shuma;*
Vremia v puti (Moscow: Tret'ia volna, 1994).

OTHER: *Plan pervogo litsa. I vtorogo,* in *Vstrechnyi khod,* compiled by Viktor Ivanovich Pososhkov (Moscow: Vsesoiuznyi molodezhnyi khizhnyi tsenr, 1989);
"Ad kak Da aD kak dA," in *Ne pomniashaia zla: Novaia zhenskaia proza,* compiled by Larisa L'vovna Vaneeva, edited by N. A. Ryl'nikova (Moscow: Moskovsky rabochii, 1990).

SELECTED PERIODICAL PUBLICATION– UNCOLLECTED:
"Strasti po literature: Manifest," *Iunost',* 9 (1994): 72.

Valeriia Narbikova belongs to the generation of young writers whose literary debuts took place during the last years of the Soviet Union. As Soviet society was undergoing complex social, cultural, and political changes under perestroika, official censorship disappeared and restrictions on publishing were lifted. Perestroika opened the way for new trends in literature that differed strikingly from the official Soviet canon. Narbikova's name figured prominently among the emerging writers and became associated closely with what critic Sergei Ivanovich Chuprinin described in the newspaper *Literaturnaia gazeta* (The Literary Gazette, 8 February 1989) as *alternativnaia proza* (alternative prose).
Alternativnaia proza, also known as *drugaia proza* (another prose), soon became a catchphrase and umbrella term for critics and readers. It referred to fiction that diverged greatly from the official critical realist model. Rather than exploring social and political issues

in a realist vein, alternative prose was preoccupied with existential problems and literary experimentation. What made it notably different, according to Chuprinin, was its effect of shock upon the reader. Unlike official Soviet literature, alternative prose did not have a strong moral orientation: its characters were entirely unheroic and frequently pitiful; it included graphic descriptions of sex and body functions; and it presented cruelty and brutality as natural phenomena in Soviet society.

Bold in its realistic description and cynical about Soviet ideals, alternative literature established itself as an innovative cultural phenomenon. Since the dissolution of avant-garde groups and the introduction of socialist realism in 1934, alternative writers were the first ones to revive the idea that literature can exist for its own sake. Alternative prose is linguistically and structurally difficult and rich in intertextual references. Born mostly in the 1950s, the authors of alternative prose came of age during the years of stagnation (mid 1970s through the early 1980s), when Leonid Il'ich Brezhnev was in power. Consciously rejecting creative and social conformism, many of these authors were resigned to a marginal position in literature and society, as well as to the idea that their works would not be published in the Soviet Union because of their provocative themes and stylistic complexity. In the mid 1990s the term *alternativnaia proza* was replaced by *postmodernistkaia proza* (postmodernist prose). Critics felt that the latter term more accurately described the new literary trends of self-reflexivity, high-language consciousness, and emphasis on the fictional basis of reality. Narbikova's generation of postmodernists was represented by authors such as Viktor Vladimirovich Erofeev, Zufar Klimovich Gareev, Viktor Olegovich Pelevin, Evgenii Anatol'evich Popov, Vladimir Georgievich Sorokin, and Tatyana Pelevin Tolstaya.

Despite Narbikova's high profile as a writer and painter from the late 1980s to the mid 1990s, her biography remains elusive. The most reliable information about her in published sources concerns primarily her

Valeriia Spartakovna Narbikova (from Ravnovesie sveta dnevnykh i nochnykh zvezd, *1990;
Doheny Memorial Library, University of Southern California)*

literary career and aesthetic views. In addition, Narbikova's own writing is a tremendous source for understanding her life as "an object of literary creation," according to Mark Lipovetsky in *Russian Postmodern Prose: Dialogue with Chaos* (1999). As she herself described in a 1998 interview with Serafima Roll, "my writing and my life form the same inseparable body." All of Narbikova's works are to a certain extent autobiographical and convey the spirit of her generation of intellectuals and artists.

Valeriia Spartakovna Narbikova was born in Moscow on 24 February 1958. She graduated from the Institut mirovoi literatury (Institute of World Literature), also known as the Gor'ky Literary Institute, and made her writing debut during the glasnost era of Mikhail Sergeevich Gorbachev. Among her teachers was the prominent writer Andrei Georgievich Bitov, who helped launch her literary career. Considered sexually provocative, her works were frequently described as scandalous, insulting, and pornographic. She was, however, a favorite of the liberal-minded critics and was nominated for several literary prizes. Her 1992 novel, *Okolo ekolo* (translated as *In the Here and There,* 1999), was nominated in 1993 for the Booker Russian Novel Prize, and her 1994 novel, *Shepot shuma* (The Whisper of Noise), received the prestigious PEN Nabokov Award in Russia in 1994. Narbikova's major works have been translated into several languages.

Her creative biography is not, however, confined to literature. Like many avant-garde writers, she is also an established artist and has participated in art shows in Russia, Europe, and the United States. Her literary work is difficult to separate from her involvement in the Moscow art scene, and the correlation between her fiction and contemporary art reflects her intimacy with Moscow art circles, which notably include Moscow conceptualists such as Il'ya Iosifovich Kabakov.

Also important for Narbikova's creative biography is her marriage to Aleksandr Davidovich Glezer, a recognized art critic, poet, publisher, art collector, and translator. One of the most prominent figures of the Moscow art and literary scenes in the 1960s and 1970s, Glezer organized many unofficial art shows and was active in samizdat, or underground, publishing. He fervently collected works of art and continued popularizing unofficial (nonconformist) art even when he left for the West during what became known, by the early 1970s, as the *tret'ia volna* (third wave) of emigration from the Soviet Union. Using his own substantial acquisitions as a base, he established museums of nonconformist art in Montgeron, France, and in New York in the mid 1970s. Glezer also founded the publishing house Tret'ia volna and a literary journal, *Strelets* (The Archer), both of which promoted the works of unofficial Russian authors. Upon his return to Russia he resumed his vigorous publishing activities in *Strelets* and Tret'ia volna. He enthusiastically supported Narbikova's creative projects, and several of her works were published by Tret'ia volna. As much as their union highlights their commitment to creative freedom, their attitudes toward the realization of this freedom are defined by the ideals of their respective generations.

Whereas Glezer's generation (he was older than Narbikova by twenty-four years) was nourished by the ideas of the *shestidesiatniki* (the 1960s generation of intelligentsia) who rebelled against the intellectual, cultural, and spiritual oppression by the state, Narbikova's generation grew up in an atmosphere of moral and spiritual crisis, during the period known as the stagnation, when—as was widely believed—the official ideology was empty and corrupt, and real moral values were possible only in the private sphere. The cultural atmosphere was stifling in the 1970s and 1980s after the dissident movement was effectively suppressed, and the hopes of the *shestidesiatniki* to gain creative and political freedoms did not materialize. The spiritual vacuum and the omnipotence of ideological falsity in Soviet life became common themes for many writers of Narbikova's generation. All works by Narbikova reflect on Russian life in the 1980s: its lack of coherence and logic, as well as its antihumanist attitude toward both the social and natural environments. Her fiction projects anxiety about the future of Russia and frequently makes use of Russian and Soviet history, as well as of Soviet political symbolism and themes.

Narbikova's first novel was *Ravnovesie sveta dnevnykh i nochnykh zvezd* (1990; translated as *Day Equals Night,* 1999), initially published in excerpted form in the literary journal *Iunost'* (Youth) in 1988. It tells about a love affair between two young people, Sana and Otmatfeian. Sana is married to Avvakum, whom she does not love and from whom she hides her adulterous relationship with Otmatfeian. After Otmatfeian accidentally hurts her feelings with a silly remark, Sana decides to leave him. She persuades her husband to accompany her to an unidentified sea resort in the south. Upset and frustrated by his breakup with Sana, Otmatfeian tries to distract himself with a business trip

(he has to inspect amateur theaters in the south). On his trip he is accompanied by his close friend, the sculptor Chiashaizhyshyn. By coincidence, the four rent the same house and eventually run into each other. From this point on the story addresses their surreal adventures. During the four friends' stay at the resort Sana and Otmatfeian become engaged, and Chiashaizhyshyn serves as their priest. Later, Otmatfeian kills Avvakum during a heated argument, and no further reference to Avvakum is made in the novel. Sana and Otmatfeian return to the city and continue their bohemian existence, their life focused mostly on sex. Eventually, they go back south and continue their carefree life there.

Throughout *Ravnovesie sveta dnevnykh i nochnykh zvezd,* the reader encounters linguistic intricacy, different layers of reality, temporal shifts, a strange assortment of characters with peculiar names, and bizarre events. Narbikova's style is pointedly nonrealist and strikingly different from the familiar language of Soviet literature, which is based on socialist realism. As Narbikova explains in her 1998 interview with Roll, socialist realism failed as a literary method because realistic language neither reflects reality nor expresses important ideas—"the further away literary language is from everyday parlance, the more vitality it has." With respect to style, *Ravnovesie sveta dnevnykh i nochnykh zvezd* confirms Narbikova's opposition to socialist realism and demonstrates her devotion to the ornamental approach of Russian fin de siècle modernist writers. In addition, because of her narrative method, the novel is hard to follow at times; it digresses frequently on topics such as ecology, the woman question, the construction of reality, and the nature of writing. *Ravnovesie sveta dnevnykh i nochnykh zvezd* also overwhelms the reader with a picture of disintegrating old values, instability, unpredictability, and ambivalence.

A sensation upon its publication, the novel was hailed by liberal critics and denounced by conservative ones. In his article "Plokhaia proza" (Bad Prose), which appeared in *Literaturnaia gazeta* (8 February 1989), Dmitrii Mikhailovich Urnov accused Narbikova of an inability to write and of linguistic pretentiousness. In his rejection of *Ravnovesie sveta dnevnykh i nochnykh zvezd,* Urnov—a respectable Soviet critic—was ignoring a nascent avant-garde trend in the U.S.S.R. of the late 1980s, one that disassociated itself from the official realist method. Especially prominent among the new avant-garde movements was conceptualism, the thematic and stylistic characteristics of which are clearly reflected in the language of Narbikova's novel. Although Narbikova never officially participated in the Moscow conceptualist movement, many of its ideas nourished her literary works.

Paperback cover for Narbikova's first novel, Ravnovesie sveta dnevnykh i nochnykh zvezd *(1990; translated as* Day Equals Night, *1999), featuring the surreal adventures of strangely named characters (Doheny Memorial Library, University of Southern California)*

The next publication by Narbikova that made waves with critics and readers alike was the novella *Plan pervogo litsa. I vtorogo* (The Plan of the First Person. And of the Second, 1989). Like her first novel, *Plan pervogo litsa* tells a story of a love triangle. A young woman, Irra (derived from the word *irratsional'nyi* [irrational]), is in a love relationship with Dodostoevsky (which translates as "before Dostoevsky"), nicknamed Dodo. When Dodo's friend, Toest'lstoy (a combination of the words "Tolstoy" and *to est'* [that is]), comes to live with them, Irra falls for him and they get married. The relationship between Dodo and Toest'lstoy becomes hostile and ends with the murder of Toest'lstoy. After killing his friend, Dodo makes a broth out of him. In an act of cannibalism, Irra and Dodo drink the broth. Shortly thereafter they are surrounded by people who try to seize them—allegedly for their crime—but Irra and Dodo fly up into the air to escape their pursuers. They finally fall down into a sandbox, and the children playing in it make two Russian Easter cakes out of them.

As with *Ravnovesie sveta dnevnykh i nochnykh zvezd,* the critical responses to this novella were divided. In his article "Pervyi i vtoroi plan Valerii Narbikovoi" (The First and Second Plan of Valeriia Narbikova), published in *Znamia* (The Banner) in 1995, the liberal writer and critic Genrikh Sapgir praises *Plan pervogo litsa* for its "celebration of the poetic word"—that is, for Narbikova's rich and innovative style. The negative criticism is encapsulated in a short article, "Bespredel" (Beyond Limits), by Andrei Vasilevsky (later an editor in chief of *Novyi mir* [New World]) and published in *Literaturnaia gazeta* in the fall of 1990. Vasilevsky describes Narbikova's story as an example of blasphemy and immorality, an insult to the feelings of Christian believers. He associates Narbikova's novella with the emerging freedom of expression and voices his strong opinion against it. Difficult to translate into English, *bespredel* describes a world free of any moral constraints, in which sex, violence, and profanation of traditional ethical values exist for their own sake. The word is frequently associated with *chernukha,* a term used mostly for cinematic and literary works, which describes ugly and immoral aspects of Soviet life. Works characterized by *chernukha* are full of despair about the present and are pessimistic about the future; they feature characters who are doomed either to a spiritual or unnatural physical death in a cruel society. Narratives depicting *chernukha* are considered adult fare because they incorporate graphic scenes of sex and violence. Whereas some readers and critics associated Narbikova's work with *bespredel,* others perceived them as examples of the emerging semigenre of *chernukha.* Both terms are important as cultural categories of perestroika. Applied to Narbikova's works, they point to her significance during the transitional stage between Soviet and post-Soviet culture.

Plan pervogo litsa, like *Ravnovesie sveta dnevnykh i nochnykh zvezd* before it, becomes a part of the cultural phenomenon of *chernukha.* It reflects a system of disintegrating moral values through the ménage à trois relationship, Toest'lstoy's murder, Irra's indifferent attitude to his violent end, and her participation with Dodo in the act of cannibalism. Narbikova's impressionist way of describing her characters intensifies the grimness of their everyday existence. Faceless and inhuman, they float through her fictional universe; she does not provide any realistic description of them but rather portrays them through their dialogues, dreams, thoughts, and actions. Among the three characters Irra is especially atypical in Soviet literature. Like the female protagonist Sana in *Ravnovesie sveta dnevnykh i nochnykh zvezd,* though to a higher degree, the character of Irra celebrates the birth of a new type of "unheroic" heroine, in contrast to the "heroic" or positive heroines of socialist realist literature. As Riitta H. Pittman comments in her 1992 contribution to *Forum for Modern Language Studies,* Irra "stands aloof from positive action"; whatever she does is permeated by "aimlessness" and devoid of any "traces of collective consciousness." In stark opposition to the socialist realist heroine, who is not only a pillar of moral strength but also an essential element of both the family and the workforce, Irra neither raises children nor holds a job. She has not a shred of loving, comforting, and motherly instincts; she cares only about herself and her own needs. Sexually emancipated, she seeks satisfaction, and acts with self-assertiveness, in her physical relationships with Toest'lstoy and Dodo. As Pittman concludes, Irra's relationship with her two partners characterizes a mature individual and reflects on her "social, psychological and moral pliability, and adaptability," unlike past heroines in Soviet literature.

Plan pervogo litsa was followed by Narbikova's second novel, *Okolo ekolo,* initially published as a trilogy of novellas in the literary journals *Iunost'* and *Znamia.* The novel retains the title of the first part of the trilogy. The two other novellas are titled, respectively, *Probeg – pro beg* (A Race–About Running, *Znamia,* 1990), and *Velikoe knia . . .* (The Great Principality . . . *Iunost',* 1991). In *Okolo ekolo,* as before, Narbikova focuses on love relationships, but this novel shows a deeper awareness of the political situation in late Soviet society than her previous works. The main heroine, Petrarka, or Petia, is in love with Boris. Although Boris loves Petia, he marries her older sister, Ezdandukta. Petia falls in love with Gleb Il. I., and together they go to an unidentified Soviet republic in the Caucasus that is, unbeknownst to the couple, on the verge of secession from the U.S.S.R. As Gleb Il. I. and Petia try to enjoy themselves on their vacation, he is approached by the leaders of the nationalist movement, who ask him to head their newly independent state. Gleb Il. I. is chosen because of his poetic vocation. In the opinion of the nationalist leaders, only a poet can create a state that is perfect in form and content—just as a poem is.

Against his will Gleb Il. I. is forced to rule a new nation. He stays there with Petia, who begins an affair with a certain Lzhedmitrii (False Dmitry). Although Petia in due time leaves Lzhedmitrii, she does not stay with Gleb Il. I. either—because of the arrival of Boris, with whom she is still in love. Boris leaves Ezdandukta, who becomes infatuated with a character named "milyi moi" (my sweetheart) and eventually marries him. "Milyi moi," however, tries to win Petia and sends Boris an insulting anonymous letter. Boris challenges "milyi moi" to a duel and meets his death in it.

Okolo ekolo is rich in intertextual layers, which bring together political realities of different historical times. Touching on many aspects of everyday life and political reality in the Soviet Union, Narbikova alludes to nationalism, Gorbachev's policies, the socialist realist falsification of reality in literature, a foreboding of the war in the Caucasus, the Soviet people's feeling of isolation in the world, and many other issues. The most striking issue, as several critics have observed, is the relationship between the artist and the state. Gleb Il. I. is doomed to poetic isolation and spiritual death when he becomes a state leader. He realizes that people want his prestige but are indifferent to his work. His subsequent career as a state leader reminds the reader of the lives of some Soviet poets and writers who became involved with the state, such as Vladimir Vladimirovich Mayakovsky and Alexandr Alexandrovich Fadeev. Another issue concerns Narbikova's use of gender. Petrarka's name, for instance, associates her with Petrarch, the great fourteenth-century Italian poet, but creates a gender ambiguity. Petrarka's diminutive name is Petia, which is also masculine. The discrepancy between the masculine name and the third-person feminine personal pronoun suggests a revision of the female role in Russian literature: Petia, a sexual adventurer like Narbikova's previous heroines, Irra and Sana, overcomes the sexual and gender passivity typical of Soviet literary heroines; her presentation in the novel as a sexual being makes her more human. A final issue in *Okolo ekolo*—one of the most sensitive topics of the Soviet legacy—is the destruction of the environment. In fact, the second word of the title, *ekolo,* hints phonetically at "ecology." Dirty streets, polluted water and air, cockroaches, flies, the disappearance of natural forests, and the extinction of birds and animals because of environmental misuse—these factors, among others, contribute to the overall misery of existence in late Soviet society.

Narbikova's latest novel, *Shepot shuma,* manifests what Lipovetsky, in *Russian Postmodernist Fiction,* calls an "aesthetic silence." He writes that authors of alternative literature "attempt to create narcissistic mythological utopias that are hermetic both philosophically and linguistically . . . They create a conflict between literary, cultural, and other contexts in order for these contexts to annihilate each other, leaving in their wake nothing but the effect of aesthetic silence." Less erotic and more meditative than her previous works, Narbikova's *Shepot shuma* explores the meaning of love, life, death, and creativity. It opens with a fatal accident. Vera, the main character, witnesses the death of a man hit by a bus. In a state of shock, she is driven home by Nizhin-Vokhov, or N.-V., and his father, Svia, both of whom subsequently engage in love affairs with Vera. She is married to an historian named Don Zhan and has a child by

Paperback cover for Narbikova's 1992 novel, Okolo ekolo, *and dust jacket for the 1999 English-language translation (left: William T. Young Library, University of Kentucky; right: Richland County Public Library)*

him. Nizhin-Vokhov leads a more complicated personal life. Though married to a beautiful woman, Snandulia, he also has a mistress, Vasil'kisa, who is forever pregnant with his baby; the fetus changes its size depending on Vasil'kisa's mood. The novel follows the characters' complex personal relationships and ends with several separations and deaths. Nizhin-Vokhov leaves Snandulia, while Vera abandons both her husband and Nizhin-Vokhov. Svia dies earlier in the novel but reappears toward the end to meet with Vera and to bury himself. Death and violence are ubiquitous in this story, which develops with the "whisper" and "noise" of nature in the background.

By the time *Shepot shuma* was published, Narbikova was already a familiar name in new Russian literature (*novaia russkaia literatura*). In the 29 June 1994 issue of *Literaturnaia gazeta* the critic Tat'iana Morozova discussed Narbikova's *Shepot shuma* as a milestone in women's literature and ranked her with Victoria

Samoilovna Tokareva, a well-established author of fiction on women's issues. *Shepot shuma,* written only five years after Narbikova's first works were labeled "bad prose" by Urnov in the same *Literaturnaia gazeta,* no longer shocks critics and readers. Morozova summarizes the literary qualities of Narbikova's novel as already familiar to the reader: well written, intertextual, erotic (though toned down in comparison with her previous works), and saturated with unusual names and the usual themes of love and art. Morozova's article acknowledges that by 1994, when the literary scene had undergone tremendous changes in just a few years, Narbikova attained sufficient literary success and popularity among the critics and readers to be firmly included among the important authors of contemporary Russian literature.

In *Shepot shuma* Narbikova continues her exploration of gender interaction. The displacement of gender roles in her works affirms the disintegration of traditional values and, concomitantly, Russia's increasing cultural identity crisis. Through her familiar device of mixing historical and fictional names and periods she creates an interplay of irreconcilable historical moments that highlights her observations on contemporary Russian society. For example, Vera's husband, Don Zhan, represents a deconstruction of Don Juan's literary identity. Instead of being portrayed as an irresistible lover and heartbreaker, Don Zhan is a domesticated cuckolded husband, faithful and vulnerable. His role suggests a transformation of conventional gender interaction in a profoundly sexist Russian society. In addition, although in *Shepot shuma* the themes of sex and the body remain important, as they are in previous works such as *Okolo ekolo* and *Plan pervogo litsa,* they are less intense and often displaced to another dimension of reality. Narbikova uses the metaphor of the body, for instance, to create a sense of the new free-market frenzy in Moscow. The bodily allusions provide a more complex perspective on the developing capitalism in Russia than would a direct criticism of the economic trend. She depicts Moscow as a filthy, rotting body, a place of degradation and disgust.

Since *Shepot shuma,* Narbikova's creative writing in the second half of the 1990s has substantially decreased. Her only notable work since 1994 is a collection of essays, *Vremia v puti* (Time in Transit, 1997), published by Tret'ia volna in a limited edition of three hundred copies. This slim book presents Narbikova's impressions of her trips abroad and reflections on life in a modern society. The subtle irony and linguistic playfulness remind the reader of her previous works; yet, *Vremia v puti* is more personal thematically and considerably less ornamental in style. It is a work of a more mature writer trying to come to grips with her changing personal life and the world outside of it. *Vremia v puti* can be characterized as a more "normal" work in an increasingly normalized literary marketplace.

In the period of transition from Soviet socialism to a new society and in the early post-Soviet years, Valeriia Spartakovna Narbikova emerged as one of the major young authors to break out of the tradition of official literature. Together with other postmodernist writers of her generation, she attempted to demythologize Soviet reality through language. Through linguistic displacements vis-à-vis the official discourse, Narbikova "de-aesthetisized" Soviet life. She portrays late Soviet society in a state of crisis, incapable of maintaining cultural integrity and of redefining its identity. Her fiction is symptomatic of the tremendous changes that Soviet society underwent during perestroika and glasnost. Narbikova's representation of sex and body functions is pioneering, and her contribution to women's literature is hard to overestimate. Not only does she play with

gender dynamics and celebrate women's sexual emancipation, but she also challenges the male-dominated representation of women in Russian literature. As someone who breaks with literary canons and established tastes, Narbikova is regarded as one of the most talented writers of early Russian postmodernist literature.

Interviews:

V. Voitov, "Interview with Valeriia Narbikova," *Stas,* 2 (1995): 114;

Serafima Roll, "Literatura kak utopicheskaia polemika s kul'turoi," in her *Postmodernisty o postkul'ture: Interv'iu s sovremennymi pisateliami i kritikami* (Moscow: R. Elinin, 1996), pp. 131–142;

Roll, "Valeriia Narbikova: A Contemporary Textual Psychology," in her *Contextualizing Transition: Interviews with Contemporary Russian Writers and Critics,* Middlebury Studies in Russian Language and Literature, volume 16 (New York: Peter Lang, 1998), pp. 85–93.

References:

Vitaly Chernetsky, "*Epigonoi,* or Transformation of Writing in the Texts of Valerija Narbikova and Nina Iskrenko," *Slavic and East European Journal,* 38, no. 4 (Winter 1994): 655–676;

Helena Goscilo, "Domostroika or Perestroika? The Construction of Womanhood in Soviet Culture under Glasnost," in *Late Soviet Culture: From Perestroika to Novostroika,* edited by Thomas Lahusen and Gene Kuperman (Durham, N.C.: Duke University Press, 1993), pp. 233–255;

Goscilo, "Speaking Bodies: Erotic Zones Rhetorized," in *Fruits of Her Plume: Essays on Contemporary Russian Women's Culture,* edited by Goscilo (Armonk, N.Y.: M. E. Sharpe, 1993), pp. 135–163;

Vadim Linetsky, "Paradoksy Narbikovoi," *Daugava,* 6 (November–December 1993): 141–147;

Mark Lipovetsky, *Russian Postmodernist Prose: Dialogue with Chaos* (Armonk, N.Y.: M. E. Sharpe, 1999);

Tat'iana Morozova, "Dama v krasnom i dama v chernom: Prodolzhaem razgovor o zhenskoi literature," *Literaturnaia gazeta,* 29 June 1994, p. 4;

Nadya L. Peterson, "Games Women Play: The 'Erotic' Prose of Valeriia Narbikova," in *Fruits of Her Plume: Essays on Contemporary Russian Women's Culture,* edited by Goscilo (Armonk, N.Y.: M. E. Sharpe, 1993), pp. 165–183;

Riitta H. Pittman, "Valeriia Narbikova's Iconoclastic Prose," *Forum for Modern Language Studies,* 28, no. 4 (October 1992): 376–389;

Larissa Rudova, "A Mindset of Present Russia: Valeriia Narbikova's Fiction," *Russian Literature,* 39 (January 1996): 79–94.

Marina Anatol'evna Palei

(1 February 1955 –)

Alexander Prokhorov
College of William & Mary

BOOKS: *Otdelenie propashchikh* (Moscow: Moskovsky rabochii, 1991)–includes "Pominovenie," "Evgesha i Annushka," "Otdelenie propashchikh," "Den' topolinogo pukha," "Skazki Andersena," "Svidanie," "Lift," "Abragam," "Lacrymosa," "Magistral'nyi bliuz," and "Virazh";

Mestorozhdenie vetra (St. Petersburg: Limbus, 1998)–includes "Kabiriia s Obvodnogo kanala," "Lenta Mebiusa," "Beskabal'noe nebo," and "Mestorozhdenie vetra";

Long Distance, ili Slavianskii aktsent (Moscow: Vagrius, 2000);

Lanch (St. Petersburg: INAPRESS, 2000).

Editions in English: "The Day of the Poplar Flakes," translated by Masha Gessen, in *Half a Revolution: Contemporary Fiction by Russian Women,* edited by Gessen (Pittsburgh: Cleis, 1995), pp. 62–69;

"Rendezvous" and "The Losers' Division," in *Lives in Transit: A Collection of Recent Russian Women's Writing,* edited by Helena Goscilo (Dana Point, Cal.: Ardis, 1995), pp. 108–110, 191–202;

"Cabiria from the Bypass Canal," in *Present Imperfect: Stories by Russian Women,* edited by Ayesha Kagal and Natasha Perova, with an introduction by Goscilo (Boulder, Colo.: Westview Press, 1996), pp. 149–168;

"Kabiriia from the Obvodnyi Canal," translated by Brian Thomas Oles in *Russian Women Writers,* 2 volumes, edited by Christine D. Tomei (New York: Garland, 1999), II: 1412–1418.

OTHER: Laura Salmon, "Moskovskie vospomonaniia," translated by Palei, *Novyi mir,* 6 (1992): 138;

Salmon, *Veer,* translated by Palei (St. Petersburg: Limbus, 1992);

"Reis," in *Chego khochet zhenshchina,* edited by Elena Trofimova (Moscow: Linor, 1994), pp. 190–221;

Martinus Nijhoff, Hendrik Marsman, and Paul van Ostaijen, "K uklonchivoi zvezde. Poems," translated by Palei and Silvana Vedeman, edited by Palei, *Novyi mir,* 7 (1997): 135–140;

Marina Anatol'evna Palei (courtesy of Nibbe & Wiedling Literary Agency)

Anfilada: Sbornik poezii, edited by Palei and Ol'ga Khvostova (Wilhelmshorst: Göpfert, 1997).

SELECTED PERIODICAL PUBLICATIONS–UNCOLLECTED: "Pavlovsk," *Istoki,* 1 (1987): 343;

"Tvoia nemyslimaia chistota," *Literaturnoe obozrenie,* 6 (1987): 61–64;

"Figurka na ogolennom pole," *Novyi mir,* 11 (1988): 245–248;

"Pust' budet dver' otkryta," *Literaturnoe obozrenie,* 2 (1988): 52–54;

"Otpechatok ognia," *Literaturnoe obozrenie,* 12 (1989): 60–63;

"Composition in Red and Blue," in *Book and Art in the U.S.S.R.,* 64 (1990): 20–22;

"The Bloody Women's Ward," translated by A. L. Tait, in *Glas: New Russian Writing. Women's View,* 3 (1992): 74–91;

"Privorotnoe zel'e," *Volga,* 12 (1993): 10–17;

"Evoliutsiia tvorcheskogo masterstva. Put'k svobode vne pola. Damskaia drebeden'," *Mariia,* 2 (1995): 175–198.

Marina Palei emerged as an important prose writer during the years of perestroika, from the mid 1980s to the early 1990s. A person of many talents, she writes prose, poetry, and criticism, as well as translates poetry from Dutch, Italian, and other languages. The recurring themes in Palei's writing include the creative freedom of the artist (usually a woman), human communication, and the liminality of existence as manifested in the interdependence of life and death, body and soul. Women's issues, such as maternity and the sexuality and physicality of women, are prominent in many of her works, which feature characters who are often homeless–both literally and in the philosophical sense of the word. According to Palei, this homelessness, together with cultural displacement, is a sine qua non condition for an individual's creative freedom.

Palei focuses on human, especially female, physiology as an indispensable part of the human condition. Merging body and spirit, she early on found an innovative way to bring the symbolic and mythic into everyday experience. This intersection textually translates into settings in threshold spaces that evoke strong existential connotations, such as a hospital or a cemetery. Palei often organizes her characters in contrasting or doubling pairs. Her longer works favor a first-person narrator who is self-aware, often ironic, and, in her later publications, increasingly sarcastic and embittered.

Palei was born Marina Anatol'evna Spivak on 1 February 1955 in Leningrad, where her parents, Ukrainian Jews, studied engineering. After her parents' divorce while she was still a child, Palei traveled with her mother and spent her teen years with her maternal grandparents in Vsevolozhsk, located in the outskirts of Leningrad. Justyna Beinek, in her contribution to *Russian Women Writers* (1999), pinpoints the main influences on Palei's identity as "psychological and material instability, various encounters with anti-Semitism, and a passion for art and reading."

In 1972 Palei began studying epidemiology at the Leningrad Institute of Medicine, from which she gradu- ated in 1978. She was unable to find any permanent job, however, because of her ethnicity, gender, and nonparticipation in the Soviet style of social networking. By this time she was also a single mother, which did not enhance her career prospects. She had to take on several temporary jobs and worked variously as a model, a cleaning woman, and a medical technician.

Palei started writing poetry in January 1984. Irina Bentsionovna Rodnianskaia, an editor at *Novyi mir* (New World) and a friend of Palei's mother, encouraged Palei to apply to the prestigious Institut mirovoi literatury (Institute of World Literature), also known as the Gor'ky Literary Institute, in Moscow. Upon enrolling, Palei studied in the workshops of Evgenii Iur'evich Sidorov and Andrei Georgievich Bitov, and after graduation she was invited to join the Union of Soviet Writers.

Palei's first publications included critical articles and reviews, many of which share two dominant themes: the fate of a woman writer and the erasure of gifted writing from cultural memory. Symptomatic of the latter theme is Palei's article "Tvoia nemyslimaia chistota" (Your Inconceivable Purity, 1987), about the forgotten (and now rediscovered) poet and translator Mariia Sergeevna Petrovykh. The theme of the woman poet and her genesis as an author likewise informs Palei's review of Tat'iana Galushko's volume of poetry, *Otpechatok ognia* (The Imprint of Flame, 1989).

Three of her early stories, "Lift" (Elevator), "Lacrymosa," and "Svidanie" (Rendezvous), initially part of a cycle called "Fabrika igrushek" (The Toy Factory) and published in her first collection, *Otdelenie propashchikh* (The Division of Lost Souls, 1991), have several common features important in Palei's style. First, the stories are set in a transitional space, such as an elevator (in "Lift"), a coffin at the cemetery (in "Lacrymosa"), and a window-computer-screen painting (in "Svidanie"). Second, the main narrator constantly subverts the binary oppositions that serve as the characters' heuristic (or problem-solving) tools. The characters of "Svidanie," who at the beginning of the story may be identified as male and female, turn out to be two cybercreatures with programmed gender identities; whether they are machines, or part-human, part-machine, is unclear. In "Lift" the self-assured yet elevator-fearing protagonist gets trapped in the "twilight zone" of an elevator, where his binary systems of coordinates cease to operate: time collapses with space; up replaces down; and motion is transformed into stasis. Through these descriptions of binary systems becoming dismantled in all three works, Palei essentially challenges the stability of her characters' identities. In "Svidanie" the male cyborg creates the female beauty, only to dismantle her and put her into storage. A moment later the male cyborg himself switches off when he attempts to execute the impossible mathematical task of division by zero. In "Lacrymosa," Mr. Van der Beidenhoff writes a treatise: every letter he produces immediately disappears. The erasure of his writing is mirrored in the erasure of his body: it lies in a coffin in a cemetery and exists only because a spider's web has delineated its vanished contours and eyes.

Erasure and memory continue to be prominent themes in Palei's later works. At the Gor'ky Institute she wrote her quasi-autobiographical novella "Pominovenie" (Remembrance of the Dead), which in an earlier draft was titled "Molenie o Dome" (A Prayer about Home, 1987). The story grew out of a student paper in Sidorov's workshop. Palei wrote an essay-improvisation on the first line of Osip Emil'evich Mandel'shtam's 1930 poem "Leningrad," which begins, "Ia vernulsia v moi gorod znakomyi do slez . . ." (I came back to my city, familiar to the point of tears . . .). Beinek contends that the autobiographical stance of this work constitutes Palei's literary credo: Palei sees "her writing growing out of what Vladimir Vladimirovich Nabokov called a 'hypertrophied nostalgia for childhood.'" The defamiliarizing gaze of the child protagonist serves as an artistic antidote to the monotony and hardships of life. Also focusing primarily on the fate of women, Palei's novella constantly emphasizes how difficult their lives are compared to those of men.

In 1990 the literary journal *Znamia* carried her novella "Evgesha i Annushka," which immediately brought her critical acclaim. It tells about the lives of two old women, Evgesha and Annushka, in a Leningrad communal apartment. The narrator, Irina, an alter ego of the author, oscillates between an intimate first-person perspective and a third-person vantage point. Annushka is a retired factory worker who is taking a rest from life. A selfless and charitable person, whose material poverty contrasts with her spiritual wealth, she tries to be helpful to people and dies a saint. Evgesha, Annushka's neighbor—and in many respects her antipode—is also retired, though six years younger than Annushka. She used to work as a hospital nurse and is still active, hardworking, and obsessed with order, discipline, and hygiene. The narrator presents Evgesha's hectic activity and Annushka's passive nature as the red herrings of the novella. Evgesha serves as a comic agent of Soviet enlightenment (her last name is Krasnova—which means "daughter of the Reds"), with its cult of reason and hygiene. Her hard work and belief in the ability to control and change one's life contrast with the narrator's depiction of unchangeable routine inside the communal apartment.

The stories from the cycle "Den' topolinogo pukha" (The Day of Poplar Down), written in the late 1980s, appeared in the volume *Otdelenie propashchikh*.

The stories are set primarily in a hospital, with the fragility of human life (suggested by the metaphor of the poplar down) as the object of narration. Each story consists of a small episode from the protagonist's medical internship and her philosophical monologue inspired by the event—a monologue that expands earthly events into mythical dimensions. The story "Skazki Andersena" (Andersen's Tales), for example, is an episode from a medical student's internship in a delivery ward. The first part of the story tells, in the third person, about the birth of a baby girl and her death at only eleven days old because of professional negligence and incompetence. The second part offers the protagonist's rereading of her own internship report, which, at best, obscures the events of her internship and, at worst, covers her own failure to save the girl's life. The protagonist questions the ability of humans to understand and express adequately what they see.

In her introduction to the cycle Palei emphasizes that her stories do not attempt to examine the deplorable state of Russian medical care; rather, they conceive of the hospital as a threshold setting that lays bare the fundamental questions of human life. She underscores the parallelism between such settings as hospital, jail, and camp barrack. As Helena Goscilo points out in *Dehexing Sex: Russian Womanhood During and After Glasnost* (1996), Palei's focus on the similarity between hospitalization and imprisonment signals an important trend in contemporary Russian women's prose: the chronotope of the women's hospital fulfills the function of a prison space and is analogous to the concentration camp in prose by Russian male writers.

In the cycle most of the hospital inmates are women, and the action of "Skazki Andersena" and "Otdelenie propashchikh," another story from the cycle, takes place in a delivery ward. Palei uses the female body as a map for women's experiences. The body as an indispensable part of individual identity has few precedents in Russian literature. Apart from the intern-narrator, nobody cares about women's emotional and physical sufferings in a hospital. Males appear only as angels of death with a medical degree; they predict the demise of patients (as in "Den' topolinogo pukha," the title story of the cycle) or inflict suffering on women's bodies (seen in "Otdelenie propashchikh").

Palei's best-known and—in the opinion of critics such as Goscilo, Sergei Borovikov, and Deming Brown—her most complex novella is "Kabiriia s Obvodnogo kanala" (initially published in *Novyi mir*, 1991; translated as "Cabiria from the Bypass Canal," 1996). Nominated for the Booker Russian Novel Prize (now the Smirnoff-Booker Prize), it tells the life story of the narrator's cousin, Raimonda, whose insatiable sexual energy ultimately symbolizes creativity and an irrepressible life force. The action is set again in Leningrad, in a gloomy communal apartment on Bypass Canal Street. Following celebrated Russian writers such as Nikolai Vasil'evich Gogol, Fyodor Dostoevsky, and Bitov, Palei adheres to the metaphorical logic of Russian language rather than to the logic of physical reality. She links the Bypass Canal with the metaphor of the heart as the life force. While everyone around Raimonda lives on the banks of the gloomy and death-driven Bypass Canal Street area, Raimonda lives through her heart and resists the deadening power of the canal.

Raimonda's congenital heart defect *(porok serdtsa),* according to the logic of Russian homonyms, leads her to become a *porochnoe serdtse* (wanton heart). Like a voracious hole, she craves anything and everything remotely phallic to fill herself up. When Palei's narrator mentions male genitalia, Raimonda—in the spirit of Gogol's lists of nose sizes and shapes—cannot stop enumerating various labels for the sacred object, from the tree of life to the crotch viper. In essence, Raimonda continues Palei's gallery of carnival characters who turn the deadening routine of contemporary urban life upside down. Palei's focus on feminine physicality, especially the "uplifting" representation of overtly manifested sexuality, constitutes a major break with both Soviet and Russian classical traditions. In her writing she inverts traditional narratives of male doctors saving women's lives and redeeming their souls—the commonplaces of masculine anxiety and suppression of female sexuality.

Both "Evgesha i Annushka" and "Kabiriia s Obvodnogo kanala" evoke the "Petersburg" tradition of Russian literature, especially its take on modernity. Since Aleksandr Sergeevich Pushkin's "Mednyi vsadnik" (The Bronze Horseman, 1833) and Gogol's *Peterburgskie povesti* (The Petersburg Tales, 1842), the Westernized imperial capital of Russia has served as the setting where the ideals of the Enlightenment, with its cult of reason and science, turn into an irrational, diabolical dystopia. Examining the bleak urban setting of "Evgesha i Annushka," Palei explicitly refers to the two Westernizers-Enlighteners of Russia, whose names are reflected in the ever-shifting identities (Petersburg/ Petrograd/Leningrad) of the city: Peter (the Great) and (Vladimir) Lenin. Vistas of a deadening metropolis dominate "Kabiriia s Obvodnogo kanala." Palei conveys her vision of modernity as a mechanized inferno through the image of a railroad station (an homage to Dostoevsky and Aleksandr Aleksandrovich Blok), where people are doomed to nonsensical consumption and excretion. A consumption that entraps the human spirit remains a key metaphor of modernity in Palei's later works, such as "Long Distance, ili Slavianskii aktsent"

Paperback cover for Palei's Long Distance, ili Slavianskii aktsent *(Long Distance, or A Slavic Accent, 2000), in which the title story explores individual identity and linguistic displacement (Collection of Mark Lipovetsky)*

(Long Distance, or A Slavic Accent, 2000) and *Lanch* (Lunch, 2000).

In 1998 Palei published a collection titled *Mestorozhdenie vetra* (Birthplace of the Wind), in which "Pominovenie," "Evgesha i Annushka," and "Kabiriia s Obvodnogo kanala" appeared together as a trilogy. She also combined stories from *Otdelenie propashchikh* ("Svidanie," "Abragam" [Abraham, 1991], and "Magistral'nyi bliuz" [Railway Blues, 1991]) with stories written after the trilogy ("Virazh" [The Curve], "Privorotnoe zel'e" [Love Potion, 1993], and "Reis" [Flight, 1994]) for a cycle titled "Lenta Mebiusa" (Möbius Strip). The cycle examines the pleasures of artistic power exercised via gazes and words.

The central story of the cycle, "Reis," constitutes a lyrical monologue by a woman who, disguised in a wig, dark glasses, and makeup, follows her former lover on a transatlantic flight. The protagonist's bittersweet pleasure emanates from her verbal art and empowering, controlling gaze. The stories "Abragam," "Virazh," and "Magistral'nyi bliuz" also favor the pleasure of a female lover and narrator; indeed, the female gaze determines the point of view in each story, in which the narrator-lover figures her creative freedom as motion, speed, and flight. In "Reis" the endless surface of the Möbius strip symbolizes the narrator's control over her gaze and words. In their monologic and highly metaphoric stance the stories border on lyrical poetry. The stories "Svidanie" and "Iz zhizni avtootvetchikov" (From the Life of Answering Machines) frame the cycle and provide counterpoint to the lyrical stance of the remaining stories. In each piece the narrator demonstrates her awareness that identity and point of view may be constructed and manipulated. For example, the protagonist-loner of "Iz zhizni avtootvetchikov" finds more emotional warmth in interacting with a high-tech answering machine than with humans. Constructed emotions outstrip unmediated human ones.

Palei's short story "Mestorozhdenie vetra," first published in *Novyi mir* (1994) and incorporated in the cycle "Beskabal'noe nebo" (The Skies of Freedom) in the 1998 collection *Mestorozhdenie vetra,* continues to examine her favorite issues of creative freedom and individual identity. Her allegory for the individual subject of resistance is a nameless clerk, with a physical handicap, who tries to learn how to ride a bicycle. The sail-like motion of his clothing captures the wind or, to be more precise, gives birth to the wind associated with the free spirit of a cyclist. This individual, irrational wind provides an outlet for the protagonist's creativity and individuality. In the process of his struggle with the bicycle—cast here as a capricious machine—the protagonist escapes the limitations of his own body and the deterministic thinking of his psychoanalyst. Palei intertwines the narrative with excerpts from the protagonist's appointments with his psychoanalyst, who pedantically explains the patient's life as a belated Oedipal anxiety—a predictable diagnosis by a representative of the medical profession functioning as a prison warden, an emotional and physical abuser.

In 1995 Palei moved to the Netherlands, and since then the subtheme of linguistic displacement has become a prominent variation on the themes of homelessness and fragmentation (of a subject's identity) in her prose. "Long distance, ili Slavianskii aktsent" exemplifies this new development in Palei's writing. In 2000 the work was published in the literary journal *Novyi mir* in two formats: it appeared in its entirety in the print version of *Novyi mir,* and an excerpt of it was offered in electronic format at the website for the journal. Simultaneous with its appearance in *Novyi mir,* "Long Distance, ili Slavianskii aktsent" was collected with other short fiction works by Palei in a volume of the same name.

"Long Distance, ili Slavianskii aktsent" examines individual identity as a trauma expressed through emotional and verbal breakdown. At the center of the narrative are the experiences of a young woman artist, an expatriate from the former Soviet Union who lives in what is vaguely identifiable as the New York area. As with much of Palei's fiction, the physical locale provides an excuse to visit a surrealistic setting in the narrator's inner world. The protagonist-narrator also adds to Palei's gallery of metaphysically homeless characters, here caught in the gap between an abandoned and despised Russo-Soviet identity and the equally despised sterility of an American middle-class identity. The protagonist is unable to fit into the "cookie-cutter" social roles of American life, as modeled by the typical middle-class American housewife or the typical Russian-Jewish denizen of an ethnic New York City neighborhood. Her identity displacement and spiritual homelessness find materialization in the absence of standard identity signs, such as a visa, an address, and a job.

The genre of "Long Distance, ili Slavianskii aktsent" mirrors the threshold, underground existence of the protagonist. Subtitled "Stsenarnye imitatsii" (Screenplay Imitations), the work constitutes a cinematically discursive narrative consisting of five loosely connected novellas. The language of these novellas attempts to visualize both the physical and the psychological space of the protagonist. For this purpose Palei intertwines her text with suggestions on how to use the camera if one wishes to film the events that transpire in the work. In addition, "Long Distance, ili Slavianskii aktsent" demonstrates Palei's mastery of verbal play and her emphasis on linguistic polysemy. The title itself brings together several meanings—above all, the ability and, simultaneously, the disability to establish contact with another human being, as well as, literally, the notion of life as a long trip. As is evident from the bilingual title, for Palei linguistic hybridity is as important as her displaced and homeless protagonist's milieu. She writes in a mix of Russian and English, and her characters speak in broken English and in Russian that sounds sometimes like a translation from English. This linguistic Tower of Babel results in communication breaks, in an inability to convey thoughts and, most importantly, feelings.

In 2000, the same year that "Long Distance, ili Slavianskii aktsent" appeared in *Novyi mir,* the literary journal *Volga* (now defunct) published Palei's *Lanch* (Lunch). Once again, her new work appeared in two versions—the full text in print and an excerpt in electronic form at the website for the journal. *Lanch* was nominated for the Smirnoff-Booker Prize.

Like "Long Distance, ili Slavianskii aktsent," *Lanch* constitutes a pastiche of texts and defies easy genre definition. The male narrator's confessional monologue frames a story titled "Ring." *Lanch* also includes the main narrator's book *Traktat*, or, specifically, the random excerpts from *Traktat* that he uses for fortune-telling. Finally, *Lanch* incorporates a palimpsest piece that the main narrator allegedly erased from the final version of his monologue—a bitter comment on contemporary academia as a guild of shameless brokers who feed on the spiritual brilliancy of genuine artists.

Power and the ability to communicate are the two major themes of *Lanch*. The male protagonist narcissistically contemplates his reflection in a silver tray, which functions as a metaphorical and narrative frame in which is unveiled the main monologue of his life—the most important part of which was devoted to writing *Traktat*, the perfect work of verbal art. The reader has access only to several random pages from *Traktat*, which renders any interpretation virtually impossible. At the end of *Lanch*, in order to avoid its cannibalistic consumption by readers and critics, the protagonist burns his magnum opus and commits suicide. The narrator-protagonist defies a finalized reading of his *Traktat* by providing the reader with only random excerpts from the work. Similarly, the final image of *Lanch*, a person on the seashore, suggests transitional space that eludes closure.

Palei, like many other Russian women writers, feels uneasy about being compartmentalized in the category of women authors. For example, she expressed her displeasure to Julia Heaton (recounted in Heaton's 1997 article for *The Slavonic and East European Review*) that her story "Otdelenie propashchikh" was published in translation in *Glas: New Russian Writing. Women's View* (1992), as "The Bloody Women's Ward," a rendering in English that is quite distant from the straightforward Russian translation, "The Division of Lost Souls." Palei views such categorization of her writing as a marginalizing practice. It finalizes and simplifies her works under one more "–ism," disempowering her as an artist.

Marina Anatol'evna Palei, however, is by no means a marginal or disempowered figure—at least in Russian cultural life. Her innovative themes and narrative stance, especially her concern with issues that are unconventional for a Russo-Soviet woman writer, such as power, identity, and bodily experience, make her an original voice in contemporary Russian literature. Her interest in self-reflexive narration and the grotesque and her focus on language as a craft link her works with the Russian tradition of self-reflexive writing—above all with the works of Gogol, Dostoevsky, Nabokov, and Bitov. Intertextual links to the prose of these writers punctuate many of Palei's texts. Premier Russian literary journals, such as *Novyi mir*, rank her among their major authors. Indeed, Palei's several nominations for the Smirnoff-Booker Prize are a deserved tribute to her verbal craft.

Biographies:

Tat'iana Mikhalovskaia, "Marina Palei," in *Dictionary of Russian Women Writers*, edited by Marina Ledkovsky, Charlotte Rosenthal, and Mary Zirin (Westpoint, Conn.: Greenwood Press, 1991), pp. 479–480;

Justyna Beinek, "Marina Palei," in *Russian Women Writers*, 2 volumes, edited by Christine D. Tomei (New York: Garland, 1999), II: 1403–1412.

References:

Helena Goscilo, *Dehexing Sex: Russian Womanhood During and After Glasnost* (Ann Arbor: University of Michigan Press, 1996), pp. 62–64, 66–67, 106–109, 122–123, 125–126;

Goscilo, "Speaking Bodies: Erotic Zones Rhetorized," in *Fruits of Her Plume: Essays on Contemporary Russian Women's Culture*, edited by Goscilo (Armonk, N.Y.: M. E. Sharpe, 1993), pp. 135–164;

Goscilo, "Women's Space and Women's Place in Contemporary Russian Fiction," in *Gender and Russian Literature: New Perspectives*, edited by Rosalind Marsh (Cambridge: Cambridge University Press, 1996), pp. 326–348;

Julia Heaton, "Russian Women's Writing–Problems of Feminist Approach, with Particular Reference to the Writing of Marina Palei," *Slavonic and East European Review*, 75, no. 1 (1997): 63–85;

Marion Michaud, "Marina Palei's Literary Style: Cabiria from the Obvodny Canal," M.A. thesis, University of Lyon, 1993;

Elena Samuelson, "Skuggor, ljusa eller dunkla: Om Marina Palej," translated by Bengt Samuelson, *Ord-och-Bild*, 101, no. 4 (1992): 53–62;

Marta Zamborova, "Ako sa sladi život," *Revue Svetovej Literatury*, 4 (1992).

Aleksei Maksimovich Parshchikov
(Raiderman)
(25 May 1954 –   )

Alexandra Smith
University of Canterbury, New Zealand

BOOKS: *Dneprovskii avgust* (Moscow, 1986)—includes "Steliannye bashni";

"Kto sluzhit vetrom . . . ," by Parshchikov, Iurii Kabankov, and Richard Nevodin (Moscow: Molodaia gvardiia, 1986);

Figury intuitsii (Moscow: Moskovskii rabochii, 1989)—includes "Ia zhil na pole Poltavskoi bitvy";

Cyrillic Light (Moscow: Zolotoi vek, 1995)—includes "Peter," "Ustritsy," and "Na ferme Kaliforniia";

Vybrannoe (Moscow: ITS-Garant, 1996);

Perepiska: Fevral' 1996–fevral' 1997, by Parshchikov and Viacheslav Nikolaevich Kuritsyn (Moscow: Ad Marginem, 1998).

Editions in English: "Poems," translated by Michael Molnar, in *Child of Europe,* edited by Michael March (Harmondsworth, U.K.: Penguin, 1990);

"Conversation Between the Editor and a Poet," "The Porcupine," "Flight," "The Woman Make-Up Artist," "New Year Verses," "Catfish," and "Mudflats," translated by Molnar, John High, Michael Palmer, and Andrew Wachtel, in *Third Wave: The New Russian Poetry,* edited by Kent Johnson and Stephen M. Ashby (Ann Arbor: University of Michigan Press, 1992), pp. 23–35;

"Poems," translated by Gerald S. Smith, in *Contemporary Russian Poetry,* edited by Smith (Bloomington: Indiana University Press, 1993), pp. 306–315;

Blue Vitriol: Poems, translated by High, Molnar, and Palmer, with an introduction by Marjorie Perloff (Penngrove, Cal.: Avec, 1994);

"Money," translated by Palmer and Darlene Reddaway; "Cow," translated by Palmer, Eugene Ostashevsky, and Reddaway; and "Prelude, Spoken to My Work Tools," translated by High, in *Crossing Centuries: The New Generation in Russian Poetry,* edited by High and others (Jersey City: Talisman House, 2000), pp. 109–112.

Aleksei Maksimovich Parshchikov, 2002
(photograph by Dmitrii Kuz'min)

OTHER: "Introduction," by Parshchikov and Andrew Wachtel, in *Third Wave: The New Russian Poetry,* edited by Kent Johnson and Stephen M. Ashby (Ann Arbor: University of Michigan Press, 1992);

"Absolute Tranquility in the Face of Absolute Trag-
edy," in Valentina Polukhina, *Brodsky through the
Eyes of His Contemporaries* (Basingstoke & New
York: Macmillan, 1992), pp. 261–275;

Michael Palmer, *SUN,* translated by Parshchikov (Moscow, 2000);

Poety-metarealisty, edited by G. Reznichenko, with contributions by Parshchikov, Aleksandr Viktorovich
Eremenko, and Ivan Fedorovich Zhdanov (Moscow: MK-Periodika, 2002).

SELECTED PERIODICAL PUBLICATIONS–
UNCOLLECTED: "Novogodnie strochki," *Literaturnaia ucheba,* 1 (1984);

"Vybor mesta," *Kommentarii,* 3 (1994): 69–83;

"Sobytiinaia kanva," *Kommentarii,* 7 (1995): 3–43;

"2000 kadrov v sekundu" and "Stikhi," *Vestnik Evropy,* 2
(2001).

Aleksei Parshchikov is a prominent Russian contemporary poet, essay writer, and translator. A natural
eccentric, Parshchikov emerged in the 1980s as one of
the most innovative poets of the period and passionately advocated a mode of writing known as *polystylistics.*
His poetic landscapes range from the Ukrainian provinces to the Crimea, Moscow, and California. An excellent photographer, Parshchikov combines his phonetic
experiments with striking visual imagery. To a great
extent his verse develops many tenets of Russian futurist poetry, including primitivist tendencies, subversive
structures, sound-painting technique, a predilection for
urbanism, and a vigorous employment of harsh words
and sounds, together with images that shock. Although
various critics label Parshchikov a metarealist poet who
displays a strong liking for metaphors, in interviews
and personal conversations he prefers to stress the
importance of fragmentation and metonymy in his
work. Parshchikov's essays and correspondence with
several poets and critics provide an invaluable insight
into the emergence of the postmodernist movement in
the Soviet Union in the 1970s and 1980s.

Parshchikov was born Aleksei Maksimovich Raiderman on 24 May 1954, in Ol'ga, a small town in Okhta
Bay in Primor'e, a region in the Far East, and spent his
childhood in Ukraine. At the age of sixteen he changed
his name from Raiderman to Parshchikov and his
nationality from Jewish to Russian; beyond providing
this information, Parshchikov avoids talking about his
parents and childhood. After graduating from school he
studied at Kiev Agricultural Academy. In 1975 Parshchikov started a creative-writing course at the Gor'ky
Literary Institute in Moscow as part of a seminar given
by the well-known critic Aleksandr Mikhailov. Upon his
graduation in 1981 Parshchikov continued to live in

Moscow and took part in various poetry readings with
his first wife–poet and psychologist Ol'ga Sviblova,
whom he married in the early 1970s–and with Ivan
Fedorovich Zhdanov and Aleksander Viktorovich Eremenko. In 1984 Parshchikov and his wife had a son,
Timofei. In the 1980s both Parshchikov and Sviblova
were members of Kirill Kovaldzhi's poetry association,
which promoted new modes of writing in Moscow. In
1987 Sviblova was celebrated in her own right for producing the documentary motion picture *Chernyi kvadrat*
(Black Square), about Soviet art, which was awarded
several international prizes. The couple divorced in the
early 1990s. Today, Sviblova is a director of the Moscow House of Photography and lives in Paris with
Timofei and her second husband.

While Mikhail Naumovich Epshtein categorizes
Parshchikov's poetry under "metarealism," or "presentism" (the poetry of presence), in the beginning of
his career Parshchikov was seen by his contemporaries
as "the Voznesensky of the 1980s," in the words of
Arina Vasil'eva in her on-line article "Istoria O." In
1989 he was invited to Scotland and Holland to take
part in international festivals. In 1990 Parshchikov–
together with Nina Iur'evna Iskrenko, Zhdanov, and
Eremenko–took part in the San Francisco International Festival. In 1993 Parshchikov undertook M.A.
studies at Stanford University, where he attended Marjorie Perloff's course on contemporary American
poetry and lectures on Russian literature delivered by
Lazar Fleishman and Viacheslav Vsevolodovich
Ivanov. In partial fulfillment of his degree Parshchikov
wrote a thesis, titled "Dmitrii Aleksandrovich Prigov v
kontekste sovetskogo kontseptualisma" (Dmitrii Aleksandrovich Prigov in the Context of Soviet Conceptualism). He worked for the journal *Druzhba narodov* (The
People's Friendship) and the newspaper *Sel'skaia molodezh* (Countryside Youth) and in 1994 joined the editorial board of the Russian journal *Kommentarii* (Commentaries). His poems and essays have appeared in
Russia, Great Britain, the United States, Denmark, and
Finland. Parshchikov has also translated the work of
American contemporary poet Michael Palmer. From
1991 to 1994 Parshchikov lived in the United States
and Switzerland; currently he lives in Germany and
occasionally in Moscow. In 1992 he married Swiss poet
and Slavic scholar Martina Huegli, from whom he has
since separated.

Parshchikov's name attracted considerable attention, both in Russia and the West, from the 1980s to
early 1990s. His work develops the futurist tradition to
a great extent, yet it is not preoccupied with
socio-aesthetic militancy and utopianism. In his scholarship on the writer, Andrew Wachtel lists Parshchikov
among the young archaists of the 1980s and highlights

some of the neoclassical tenets of Parshchikov's writing. Russian critic Konstantin Kedrov labels Parshchikov a "metametaphorist." According to Michael Molnar in his contribution to *The Reference Guide to Russian Literature* (1998), however, Parshchikov considers fragmentation and metonymy the core elements of his poetics. Molnar also indicates the presence of baroque elements in Parshchikov's poetry. In the essay "Sobytiinaia kanva" (Chronological Description of Events), published in 1995 in *Kommentarii,* Parshchikov highlights the role of playfulness and parody in his poetry. "The psychology of the moron," Parshchikov explains, "which is devoid of determinism, was adopted by my generation as the literary norm of a character's self-consciousness. It was honest because it was not prejudiced. This psychology was real and parodic; it was a kind of revenge on the official [propaganda]." According to Barrett Watten in his article for the online journal *Postmodern Culture,* Parshchikov's poetry shares features with Russian conceptualist art, especially because of the post-Soviet subjectivity manifested in Parshchikov's work. Reviewing the cultural scene in 1990s Russia, Watten states: "A prospective conclusion is that contemporary post-Soviet culture, once it had expanded to integrate both unofficial and international influences, does not simply mean an uncritical embrace of Western postmodernism, but reveals a post-Soviet subjectivity that is not simply reducible to the various national identities now contesting the ground of the former Soviet state."

Aleksei Tumol'sky sees Parshchikov, together with Arkadii Timofeevich Dragomoshchenko and Il'ia Kutik, as one of the representatives of the southern Russian school of writing; these writers were widely discussed in the Russian media in the 1980s. The southern school emerged from Ukrainian underground literature and includes poets who belong to the generation of the 1970s. Their links with underground culture are based on their aesthetic: they were alien to the restrictive practices of socialist realism. Parshchikov's first significant poem was published in *Literaturnaia ucheba* (Literary Education) in 1984. His main publications appeared in such journals as *Mitin zhurnal* (Mitia's Journal) and *Kommentarii,* which are famous for their radical shift from socialist realism. The impersonal nature of Parshchikov's poetic persona is already evident in his 1980s cycle "Stekliannye bashni" (Glass Towers, 1986). In his poem "Poet i Muza" (Poet and Muse), included in this cycle, he plays the role of an archetypal Romantic poet who needs his muse as a source of inspiration: "The more agitated the poet becomes, / The louder the woman's head whistles in his thoughts." In "Svobodnye stikhi" (Free Verse), another poem from the same cycle, the image of the beloved is portrayed in an extremely detached manner as well—as if she is just a robot, acting out the role of a woman in love: "My beloved acquired a passion in response to my love." The poetic persona seems to enjoy his freedom from the self and perceives life as a playful theatricality: "In this free space, i.e. without any tension / I live enjoying my entertainments. . . . If you like this game, you could acquire it for yourself, too." The title "Svobodnye stikhi" suggests that this poem is not just a vers libre (free verse) but also a kind of new poetry that preaches free love and freedom from politicized discourse. Written in 1985 and concluding with a line that alludes playfully to the ribbons in the Soviet coat of arms, it marks both the fall of the Soviet man and the beginning of the new drama of anonymity.

Parshchikov's poetry also reinvents the image of the poet as prophet in the modernist tradition and as a moral voice in socialist realism. In his verse he presents a depersonalized self of the creative human object that encompassess various historical periods and transgresses geographical boundaries. Since one of Parshchikov's favorite devices is the palimpsest, his lyric hero appears to exist in several temporal and spatial dimensions, simultaneously speaking in a multitude of voices. Thus, in "Zemliatriasenie v bukhte Tse" (The Earthquake in the Bay of Tse) he not surprisingly refers to himself as the reinvented "collective self," a nameless spirit possessing cultural memories from the past:

. . . smykaia soboi predmety.
ia stal sredoi obitaniia
zreniia vsei planety.
Trepetanie, trepetanie. . . .

(. . . my self molds together objects,
I have become the environment
Of the whole planet's vision.
Tremors, tremors. . . .)

Parshchikov's verse displays the same sense of theatricality found in baroque art: many of the titles for his poems feature actors, makeup artists, and theatrical performances—such as "Stsena iz spektaklia" (Scene from a Play), "Dve grimiershi" (Two Female Make-Up Artists), and "Udody i aktrisy" (Hoopoes and Actresses), all of which appear in his 1980s cycle "Stekliannye bashni." Parshchikov's poetic landscapes, which range from Kiev, the Crimea, and Moscow to San Francisco and Los Angeles, are permeated with the same sense of estrangement as the everyday material presented in baroque art. They construct space as part of some global theatrical performance. Thus, in his poem "Korova" (Cow) Parshchikov brings together in an unexpected manner Rome, Athens, Paris, and Kiev, as if these cities belong to the same archetypal sacred mother cow:

> Rashitaia, rel'efnaia, v shagu raskleshennaia korova,
> raz'iataia na 12 chastei.
> Tebia kupaet formalin,
> Ot vymeni k zobu ne piatitsia maslianyi shar.
> Slovno apostoly, chasti tvoi, korova.
> razbrelis'. Prodolzhaia svoi rost,
> legkim pravym i levym Kiev osnovan,
> vydokhnuv Lavru i svarnoi most.
> Tvoim vzgliadom poslednim Rim zakoldovan,
> Afiny, Parizh,
> Kazhdyi tvoi pozvonok, korova, –
> Prozrachnoi pagody etazh.
>
> (O cow, embroided, embossed, bellbottomed at the foot,
> Anatomized into twelve parts –
> Formalin bathes you,
> Between udder and craw the buttery ball stays put.
> Like the apostles, your parts, O cow,
> Scattered, expanding continuously.
> Kiev arose from your right and left lung,
> Exhaling the Lavra and the welded bridge.
> Your last glance mesmerized Rome,
> Athens, Paris –
> Each of your vertebrae, O cow –
> Forms one floor of a limpid pagoda).

In a radical manner Parshchikov also destabilizes the perception of language. Thus, for example, in some poems references to linguistic terms that are brought to life are encountered in an unusual context, as seen in these lines: "In front of you there is darkness with the infinitive, / Where the muscles of the sand protect us"; "The head is pecking the tub / Like the letter 'Iat'"; and "They cut the alphabetical watermelon and give everyone slices."

The most important achievement of Parshchikov's poetry to date is the *poema* (long narrative poem) "Ia zhil na pole Poltavskoi bitvy" (I Lived on the Battlefield of Poltava), first published in *Mitin zhurnal* in 1985 and awarded the Andrei Bely Prize in the same year. The *poema* was included in Parshchikov's 1989 verse collection *Figury intuitsii* (Figures of Intuition). "Ia zhil na pole Poltavskoi bitvy" reveals Parshchikov's baroque techniques and his strong interest in historical themes (his consideration of the Poltava battle as an important event in Russian and European history, for example). It also includes some autobiographical overtones: he lived in a house, located between Poltava and Dikan'ka in Ukraine, which he inherited from his relatives. The *poema* incorporates archaic elements mixed with references to contemporary Russian life—such as its use of hexameters, which are associated with Greek and Latin poetry. Parshchikov's reference to the battle of 1708 also alludes to Alexander Sergeevich Pushkin's 1829

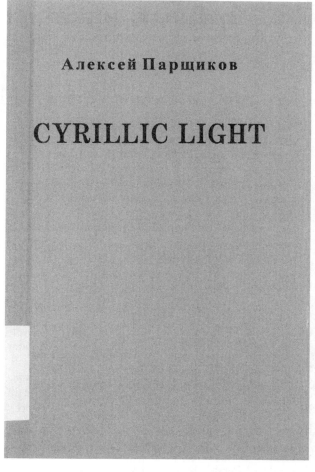

Paperback cover for Parshchikov's 1995 poetry collection, which includes poems about Peter the Great, Moscow, and a farm in California (Jean and Alexander Heard Library, Vanderbilt University)

poema "Poltava." Parshchikov's metapoetic invocation of his craft ("Run, my verse, my hound—fetch it!—and come back to my heel / With the branch clasped in your jaws, again serve the arc") also weaves in a paraphrase of Boris Leonidovich Pasternak's 1931 poem "Stikhi moi, begom, begom . . ." (My poems, run, run over there . . .). Here, Parshchikov brings to life the whole poetic tradition of addressing the poet's tools, exemplified most vividly in Pushkin's "Moei chernil'nitse" (To My Inkwell, 1820) and in Marina Ivanovna Tsvetaeva's "Stol" (My Desk, 1934). It highlights the poet's preoccupation with language itself and with the poetic tradition to which he belongs, rather than with the truthful depiction of an historical event. Parshchikov's juxtaposition of the poetic craft with the battlefield ("Letters, you are my army, / Become blind and wandering along the edge of two epochs") alludes to the experiments of Vladimir Vladimirovich Mayakovsky, whose famous

On the book cover:

Алексей Парщиков

CYRILLIC LIGHT

slogan, "I want my pen to be equated to the gun," is playfully redefined in Parshchikov's poem.

In his "Pervoe liricheskoe otstuplenie" (First Lyric Digression), a chapter from "Ia zhil na pole Poltavskoi bitvy," Parshchikov writes:

Rebenki – zaitseoobrazny: snizu dva zuba, a shcheki! Tak zhe i zaitsy – detopodobny.
Zlobny zaitsy i nepredskazuemy, slovno oskolki sery chirknuvshei spichki.
Vperedi mototsikla i szadi – pryg-skok! – zhivye kavychki!

(Kids are hare-like: two teeth below and cheeks! While hares are kid-like.
Hares are nasty and unpredictable, like bits of sulphur from a struck match.
Out front a motorcycle and in back – hop-skip! – living!).

Parshchikov states from the beginning that his *poema* is a mock epic of metatextual quality. Taking into account that in Russian folk tradition a hare is a bad omen, bringing disaster and misfortune, Parshchikov's observation suggests a highly allusive denunciation of Peter the Great's reforms and a challenge to Pushkin's glorification of the tsar in "Poltava." This Parshchikov *poema* contributes to the collapse of the grand narrative in Russia, giving way to the expression of the poet's post-Soviet subjectivity. Such a parodic depiction of history has all the marks of postmodernist discourse, which places the past critically in relation to the present. The title of Parshchikov's mock epic "Ia zhil na pole Poltavskoi bitvy" paradoxically depicts the presence of the past: it creates a present modern narrator engaged in generic ironic play on nineteenth-century authoritative discourses (expressed mainly through references to Pushkin's narrative poems). In an ironic manner Parshchikov refers to St. Petersburg not as a window upon Europe—as immortalized in Pushkin's "Mednyi vsadnik" (The Bronze Horseman, 1833)—but as Peter's "eternal and gloomy city, a little window, covered with newspaper."

While Parshchikov's soldiers are resurrected to fight again in the present, present-day patients in a nearby mental hospital re-create the battle, too. In other words, Parshchikov's text presents a playful palimpsest, consisting of various historical and metatextual planes. This device allows the poet to juxtapose himself both with Peter the Great and with Pushkin. The poetic persona, created in Parshchikov's mock epic, is given an opportunity to create various points of view, based on several self-representations. Parshchikov appears to be the creator of the new text, as well as a beholder of the collective memory, who happens to cross the well-known battlefield every day by bicycle—"I'll recollect all

of them, while crossing the field triumphantly on my bike"–and a participant in literary history.

In *Figury intuitsii* Parshchikov defines his newly invented poetic persona as a figure of intuition who exists separately from the poet. Thus, for example, in his poem "Den'gi" (Money) Parshchikov states:

Figury intuitsii! V pustyne
oni zhivut, protknuv zrachki
koliuchkami. Sviatye
kommuny ikh v verkhoviiakh reki
vremien. U nas est' krugozor i pochta,
ob'iat'ia i zemlia, i molniia v brikete . . .
U nikh net nichego, togo, chto
stanovitsia priobreten'em smerti.
Oni est' motsarty trekhletnie.
Noch'. Vys' vzyskatel'na. Zaborista toska.
Togda figura intuitsii zametnee:
ona idiet odna, no s dvukh kontsov mosta.

(Figures of intuition! They live
In the desert, their pupils pierced
By spikes. Their holy
Communes sit high toward the source
Of time's river. We have vistas and e-mail,
Embraces and earth, and lightning in a bottle.
Death can't afford
What they have to sell.
They are three-year-old Mozarts.
It's night, the heights exacting, the yearning brute.
Now the figure of intuition grows more visible.
It walks alone from both ends of the bridge).

Parshchikov aspires to canonize the impersonal gaze as the most sacred mode of writing. If history is a sack—an abyss of money inside it—the subject who could "carry the powerful centuries on a stick," as Parshchikov's poem suggests, dissolved itself. In a provocative manner the poet admits his amnesia: "And who was a figure of intuition to whom?"

A negative view of Peter the Great is also embedded in Parshchikov's poem "Peter," which appears in his collection *Cyrillic Light* (1995). In this poem the persona encounters the tsar's living spirit, seen as dust from the road in the shape of "burning digits nine," thereby alluding in an allegorical manner to the apocalyptic number 666, presented here upside down. Discussed in the Bible in Revelations, this number represents the demonic beast with ten horns and seven heads, the new object of worship in apocalyptic times. In "Peter" Parshchikov advocates the validity of the little man, whose role in history is overshadowed by tyrants and by heroes. He states: "I say that between the stone and water / The worm represents the void of horror. Besides– / The worm is a measure of time and blood." Here he expresses his sympathy with the image of the little man crushed by advancing modernity, as depicted in Pushkin's other narrative poem "Mednyi Vsadnik." Parshchikov's image of the worm also recalls Gavrila Romanovich Derzhavin's ode "Bog" (God, circa 1792), in which the significance of his human self is reaffirmed: "I am king–I am slave; I am worm–I am god!"

In the humorous poem "Ustritsy" (Oysters), published in *Cyrillic Light*, Parshchikov makes fun of the modern image of a Moscow available for consumption: "Moscow-croak-croak. The capital / Could easily be put inside any oyster." Yet, now the poet's self-image is also rooted in the culture of exhibitionism and consumption. Thus, in "Na ferme Kaliforniia" (At the Farm, in California), also a poem from *Cyrillic Light*, Parshchikov's self-representation draws on images of mass consumption: "In the striped dressing gown, just like bacon, I'm flying in between warm garages."

Parshchikov's poetry conveys many aspects of the postmodernist worldview. The most important feature of his poetics is its engagement in a kind of double consciousness: it aspires to close the gap between high and low art forms by mixing references to them in a playful manner. Hence, in another poem from *Cyrillic Light*, "Domovoi" (House Spirit), Parshchikov writes: "Vrubel's Demon and Michael Jackson are mixed up / On my wall. Everyone is chewing painkillers. / Was this time envisaged by someone else? I sat around the infra-red graves." Here, Parshchikov ponders the nature of mass-produced images in photography, asserting his individuality through repetitive references to the self: "I opened up myself, I saw, I knew, I sought / The imperative of these incredibly light columns." These metaphysical and philosophical overtones create a sense of physical displacement from Russia that can be seen as a metaphor for Parshchikov's poetic fate. By blending images of modernity with archaic elements, he arguably creates intentional parallels with the baroque poetry of Derzhavin and resurrects outmoded genres such as the solemn ode, the mock epic, and the lyrical epic poem. Both Parshchikov and Derzhavin share a revolutionary attitude toward language and established tradition.

American readers welcomed the publication in 1994 of Aleksei Maksimovich Parshchikov's *Blue Vitriol*, the first collection of his poetry in English translation. Poet and translator Lyn Hejinian heralded the volume as an important occasion and a new source of inspiration for American poets. In addition to his poetry, Parshchikov's essays and book reviews, as well as his correspondence with Viacheslav Kuritsyn, *Perepiska:*

Fevral' 1996–fevral' 1997 (Correspondence: February 1996–February 1997, 1997), are helping to shape the postmodernist aesthetic in twenty-first-century Russia.

Interviews:

John High, "An Interview with Aleksei Parshchikov," *Five Fingers Review*, 8/9 (1990): 39–46;

Ivan Davydov, ". . . Dlia pishushchego po-russki zhit' v Kel'ne – vse ravno chto zhit' gde-nibud' v Zaporozh'e," *Russkii zhurnal* (26 October 1998) <http://www.russ.ru/journal/persons/98-10-26/david.htm>;

Igor' Shevelev, "Russkii poet na randevu: Poet Aleksei Parshchikov," *Vremia* (10 July 2002);

Aleksandr Shatalov, "'Put' poezii -ot vneshnei formy k vnutrennei': Besedy v programme 'Grafoman'," (2 February 2003) <http://www.tvkultura.ru/news.cfm?nws_type=2&news_id=8642&date=2003-02-02>.

Biography:

Iurii Orlitsky, "Parshchikov Aleksei Maksimovich," in *Russkie pisateli 20 veka. Biograficheskii slovar'*, edited by Petr Alekseevich Nikolaev (Moscow: Bol'shaia Rossiiskaia Entsiklopediia, 2000), p. 539.

References:

Mikhail Naumovich Epshtein, "Metamorfoza," in his *Paradoksy novizny* (Moscow: Sovetskii pisatel', 1988), pp. 139–179;

Epshtein, "Theses on Metarealism and Conceptualism," in *Russian Postmodernism: New Perspectives on Post-Soviet Culture*, edited by Epshtein and others (New York & Oxford: Berghahn Books, 1999), pp. 105–112;

Konstantin Kedrov, "Metametafora Alekseia Parshchikova," *Literaturnaia ucheba*, 1 (1984);

Aleksei Tumol'sky, "Russkie evropeitsy iz Ukrainy" <http://nlo.magazine.ru/dog/gent/main21.html> [accessed 17 June 2003];

Andrew Wachtel, "The Youngest Archaists: Kutik, Sedakova, Kibirov, Parshchikov," in *Rereading Russian Poetry*, edited by Stephanie Sandler (New Haven & London: Yale University Press, 1999), pp. 270–286;

Barrett Watten, "Post-Soviet Subjectivity: Arkadii Dragomoshchenko and Ilya Kabakov," *Postmodern Culture*, 3, no. 2 (January 1993) <http://www.iath.virginia.edu/pmc/text-only/issue.193/watten.193>.

Viktor Olegovich Pelevin

(22 November 1962 –   )

Gerald McCausland
University of Pittsburgh

BOOKS: *Sinii fonar'* (Moscow: Tekst, 1991)–includes "Zatvornik i Shestipalyi," "Zhizn' i prikliucheniia saraia Nomer XII," "Prints Gosplana," "Khrustal'nyi mir," "Deviatyi son Very Pavlovny," "Problema vervolka v Srednei polose," "Spi," and "Mittel'shpiel"; translated by Andrew Bromfield as *The Blue Lantern and Other Stories* (New York: New Directions, 1997)–includes "Hermit and Six-Toes," "The Life and Adventures of Shed Number XII," "Crystal World," and "Mid-Game";

Omon Ra: Povest', rasskazy (Moscow: Tekst, 1992)–includes *Omon Ra,* translated by Bromfield (London: Harbord, 1994; New York: Farrar, Straus & Giroux, 1996);

Chapaev i Pustota (Moscow: Vagrius, 1996); translated by Bromfield as *The Clay Machine-Gun* (London: Faber & Faber, 1999); republished as *Buddha's Little Finger* (New York: Viking, 1999);

Zhizn' nasekomykh: Romany (Moscow: Vagrius, 1997)–includes *Zhizn' nasekomykh,* translated by Bromfield as *The Life of Insects* (London: Harbord, 1996; New York: Farrar, Straus & Giroux, 1998);

Zheltaia strela: Povesti i rasskazy (Moscow: Vagrius, 1998)–includes *Zheltaia strela,* translated by Bromfield as *The Yellow Arrow* in *Omon Ra* (London: Harbord, 1994);

Generation "P" (Moscow: Vagrius, 1999); translated by Bromfield as *Babylon* (London: Faber & Faber, 2000); republished as *Homo Zapiens* (New York: New Directions, 2002).

Editions in English: *The Yellow Arrow,* translated by Andrew Bromfield (New York: New Directions, 1996);

A Werewolf Problem in Central Russia and Other Stories, translated by Bromfield (New York: New Directions, 1998)–includes "A Werewolf Problem in Central Russia," "Vera Pavlovna's Ninth Dream," "Sleep," "Tai Shou Chuan USSR (A Chinese Folk Tale)," and "Prince of Gosplan";

4 by Pelevin, translated by Bromfield (New York: New Directions, 2001).

Viktor Olegovich Pelevin (from the cover for Chapaev i Pustota, *1996; Howard Tilton Memorial Library, Tulane University)*

Editions and Collections: *Sochineniia,* 2 volumes (Moscow: Terra, 1996);

Zhizn' nasekomyk, introduction by Viacheslav Kuritsyn (Moscow: Vagrius, 1997);

Sobranie sochinenii, 3 volumes (Moscow: Vagrius, 1999);

Omon Ra (Moscow: Vagrius, 2000);

Zhizn' nasekomykh (Moscow: Vagrius, 2000);

Zheltaia strela: Sbornik (Moscow: Vagrius, 2000);

Zatvornik i Shestipalyi (Moscow: Vagrius, 2001);

Vstroennyi napominatel' (Moscow: Vagrius, 2002).

SELECTED PERIODICAL PUBLICATIONS–
UNCOLLECTED: "Koldun Ignat i liudi," *Nauka i
     religiia,* 12 (1989): 29;

"Zombifikatsiia sovetskogo cheloveka," *Novyi zhurnal,*
     179 (1990): 324–328;

"Pod sinim fonarem," *Nezavisimaia gazeta,* 20 January
     1993, p. 5;

"Papakhi na bashniakh," *Ogonek,* 42 (1995): 62–66;

"Ultima Tuleev, ili Dao vyborov," *Nezavisimaia
     gazeta-Stsenarii,* 3 (1996).

One of the most successful Russian writers who emerged in the post-Soviet literary scene during the 1990s, Viktor Pelevin has managed to bridge that most unbridgeable of gaps in Russian culture–the one existing between so-called genuine literature and popular fiction for a mass readership. His novels and short stories are read and discussed by intellectuals and teenagers, journalists and academics alike. The broadness of the reception of his writings is matched by the range of his subject matter and the pretensions of his style. His works juxtapose rock culture, Soviet kitsch, and socialist-realist clichés with Continental philosophy and Eastern mysticism. All of these elements are tossed together with a distinctive style and tone that is pervaded by both a sense of gravity and an almost flippant ironic distance. His reputation for reclusiveness belies a keen sense of the authorial image, which he is careful to maintain and manage. The writer who "never gives interviews" is constantly quoted, and the quotes sharply contradict each other in such a way as to give the biographical Pelevin an aura of mystery and complexity befitting a cult figure of the outgoing twentieth century. As a result, there is more misinformation than information regarding Pelevin's biography. Inasmuch as he has a public persona, it is that of a mystic recluse. Various biographical facts such as his marital status, for example, are simply unknown since they are unimportant for the image he so carefully projects.

Viktor Olegovich Pelevin was born on 22 November 1962 in Moscow. His father, Oleg Anatol'evich Pelevin, was a military officer. His mother, Zinaida Efremovna Pelevina, taught English in the same *spetsshkola* (special school) in which Pelevin himself studied in his youth. Despite Pelevin's rather elite primary and secondary schooling, his childhood does not seem to have been in any way extraordinary for a

boy growing up in the Soviet Union of Leonid Il'ich Brezhnev's regime. Pelevin's higher education consisted of two complete courses of study. First, he graduated from the Moscow Energy Institute, where he received a technical education, and then from the Gor'ky Literary Institute, where young Soviet writers were trained to create in the spirit of socialist realism. Pelevin seems to have been a mediocre student at best, but his talent as a creative artist began to manifest itself at this same time. He participated in several more-or-less formal groups of writers, particularly those writing in the science-fiction genre. He was employed in various capacities: as a journalist, an editor, and a publisher of literary works. He also translated works of occultism and New Age spirituality into Russian. During these formative years he had almost no contact with writers only slightly older than he, such as Viktor Vladimirovich Erofeev or Vladimir Georgievich Sorokin, figures who became known as the creators of Russian literary postmodernism. The first of his own works to be published, a short prose piece titled "Koldun Ignat i liudi" (The Sorcerer Ignat and People), which appeared in the journal *Nauka i religiia* (Science and Religion) in 1989, showed few of the distinctive traits that later came to be known as inherent to his style.

One of the first significant publications of the young Pelevin was not a literary work at all but a work of social theory. "Zombifikatsiia sovetskogo cheloveka" (The Zombification of Soviet Man, published in *Novyi zhurnal* [The New Review], 1990), subtitled "Opyt svavnitel'noi antropologii" (An Experiment in Comparative Anthropology), purports to describe the indoctrination of the individual in the Soviet Union in terms appropriate to primitive societies. Telling of Soviet spies in Haiti, Ian Fleming's novel *Live and Let Die* (1954), a part of the James Bond series, serves as a rhetorical device that allows Pelevin to establish an otherwise arbitrary allegorical relationship between the ritual voodoo practices of an aboriginal tribe and the ideological system in place during the late Brezhnev years of the Soviet Union. The connection between the two systems has little to do with any symbolic structural homologies, shared ritual practices, or external similarity of appearances. Neither the herbal poisons employed by the voodoo magicians nor the institutional apparatus of Soviet repression explains the transformation from a human into a "zombie." The zombification of the Soviet individual begins in early childhood and takes place through the effect of various "magical" designations (October), objects (red ties), and incantations ("Pioneer's Honor!"). The psychic background of the individual and the social function of these external phenomena create the magic at work in the creation of the zombie.

Pelevin's principal interest in this article is the demonstration of this particular interaction. The external structures of society have no power of indoctrination in and of themselves. They are given their power by the psychic state of the individuals that partake in them. The principal value of "Zombifikatsiia" for the literary biography of the author is the evidence it provides of Pelevin's strong interest in human consciousness, mysticism, and political practice from the beginning of his creative activity.

Many of the most distinctive features of Pelevin's literary writing style are already present in his earliest short stories and novellas. In "Zatvornik i Shestipalyi" (first published in *Khimiia i zhizni'* [Chemistry and Life], 1990; translated as "Hermit and Six-Toes," 1997) the story begins with a conversation between a simpleton named Shestipalyi, socially outcast because of his physical deformity, and a rather arrogant intellectual and mystic with the fitting name of Zatvornik, the Russian term for hermit. The setting is a nondescript desert with debris that seems to evoke the image of an abandoned construction site. The unlikely pair develops a rapport over the course of several days as Zatvornik begins to explain the mysteries of the natural and social world to Shestipalyi, who earnestly strives to comprehend the incomprehensible. Shestipalyi, for his part, explains his conception of the world to Zatvornik, and his description is the first clear, concrete indication to the reader that the setting of the story is much more than simply an abandoned wasteland beyond human society. In the society from which Shestipalyi has been banished, high social standing is rewarded through proximity to the "combined feeding-trough and drinking-trough," and the community is led by the "Twenty Closest." This community is physically enclosed within the "Wall of the World," beyond which lies only the "Mystery of the Ages." These terms define the extent of Shestipalyi's knowledge of the universe. Zatvornik, who has observed nature for some time and gained perspective, explains to Shestipalyi that the "world" is merely one of seventy such worlds that travel through space upon a large black belt within a universe that carries the name "Lunacharsky Broiler Factory." It turns out that the two heroes of the story are chickens being raised for food, and as the action of the story begins in earnest, the end of the world is nigh as the chickens are less than twenty-four hours away from being slaughtered.

This method of indirectly introducing the characters and setting of a story is a trademark of Pelevin's artistic style. The reader sees details without at first comprehending the context. Pelevin's prose is a study in the process of perception. The reader's slow progress in putting the details of the description and dialogue together parallels the progress of the main characters in their gradual enlightenment. This effect is the source of much of the pleasure of a Pelevin text: the experience of reading is a reenactment of the experience depicted in the story told by the text itself.

The story told in "Zatvornik i Shestipalyi" is the passage to freedom in both its physical and spiritual sense. While escape from the mechanized chicken farm is always possible, the birds are able to attain true freedom only through the gradual development of their powers of perception, insight, and ultimate enlightenment. Reminiscent of Socratic dialogue, this process of enlightenment progresses through the intellectual work of a master and a pupil. Shestipalyi first sees Zatvornik as a particularly intelligent and inquisitive companion, but the latter soon reveals himself to be as much a spiritual guide as a clever interlocutor. His knowledge of the gods comes not merely from careful observation but from mystical insight. Perception and understanding have much more to do with the inner workings of the individual mind and consciousness than with the external world. As Zatvornik remarks to Shestipalyi, "what matters is not what is said, but who says it." Significantly, the intellectually inferior Shestipalyi is the one who discovers, through a power from within himself, the mechanics of flight and thus the route to escape from the poultry factory.

Pelevin develops his views on the nature and power of individual consciousness even further in the 1991 story "Zhizn' i prikliucheniia saraia Nomer XII" (translated as "The Life and Adventures of Shed Number XII," 1997). Just as ancient folklore imagined inanimate objects in nature to possess souls, so does Pelevin depict the consciousness of a storage shed. The shed has no specific moment of birth and, as it turns out, no specific moment of death. It comes to consciousness gradually over time and carries within itself only dim, formless memories of freshly cut plywood lying in neatly piled stacks. Becoming conscious only after construction, the shed incorporates into itself the consciousness of the objects stored within its walls. The consciousness of two bicycles teaches the shed to attain freedom as it lives the vicarious life of the bicycles racing endlessly through the streets of the city, the paths of the countryside, or the depths of the forest. In short, the bicycles free the shed from the tethers of its physical existence. After the shed is apparently rented to a grocery seller, a barrel of brine in which cucumbers are pickled replaces the bicycles. The rot and stagnation of the barrel replace the life-giving freedom of the bicycles. The barrel attempts to fill the consciousness of the shed in the same way that the bicycles and other objects had done earlier.

The resulting struggle makes up the main philosophical content of the story as the shed fights to maintain its individuality against the force of death attempting to replace it. The shed prevails against the barrel only by committing suicide, after which its spirit lives on in the form of a spectral bicycle that haunts the grocery seller in a closing scene reminiscent of Nikolai Vasil'evich Gogol's "Shinel'" (The Overcoat, 1842). The reader is left to decide, however, what this story asserts about the formation of human identity, the nature of spiritual freedom, and the ability of the individual to offer resistance to the outside factors that influence individual development so strongly.

Besides "Zhizn' i prikliucheniia saraia Nomer XII," several of Pelevin's other best-known stories were published in 1991. "Prints Gosplana" (translated as "Prince of Gosplan," 1998), which first appeared that year in the journal *SOS: Serial Ostrykh Siuzhetov* (SOS: Periodical of Provocative Subjects) before its publication in the collection *Sinii fonar'* (The Blue Lantern, 1991; translated as *The Blue Lantern and Other Stories*, 1997), is the first story among Pelevin's works that illustrates his fascination with computer technology and its effect on human consciousness. The hero of the story, a bureaucrat in a state enterprise, lives simultaneously in two "places": his everyday life and his computer life—that is, within the adventures created by his favorite computer game, in which he must progress through a series of skill levels before he "attains the princess." He does not seem to know where one life ends and the other begins. This uncertainty is soon revealed as an ontological one precisely within the text of the story. The narrative moves among several modes that serve to anchor the story to various, mutually exclusive realities. The characters of the story, the hero and his coworkers, friends, and acquaintances, seem to be, by turns, players (that is, consumers) of the computer games; programmers (that is, creators) of the computer games; figures within the imaginary world of the games; and even projections into an external reality from within the world of the games. The text refuses to settle upon one or another of these "anchors" of reality. The life of the hero is suspended in an intermediate realm, giving the reader no basis on which to decide what the actual content of the tale is supposed to mean or in what "reality" the hero exists. This shift of virtual reality into the narrative, into the texture of the text, has become a recognizable trait of Pelevin's style.

Pelevin's early short stories are characterized by a highly developed sense of fantasy and imagination. Their contact with the Soviet and post-Soviet reality in which he lives is limited largely to the linguistic clichés that filled much of Soviet ideological discourse. "Khrustal'nyi mir" (first published in *Znanie – sila* [Science Is Knowledge], 1991; translated as "Crystal World," 1997), however, departs from this general ten-

dency. The story takes place on a specific—and, for Russia, significant—date in history: 24 October 1917. Two army sentries have been placed on duty to prevent Vladimir Lenin, the Bolshevik leader, from reaching the Smolny Institute, from where he will lead the insurrection that topples the Provisional Government. Lenin attempt to pass in various, wildly absurd disguises, giving the story a significant element of humor. A stronger presence in the story is the somewhat incongruous historicophilosophical discussions between the two sentries—discussions that range from Rudolf Steiner's notion of anthroposophy (the belief that only those of the keenest minds can attain a sense of the spiritual) to the metaphysical teachings of Oswald Spengler. The inclusion of such unlikely metaphysical discussions and disquisitions, which seem to interrupt the narrative flow of the story, is an element of Pelevin's style on which critics are sharply divided. While one point of view asserts that a philosophical dimension has always been one of the most distinctive traits of Russian literature, others refer to these speculative tangents as the artistic flaw of an undisciplined writer. The particular content of the philosophical passages in "Khrustal'nyi mir" are, in any case, not foreign to Pelevin's characteristic issues of concern. They encompass the meaning of history, the ability of the individual to orient himself in a fleeting and changing world, and the ephemeral nature of all human culture. The two heroes of the story explore these questions not only with the help of contemporary philosophers and artists but also with the aid of hallucinogenic drugs—another recurrent motif of Pelevin's fiction. Through knowledge and insight, the two arrive at the joyless conclusion that the old, familiar world is ending. This cultural pessimism was indeed characteristic of much of the St. Petersburg intelligentsia on the eve of the Bolshevik Revolution. For the contemporary reader, who knows quite well to what extent the entire reality of St. Petersburg was about to end in October 1917, Pelevin's particular philosophy of history is more than simple intellectual game playing.

Even more firmly anchored in the daily reality of its Russian readers is the story "Deviatyi son Very Pavlovny" (1991; translated as "Vera Pavlovna's Ninth Dream," 1998). The setting for the action in this narrative is a public lavatory that, during the economic changes of perestroika, is ultimately transformed into a store where clothing and jewelry are sold on commission. The story is told as seen through the mind of Vera, the washerwoman of the men's lavatory, who is firmly convinced that she is the sole cause of all the massive changes affecting her country during the years of Mikhail Sergeevich Gorbachev. She and the washerwoman Maniasha—from the adjoining lavatory—compose yet another of Pelevin's pairs of pupil and spiritual

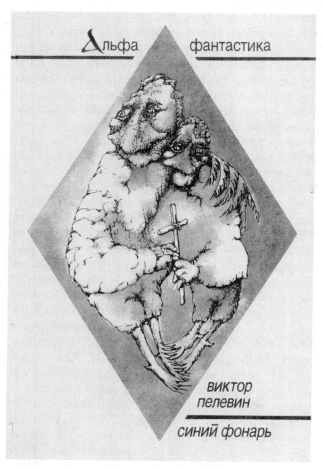

Front cover for Pelevin's Sinii fonar' (1991; translated as The Blue Lantern and Other Stories, 1997), in which the title story depicts his fascination with computers and their effect on human consciousness (Tulsa City-County Library)

phorical terms what happens to that country—while what happens to the country is made up of thousands of separate lives." This statement comes close to laying bare the artistic potential of Pelevin's intellectual worldview. His short stories never fall into simple solipsism. The indeterminacy of human consciousness and its relation to the external world and to the formation of human society give the storyteller's imagination limitless possibilities for creativity. Pelevin's style is unmistakable without ever becoming monotonously repetitive, a charge sometimes leveled at his well-known contemporaries such as Sorokin or Valeriia Spartakovna Narbikova. In the case of Vera, the story ends in a clever textual turn toward a novel by the nineteenth-century revolutionary Nikolai Gavrilovich Chernyshevsky, *Chto delat'?* (What Is to Be Done? 1863), to which Vera has been banished as a consequence of her "third-degree solipsism." The choice of *Chto delat'?* is not arbitrary; it is perhaps the most famous Russian literary example of the revolutionary pathos that attempted to create a new world out of the will and consciousness of certain "new people."

"Deviatyi son Very Pavlovny" appeared in Pelevin's first book publication, *Sinii fonar'*. The stories in this collection brought a new level of renown to Pelevin, who until this point had published mostly in the fiction sections of popular-science journals. Taken together, these stories make clear that Pelevin is much more than a writer of traditional science fiction. Several of the stories have become well known and show the depth of his interest in the themes already manifest in his first publications.

The mysteries of individual identity and human consciousness are explored in almost every story of *Sinii fonar'*. "Problema vervolka v Srednei polose" (first published in *Sinii fonar'*; translated as "A Werewolf Problem in Central Russia," 1998) depicts the transformation of a young man into a werewolf, whereby the main interest is not the physical transformation itself but its significance for his sense of self. In his new werewolf existence the hero comes to know a freedom he had never experienced as a simple human being; he becomes confident in who he is and in the meaning of his life.

"Spi" (translated as "Sleep," 1998) chronicles the discoveries of another young man who finds that he can live his life in a much more satisfying manner if he sleeps through it, a method that almost everyone around him had adopted before he himself was aware of it. The hero, Nikita, finds himself in a situation paralleling that of a dissident in the last years of the Soviet Union—he is a misfit who bravely struggles to understand why he is the only person who can see that everyone is going through life in a state of sleep. The story

guide. In this case Maniasha initiates Vera into the conviction that the external world is merely a projection of one's inner soul. Vera is oblivious to Maniasha's warnings that abuse of this insight might have unforeseen consequences. Vera at first takes delight in the changes wrought upon Russia by mere changes in her internal consciousness. Her desire to adorn her lavatory with pictures on the wall and background music bring with them the changes that destroyed the Soviet Union.

Under the guidance of Maniasha, Vera discovers that her own consciousness is the source of all reality and that changes in her internal world manifest themselves in the external world of material things. She understands only too late that the external world must answer back, for, in the words of Maniasha, "from one point of view, we really do create our own surroundings, but from another, we ourselves are merely the reflection of all that surrounds us. And therefore the fate of any individual in any country repeats in meta-

ends with his final surrender to existence in an eternal dream state. A similar theme is touched upon in the title story of the collection. In "Sinii fonar'," a group of boys attempts to frighten each other in the night with tales of corpses that do not realize they are dead. The story ends with the open-ended question: how do people know whether they are truly alive or are simply corpses that do not realize they have died?

Many of these stories are extremely suggestive of political allegories, but as seen in still other stories, Pelevin does not seem interested in portraying the mundane daily life of Soviet or post-Soviet people. An interesting exception to this general trend is "Mittel'shpiel" (first published in *Sinii fonar'*; translated as "Mid-Game," 1997), which has become one of Pelevin's best-known stories. The story is embedded in the milieu of perestroika and centers on the adventures of two hard-currency prostitutes and their nearly fatal encounter with a pair of serial killers. Only after the main action of the story is the truth about these four characters revealed: they are all transsexuals. The transformations in Russian society during the 1980s have required equally radical transformations in the Russian people. The change from party functionary to entrepreneur is typical of the real-life challenge faced by individuals raised as Soviet citizens, but in his distinctive manner of the grotesque, Pelevin materializes this change in the most radical kind of physical transformation. The resulting alteration revisits the question of individual identity and consciousness seen in almost everything that Pelevin writes. The two women in "Mittel'shpiel" have thoroughly adjusted to their new lives. In the political language of the time, they have completely and successfully *perestroilis'* (restructured themselves), from the verb *perestroit'sia* (to restructure oneself or to be restructured). They have become different persons. Nevertheless, the echoes of their former identities continue to exist within their consciousness and are capable of rising to the surface at any time.

Pelevin's first long work of fiction, the novella *Omon Ra* (translated, 1994), was published in 1992. This book has done more than any other single work to establish Pelevin's image and reputation among his Russian readership. The work is also his most personal, as it displays much that is autobiographical in the character of his protagonist, Omon Krivomazov. The name of the hero immediately calls forth associations with both contemporary Russian reality ("OMON," or *otriad militsii osobogo naznach-eniia* [militia special forces unit], is a paramilitary division of the Soviet and post-Soviet police forces) and classical Russian literature (Krivomazov echoes the family name at the center of Dostoevsky's 1879–1880 novel, *Brat'ia Karomazovy* [The Brothers Karamazov]). The young hero's adopted

name, Ra, is the name of an Egyptian god and adds yet another layer to the complex and ambitious artistic agenda of this work.

Upon its initial publication in the prestigious monthly literary journal *Znamia* (The Banner), the work was interpreted by most readers as an exceedingly clever and biting satire of the Soviet space program. At one level, this interpretation is certainly accurate. Omon, the boy who dreams of flying into outer space, seems close to realizing his dream only to discover that the entire Soviet space program is nothing but a cleverly staged fiction constructed for domestic and foreign consumption. There is much more to the work, however, than mere political satire. It addresses most of the issues seen in Pelevin's shorter texts in a tightly integrated and highly engaging prose style that makes *Omon Ra* one of his most successful works.

The story takes place during the childhood and youth of the protagonist, and many of its themes are introduced with a child-like inflection. The boy experiences the adult world as stultifying and vaguely oppressive, and he quickly discovers that escape into fantasy makes life much more bearable and interesting. His fascination with flying is linked with his desire to flee the mundane world of his everyday existence—that is, he yearns for freedom. Yet, as seems clear from the start of the story, freedom in this case is more than simply freedom from the material constraints of society. Early in his childhood, Omon finds out for himself that freedom can be found within his own imagination. While watching a film about fighter pilots, he realizes that "I can look out from inside myself like looking out of a plane, it doesn't really matter at all where you look out from, what matters is what you see." Once the boy has learned the power of his own consciousness, he decides that he has no need to depend on the external world for his individual experience. In his childish imagination, he can go anywhere he likes, under his own power, at any time he wishes.

From the time that he begins his cosmonaut training, however, Omon seems to be caught in the tight and deadly grip of external reality. He soon learns that Soviet technology does not allow for manned space flights, and thus the flights are all automated. For reasons that are never explained, these automated flights still require a crew, the members of which can never return to Earth; thus, they die at the end of their missions. Omon's realization of his dream to fly into space is thus his death sentence. His particular assignment will be to fly to the moon and explore its surface in a motorized vehicle, after which he will leave a beacon and shoot himself in a last heroic act of self-sacrifice. At no point during his training does he ever doubt that he will indeed be launched into space and land on the

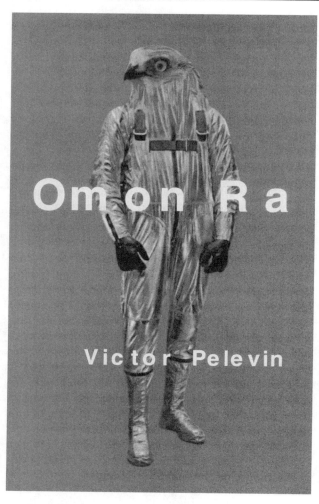

Dust jacket for the 1996 English-language edition of Pelevin's 1992 novella, an exploration of individual and collective human consciousness in the context of the Soviet space program (Richland County Public Library)

"Remember, Omon, although man, of course, has no soul, every soul is a universe. That's the dialectic. And as long as there is a single soul in which our cause lives and conquers, that cause will never die. . . . Just one pure and honest soul is enough for our country to take the lead in the conquest of space; just one pure soul is enough for the banner of triumphant socialism to be unfurled on the surface of the distant moon. But there must be one pure soul, if only for a moment, because the banner will be unfurled within that soul."

This confession of faith by the old colonel links the political satire of the story with Pelevin's larger metaphysical concerns. Omon must participate in the mission believing in the reality of his trip to the moon, for only in his consciousness can the trip ever take place. In turn, if the trip takes place in his consciousness, then it takes place in reality in the same way as the young boy once believed that he could fly simply by using his imagination.

A concern with socialist realism and its project of constructing a new socialist reality was the intellectual stimulus behind the development of an artistic movement in late-twentieth-century Russian culture that is usually subsumed under the rubric of "postmodernism." A movement called "sots-art" specifically looks at the power of Stalinist imagery and discourse in order to analyze its power to construct the Soviet consciousness. In *Omon Ra* Pelevin's meditations on the nature of human consciousness intersect with these experiments in postsocialist art. While his earlier parody of Soviet reality was often limited to the quotation of linguistic clichés to humorous effect, his use of Soviet clichés, images, and rituals in this text approaches the style of the sots-art writers. One particularly clever joke is the insertion into the story of the canine Laika, the "first Soviet cosmonaut." In a characteristic touch, however, Pelevin's Laika has developed both diarrhea and a drinking problem, thus deviating from "pure" sots-art and approaching the burlesque.

Pelevin's dedication, "Geroiam sovetskogo kosmosa," in *Omon Ra* is rendered into English as "For the Heroes of the Soviet Cosmos." This "kosmos" is not to be understood as the cosmos "up there" but as the entire Soviet space: physical, cultural, and metaphysical. *Omon Ra* shows much more clearly than any of Pelevin's earlier works both the degree to which the realm of individual and collective human consciousness was refracted by the Soviet political regime and the resulting cultural milieu, and the degree to which that consciousness then projected itself back upon reality, transforming it into something much more than simple external reality. The verisimilitude that Pelevin maintains throughout the story depends on the child-like faith that the protagonist maintains until its last page, when he

moon, despite many clues to the contrary that even the attentive reader is likely to miss. The fact that Omon, sealed in the capsule of his rocket ship, will never leave Earth is revealed only at the end of the story. The only thing real in the entire production is the gun with which Omon is to end his own life, in the belief that shortly he will suffocate, in any case, on the surface of the moon.

The narrative leaves unexplained why several young men must participate in a staged fantasy for which the authorities could easily have hired actors. Indeed, apparently the authorities have proceeded in exactly this manner for other aspects of the Soviet "space program." Colonel Urchagin, the wheelchair-bound KGB officer who supervises the training of young cosmonauts, indirectly explains this approach. On the eve of his purported space flight, Omon is called aside by Urchagin, who gives him a kind of final blessing:

attempts to find out "where exactly on the red line" he is. The implication of *Omon Ra* is that no one in "Soviet space," much less its heroes, knows yet exactly where on the red line they would find themselves, if they knew where and, more important, how to look.

After the publication of *Omon Ra* Pelevin was widely acknowledged as a major new contemporary writer. Mere weeks into 1993, *Nezavisimaia gazeta* (The Independent Gazette) published a suite of essays by Pelevin under the general title "Pod sinim fonarem" (Under the Blue Lantern). The essays address contemporary philosophical, cultural, and political issues. "Ikstlan–Petushki" (From Ixtlan to Petushki) juxtaposes a Mexican tale by Carlos Castaneda with Venedikt Vasil'evich Erofeev's renowned work *Moskva–Petushki* (1977; translated as *Moscow to the End of the Line,* 1980). Pelevin ruminates on the nature of the journey home, concluding with the wry remark that all roads in fact lead nowhere. The essay "Dzhon Faulz i tragediia russkogo liberalizma" (John Fowles and the Tragedy of Russian Liberalism) suggests that *Homo sovieticus* (Soviet Man) is no more than a generalized version of what in capitalist societies might be considered a social misfit or naive idealist. This type had simply grown fruitful and multiplied in the conditions of life in the Soviet Union. "GKChP kak tetragrammaton" (GKChP as Tetragrammaton) is a playful meditation on the mystical powers of the Soviet mania for abbreviations. Pelevin's observations in the three small essays are both brilliant and undisciplined, both insightful and insignificant. Most important, they demonstrate that however interesting one might consider the philosophical or metaphysical aspect to Pelevin's writing, he remains first and foremost a creator of imaginative prose whose great talent and primary interest is in dreaming hitherto unimagined possible worlds in which to bring his notions to life.

Pelevin's reputation continued to grow during the year 1993. The collection *Sinii fonar'* was awarded the Malyi Booker Prize, the "Little Booker," that year for the best collection of short stories. At about the same time, several of Pelevin's short stories were published for the first time in English translation, giving readers throughout the English-speaking world their first glimpse of this new and different voice from Russia. This publication had significance for the author's career and reputation inside, as well as outside, Russia. The translations appeared in the literary journal *Glas,* which originally was intended to appear in both English and Russian editions in order to showcase the most interesting new Russian writers. By the time Pelevin's stories appeared, however, the journal was being published only in English, but its editors, Natasha Perova and Arch Tait, had already demonstrated their knack for finding the most talented writers of various literary gen-

erations for the magazine. Pelevin's inclusion in the fourth issue of *Glas* constituted his admission to the still rather exclusive club of new and serious Russian writers. This was important for the young author not merely for the prestige that it gave him but also because Russian writers during the 1990s were finding they could no longer live on earnings from their work regardless of their talent. This realization was the result of both the general economic depression of those years in Russia and the fluctuation of the book market, which had been flooded initially with publications of repressed Soviet-era greats and then with cheap detective fiction and romance novels, patterned mostly after foreign models. One of the few ways that a Russian writer could survive without abandoning his or her craft was to publish abroad and thus earn hard currency. Pelevin's publication in *Glas* paved the way to publication abroad and the prospect of one day living exclusively from his published writings.

In the spring of 1993 *Znamia* brought out Pelevin's second long work, the full-length novel *Zhizn' nasekomykh* (first published in book form, 1997; translated as *The Life of Insects,* 1996). At its simplest level this novel seems to consist of a single extended joke. It comprises several episodes loosely linked together and set in a small Crimean resort town. The characters in the novel appear at times as human beings and at times as various species of insects. The choice of insect species is not arbitrary; it is clearly meant to portray various segments of human society. This social portrait easily depicts the chaos of post-Soviet Russia. Mosquitoes, for example, embody the new entrepreneurs—both foreign and domestic; dung beetles and flies are found around the filth and refuse of society; moths are both intellectuals and mystics; ants are the laborers who live their dreary lives by sheer instinct; and cicadas are the nonconformists and dissidents.

Zhizn' nasekomykh was soon followed by another notable publication, the novella *Zheltaia strela* (first published in *Sochineniia,* volume 2, 1996; translated as *The Yellow Arrow,* 1996). This work was Pelevin's first to appear in *Novyi mir* (New World, 1993), a highly respected journal that is identified with, and traditionally read by, the Russian urban intelligentsia. The novelty in this story is not so much the content but the setting. As so often happens in Pelevin's prose, the opening pages do not immediately reveal where the action is taking place. What seems at first to be a Soviet workers' dormitory turns out to be the inside of a train that is traveling "toward a ruined bridge." The entire world is portrayed as a single train, the Yellow Arrow, and the protagonist is a young man who has come to see "the world" for what it really is.

Dust jacket for the 1998 English-language edition of a collection
of short fiction by Pelevin, in which the hero of the title story
undergoes a physical and psychological transformation
(Richland County Public Library)

This device allows Pelevin to concentrate much of his philosophy into the small space of the work. The protagonist, Andrei, comes to recognize the world through the help of an older and wiser friend, Khan, a man of undetermined Eastern heritage—a student-teacher interaction that patterns many of Pelevin's early works. Khan explains that most people in the world are mere "passengers," having no consciousness of where they are or of where they are going. Despite their ability to see out the windows of the train, they have no desire to understand what lies beyond them or to go there themselves. For passengers, everything outside of the train is the land of the dead. The various compartments and segments of the train provide a cross-section of contemporary Russian society as well as, apparently beyond the border, of the near and far abroad. The passengers include workers, black marketeers, criminal gangs, and even the homeless. By contrast, Andrei, who has come to consciousness, realizes that his destiny lies beyond the confines of the train. The story ends when,

in the dead of night, the train comes to a stop and Andrei forces the door open and walks into an uncertain future.

After *Zheltaia strela* Pelevin did not publish anything new until 1995, when his story "Papakhi na bashniakh" (Towers in Cossack Fur Hats) appeared in *Ogonek* (The Flame), a popular weekly magazine. In this narrative Pelevin turns his humorous talents to what can hardly be called a joking matter. Published during the first Chechen conflict, the story takes an ironic view of the relations between Russians and their Caucasian neighbors. The protagonist of the story bears the name of a real-life Chechen terrorist leader, Shamil Basaev, as well as other details recognizable from his biography. Pelevin's Basaev leads a successful campaign to occupy the Kremlin, a feat that goes virtually unnoticed by the inhabitants of the Russian capital. In an attempt to gain attention, the Chechen occupants decide to take hostages. Basaev's conviction that they will find volunteer hostages turns out to be justified. The Kremlin is soon filled with show-business figures, journalists, and entrepreneurs of various sorts all looking to serve their own ends by being at the center of a public event. The mass media and the commercial interests linked with them begin to take control of the situation, and Basaev himself finds that he has lost control over both the Kremlin and his own band of fighters as the entire territory becomes one huge television studio with the atmosphere of a three-ring circus.

This story is Pelevin's most daring attempt to touch upon a contemporary political situation, although its message softens the edge of this "hot" topic. "Papakhi na bashniakh" is his first extensive treatment of the power of the mass media in contemporary society. The media and the interests that control it are portrayed not only as the true center of power in the story but also as the producers of reality. The terrorists had hoped to gain attention by manipulating the media, but they soon find that they themselves have become hostages to the image makers. Pelevin's highly artistic prose is here free of the heavy metaphysical overlay characteristic of many of his other texts; but, paradoxically, it skillfully illustrates the French philosopher Jean Baudrillard's understanding of modern media and its power to influence society. Modern media technology enables the production and proliferation of simulacra, which, according to Baudrillard in *Simulacres et simulation* (1981; translated as *Simulacra and Simulation,* 1994), are "copies without originals." Baudrillard provocatively asserts, for example, that the Gulf War never occurred, because television images of smart bombs hitting their targets construct a sanitized Gulf War that never took place in reality but that replaces reality for the viewers. In the same way, Pelevin turns Shamil Basaev into a "virtual terrorist"; his real existence waxes and wanes according to the mass appeal of his television image, which threatens to replace him totally. Whether Pelevin's portrayal of Basaev is true to reality is pointless to argue, for there is no reality beyond the portrayal.

"Papakhi na bashniakh" was Pelevin's only significant publication in 1995, during which he was presumably devoting himself to writing his largest and most ambitious novel to date. *Chapaev i Pustota* (1996; translated in the United Kingdom as *The Clay Machine-Gun,* 1999; republished in the United States as *Buddha's Little Finger,* 1999) is in many ways a kind of summation of the themes that Pelevin developed over the course of the preceding six years. The two protagonists of the novel form another of the teacher-protégé pairs so typical of Pelevin's works. Both of these characters, however, are constructed in such a way that they lack any real substance. Petr Pustota (renamed Pyotr Voyd in the published English translations, thus preserving the meaning of *pustota,* the Russian word for "emptiness") not only strives for emptiness at the end of the novel but from the opening pages of the novel demonstrates this concept through his vacuous personality. Pelevin's Chapaev, like Basaev in the earlier story, has little to do with the legendary commander immortalized in Dmitrii Andreevich Furmanov's novel *Chapaev* (1923). Rather, Pelevin's Chapaev bears the name and thus a virtual contact with the Chapaev of Furmanov's novel, the still quite popular 1934 movie by Georgii Nikolaevich Vasil'ev and Sergei Dmitrievich Vasil'ev (the "Vasil'ev Brothers"), and the myriad Chapaev jokes that formed such a vital part of Soviet popular culture. At the same time Pelevin's Chapaev is remade into a Buddhist mystic, a spiritual teacher who will guide Pustota on his ultimate journey to "Inner Mongolia."

Chapaev is only one of the forces vying to claim the void that is Pustota's personality. The reader soon learns that Pustota exists in a temporal void as well. His personality oscillates between the era of the Russian Civil War and the post-Soviet Russia of the early 1990s. The scenes taking place in 1919 alternate between the city of Moscow and the field marches of Chapaev's army. The scenes from 1991 occur in a psychiatric ward, where Pustota is undergoing treatments for apparent schizophrenia, which involve something akin to group therapy: four patients are administered psychotropic drugs that allow them to share their delusional fantasies over a kind of empathic network. The result is that both protagonist and reader are left in a state of epistemological and ontological uncertainty similar to what was seen in works such as *Zhizn' nasekomykh* and "Vera Pavlovna's Ninth Dream."

As almost all reviewers of the novel have observed, the dreams of the various mental patients represent a sort of menu of possibilities out of which Russia might construct a new identity for itself in the post-Soviet void of the 1990s. These dreams occupy a significant part of the novel as a whole. The first tells of the union between Arnold Schwarzenegger and Simply Maria, the heroine of a Mexican soap opera wildly popular in Russia in the mid 1990s. The second tells of an encounter with the East in the figure of a Russian youth who goes to work for a Japanese businessman; a downturn in business requires atonement in the form of hara-kiri, the ritual suicide. The third dream portrays a group of new-Russian mobsters discussing metaphysics in a language laced with gangster slang. These dreams stand for the various "faces" of contemporary Russia: the mass culture of cheap western television images, the New Age interest in Eastern occultism, and the amorality of a new lawless class. Their separation into individual dreams is artificial, for they all enter into the cultural morass of post-Soviet Russia and into the chaotic "soup" of Pustota's mind.

Chapaev i Pustota is Pelevin's most postmodern work in that it juxtaposes various cultural models in a temporal and spatial suspension. Unlike most works of postmodernism, however, the novel seems to stake out a philosophical (if not an ideological) position of its own. Pustota's conversations with Chapaev and Anna the machine gunner are the most detailed working-out of the philosophy of Zen Buddhism, a metaphysical stance that has served as one of Pelevin's points of orientation for most of his writing career. Through the character of Chapaev, Pelevin's metaphysic is pushed to the limits of its logic: Chapaev insists on the ephemeral nature of all material reality and on the necessity of achieving true freedom through a renunciation of that reality. The novel is suffused with allusions to the proposition that the material world is in a state of passing away. It has no more permanence than a dream. To embrace the emptiness—to reach the metaphorical "Inner Mongolia"—is simultaneously to check out of the insane asylum and to reach complete freedom.

Not all critical reaction to *Chapaev i Pustota* was positive. While many readers welcomed yet another example of Pelevin's particular brand of intellectual prose, some reviewers held that the philosophical content of the text weighed it down, to the detriment of the story. Furthermore, the ideas espoused by the author seemed to have reached a natural limit. In an interview Pelevin himself described the novel as "the first novel in world literature, the action of which takes place in absolute emptiness." Although this quip is in the spirit of almost everything written by Pelevin up to this point, the maximalism of *Chapaev i Pustota* seems to lead to a dead end. On the other hand, the ludic quality of Pelevin's writing does not fail him even here as, after

Dust jacket for the 1998 English-language edition of Pelevin's novel Zhizn' nasekomykh *(1997), in which the characters appear variously as human beings and as insects (Richland County Public Library)*

Pustota's enlightenment toward the end of the novel, a taxi driver remarks that "pretending that you doubt the reality of the world is the most cowardly form of escape from that very reality. Squalid intellectual poverty, if you want my opinion." Despite the controversy, Russian readers and critics generally agreed that the publication of *Chapaev i Pustota* was the most important literary event of 1996. Many therefore considered the omission of the novel from the shortlist of the Booker Russian Novel Prize that year to be a scandal.

Now that he had questioned the mere existence of material reality in *Chapaev i Pustota,* Pelevin turned again to the creation of virtual reality. During the presidential election campaign of 1996, he used computer technology to construct a composite picture based on the physical characteristics, political image, and popularity ratings of the six leading candidates. In "Ultima Tuleev, ili Dao vyborov" (Ultima Tuleev, or the Tao of Elections), an article published in 1996 in *Nezavisimaia gazeta-Stsenarii* (The Independent Gazette-Screenplay) in which Pelevin names his virtual president "Ultima Tuleev," he celebrates the power of modern technology to construct a reality that would materialize the collective consciousness of the nation and relieve voters of the necessity of choosing among unsatisfactory alternatives.

This playful exploration of the potential of media technology is merely a prelude to the much more detailed treatment that Pelevin gave the topic in his next long literary work, the novel *Generation "P"* (1999; translated in the United Kingdom as *Babylon,* 2000; republished in the United States as *Homo Zapiens,* 2002). Verging on a bildungsroman, *Generation "P"* tells the story of a young man's education and maturation. Vavilen Tatarsky begins his development as an already unsuccessful writer of fiction who, through a stroke of good fortune, lands a job at an advertising agency. He is phenomenally successful in his new profession and, in the new market economy of Russia, quickly masters the art of manipulating mass consumers with slogans and jingles. He progresses from the writing of advertisement slogans to engaging in "black public relations" in the virtual economy. By the end of the novel he has become a member of a secret society that manipulates the country through total control of the mass media. The entire political life of Russia turns out to be a fiction created through television.

The language and style of this work is significantly different from that of Pelevin's earlier publications. Small but significant parts of the text are in English, and much of the rest of the Russian text is permeated with foreign words and phrases, many of them in the form of advertising jargon. The text reveals the growing dominance of English in certain spheres of modern urban life in Russia. The competition between the two languages is only one of several stylistic contrasts in *Generation "P,"* which is made up of the juxtaposition of numerous discourses—including ones about Eastern mysticism and ancient mythology, subjects that have long interested Pelevin and appeared in many of his works already. Pop psychology plays a much larger role in this novel than in earlier works, as the hero tries to teach himself the art of manipulation through language. This mixture of discourses echoes the strategy used in *Chapaev i Pustota;* whereas in the earlier novel the various discourses remained distinct, *Generation "P"* gradually brings them together in a whimsical synthesis that reaches its peak when Tatarsky summons the spirit of Che Guevara. The Latin American revolutionary's disquisition references both Eastern spirituality and Western mass culture as it describes the ways in which the individual psyche can be manipulated by stimulating the various "wow-impulses," a linguistic pun on the word "vau," which is used by contemporary Russian urban youth.

Zen Buddhism, drug-induced euphoria, and metaphysical inquiries into the nature of existence all find their place in *Generation "P."* The most significant new theme is the treatment of the mass media and its power over the individual and society. In Pelevin's portrayal this power is absolute and irresistible. There is no way out of the virtual world of created reality. The end of Tatarsky's education is marked by his full and complete acceptance of this fact. He, in fact, becomes a "living god." As Tatarsky is initiated into the secrets of the guild that controls the media, all of the discourses and signifiers of the text come together. In this way the novel is not to be interpreted as a message of resignation to the hopelessness of resistance. It is yet another expression of Pelevin's basic message: the insubstantiality and impermanence of the material world in which people believe themselves to live.

Generation "P" has been followed by another period of relative silence. As of this writing, many avid readers look forward to the appearance of another lengthy work presumably under construction. Viktor Olegovich Pelevin's reputation was made by his short fiction, much of it brilliant, clever, provocative, and novel. His continuing importance seems to rest on his ability to create larger works of fiction. As so many Russian writers of the nineteenth and twentieth centuries are now remembered principally for their long novels, so Pelevin has secured himself a place in Russian literary history with his four major novels, of

which casual reviews have given way to more serious and extended scholarly treatment. Whatever his ultimate role in the creation and formation of a new, post-Soviet, Russian literary tradition, Pelevin's name will certainly not soon fade into the oblivion he depicts so well in his prose.

Interviews:

Sally Laird, "Viktor Pelevin," in *Voices of Russian Literature: Interviews with Ten Contemporary Writers,* edited by Laird (Oxford: Oxford University Press, 1999), pp. 178–192;

Jason Cowley, "Gogol À Go-Go," *New York Times Magazine,* 23 January 2000, pp. 20–23;

Sergei Kuznetsov, "Viktor Pelevin: Tot, kto upravliaet etim mirom," 20 May 2003 <http://sharat.co.il/krok/pelevin.htm>.

Bibliographies:

Sergei Nekrasov, "Viktor Pelevin: Opyt bibliografii," *Bibliografiia,* no. 3 (1999) <http://pelevin.nov.ru/stati/o-bibl/1.html>;

Igor' Kondakov, "Pelevin Viktor Olegovich," in *Russkie pisateli 20 veka: Biografichesky slovar',* edited by Petr Alekseevich Nikolaev (Moscow: Bol'shaia Rossiiskaia Entsiklopediia, 2000), pp. 543–545.

References:

Sally Dalton-Brown, "Ludic Nonchalance or Ludicrous Despair? Viktor Pelevin and Russian Postmodernist Prose," *Slavonic and East European Review,* 75 (1997): 216–233;

Alexander Aleksandrovich Genis, "Borders and Metamorphoses: Viktor Pelevin in the Context of Post-Soviet Literature," *Russian Postmodernism: New Perspectives on Post-Soviet Culture,* edited by Mikhail Naumovich Epshtein, Genis, and Slobodanka Vladiv-Glover (New York: Berghan, 1999), pp. 212–224;

Mark Lipovetsky, "Goluboe salo pokoleniia, ili Dva mifa ob odnom krisise," *Znamia,* 11 (1999): 207–215;

Gerald McCausland, "Viktor Pelevin and the End of Sots-Art," in *Endquote: Sots-Art Literature and Soviet Grand Style,* edited by Marina Balina, Nancy Condee, and Evgeny Dobrenko (Evanston, Ill.: Northwestern University Press, 2000), pp. 225–237;

Andrew Meier, "Post-Soviet Surrealism: Viktor Pelevin's Fantastic Novels Speak to the Sense of Alienation Felt by Young Russians," *Time,* 153 (5 April 1999): 13.

Ludmila Petrushevskaya

(26 May 1938 –   )

Helena Goscilo
University of Pittsburgh

BOOKS: *Sbornik odnoaktnykh p'es* (Moscow: Sovetskaia Rossiia, 1979);

Skazki bez podskazki (Moscow: Detskaia literatura, 1981);

P'esy, by Petrushevskaya and Viktor Slavkin (Moscow: Sovetskaia Rossiia, 1983)–includes *Uroki muzyki,* translated by Stephen Mulrine as "Music Lessons," in *Cinzano: Eleven Plays* (London: Nick Hern, 1991), pp. 47–134; and *Lestnichnaia kletka,* translated by Alma H. Law as *The Stairlanding* (Scarsdale, N.Y., 1983);

Zaiachii khvost, with illustrations by M. V. Kurchevskaia (Moscow: Tvorcheskoe ob"edinenie Kinotsentr, 1987);

Pesni dvadtsatogo veka (Moscow: Soiuz teatral'nykh deiatelei RSFSR, 1988)–includes *Tri devushki v golubom,* translated by Liane Aukin and Michael Glenny as "Three Girls in Blue," in *Stars in the Morning Sky: Five New Plays from the Soviet Union* (London: Nick Hern, 1989); *Kvartira Kolumbiny,* translated by Law as *Columbine's Apartment* (Scarsdale, N.Y., 1988); *Monologi; Temnaia Komnata,* translated by Mulrine as "The Dark Room," in *Cinzano* (London: Nick Hern, 1991); and *Den' rozhdeniia Smirnovoi;*

Bessmertnaia liubov' (Moscow: Moskovskii rabochii, 1988)–includes "Prikliucheniia Very," "Strana," "Smotrovaia Ploshchadka," "Takaia devochka, sovest' mira," "Mania," and "Skripka," "Svoi krug"; translated by Laird as *Immortal Love* (London: Virago, 1995; New York: Pantheon, 1995)–includes "The Adventures of Vera," "Another Land," "The Lookout Point," "This Little Girl," "Manya," "The Violin," and "Our Crowd";

Tri devushki v golubom (Moscow: Iskusstvo, 1989);

Svoi krug (Moscow: Ogonek, 1990);

Lechenie Vasiliia i drugie skazki (dlia detei) (Moscow: Tvorcheskoe ob"edinenie Kinotsentr, 1991);

Po doroge boga Erosa (Moscow: Olimp, 1993)–includes *Vremia noch',* translated by Sally Laird as *The Time: Night* (London: Virago, 1994; New York: Pantheon, 1994);

Ludmila Petrushevskaya (from the dust jacket for Immortal Love, *1995; Richland County Public Library)*

Taina doma (Moscow: Kvadrat, 1995)–includes "Novyi raion" and "Taina doma";

Bal poslednego cheloveka (Moscow: Lokid, 1996);

Sobranie sochinenii, 5 volumes, edited by Inna Borisova (Moscow: AST, 1996; Khar'kov: Folio, 1996);

Natoiashchie skazki (Moscow: Vagrius, 1997);

Skazka pro Azbuku (Moscow: Nauka, 1997);

Dom devushek (Moscow: Vagrius, 1998)–includes "Belye doma" and "Dom devushek";

Karamzin derevenskii dnevnik (St. Petersburg: Pushkinskii fond, 2000)–includes "Karamzin derevenskii dnevnik";

Koroleva lir (St. Petersburg: Zlatoust, 2000);

Naidi menia, son (Moscow: Vagrius, 2000);

Chemodan chepukhi (Moscow: Vagrius, 2001);

Most Vaterloo (Moscow: Vagrius, 2001);

Rekviemy (Moscow: Vagrius, 2001);

Schastlivye koshki (Moscow: Vagrius, 2001);

Chernoe pal'to (Moscow: Vagrius, 2002);

Gde ia byla (Moscow: Vagrius, 2002);

Kak tsvetok na zare (Moscow: Vagrius, 2002);

Sluchai v Sokol'nikakh (Moscow: Vagrius, 2002);

Takaia devochka (Moscow: Vagrius, 2002).

Editions and Collections: *Monologi. Temnaia komnata* (Moscow: Soiuz teatral'nykh deiatelei RSFSR, 1988);

Nastoiashie skazki (Moscow: Vagrius, 1999);

Vremia-noch' (Moscow: Vagrius, 2001).

Editions in English: *Four,* translated by Alma H. Law (New York: Institute for Contemporary Eastern European Drama and Theater, 1984)—comprises "Love," "Come into the Kitchen," "Nets and Traps," and "The Violin";

Clarissa and Other Stories, translated by Law (Scarsdale, N.Y., 1985);

The Observation Platform: A Monolog for an Actress, translated by Law (Scarsdale, N.Y., 1987);

Cinzano: Eleven Plays, translated by Stephen Mulrine (London: Nick Hern, 1991)—includes "Cinzano," "Smirnova's Birthday," "Music Lessons," "The Stairwell," "Love," "Nets and Snares," "The Dark Room," "The Execution," "The Meeting," "A Glass of Water," and "The Isolation Box."

PRODUCED SCRIPT: *Skazka skazok,* by Petrushevskaya and Iurii Norshtein, Soiuzmul'tfil'm, 1979.

PLAY PRODUCTIONS: *Uroki muzyki,* Moscow State University Theater, 1978;

Tri devushki v golubom, Lenin Komsomol Theater, 1985.

An existentialist who conceives of human life as an unrelievedly punitive condition, Ludmila Petrushevskaya has produced a sizable body of fiction and drama that casts her tragic vision in a unique synthesis of sordid plots and sophisticated form. With minor exceptions, her work charts the daily psychic monstrosities of a spiritual waste-land populated by victims and victimizers bound by an endless chain of universal suffering and abuse. These Dostoevskian "lacerations," which transpire in a world devoid of God and hope for transcendence, are conveyed through the highly rhetorical, manipulative voice of Petrushevskaya's female narrators, whose strategic juggling of repression and expression constitutes her authorial signature. Despite her venturesome exploration of an

impressively wide array of genres and fictional hybrids during the thirty-five years of her literary career, Petrushevskaya has not deviated from her essentially desolate perception of human life as purgatory.

Her work coheres into a single and singular vision that has undergone only minor modifications, primarily in genre experimentation, throughout her professional life. From her first published stories in 1972 to–approximately twenty years later–her longest and most complex narrative, *Vremia noch'* (first published in *Novyi mir* [New World], 1992; translated as *The Time: Night,* 1994), several features have indelibly and consistently stamped her prose and drama the way a watermark individualizes paper. These features include a relentlessly, even aggressively, wintry vision of life, from which she denies respite to her personae and readers alike; the exploration of topics traditionally taboo in Soviet Russia, such as alcoholism, physical violence, inveterate mendacity, murder and suicide, and sexuality in all its manifestations (including prostitution, casual copulation, rape, incest, pedophilia, impotence, and homosexuality); situational leitmotivs and character types that compactly signal comprehensive psychological and physical desperation; complex narrative strategies à la Fyodor Dostoevsky, particularly the *skaz* (a nonauthorial narrator's stylized, digressive, colloquial discourse) of Petrushevskaya's preponderantly female narrators; a highly rhetorical discourse patching together words and structures from disparate and usually incompatible walks of life; and a chronotope (the inescapable symbiosis between represented time and space) in which temporal diffusion operates in tandem with precise, semantically freighted spatial specification.

Though relatively few personal details about her life are known, Petrushevskaya's chillingly forlorn view of the world doubtless stems from her childhood, which reads like a paradigmatic horror story of the Stalinist era. Born on 26 May 1938 in Moscow during Joseph Stalin's purges and shortly before the upheaval of World War II, Petrushevskaya underwent not only personal family traumas but also the psychological and material devastation and hardships of indigence, displacement, near starvation, and perpetual fear endured by many Russians throughout that historical nightmare. Her maternal relatives perished in Stalin's terrorist campaign; her father abandoned the family before Petrushevskaya was born; and in 1943 her penniless mother moved with her parents and sister to Samara (then Kuibyshev), where she temporarily placed Petrushevskaya in a children's home—presumably to ensure her daughter's survival amid desperate circumstances. The family returned to Moscow in 1948. Three years later Petrushevskaya's linguist grandfather, Nikolai Iakovlev, was branded an enemy of the people. This status doomed not only him but also his relatives to public ostracism and contempt, abject poverty, impossibly cramped living quarters in a communal apartment, and constant domestic tension. As respite from the horror of witnessing his rapid descent into insanity in the single room ("a mini-Gulag," as Petrushevskaya calls it in an interview featured in Sally Laird's *Voices of Russian Literature: Interviews with Ten Contemporary Writers* [1999]) that he shared with her and her mother, Petrushevskaya spent entire days in the library, the sole sanctuary available to the literate during late Stalinism. After four years of study (from 1956 to 1960) in the journalism department at Moscow State University, Petrushevskaya married, had a child, became widowed (her husband contracted a terminal illness that paralyzed him for years before his death), remarried, and gave birth to two more children.

With three offspring to feed, Petrushevskaya accepted what employment she could find to protect them from the deprivation that had blighted her own childhood. She worked as a journalist, radio announcer, television editor, and translator (from Polish), writing her own fiction in the kitchen at night while the family slept—a scenario revisited three decades later in her novel *Vremia noch'*. After several insignificant publications dating from 1961, her promising literary debut in 1972 with the two stories "Istoriia Klarissy" (Clarissa's Story) and "Rasskazchitsa" (The Storyteller), published in the Leningrad journal *Avrova* (Aurora), was followed by roughly two decades of virtual silence. The dark pessimism and unconventional narrative tone of her prose violated expectations not only of women's fiction but of Soviet writing in general. Although editors such as Aleksandr Tvardovsky (of *Novyi mir*), to whom she submitted her first stories in 1969, sat up and took notice upon receiving her manuscripts, they did not risk publication. Instead, *Novyi mir* offered material support by assigning her reviews and book reports. The plays that Petrushevskaya began to write during 1973 to 1974—such as *Uroki muzyki* (1983; translated as "Music Lessons," 1991), *Chinzano* (published in *Teatral'naia zhizn'* [Theater Life], 1988; translated as "Cinzano," 1986), and *Vstrechi druzei* (Meetings of Friends, published in *Sovremennaia dramaturgiia* [Contemporary Dramaturgy], 1989)—fared better: university groups and an underground theater performed them under the guise of "creative evenings." The flamboyant director Roman Viktiuk's staging of *Uroki muzyki* in 1978 and the production of *Chinzano* in the 1980s by the talented studio group Chelovek brought her to the public eye. Mainstream theaters and journals, however, continued to reject her persistent submissions.

Glasnost finally liberated Petrushevskaya from this professional limbo. The ban on her major play, *Tri devushki v golubom* (first published in *Sovremennaia dramaturgiia* [Contemporary Dramaturgy], 1983; translated as "Three Girls in Blue," 1989), was lifted in 1985. That year, Mark Zakharov's production of the play in the

Lenin Komsomol Theater was greeted with fervent enthusiasm. This production explored the dramatic potential of the play as a contemporary revision of Anton Pavlovich Chekhov's *Tri sestry* (Three Sisters, 1901). Petrushevskaya began to gain steady, though controversial, recognition from critics and general readers alike. Whereas the radical changes in the production, dissemination, and consumption of literature ushered in by the erosion of the Soviet cultural infrastructure curtailed many writers' careers, the process of "desovietization" eventually brought Petrushevskaya international renown, many invitations, and coveted national rewards, including the prestigious Pushkin Prize in 1990. In fact, during 2001 the Leonid Shishkin Gallery in Moscow combined Petrushevskaya's reading from her works with an exhibit and auction of her watercolors (mainly flowers and self-portraits), "fumages," as she calls them, and "homages," some of which also illustrate her volumes published by Vagrius. Such is Petrushevskaya's cultural stature today that a musical concert may well be in the offing—for she boasts an excellent singing voice, an unerring ear (evident in her narrative tone), and a fine knowledge of opera.

Since Petrushevskaya's prose never passed through what Nabokov compassionately calls the "writer's vernating stage" (*vernate* is an obsolete term, meaning "to become young again"), but emerged fully formed at the outset, its defining features already characterized her first publication, "Rasskazchitsa," and have merely intensified and multiplied with time. Since the 1990s she has experimented with such genres as the parable and fairy tale, evidenced by the collection *Skazki dlia vzroslykh* (Fairy Tales for Adults, published in *Iunost'* [Youth], 1990); a hybrid of *sluchai* (incident) and horror story (exemplified by the cycle "Pesni vostochnykh slavian" [Songs of the Eastern Slavs], published in *Novyi mir*, 1990); and poetry (*Karamzin derevenskii dnevnik* [Karamzin-Countryside Diary], 2000). Yet, the majority of her texts rely on the tried and true methods she pioneered at the outset to convey her tragically grisly view of the world.

"Istoriia Klarissy," one of Petrushevskaya's two inaugural publications in 1972, contends that a woman's imperative is "to stand up for herself and make her solitary way through a hostile world," a sentiment echoed later in "Prikliucheniia Very" (1988; translated as "The Adventures of Vera," 1995), which dramatizes people's need "somehow or other to fight their lone solitary life." This worldview receives its clearest elaboration in the gnomic story "Cherez polia" (published in *Avrora*, 1983; translated as "Crossing the Field," 1995), astutely singled out by the Russian critic Natal'ia Ivanova in her 1993 article as a cornerstone text for grasping Petrushevskaya's philosophy. Stripped to bare essentials, the vestigial plot of the story recounts the female narrator's walk with a male acquaintance from the railway station to a house where their friends await them. This ostensibly banal experience analogizes the physical journey with a traversal through life—a conceit rooted in folklore and popular since antiquity, as illustrated by Mikhail Bakhtin's study of the chronotope of the road in *Voprosy literatury i estetiki* (Questions of Literature and Aesthetics, 1975; translated as *The Dialogic Imagination,* 1981). The mythic nature of the passage through natural-historical space undertaken by Petrushevskaya's duo may be inferred from the cosmic elements that symbolize the couple's encounter with both nature and history: the forest, the empty fields, the lightning-streaked thunderstorm that washes over them, and the cultivated earth that has yet to yield any fruit. In "Cherez polia" this confrontation with life and death, which lays bare the individual human essence, catalyzes the narrator's realization that under different circumstances her companion would be her ideal life mate. The terms of that insight become extended (that is, they encompass a broader social spectrum) with the couple's eventual "Hansel-and-Gretel-like" arrival at their destination—a *teplyi dom* (warm house), which has food, drink, and a cozy conviviality; here, the narrator warms her "soul after the long, hard stretch of life's journey."

Starting with her early works, such as the one-act play *Liubov'* (published in *Teatr* [The Theater], 1979; translated as "Love," 1984), Petrushevskaya achieves some of her strongest effects through her unaccommodating depiction of family members, or "loved ones," as people who rely on their socially sanctioned roles to legitimate their relentless, pragmatic abuse of those whom they proclaim to love. Works throughout the 1980s (such as "Svoi krug" [Our Circle], published in *Novyi mir,* 1988; translated as "Our Crowd," 1995) and into the 1990s (including *Vremia noch'* and "Malen'kaia Groznaia" [Little Groznaia], published in *Znamia* [The Banner], 1998) highlight aspects of domestic strife. The self-serving brutality of family members from whom one traditionally expects humaneness accounts in large measure for the bleak aura of thwarted hope and inevitable loss in these works. Invariably equated with suffering innocence, children are the only ones in Petrushevskaya's works who are exempt from what otherwise appear as universal (self-)destructive urges, although their very existence imposes intolerable burdens on parents, who for the most part are single, divorced, or abandoned mothers. Relations between mothers and daughters, which Petrushevskaya mistakenly believes is a topic "virtually taboo in literature" (demonstrating her ignorance of not only Western but also Russian contemporary women's fiction), figure most prominently and dispiritingly in her family dynamics as a battleground on which egos clash and resentment, envy, and distrust flourish.

Paperback cover for Petrushevskaya's Svoi krug *(Our Circle); the title story offended many Soviet readers because of its graphic representation of physical abuse and bodily functions (Collection of Mark Lipovetsky)*

Whereas Petrushevskaya's early works capture the doomed search for an existential "home," her narratives and plays of the 1980s and 1990s "spatialize" the perversion of conventionally hallowed bonds by transforming the notion of house as home and harbor into either an enclosure or a defensive stronghold against those sharing that space—hence, the frequency in these publications of liminality, of thresholds (similar to Dostoevsky's use of them), and of barred and locked doors, which betray the psychological need for self-protection from ostensible intimates, while simultaneously locating people, metaphorically, on the existential edge of a precipice. In terms of Bakhtin's chronotope, Petrushevskaya meticulously, even insistently, delineates space, even as she regularly blurs temporal markers. Time matters little in her literary universe, for the latter explores eternal questions of human existence. The titles of her prose and drama repeatedly advert to a locus that functions centrally in the text: *Lestnichnaia kletka* (translated as *The Stairlanding,* 1983); "Strana" (1988; translated as "Another Land," 1995); *Temnaia komnata* (1988; translated as "The Dark Room," 1991); "Izolirovannyi box" (published in *Novyi mir,* 1988;

translated as "The Isolation Box," 1991); "Smotrovaia Ploshchadka" (published in *Druzhba narodov* [The People's Friendship], 1982; translated as "The Lookout Point," 1995); "Novyi raion" (The New Area, first published in *Novyi mir*, 1990); "V malen'kom dome" (In the Little House, *Novyi mir*, 1990); "Belye doma" (White Houses, first published in *Druzhba narodov*, 1996); "Taina Doma" (The Mystery of the House, 1995), and "Dom Devushek" (The Girls' House, first published in *Znamia*, 1996). The title of *Vremia noch'*, on the other hand, refers to a perpetual, mythic time that makes a trope of the protagonist's psychological state without enabling the reader to determine the sequence of events, the protagonist's exact age, and other comparable information.

Yet, although many of Petrushevskaya's plays and stories take place in an apartment, a hospital ward, an office, or a city street, two texts—"Nikogda" (Never, published in *Znamia*, 1998) and the poetic work "Karamzin derevenskii dnevnik"—reflect the extension of her grim purview to the countryside, registering a key moment in Petrushevskaya's development. The primordial, uncomprehending atavism portrayed in "Nikogda" adds a new, terrifying note to the customary Petrushevskian scenario of visceral animosity toward one's fellow humans that dominates the majority of her works. Just as home is synonymous with prison or torture chamber, so do the dinners, parties, and gatherings of family members and intimates presumed as camaraderie and celebrations become carnivalized into scenes of psychic evisceration, hysteria, and physiological debasement. In the spirit of Dostoevsky, group scenes at table culminate and disintegrate in scandals, exposés, beatings, drunken vomiting, and the dissolution of marriages. "Svoi krug," which Petrushevskaya has characterized as a narrative marking the end of love, captures with special vividness the inverted nature of Petrushevskaya's pseudofestivities: a pattern of epic inebriation, vicious arguments, sexual titillation, and scapegoating bonds the attendees not through affection but through concerted enmity toward one or more of their putative friends or (former) spouses. Virtually all "parties" in Petrushevskaya's works end with disaster, the breakdown of a relationship, or unspeakable acts. The "country" dimension of Petrushevskaya's purview, however, adds the ax and the dark realm of daily animal existence to the grab bag of horrors unfolded in her fiction.

Petrushevskaya's transgressive treatment of physicality may account in part for her exclusion from print in the years before glasnost. Her texts of the 1970s and 1980s directly acknowledge an entire range of physical phenomena that other Soviet writers for decades shrank from contemplating. Prostitutes, alcoholics, nymphomaniacs, suicides (who all, in a sense, violate their bodies) populate her works, which matter-of-factly record how people urinate (or more) outside the toilet (as in the story "Ali-Baba," published originally in *Avrora*, 1988); vomit (as in "Svoi krug"); and arouse one another "with intent" and subsist on a regular diet of sexual surrogates (as in "Takaia devochka" [A Girl Like That]; translated as "This Little Girl," 1995). Although the stark grimness of her vision daunts many readers, some Russians' discomfort with or distaste for Petrushevskaya's works stems from the long-standing habits of Soviet prudishness regarding literary physiology. Like many writers of the post-Soviet era, but at least a quarter century earlier, Petrushevskaya in the 1970s began exploring, profoundly and productively, the textual possibilities of the narrated body. Suppressed by the Soviet authorities' cult of fastidious, if hypocritical, propriety, by the time the explicitly inscribed body surfaced (during "desovietization"), it had acquired enormous rhetorical power through decades of euphemism and neglect. A work such as "Svoi krug" registers the body as significant in ways central to human experience and to literary representation. Written in 1979 but published in 1988, at the height of perestroika, "Svoi krug" nonetheless offended many Soviet readers. In addition to illustrating the above categories, it refers regularly and repeatedly to false eyes rolling out of sockets, knocked-out teeth, a ripped-up body with a hole in the stomach, a bleeding nose, a ruptured maidenhead, dildos, D-cup breasts, impotence, one-night stands, incestuous relations between parents and children, group sex, sexual experimentation between children, near rape, bed-wetting, and child beating. Here, as elsewhere, Petrushevskaya conceives of the body as a site of violence, of hyperbolized ingestion and regurgitation—the ins and outs of every sort through all available orifices.

Beginning with the 1980s, Petrushevskaya's publications, including "Svoi krug" and *Syraia noga* (A Raw Leg, published in *Sovremennaia dramaturgiia*, 1989), a revised version of *Vstrecha druzei*, reveal two-directional aspects of the body (mimicking the sexual act and the biological sequence of eating and excreting, drinking and urinating or vomiting) as one of Petrushevskaya's major stratagems. The device enables her to structure the tonality of narrative and dialogue that conceal in the midst of disclosure and vice versa; to infuse horror with comedy; and to punctuate periphrasis, bordering on abstraction, with a single concrete detail, so that reinforcement through contrast struggles with semierasure. As a consequence, presence may dissolve into insignificance, while absence acquires tremendous force. Unlike writers who tend to foreshadow instances of physiological dysphemism (the use of offensive wording in place of an agreeable expression) and sexual explicitness through framing and an assortment of other textual signals, Petrushevskaya achieves dramatic effects by purveying formerly bypassed details of the body abruptly and explicitly, but neutrally. What another author might contextualize in an emotional aura, which anticipates the horrifying or the shocking, Petrushevskaya records in a bland tone indistinguishable from descriptions of a cactus or the weather. The technique results in a leveling: it strips the body of illusion, demystifying and uncovering it to expose its parts and its activities as a commodity—as merely another item in a potentially infinite series (which enables the paronomasia of such titles as *Syraia noga* in a play where people's flesh does, indeed, get treated as meat).

This process of dehumanization externalizes the spiritual violation and suffering that are Petrushevskaya's dominant concerns. If nineteenth-century Russian literature discoursed freely on the soul and eschewed corporeality (likewise slighted by Soviet ideological aesthetics), the erstwhile taboo body is, paradoxically, Petrushevskaya's euphemism for the devastation of the psyche. Inverting hardy conventions by rigorously eliminating displays of the inner self and unconstrainedly recording externals, she discloses repellent physical minutiae (signifiers) so as to camouflage what is truly obscene—psychological and spiritual pain and desolation (signified). Her truly obscene narratives communicate through displacement onto the body and a perpetual deferment of the correspondence between the named and the unarticulated or unrepresentable. On a rhetorical level, then, Petrushevskaya duplicates the in/out movement of her personae. Her characters and narrators speak in a casual, disengaged tone about abortions, miscarriages, sickness and death, rotting limbs and dismemberment, and beatings, while either omitting or deflecting through irony all mention of shame, humiliation, pain, love, and other emotions. By making the expression of feelings and a genuine analysis of psychological motives a taboo, Petrushevskaya casts the body as the materialization of psychic trauma, of the otherwise "unsaid." She treats the invisible, emotional aspect of human experience as the unmentionable, substituting body language as her medium of permissible communication.

Petrushevskaya's seemingly programmatic commitment to dysphemism draws attention all the more forcibly to those moments when she has recourse to its opposite, euphemism, particularly because she intensifies the impact through repetition. Her strategic reticence often assumes the form of a familiar trope, as in the story "Mania" (published in *Druzhba narodov,* 1973; translated as "Manya," 1995), in which Petrushevskaya develops in her typically tautological manner the familiar synecdoche of hair as a clue to female sexuality or seductiveness. Alternatively, she may substitute a purposely nebulous phrase (rendered meaningful only by maximal contextu-

alization) for a more precise and explicit expression. For example, the narrator in "Takaia devochka" has no scruples about recounting her husband's sundry infidelities, her own pleasurable interest in the specifics of his conquests, and the alleged readiness with which their neighbor, the former prostitite Raisa, has sex with any stranger who knocks on her door. Yet, Petrushevskaya not only invokes euphemism when referring to sexual intercourse but, of the terms at her disposal, chooses the most semantically vague and blatantly circumambient: *eto delo* (that business), which, outside of the context of the story, could refer to anything. The code words render the activity as something unnameable and enshrouded in coyness, partly because behavior of a more questionable order is spoken of freely and directly.

With her literary debut in the early 1970s, Petrushevskaya renewed the narrative mode of orality in contemporary Russian literary prose, for the overwhelming majority of her stories and tales proceed from a "chatty" and catty narrator whom one might meet on the subway or tram, at the local store or hospital, or waiting in line on the street. In her interview with Laird, Petrushevskaya calls Russia "a land of women Homers . . . who tell their stories orally, just like that, without inventing anything." Various critics' claims that no one listens to anyone else in Petrushevskaya's works are not only inaccurate but also insensitive to the motivation behind the sui generis tale spinning of her colloquial female Homers. One of three psychological impulses most frequently propels her narrators to produce stories: the urge to unburden the lonely self (as in "Medeia" [Medea], which appeared in *Al'manakh "Aprel'"* [The Almanac "April"], 1990); the desire to forge temporary bonds with an audience or interlocutor while asserting one's own illusory superiority through the controlling act of "telling" (the syndrome of the fleeting encounter that allows time for rapidly describing a *sluchai* in a gossipy mode saturated with dark hints and nasty presuppositions, as in the story "Skripka," published in *Druzhba narodov,* 1973; translated as "The Violin," 1995); and, in first-person narratives, the aggressive yet defensive need for self-exculpation (seen in "Takaia devochka" and *Vremia noch'*). The majority of Petrushevskaya's stories open in medias res, as though the narrator is resuming a suspended conversation, and develop as an exfoliation of incompletely clarified references, events, and suggestive suppositions, all confided in a disconcertingly snide or knowing tone. Selectivity of detail and flaunted vagueness, along with such sweeping generalizations as "everyone knew" (also, "everyone thought" and "everyone realized") or "no one heard" (also, "no one saw" and "no one wanted") spotlight omissions, unwarranted conclusions, exaggerations, and suppressions—all of which undermine the narrator's veracity and, above all,

Paperback cover for a 1991 English-language edition of Petrushevskaya's plays, some of which were staged (in Russian) by university groups and underground theaters in Moscow in the 1970s (Thomas Cooper Library, University of South Carolina)

increase readers' awareness of the subjective power that inheres in any narration.

Although Petrushevskaya repeatedly has declared her passion for the fairy tale as a genre, she began creating narratives that explicitly bear this label only after "desovietization." Her penchant for grouping her works according to genres has prompted some commentators (such as Sally Dalton-Brown and Nina Kolesnikoff) to focus on the constitutive features distinguishing a story from a fairy tale for adults or a dialogue from a monologue. Yet, Petrushevskaya alters her own taxonomy, and, indeed, her plays are "dialogic" only in the most obvious and reduced sense of having characters speak in sequence, whereas her monologues and most of her short narratives develop in genuinely (that is, internally) dialogized fashion as defined by Bakhtin: the speaking voice anticipates, answers, and polemicizes with voices

(or perspectives) that remain unidentified and have no discrete, palpable existence in the given works. Her *nastoiashchie skazki* (real fairy tales), like her *zhivotnye skazki* (animal fairy tales), both of which date from the early 1990s, display characteristics of the genuine folkloric genre but deviate stylistically from it in multiple ways. Unlike quintessential fairy tales, they synthesize plots centering on familiar folkloric characters, such as Elena the Beautiful and various princesses, with Petrushevskaya's typical ironic observations about human conduct; these narratives lack verbal formulas, indulge in description, and sometimes end far from happily. They never attain the magical charm that imbues her screenplay for Iurii Norshtein's award-winning animated film, *Skazka skazok* (The Tale of Tales, 1979). Purportedly Petrushevskaya's favorite form, the fairy tale–like the majority of her narratives–undergoes generic metamorphosis in her hands. Just as Petrushevskaya's poetry is more prosaic than her prose, so her fairy tales seem less enigmatic and "flat" on the surface than her short stories.

Thus far, Petrushevskaya's most substantive and complex narrative is *Vremia noch'*, a nuanced, chilling investigation of totalitarian pseudonurture and a veritable encyclopedia of Petrushevskiana. *Vremia noch'* ostensibly recounts the noble endeavors of Anna Andrianovna, a woman in her late fifties, to sustain–both morally and economically–her family members: her mother, Sima, son, Andrei, daughter, Alena, and grandson, Timochka. In accordance with her principle of condensation, Petrushevskaya distributes among these four generations virtually all of her favorite synecdochic signs of existential horror. Sima, presumably a schizophrenic (though only a fraction more insane than anyone else in the story), has been committed by her daughter to a psychiatric hospital, and when in the course of the narrative Anna Andrianovna has her mother transferred to a mental asylum, the incontinent old woman with a persecution mania helplessly urinates where she stands, waiting for transportation. Andrei, who served a term in prison, where he submitted to presumably forcible homosexual advances, brings two women off the street to his mother's room and there proves his manhood, to the rhythm of Anna Andrianovna's discreet tapping on the door. Permanently maimed through leaping out of a second-story window after an argument with his wife, Andrei, like many men in Petrushevskaya's stories, is an alcoholic who steals money from his mother to appease his constant craving. Alena, who abandoned her older child, Timochka, to her mother's care, left behind a notebook graphically detailing her sexual experiences with her married boss, by whom she had another baby; she now lives with her boss and is expecting a third child. Anna Andrianovna alternates between tears of self-pity and vicious contempt; Andrei pilfers and drinks; Alena breeds; and Timochka at six has a nervous tic from all of his psychological traumas. Indigent, close to starvation, torn by hysterical jealousy and loathing for one another, the family corroborates Leo Tolstoy's dictum in *Anna Karenina* (1875–1877) that every family is unhappy in its own way. The references to Tolstoy's novel, which Petrushevskaya intersperses throughout her narrative, point to fundamental parallels between *Vremia noch'* and *Anna Karenina*—above all, to the focal problem of a breakdown in family structure.

Anna Andrianovna promotes her own image as an extraordinary paragon of martyred largesse, a rock of dependability in a morass of irresponsible self-indulgence ("Andrei came back from camp and ate my herring, my potatoes, my black bread, drank my tea, and devoured my mind as always and sucked my blood . . . I said nothing"). As she repeatedly reminds everyone, while earning a mere pittance through her poetry readings, she nevertheless maintains the household, shelters her self-destructive offspring ("I'm all they've all got, have to rescue the lot of them, I saved my son's life"), cooks, launders, and denies herself even minimal necessities for the sake of her beloved grandson, who accompanies her everywhere ("Always and everywhere it's been just you and me and that's the way it's going to stay!"). Overly conscious self-sacrifice usually originates in less than admirable motives, or, as the irreverent maxim of Albert Camus's skeptical Clamence in *La Chute* (The Fall, 1956) maintains: People climb crosses so as to be seen from long distances.

Indeed, a close scrutiny of double voicing in the text unmasks Anna Andrianovna's apparent Christian self-sacrifice as a mode of sadistic, egomaniacal control and vampirism—all in the name of love, which she trumpets as "the most important thing in life." She histrionically refers to her son—who calls her "bitch"—as "the sun of my whole life"; she says of her daughter, "my beauty Alena, my quiet little nestling, who was such a comfort to me"; and she addresses her grandson with the capitalized terms "He" and "Angel," and as "holy infant" and "my star, my darling." Much like Dostoevsky's two Katerina Ivanovnas—in both *Prestuplenie i nakazanie* (Crime and Punishment, 1866) and *Brat'ia Karamazovy* (The Brothers Karamazov, 1879–1880)—Petrushevskaya's Anna Andrianovna "theatricalizes" her role of self-abnegator (through tears, clasped hands, hyperbolic entreaties, and invidious comparisons between self and others) and exacts a crushing psychological price for all of her "kindnesses," prompted by bottomless pride. An authority on all questions ("I know children's hearts," she says at one point), she deems herself a voice articulating a higher Truth:

Bringing enlightenment, the light of the law, to these benighted folk, these swarming masses! The dark conscience incarnate of simple people speaks within me and I'm no longer myself, I'm an oracle, I lay down the law. The children who hear me speak—in schools, in summer camps, in clubs—they all shrink and tremble, but they never forget!

As she asserts even earlier in the novel, "I spend my whole life saving children! I'm the only one in the entire neighborhood who stays alert at night, listening and listening to hear whether anyone's crying out!"

To anyone conversant with Dostoevsky's works, from *Bednye liudi* (Poor Folk, 1846), through *Zapiski iz podpol'ia* (Notes from Underground, 1864), to the big novels, the Dostoevskian elements in Petrushevskaya's fiction are instantly apparent. Fundamental and wide-ranging, they operate on both horizontal and vertical planes. Both writers explore above all the enigma of the human personality, particularly its capacity for evil in infinite guises, with the significant difference that Dostoevsky credits the possibility of goodness (and in *Idiot* [The Idiot, 1868] attempts to portray its incarnation), whereas Petrushevskaya manifestly shares Graham Greene's expressed conviction that human nature is not black and white, but "black and grey." In addition, for both Dostoevsky and Petrushevskaya the suffering of children offers the most intolerable and compelling evidence of cosmic injustice (and for Ivan Karamazov in *Brat'ia Karamazovy*, it is irrefutable justification for rejecting God and his world); as Anna Andrianovna observes in *Vremia noch'*, "Children are conscience personified." Not unlike the Greek tragedians, both writers also anatomize the heritage of evil and its infinitely subtle variations through the resonant trope of the family. Moreover, perhaps more obtrusively in Petrushevskaya's world but also in Dostoevsky's, disease functions as a key metaphor for psychological and spiritual states. In contrast to Dostoevsky's predilection for brain fever, epilepsy, and possession—afflictions that signal a breakdown in rational faculties and harmony—Petrushevskaya remains resolutely physiological in her emphases. Like Dostoevsky, she also recognizes the drive to assert the unaccommodated subjective self and the demand that it be fully acknowledged as intrinsic to human psychology. Neither writer denies appetite as a springboard to action, insatiability as commonplace, and sensuality as a fact of life. Masochism, hysteria, voyeurism, and their relatives all receive their due in the texts of both. Finally, both Dostoevsky and Petrushevskaya show the human tendency for self-entrapment; they not only inscribe it in compulsive behavior (a kind of *perpetuum mobile* [in constant movement], flaunted in the Underground Man's mode of argumentation in *Zapiski iz podpol'ia*) but also spatialize it through cramped quarters—

Dust jacket for the 1994 English-language edition of Petrushevskaya's
Vremia noch', *her longest, most complex narrative*
(Richland County Public Library)

such as the coffin of Raskol'nikov's room in *Prestuplenie i nakazanie* and the tiny, locked or barricaded rooms in Petrushevskaya's plays and stories. Thresholds, locks, and screens suggest both borderline states and a fatal, self-protective retreat into one's inner being—into an ever-diminishing self.

Her debt to Dostoevsky notwithstanding, two significant traits decisively distinguish Petrushevskaya's prose from his. Above all, Petrushevskaya's purview is overwhelmingly gynocentric: her narrators and protagonists are female, and the concrete problems ceaselessly beleaguering them (pregnancy, abortion, child care, and feeding, for example) belong to the spheres of reproduction and caretaking—vocations traditionally associated with women. Men are relegated to secondary status, although their promiscuity, selfishness, infantilism, and propensity to violence account for much of women's misery. Unfaithful and irresponsible as husbands, men tend

to be absent fathers or inclined to inappropriate (violent or incestuous) interest in their daughters. They remain, however, if not on the periphery of Petrushevskaya's fictional world, then certainly outside its center.

Second, Petrushevskaya's writings utterly lack Dostoevsky's habit of stuffing novels with philosophizing and protracted argumentation. Her narrative mode follows a kind of iceberg principle, whereby the visible or compactly articulated only hints at that which is submerged but most significant. She narrates and dramatizes where Dostoevsky would sooner have a character expound a theory or viewpoint—hence the extraordinary condensation of her prose, which, moreover, unfailingly proceeds as oral narrative, intensifying the subjectivity of her discursive strategies. Petrushevskaya's prose, in fact, eliminates entirely the omniscient/objective narrator who lends Tolstoy's fiction its comforting, if infuriating, aura of authority. Her writing also cleverly combines repetition with laconicism in a unique manner that leaves no doubts about Petrushevskaya's familiarity with such Freudian concepts as obsession, guilt, repression, and fetishism.

After more than three decades of struggle, Ludmila Petrushevskaya finally has received condign recognition; yet, she continues to unsettle critics and readers not only because of the unrelieved bleakness of her vision (Greek tragedy without catharsis) but also because the Russian, and especially Soviet, tradition taboos negation by women, whose social and literary function is to support and encourage, to wax optimistic, and to provide emotional bandages to those endowed with the inborn right to gloom—men. Furthermore, her unflinching acknowledgment of what in the Soviet context would qualify as anomalous sexuality (some have dubbed it pathology), whether on the level of potential or praxis, has offended or horrified even liberal critics and readers. Admirers of her authorial skills, while applauding her tireless experimentation with genre, occasionally find her seemingly uncontrollable knee-jerk insistence on "the worst of all possible worlds" and on the tiresome invocation of such types as the hospitalized mother—worn threadbare through merciless repetition—inadvertently comic. Interviews with Petrushevskaya leave no doubts that she envisions herself as a creative crusader with a moral teleology, intent on awakening people's consciences. Among contemporary writers, Petrushevskaya more than any other prosaist may be considered Dostoevsky's true, if undutiful and unloved, daughter. Whereas she has had to pay a professional price for that status in Soviet and post-Soviet society, readers have been the rich beneficiaries.

Interviews:

Antje Leetz, "Gesprach mit Ludmila Petruschewskaja," *Sinn und Form,* 3 (1990): 533–544;

Sally Laird, "Lyudmila Petrushevskaya," in *Voices of Russian Literature: Interviews with Ten Contemporary Writers,* edited by Laird (Oxford: Oxford University Press, 1999), pp. 23–48.

Biographies:

Sigrid McLaughlin, "Petrushevskaya, Liudmila Stefanovna," in *Dictionary of Russian Women Writers,* edited by Marina Ledkovsky, Charlotte Rosenthal, and Mary Zirin (Westport, Conn. & London: Greenwood Press, 1994), pp. 504–507;

Melissa T. Smith and Nyusya Milman, "Liudmila Petrushevskaya," in *Russian Women Writers,* 2 volumes, edited by Christine D. Tomei (New York: Garland, 1999), II: 1421–1427;

Jane A. Taubman, Petrushevskaya bibliography (1 February 1999) <http://www.amherst.edu/~russian/resource/petru/russbib. html>;

T. A. Sotnikova, "Petrushevskaya, Liudmila Stefanovna," in *Russkie pisateli 20 veka. Biograficheskii slovar',* edited by Petr Alekseevich Nikolaev (Moscow: Bol'shaia Rossiiskaia Entsiklopediia, 2000), pp. 551–552.

References:

N. Agisheva, "Zvuki 'My' (o dramaturgii Petrushevskoi)," *Teatr,* 9 (1988): 55, 64;

L. Antokol'sky, "Nuzhnoe slovo: Nravstvenno-filosofskie poiski na primere rasskaza L. Petrushevskoi 'Seti i lovushki,'" *Voprosy literatury,* 10 (1975): 73–102;

Mikhail Bakhtin, *Voprosy literatury i estetiki* (Moscow: Khudozhestvennaia literatura, 1975); translated by Caryl Emerson and Michael Holquist as *The Dialogic Imagination* (Austin: University of Texas Press, 1981);

Adele Barker, "Women Without Men in the Writings of Contemporary Soviet Women Writers," in *Russian Literature and Psychoanalysis,* edited by Daniel Rancour-Laferriere, Linguistic and Literary Studies in Eastern Europe, volume 31 (Amsterdam & Philadelphia: J. Benjamins, 1989), pp. 431–449;

Patricia Carden, "The Art of War in Petrushevskaya's 'Our Crowd,'" *Studies in Short Fiction,* 34 (1997): 39–54;

Sally Dalton-Brown, *Voices from the Void: The Genres of Liudmila Petrushevskaia* (New York & Oxford: Berghahn, 2000);

Elena Gessen, "Kto boitsia Liudmily Petrushevskoi?" *Vremia i my,* 81 (1984): 109–119;

Helena Goscilo, "Mother as Mothra: Totalizing Narrative and Nurture in Petrushevskaya," in *A Plot of Her Own: The Female Protagonist in Russian Literature,* edited by Sona Hoisington (Northwestern, Ill.: Northwestern University Press, 1995), pp. 102–113, 157–161;

Goscilo, "Speaking Bodies: Erotic Zones Rhetoricized," in *Fruits of Her Plume: Essays on Contemporary Russian Woman's Culture,* edited by Goscilo (Armonk, N.Y.: M. E. Sharpe, 1993), pp. 135–164;

Natal'ia Ivanova, "Bakhtin's Concept of the Grotesque and the Art of Petrushevskaia and Tolstaia," in *Fruits of Her Plume: Essays on Contemporary Russian Woman's Culture,* edited by Goscilo (Armonk, N.Y.: M. E. Sharpe, 1993), pp. 21–32;

Maya Johnson, "Women and Children First: Domestic Chaos and the Maternal Bond in the Drama of Liudmila Petrushevskaia," *Canadian Slavonic Papers,* 34 (March/June 1992): 97–112;

Nina Kolesnikoff, "The Absurd in Ljudmila Petruševskaja's Plays," *Russian, Croatian and Serbian, Czech and Slovak, Polish Literature,* 43 (15 May 1998): 469–480;

Kolesnikoff, "The Generic Diversity of Ljudmila Petruševskja's Plays," in *Slavic Drama: The Question of Innovation,* edited by Andrew Donskov and Richard Sokolski (Ottawa: University of Ottawa, 1991), pp. 221–225;

Kolesnikoff, "The Generic Structure of Ljudmila Petrusevskaja's 'Pesni vostochnyx slavjan'," *Slavic and East European Journal,* 37 (Summer 1993): 220–230;

Kolesnikoff, "The Narrative Structure of Liudmila Petrushevskaia's Short Stories," *Canadian Slavonic Studies,* 4 (1990): 444–456;

Irina Murav'eva, "Dva imeni (T. Tolstaia i L. Petrushevskaia," *Grani,* 152 (1989): 99–133;

E. Nevzgliadova, "Siuzhet dlia nebol'shogo rasskaza," *Novyi mir,* 4 (1988): 256–260;

I. Shagin, "Posleslovie k publikatsii p'esy *Syraia noga,*" *Sovetskaia dramaturgiia,* 2 (1989): 53–74;

Alexandra Smith, "In Populist Clothes: Anarchy and Subversion in Petrushevskaya's Latest Fiction," *New Zealand Slavonic Journal* (1997): 107–125;

Melissa T. Smith, "In Cinzano Veritas: The Plays of Liudmila Petrushevskaia," *Slavic and East European Arts,* 3 (Winter/Spring 1989): 247–252;

M. Stroeva, "Mera otkrovennosti: Opyt dramaturgii Petrushevskoi," *Sovremennaia dramaturgiia,* 2 (1986): 218–228;

I. Vladimirova, "Svoi golos: Literaturnaia kritika (O rasskaze L. Petrushevskoi 'Seti i lovushki')," *Neva,* 3 (1977): 159–166;

Slobodanka Vladiv-Glover, "The Russian Anti-Oedipus: Petrushevskaya's *Three Girls in Blue,*" *Australian Slavonic and East European Studies,* 12 (1998): 31–56;

Josephine Woll, "The Minotaur in the Maze: Remarks on Liudmila Petrushevskaia," *World Literature Today,* 67 (Winter 1993): 125–130.

Evgenii Anatol'evich Popov

(5 January 1946 –   )

Robert Porter
University of Glasgow

BOOKS: *Vesel'e Rusi* (Ann Arbor, Mich.: Ardis, 1981);
Ptitsy v gorode (Leningrad: Sovetskii pisatel', 1989);
Zhdu liubvi neverolomnoi (Moscow: Sovetskii pisatel', 1989)–includes "Zhdu liubvi neverolomnoi," "Barabanshchik i ego zhena, barabanshchitsa," and "Svinye shashlychki";
Prekrasnost' zhizni: Glavy iz "romana s gazetoi," kotoryi nikogda ne budet nachat i zakonchen (Moscow: Moskovskii rabochii, 1990);
Samolet na Kel'n (Moscow: Orbita, 1991);
Nakanune nakanune (Moscow: Tekst, 1993);
Dusha patriota, ili, Razlichnye poslaniia k Ferfichkinu, with illustrations by Viacheslav Sysoev (Moscow: Tekst, 1994); translated by Robert Porter as *The Soul of a Patriot or Various Epistles to Ferfichkin* (London: Harvill, 1994);
Podlinnaia istoriia "Zelenykh muzykantov": Roman-kommentarii (Moscow: Vagrius, 1999);
Tikhokhodnaia barka "Nadezhda" (Moscow: Vagrius, 2001)–includes "Maliulen'ki";
Master Khaos (Moscow: MK-Periodika, 2002).
Editions and Collections: *Nakanune nakanune* (Moscow: Gelios, 2001);
Podlinnaia istoriia "Zelenykh muzykantov": Roman-Kommentarii (Moscow: Vagrius, 2001);
Tikhoradkaia barka "Nadezhda" (Moscow: Vagrius, 2001);
Vesel'e Rusi (St. Petersburg: Amfora, 2002).
Edition in English: *Merry-Making in Old Russia,* translated by Robert Porter (Evanston, Ill.: Northwestern University Press, 1997)–includes "I Await a Love That's True," "The Drummer and the Drummer's Wife," "Merry-Making in Old Russia," "The Reservoir," and "Pork Kebabs."

OTHER: *Metropol': Literaturnyi al'manakh,* edited by Popov, Vasilii Pavlovich Aksenov, Andrei Georgievich Bitov, Viktor Vladimirovich Erofeev, and Fazil' Abdulovich Iskander (Moscow & Ann Arbor, Mich.: Ardis, 1979);
"Oblaka," "Pivnye drozhki," "Sir'ia, Boris, Laviniia," "Vechnaia vesna," "Vo vremena moei molo-

Evgenii Anatol'evich Popov (courtesy of the author)

dosti," and "Katarsis," in *Katalog,* compiled by Filipp Berman (Ann Arbor, Mich.: Ardis, 1982);
"Sluchai s Venediktom," in Venedikt Vasil'evich Erofeev's *Moskva-Petushki: Bessmertnaia poema Venedikta Erofeeva,* edited by Eduard Vlasov (Moscow: Vagrius, 2000), pp. 5–12;
Zolotoi vek = The Golden Age: Izbrannoe, edited and compiled by Popov and Vladimir Salimon (Moscow: Manezh, 2001).

SELECTED PERIODICAL PUBLICATIONS–
UNCOLLECTED: "Dva rasskaza," *Novyi mir,* 4 (1976): 164–172;

"Rasskazy," *Novyi mir,* 10 (1987): 97–120;

"Rasskazy" and *Avtovokzal, Volga,* 10 (1988): 72–112;

Billi Bons: Povest', Vest' (1989): 111–137;

"Rasskazy," *Zerkala* (1989);

"Rasskazy," *Volga,* 3 (1990): 39–61;

"Sady Allakha," *Soglasie,* 3 (1991);

"Restoran 'Berezka': Poema i rasskazy o kommuni-
        stakh," *Znamia,* 3 (1991): 133–159;

"Kholoda (rasskazy)," *Volga,* 3 (1991): 5–24;

"Udaki: neskol'ko kratkikh istorii o k sozhaleniiu vse
        eshche vstrechaiushchikhsia v nashei zhizni vre-
        menami vsegda otdel'nykh nedostaykakh,"
        Druzhba narodov, 1 (1992): 3–27;

"A chto vse eto znachit? Proisshetsviia poslednikh let,"
        Kontinent, 74 (1993);

"Magazin 'Svet,' ili Sumerki bogov," *Druzhba narodov,* 12
        (1993);

"The Silhouette of Truth," *World Literature Today,* 67,
        no. 1 (1993): 37–39;

"Liumpeny," *Znamia,* 5 (1994);

"Loskutnoe odeialo. Rasskaz-entsiklopediia," *Kontinent,*
        83 (1995);

"Chitaiushchii pisatel'," *Znamia,* 1 (1996);

Tri pesni o perestroike s prologom, epilogom, i epigrafom,
        Oktiabr', 1 (1999): 56–73;

"Otsutvie otsutstviia," *Inostrannaia literatura,* 5 (1999);

"Triumf voli Dzheimsa Dzhoisa," *Novoe vremia,* 32
        (1999): 38–39;

"Kto-to byl, prikhodil i ushel," *Oktiabr',* 9 (2000);

"Kul'tpokhod v Kreml'," *Vestnik Evropy,* 2 (2001);

"Volga vpadaet v Kaspiiskoe more," *Voprosy literatury,* 3
        (2001);

"Pugovitsy ot novykh shtanov," *Inostrannaia literatura,*
        11 (2001).

Evgenii Anatol'evich Popov was born in Krasnoiarsk in Siberia on 5 January 1946. Popov's father,
Anatolii Evgen'evich Popov, was a professional soccer
player who later became a major in the Ministry of
Internal Affairs. His mother, Galina Aleksandrovna
(Mazurova) Popova, was a kindergarten teacher. One
of two children, Popov has a sister, Natal'ia.

Popov moved to Moscow in 1963 to study, but
his attempts to enroll in humanities courses (literature,
cinematography, and even Oriental languages) failed,
and he finally entered the Ordzhonikidze Geology and
Prospecting Institute. He graduated in 1968 and at the
time was a Muscovite in all but name. On several occasions Popov speaks of having two hometowns, Krasnoiarsk and Moscow; similarly he also had, in the
1960s and early 1970s, two professions, geology and literature. He had been publishing in a minor fashion
from the age of sixteen. Moscow in Popov's student
days was a most invigorating experience for any aspir-

ing writer, for the volatile and relative freedom of the
Nikita Sergeevich Khrushchev era (1953–1964) was
ending. The era of Leonid Il'ich Brezhnev (1964–1982)
was, to use the word of the narrator in Popov's *Dusha
patriota, ili, Razlichnye poslaniia k Ferfichkinu* (first published
in *Volga,* 1989; translated as *The Soul of a Patriot or Various
Epistles to Ferfichkin,* 1994), *slozhnyi* (complicated). The
arrest in late 1965 and trial in February 1966 of Yulii
Markovich Daniel' and Andrei Donatovich Siniavsky
for publishing their works abroad represented a return
to Stalinist ways. Yet, beginning in 1966, Mikhail
Afanas'evich Bulgakov's masterpiece *Master i Margarita*
(1966–1967; translated as *The Master and Margarita,*
1967), which by no means was dissimilar in spirit to the
phantasmagoric prose of Daniel' and Siniavsky,
appeared–though in truncated form and many years
after Bulgakov's death. All these events were taking
place against the backdrop of the "young prose" movement in Russia, at whose head stood Popov's future
comrade in arms, Vasilii Pavlovich Aksenov.

As was the practice in Soviet times, a recently
qualified geologist had little choice but to work–when
and where the state chose–as a geologist, no matter
what other professional inclinations he might have had.
In 1968 Popov returned to Siberia, where he worked as
a prospector until 1975. For young healthy men and
women such a life had its attractions: it was extremely
well paid; there were periods of leave in the big cities;
and "in the field" there was, above all, freedom. The
tough conditions of the prospecting camps and the
larger-than-life characters and events that Popov came
across in those years provided material for more than a
few stories. There were also trips back to Moscow, and
a good amount of Popov's writing plays on the contrasts between the capital and the backwoods, between
the ostensibly sophisticated intellectuals of European
Russia and the apparently simple folk of Siberia–be
they boorish, violent, simpleminded, or simple hearted.

In 1975 Popov finally moved back to Moscow,
or, rather, to the small town of Dmitrov, some sixty-
five kilometers north of the capital, where, in exchange
for his apartment in Krasnoiarsk, he obtained accommodation in a modest house, in a modest part of town,
known to the locals as "nigritianskii poselok," or
"Negro Village." He commuted to Moscow a couple of
times a week to attend to literary matters. His actual
writing debut occurred in April 1976 with the publication in *Novyi mir,* the leading literary monthly, of two
short stories–"Zhdu liubvi neverolomnoi" (collected in
book form, 1989; translated as "I Await a Love That's
True," 1997) and "Barabanshchik i ego zhena, barabanshchitsa" (1989; translated as "The Drummer and the
Drummer's Wife," 1997). The immensely popular
writer and motion-picture actor Vasilii Makarovich

2.

ОПУСТИЛИСЬ, вот что произошло, и с этой точки зрения следует
рассматривать все остальное, производное: развал экономики, кро-
вавые войны на окраинах бывшей советской империи, международное
нищенство, ~~массовую~~ эмиграцию на Запад и даже взрыв на Чернобыль-
ской АЭС, запрограмированный революцией 1917 года с ее людоедским
лозунгом " весь мир насилья мы разрущим до основань..." *идеолого*

В люмпенизации сознания - суть психологии ~~плакатного~~ *того* нового
"о котором нам талдычили прежде"
советского человека, и в этом смысле мы имеем в нашей стране лох-
мотья наций, профессий, сословий, полов, объединенных единым созна-
нием ЗОНЫ, в которой нужно не жить, а выживать. Где " вся-то наша
жизнь есть борьба", как утверждают строки ~~знаменитой~~ *советской* революционной
песни, а формы этой борьбы разнообразны, но не суть важны. Будь это
танки, посланные на улицы Праги в 1968 году,   возведение царских
дворцов для "слуг народа" или звериная потасовка в очереди у
лотка с мясом.

Люмпен-пролетариат, люмпен-крестьянство, люмпен-интеллигенция...
Вторая часть определения практически исчезла, как хвост у эволюци-
онировавшего животного, ~~и возникла странная персона СОВЕТСКОГО
ЧЕЛОВЕКА.~~

Простые люди всегда все ~~знали, знают и будут~~ *поминать* знать. Но жить -то
все-таки нужно, хотя и ценою люмпенизации, пауперизации, огрубления
и бескультурья.

Жить нужно потому, что есть женщины, старики и дети. И как бы
низко ни пали мы, в каком бы дерьме ни барахтались, но это и есть
та ПОЧВА, которая дана нам на сегодняшний день, и иной у нас нет.

Вот почему воспоминания о победоносной войне для многих не
прошлое, а тот островок реальности, которого жаждет измученное соз-
нание, не способное совладать с океанскими волнами окружающего
жизненного бреда.

Особенно для женщин. Женщины вообще лучше, чем мужчины. Ведь

Page from the revised typescript for "Transformatsiia plakata" (Transformation of the Placard),
published in 1995 (courtesy of the author)

Shukshin, himself a Siberian, wrote the preface to these stories, which were published after Shukshin's death. He accurately predicted that Popov's literary path would not be easy.

By late 1970s Popov had written possibly as many as two hundred stories, but only a tiny fraction had been published. A contract was signed with a Krasnoiarsk publishing house to bring out a collection, which was duly prepared. These events were overtaken, however, by *Metropol': Literaturnyi al'manakh* (Metropolis: A Literary Almanac, 1979), in which Popov's work was published, resulting in an appearance more explosive than his debut in *Novyi mir*. Throughout 1978, in collaboration with Aksenov, Andrei Georgievich Bitov, Viktor Vladimirovich Erofeev, and Fazil' Abdulovich Iskander, Popov compiled and edited a large anthology of works by twenty-six writers (including the editors themselves), pasted it up in an outsized single volume, and produced a print run of twelve copies. Acting in a devil-may-care fashion, the conspirators, as these writers were considered in Soviet times, planned a "launch," requesting simultaneously that the book be published officially without the usual cumbersome procedures involving delays, censorship, and untoward editorial interference. The unorthodox impudence and playfulness on display were reflected typographically in the title, which suggested that the stress should fall, erroneously, on the second syllable: *Metr-o-pol'*.

The proposed "launch" in January 1979 was thwarted by the authorities, the ringleaders were hauled in for questioning, and Popov—together with Erofeev—was expelled from the Union of Soviet Writers, or writers' union, to which he had been admitted only eight months previously. The book was promptly brought out by the publisher Ardis in the United States. The chief hatchet man was the first secretary of the Moscow Writers' Organization, Feliks Feodos'evich Kuznetsov. Later, in post-Soviet times, he tried to pass himself off as a liberal who had managed to avert worse retribution for the *metropol'tsy* (as the *Metropol'* editors were called). A furious Popov fought and won a legal battle to have Kuznetsov return an original copy of *Metropol'*, which the latter had paraded on television.

In 1981 Ardis brought out a collection of Popov's stories, *Vesel'e Rusi* (the title story of which was translated as "Merry-Making in Old Russia," 1997). In the wake of his involvement in a second unofficial anthology, *Katalog* (Catalogue, 1982), ostensibly compiled by Filipp Berman (the "frontman" for what was actually a joint effort) for publication by Ardis, Popov and others were subjected to a ten-hour-long house search in November 1981 (at the time he was living in the studio of the sculptor and writer Fedot Fedotovich Suchkov in

Moscow). All his manuscripts were seized, as were three typewriters—his own and those of his wife and his landlord. Subsequently, he became a nonperson, surviving on hackwork written under pseudonyms and avoiding contact with the foreign press but far from idle on the literary front. He was also much in the eye of literary scholars abroad.

Few could have guessed in these years just how imminent were the transformation and then collapse of the Soviet system. Brezhnev died in office in November 1982, succeeded first by Yurii Vladimirovich Andropov, who died in office in February 1984, and then by Konstantin Ustinovich Chernenko, who died in office in March 1985. Mikhail Sergeevich Gorbachev's policies of glasnost (openness) and perestroika (restructuring) made Russian literature freer than it had ever been but quickly led to economic instability, a massive rise in crime, and eventually the breakup of the Soviet Union, which formally ceased to exist in 1991. These events made a dramatic impact on millions of lives and careers, not least Popov's.

He was readmitted to the writers' union in 1988, became a founding member of the Moscow branch of the PEN Club, and was for a time its vice president. Widely published at home and abroad and free to take up several invitations to lecture or be a writer in residence, Popov led a hectic but rewarding life. By this time he was married to Svetlana Anatol'evna Vasil'eva, whom he had met in 1979 and wed in 1981. Popov and Svetlana were blessed with a son, Vasilii, in 1989.

Some of the turmoil and excitement of the late 1980s is anticipated in Popov's first novel, *Dusha patriota*, which was written in the winter of 1982 and 1983. At first sight the work appears chaotic combining anecdotes from the author's own biography and family history with impressionist snapshots of the literary world in the late Brezhnev era. Events are recounted through the words of a narrator who is avowedly unreliable, in the mode of many of the storytellers found in Mikhail Mikhailovich Zoshchenko's fiction. Yet, the whole is deftly pulled together with the death of the character— "TOT, KTO BYL" (HE WHO ONCE WAS)—clearly Brezhnev, although he is never named. At this point in the text, current affairs then cut across the narrator's mental ramblings, which parallel his geographical ramblings through the streets of Moscow. He is accompanied by poet and artist "D. A. Prigov" (named after the actual writer, Dmitrii Aleksandrovich Prigov), and together they arrive close to "the epicentre of world history"—Brezhnev's lying in state in the Hall of Columns in the House of Unions. The entire text of *Dusha patriota* is heavily laden with historical and literary allusions, this particular episode no less so: the two protagonists suggest to each other that they "remember this all their lives." The reader is obliquely reminded that Alexander Herzen (Aleksandr Ivanovich Gertsen) and Nikolai Platonovich Ogarev made a vow on the Sparrow Hills never to forget the 1825 Decembrist uprising.

The episode is also marked by a blend of banality and seriousness that punctuates the whole text. Sensing that history is on the move, the two itinerant Muscovites simultaneously feel as if they are sitting "in a Russian Soviet kitchen of a one-room apartment." Near the start of the novel is a story about the narrator's Uncle Kolia astounding the city of Vienna by preparing in its finest restaurant the most mundane of Russian dishes. At the end of the book is an account in note form of Brezhnev's funeral as seen on television. The pomp and grandeur are deflated by the casual asides of the viewers. Typographically the text "thins out," as if to underpin the hypocrisy of the ceremony—religious in all but name—before concluding with a Christmas toast to all the characters mentioned in the work (with the exception of Joseph Stalin).

The book edition of the novel (1994) was copiously illustrated by Viacheslav Sysoev with witty and irreverent cartoons, in a way building on the two deliberately useless sketch maps that Popov provided for the initial publication of *Dusha patriota* in the journal *Volga* in 1989. Prigov supplemented the text with examples of his own postmodernist verse. The aim was to "lighten" the text, which has been compared to Laurence Sterne's *The Life and Opinions of Tristram Shandy, Gentleman* (1760–1767), also known as *Tristram Shandy*. Its anarchic comedy notwithstanding, *Dusha patriota* demands of the reader much inside knowledge and arguably lacks the immediacy of many of Popov's short stories and other works.

Popov's largest work to date is *Prekrasnost' zhizni: Glavy iz "romana s gazetoi," kotoryi nikogda ne budet nachat i zakonchen* (The Splendour of Life: Chapters from a "Novel with a Newspaper" That Will Never Be Started or Finished, 1990). The title has an untranslatable pun (*roman* can mean either love affair or novel in Russian), and therein lies the clue to this ostensibly highly structured work. Each "chapter" is titled by year—starting with 1961 and running consecutively through 1985—and, as the author says in his preface, includes a text written by him (dating from the year of the title), as well as extracts from the Soviet press from that year and a text dating from the first half of the 1980s. The book reproduces the manner of the Soviet press in all its leaden rhetoric—even typographically, including block (capital) letters, italics, and bold type (exclamation marks abound), all of which contrasts with Popov's own ironic absurdist narratives. There would appear to be a never-ending duel: on the one hand there is officialese—which purports to be factual, realistic, and

objective—yet, as presented by Popov, it is anything but these things; on the other hand is Popov's seemingly pointless anecdotes and feeble-minded characters, which, to borrow a phrase from one of his articles as it appeared in English translation, offer us a "silhouette of truth." The subtitle of the work underscores the *perpetuum mobile* (perpetual motion) of the struggle, while its comedy, at times dark and mysterious and often richly ironic, testifies to the creative writer's eternal superiority. As Popov tells the reader of *Prekrasnost' zhizni* in a section titled "Vmesto epiloga" (Instead of an Epilogue): "In finishing this work the author has suddenly thought with anger why should he have started singing his head off like this when objective reality and the experience of the life he has led have taught him he should do quite the reverse." Such wry sentiments should be set against, for example, Kuznetsov's lengthy diatribe leveled at *Metropol'*, which is included in the volume.

Parody, as demonstrated particularly in *Dusha patriota,* is one of the hallmarks of Popov's prose and indeed is the basis of his third novel, *Nakanune nakanune* (On The Eve of On The Eve, 1993). Intertextuality of the kind encountered in this work was a frequent feature of literature in the glasnost era, as seen in Viacheslav Alekseevich P'etsukh's *Novaia moskovskaia filosofiia* (The New Moscow Philosophy, 1989), a reworking of Fyodor Dostoevsky's *Prestuplenie i nakazanie* (1866; translated as *Crime and Punishment*, 1886). Insanakhorov, the hero in Popov's pastiche of Ivan Sergeevich Turgenev's novel *Nakanune* (1860; translated as *On The Eve: A Tale,* 1871), is an amalgam of Andrei Dmitrievich Sakharov (the human rights activist and, to Soviets, the father of the atomic bomb) and an "Aleksandr Isaevich Solzhenitsyn-like" dissident who is in exile in the West but who returns to Russia after the collapse of Communism. Shrinking dramatically in size after a prolonged illness, Insanakhorov is transported across the border in a matchbox by his wife. This knockabout comedy, in which three drunken loutish writers—Popov, Erofeev, and Prigov—make sporadic appearances, is couched in the manner of Turgenev's decorous, nineteenth-century narrative style, while simultaneously plummeting into the vernacular and bawdy. The heroine smuggles her husband across the border in her most private part. The narrator also finds time to poke fun at postmodernist theorizing (to which Popov is not infrequently subjected, of course): "Nobody knows what postmodernism is but they all pretend that they do." Later, the reader is told that it was invented by the Komitet gosudarstvennoi bezopasnosti (KGB, State Security Committee). The serious side to the work resides in its implication that freedom of speech in Russia also means freedom for fanatics and for ineffectual romantics.

Each of Popov's major novels displays a startling formal inventiveness: the epistolary diary resulting in *Dusha patriota,* the admixture of newspaper collage and fiction that is *Prekrasnost' zhizni,* and the mock nineteenth-century narration of *Nakanune nakanune.* Popov's next novel, *Podlinnaia istoriia "Zelenykh muzykantov": Roman-kommentarii* (The True Story of "The Green Musicians": A Novel and Commentary, 1999), is no exception. Sixty pages of conventional narrative are swamped by some 250 pages of footnotes and an appendix that lists all the people mentioned in the commentary, together with apologies for any omissions and an invitation to anyone willing to include himself or herself in the list. The protagonist Ivan Ivanych is an aspiring young writer whose story about the theft of a bicycle is published in a provincial newspaper. His stated aim is that the piece may prick the conscience of the thief and the bicycle will be returned. The story, much amended, appears, and Ivan becomes obsessed with literature and is thrown out of college for failing his exams. The literary group, of which he was a member, folds, while his relationship with his girlfriend Liudmila breaks down, and the drunken journalist Vasilii Popugasov, who published him, is fired. Vasilii claims to be writing a novel called *BICH* (The Dropout), for which his dissolute lifestyle is providing the raw material. By contrast, the material that Ivan collects from his mundane job at a vegetable depot (storage facility) does not interest him, and his creative work is performed while he is lounging on the divan at home: "Vsiakaia zelenaia mut'" (All sorts of green murk) float through his mind.

The climax of the narrative occurs when the hero, in a drug-induced dream, is introduced by a "Golos" (Voice) to a scene in which Soviet writers are balancing and dancing on threads and wires–the higher they get, the safer they are. This spectacle contrasts with those of all of Ivan's relatives and acquaintances, along with Leo Tolstoy, Dostoevsky, Nikolai Vasil'evich Gogol, and other great classic Russian writers–in short, the "Narod" (People)–in a dim dark place, and elsewhere the "ZELENYE MUZYKANTY" (GREEN MUSICIANS) writhing around in slime, with no one helping them. The Voice tells Ivan that the green musicians must climb out by themselves, just as Tolstoy and Dostoevsky did. Ivan wakes up, resumes his studies, starts a family with Liudmila, and eventually becomes a highly successful factory manager. He enjoys reading and talking about literature but forgets about the green musicians. The drunken journalist mends his ways, provides the author with the narrative just read, and posits to him the notion that Ivan missed a rare oppor-

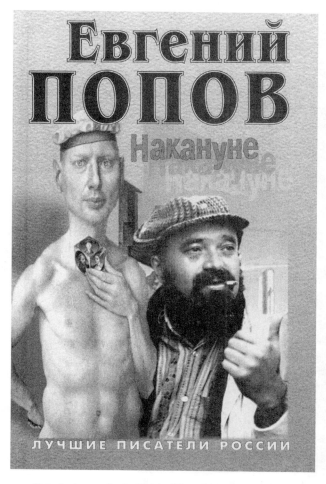

Paperback cover for the 2001 edition of Popov's Nakanune nakanune (On the Eve of on the Eve), a comic novel in which he and writers Viktor Vladimirovich Erofeev and Dmitrii Aleksandrovich Prigov make periodic appearances (Collection of Mark Lipovetsky)

tunity, that possibly "at the back of all this there was a tragedy that might have shaken the world."

As with *Dusha patriota, Podlinnaia istoriia "Zelenye muzykanty"* displays much incidental factual information: Popov writes his novel in Berlin in the villa of Otto Grotewohl, the former president of the German Democratic Republic, throughout the summer of 1997, and the title dates from an unpublished work of 1974; Popov was once seriously ill with jaundice, after receiving at work an injection with a dirty needle; as a geologist he was supplied with maps that, for security reasons, were doctored on a "need-to-know" basis; Popov tells the reader that he deeply loves Svetlana, his third wife, and admires her writing; the *Metropol'* affair is aired several times; and his relationships with various literary figures ranged from close friends (Aksenov, Erofeev, and Prigov) to enemies, scoundrels, and hacks. There are also anecdotes, bawdy ditties, and fanciful asides. The word *odnako* (however) is footnoted at some length and is defined as "a buffer between civilization and the harsh surrounding reality." There are light-hearted references to postmodernism, the "new Russians," and mention is made of the war in Chechnia.

In addition, the commentary to the novel tells the reader that James Joyce's *Ulysses* (1922) can be considered an *uchebnik zhizni* (textbook of life) for those who are striving to live *razumno* (sensibly) and that Dedalus and Bloom are engaged in a *permanentnyi uvazhitel'nyi dialog* (permanent, respectful dialogue) no less than Chapaev and Pet'ka (the subjects of countless anti-Soviet jokes concerning the Russian Civil War). In the commentary rock music and jokes stand in defiance of totalitarianism. There are also fragments from an unfinished work by Popov called "Mina" (The Land Mine) in the commentary. *Podlinnaia istoriia "Zelenykh muzykantov,"* which can be read from cover to cover episodically, or by skipping to the "appropriate" annotation and back again, provides an authentic notion of the modern world, which the most gifted and honest of Ivan Ivanyches (that is, mediocre writers) could never hope to match. Nikolai Klimontovich called the melody that the book emits a Russian synonym for "the unbearable lightness of being."

Popov's latest novel, *Master Khaos* (Master Chaos, 2002), opens with the hero temporarily losing his passport. His consequent statelessness causes him to launch into reflections on various countries of Europe (their recent history and culture), and the whole mosaic is neatly pulled together at the end with the appearance of a specialist in complex systems.

Popov established his reputation among discerning readers initially through his short stories, ensuring only minimal publication under the Communist regime. In interviews and in *Podlinnaia istoriia "Zelenykh muzykantov"* he recounts how one well-meaning editor suggested that she could get his work into print if he relocated his narratives in America. Certainly, the seamy side of Russian life (immoderate drinking, criminality, promiscuity, poverty, ignorance, corruption, and incompetence in officialdom) is paraded in much of Popov's fiction. He says in *Podlinnaia istoriia "Zelenykh muzykantov"* that "drop-outs" (or "unemployed alcoholics"—known as *bichi,* a term generally thought to derive from "byvshii intelligentnyi chelovek" [a former *intelligent*]) were his Arina Rodionovna (Pushkin's story-telling nurse-muse). Mere social protest, however, is quite the least of Popov's preoccupations. Rather, his short stories owe much to the modernist and absurdist experiments of the 1920s, found notably in the works of Daniil' Ivanovich Kharms and Zoshchenko. Characters

behave irrationally, thinking and talking nonsense of varying degrees; the "endings" of these works, if they can be said to have endings, which is not always the case, are unsettling. All this was completely at variance with the tenets of socialist realism, whereby under the Communist regime writers were required to educate readers in the spirit of socialism and display some faith in the crude and materialist rationality of mankind and in historical determinism.

Parody and inversion are two of the distinguishing features of Popov's prose. The stories set in Siberia can frequently be read as a counterweight to the officially tolerated village prose, in its heyday in the 1960s and 1970s. Several such writers, many of them Siberians like Popov, portrayed rural life as tough; but their heroes and heroines were flesh-and-blood characters; stoic loyal citizens; and, finally, patriots—despite the drunkenness and ignorance that beset them. The villains of village prose—the wastrels and thieves—take center stage in Popov's fiction, and any authorial moralizing is heavily laced with irony. The grandeur and natural resources of Siberia, in Popov's narratives, are reduced to banality.

The mock-heroic tone of his stories is echoed in intricately wrought, extended sentences, where several participles and subordinate clauses house demotic epithets and convey images of human crassness and triviality. Block capitals and other typographical devices are deployed to parody Soviet rhetoric, while listing and itemizing are commonplace. Several of the short stories are deliberate inversions of the traditional fairy tale, beginning with phrases such as "Once upon a time . . ." and showing events that happen in threes. Yet, in Popov's approach, a Little Red Riding Hood type is likely to end up trapped in a marriage to a wolf who has moved in with her and her grandmother.

Throughout Popov's prose one finds the same minor characters and locations recurring, creating an impression of familiarity and even inevitability, rather than adventure and heroism. For example, a character known as Fetisov features as a hack writer or minor white-collar worker in the short stories. In playing to this alter ego Popov is doing no more than many other serious writers of his generation and insisting on his own autonomy, celebrating his freedom to write and create according to his own instincts. Fetisov's literary offerings are deliciously inept.

Which of Popov's many stories will emerge as "classics" of his canon is too early to say, but several works have been anthologized and translated often enough to give some indication. "Vodoem" (translated as "The Reservoir," 1996) first appeared in *Metropol'* in 1979. At a provincial holiday resort a visiting gay couple comes to the attention of the ultraorthodox residents—the local girls adorn one of the pair with a bra and some makeup. The couple quarrel and are drowned in the reservoir, only to return at midnight as skeletons copulating on the raft from which they fell. The extremely conservative Colonel Zhestakanov, a war hero who tried to save them so that they could stand trial, is consequently driven to seek psychiatric treatment, while the other residents, all likewise seeing the skeletons, eventually move away. Homosexuality was illegal in the Soviet Union and was almost never mentioned officially, except in clinical terms. At least one subtext of the story might be that while the fantastic in Russian literature has enjoyed such a strong tradition, albeit emasculated in Soviet times, the perfectly real, though socially and legally unacceptable, has not.

"Svinye shashlychki" (1989; translated as "Pork Kebabs," 1996) can be read as one of the best paradigms of a Russian age-old predicament—namely, whether to live peaceably with a comfortable falsehood or face reality and all the disaffection that falsehood might bring. In this story a restaurant runs well and the customers are happy until they find out that the proprietor has been serving dog meat, not pork. After his arrest and the reopening of the establishment, where smaller and tasteless portions are served, the customers argue as to which situation is better, until a pop song diverts their attention. The narrator is similarly distracted; he promises the reader another story—this time about a man who fell into a vat of beer. Significantly, "Svinye shashlychki" ends in the summer of 1967, the fiftieth anniversary of the Russian Revolution, but Popov's text suggests an altogether different set of priorities.

In his narratives Popov rarely resorts to the blatantly fantastic (as "Vodoem" does), preferring to "explain" improbable or impossible events in terms of dreams, intoxication, or hallucinations and by relying on eccentrics and yarn spinners. Yet, the macabre and violent are seldom far away, as in "Maliulen'ki" (Little 'Uns, 2001), in which the reader hears of a Siberian woman offering a good home to a neighbor's pet dog and an hour later its hide is drying out on a rope, fresh blood dripping from it. Popov admires the capacity of the everyday to provide horror, wonder, entertainment, and personal freedom, while he has nothing but disdain for the officially sanctioned myths and fantastic promises that politicians peddle.

Tikhokhodnaia barka "Nadezhda" (The Slow Wooden Barge "Nadezhda," 2001), includes more than twenty stories hitherto unpublished or, in some cases, published only in the United States, when Popov was proscribed at home. On the surface, none of them owes much in particular to the post-Soviet era, and they achieve a degree of universality. The fantastic element is glimpsed in "Polet" (Flight), in which the narrator

Front cover for the 2002 edition of Popov's Vesel'e Rusi *(Merry-Making in Old Russia), one of his best-received works (courtesy of the author)*

falls off the balcony of a high-rise while hanging out his washing and is able to detail what he sees at each floor during his descent; he lands safely in a heap of fiberglass insulation material. In "Naschet dvoinikov" (Talking of Doubles) one character claims to have seen three of his doubles: two on television at Wembley Stadium in 1966 (one was Queen Victoria and the other a hooligan), while the third, an Egyptian scribe, was in a book about the ancient world. There is a GEN Club for tracing doubles, which insists to the hero that his double is Jesus Christ, since all people are the children of Abraham.

In the last fifteen years, Evgenii Anatol'evich Popov has established himself as one of the foremost writers of Russia. In addition to his fiction, he has published, though has not performed, several plays. The writer Veniamin Aleksandrovich Kaverin was apparently convinced that Venedikt Vasil'evich Erofeev's masterpiece, *Moskva-Petushki* (1977; translated as *Moscow to the End of the Line,* 1980), was in fact written by Popov; thus, that he has written the preface to the new, extensively annotated edition of this novel is doubly appropriate. Popov is a frequent guest at literary events at home and abroad. His irreverence and probity make for a healthy and stabilizing voice in Russia today.

Interviews:

Evgenii Shklovsky, "Chelovek nikogda ne byvaet schastliv," *Druzhba narodov,* 6 (1998);

Shklovsky, "My plyvem na rezinovoi lodke po gornoi rechke," *Trud,* 14 February 1998;

"Evgeny Popov," in *Voices of Russian Literature: Interviews with Ten Contemporary Writers,* edited by Sally Laird (Oxford: Oxford University Press, 1999), pp. 118–142.

Biography:

Viacheslav Kuritsyn, "Popov Evgenii Anatol'evich," *Russkie pisateli 20 veka. Biograficheskii slovar',* edited by Petr Alekseevich Nikolaev (Moscow: Bol'shaia Rossiiskaia Entsiklopediia, 2000), pp. 567–568.

References:

Sergei Borovikov, "Evg. Popov bez i dr.," *Druzhba narodov,* 12 (1991): 231–240;

Borovikov, "Evg. Popov kak natsional'nyi pisatel'," *Volga,* 2 (2000): 135–136;

K. Engel', "Rossiia mezhdu raem i adom: Roman Evgeniia *Popova Nakanune nakanune,*" *Russian Literature,* 49 (2001): 129–142;

A. Kasymov, "Shchiglia: Evgenii Popov: Desiat' let tomu vpered," *Znamia,* 7 (2000): 200–205;

Nikolai Klimontovich, "O 'Zelenykh muzykantakh' i spelom avtore," *Russkii telegraf,* 24, no. 8 (1998);

A. Kolobrodov, "Evgenii Popov: "Podlinnaia istoria 'Zelenykh muzykantov'," *Volga,* 9 (1998): 133–135;

Mark Lipovetsky, *Russian Postmodernist Fiction: Dialogue with Chaos* (Armonk, N.Y.: M. E. Sharpe, 1999), pp. 184–197;

Andrei Nemzer, "Zlye velikany ushli," *Vremia MN,* 24, no. 7 (1998);

Robert Porter, *Russia's Alternative Prose* (Oxford: Berg, 1994), pp. 88–137;

Anthony Vanchu, "Cross(-Dressing) One's Way to Crisis: Yevgeny Popov and Lyudmila Petrushevskaya and The Crisis of Category in Contemporary Russian Culture," *World Literature Today,* 67, no. 1 (Winter 1993): 107–118;

Anatoly Vishevsky, "Creating a Shattered World: Towards the Poetics of Evgeny Popov," *World Literature Today,* 67, no. 1 (Winter 1993): 119–125;

Vishevsky, "O poeticheskom mire Evgeniia Popova," *Russian Language Journal,* 45, nos. 151–152: 185–225;

Mikhail Zolotonosov, "888 kommentariev k Ivanu Ivanovichu: Politicheskii roman Evg. Popova kak simptom literaturnogo protsessa," *Moskovskie novosti,* 35 (1998): 22.

Dmitrii Aleksandrovich Prigov

(5 November 1940 –)

Evgeny Dobrenko
University of Nottingham

(Translated by Seth Graham)

BOOKS: *Stikhogrammy: Graficheskie stikhi* (Paris: A-Ia, 1980);

Slezy geral'dicheskoi dushi (Moscow: Moskovskii rabochii, 1980);

Piat'desiat kapelek krovi (Moscow: Tekst, 1993);

Zapredel'nye liubovniki: Stikhi (Moscow: Argo-Risk, 1994);

Iavlenie stikha posle ego smerti: Stikhi (Moscow: Tekst, 1995);

Sobstvennye perepevy na chuzhie rifmy (Moscow: Muzei Vadima Sidura, 1996);

Sbornik preduvedomlenii k raznoobraznym veshcham (Moscow: Ad Marginem, 1996);

Militsaner i drugie (Moscow: Obscuri Viri, 1996);

Sovetskie teksty 1979–1984 (St. Petersburg: Ivan Limbakh, 1997);

Podobrannyi Prigov (Moscow: RGGU, 1997);

Napisannoe s 1975 po 1989 (Moscow: Novoe literaturnoe obozrenie, 1997);

Napisannoe s 1990 po 1994 (Moscow: Novoe literaturnoe obozrenie, 1997);

"Evgenii Onegin" Pushkina (St. Petersburg: Krasnyi matros, 1998);

Zhivite v Moskve: Rukopis' na pravakh romana (Moscow: Novoe literaturnoe obozrenie, 2000);

Ischisleniia i ustanovleniia: Stratifikatsionnye i konvertatsionnye teksty (Moscow: Novoe literaturnoe obozrenie, 2001);

Tol'ko moia Iaponiia: Nepridumannoe (Moscow: Novoe literaturnoe obozrenie, 2001);

Ditia i smert' (Moscow: Logos, 2002).

Collections: *Sobranie stikhov,* 2 volumes, Wiener Slawistisher Almanach, no. 42 (Vienna: Gesellschaft zur Förderung slawistischer Studien, 1996, 1997);

Izbrannye proizvedeniia (Moscow: ZebraE/EKSMO, 2003).

Edition in English: *Texts of Our Life,* selected, with an introduction, by Valentina Polukhina (Keele, U.K.: Essays in Poetics, 1995).

OTHER: "Moskva i moskvichi," in *Molodaia poeziia 89. Stikhi. Stat'i. Teksty,* compiled by Arkadii Vasil'evich Tiurin and Sergei Migranovich Mnatsakanian (Moscow: Sovetskii pisatel', 1989);

"Poems, Moscow Conceptualism," in *Novostroika=New Structures,* edited by Martin Walker (London: Institute of Contemporary Arts, 1989);

"Stikhi," in *Ponedel'nik. Sbornik stikhov,* compiled by Prigov (Moscow: Prometei, 1990);

"Come In If You Can," in *Re-entering the Sign: Articulating New Russian Culture,* edited by Ellen Berry and Anesa Miller-Pogacar (Ann Arbor: University of Michigan Press, 1995);

"Stikhi, Zvezda plenitel'naia russkoi poezii, Evgenii Onegiin Pushkina," in *Shinel' Pushkina: Sbornik k 200-letnemu iubileiu Pushkina,* edited by Mikhail Berg (Moscow: Pentagraphic, 2000).

SELECTED PERIODICAL PUBLICATIONS—UNCOLLECTED: "Gde nashi ruki, v kotorykh nakhoditsia ashe budushchee?" *Vestnik novoi literatury,* 2 (1990);

"Apofeoz militsanera," *Druzhba narodov,* 4 (1990);

"Chto russkomu zdorovo—to emu i smert'," *Kol'tso A* (1993–1994);

"Integral drozhashchii," *Voprosy literatury,* 4 (1994);

"Kniga o schast'e," *Znamia,* 4 (1994);

"Manifesty," *Wiener Slawistischer Almanach,* no. 34 (1994).

Dmitrii Prigov is a poet, prose writer, and artist who works in graphic, installation, and performance media. He is one of the leading representatives of Moscow conceptualism and is also associated with sots-art, a

Dmitrii Aleksandrovich Prigov (photograph © Eberhard Schorr)

movement that developed in the U.S.S.R. and the West in the 1970s and 1980s. Other practitioners of sots-art include the poets Lev Semenovich Rubinshtein, Timur Iur'evich Kibirov, and Igor' Moiseevich Irten'ev; the prose writers Vladimir Georgievich Sorokin and Evgenii Anatol'evich Popov; and the painters Eric Vladimirovich Bulatov, Vitalii Anatol'evich Komar, Aleksandr Danilovich Melamid, Il'ia Iosifovich Kabakov, Aleksandr Kosolapov, and Grisha Bruskin.

Prigov was born on 5 November 1940 in Moscow, where he also grew up. His father was an engineer and his mother a pianist. In 1966 he graduated with a major in sculpture from the Industrial Art Institute (formerly the Stroganov Academy) and subsequently worked in the Central Architectural Administration. He became a member of the Soviet Artists' Union in 1975 and joined the Union of Russian Writers and the Russian PEN Club in 1991. He was awarded the Pushkin Prize in 1993.

Until 1988 Prigov's works were published underground in the U.S.S.R. (as samizdat) and in the West (as *tamizdat,* a variation of samizdat that emphasizes publication "there" [*tam*]—away from, or out of, the U.S.S.R.). His poems have been translated into English, French, German, Italian, Finnish, and Swedish. During perestroika he began to publish his verse openly in major Soviet literary journals such as *Novyi mir* (New World), *Iunost'* (Youth), *Druzhba narodov* (The People's Friendship), *Rodnik* (The Creek), *Ogonek* (The Flame), and *Volga*. Since 1987 he has participated in artistic exhibitions in Russia, England, Germany, Holland, Italy, France, Sweden, and the United States.

The majority of Prigov's texts, which total more than twenty thousand, are parts of cycles such as "Scenes from Private and Public Life," "The Fifth Thousand," "Representatives of Beauty in Russian History and Culture," "Verses for Every Day," "A Proposal," "Terrorism with a Human Face," "Opisanie ob"ektov" (Description of Objects), "Cockroachomachy," "40 Banal Arguments on Banal Topics," "Obituaries," "Apofeoz militsanera" (Apotheosis of a Militiaman, 1990), "Moscow and the Muscovites," "Play and Ranks," "Tears of the Heraldic Soul," "Slogans," "Complete and Decisive Victory," "The Image of Reagan in Russian Literature," "My Russia," "Where They Tore off Mishka's Paw," and "A Hard Childhood." These cycles are the most representative examples of Moscow conceptualism.

Prigov's poetry is also the most representative expression of the aesthetics and poetics of literary sots-art, the Russo-Soviet variety of conceptualism. Sots-art was perceived by late Soviet culture as a strategy for destroying the Soviet myth, and it turned out to be the last style to be completely formed in Russian literature after socialist realism. The fundamental purpose of the socialist-realist aesthetic—the coinciding of "life and the ideal"—was the starting point of sots-art and not merely an object of citation but also of endless transformations. Sots-art mimesis is practically indistinguishable from that of socialist realism: a similar "reflective" mechanism operates in both cases. In the socialist-realist aesthetic, however, the object of reflection is recognized as a particular reality constructed according to a politico-aesthetic template, while in sots-art that reality is the socialist-realist text itself. In its work with Soviet quotations (of various levels, from the textual to the mental) sots-art presupposes a reality and an "identifiability" of ideological contexts to which those citations must refer. The author (and beyond him the reader and the spectator) who works with ideological signs encounters a basic problem: he or she can take from the past only a skeleton of meaning that is almost completely picked clean of the flesh of social meanings. The author's task, however, entails precisely the reconstruction of those meanings and the reanimation of overtones within the ideological sign—overtones of which the consumers of the ideology were often unconscious.

In this context one might better understand, for example, the genre of the *azbuka* (alphabet or ABCs), which Prigov created in the 1970s (since that time he has composed eighty-six "ABCs"). An alphabet is not merely a form but also a form of a form—a kind of quasi form, or a micromodel, of the sots-art inventory of the Soviet world. An alphabet is itself an inventory of language signs. For this reason it is a convenient form for Prigov to fit into the hollow cells of the Soviet "fundamental lexicon" (as a celebrated painting by fellow conceptualist Grisha Bruskin was titled). Prigov, like his sots-art colleagues, constantly says that his artistic task is to "escape the imprisonment of language": "the artist's mission is freedom, the image of freedom, a thematicized freedom," "an articulated freedom."

> Art's main task, its purpose in this world, is to display a certain freedom, with all its dangers. . . . I took the Soviet language as the most functional, obvious and accessible language at the time; it represented the ideology and passed itself off as absolute truth descended from the heavens. A person was crushed by this language not from without, but within himself. Any ideology that aspires to own you completely, any language, has a totalitarian ambition to capture the entire world, cover it with its own terminology, and show that it is the absolute truth. I wanted to show what freedom is. Language is just language, not absolute truth, and once we understand that, we achieve freedom.

Roland Barthes claimed that language is a symbol of the coercive activity of power and that literature effects a breach toward "anarchy." In this situation, suggests Barthes, "there is nothing left except to joke with language, to make a fool of the language. This saving knavery, this slyness, this brilliant deception that allows the sound of the disempowered language to be heard in all the majesty of the incarnated parchment of the revolutionary word, I for my part call 'Literature.'" Prigov, in turn, suggests that "the exposure, deconstruction and objectification of contemporary art's inner pathos and aspirations towards being a quasi-religion" are a "second secularization." He defines postmodernism as "a frozen, dependent time" and sees its features in eclecticism, quotation, and an absence of a preferable axiology, positions and language that result from the removal of dramaturgy, from "dramaturgilessness." According to Prigov, "The unthinkable population of the surrounding space by verbal texts" forces one to view the world as nature is viewed—"that is, as the source from which the artist can and must derive material for his works."

Prigov argues that the main pathos of artistic activity is the uncovering of "the dramaturgy of the mutual relationship between the object and the language of description." In connection with this Prigov considers himself a "passive observer of the logoses of language," of archetypes for thought, myths, languages, and a "scenographer and registrar," and he considers his texts merely "materialized imagistic gestures." Working with quotation has its own logic: by "remythologizing" the Soviet social consciousness and constantly "quoting" Soviet linguistic and mental clichés, Prigov and sots-art in general present Soviet ideological signs in an exaggeratedly lifeless form. The worn-out quality of Soviet ideological clichés, however, is relative. In and of itself that kind of quotation is not dead because the process of its wearing out lasted seven decades; but at the same time these clichés are worn out precisely because they were imprinted on the Soviet consciousness too deeply (and, not insignificantly, via the traumatic experiences of Soviet history). Consequently, sots-art does work with stylistically worn (and in this sense lifeless) but historically living sociocultural codes.

The aesthetics of sots-art in general—and of Prigov in particular—is the creation of a particular kind of mirror in which the socialist-realist text is inverted. Here, a more complicated artistic task than the simple "discovery of a second reality" under the socialist-realist text is fulfilled. That is, the conflict—the catastrophic incongruity—between style and events is laid bare. Quotation is where the "defamiliarizing" of socialist realism takes place. For socialist realism, with its aspirations toward being a "reflection of the truth of life" and in the "forms of life itself," this means total destruction.

The aesthetic model that Prigov employs in creating "Soviet texts" is best illustrated by his cycle "Opisanie ob"ektov." It consists of nine texts that accurately describe an array of objects, giving them a "portrait-like recognizability," with the intent of "demystifying" them. Each object–egg, cross, pillow, pole, scythe, wheel, monkey, woman, and hammer and sickle–is described using the same expressions: each of them "is among the most common objects in man's everyday social and professional experience"; each has "a size ranging from 20 mm to endlessly long"; each has some sort of "everyday utility" (a scythe is used "for reaping, cutting, sharpening, fighting, popular war, etc.," while a monkey can be used "as a zoo exhibit, for scientific research, for name-calling, etc."); and the "historical origin" of each is associated with something that is "absolutely incorrect from the Marxist point of view." Each object is "practically irreproducible. For the reasons stated above the real existence of the object is considered improbable."

In his cycle "V pomoshch' izushchaiushchim russkuiu literaturu" (To Help Those Studying Russian Literature), Prigov describes literature itself in a similar way, using a wide spectrum of Soviet discourse about literature–from school compositions to scholarly works. The "objects" described are Aleksandr Sergeevich Pushkin, Mikhail Iur'evich Lermontov, Nikolai Alekseevich Nekrasov, Maksim Gor'ky, Vladimir Vladimirovich Mayakovsky, Nikolai Alekseevich Ostrovsky, and Mikhail Aleksandrovich Sholokhov. The means of description are the same even here: the "life and works," "creation of the novel," and "blossoming of talent" coincide with either a "striking, difficult" or "dark, tragic" "period of Russian history." Similarly, Prigov inserts phrases such as "These were the years" "of cruel reactionism and the police state," "revolutionary struggle," and "when the last thunderous volleys of the Civil War had only just faded."

A particular aspect of the poetic world created by Prigov is an emphasis on the creation not so much of a text but of an "image of the poet." In this departure from the "literary raw" into the "literary environment," the avant-garde impulse is apparent. The image of the Soviet graphomaniacal poet–created by Prigov–and the "production of texts," resulting from the effort to encompass every socialist-realist genre, motif, image, stylistic move, and cliché of Soviet speech and thought, grow out of a constant appeal to the "artistic output" of socialist realism in both qualitative and quantitative dimensions.

Prigov rarely appeals directly to socialist-realist texts, since what is constructed is not so much a simulacrum of the text as of its author–the poet, the life

teacher–who is close to the people and shares their interests, opinions, values, and tastes; he is thus able to embody a higher spiritual authority for them. Fulfilling the requirements of the socialist-realist aesthetic, however, Prigov reproduces "Soviet ideology" in the same way that it was assimilated by, and existed in, the mass consciousness rather than in correspondence with the official ideological code. This reproduction is the source of the tautological nature of his texts: Soviet reality is reproduced in full correspondence with the "proper speech" of socialist realism. The second reality is completely "removed." The resulting effect is a complete absence of reality.

The repetition of rhetorical figures from the "fundamental lexicon" of Soviet culture is a dissection of their internal tautology. This is easily detected in Prigov's poetic devices, the most characteristic of which is the rhyming of identical words ("people," for example, is rhymed with "people"). As a result of this device, the meaning of an utterance is reduced to the duplication of the initial premise, a duplication that is abundantly emphasized:

> Narod on delitsia na nenarod
> I na narod v bukval'nom smysle
> Kto ne narod – ne to chtoby urod
> No on – ubliudok v vysshem smysle
> A kto narod – ne to chtoby narod
> No on naroda vyrazhen'e
> Chto ne ukazhesh' tochno – vot narod
> No skazhesh' tochno: est' narod!

> (The people he divides into non-people
> And people in the literal sense
> Whoever is not people is not exactly a deformed person
> But he is a mongrel in the highest sense
> And who is the people is not exactly the people
> But an expression of the people
> Which you cannot point to exactly–there is the people
> But you will say exactly: there exists a people!)

The tautological nature and fundamental ambiguity are included not only in the author's position but also in the position of the recipient: the Soviet mass consciousness, made profane by sots-art, exhibits an absolute emptiness. This emptiness is the result of the reflection or, more precisely, the doubling of official Soviet discourse, in which, instead of a multiplication of meaning, there is an actual void of meaning. In part, the emptiness is connected to the precise nature of official organs of discourse, with their unambiguous correctness and proscription of multiple readings. Prigov's text, however, dissects the hidden functionality of official discourse: official meanings themselves are predisposed to reflection–that is, doomed to tautology in the process of mass consumption:

Urozhai povysilsia
Budet bol'she khleba
Budet bol'she vremeni
Rassuzhdat' pro nebo
Bol'she budet vremeni
Rassuzhdat' pro nebo
Urozhai ponizitsia
Men'she stanet khleba

(The harvest yield has increased
There will be more bread
There will be more time
To discuss the sky
More time will there be
To discuss the sky
The harvest yield will decrease
There will be less bread.)

Pust' vse umrut, kak ia zastavil
Tak pobediat segodnia russkie
Ved' neplokhie parni russkie
Oni stradali mnogo, russkie
Terpeli uzhasy nerusskie
Tak pobediat segodnia russkie

(Let everything be as I have conceived it
Let everyone live as I have compelled them
Let everyone die as I have compelled them
This time the Russians will be victorious
The not-so-bad Russian fellow
And the not-so-bad Russian wenches
They suffered greatly, the Russians
Endured horrors that were un-Russian
Thus today the Russians will be victorious.)

The function of power is constantly to demonstrate its immutable abundance. Like any abundance it is always empty inside, tautological. Prigov essentially only reproduces its logic. Like sots-art in general, he perceives and re-creates the Soviet world as an enormous construct made of words. The desacralization (removal of sacred traits) of ideology is possible via the desacralization of style. The aestheticization of the Soviet social consciousness—of the world of Soviet "visual agitation, of mass media, of ideological speech, of the aesthetic of the poster and the slogan, of mass propaganda literature, and of 'isoproduction'"—is, in Boris Efimovich Groys's definition, a process by which its worn-out quality is overcome. Sots-art perceives this worn-out quality as a central aesthetic value and applies to it a strategy not of substitution or "vivification" (as in the traditional social novel) but of cultivation. This is the definition of the aesthetics of quotation. The text becomes transparent: it is woven only in order to make visible the ideologemes, myths, literary clichés, and propagandistic matrices that lie behind it. Sots-art "remythologizes" reality and, consequently, "demythologizes" it. In this respect the sots-art quasi myth is fundamentally different from traditional myths.

Prigov's remythologizing strategy is reduced to the "completion" of myth, but the process itself of "myth-creation" exposes the demythologizing emphasis of sots-art, which leads to the destruction of the artificially created epic timelessness of myth. Prigov completely "lays bare the device" in the long poem "Kulikovo," in which the author presents himself in the form of a demiurge and history (in this case the battle of Kulikovo of 1380 between the Mongols [Tartars] and the Russians, led by Prince Dmitrii) in the form of theater:

Pust' budet vse, kak ia predstavil
Pust' vse zhivut, kak ia zastavil

The author unexpectedly changes his mind: "But nevertheless the Tartars are nicer / And their names are nicer / And their voices are nicer / And their habits are nicer / Although the Russians are even nicer / But nevertheless the Tartars are more nice." A solution then arises—"So let the Tartars be victorious / This way everything will be visible to me / So the Tartars will be victorious"—after which comes the final line, "But anyway tomorrow we'll see."

Here the author constructs not an exposition of the coming battle so much as an exposition of himself. The bared "myth-creation" is already demythologized. The myth is destroyed for several reasons: first, it suddenly acquires a sort of demiurge in the person of the author (myth in principle cannot be authored; the personification of myth is the act of its destruction); second, myth cannot withstand variability (as seen in the lines "Thus today the Russians will be victorious"; "So the Tartars will be victorious"; and "But anyway tomorrow we'll see"); third, myth does not have a history (the disclosure of the genealogy of a myth is by definition a demythologization). What occurs here is precisely a history of how one (some author) moves aside the set decorations of myth, an exposure of the "kitchen" of myth-creation, or the demystification of the primary mystery of myth—its birth.

The process of "completing construction" on a myth turns out to be its destruction every time: a myth cannot be "completed"; it is by definition absolute and finished (unfinished, myths do not exist). For this reason, when Prigov constructs his texts (such as his cycle of verses about the Militiaman, "Apofeoz militsanera") as a means for completing construction on myth, he does not complete the edifice but rather imposes on it constructs (at first glance unworthy and completely unnecessary ones) that invariably doom it to collapse.

The solution to this task is accomplished by erasing the boundaries between the personal and role-playing and the conclusive transformation of social roles into the per-

Prigov at the Andy Warhol Museum in Pittsburgh, May 2002 (photograph by Mark Lipovetsky)

sonal. As a result, the author of a socialist-realist text (power, state) becomes its distinctive "lyrical hero." In the cycle about the Militiaman the experiment achieves maximum purity, which makes the cycle one of Prigov's most popular.

In "Apofeoz militsanera" the reader can detect the state of the subconscious. That the Militiaman sleeps on the subway, for example, is not important. The passengers know that "something in him is invisibly awake, the Militiaman in him." This "something" is an emanation of the state, of power. It is what stands at the "post" in the person of the Militiaman:

Kogda zdes' na postu stoit Militsaner
Emu do Vnukovo prostor ves' otkryvaetsia
Na Zapad i na Vostok gliadit Militsaner
I pustota za nimi otkryvaetsia

I tsentr, gde stoit Militsaner –
Vzgliad na nego otvsiudu otkryvaetsia
Otvsiudu viden Militsaner
S Vostoka viden Militsaner
I s Iuga viden Militsaner
I s moria viden Militsaner
I s neba viden Militsaner
I s-pod zemli . . .
Da on i ne skryvaetsia.

(When the Militiaman is standing here at his post
The whole space up to Vnukovo opens up before him
To the West and the East looks the Militiaman
And emptiness opens up beyond them
And the center, where the Militiaman is standing—
The view onto it opens up from here
The Militiaman is seen from everywhere
The Militiaman is seen from the East
And the Militiaman is seen from the South

And the Militiaman is seen from the sea
And the Militiaman is seen from the sky
And the Militiaman is seen from underground . . .
Not that he's hiding.)

"The center, where the Militiaman is standing" is the center of the space of total observation created by the authorities, a space in which "He rises as a visible example / Of the State system." The criminal, the enemy, and the terrorist are the people who must hide. If, for example, a terrorist threatens the Militiaman's life, the threat is merely empty: the Militiaman cannot be killed. He is not so much a person as a living hypostasis of the State. "Metaphysical dimension" in Prigov's presentation of the Militiaman refers to the laws of State, which are certainly more significant than "the secret laws of the universe." These metaphysics saturate every action of the Militiaman (authority), even the questioning of suspects: "Est' metafizika v doprose . . ." (There is a metaphysics in interrogation . . .). To be "in the law" means to connect earth and heaven. In addition, if, for example, the Militiaman communicates over his police radio, he is certainly communicating with God himself. The conversation between the Militiaman and the Heavenly Power, pictured in one of Prigov's poems, is also a conversation between two lawmakers—the State and Heaven. Moreover, in Prigov's world the "Heavenly Power" (which "communicates" with Stalin frequently) sees the Militiaman not just as an equal but even with a kind of wariness.

When the Militiaman addresses people, he speaks not "in the name of," not as a middleman, but with full recognition of the authority entrusted to him by the Heavenly Power—the State. The State, in the person of the Militiaman, "is full of love and fulfillment of duty," and for that reason whatever may happen in "this" (everyday) life is only a manifestation of private (not metaphysical) chaos. Somehow "the plumber will ruin the toilet, the gasman will ruin the gas, the electrician the electricity, the fireman will start a fire, and the messenger will do something mean," but "pridet Militsaner, skazhet im: ne balovatsia!" (The Militiaman will come, he will say to them: don't play pranks!).

Prigov purposely removes the "cultured" and refined quality of Soviet mythology. That mythology is perceived through the prism of his "lyrical hero"—the State as something completely, organically natural. For this reason the Militiaman, no matter where he is or what he does—"strolling in the park," "standing at his post," "sleeping in the subway," or drinking beer in the "House of Writers cafeteria"—is the omnipresent State, the major "lyrical hero" of Prigov's epic. The hero's main intention is to establish spaces of surveillance, control, and normalization. Everything that ends up

inside that power field is full of harmony and consequently devoid of ambiguity. Everything that violates this principle, that does not enter the space of control and surveillance, and that is spontaneous is subject to change, replacement, or destruction.

The main task—articulating the Soviet subconscious—dictated Prigov's choice of a new optical strategy: "the reflection of life in the forms of life itself." This optical approach is born at the intersection of mass and official consciousness. Both layers are reduced to a kind of extensive utterance of half-boiled ideology. Although Prigov himself claims that he works "with pop images, pop forms, and pop representations of culture," one can say that the basic field of transformation of these "pop images" originates precisely on the border of the mass and the official.

"Washing" and cleansing Soviet myth "in correspondence with historiosophic concepts of our time," Prigov arranges the myth in an already "displaced" chronotope. The relationship of the myth to this chronotope is full of bewilderment and confusion. Furthermore, the appeals in "Apofeoz militsaner" to something otherworldly, or something lying beyond the limits of comprehension, combine to form the image of the "little man." This potential mask is one of many masks ("images") that Prigov has tried on during the course of three decades of writing poetry. His main mask—that of state poet Dmitrii Aleksandrovich Prigov, who is composing the Soviet epic—is different. As a result Moscow becomes the natural habitat for the epic to unfold in.

The antiquity of Moscow is not considered here; the city "stands bashfully reflected" on the banks of a "bluish gulf" and "reads the dreams of Ashurbanipalo." Its neighbor is a desert, as well as "snow-capped mountains from which the eagle rises." The city is sprawled at the foot of a fairy-tale mountain, and the Muscovites observe the capture of the eagle and the snow leopard "and welcome the victor: Hoorah!" Myth is overgrown with history: "When in this place Ancient Rome / Affirmed the laws and the State / Then the Muscovites went to the senate in togas / Crowned with laurel wreaths."

Even now, in "little skirts and jeans," Muscovites—with their hearts beating proudly—bear envy toward the whole world. To this day, in these proud hearts, lives the idea of a "separatist Moscow" and burns the "crazy flame of Muscovite national pride." Prigov populates with people the magnificent projects of the "majestic capital" that were published extensively in the pages of the magazine Architecture of the U.S.S.R. from the 1930s to the early 1950s, or he animates the scale models employed in Aleksandr Ivanovich Medvedkin's 1938 film New Moscow. Moscow is not simply an eternal city but the pra-mother of the human race, and the Muscovites themselves are humankind.

The prominence of Moscow in Soviet mythology—the emphasis on its antiquity and primordial status—goes back to the centripetal nature of totalitarian cosmology and "historiosophy." Moscow is not merely the center of the Soviet topos; it essentially takes onto itself the basic characteristics of that topos, the main one of which is expansiveness. Moscow in Prigov's epic is not even the Third Rome ("I don't see a Fourth anywhere") but a kind of expanding space—from the Mausoleum, the Spasskaia Tower, Vnukovo, and the Bolshoi and Malyi Theaters to the Militiaman standing at his post—located somewhere in the heavens.

Reflecting on the structure of myth, Barthes defines its nature in the following way: "Myth hides nothing and flaunts nothing: it distorts; myth is neither a lie nor a confession: it is an inflexion. . . . Myth is speech *stolen and restored*. Only, speech which is restored is no longer quite that which was stolen: when it was brought back, it was not put exactly in its place. It is this brief act of larceny, this moment taken for a surreptitious faking, which gives mythical speech its benumbed look." Correspondingly, the reverse process is to pinpoint the exact place from which speech was stolen. To do this directly is the task of the historian. Prigov does not pinpoint the correct place, but in his gesture of "removing the worn-out quality" of myth he exposes the nonconformity of the word to its "place": "the brief act of larceny" is made obvious. Thus, called into question is not only the sojourn of the given speech in "this place" but the precise possibility in the world of "exact speech" in general. This question is generally the basis of postmodern skepticism toward any description of the world.

In the 1990s Prigov not only addressed Soviet language and the mask of the Soviet state poet but also created the image of the "female poet," as well as exemplary models of "homosexual poetry." Expounding on this theme, Prigov says: "after playing with Soviet language and Soviet myths . . . I worked in the public personae of the ecstatic poet, the philosophical poet and others. The sum of all these stylistics and images creates my directorial image, so to speak."

The sphere of citations and distinctive parody now included not only Soviet but also classical Russian literature, seen as the prototext of Soviet culture. All this enhances the element of not so much a postmodernist aesthetic but a modernist aesthetic (which as a whole is the subject of sots-art citation and parody). Discussing the genealogy of "avant-garde artistry," Prigov divides it into "ages": the "futurist-constructivist" age, which gave way to a "reaction against its mechanistic nature and euphoria for projects" and an attempt to

prove "the absurdity of language on all levels"; but still those figures (the *Oberiuty,* who belonged to OBERIU [Association of Art]) were also, according to Prigov, "murky, unreflective carriers of the avant-garde ideology of the first age." Only in the "third age," the "pop-art-conceptualist" age, was there a "completion of the triad," a "displacement of the mutually-opposed language positions of the first two ages . . . an affirmation of the truth of every language within the boundaries of its own axiomatics . . . and an announcement of its untruthfulness and totalitarian ambitions."

Meanwhile, in his attempts to reread the Russian classics—for example, in the cycles "Vnutrennie razborki" (Infighting, 1993) and "Siuzhety" (Plots, 1993), in his "Kniga o schast'e" (Book of Happiness, published in *Znamia* [The Banner], 1994), or in texts in which he creates the "image" of a prophet or a female poet, specifically modernist strategies of working with a text are developed. Such a method of working with "any language" has been viewed as dubious by many critics. In "Mezhdu imenem i imidzhem. Dialog" (Between Names and Images. A Dialogue), published in *Literaturnaia gazeta* (The Literary Gazette, 12 May 1993), Sergei Markovich Gandlevsky, for instance, notes:

> It baffles me when you treat Pasternak's "August" or Lermontov's "Dream." It's not that I'm a flustered noblewoman who flops into a faint from blasphemy. I just don't think that kind of treatment is fruitful. In the case of works that show, to put it mildly, talent, the form explains little. What does it mean to say that Pasternak's poems are typical of the 1950s confessional lyric, etc.? It is not those parameters that make the poems remarkable. Your method doesn't take the rest of it into account, and it is the rest of it that is precious, genius.

Since the mid 1990s the pessimistic element in Prigov's work has become noticeably stronger. Many texts of this period are dominated by an aesthetic of the ugly, the horrible, and the cruel. The irony of sots-art has given way to a "poetics of the absolute minus," in the words of Elena Trofimova (*Russkie pisateli 20 veka: Biograficheskii slovar'* [Russian Writers of the Twentieth Century: A Biographical Dictionary], 2000) with reference to *Piat' desiat kapelek krovi* (Five Droplets of Blood, 1993). For Prigov this is yet another "mask"—this time the mask of the demonic existentialist poet. Such total relativism has been met with different reactions, often rather sharp.

In 2000 Prigov took on a new role as a memoirist. His novel *Zhivite v Moskve* (Live in Moscow, 2000) is, on the one hand, a continuation of his poetry cycle "Moskva i moskvichi" (Moscow and Muscovites,

1989), while it develops, on the other hand, the tradition of Venedikt Vasil'evich Erofeev, Sasha Sokolov, and Evgenii Anatol'evich Popov. Moscow appears as the global center of catastrophic, almost cosmogonic, events. In 2001 Prigov published *Tol'ko moia Iaponiia* (Only My Japan), a book written in the form of a travel journal that tells the story of his stay in Japan. The narrative whimsically combines ethnographic details with the fantastic and a thorough, reliable description of everyday life among the Japanese with the grotesque.

Prigov's theoretical pieces are as important an aspect of his work as his artistic exhibitions and installations. He has produced many articles, manifestos, *preduvedomleniia* (forewarnings–a special genre that he invented to accompany his cycles and installations), and interviews in which he not only develops the theoretical bases of conceptualism but also conducts an active polemic on intraliterary problems, as well as problems of a wider scope regarding general aesthetics and sociopolitical topics. These materials have appeared in newspapers, magazines, and journals both in Russia and in the West. Portions of them have been published in *Wiener Slawistischer Almanach* (1994), *Sbornik preduvedomlenii k raznoobraznym veshcham* (A Collection of Forewarnings of Diverse Things, 1996), and in a book of interviews, conducted by Irina Balabanova, titled *Govorit Dmitrii Aleksandrovich Prigov* (Dmitrii Aleksandrovich Prigov Speaks, 2001).

Dmitrii Aleksandrovich Prigov is a central figure both in the Soviet underground of the 1970s and 1980s and in post-Soviet literature as a whole. His works demonstrate, in the words of the poet himself, "the radical aesthetic practices" of working with the Soviet language and–more broadly–with Soviet civilization. Those aesthetic strategies, which came to maturity during the twilight of the Soviet era, have had an enormous influence on all of post-Soviet culture, the contents of which are essentially an ironic reworking of "Soviet cultural heritage."

Interviews:

Prigov and Sergei Markovich Gandlevsky, "Mezhdu imenem i imidzhem. Dialog," *Literaturnaia gazeta*, 12 May 1993, p. 5;

Irina Balabanova, *Govorit Dmitrii Aleksandrovich Prigov* (Moscow: OGI, 2001).

Bibliography:

Mary Nicholas, "Dmitrij Aleksandrovich Prigov: Selected Bibliography," *Russian Literature*, 93, no. 1 (January 1996).

Biography:

Elena Trofimova, "Prigov D. A.," in *Russkie pisateli 20 veka: Biograficheskii slovar'*, compiled by P. A. Nikolaev (Moscow: Bol'shaia Rossiiskaia Entsiklopediia, 2000), pp. 570–571.

References:

Mikhail Natanovich Aizenberg, "Nekotorye drugie," *Teatr*, 4 (1991);

Evgeny Aleksandrovich Dobrenko, "Nashestvie slov. Dmitrii Prigov i konets sovetskoi literatury," *Voprosy literatury*, 6 (1997): 36–65;

Dobrenko, "Preodolenie ideologii. Zametki o Sots-Arte," *Volga*, 11 (1990): 164–184;

Mikhail Naumovich Epshtein, "Kontsepty . . . Metaboly: O novykh techeniiakh v poezii," *Oktiabr'*, 4 (1988);

Viktor Vladimirovich Erofeev, "Pamiatnik dlia khrestomatii," *Teatr*, 1 (1993): 139;

Boris Efimovich Groys, *The Total Art of Stalinism: Avant-Garde, Aesthetic Dictatorship, and Beyond* (Princeton: Princeton University Press, 1988), pp. 95–99;

Viacheslav Nikolaevich Kuritsyn, "Ocharovanie neitralizatsii," in *Tirazh 300 EKZ: Kniga o postmodernizme* (Ekaterinburg, 1992), pp. 73–85;

Kuritsyn, "Postmodernizm–novaia pervobytnaia kul'tura," *Novyi mir*, 2 (1992);

Kuritsyn, "Prigova mnogo," *Teatr*, 1 (1993): 136–139;

Mark Lipovetsky, "Kak chestnyi chelovek . . . ," *Znamia*, 3 (1998);

Aleksei Medvedev, "Kak pravil'no srubit' suk, na kotorom sidish'," *Teatr*, 1 (1993): 140–143;

Mary Nicholas, "Dmitrij Prigov and the Russian Avant-Garde, Then and Now," *Russian Literature*, 93, no. 1 (January 1996);

Vol'f Shmidt, "Slovo o Dmitrii Aleksandroviche Prigove," *Znamia*, 8 (1994);

Elena Trofimova, "Moskovskie poeticheskie kluby 1980-kh gg," *Oktiabr'*, 12 (1991);

Trofimova, "Stilevye reministsentsii v russkom postmodernizme 90-x godov," *Obshchestvennye nauki i sovremennost'*, 4 (1999).

Dina Il'inichna Rubina

(19 September 1953 –)

Marina Adamovitch
Kontinent (Paris-Moscow)

BOOKS: *Kogda zhe poidet sneg?* (Tashkent: Esh gvardiia, 1980)—includes "Po subbotam" and "Etot chudnoi Altukhov";

Dom za zelenoi kalitkoi (Tashkent: Gafur Guliam, 1982);

Otvorite okno! (Tashkent: Gafur Guliam, 1987)—includes *Zavtra, kak obychno;*

Dvoinaia familiia (Moscow: Sovetskii pisatel', 1990)—includes *Dvoinaia familiia,* translated by Marian Schwartz as *The Double-Barreled Name, Nimrod,* 33, no. 2 (Spring–Summer, 1990); and "Liubka," translated by Schwartz, *Stories,* 25 (1991): 25–37;

Odin inteligent uselsia na doroge (Jerusalem: VERBA, 1994)—includes *Vo vratakh Tvoikh;*

Kamera naezzhaet, with a foreword by Lev Anninsky (Moscow: Ostozh'e, 1996);

Vot idet Messiia! (Tel Aviv, 1996); translated by Daniel M. Jaffe as *Here Comes the Messiah!* with a foreword by Jaffe (Brookline, Mass.: Zephyr, 2000);

Uroki muziki (Jerusalem, 1996);

Poslednyi kaban iz lesov Pontevedra (Jerusalem: Pilies Studio, 1998);

Vysokaia voda venetsiantsev (Jerusalem: LIRA, 1999);

Chem by zaniat'sia? (St. Petersburg: RETRO, 2001);

Ternovik (St. Petersburg: RETRO, 2001);

Voskresnaia messa v Toledo (Moscow: Vagrius, 2002).

Collections and Editions: *Angel konvoinyi* (Moscow: Medzhibozh, 1997);

Uroki muziki (Moscow: Gudial, 1998);

Odin intelligent uselsia na doroge (St. Petersburg: Simpozium, 2000);

Poslednyi kaban iz lesov Pontevedra (St. Petersburg: Simpozium, 2000);

Pod znakom karnavala (Ekaterinburg: U-Faktoriia, 2000);

Kogda vypadet sneg (Ekaterinburg: U-Factoriia, 2000);

Vysokaia voda venetsiantsev (Moscow: Vagrius, 2001);

Glaza geroia krupnym planom (Moscow: Vagrius, 2002);

Neskol'ko toroplivykh slov liubvi (St. Petersburg: RETRO, 2003).

Editions in English: *On Upper Maslovka* [excerpt], translated by Marian Schwartz, *Glas,* 13 (1996): 109–137;

Dina Il'inichna Rubina (photograph by Sergei Bogdanov)

"Apples from Shlitzbutter's Garden," translated by Daniel M. Jaffe, in *With Signs and Wonders: An International Anthology of Jewish Fabulist Fiction,* edited by Jaffe (Montpelier, Vt.: Invisible Cities, 2001).

PLAY PRODUCTION: *Chudesnaia Doira,* by Rubina and Rudolph Barinsky, Uzbeksky Gosudarstvennyi Teatr Dramy, 1982.

PRODUCED SCRIPT: *Nash vnuk rabotaet v militsii,* motion picture, Uzbekfil'm, 1984.

OTHER: Marina Moskvina, *Izgolovie iz travy,* with a foreword by Rubina (St. Petersburg: RETRO, 2002).

SELECTED PERIODICAL PUBLICATIONS–
UNCOLLECTED: "O sebe. Ia–ofenia," *Znamia,* 4 (1997);

"Nash kitaiskii biznes," *Znamia,* 7 (1999);

"O proze realnoi i virtual'noi," *Druzhba narodov,* 11 (1999);

"Monologi," *Druzhba narodov,* 4 (2000);

"Natsional'naia spetsifika literatury–anakhronizm ili neot'emlemoe kachestvo?" *Znamia,* 9 (2000);

"Rasskazy," *Druzba narodov,* 2 (2001);

"Ierusalimtski (chetky)," *Druzhba narodov,* 7 (2002);

"Neskol'ko torophlivikh slov o lubvi," *Novyi mir,* 1 (2003).

Dina Rubina is one of the best-known names among modern Russian writers. Starting with her first novels, which appeared in the 1980s in *tolstye* (thick) literary magazines, she attracted attention from serious Moscow critics. Some characterized Rubina as one of the representatives of "women's prose," while others saw in her a successor to Iurii Valentinovich Trifonov and his style of social psychological writing. All admitted the brilliance and strength of her talent. Today, Rubina is rightfully one of the most popular authors of the Russian diaspora.

Dina Il'inichna Rubina was born on 19 September 1953 in Tashkent, Uzbekistan. Her father, Il'ia Davidovich Rubin, was an artist, and her mother, Rita Aleksandrovna Rubina, was a history teacher. Both her parents were Ukrainian Jews whose families had arrived in Tashkent in their own ways: Rubina's mother came with waves of refugees from Poltava, in central Ukraine, while her father returned from service during World War II, to his parents, who had been evacuated to Tashkent from Khar'kov, in northeastern Ukraine. Both families told colorful stories about their ancestors. Rubina's maternal great-grandfather was a rabbi, and her paternal great-grandfather was a drayman in Warsaw, a man of such unbridled temper that his son (her grandfather) had to run away from home and never came back to his family.

Rubina's childhood was filled with family love but suffered from a lack of space; the family lived in small apartments with scarcely any room for children, let alone a girl. One room was always reserved for her father's studio, with Rubina's folding bed stuck among canvasses and tubes of paint. As she writes in *Kamera naezzhaet* (The Camera Zooms In, 1996), "One of the nightmares of my childhood was that in the middle of the night I would bump my leg, or arm, on the latest portrait of Karl Marx, commissioned from my father by the . . . kolkhoz . . . and it would fall down on me." The cramped spaces, both physical and social, and the family's limited circumstances probably inspired Rubina's first stories, which feature motifs of escape (in search of freedom) and the yearning for unbound space and absolute independence (from the social to the metaphysical).

Rubina's first story, "Bespokoinaia natura" (A Fidgety Nature, 1971), was accepted for publication by the humor department of the national magazine *Iunost'.* Quite soon after the appearance of "Bespokoinaia natura," Rubina began to write serious stories for the prose department at *Iunost,'* and the "fidgety natures"– characters from Rubina's other early stories such as "Po subbotam" (On Saturdays, 1974; collected, 1980) and "Etot chudnoi Altukhov" (This Strange Altukhov, 1976; collected, 1980)–were also introduced to the readers of the magazine. In 1977 she wrote a novella, distinct for its lyrical intonation, titled *Kogda zhe poidet sneg?* (So, When Will It Snow?, 1980). The main character Nina is gravely ill, but warm, lucid feelings of first love help her to conquer her fear of nonexistence. Rubina's earliest novellas already showed examples of subtle psychological prose.

In 1977, upon graduation from the Tashkent Conservatory (where she had studied piano since 1972), Rubina began working at the Institute of Culture. Her music students were "the children of mountain shepherds," as she calls them in *Kamera naezzhaet,* who were supposed to grasp and then impart European culture to the rural *auls* (mountain villages) of Uzbekistan. She soon left her music-teaching career and tried to earn a living by translating the works of Uzbek writers. In 1982 Rubina won an award for the play *Chudesnaia Doira* (The Magic Doira [an Uzbeki musical instrument]), which she co-authored with Rudolph Barinsky, from the Uzbek Ministry of Culture; the play, though never published, was staged that same year at the Uzbesksky Gosudarstvennyi Teatr Dramy (Uzbek State Theater of Drama). Later, Rubina wrote another play, loosely based on her earlier novel *Kogda zhe poidet sneg?* Performed on radio and television, it reached the national audience with great success. She considers this episode of her biography, however, with some skepticism: "To produce my works in theater or cinema is as impossible as those of Iskander or Dovlatov. The prose of writers with a clearly expressed authorial intonation cannot be transferred to the movie screen or to the theater stage. One must humbly accept this," as Rubina recounted in a personal interview in January 2001. In 1984 the motion picture studio Uzbekfil'm made a movie, *Nash vnuk rabotaet v militsii* (Our Grandson Works for The Police), based on Rubina's *Zavtra, kak obychno*

Rubina in Tashkent, 1984 (courtesy of the author)

(Tomorrow As Usual, first published in *Iunost'* [Youth] 1984; collected, 1987), an early novella about the work of homicide detectives; Rubina wrote the screenplay for the movie. She subsequently recalled this event as a genuine creative failure. Yet, the story of making a movie becomes a topic of her later, much more successful, novella *Kamera naezzhaet,* in which Rubina clearly defines a main theme of her works: a person's right to freedom and self-expression, which the forces of everyday personal and social circumstances suppress to tragic effect.

The stuffy, miserable atmosphere of life in Uzbekistan suffocated Rubina, now married and the mother of a son. In the mid 1980s she moved with her son, Dmitry, to Moscow and, writing on a freelance basis, began publishing her work regularly. She started a new family with a famous artist, Boris Karafelov, and had a second child, a daughter named Eva. The circle of her Moscow acquaintances expanded considerably during these years

and included musicians, artists, and writers. Rubina felt the same claustrophobic pressure in Moscow, however, that she did in Tashkent—an intellectual, political, and cultural stifling. She was dispirited especially by the ideological cynicism that governed Moscow—by the Orwellian doublethink that slowly transmuted into personal immorality and social conformism.

Rubina's works of that period come close to Trifonov's tradition of social psychological prose. In her story "Liubka" (1989; collected, 1990) the heroine, whose name is the same as the title, is the head of a gang, a professional thief, and a criminal. Yet, Liubka turns out to be the only decent character in the narrative: she does not betray Irina Mikhailovna, a young Jewish doctor who suffers alienation and persecution during the so-called Doctors' case, when Soviet special services in the early 1950s revealed a plot by several well-known Jewish doctors to kill key government officials. Later in Rubina's works, ideological cause gave way to ethnic identity and psychological issues, but "Liubka" reflected the distinctive sociocultural atmosphere in the early years of perestroika that invaded Russian literature with bits of political and ideological conflicts. The "Jewishness" of Irina serves as a social sign of alienation for Rubina, who also suffered rejection because of her Jewish heritage. Remembering the Soviet past in *Kamera naezzhaet,* for example, Rubina gives a heart-wrenching description of herself as someone who is "imprisoned in a zone." She names her guardian angel as the "camp guard":

> I picture my guardian angel as a camp guard, balding, with the unclear eyes of a drunkard, in thick-wadded pants that smell like tobacco and disinfected train-station restrooms. . . . On an attempt to escape from this zone called life, my guardian angel grabs me by the collar and drags me through a stage of living, twisting my arms and kicking me. And this is the best he can do.

In search of the genuine foundations of human existence, Rubina referred to her family's ethnic background, and her search overlapped with the overall context of changes happening in Russian literature during perestroika—such as the increasingly audible theme of national identity. In addition, the idea of forgotten, abased Jewishness became more and more persistent in Rubina's prose. The motif of alienation from the surrounding world, present in Rubina's initial stories, assumed by the early 1990s the more concrete theme of national Jewish ostracism and expulsion. Continuing to base her narratives on the psychological elaboration of her characters, while working inside the tradition of the Moscow school of sociopsychological prose, as represented by Trifonov and other "forty-year-old" writers, Rubina began to romanticize ethnicity and ethnic culture in her fiction.

In 1990 Rubina repatriated to Israel with her family, a move that was profoundly deliberate and carefully pondered, yet still quite dramatic for her, since it meant crossing creative and personal boundaries. The crisis that resulted from her repatriation is depicted in *Vo vratakh Tvoikh* (At Thy Gates, first published in the journal *Novyi mir* [New World] 1993; collected, 1994): "The first weeks of emigration seemed like a serious disease: typhoid or cholera, with a fever, delirium, not being in one's own bed, but in the heated goods wagon of a furious train that goes at full speed, the devil knows where."

Henceforth, Rubina's émigré experience became a key idea in her writings. "The circle was formed," writes Rubina in the novel *Vot idet Messiia!* (1996; translated as *Here Comes the Messiah!,* 2000). "She felt suddenly such an endless orphanhood; homelessness; misfortune and nauseating fear; she felt how a spiritless

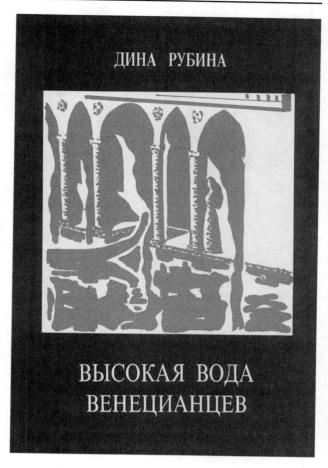

Front cover for Rubina's 1999 Vysokaia voda venetsiantsev (The Venetians' High Tide), a collection of new and previously published works (courtesy of the author)

hand moved apart the tissues of her body, is penetrating inside, into the thorax, emptying the tumor of her soul with the metastases of the past." *Vot idet Messiia!* is probably Rubina's most important and complex creation. Her previous heroine—one of a "fidgety nature," appearing in several earlier works—splits here into two, and the story line moves forward with two protagonists. The novel also splits into two separate plots, developing parallel to each other and converging in the death scene, toward the end, of one of the heroines.

The life of one of the protagonists, Ziama, the émigré, is typical for an expatriate of the Soviet Union: threat of unemployment; an almost nonexistent salary; work at a minor Russian émigré newspaper; and a difficult and dangerous daily existence in a village situated in a free territory surrounded by hostile Arab settlements. But this "small woman with a neck like a swan's" endures all hardships quietly and complacently because, for the first time in her life, she does not feel like an orphan or an alien. The feeling of kinship and

Front cover for Rubina's Neskol'ko toroplivykh
slov liubvi (*A Few Hurried Words of Love*),
published in 2003 (courtesy of the author)

the idea of having blood ties with other people of a common history and heritage make Ziama intensely happy. Rubina creates archaic wonders that are nonetheless full of poetic beauty and ethnic characters that Ziama, as well as Rubina herself, "loves calmly, strongly, bitterly." As if crowning her heroine with a romantic halo, Rubina writes, "This woman was afraid of the dark and the bullet, but was not frightened by the face of her people." She poeticizes Ziama's image in creating a legend about a wayward daughter who has found, finally, her parents' house. Therefore, not coincidentally, the death of Ziama is presented by the author as the metaphorical offering of the godly lamb—as a sacrifice making possible the future renaissance of the people of Israel.

More than once, critics made note of the autobiographical nature of Rubina's perennial heroine. In 1999 in an interview that appeared in the journal *Voprosy literatury* (Questions of Literature), Rubina admits: "My heroes peer from behind my shoulder. . . . They are concerned about me without any reverence—maybe they know that I am only one of them, neither better nor worse." The short distance between the author and the protagonist is a typical trait of Rubina's prose. Read-

ers are prompted to look at the "promised land" with Ziama's meek glance and to try to experience the pain and joy she derives from her complete existence. But the narrator does not ensure the identity of the protagonist for the duration of the entire novel. In its last pages the distance between the narrator and the protagonist expands to the level of "heaven-and-earth." The narrator's voice sounds the divine prophecy of a coming messiah: "And when I come, when I appear, at last, to the rebellious house—recalcitrant tribes,—I will, as promised, raise her from the dead. . . . She is my substitute, she is my alternate, and she is my redemption."

The metaphysical aspect of *Vot idet Messiia!* is one of its fundamental elements. Israel is envisaged by Rubina as a truly "promised land," the land of Moses and the Ten Commandments—where one awaits the Messiah, and people of the three great religions spar in a protracted argument about God. The high stakes of this argument determine both the existence and self-understanding of the people who live in this disputed land. For these reasons Rubina believes that the undemanding, everyday story of the life and death of Ziama lies within the parameters of a parable about a heroine sacrificed "for the people, for their sins, for their lives, for their land. . . . Any other kind of sacrifice is simply meaningless. . . ."

The second plot of the novel is created on a philosophical-psychological level. It relates the story of another émigré from Russia, the writer N., the second voice in the narrative and a second hypostasis of the "fidgety nature." N. is planning to write a novel about a heroine sacrifice. Unexpectedly, this project embodies a reality: the idea of a new novel is incarnated as Ziama's real life and death before the novel is even written.

The writer N.—like every genuine artist—is an individual without borders and relationships; he stays on the outside of nation, history, and law. This artist is a citizen of the universe, which is why he is doomed to eternal solitude. "The creative work as well as death—they both are like solitary acts," Rubina suggested in the 1999 interview with Denis Golovanov. "The writer's motherland is a prohibited inner space, bordered and secured by the watch-dogs of her habits, complexes, preferences, loves,—the goods of the wanderer that she never refuses and that she keeps inside very, very deep." These definitions have self-referential meanings as well, as described in Rubina's "O sebe. Ia—ofenia" (About Myself. I—Am a Peddler, published in *Znamia* [The Banner], 1997): "I am kind of a peddler . . . this is some kind of vagrancy—there you pick up a word, here you grab a picture, there you notice a human type. . . ."

After moving from Russia to Israel, Rubina started not only a new phase in her personal life but also a new period of creative work. Yet, critics in Russia did not understand the changes that had happened to her. By placing her in the category of traditional émigré fiction, they characterized Rubina's prose as "female"–filled with sentimentality and exciting Eastern exoticism. In measuring her books, published chiefly in Jerusalem, by the scale of works put out in Moscow by Trifonov and other writers of his generation, critics in Russia did not notice that Rubina was trying to work on a new, untouched continent and with fresh clay, "from which the literary Golem is being created," as she expressed in the 1999 interview. The mass emigration from the Soviet Union that took place in the last third of the twentieth century complicated the character of Russian-language literature abroad. In particular, the large population of Russian-speaking émigrés in Israel not only brought to life a serious, independent political and social movement but also served as a foundation for the development of a special "Russian-Israeli literary cocktail," for which Rubina provides the recipe:

> Let us take the Jewish national temperament, add a large portion of Soviet mentality, pour into the mixture a full spoon of spicy émigré problems, a handful of grains of regular human vanity, half a cup of existential prophetic itch, then pour in an unsparingly sincere love of Russian word and culture, heat it all on Jerusalem's sun.

Rubina's Jerusalem texts are constructed with precious, primary artistic material. This "Golem" consists of the complex context of both Russian and Jewish literary and cultural traditions. She concentrates on the closed "domestic world," the internal space and the static, "eternal" time of the "promised land" that is squeezed "not only by the borders, . . . but by a constant threat . . . that tomorrow . . . the whole nation . . . can cease to exist," as she told Golovanov. Speaking in this same interview she said that "the hidden tragedy of existence" in this dense nation-family is what burdens her conscience and defines the structure of her narration.

Although Rubina continues to write in Russian and her emotional connection with Russian literature has not been interrupted, her location in Israel and its Hebrew linguistic environment form supplementary visual and auditory overtones in her work. As her later writings show, she becomes increasingly engaged in wordplay. The linguistic noise of Israel and the powerful verbal layer of the grinning East are now intertwined with the subtle irony of her prose, which has been justly compared to that of Sholom Aleichem, Sergei Donatovich Dovlatov, and Fazil Abdulovich Iskander.

Dina Il'inichna Rubina has been working productively since the early 1990s. In 1990 she received the Arie Dulchin Prize for Literature for her book *Odin inteligent uselsya na doroge* (An Intellectual Sat Down in the Road, 1994). *Vo vratakh Tvoikh* was nominated for the Booker Russian Novel Prize in 1994. In 1995 she received an award from the Israel Writers' Union for her book *Vot idet Messiia!*, which in 1997 was also nominated for the Booker Russian Novel Prize. Rubina is the author of almost twenty books; her works have been translated into twelve European languages and are well known all over the world. Her novella *Dvoinaia familiia* (1990; translated as *The Double-Barreled Name,* 1990) was translated into French in 1996 and recognized by a network of bookstores in France as the best book of that year.

Interviews:

Denis Golovanov, "Ni zhesta, ni slova," *Voprosy literatury,* 5–6 (1999);

Olga Dunaevskaia, "Lubimaia igra Dini Rubinoi," *Moskovskie novosti,* no. 1089, 29 May 2001;

Aleksandr Melikhov, "My ne v proigrishe," *Neva,* 12 (2002): 180.

Biographies:

G. G. Branover, *Rossiiskaia evreiskaia entsiklopediia,* 3 volumes (Moscow: Rossiiskaia akademiia estestvennykh nauk: Rossiisko-izrail'sky entsiklopedichesky tsentr: "EPOS", 1994–1995), II: 505–506;

Vasillii Litvinov, "Rubina Dina Il'inichna," in *Russkie pisateli 20 veka. Biografichesky slovar',* edited by Petr Alekseevich Nikolaev (Moscow: Bol'shaia Rossiiskaia Entsiklopediia, 2000), pp. 603–604.

References:

Lev Anninsky, "Byt' evreem evreiu slozhno . . . ," *Druzhba narodov,* 6 (1997): 220–   ;

Anninsky, "Otsecheno? Otrubleno? Otrezano?" *Druzhba narodov,* 10 (1996): 218–   ;

Dmitrii Bykov, "Kamera pereezzhaet," *Novyi mir,* 7 (2000): 200–203;

Alla Marchenko, "S prekrasnym vidom na Ershalaim," *Novyi mir,* 3 (1997): 217–221;

I. Pitlyar, "Do smeshnogo zhal'," *Novyi mir,* 5 (1995): 238–241;

Sait Diny Rubinoi (The Dina Rubina Site) <http://www.dinarubina.com> [accessed 25 July 2003];

Evgenii Shklovsky, "Nashi," *Oktiabr',* 7 (1997): 171;

Gleb Shul'piakov, "Nebesnyi konvoi," *ExLibris NG,* 22 January 1998, p. 2–;

Leonid Zhuhovitsky, "Otkrytiia-vperedi," *Iunost',* 11 (1983).

Lev Semenovich Rubinshtein

(19 February 1947 –   )

Mark Lipovetsky
University of Colorado at Boulder

BOOKS: *Eto interesno. Kulturpalast: Neue Moskauer Poesie & Aktionskunst,* edited by Gunther Khirt and Sascha Wonders (Wuppertal, Germany: S-Press, 1984);

Malen'kaia nochnaia serenada (Moscow: Renaissance, 1992);

Mama myla ramu (Moscow: Renaissance, 1992);

Poiavlenie geroia (Moscow: Renaissance, 1992);

Vse dal'she i dal'she: Iz "Bol'shoi kartoteki," afterword by Khirt and Wonders (Moscow: Obscuri viri, 1995);

Reguliarnoe pis'mo (St. Petersburg: Ivan Limbakh, 1996);

Voprosy literatury (Moscow: ARGO-RISK, 1996);

Sluchai iz iazyka (St. Petersburg: Ivan Limbakh, 1998);

Domashnee muzitsirovanie (Moscow: Novoe literaturnoe obozrenie, 2000)—includes "Imperativnaia programma 'Novogo antrakta,'" "Ocherednaia programma," "Programma sovmestnykh perezhivanii," and "35 novykh listov."

Editions in English: "Statement. A Little Nighttime Serenade. From Thursday to Friday," translated by Gerald J. Janecek in *Third Wave: The New Russian Poetry,* edited by Kent Johnson and Stephen M. Ashby (Ann Arbor: University of Michigan Press, 1992), pp. 137–150;

"The Six-Winged Seraph," translated by Andrew Reynolds, in *The Penguin Book of New Russian Writing: Russia's Fleurs du Mal,* edited by Reynolds and Victor Erofeev (London: Penguin, 1995), pp. 300–308;

"What Can One Say?" translated by Janecek, in *Reentering the Sign: Articulating New Russian Culture,* edited by Ellen E. Berry and Anesa Miller-Pogacar (Ann Arbor: University of Michigan Press, 1995), pp. 212–216;

"Sonnet 66," translated by Michael Molnar, and "Melancholy Album," translated by Janecek, in *Crossing Centuries: The New Generation in Russian Poetry,* edited by John High, Vitaly Chernetsky, Thomas Epstein, and others (Jersey City: Talisman House, 2000), pp. 51–57;

Lev Semenovich Rubinshtein (photograph © Eberhard Schorr; courtesy of the author)

Here I Am: Performance Poems and Essays, translated by Joanne Turnbull, *Glas,* no. 27 (2001)—comprises "A Catalog of Comical Novelties," "From Beginning to End," "An Elegy," "First It's This, Then It's That," "Thursday Night, Friday Morning," "Communal Function," "The Hero Appears," "The Cat Wore a Hat," "The Smoke of the

Fatherland, or a Filtered Gulag," "That's Me," and "Here I Am."

OTHER: Vladimir Georgievich Sorokin, *Pel'meni*, with an introduction by Rubinshtein, *Iskusstvo kino*, 9 (1990);

Lichnoe delo #__, compiled and edited by Rubinshtein (Moscow: Soiuzteatr, 1991);

"What Can One Say?" in *Re-entering the Sign: Articulating New Russian Culture*, edited by Ellen E. Berry and Anesa Miller-Pogacar (Ann Arbor: University of Michigan Press, 1995);

Poety-kontseptualisty: Dmitrii Aleksandrovich Prigov, Lev Rubinshtein, Timir Kibirov, edited by G. Reznichenko (Moscow: MK-Periodika, 2002).

SELECTED PERIODICAL PUBLICATIONS–UNCOLLECTED : "Eto vse" [samizdat], *37*, no. 15 (1978);

"Eto vse" [fragments], *A-Ia*, 1 (1979);

"Eto vse," *Kovcheg*, 6 (1981): 84–93;

"Iz neizdannogo," *Literaturnoe obozrenie*, 10 (1989): 87–90;

"Sobytie bez naimenovaniia," *Iskusstvo*, 1 (1990): 47;

"Chto tut mozhno skazat' . . . ," *Index* (1991): 343–346; *Lichnoe delo #__* (1991): 232–235;

"Poeziia posle poezii," *Oktiabr'*, 9 (1992): 84–87;

"O poteriakh," *Itogi*, 25 May 2000;

"Gitler s Piskarevki," *Itogi*, 5 September 2000;

"O imena, o nravy," *Itogi*, 12 October 2000;

"Yantsy ot pechki," *Itogi*, 31 October 2000;

"Sindrom Shveika, ili K istorii voprosa," *Ezhenedel'nyi zhurnal*, 00 (2001);

"Podderzhanie razgovora," *Ezhenedel'nyi zhurnal* (2001);

"Zametki fenologa," *Ezhenedel'nyi zhurnal*, 1 (2002);

"Idushchie Zusammen," *Ezhenedel'nyi zhurnal*, 2 (2002);

"Politgramota," *Ezhenedel'nyi zhurnal*, 5 (2002);

"Pogonia za shliapoi," *Ezhenedel'nyi zhurnal*, 9 (2002);

"Kuzen tarakanak," *Ezhenedel'nyi zhurnal*, 9 (2002);

"Nad bednoi nianeiu moei," *Ezhenedel'nyi zhurnal*, 10 (2002);

"Istoriia odnoi borody," *Ezhenedel'nyi zhurnal*, 13 (2002);

"Chuzhie pis'ma," *Ezhenedel'nyi zhurnal*, 14 (2002);

"Lokhovozka," *Ezhenedel'nyi zhurnal*, 16 (2002);

"Byloe i dumy," *Ezhenedel'nyi zhurnal*, 18 (2002);

"O satire i iumore," *Ezhenedel'nyi zhurnal*, 20 (2002);

"I kukarekal, kukarekal. . . ," *Ezhenedel'nyi zhurnal*, 22 (2002);

"Usad'ba Nabokova, ili Mozhno vezde," *Ezhenedel'nyi zhurnal*, 25 (2002);

"V zharkikh ob'iati'iakh Tsel'siia," *Ezhenedel'nyi zhurnal*, 32 (2002);

"V shkolu s roditeliami," *Ezhenedel'nyi zhurnal*, 34 (2002);

"Nam potrebny zlatye kumiry," *Ezhenedel'nyi zhurnal*, 38 (2002);

"Naprasnaia ispoved'," *Ezhenedel'nyi zhurnal*, 40 (2002);

"Komediia polozhenii," *Ezhenedel'nyi zhurnal*, 42 (2002);

"Beskhoznye den'gi," *Ezhenedel'nyi zhurnal*, 45 (2002);

"Krupnaia kala," *Ezhenedel'nyi zhurnal*, 52 (2003);

"Chelovek v futliare," *Ezhenedel'nyi zhurnal*, 56 (2003).

Lev Semenovich Rubinshtein is one of the most prominent poets of Russian conceptualism and postmodernism. His importance is complemented by his close friendship with two other prominent authors, Dmitrii Aleksandrovich Prigov and Timur Iur'evich Kibirov. Rubinshtein has invented a distinctively personal literary genre, a kind of multirhythmic and multidiscursive poem in the form of the card catalogue. These seemingly spontaneous, yet thoroughly arranged, collections of enigmatic fragments and citations are provisional and aleatory "language cases" (a phrase that serves as the title of one of his books). The poem cards fuse various styles and microgenres within a single work and generate an effect comparable to the "symphonism" of contemporary Russian composers such as Alfred Shnitke or Sofia Gubaidullina. Rubinshtein's poetry bridges the gap between the postmodernist-conceptualist deconstruction of various literary, cultural, political, and colloquial discourses and the tradition of Russian philosophic (metaphysical and existentialist) lyrics. He deconstructs and mocks this tradition while at the same time vitalizing and resurrecting it in new cultural and historical contexts.

Lev Semenovich Rubinshtein was born in Moscow on 19 February 1947 into a family of Jewish intelligentsia. His father, Semen L'vovich Rubinshtein, was a construction engineer. His mother, Elena Mikhailovna Rubinshtein (née Kogan), though educated as a railroad engineer, devoted her life to her family. Along with their many relatives (ranging in number from five to fifteen at different periods of time), the Rubinshteins shared two rooms in a Moscow communal apartment that belonged to the poet's grandmother. In part, because of a shortage of living space, Rubinshtein and his parents spent a significant part of their time outside of Moscow in the village of Taininka, where he attended school. Only when ill and during school breaks did Rubinshtein spend time in Moscow with his grandmother. His family moved to the Moscow outskirts of Liubertsy only when he became a high-school student.

In 1965 Rubinshtein was accepted to the Moscow State Pedagogical Institute (now Moscow State Pedagogical University) at the school of philology. While a student, he began to write poetry. His poetic taste differed from the interest in versified sociopolitical criticism dominant among the generation of the 1960s, a generation inspired by the liberalization brought by the Thaw that Nikita Sergeevich Krushchev initiated. Rubinshtein's first strong poetic impressions came from the works of Boris Leonidovich Pasternak. His early poems (which remain unpublished) combined, however, the influences of two other, highly incompatible poets of the twentieth century—Velemir Khlebnikov, a daring avant-gardist, and Osip Emil'evich Mandel'shtam, a neoclassical lyricist. In 1971 Rubinshtein graduated from the Institute with a diploma in Russian language and literature instruction. Yet, he never taught. While still a student, he started working at the Institute library as a bibliographer; he remained at this position until 1992, serving as a librarian for more than twenty years. Although he began writing poetry at the end of the 1960s, he considers the year 1974 to be a turning point in his literary career. At that time he created his first "catalogue"—"Novyi antrakt" (A New Intermission)—which to date remains unpublished. Rubinshtein describes his initial impulse to use this highly unorthodox form for his poetic experiments as a desire to combine visual and verbal media. Between 1973 and 1974 Rubinshtein created several visual compositions that included wall graffiti, texts written on matchboxes, and bottle labels. In the 1970s, quite characteristically, he often "demonstrated" rather than read or recited his catalogues at underground home concerts. From 1976 to 1977 the Moscow conceptualist circle was formed as an informal group of underground artists (Il'ia Iosifovich Kabakov, Erik Vladimirovich Bulatov, Viktor Pivovarov, Vitalii Anatol'evich Komar, Aleksandr Danilovich Melamid, Nikita Alekseev, and Valerii Gerlovin), poets (Rubinshtein, Prigov, and Vsevolod Nikolaevich Nekrasov), and theorists (Boris Efimovich Groys and Andrei Monastyrsky). The group usually gathered for readings and small exhibits, followed by a discussion, in the Moscow apartment owned by Aleksandr Chachko. Rubinshtein became known among Moscow intelligentsia as an active poetic voice of this group. From 1978 to 1981 his first publications appeared in the samizdat journal 37 (edited by Viktor Borisovich Krivulin) and the Paris-based magazines A-Ia and Kovcheg (The Ark). These publications by Rubinshtein accompanied larger presentations of the entire conceptualist circle and poetic "illustrations" to artworks, as well as to the manifesto by Groys, "Moskovskii romanticheskii kontseptualizm" (Moscow Romantic Conceptualism, published in A-Ia in 1979). In the early 1980s Rubinshtein had an opportunity to read his texts during a concert in the Fyodor Dostoevsky Museum in Leningrad, an event organized by the "Club '81'"—a group of underground writers who were accepted, to a certain extent, by the literary authorities. Another public reading happened in 1983 in the Tsentral'nyi Dom Rabotnikov Iskusstva (Central

Moscow House of the Arts). In 1984 his first book was published in Western Germany as a result of the enthusiastic support of Gunther Hirt and Sascha Wonders.

In 1986 Rubinshtein became a member of the club "Poeziia" (Poetry) along with other Moscow conceptualists, Prigov and Kibirov, as well as authors such as Sergei Markovich Gandlevsky, Mikhail Natanovich Aizenberg, Evgenii Anatol'evich Popov, Viktor Vladimirovich Erofeev, Mikhail Naumovich Epshtein, and Nina Iur'evna Iskrenko. Together with some of these poets Rubinshtein participated in several performances titled Almanakh (Almanac). These performances were perceived by both the public and the critics as the powerful beginnings of a new poetic style and a new poetic generation. Later, the materials of these performances were compiled and edited by Rubinshtein in the collection Lichnoe delo #__ (Personal Case No.__) in 1991.

Overall, perestroika dramatically changed Rubinshtein's life as a poet. If before 1987 he was an underground poet—and thus, according to a saying of the time, "widely known in narrow circles"—then during the years of perestroika he obtained a status as one of the greatest representatives of postmodernism in literature. If earlier his performances were limited to occasional readings in private apartments, during this period he performed regularly, in different cities and concert halls. His recitations were recorded and transmitted by radio stations such as the British Broadcasting Company, German Wave, and Radio Liberty. Yet, what is more important, his poetry began to be published in the Soviet Union. At first, his selected compositions appeared in lesser-known journals, including Daugava (Riga) and Literaturnoe obozrenie (The Literary Review). Collections of his poetry became published in anthologies or collections with small circulations, such as Ponedel'nik (Monday, 1990), Index, and Lichnoe delo #__; these books encompassed his texts written much earlier, in the 1970s and early 1980s. Between 1994 and 1996 his new texts were initially published in the so-called tolstye (thick), or the most authoritative, journals—Novyi mir (New World) and Znamia (The Banner), for example. Simultaneously, his own books started to appear: at first small ones, which included from three to five compositions, such as Malen'kaia nochnaia serenada. Mama myla ramu. Poiavlenie geroia (A Little Nighttime Serenade. Mom Washed a Window. The Hero's Appearance, 1992); Vse dal'she i dal'she: Iz "Bol'shoi kartoteki" (Ever Onward: From the "Big Card File," 1995); and Voprosy literatury (Questions of Literature, 1996). Then followed the books that included almost all of Rubinshtein's major poetic texts: Reguliarnoe pis'mo (Regular Writing, 1996) and the most complete collection to date, Domashnee muzitsirovanie (Home Music-Playing, 2000). In a sense, however, all of his books did not reflect the recent developments of a

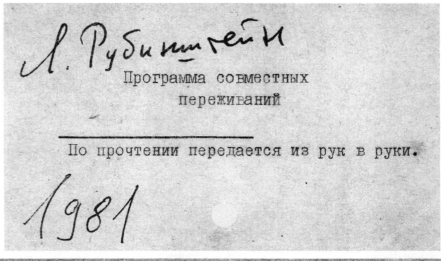

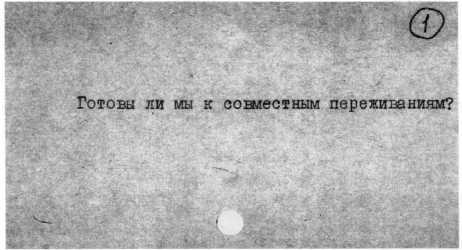

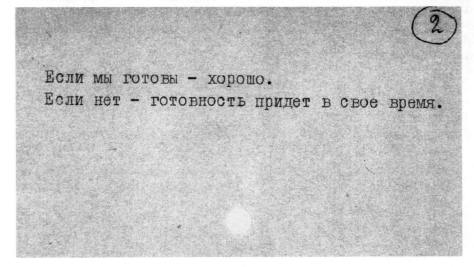

Three of the catalogue cards on which Rubinshtein, who started out as a librarian, wrote his 1981 work "Programma sovmestnykh perezhivanii" (A Program of Joint Feelings), published in his Domashnee muzitsirovanie *(Home Music-Playing, 2000), the fullest collection of his writings. The title card (top) is signed by Rubinshtein (from* Domashnee muzitsirovanie, *2000; Collection of Mark Lipovetsky).*

poet, as usually happens with poetic publications, but represented his creative path as a ready-made system: works composed decades ago were published next to the latest texts by Rubinshtein, though for a reader they all were new, more or less. This paradoxical situation was typical for many authors who evolved within the underground subculture.

Extensive publication of Rubinshtein's works brought his poetry to the center of critical discussions. All the critics focus on the nature of Rubinshtein's original genre—a catalogue, which serves as a universal form for all his poetic compositions. Some critics suggest that his job as a librarian indirectly affected his invention of the poetic genre of the catalogue, written on index cards that were customarily used for bibliographic records. In this form of poetic composition, he found a postmodernist metaphor for the world and for personality as a combination of texts and textual references; that is, a library. According to Groys in his contribution to *Endquote: Sots-Art Literature and Soviet Grand Style* (2000), "The texts of Lev Rubinshtein appear like unique library catalogues, describing his individual—and furthermore virtual, rather than real—library. . . . Each separate line of Rubinshtein's text refers to a certain virtual book kept in the inner space of his memory, in which each line must receive its full deciphering."

In his articles about the new poetry written in the 1980s, Epshtein compares Rubinshtein's cards with the visual works of Kabakov, a comparison Epshtein justifies on the basis that both of them satirize linguistic garbage and thus clear out the "deadwood" of language. In his polemic with Epshtein, published in *Daugava* in 1989, V. Lettsev showed that Rubinshtein's vulgar speech formations served as a trampoline for leaping beyond the boundaries of rationalistic discourse comparable to "Zen koans: paradoxical questions, riddles, and problems that have no logical solution on a level of discursive thought." Andrei Leonidovich Zorin, whose 1989 article, "Katalog," accompanied one of Rubinshtein's first publications in the Soviet Union, wrote that the "card" structure of Rubinshtein's texts has a world-modeling function, giving rise to a "model that disregards connections between cause and effect. . . . His cosmos turns out to be populated by voices calling out to each other in a bodiless void." Aizenberg, a poet and critic who belonged to the Moscow conceptualist circle and has written about Rubinshtein's poetry since the early 1980s, emphasizes "rhythmicality" as the main vehicle of meaning in his poetry.

Rubinshtein himself feels that the term "intergenre" fits his invention better that any other word. His text, he writes in the introduction to the collection *Reguliarnoe pis'mo,* may be read

. . . to kak bytovoi roman, to kak dramaticheskaia p'esa, to kak liricheskoe stikhotvorenie i t.d., t.e. skol'zit po granistam zhanrov i, kak zerkalo, na korotkoe mgnovenie otrazhaet kazhdyi iz nkh, ni s odnim ne otozhdestvliaias'. . . . Geroiami kazhdogo moego teksta iavliaiutsia nekie drugie teksty. Mozhno nazvat' ikh "protekstami." Eti proteksty (kak i geroi) rozhdaiutsia, zhivut, vstupaiut v slozhnye igry drug s drugom, sozdaiut dramaticheskuiu intrigu, uniraiut, snova rozhdaiutsia i t.d.

(. . . as a novel or a play, or a lyric poem and so on, that is, it slides along the borders between genres, and like a mirror, for the short moments reflects each of them, without identifying itself with any of them. . . . The main protagonists of these texts are other texts. These about-texts [like literary characters] are born at some point, they live their lives, communicate through complex games with one another, create dramatic intrigues, die and resurrect, and so on).

Even more telling than these statements are Rubinshtein's frequent attempts—suggestive rather than assertive—to define the essence of his compositions within the larger scope of his poetic texts. Sometimes these statements develop into separate "cards," which are self-sufficient text segments, as seen in the following excerpts: "What kind of 'spontaneous writing' do you mean?! Everything is calculated to the last dot. . . . Every seemingly elementary utterance leans towards sacralization when it is located among other utterances whose homogenous qualities may be sensed intuitively rather than defined by rational efforts" (from "Iz dnevnykh zaniatii" [Daytime Activities], 1984); "Under investigation is the mechanism of spontaneously emerging and self-destructing communications. . . . The so-called 'live' zones of language expose signs of decay, while those which were supposed to be deceased for quite a while, suddenly sprout with little sticky green leaves" (from "Vremia idet" [Time Goes By], 1990); and "Everything here reminds us of something, points out at something, and refers to something. When you are just beginning to understand what's going on, it's time to leave" (from "Vse dal'she i dal'she" [Ever Onward], 1984).

Apparently, Rubinshtein perceives his own poetic works as ones revealing hidden layers, forces, and processes of language—both structural and communicative. His seemingly chaotic compositions perform a ritual of linguistic resurrection. Ideally, each of his texts creates provocation within the realm of language, forcing dead elements to revive and expose the automatization (cultural death) of seemingly active discursive forms. Especially illuminating is Rubinshtein's remark on *iazykovaia misteriia* (a linguistic mystery, or a miracle play of language) from "Sonet 66" (Sonnet 66, 1987). The generic plot of medieval miracle plays necessarily embodies a story of Christ's suffering and resurrection, which, in turn, is based on the archetypal model of transformation of chaos into cosmos, essential for any archaic ritual. Rubinshtein employs the same archetypal model in the compositions of his poetic catalogues.

Each of Rubinshtein's catalogues begins with a more or less chaotic superimposition of various linguistic, discursive, and stylistic forms, as well as quotations and quasi-quotations. These forms are dissociated from their "native" contexts and comically estranged by such dissociation. Provisional and aleatory movements of these cultural fragments, however, create new and unpredictable relations between them. These newly emerging and dissipating associations express themselves first and foremost in the rhythmic organization of Rubinshtein's texts. These rhythms at first sound parodical because they are based on formal repetitions, which emphasize the chaotic nature of the content. Step-by-step and card-by-card, these rhythms become more complex and meaningful yet preserve their elusive and provisional nature. Rubinshtein's texts usually reach their rhythmical climax in the finale, or, alternatively, as the last cards intentionally dissolve and downplay the rhythmic "epiphany" achieved just before the ending. The search for the rhythm is extremely significant because it corresponds to the search for order and harmony.

For paradoxically simplistic configurations of rhythmic organization, Rubinshtein frequently employs anaphoric beginnings, in which the same word is repeated at the start of consecutive expressions or phrases: "Mozhno . . ." (variously translated: You could, You may, or It is possible) in "Katalog komediinykh novshestv" (1976; translated as "Catalogue of Comical Novelties," 2001); "Inogda . . ." (Sometimes) in "Elegiia" (Elegy); "Dorogoi drug!" (Dear Friend!) in "Druzheskie obrashcheniia 1983 goda" (Friendly Addresses of 1983); and "Snilos' / Prisnilos' . . ." (I was dreaming / I dreamed) in "S chetverga na paitnitsu" (From Thursday to Friday). He also often uses syntactical parallelism, such as "To odno, to drugoe" (First it's this, then it's that) and "Esli . . . to" (If . . . then). Frequently the series of cards is united with primitive rhyme and meter, or "empty" cards appear marked with numbers only. The repetition of refrains is constituted either by simple speech commands (such as "tak," "nachali," "dal'she," "tikho!" "davai," "tri-chetyre," "i vot") or by a theme with complex variations and modifications (different endings to the line beginning with the words "Zhizn' daetsia cheloveku . . ." [Life is given to a man . . .] in the text "Vsiudu zhizn'" [Life Is Everywhere]).

More complex and subtle rhythms, which typically appear in the second half of Rubinshtein's texts, are organized by the distanced—and not necessarily the literal—reiteration of the same, or similar, words,

phrases, motifs, or images. These cards become engaged in invisible and indirect dialogues. Thus, the text "Voprosy literatury" (Questions of Literature, 1992) consists of two uneven parts. The first (and longest) part, comprising cards 1–99, starts with the words "I vot ia pishu . . ." (And so I'm writing . . .), while the second (and shorter) part, encompassing cards 100–115, begins with "I vot my chitaem . . ." (And so we're reading . . .). With the exception of the first seven cards, all the cards in the first part consist only of interrogative constructions. Some of these mock textbook "questions for discussion" are applicable to any given work of literature, whereas others express unnamed, yet clearly troubling, feelings of loss and confusion that gradually become dominant. In the second part the intonation changes drastically, and the descriptions of exaltation and excitement replace suggestive motifs of despair:

111. Odnim slovom, vseobshchemu likovaniiu ne bylo granits.
112. V tot mig kazhdym iz nas ovladelo otchetlivoe chuvstvo, chto vse strashnoe i tiazheloe vo vsei nashei zhizni ushlo bezvozvratno.
A vperedi lish' beskonechnaia radost'.
113. Radost' navsegda.

(111. To sum it up, the universal rejoicing was boundless.
112. At that moment each of us experienced a clear sensation that everything scary and heavy in the whole life was gone for good.
And ahead of us was only endless joy.
113. Joy forever).

This sudden change in tone is not as unmotivated as it seems. The cards that follow "I vot my chitaem . . ." describe the conditions in which the reading takes place and literally repeat the first seven cards of the composition, which refer to the conditions of writing. Both writing and reading happen in the background of a storm, "nauseating sadness," and sarcastic views of people. Yet, both writing and reading strive to overcome, or at least disregard, these catastrophic conditions.

Another powerful means enabling Rubinshtein to transform the chaos of linguistic fragments into a complex musical, rather than literary, composition is his system of intertextual references. Along with obvious and worn-out classical quotes, Rubinshtein frequently locates his own text in the background of other, less trivial, classical texts. Usually, this "master intertext" is disclosed in the title of the composition: for example, "Shestikrylyi serafim" (The Six-Winged Seraph, 1984) includes an obvious and direct reference to Aleksandr Sergeevich Pushkin's "The Prophet," and "Sonet 66" suggests a direct link to William Shakespeare's masterpiece of the same title, which starts with

Paperback cover for Rubinshtein's Reguliarnoe pis'mo *(Regular Writing, 1996), in which the title essay focuses on the processes of reading and writing (Collection of Mark Lipovetsky)*

the line, "Tired with all these, for restful death I cry"; both compositions are included in Rubinshtein's book *Reguliarnoe pis'mo*. By this means intertextual tension is created from the first cards of Rubinshtein's composition. His intertextual "promise," however, leads to occurrences of famous lines and images in improper contexts, as in "Shestikrylyi serafim," or it may not express itself in any visible quotations, as seen in "Sonet 66." Nevertheless, both texts are designed as intertextual reassessments of models of tragic harmony embodied by Pushkin and Shakespeare, respectively. This correlation creates a framework not within but outside Rubinshtein's text, in the mind of the reader—who is cued by the title to look for elements of composition that might echo or argue with classical intertexts.

Thus, in "Shestikrylyi serafim" the lines that directly or indirectly refer to Pushkin's prophet are scattered among irrelevant textual fragments. These lines anticipate the final "card," which may be read as a summary of the entire text as well as a renewed story of the death and resurrection of Pushkin's prophet. In Rubinshtein's composition, immersion in the everyday chaos

of aleatory and incoherent voices replaces the solemn encounter of Pushkin's hero with the six-winged seraph. In both Pushkin's and Rubinshtein's cases, however, the hero's eyes and ears are opened to the sensations of the whole universe in its poetic-harmonic (Pushkin) and prosaic-chaotic (Rubinshtein) registers.

In "Sonet 66" the relation of the entire composition to the "title" text in fact shapes the main intellectual intrigue of the composition. Only one line refers directly to Shakespeare's sonnet 66: "Drugu budet trudno bez menia" (Pasternak's translation of "Save that to die, I leave my love alone," the last line of Shakespeare's poem). The other line, "Khotelos' by zabyt', zasnut'" (an inexact quotation from Pasternak's translation of the line, "To die,—to sleep,—No more . . . ," in Hamlet's soliloquy "To be or not to be . . . ," from the eponymous play, published in 1603), belongs to the same intertextual sphere, especially since "To be or not to be . . ." and sonnet 66 were frequently compared to each other in Soviet studies of Shakespeare. Yet, what Rubinshtein's text actually refers to is the structural movement from desperation and death to the will to live (equivalent to resurrection), which is epitomized by Shakespeare's sonnet 66. Rubinshtein's composition runs this movement through a whole gamut of emotions, such as an optimistic hope to overcome the inevitable physical destruction by spiritual effort and a philosophical belief that "life begins from non-existence"–that dust engenders (*rozhdaiutsia iz prakha*), as well as refrain, a desperate scream: "Neuzheli bol'she nikogda?" (Can't believe that it will ever happen again?). Yet, the dominant intonation of the text (and especially the combinations of enthusiastically banal rhymed text with sarcastic prose interventions) clearly demonstrates the inapplicability of Shakespearean wisdom–an intellectual model sanctified by the "high literature" canon–directly to prosaic existence. According to Rubinshtein's poetic logic, literary discourse–ranging from flat truism to Shakespeare's masterpiece–always tries to conceal the gap between cultural idioms and existential presence, but it inevitably fails to overcome the trauma of existence (and death), even when directly addressing the most tragic questions of being. Paradoxically, the only feasible realm where death and deadly desperation can really produce a new life and resurrection is the realm of language itself.

Symptomatically, for the construction of these complex and meaningful rhythmic and intertextual compositions, Rubinshtein almost invariably employs trivialized or merely meaningless textual segments. Banal phrases, incomplete sentences, interrupted scenes and plotlines, and even blank cards are his favorite "materials." The lack of independent meaning in these elements, however, serves as a powerful means to produce new meanings in Rubinshtein's texts. On the back cover for *Here I Am: Performance Poems and Essays* (2001) the critic Ekaterina Degot insightfully compares Rubinshtein's poetics with "computer hyper-texts, where each message conceals a larger context and where you unavoidably leave certain files unopened on each page as you go on. His poetics can be described as that of fatally missed opportunities and in this sense reminiscent of Chekhov, a fact that has been noted by many critics." This comparison with Anton Pavlovich Chekhov is as valid in this context as is a comparison with the "transrational" poetry (*zaum'*) of early Russian avant-garde poets. These mostly formal parallels may overshadow the fact that the constant deferral of meaning and endless postponement of the statement becomes the central theme of Rubinshtein's poetry, which makes his verse especially significant in the context of postmodernist aesthetics. Jean-François Lyotard's definition of the postmodernist sublime, as presented in his essay "Answering the Question: What is Postmodernism?" (1984), may be directly assigned to any of Rubinshtein's texts, since they all in actuality "put . . . forward the unpresentable in presentation itself; that which denies itself a solace of good forms,

the consensus of taste which would make it possible to share collectively the nostalgia for the unattainable. . . ."

A certain evolution may be detected in the development of this theme in Rubinshtein's works from the 1970s to the 1990s. In his early compositions, "Novyi antrakt," "Imperativnaia programma 'Novogo antrakta'" (The Imperative Program of "The New Intermission," 2000), and "Ocherednaia programma" (The Next Program, 2000)–both of which were written in 1975–and "Katalog komediinykh novshestv," Rubinshtein explores the process of producing various meanings through abstract grammatical structures, speech situations, and models. The detected models are so universal that in fact they can produce a variety of meanings, including ones that are opposite each other and may annihilate one another. In his contribution to *Endquote: Sots-Art Literature and Soviet Grand Style* Gerald Janecek argues that in the early Rubinshtein texts ". . . we are confronted with what could be interpreted as a very pessimistic view of the world and human activity as merely a process of going through the motions provided by the grammar of language–a mechanical, exitless, limited existence. . . . Suggested also are the limits and rigidities of language where a user is condemned to filling in the blanks of predetermined linguistic structure."

Janecek remarks that in "Ocherednaia programma" the grammar structures and speech models–or, in other words, the text itself–"creates the role of the author in its writing, goes through the process of composition step by step, places the author in an explicit, though complex, relationship with a readership and with external reality, and reminds us regularly and, especially in the end, that we are dealing with a highly artificial object." This observation is especially true in regard to Rubinshtein's "Programma sovmestnykh perezhivanii" (A Program of Joint Feelings, 2000) and "35 novykh listov" (35 New Sheets of Paper, 2000), both of which were written in 1981, in which he constructs flexible communication between the author and his readers, all of whom are united by nothing but sheer and seemingly meaningless models of communication, or pure and abstract discourse. The author's "presence" in these texts turns out to be unpresentable, appearing as an empty center (signifier) of these communicative practices.

Having detected the "limits and rigidities" of language ("the unpresentable in presentation itself," as Lyotard says) in his early works, Rubinshtein consistently tries to cross these boundaries in his later compositions. Beginning with texts such as "Malen'kaia nochnaia sereneda" and "Usloviia i primety" (Conditions and Omens, 1983) and works such as "Privyhcka iz vsego delat' tragediiu" (The Habit to Make a Tragedy Out of Everything, 1986), "Domashnee muzitsirovanie," and "Vsiudu zhizn'," the textual "noise" (the assembling of linguistic structures without content or discursive fragments) appears as a postmodernist metaphor of existence by presenting it as a chaotic whirlwind of signs, textual fragments, intertextual references, and communicative mechanisms—which either annihilate each other or produce contingent and absurd combinations, lacking any tangible order or center. Various attempts to define the meaning of "vse eto" (all this), which begins every segment of the text, bring the author to the notion of death, disappearance, lack of meaning, and silence. In these texts Rubinshtein translates the limits of textuality—the unrepresentable—into an artistic equivalent of death. Accordingly, the interrupted, incomplete, or fractured utterances that make up these texts suggest a constant deferral of the meaning of life in the process of existence.

For example, at the end of *Malen'kaia nochnaia serenada* the announcement of death emerges as the result of attempts to define the meaning of life: "85. A human cannot live / Without suffering. 86. A human cannot live, / If he doesn't have at all! 87. A human cannot live / Without dying! 88. A human cannot live! / A human cannot live! 89. (Applause)." The "figure of death" immediately translates into an acknowledgment of meaninglessness in the text: "90. –It's not clear. 91. –What is not clear? 92. –Nothing is clear! 93. –What does it mean "nothing"? 94. –Nothing is nothing. That's that. 95. It's strange." Such a juxtaposition of existential and textual "nothingness," however, produces a moment of tension and then sudden relief: "96. (Long pause). 97. (Applause)."

By substituting the existential meaninglessness of a postmodern worldview with its linguistic models, Rubinshtein also adds existential dimension to his seemingly formal search for rhythmicity. The textual movements of these compositions indicate a constant desire to penetrate into or beyond the unpresentable—to detect the moment after the end of precisely these movements, textual as well as existential. For instance, in "Druzheskie obrashcheniia 1983 goda" he writes: "After the times about which it is said that they are the last, may follow the others, about which nobody knows what to say." Obviously, the text cannot achieve the task to go beyond the presentation; persistent surfing on the brink of the "unpresentable," however, is the most important generator of rhythmicity in Rubinshtein's works—the impossibility of going further, beyond the end, produces recurring cyclical trajectories that are detected as rhythmical. Characteristically, the complex rhythms in Rubinshtein's works usually begin to appear after the clear articulation of such motifs as death, emptiness, disappearance, and void.

The desperate and senseless attempts to detect the limits of language and existence and the absurd striving to go beyond these boundaries—a striving that inevitably ends in comical failure—serve in Rubinshtein's text as the only possible way to reveal rhythm that is a subjective and tentative order within the existential-cultural chaos. As a rule, not one single fragment but rather the entire structure of the composition renders evident Rubinshtein's philosophic concept. "Vsiudu zhizn'" presents a highly characteristic example of mutual correspondence between structural and philosophic movements in Rubinshtein's poetry. "Vsiudu zhizn'" consists of several "voices." The first one is represented by the rhymed truisms on the meaning of life, invariably beginning with the words "Zhizn' daetsia . . ." (Life is given . . .). This voice is constantly interrupted by the "director's" commands, "Stop! Begin! Go on! OK! Great! Come on!" and similar expressions that constitute the second voice of the text. The third voice may be defined as collective since it encompasses fragments of various conversations, which are incomplete but suggestive: "Well, gentlemen, the tea is getting cold . . ."; "Who is cute? This mustached macaque is cute? Come on! . . ."; "One intern there, he is very cool. He looks at you so-ooo. . . ." Gradually, the third voice takes over the rhymed maxims on the meaning of life, and the fragmented pieces of conversation begin to form microplots, all varying the motif of rejection of the search for the meaning of life: "Let me see: 'Bha-ga-vat-gi-ta' . . . What the fuck is this? . . . 'All is a game'–who said this? . . . There are several reasons here. The first is the System itself. . . . My god, they are all guilty. Take this one for example. . . ." After these statements appears a textual segment that may be read both as an autoreferential metapoetic statement and the author's own answer to the philosophical question, "Do you know what crossed my mind? In order to resurrect a cadaver,–in the aesthetic terms, of course,–one must kill it first. The main thing is to find a way to do so . . . Not clear? Well–later. . . ." In other words, to supplement the lack of the meaning of life or of the text interchangeably, which was substituted either by "poetic" truisms or by prosaic cynicism, one needs to experience death or, in aesthetic terms, to transgress the unrepresentable.

The segment of the text that immediately follows this statement–at first vaguely and then more and more distinctively–develops the motif of sudden death that cancels any life plans and drags the survivors to the edge of yawning emptiness. The cards representing this textual movement alternate with those that vary the motif of unpredictability and the incomprehensibility of existence. Step-by-step, these prosaic as well as rhymed fragments deconstruct the model of life represented by the first (optimistic) and third (cynical) "voices." In this part the bitter vision of existential chaos replaces both "high" and "low" discourses, which reveal their comic impotence next to the notions of death. In this context the second voice—the "director's" commands—acquires a new meaning. It begins to be perceived as the voice of God who, with a teacher's persistence, brings the reader back to the sober and hopeless understanding of the chaotic nature of existence: "Stop! Once again! All together: Stop! From the very beginning!"

The message of the chaotic senselessness of existence, however, contradicts the enhanced rhythmicity of the finale, wherein prosaic and rhymed voices merge in their attempt to find the most appropriate ending to the phrase "Our life all by itself, runs across the waves. . . ." Such variants as "with an unruly head," "with an incomprehensible head," and "with an impossible head" are rejected altogether. Only the version "Our life all by itself runs across the waves. With infinite ennui" receives the "director's" approval: "All right. That's it. Enough. Thank you." The juxtaposition of extreme pessimism with the highest degree of rhythmicity clearly demonstrates that ridiculous and desperate attempts to detect the meaning of life—and by this means to transgress death—can only confirm once again the lack of meaning. Yet, these attempts produce a certain rhythm and order within the chaos of language and existence, making both at least merrier.

The constitution of the poet's subjectivity occupies a primary place in Rubinshtein's compositions of the 1990s. Almost all of them are focused either on processes of writing and reading, as seen in "Chistaia lirika" (Pure Lyrics, 1989), "Voprosy literatury," and "Reguliarnoe pis'mo" (1994), or they directly address the problem of self-representation, demonstrated in "Drugoe imia" (Another Name, 1990), "Vremia idet" (1990), "'Ia zdes'" (1994; translated as "Here I Am," 2001), and "'Eto ia'" (1995; translated as "That's Me"). Similar motifs began to appear in Rubinshtein's texts from the 1980s, however, as evidenced in "Shestikrylyi serafim," *Poiavlenie geroia,* "Sonet 66," and *Mama myla ramu* (translated as "The Cat Wore a Hat," 2001). In all these texts the self collides with others, and the presence and the absence of "I" are joined.

Quite characteristically, two of the last texts from this "series" are named almost tautologically: "'Ia zdes'" and "'Eto ia.'" In both titles, the presence of "I" in quotation marks renders obvious that identity may manifest itself only through a quotation, by something borrowed from "others." "'Eto ia'" occasions a sort of summary of Rubinshtein's poetry as a whole. The interaction between the photographs (or photographic cards) from the family album and the bibliographical cards shapes the plotline of the entire "'Eto ia.'" The names mentioned in the first half of the text as people pictured in the family photos become the authors of books and articles in the

Лев Рубинштейн
Случаи из языка
ИЗДАТЕЛЬСТВО ИВАНА ЛИМБАХА

Paperback cover for Rubinshtein's Sluchai iz iazyka *(Happenings of Language, 1998), for which he received the Andrei Belyi Literary Prize in 2000 (Collection of Mark Lipovetsky)*

second half. Another pivotal point is that all these names first appear after "Sitting" and "Standing" in the "photographic" part. A certain group photograph from a family archive comes to life before the reader's eyes. Seemingly, any autobiographically colored elements that could be the bearers of the self-consciousness of "I" are completely absent. In fact, the "I" here is manifested indirectly through "others." Only the consciousness and portrayal of "I" continually appearing next to those of "Govendo T. Kh." and "the aforementioned A. V. Sutiagin" unites these characters in the general space of the text—in a single scene of the text, actually—from which they all gradually exit. The remarks they pronounce may puzzle one only outside of the general semantic field of the text.

Thus, A. P. Gavrilin says: "We, for example, say: the wind is making noise. Right? . . . Yet, it is not the wind at all, but rather that which falls in its path: tree branches, roofing tin, stove chimneys. The wind, Liubochka, is not making noise. What can it make noise with?" This explanation directly refers to the ability of the "I" to manifest itself in the poem, a problem with which the structure of the text constantly plays. "I" is the wind, incarnating itself only in something else or through others, but not reduced to roofs, chimneys, and trees, remaining in some way separate from them.

By no accident—when everyone exits before the finale—does "I," nevertheless, not disappear. The rhythm of the final part (cards 103–119) returns to the rhythm of the initial fragment. Yet, the rhythmicity of the final fragment is much greater. Here, the same phrase is distinctly repeated—"And that's me"—whereas in the beginning "I" was invoked through variations. The repeated maxim in its turn is anaphorically linked with phrases about others. Here, too, these phrases shape a text with verse rhymes, but now the composition is no longer torn apart by the refrain "And that's me"; on the contrary, the refrain becomes an integral part of the particular and tangible rhythmic design. There truly is an occurrence of "I," dissolved in signs of the existence of others.

Rubinshtein's autobiographical "I" is freed of any individual biographical or even external characteristics. At the same time this "I" turns out to be an unrepeatable combination of alien and repeated elements of existence, from people and words to things and signs. The search for this combination, the elaboration of its design, is actually the meaning of life; the definitive discovery of "I" is the result of one's life. When this search is completed, one can only exit.

That all the characters, including "I," eventually exit connects this composition with Rubinshtein's works of the second period, which focus on attempts to transgress the unrepresentable—death, absence, and silence. In "'Eto ia'" Rubinshtein does not try to cross this invisible boundary. Furthermore, the "exit" remark appears when the part played by the character on the textual stage is completed. The absence and the exiting justify that the presence, albeit elusive and arbitrary, has occurred. In fact, the "exit" becomes the main proof of the character's life, the "I" notwithstanding. This finale echoes with that of the composition "'Ia zdes'" in which the protagonist's futile attempts to announce his presence ("I vot ia zdes' . . .") are constantly interrupted by somebody's voices, impersonal description of other people and their lifestyles, scenes from somebody else's everyday dramas, and so forth. Only in the final part of the composition (cards 81–97) the last announcement "Itak, ia zdes'!" ("And so, I'm here!") generates a stream of poetic images united

with feelings of parting and disappearance, which reach their climax in the last four cards repeating the same phrase: "Ukhodim vroz', ne zabyvai menia" ("We go our separate ways, don't forget me").

The structure of Rubinshtein's texts written in the 1990s becomes a plastic model of the "I," a model of moving (self-) consciousness. Its rhythmic structure acquires a special, philosophical meaning. The segments of the text, united by a single rhythm, manifest—not biographical but, rather, metaphysical—phases of the formation of the "I." The rhythmic organization turns this text into a condensed synopsis of a bildungsroman. The concept of the creative "I" is born as a result of the attendant short-lived systems characterizing the unstable correlation of the "I" and the Other. The "I" is also a dynamic unity of these unstable rhythms, which join "I" and the Other in such diverse and contradictory ways.

"'Eto ia'" and "'Ia zdes'" are the last published and—according to the poet's confessions—last written poetic compositions. Paradoxically, the decline of Rubinshtein's poetic activity occurred at the time when he had become widely acknowledged as one of the most original contemporary Russian poets. In 1992 and 1994 he was awarded several prestigious German literary prizes. In 1992 he became a member of the Russian PEN Center. His texts were used by composers such as Anton Batagov, Vladimir Martynov, and Aleksei Aigi for various music performances, in which the poet frequently participated. In 1998 well-known conceptualist artist Grisha Bruskin created a series of porcelain plates, "Na kraiu" (On the Edge), that combined stylized visual images with fragments from Rubinshtein's texts placed on the plates' borders or edges. Rubinshtein is regularly invited to various European and American universities to give poetry readings.

After a period of virtual silence, in the late 1990s Rubinshtein started to write and publish prose. The author's prose is closely connected to his newly acquired career as a journalist. He worked as a staff member of the newly organized magazine *Itogi* (Summing Up, a joint project with *Newsweek*), from 1996 to 2001. In 2001, after a forced change in management, Rubinshtein—together with other staff members—left *Itogi*. In 2002 the entire group organized a new magazine, *Ezhenedel'nyi zhurnal* (A Weekly Journal), for which Rubinshtein wrote until 2003, when he left to work as a columnist for the new magazine, *Politburo*. Rubinshtein's assignments include "columns," interviews, and book reviews. Soon after their first appearance, his columns, however, surpassed the limits of the journalistic "free genre." In 2000 Rubinshtein was awarded the prestigious Andrei Belyi Literary Prize, in the category of literary criticism, for his prose collection *Sluchai iz iazyka* (Happenings of Language, 1998). Paradoxically, how-

Rubinshtein in Moscow, June 2003

ever, none of the texts included in *Sluchai iz iazyka* could be categorized reasonably as "literary criticism." Rubinshtein had created a genre of his own. The short nonfictional stories of *Sluchai iz iazyka,* with their distinct comical twists, focus on the deconstruction of social and personal mythologies reflected mostly through language. This new genre is not opposed to Rubinshtein's poetic works. In actuality, it represents the logical development of his interest in nonfictional discourse as manifested in his compositions of the 1990s. That the fullest collection of Rubinshtein's poetic texts, *Domashnee muzitsirovanie,* also includes six of his nonfictional stories confirms that a significant correlation exists between his prose and his poetry. A similar principle of organization is used in *Here I Am,* since that book consists of two prosaic texts and nine poetic compositions.

In his first book of prose, *Slauchai iz iazyka,* Rubinshtein invariably addresses subjects that, in different respects, reflect the most popular or authoritative discourses and mythologies of the current and recent epochs. He writes about the Soviet mythologies surrounding Vladimir Lenin, as seen in "V Mavzolei tvoiu" (Into Your Tomb) and Pushkin, as shown in "Ostorozhno – Pushkin" (Caution: Pushkin). He comically describes channels of artificial mythologization, exemplified by the pieces, "Narmud – éto Shprit dlia naroda . . ." (Narmud is Shprit for the people . . .) and "Liniia otryva" (The Line of Detachment). He discusses transmutations of language–as in "OPEN ili ne OPEN," "Im pishet vsiakii" (Everyone Writes with It), and "U menia zazvonil telefon" (A Phone Rings at My Place)–and perceptions of the West in Soviet and post-Soviet times, shown in "Uzhe kak doma" (Already As If at Home) and "Vnuki starika Khottabycha, ili Mal'chik u Khrista na elke" (Grandchildren of the Old Genie Khottabych, or A Boy at the Christmas Party). He is interested in the semiotics of "monumental propaganda," crises of authorship, the collapse of literary hierarchies, and the mythology of a road. He is intrigued by the paradoxes of Russian femininity, as well as by the resurrection of the Soviet anthem and imperial symbolism in general. He develops his autobiographical discourse through an investigation of the mythologies of childhood, as in "O strakhakh" (On Fears) and in "O poteriakh" (On Losses). Some of his texts may be read as condensed symbols of entire epochs: "Kommunal'noe chtivo" (translated as "Communal Fiction") pictures the mythology of a communal apartment as the epitome of the Soviet way of life. The spirit of the early 1980s with its endless funerals of the Communist bosses is pinpointed in the absurdist "Vospominanie o vozdaianii" (Reminiscence on Retribution). In contrast, the fantastic nature of perestroika is captured in "Razbor poletov, ili desiat' let spustia" (Discussion on Flights, or Ten Years Later), Rubinshtein's recollection about Matias Rust, the young German who landed his one-man plane on Red Square.

Regardless of the scale of his subject, Rubinshtein pictures it as unnoticeable molecules of the cultural landscape through minute and comprehensive, anecdotal details and paradoxes. Thus, in his text "Dym otechestva, ili Gulag s fil'trom" (2000; translated as "The Smoke of the Fatherland, or a Filter Gulag," 2001) he discusses the reappearance of an old and coarse brand of cigarettes, "Belomor," on the post-Soviet free market. At first he sarcastically defamiliarizes "automatized perceptions" of the brand name: "The most portentous aspect of a Belomor is its name, which has survived everything. Imagine a German cigarette called Auschwitz or Buchenwald. Consider as well the smoking chimneys and the similarity becomes ridiculous. You could split your sides laughing." Subsequently, he pays attention to a small detail that distinguishes the new Belomor from its prototype: the former is filtered, more "civilized," more refined, yet with "the same sickeningly familiar picture on the pack." Rubinshtein immediately detects in this seemingly unnoticeable transformation the emblem of the newly born post-Soviet, nostalgic mythology of history.

Out of all Rubinshtein's prosaic texts, this essay is probably one of the most serious by its intonation. Usually his "deconstructions" of popular mythologies are hilariously funny rather than sarcastic. He does not satirize but observes the paradoxes of mythological mentality, as a rule, through the prism of linguistic formulas. Thus, the horror-movie nature of the cult of Lenin is exposed in a story about a boy who returns home from kindergarden, completely in tears, as shown in "V mavzolei tvoiu": "'I am afraid of Lenin,' in a trembling whisper said the boy. 'What do you mean?' Mom got scared no less than her son. 'Galina Nikolaevna told us that Lenin died but he is still alive and loves children very much!'"

Rubinshtein's laughter–his ability to detect absurdities of mentality petrified in language–is opposed to "mass didacticism," which he defines as a dominant factor in Russian cultural mentality. In "Uchitelia bez uchenikov, ili Iz-pod glyb" (Teachers without Students, or From beneath the Rocks, 1998) he defines it as "a seemingly civilized form of violence and aggression, which deeply penetrated the atmosphere of public and private life." The ability to laugh and to distance oneself from mythological formulas and beliefs, suggests the multiple and relative natures of any truth, of any statement, and thus undermines any possibility of judgment. Rubinshtein trusts the logic of language that, sooner or later, unintentionally brings any seriousness and any dogma to the point of absurdity. At these moments language ceases to serve as a "vehicle for ideas" and starts to mock its own "content." The nonfictional documentation of these particular moments, these everyday involuntary "deconstructions," constitutes the main goal of Rubinshtein's prose.

Through his works and his lifelong performance Lev Semenovich Rubinshtein bridges two epochs of Russian cultural history. As one of the leaders of underground literature in Moscow, he managed to preserve his idiosyncratic place within new cultural conditions after the collapse of Communist rule. Unlike many other underground authors, he did not join the post-Soviet literary establishment (he has more literary honors and awards from abroad than from Russia). He also avoided the danger of self-repetition and even reinvented himself as a prose writer. Neither an ideologist nor an entertainer, Rubinshtein almost entirely alone represents a philosophical trend within Russian postmodernism. This trend focuses on the playful, yet emotionally charged, deconstructions of existential and unrepresentable aspects of various discursive practices and language. This kind of literary deconstruction surpasses the limits of the critique of totalitarian ideology and its language, defining factors for Moscow conceptualism and sots-art (postmodernist mockery of socialist realism discourses). Therefore, the increasing historical remoteness of Soviet cultural mythologies does not undermine the significance of Rubinshtein's works but, on the contrary, reveals in them new philosophical dimensions echoing the poststructuralist critique of the logocentrism and metaphysics of presence.

Interviews:

Holt Meyer, "Iazyk-pole bor'by i svobody," *Novoe literaturnoe obozrenie*, 2 (1993): 306–311;

"It Is the Time and It Is the Record of the Time," *Khudozhestvennyi zhurnal*, 7 (1995);

Zara Abdullaeva, "Voprosy literatury," *Druzhba narodov*, 6 (1997): 176–184;

Sergei Shapoval, "Chistaia lirika," *Ural'skaia nov'*, 2 (1998);

Tatiana Voskovskaia, "Dlia menia liuboi tekst sposoben v kakoi-to moment stat' poéziiei," *Russian *Journal* (21 April 1998) <http://www.russ.ru/journal/inie/98-04-21/voskov.htm>.

References:

Mikhail Natanovich Aizenberg, "Nekotorye drugie," *Teatr,* 4 (1991): 98–111;

Aizenberg, "Vmesto predisloviia," in *Pondel'nik: Sem' poetov samizdata,* compiled by Dmitrii Aleksandrovich Prigov (Moscow: Prometei, 1990), pp. 7–26;

Aizenberg, "Vokrug kontseptualizma," in his *Vzgliad na svobodnogo khudozhnika* (Moscow: Gendalf, 1997), pp. 128–154;

Dmitrii Bavil'sky, "Kartochnyi domik," *Arion,* 3 (1998);

Mikhail Berg, "Poslednie tsvety L'va Rubinshteina," *Novoe literaturnoe obozrenie,* 30 (1998): 343–348;

Mikhail Naumovich Epshtein, "On Olga Sedakova and Lev Rubinshtein," in *Russian Postmodernism: New Perspectives on Post-Soviet Culture,* by Epshtein, Aleksandr Genis, and Slobodanka Vladiv-Glover (New York: Berghahn Books, 1999), pp. 113–117;

Michael Fleischer, "Das Fragment und die Bedeutung: Eine besondere Textsorte," in *Probleme der Textlinguistik/ Problemy lingvistiki teksta: Gemeinschaftsarbeit von Wissenschaftlern der Partneruniversitaten Bochum and Minsk,* edited by Helmut Jachnow and Adam E. Suprun (Munich: Sagner, 1989), pp. 141–172;

Mikhail Leonovich Gasparov, "Russkii stikh kak zerkalo postsovetskoi kul'tury," *Novoe literaturnoe obozrenie,* 32 (1998): 77–83;

Boris Efimovich Groys, "Moskovskii romanticheskii kontseptualizm," in his *Utopia i obmen. Stil' Stalin. O novom* (Moscow: Znak, 1993), pp. 260–274;

Groys, "Text as a Ready-Made Object," *Endquote: Sots-Art Literature and Soviet Grand Style,* edited by Marina Balina, Nancy Condee, and Evgeny Dobrenko (Evanston, Ill.: Northwestern University Press, 2000), pp. 32–45;

Gerald Janecek, "Lev Rubinshtein's Early Conceptualism: The Program of Works," in *Endquote: Sots-Art Literature and Soviet Grand Style,* edited by Balina, Condee, and Dobrenko (Evanston, Ill.: Northwestern University Press, 2000), pp. 107–122;

Naum Leiderman and Mark Lipovetsky, *Sovremennaia russkaia literatura. Kniga 3. V kontse veka* (Moscow: Editorial URSS, 2001), pp. 22–26;

V. Lettsev, "Kontseptualizm-chtenie i ponimanie," *Daugava,* 8 (1989): 107–113;

Lipovetsky, "Konets veka liriki," *Znamia,* 10 (1996): 206–216;

Alessandro Niero, "O 'kartotechnoi' poezii L'va Rubinshteina," *Slavica Tergestina,* 7 (1999): 123–144;

Irina Stepanovna Skoropanova, "Iazykovye matritsy massovogo soznaniia: Lev Rubinshtein," in her *Russkaia postmodernistskaia literatura* (Moscow: Flinta, 1999), pp. 203–209;

Andrei Leonidovich Zorin, "Al'manakh–vzgliad iz zala," *Lichnoe delo #__,* pp. 246–271;

Zorin, "Katalog," *Literaturnoe obozrenie,* 10 (1989): 90–92;

Zorin, "Muzy iazyka i semero poetov," *Druzhba narodov,* 4 (1990): 240–249;

Zorin, "Stikhi na kartochkakh: Poeticheskii iazyk L'va Rubinshteina," *Daugava,* 8 (1989): 100–102.

Nina Nikolaevna Sadur

(15 October 1950 –   )

Birgit Beumers
University of Bristol

BOOKS: *Chudnaia baba,* with an afterword by Viktor Sergeevich Rozov (Moscow: Soiuzteatr, 1989)—includes *Chudnaia baba, Ulichennaia lastochka, Ekhai, Zaria vzoidet, Sila volos, Zamerzli,* and *Nos;*

Ved'miny slezki: Kniga prozy (Moscow: Glagol, 1994)—includes *Chudesnye znaki spasen'ia, Almaznaia dolina, Iug,* "Veter okrain," and "Bessmertniki"—comprises "Severnoe siianie," "Bezotvetnaia liubov'," "Utiugi i almazy," "Tsvetenie," "Blizhe k pokoiu," "Motyl'ki Soldaii," "Pechal' ottsa moego," and "Zanebesnyi mal'chik"; translated by Cathy Porter as *Witch's Tears and Other Stories* (London: Harbord, 1997)—includes "Unrequited Love," "Flowering," "Closer to Rest," "Star-Boy," "The South," and "The Wind from the Suburbs";

Sad (Vologda: Poligrafist, 1997);

Obmorok (Vologda: Poligrafist, 1999)—includes *Krasnyi paradiz, Morokob,* and *Chardym;*

Chudesnye znaki spasen'ia (Moscow: Vagrius, 2000);

Vechnaia merzlota (Moscow: ZebraE/EKSMO, 2002).

Editions in English: "Witch's Tears," translated by Alexander Maidan, in *Women's View,* edited by Natasha Perova and Andrew Bromfield (Moscow: Glas, 1992);

"Irons and Diamonds," translated by Bromfield, in *Jews and Strangers,* edited by Perova (Moscow: Glas, 1993);

"Frozen," translated by Catriona Kelly, in *An Anthology of Russian Women's Writing, 1777–1992,* edited by Kelly (Oxford & New York: Oxford University Press, 1994);

"Touched," in *Half a Revolution,* edited and translated by Masha Gessen, with a preface by Olga Lipovskaya (Pittsburgh: Cleis, 1995)—includes "It Glistened," "Mean Girls," "Rings," "Silky Hair," "The Bad Seed," "The Blue Hand," "The Cute Little Redhead," "They Froze," and "Two Fianceés";

"Worm-Eaten Sonny" and "Wicked Girls," in *Lives in Transit,* edited by Helena Goscilo (Dana Point, Cal.: Ardis, 1995).

Nina Nikolaevna Sadur (photograph by Vasily Dorofeev © Vagrius)

PLAY PRODUCTIONS: *Chudnaia baba* and *Nos,* Moscow, Theater Studio "Benefice," 1987;

Chudnaia baba, Moscow, Center Debut, 1987; Moscow, Ermolova Theater, 10 October 1987; Vilnius, Russian Drama Theater, 1988;

Pannochka, Moscow, Studio Theater Chelovek, 1988;

Liubovnye liudi, Leningrad, Theater Studio of L. Malevannaia, 1991;

Sobor"iane, Moscow, Vakhtangov Theater, 1991;

Pannochka, Omsk, Academic Drama Theater, 16 June 1992;

Lunnye volki, St. Petersburg, Fontanka Theater, 1993;

Cherty, suki, kommunal'nye kozly, Moscow, MGU Theater, 1993;

Ubliudok, Moscow, Theater Model, 1993;

Brat Chichikov, Saratov, Academic Drama Theater, 1996; Omsk Drama Theater, 15 May 2002;

Ulichennaia lastochka, Moscow, Theater Studio "Benefice," 1996;

Zamerzli, Ulan-Ude, Youth Theater, 1998;

Chardym, St. Petersburg, Baltic House Theater, 4 May 1998;

Zovite Pechorinym, Moscow, Pushkin Theater, 15 October 1999;

Mistifikatsiia (Brat Chichikov), Moscow, Lenkom Theater, 5 January 1999.

PRODUCED SCRIPTS: *Star Boy,* radio, BBC, 1996; *Ekhai,* radio, BBC, 1998.

OTHER: "Pronikshie," in *Nepomniashchaia zla,* edited by Larisa L'vovna Vaneeva (Moscow: Moskovsky rabochii, 1990);

"Krasnyi paradiz," in *Novye amazonki,* edited by Svetlana Vasilenko (Moscow: Moskovsky rabochii, 1991).

Nina Sadur began her career as a playwright. During the latter years of perestroika Sadur's plays were circulated and staged initially at small studio theaters before they were added to the repertoire of more-established theaters. Her plays are powerful in their structure, their use of language, and their combination of folk beliefs and ritual with Soviet reality. By anticipating the prominence of ritual through her dramatic works of the 1990s, Sadur influenced the development of Russian theater aesthetics. She shares with conceptualists a concern for the power of language, which she undermines in her writings by pointing up the failure of language to convey meaning. Sadur's phantasmagoric worlds are not constructed through language but through characters, and as such they are far more tangible than linguistic constructs. Her thematic approach lies with the meaning of human existence in an open space and with the nature of evil. Sadur's creative career as a playwright effectively ended, however, around 1987. By the early 1990s she had moved away from playwriting toward prose, first publishing stories in collections before producing longer prose works in the latter half of the 1990s. Sadur's reputation as a playwright is nonetheless significantly stronger and more substantive than her role as a prose writer.

Nina Nikolaevna Sadur was born on 15 October 1950 in Novosibirsk to a family engaged in the literary life: her mother worked as a teacher of Russian; her father was a poet. Sadur arrived in Moscow in 1977 to study at the Gor'ky Institute of World Literature, from which she graduated in 1983. Sadur studied at the Literary Institute under Viktor Sergeevich Rozov, a distinguished playwright. Sadur demonstrates an extraordinary grasp of theatrical conditions in her plays: she both conforms to theatrical tradition and innovates it from within, breaking free from the constraints of psychological realism in her vision of a new kind of theater. While her full-length plays testify to her awareness of the conventions of Soviet theater of the time, she was quick to develop her own theater language and patient enough to wait for theaters and directors to find the most appropriate scenic language for her texts. Her first play, *Chudnaia baba* (The Weird Peasant Woman, 1989) written in 1982, enjoyed great popularity among the studio theaters that flourished in Moscow during the mid 1980s. The proper scenic expression for its combination of Soviet reality with universal absurdity came about when Vladimir Tumanov staged *Chudnaia baba* in Vilnius, Lithuania, in 1988.

Chudnaia baba established Sadur as a leading playwright of the "new wave" of Soviet dramatists, alongside Liudmila Petrushevskaya, Viktor Iosifovich Slavkin, and Liudmila Nikolaevna Razumovskaia. It consists of two plays, "Pole" (The Field) and "Gruppa tovarishchei" (A Group of Comrades). In "Pole" the reader encounters Lidiia Petrovna, lost in an open field—an image that recurs in many of Sadur's plays of the period. She meets an old peasant woman, who appears from nowhere, and asks her for directions to the field where she is supposed to harvest potatoes with her colleagues from work. Yet, instead of receiving instructions, Lidiia begins to pity the old woman for wearing no socks, and she pledges her help. The woman's surname, Ubienko (from *ubit',* or to kill), does not startle Lidiia, even though her heart suddenly starts aching. Identifying herself as the evil of the world, the old woman soon emerges as the force that probably led Lidiia astray in the first place. The woman offers to play a game, in which Lidiia has to catch her and thus rid the world of all evil. Lidiia fails to hold the woman: she is afraid of sacrificing her own life, although the reward is paradise on earth. She falls into a black hole, and the upper skin of the earth is peeled away, so that all life disappears, except for Lidiia. Now that she is the remaining company for the old woman, Lidiia no longer wants to live; in order to entertain her only companion, the old woman creates an exact replica of the world that has disappeared.

In the second play, "Gruppa tovarishchei," Lidiia Petrovna is back in her Moscow office, convinced that everybody around her is a mere reflection of the real person, and only she is alive. She believes herself responsible for the disappearance of the whole world and tells her coworkers what happened. As a result, none of Lidiia's colleagues can prove that they really exist—not even through confessions of hitherto unknown deeds (theft) and emotions (love and hatred). Eventually, they turn against Lidiia by alleging that she has died and has been unwilling to sacrifice her life for the happiness of the world. Here, Sadur plays with an inversion of perspectives and viewpoints, gradually shifting the point of view of the drama. At a point when the audience verges on perceiving Lidiia's experience as a dream, one of her coworkers receives a call from the old woman, who asks after the socks that Lidiia promised her.

In *Chudnaia baba* Sadur explores folk beliefs (such as the myth of the world standing on three whales) and mingles them with philosophical views (the phenomenal world as a mere reflection), while all the time addressing issues of immortality and of the meaning of life. By setting the play in an open field in the first part of *Chudnaia baba* and then switching to the enclosed space of a Moscow office, she reveals her extraordinary capacity to combine an abstract setting with the realia of Soviet life. Her characters use folk language mixed with colloquialisms or local dialect. Yet, language fails as a means of communication: Lidiia Petrovna is taken nowhere by the old woman, and she cannot convince her colleagues about what has really happened. As Catriona Kelly asserts in regard to *Chudnaia baba* in *A History of Russian Women's Writing, 1777–1992* (1994), "But if Sadur is arguing here that language creates reality, she is equally concerned with the limitations of language. In the second part of 'The Weird Peasant Woman,' Lidiya Petrovna . . . fails to persuade her colleagues of the momentous cosmic change that has taken place." Sadur thus undermines the power attributed to language by many of her contemporary writers, such as Vladimir Georgievich Sorokin and Viktor Olegovich Pelevin.

Ulichennaia lastochka (The Trapped Swallow, 1996), written in 1982, is a full-length play that explores a couple's relationship, as well as their association with Daria, a psychotherapist at a clinic. Daria tries to cure Alla, the wife, of memory loss but in fact strips Alla of her identity and individuality. In the first act Daria isolates Alla in an apartment, hoping to create a vacuum around her in order to induce a recovery of memory by making Alla feel anxious about her loneliness. At the same time, Daria alleges the existence of a relationship between Alla's husband, Andrei, and their adopted daughter. In the second act Daria makes Alla responsible for the death of Daria's nephew Vasia, with whom Alla had an affair. Daria then manipulates Andrei into thinking that Alla killed Vasia, after accusing him first of the murder. She then finds out that Alla only pretends to have lost her memory and that Alla did indeed kill Vasia and has taken the keys to the apartment from an inmate in the clinic. As Daria compares her to an imprisoned swallow, Alla "flies" out of the window to her death. On the level of a detective story, Daria's discovery drives Alla to suicide, which may be an indication of her guilt. Yet, the isolation that Daria imposed on Alla makes impossible Alla's return to her former life. Daria composes roles for everybody around her, and ultimately she acquires authority and the meaning of life only through her victims. *Ulichennaia lastochka* is a fine example of Sadur's playful exploration of the human psyche and issues of power and authority; it also examines language as a force that creates and manipulates people and reality.

Ekhai (Drive On, 1998), written in 1983, is one of Sadur's most popular plays. Set in the "open space" of the stage, it depicts an encounter between a *mashinist* (in this case, a train engineer-driver) and a *muzhik* (man): as the man attempts to kill himself on the rails, the driver stops the train and tries to make the man move. Angry that his timetable will get muddled, the driver appeals to the man to think of the passengers on the train. The man, in turn, tries to convince the driver to run over him: he encourages the driver to think of him as an enemy—so as to make the job of running over the man easier for the driver. Then the driver tells the man about his own life and colleagues in the hope that once the man learns of the driver's travails, he will change his mind about committing suicide. Eventually, the driver suggests taking the man to a doctor who can offer professional help in solving the man's problems. The man mentions that "his woman" did not give him money for wine, and he therefore wants to kill himself; the driver instantly offers the money. At this point an old woman (*babka*) arrives, looking for her goat. Although the man is not from her village and speaks a different dialect he finds a common language with the woman, who accepts him despite all his foibles. Though the *mashinist* warns the couple otherwise, the *muzhik* and the *babka* march off together. Sadur cleverly shifts power and dominance from the driver to the man, while undermining the force of language: the stories about himself that the driver tells the man have no effect, while ultimately the unstructured and repetitive use of folk wisdom by the old woman has a lasting impact. Language serves to invent reality, not to pin it down. The identity of the man is also veiled in mystery: he could be a former convict, he could be a simple peasant–Sadur leaves his identity undefined to the end.

Zaria vzoidet (Dawn Rises, 1989), written in 1983, consists of two parts: "Ubliudok" (The Mongrel) and "Lunnye volki" (Lunar Wolves). "Ubliudok" explores the relationship between Viktor, Zoya, and their adopted son, Egor, who supports them in both financial and moral ways. Egor once saved Viktor, who has begun drinking after seeing a wolf on the street–a fact that Zoya tries to explain by inverting the order: according to her, Viktor first came under the impact of alcohol, then saw the wolf. This inversion makes the mysterious and supernatural acceptable; a character's manipulation of reality through language is a common device in Sadur's work. Finally, Zoya asks Egor to free Viktor from her presence and kill her: she is incapable of combining the real and the supernatural–not unlike Lidiia Petrovna (in *Chudnaia baba*), who is taken to an asylum at the end of the play, or Alla (in *Ulichennaia lastochka*), who commits suicide.

"Lunnye volki" explains why Egor is called a mongrel: he lives with wolves. One day he encounters the old woman Motia, whom he asks for a sheep to take to the wolves but which she refuses to give. Old age and youth are blurred in Egor's character: he is both a boy and an adult. Such blurred lines between youth and old age occur in Sadur's prose as well–notably exemplified by the character Anna Ivanovna in the story "Veter okrain" (1994; translated as "The Wind from the Suburbs," 1997)–and serve to illustrate the vague and indefinite nature of reality when compared to memory and dreams. Eventually Motia seizes a gun, ready to arrest Egor, whose destruction of Viktor was a result of his interference in an experiment with a wolf. Once Egor is dead, the sun will rise again. The play has allegorical overtones about the Soviet system. Its references to the sheep, herds, and wolves that are hunted also appear in the work of poets such as Sergei Aleksandrovich Esenin and Vladimir Semenovich Vysotsky, who felt persecuted by the Soviet system. Yet, the setting is in an open, undefined space, while references to folk beliefs and superstitions (the behavior of wolves) are mingled with Soviet reality (the life of Viktor and Zoya). The two worlds coexist: the mysterious develops from a seemingly perfect, normal setting (an old woman feeds a boy by the fire) and interferes with reality (the broken relationship between Zoya and Viktor), while evil is embodied by a boy (Egor) who wishes to do good but wreaks havoc.

Written in 1984, *Sila volos* (The Power of Hair, 1989) clearly is not written for the stage. Imitating the style of Evgenii Vladimirovich Kharitonov, to whom it is dedicated, the play consists of conversations conducted by hair–at times in single voices, at others in a chorus of voices–lamenting that the man on whose head they grow has fallen in love with a woman, whose hair they are not compatible with. In fact, the woman–apparently noticing the jealousy of the man's hair toward hers–sets a louse into his hair. The piece is interesting for its poetic and rhythmic use of language reflecting the movement of hair, as well as the formation of single voices into a chorus. The play also demonstrates Sadur's ability to create nonhuman characters that are endowed with human features (love and jealousy) in the tradition of Nikolai Vasil'evich Gogol's "Nos" (The Nose, written in 1833, published in 1836).

Indeed, Sadur's own play *Nos* (The Nose, 1989), written in 1986–though less concerned with certain "Gogolian" themes–alludes to Gogol's work even more explicitly. Irma has invited her former friends from college for a visit: Natasha and Volodia, who are getting married, and Marina and Tolik. They are all afraid of Irma because of her evil looks, her black eyes, and her resemblance to a witch; Irma has tried to rectify these physical shortcomings by having cosmetic surgery on her nose. Irma says that she is studying kindness as a way to cure people of illnesses, but she is lying; she claims that she dreams of everybody she knows–also a lie. When her friends realize that they have started to quibble because of Irma, they leave; suddenly, Irma threatens that her brother will kill them when he is released from prison. In *Nos,* Sadur weaves together numerous features of her earlier work: her concern with the supernatural and the mysterious and the theme of evil beings doing good are presented alongside the manipulation of reality (Irma's lies). Sadur also brings in a new element: the evil deed becomes dissociated from the supernatural world and enters the criminal world.

Sadur's full-length plays of this period also include *Novoe znakomstvo* (New Acquaintance, 1986), a two-act play set in a provincial town, in which the police officer Grachev tries to bring order to the apartment block where he grew up. Grachev is apparently fond of Larisa, who has been living with her brother, Misha, since the two were orphaned. Fearing the loss of his sister's affection, Misha destroys a neighbor's car in rage and verbally abuses other neighbors; eventually, his abuse causes the neighborhood caretaker, whom he sees as a father figure, to have a heart attack. Grachev follows Misha's behavior and realizes the difficulty of his job as a policeman: he has to separate his love for Larisa from the job of containing Misha's aggression, which evidently results from Grachev's affection for Larisa. This play develops further the theme of psychological terror first seen in *Ulichennaia lastochka* but remains within the boundaries of late-1980s conventions of Russian theater the concern for

Front cover for Sadur's Ved'miny slezki *(translated as* Witch's Tears and Other Stories, *1997), a collection of short prose works, many of them organized in cycles (Jean and Alexander Heard Library, Vanderbilt University)*

one's social environment, love and hatred, and the betterment of society are common Russian cultural themes of this time.

Zamerzli (1989; translated as "Frozen," 1994) is a *p'esa-maliutka* (miniature play), according to Sadur's genre definition. She took up the theme of this play in a story of the same title in the cycle "Pronikshie" (Penetrated, 1990; translated as "Touched," 1995). *Zamerzli* explores the situation of Nadia, whose mother dates young boys and does not give her any pocket money. Nadia is thus forced to take a job as a custodian in a theater, where she meets, and works with, Leila. Leila, from Daghestan, is educated but not pretty—she was beaten by her father—and has bad hearing. The girls observe Uncle Leva, an "evil man" who works in the theater, while Leila tells Nadia about the theater, its spells and mysteries, and her dreams of a house and a family. They see a cross with a Christ figure being car-

ried out from the theater storage room, and Nadia, upset about the state of the cross, brushes off the snow and waves at Uncle Leva in a mocking way, which prompts him to throw a stone at her. Nadia wakes up at home. In the story Nadia is alone; she has nobody to talk to; and the narrative presents her isolation. The dialogue with Leila, the southern girl, feeds into the novel *Almaznaia dolina* (Diamond Valley), which appeared in the 1994 collection *Ved'miny slezki: Kniga prozy* (Witch's Tears: A Book of Prose).

Next, Sadur wrote two short plays set in the town of Sudak in the Crimea. "Krasnyi paradiz" (Red Paradise), which came out in 1990 in the journal *Siuzhety* (Subjects), tells about two men and a woman who visit and search the Soldai fortress in the hope of finding some treasure. The woman lures the men into a cave—a torture chamber of sorts—where death is impossible despite the inhuman abuses that all three inflict upon one another. Eventually they discover that they can die if they stop wanting to live. Combining the supernatural with the fantastic, the play transports the characters into a mysterious and historical setting. The title of the other short play, *Morokob,* also published initially in *Siuzhety* in 1990, inverts the word in Russian for fainting or swooning, *obmorok.* Sadur situates the action of the play on the Black Sea coast, where the Latvian sailors Agris and Imant and the Yakutian girl Sardana dwell with the local people. As the sailors measure the fish from the sea, they hear mysterious stories about the landlord, allegedly a mere ghost, and about the neighbor, who gives birth to cats. In the course of their pursuits Agris, Imant, and Sardana fall into a ditch, which turns out to be the opening of a giant fish; they travel through its intestines and end up at the front door of the house, strengthened in their friendship. The play features characters of different ethnic origins, a theme more prominent in Sadur's prose. Both plays rely more on the originality of the situation than on that of the language: the characters in them are actively engaged in the penetration of the supernatural world (such as a torture chamber or a giant fish), and language no longer plays a key role in the creation of these worlds. From the point of view of performance, these plays are not theatrical but, rather, cinematic because of their emphasis on unreal journeys into animals and historical mysteries.

Cherty, suki, kommunal'nye kozly (Devils, Bitches, and Communal Goats), published in *Teatr* (Theater) in 1992, is a stage version of *Almaznaia dolina* and explores life in a communal apartment. Another adaptation of a prose work is the play *Chardym* (1999), which transposes some characters from Sadur's novel *Sad* (The Garden, 1997) onto the island Chardym in the river Volga.

Although Sadur's prose work began being published only in the 1990s, she has written prose since at least 1981. "Devochka noch'iu" (The Girl at Night, written in 1981) and "Chto-to otkroetsia" (Something Opens Up, written in 1982) testify to her early engagement with prose. Sadur's prose is more autobiographical than her plays, and certain characters recur in both her plays and stories. Her works in prose consist largely of short fiction, which displays well her technique of shifting narrative stances and her preoccupation with the theme of escape—in particular from dull, everyday reality (often of communal life) into the world of folk beliefs and the supernatural.

Sadur's cycle "Pronikshie," written in the late 1980s, consists of ten short stories. The cycle opens with "Blesnulo" (A Flash of Light; translated as "It Glistened," 1995), which introduces the theme of supernatural forces. Ol'ga foresees everything that happens to Alik, and for that reason she does not marry him. Instead, she marries another man, whom she subsequently divorces. Meanwhile, Alik becomes paralyzed, just as Ol'ga foresaw. Sadur emphasizes how love enables one to have the strength to look into the future, while the action that results from this vision leads often to a "secure" yet uninteresting life. She shifts the narrative in such a way that perfectly normal events appear sinister. In "Milen'kii, ryzhen'kii" (translated as "The Cute Little Redhead," 1995), first published in *Teatr* in 1992, the student Natasha rents a room from an old woman. At night Natasha hears voices and sees a strange cat. One night, the costume for her study project disappears and is worn by a figure that appears the following night. Natasha leaves the apartment quickly and gets married. The story further explores supernatural forces and demonstrates how the girl guards herself against these powers.

While the first two stories assess how a character's involvement in the supernatural world can be avoided, the third and fourth explore the positive and negative sides of supernatural forces. "Shelkovistye volosy" (translated as "Silky Hair," 1995) concerns a sick little boy whose mother, seeking a cure for her son, is advised to bury a button under a tree in a friend's garden. She goes to the garden and discovers that her friend's child will become sick if she throws the button away. Yet, she decides to save her own child. Sadur shows the dangers of engaging with the supernatural: health and wellness can be reinstated by acts of superstition, while a curse cannot be lifted without it falling upon somebody else. The threshold between curing and making ill—between acting for the good of one's child and inflicting harm on another—is addressed. "Kol'tsa" (translated as "Rings," 1995) is a first-person narrative told by Larisa in colloquial language about her friend Liubka, who has found a valuable ring. This theme serves as a backdrop for the story of the boy Levan, in whom Larisa seems interested. Married and much older than she, he sports a ring that resembles a split snake. Larisa has several dreams about this ring, and through them she realizes that nothing will come of her relationship with him: the future holds no love for her—only disillusionment. Sadur dwells on the significance of symbolic objects and their stifling effect on Larisa.

The next two stories illustrate that characters were right in trusting their instincts about superstitions. "Zamerzli" (translated as "They Froze," 1995), which has the same title as Sadur's 1989 play, is told by a first-person narrator who tries to earns money for a pair of jeans by working as a custodian in a theater. She encounters the imbecile Uncle Leva, who scares her. As she brushes the snow off a Christ figure on a cross (actually a theater prop), Leva throws a stone at her, and this act confirms for the reader the "evil" side to his nature. In "Dve nevesty" (translated as "Two Fiancées," 1995) an Afghan veteran kills himself when his fiancée finishes her relationship with him and marries another man. At his funeral the information that the Afghan had "insured" himself against such a mishap—that he in fact had two fiancées—is revealed. On both occasions, no harm is done to anyone, but superstitions turn out to have been justified.

The ensuing three stories in the cycle "Pronikshie" form a triptych on the power of evil. "Siniaia ruka" (translated as "The Blue Hand," 1995) addresses the supernatural elements that intrude in the everyday life of two women. Valia hates Mariia Ivanovna, her neighbor in the communal apartment where Valia lives; she suffers physically from Mariia Ivanovna's presence—a sickness that manifests itself in a stiff neck and blue hands. One night Mariia Ivanovna gives Valia pancakes as a gesture of kindness, and afterward, during the night, Mariia Ivanovna is killed by a blue hand, while Valia disappears. "Chervivyi synok" (The Worm-Ridden Lad; translated as "The Bad Seed," 1995; also translated as "Worm-Eaten Sonny," 1995) is a diatribe against men: they deserve to be treated like servants, since they merely sport a mask to cover their maggot-infected brains. Finally, once again women make use of supernatural powers in "Zlye devushki" (translated as "Wicked Girls," 1995). The young man Harry leaves his wife and family to live with Emma. When they move into an apartment of their own, they find a box with two chocolates. Harry eats one of the chocolates, and he discovers the next day that it has been replaced overnight. Obsessed by this sequence of events, Harry loses interest in life—until Emma's friend puts an end to the spell by devouring both chocolates at once, thus attracting Harry's attention at last (even though this friend is aware of how poorly Harry treats Emma). "Siniaia ruka" and "Zlye devushki" explore the interconnectedness of two things: the hatred of one woman is so strong that one gesture—whether it is the offer of pancakes or chocolates—can trigger annihilation.

The final story in "Pronikshie" is "Ved'miny slezki" (translated as "Witch's Tears," in *Women's View*, 1992), a third-person narrative about a girl, Nadia, who wishes to curse a young man for leaving her. She visits a witch and follows her to a river, where the witch makes the spell rebound and turns the girl into an old woman/ water spirit. The story addresses the issue of suffering, which seems to constitute the meaning of the girl's life; Nadia's suffering causes her to turn evil—as when she desires to curse the young man. The story also draws on folk belief and superstition, which Sadur harmoniously blends into a decidedly modern and contemporary plot.

The stories of the cycle "Pronikshie" display several biographical features. Like the first-person narrator in "Zamerzli," Sadur worked as part of the custodial staff at the Pushkin Theater shortly after arriving in Moscow in the 1970s. The story "Siniaia ruka" illustrates the nightmare of living in a communal apartment, an experience that Sadur also had during her early years in Moscow. Overall, the cycle demonstrates Sadur's characteristic way of bringing the supernatural into the real world without drawing a line between the two, as well as her view of the supernatural as both a positive and negative force.

The cycle "Bessmertniki" (Immortals), written around 1990 and published in 1994 in *Ved'miny slezki,* comprises eight short stories. The first two stories, "Severnoe siianie" (Northern Lights) and "Bezotvetnaia liubov'" (translated as "Unrequited Love," 1997), initiate the theme of contrasts in the cycle, particularly between light and dark and between love and hatred; the stories also explore the idea of noncommunication, which occurs, in the first instance, because of a wrong telephone connection and, in the second, because of work schedules.

The next three stories in the cycle explore old age and death. "Utiugi i almazy" (first published in *Soglasie* [Consent], 1993; translated as "Irons and Diamonds," 1993) is a story about a Jewish family who wishes to immigrate to Israel and sell their possessions in order to buy diamonds, an illegal undertaking. After they buy the diamonds, the eldest family member, Uncle Isaiah, hides them under a tile. When robbers raid the apartment and torture the family members with hot irons, Uncle Isaiah eventually reveals the hiding place. A simple narrative, the story thematically

links the torture of Jews during the Holocaust to their continuing torture by subsequent systems and other people. In "Tsvetenie" (translated as "Flowering," 1997) the first-person narrator buys some twigs for herself and for the old woman, Khazina, who lives in the same communal apartment. The narrator dreams of the older woman's death, and the next morning she removes the now blossoming twigs, destroying all life in Khazina's room and symbolically taking life away from the old woman. The idea of dreams becoming enacted appears here alongside the idea of death: on the one hand, the story expresses the desire to conquer age and isolation through the narrator's personal contact with Khazina; on the other, it shows the narrator's impulse to take life (symbolized by the flowers) away from her elderly neighbor. Finally, "Blizhe k pokoiu" (translated as "Closer to Rest," 1997) takes the form of a dialogue rendered in indirect free style. Two old women, Lena and Marina, visit a cemetery in Leningrad and converse on life and death. Eventually, Lena returns to her family in Moscow. These three narratives develop the theme of death: in the first, death is a threat that is avoided; in the second, it instills fear in the young; and in the third story, death is a part of life for the old women.

The next two stories in the cycle concern threats to the relationship between a parent and a child. "Motyl'ki Soldaii" (The Butterflies of Soldai) is set in the Black Sea town of Sudak, where the male first-person narrator, Vladimir, rents out a room to two women, a mother and daughter. He seduces the mother to drink, taking her attention away from her daughter. "Pechal' ottsa moego" (My Father's Sadness) deals with a father and his four-year-old son. The father, who adores his son, fails to appreciate how small and young he is and takes him to see dolphins. The boy falls into a coma from exhaustion; Sadur suggests that the father's love overburdens his son, potentially disabling him.

Although the final piece of *Bessmertniki* embodies certain ideas that connect it to the cycle—such as immortality and the inability to come to terms with death and disappointment—it also stands apart from the other stories. "Zanebesnyi mal'chik" (translated as "Star-Boy," 1997) tackles the themes of cosmos and infinity. The first-person narrator, Oktiabrina, is the mother of Yuri Gagarin, the first man ever to travel in space. Oktiabrina suffers because her son found nothing in the cosmos but emptiness, and upon his return he spat on Leonid Ilyich Brezhnev for making the nation believe that there was a "content" to be conquered in space. The story debunks the myth of the Soviet appropriation of the cosmos as meaningful space; it addresses the glaring emptiness that the cosmos offers and thus its failure to provide meaning. Oktiabrina feels threatened by the expanse and emptiness of space and believes that during his flight Gagarin pierced a hole in the membrane of the earth, through which infinity trickles and infects people. The theme of emptiness dominates the narrative until the Dyrdybaevs–Faina and her son Felix–intrude. The Dyrdybaevs are southern people, and the darkness of their skin is related to their proximity to the center of the earth. For Sadur, dark people represent a source of life and energy; they are at once envied, admired, and hated by the narrator of "Zanebesnyi mal'chik." This ambiguous relationship with southern people emerges in Sadur's later works with a nationalistic slant. "Zanebesnyi mal'chik" intersperses symbolic dreams with reality. Dreams function as an escape from reality–as a world that renders reality comprehensible and manageable, which is reminiscent of what is said in "Blizhe k pokoiu": "you've got an excellent mental illness which melts the cruelty of our life into the land of milk and honey."

Sadur's longer fiction consists of several novellas and novels. Her first novel, *Chudesnye znaki spasen'ia* (Miraculous Signs of Salvation, written in 1989; published in 1994), revisits her characteristic setting of a communal apartment, where the female first-person narrator is visited by a Leningrad poet to whom she is indifferent. Later, however, upon learning about his suicide, she develops a guilt complex that manifests itself through his appearance in her dreams. Her indifference toward him turns into hatred for, and thus a more engaged relationship with, her neighbors. The narrative moves in circles, reflecting the enclosed nature of the protagonist's guilt. *Chudesnye znaki spasen'ia* does not stand up to the sophistication of Sadur's earlier short works of prose, and its literary merit is hampered further by the transparent reference to the late rock star and poet Aleksandr Bashlachev.

Almaznaia dolina is told from narrative perspectives that are constantly shifting between third-, second-, and first-person points of view (she, you, we, and I). Serving a cinematic purpose, the device of multiple viewpoints allows crosscuts from the protagonist, Vera, to her neighbors–either to support or counter Vera's actions. Vera is forced out of her job and is lonely. Trained as an engineer, she lives in a communal apartment and now works as a custodian at a theater. The story is dominated, on the one hand, by her squabbles with her neighbors and, on the other, by her relationship to her brother, a layabout who saves a child in a fire. She condemns her brother for his youthful exploits and for betraying his wife; he does not live up to his sister's expectations of a hero. Vera inflicts evil, on a small scale, upon others in revenge for her own unhappiness. The story touches on many central themes in Sadur's work: the experience of communal living, the vitality of

Front cover for Sadur's 1997 novel, Sad *(The Garden),*
which displays her continuing obsession with race
(Howard-Tilton Memorial Library,
Tulane University)

southern people, and the fine line between good and evil. Most interesting here, however, is the narrative strategy. Vera punishes her brother for not living up to her expectations. Her flaw–the assumption that people should meet her expectations–is implied by the title, which is her misreading of the wine label "Alazanskaia" for "Almaznaia."

The novella *Iug* (first published in *Znamia* [The Banner], 1992; translated as "The South," 1997) is a first-person narrative about a woman, Olia, who travels south. Lifeless and listless, she is in need of a rest, and she identifies the dark-skinned people of the southern region with energy. Olia is attracted to the landlady's son, Kostia, and his warm personality; she shares her bed with him and is expelled from the hotel. The story suddenly shifts to another female first-person narrator and follows three women–Valia, Maria, and Tonia–on their last journey. The themes of weakness and death—the departure of one's life force—dominate this story.

The novel *Sad* consists of three parts, the first of which was published separately as "Veter okrain," followed by "Zaikushka" (The Stammer) and "Slepye pesni" (Blind Songs). These sections are concerned with characters who change their age and shift their identity but carry the same names. "Veter okrain" is narrated in first person by the singer Anna Ivanovna, who loves the "dark-skinned" Dima Dyrdybaev; Dima is often visited by his friend Alesha, who stutters. Anna's identity is fluid—at times the Anna character is a mother, at times a daughter. She is both alive and dead: in one part of "Veter okrain," waking up in Moscow, she has no milk for her son, Alesha; in another part, she is in Siberia and has just been killed while carrying milk. Milk stands for the feebleness found in northern people. Sadur blurs the line between dream, or hallucination, and reality and between past and present and thereby deprives the story of coherence. Moreover, these dreams seem more like drug- or alcohol-induced hallucinations than stories with a supernatural twist. Dima and Alesha reappear in "The Stammer," in which they kill Anna Ivanovna, now an old woman. In the final part of the novel drunkards of the street join the cast of characters. Overall, *Sad* exhibits a complexity that stems exclusively from the hallucinations of the Dyrdybaevs. Continuing Sadur's obsession with race, it alternates comments on the admiration and hatred of the physical strength of the "dark," southern people with speculations about the weakness of northern tribes.

Sadur's writing is distinguished in two important ways: it avoids using an omniscient narrator and it employs a shifting narrative stance that often moves from first to third person in order for a character to view the self from the outside and for the purpose of introspection. The shift between "I" and "she," and "we" and "you," may also, however, speak of dissociation and association with a character or the surrounding world and as such give a clue to the state of intoxication or hallucination of which many characters can be suspected. These shifts are therefore less easily transposable to cinematic movements than may appear at first sight. By working both in the dramatic and prose genre, Sadur shifts her own position and her own view of events just as much as she shifts narrative stances and viewpoints in her stories. Her use of language is often colloquial, and reminiscent of the *skaz* technique,

whereby the narrator imitates the colloquial language of the characters in order to offer an insight into the characters' thoughts.

Sadur's plots often focus on an irrelevant detail rather than a main theme. Her shift in emphases makes the normal appear sinister and the supernatural normal. This decentered approach to emphasis makes finding out what happens difficult for the reader. The themes that dominate Sadur's prose concern the energy and life force of the southern people, who are envied—almost hated—for their vitality; in this sense Sadur's perspective borders on nationalism. Northern people are white and unable to survive, and the whiteness of the Russian people reflects a weakness. In her later works dreams and hallucinations are associated with alcohol consumption.

In general, Nina Nikolaevna Sadur's work as a prose writer offers less of a contribution to Russian fiction in the 1990s than her work as a dramatist. Since the late 1990s Sadur has focused more on works for the stage. Her plays show innovative dramatic writing and push the boundaries of the performing arts, thus opening the path for a new generation of Russian dramatists. In particular, her adaptations of prose fiction for the stage, largely commissioned by theater companies, stand out—such as *Zovite Pechorinym* (Call Me Pechorin, 1999), inspired by Mikhail Iur'evich Lermontov's *Geroi nashego vremeni* (A Hero of Our Time, 1840) and commissioned by the Pushkin Theater.

Interview:
Nataliia Pashkina, "Pisat', znachit zhit'," *Teatral'naia zhizn'*, 2 (1988): 32.

References:
Vladimir Bondarenko, "Den' zavtrashnii," *Sovremennaia dramaturgiia*, 1 (1986): 255–262;

Oleg Dark, "Zhenskie antinomii," *Druzhba narodov*, 4 (1991): 264–265;

Catriona Kelly, "Nina Sadur," in *A History of Russian Women's Writing, 1777–1992* (Oxford: Oxford University Press, 1994): 433–442;

Nataliia Pashkina, "Magiia tvorchestva," *Sovremennaia dramaturgiia*, 3 (1990): 245–247;

Serafima Roll, "The Death of Language and the Language of Death in Nina Sadur's 'Echaj,'" *Russian Literature*, 34 (1993): 187–206;

Alena Solntseva, "Te, kto prishel posle," *Sovetsky teatr*, 4 (1987): 36–41.

Vladimir Aleksandrovich Sharov

(7 April 1952 –   )

Thomas Epstein
Boston College

BOOKS: *Do i vo vremia* (Moscow: Nash dom/L'Age d'Homme, 1995);
Stikhi (Moscow: Nash dom/L'Age d'Homme, 1996);
Sled v sled (Moscow: Nash dom/L'Age d'Homme, 1997);
Repetitsii; "Mne li ne pozhalet'" (Moscow: Nash dom/L'Age d'Homme, 1997);
Staraia devochka (Moscow: Nash dom, 2000);
Voskreshenie Lazaria (Moscow: Vagrius, 2003).
Edition: *Sled v sled* (Moscow: OLMA, 2001).

SELECTED PERIODICAL PUBLICATIONS–
UNCOLLECTED: "'Realisticheskie' soobrazhenia," *Znamia,* 4 (2000);
"Eto ia – prozhil zhizn' . . ." *Druzhba narodov,* 12 (2000);
"Neskol'ko myslei v zashchitu liberalizma," *Druzhba narodov,* 10 (2001).

The task of contextualizing Vladimir Sharov's novels is in many ways as complicated as analyzing his novelistic strategy. Sharov's fictions are at once a profound meditation on, and a parody of, the eschatology of Russian history and Russian-Jewish history; an aggressive experiment in postmodern Russian prose; and a bewildered cry of the eternal human condition. His combination of playfulness and seriousness, of parody and lyric, and of the sacred and profane not only complicates the reader's interpretive task but also suggests that Sharov has assimilated, perhaps more than any of his contemporaries, the artistic and philosophical legacy of *both* the nineteenth and twentieth centuries of Russian literature.

Vladimir Aleksandrovich Sharov was born in Moscow on 7 April 1952. His grandparents were, in his own words from a personal interview, "professional revolutionaries," and his parents important liberal Soviet intellectuals. His father, Aleksandr Israilevich Sharov (or Shera, as his friends called him), was a geneticist by training. A member of the Communist Party, he turned to writing in the 1960s and became a noted author of fairy tales; their insufficiently

Vladimir Aleksandrovich Sharov (from the cover for
Voskreshenie Lazaria, *2003; Collection
of Mark Lipovetsky)*

ideological stance made publication difficult. Sharov's mother, Anna Mikhailovna Sharova, a physicist, was also a writer—in her case, the author of several works popularizing contemporary physics. Sharov married Ol'ga Dunaevskaia in 1974. In 1976 he graduated from Voronezh State University with a degree in history. A father of two, he devotes himself exclusively to writing. He and his family live in Moscow.

Sharov began his literary career not as a novelist but as a poet. Significantly, despite the association of his prose with Russian postmodernism, neither in style nor in subject matter do his poems have anything essentially in common with the Moscow conceptualists, whose aesthetics have been most closely identified with Russian postmodern poetry. Instead, Sharov's poems—written in the 1970s and 1980s but not published until 1996—are, for the most part, exquisitely crafted depictions of landscape, with or without human presence. They are brief and often mysterious evocations, suggesting neither nihilistic meaninglessness nor enclosure within language but rather real, if hidden, metaphysical depths. Such poems, at once authentically contemporary and reminiscent of the subdued metaphysico-mystical visions of Afanasii Afanas'evich Fet and Fedor Ivanovich Tiutchev, would be inconceivable from the more militant postmodern poets, such as Lev Semenovich Rubinshtein and Dmitrii Aleksandrovich Prigov. This undisguisedly lyrical and religiophilosophical element, which provides Sharov with a link both to the nineteenth century and to the Russian religious revival at the turn of the twentieth century, sets him apart from many of his immediate contemporaries.

Sharov's first novel, *Sled v sled* (Step for Step), was written between 1978 and 1984 but, because of censorship, not published until the end of the Soviet period. It appeared initially in 1991 in the journal *Ural* and in book form in 1996. *Sled v sled* is both his most formally experimental work—encompassing various notes, supposed archival material, an inserted novella, and a plethora of narrative strands—and his most historically ambitious. It constitutes a kind of quasi-biblical genealogy of a Judeo-Russian clan whose roots reach back to the times and family of Jesus Christ and forward to the various gulags of Soviet Russia. The central narrative strand tells the exemplary story of the family of Moses Sheikman, who lived from the 1830s to 1901, a Jew converted to Russian Orthodoxy and ultimately called to the priesthood. Sheikman, according to the narrator, is obsessed with two subjects: the biblical story of Abraham, Isaac, and Jacob (which for him means the creation of a chosen people by its separation from its ancestors—in this sense, analogous to his own life) and Russian history. These two themes prove key to an understanding of both his family and of "Russianness" itself. As in the Pentateuch, *Sled v sled* is a story of families, of wanderings and exile, of deaths and births, and of the unequal relationship between a Creator and his creation. Read as a psychological or character-based novel, *Sled v sled* can be called a failure: it is porous, schematic, and allegorical. But this "failure" becomes one of Sharov's strengths and is a means to his artistic success; in a world (in the Russian world) overdetermined by history and Hegelian *Geist* (spirit), psychological characterization is inadequate if not irrelevant. The Soviet Russian is not so much a psychological entity as an historical atom whirling through time and space. What results, in literary terms, is not a bildungsroman nor a psychological study but the great arc of Russian and Soviet-Russian history, with all its biblical parallels: "chosenness," exile, revolution, the burden (and absurdity) of history. Fiction and imagination give these parallels meaning, creating a world (and the people in it) that ramifies like the branches of a tree.

The second of Sharov's novels, *Repetitsii* (Rehearsals), was written between 1986 and 1988 and first published in 1992 in the journal *Neva*. It remains the author's favorite. As with all his novels, Sharov's strategy in *Repetitsii* centers on the conflation of secular and sacred history, fact and myth, reality and imagination—all of which for him define the parameters of Russian and Soviet-Russian history. Significantly, *Repetitsii* begins with a quote from the Apostle Peter and then immediately launches into an historical-biographical portrait of the putative author of the book, an anthropologist by training. Born in 1958 and thus himself a product of the vagaries of Soviet history, the unnamed narrator ends up in Tomsk, Siberia, where he manages to become the favorite graduate student of V. N. Suvorin, a renowned historian of Siberia and theorist of the special destiny of Russia: the re-creation of Jerusalem on Russian soil.

After Suvorin's death the narrator inherits the historian's legacy and his archives, which leads him to the discovery of a seventeenth-century Breton manuscript written by Jacques Sertan. An itinerant French actor who wound up in Russia, Sertan eventually came under the thumb of the Archimandrate Nikon, the ecclesiastic whose reforms resulted in the 1666 schism of the Russian Orthodox Church. Nikon confesses to Sertan his plan to re-create his New Jerusalem in Siberia. Because of his experiences as a professional actor, Sertan is chosen by Nikon to carry out these plans, reenacting the Mystery that is Christ's incarnation on a life-size stage. Commenced thus as an imitation, the play—whose purpose is to compel the Second Coming—takes on a life of its own; the peasant actors are swallowed up by their roles and begin to take Sertan for their Teacher. Ultimately, Sertan himself begins to believe in this fiction, and Nikon's New Jerusalem becomes a mere decoration for the repetition of Christ's real passion. This attempt to re-create Christ's Passion, his Crucifixion, and the Second Coming constitutes the foundation of the endlessly repeating story of this mythical sectarian group (a potential symbol of Russia itself), which is followed all the way to 1939, when the "last Jew" is killed and secular history finally "begins." This last event, obviously not part of the historical record, suggests instead that Russian history is not so much a material fact as a combination of myth, nightmare, and wish fulfillment. The country must be read as allegory, the latecomer nation to Western and Christian civilization obsessed with its marginality, its distinctiveness, and its eschatological role in a world from which Christa is absent:

> . . . five days later he [Sertan] began with tryouts and an initial allocation of roles. Then came time for memorizing lines. This was the most trying time for Sertan; he worked with the actors for days on end and almost never slept. The peasants were illiterate and learned their roles strictly by listening. There was no one on whom he could call to help him in this: neither on the monks nor on others who could read. Moreover, it was not merely a matter of their difficulty in memorizing their lines (although that was difficult enough: their memories being weak and untrained, they could fairly easily summarize the text but could memorize it only with the greatest difficulty); the greater difficulty was that the words, concepts, and relations among the people and world were completely unknown and alien to them, and even when they understood the words they were frequently unable to grasp their significance. Thus, this joint reading and memorization became simultaneously a rehearsal and an explanation—indeed it was everything imaginable *except* a simple memorization. But his efforts were not in vain; working with the actors day after day, he could see how the words slowly and gradually began to affect them, he could see how words change men.

Sharov's allegory, here and in all his novels, is neither total nor pure: the real and fantastic, the historical and mythical, and the seventeenth century and the twentieth century blur to an almost indistinguishable broth. Unlike in the more archetypically postmodern historical phantasmagorias of his contemporaries Pelevin and Sorokin, however, Sharov seeks neither to mystify, demystify, nor ridicule Russian history. His characters are not imprisoned in a language without a signified, but, rather, as Russians (and thus cut off from a recognizable origin), they require allegory as a primary, not to mention tragic, mode of self-knowledge. Unable to ground itself in time, Russia is engaged in a never-ending and self-defeating (because unrealizable) "rehearsal" for the end of time in which thing and symbol, thought and being, will once more merge. For those individuals "in" time—that is, all people—the results are monstrous: a hatred of the Creator, confusion of the sacred and secular, an eternal repetition of chosenness, exile, and slaughter.

Sharov's third novel, *Do i vo vremia* (Before and During), first appeared in the journal *Novyi mir* (New World) in 1993 and came out in book form in 1995. It is by far his best-known and most controversial work. *Do i vo vremia* provoked immense debate, most notably from a group of conservative editors within *Novyi mir*. Their collective attack, published in the journal as "Sor iz izby" (Dirty Linen, 1993), focused not only on the "deficiencies" of the novel but attacked Sharov as

Dust jacket for Sharov's second novel, Repetitsii *(Rehearsals, 1997), in which a seventeenth-century itinerant actor re-creates Christ's passion to bring about the Second Coming (Collection of Mark Lipovetsky)*

a person and the editors who allowed "such garbage" to be published. Many articles and several public meetings, either in support or condemnation of Sharov, followed. Most of the leading critics—including Sergei Sergeevich Averintsev, Natalia Borisovna Ivanova, Viacheslav Nikolaevich Kuritsyn, Mark Lipovetsky, Irina Bentsionovna Rodianskaia, and Karen Ashotovich Stepanian—had their say. While in retrospect the controversy generated much more heat than enlightenment, it demonstrated both the high stakes of Sharov's "historiosophy" (the study of the wisdom or ultimate meaning of history) and the seriousness with which Russian critics continue to approach literary art.

Like *Sled v Sled, Do i vo vremia* is quite difficult to summarize in any meaningful way. The novel opens, or at least as the narrator says "it seems to," on 17 October 1965. The narrator, a Bolshevik-sympathizing journalist (in mock allusion to the work of Marcel Proust, the reader is told that the journalist's enthusiasm for Bolshevism derives from his childhood association of communism with the sweet smells that came from the Pravda pastry factory), is wandering, half lost, on the outskirts of Moscow in search of a psychiatric clinic where he is to receive—although he is ambivalent about it—treatment for his "problem." This problem turns out to be a strange form of amnesia—for weeks at a time he forgets everything and disappears from family and friends only to reappear disheveled and bloodied in one provincial police station or another. Placed as it is at the beginning of the novel, and especially in light of what is to follow, the theme of the untrustworthiness of memory and the relationship of past memory to present need and desire cannot be overemphasized. Indeed, much of the outrage and misunderstanding provoked by the novel seem to stem from its having been read as a narrowly polemical, and somehow "objective," diatribe on Soviet Russian history. This kind of reading, however, violates Sharov's literary epistemology, according to which "knowing" Russian history and the Russian person is possible only through the *in*direction of metaphor, imagination, and always foundering allegory.

The narrator is admitted to this clinic, which is actually a repository, or dumping ground, for senile former party cadres and prominent Bolsheviks. The narrator, Aleksei by name, who is burdened with a feeling of personal historical guilt and a sense of being a *samozvanets* (impostor), had intended to continue the work of repentance initiated, according to legend, by the sixteenth-century Russian Tzar Ivan the Terrible in his *Sinodika opal'nikh* (Synodia of the Disgraced) by writing his own *sinodika* of forgotten members of his own family and the remarkable people whom he has met in his life. Yet, hospitalized and separated from his personal memories, he finds the continuation of such a project impossible and decides to turn to, indeed to save in an act of memory, the patients inside the clinic. What he gets from his primary informant, a man called Ifraimov, is a picture of Christianity and post-Alexandrian Russia that in many ways coincides with the views of the "heretical" Russian thinker Nikolai Fedorovich Fedorov, who transformed the Russian religious ideal of *sobornost'*, that is, spiritual experience understood as an organic collectivity of humans under God, into a social and scientific obligation to be realized by humans alone. Fedorov believed, among other things, that the holiest duty of humanity was, via technology, to resurrect the dead.

After an excursus on prerevolutionary Russia (neatly divided into maximalist and minimalist camps: Fedorovians and Russian Revolutionaries); an aside on God's silence; and a deconstruction of the iconic Leo Tolstoy (supplied by several of the clinic Bolsheviks who, not surprisingly, started out as followers of Tolstoy and who reveal that Tolstoy lived not one but two lives—his own and that of his son, Lev L'vovich Tolstoy), the narrative then turns to its central strand: the three lives of Germaine de Staël—her pollination, or various forms of sexual reproduction, of Russian history. Once more combining true historical memory with fantastic and phantasmagorical layers of experience, the obviously false with the merely speculative, the narrator's informant takes us from the supposed half-Sephardic Jewish roots of Madame de Staël to her father, Nekker, and into the salons of revolutionary Paris, where the historical Madame de Staël dreamed of gaining absolute power and transforming the world. Frustrated in her attempt but having learned the secret of self-propagation, she gives birth to herself a second time, in the form of a liberal-minded landowner by the name of Evgeniia Frantsevna Stal'. Traveling the countryside in a glass-enclosed post chaise, in which she also sleeps (the glass enclosure suggests both Vladimir Lenin's mausoleum and a fairy tale), she encounters a young man who takes her for Sleeping Beauty. This man is actually Fedorov himself. Longing to wake her from slumber and return her to life as if he were a Prince Charming, he comes to her night after night to lie by her glass coffin, trying to awaken her with his repressed and frustrated sexual passion. Soon Stal', who is ever seeking a material embodiment for her dream of total power, begins to lust for Fedorov and uses opium to entrance and then have sex with him: this encounter becomes the basis for Fedorov's idea of literally resurrecting the fathers, correcting the creation and turning Humanity toward itself instead of toward a transcendent God.

In her third life Madame de Staël becomes both mother and lover to Joseph Stalin (here, the earlier parody on Tolstoy's enlightened landowner turns into a travesty of Maksim Gor'ky's *Mat'* [Mother], 1906), in whom she sees the ultimate incarnation of her revolutionary fantasies. Staël's Stalin is unlike the historical Stalin. He is depicted here as a sensitive and somewhat weak figure in the tradition of the "superfluous man"—until he encounters Fedorov's doctrines: believing now that all will be resurrected at the end of time, Stalin will later feel justified in his reign of terror. Participating in the revolutionary struggle, Stal' also has a love affair with the composer Aleksandr Nikolaevich Skriabin, who takes over the leadership of Fedorov's group. Living in Geneva, Skriabin meets up with, and is depicted as holding intellectual sway over, Lenin: indeed, the latter revolutionary's philosophy turns out to be based largely on Skriabin's scores. Throughout this phantasmagoria, which reads something like an apocryphal book out of a canonic New Testament of a secular apocalypse, temporal chronology is frequently and obviously violated: for instance, both Fyodor Dostoevsky and Vladimir Sergeevich Solovyov are depicted as alive in 1905. Real and fantastic events fall one upon another. Finally, as the novel ends, the reader finds Fedorov, who turns out to be a patient at the clinic, with a resentful Madame de Staël at his side (she, too, is a patient), setting sail as a modern-day Noah on the sea of a new flood, which may well symbolize early 1990s Russia.

As mentioned above, *Do i vo vremia* incited much protest. Communists were scandalized by the profanation of their Revolution: rather than an act of reason, Sharov depicts the Revolution as the triumph of delirium, as a combination of avant-garde art, sexual repression, and religiomystical madness. Liberals were made uncomfortable by the picture of Russia as a sick and unreal culture. Contemporary Fedorovians and other mystics—a not negligible group—could not accept the idea of the Russian Revolution as an embodiment of Fedorov's project. Sharov's supporters, by contrast, hailed the novel precisely for its transgressions against canonicity both in form and content.

Sharov's fourth novel, *"Mne li ne pozhalet' . . ."* ("Should I Not Pity . . . ," 1998), was first published in 1996 in the journal *Znamia* (The Banner). Its title is taken from the Old Testament Book of Job, which quotes God's response to Job's reproach of him for having saved an unworthy people. Like his other novels, *"Mne li ne pozhalet' . . ."* has an extremely complex and somewhat schematic plot. It begins with an eight-page set piece—a kind of prologue—in which the lives of various "Leptagovs" are told by three Leptagov sisters who, the reader learns, may or may not be sisters or even Leptagovs. This set piece is followed by the story of still another (or the same?) Leptagov, Sergei Ivanovich, the protagonist of the novel. His story is actually that of a secular saint's *zhitie* (life), written by A. L. Trept by order of the Central Committee of the Communist Party, which has decided to create a Third Testament (an obvious parody of the role of the Russian writer under Soviet power). As a disciple of Leptagov, Trept sings his story to the narrator—"sings" it, because Leptagov ended his life as a choirmaster (the choir itself, as shall be seen, is an allegory of the Soviet-Russian people).

The stages of his progress, which are many, cannot be easily summarized. Originally a modernist composer (his Promethean oratory *Titanomachia*, per-

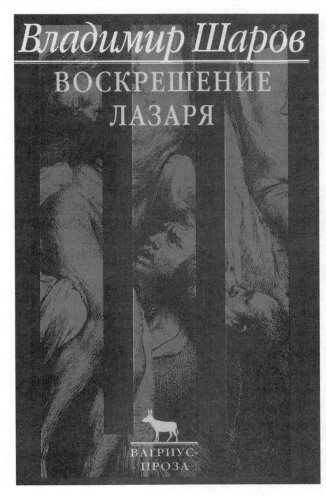

Front cover for Sharov's epistolary novel, Voskreshenie Lazaria *(The Raising of Lazarus, 2003), which spans the biblical era to revolutionary and contemporary times (Collection of Mark Lipovetsky)*

formed on a ship in 1914, supposedly caused the sinking of the real *Titanic*), Leptagov soon comes to understand that not "instrumental music" but the chorus is the center of modern music and that he must transform himself into a choirmaster, whose job will be to create, at the request of the chorus members themselves, the Single Church of the Single God. At this point Leptagov, a modern-artist-as-revolutionary (or vice versa), makes his leap from "composer to choirmaster or, more precisely, to builder and architect." With the help of his "all-Russian chorus," consisting of Socialist Revolutionaries (SRs), high school students (also known as the *nevinnye* [guiltless]), and sectarian Castrators, Leptagov begins to build churches with the sheer power of their voices—building new ones and destroying old ones, destroying and building endlessly.

With the introduction of the characters Kraus and Balmenova, the novel bifurcates into two strands: Leptagov's relationship with the choir (including Balmenova) and Balmenova's own story, which in some ways becomes the center of the novel. Kraus and Balmenova, the "perfect" revolutionary couple, begin as SRs who are exiled to Kimry, where Leptagov himself has taken refuge, in the early 1910s. In Kimry they are married, by order of the party. They do not consummate their marriage—Kraus sees no reason to—but Balmenova, as a modern woman, is driven half-mad with lust for him. In her frustrated desire she is drawn to the Castrators in the chorus (she is herself of Old Believer stock) and "infiltrates" them in order to bring them over to the Revolution—but she is transformed by her encounter with them and becomes not only a *khlyst* (flagellator) but a new Mother of God. Ultimately, the SR-Castrator alliance leads to the Russian Revolution (the Bolsheviks are depicted as their puppets). In the ensuing social catastrophe Kraus becomes a priest near Kimry, while Balmenova turns party prosecutor in her unwillingness to consent to a "Virgin Mary" role—to give her only son up for crucifixion. The party leadership, by contrast, hopes that he will become the Christ and take away their sins. He is, in fact, sent to the desert of Central Asia on an archaeological expedition, walks on water, follows a water spout, meets with Seventh-Day Adventists, and is tempted by the devil, but he cannot become the Christ that all wish for. Meanwhile, Kraus leads a rebellion of *skot* (cattle) against Man and the City (including Kimry). After Soviet troops put down their rebellion, Balmenova prosecutes the case. All the while, Leptagov and his growing chorus line the banks of the Volga, singing for forgiveness.

The last pages of the novel (the actual body of the Third Testament) depict the sacred transformation of the Soviet people. In February 1939 there arises the Great Forgiveness: the party confesses its sins, plans to let Stalin step down (but lead the repentance), and repatriate the kulaks. All their property is returned to them by the repenting peasants. Then the kulaks themselves repent. Finally, everyone repents—the entire country becomes one great chorus of repentance and expiation. Leptagov then leads the people into a burning turf swamp to meet God. As with the prophet Jonah, God puts Leptagov to sleep under a tree that he then destroys. The novel ends with Jonah-Leptagov's angry and bewildered conversation with God, whose love for an "undeserving" people he cannot understand.

"Mne li ne pozhalet' . . ." is in some ways Sharov's most accomplished novel. Read as a commentary on the madness of the Russian Revolution, it is simulta-neously hilarious, disturbing, and profound, comparable to the novels of Mikhail Afanas'evich Bulgakov and Andrei Platonovich Platonov. It can also be read as an allegory on the sickness itself of excessive allegorizing. In *"Mne li ne pozhalet' . . ."* Sharovian allegorizing reaches its peak: the symbolism becomes so heavy-handed—and yet evanescent, everything cannibalizing everything else—that the allegorical form functions as a kind of critical self-commentary. In Leptagov's (that is, Revolutionary Russia's) excessive desire to create a transcendent, timeless meaning for himself (itself), Leptagov-Russia loses itself in the maze of the overdetermined symbols that it created.

Sharov's fifth novel, *Staraia devochka* (The Old Maiden, 2000), though ultimately no less ambiguous and ambitious than the others, has a somewhat simpler plot than the preceding four. It tells the story of Vera Andreevna Radostina, a true believer in the Communist utopia, who loses her faith (her first name means "faith," while her last name suggests joy) after the arrest and execution of her no less true believing husband, Iosif Berg, in 1937. In despair, and with the help of a daily diary that she has kept for years, Vera decides to "go backward" in time, hoping to find her lost life. This project sets the entire Soviet apparatus—including Stalin, who, along with everyone else, is in love with her—into a panic: they must find a way to stop her, for hers is a "temptation" that might affect the entire Soviet people. The bulk of the novel follows the investigation by the secret police into the lives of all the people whom Vera (faith) has touched. In the end the narrator himself recounts his crucial encounter with Vera in the 1960s, when she was a little girl whom he met—and fell in love with—at his family's summer dacha.

Although Sharov's dazzling imagination and mastery of Russian prose style by now have been almost universally acknowledged, his work is still seeking its place in the contemporary Russian literary canon. The extremely small press runs of his novels are one indication of this, but the greater difficulty lies in the complexity of his art. The former problem has now perhaps been resolved with the publication of Sharov's sixth novel, *Voskreshenie Lazaria* (The Raising of Lazarus, 2003), by the mainstream Moscow publisher Vagrius. *Voskreshenie Lazaria* is an epistolary novel featuring the now familiar conflation of Biblical, revolutionary, and contemporary eras.

For the partisans of Russian postmodernism, the novels of Vladimir Aleksandrovich Sharov appear to be insufficiently decentered. While not without metanarrative games, they deliver too much meaning, too much history, and too much humanity and God. For the opponents of postmodernism, Sharov's novels suffer from the opposite failing: they seem *excessively* decentered. Neither allegory nor realism hold: unfinished story gives rise to unfinished story; characters come and go; one idea becomes its opposite; and different eras cohabit in the same moment. But the disappointment occasioned by such seeming chaos is a result of expecting from Sharov something he cannot deliver: an "unbroken world." Consumed by the sinfulness of humanity and the horrors of history, he depicts men and women who are seeking to put back together the broken pieces of their fallen humanity, wherever they may fit. Faced by divine silence, his narrators give not a final, privileged answer but provide their own error- and desire-filled, tentative ones. Secular and sacred, real and imaginary, crucifixion and resurrection, Jew and Russian—Sharov depicts these ironic intertwinings. This structural weakness thus becomes a functional strength: it embodies the anguishing, estranging, and, at times, self-mocking truth of Sharov's world. Like Dostoevsky, he is excessive not in order to deny, misrepresent, or flee reality but, rather, to capture it more accurately. The unique discomfort provoked by his novels is eloquent testimony to how close to the bone he strikes.

References:

Dmitrii Bak, "Filosifiia obshchego tela. Eshche raz pro roman Vladimira Sharova," *Nezavisimaia gazeta,* 16 July 1992, p. 7;

Sergei Kostyrko, Irina Rodianskaia, and Andrei Vasilevsky, "Sor iz izby," *Novyi mir,* 5 (1993): 186–190;

Vladislav Kuritsyn, "Tropik pamiati," *Literaturnaia gazeta,* 9 June 1993, p. 4;

Naum Leiderman and Mark Lipovetsky, "Zhizn' posle smerti, ili novye svedeniia o realizme," *Novyi mir,* 4 (1994): 233–253;

Lipovetsky, "Privet iz Khaosmosa," *Literaturnaia gazeta,* 31 May 1995;

Mikhail Nekhoroshev, "Istoriia Model' i Lichnost'," *Neva,* 4 (1994): 260–274;

Karen Stepanian, "Nazovu sebia Tsvayshpatsiren," *Znamia,* 11 (1993): 184–195;

Viktor Toporov, "Tysiacha let odinochestva," *Nezavisimaia gazeta,* 16 July 1992, p. 7;

Galina Vasil'eva, "My nash. My 'Novyi mir' possorim . . . ," *Komsomol'skaia Pravda,* 29 June 1993, p. 3.

Galina Nikolaevna Shcherbakova
(10 May 1932 –   )

Maria Litovskaia
Ural State University

(Translated by Seth Graham)

BOOKS: *Sprava ostavalsia gorodok* (Moscow: Sovetskii pisatel', 1979);

Roman i Iul'ka (Moscow: VAAP-Inform, 1982);

Vam i ne snilos' (Moscow: Molodaia gvardiia, 1983)– includes "Vam i ne snilos'";

Otchaiannaia osen' (Moscow: Molodaia gvardiia, 1985);

"Fe Li Ni": Fedoseeva Lidiia Nikolaevna (Moscow: Soiuz kinematografistov SSSR, 1989);

Krushenie (Moscow: Sovetskii pisatel', 1990)–includes *Krushenie,* "Diadia Khlor i Koriakin," and *God Aleny;*

Anatomiia razvoda (Moscow: Molodaia gvardiia, 1990)– comprises *Mandarinovyi god (Ideal'nyi variant)* and *God Aleny (Ironicheskii variant);*

Do skoroi smerti, madam! (Moscow: VECHE, 1996);

Prichudy liubvi (Moscow: AST, 1997);

Armiia liubovnikov (Moscow: AST, 1998)–comprises "Armiia liubovnikov";

Kto smeetsia poslednim (Moscow: EKSMO, 1998);

Aktrisa i militsioner (Moscow: AST, 1999);

Podrobnosti melkikh chuvstv (Moscow: Vagrius, 2000)– includes *Voskhozhdenie na kholm tsaria Solomona s koliaskoi i velosipedom;*

Utkomest' (Moscow: Vagrius, 2001);

Molenie o Eve (Moscow: Vagrius, 2001).

Collections: *God Aleny* (Moscow: Vagrius, 1996);

Zhenshchiny v igre bez pravil (Moscow: Bukmen, 1996);

Dver' v chuzhuiu zhizn' (Moscow: AST, 1997);

Mandarinovyi god (Moscow: Lokid, 1997);

Provintsialy v Moskve (Moscow: Lokid, 1997);

Love-storiia (Moscow: OLMA, 1999);

U nog lezhachikh zhenshchin (Moscow: Vagrius, 1999);

Krovat' Molotova (Moscow: Vagrius, 2001);

Mal'chik i devochka (Moscow: Vagrius, 2001).

Edition in English: "The Wall," in *Balancing Acts: Contemporary Stories by Russian Women,* edited by Helena Goscilo (Bloomington: Indiana University Press, 1989).

Galina Nikolaevna Shcherbakova (from the paperback cover for Krushenie, *1990; Doe Library, University of California, Berkeley)*

PRODUCED SCRIPTS: *Vam i ne snilos',* motion picture, Gor'ky Film Studio, 1980;

Karantin, motion picture, Gor'ky Film Studio, 1983;

Lichnoe delo sudi Ivanovoi, motion picture, Gor'ky Film Studio, 1985;

Dvoe i odna, motion picture, Gor'ky Film Studio, 1988;
Pust' ia umru, Gospodi . . . , motion picture, Gor'ky Film
    Studio, 1988.

SELECTED PERIODICAL PUBLICATIONS–
UNCOLLECTED: "Neskol'ko epizodov iz zhizni
    devochki," *Iskusstvo kino,* 10 (1984);
"Emigratsiia po-russki," *Ogonek,* 9 (1991);
"Ubikvisty," *Soglasie,* 2 (1992);
"Edinstvennaia, nepovtorimaia," *Don,* 3–4 (1992);
"Rol' pisatelia P'etsukha v zhizni prodavshchitsy kol-
    basy Vali Veretennikovoi," *Ogonek,* 6 (1992);
"Trem devushkam kanut'," *Zhurnalist,* 4–5 (1993);
"Obraz ada," *Zhurnalist,* 1–2 (1995);
"Tol'ko mertvye znaiut vse," *Zhurnalist,* 6–7 (1996).

Galina Shcherbakova is one of the most widely
published Russian prose writers. Her fiction became
popular because of her ability to react quickly to the
most urgent social problems of her time, such as teenage sexuality, the transformation of gender stereotypes,
the disintegration of traditional family relationships,
and the rapid growth of social aggression. Shcherbakova's gift as a writer lies in the ways in which she
responds to these problems; she also makes them
acceptable as topics for the broadest readership. Her
short stories and novels, written in a clear and accessible manner, are entertaining for their use of plot and
distinct in their use of witty and observant narratives
from the perspective of an experienced, and tolerant to
human weakness, woman.

Galina Nikolaevna Shcherbakova was born on
10 May 1932 in the small industrial town of Dzerzhinsk
in Ukraine. Her mother, Valentina Fedorovna Ste-
tsenko, a housewife, divorced Shcherbakova's father,
Nikolai Sergeevich Ludenko, a well-paid accountant,
when their daughter was four years old. Later
Valentina Fedorovna married a mining engineer, Viktor
Alekseevich Funin, who was a father figure for
Shcherbakova. Shcherbakova spent her childhood in a
small mining town located in the Don coal basin. In
1950 she enrolled in the School of Philology at Rostov
State University. While a sophomore, she married and,
following her journalist husband, Aleksandr Scherba-
kov (who eventually joined the staff of the journal
Ogonek [The Flame]), with whom she had two children,
Aleksandr and Ekaterina, moved to Cheliabinsk, a
large industrial city in the Urals. She then transferred to
the history-philology department of the local pedagogical college, from which she graduated in 1955. After
graduation, for three years she worked as a teacher of
Russian language and literature in the Cheliabinsk
schools. In 1958 her articles began appearing in local
newspapers, and soon she gave up teaching and

became a professional journalist. Her first affiliation
was with the Cheliabinsk *Komsomolets* (The Komsomol
Member), the newspaper for the Russian Communist
youth organization, for whom she wrote from 1958 to
1969. After this association she worked for several
other newspapers in Rostov, Volgograd, and Moscow.
At first she combined journalism with prose writing,
but since 1969 she has focused entirely on her prose
and scriptwriting.

Shcherbakova first attracted widespread attention
with her "adolescent" novella *Vam i ne snilos'* (You
Haven't Seen It Even in a Dream, 1983). The protagonists, Roman and Iul'ka (which are the Russian versions of the names Romeo and Juliet), are Moscow
high-school students who find themselves in a situation
similar to that of their Shakespearean peers: young love
is ignited despite familial hostilities. The long-held,
unrequited love of Roman's father for Iul'ka's mother,
Liudmila Sergeevna, continues to smolder within him
yet still evokes only annoyance in her. Suspecting that
the son is as tiresome as his father, she tries to keep
Roman away from her daughter. Roman's mother,
Vera Georgievna, expects her son's beloved to prove as
cruel-hearted as her mother. The two teenagers are sent
to different cities to prevent their meeting. Transferred
to a new school under a false pretext, Roman is later
sent to Leningrad to care for his supposedly infirm
grandmother. The more obstacles that the young lovers
encounter, however, the stronger and more desperate
their emotions become. Finally, Iul'ka's mother recon-
ciles herself to her daughter's feelings and gives the girl
her blessing to go to Leningrad. She arrives just in time
to see Roman, who, upon discovering that his parents
have deceived him, jumps from a third-floor window
and lands on a pipe hidden in the grass.

These earnest young characters, unable to hide
their feelings or even to see the necessity of doing so,
become the victims of the excessive paternalism of the
adults, whose imagined future for their children is a
product of their own personal experiences and firmly
held stereotypes. Vera Georgievna's unthinking, egotistical desire to control her son's internal world spurs her
on even after everyone sees how perniciously her
actions are affecting Roman. Yet, none of the other
characters takes it upon him- or herself to stop her,
since that would mean interfering in someone else's private life. Thus, the good intentions of each player in the
love story contribute to the tragic conclusion.

In the opinion of critics the novella satisfied readers' expectations, since it was, in the words of Tat'iana
Kravchenko in her 1997 article in *Literaturnaia gazeta*
(The Literary Gazette), "halfway between melodrama
and contemporary drama." It provoked heated discussions among youths and teachers, primarily for its

Paperback cover for Shcherbakova's collection Krushenie
*(Downfall, 1990), in which the title novella is an exposé
of corruption among Communist Party cadres (Doe
Library, University of California, Berkeley)*

depiction of "adult" love between adolescents. The novella was adapted by Shcherbakova for a movie of the same name in 1980, directed by Il'ia Frez.

Shcherbakova portrays puberty as a period of rapidly emerging emotions, against which young people are usually defenseless. They have not yet developed fully—as most adults have—the ability to hide one's feelings and to react with calm indifference to situations that experience has taught adults to recognize as common, ordinary life events. The plot of the novella *Otchaiannaia osen'* (Desperate Autumn, 1985) involves a quadrangle of unrequited love among four classmates: Misha loves Irina, Irina loves Sasha, Sasha loves Shurka, and Shurka loves Misha. They feign indifference, chase after one another, make open declarations of love and hate, get into fistfights, and do inexplicable things, such as locking the school director in her office.

In the novella *Dver' v chuzhuiu zhizn'* (Door to Another Life, 1985) Pavlik and Masha, who have come to Moscow from the remote provincial city of Seversk, meet their new neighbor, Mila, who tries with all her might to impress them with how well-off her family is. She rails against the poorly dressed Pavlik's incomprehensible principles and ends up falling in love with him.

From the adults' perspective adolescents can behave correctly or incorrectly, but Shcherbakova emphasizes common traits in all of her young protagonists: their immature amorphousness of character; the ease with which they go from anger to delight and from self-confidence to desperation; and their capacity for rash, foolhardy, even suicidal behavior. The disturbed teens, inexperienced but not stupid, are surrounded by mostly intelligent adults—typically parents and teachers—who are conscious of their own motives and sincerely want the best for their children and students. Young people in Shcherbakova's works are never depicted in confrontation with parents or teachers. On the contrary, they are quite trusting of the advice that they receive, though they instinctively sense where guileless love ends and egotistical moralizing begins.

Shcherbakova's adult characters, despite their individual differences, can be divided into two types. Adults of the first type recognize children's right to act independently even when their actions are obviously irrational (their credo is expressed by Anna Sergeevna, the school director in *Otchaiannaia osen'*: "Sinite parvulos!" [Permit the children!]) and understand that life in general is difficult, that suffering enriches the soul and is unavoidable. Those of the second type compose for themselves strict rules for living and judge the behavior of adolescents based on the world that they, the adults, have conceived. Such adults are prepared to pave the way for children and do not understand that children want to find their own path and will avoid the safety zones created by their guardians, encountering tragically insoluble situations. Both types of adult are correct in their own way, as are the adolescents.

In order to emphasize the "multiplicity" of reality, and the unavoidability of conflict in any situation involving various wills and ideas about life and conflict resolution, Shcherbakova uses a device in her early stories that becomes formally central to her later work: she constructs her narrative so that the consciousness of each character is presented in the form of certain relatively independent fragments, typically separated from one another by gaps. The alternation of such fragments allows her to look at a single fact from various perspectives. Thus, the chance acquaintance of provincials and Muscovites in *Dver' v chuzhuiu zhizn'* is shown from the point of view of several characters, united by the links to the Mikhailovs' house. One of these characters is

Katia, who in her youth briefly lived in this house, when a college student named Kolia Mikhailov brought her there from faraway Seversk, and who was tossed out two days later, pregnant and with a suitcase full of nice things and a savings account opened by Kolia's parents for Katia. Now Katia, together with her children, Masha and Pavlik, is visiting Moscow and thanks to the help of her girlfriend Zoia finds herself in an apartment neighboring the Mikhailovs' home. Among the narrators are the following: Katia's friend Zoia, who is happy to have arranged such a comfortable place to live for her hometown friend and her children; Masha, Katia's daughter, amazed by Mila's expensive things and at the same time zealously defensive of her own independence; Pavlik, Katia's son, intrigued by the strange neighbor girl; Mila, who wants the silly boy to like her but also wants to take revenge on him; Mila's mother and Kolya Mikhailov's wife, Larisa, who loves her daughter but is annoyed by her insatiable consumerism and snobbishness; and finally the Mikhailovs' friend Timosha, who always tries to smooth over conflicts and is the only person who knows the full truth about the situation: that Pavlik and Mila have the same father. Multiple vantage points according to Shcherbakova constitute the pattern of life, in which the multiple truths of multiple people coexist—although the main truth of life, she suggests, is that everyone must be given the opportunity to live out his or her own destiny.

During perestroika, when exposé literature came to the fore, Shcherbakova actively participated in the trend. The target for exposure in her novella *Krushenie* (Downfall, 1990) is the system of principles by which leading Party cadres were chosen and assigned. The protagonists hail from the same city. Viktor Ivanovich, a former schoolteacher, has made a successful career in the Party in an unusual way—by shoring up the support of his hometown friends Valentin Kravchuk and Nikolai Zinchenko. Kravchuk is a journalist who, on the advice of his protector, Viktor, specializes in creating images of positive heroes, which helps him receive a transfer to the capital and an appointment as editor of a "second-tier but respectable" Moscow magazine. Zinchenko, a former collective-farm clerk who harbors a lifelong loathing of the weak intelligentsia, rises with Viktor's help to a top post in cultural administration. All three friends are surprisingly respectable in public, but their private lives betray internal strife. Viktor devotes all of his energy to monitoring the slightest changes in the opinions of his superiors. Kravchuk's wife never adapted to her new life in Moscow and as a result has become an alcoholic. Zinchenko is despised by his wife and children, who want nothing to do with their father, and his son-in-law, a restorer, refers to him

as "my invincible enemy." The three friends are driven solely by their hateful memories of their impoverished postwar childhood and their desire to go from rags to riches by any means. Zinchenko accepts bribes in exchange for college admissions or assignments to warm climes, precisely in order to feel powerful over the kind of people who humiliated him as a child. His betrayal of his past, however, and his indulgence of his own spite and indifference result in the collapse of the hometown alliance. The bureaucrats, internally damaged and focused on the complexes they brought with them from home, further the ruin of the government they are supposed to serve; they see their jobs merely as a means of self-affirmation.

Such a critical tendency is uncharacteristic, however, in Shcherbakova's works. More often, her fictional worlds move toward restored harmony despite all of their shortcomings, dramas, and even tragedies. At times this tendency takes on an almost fantastic quality. In the short story "Diadia Khlor i Koriakin" (Uncle Khlor and Koriakin, 1990), for example, Koriakin, a lonely photojournalist who married at the age of forty-three suddenly becomes a widower. After his late wife's funeral her relatives decide to send Ol'ga, her daughter from her first marriage, whom the relatives want nothing to do with, to live with her father. A working-class rambler by nature, Koriakin has never laid eyes on the girl; to himself he calls her his "so-called daughter." Frolov, the widower, has developed an attachment to the girl, however, and writes Koriakin a letter requesting permission to adopt her. This awakens a proprietary feeling in Koriakin, and he comes to take Ol'ga away, but he lingers at Frolov's place, fixing faucets, cooking meals, and renovating the apartment. Ultimately, the two bachelors grow so accustomed to each other that they decide to become roommates and raise Ol'ga together.

In the 1990s Shcherbakova tried her hand at the detective-story genre—such as "Trem devushkam kanut'" (Three Women Will Vanish, first published in *Zhurnalist* [The Journalist], 1993) and "Tol'ko mertvye znaiut vse" (Only the Dead Know It All, first published in *Zhurnalist,* 1996)—but readers and critics considered her an author of "women's prose," with its focus on the fates of women and the personal problems of female existence. In 1990 Shcherbakova published *Anatomiia razvoda* (Anatomy of a Divorce). This bipartite work comprised two novellas as two versions of divorce—*Mandarinovyi god (Ideal'nyi variant)* (The Tangerine Year [The Ideal Version]) and *God Aleny (Ironicheskii variant)* (The Year of Alena [The Ironic Version]), which was also included in the collection *Krushenie. Mandarinovyi god* tells about the divorce of a middle-aged engineer, Aleksei Nikolaevich, from his wife, Anna Antonovna, who

Hardback cover for Shcherbakova's Anatomiia razvoda
*(Anatomy of a Divorce, 1990), comprising two novellas,
each giving a different portrait of a failed marriage
(Davis Library, University of North
Carolina at Chapel Hill)*

is a teacher. As in many Soviet families who must continue to live together because of the scarcity of housing, the divorce between Aleksei and Anna is stalled by the issue of how to divide the apartment. Aleksei's lover, Vika, proposes that he move his wife and daughter into Vika's beautifully furnished two-room apartment and that Vika herself move into the three-room apartment where Aleksei's family currently lives. Anna does not want to leave the apartment to which she has grown accustomed and suggests that her husband move in with his mistress. The tale of divorce eventually develops into a tale of apartment redistribution. Each woman considers her solution to be "ideal" and endlessly convenient for all; neither sincerely understands why the other side will not accept it. The mild-mannered and delicate Aleksei goes back and forth between the two women in attempts to reconcile them. Ultimately, however, he cannot bear it, and he dies. Thus, a fateful irony leads to an ideal resolution: Aleksei is dead and thus free from further torment; Anna becomes a widow rather than a divorceé, which she sees as an improvement in her status; and Vika continues living in her beautifully furnished apartment and is able to join the Communist Party, since she did not end up playing the role of a homewrecker (Party membership is essential to her career development). The apartment-exchange motif, which in Iurii Valentinovich Trifonov's novella *Obmen* (The Exchange, 1969) leads to the exposure of the characters' hidden moral defects, is resolved by Shcherbakova as the collision of multiple petty truths, resulting in a more human life.

God Aleny depicts a year in the life of a long-divorced woman named Nina, who is the mother of a grown daughter, lives with her former mother-in-law, and is temporarily taking care of a deceased girlfriend's daughter, Alena, who is also divorced. Alena is cheerful and brazen, attractive and coquettish, and her appearance sparks a series of dramatic events in Nina's measured life—both Nina's former husband and son-in-law began to court Alena openly. But all these potential conflicts involving Alena turn out to be invented: Alena does not seduce anyone; she gives birth to a baby boy fathered by her married boss, and she gathers around the new would-be grandson a group of aging people who, because of his birth, feel as if their lives have been given meaning and have entered a new stage. Alena, the potential disturber of the peace, turns out to be the benefactor of all, and once again precedent proves more valuable than the letter of the law.

A central theme in Shcherbakova's works—the impossibility of shifting a full-blooded, diverse life into the narrow confines of preplanning and codification—expanded in the 1990s when she began depicting the physiological aspects of her characters' lives, which had been impossible under conditions of censorship. A characteristic work in this regard is the novella "U nog lezhachikh zhenshchin" (At the Feet of Recumbent Women, first published in *Novyi mir* [New World], 1996). Three elderly neighbors—Soroka, Panin, and Shprekht—who previously had not spoken to one another for years, gather on the street every day to exchange news and wisecracks, after which each of them heads home to his paralyzed wife. Soroka, a local Party worker, snitch, and con-man; Shprekht (whose real name is Shpekov), a simple-minded mining engineer; and Panin, a mine surveyor who was repressed in his youth, selflessly care for their wives, who are, respectively, Zinaida, an obese former pilot; Varvara, a machinist; and Liudochka, a meek schoolteacher. The first woman is immobile and mute, the second a quadriplegic and a hysteric, and the third—in addition to her paralysis—is also somewhat mentally ill. But they all have their own inner lives, about which their husbands have no idea. They dream, reminisce, think about their loved ones, and even make plans. The male characters are capable of great love, but it manifests itself in empty remarks and the unaesthetic daily routines of changing diapers and preventing bedsores, for example. They know all about each other's "constipation and putrid sinuses," and, according to Shcherbakova, this conjoining of the down-to-earth (that is, the carnal) with the spiritual constitutes real, "living" life.

Beginning in the mid 1990s, apart from focusing more on the physiology of her characters, Shcherbakova changed her poetics as well. The image of a smart, experienced, sensible female narrator started appearing in her works. "Shcherbakova tells stories simply. Intelligently. Ordinarily . . . Trustingly. With captivating details . . . With wit, and without shying away from current slang. She plays at condescension toward her characters, her readers, herself," remarks Andrei Nemzer in his 5 March 1996 article in *Segodnia*. The writer herself said that "writing in the first person is incredibly liberating," as she was quoted in a 1999 interview with Mikhail Butov. In the works written in this new manner—the novel *Armiia liubovnikov* (Army of Lovers, first published in *Novyi mir,* 1998) and *Aktrisa i militsioner* (The Actress and the Policeman, first published in *Novyi mir,* 1999)—her narrator is an inexhaustible font of everyday situations, the sheer number of which allows her to rearrange them for ease of comprehension and to draw equally everyday conclusions from them. The main conclusions are love exists in the world despite everything, and everyone's fate is predetermined.

Utkomest' (Hidden Vendetta, 2001) is a novel of three beautiful women who have been friends since childhood—Sasha, a school director; Raisa, a saleswoman and former construction engineer; and Ol'ga, editor of a women's magazine—and their envious rival, a writer named Polina Nashchokina. In 1979, as a novice correspondent for the newspaper *Pionerskaia pravda* (Pioneer's Truth), the homely, impoverished Nashchokina was slogging along a dirty Moscow street on an assignment. The sole of her shoe had come off, and she tried to go into a restaurant but was not admitted—even though she had just watched the three beautiful and, to her, successful girlfriends walk right in. Her foot froze in the torn shoe as a result, and she has harbored a secret spite for them ever since. She meets them twenty years later, and they look just as beautiful and, apparently, as fortunate as ever. She follows one of them, Raisa, and catches up with her just as she is being attacked by a military officer, to whom Raisa has given a bribe so that her son will not be conscripted into the army. Raisa breaks free of the would-be rapist and, in a

state of temporary insanity, hits Nashchokina over the head with a bottle. Nashchokina is hospitalized, and her feeling of "hidden vendetta" grows stronger, but the efforts of Raisa's girlfriends resolve the situation: Raisa, temporarily paralyzed after her crime, begins to recover; Ol'ga and Sasha become even closer when their children get married; and they are occupied by maternal duties and by love for their common grandson, Adam. In addition, Nashchokina writes a novel about her spite and hatred, titled *Utkomest',* for which she receives a literary prize. Nashchokina's novella is written from the perspective of each of the four female characters, a device that allows Shcherbakova to underscore the common threads of misfortune and prosperity among the women—all of whom cultivate happiness out of unhappiness. All the emotions in the story, even such un-Christian emotions as mistrust and hatred, are recast over time into sympathy (Ol'ga), understanding (Sasha), insight (Raisa), and even literary talent (Nashchokina).

The novella *Voskhozhdenie na kholm tsaria Solomona s koliaskoi i velosipedom* (The Ascent of King Solomon's Hill with Carriage and Bicycle, 2000) combines the stories of several women connected by familial ties: the peasant Rudenchikha, who died one hundred years earlier en route from Pushchi-Voditsa to Kiev, where—though uninvited—she was headed to see her sister; her great-granddaughters, Liliia, Astra, and Mariia; and other relatives in addition to Rudenchikha's direct descendants. The female members of Rudenchikha's family tree are overtaken in old age by an irresistible urge to flee their familiar places of residence in search of what seems like happiness but which, in reality, is death. This passion manifests itself differently in each character. Rudenchikha hurries to see her sister, ostensibly to help her but actually to pray for her own "sinister fate" and to see the beauty of Kiev, but she dies on the way and is buried by the side of the road by a passerby, Khaim. Liliia and Astra's mother in her old age rushes back and forth between her eldest and youngest daughters, one of whom is about to get married and the other divorced, and neither of whom has any plans to spend her life with her mother. In the end their mother dies at a train station between the two cities where the daughters live, and is buried in the local cemetery. Liliia runs away from her daughter and granddaughter, and from the apartment she acquired with difficulty from her fourth husband, to nowhere, for she vanishes somewhere in the expanse of Russia. Astra explores her Jewish roots and goes to Israel to visit her son, dreaming of emigration herself, and dies at a bus stop despite the efforts of a doctor, also named Khaim. The mundane story of divorce, marriage, apartment exchanges, adultery, and children's problems transforms into a situation of predetermination and the impossibility of transcending the limits that fate assigns a person. If Mariia, the last great-granddaughter, is predestined to be the family's unifier, then no matter how she tries to hide from her fate, sitting quietly in her hospital laboratory, she cannot avoid her renewed acquaintance with her cousins after decades of separation, or the trip to Israel to see the grave of Astra, or the chance encounter with a German, Franz, who was once in love with her mother. She restores the family's past, the link between its long-lost chapters. People in Shcherbakova's works do not recognize their kinship roles, but they are prepared to fulfill them when necessary, in obedience to some unseen force.

Critical interest in the works of Galina Nikolaevna Shcherbakova has grown, and although critics, such as Butov and Tat'iana Morozova, have noted her mature craftsmanship and inexhaustible optimism, she is still discussed only within the boundaries of "women's prose." Despite the fact that Shcherbakova's prose rarely becomes a subject for critical and scholarly analysis, her works are popular, primarily among women readers. Living in Moscow and continually publishing new works, Shcherbakova has asserted that "People don't live long enough to hear all the stories I want to tell them."

Interviews:

Mikhail Butov, "Liudi stol'ko ne zhivut, skol'ko ia khochu rasskazat': S Galinoi Shcherbakovoi beseduet Mikhail Butov," *Novyi mir,* 1 (1999): 224–229;

"Mne komfortno bezumnom segodnia: beseda s izvestnoi pisatel'nicei," *Trud,* 30 June 2000: 5;

"Kol'tsa i manka – sakral'nye poniatiia moei zhizni," *Uchitel'skaia gazeta,* 29 August 2000, p. 24.

References:

N. Anisimova, "Semeinyi krug," *Literaturnoe obozrenie,* 9 (1980): 54–55;

Nina Barmina, "266 stranits pro liubov'," *Zhurnalist,* 10 (1980): 45–47;

N. Bolonina, "Nam i ne snilos'," *Sobesednik,* 11–12 (1994): 11;

A. Gorlovsky, "O Shekspire liubvi i romeo-julietstve," *Detskaya literatura,* 10 (1980): 7–11;

Tatiana Kravchenko, "Eshche odna 'Love-storiia': O povesti G. Shcherbakovoi 'Mitina liubov'," *Literaturnaia gazeta,* 15 (1997): 11;

V. Lisovsky, "Liubov' i nravstvennost'," *Detskaia literature,* 10 (1980): 11–14;

Tatiana Morozova, "My uvidim nebo v polosochku," *Literaturnaia gazeta,* 18 (2000): 10;

Morozova, "Prigovorennaia k liubvi: Novoe staroe imia: Galina Shcherbakova," *Literaturnaia gazeta,* 3 (1999): 10;

Andrei Nemzer, "Kak, s chego nachat' moiu istoriiu? . . . ," *Segodnia,* 5 March 1996;

L. Novikova, "Telo protiv pustoty," *Znamia,* 9 (1998): 225–226;

Maria Remizova, "Bab'ia dur'," *Nezavisimaia gazeta,* 10 (1999): 7;

T. Serebriakova, "Retsepty liubvi – eto 'Vam i ne snilos'," *Rossüskaia gazeta,* 26 March 1999, p. 31;

Irina Vasiuchenko, "Dobryi urok," *Oktiabr',* 10 (1984): 203–204.

Sasha Sokolov
(Aleksandr Vsevolodovich Sokolov)
(6 November 1943 –)

Anna Brodsky
Washington and Lee University

BOOKS: *Shkola dlia durakov* (Ann Arbor, Mich.: Ardis, 1976; revised, 1983); translated by Carl Proffer, with an introduction by D. Barton Johnson, as *A School for Fools* (Ann Arbor, Mich.: Ardis, 1977; New York: Four Walls Eight Windows, 1988);

Mezhdu sobakoi i volkom (Ann Arbor, Mich.: Ardis, 1980);

Palisandriia (Ann Arbor, Mich.: Ardis, 1985); translated by Michael H. Heim as *Astrophobia* (New York: Grove Weidenfeld, 1989);

V ozhidanii Nobelia, ili Obshchaia tetrad' (St. Petersburg, 1993);

Palisandriia. Roman. Esse. Vystupleniia, with an essay by Boris Groys (St. Petersburg: Simpozium, 1999).

Editions and Collections: *Shkola dlia durakov; Mezhdu sobakoi i volkom* (Moscow: Ogonek, 1990);

Shkola dlia durakov; Mezhdu sobakoi i volkom, with an introduction by Aleksei Tsvetkov (St. Petersburg: Simpozium, 1999);

Russkie tsvety zla, compiled by Viktor Vladimirovich Erofeev, with contributions by Erofeev, Sokolov, Sergei Donatovich Dovlatov, Venedikt Vasil'evich Erofeev, and others (Moscow: Zebra E/EKSMO, 2001).

OTHER: Vladimir Pomeshchik, *Polia poigrannykh srazhenii,* with a foreword by Sokolov (Smolensk: TRAST-IMAKOM, 1993);

Proza russkogo zarubezh'ia, volume 3, compiled by O. I. Dark, with contributions by Sokolov (Moscow: Slovo, 2000);

Benedikt Erofeev. Valerii Popov. Sasha Sokolov: Sbornik, with contributions by Sokolov (Moscow: Zebra E/EKSMO, 2002).

SELECTED PERIODICAL PUBLICATIONS—
UNCOLLECTED: "V dome poveshennogo," *Literaturnyi kur'er,* no. 10 (1983), pp. 4-6;

"Portret khudozhnika v Amerike: V ozhidanii Nobelia," *Almanakh Panorama,* no. 254 (1986), pp. 30-31.

Sasha Sokolov is one of the premier writers of the late–and post–Soviet period. His body of works is quite small but of outstanding quality, as recognized early in Sokolov's career by Vladimir Vladimirovich Nabokov. Sokolov's postmodernist novels explore the themes of identity, history, and stagnation.

Aleksandr Vsevolodovich Sokolov was born on 16 November 1943 in Ottawa, Canada, where his father, Major Vsevolod Sokolov, had been transferred for work in the Commercial Counselor's section of the Soviet embassy. The Sokolovs returned to Moscow in 1946. As part of the government elite, Sokolov's father was able to provide his family with a comfortable life in Russia. D. Barton Johnson writes in "Sasha Sokolov: A Literary Biography" (*Canadian-American Slavic Studies,* 1997) that Sokolov was a "dreamy schoolboy," and at one time his parents considered placing him in a special school. Instead, he was extensively tutored as a boy. From about the age of twelve he began writing comic pieces to amuse his fellow students. After finishing high school in Moscow in 1961, Sokolov worked briefly as a morgue attendant and then as a lathe operator. In 1962 he entered the Military Institute of Foreign Languages, where he studied English and Spanish while working on fiction, but did not graduate. In 1965 he became a member of a Moscow literary group, Samoe Molodoe Obshchestvo Geniev (Society of the Youngest Geniuses)—better known by their initials, SMOG, which also spell the Russian word for "I was able."

In 1966 Sokolov enrolled in the journalism department at Moscow State University and five years later received his degree in journalism. Throughout the 1960s and early 1970s he published several short stories and sketches for Soviet magazines and newspapers. A heavily edited version of his short story "Staryi shtur-

Sasha Sokolov in Alanya, Turkey, 2003 (courtesy of the author)

man" (The Old Helmsman) was published in May 1971 in *Nasha zhizn'* (Our Life), a periodical for the blind. It won first prize from the magazine as the best story about the blind.

During 1972 to 1973, while working on his first novel *Shkola dlia durakov* (1976; translated as *A School for Fools*, 1977), Sokolov lived in the Kalinin region by the Volga River and worked as a game warden in a hunting preserve for the Soviet elite. (His experiences on the Volga eventually provided the foundation for his second novel, *Mezhdu sobakoi i volkom* [Between Dog and Wolf], 1980.) In the spring of 1973 he completed *Shkola dlia durakov*. The novel did not conform to the officially prescribed norms of socialist realism and therefore could not be published in the Soviet Union. Sokolov sent the novel to publishers in the West, and in 1975 he himself emigrated from the Soviet Union. Finally, *Shkola dlia durakov* was published by Ardis Press in 1976 and received a highly enthusiastic response from Vladimir Vladimirovich Nabokov, who wrote in a 17 May 1976 letter to Carl Proffer, one of the founders of

Ardis: "I have now read Sokolov's *Shkola dlia durakov,* an enchanting, tragic, and touching book. . . . It is by far the best thing you have published in the way of modern Soviet prose." Nabokov's accolade was used to promote the English translation of the novel.

Shkola dlia durakov is situated within a rich tradition of Russian and European literature. As a narrative about a boy's life, it can be included in the long Russian tradition of books about childhood–such as Sergei Timofeevich Aksakov's *Detskie gody Bagrova-vnuka* (Childhood of Bagrov's Grandson, 1856); Leo Tolstoy's *Detstvo* (Childhood, 1852), *Otrochestvo* (Boyhood, 1854), and *Iunost'* (Youth, 1857); Andrei Bely's *Kotik Letaev* (1922); and stories by Andrei Georgievich Bitov. Notwithstanding its accomplished and confident artistry, *Shkola dlia durakov,* Sokolov's first novel, is plainly a youthful work. Its subject is a young author's artistic maturation–the difficulties of writing, the pains of being different, and the rebellion of a sensitive soul against the stale and oppressive world of Soviet reality. The book is narrated from the point of view of a boy with a complex psyche. He sees himself as two people, and at times the story is told as an ongoing dialogue between his two selves.

Rather than a linear narrative, the episodes of *Shkola dlia durakov* form a kind of mosaic. The reader learns about the many facets of the boy's world, such as his summer dacha; his love of nature; his hatred of school; and his unsettled relationships with his parents, his psychiatrist (Dr. Zauze), and his neighbor (Sheina Trachtenberg). The novel is suffused with lyrical evocations of nature, trains, weather of every kind, and the emotions of love, tenderness, and loss.

Yet, *Shkola dlia durakov* is not only a book about youth. A highly self-conscious work, the novel exemplifies the process of writing; creation is the overarching theme of the book. It starts with the narrator's musings on how to begin writing a book and ends with his completion of the narrative, which he is compelled to finish because he has run out of paper. As a book about writing and the development of a writer, *Shkola dlia durakov* resembles Ivan Alekseevich Bunin's *Zhizn' Arsen'eva* (The Life of Arsen'ev, 1930), as well as Nabokov's *Dar* (1937–1938; translated as *The Gift,* 1963). Sokolov's self-consciousness in this novel is charged with a deep sense that the writing of fiction holds profound political significance in a country where freedom of speech is nonexistent. In an address in honor of Proffer, Sokolov expressed his conviction in the political and moral mission of Russian literature: "It happened in Russia where literature is a matter of honor. . . . It is also a holy deed. It is also a cornerstone of culture. And if during the time of economic mishap the word replaced currency, in the years of laggard repression it replaced bullets." Critics, too, have pointed out the political implications of the book. As Ludmilla Litus notes in her 1997 article for *The Slavic and East European Journal,* "Although the primary focus in the novel is on literature and the creation of literature, questions that deal with creative writing, repressive society and 'artistic freedom' are equally important."

In an essay titled "V dome poveshennogo" (In the House of a Man Who Was Hanged in Literaturnyi) Sokolov describes at some length the hero of his first novel, particularly the dissident and anarchist sides of him:

> This is a book about a subtle and strange boy, suffering from a double personality, about a student So-and-so who cannot reconcile himself with existing reality. Anarchist by nature, he protests against everything and finally concludes that nothing exists in the world, absolutely nothing but the wind. The author is sympathetic to his hero. Their outlook on human rights in general and on the rights of Russians in particular coincides with the view of a . . . more renowned dissident.

One way that Sokolov's youthful hero resists the establishment is by satirizing it, not only lampooning his oppressors, but also destroying the linear flow of time as prescribed by Marxist views of history, which essentially led to the then-current Soviet regime. Moreover, Sokolov undermines the dominant language imposed by official ideologies by freely mixing it with the idiosyncratic language of the narrator's poetic vision. He abandons conventional syntax and sentence structure, merging different voices into one utterance and, conversely, breaking the speech of one character into a dialogue.

In writing about *Shkola dlia durakov* in their article for *Literaturnoe obozrenie* (The Literary Review, 1993), Petr L'vovich Vail' and Aleksandr Aleksandrovich Genis assert that "Reality respectfully and quietly made way for literature, enabling the creation of a unique book in which the literary game and the writer's style are everything." Modernist writers had also resisted the brutality of history by creating an idiosyncratic time and space for their characters. What distinguishes Sokolov from his modernist forebears, however, is that he does not isolate his character from the destruction of time and space. Instead, his protagonist, is as fully destabilized as the world around him; he does not triumph over the world. In a climactic moment in the novel, the narrator sees himself dwindle and diminish in "one of his stages of disappearing" and gradually becomes transparent, merging with the world around him. This transformation marks a striking departure from the heroization of the artist in modernist works such as Nabokov's *Dar,* Bunin's *Zhizn' Arsen'eva,* Mikhail Afanas'evich Bulgakov's *Master i Margarita* (The Master and Margarita, written, 1929–1940; published, 1966–1967), or Boris Leonidovich Pasternak's *Doktor Zhivago* (1957). Though creative, the voice of Sokolov's narrator will never become the voice of authority, or even an alternative power to the political authority. While destroying the world of oppression, Sokolov—unlike his modernist predecessors—leaves no alternative hierarchy. That his hero never grows up is significant in this regard; his mere age makes him a traditionally defenseless character.

After emigrating from the Soviet Union in 1975, one year before *Shkola dlia durakov* was published, Sokolov resided in Austria for a time and in 1976 came to the United States. In 1977 he moved to Canada, the place of his birth, and was granted Canadian citizenship. From 1975 to 1978 he received a stipend from the Readers' Fund for Sasha Sokolov's Work. Its founders considered Sokolov's books a distinctive phenomenon in Russian literature and instituted the fund to help the author devote all his time to writing.

*Sokolov at the University of Southern California, 1981, during a conference
of Russian émigré writers (photograph by Craig R. Dietz)*

At the time of his arrival in North America, Sokolov was working on *Mezhdu sobakoi i volkom,* which he completed in 1979, and it was published in 1980. The Leningrad samizdat (underground) journal *Chasy* (The Clock) gave the novel its Andrei Bely Award for the best work of Russian prose for 1981. The award was voted upon by the editorial board of the journal and approximately a hundred dissident writers.

Mezhdu sobakoi i volkom is Sokolov's second novel and perhaps the most enigmatic and difficult of his works. It has virtually no plot, and its language throughout consists of verbal puns and allusions to art and history. In her contribution to the special Sokolov issue of *Canadian-American Slavic Studies* (1987), Barbara Heldt writes that in this novel "Each character is more than one character and each word is the history of the Russian literary and spoken language." Despite the abstract nature of the novel, it is, like all of Sokolov's works, deeply rooted in personal experience—specifically, the years that he spent working as a forester in the Volga region. *Mezhdu sobakoi i volkom* is ultimately about the author's lyrical evocation of Russia, its landscape, its poverty, its poetry, and its lore.

The title of the novel refers to Aleksandr Sergeevich Pushkin's poetic lines from *Evgeny Onegin* (1825–

1832), which describe twilight as the time of day when a herdsman or a hunter cannot tell the difference between a dog and a wolf. As Johnson has pointed out in "Sasha Sokolov's Twilight Cosmos: Themes and Motifs" (*The Slavic Review,* 1986), twilight crystallizes the poetics of the novel. First, just as the title of *Mezhdu sobakoi i volkom* evokes Pushkin's idea of twilight as a time when images become blurred, so is the genre of the work also unclear or ambiguous. Although the work is largely a prose narrative, its main themes are captured in poems that follow each of its sections. The disintegration of the narrator, seen previously in *Shkola dlia durakov,* continues in Sokolov's second novel. *Mezhdu sobakoi i volkom* features several narrators whose voices are not always distinct from one another. Apparently two narrator-protagonists are at the center of the story: on the one hand, there is Iakov Palamakhterev—a young huntsman who may be the author of the poems interspersed in the book and whose narrative makes sophisticated allusions to European art and history—and, on the other hand, there is Il'ia Zynzyrella, an older huntsman who is possibly Palamakhterev's father and whose narrative is distinguished by a greater folksiness.

Also in keeping with the "twilight" nature of the book, Sokolov obliterates the differences between past, present, and future. The different characters intermingle with one another; the same story is narrated in completely different ways; and the mere concept of "truth" becomes irrelevant. The novel presents a continuous flux of metamorphoses: a legless cripple becomes an expert skater; the mute speak; a man becomes a fox; a son becomes a father; and a mother becomes a girl as well as the son's mistress. The characters' names also change, as Fedor becomes Peter and Peter becomes Egor.

In *Mezhdu sobakoi i volkom,* Sokolov looks back at Russia with the eyes of an émigré, and what he sees is not an actual Russia but a mythic one, cleansed of its political reality. The action is set in the land of Zaitil'shchina, whose name is derived from Itil', the mythic name for Volga. Although the narrative lacks a clear, main plot to guide the reader through the densely woven poetic imagery, some plotlines can be discerned nonetheless within the intricate linguistic web of the story. Zynzyrella, one of the primary narrative voices, is writing a complaint to a state official about the theft of his crutches. They were stolen in retaliation for his use of them to beat a dog, whom he, in a drunken haze, had mistaken for a wolf. The dog belongs to Palamakhterev, the one who actually stole the crutches. By the end of the book the reader discovers that the crutches were not stolen but were placed accidentally into the coffin of a drowned huntsmen. Zynzyrella's life story emerges in various fragments throughout the text of the narrative. He pines for a woman named Orina, whom he met while still a young man. They had a child, Iakov (Iasha), together, but Zynzyrella no longer knows his whereabouts or those of Orina.

Another plotline narrates the story of Orina, a promiscuous woman who sleeps with men for pleasure, for small presents, and out of pity. One day, Orina's jealous lovers catch Zynzyrella and tie him to the train tracks. Orina loses her life trying to rescue him, and Zynzyrella loses a leg, or possibly both legs. In another version of the story Zynzyrella is not the one tied to the tracks but, rather, Orina's fox—a present from a local hunter. In yet another alternative version, Orina moves away with her son Iasha and changes her name so that Zynzyrella will not be able to find her. Iakov—Zynzyrella's son—is the other "narrator" (although his narrative really takes the form of daydreams and constantly shifting recollections). At one point Iakov recalls his attraction to a dim-witted girl who might be Orina, thus effacing the distinction between father and son.

This account of the story, however, offers these two narrators rather more definition than they possess within the novel. Sokolov is at pains to thwart the reader's expectations of distinct, autonomous charac-

ters. For example, the spelling of "Zynzyrella" keeps changing throughout the novel: different spellings also include Dzynzyrella and Dzyndzyrella. This character also receives letters from an "I. P. Sinderela." While a sudden comic allusion to "Cinderella" springs up in Russian, the name also imitates the ringing of a bell (*dzyn-dzyn*). In other words, Sokolov's use of Zynzyrella as a name suggests that it is not a name at all—it is nothing but a sound. In *Mezhdu sobakoi i volkom,* names seem to vanish into thin air, and the characters whom the readers thought were named turn out to exist only as naught.

Sokolov mythologizes Russia in his second novel (for example, he calls the country a "she-wolf." This alludes to the nickname of Moscow as the Third Rome by recalling the well-known myth of the wolf who suckled Romulus, the legendary founder of Rome). At the same time, however, he mocks the mere idea of mythologizing Russia. The narrator compares the citizens of this Russia-as-she-wolf to the fleas that the wolf bites, one after another, while on the run. In addition, Sokolov does not structure narrative time according to some mythological model of cyclical time. Winter is the predominant season. There are no grand, easily comprehensible orders. Chapters seem to visit and revisit the same subject matter in a random, unpredictable way. Thus, when the reader encounters a chapter titled "Zaitil'shchina" for a third time, or a chapter titled "Pictures from an Exhibition" for a second time, the sense of motion itself is undermined.

Zaitil'shhcina, a world without time, is deeply mysterious and ultimately confusing for the reader. Yet, the reader is compelled to recognize this world as his own, for it is as familiar as it is strange. Sokolov builds this world up from many familiar phrases, quotations from literature and poetry, popular songs, and literary and colloquial clichés. What helps orient the reader in this twilit, ambiguous, and timeless world are the familiar literary materials from which it is constructed. In and of themselves, these allusions, whether to famous poems or famous paintings, have little sentimental value. When situated in the disorienting cosmos of Sokolov's novel, however, they afford the joy of recognition, the pleasure of a fresh reunion with something once dear or familiar and now either hackneyed or forgotten. *Mezhdu sobakoi i volkom,* therefore, can be viewed as the ultimate novel of nostalgia, falling within the tradition of Russian novels about the homeland written in exile. The novel met with a puzzled response by critics, who found the text terrifically complex. As Johnson points out in "Sasha Sokolov: A Literary Biography," Carl Proffer—the owner of Ardis Press and the publisher of *Mezhdu Sobakoi i volkom*—wrote that he did not understand the book. Even a distinguished and sympa-

Paperback cover for the 1988 English-language edition of Sokolov's first novel, Shkola dlia durakov *(1977; revised, 1983), a work about youth and the process of writing* (www.amazon.com)

thetic reader such as Nina Berberova was perplexed, according to souces cited by Johnson.

In 1983 Sokolov completed his third novel, *Palisandriia* (1985, translated as *Astrophobia,* 1989), which—like his earlier books—was published by Ardis. By the time that *Palisandriia* appeared, Sokolov had perfected his style to combine fragments of various discourses while using intertextuality to create evocative and stunning new imagery. The linguistic fabric in *Palisandriia* embraces almost the entirety of the Russian language—from Church Slavonic to the elegant literary language of the nineteenth century to Soviet lingo. The effect is both comic and tragic.

In this novel Sokolov also revisits many of the themes from his previous works—above all, the relation between the poet and power—but, as *Palisandriia* shows, these ideas have been thoroughly reconsidered. For example, *Shkola dlia durakov* is about the struggle for cre-

ative freedom, particularly the freedom to use the Russian language in ways not in accordance with Soviet literary doctrine, whereas in *Palisandriia* Sokolov plainly achieves an unprecedented degree of verbal freedom. This verbal liberty is mirrored in the freedom of travel enjoyed by the protagonist Palisander, who journeys unfettered not only from place to place but also from time to time, sex to sex, and species to species. Despite this artistic mobility, however—an artistic culmination merely glimpsed in Sokolov's first novel—*Palisandriia* promotes a much more tragic sensibility than *Shkola dlia durakov.* As the poet Aleksei Tsvetkov writes in his introduction to Sokolov's 1999 collection *Shkola dlia durakov; Mezhdu sobakoi i volkom,* "The novel, written in the best tradition of parody is laugh-out-loud funny, but unlike the earlier novels, its humor is entirely icy." The two works also share suggestive train imagery. In *Shkola dlia durakov* the image of the train occasioned lyrical musings about the limitless possibility of the imagination. In *Palisandriia,* however, the train assumes apocalyptic significance and thus harbingers the end of the world. Palisander has gathered the bodies of deceased émigrés and is bringing them back by train to their homeland. To the crowds that come to greet him, he promises to build more and more cemeteries. For Sokolov, by the time that he writes *Palisandriia* the train has lost its association with a child's fantasy and has become a portent of global calamity—not unlike trains in the works of Tolstoy and Fyodor Dostoevsky.

The endings of the two novels also invite comparison. As *Shkola dlia durakov* closes, the narrator walks out to buy more writing paper—a youthful promise of works to come. At the end of *Palisandriia,* however, the narrator (who is specifically referred to as *avtor* [the author]) rushes, in the throes of despair, to a staircase, where—instead of a sweeping Romantic gesture such as committing suicide—he merely and anticlimactically vomits.

These comparisons between Sokolov's first and last novels point to the thematic trajectory of his work. In *Shkola dlia durakov,* human misery appeared contingent, the result of specific (and curable) historical conditions. The novel depicted a sturdy hierarchy of good and evil. In *Palisandriia,* Sokolov's reach is much more embracing: it extends far past Soviet Russia, seeming to encompass the entirety of the world. He creates a world without borders, but this artistic culmination now supports a brooding, pessimistic message. Sokolov presents a world without historic motion or development. The intense lyricism that had always been at the heart of his writing is now inextricable from a deep sense of the absurdity and inherent misery of life. In fact, his main themes in *Palisandriia* are the absurdity of history and the absurdity of art. A consummate work of literary art,

Sokolov's third novel ruthlessly, and with astonishing invention, subverts the mere idea of art.

As in *Shkola dlia durakov* and *Mezhdu sobakoi i volkom,* the narrative of *Palisandriia* resists a straightforward summary. The Russian title is meant to invoke epic: just as Virgil's *Aeneid* (29?–19 B.C.) is an epic about Aeneas, so *Palisandriia* is a mock epic about Palisander—namely, Palisander Aleksandrovich Dahlberg. This fantastic creature is the grandson of Rasputin, the grandnephew of Lavrentii Pavlovich Beriia (director of the Soviet secret police), a protégé of Joseph Stalin, and a favorite of Leonid Il'ich Brezhnev. The book purports to be a biography of Palisander, but Palisander is hardly more than a figment of language: Sokolov completely dissolves the idea of an autonomous, well-defined individual and offers instead the lyric pleasures of metamorphosis. Palisander is ultimately impossible to locate in any historical era—he is now male, now female. Indeed, since he was once Catherine the Great's horse, he has a precarious grip on being human.

Palisander ultimately has no identity. Not only can he not be tied down to a specific era, gender, or species, he flows in and out of other characters. At times he seems to be a double of the enigmatic Iasha Nezabudka. Iasha, whose name suggests the diminutive form of the personal pronoun *ia* (I) in Russian, is the Kremlin *chasovoi* (sentry), while Palisander belongs to the order of the *Chasovshchiki* (the Clockmasters). Iasha's last name, Nezabudka, speaks of "never forgetting" (*nezabudka* is also the term for the flower forget-me-not). Palisander thinks of himself as a "khroniker tekushchego vremeni" (chronicler of the current time). Iasha, like Palisander, eventually finds himself in a nursing home, and the two (but are they really two people?) were born on the same date, month, and year.

The novel *Palisandriia* exemplifies an assault on the idea of the self–a violation that is closely related to Sokolov's attitude toward history in the novel. History traditionally has been an important foil for art. Many modernist writers, as well as Sokolov himself in his earlier works, claimed that their art escaped the ravages of history–its brutality, banality, and blindness. Indeed, the transcendence of history was the goal and the measure of these writers' art.

Palisandriia, in contrast, does not transcend history but, rather, addresses it directly. Essential to this effect of transcendence is the presence of actual historical figures (such as Beriia and Brezhnev) who typically rank among the most colorful characters of the novel. Sokolov makes history seem absurd, and by doing so he negates its impact as the terrifying enemy that only a supreme artist can confront and subdue. *Palisandriia* is a great leveler of things. For the embattled relation between art and history, it substitutes a level playing

Dust jacket for the 1989 English-language edition of Sokolov's third novel, Palisandriia *(1980), in which the protagonist travels in time and space, changing his gender and species as necessary (Richland County Public Library)*

field on which artists and politicians alike are ridiculous. A work of art played as a "no trump," *Palisandriia* completely renounces the claim that art has the upper hand on reality, for it makes reality look as fully fantastic as art. The novel met with an enthusiastic response by readers in the United States–including Johnson and Olga Matich.

In addition to his novels, Sokolov has also written several essays, most of which have been collected in book form in *Palisandriia. Roman. Esse. Vystupleniia* (Palisandriia. A Novel. Essays. Speeches, 1999). Some of the writings included in this edition were initially presented at conferences or public readings–such as the essay titled "V dome poveshennogo" and first presented as a speech in 1983 at a conference on human rights at Emory University in Atlanta, Georgia, and "Portret khudozhnika v Amerike: V ozhidanii Nobelia" (The Portrait of an Artist in America: In the Expectation of the Nobel Prize) first given as a speech in 1985 at the University of Santa Barbara, California. Most of his essays are devoted to highly personal and poetic

Page from the manuscript for Sokolov's unpublished work "Ptitsezrets" (The Bird Watcher), which he began writing in 2001 (courtesy of the author)

meditations on the nature of literature, his own fate as an émigré writer, and topics of political and creative freedom. In his essays written in the early 1980s, Sokolov posits that writing literature is a heroic act and, as such, valorous and honorable. In "Trevozhnaia Kukolka" (An Anxious Cocoon) he describes the artist as a transcendent figure, able to free himself from the brutal restraints of history and actual life. In another essay, "V dome poveshennogo," Sokolov—already departed from the Soviet Union—expresses a joyous sense of freedom and seems to believe that perfect freedom is attainable in the West. Freedom, he writes, is the measure of every man, and if freedom—the only condition for writing and thinking—does not exist in one's homeland, the only choice is to leave.

The mood of Sokolov's essays changes drastically by the end of the 1980s, for he has become disillusioned by the West and its indifference to art. In "Znak ozaren'ia" (A Sign of Revelation), written in 1991 and included in the 1999 edition of *Palisandriia*, Sokolov rejects the whole idea of literature in the contemporary world, claiming that it is neither useful nor viable. The essay is partly fictional and partly autobiographical. In

it, the protagonist (who is also the author of the essay) admires a great lyric poet, whose works he learns by heart. He follows the poet's life and eventually merges with him entirely (the great lyric poet in the essay is apparently Pasternak, whose poetry is woven into Sokolov's text, along with quotations from Aleksandr Aleksandrovich Blok and Osip Emil'evich Mandel'shtam). This merger is the protagonist's great achievement, but, at the same time, he understands that he will never return to the ranks of poets and writers. He writes that he has used up language and all of its quotations. He uses the image of a library now plunged in darkness after the candles and lights have burned out. Sokolov employs this image in *Palisandriia;* it expresses more than his own personal sense of frustration. In "Znak ozaren'ia" he calls his contemporaries the "apocalyptic generation" and writes that literature is of no use to them.

Since the collapse of the Soviet Union in 1991 Sokolov has made several brief visits to Russia. In 1996 he received the Pushkin Prize, established by the German fund of Alfred Topfler in Russia, for his literary accomplishments. Sokolov's three major novels share distinct stylistic features, among which is the combination of various kinds of discourse—official Soviet lingo, nineteenth-century literary language, contemporary colloquialism, and scholarly language. All or any of these discourses can coexist in the space of a single passage or even a single sentence. All three of the novels, moreover, are rich in references to other literature. Sokolov weaves into his texts many quotations from Russian and foreign prose, poetry, and song. Finally, in each of his novels he rejects linear time and represents it, rather, as amorphous, lacking cohesion and firm outlines. Sokolov's literary influences include Pushkin and Nikolai Vasil'evich Gogol, as well as Bunin, Pasternak, Nabokov, and Bitov. In addition, critics have compared his prose to that of Bely and Andrei Platonovich Platonov, among Russian writers, as well as James Joyce, Italo Calvino, and Jorge Luis Borges from the West.

At the turn of the millennium Sasha Sokolov seems concerned with the staleness and tedium of life. Yet, just as important for him are the potent forces of rejuvenation inherent in language. These forces derive their power in large part from the endlessness of language and the multitude of discourses it is capable of generating. Sokolov's liberating irony thwarts any kind of official discourse. It makes a mockery of Soviet authority, of course, but also of the self-mythologization of art. While his novels are important works of art, their accomplishment does not consist of some purported transcendence of history. They constitute, rather, supremely inventive and linguistically agile broodings on the inescapability of time. In Sokolov's writings art emerges as the incomparably deft meditation of our thorough immanence.

Interviews:

A. Polovets and S. Rakhlin, "Sasha Sokolov govorit," *Al'manakh Panorama*, 3 September 1981, pp. 8–9, 12;

K. Sapgir, "V *Russkoi mysli* – pisatel' Sasha Sokolov," *Russkaia mysl'*, 12 November 1981, p. 11;

Sergei Rakhlin, "Pisatel'– vezde chuzhoi," *Al'manakh Panorama*, 29 May–6 June 1982, p. 10;

A. and N. Voronel', "Ia khochu podniat' russkuiu prozu do urovnia poezii . . . (Beseda s Sashei Sokolovym, SShA, 1983 g.)," *Dvadtsat' dva*, 35 (1984): 179–186;

Olga Matich, "Russian Writers on Literature and Society," *Humanities in Society*, 7 (1984): 221–223;

Matich, "Beseda s Sashei Sokolovym: 'Nuzhno zabyt' vse staroe i vspomnit' vse novoe . . . ,'" *Russkaia mysl'*, 31 May 1985, p. 12;

Matthias Rosenthal, "An Interview with Sasha Sokolov. The Writer as Free Spirit," *Daily Nexus*, 21 November 1985, pp. 4A, 6A;

Russell Harris, "Sasha Sokolov," *Zero*, 1 (1986): 78–80;

Viktor Erofeev, "Vremia dlia chastnykh besed . . . ," *Oktiabr'*, 8 (1989): 195–202;

John Glad, *Conversations in Exile: Russian Writers Abroad* (Durham, N.C.: Duke University Press, 1993), pp. 174–185.

Biographies:

D. Barton Johnson, "Sasha Sokolov: A Literary Biography," *Canadian-American Slavic Studies*, 21 (1987): 203–230;

E. Zubareva, "Sokolov Sasha," *Russkie pisateli 20 veka. Biograficheskiy slovar'*, edited by Petr Alekseevich Nikolaev (Moscow: Bol'shaia Rossiiskaia Entsiklopediia, 2000), pp. 653–654.

Bibliography:

D. Barton Johnson, "A Selected Annotated Bibliography of Works by and about Sasha Sokolov," *Canadian-American Slavic Studies*, 21 (1987): 417–428.

References:

Laura Beraha, "The Last Rogue of History: Picaresque Elements in Sasha Sokolov's *Palisandriia*," *Canadian-Slavonic Papers-Revue Canadienne des Slavistes*, 35 (1993): 201–220;

Aleksandr Boguslawski, "Vremia Palisandra Dal'berga," *Russian Language Journal*, 42 (1988): 221–229;

Edward J. Brown and D. Barton Johnson, "Forum: The Third Wave," *Slavic & East European Journal*, 30, no. 3 (Fall 1986): 380–419; no. 4 (Fall 1986): 509–552;

Canadian-American Slavic Studies, special Sokolov issue, 21 (1987);

John Fridman (Friedman), "Vetru net ukaza: Razmyshleniia nad tekstami romanov *Pushkinsky dom* Bitova i *Shkola dlia durakov* S. Solokova," *Literaturnoe obozrenie*, 12 (1989): 14–16;

Johnson, "The Galoshes Manifesto: A Motif in the Novels of Sasha Sokolov," *Oxford Slavonic Papers*, 22 (1989): 155–179;

Johnson, "Sasha Sokolov: The New Russian Avant-Garde," *Critique. Studies in Contemporary Fiction*, 30 (1989): 163–178;

Johnson, "Sasha Sokolov and Vladimir Nabokov," *Russian Language Journal*, 41 (1987): 153–162;

Johnson, "Sasha Sokolov's *Palisandrija*," *Slavic & East European Journal*, 30 (Fall 1986): 389–403;

Johnson, "Sasha Sokolov's Twilight Cosmos: Themes and Motifs," *Slavic Review*, 45 (1986): 639–649;

Johnson, "Vladimir Nabokov and Sasha Sokolov," *Nabokovian*, 15 (Fall 1985): 29–39;

Vladimir Kravchenko, "Uchitel' derzosti v shkole dlia durakov," *Literaturnaia gazeta,* 15 February 1995, p. 3;

Mark Lipovetsky, "Mifologiia metamorfoz: Poetika *Shkoly dlia durakov* Sashi Sokolova," *Oktiabr',* 7 (1995): 183–192;

Lipovetsky, "Self-Portrait on a Timeless Background: Transformations of the Autobiographical Mode in Russian Postmodernism," *Auto-Biography Studies,* 11 (Fall 1996): 140–162;

Ludmilla L. Litus, "Sasha Sokolov's *Shkola dlja durakov:* Aesopian Language and Intertextual Play," *Slavic & East European Journal,* 41 (1997): 114–134;

Litus, "Sasha Sokolov's 'Shkola dlja durakov': Form, Language, Intertext, and Allusion," dissertation, University of Michigan, 1991;

Olga Matich, "Sasha Sokolov's *Palisandriia:* History and Myth," *Russian Review,* 45 (1986): 415–426;

Karen Rice McDowell, "The Reemergence of Medieval Word-Weaving in Sasha Sokolov's 'Shkola Dlia Durakov': Invoking the Word," dissertation, University of Virginia, 1997;

Arnold McMillin, "Aberration or the Future: The Avant-Garde Novels of Sasha Sokolov," in *From Pushkin to Palisandriia: Essays on the Russian Novel in Honor of Richard Freeborn,* edited by McMillin (New York: St. Martin's Press, 1990), pp. 229–243;

Karen L. Ryan, "Sokolov's *Palisandriia:* The Art of History," in *Selected Papers from the Fifth World Congress of Central and East European Studies (Warsaw, 1995),* edited by Ryan and Barry P. Scherr (Basingstoke, U.K.: Macmillan / New York: St. Martin's Press, 2000), pp. 215–227;

Ulrich Schmid, "Flowers of Evil: The Poetics of Monstrosity in Contemporary Russian Literature: Erofeev, Mamleev, Sokolov, Sorokin," *Russian Literature,* 48 (2000): 205–222;

Cynthia Simmons, "Incarnations of the Hero Archetype in Sokolov's *School for Fools,*" in *The Supernatural in Slavic and Baltic Literature: Essays in Honor of Victor Terras,* edited by Amy Mandelker (Columbus, Ohio: Slavica, 1988), pp. 275–289;

Simmons, *Their Father's Voice: Vassily Aksyonov, Venedikt Erofeev, Eduard Limonov, and Sasha Sokolov* (New York: Peter Lang, 1993);

Igor P. Smirnov, "Geschichte der Nachgeschichte: Zur russisch-sprachigen Prosa der Postmoderne Niemeyer," in *Modelle des literarischen Strukturwandels,* edited by Michael Titzmann and Georg Jager (Tübingen: Niemeyer, 1991), pp. 205–219;

Alexander Suslov, "The 'New Art' Tradition in Modern Russian Prose," dissertation, Georgetown University, 1984;

Vladimir Tumanov, "A Tale Told by Two Idiots: Krik idiota v *Shkole dlia durakov* S. Sokolova i v *Shume i iarosti* U. Folknera," *Russian Language Journal,* 48 (1994): 137–154;

Petr L'vovich Vail' and Aleksandr Aleksandrovich Genis, "Uroki shkoly dlia durakov," *Literaturnoe obozrenie,* 1–2 (1993): 13–16;

Jasmina Vojvodic, "Otkliki simul'tanizma v postmodernistskoi proze (*Shkola dlia durakov* Sashi Sokolova)," *Russian Literature,* 51, no. 3 (April 2002): 273–294;

Mikhail Volgin, "Bessmertnoe vchera: Chekhov i Sasha Sokolov," *Literaturnoe obozrenie,* 11–12 (1994): 13–15;

Kevin Windle, "From Ogre to 'Uncle Lawrence': The Evolution of the Myth of Beria in Russian Fiction from 1953 to the Present," *Australian Slavonic & East European Studies,* 3 (no. 1) (1989): 1–16;

Andrei Zorin, "Nasylaiushchii veter," *Novyi mir,* 12 (1989): 250–253.

Papers:

Some of Sasha Sokolov's papers can be found in the Department of Special Collections at Davidson Library, University of California, Santa Barbara. This collection, known as the Sasha Sokolov Collection, Mss 117, includes his correspondence with Ardis Press; all three of his novels in both typescript and proof versions; interviews and speeches; and two audiocassettes. Photographs and drawings of Sokolov are also kept in this collection.

Vladimir Georgievich Sorokin

(7 August 1955 –   )

Konstantin V. Kustanovich
Vanderbilt University

BOOKS: *Ochered'* (Paris: Sintaksis, 1985); translated, with an introduction, by Sally Laird as *The Queue* (New York & London: Readers International, 1988);

Vladimir Sorokin: [Sbornik rasskazov], with an introduction by Dmitrii Aleksandrovich Prigov (Moscow: Russlit, 1992)–includes "Kiset";

Mesiats v Dakhau (Moscow, 1992); translated by Jamey Gambrell as *A Month in Dachau* in *Grand Street,* 48 (1994);

Norma (Moscow: Obscuri viri/Tri kita, 1994);

Roman (Moscow: Obscuri viri/Tri kita, 1994);

Tridtsataia liubov' Mariny (Moscow: R. Elinin, 1995);

Dostoevsky-Trip: P'esa (Moscow: Obscuri viri, 1997);

Sobranie sochinenii (2 volumes, Moscow: Ad Marginem, 1998; enlarged, 3 volumes, 2002)–includes "Vozvrashchenie," "Pervyi subbotnik," *Serdtsa chetyrekh, Pel'meni, Russkaia babushka, Zemlianka, Doverie, S Novym godom, Iubelei, Dismorfomania, Shchi,* and *Hochzeitsreise;*

Goluboe salo (Moscow: Ad Marginem, 1999);

Pir (Moscow: Ad Marginem, 2001)–includes "Nastia," "Konkretnye," "Den' russkogo edoka," "Sakharnoe voskresen'e," and "Pepel";

Led (Moscow: Ad Marginem, 2002).

Editions and Collections: *Norma* (Moscow: BSG-PRESS, 1999);

Tridtsataia liubov' Mariny. Ochered' (Moscow: BSG-PRESS, 1999);

Serdtsa chetyrekh (Moscow: Ad Marginem, 2001)–includes *Dostoevsky-trip, Pel'meni,* and *Hochzeitreise;*

Pervyi subbotnik (Moscow: Ad Marginem, 2001);

EPS, with contributions by Sorokin, Viktor Vladimirovich Erofeev, and Dmitrii Aleksandrovich Prigov (Moscow: ZebraE, 2002);

Utro snaipera (Moscow: Ad Marginem, 2002).

PLAY PRODUCTIONS: *Hochzeitsreise,* Berlin, Prater, 2 November 1995;

Dismorfomaniia, Vienna, Schauspielhaus, November 1996;

Pel'meni, Munich, Kammerspiele, Werkraum, 23 February 1997;

Shchi, Moscow, Teatr na Iugo-Zapade, 2 March 1999; Cottbus, Germany, Staatstheater Cottbus, 1999;

Dostoevsky-Trip, Moscow, Teatr na Iugo-Zapade, 24 November 1999.

PRODUCED SCRIPTS: *Moskva,* motion picture, by Sorokin and Aleksandr Zel'dovich, Studio Telekino, 1999;

Kopeika, motion picture, by Sorokin and Ivan Dykhovichnyi, Skarabei Films and Volya Film Company, 2002.

SELECTED PERIODICAL PUBLICATIONS– UNCOLLECTED: "A Business Proposition," translated by Jamey Gambrell, *Glas: New Russian Writing,* 2 (1991);

Cashfire, by Sorokin, Aleksandr Zel'dovich, and Oleg Radzinsky, *Iskusstvo kino,* 4 (2002): 103–141.

The Russian writer who has violated the tenets of Russian literature the most is arguably Vladimir Sorokin. In his books Sorokin subverts the traditional ideological and representational functions of the literary profession in Russia; he creates words and sentences on paper with no communicative purpose. In the context of the two-century history of Russian literature as the soul and conscience of Russian society, Sorokin's writings are shocking and, for many, as blasphemous as the unraveling of the Soviet Union in the late 1980s and early 1990s. Not by mere chance do these two phenomena–the formation of the writer Sorokin and the reformation of Russia–coincide. Both are products of the forces that were at work in the Soviet Union in the 1970s and the 1980s–forces that developed gradually, hidden from the public eye in the depths of Russian life. Yet, when they surfaced, they marked the end of two opposing totalitarian systems: literature and the state. In the Soviet Union and in nineteenth-century Russia as well, literature was the one of the few possible means

Vladimir Georgievich Sorokin (Associated Press)

of alleviating the stifling pressure of the all-pervasive and omnipotent official ideology. For this reason Russian literature and its creators achieved an unprecedented degree of social and political influence. Sorokin, however, seems to detest the power of literature as much as the power of any oppressive system. His work is a continuous verbal attack on literary tradition and, at the same time, an attempt at creating a nonrepresentational alternative to it.

Vladimir Georgievich Sorokin was born on 7 August 1955 in the little town of Bykovo in the Moscow suburbs. His father was a professor of metallurgy and his mother, a housewife. After the ravages of World War II and the postwar famine of 1946 to 1947, life in the Soviet Union gradually approached something resembling normalcy. The traumas during the era of Joseph Stalin—such as the attack by Andrei Aleksandrovich Zhdanov on the arts in 1946 and the anticosmopolitan (anti-Jewish) campaign from 1948 to 1953, which resulted in a new wave of purges and executions—began to heal after the leader's death in 1953. The country was on the threshold of the "Thaw" period initiated by Nikita Sergeevich Khrushchev. Although the population still experienced shortages of

even essential staples and queues snaked endlessly down city streets, people did not starve. Besides, Moscow and Leningrad were much better supplied than both the countryside and other Soviet cities.

Yet, because of peculiarities in the Soviet social system and certain objective historical factors, many children—even children from stable families—were exposed to the extreme cruelty and explicit promiscuity that poverty and crowded conditions often engender. During World War II, Russia lost twenty million people, mostly men, and millions more perished in Stalin's labor camps. As a result, scores of children were fatherless; their mothers were utterly and routinely exhausted by their jobs, domestic chores, and endless queues for food and supplies. Many children, practically abandoned, became dependent on whatever peers or other adults were available. In 1953, after Stalin's death, the Soviet government granted a general amnesty but excluded political prisoners. Hundreds of thousands of criminals returned to their hometowns; streets and neighborhoods were infested by gangs.

Like other urban children, Sorokin as a boy lived and grew up in an environment that did not provide sufficient protection for his psyche. Almost certainly, he was a sensitive boy with an early sexual awareness. He remembers an episode at a child-care center when a teacher caught him playing with himself. The teacher became extremely angry with him and threatened to cut off his penis should he be caught again. After that Sorokin started stuttering. In Crimea, where his father took him for a vacation, he witnessed an incident of senseless cruelty when he saw his family's neighbor beat up his father-in-law, an old man. As recounted in Serafima Roll's contribution to *Postmodernisty o post-kul'ture: Interv'iu s sovremennymi pisateliami i kritikami* (The Postmodernists on Postculture: Interviews with Contemporary Writers and Critics, 1996), the young Sorokin heard the victim ask his son-in-law, "Why do you beat me?" The answer was, "Simply because I like it." This violent act made such a strong impression on the boy that the story line of a father taking his child on a vacation in Crimea appears later in one of Sorokin's novels, *Tridtsataia liubov' Mariny* (Marina's Thirtieth Love, 1995). Here, however, Crimea is the locus of a much more horrific crime: the rape of a ten-year-old girl by her father.

Early in his life Sorokin developed a passion for drawing. At the age of eight he attended an art studio at the Pushkin Museum in Moscow, where he continued his studies for five years. At fourteen he tried to write fiction but soon abandoned this pursuit because, as he remembers, it was too easy and did not provide enough challenge. He soon enrolled in the Moscow Institute of Petroleum and Gas, from which he graduated in 1977, but he never went on to work in this field; instead, he earned his living as a book designer. In 1977 he married a music teacher, Irina, who gave birth to their twin daughters, Anna and Maria, in 1980.

In the mid 1970s Sorokin joined a circle of Moscow artists and poets known as the Moscow conceptualists. He befriended Dmitrii Aleksandrovich Prigov, Lev Semenovich Rubinshtein, Eric Vladimirovich Bulatov, Andrei Monastyrsky, and the group known as the Meditsinskaia germenevtika (Medical Hermeneutics). At that time he returned to literary work; as he states in an interview with Sergei Vladimirovich Shapovalov, published in Sorokin's *Sobranie sochinenii* (Collected Works, 1998), literature "clenched its teeth on him in a deadly grip," never to release him again. Sorokin's friends encouraged him in his first literary endeavors, which apparently fit the main principles of conceptualism. One of these principles is the rejection of the traditional art of representation because, as conceptualists contend, free and independent representation of reality is impossible. One's mind is controlled by many discourses that constitute the context of a life. History, great teachings—or metanarratives—literature, and even language determine the way one's mind

works, leaving no individual space or subjective freedom in any artistic creation.

Conceptualists try to extricate themselves from the prison of discourse. One way to do this is to subvert the representational function of language. Instead of depicting reality, the artist creates a "hyperreality," or (in the words of the philosopher Jean Baudrillard) "simulacra"—signifiers without signifieds, objects behind which there are no ideas. Mikhail Naumovich Epshtein, a scholar of Russian postmodernism and, in particular, of conceptualism, writes in *After the Future: The Paradoxes of Postmodernism and Contemporary Russian Culture* (1995) that "conceptualism tries to wrench out of the word any meaning whatever, leaving an empty, echoing shell: a senseless cliché that says nothing." Moscow Conceptualists employ different techniques to strip the contents of their works of any meaning. One of these techniques is to present an object outside of any context—historical, ideological, or cultural—thus depriving the recipient of any referents and consequently of the possibility of interpretation. The artist's task is reduced to creating "clichés," that is, portraying not the reality but the language itself. Through such an approach, language depicts language, and art depicts art. As a result, conceptualists expect the user to have no ideological or emotional response to their works.

Conceptual art also exemplifies one of the main tenets of art in the postmodern era: the death of the author. Expounded upon by Roland Barthes, Michel Foucault, and Jacques Derrida, the idea of reducing the role of the author to that of a "scriptor," who is engaged in mere textual play with existing discourses, finds its practical realization here. The traditional author attempts to control the reader with the totalitarian power of his or her book. The scriptor's writing avoids any ideational influence by relinquishing the claims of logic or textual originality. This is what lies behind the frequent use of "ready-mades" in conceptual works. In the narrow sense, a "ready-made" can be any object presented as an object of art, such as Marcel Duchamp's *Fountain*, a urinal that he attempted to exhibit in New York in 1917. In a broader sense, which is relevant to Sorokin's work, a "ready-made" can be a familiar discourse (artistic, literary, or linguistic) recreated in a new work.

The principles and aesthetics of conceptualism have found an ardent practitioner in Sorokin. In the introductory section of part 7 in his book *Norma* (The Norm, 1994) Sorokin lists the most important twentieth-century avant-garde figures whose works and ideas have influenced him. Western conceptualism "struck him with the simplicity of its idea," and Duchamp is for him "the highest phenomenon of human culture of all times." In the late 1970s and early 1980s Sorokin simultaneously worked on several pieces, adopting the conceptualist aesthetics of producing "senseless clichés." His first published work was *Ochered'* (1985; translated as *The Queue*, 1988), the purest conceptual work by Sorokin. In other works of the same period he combines the conceptualist practice of reproducing artistic codes with other artistic and ideological goals.

Sorokin worked on *Ochered'* from 1982 to 1983, during the same period that he wrote his short stories, *Norma*, and *Tridtsataia liubov' Mariny*. There may be several reasons why the Paris-based, Russian émigré journal *Sintaksis* chose to publish this text; other works that Sorokin wrote in the early 1980s only appeared in print seven to nine years later. *Ochered'* is probably Sorokin's most "interpretable" work. Many critics saw in it a social commentary on the Soviet phenomenon of constant shortages and long lines. Moreover, its narrative structure is more simple in comparison to some of his other works, in which clashing discourses make for difficult reading. Finally, *Ochered'* shocks the general reader perhaps the least out of all of Sorokin's writings during this time: although there are plenty of obscenities in the text, his favorites—graphic descriptions of dismemberment, cannibalism, and all kinds of human excretion—are absent, except for an innocuous urination in the courtyard.

The text of *Ochered'* consists of a stream of utterances, not unlike what is found in the writings of Rubinshtein, produced by people standing in a long line for some item of clothing. Sorokin never makes clear what the object of their desire is. At first they seem to be waiting for shoes, then some kind of lined jacket, and then, most probably, imported jeans. People stand in line for two days. For about 150 pages the text has not a single word of the narrator's speech and consists only of dialogue between characters standing in line. The reader can discern the central character, Vadik, and even figure out what happens to him through these long hours in line. He picks up a girl, Lena, who stays with him for some time but later leaves for a more refined and educated man. He befriends other men, and they pool their money twice to buy vodka and drink it in a courtyard. There, in a drunken stupor, Vadik falls asleep on the grass. At the end of *Ochered'* he finds himself in the apartment of one Liudmila, with whom, after a brief supper, he has passionate sex. In the morning she brings him to the warehouse where she works and where Vadik eventually obtains the desired, yet still unnamed, product.

Sorokin justifiably rejects the interpretation of this work as an exposé of Soviet life. As with his other works, his primary interest lies in the depiction of discourse. A Soviet-era queue is a distinctive public space where people of different social groups and professions come into close contact for a long time. Such social gatherings provide Sorokin with rich material of many different discourses. The reader "hears" a learned scholarly exchange between two scientists and a much less sophisticated comparison of vodka to cheap fortified wines; trite remarks about the ineffectiveness of the police and the insolence of Georgians; a pseudoprofound discussion of the Israeli-Arab war; news about the latest developments in Western rock music shared by youths; and crude comments about the dimensions of some man's penis and the effect that it produces on his girlfriend or wife. To depict a roll call in the line, Sorokin lists about six hundred names, following each with the response, "Here." Pages of "A-a-hs" and "O-o-hs" and "A-a-a-a-as" render the discourse of unrestrained sexual intercourse, and Vadik's nap on the grass is presented simply as a blank page. In *Ochered'* Sorokin enjoys language without striving to produce ideas.

In the late 1970s and early 1980s Sorokin also wrote a collection of short stories, *Pervyi subbotnik* (The First Working Saturday, 1992). Some of these stories, including the eponymous "Pervyi subbotnik," appeared in 1992 in the modest-sized volume *Vladimir Sorokin: [Sbornik rasskazov]*—the first book of his to be published in Russia. The full text of this book, however, appeared only in Sorokin's two-volume *Sobranie sochinenii*. The title "Pervyi subbotnik" is laden with significance for the Soviet reader and thus deviates from the ideational detachment of pure conceptualism that is characteristic of *Ochered'*. *Subbotnik* (a working Saturday) refers to the practice of the Soviet government to "extort" extra working days from workers without pay. The practice goes back to the early 1920s; Lenin hailed it in his article "Velikii pochin" (The Great Initiative, 1919). The official propaganda and socialist realist literature presented these working Saturdays (*subbotniki*) as the product of workers' conscientiousness and as a completely voluntary initiative.

In "Pervyi subbotnik" Sorokin employs an artistic method that became his trademark in many later works. The style and ideological makeup of the story resemble a typical socialist realist treatment of a factory theme. A group of workers come on Saturday to their factory for the *subbotnik*. They are happy, the weather is good, and their assignment of raking leaves is pleasant. The thought that they are continuing the great tradition of volunteering their labor for the country makes them even happier. Their young comrade, a new worker, is slightly late because he missed his train, but since everybody is in a great mood he is easily forgiven. The old worker remarks on the good clothes that the lad is wearing. The reader is supposed to conclude that the *subbotnik* is a festive event for the young man but this *subbotnik* is his first. His comrades congratulate him; they feel how important this day should be for the young worker. There is a reason for celebration.

In the story "Pervyi subbotnik" Sorokin re-creates the "sacred" genre of socialist realism, which various critics have written about. Margarita Tupitsyn attributes to conceptualism the function of "dismantling the system of sacred referents of totalitarian culture without abandoning its generic features and mythical language." The conceptualist author accomplishes a subversion of these "sacred referents" by placing them into an alien cultural context or by combining them with profane elements in the same text. According to Emile Durkheim, the sacred and profane are two opposite spheres of human existence, which in a traditional social environment never mix or meet. Durkheim writes in *Les formes elementaires de la vie religieuse* (1912; translated as *The Elementary Forms of Religious Life,* 1995) that "the sacred and the profane are always and everywhere conceived by the human intellect as separate genera, as two worlds with nothing in common." When these two worlds are put together, the sacred ceases to be such.

In the context of the years immediately preceding and following the collapse of the Soviet Union, when "Pervyi subbotnik" was written, published, and read, the extreme ideological cynicism of the era already undermines the sacredness of the text. Sorokin proceeds, however, to combine the sacred theme and style with the profane elements within the text itself. At the end of the story, to salute the first *subbotnik,* the workers—one by one—"fire salvos" by passing gas. The veteran worker delivers the longest and loudest "salvo." These concluding paragraphs completely dismantle the socialist realist fabric of the story. Thus, one can refer to the first part of the story as a "model" of socialist realism; the second part is the "killer" text that utterly profanes the sacred character of the first part.

This bipartite structure has become a trademark of Sorokin's prose. In some stories, as in "Pervyi subbotnik," the second, destructive discourse is relatively innocent; in others it surpasses all possible limits of imagination in its depiction of bodily excretions, mutilations, and uncommon sexual practices. The two discourses—the "model" text and the "killer" text—are most often separated by a sudden transition toward the end of the text. At some point the innocent reproduction of the socialist realist cliché turns into a monstrous conglomerate of shocking images and words. Less frequently, the destructive discourse intermittently penetrates the text throughout the entire story. Thus, "Vozvrashchenie" (Coming Home), which appeared in the 1998 *Sobranie sochinenii,* re-creates a typical Soviet literary stereotype of first love: two innocent young people, timid but tender, are deeply in love with each other

but do not engage in sexual relations—as is the norm in socialist realist literature. They are students on a break, and he invites her to visit his family. His mother is a kind, middle-aged housewife, and his younger brother is a strong youth with an inclination for science (he assembles his own telescope); together they constitute the archetype of a good Soviet family. No father is mentioned in the narrative; either he is dead or, if alive, may be still at work fulfilling a production quota. Sorokin skillfully and lovingly reproduces minute details of character depictions and styles that are extremely familiar to the Soviet reader. From time to time, however, these innocent characters utter outrageously obscene phrases in the course of their polite table talk; the couple's romantic dialogue, when they are alone, is also interspersed with shocking obscenities, after which the conversation returns to its routine flow of clichés.

More often, the break in the established discourse occurs through a sudden transition to a different, extremely violent and offensive discourse in the second part of the story. Methods of developing the "killer" text vary. One way is to undermine the "model" text—the first part of the narrative—on the level of language itself. Sorokin either introduces linguistic units traditionally unacceptable in Russian literature, such as the obscenities in the story "Vozvrashchenie," or he writes in such a way that language completely disintegrates toward the end of the story. In "Kiset" (The Tobacco Pouch), published in the 1992 collection, *Vladimir Sorokin,* a beautiful girl gives a tobacco pouch to a young soldier who is passing by her village with retreating troops. He keeps the pouch over his heart for four years of the war and then for eleven years in the Stalin camps. The pouch helps him to carry on and survive all the ordeals that he goes through. Finally, sixteen years after their meeting in that village the soldier finds the woman who gave him the pouch. At this point the story falls apart. In the last three pages, sentences become disjointed; the syntax breaks; new, heretofore nonexistent, words appear; and the theme of the narrative is impossible to establish—although in three separate paragraphs of ten, thirteen, and twenty-one lines the reader finds some resemblance of cohesive miniplots. These subplots have no relation to the story of the pouch, and their contents are by themselves quite repugnant: the first portrays the charred corpse of a woman and a battle with a giant worm feeding on her corpse; the second presents a canal filled with tons of swarming lice; and in the third a woman gives birth to a monster baby.

In the story "Proezdom" (Passing By, 1992) a department head from a regional party committee, Georgii Ivanovich, drops in on his colleagues from the district party committee. At an impromptu meeting he

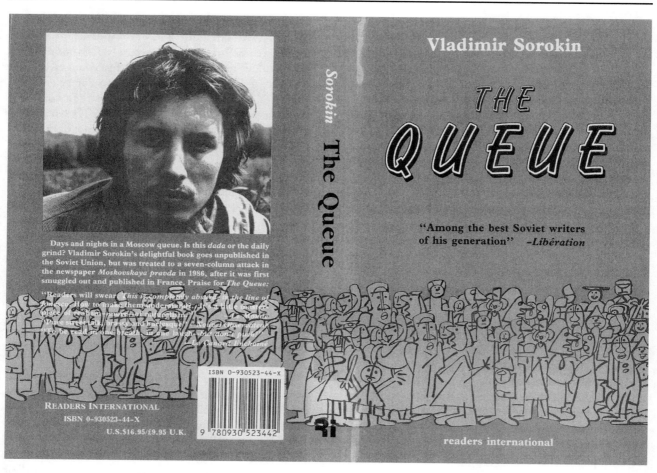

Dust jacket for the 1988 English-language edition of Sorokin's 1985 novel, Ochered',
considered his most purely conceptual work (Richland County Public Library)

praises them for their good work and discusses their plans for the future. At the end of his visit he stops at the office of Vladimir Ivanovich, the head of the Propaganda Department, who is flattered by this visit. Suddenly, in the course of their conversation, Georgii Ivanovich climbs on the desk, drops his pants and underwear, and begins defecating. The bewildered Vladimir Ivanovich has no alternative but to catch the feces in his hands to save important materials on the desk. Having finished, Georgii Ivanovich pulls his pants up, jumps off the desk, makes a telephone call, and in a business-like manner leaves the office. The contrast between the core of the story—a brilliant rendering of an archetypal socialist realist narrative—and its ending in Vladimir Ivanovich's office is all the more shocking; the description of the process of defecation is meticulous, resembling a blow-up in a movie script. With virtually each subsequent work Sorokin seeks drastic, shocking measures to dissipate the monotony of derivative art. The tension caused by the sudden invasion of a "killer" discourse is analogous to the intensity of many "scandal" scenes in Fyodor Dostoevsky's novels.

There is little that is derivative about *Norma,* a work consisting of eight parts, none of which is connected to the others in any way; in reading *Norma* one is immediately faced with the problem of defining the genre of the book. Part 1 is a collection of short sketches that capture brief moments in the lives of an entire gamut of Soviet social types. Here, Sorokin manifests his predilection for the visual arts; each little story or sketch "behaves" like a painting, lacking chronological development and a complete plot. Although the episodes are not connected to one another by the same characters or shared elements of plot, one element in each episode is common to all and, in fact, gives the book its title: all the adults in these stories have to consume their daily "norm," a small, factory-produced briquette of human feces.

Parts 2 and 6 exhibit the minimalist aesthetics frequently encountered in conceptual works. The second part depicts a "normal" human life simply by listing nouns appended by the adjective "normal." This part starts with the phrase "normal birth," continues with "normal boy," and then goes on to mention more than 1,600 such phrases, providing a detailed account of the typical life of an urban Soviet man in the 1960s or 1970s. The section then ends with the phrase "normal death." Going through this list, the reader learns that the protagonist went to a vocational school, had his share of drinking and sex while in his teens, served in the army, became a bus driver, married a woman named Marina, had children, engaged in extramarital affairs, became a grandfather, retired, received dentures, developed heart disease, and, finally, died. Part 6 has only twenty-eight phrases—brief statements with the word "norm" or its derivatives, such as "Everything is normal between Vasia and Lena," or "The legal norms have been observed," or "The Georgian tea 'Norm' is popular."

Part 3 of *Norma* exemplifies Sorokin's practice of conceptualism. It includes two stories that oppose one another in style, language, mood, intonation, characters, actions, and events. The first one describes a man, Anton, coming back to his native village, where he spent his childhood and youth. In a little box buried in his orchard, Anton finds a letter written by the nineteenth-century Russian poet Fedor Ivanovich Tiutchev and discovers that he is Tiutchev's direct descendant. A nostalgia for the Russia of bygone years pervades the story. The action in the second story also takes place in a Soviet village, but the reality is completely different. The melancholic nostalgia and beauty permeating the first story has given way to images of decay, filth, and violence. Instead of the beautiful language of nineteenth-century Russian prose, the most obscene parlance characteristic of drunken hoodlums is expressed. Blurring the boundary between reality and fiction, Sorokin also plays with the notion of authorship in the third part; he illustrates Foucault's idea that the author must be erased in favor of forms characteristic of discourse.

In Part 5 of *Norma,* Sorokin experiments with discourse by representing the correspondence of a man with a professor who is his distant relative. The man takes care of the professor's dacha and garden. In his messages to the professor, he complains about mutual relatives, who come to the dacha to relax but refuse to share the labor, and describes his daily life around the dacha (including making repairs and planting vegetables and strawberries). These messages reproduce the discourse typical of a not-so-well-educated, middle-aged veteran of World War II. The narrative progresses not through plot developments but through changes in the language of the correspondence. First, toward the end of the messages the tone becomes aggressive. Then the

man starts cursing his correspondent, and the obscenities grow in number and strength. Later, sentences become less and less cohesive as the man uses nonexistent words more frequently—until only the greeting and one or two obscene sentences at the beginning are rendered in Russian. Lines of random letters with no spaces between them follow. The last ten messages consist only of several lines of the letter *a*.

The texts in Part 7 are purely conceptual pieces, each including a "ready-made"—a song or a poem from Soviet popular culture, each of which is incorporated into the body of the piece, or story, with an easily recognizable socialist realist plot. The monological text of a poem is presented as a dialogue in prose. The original text is broken further by the narrator's remarks, additional utterances of the interlocutors, and a description of their appearances and actions. Many stories deal with war themes: a soldier bidding farewell to his sweetheart before departing to the front; a captain writing a letter from the front to his wife; a division commander making the rounds in the trenches; and navy sailors toiling on their difficult sea voyages. Other stories borrow from plots describing socialist construction projects or lives on collective farms.

Part 8 describes a staff meeting at some organization—perhaps a journal—at which the participants discuss two forthcoming issues. The third-person narrative style is reminiscent of socialist realist production prose, with its descriptions of factory workers, mandatory meetings, and clichéd speeches of party leaders, but the direct speech of the participants consists mostly of neologisms invented by Sorokin. These otherwise nonexistent words do not make up a new language, however, since they utterly lack meaning. Yet, Sorokin manages to create the general atmosphere of a meeting and to suggest the familiar intonation of its participants' remarks by intermittently inserting semantic links—meaningful phrases that fuse the text into one whole. *Norma* may be considered an "experimental laboratory," in which Sorokin tries future literary techniques. All the motifs, themes, and devices found in *Norma* appear in his later works.

Sorokin's novel *Tridtsataia liubov' Mariny* deviates from his typical bipartite structure of creating a "model" text in the style of a known literary discourse, followed by a "killer" text. Although the work consists of two contrasting parts, the first one does not imitate any established literary style. As in Part 1 of *Norma,* Sorokin creates in *Tridtsataia liubov' Mariny* his own narrative describing the life and sexual escapades of a thirty-year-old music teacher, Marina Alekseeva. At ten, she was raped by her own father, who then committed suicide; at twelve, she was raped again by a summer-camp counselor; and at fifteen, she was seduced by an older woman. During the intervening fifteen years Marina has many sexual encounters with men, but they do not provide the gratification that she so desperately seeks, nor does she ever experience an orgasm with a man. She finds satisfaction and orgasms only in *rozovaia liubov'* (rose love), a Russian slang expression for lesbian love.

Marina's story is told in flashbacks that lead to her present life as a beautiful, thirty-year-old woman with rich experiences in sex, drinking, and, occasionally, pot smoking. The current events in the novel take place in 1983, when the secretary general of the Soviet Communist Party was Iurii Vladimirovich Andropov. Like many members of the Soviet intelligentsia at that time, Marina is moderately dissident, moderately religious, and moderately pro-Western. In her secret drawer she keeps the Bible and books by Aleksandr Isaevich Solzhenitsyn, George Orwell, and other banned authors. Despite her unsatisfying experiences with men, she believes that there is one man who could give her happiness, and she often fantasizes about meeting him. This man is Solzhenitsyn; his portrait hangs on the wall in her room next to the paintings by the dissident artists who are her friends.

One day Marina has a prophetic dream in which Solzhenitsyn, who appears to her as a Supreme Being, chastises Marina in a thunderous voice for living without love. She has had many lovers but has not loved anyone or anything. "But what am I to do?" she asks him. The answer is "To love." Her question "Whom?" however, receives no answer. Marina awakens from the dream transformed, although she still does not realize what is happening to her. She chases out her twenty-ninth lesbian lover, throws away a little sack of marijuana, and one by one breaks her ties with the black marketeers, the hippies, and her American friend Tony—in a word, with her entire past.

Two days later she meets Sergei Nikolaevich, a man who bears a striking physical resemblance to her hero, Solzhenitsyn. But Sergei is the polar opposite of the dissident writer: a devout Communist, he serves as the secretary of the party committee at a compressor factory. He is a patriot of the Russian people and the Soviet Union; he hates dissidents, Jews, and Americans, believing that they are responsible for shortages and other imperfections in Soviet life. Meeting Sergei is the turning point in Marina's life, as well as in the literary structure of the novel. She discovers in him a powerful spiritual force—so powerful that her metamorphosis, which started several days earlier in the form of her prophetic dream, is completed during her first sexual encounter with him. On that night she has an explosive orgasm, her first with a man. In the morning she takes Solzhenitsyn's portrait from the wall (his face is con-

torted now in a devilish grimace) and throws the portrait, together with her dissident books, into the fire. She then goes with Sergei to his factory and on the same day starts a job there as a lathe operator, leaving behind her profession, her dissident past, and her lesbian loves.

The remaining seventy pages, more than one-third of the entire novel, represent not only Marina's metamorphosis from a social, bohemian Muscovite into a conscientious factory worker but also the complete transformation of a realistic portrayal of a decadent life into a conceptualist text. At first, the reader notices this transformation only in Marina's unorthodox actions. Sorokin still preserves the realism of direct discourse in the dialogues between Marina and her new coworkers. Gradually, however, their speech increasingly resembles lines from the Soviet press; the characters no longer address each other by their first names but as "comrades" or "comrade Alekseeva." The narrator's remarks, which had attributed lines from the dialogue to concrete characters, disappear; the dashes separating the lines of one character from those of another also disappear. The last twenty-two pages represent one paragraph consisting of lines borrowed directly from Soviet newspapers of the period. All that remains in the novel is socialist realism in its pure form, without plot or characters. The novel disappears, yet the discourse remains.

In Sorokin's next large work, *Roman* (Roman, 1994), which he wrote from 1985 to 1989, the disintegration of the novel assumes an even more extreme form. The title itself is ambiguous. The Russian word *roman* can mean "novel," or it can be a man's name. Indeed, the protagonist of *Roman* is named Roman. The use of a protagonist's surname as the title of a novel is not unusual in the Russian literary tradition, which includes Aleksandr Sergeevich Pushkin's *Evgenii Onegin* (1825–1832) and *Dubrovsky* (1841); Ivan Aleksandrovich Goncharov's *Oblomov* (1859); and Dostoevsky's *Brat'ia Karamazovy* (The Brothers Karamazov, 1879–1880). Yet, there is no novel in Russian literature titled solely with the male protagonist's first name—unless the main character is a tsar, as in Dmitry Sergeevich Merezhkovsky's *Petr i Aleksei* (Peter and Alexis, 1905). There is also no single work whose main title is a term for a literary genre—only collections of short stories or poems by one author. Thus, the word *roman* on the cover of a Russian book has no established meaning and only puzzles the reader. Sorokin gives his novel such an ambiguous title to suggest that the book is not only about the protagonist Roman but also about literature itself.

Roman follows the usual paradigm of the bipartite structure, but the contrast between its two parts is much more dramatic than in Sorokin's other works. This text is Sorokin's longest, and its lengthiness enables him to construct a full-size novel in the first part. The longer the first part, the deeper is the reader's engagement with it and the stronger is the effect produced by the second, contrasting part. Moreover, the re-created style in Part 1 is not socialist realism, whose desecration appeared in the eyes of the Russian intelligentsia as a legitimate process of obliterating the legacy of Soviet ideology. The model for the first part of this book is the discourse of Russian classical prose—the "holy of holies" of Russian culture, the source of truth and liberal ideas, and the inspiration for opposition to the government. Russian literature has kept the nation under its sway for almost two centuries. Because of the social importance, far-reaching influence, and tremendous power of literature, its profanation in the second part of Sorokin's novel cannot help but come across as extreme blasphemy. *Roman* is one of his most resolute attacks on Russian literature as a totalitarian system controlling the minds and hearts of the Russian people.

The first part begins with a prologue written in the melancholic tone of Nikolai Mikhailovich Karamzin's *Bednaia Liza* (Poor Liza, 1796). Then there follows the traditional motif of a young landlord returning to his estate, from which he has been long absent. Further along in the text one finds descriptions of hunting, mowing, endless feasts, and long soul-searching conversations—the entire inventory of social interactions in a classic Russian novel. The reader also recognizes familiar characters: a misanthropic doctor; a lonely village teacher; a disappointed and cynical young woman; and a kind and romantic woman—the typical type of heroine found in the fiction of Ivan Sergeevich Turgenev. Roman's courtship and marriage to Tania, the female protagonist, remind the reader of the story of Kitty and Levin in Leo Tolstoy's *Anna Karenina* (1875–1877). These familiar characters, themes, motifs, and stylistic features engage the reader in a nostalgic trip through nineteenth-century Russian literature by invoking works by authors ranging from Karamzin to Anton Pavlovich Chekhov. Some episodes allude to works of twentieth-century Russian literature, but only to those that continue the tradition of nineteenth-century prose of moral guidance and philosophical exploration.

By implanting these literary references into his novel, Sorokin strengthens its connection with classic Russian literature, a tie that he painstakingly cultivates. Yet, after approximately 290 pages and 70 pages before the end—following Roman's wedding to Tania—the smooth and warm fabric of this literary model is suddenly ripped apart by the drawn-out rendering of a murder reminiscent of Raskol'nikov's crime in Dostoevsky's *Prestuplenie i nakazanie* (Crime and Punishment,

1866). Roman hacks the entire village population to death with an ax, walking with his young bride from house to house while she keeps ringing a little bell. The murders have no logical explanation or textual justification; the reader obviously deals here with Sorokin's usual device of colliding two discourses. After all the murders are completed, Roman disembowels the corpses and brings the intestines into the church. Then, in the same order, he beheads each corpse and takes the heads to the church. He conducts other, even less tolerable manipulations with the bodies outside, and then inside, the church. Then he kills Tania (in the process, she still rings her little bell) and for some time is preoccupied with her body.

As Roman undergoes the sudden transformation from an idealistic young man to a monstrous murderer, the *roman* (the novel) undergoes its own, already familiar metamorphosis: it begins to disintegrate quickly. At first, each murder is described in detail; descriptions then become more and more simple until sentences are reduced to just several words—subject, predicate, and one or two direct or indirect objects. In the end, only two words remain in each sentence—the subject (Roman) and the predicate: "Roman crawled. Roman cried. Roman laughed." Sorokin also destroys in the second part of the novel all major features of literary discourse. The actions that Roman performs on his victims are described in repeated sentences; only the names of the victims change. As a result, the concept of a literary style, which typically does not bear repetitions even of individual words, let alone entire sentences, is no longer applicable here. A literary work becomes a list—a common feature in postmodern literature. A list, obviously, lacks any subjectivity, and therefore the authorial point of view is completely removed from the text—the ultimate method of doing away with the author. The main requirement of a list is its completeness, and Sorokin truthfully fulfills this requirement by selecting forty names and repeating the description of each action for each victim. This approach undermines another important feature of literary discourse—compactness.

Thus, in the dramatic conflict between two discourses, the first one (the nineteenth-century novel) receives a fatal blow, not only because it cannot withstand the monstrosity of its protagonist's actions but also because its complex and beautiful organism degenerates into a simple list, "returning to [the] dust" of separate words. The novel ends with a meaningful sentence "Roman umer"—Roman (the protagonist or the novel) died. These words also spell out the death sentence for literature and its lofty function in Russian society.

Soon after completing *Roman*, Sorokin wrote *Mesiats v Dakhau* (1992; translated as *A Month in Dachau*, 1994), the story of a Russian writer, named Vladimir

Sorokin, who travels to Germany to spend his vacation in a Nazi concentration camp. Upon his arrival in Dachau, Sorokin (the protagonist) undergoes a series of horrific physical and mental tortures. The executioners pull his fingernails out, beat and whip him, hound him with dogs, urinate and defecate on him, and starve and rape him. Perhaps the most harrowing of the tortures is when the starved protagonist is offered, and consumes with great zest, choice dishes prepared first from a young Russian girl, Lena Sergeeva, and then from a Jewish boy, Osia Blumenfeld.

This short text of fifteen pages constitutes an important closure in Sorokin's work and his search for new artistic paths. With this work, the prolific 1980s came to an end, and he left behind his method of dramatic opposition between the "model" and "killer" texts. *Mesiats v Dakhau* has no bipartite structure but is based instead on a continuous plot. In its emotional, almost affected style one recognizes features of Russian symbolist prose; yet, Sorokin does not make symbolist discourse the protagonist of his text only to destroy it toward the end, as he did in previous works. In any event, this task would have been difficult since symbolist discourse left a much weaker trace in the Russian cultural consciousness than did nineteenth-century realist literature or socialist realism. For this reason, recognizing the target of the author's attack would be difficult for the reader.

The continuous plot of *Mesiats v Dakhau* unfolds properly from the beginning to the end as a sequence of events in the life of the protagonist. This approach to the story line becomes even more pronounced in Sorokin's next, longer work, *Serdtsa chetyrekh* (The Hearts of the Four, published in 1998 in *Konets veka* [End of the Century]; excerpt translated as *Four Stout Hearts*, 1991). In this novel written in 1991 Sorokin continues working with new structural elements introduced in *Mesiats v Dakhau*. He writes an original science-fiction story, a genre he had long dreamed of exploring. The plot describes a scientific project carried out by four protagonists: Ol'ga, a young woman of twenty-six; thirty-five-year-old Sergei Rebrov; Genrikh Ivanovich Schtaube, a man of sixty-six; and a teenage boy, Serezha. A dangerous and gruesome endeavor, the project involves several assassinations committed by the protagonists—including the murders of Serezha's and Rebrov's own mothers; shootouts with the army, militia, and the Komitet gosudarstvennoi bezopasnosti (KGB, State Security Committee); and ambushes, tortures, and similar kinds of activities. Ol'ga is a member of the Russian Olympic target-shooting team and for this reason is designated to be the hit woman for the group. The book reads more as a script for an action movie rather than as a science-fiction story.

In *Serdtsa chetyrekh,* to compensate for the lost tension between the model text and the "killer" text, which is absent here, Sorokin increases the intensity of the clash between the reader's expectations of what a literary text should be and the actual text. The degree of gore in this novel (the dismembering, cutting up, grinding, cooking, eating, juicing, and sucking of human bodies) surpasses even the ending of *Roman* and the description of the various means of torture in *Mesiats v Dakhau*. The carnage also affects the reader much more strongly because the relatively cohesive plot creates an illusion of reality. The trials and tribulations of the protagonists have a "happy" ending. They mount four steel platforms of a press (a machine used to form metal parts under pressure), lie down, and smile happily as steel bars enter their skulls, shoulders, stomachs, and legs. Knives start spinning, freon starts flowing, and the heads of the press cover the platforms. Twenty-eight minutes later the press produces four dice; these are four hearts—compressed, frozen, and shaped into cubes.

However, *Serdtsa chetyrekh* is still a conceptual work. Although Sorokin creates his own plot and carries it throughout the entire book without subverting it with a "killer" text, he does not bother to explain the purpose of the protagonists' actions, who their opponents are, or the reason for each confrontation. This lack of vital information underscores the conceptual function of the text: its primary purpose is to create a model of a science-fiction work with the added element of extremely violent action. Reality is indecipherable here.

Besides prose, Sorokin also has written several plays and collaborated on movie scripts. Perhaps more than his prose, these texts reflect the changes that took place in Russia in the late 1980s and 1990s. The plays *Pel'meni* (Ravioli, 1998), *Russkaia babushka* (Russian Grandma, 1998), *Zemlianka* (The Dugout, 1998), *Doverie* (Trust, 1998), *S Novym godom* (Happy New Year, 1998), *Iubilei* (The Jubilee, 1998), and *Dismorfomaniia* (Dismorphomania, 1998) bear traces of Soviet reality, while *Shchi* (The Cabbage Soup, 1998), *Hochzeitsreise* (Honeymoon Trip, 1998), *Dostoevsky-trip* (Dostoevsky Trip, 1997), and the script *Moskva* (Moscow, 1999) show Sorokin's interest in the discourse and realia of a new social group, the "New Russians," which emerged in the chaotic years of post–Soviet Union democracy. This group represents the nouveau riche, most of whom accumulated their wealth from racketeering and illegal financial operations, or the theft of natural resources, military equipment, and nonferrous scrap metal. A devoted connoisseur of various discourses in the Russian language, Sorokin could not pass up the opportunity to delight in a completely new linguistic phenomenon, which he does most successfully in *Shchi,* staged in the late 1990s in both Moscow and Germany, and in *Moskva*.

Since his forte is direct speech and since many of his prose works have little or no narration, Sorokin's interest in playwriting is not surprising. In an interview, he once noted that he turned to writing plays because he hated them—a paradoxical statement at first glance, but, if one remembers that his unceasing campaign against literature led to creating his own literature, then his words do not appear so odd. Sorokin's plays exhibit a similar emphasis on discourse and employ techniques similar to those found in his prose. The reader becomes engaged not in the actions and fates of the characters but in their speech. In the play *Zemlianka* four Soviet army officers eat, drink, and chat during a short respite from combat. One of them also reads a newspaper aloud for his comrades. The officers seem to have a continuous, meaningful conversation, but often their rejoinders only begin as responses to their interlocutors' remarks, after which they stray to a different subject. Sorokin creates here a model for leisurely conversation between several people who kill their time by exchanging superficial remarks. The model reproduces the living speech of less educated people, which is garnished with obscenities, slang, and pseudoprofound utterances.

In his plays, as in his prose, Sorokin liberally uses "ready-made" inserts—excerpts from previously published, well-known works. *Iubilei,* for example, is a play within a play; paying special homage to Chekhov, Sorokin borrows several lines from his plays for the play within a play. This hybrid play is staged at a factory that manufactures "chekhovoprotein" from thousands of living Chekhovs in order to increase the level of culture in the country. Similar factories process Pushkins, Turgenevs, Tolstoys, Dostoevskys, and other renowned Russian writers. The play *Dismorfomaniia* makes use of William Shakespeare's *Hamlet* (1603) and *Romeo and Juliet* (1597), while *Dostoevsky-trip* includes extensive quotations from Dostoevsky's *Idiot* (The Idiot, 1868).

Perhaps the most traditional play—the one that engages the reader and spectator alike with its characters and their plight—is *Hochzeitsreise,* a love story between Gunter, the son of a Nazi *Shutzstaffel* (SS, the protection staff responsible for intelligence, security, the police, and mass extermination under the Nazis) general, and Masha, the daughter of a female major in Stalin's secret police, the Narodnyi komissariat vnutrennykh del (NKVD, People's Commissariat for Internal Affairs). Gunter is ridden with guilt about the atrocities committed by his father—a guilt that results in extreme neurasthenia and a penchant for collecting Jewish artifacts. Masha feels no guilt for her mother's actions, but she falls in love with Gunter and tries to help him. A treat-

ment suggested by Masha's friend, the psychiatrist Mark, seems to work: Gunter and Masha, dressed in their parents' respective uniforms, drive through contemporary Germany subjecting themselves to anger, insults, and sometimes cheering from other travelers. This psychological torture cures Gunter's stuttering and makes him capable of intercourse with Masha, but when the happy couple drives to the chapel to get married, an accident involving a meat truck—which symbolically carries Masha's and Gunter's parents' names on its side—reverses Gunter's cure. The conclusion of *Hochzeitsreise* is that one cannot escape the past.

Similarly, the pieces written in the mid and late 1990s, such as *Shchi* and *Moskva,* have well-developed plots and allow readers to identify with the characters. These plays and scripts indicate a certain shift in Sorokin's work toward more representational writing and away from his purely conceptual emphasis on discourse, a shift also observed in the full-size novel *Goluboe salo* (Blue Lard, 1999) and shorter pieces collected in the book *Pir* (Feast, 2001).

In the 1990s Sorokin's work began receiving long overdue national and international recognition. In 1992 he received a grant from the Deutscher Akademischer Austauschdienst (German Academic Exchange Service), also known as DAAD, and in 1997 he was invited to participate in a literary colloquium in Berlin. In October 1997 the Mannheim Slavic Seminar conducted an international symposium dedicated to Sorokin's prose, film, and drama, the proceedings of which were published in 1999 in book form. In 1998 Sorokin became the first Samuel Fischer Visiting Professor of Literature at the Institute for General and Comparative Literature at Free University in Berlin. There he taught a seminar on Moscow conceptualism. On many occasions he was invited to read his works or participate in readings of their German translations. Many of his plays were staged in Berlin and other German cities, as well as in Vienna. From 1998 to 2000 he also taught at the Foreign Institute in Tokyo.

These events and responsibilities might explain why Sorokin was not as prolific in the 1990s as he had been during the previous decade. After finishing *Mesiats v Dakhau* and *Serdtsa chetyrekh,* he wrote three plays, several screenplays, and several short pieces, later included in the collection *Pir.* Only in the late 1990s did he return to long prose and publish his new novel, *Goluboe salo* (Blue Lard, 1999).

In *Goluboe salo,* as in *Serdtsa chetyrekh,* Sorokin turns to the genre of science fiction to connect the future and the past in a time-travel plot. The novel opens in the year 2068 at a scientific station in eastern Siberia. Although one can recognize Russian roots in many of the employees' names, the scientists are not Russians but Eurasians.

They speak Russian, but their Russian includes new words and words from other languages, mostly Chinese and some German, English, and French. The project at the station is to clone and nurture the Russian writers and poets Chekhov, Dostoevsky, Pasternak, Tolstoy, Anna Andreevna Akhmatova, Andrei Platonovich Platonov, and Vladimir Vladimirovich Nabokov. In no way, however, are the scientists interested in Russian literature. In fact, writers are now called "scriptors," and writing literature is referred to as a "script-process." The clones do produce texts—and Sorokin includes them in the book, yet again displaying his talent for imitation—but they are simply by-products of growing "blue fat" on the clones' bodies. This fat has unique thermodynamic properties: it is indestructible and never changes its temperature. When the cloning of each "object" is completed, the clones receive pens and paper, do their "scripting," fall into hibernation, and start growing the blue fat in their incubators. For some mysterious reason, only the lard of "scriptors" has these unique properties.

The futuristic part of the book ends in a vicious attack on the station by a band of *zemleeby* (Earth-Fuckers), a male tribe that rejects the fruits of progress and civilization and worships Mother Earth by literally copulating with her. They murder the scientists at the station, cut out the blue fat from the clones' bodies, and rush it to their base. From there, the blue fat is sent on a time machine to a fictitious Soviet Union of 1954. In Sorokin's rendering of this era, World War II was won by an alliance of the Soviet Union and Germany against the United States and England, which were destroyed by a nuclear attack. Stalin is still alive and rules the country together with all his henchmen—Lavrentii Pavlovich Beriia, Viacheslav Mikhailovich Molotov, Georgii Maksimil'ianovich Malenkov, Lazar Moiseevich Kaganovich, Klim Efremovich Voroshilov, and others. Nikita Sergeevich Khrushchev is also there, but he is ousted and retreats to his country fortress, where he frequently receives Stalin as his lover. Stalin's wife, Nadezhda Sergeevna Alilueva, sleeps alternately with Pasternak and her stepson, Stalin's older son Iakov. Also present are prominent Soviet writers, some of whom, such as the poet Osip Emil'evich Mandel'shtam, are supposed to be dead (Mandel'shtam died sometime in the late 1930s), and others of whom, such as Aksenov, Brodsky, and Yevtushenko, should not be writers yet.

After the blue fat arrives from the future, Stalin and Khrushchev spirit it to Germany, where they are most heartily received by Adolf Hitler, his wife, Eva, and his cohorts, who include Heinrich Himmler, Hermann Göring, and Martin Bormann. The Germans know the secret of the blue fat: those who are injected with its essence will find themselves in Eden. A harmonious dinner, however, ends in skirmishes and shootouts, and only Stalin survives. He manages to inject himself through the eye (a fatal mistake) with the essence, after which his brain begins to grow uncontrollably. It destroys Hitler's castle, the earth, the sun, and the universe, and then becomes a black hole and finally begins shrinking. Thirty-five billion years later it has shrunk to the natural size of Stalin's brain. The book ends in 2068, the same year in which it began. Now Stalin is a tailor in the service of a young man who is getting ready for an Easter ball. Stalin has just finished making his cape from the blue fat.

This novel marks the completion of the shift from conceptualism to traditional mimetic literature that Sorokin began in *Mesiats v Dakhau* and developed in *Serdtsa chertyrekh*. While conceptualist function is practically reduced to naught, the author's iconoclastic fervor reaches its apogee here. Not only socialist realism but all the major classics of Russian literature are denigrated—they are portrayed as repulsive, deformed clones. The living writers depicted in the second part of the book are even more repelling. They appear under initials or first names but are easily recognizable by anyone familiar with Russian literature of the twentieth century. Akhmatova is an old obese woman, a kind of holy fool; she licks Stalin's boots in a paroxysm of self-abasement and slavish love for the leader. Mandel'shtam, one of the greatest Russian poets who died in the camps—presumably driven to madness and starvation—appears here as a murderous hoodlum, hungry only for drugs, gambling, and prostitutes. The 1960s writers and poets of the new wave, which include Aksenov, Yevtushenko, and Andrei Andreevich Voznesensky, are presented as cowardly sissies who are attacked and robbed by their contemporaries, the underground poets Genrikh Sapgir and Evgenii L'vovich Kropivnitsky. These two receive a sympathetic characterization from the author, who portrays them as bold, streetwise toughs. By the end of *Goluboe salo*, Russian literature is effectively dead. Blue fat—a magic substance that can be produced only from the clones of great Russian writers, a substance so powerful that it sweeps cities off the surface of the Earth and destroys the universe—is grown by scientists of the future for no other purpose than using it as a fabric for a fop's masquerade costume.

The book *Pir* collects works that are thematically united by their references to food. The first story, "Nastia," imitates the Chekhovian portrayal of endless table discussions and mingled love affairs at a prerevolutionary country estate. Yet, this familiar portrait is used only as a groundwork for the author's own "feasting" on sumptuous routines of a Russian dinner. Following the rich tradition of feast descriptions in Russian literature, whose authors range from Nikolai Vasil'evich Gogol to Bulgakov, Sorokin creates an atmosphere of love and neighborly harmony around the dinner table, disturbed only by the knowledge that, for the main course, the hosts and guests are enjoying the hosts' baked daughter, whose sixteenth birthday they all are celebrating.

Eating is an extremely important part of Russian culture. The mythic cult of food is as strong as the mythic cults of literature and high culture, but unlike the latter cults, which are characteristic of only the intelligentsia, the former is universal in Russian society. This affectionate attitude toward food can be compared with attitudes toward erotic experiences. People look forward to a holiday rendezvous with food and often make great sacrifices to ensure that the holiday table is full of rare delicacies and that the guests are happy. Russians, especially when in a festive mood, refer to the items on the table by using diminutive, or endearing, forms of nouns. Hosts show their love and respect for guests by insisting that they have yet another helping, and to refuse does not signal the guest's satiation but, rather, a dislike of the hosts' disposition toward the guests. Food and eating therefore make up a semiotic system, a "language" for expressing various degrees of relationships in Russian culture. Thus, in devoting his book to food, Sorokin again creates a conceptualist representation of "language" rather than of reality.

In *Pir* Sorokin also continues his exploration of science fiction, liberally spicing it up with mysticism, Asian motifs, and the language and realia of the Russian mafia. The characters in "Konkretnye" (The Concrete Ones) speak a strange language—a combination of Russian, Chinese, English, and German—and use high-tech devices to enhance their sexual pleasure. For a more "spiritual" kind of entertainment they "devour" masterpieces of world literature by somehow being transposed into fictional reality and literally devouring characters and objects in Herman Melville's *Moby-Dick* (1851), Tolstoy's *Voina i mir* (War and Peace, 1868–1869), and other novels. The consumed and digested people and items are immediately excreted from their bodies in an avalanche of feces. The language of the characters and the scorn for literature in this story echo the ideas that Sorokin promotes in *Goluboe salo*. In that novel, great Russian writers produce a substance that is good only as a fabric for masquerade costumes. Here, in "Konkretnye," the sentence is even harsher: the place for world literature is the sewer.

Sorokin also finds new blasphemous topics, ones not explored in previous works. In the story "Den' russkogo edoka" (A Day in the Life of a Russian Eater) he portrays six ugly and greedy Jews whose goal is to rob Russia and enslave the Russian people. Another story, "Sakharnoe voskresen'e" (Sugar Sunday), ridi-

Front cover for Sorokin's 1999 novel, Goluboe salo *(Blue Lard), about the cloning of Russian writers (Collection of Mark Lipovetsky)*

cules one of the most tragic days in Russian history—the so-called Bloody Sunday—when scores of peaceful demonstrators were massacred by tsarist troops on 9 January 1905. "Sakharnoe voskresen'e" is a grotesque spoof that presents all the participants—the workers, the intelligentsia, the writer Maksim Gor'ky, the renowned basso Fedor Ivanovich Shaliapin, Prime Minister Petr Arkad'evich Stolypin, and the tsar's family—as idiotic parodies of historical figures. But as in previous works, these blasphemous images are not present to convey the author's ideas but to create an aesthetic tension within the text and launch still another attack on moral and literary mythologies.

Pir confirms that Sorokin's rebellious ardor has subsided after almost a quarter of a century of his incessant rage against the oppression of the common value system. Although the unifying theme of food in the collection enables him to exploit two of his favorite topics, cannibalism and defecation, the imagery in this book and in other works of the mid and late 1990s, such as *Goluboe salo, Hochzeitreise, Shchi,* and *Moskva,* is far more mild than in earlier works. Perhaps the most unappetizing episode in *Pir* is a wrestling match in the story "Pepel" (Ashes); yet, the description of two wrestlers—covered with open sores, scabs, and carbuncles, ripping each other's flesh with their teeth and hands—cannot compare with the degree of carnage and sacrilege that one finds in *Roman* and *Serdtsa chetyrekh.* The more tension Sorokin creates within the original plot, the fewer horrifying images he needs in order to produce a dramatic effect. Fighting the omnipotent authority of literature has become inconsequential, since literature has little authority in the new Russia.

Led (The Ice, 2002), the novel that Sorokin published after *Pir,* completes his transition to representational fiction. Whereas *Goluboe salo* and *Pir* still rely on blasphemous images to create the tension between the reader and the text, *Led* is a work of pure science fiction in which the conflict is confined strictly to the text, and the author abandons both his conceptualist games and his crusade against literary and cultural mythology. One still finds foul language and a few descriptions of torture, drugs, and sex here and there in the novel, but they do not target the reader's moral sensibilities. In view of the latest tendencies in Russian literature these narrative elements can no longer shock and appall the sophisticated reader. And Sorokin uses them not for this purpose but simply for the development of the story. He himself declares that *Led* is his first novel in which content is more important than form.

The novel uses the motif of the Tunguska meteorite, popular in Soviet science fiction, and combines it with mythic motifs of creation and apocalypse. The story tells of twenty-three thousand distinctive people living on Earth. They are actually rays of primordial eternal light, but by a tragic mistake they are scattered now among regular humans. Their hearts are sleeping and they are not aware of their special nature, but they can be awakened when their chests are pounded upon with a hammer made of ice. The ice is also special: to awaken the heart, the ice must be taken from a huge ice block buried in the Siberian taiga and known as the Tunguska meteorite. Once awakened, these "ray people" can communicate with each other through their hearts. To do this they press their bare chests to one another and remain still for long periods of time, going through some kind of extremely pleasant, orgasmic experience. Gender, age, and appearance make no difference in this process of communication through hearts.

Immediately after awakening a ray person goes through a seven-day period of extreme depression and uncontrollable sobbing, which serves as a ritual of initi-

ation. The ultimate goal is to awaken all twenty-three thousand hearts, form a circle of twenty-three thousand people, and say twenty-three magic words, after which the Earth will cease to exist and the twenty-three thousand rays will return to the eternal light.

Sorokin's novel resembles a traditional romantic story about noble heavenly creatures, although he is not shy about presenting them occasionally as extremely cruel, pitiless beings. For them regular people are but "meat machines," and if the hammering on the chest does not produce the response indicating that the tested person belongs to the ray community, he or she is hammered to death. A promise to, or an agreement with, a "meat machine" has no significance either: as soon as "it" is no longer needed the promise will be ignored and "it" will be murdered and discarded. Thus, in this novel Sorokin portrays a kind of *über-mensch* race; and the fact that the ray people are all blond with blue eyes may indicate his continuing fascination with the Nazi theme. Some of the most active ray people are high-ranking officers either in the SS or the NKVD.

In *Cashfire* (2002), the movie script that Sorokin co-authored with Oleg Radzinsky and Aleksandr Zel'dovich, he turns to the popular postmodernist theme of the postmodern human losing his grip on reality. The Baudrillardian notion of reality as a simulacrum created by the media is expanded here to include other simulacra: the crooked world of Wall Street and the cold, impersonal, and voyeuristic world of the Web. The protagonist, the Russian émigré Sasha Cohen, is a successful Wall Street trader. Her move to the West and adjustment to the demands of her profession have already forced her to give up a greater part of her soul: she shuns deep emotions, reducing intimate relationships to superficial sexual encounters; she shuts off her memory, avoiding nostalgic recollections of her Russian past; and even her current name, the American-Jewish Cohen, stands in meaningful opposition to her poetic Russian maiden name, Kedrova, derived from the word *kedr*—cedar, a tree that grows in Russia in the Urals and Siberia.

On Wall Street she constantly has to negotiate between her moral convictions and the relative values of multiple realities with which she has to deal in her professional life. Sasha still believes that people's individual decisions and actions should make a difference, but she lives in a world controlled by pure chance; it is a world of probabilities rather than of individual choices. Everything is in flux in this world: the stock market, media opinions, and people's fates. Those who cling to absolute values are out of place here. They are caught in the "grinder" of cynical manipulations and perish. At the end Sasha symbolically goes up in flames together with bundles of old canceled banknotes.

Vladimir Georgievich Sorokin's critics note that his impersonal and amoral conceptualist methods gradually yield to mimetic practices in the later works. Works such as *Led* and *Cashfire* show Sorokin merging with the mainstream literature of representation. Moving in this direction, he may arrive at the bosom of mainstream representational literature, an area in which he would face stiff competition not only from his contemporaries but also from the literary tradition of the past. He does not have to fear this competition, however. With his distinctive talent for grasping various social discourses and his capacity for a cinematic visualization of reality, he will have little problem in finding his own niche in a world of new social realities and rapidly developing television, cinema, and computerized media.

Interviews:

Tat'iana Rasskazova, "Tekst kak narkotik," in *Vladimir Sorokin: [Sbornik rasskazov]* (Moscow: Russlit, 1992), pp. 119–126;

Serafima Roll, "Vladimir Sorokin: Literatura kak kladbishche stilisticheskikh nakhodok," in *Postmodernisty o postkul'ture: Interv'iu s sovremennymi pisateliami i kritikami,* edited by Roll (Moscow: R. Elinin, 1996), pp. 119–130;

Sergei Shapovalov, "'V kul'ture dlia menia net tabu. . . .' Vladimir Sorokin otvechaet na voprosy Sergeia Shapovalova," in Sorokin's *Sobranie sochinenii,* 2 volumes (Moscow: Ad Marginem, 1998), pp. 7–20;

Sally Laird, "Vladimir Sorokin," in her *Voices of Russian Literature: Interviews with Ten Contemporary Writers* (Oxford: Oxford University Press, 1999), pp. 43–62.

References:

Svetlana Beliaeva-Konegen, "Khoroshee zabytoe, ili Rasstreliat' bez suda (o proze Vladimira Sorokina)," *Strelets,* 2 (1992): 150–153;

Ekaterina Bobrinskaia, *Kontseptualizm* (Moscow: Galart, 1994);

Dagmar Burkhart, ed., *Poetik der Metadiskursivität: Zum postmodernen Prosa-, Film- und Dramenwerk von Vladimir Sorokin* (Munich: Otto Sagner, 1999);

Mikhail Naumovich Epshtein, *After the Future: The Paradoxes of Postmodernism and Contemporary Russian Culture,* translated, with an introduction, by Anesa Miller-Pogacar (Amherst: University of Massachusetts Press, 1995);

Aleksandr Genis, *Ivan Petrovich umer* (Moscow: Novoe literaturnoe obozrenie, 1999), pp. 72–81, 113–122;

Mark Lipovetsky, "Goluboe salo pokoleniia, ili Dva mifa ob odnom kruzise," *Znamia,* 11 (1999): 207–215;

Lipovetsky, "Novyi 'moskovsky' stil': *Moskva* Sorokina i Zel'dovicha i *Kul'tura Dva* Papernogo—opyt parallel'nogo chteniia," *Iskusstvo Kino,* 2 (1998): 87–101;

Lipovetsky, *Russian Postmodernist Fiction: Dialogue with Chaos,* edited by Eliot Borenstein (Armonk, N.Y.: M. E. Sharpe, 1999), pp. 197–219;

Serafima Roll, "Stripping Socialist Realism of its Seamless Dress: Vladimir Sorokin's Deconstruction of Soviet Utopia and the Art of Representation," *Russian Literature,* 39 (1996): 65–78;

Mikhail Ryklin, "Medium i avtor: O tekstakh Vladimira Sorokina," in *Vladimir Sorokin: Sobranie sochinenii v dvukh tomakh* (Moscow: Ad Marginem, 1998), pp. 737–751.

Tatyana Tolstaya

(3 May 1951 –   )

Helena Goscilo
University of Pittsburgh

BOOKS: *"Na zolotom kryl'tse sideli . . ."* (Moscow: Molodaia gvardiia, 1987)–comprises "Liubish'–ne liubish'," "Reka Okkervil'," "Milaia Shura," "'Na zolotom kryl'tse sideli . . . ,'" "Okhota na mamonta," "Krug," "Chistyi list," "Ogon i pyl'," "Svidanie s ptitsei," "Spi spokoino, synok," "Sonia," "Fakir," and "Peters"; translated by Antonina Bouis as *On the Golden Porch and Other Stories* (London: Virago, 1989); republished as *On the Golden Porch* (New York: Knopf, 1989)–comprises "Loves Me, Loves Me Not," "Okkervil River," "Sweet Shura," "On the Golden Porch," "Hunting the Wooly Mammoth," "The Circle," "A Clean Sheet," "Fire and Dust," "Date with a Bird," "Sweet Dreams, Son," "Sonya," "The Fakir," and "Peters";

Liubish'–ne liubish', with an introduction by Vladimir Novikov (Moscow: Oniks, 1997)–includes "Noch'," "Plamen' nebesnyi," "Samaia liubimaia," "Serafim," "Vyshel mesiats iz tumana," "Poet i muza," "Siuzhet," "Limpopo," "Somnambula v tumane," and "Reka Okkervil'";

Sestry, by Tolstaya and Nataliia Nikitichna Tolstaia (Moscow: Podkova, 1998)–includes (by Tolstaya) "Interv'iu," "90 x 60 x 90," "Belye steny," "Neugodnye litsa," "Anastasiia," "Nebo v almazakh," "Dolbanem krutuiu popsu!" "Politicheskaia korrektnost'," "Nozhki," "Bonjour, moujik! Pochiol von!" "Vot tebe, baba, blinok!" "Intelligent," "Glavnyi trup," "Pamiati Brodskogo," "Riazhenye," "Lilit";

Reka Okkervil' (Moscow: Podkova, 1999)–includes "Turisty i palomniki (esse)," "Zhensky den' (esse)," "Noch' Feniksa," and "Iorik";

Kys' (Moscow: Podkova, 2000); translated by Jamey Gambrell as *The Slynx* (Boston: Houghton Mifflin, 2003);

Den': Lichnoe (Moscow: Podkova, 2001)–includes "Russkii mir";

Dvoe: Raznoe, by Tolstaya and Tolstaia (Moscow: Podkova, 2001);

Tatyana Tolstaya (photograph © by Jerry Bauer; from the cover for The Slynx, *2003; Richland County Public Library)*

Izium (Moscow: Podkova, 2002).

Edition and Collection: *Noch': Rasskazy* (Moscow: Podkova, 2001);

Reka Okkervil' (Moscow: Podkova, 2002).

Editions in English: *Sleepwalker in a Fog,* translated by Jamey Gambrell (New York: Knopf, 1992)–comprises "Sleepwalker in a Fog," "Serafim," "The Moon Came Out," "Night," "Heavenly Flame," "Most Beloved," "The Poet and the Muse," and "Limpopo";

Pushkin's Children: Writings on Russia and Russians, translated by Gambrell (Boston: Houghton Mifflin,

2003)—includes "On Joseph Brodsky" and "The Making of Mr. Putin."

OTHER: *Beyond the Fall: The Former Soviet Bloc in Transition, 1989–99,* by Tolstaya, Anthony Suaua, and Jacques Rupnick (New York: Liaison Agency, 2000);

Andrei Platonovich Platonov, *The Fierce and Beautiful World,* translated by Joseph Barnes, with an introduction by Tolstaya (New York: New York Review of Books, 2000);

Tat'iana Tolstaia. Evgenii Popov. Anatolii Gavrilov: Sbornik, with contributions by Tolstaya (Moscow: Zebra E/EKSMO, 2002).

SELECTED PERIODICAL PUBLICATIONS–
UNCOLLECTED: "Notes from the Underground," translated by Jamey Gambrell, *New York Review of Books,* 37 (31 May 1990): 3–7;

"In Cannibalistic Times," translated by Gambrell, *New York Review of Books,* 38 (11 April 1991): 3–6;

"The Golden Age," translated by Gambrell, *New York Review of Books,* 39 (17 December 1992);

"The Age of Innocence," translated by Gambrell, *New York Review of Books,* 40 (21 October 1993): 24–26;

"Boris the First," *New York Review of Books,* 41 (23 June 1994);

"Russian Lessons," *New York Review of Books,* 42 (19 October 1995): 7;

"The Way They Live Now," *New York Review of Books,* 44 (24 April 1997);

"Love Story," *New York Review of Books,* 44 (20 November 1997);

"Missing Persons," *New York Review of Books,* 45 (15 January 1998): 10, 12;

"Russian Roulette," *New York Review of Books,* 45 (19 November 1998);

"Out of This World," *New York Review of Books,* 47 (13 April 2000).

Though a controversial figure in her own country, during the second half of the 1980s Tatyana Tolstaya impressed Western readers as the uncontested premier Russian prosaist of a new era. For many, both her rhetorically exuberant, apolitical stories and her opinionated outspokenness in speeches on any and all topics during visits to the United States—delivered, moreover, in English—epitomized the policy of glasnost instituted by Mikhail Sergeevich Gorbachev (who was general secretary of the Communist Party from 1985 to 1991). Until her debut as a novelist in 2000, Tolstaya's fiction consisted of twenty-one short narratives—published between 1983 and 1991, immediately translated into approximately a dozen languages, and read by academics, fellow authors, and general readers throughout the world. This relatively small corpus rapidly secured Tolstaya the international reputation she still enjoys, in a cultural atmosphere inconceivably remote from the expectant euphoria of perestroika. While she has ascribed her accelerated success largely to timing, the sheer novelty and zest of her fiction chiefly accounted for its enthusiastic reception in multiple quarters.

A writer of impeccable literary pedigree, Tolstaya claims descent from such noted literati as the nineteenth-century novelist Leo Tolstoy (her great-granduncle), the Stalin Prize–winning Soviet author Aleksei Nikolaevich Tolstoy (her paternal grandfather), the poet Natal'ia Vasil'evna Krandievskaia (her paternal grandmother), and Mikhail Leonidovich Lozinsky (her maternal grandfather), the acclaimed translator of William Shakespeare, Molière, Dante Alighieri, and Miguel de Cervantes. Within her privileged, close-knit immediate family, a profound respect not only for culture and education but also for multilingualism and the power of language constituted Tolstaya's formative values, along with humor, energy, and an irreverent irony for the conventions of Soviet ideology and decorum. She acquired fluency in both English and French, and among the many volumes she consumed nonstop she particularly favored Nikolai Al'bertovich Kun's *Chto rasskazyvali drevnie Grekhi o svoikh borakh i geroiakh* (What the Ancient Greeks Told about Their Gods and Heroes, 1940; also known as *Legendy i mify Drevnei Gretsii* [The Legends and Myths of Ancient Greece]). Not surprising for a family with such literary and linguistic interests, Tolstaya's sister Natal'ia Nikitichna Tolstaia teaches Scandinavian literature at St. Petersburg University, while her brother Ivan Tolstoi, who works for Radio Free Europe/Radio Liberty in the Czech Republic, is an expert on Vladimir Vladimirovich Nabokov.

Tatyana Tolstaya was born on 3 May 1951, one of seven children born during late Stalinism to Leningrad professor of physics Nikita A. Tolstoy and his wife. She studied classics at Leningrad State University from 1968 to 1974 before marrying her Muscovite fellow student Andrei Lebedev, a classicist specializing in pre-Socratic philosophy, with whom she had two sons. Upon moving to Moscow in 1974, she worked for eight years at the publishing house Nauka, in the division of oriental literature. Shortsightedness indirectly led to her literary debut. In 1983, bored by contemporary Russian literature and forbidden to read for three months after undergoing an eye operation at Sviatoslav Fedorov's clinic, which famously pioneered corneal laser surgery to correct myopia, she decided to test her own writing abilities. The result led to the publication

*Dust jacket for the 1989 English-language edition of Tolstaya's "Na zolotom kryl'tse sideli . . ." (1987),
a tale of lost innocence and elegiac reminiscences (Richland County Public Library)*

later that year of her first story, "'Na zolotom kryl'tse sideli . . .'" (translated as "On the Golden Porch," 1989), in the Leningrad journal *Avrora* (Aurora). After her sixth published story, "Peters" (translated as "Peters," 1989), appeared in the prestigious liberal Moscow monthly *Novyi mir* (New World) in 1986, critics at home and abroad hailed Tolstaya as a boldly original poetic voice, whose verbal pyrotechnics starkly contrasted with the predictable, gray lexicon and nerveless rhythms of late-Soviet prose. A year later, when the Soviet publisher Molodaia gvardiia published the slim paperback volume titled *"Na zolotom kryl'tse sideli . . . ,"* which encompassed thirteen of her stories, all sixty-five thousand copies sold out in an hour.

Critics accustomed to ferreting out political relevance or social commentary in Soviet literature found themselves at a loss upon encountering Tolstaya's prose. A fascination with time, memory, imagination, and yearning presides over her fiction, which instantly rivets the aesthetically inclined reader through its dazzling tropes, preciseness and sensuality of descriptive detail, fusion of plangent and satirical registers, and

wealth of cultural echoes from literature, myth, and folklore. Stylistically rooted in the modernism of Andrei Bely, the ornamental prose of Iurii Karlovich Olesha, and the elaborate allusiveness of Nabokov, her stories, despite the proliferation of contemporary idioms and colloquialisms, recall an earlier, verbally richer period of Russian literature–above all, the experimental 1920s. Although the slightness of Tolstaya's plots and her almost Gogolian penchant for apparent digressions initially create the illusion of narrative and verbal profligacy, a more discriminating, or attentive, reading soon reveals maximal condensation as one of her salient authorial features. Within the space of a dozen pages she manages to establish the texture and trajectory of an entire life.

The two stories that inaugurated Tolstaya's literary career, "'Na zolotom kryl'tse sideli . . .'" and "Svidanie s ptitsei" (1983, published in *Oktiabr'* [October]; translated as "Date with a Bird," 1989), adopt the lapsarian myth (the myth of the Fall, the first transgression committed by Adam and Eve) as an algorithm to trace their child protagonists' initiation into the world of adulthood. In both, the passage of time entails not maturation but loss of innocence, as emotional and sensual sclerosis sets in. Through observing the marital fate of her ostensibly nondescript neighbor Uncle Pasha and her own bifocal perception of him, the first-person narrator of "'Na zolotom kryl'tse sideli . . .'" realizes that with the passage of time the luminous, transformative vision vouchsafed by childhood and the euphoria of reciprocated romantic love, which convert every experience and phenomenon into a magical Aladdin's cave, vanish together with Edenic freedom from self-consciousness. People age, and love wanes, sours, or evaporates. Whereas childhood is a timeless paradise of wondrous creativity and sensation, adulthood sentences one to the banality and anguish of mortality—the inevitable submission to empirical forces that eventually relegate one to the sidelines of life and culminate in death.

The luxurious prose of "'Na zolotom kryl'tse sideli . . .'" absorbs such diverse elements as children's counting rhymes; citations from Aleksandr Sergeevich Pushkin, Guillaume Apollinaire, and Mikhail Afanas'evich Bulgakov; references to Greek myth, folklore, and Ludwig van Beethoven; and multiple images of temporality so as to evoke the human joys tragically fated to evanescence. Memory alone redeems and resurrects the inestimable value of individuals and experience that otherwise would forever sink in Lethe. This idea, which recurs throughout Tolstaya's writings—for example, in "Sonia" (1987; translated as "Sonya," 1989), "Samaia liubimaia" (1997; translated as "Most Beloved," 1992), "Milaia Shura" (1987; translated as "Sweet Shura," 1989), and "Limpopo" (1990, published in *Sintaksis* [Syntax]; translated, 1992)—especially dominates the early stories. The narrative of "'Na zolotom kryl'tse sideli . . .'" enacts a perceived truth articulated by Tolstaya in sundry interviews—that the past has more legitimate claims to reality than do the present and the future, for it alone lies within one's powers of imperfect retrieval. Characteristically, elegiac reminiscences of irreclaimable perceptions and sensations—when each day comprises adventures, discoveries, and delights—interweave with vivid, palpable inscriptions of the bounties of life, captured in such objects as a lamp, an egg, an antiquated clock, and a bed, which the prelapsarian imagination invests with mesmerizing enchantment. While the story traces evanescence (of the narrator's childhood and uncorrupted vision, of Uncle Pasha's life, and of an entire worldview), its density of coruscating images, flights of fantasy, temporal and spatial leaps, as well as radical shifts in tone, cohere into a text that pulsates with irrepressible energy and poetry. As in her later works, Tolstaya's verbal largesse metamorphoses melancholy and gloom

into a voyage through wonderland—which explains why in the late 1980s Fazil' Abdulovich Iskander astutely noted that Tolstaya's style, and, above all, her lush language, in a sui generis strategy of displacement, compensates the reader for her characters' sorrows and travails.

"Svidanie s ptitsei" similarly charts the boy Petia's disillusionment, in a confrontation with the frailty of flesh as he simultaneously copes with his grandfather's death and the discovery that his ideal, Tamila—the source of a wondrous universe teeming with seductive plots and enigmatic objects—is his repellent Uncle Boria's sexual plaything. Tolstaya inserts such fairy-tale topoi as the dragon, the princess residing on a crystal mountain, magic rings, seeds, and eggs—clustered around Tamila—while also evoking the mythic birds of paradise, Sirin and Alkonost, as agents of death and melancholic yearning. These interpolations enable a modulation to Petia's dream, where Tolstaya brilliantly translates a sense of anxiety, premonitory fear, and unanchored guilt into a symbolic narrative of underground flight, capture, and exposure that in turn prepares the reader for the shattering discovery that plunges Petia into misery and the compromised realm of postlapsarian cognition ("the dead empty world was filled with gray thick oozing depression. Everything was a lie"). A tight structure; a network of matrix tropes (particularly the symbols of the egg, tree, and ring); the myths of Atlantis and the Flying Dutchman; and the trappings of folklore that regularly undergird Tolstayan narratives—including "'Na zolotom kryl'tse sideli . . . ,'" "Poet i muza" (1986, published in *Novyi Mir* [New World]; translated as "The Poet and the Muse," 1992), and "Somnambula v tumane" (1988, published in *Novyi Mir*; translated as "Sleepwalker in a Fog," 1992)—transform this deceptively compact story into a full-fledged allegory of the initiation of the soul into a fallen world.

Whereas Tolstaya's debut stories embrace folklore, the Edenic myth, and the traditional concept of childhood as sunlit, carefree play, "Liubish'—ne liubish'" (1987; translated as "Loves Me, Loves Me Not," 1989) and "Noch'" (published in *Oktiabr'* [October], 1987; translated as "Night," 1992) expose the shadowed side—the underbelly—of childhood as vulnerability and terror. Both works show the child held hostage to sickness, dependency, nocturnal fears, and incomprehension, ultimately alienated from the world of grown-ups through language. The dualism that marks the majority of Tolstaya's narratives, adumbrated in the title of "Liubish'—ne liubish'," pits the animistic, tactile world of the recalcitrant narrator, a five-year-old girl, against the pretentiously exalted effluvia of Maria Ivanovna (which Tolstaya contracts to Maryvanna, a pun on marijuana), the sentimental governess who is terminally immersed in grandiloquent reminiscences of her own past. Their inimical relationship finds expression in a contrast of discourses. The repeated recitations by Maryvanna of her former lover's (her uncle's) abstruse quasi-symbolist poetry, filled with ready-made phrases about death, sexuality, and melodramatic incidents, frighten the little girl ("after hearing a poem like that, who'd be brave enough to lower her feet from the bed, to use the potty, say?"). The language of the child narrator is studded with neologisms and results from passionately felt, immediate reactions to concrete experiences ("'*Bad*-bye!'" and "'*No* revoir'" are two examples). Animal struggles against anima. Typically, the robust humor with which Tolstaya infuses the manifold illustrations of the little girl's willful obstinacy alternates with her poignant inner cries of existential anguish: "Lord, the world is so frightening and hostile, the poor homeless, inexperienced soul huddling in the night wind. Who was so cruel, who filled me with love and hate, fear and depression, pity and shame, but didn't give me words: stole speech, sealed my mouth, put on iron padlocks, and threw away the keys."

These words provide a fitting epigraph for Tolstaya's "Noch'," an affective, disturbing portrayal of a middle-aged male who suffers the status and intellectual level of a child because of Down's syndrome. Proceeding largely from the viewpoint of the mentally hampered Aleksei Petrovich, the narrative highlights the primacy of language as a means of penetrating the mysteries of life and of inscribing oneself in the world. Cut off from the full spectrum of human experience and protected from everyday reality by the physically ungainly fortress of his mother's care, Aleksei dwells in the nocturnal darkness of primitive response and discursive alienation. Humans and objects appear to him only as undifferentiated primal categories: Men, Women, Legs, Tobacco. Deluded into fantasies of writing poetry, despite his inability to distinguish individual words correctly or to grasp the conventions of social intercourse in an "incomprehensible, unnavigable world," Aleksei retreats into the maternal burrow of animal nurture (just as the little girl in "Liubish'—ne liubish'" seeks refuge with the wisely simple Nanny Grusha, who can warm her "frozen, lost, bewildered heart"). Aleksei's creativity stops—and the story ends—with the word summarizing his cognitive condition: *night*. Tolstaya's hallmark mélange of the tragic and the touching rests on the rudimentary but effective device of chopping up the words of Pushkin's lyric "Zimnii vecher" (Winter Evening, 1825) into nonsensical word fragments, thereby conveying the distorted form in which Aleksei apprehends his environment ("A pall the storm casts on the sky" becomes "Apall thus tormcas tson thus ky").

Three of Tolstaya's narratives—"Sonia," "Milaia Shura," and "Samaia liubimaia"—explore resurrection through memory, one of her key notions and an example of binarism. A mainstay of Tolstaya's fiction, binarism—as posited by the late structuralist scholar Iurii Mikhailovich Lotman—is a constitutive feature of Russian culture and forms the conceptual backbone of several of Tostaya's stories from the mid 1980s, in which Metaphysics and Materialism, Idealism and Empiricism, and Soul and Body, for example, are pitted against each other. Whatever the differences among "Sonia," "Milaia Shura," and "Samaia liubimaia," these three stories assert the primacy of spirit, self-sacrifice, and generosity in plots constructed around women whose bizarre physical appearances elicit ridicule, compassion, or condescension in those unable to appreciate their profoundly humane, salvatory capacities.

"Sonia" balances the eponymous heroine's exterior and her tactless social behavior with traits that cumulatively presage her final function of guardian angel. Her resemblance to an ill-clad horse, "with a sunken chest, legs so fat they looked as if they came from a different person's set, enormous feet," disconcerts observers and invariably invites scorn, but in her role of museum curator she preserves culture, just as she sustains the next generation through feeding, sewing for, and taking care of others' children.

In "Sonia" the retrospective movement of the narrative fictionally resuscitates the protagonist only to confirm her physical death, an idea that likewise shapes "Milaia Shura." The decrepit Aleksandra Ernestovna, nicknamed Shura, dies as soon as her exuberant reminiscences of her amours and marriages converge into the illusion of a knowable and thus communicable life. This instantiation of missed opportunities—that is, the narrator's brief absence from Moscow precisely at the time of Shura's death—employs the broader elegiac theme of the passage of time ("And then? Why keep asking and then, and then? Life passed, that's what happened then!"). Two incidents mirror this unrealized moment in the narrative present: Shura's elegiacally treated failure many years ago (in the narrated past) to meet her beloved Ivan Nikolaevich at the railroad station in the Crimea, which leaves him "lost in time . . . on the other side of the years"; and the failure (in the "subjunctive" mood of fantasy and cast in a comic register) of the twenty-six-year-old violinist, who "kept silent all the time he lived at Aleksandra Ernestovna's," to declare his passion for the indomitable octogenarian. In "Milaia Shura," while psychological processes immobilize people, life passes and passes them by.

A process of reconstitution, conducted piecemeal and for the most part achronologically, structures "Samaia liubimaia," in which the gradual dilapidation of a dacha images the aging process of its protagonist, the endearing, gargoyle-like Evgeniia Ivanovna, nicknamed Zhenechka. Seasons function as biographical stages in the narrator's recollections of her childhood, when she was under Zhenechka's devoted tutelage. An object of mockery for her charges, Zhenechka epitomizes the efficient, generous nurturing that enables children's emotional growth (the mute boy she tutors partially regains his speech)—a nurturing that Tolstaya metaphorized in her tending of the garden that blooms luxuriantly under her strong, patient care ("In her hands, flowers seem to soar"). In her orbit both nature and people perpetuate themselves. Moreover, her unstinting dedication to several generations and her tireless vigor at the service of others intimate the possibility of combating the inexorable flow of time through spiritual vitality and emotional engagement ("She meant to live forever . . . we, too, were certain of her immortality").

No reader could accuse Tolstaya of fictionally idealizing or poeticizing women. In fact, her female characters fall into several unprepossessing, pitiable, or ice-veined types: the kindly, wheezing, flat-footed dinosaur of a woman sustained by poetic reminiscences and a bounteous spirit encased in an unwieldy physique; the maladroit female outsider, bypassed by experience, whose romantic daydreams improbably clash with a hapless, unappetizing demeanor; and self-centered, pragmatic sirens confident of enslaving admirers solely through their physical charms. Tolstaya's fictional women invariably illustrate the divergence between interior qualities and exterior assets, normally in reverse proportion to one another. Such discontinuity receives humorous but chilling treatment in two of her most ironic stories: "Okhota na mamonta" (1985, published in *Oktiabr'*; translated as "Hunting the Wooly Mammoth," 1989) and "Poet i muza," which map the course of their self-deluded beauties' successful, cold-blooded campaigns to trap and tame their defenseless male prey.

Both stories exchange one gender stereotype for another: in the immemorial myth of romantic seduction, Tolstaya replaces the male hunter's pursuit of the fleeing virgin with female predators who stalk and secure their victims through quasi-military means. Tolstaya figures the primitiveness of Zoia's relentless manipulation of Vladimir into matrimony as the capture of the wooly mammoth—a metaphor concretized by Vladimir's artist friend in a painting that shares the title of "Hunting the Wooly Mammoth." Intent on her goal of ensnaring Vladimir, Zoia resorts to the hackneyed

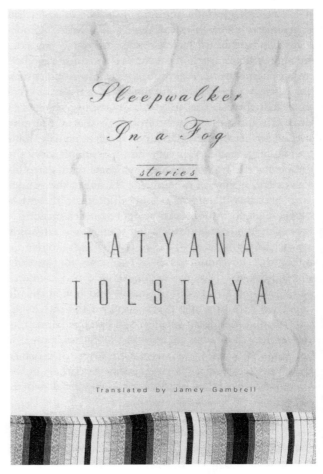

Dust jacket for the 1992 English-language edition of a collection of Tolstaya's stories (Richland County Public Library)

ploys of simulating mystery and fragility (playing a princess, a fairy, a femme fatale) while simultaneously domesticating the wayward engineer through the tried-and-true method of commandeering all aspects of his life: she accompanies him everywhere, inserts her photograph in his wallet, purchases slippers for him when he moves in with her, feeds him, and subjects him to the psychological pressure of her silent but obtrusively displayed dissatisfaction. At the end of the story her pyrrhic victory is complete: the "heavy, quick, hairy, insensitive animal"—her vitriolic, resentful image of Vladimir—settles into "the blissful thick silence of the great ice age." Passages encapsulating Zoia's fantasies about hypnotizing various audiences with her presumably incomparable beauty emphasize the cliché against which Western feminists have agitated for a quarter century: namely, that a woman's looks are her passport to a paradise of plenty.

An identical delusion propels Nina's merciless exertions in "The Poet and the Muse," which complicates the gender warfare through an intersecting conflict between the methodical ruthlessness of the medical and military mentalities and the carefree, bohemian expansiveness of artists. Tolstaya casts the doctor Nina as a closed, self-preoccupied pragmatist, determined to possess the handsome janitor-poet Grisha as a trophy earned by her beauty—the fabled quality requisite for a great poet's muse. Denying him all subjectivity, she eliminates the friends and fellow artists who share his values and inspire him (above all, Lizaveta, the painter who practices "talonism"), and suffocates him with a bland regimen of domesticity, doused in jealousy. In a cross-gendered replay of Samuel Richardson's *Clarissa: or, the History of a Young Lady* (1747–1748), under an attack that he cannot repel, Grisha opts for freedom through death. Tolstaya juxtaposes the two diametrically opposed spheres of bourgeois and bohemian life as surface, control, and practicality, on the one hand, and spiritual richness, warmth, and carefree camaraderie, on the other. Nina emerges as a merciless oppressor and censor, dictating the acceptable terms of Grisha's creativity, dismissing his companions as garbage to be vacuumed out of their shared apartment, and depriving Lizaveta of her residence.

A cynical male counterpart of Zoia and Nina, Vasily Mikhailovich in "Krug" (1987, published in *Oktiabr';* translated as "The Circle," 1989) likewise instrumentalizes lovers, largely to defer confrontation with his mortality. The story, which traces his ineluctable movement toward death, retrospectively catalogues his various liaisons and dwells on his failure to appreciate the genuine love of his child-like Isolde, "happy to sit forever at his side, burning like a wedding candle, burning without extinguishing with a steady quiet flame." Unable to fulfill his reciprocal role of Tristan, he restlessly seeks other modes of deferment and self-oblivion, "grimly smothering all the sparks that flashed on the way" until the final oblivion of "his well-earned cup of hemlock." Ironing the myth of Tristan and Isolde in an intertextual way, "Krug" inscribes Tolstaya's favorite thematic clusters of loss and memory, spirit and matter, and naive affirmation and selfish skepticism. A gratifyingly rich, resonant metaphor, the circle of the title evokes not only entrapment and closure but also divine perfection and its corollaries, such as the halo of sainthood, consummate union, and protection against hostile forces.

As in her exploration of childhood, Tolstaya spotlights romantic love from multiple angles. Whereas Vasily Mikhailovich fails to appreciate an abiding and devoted passion, two of Tolstaya's luckless protagonists—Natasha in "Vyshel mesiats iz tumana" ("The Moon Came Out," 1987) and the eponymous Peters—nurture futile visions of romance projected onto individuals who either scorn them or remain unaware of their feelings. "Peters" and "Vyshel mesiats iz tumana" essentially offer gender variations on a single plot: the hapless, physically unattractive childhood of a "loser" modulates to an adolescence stifled by an omnipotent grandmother and tormented by inarticulate romantic (sexual) aspirations that never become actualized, vanishing with the onset of middle age and its melancholy resignation. Poetic, metaphor-laden flights of fantasy alternate here, as elsewhere in Tolstaya's fiction, with imagery suggestive of incarceration, stagnation, and death, as both protagonists shuttle between extravagant, groundless hopes and grimly humiliating reality.

Seduced and betrayed by their powers of illusion, Tolstaya's risible "failures"—characters who harbor hopes of an eternal, impossible love—overlap with her beneficiaries and victims of art. One of her most complex and skillfully paced stories, "Reka Okkervil'" (1985; translated as "Okkervil River," 1989) inextricably welds the myth of St. Petersburg to a plot of psychological enslavement through the eroticization of art. Both the phantasmagoric city and Vera Vasil'evna's sirenic performance of romances, preserved on vinyl, entail imaginative creation. For the common denominator in their inexplicable enchantment Tolstaya chooses the symbol of rushing water: just as the river periodically overspills its banks, so the irresistible singing voice drowns out all thoughts and doubts, obliterating everything on its wayward course. Blending literary echoes, urban romance, Mikhail Iur'evich Lermontov's lyrics, and historical references, the story highlights the capacity of art not only to triumph over quotidian reality but also to breed and feed obsession. The isolated, worshipful translator Simeonov endows Vera Vasil'evna the chanteuse with all the alluring traits of womanhood; her voice generates his hackneyed visions of personal trysts with her as a femme fatale. Although Simeonov's confrontation with the lumbering, mustached whale of her physical self briefly disillusions him, his repulsion dissipates under the spell of her enthralling recordings, which bring him back, metaphorically, to his knees.

A kindred disillusionment awaits Galia in the aptly titled story "Fakir" (1986; translated, 1989), in which Filin's unique flair for elegant style and beauty completely captivates Galia. She reveres him as a "handsome, giving, hospitable" magician, literally and figuratively ensconced above the crude practicalities of everyday humdrum pursuits, who regularly orchestrates an "evening of miracles." Once removed from the "golden atmosphere of the lofty and the beautiful" established in the theater of his exquisitely appointed apartment, however, Filin becomes diminished in her eyes into a "pretender," a "clown in a shah's robe." Her disbelief no longer suspended, the metamorphosis in her perspective on Filin pulls Galia down from the transcendent heights of aesthetic stimulation to the harsh discomfort of petty domestic concerns. "Fakir" essentially revives Marcel Duchamp's cardinal demythologizing principle of contextualization: like Duchamp's urinal exhibited in a museum, Filin belongs to art as long as he remains on the stage of his high-rise dwelling. Wrenched from this setting, however, he becomes relegated to the lesser category of mortal (indeed, middling) man—just as a urinal no longer displayed in a museum reverts to its lowly function as a receptacle for bodily fluids.

Virtually all these stories share a core fund of devices that Tolstaya subjects to endless permutations: binarisms; value-laden chronotopes; uneven pacing; incessant spatial and temporal zigzags; narrative beginnings in medias res; quicksilver shifts in voice, tone, and viewpoint; and fragmentariness, with metaphor or chance memory alone forging fragile transitions between discrete narrative units. Her prose relies on a wealth of verbal ingredients subjected to unusual, enticing arrangements. Metaphor, above all, and multiple stylistic levels glutted with songs, poems, romances, clichés, and (often submerged) references to literature, folklore, and historical events account for the vivid textual opulence in which Tolstaya's admirers revel and her detractors deplore as ostentatious and self-indulgent. Tolstaya's tonal range, her penchant for moving swiftly from elegiac pensiveness to ironic summation, to indulgent humor, to tragic philosophizing, to wistful lyricism, is extraordinary, and the succession of strongly marked, disparate registers partly explains why on the basis of her fiction various readers puzzle over Tolstaya's stance on art, religious issues, heterosexual relations, and so forth. Hers is a maximally rhetorical prose, replete with apostrophes, questions, repetition, self-commentary, and embedded and highlighted citations. It teems with tropes whose extravagant elaboration recalls Homeric similes.

The formula "less is more" to some extent may be applied to Tolstaya's writing practices. As several of her stories and particularly her novel attest, the shorter her narratives, the better. Brevity calls upon one of Tolstaya's most admirable talents as a writer—an uncanny aptitude for drastic condensation whose rewards are most conspicuous in her breathtaking early prose, which, not coincidentally, could be scanned as poetry if broken down into parallel lines. Her longer works—those written in the late 1980s and thereafter—suffer from shaky structure and occasionally create the impression of aimlessness or impasse. Endings, likewise, are problematic for Tolstaya, at their weakest con-

sisting of little more than a fade-out or a sentence manifestly superimposed to provide an illusion of closure. These unpersuasive tactics substantiate Chekhov's famous pronouncement that endings are the place where an author is most apt to "lie."

Three of Tolstaya's stories—"Chistyi list" (A Blank Sheet, published in *Neva*, 1984), "Serafim" (1986, published in *Novyi Mir;* translated, 1992), and "Spi spokoino, synok" (1986, published in *Avrora;* translated as "Sweet Dreams, Son," 1989)—opt for a philosophical grotesque that initially seems promising but ultimately fails to salvage these texts that are overly eager to "convey a message" and in so doing expose their own seams. All three in varying degrees thematize identity, moral choices, and their consequences. "Chistyi list" echoes Evgenii Ivanovich Zamiatin's *My* (written in 1920, published in 1952; translated as *We,* 1924) in its gruesome portrayal of a fantastic operation that excises the human heart and soul, thereby liberating patients from emotions and suffering but also depriving them of what presumably makes one quintessentially human. "Serafim" portrays the paradoxical figure of a cold, narcissistic "angel" intent solely on preserving his pure facade of seraphic beauty, which utterly contradicts his vicious, rotten inner impulses. "Spi spokoino, synok" interweaves two parallel but contrasting plots: that of the adult, orphaned Sergei's thwarted struggle to discover his past and his origins (who his parents were), and his mother-in-law's re-creation of a past that she most probably manufactures. The first seeks to uncover "truth," while the second strives to hide it through deception and self-delusion. While not devoid of Tolstaya's bold rhetorical strategies, sardonic skepticism, and poetic effects, these stories leave little for the reader to ponder.

The year 1988 marked two radical turns in Tolstaya's life: upon her third nomination, Tolstaya finally was accepted into the Moscow Writers' Union, and the University of Richmond invited her to spend a year on its campus as writer-in-residence. During her tenure there, the university organized a conference devoted to her fiction; magazines and newspapers published her book reviews and interviews; and sundry media solicited her opinion on Russian-related issues, which ranged from the anticipated consequences of perestroika to the status of women at home and abroad. Tolstaya proceeded to give lectures and interviews across the country as she accepted offers from the University of Texas and, later, Texas Tech University to join their Slavic departments in the capacity of visiting scholar. She quickly earned a reputation as a vehement critic of Western feminism, American society, and especially the system of advanced education in the United States. While lambasting American univer-

Татьяна Толстая
ДЕНЬ

личное

Front cover for Tolstaya's Den': Lichnoe *(Day: Personal, 2001), a collection of articles and essays written during the 1990s (Collection of Mark Lipovetsky)*

the volatile male poet Lenechka wishes to conceive a Pushkin, or a child of Pushkin's genius, with the African student Judy, newly arrived in Russia to train as a veterinarian, but the retrospective story meanders through a patchwork quilt of discrete episodes whose antic humor cannot disguise their author's loss of focus. "Siuzhet" (on the last page dated "June 1937, St. Petersburg," four months after Pushkin's death) likewise separates into frequently amusing but weakly connected scenes as a Pushkin who survived his duel becomes privy to watershed events and great figures in Russian history and culture up to the emergence of Joseph Stalin. Both "Siuzhet" and "Limpopo," loosely constructed around the distinctive idolatry of Pushkin in Russia, lack plot continuity and coherence; their digressions showcase bravura linguistic performance without surmounting authorial disorientation. Whereas Tolstaya's early stories impress by their stunning integration of all narrative elements, her works of the late 1980s and early 1990s sooner reveal a clever, erudite author at a creative crossroads.

Tolstaya's efforts to summarize the course of Russian culture find their fullest realization in *Kys'* (2000; translated as *The Slynx,* 2003), the novel that appeared after a decade of no new fiction writing, constant travel, and changes in institutional affiliation. During 1991 and 1992 at Goucher College and in 1993 at Princeton University, she taught Soviet literature; in 1994 she accepted an appointment as an associate professor in the English department at Skidmore College, entrusted with courses in creative writing and Soviet literature. At this time her name virtually disappeared from the United States press, which earlier had tenaciously tracked developments in her literary career. The general public therefore did not learn of Tolstaya's sojourn at Oxford University, her purchase of a house just outside Princeton, and her acquisition of the green card that now enables her to travel freely as a permanent resident of the United States (although she lives principally in Moscow). A figure frequently encountered in the Russian media, Tolstaya has captured the attention of the Russian capital through her television appearances; her journalism in *Moskovskie novosti* (Moscow News) and *Russky telegraf* (Russian Telegraph); and her novel, which garnered sufficient attention to rationalize a republication of her short stories—which appeared as the collection *Noch'* (Night, 2001)—and the book publication of the journalism pieces she produced primarily in the 1990s, *Den': Lichnoe* (Day: Personal, 2001).

Tolstaya's journalism, which represents a sizable portion of her comparatively modest output, consists mainly of Russian and Anglophone articles and reviews. Associated chiefly with *Moskovskie novosti,* the

sities, Tolstaya continued to address their audiences in paid talks arranged by her agent and to participate in academic conferences.

This period witnessed a perceptible change in Tolstaya's shrinking number of publications. The encroachment of contemporary concerns upon her prose resulted in unexpected detours and formal shifts. Folklore, a salient characteristic of her earlier fiction, yielded to political relevance and national mythologies, while the increasing length of her stories worked against their hallmark condensation. Insistent allegorizing (with Pushkin as the matrix signifier) and structural slackness characterized this new direction, exemplified to varying degrees in "Somnambula v tumane," "Limpopo," and "Siuzhet" (The Plot, published in *Sintaksis,* 1991). "Somnambula" retains many of Tolstaya's earlier fictional strategies (use of folklore, mirroring techniques, and unstable narrative voice) and dominant preoccupations (memory, terror of oblivion, and conflicting impulses) but suffers from repetition and longueurs. "Limpopo" rests on the absurd premise that

Russian items subscribe to the elastic genre of brief thoughts on contemporary concerns, while their English-language counterparts incline to the essay format favored by digressive, lengthy book reviews. The differences between these two culture-specific categories attest to Tolstaya's awareness of distinctions in readership. Writing for a Russian audience, Tolstaya relies on opinion heavily laced with irony, providing acerbic commentary on, for example, glasnost, Soviet women, feminism in the United States, the intelligentsia, and the consequences of market reforms. As in interviews, whenever the topics of academic and contemporary life in the United States, feminism, and political correctness surface, Tolstaya's impassioned attacks smack of diatribe, fueled by quite startling oversimplification. Reviews, such as those of books by Iskander and Aleksandr Aleksandrovich Genis and of Aleksandr Sokurov's motion picture *Telets* (Taurus, 2000), favor personal ruminations over rigorous assessment of the work in question. Her more fact-based, substantial reviews in the Western press, however, usually benefit from a strong dose of logical argumentation and resort less frequently to the rhetorical strategies of impressionism, which presupposes a single, quick perusal by readers more responsive to the wit, rather than the weight, of an author's viewpoint and the persuasiveness of her adduced evidence. Perhaps the most memorable and multifaceted reviews include those that first appeared in *The New York Review of Books;* Tolstaya wrote on Aleksandr Isaevich Solzhenitsyn's *"The Russian Question" at the End of the Twentieth Century;* Joyce Toomre's 1992 English translation of Elena Molokhovets' celebrated *Classic Russian Cooking* (1861); Robert Conquest's *The Great Terror: A Reassessment* (1991); and two illustrated volumes on Russian photography, David King's *The Commissar Vanishes* (1997) and *Eyewitness to History: The Photographs of Yevgeny Khaldei,* by Alexander and Alice Nakhimovsky (1997).

Provocation is Tolstaya's forte, and the flexibility of the essay genre permits her to give it full rein. In its proclivity to hyperbole, polemical, unexpected twists of thought and formulation, and a sardonic tone that occasionally sharpens into sarcasm or congeals into archness, Tolstaya's domestic journalism overlaps with her fiction. Anecdotes and vignettes structured around absurd, idiosyncratic personae or circumstances enliven these short, fugitive texts. By contrast, her more leisurely book reviews in the West, almost exclusively of volumes addressing issues of history, occasionally border on the academic in the scrupulous attention paid to historical context and detail. Predictably, Tolstaya lauds Conquest's meticulously documented study and ridicules Solzhenitsyn's sententious pronouncements. She uses both occasions to air her views on the triumphs and travails of Russia, as well as Western perceptions (which are, invariably, misperceptions) of them, and treats readers to her signature blend of flamboyant metaphors and sweeping generalizations. Her most scathing review, of Gail Sheehy's thick tome on Gorbachev (*The Man Who Changed the World: The Lives of Mikhail S. Gorbachev,* 1990), appeared in *The New Republic* (27 May 1991). It showcases Tolstaya's rhetorical panache and her bilious enmity toward Western analysts of Russian culture who have neglected their homework.

With the new millennium, Tolstaya entered a long-heralded phase of her literary career: she finally published her vigorously advertised first novel, which, according to her own testimony, she had been writing for more than a decade. *Kys'* elicited mixed critical reactions, ranging from irritated bewilderment or disappointment (from reviewers such as Andrei Nemzer, Nikita Eliseev, and Viacheslav Kuritsyn) to hosannas proclaiming it "an encyclopedia of Russian life" (Dmitrii Ol'shansky) and "The Great Russian Novel" (Lev Danilkin) that has elevated its author into a "classic of Russian literature" (Boris Paramonov).

Tolstaya's ambitions for the novel may be inferred from the titles that she assigns its thirty-three chapters: they consist of the Church Slavonic alphabet (from "Az" to "Izhittsa" [A to Z]), with a preference for those variants that double as modern Russian words (such as "Cherv'" [worm] rather than "Cha"). The device connotes comprehensiveness, adverts to origins (or regression), and introduces a comic element—all functions in which the text itself is implicated. Critics have read the novel diversely, for the simple reason that it invites (and thematizes) multiple interpretations: as a dystopian summation of Russian cultural obsessions; more narrowly, as a satire on post-Soviet Russia; and, most broadly, as a deconstruction of the signifying capacities of language. Though not necessarily to everyone's taste, the sumptuous language of *Kys',* with its shifting stylistic levels, is a genuine tour de force, and, as typically obtains in Tolstaya's prose, it ultimately reigns as the triumphant though ambiguous (indeed, polysemous) protagonist of the text.

Probably the most accessible aspect of *Kys'* is its dystopian layer, which generally reproduces many of the situational elements codified by that genre (recalling, above all, Zamiatin's novel *My*). Tolstaya's plot follows the standard dystopian paradigm, with capitalization indicating the significance of key phenomena and events that reflect or have produced the temporally unidentified Here and Now. As a Consequence (*Posledstvie*) of an Explosion (*Vzryv*) that occurred more than two centuries ago, the population of Fedor-Kuz'michsk has mutated into humanoids whose bodies display animal features (a tail, claws, and gills, for instance), as well as multiplication and relocation of physical parts. In some, ears of sundry shapes and sizes sprout from knees, feet, armpits, and head; others have feathers protruding from skulls and eyes, and so forth, in endlessly grotesque permutations. Residing in what formerly was called Moscow (built on seven hills) but now consists of huge, desolate provincial expanses with forests to the north and Chechens to the south, the inhabitants eat enigmatic "ognetsy" (firelings), worms, and mice (the last doubling as currency); smoke and drink rust (also boiled for ink); and communicate in a substandard language that transparently deforms conventional contemporary Russian. Tolstaya renders their speech phonetically: "mogoziny" stands for *magaziny* (stores), "abrazavanie" for *obrazovanie* (education); this device emphasizes the people's unfamiliarity with the printed word. Within this surreal universe, from which the general skill of writing has entirely disappeared, hares fly, chickens lay poisonous eggs, and wooden pillars named after Moscow streets and metro stations have replaced monuments–memorials to bygone eras erected not by institutional decree but on the anomalous whim of a single individual, Nikita Ivanych.

A minority of impossibly aged *Prezhnie* ("Oldeners," as Jamey Gambrell renders this term in *The Slynx*) retain memory of the past, about which the average citizen or *Pererozhdenets* (Reborn) has no inkling, for universal amnesia reigns over the "nation." Despite the communal services that approximate socialist institutions, such as the *Stolovaia Izba* (Food Hut), *Raboch'ia Izba* (Skills Hut), and *Sklad* (Warehouse), a rigid social hierarchy divides citizens into the powerful *Sanitorions* (Orderlies) and the average *golubchiki* (golubchiks or little dears). Fyodor Kuzmich (from whom the town gets its name), the "cult of personality," absolute ruler (the *Nabol'shii Murza* [Greatest Murza]–the latter a word of Tatar origin denoting a feudal lord during the fifteenth century), whose name, when mentioned, requires the automatic mantra "glory to him," has arrogated to himself all past and present verbal production, including others' poetry. His wise words and lyrics, reproduced by human copiers who resemble Nikolai Vasil'evich Gogol's Akakii Akakievich, a protagonist of "Shinel'" (The Overcoat, 1842), circulate in an illiterate society that prohibits the possession of books, which are reputed to be fatal to citizens' health, presumably because of radiation. True to dystopian formulas, the novel traces the eloquently named Benedict's subversive quest for the forbidden–here, the printed Word. That search culminates in his discovery of an enormous library, and subsequently, the realization that Fedor Kuz'mich, a cowardly dwarf, merely plagiarizes all of Russian literature and generates self-promoting decrees. By no accident is his surname Kablukov (heel), which alludes to the idiom for repressive control, "byt' pod kablukom" (to be under someone's thumb–literally, a heel). Once installed as Fedor Kuz'mich's successor, Benedict's father-in-law and former Chief Orderly, Kudeiar Kudeiarov, the ostensible liberator, replays his deposed predecessor's totalitarian scenario. Kudeiar Kudeiarov's noxious halitosis and his association with the brigand made popular by the folksong "Kudeiar" ("Zhili dvenadtsat' razboinikov . . ." [There lived twelve robbers . . .]) offer early clues to his rank "inner nature," which his rhetoric camouflages.

Readers interpreting the novel as a metaphor for post-Soviet transformations would have no difficulty linking the genesis of *Kys'* and its pivotal event with the Chernobyl disaster (the Explosion in the novel), when Tolstaya did, indeed, begin work on the text. Various features in *Kys'* reflect key aspects of the 1990s: the prominence of a corrupt, self-serving oligarchy; the marginalization of high culture; the emergence of New Russians' "blia" (in-speak, or jargon, which figures prominently in the novel), which violates every conceivable grammatical rule; wholesale national amnesia, paradoxically coexisting alongside an orgy of retrieval via reinstatement of old street names, institutions, and Europeanized terminology; the devaluation and degradation of peoples' living standards; and the exposure of an ostensible benefactor as a despot. In short, an atmosphere of chaos–of the cultural and political, apocalyptic incoherence that beleaguered Russia in the 1990s– permeates the novel. In an essay titled "Russkii mir" (translated as "The Russian World," *The Guardian*, 1993), published in book form in *Den'*, Tolstaya dubs Russia a huge insane asylum embracing one absolute (relativism) and one constant (chaos). Russia, she argues, exists in mythological time, wherein all events occur simultaneously, and the world of *Kys'* amply illustrates the bewildering disorder within the *perpetuum immobile* endemic to both utopia and dystopia.

Tatyana Tolstaya's modernist stylistics, her juxtaposition of elements from high and popular culture–of tragic and trashy, heinous and hilarious–tempt critics to situate her within Russian postmodernism. What militates against such a niche is Tolstaya's impassioned allegiance to humanistic values, her all too patent reverence for culture, literature, and language, and her unmistakable respect for generosity, integrity, and decency. Noncommittal linguistic games, a juggling of equally ironized and ultimately discredited positions, and the absence of an implicit center have little place in Tolstaya's body of works, which, on the contrary, celebrates culture and its perceived achievements while mourning their erosion in the contemporary world.

Dust jacket for the 2003 English-language edition of Tolstaya's Kys' *(2000), her first work
of fiction in ten years (Richland County Public Library)*

Her intertextual prose requires slow, assiduous rereading, for what matters most often lies buried among multiple layers of verbal display. Making sense of Tolstaya's texts entails an archaeological excavation, and for that reason one might expect a trained Freudian with ready recall of the entire gamut of Russian literature to be her most adept reader. If the West lionized Tolstaya in the 1980s and early 1990s on the basis of her early fiction, at home her current popularity may be attributed to enthusiasm for her novel. Whatever the vagaries of her reputation, Tolstaya has firmly installed herself in the canon of Russian literature.

Interviews:

Olga Martynenko, "A Little Man Is a Normal Man," *Moscow News,* 8 (1987): 10;

Elena Svetlova, "Chetvertoe izmerenie," *Moskovskii komsomolets,* 29 November 1987, p. 2;

Andrei Mal'gin, "'Eto bylo tak legko–ne uchit'sia,'" *Moskovskie novosti,* 21 (1988): 10–11;

Aleksandr Shchuplov, "'Poidite navstrechu chitateliu! . . . ,'" *Knizhnoe obozrenie,* 1 January 1988, p. 4;

Aleksandr Glezer, "'Idei glasnosti i perestroiki intelligentsiia podderzhivaet': Beseda s Tat'ianoi Tolstoi," *Strelets,* 1 (1989): 161–173;

Peter I. Barta, "The Author, the Cultural Tradition and Glasnost: An Interview with Tatyana Tolstaya," *Russian Language Journal,* 147–149 (1990): 265–283;

Elena Svetlova, "My ne malen'kie," *Sovershenno sekretno,* 4 (1990): 4–5;

S. Valentinova, "'Zhizn' beskonechna v tu i v druguiu storonu,'–ubezhdena Tat'iana Tolstaia," *Zhenshchina do i posle,* 18 (1991): 8–9;

Tamara Alagova and Nina Efimov, "Interview with Tatyana Tolstaya," translated by Michael A. Aguirre, *World Literature Today,* 67 (1993): 49–53;

Elena Veselaia, "Otplyvaiushchii ostrov," *Moskovskie novosti* (6–13 March 1994): 2; translated by Elena Vesyolaya as "An Island Sailing Off," *Moscow News,* 10 (11–17 March 1994): 12;

Elisabeth Rich, "Tatyana Tolstaya," *South Central Review: The Journal of the South Central Modern Language Association,* 12 (1995): 84–91;

Serafima Roll, "Writing as a Passage into Another Reality," *Contextualizing Transition: Interviews with Contemporary Writers and Critics,* edited by Thomas R. Beyer Jr., Middlebury Studies in Russian Language and Literature, volume 16 (New York: Peter Lang, 1998), pp. 95–113;

Sally Laird, "Tatyana Tolstaya," in *Voices of Russian Literature: Interviews with Ten Contemporary Writers,* edited by Laird (Oxford: Oxford University Press, 1999), pp. 95–117.

Biographies:

Frank Magill, ed., "Tatyana Tolstaya," in *Great Women Writers* (New York: Holt, 1994);

Sophia Wisniewska, "Tat'iana Tolstaia," in *Russian Women Writers,* 2 volumes, edited by Christine D. Tomei (New York: Garland, 1999), II: 1477–1484;

Natal'ia Ivanova, "Tolstaia Tatiana," in *Russkie pisateli 20 veka: Biograficheskii slovar',* edited by Petr Alekseevich Nikolaev (Moscow: Bol'shaia Rossiiskaia Entsiklopediia, 2000), pp. 687–688.

References:

Leonid Bakhnov, "Chelovek so storony," *Znamia,* 7 (1988): 226–228;

Adele Barker, "Are Women Writing Women's Writing in the Soviet Union Today? Tolstaya and Grekova," *Studies in Comparative Communism,* 31 (1988): 357–364;

Sally Dalton-Brown, "A Map of the Human Heart: Tatyana Tolstaya's Topographies," *Essays in Poetics,* 21 (1996): 1–18;

Aleksandr Aleksandrovich Genis, "Risunki na poliakh: Tatiana Tolstaia," in his *Ivan Petrovich umer: Stat'ii rassledovaniia* (Moscow: Novoe literaturnoe obozrenie, 1999), pp. 66–71;

John Givens, "Reflections, Crooked Mirrors, Magic Theaters: Tat'iana Tolstaia's 'Peters,'" in *Fruits of Her Plume: Essays on Contemporary Russian Women's Culture,* edited by Helena Goscilo (Armonk, N.Y.: M. E. Sharpe, 1996), pp. 250–270;

Helena Goscilo, *The Explosive World of Tatyana N. Tolstaya's Fiction* (Armonk, N.Y.: M. E. Sharpe, 1996);

Goscilo, "Monsters Monomaniacal, Marital, and Medical. Tatyana Tolstaya's Regenerative Use of Gender Stereotypes," in *Sexuality and the Body in Russian Culture,* edited by Jane T. Costlow, Stephanie Sandler, and Judith Vowles (Stanford: Stanford University Press, 1993), pp. 204–220;

Goscilo, "Perspective in Tatyana Tolstaya's Wonderland of Art," *World Literature Today,* 67 (1993): 80–90;

Goscilo, "Tat'iana Tolstaia's 'Dome of Many-Coloured Glass': The World Refracted through Multiple Perspectives," *Slavic Review,* 47 (1988): 280–290;

Goscilo, "Tolstaian Times, Traversals, and Transfers," in *New Directions in Soviet Literature,* edited by Sheelagh Duffin Graham (New York: St. Martin's Press, 1992), pp. 36–62;

Goscilo, "Tolstajan Love as Surface Text," *Slavic and East European Journal,* 34 (1990): 43–52;

Goscilo, ed., *Fruits of Her Plume: Essays on Contemporary Russian Women's Culture* (Armonk, N.Y.: M. E. Sharpe, 1996), pp. 59–84, 135–163;

Natal'ia Ivanova, "Bakhtin's Concept of the Grotesque and the Art of Petrushevskaia and Tolstaia," in *Fruits of Her Plume: Essays on Contemporary Russian Women's Culture,* edited by Goscilo (Armonk, N.Y.: M. E. Sharpe, 1993), pp. 21–32;

Mark Lipovetsky, *Russian Postmodernist Fiction: Dialogue with Chaos* (Armonk, N.Y.: M. E. Sharpe, 2000), pp. 127–138;

Lipovetsky, "Sled Kysi," *Iskusstvo kino,* 2 (2001): 77–80;

Elena Nevzgliadova, "Eta prekrasnaia zhizn'," *Avrora* (October 1986): 111–120;

Elena Petrusheva, "Tatiana Tolstaya," *Soviet Literature,* 2 (1987): 169–174;

Svetlana Piskunova and Vladimir Piskunov, "Uroki zazerkal'ia," *Oktiabr',* 8 (1988): 188–198;

Daniel Rancour-Laferriere, Vera Loseva, and Aleksej Lunkov, "Violence in the Garden: A Work by Tolstaja in Kleinian Perspective," *Slavic and East European Journal,* 39 (1995): 524–534;

Raisa Shishkova, "Nich'i babushki na zolotom kryl'tse," *Kontinent,* 56 (1988): 398–402;

K. A. Simmons, "Zhenskaia proza and the New Generation of Woman Writers," *Slovo: A Journal of Contemporary and East European Affairs,* 3 (May 1990): 66–77;

Petr Spivak, "Vo sne i naiavu," *Oktiabr',* 2 (1988): 201–203;

Karen Stepanian, "Golos, letiashchii v kupol," *Voprosy literatury,* 4 (1988): 78–105;

Petr L'vovich Vail' and Aleksandr Aleksandrovich Genis, "Popytka k begstvu. II: Gorodok v Tabakerke–Proza Tat'iany Tolstoi," *Sintaksis,* 24 (1988): 116–131;

Andrei Vasilevsky, "Nochi kholodny," *Druzhba narodov,* 7 (1988): 256–258;

Sophia Teresa Wisniewska, "Narrative Structure in the Prose of Tat'jana Tolstaja," dissertation, Bryn Mawr College, 1992;

Mikhail Zolotonosov, "Mechty i fantomy," *Literaturnoe obozrenie,* 4 (1987): 58–61.

Lyudmila Ulitskaya

(2 February 1943 –)

Maria Litovskaia
Ural State University

(Translated by Seth Graham)

BOOKS: *Skuchnaia shuba* (Moscow: Malysh, 1982);
Sto pugovits (Moscow: Detskaia literatura, 1983);
Moi vnuk Veniamin (Moscow: VAAP-inform, 1988);
Taina igrushek (Moscow: Kinotsentr, 1989);
Bednye rodstvenniki (Moscow: Slovo, 1994)—includes "Sonechka" and "Doch' Bukhary"; translated by Arch Tait as "Sonechka" and "The Daughter of Bokhara" in *Sonechka and Other Stories,* New Russian Writing, volume 17 (Moscow: GLAS, 1998);
Medeia i ee deti (Moscow: Vagrius, 1996); translated by Tait as *Medea and Her Children* (New York: Schocken Books, 2002);
Veselye pokhorony (Moscow: Vagrius, 1998); translated by Cathy Porter as *The Funeral Party,* edited by Tait (London: Gollancz, 1999; New York: Schocken Books, 2001);
Lialin dom: Povesti, rasskazy (Moscow: Vagrius, 1999);
Kazus Kukotskogo (Moscow: Vagrius, 2000);
Tsiu-iurikh: Roman, rasskazy (Moscow: EKSMO, 2002);
Vtoroe litso (Moscow: EKSMO, 2002)—includes "Vtoroe litso";
Pervye i poslednie (Moscow: EKSMO, 2002);
Skvoznaia liniia (Moscow: EKSMO, 2003)—includes "Skvoznaia liniia."
Collections and Editions: *Pikovaia dama i drugie rasskazy* (Moscow: Vagrius, 2001);
Bednye, zlye, liubimye: Povesti, rasskazy (Moscow: EKSMO, 2002);
Bednye rodstvenniki: Rasskazy (Moscow: EKSMO, 2002);
Devochki: Rasskazy (Moscow: EKSMO, 2002);
Sonechka: Povesti i rasskazy (Moscow: EKSMO, 2002).

PRODUCED SCRIPTS: *Sto pugovits,* motion picture, Soiuzmul'tfil'm, 1983;
Lenivoe plat'e, motion picture, Soiuzmul'tfil'm, 1987;
Taina igrushek, motion picture, Soiuzmul'tfil'm, 1987;
Sestrichki liberti, motion picture, Gor'ky Film Studio, 1990;

Lyudmila Ulitskaya (photograph by Yasov Titov © Vagrius)

Umirat' legko, by Ulitskaya, Ivan Biriukov, and Grigorii Riazhsky, motion picture, NTV-Profit and Patmos-Media, 1999.

Lyudmila Ulitskaya has become one of the most popular authors in Russia. Located between mass culture and experimental, or "high" literature, her works exemplify contemporary belles lettres. Her novels, novellas, and short stories are written in the traditionalist manner and tell the stories of ordinary people who find their happiness and the significance of life not in social service but in the sphere of private existence. Ulitskaya actualizes Russian classical tradition by focusing on traditional concepts of guilt and faith and the meaning of life and consciousness. Yet, she constantly innovates this tradition by describing characters whose lives vacillate between normality and insanity and between the real and the imaginary—characters whose acts of generosity and meekness invite the reader to question certain customary assumptions about human behavior.

Ulitskaya was born in the town of Davlekanovo in Bashkiriia, an autonomous republic within the Russian Federation, to which her family had been evacuated from Moscow during World War II. The family left Moscow, because as Jews they would have been in considerable danger had the city been captured. Her parents belonged to Moscow families with long-standing intelligentsia traditions. Ulitskaya's father worked as a biochemist, while her mother was an agricultural engineer. After the end of the war the family returned to Moscow, where they lived in an overcrowded communal apartment. Ulitskaya's parents divorced when she was still a schoolgirl. She entered Moscow State University in 1962 and graduated from the biology department in 1967. From 1968 to 1970 she was employed at the Institute of General Genetics of the Academy of Science. During these years she started writing prose, but it remained unpublished until the late 1980s. Her interest in literature and the arts brought her to the newly organized Jewish Chamber Theater, where she worked as the head of the literary section from 1970 to 1982. Ulitskaya was married three times—first to a physicist; then to a geneticist, with whom she had two children, Aleksey and Pyotr; and lastly to Moscow artist Andrei Krasulin. In 2000 Krasulin exhibited in Manezh a series of his etchings made from the pages of Ulitskaya's rough drafts.

Ulitskaya began her career as an author by writing children's literature. She based her works on her own childhood memories and also wrote stories about Jewish life. She became well known after the journal *Novyi mir* (New World) published her *povest'* (novella) "Sonechka" (1992; translated, 1998) and story "Doch' Bukhary" (1993; translated as "The Daughter of Bokhara," 1998). The first story is based on a protonarrative popular in intellectual circles about the peaceful coexistence of a prominent artist's faithful wife and young mistress. The wife, Sonechka, is a homely librarian who resembles a "young camel" and tends to shut herself off from the real world by reading books. She marries the aging artist Robert Viktorovich, a man of great talent who is perse-

cuted by the Soviet authorities. Sonechka zealously fulfills her duties as wife, mother, and caretaker (of the rooms that the family calls home) and displays a reverent attitude toward her husband's talent and her daughter's upbringing. With their experiences of surveillance and poverty behind them, the family is gradually building a peaceful and materially prosperous life when Iasia, a girlfriend of the daughter, moves in and becomes the artist's mistress. While maintaining warm relations with his wife, Robert Viktorovich tries with Iasia's help to regain the artistic energy of his youth and to solve the riddle of the color white. Sonechka realizes, primarily from the changes in his art, that her husband is having an affair and accepts the fact that the white-skinned, fair-haired Iasia is indispensable to him. Iasia in turn feels deep gratitude toward the family for taking her in, and because of her particular biographical history and psychology she does not feel awkward around Sonechka. To the bewilderment of outside observers, this love triangle exists harmoniously right up until the artist's death, and at his funeral both wife and mistress—like Leah and Rachel in the Book of Genesis—stand at the coffin. Afterward, Sonechka, again engrossed in reading, remains on good terms with Iasia, who marries a well-off Frenchman.

Ulitskaya's Sonechka resembles all the Sonechkas in Russian literature—beginning with Fyodor Dostoevsky's characters—in that she is kind and magnanimous. Endowed with a simple and expansive view of life, she knows that what is important to her is that she loves: she accepts her treatment by others, including her loved ones, as it comes and does not aspire to anything more. Because of Sonechka's worldview, which gives her much wisdom, she does not lose her sense of self to external sufferings; she preserves her full, tranquil inner life in the face of all adversity.

The *povest'* was short-listed for the Booker Russian Novel Prize in 1993 and garnered three awards for best translated novel—the Medici Prize in France in 1995, as well as the Penne Prize (1997) and the Giuseppe Acerbi Literary Award (1998) in Italy. In 2002 "Sonechka" was presented as a play, directed by Marina Brusnikina, at the Moscow Art Theater named after Anton Pavlovich Chekhov, also known as the MkhT.

"Doch' Bukhary" is based, though in a modified way, on the popular motif of the "spouse-nanny." A major from a medical unit brings home a beautiful Eastern war bride named Alechka, to whom the neighbors give the nickname Bukhara. The meek Alechka is from a refined Uzbek family of academics and was raised in the traditions of Eastern obedience. She quietly joins the family of Russian doctors and gives birth to a daughter named Milochka, who has Down's syndrome. The birth of the afflicted girl immediately causes the family to fall apart, and the mother raises her daughter alone. After

Bukhara becomes terminally ill, she uses her knowledge of certain medicines to prolong her life by six years so that she can secure her daughter's future. Before dying, she sends her daughter to learn a simple craft and finds her a similarly disabled, quiet husband.

Ulitskaya herself has said in a 1991 interview with the magazine *Stolitsa* (The Capital) that she wanted to show "the remote provinces of life," where the "lofty movements of the soul" are revealed through "absolutely mundane acts. . . . Bukhara arranges her daughter's life as if she's choreographing the girl's fate from beyond the grave." The people "outside our social consciousness: the sick, the elderly, the disabled, the insane," contends Ulitskaya, have their own lives, in which they find room for happiness, selflessness, and depth of feeling.

These and subsequent stories earned Ulitskaya a reputation among critics as a formidable fiction writer with an affinity for "neo-sentimentalism," as Mikhail Naftal'evich Zolotonosov wrote in *Moskovskie novosti* (Moscow News, 1993), and for "artistic paraphrase," as described by Alla Kuzicheva in her contribution to *Knizhnoe obozrenie* (The Book Review, 1993). She became known as an author who pays attention to details and is skilled at constructing plots that hold the reader's attention. The harshest critics, such as Efim Liamport in *Nezavisimaia gazeta* (The Independent Gazette, 1993), labeled her works "literature for housewives" because of her penchant for melodramatic situations and tranquil endings.

As can be seen from Ulitskaya's first published works, she likes to depict her characters' life histories, and one of her central themes is the common fates shared by characters belonging to the same family. Not by accident are Ulitskaya's next works–*Medeia i ee deti* (1996; translated as *Medea and Her Children*, 2002), *Veselye pokhorony* (1998; translated as *The Funeral Party,* 1999), and *Puteshestvie v sed'muiu storonu sveta* (Journey to the Seventh Side of the World, 2000) (also known as *Kazus Kukotskogo* [The Kukotsky Case, 2000] in book form)–situational sociopsychological novels in which the biographies of the members of a single family (and the people associated with them) are played out against the background of historical realia. Ulitskaya rejects linear chronology; while on the whole the narrative moves from the past to the future, from the characters' births to their deaths, there is also constant retrospection in the form of prehistories for newly introduced characters. Social and political events–history on a large scale–are invariably placed on the periphery of the narrative, while the center is occupied by psychological portraits of the characters, who are engrossed mostly in their own private problems. Ulitskaya invariably affirms in her fiction the significance of the "private" lives of people who for a variety of reasons (such as conscious escapism, mental illness, or

Paperback cover for the 1998 English-language edition of a collection of short fiction by Ulitskaya (Thomas Cooper Library, University of South Carolina)

domestic circumstances) do not take active roles in shaping the world, although they exist within it, adapting it to their daily needs and themselves adapting to the world.

The novel *Medeia i ee deti,* short-listed for the Booker Russian Novel Prize in 1997 and similar to Ulitskaya's previous works because of its "transparent, tireless, compact narrative," as Mikhail Karapetian wrote in his 1998 review in *Kul'tura* (Culture), tells the story of a Greek woman, Medeia Sinopli, and her relatives, who have been scattered across the globe by time and history. The thirteen Sinopli siblings were adopted by various relatives after their father's death in 1916: some ended up in Tbilisi, some in Marseilles, and some in Vilnius. Two brothers died in the Russian Civil War and two in World War II; one became an elder at a Mount Athos monastery; and one sister, Aleksandra, settled in Moscow, while two others, Anel'ia and Anastasiia, went to live in Tbilisi. Medeia settled in the Crimea and has lived her whole life there. She and her husband never had children of their own, but every year their home serves as a place of reunion for her siblings, nephews, nieces, grandnephews, grandnieces, and their various offspring and houseguests from Tbilisi, Moscow, and Lithuania. The degree of familial relations between them all is at times hard to determine, but they consider themselves members of a single clan, at the center of which is Medeia, a physician's assistant who has spent her whole career in one local hospital and is long set in her simple ways. She might appear to be of little interest to the younger members of the family, but they consider the contact with her to be restorative and respect her as the personification of family unity—of the clan's inexplicable strength—although many of them no longer have the surname Sinopli. Medeia is pious, reserved, smart, and observant. Her guiding principle is that "intelligence makes up for any shortcoming," and she makes penetrating, but nonjudgmental, observations about her relatives that do not interfere with her sincere love for them. She is strict in her own behavior but forgives her younger sister Sandrochka, who has flitted from one man to another her whole life, even when Sandrochka has an affair with Medeia's own husband. Readers were struck by the impeccably positive character of the heroine, whom Sandrochka calls a righteous woman and who was compared by the critic Leonid Bakhnov, in his 1996 article for *Druzhba narodov* (The People's Friendship), to the character of Matrena in Aleksandr Isaevich Solzhenitsyn's "Matrenin dvor" (1962; translated as "Matryona's Home," 1962).

The external bonds between Medeia's extended and scattered family members depend on their nearly obligatory gatherings in the Crimea during spring and summer vacations. Ulitskaya underscores the profound internal kinship of the family, which remains intact even though members might not see each other for decades. Medeia has inherited from her ancestors, and transmits to their descendants, a distinctive spiritual aristocratism, an inner freedom, as well as an inner drive to follow one's natural, innate destiny—be it the gift of a kind soul, poetic talent, or sense of humor—and to recognize the right of others to follow their own natural destinies. This deep self-respect helps the characters withstand the most delicate life situations with dignity. For example, Nika and Masha—aunt and niece, respectively, of the same age—become involved with the same man, and Georgii, who lives with his family in Medeia's house after her death, discovers that Medeia has willed her property to a Tatar family whom he does not know. But all such situations in the Sinopli family are resolved without inflicting moral injuries on anyone. Medeia and her children recognize the rights of others and are prepared to make any necessary sacrifices. Their attitude ultimately proves successful: relationships are preserved, or a new home is built. The characters' willingness to be themselves even helps them survive the onslaught of history—wars, revolutions, and emigration—although on the surface the temporal bonds appear almost broken (the old and young members of the family dress differently, express their opinions differently, and are interested in different things). Yet, in the end people do not change much with the years: they all love their children and are internally prepared for whatever creative work might present itself. The long span of time portrayed in the novel helps underscore the constancy and harmony of human nature that shows through external changes in society.

Ulitskaya has said more than once in various interviews that "the values of private life are more significant and vital than the values of one's inner world," that the space occupied by private life "is the space of women's life," and that the central image of her work is "the image of a large family, of large problems that are solved within a small circle of people." This focus of Ulitskaya's works has led some critics, such as Liamport and Pavel Basinsky, to classify her as an author of so-called pedestrian fiction that focuses on the problems of everyday life with its private loves and domestic troubles. Others, including Ol'ga Slavnikova and Aleksandr Vial'tsev, have insisted that Ulitskaya is a writer of serious literature. Vial'tsev argues that *Medeia i ee deti* is "the largest step in recent years in the direction of the classic Russian novel," and that her works are "contemporary saints' lives against a backdrop of a humanity mired in passion and lechery and free from the fear of life."

The novel *Veselye pokhorony* depicts the last days of a happy, intelligent man named Abram (better known as Alik), a talented, if not overly successful, artist who emigrated from the Soviet Union. He is surrounded by various people who once loved him, who love him still, or who simply want to help him: his former wife and current wife; his mistress; a female doctor from Byelorussia; a female translator from Rome; a local Orthodox parish priest; an Israeli rabbi teaching Judaism in the United States; musicians from Latin America who sing outside the dying man's window; a teenage girl; and a female engineer from Moscow who has gravitated to the Russian-speaking community. Although the novel takes place in August 1991 during the coup that preceded the collapse of the Soviet Union, it includes flashbacks to the characters' pasts, showing how they are linked—either directly or indirectly—by love or friendship to the dying master of the house. Alik has a talent for making people happy, and everyone gratefully shows him their best side. He is such a luminous figure that even his tortuous death ceases to be terrible, transforming his last days into a series of meetings and a demonstration of fine human motives and qualities. In service to the dying man, people who are seemingly incompatible are united: wives and mistress; clergy of different religions; the successful and the unsuccessful; and the rich and the poor. Even after his death Alik finds a kind word for everyone. Displaying his extraordinary inner freedom in a videotaped speech that is viewed at his wake, he gives his blessing for the future lives of his loved ones, near and far, and after the funeral new bonds are formed between the living characters.

The concept of the other—someone of a different nationality, age, or psychology—is important to Ulitskaya, and in *Veselye pokhorony* she shows how, faced with the death of a good person, people are capable of overcoming class, religious, and gender stereotypes and of demonstrating their commonality. Although the narrative is fraught with internal drama, born of the presence of death and the diversity of the characters, conflict fades away and is resolved in universal reconciliation—the temporary nature of which, incidentally, is hinted at in the concluding dialogue between Alik's former wife and their daughter. Critics considered *Veselye pokhorony* a partial success, noting, on the one hand, its meaningful depiction of death as a part of life and thus as something not hostile to human beings and, on the other, its flawed composition, according to Slavnikova in her 1999 contribution to the journal *Ural,* and its naturalism, as seen in Vadim Iuzbashev's 1998 article for *Znamia* (The Banner).

In the novel *Kazus Kukotskogo* the historicism that characterizes Ulitskaya's artistic thinking is even more apparent. Awarded the Smirnoff/Booker Prize (formerly the Booker Russian Novel Prize) for the best novel of 2001, it is constructed around the family history of the Kukotskys. The head of the family, Pavel Andreevich, is a gynecologist who comes from a long line of doctors in the family. During World War II he became a member of the prestigious Academy of Science, and his high position obligates him to be not only a private person but also a public figure. He attempts to influence the course of Soviet state politics by proposing a project for the organizational reform of Soviet obstetric and gynecological services. His best friend, the geneticist Il'ia Iosifovich Gol'dberg, is in constant, active opposition to the Soviet regime—thanks to his profession as well as his hot temper—and as a result has spent much of his life in exile or in prison camps. A public figure is not necessarily a person who must think from the perspective of the state but, rather, anyone who thinks about the good of humanity and who makes efforts toward the achievement of that good. Both Kukotsky and Gol'dberg argue over the philosophy of the state, about its future paths, and about ways to communicate with it, but the characters' ideas about government are partially put into practice only many years later by others who do not have a clue as to who first proposed the measures they now are taking. The ideas produced by the protagonists grow and bear

Front cover for Ulitskaya's 1996 novel, Medeia i ee deti *(translated as* Medea and Her Children, *2002), about a Greek woman and her large, scattered family (Jean and Alexander Heard Library, Vanderbilt University)*

fruit after they themselves have already lost interest in them. Thus, historical circumstances in the novel cease to be a mere backdrop, and the characters' fates are not simply linked to whatever phase the regime happens to be in. Kukotsky and Gol'dberg try to influence events, and in the end each of them in some way succeeds in achieving what he wanted. Yet, in Ulitskaya's fiction, forms of government manifest themselves primarily via private life. The upheavals in the family lives of Kukotsky, Gol'dberg, and their children—Tania, Kukotsky's daughter, and Gol'dberg's two sons—reflect the history of the country: times of hunger and times of bounty; favorite books and movies; the organization of everyday routines, fashions, and a system to define the permissible and the forbidden, all of which, directly or indirectly, influence the life of every person living in the here and now.

Ulitskaya underscores in the novel, however, not only the historicity but also the metaphysical nature of

Front cover for Ulitskaya's Veselye pokhorony *(1998; translated as* The Funeral Party, *1999), a novel about the final days of a Soviet émigré artist (Jean and Alexander Heard Library, Vanderbilt University)*

general circular movement of humanity in search of a beautiful melody formed from passion, suffering, and goodness. Elena senses the significance of the dream, although she cannot interpret its symbolism, and she remains in the dream world. This world, like Gol'dberg's scandals, Kukotsky's drunkenness, and Tania's deviations from the ingrained traditions of her family, enables Elena to escape her oppressive reality.

Despite the dramatic events of the novel, its pathos is undeniably optimistic, and it is an optimism of universal scope. Ulitskaya operates on the premise that the world is basically constructed in a rational and delicate way, although human beings are never able to grasp fully the essential duality (the delicate spirituality and the rational corporeality) of the world. Her characters perceive the corporeality of the world as a blueprint (Elena), as an endless reproduction of people like ourselves (Kukotsky), or as the play of genes (Gol'dberg). But they also sense a certain inexpressible essence, which appears to Elena in a prophetic dream-parable; to Kukotsky in his clairvoyance and his thoughts on the mutual links between the cosmos and conception; and to Gol'dberg in his insights into the laws of genetics, which is incarnated in the earnest prayers of the illiterate Vasilisa, compiled by her from the fragments of psalms that she knows. Despite the inexpressibility of this thought, it penetrates the characters' lives, which may develop through evolution or revolution, either progressively or regressively, but always from one good to the next. No historic cataclysms prevent Kukotsky from sending money and packages to the needy, and the drunkenness that he cultivates in himself as a means of escaping the unbearable circumstances of his existence does not prevent him from being a fine doctor or a brilliant, profound man. Nor is Gol'dberg prevented from energetically and emotionally asserting his own innocence, thereby paradoxically saving himself from even harsher punishment on the part of the public and earning him political capital as a dissident.

Even when the whole world appears on the verge of collapse (loved ones are dying, freedoms are being taken away, and work no longer holds interest), Ulitskaya's characters do not lose their dignity. Indifferent to material values, they are tidy inside and out and honest to themselves and others—however strange their behavior may be (as exemplified by Tania's crisis, her parents' internal family dramas, and the strange relationship between Tania and the Gol'dberg brothers). Ulitskaya suggests that this basic principle of self-respect is what holds the world together. Even secondary characters and characters who at first glance are morally dubious (such as the ballerina Poluektova, for whom everyone has contempt) behave impeccably at critical moments: Poluektova takes care of her former husband when he becomes a widower, and the

private life, represented in her previous texts by references to mythological images such as Eden, Leah and Rachel, and Medea. These references move the plots and characters beyond the frame of their specific historical times and places them into a world of existential universals. The central moment of *Kazus Kukotskogo* is the description of Elena's dream. Like many of Ulitskaya's characters, Elena goes mad, but her incisive husband perceives in her insanity a defense mechanism against the surrounding world and a vision of a future with which she does not want to cope. The dream that initiates Elena's madness is manifested as an allegorical portrait of the current real-life drama she is experiencing (the suppression of what is pure and sincere in the self by a hard layer of unnecessary obligations and prejudices) and of a future tragedy in her family (the death of her daughter). The allegorical dream is also a portrait of the

gesture earns her the lasting respect of the general who plans to marry her. Goodness spawns goodness, and evil is a transient force in a world where there are no national borders (questions of nationality are of no interest to the characters), the provincial blends with the urban, different generations find unexpected points of contact, and a high value is placed on creativity and professionalism.

Kazus Kukotskogo caused little discussion among critics following its journal publication. When the novel was awarded the Smirnoff/Booker Prize in 2001, however, some critics expressed indignation because the prize committee was honoring a work of such lowbrow content. Others reviewers, among them Galina Ermoshina, supported this choice and viewed it as way of closing the gap between "high" and "low" literature.

The short stories and novellas published since *Kazus Kukotskogo*—*Tsiu-iurikh* (2002) "Vtoroe litso," (The Second Face, 2002), and "Skvoznaia liniia" (The Through Line, 2003)—have been largely ignored by the critics. Possibly, a new novel is expected from Ulitskaya, and these smaller texts could be perceived as a "warming-up" for a more significant work. In these shorter pieces Ulitskaya continues to explore the world of Russian emigration and the vast theme of Russians abroad. She introduces a new theme, however, with the presentation of deception as a creative force in the routine of life. The false tales of the heroine of "Vtoroe litso" may sound terrifying (she lies about the deaths of her children), yet by these fantasies she manages to transform her mundane reality into a kind of modernist (tragic and subverted) literary work.

Many critics characterize the pathos of Lyudmila Ulitskaya's prose using Bunin's metaphor *legkoe dykhanie* (light breathing). Despite the dramatic and tragic circumstances depicted, her works are devoid of sudden shocks: death, illness, separation, and betrayal are valuable parts of life, and the characters who live that life are, in the words of Karapetian, "deep-down good people, with God in their hearts, but on the surface quite sinful, even excessively so" (*Kul'tura*, 1998). The ruin wrought by time cannot break the bonds of love and goodness; these central themes of Ulitskaya's work are amazingly resonant in the consciousness of a society in search of something on which to rely, as Ulitskaya says in an interview with Anastasia Gosteva: "life is full of precious gems, of feats of love . . . We're living in a time of monstrous demolition, but there are fundamental values that cannot be destroyed."

Interviews:

E. Gushchina, "'Ia pishu v shkaf': beseda s pisatel'nitsoi L. Ulitskoi," *Stolitsa*, 46–47 (1991): 118–119;

M. Riurikova, "Mne interesna zhizn' 'serykh' liudei," *Literaturnaia gazeta*, 20 September 1995, p. 3;

V. Amurskaia, "Moi dom – moia krepost'," *Moskovskie novosti*, 21 February 1996, p. 36;

Amurskaia, "Literatura proiskhodit iz zhizni . . . ," *Russkaia mysl'*, 16 April 1996, p. 16;

Anastasia Gosteva, "Prinimaju vs'o, chto daets'a," *Voprosy literatury*, 1 (2000);

I. Tsiporkina, "Tvorets znal, chto delal," *Knizhnoe obozrenie*, 33 (14 August 2000).

References:

Leonid Bakhnov, "Genio loci," *Druzhba narodov*, 8 (1996): 178–180;

Pavel Basinsky, "Nesvarenie dushi," *Literaturnaia gazeta*, 24 September 1997, p. 3;

Galina Ermoshina, "Forma bor'by so vremenem—pechal'nai popytka ego unichtozheniia," *Znamia*, 12 (2002): 201–203;

Vadim Iuzbashev, "Parallel'naia literatura," *Znamia*, 11 (1998): 221–222;

Mikhail Karapetian, "Aristokraty dukha, brazhniki i bludnitsy: 'Legkoe dykhanie' geroev L. Ulitskoi," *Kul'tura*, 23–29 July 1998, p. 10;

T. Kazarina, "Bednye rodstvenniki," *Preobrazhenie*, 4 (1996): 169–171;

C. Keller, "Die kinderlose Medea und das geloschte Itedachtnis," *Weltwoche*, 29 (1977): 41;

Alla Kuzicheva, "V spiskakh zhachitsia . . . 'Vechnaia Sonechka'?" *Knizhnoe obozrenie*, 50 (1993): 13;

Efim Liamport, "10 000 funtov likha," *Nezavisimaia gazeta*, 12 August 1993, p. 8;

Tatiana Morozova, "Rezh' da esh': O romane L. Ulitskoi 'Medeia i ee deti'," *Literaturnaia gazeta*, 19 June 1996, p. 4;

Christina Parnell, "Hiding and Using Sexuality: The Artist's Controversial Subject in Modern Russian Women's Literature," in *Gender and Sexuality in Russian Civilization*, edited by Peter Barta (London: Routledge, 2002), pp. 311–324;

D. Savostin, "Vek-volkodav po Liudmile Ulitskoi," *Delovoi mir*, 13 February 1997, p. 6;

Ol'ga Slavnikova, "Nedolet ukazyvaet na tsel'," *Ural*, 2 (1999): 183–186;

Aleksandr Vial'tsev, "Nezamyslovatye zhitiia sovremennykh sviatykh: L. Ulitskaia i ee kritiki," *Literaturnaia gazeta*, 4 March 1998, p. 11;

Mikhail Naftal'evich Zolotonosov, "Chuvstvovat' s pristavkoi 'neo'," *Moskovskie novosti*, 10 February 1993), p. 5B.

Petr L'vovich Vail'

(29 September 1949 –   )

and

Aleksandr Aleksandrovich Genis

(11 February 1953 –   )

Ivan Tolstoi
Radio Free Europe/Radio Liberty

(Translated by Andrei Tolstoi)

BOOKS (BY VAIL'): *Genii mesta,* with an afterword by Lev Losev (Moscow: Nezavisimaia gazeta, 1999); *Karta Rodiny* (Moscow: Nezavisimaia gazeta, 2003).

OTHER (BY VAIL'): Joseph Brodsky, *Rozhdestvenskie stikhi; Rozhdetstvo: Tochka otscheta: Beseda s Petrom Vailem,* compiled, with an afterword, by Vail' (Moscow: Nezavisimaia gazeta, 1992; enlarged, 1996);

Brodsky, *Peresechennaia mestnost': Puteshestviia s kommentariiami,* compiled, with an afterword, by Vail' (Moscow: Nezavisimaia gazeta, 1995);

"Bez Dovlatova," in *Maloizvestnyi Dovlatov,* edited by Andrei Ar'ev (St. Petersburg: Zvezda, 1995), pp. 451–464;

"Professiia: Navigator," in Boris Grebenshchikov, *Sobranie sochinenii v 2-kh tomakh* (Tver': LEAN, 1997), I: 4–6;

"Rifma Brodskogo," "Vsled za Pushkinym," "Stikhi riadom s molokom i aspirinom," and "Poety s imperskikh okrain," in *Iosif Brodsky: Trudy i Dni,* edited by Vail' and Lev Losev (Moscow: Nezavisimaia gazeta, 1998), pp. 5–9, 24–28, 67–79, and 248–255;

"Poslednee Stikhotvorenie Iosifa Brodskogo," in *Iosif Brodsky: Tvorchestvo, lichnost', sud'ba* (St. Petersburg: Zvezda, 1998), pp. 3–5;

"Formula liubvi," in *Sergei Dovlatov: Tvorchestvo, lichnost', sud'ba,* edited by Ar'ev (St. Petersburg: Zvezda, 1999), pp. 183–186;

"Veselyi Stol," in *Kukhnia veka,* by Vil'iam Vasil'evich Pokhlebkin (Moscow: Polifakt, 2000), pp. 7–8.

BOOKS (BY GENIS): *Amerikanskaia azbuka* (Tenafly, N.J.: Hermitage, 1994; Ekatinburg: Izdatel' stvo Ural'skogo Universiteta / St. Petersburg: Letnii Sad, 2000);

Vavilonskaia bashnia: Iskusstvo nastoiashchego vremeni (Tallinn: Aleksandra, 1996; Moscow: Nezavisimaia gazeta, 1997)–includes *Khorovod;*

Portrait of the Poet. Joseph Brodsky 1978–1996, with a preface by Lev Losev and photographs by Marianna Volkov (New York: Slovo, 1998);

Temnota i tishina: Iskusstvo vychitaniia, with illustrations by Aleksandr Zakharov (St. Petersburg: Pushkinskii fond, 1998);

Dovlatov i okrestnosti (Moscow: Vagrius, 1999)–includes *Dovlatov i okrestnosti: Filologicheskii roman, Brodskii v New Yorke,* and *Temnota i tishina;*

Ivan Petrovich umer: Stat'i i rassledovaniia, with an introduction by Mikhail Naumovich Epshtein (Moscow: Novoe literaturnoe obozrenie, 1999)–includes selected bibliography;

Bilet v Kitai (St. Petersburg: Amfora/Evrika, 2001)–includes translations of Leo Tolstoy's works;

Peizazhi (St. Petersburg: Pushkinskii fond, 2002);

Trikotazh (St. Petersburg: Ivan Limbakh, 2002).

Collection: *Raz! Dva! Tri!* with a foreword by Tatyana Tolstaya (Moscow: Podkova/EKSMO, 2002)–comprises volume 1, *Kul'turologiia;* volume 2, *Rassledovaniia;* and volume 3, *Lichnoe.*

Editions in English: *Russian Postmodernism: New Perspectives on Post-Soviet Culture,* by Genis, Mikhail Naumovich, Epshtein, and Slobodanka Vladiv-Glover (New York & Oxford: Berghahn, 1999);

Petr L'vovich Vail' (from the dust jacket for Genii mesta, *1999; Collection of Mark Lipovetsky)*
and Aleksandr Aleksandrovich Genis (courtesy of the author)

Red Bread (Chicago: Ivan R. Dee, 2000)–includes "USA from A to Y" and "Darkness and Silence: The Art of Subtraction."

OTHER (BY GENIS): "Na urovne prostoty," in *Maloizvestnyi Dovlatov,* edited by Andrei Ar'ev (St. Petersburg: Zvezda, 1995), pp. 465–473.

SELECTED PERIODICAL PUBLICATIONS (BY GENIS)–UNCOLLECTED: "Khleb i zrelishche," *Zvezda,* no. 1 (2000);
"Modernizm kak stil' dvadtsatogo veka," *Zvezda,* no. 11 (2002).

BOOKS (BY VAIL' AND GENIS): *Sovremennaia russkaia proza,* with an introduction by Paul Debreczeny (Ann Arbor, Mich.: Ermitazh, 1982);
Poteriannyi rai: Emigratsiia: Popytka avtoportreta (Ramat Gan: Moskva-Ierusalim, 1983);
Russkaia kukhnia v izgnanii, with an introduction by Lev Losev (Los Angeles: Almanac, 1987; Moscow: PIK, 1990);
60-e: Mir sovetskogo cheloveka (Ann Arbor, Mich.: Ardis, 1988; with an afterword by Lev Anninsky, Moscow: Novoe literaturnoe obozrenie, 1996);
Rodnaia rech', with an introduction by Andrei Donatovich Siniavsky (Tenafly, N.J.: Ermitazh, 1990; Moscow: Nezavisimaia gazeta, 1991); revised as *Rodnaia rech': Uroki iziashchnoi slovesnosti* (Moscow: Nezavisimaia gazeta, 1995; revised again, 1999);

Amerikana, with an introduction by Ol'ga Timofeeva (Moscow: Slovo, 1991).
Editions: *60-e: Mir sovetskogo cheloveka* (Moscow: Novoe literaturnoe obozrenie, 1998);
60-e: Mir sovetskogo cheloveka (Moscow: Novoe literaturnoe obozrenie, 2001).

SELECTED PERIODICAL PUBLICATIONS (BY VAIL' AND GENIS)–UNCOLLECTED: "Na avrale: Pisateli i mir," *Vremia i my,* no. 31 (1978);
"Shampanskoe i politura," *Vremia i my,* no. 36 (1978);
"V poiskakh utrachennykh istin," *Tret'ia volna,* no. 5, (1979);
"Metropol'naia kultura," *Ekho,* nos. 2–3 (1979);
"Literaturnye parodii," *Ekho,* nos. 2–3 (1979);
"Kubiki Maramzina," *Tret'ia volna,* no. 6 (1979);
"My – s Braiton Bich," *Vremia i my,* no. 40 (1979);
"Zagovor protiv chuvstv: Besedy s Zinov'evym," *Kontinent,* no. 24 (1980);
"Razgrom: Istoriia emigratsii pisatelia Aksenova, avtora romana *Ozhog,*" *Grani,* no. 61 (1981);
"Skazki o Germanii: Iz knigi *Okno v Evropu,*" *Grani,* no. 137 (1985);
"Printsip matreshki," *Novyi mir,* no. 10 (1989);
"Gorodok v tabakerke: Tatiana Tolstaia," *Zvezda,* no. 8 (1990);
"Otrazhenie v Samovare: Alexei German," *Teatral'naia zhizn',* no. 6 (1992);
"Uroki shkoly dlia durakov," *Literaturnoe obozrenie,* nos. 1–2 (1993).

Petr Vail' and Aleksandr Genis, who started out as journalists in their native Latvia, pioneered a brand of writing that came to be known as "essayism," a specific genre combining a lyrical style with methods used in cultural studies. The writer Sergei Donatovich Dovlatov, who was a close friend and colleague to Vail' and Genis, described them as "perhaps, the only writers in emigration that concentrated almost exclusively on essayism. Therefore one can only judge them as writers using the criteria applicable to essayism, while not forgetting the qualities that are typical for this genre—the originality of judgment, fluidity, and humor. In their work, they have incorporated traits that are very typical for the Western and American tradition of quality—wordplay, wit, and precision." Yet, Dovlatov did not foresee in the pair's witty style a natural striving for the independence that eventually led them away from literary criticism and the interpretation of the works of others to their own original writings. Having started their careers by exploring worlds created by other writers, Vail' and Genis came to find worlds of their own when, in 1976, while still living in the U.S.S.R., they began to write original works together. Later, after emigrating, they acquired a prestigious reputation in New York. In 1990, after their works began getting published in the Soviet Union during the era of perestroika, they decided to part ways and develop individual perspectives and styles. Both consider the experiment of working autonomously to be a successful one. According to Vail' in a 1999 interview with Ivan Tolstoi, "One author became three."

Petr L'vovich Vail' was born in Riga, Latvia, on 29 September 1949. His father, Lev Maksimovich, was an engineer, and his mother, Vera Mikhailovna, was a surgeon. In 1976 he completed his studies, by correspondence, in the editorial department of the Moskovskii Poligraficheskii Institut (The Moscow Polygraphical Institute), where he had worked since 1972. By this time he had been contributing regularly to the Riga edition of the newspaper Sovetskaia molodezh (Soviet Youth), subsequently becoming its executive secretary until he was fired in 1977 for "ideological disparity." The following year Vail' immigrated to the United States, passing through Vienna and Rome before landing finally in New York.

Aleksandr Aleksandrovich Genis was born in Ryazan' on 11 February 1953. Genis's father, Aleksandr Arkad'evich Genis, was a professor of computer science, and his mother, Angelina Filippovna (née Buzinova), was an engineer. (Both of his parents now live in the United States.) He completed a course in Russian philology at the Latviiskii gosudarstvennii universitet (Latvian State University). His first published work—"Svetlyi Sever" (The Bright North), an essay about

Solovki, an island in the White Sea, where a fifteenth-century Russian Orthodox monastery was converted into a gulag—appeared in Sovetskaia molodezh in 1970. Genis married his fellow student Trina Veniaminovna (née Sergeeva) in 1973; they have one son, Daniel (born 1978), who was born in the United States. Genis contributed to the weekly newspaper Rigas Vilni (Riga's [Air] Waves) and the samizdat magazine Evreiskaia mysl' (Jewish Thought) before immigrating to the United States in 1977, one year before the arrival of Vail'.

The first piece that Vail' and Genis co-authored was a review of Valerii Georgievich Popov's short-story collection Normal'nyi khod (The Normal Flow, 1976), published in Sovetskayia molodezh (Soviet Youth) the same year as Popov's book, shortly before their emigration. Once both Vail' and Genis were in New York, they collaborated again and produced essays, reviews, and critiques on Soviet cinematography, literature, and other aspects of Soviet cultural life. Their work appeared initially in Novoe russkoe slovo (The New Russian Word), a Russian-language daily newspaper published in New York City, and later in Tret'ia volna (The Third Wave), Kontinent (The Continent), Ekho (The Echo), and Vremia i my (Time and Us), where their best-known article, "My – s Braiton Bich" (We Are From Brighton Beach), was published in 1979. This article expressed the basic principles of the émigré life that Vail' and Genis were leading, whereby the concept of "Brighton Beach" (a neighborhood in Brooklyn, New York, where many Soviet émigrés settled upon their arrival in the United States) was broadly interpreted as an idea of freedom undefined by religious, intellectual, or civic currents. Thus, from the authors' point of view, their "first Brighton Beach" had been Ostia, Italy, a place dating back to ancient Rome; in the 1980s Ostia was the site of a busy Soviet Jewish refugee resettlement site. In a piece for Krug (The Circle) in 1979, however, G. Mordel', an Israeli journalist, denied the claims of freedom made by Vail' and Genis in their article and denounced "My – s Braiton Bich": "We are really worrying because of our government's political and economic mistakes. . . . The inhabitants of Brighton Beach will always remain alien in America, and alien to us. Meanwhile, we're talking about Jewish feelings. Using the same Russian language we're talking in different languages. This is evident from Vail' and Genis's article."

Since their first publications, when discussing literature Vail' and Genis, writing in their article "Metropol'naia Kultura" (Metropolitan Culture) (Ekho, 1979) developed the idea of a fertile "third" cultural power—the aesthetic samizdat that was opposed equally to Soviet and anti-Soviet dissident literature: "Balancing under the censor's vigilant eye is not just a technical trick, it's the author's conduct, moreover his style, and even more than that—often a view of the world. It is some sort of Archimedes's law of censure: pressuring content. Nevertheless, the essence brings the diversity of artistic form to the surface of literature, and the form itself turns into the protesting essence." Yet, when their uncensored almanac, *Metropol'* (Metropolis), appeared in samizdat in the Soviet Union from 1979 to 1980, the critics started to question their favorite concept: the fertile "third" cultural power. *Metropol'* "wanted to claim the existence of a special 'third culture' [a nonpolitical underground]—not one based on lies like the first [an official power], and not so intimidating to the supremacy like the second [a highly political underground]. We have to admit: this didn't work—neither in terms of literature, nor tactics. The literature in *Metropol'* undergoes a common literary trial, and its authors have already begun to encounter common Soviet troubles—threats, lectures from the supremacy, and expulsions," as they wrote in "Metropol'nia Kultura."

The search for an unengaged literary path brought Vail' and Genis closer to the perspective of Dovlatov, the editor in chief of the weekly newspaper *Novyi amerikanets* (The New American), where the duo was offered a job in 1980. Approximately 170 of their works were published in *Novyi amerikanets*—under their own names as well as under pseudonyms, which included Andrei Dvinsky, Efim Vishniakov, Yurii Avgustinsky, Vitalii Kogan, Mikhail Bernovich, Vladimir Shifrin, S. Zapolskaia, Richard Sheikin, Ar'e Zamir, Gennadii Snegin, and Vitalii Borovitsky. (Before 1988 Vail' and Genis signed all of their works as coauthored, even if only one of them had written the work.) *Novyi amerikanets* folded in 1983, at which point Vail' and Genis began editing *Sem' dnei* (Seven Days), a weekly magazine. A year later the pair additionally began working freelance for Radio Liberty. For *Sem' dnei* the pair wrote on topics as diverse as émigré literature, a New Year's celebration in Brazil, the author George Orwell, the city of New York, crime in the United States, and their travels in Japan and Yeti. Two of their regular features for the magazine were a "Khronika" (Chronicle) and an historical calendar. When *Sem' dnei* ceased operations because of funding problems, Vail' and Genis began work as columnists for *Panorama*. From 1985 to 1992 they co-authored more than 350 articles for *Panorama*, including the rubric titles "Pis'ma s Beregov Gudzona" (Letters From the Banks of the Hudson River), "New Iorkskii Reportazh" (The New York Report), and "Manhettenskie Zapiski" (Manhattan Notes), some of which were collected in *Amerikana* (Americana, 1991), as well as chapters that appeared later in their books *Russkaia kukhnia v izgnanii* (Russian Cuisine in Exile, 1987), *Rodnaia rech'* (Mother Tongue, 1990), and *Amerikana*. Several times they also

tried writing fiction together. Such pieces include "Roundtrip: Kinopovest' ob emigrantakh" (Roundtrip: A Cinematic Novella on Emigrants); "Literaturnye Parodii" (Literary Parodies) on Dovlatov, Aleksandr Zinov'ev, Iurii Mamleev, and Eduard Limonov, both of which were published in *Sem' dnei;* and satirical poetry, such as that published in *Tret'ia volna* under the pen name Dvinsky.

The first book on which Vail' and Genis collaborated was *Sovremennaia russkaia proza* (Contemporary Russian Prose, 1982), a compilation of essays dedicated to the "Russian literary decadence of the 1970s," or the "new baroque." For Vail' and Genis, as they make clear in *Sovremennaia russkaia proza*, Russian literature and "ideological systems" in general at that time were in a state of crisis. In such a context, "in the wake of the first uncertain experiments, something begins to surface, something that has come to change the great literature of ideas to a literature of games. . . . Games instead of struggles, fiction instead of truth, rhythm instead of sense, chatting *[poliv]* instead of prose, ornaments instead of reforms, and baroque instead of the natural school. . . ." The closing phrase of this quotation not only predefined the future of Russian literature but also served as a declaration of the pair's personal vision of art—the central theme of their writings for many years to come.

Igor' Efimov, who published *Sovremennaia russkaia proza*, changed its title from the original "Sovetskoe Barokko" (The Soviet Baroque), with which the authors had intended to attract an academic readership; all that was left subsequently from the original design of the book was a painting by Francisco Goya on its cover. *Sovremennaia russkaia proza* includes chapters on Zinov'ev, Aleksandr Isaevich Solzhenitsyn, Fazil' Abdulovich Iskander, Georgii Nikolaevich Vladimov, Venedikt Vasil'evich Erofeev, Vladimir Nikolaevich Voinovich, Andrei Donatovich Siniavsky, and Vasilii Pavlovich Aksenov. It also has a chapter titled "Effekt Populiarnosti" (The Effect of Popularity), which provides a brief overview of the works of *derevenshchiki* (village prose writers), Limonov, Vladimir Emelianovich Maksimov, Yurii Valentinovich Trifonov, the brothers Boris Natanovich Strugatsky and Arkadii Natanovich Strugatsky, Efraim Sevella, Yuz (Iosif Veniminovich) Aleshkovsky, as well as excerpts from the essay "Shampanskoe i politura" (Champagne and Politura, published originally in 1978 in *Vremia i my*), about the actor and singer Vladimir Semenovich Vysotsky. (*Politura* refers to a cheap form of alcohol that is extracted from polishing solutions.) The chapters that close out the book are "Emigrantskaia periodika" (a short survey of the magazines of the "third wave" emigration) and "Literaturnye mechtaniia" (Literary Dreams), in which

Vail' (right) and Genis (center) with Sergei Donatovich Dovlatov in New York City, 1979 (from Maloizvestnyi Dovlatov, *1995; University of Massachusetts, Amherst Libraries)*

the authors show the traits of a new artistic strand of thought, which came to replace the aging forms, through excerpts from the works of contemporary Russian artists such as Dovlatov, Popov, Andrei Georgievich Bitov, and Sasha Sokolov.

In his "Predislovie" (Foreword) to *Sovremennaia russkaia proza* Paul Debreczeny compares Vail' and Genis with famous Russian critics such as Vissarion Grigor'evich Belinsky, Innokentii Fedorovich Annensky, Mikhail Mikhailovich Bakhtin, and Arkadii Viktorovich Belinkov. Debreczeny remarks, "Vail' and Genis don't analyze the content of literature as much as they discuss it. With a lyrical raid, they try to reconstruct the atmosphere of the reviewed piece. Most valuable are those pages in the book where the authors criticize the faults of well-known pieces, because what uncensored literature needs most is an unbiased, and professional, dissection of literary qualities." *Sovremennaia russkaia proza* already showed signs of what was later recognized as the main traits of the co-authors: their comprehensible, fearless humor and their use of aphorisms. Nevertheless, the book was criticized in several reviews. For example, Valerii Golovskoy, writing in 1984 for *The Russian Literature Journal,* did not agree with the postulate ("the main problem of new Russian literature is the

new literary form") put forth by Vail' and Genis and criticized the authors' passion for "literature for literature's sake." Golovskoy regarded their literary analysis as "one-sided" and "entirely aesthetical." According to him, "Vail' and Genis themselves cannot endure this method, quite often descending from the aesthetical heavens to the social, common earth." Although Neil Cornwell in his 1985 contribution to *Irish Slavonic Studies* appreciated the co-authors' terminology describing the nature of artistic prose, he noted their "little heed to recent scholarship—either (whether it exists) Soviet, or western." According to critic John B. Dunlop in his 1983 article for *The Slavic Review,* what Vail' and Genis "have to say about the new 'decadence' is often illuminating and apt. Their enthusiasm for the tendency, however, at times leads them to be less than fair toward the so-called 'realists.'"

Another theme that Vail' and Genis develop in their writings is that of the Stalinist generation and its experiences of emigration from the Soviet Union to the United States. *Poteriannyi rai: Emigratsiia: Popytka avtoportreta* (Paradise Lost: Emigration: An Attempt at Self-portrait, 1983) addresses such a theme. Designed by the well-known conceptualist artist Vagrich Bakhchinan (and including eighteen of his self-portraits), the book depicts a "group picture" of the third-wave emigration. Its chapters are titled "Na smert' slova" (To commemorate the Death of the Word), "Tam" (There), "Vpered na zapad" (Forth to the West), "Etiud v nastoiashchem vremeni" (An Essay in Present Tense), "Golos iz zapovednika" (The Voice from the Wildlife Reserve), "Zdes'" (Here), and "Poteriannyi rai" (Paradise Lost).

In his 1984 review of *Poteriannyi rai* for *Panorama* Grigorii Ryskin wrote that the book resembles an encyclopedia "of here-ish and there-ish life. Its composition is symmetrical: possessions, work, holidays, love, mass culture, language. . . . The authors attempt to answer three questions: who were we, who did we become, and who will we be? To us, the answers are inauspicious, insulting, and ironic. But they are the truth." According to Ryskin, the thesis of *Poteriannyi rai* cannot be understood without alluding to the 1960s as "the short Renaissance," a fragment of time between the Soviet invasion of Hungary (1956) and the Prague uprising (1968), because this period "is when the road to the West began for us, and this is when America came before us." When describing *Poteriannyi rai* as "filled with talent and humanity," he especially praises the sections that concern the destruction of mythological temptations facing many émigrés—mainly those temptations spawned by Judaism and anti-communism. Vail' and Genis show that Soviet émigrés of the 1970s did not, as a whole, turn to any religion or join any political movement. Ryskin argues that for Vail' and Genis, "The purpose of our existence . . . is more important and elevated. . . . We have lost more than we have gained, because delusions are always sweeter than the truth. Geography has come to an end, and a lengthy and complicated science of reconstruction has begun. And there is only one way to go—from a Soviet man to simply a man." Another reviewer, Mark Popovsky, writing in 1986 for *Grani* (Facets), complimented sections of the book in which Vail' and Genis comment on the "social immaturity" of émigrés, yet criticized them for prioritizing their main stylistic traits: "Attempts to use wit on every page, insert a joke in every paragraph . . . Constant jokes and irony to everyone and everything make the reader doubt his trust in the authors."

Russkaia kukhnia v izgnanii, the third book on which Vail' and Genis collaborated, was initially published, chapter by chapter, in *Panorama*. It was the first work of theirs to become extremely popular; despite being published four times already in various periodicals, it was later republished in many Russian and émigré newspapers and magazines. Dispensing practical culinary advice in a humorous presentation, *Russkaia kukhnia v izgnanii* eventually was perceived as a successful guide to life and a psychological "self-help" book (particularly in regard to arrogance and depression).

"Poetika kukhni," the introduction to the book written by literary scholar and poet Lev Losev, is a brief survey of Russian cuisine from the time of the seventeenth-century tsar, Aleksei Mikhailovich, to the modest meals eaten by Solzhenitsyn. At the same time the introduction prepares the reader for a completely different book. Vail' and Genis had not intended to praise famous literary heroes (in the works of Aleksandr Sergeevich Pushkin, Leo Tolstoy, Anton Pavlovich Chekhov, and Nikolai Vasil'evich Gogol) who partake of food but, rather, their own appetite and talent for making soup. In the framework of "how to" books or manuals, they offer new émigrés lessons of patience, curiosity, and creativeness, but the irony of their approach is evident from the start, especially in regard to the design of the book cover, the subtext for which is Gleb Struve's *Russkaia literatura v izgnanii* (Russian Literature in Exile, 1956). The cover for Struve's book has been morphed into a cover of satirical, unemotional dimensions for *Russkaia kukhnia v izgnanii*. In Bakhchinian's cover design, Alenushka, a Russian girl usually depicted in a fairy woodland by painter Viktor Vasnetsov, is crying, sitting on a hamburger as if it were a hassock in her living room.

Despite the great popularity of *Russkaia kukhnia v izgnanii,* however, there are few reviews of it, perhaps owing to the majority of literati who regarded the book as only a collection of recipes; moreover, reviewing a book about food was not popular in Russia. Among the few people who reviewed the book was the poet and essayist Lev Semenovich Rubinshtein. Rather than concentrating on the stylistic qualities of the work, Rubinshtein, writing in *Itogi* (Summing Up), focused on its new "social address." He argued that because people who could afford all of the ingredients mentioned by Vail' and Genis were rather scarce, *Russkaia kukhnia v izgnanii* was generally a book for the "upper class," or nouveau riche Russians. When, in the late 1990s, people found themselves able to afford and buy more and more things, the audience for the book grew immensely. Of the handful of critics who wrote on the book, Ivan Davydov produced the review that was closest to the authors' perspective. Noting that *Russkaia kukhnia v izgnanii* was "more than a cookbook (food in Russia is much more than just food)," Davydov viewed it as a repository of memories, an exploration of culture, and a poem—"not only because a part of the book is poetry, but because the authors are literally extolling food." For example, "In the chapter concerning the crimes of the West against Russian cuisine, Vail' and Genis curse the authors of foreign books about 'good and healthy food.'" Davydov also highlighted the humorous nature of the work, adding that "Besides all that, it is a philosophical composition about the meaning of life."

The fourth book that Vail' and Genis wrote together was a cultural study titled *60-e: Mir sovetskogo cheloveka* (The 1960s: The World of the Soviet Man, 1988). Here they take a step back from *Russkaia kukhnia v izgnanii* and analyze the era that preceded emigration. Vail' and Genis remark that the epoch they describe cannot be confused with the overlapping period of the Thaw, which took place from 1956 to 1964, the years of Nikita Sergeevich Khrushchev's rule. In their opinion the 1960s "began in 1961 with the Twenty-Second Congress of the Communist Party that accepted the program of building communism and ended in 1968 with the occupation of Czechoslovakia, interpreted in the U.S.S.R. as an end to all hopes." In *60-e* Vail' and Genis comment on their approach to the historical subjects: "a rational analysis of modern history is in many cases helpless. Only through the wholesome artistic impression can we capture the rooted, mythological basis of our time."

Efimov, a publisher of previous works by Vail' and Genis, was the first to review *60-e*. Listing the subjects that the authors had avoided, he asked in a review titled "Portret epokhi nariade i z slov," published in *Almanakh Panorama* (Panorama Almanac, 23–30 June 1989), "Where is the ignorance of human rights? Where is the impoverishment of the countryside and the growth of corruption? Where is the demolition of churches and the persecution of the faithful? Where is the governmental anti-Semitism, the Russification of Baltic and Caucasian nations, and the pollution of the environment?" Indeed, Vail' and Genis refrain from discussing these issues out of their preference for investigating the psychology of the 1960s generation. They concentrate on describing only one-tenth of the Soviet people, claiming that the other nine-tenths are unresearchable. The goal that they set for themselves is to re-create the atmosphere of the 1960s—"the customs, the ways of life, the social ideas, and the style of the era." The vision introduced earlier in *Poteriannyi rai* is reemphasized in *60-e:* it is the interrelation between the cult of literature in Russia and the Soviet Union as the manifestation of the Truth, and the psychological phenomenon whereby "the word is the deed."

Disagreeing with this idea, Efimov writes that *60-e* is a book about lingual mythology, or about the mythologization of words and the role that these mutually cooperating phenomena played in the lives of the Soviet people. The authors, however, consciously refuse to approach this subject analytically. Efimov argues that in the view of Vail' and Genis one describes a myth only

by creating its duplicate. *60-e* essentially embodies a myth creation—a retrospective myth that attempts to recapture the colors and harmonies of an era that has passed already. When Vail' and Genis write about contemporary or classical Russian literature, they end up with an artistic narrative dressed up in the costume of literary criticism. When they write about an event or a time period in history, they create a story that reads more like an excerpt from Jonathan Swift's *Gulliver's Travels* (1726) than one from Sergei Mikhailovich Solov'ev's *Istoriia Rossii s drevneishikh vremen* (A History of Russia from Ancient Times, 1854–1858). For this reason, Efimov writes, one cannot judge their books according to the criterion of "right or wrong." The only measures applicable to works by Vail' and Genis are "brighter or paler," "original or banal," and "interesting or monotonous."

Despite Efimov's criticisms, *60-e* received many positive reviews when the book was published in Russia in 1996. Critics such as Linor Goralik and Viacheslav Kuritsyn (1996) commented on the authors' interest in "the semiotics of everyday life," their "masterful wit," and their "imagination and magnificence." Special emphasis was put as well on the structure of the book, which consists of a series of "descriptive analyses, basic concepts, values, and names" that gnawed at the minds of the Soviet people during the 1960s—including "communism, outer space, Cuba, America, romantics, dissidents, bohemians, sport, Solzhenitsyn, Jews, Prague," as Ol'ga Kabanova describes it. Almost all the reviewers of *60-e* noted the elegance of the aphorisms employed by Vail' and Genis, such as "It is easier to live with your sleeves down when you're wearing a sweater, than when you're wearing a jacket"; "People who don't know what they live for are still more acceptable than those who know it for sure"; "At the beginning of the 1960s the question 'Is there a God?' seemed ridiculous when compared to one such as 'Is there life on Mars?'"; and "Instead of the question, 'What is the future of the Soviet Union?' the intelligentsia is more concerned with the question 'What will its past be like?'" In general *60-e* resembled a manual, necessary for the understanding of the mentality of the decade and the upcoming years of Soviet reign and perestroika. The book was published once in the United States and three times in Russia.

Vail' and Genis purposely gave their next joint effort the infantile title of *Rodnaia rech'*, which was what primers in Russian elementary schools were called for more than a hundred years. By this title the authors announce a new approach to their classical heritage—an approach that is not marred by ready-made ideological structures. "Russian literature is a very entertaining subject," Vail' and Genis claim, "and one should speak of it playfully and light-heartily." In

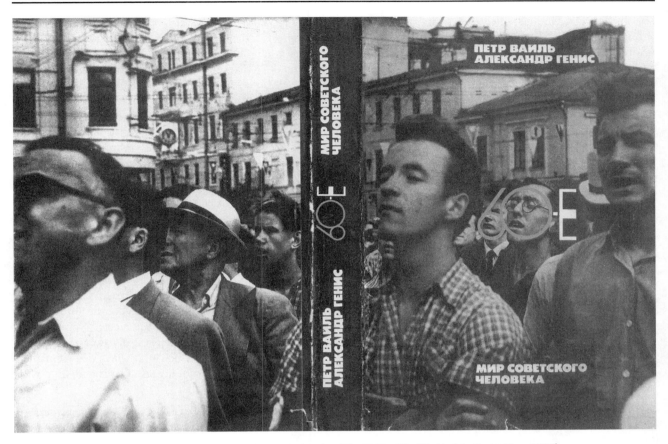

Dust jacket for 60-e: Mir sovetskogo cheloveka *(The 1960s: The World of the Soviet Man, 1988),*
Vail' and Genis's fourth collaboration (Collection of Mark Lipovetsky)

his introduction to *Rodnaia rech'* Andrei Donatovich Siniavsky writes, "This renovation of the language prompts the reader, no matter what his intellect, to reread all literature from the school curriculum. This long-known technique is called defamiliarization. Using it does not require a lot, only a small effort to take an unbiased look at the piece of work. As if you are reading it for the first time. And you'll see—behind every classic there lies a live, newly discovered idea. One that you want to play with." *Rodnaia rech'* is strictly structured in accordance with the Soviet school curriculum, and its characters are only those writers whose works are studied in school—among them, Belinsky, Nikolai Mikhailovich Karamzin, Denis Ivanovich Fonvizin, Aleksandr Nikolaevich Radishchev, Aleksandr Sergeevich Griboedov, Pushkin, Mikhail Iur'evich Lermontov, Gogol, Aleksandr Nikolaevich Ostrovsky, Ivan Sergeevich Turgenev, Ivan Aleksandrovich Goncharov, Nikolai Gavrilovich Chernyshevsky, Nikolai Alekseevich Nekrasov, Mikhail Evgrafovich Saltykov, Tolstoy, Fyodor Dostoevsky, and Chekhov. Pushkin, Lermontov, Gogol, and Chekhov take up two chapters each.

Readers of the book were divided in their sentiments toward it: one was either a devoted follower of the ideas expressed in *Rodnaia rech'* or in determined opposition to them. Those who liked the book, such as Iurii Karabchevsky, noted its "briefness," "the intense rhythm of the presentation, which is filled with unexpected and energetic formulas and unambiguous conclusions" and carried out like "an honorably endured" test from the school curriculum. The opposition, led by Tatiana Ivanova, who wrote about *Rodnaia rech'* in 1991 for *Znamia* (The Banner), pointed out that Vail' and Genis present Russian classics as a collection of entertaining, if not playful, texts and ignore the ideas of freedom as the main legacy of the classical heritage. Sergo Lominadze, an editor at the Soviet academic journal *Voprosy literatury* (Questions of Literature), was appalled that Vail' and Genis were teaching the reader not to seek "answers" from the classics but to try to understand their "lessons." Lominadze was critical mostly of the chapters concerning Lermontov's poetry and Dostoevsky's *Prestuplenie i nakazanie* (1866; translated as *Crime and Punishment*, 1886). Writing in *The Slavic and East European Journal* in 1992, the American scholar

Maxim Shrayer, who classified the co-authors' style as "ironic story-telling," welcomed their opinion of Ivan Andreevich Krylov as a major literary figure; their interpretation of Nekrasov's lyric works as a triangle encompassing "the poet, his sister (the muse), and their brother—the people"; their depiction of the people as a rhetorical figure in the works of Radishev; and many other concepts. Yet, at the same time Shrayer criticizes Vail' and Genis for their "lack of critical methods" and "absolute unfamiliarity with modern interpretations of literature." Finally, Sergei Kormilov, an expert in nineteenth-century Russian literature, gave his 1994 review of *Rodnaia rech'* in *Literaturnoe obozrenie* (The Literary Review) the title "Antiuchebnik" (The Anti-Textbook), incorporating both positive and negative comments into his article. Kormilov was certain that the book would receive negative reviews from scholars of Pushkin, Lermontov, Nekrasov, and Dostoevsky but nonetheless complimented Vail' and Genis for prompting serious thought through their book, particularly since it concerns a popular theme.

In 1990 Vail' and Genis prepared their third book for publication by a Moscow publishing house, Sovetskii pisatel' (Soviet Writer), but it ended up unpublished because of financial strain. "Popytka k begstvu" (An Attempt at Escape) at any rate was reviewed in manuscript form by a renowned Russian critic and literary journalist, Sergei Ivanovich Chuprinin, though the review was also unpublished. He wrote of Vail' and Genis that "They are talented with words: temperamental, strictly organized, often witty and aphoristic. . . . Because of this, they are also talented in selecting their subjects, which makes this book, which discusses the works of several modern writers, if not an exhaustive, then at least a self-sufficient, characteristic of the past decade as a whole."

The last book that Vail' and Genis co-authored, *Amerikana* was a collection of lessons that anyone traveling for the first time to the United States should learn before arriving there. *Amerikana* depicts an émigré's "America." If the previous parts of the trilogy address the themes of departure and what is left behind, in the sense of "this is where we left from," then *Amerikana* explores the ideas of arrival and resettlement, in the sense of "this is where we came to." Previously published in *Panorama*, these essays about cultural history carry titles such as "O reklame" (On Commercials), "O druzhbe s amerikantsami" (On Friendship with Americans), "O plemeni slavistov" (On the Slavic Tribe), "O neboskrebakh i utiugakh" (On Skyscrapers and Irons), "O iuzhanakh i iuge" (On the Southerners and the South), and "Ob odinochestve Charli Chaplina" (On Charlie Chaplin's Loneliness). *Amerikana,* which comprises fifty-seven essays, received mixed reviews. In his 1992 piece for *Novoe russkoe slovo* Popovsky criticized the authors for their total indifference to moral and religious issues. Ol'ga Timofeeva, in her introduction to the book, remarked that the co-authors' beloved genre of essayism is most applicable to *Amerikana:* "With their natural, lively persistence, P. Vail' and A. Genis have grasped the familiar (to them) science of emigration—coinhabitance. The protagonists of the story will never become Americans (something they do not regret): while remaining Russian, they seek a common language with America."

After 1990 Vail' and Genis did not write or publish as co-authors, and throughout the decade Russian literati discussed why the pair stopped producing works together. Some believed that the reason lay in the completeness of their co-authored projects and their unwillingness to apply the same literary techniques to a new historical environment. Galina Iuzefovich wrote in *Ezhenedel'ny zhurnal* (Weekly Review) of the "break-up of the star-like duet" and its consequences: "Nobody won and nobody lost—there was just a division of property. Each one left with what he came with. Vail' remained with his journalistic magnificence. Genis ended up with depth and lyricism."

In the first few years after their partnership ended, Vail' paid tribute to other peoples' books—primarily those of Joseph Brodsky. Vail' came up with the idea for, and compiled, Brodsky's *Rozhdestvenskie stikhi; Rozhdestvo: Tochka otscheta: Beseda s Petrom Vailem* (Christmas Poetry; Christmas: The Reference Point: A Conversation with Petr Vail', 1992), in which, as a supplement, he published an interview with the poet. He repeats the role of interviewer in Brodsky's *Peresechennaia mestnost': Puteshestviia s kommentariiami* (Cross-Country: Travels with Commentaries, 1995), a selection of poems written between 1972 and 1983 that are thematically unified by the idea of travel. Vail' organized the book by place (the United States, Europe, and Italy) and offered commentary based on his conversations with Brodsky. One critic, Aleksandr Sumerkin, considers *Peresechennaia mestnost'* a key work in the understanding of Brodsky's use of metaphysics, time, and space in his verse. The third work that Vail' published about Brodsky was written with Losev. *Iosif Brodsky: Trudy i Dni* (Joseph Brodsky: Works and Days, 1998) describes the poet's life after his immigration to the United States in 1972. As Gleb Shul'piakov noted in the journal *Vinnaia karta* (Wine Cart, 1999–2000) in his article about the book, *Iosif Brodsky* "is about how Brodsky lived as an émigré . . . how he had visited England, and how he got along with other Nobel Prize winners. . . . This book mythologizes how he captivated his students at Amherst College, how closely his poetry was knit with milk and aspirin, and how he accepted the Nobel Prize."

The first book that Vail' wrote on his own, *Genii mesta* (Genius Loci, 1999), revealed how much the author had surpassed his usual role of commentator and grew into an independent trendsetter of culturological judgments. Sergei Markovich Gandlevsky referred to this book as "literary research with a human face." According to the author

the main point of each chapter of this book is in the double comparison or contrast. Every city that is interpreted through a creative personality is parallel to the other pair 'the genius—the area.' Los Angeles does not just become more intelligible because of Chaplin, but vice versa, and the next pair, San Francisco and Jack London, gives an additional perspective. There are thirty-six of these pairs. . . . The genre of essay assumes a wide variety of associations, among them are those of a recollective character. So, when reading about Rome and Petronius, you will come across the memory of how I worked in Rome as a fireman; in the discussion about Rimini and Fellini, a lot of room is taken up by Spielberg; in the chapter about Venice and Carpaccio, there is plenty of discussion about Othello and Iago; and the story about Seville and Merime mixes with stories of what people used to eat and drink in my youth.

Genii mesta received dozens of positive reviews. Shul'piakov, in his article "Proportsii Vailia" (*Novyi mir* [New World], 1999) voiced the opinion of many when he wrote, "This is a genre that, we hope, will be referred to from now on, as *Vail'*." In his reception of the book Losev compared Vail' to intellectual writers such as V. S. Naipaul and Derek Walcott. On the other hand, in her 1999 review of the book for *Znamia,* Elena Ivanitskaia criticized the rather muted, secretive presence of Russian history and culture in the book and the excessive attention to gastronomical themes, to which Vail' replied that "Distinguishing, by taste, between twenty-six types of olives shows as much culture as distinguishing, by ear, between Mozart's forty-one symphonies."

His second book, *Karta Rodiny* (The Map of the Motherland, 2003), is another work that combines autobiography, travel notes, lyricism, and journalism. Vail' travels in search of the country in which he was born and that he left; he goes to the new countries that were formed after the breakup of the Soviet Union; and he investigates his personal roots and the history of his life. Among the chapters of the book are "Solovetskaiia noch" (The Night in Solovki); "Evropeiskaiia chast'" (The European Part [of Russia]); "Bespokoiiashchii ogon'" (The Troubling Fire), a piece about Chechnya; and "Velikii gorod, dal'niaia okraina" (The Great City, the Far Outskirts), which focuses on the Russian New York. According to Tatyana Tolstaya as she wrote in

Dust jacket for Genii mesta *(The Genius of Place, 1999), the first book Vail' wrote after ending his collaboration with Genis in the early 1990s (Collection of Mark Lipovetsky)*

Europa Center (1996), "Vail did not only travel around the world and depict it with his wise and fluent quill. Distant from Russian arrogance ('we want to go to a museum and not a restaurant'), Vail has experienced both the spiritual food of our world as well as its earthly dishes."

Genis's first solo book was *Amerikanskaia azbuka* (1994; selected chapters translated as "USA from A to Y," 2000), a long essay in the genre of lyrical cultural studies. Organized alphabetically, starting from "automobile" and ending with "yacht," the book is sequentially ordered like an encyclopedia and filled with articles about terms that are key to American life (such as "bank," "mall," "mail," and "sex shop"). The second edition of the book, published in 2000, was illustrated with digital compositions by Zhenia Scheff.

Genis's second book, *Vavilonskaia bashnia: Iskusstvo nastoiashchego vremeni* (The Tower of Babel: The Contemporary Art Form, 1996), was a collection of essays in which he applied the method of lyrical cultural studies to the whole history of culture and thus served as some-what of a sequel to *Amerikanskaia azbuka*. According to Genis, "the goal that contemporary art forms have is to load the moment with meaning and give it maximum weight." While analyzing the subtitle of the book in a piece for *Itogi* (6 May 1997), Rubinshtein noted that "besides its direct meaning, 'contemporary art' also implies the idea that one must capture the most elusive state which we call the 'present tense.' . . . It is presented to us as chaos and noise. Accepting and realizing this, is not yet everything. The role of the artist is to find, in this noise, if not order, then at least a possibility of order."

The protagonists of *Vavilonskaia bashnia* are mass culture, tourism, art and the interpretation of dreams, poetry of the East and the West, and the reign of video images. Other important concepts under discussion are the paradigm of a cabbage (art, like cabbage, hides in itself the core-truth) and the paradigm of an onion (in which there is no secret concealed in the core, just as there are no insignificant layers—each layer is equally valuable). The title of the book reflects a concept quite important to Genis, that of "cultural co-authorship": "The Babylonian tragedy was the revenge for the exces-sive trust invested in the language. This is why a new tower can only be erected in a world that would learn to respect and appreciate non-verbal culture. It is often eas-ier to agree without words." Genis's book also analyzes the phenomenon of man's journey from trust in educa-tion, science, and knowledge to archaic values that had been forgotten in the twentieth century: living outside of industrial cities, the voluntary concession of many con-quests by civilization, and the interest in religion.

Increasingly fond of Eastern cultures, especially Zen Buddhism, Genis gathered his reflections in *Bilet v Kitai* (A Ticket to China, 2001). China attracted Genis not only intellectually and aesthetically but also as a major partner of the West in the twenty-first century. The book ends with excerpts from Lao-Tzu in free translations by Genis, so that *Bilet v Kitai* is both an essayist and artistic piece—a combination to which he pays more and more attention. An earlier book, *Temnota i tishina: Iskusstvo vychitaniia* (1998; translated as "Darkness and Silence: The Art of Subtraction," 2000), falls into such an artistic category, since its genre may be defined as philosophical poetry in prose. In *Temnota i tishina* Genis claims that "Darkness and silence are the model-ing clay of literature. Not ink and paper, not others' books and one's own experience, not images and com-parisons, but darkness and silence—this is what litera-ture is made of."

Another one of Genis's prosaic works is a book called *Peizazhi* (Landscapes, 2002), what the author calls "the sawdust of everyday observations" that are bound by the central theme of depicting a landscape under a strictly defined angle. Examples are the chapter titles "Zelenyi peizazh. Wabi-Sabi" (The Green Landscape. Wabi-Sabi), "Chernyi peizazh. Teni v N'iu Iorke" (The Black Landscape. Shadows in New York), "Pestryi Pei-zazh. Syroe i varenoe" (The Colorful Landscape. Raw and Boiled), "Muzhskoi Peizazh. Ian'" (The Male Land-scape. Yang), "Zhenskyi Peizazh. In'" (The Female Land-scape. Yin), and several others. Genis's last book in this genre is the novel *Trikotazh* (Knit, 2002), a collection of lyrical, autobiographical stories in which chronology and life sequence are replaced with the logic of dreams and the poetry of recollection. Knitted from every strand, the fabric of life (the author's key metaphor) forms the intri-cate design, which one can marvel at endlessly, untangle, and search for knots and holes of fate.

Contemporary literature is another key subject for Genis. His book *Dovlatov i okrestnosti: Filologicheskii roman* (Dovlatov and His Environs: A Philological Novel, 1999), published in *Dovlatov i okrestnosti,* includes stories about famous literary figures, émigré life in New York, and the first attempts to organize an independent Rus-sian newspaper. The book is also filled with what Stanislav Rostotsky called in his article for *Vremia MN* (Time-Moscow News, 19 May 1999) "a drunkish touch of drama that is hard to explain." Following in the foot-steps of Arkadii Viktorovich Belinkov, who wrote a "lit-erary research novel" about Iurii Karlovich Olesha called *Sdacha i gibel' sovetskogo intelligenta* (Resignation and Death of the Soviet *intelligent,* 1976), Genis created the genre of "philological novels." In *Khorovod* (Round Dance), pub-lished in *Vavilonskaia bashnia,* he describes the genre as one that allows an author to compose a piece in which "he is given as much freedom to say irresponsible and unprov-able things as the characters of fiction." An example of irresponsibility, pointed out by Genis himself, is the choice of the main character for *Dovlatov i okrestnosti*. This character is, controversially, Genis and not Dovlatov, whom Genis uses as a reason to talk about himself and "significant metaphysical worries."

Lilia Pann, writing in *Literaturnaia gazeta* (30 Octo-ber 1996), discusses how Genis, with Dovlatov's help, gets to know himself in *Dovlatov i okrestnosti:* "We already know, from his [Genis's] lyrical culturology, that he [Genis] sees the world as an organic whole, the people as all coming from the same roots, but only in a book con-cerning a different theme, can we experience his 'meta-physical worries.'" Disagreeing with Genis on several counts, Irina Sluzhevskaia denied his claims that Dovla-tov was "asocial" and "free from morals." She uses as her source Nikita Eliseev, who wrote in an unpublished manuscript that Dovlatov's sense of morals was "impec-cable" and that "all of his stories are dedicated to the theme that there is a line that no decent person crosses."

Mark Lipovetsky approached *Dovlatov i okrestnosti* in a manner that the author had wished for in the subtitle—precisely as "a philological novel." Dedicated to the philological aspect of the book, Lipovetsky wrote in "Kritika kak priem" (Criticism as Device), published in 2000 in *Novoe literaturnoe obozrenie* (New Literary Review), that "Genis has quite sequentially reconstructed the model of Dovlatov's aestheticism," which in Lipovetsky's opinion the author often mimics. In discussing the novelistic aspect of the book Lipovetsky notes that Genis "revives the traditions of modernist metafiction" and brings the book closer to its predecessors—among which Lipovetsky lists Siniavsky's *Progulki s Pushkinym* (1975; translated as *Strolls With Pushkin,* 1993), which Siniavsky wrote as Abram Tertz, and Valentin Petrovich Kataev's *Almaznii moi venets* (My Diamond Crown, 1977), both of which were criticized "in different circles of liberal intelligentsia" for the same reasons that readers criticized Genis for *Dovlatov i okrestnosti.*

In his next book, *Ivan Petrovich umer: Stat'i i rassledovaniia* (Ivan Petrovich Has Died: Articles and Investigations, 1999), Genis goes from his own philological fiction to the critical examination of fiction by other writers. The book compiles essays written over the course of ten years and is organized in several sections. "Besedy o novoii slovestnosti" (Conversations about New Literature) examines contemporary writers such as Dovlatov, Erofeev, Siniavsky, Tolstaya, Vladimir Semenovich Makanin, Viktor Olegovich Pelevin, Sasha Sokolov, and Vladimir Georgievich Sorokin. The section titled "Shvy vremeni" (The Seams of Time) has survey articles on subjects such as the literary history of perestroika, the paradigms of contemporary culture, and the culinary aspects of Soviet civilization. The subdivision under the title "Chastnyi sluchai" (An Individual Case) encompasses essays about Gandlevsky, Dmitrii Galkovsky, Gerald Durrell, Wallace Stevens, and Ezra Pound, for example.

The title of the book signifies Genis's denial of the "life-like" poetics that is, in his opinion, incompatible with the world today, in which everything is already said: "How immense an opinion of the self does one need to have," Genis writes, "to write 'Ivan Petrovich got up from the squeaky chair and walked up to the open window.' In order not to feel ashamed of plagiarizing, one must make himself forget about all the previous and upcoming Ivan Petroviches, squeaky chairs, and open windows. One must firmly and zealously believe in his reign over the world to think that he is depicting life as it is." Ivan Petrovich, according to Pann, writing in *Znamia* (2000), is a "common noun" for "the typical representative of the literature of socialist, and critical, realism. . . . In general, Ivan Petrovich is

Paperback cover for Genis's Bilet v Kitai *(A Ticket to China, 2001), a product of his fascination with Eastern cultures and Zen Buddhism (Collection of Mark Lipovetsky)*

any protagonist that has not realized his conventionality."

In 1999, in collaboration with Mikhail Naumovich Epshtein and Slobodanka Vladiv-Glover, Genis published a book in English about Russian literature titled *Russian Postmodernism: New Perspectives on Post-Soviet Culture.* The majority of his contributions to the book are identical to what he wrote in *Ivan Petrovich umer.* From 2000 to 2001 Genis was the author and host of a television series, "Alexander Genis: Pis'ma iz Ameriki" (Letters from America), which was screened on the Russian channel Kultura (Culture). Svetlana Taroshchina, a television critic, noted that the series was "an attempt at a sober perspective on the phenomenon of a country where people came at different times to start life on a new page."

After fifteen years of co-authorship and twelve years of writing and publishing individually, Petr L'vovich Vail' and Aleksandr Aleksandrovich Genis have shown that despite many common themes (Brodsky, Dovlatov, food writing, and travel), they each have an individual path in literature. Genis has expounded on cultural research and the study of Eastern influence on Western civilization, while Vail' writes in depth about Western European art and the satirical depiction of the unchangeable absurdities of everyday Russian life. Yet, no matter how diverse, the end product from Vail' and Genis is always well-written prose.

Interviews:

Natalia Morozova, "Svoboda eto 'absoluntyi nol','" *Sovetskaia molodezh* (Riga), 2 June 1990;

Evgenia Podberezina, "Petr Vail i Aleksandr Genis: My pochti kak kentavry," *Rigas balls*, 8 June 1990;

Maksim Maksimov, "Sovietskie 'amerikano,' Ili nashe otechestvo—rodnaia Rech'," *Smena*, 9 January 1992;

Elena Iakovich, "Odinokie stranniki s pachki Pamira: Razgovor Petra Vailia i Aleksandra Genisa s Sergeem Gandlevskim i Timurom Kibirovym v gostinnitse 'Pekin' pod Novyi god," *Literaturnaia gazeta*, 15 January 1992;

Tatiana Andriasova, "Pripodniataia tselina," *Moskovskie novosti*, 28 January 1992;

Aleksandr Shchuplov, "Soavtorstvo—takoi slozhnyi i intimnyi institut . . . ," *Knizhnoe obozrenie*, 7 February 1992;

Natalia Kozlova, "Piknik na obochine: Interv'iu s Petrom Vailem i Aleksandrom Genisom," *Novoe russkoe slovo*, 5 May 1992;

Maksim Maksimov, "Vezde gde mozhno zhit', mozhno zhit' khorosho," *Nedelia*, no. 8 (1992);

Andriasova, "Ugroza svobody," *Moskovskie novosti*, 24 January 1993;

Vladimir Iarmolinets, "Petr Vail': 'Rossiia eshche dolgo budet eto raskhlebyvat','" *Novoe russkoe slovo*, 7 April 1995;

Lilia Pann, "My uzhe ne zhivem v epokhu geroev i geniev," *Literaturnaia gazeta*, 30 October 1996;

Sergei Iur'enen, "Petr Vail': Zhanr—svobodnoe bluzhdaniie mysli po bumage," *Evropa tsentr*, no. 14 (1996);

Iulia Kantor, "Chelovek dolzhen byt' zhiv, syt, i svoboden," *Nevskoe vremia*, 29 November 1996;

Nikolai Khalezin, "Puteshestvie vo vremeni," *Imia*, no. 3 (1997);

Konstantin Donin, "Aleksandr Genis: Gliadia iz 'Boinga,'" *Bostonskoe vremia*, 25 April 1997;

Tatiana Vol'tskaia, "Moloko, koneshno skislo, no . . . ," *Literaturnaia gazeta*, no. 23 (1998);

Ivan Tolstoi, "Bespechnyi pedant, ili Doverije k potoku: K 50-letiju Petra Vailia," *Zvezda*, no. 9 (1999);

Gleb Shul'piakov, "Petr Vail' O vine: Chem men'she vperedi let, tem bol'she vremeni," *Vinnaia karta*, 15 December 1999–15 January 2000;

Marina Adamovich, "Novyi arkhipelag, ili konets emigrantskoi literatury," *Kontinent*, no. 102 (2001);

Tolstoi, "Ya pisal by texty dazhe vniz golov: k 50-letiju Aleksandra Genisa," *Zvezda*, no. 2 (2003).

References:

Mikhail Aizenberg, "V kontse priamoi," *Itogi*, 5 May 1998;

Andrei Bychkov, "Puteshestvie iz New Yorka v Lkhasu," *Obshaia gazeta*, nos. 2–11, June 1997;

Ellen Chances, "Petr Vail and Alexander Genis. *Sovremennaia russkaia proza*," *Slavic and East European Journal*, 28, no. 2 (1984);

Neil Cornwell, "Pyotr Vayl' and Aleksandr Genis, *Sovremennaia russkaia proza*," *Irish Slavonic Studies*, no. 6 (1985);

Ivan Davydov, "Petr Vail', Aleksandr Genis, *60-e: Mir sovetskogo cheloveka*," *Russkii Zhurnal* (26 December 1997) <http://www.russ.ru/journal/zloba_dn/97-12-26/david.htm>;

Davydov, "Russkaia kukhnia v izgnanii," *Russkii Zhurnal* (4 April 1998) <http://www.russ.ru/journal/kniga/98-04-04/david.htm>;

Sergei Donatovich Dovlatov, "Kto takie Vail' i Genis? Popytka utochneniia," *Panorama*, 18–25 August 1989;

John B. Dunlop, "*Sovremennaia usskaia proza*. By Petr Vail' and Alexander Genis," *Slavic Review*, 42, no. 4 (1983);

Valerii Golovskoy, "Petr Vail, Alexander Genis, *Sovremennaia russkaia proza*," *Russian Literature Journal*, nos. 129–130 (1984);

Linor Goralik, "Petr Vail', Aleksandr Genis. *60-e: Mir sovetsokgo cheloveka*," *Russkii Zhurnal* (26 October 1999) <http://www.russ.ru/krug/razbor/19991022.html>;

Elena Ivanitskaia, "Suita v proze," *Znamia*, no. 10 (1999);

Tatiana Ivanova, "Pervaia edinstvennaia–i posleniaia nadezhda," *Znamia*, no. 5 (1991);

Ol'ga Kabanova, "Obretennoe pokoleniie (Poslednee issledovanie o shestidesiatykh)," *Kommersant Daily*, 21 August 1996;

Iurii Karabchevsky, "Zhivaia rech'," *Knizhnoie obozrenie*, no. 5 (1991);

Natalia Kisis, "V soprovozhdenii velikikh gidov," *Diena*, 17 July 1999;

Nikolai Klimontovich, "Vagner, Florentsiia, Baikal i Makiavelli," *Russkii telegraf*, no. 1, 1997;

Sergei Kormilov, "Antiuchebnik," *Literaturnoe obozrenie,* no. 12 (1994);

Leonid Kostiukov, "Treshchiny na mramore: Brodsky, o Brodskom i okolo Brodskogo," *Russkii telegraf,* 4 March 1998;

Viacheslav Kuritsyn, "Niotkuda s liuboviu: Kul'turologicheskii roman P. Vailia i A. Genisa o shestidesiatykh," *Literaturnaia gazeta,* 25 September 1996;

Kuritsyn, "Prinesennye Vetrom. Pamiati Vailia i Genisa," *Literaturnaia gazeta,* no. 30, 1994;

Alla Latynina, "Nabliudatel'nyi Punkt Genisa," *Vremia MN,* 22 May 2002;

Mark Lipovetsky, "Kritika kak priem," *Novoe literaturnoe obozrenie,* no. 44 (1999);

Lev Losev, "Aleksandr Genis, *Dovlatov i Okrestnosti,*" *Znamia,* no. 10, 1999;

David Macfadyen, [On Russian Postmodernism], *World Literature Today,* Winter 2001;

M. Mondello, "Step Back from Life's Canvas," *Moscow Times,* 27 July 2001;

G. Mordel', "Kilogrammy schast'ia na Brighton Beach," *Krug,* 4 (10 July 1979);

Lilia Pann, "U Petrovicha," *Znamia,* no. 4 (2000);

Mark Popovsky, "Pisateli i Amerika," *Novoe russkoe slovo,* 14 April 1992;

Popovsky, "Predely ironii", *Grani,* no. 136 (1986);

Stanislav Rostotsky, "Smekh i trepet," *Vremia MN,* 19 May 1999;

Lev Semenovich Rubinshtein, "Khudozhestvennaia diagnostika dukha vremeni," *Itogi,* 6 May 1997;

Rubinshtein, "Usadiv dve kul'tury za obshchim stolom," *Itogi,* 31 March 1998;

Grigorii Ryskin, "Ot 'gomosovetikusa' k cheloveku," *Panorama,* no. 151 (1984);

Elin Schoen, "The Russians Are Coming! The Russians Are Here!" *New York Times,* 7 September 1980;

Maxim Shrayer, "Petr Vail', Aleksandr Genis. *Rodnaia rech'.* S predisloviem Andreia Siniavskogo," *Slavic and East European Journal,* 36, no. 4 (1992);

Gleb Shul'piakov, "Proportsii Vailia," *Novyi mir,* no. 12 (1999);

Svetlana Taroshchina, "O peizazhakh dushi," *Vremia MN,* 26 October 2001;

Abram Tertz [Andrei Donatovich Siniavsky], *Progulki s Pushkinym* (London: Overseas Publications Interchange, 1975; St. Petersburg: Vsemirnoe slovo, 1993); translated by Catherine Theimer Nepomnyashchy and Slava I. Yastremski as *Strolls with Pushkin* (New Haven: Yale University Press, 1993);

Tatyana Tolstaya, "Kot i okrestnosti," *Obschhiaia gazeta,* 29 July–4 August 1999.

Svetlana Vladimirovna Vasilenko

(24 January 1956 –)

Elena Prokhorova
George Washington University

BOOKS: *Zvonkoe imia: Videopoema i rasskazy* (Moscow: Molodaia gvardiia, 1991)–includes "Shamara" and "Bobochka";

Durochka. Roman, povest', rasskazy (Moscow: Vagrius, 2000);

Bryzgi shampanskogo (Moscow: AST-Olimp, 2002).

Edition: *Shamara: Povest'* (Moscow: Stolitsa, 1991).

Editions in English: "Shamara," translated by Andrew Bromfield, in *Women's View,* edited by Bromfield and Natasha Perova (Moscow: Glas, 1992), pp. 26–50;

"Going After Goat-Antelopes," translated by Elisabeth Jezierski, in *Lives in Transit: A Collection of Recent Russian Women's Writing,* edited by Helena Goscilo (Ann Arbor, Mich.: Ardis, 1995), pp. 46–68;

"Piggy," translated by Bromfield, in *Present Imperfect: Stories by Russian Women,* edited by Ayesha Kagal and Perova, with an introduction by Goscilo (Boulder, Colo.: Westview Press, 1996), pp. 26–40;

Shamara and Other Stories, translated, with an introduction, by Goscilo–includes "The Gopher" (Evanston, Ill.: Northwestern University Press, 2000).

PRODUCED SCRIPTS: *Goriachev i drugie,* television, ORT, 1994;

Shamara, motion picture, Dovzhenko Film Studio, 1994;

Nekrasivaia, motion picture, Mosfilm/Debiut, 1994;

Koroli russkogo syska, television, RTR, 1995;

Posle voiny, motion picture, screenplay by Vasilenko and Arkadii Iakhnis, Gloriia-Film, 2001;

Mesto, motion picture, Chelovek i vremia, 2001.

OTHER: "Khriusha," in *Kitaigorodskaia stena: Rasskazy molodykh moskovskikh pisatelei,* compiled by Nikolai Ivanovich Doroshenko and Valerii Anatol'evich Semenov (Moscow: Sovremennik, 1988), pp. 290–305;

"Suslik," "Za saigakami," "Zvonkoe imia," "Schast'e," "Kto ikh poliubit," and "Tsaritsa Tamara," in *Zhenskaia logika: Povesti, rasskazy. Sbornik zhenskoi prozy,* edited by Liudmila Vladimirovna Stepanenko and Aleksandr Vladimirovich Fomenko (Moscow: Sovremennik, 1989), pp. 100–204;

"Gen smerti," in *Vstrechnyi khod,* compiled by V. I. Pososhkov (Moscow: Stil', 1989), pp. 158–185;

"Zvonkoe imia," in *Chisten'kaia zhizn': Povesti i rasskazy,* compiled by Anatolii Shavkuta (Moscow: Molodaia gvardiia, 1990), pp. 121–158;

"Duratskie rasskazy," in *Novye amazonki,* compiled, with an introduction, by Vasilenko (Moscow: Moskovskii rabochii, 1991), pp. 311–322;

Osip Emil'evich Mandel'shtam, *Sobranie proizvedenii: Stikhotvoreniia,* edited by Vasilenko and Iu. L. Freidin (Moscow: Respublika, 1992);

Irina Mikhailovna Semenko, *Poetika pozdnego Mandel'shtama: Ot chernovykh redaktsii k okonchatel'nomu tekstu,* compiled by Vasilenko and P. M. Nerler, with an introduction by Lidiia Ginzburg (Moscow: Vash Vybor TSIRZ, 1997);

Zhenshchiny: Svoboda slova i svoboda tvorchestva, compiled, with an introduction, by Vasilenko (Moscow: Eslan, 2001);

"O sebe" <http://www.m-m.sotcom.ru/11-13/vasilen1.htm> [accessed 21 July 2003].

SELECTED PERIODICAL PUBLICATIONS–UNCOLLECTED: "Dva rasskaza," *Novyi mir,* 9 (1997): 43–53;

"Rusalka s Patriarshikh prudov," *Literaturnaia gazeta* (February/March 1998);

"Krasnye flamingo" [fragment], *Slovo,* 21 (2000): 54–65.

Svetlana Vasilenko belongs to the generation of Russian writers who began their literary careers in the interregnum between the late Stagnation–the end of Leonid Il'ich Brezhnev's rule–and perestroika, when Mikhail Sergeevich Gorbachev was in power. Her outspoken and self-conscious female characters, the personal tone of her narration, and her masterful use of metaphorical language instantly made her a name among critics and colleagues. Vasilenko's focus on the everyday grind of Russian life was deemed problematic, however, and for several years delayed her recognition as a writer. She has been labeled a "tough prose" writer by Deming Brown, a writer of "trench-truth" by Nikolai Shipilov and even a writer of "naturalism" by Pavel Basinsky.

Since the late 1980s Vasilenko's works have been a noticeable presence in the post-Soviet literary scene. She was nominated for the Booker Russian Novel Prize, the most prestigious literary award in Russia, in 1998 for *Durochka* (Little Fool, 2000), thus far her only novel, which had appeared in *Novyi mir* (New World) that same year. In addition to prose, Vasilenko also writes movie scripts. In addition, as head of the Russian Writers' Union and a member of the Russian PEN Club, she is actively involved in the cultural life of her country, organizing symposia and editing collections of women's writing.

Vasilenko was born Svetlana Vladimirovna Moreva on 24 January 1956 in the Astrakhan region, in the town of Kapustin Iar–the Russian equivalent of Cape Canaveral. Kapustin Iar was the place where the first Sputnik was launched and had been visited by Iurii Gagarin and Valentina Tereshkova, the first male and female cosmonauts. Vasilenko's mother, Maria Savel'evna Vasilenko, a Ukrainian by birth, came from a family of veterinarians who moved from Ukraine to Russia in 1933 in order to escape famine. Vasilenko's father, Vladimir Georgievich Morev, an officer specializing in rockets, was constantly absent from home and eventually abandoned his family. Vasilenko has represented both of her parents in her works, yet as polar opposites: the father's profession is linked with destruction and death, while the mother appears as a symbol of life. She dedicated her first collection of works to her mother, whose last name she adopted.

The town Kapustin Iar, populated only by young officers and their families, was not listed on any map. In the introduction to her collection, *Zvonkoe imia: Videopoema i rasskazy* (A Resounding Name: A Video-Narrative Poem and Stories), Vasilenko refers to the years spent in the security zone as her "cosmic childhood." By her own admission her father could have been the one designated to "press the button" during the 1962 Cuban Missile Crisis. Many memories from this time found their way into her prose. One of the most striking images, occurring at the end of *Durochka*, is of a teacher who tells schoolchildren that they should be proud of being "nuclear hostages": after all, rockets from all over the world are targeting their town. The feeling of exposure to the evil of the world permeating Vasilenko's writing originates in her childhood experiences. The impressions of these early years also account for the strong autobiographical bent of

her works, as well as for what Helena Goscilo, in her introduction to *Shamara and Other Stories* (2000), a collection of Vasilenko's fiction in translation, calls the writer's "impassioned feminism."

Vasilenko began to write when she was eight years old. In 1973 some of her poetry was published in a major Soviet youth newspaper, *Komsomol'skaia pravda* (Komsomol' Truth). She received hundreds of letters from all over the Soviet Union, and the Komsomol' authorities in Kapustin Iar reprimanded her for giving away her street address in a town that was a secret location. After graduating from high school, Vasilenko–who says in "O sebe" (About Myself, published online at <http://www.m-m.sotcom.ru/11-13/vasilen1.htm> that she "wanted to write like Dostoevsky"–came to Moscow and attempted to enter, first, the Department of Psychology at Moscow State University and, then, the Institut mirovoi literatury (Institute of World Literature), also known as the Gor'ky Institute. Administrators at the latter institution advised her to work for two years before becoming a student. For approximately a year she worked at a synthetic-fibers plant in the Volgograd region in a town that turned out to be a prison zone. The town and its inhabitants later served as, respectively, the setting and characters for Vasilenko's novella "Shamara" (1990).

After returning to Moscow, Vasilenko supported herself by working at several odd jobs; she hauled fruit, delivered mail, and toiled in a few other positions that were available to non-Muscovites. From 1978, when she entered the Gor'ky Institute, until 1983, the year that she graduated, she studied prose writing there under Grigorii Iakovlevich Baklanov. Her favorite writers at the time were Knut Hamsun and Thomas Mann, as well as Iurii Valentinovich Trifonov. In addition to her literary studies at the institute, Vasilenko took classes in motion-picture directing and in 1989 graduated from the Workshop for Movie Directors and Scriptwriters. The following year she began working with Andrei Sergeevich Konchalovsky on the movie *Tristan and Isolde*. During this time Vasilenko also joined the Writer's Union (in 1989) and the PEN Club (in 1990).

In 1982, while still a student at the Gor'ky Institute, she published her first story, "Za saigakami" (translated as "Going After Goat-Antelopes," 1995), in the journal *Literaturnaia ucheba* (Literary Education). The story is about a young woman (the first-person narrator) and her girlfriend flirting with two officers at a restaurant. The unexpected appearance of the heroine's male childhood friend disrupts the predictable narrative, as the two steal out of the restaurant and go for a ride. A series of foreshadowing devices–such as a broken champagne glass, dead lobsters on the dinner table,

Svetlana Vladimirovna Vasilenko (courtesy of Vagrius Publishing)

and a baby antelope that they run over—anticipates the tragic outcome: the woman's male friend dies in a car accident. Two aspects of "Za saigakami" influenced Vasilenko's later techniques. First, the sensuality and richness of the heroine's experience contrast with the banal and predictable script. Second, the resistance to finalizing this experience in a single plot inspires Vasilenko to explore alternative narrative lines. For instance, the incident with the baby antelope is framed neither as a dream nor as a memory but is marked as a moment when the boundary between the closed fictional world and infinite human experience becomes erased: "Somewhere here the lie begins, I myself don't know where."

"Za saigakami" created a stir among literati and was named among the best works of the year. Despite this recognition, however, Vasilenko remained unpub-

lished and virtually unknown to the reading public for a long time. Her second story, "Zvonkoe imia" (A Resounding Name), appeared in the journal *Iunost'* in 1988 and established Vasilenko's reputation. The story recounts two days in the life of a postal worker, Natka, who has come to Moscow from a provincial town in search of love and a residence permit. The narrative starts when her friend's husband returns to Moscow from a resort without his wife and pays Natka a visit. The two embark upon an affair and spend the next day in an amusement park. For Natka, haunted alternately by a dream of "true love" and by thoughts of the cheated wife's rage, this walk turns into a nightmarish vision of sweaty crowds in a heat-crazed, apocalyptic city.

"Za saigakami" and "Zvonkoe imia" already include many features that have since become staples of Vasilenko's prose: a subjective mode of narration, the identification of the implied author with the female protagonist, and the alternation of a confessional tone with "cinematic" passages when the events are narrated from a detached perspective. The narrated events are trivial and follow the predictable pattern of seduction and cheating-on-your-best-friend. Yet, within Natka, under this surface banality seethes an array of emotions—guilt, desire, fear, and hope. The sense of internal division is, indeed, almost Dostoevskian, and that men (including Sasha in "Zvonkoe imia") are completely blind to the complex emotions that they stir in women complicates such inner conflict.

Despite her gynocentric vision, Vasilenko does not idealize her women characters. The heroine-narrator of the story "Khriusha" (1988; translated as "Piggy," 1996), for instance, enters the narrative with words of spite that are worthy of Fyodor Dostoevsky's "underground man": "I hated the pig from the very first day." The heroine insists that her mother kill the pig; for the daughter it symbolizes all the dirt and humiliation that her widowed mother experiences among the arrogant and mercantile wives of officers stationed in the town. For the mother, however, the pig is her sole life companion. Vasilenko lays bare her heroine's "self-exculpating strategies," according to Goscilo's introduction, by interspersing the first-person narrative with "authorial" remarks, thus transforming the narrator into an object of scrutiny. Only after Vasilenko gives a striking and naturalistic description of the pig's slaughter do the reader and the heroine realize that the harrowing spectacle has been witnessed by the heroine's young son. Seeing the event through his terrified eyes brings catharsis to the heroine. The sacrificial meaning of the slaughter is played out on two levels: first, through the traditional symbolism of redemptive blood and, second, as a means of laying bare the oppressive nature of a hygienic, rational view of the world.

Like Lyudmila Petrushevskaya's work, Vasilenko's narratives demolish the stereotype that women's prose is, or should be, sentimental—or at least life-affirming. Vasilenko's texts decidedly lack sentimentality, even in their treatment of the most sacred topics. The story "Gen smerti" (The Death Gene, 1989), for instance, is set in an abortion clinic and describes a community of women who have nothing in common but their decision to end unwanted pregnancies. As they try to distract themselves from disturbing thoughts, one of the women, Tamara, who has already had twelve abortions, lays bare the truth behind the banality of the hospital setting: "Laughing, eh? You came here in your house robes, and later you'll fry potatoes in your robes! To a funeral—in robes!" Like the narrator of "Khriusha," the protagonist Natal'ia is a biologist and extreme rationalist. She has devoted her life to finding the "gene of death"—a goal she set for herself after her officer father died when she was a child. "Biology," or "the dark force," as she defines it, represents everything that cannot be analyzed and explained. Natal'ia feels threatened and disgusted by her own unexpected pregnancy, by the involuntary closeness of bodies in the hospital room, and by the intimate confessions of other women. Yet, precisely this closeness and the surrogate community of women afford her a sense of consolation after the abortion. As she listens to Tamara's life story of losses and betrayals, for a moment the disjointed and illogical world is restored to its meaning and beauty, and at the center of this world stands Woman as a life-giving force.

One of Vasilenko's impressive achievements as a storyteller is her adeptness in capturing complex and often contradictory feelings in concise narrative form. "Schast'e" (Happiness, 1989) is a four-page story about a young woman, now married, who goes to visit her longtime love, whom she has not seen for several years. As she hugs him, she realizes that his face was badly burned and disfigured in the Afghan war. With no prospects of having a family or normal communication with people, he works at a slaughterhouse, where, before killing cattle, he names them after the Soviet party and military leaders responsible for the war. The stories "Suslik" (1989; translated as "The Gopher," 2000) and "Babochka" (The Butterfly, 1991), each of which does not exceed two pages, capture the magic and fragility of the world in condensed images. In "Suslik," for instance, schoolchildren collect animal skins and pour chlorinated water into gophers' burrows. The natural landscape recalls a postapocalyptic desert; what is contaminated, however, is the human element. Through a metaphor—"chlorinated water" becomes "chlorinated spite"—Vasilenko attempts to fuse the physical and the emotional, the material and the metaphysical.

In 1990 Vasilenko published one of the most interesting of her works, the novella "Shamara," which in 1994 she adapted into a motion picture. The heroine of "Shamara" lives in a prison *zona* (zone), a town populated by convicts who work at a chemical plant. Gang-raped several years ago, Shamara refused to testify against one of her offenders and married him. She then put him in jail for drinking and abuse and, like the wife of a Decembrist (one of a group of revolutionaries who rose up against Tsar Nicholas I unsuccessfully in December 1825), followed him to his place of incarceration, a labor camp. All these events notwithstanding, Shamara's irrational love for her abuser and the magic of the word *husband* define her whole existence. In the name of this unrequited love she sleeps with a parole officer and is ready to kill her rival, a "clean" city girl.

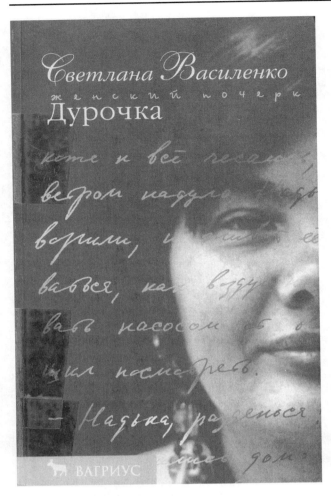

Front cover for Vasilenko's only novel, Durochka
*(Little Fool, 2000), which takes place in two
different time periods, the 1930s and the
1960s (Skokie Public Library)*

Subtitled "Videopoema" (video-narrative poem), "Shamara" indeed displays certain cinematic narrative techniques: a montage-like sequencing of episodes, the abrupt appearance of characters without backgrounds or prehistories, and the narrator's refusal to provide psychological commentary. In a sense the selection of characters itself—from ill-educated and violent criminals and guards to barren and hysterical girlfriends, all of whom live with radiation from chemical waste—invites such a detached style. The detachment, on the one hand, allows Vasilenko to avoid melodramatic excess; on the other, it underscores the characters' rootlessness and an absence of values rather than any "essential" flaws. Matter-of-fact, dispassionate narration constructs both the mores of the violent town and the dysfunctional behavior of its population as typical (that is, symptomatic) of the broader social and ethical dead end. For instance, food shortages force people to stand

in line to buy their portions of whale meat. The reference to "whale fish" invokes the Russian legendary belief that the earth rests on three whales. Typically for Vasilenko's writing, the image simultaneously operates on ecological, social, and metaphorical levels (humanity is devouring its own life foundation).

Yet, Shamara, like many of Vasilenko's female characters who at once are conditioned by their environment and resist it, is capable of regeneration. This split produces the strong antirationalist bent in Vasilenko's narratives. She writes not about a lost or false subjectivity but, rather, a displaced one—a subjectivity burdened with layers of lies, myths, and false hopes. In the end, however, the subject does emerge—in pain, in hope, and in a sudden realization of its own cruelty and senseless existence. At the end of the novella, Shamara—betrayed, beaten, and recovering from a barbaric abortion—sails on a boat into the unknown. Perhaps because of a childhood spent in the steppe, rivers carry a liberating and redemptive meaning in many of Vasilenko's works.

Unlike the heroines found in the works of Petrushevskaya or Marina Anatol'evna Palei—heroines who, however disenfranchised, still belong to a family or establish their identity through sexual acts—Vasilenko's female characters lack such connections. Her heroines are not only socially marginal but also extremely lonely. On the one hand, they are geographically and socially displaced and uprooted. On the other, they live in surrogate communities—dorms, communal apartments, orphanages, and clinics. Sexual experience, whether narrated by a character (as in "Gen smerti") or graphically represented (as seen in "Zvonkoe imia" and "Shamara"), does not bring happiness and satisfaction. Quite often it resembles rape and almost always lacks emotional response from male partners.

The majority of Vasilenko's publications from the late 1980s to the early 1990s came out in journals and collections of women's prose. The first of these collections, *Ne pomniashchaia zla: Novaia zhenskaia proza* (She Who Bears No Grudge: New Women's Prose), appeared in 1990 and was followed by *Novye amazonki* (The New Amazons, 1991), which became notorious among male critics for its "naturalism." As the journalist Nadezhda Azhgikhina remarks in her 1994 book *Novaia volna* (The New Wave), the distinctively feminine point of view and experience offered by "women's prose" did not fit easily into familiar categories and were channeled into derogatory clichés of criticism. Along with other contributors, Vasilenko was labeled a purveyor of *chernukha*—the use of naturalistic and violent scenes for sensationalist effect. The qualms voiced by the liberal male critics were the same as those expressed by the Soviet literary establishment—namely, an excessive focus on the underbelly of Russian life: crowded dorms, violence in dirty streets, and adulterous episodes framed by the decay of communal apartments. This accusation, in the writer's words, has always surprised Vasilenko: she believed that she was writing about everyday Russian life, which most Russians live and consider normal.

Vasilenko's first book of collected stories, *Zvonkoe imia: Videopoema i rasskazy,* appeared in 1991. In her autobiographical introduction to the book, "O sebe" (About Myself), Vasilenko refers to Russia as a primitive society, in which ideology has been substituted for spirituality, represented in particular by religion and philosophy. The subject of her fictional universe is standing "in the middle of the world where nature and history rage, where one is irradiated—both physically and spiritually, one believes in nobody and nothing . . . On one's lips are several words: 'give,' 'I want,' 'kill,' 'I love,' 'I hate,' and several obscene expressions, with which one can convey all one's feelings. . . ." Vasilenko refers to herself as "the first writer of the primitive society" described in her essay, a writer who is searching for grains of humanity amid man-made spite and self-inflicted pain.

This primitive society is the protagonist of Vasilenko's minicycle "Duratskie rasskazy" (Silly Stories, 1991), which is absurdist in the tradition of Nikolai Vasil'evich Gogol and Daniil Ivanovich Kharms. As in Gogol, anything might, and does, happen, and what happens is born out of language: chopped, banal phrases and clichés seem to generate miscommunication. The brief narratives and dialogues of the cycle are reminiscent of conceptualist poetry, in particular of Dmitrii Aleksandrovich Prigov's work, in that both Vasilenko and Prigov approach ideological discourse and cultural stereotypes as artifacts that, once produced, shape the reality around them. However, for Vasilenko, as for Kharms, nonsensical events have their sinister logic. For instance, "Skazka o dobrykh i chestnykh liudiakh, ob obez'ianakh i o tom, kak poiavilis' Adam i Eva" (A Tale About Kind and Honest People, About Apes, and About How Adam and Eve Appeared), the longest of the "Duratskie rasskazy," is an allegory of Soviet enlightenment. The protagonist of the story collects and studies plants by eating them. His goal is to grow Chesdobr —the plant of *chest'* (honesty) and *dobro* (kindness). But as Chesdobr multiplies and all people on earth become honest and kind, other plants and animals die out and are replaced by stone monuments. Lacking nourishment, the population of the earth disappears—except for two youths, Adam and Eve, who did not ingest the Chesdobr with their mother's milk. Vasilenko's criticism of Soviet enlighten-

ment is of an ecological and anthropological, rather than political or ideological, nature.

From the mid 1990s Vasilenko has been working in cinema. Among the finished productions for which she wrote scripts are a short motion picture, *Nekrasivaia* (A Homely Woman, 1994), based on Iurii Pavlovich Kazakov's 1956 story by the same title, and *Posle voiny* (After the War, 2000), which recounts life in a small Jewish settlement in the first month after World War II. In addition, she has written scripts for two television series, *Goriachev i drugie* (Goriachev and Others, 1994), which aired on *Obshchestvennoe Rossiiskoe Televidenie* (Russian Public Television), and *Koroli russkogo syska* (Kings of Russian Detection, 1995), which aired on *Rossiiskoe televidenie* (Russian Television Channel).

Vasilenko's interest in the cultural construction of feminine identity found full expression in the novel *Durochka*. Published in 1998 in the journal *Novyi mir,* *Durochka* recaptures many of Vasilenko's earlier themes and motifs. At the same time, the central theme of this longest and most complex of her works to date, is Russo-Soviet national mythology. The heroine of the novel is a mad, mute girl with a double name—Ganna and Nadezhda (Hope), who "sails" into the narrative brought in by the river as an orphan on a raft and at the end ascends to heaven. The narrative unfolds in two temporal dimensions (the 1930s and the 1960s) and combines historical events (the purges and famine of the 1930s and the Cuban Missile Crisis of the early 1960s) with myths and legends.

Ganna Nadezhda embodies two of Vasilenko's central archetypal figures: she is both an abused woman-child and a redeeming force. Both her vulnerability and her power are linked to the Russian idea of kenoticism, which advocates the piety of uncomplaining suffering—especially of undeserved suffering. Like kenotic saints (who are traditionally male), Ganna follows the example of Christ; she rejects violence and heals through love. Because of her madness and muteness (which is not absolute, since she sings beautifully and reacts to violence with animal-like cries) Ganna is also associated with Russian *Iurodivyi* (fools-in-Christ). According to Russian cultural mythology, although their speech was incomprehensible, fools-in-Christ were able nonetheless to reveal the truth and predict the future. At the end of the novel Ganna enacts the Apocalypse, or Second Coming: she averts an American nuclear attack and ascends to heaven.

As in Vasilenko's short stories, the narrative voice in *Durochka* shifts from character to character, switching from third- to first-person narration. Ganna stands at the intersection of these voices, which are predominantly male, yet she herself lacks one. Her muteness, starkly contrasted to the ideological, or cultural, clichés of other characters in *Durochka,* reflects Vasilenko's skepticism of "rational" discourse. As Ganna "passes over" from one community and time to another, she identifies with the roles imposed on her but always transcends their meaning. In the end the traditional oppositions between normalcy and madness, "reality" and legend disappear. National destiny in *Durochka* becomes inseparable from womanhood—not in a biological but in a spiritual and metaphysical sense. In 1998 *Durochka* was nominated for the Booker Russian Novel Prize and was recognized by *Novyi mir* as the best Russian novel of the year. Vasilenko plans to adapt *Durochka* for the screen, and as part of this project, she has completed a documentary movie, *Mesto* (Place, 2001), which portrays the world from the viewpoint of a mentally challenged boy who lives in her hometown of Kapustin Iar.

Vasilenko has been at work on a novel, "Krasnye flamingo" (Red Flamingos), which she started after her stay at an artists' colony located in Saratoga Springs, New York. A chapter from the manuscript was published by *Literaturnaia gazeta* (The Literary Gazette, February/March, 1998) as "Rusalka s Patriarshikh prudov" (Mermaid from Patriarshii Ponds), as well as in the New York–based émigré almanac *Slovo* as "Nachalo romana 'Krasnye Flamingo'" ("The Beginning of the Novel 'Red Flamingos'"). The heroine of the novel meets a young woman, Nina, while both are getting a divorce. The two of them go on a drinking binge in a park, during which the protagonist witnesses Nina dragging three policemen underwater and drowning them. She spends the night in Nina's room in a large communal apartment. As she tries to leave, the labyrinth of passageways and doors turns into a magic forest, where the neighbors are fairy-tale characters, such as a mermaid, and Baba Yaga, a witch who devours her victims. This introduction of magic does not signal breaches in reality, as it does in the stories of Nina Nikolaevna Sadur; rather, it is a product of the heroine's psyche. The tangible nature of these visions is, therefore, more terrifying.

In 2001 Vasilenko co-edited (with Azhgikhina) a collection of articles titled *Zhenshchiny: Svoboda slova i svoboda tvorchestva* (Woman: Freedom of Speech and Freedom of Creativity), the product of a seminar on women, mass media, and literature. Representing an array of positions on the issues concerning the role of women in contemporary culture, the collection gives voice both to Russian feminists and to women writers and journalists with more traditional views.

The narratives of Svetlana Vladimirovna Vasilenko are feminist, in that they center on feminine consciousness, and they are postmodernist, in that they deconstruct both ancient and quite modern myths. Yet, just as her women characters resist a stable identification, Vasilenko's narratives cannot be pinned down easily in terms of genre or ideology. She avoids fashionable topics and trendy exposés, choosing instead the thorny path of a "human ecologist" and a bold blend of high and low subjects. Such a position makes Vasilenko an uncommon phenomenon in the perpetually transitional Russian culture of today.

Bibliography:

[Svetlana Vasilenko Bibliography] <http://www.m-m.sotcom.ru/11-13/vas-bibl.htm> [accessed 21 July 2003].

Biography:

Elena Trofimova, "Vasilenko, Svetlana Vladimirovna," in *Dictionary of Russian Women Writers,* edited by Marina Ledkovsky, Charlotte Rosenthal, and Mary Zirin (Westport, Conn.: Greenwood Press, 1991), p. 690.

References:

Nadezhda Azhgikhina, "Paradoksy 'Zhenskoi prozy,'" in *Novaia Volna* (Moscow: Moskovskii rabochii, 1994), pp. 82–86;

Pavel Basinsky, "Pozabyvshie dobro?" *Literaturnaia gazeta,* 20 February 1991, p. 10;

Deming Brown, *The Last Years of Soviet Russian Literature: Prose Fiction, 1975–1991* (Cambridge: Cambridge University Press, 1993);

Helena Goscilo, *Dehexing Sex: Russian Womanhood during and after Glasnost'* (Ann Arbor: University of Michigan Press, 1996), pp. 91–95, 104–106;

Goscilo, "Speaking Bodies: Erotic Zones Rhetoricized," in *Fruits of Her Plume: Essays on Contemporary Russian Women's Culture* (Armonk, N.Y.: M. E. Sharpe, 1993), pp. 137–138;

Nikolai Shipilov, "Okopnaia pravda Svetlany Vasilenko," in Vasilenko, *Zvonkoe imia: Videopoema i rasskazy* (Moscow: Molodaia gvardiia, 1991), pp. 261–265.

Mikhail Mikhailovich Zhvanetsky

(6 March 1934 –   )

Seth Graham
University of Pittsburgh

BOOKS: *Vremia bol'shikh peremeshchenii,* Samodeiatel'nyi teatral'nyi Repertuar i metodika, no. 18 (Moscow: Iskusstvo, 1977);

Vstrechi na ulitsakh (Moscow: Iskusstvo, 1980);

Sobranie sochinenii, 14 volumes (Nizhnyi Tagil: Privately printed, 1983–2000);

God za dva, with an introduction by Andrei Georgievich Bitov (Moscow: Iskusstvo, 1989; revised edition, Leningrad: Leningradskii komitet literaturov, 1991);

Monologi (N.p.: Oner, 1990);

Staroe i novoe (Krasnoiarsk: Krasnyi rabochii, 1991);

Kogda nuzhny geroi (N.p., 1992);

Moia Odessa (Moscow: Olimp, 1993)–includes "Nachalo";

Sobranie proizvedenii, 4 volumes (Moscow: Vremia, 2001)–comprises volume 1, *Shestidesiatye;* volume 2, *Semidesiatye;* volume 3, *Vos'midesiatye;* and volume 4, *Devianostye.*

Edition in English: *Rasskazy/Stories,* translated by Brian Baer and Irina Barskova (New York: Slovo, 1994).

PRODUCED SCRIPT: *Ves' Zhvanetsky,* television, NTV, 1998–1999.

RECORDINGS: *Roman Kartsev, Viktor Il'chenko, Mikhail Zhvanetsky,* by Zhvanetsky, Kartsev, and Il'chenko, Melodiia, 1973;

Riskovannye shutki, Russian and International Songs, 1982;

Diskoteka smekha, by Zhvanetsky, Kartsev, and Il'chenko, Melodiia, 1986;

Mikhail Zhvanetsku, 1990;

Privet, elektorat! Vtoroe vnezapnoe obrashchenie Mikhaila Zhvanetskogo k naseleniiu, Solyd Records, 1996;

Odesskii telefon, 1998.

SELECTED PERIODICAL PUBLICATIONS–UNCOLLECTED: "Ni sekundy ne poterial!" *Avrora,* no. 1 (January 1972): 79;

"Chto vneshnost?!" *Literaturnaia gazeta,* no. 5, 1975;

"Visions of America Plenty," *New York Times,* 11 March 1990, p. 3;

"Opiat' svoboda," *Leningradskaia Pravda,* 22 December 1990;

"Iz Odessy s privetom," *Knizhnoe obozrenie,* 28 December 1990, p. 3;

"Obnimemsia, brat'ia!" *Gudok,* 1 January 1991;

"Strakh ispytyvat' mozhno. Boiat'sia ne nado!" *Moskovskie novosti,* 3 February 1991, p. 10;

"Vospominanie o ede," *Moskovskii komsomolets,* 13 July 1991;

"Vs-s-stuplenie . . . ," *Literaturnaia gazeta,* 31 July 1991, p. 16;

"Telefonnyi razgovor; V ritme tango," *Stolitsa,* no. 10 (1994): 47–48;

"Rasskaz," *Ogonek,* no. 14 (April 1995): 41–42;

"Laughter and Tears," *Moscow Times,* 18 May 1996;

"On Ourselves," *Moscow News,* 16–22 February 2000, p. 9;

"On prishel ko mne s tonometrom," *Meditsinskaia gazeta,* 17 May 2000, p. 16;

"Pishushchemu i pokazyvaiushchemu," *Moskovskie novosti,* 18–25 September 2000, pp. 1, 12; translated as "To: Writers and Anchors," *Moscow News,* 20 September 2000, p. 1.

Mikhail Zhvanetsky is the most popular Russian satirist of the late-Soviet and post-Soviet periods. After spending the first decade of his career in virtual anonymity, writing monologues and sketches for performance by others, he developed an immense following as a performer of his own material in the 1970s. Zhvanetsky's readings of his sharp, irreverent miniatures became legendary events during the second half of Leonid Il'ich Brezhnev's eighteen-year rule (1964–1982), a time of socio-economic and cultural stagnation and political cynicism within the educated public. The unflinching contemporary topicality and ironic double meanings that characterize Zhvanetsky's satire guaranteed that he would have periodic run-ins with the authorities and could not perform in large venues or publish in mass print runs. Nevertheless, he became a household name, in large part because his readings were informally recorded on tape and circulated widely in homemade copies.

Mikhail Mikhailovich Zhvanetsky (from The Mikhail Zhvanetsky Official Site, www.jvanetsky.ru)

Although he has published several collections of his works and many stories in national periodicals (the majority of them since the end of Soviet censorship in the late 1980s), Zhvanetsky continues to be known primarily as an "author-performer" whose literary output is ideally conveyed in oral, rather than written, form: Zhvanetsky himself reads aloud from the page. Most of his Soviet-era compositions were published only years—or even decades—after they were written and first performed. His colloquial, conversational style and his various idiosyncratic narrators place much of his work in the narrative tradition of Russian *skaz,* to the past masters of which (especially Mikhail Mikhailovich Zoshchenko) he is often compared.

Mikhail Mikhailovich Zhvanetsky was born on 6 March 1934 in Odessa (in present-day Ukraine), a port on the Black Sea, with a reputation as a fertile source of literary, comedic, and musical talents. Many famous Odessites, including Zhvanetsky, have been part of the large Jewish population of the city (among his best-known predecessors in this regard are the early-twentieth-century writers Isaak Emmanuilovich Babel' and Il'ia Arnol'dovich Il'f). Both his father, Emmanuil Moiseevich Zhvanetsky, and his mother, Raisa Iakovlevna Zhvanetskaia, were doctors, a fact that made particularly sharp Zhvanetsky's memory of the 1953 "doctors' plot" (or "doctors' case")—

a false conspiracy accusation that was a pretext for the repression of several Jewish physicians by the regime of Joseph Stalin. Doctor-patient encounters as well as Jewish life became prominent themes later in his writing.

Zhvanetsky attended the Odessa Institute of Naval Engineering from 1951 to 1956. There he cofounded an amateur theater troupe, Parnassus-2, with fellow students Viktor Il'chenko and Roman Andreevich Kartsev (both of whom later became famous comedians). The sketches and monologues that Zhvanetsky wrote for the troupe during this period formed the basis for much of his later work, especially the many pieces about his beloved Odessa, where, Zhvanetsky wrote in "Nachalo" (Beginning), published in *Moia Odessa* (My Odessa, 1993), a writer "doesn't have to write anything. He just has to open the window and start taking notes."

After graduation Zhvanetsky worked as a mechanic and an engineer at the port of Odessa. Kartsev and Il'chenko also took full-time jobs, but the trio of friends continued their theatrical activities. The cultural renaissance of the post-Stalinist "Thaw" in the late 1950s inspired a formidable amateur-theater movement in the U.S.S.R. and made stars of the comedians, actors, and musicians that appeared in the growing mass media. Zhvanetsky later recalled how he and Il'chenko listened to recordings or radio broadcasts of the legendary comedian Arkadii Isaakovich Raikin while working the night shift at the port. When their troupe visited Leningrad as part of an amateur-theater exchange in 1958, Zhvanetsky and Il'chenko went to the Leningrad Miniatures Theater, where Raikin was the artistic director, and asked to perform for their idol. Recalling years later his first meeting with Zhvanetsky, Raikin remarked that he was impressed by the young satirist. When Raikin's own troupe passed through Odessa while on tour in 1960, he watched another performance by Parnassus-2. This time he was particularly impressed by Kartsev's pantomime and monologue skills, so much so that Raikin offered him a position in his company. Kartsev accepted and moved to Leningrad, where Il'chenko—whom Raikin hired later that year—soon joined him.

Left alone in Odessa without his creative partners, in 1964 Zhvanetsky took the bold step of quitting his job and moving to Leningrad himself, where he took a low-paying writing job at a food-industry *dom kul'tury* (house of culture). Although Raikin had not hired him, he continued to write satirical shorts and frequented the Miniatures Theater to observe his role model at work. He would show his compositions to Raikin, who sometimes chose small pieces for the theater repertoire. Zhvanetsky was especially encouraged after Raikin accepted a large monologue titled "Dnevnik" (Diary, 1964). This early piece includes many formal and thematic trademarks of Zhvanetsky's later work: the one-sided dialogue in which the narrator responds to unheard, unseen interlocutors; a speech by an authority figure constantly interrupted by spontaneous, informal comments (in this case a teacher attempting to impart advice to his rowdy students); and a simple-hearted, uneducated narrator confounded by modern technology (the diarist recalling his first day on a factory job: "something started honking and clanging and everyone took off. I ran to the left, to the right, knocked three guys over, and when they finally caught me it turned out it was the lunch bell").

Though still not employed by the theater, Zhvanetsky had begun to accompany Raikin's troupe on tour at his own expense. After three years of sparse living, however, Zhvanetsky told Raikin in 1967 that he was returning to Odessa because he could no longer afford to live in Leningrad. Raikin immediately offered him a contract to script an entire show, which allowed Zhvanetsky to stay in his adopted city. The result, a production called *Svetofor* (Traffic Light), premiered in 1967 to great acclaim. It was a triumph especially for Raikin himself, whose performances of Zhvanetsky's pieces for the show—including the monologues "V vek tekhniki" (In the Age of Technology, performed in 1967) and "Defitsit" (Shortage, 1966) and the sketch "Avas" (And You, performed in 1967)—became Raikin classics. Zhvanetsky was

finally invited to join the theater on a more permanent basis. He was hired as an actor but soon became the *zavlit* of the theater—the person in charge of the literary portions of the repertoire.

In Zhvanetsky's output during his years with Raikin the themes that eventually came to define his post-Raikin work were already present, though with a more broadly comedic tone than that of his later, more pointed satire. "V grecheskom zale" (In the Greek Sculpture Gallery, performed in 1966) is a monologue from the perspective of a working-class man determined to spend his precious day off in his preferred way—getting drunk, eating, and reading the paper—even though his wife has dragged him to the Hermitage Art Museum in Leningrad. He adapts the ancient sculpture gallery to his own purposes for an impromptu drinking session. In "Defitsit," written in a similar style, the narrator defends the beneficial social effects of consumer-goods shortages, which in the abundant future, he predicts, will themselves be a scarce, prized commodity to be shared behind closed doors with close friends (Raikin gave the monologue a less satirical, more comedic tone by performing it with a Georgian accent). In "V vek tekhniki" a narrator reminiscent of the confused factory worker in "Dnevnik" is sent to an international exhibition in Paris to demonstrate the latest Soviet technological marvel—a machine of some sort—with (literally) explosive results. These and other pieces from the 1960s exemplify the theatricality of Zhvanetsky's Raikin-era output, as well as his use of "pure" *skaz,* in which the style imitates a character's oral speech: no authorial voice is present and the narrator is unreliable and uneducated.

The satire of Zhvanetsky's early work is pointed but aimed at safely broad targets (shortages, bureaucracy, drunkenness) and imbued with an optimism that is only partly ironic. "Beregite biurokratov" (Save the Bureaucrats, performed in 1967), for instance, encourages Soviet citizens to unite "to prevent the extinction of bureaucrats," reasoning that people would become weak and lazy if they did not have to deal with the constant resistance and complications encountered at every level of the bureaucracy. Some of Zhvanetsky's work for Raikin was not satirical at all and even tended toward sentimentalism. "Dai ruchku, vnuchek!" (Give Me Your Hand, Grandson!, performed in 1968), for example, is a bittersweet, lyrical scene of an old man walking with his three-year-old grandson, gently giving him advice. That piece is a good example of Zhvanetsky's use of the genre known as the *repriza* (from the French *reprise*), in which humorous lines are interspersed with nonhumorous text to achieve a deft balance of comic and lyric tones.

Raikin selected only some of Zhvanetsky's miniatures for inclusion in the theater's repertoire. In 1968 Zhvanetsky himself began to perform material not chosen

Zhvanetsky, left, with comedian Arkadii Isaakovich Raikin, right, for whom he wrote material during the 1960s (from The Mikhail Zhvanetsky Official Site, www.jvanetsky.ru)

by Raikin at small, closed readings in "Houses of Scholars," "Houses of Writers," and other such venues not open to the public and reserved as perquisites for members of prestigious professional unions. At these events he read material that he knew skirted the boundaries of the ideologically permissible, but he felt that his affiliation with one of the most popular theaters in the country—and especially with the legendary, beloved Raikin—afforded him a degree of immunity. In 1969, however, another member of the troupe told Zhvanetsky that Raikin himself was becoming averse to the increasingly pessimistic, politically caustic tone of Zhvanetsky's satire and wanted him to leave the theater. Zhvanetsky was puzzled to hear this news and even treated it as a joke by slipping an ironic "letter of resignation" between the pages of the next manuscript he submitted. To Zhvanetsky's amazement and horror, Raikin took the letter seriously and signed it. Later, Zhvanetsky always referred to his reluctant departure from the Miniatures Theater as a de facto dismissal. Kartsev and Il'chenko also left Raikin's theater soon thereafter.

Both Raikin and Zhvanetsky later acknowledged that their relationship had become strained and that the break was not entirely amicable. Zhvanetsky took the separation quite hard, and relations between the two were cordial at best for years to come. Occasionally, Zhvanetsky still showed his new material to Raikin, but Raikin performed a new Zhvanetsky monologue only once more, in 1978. Still, on the occasion of Raikin's seventieth birthday in 1981 Zhvanetsky called him "my first love," and in his memoirs Raikin speaks kindly of his former protégé, characterizing their split as a simple parting of the ways between two professional artists. Their split was also emblematic of the generational shift from the light satirical treatment of everyday life and human foibles that characterized Soviet satire in the late 1950s and 1960s and the more politically pointed, intellectual, ironic satire of the "era of stagnation" that followed.

After leaving Raikin's troupe Zhvanetsky, Kartsev, and Il'chenko, now seasoned professionals, returned to Odessa, where they founded the Odessa Miniatures Theater in 1970. In the course of the next few years Zhvanetsky wrote both for the new theater and for his own increasingly popular solo concerts. During this period he developed his trademark stage presence: the writer alone, in street clothes, standing at a microphone, pulling wrinkled, marked-up pages out of a worn leather briefcase (an accessory that became as indispensable to his image, he says, as "Churchill's cigar") and reading them aloud in his fast-paced Odessa accent. He is considered the inventor of his own genre, related to comic miniatures and monologues for the circus and variety stage, but with no costumes, makeup, or other theatrical concealments of the author-performer's identity. This absence of a literal mask was accompanied by a related difference from his earlier work as well as from his predecessors in the *skaz* tradition; in contrast to Zoshchenko (and to Raikin for that matter) Zhvanetsky often collapses the distance between author and narrator so that the *skaz* style becomes not an instrument for satirizing a risible narrator's lack of cultural or intellectual sophistication—a sort of verbal slapstick—but a medium for the author's own more-or-less direct (though markedly "artistic") discourse.

One of Zhvanetsky's best-known monologues in this regard is "Ikh den'" (Their Day, performed in 1974), inspired by a characteristically optimistic televised speech by the Soviet minister of meat and dairy production at a time when such products were in short supply. The piece is a good example of the increasingly frequent autobiographical perspective in Zhvanetsky's work, as well as the essayistic tendency that made his one of the leading voices among the creative intelligentsia during perestroika. In the monologue Zhvanetsky ironically addresses the incongruity between everyday reality as described in the mass media and the same as experienced by the average Soviet citizen, as well as the privileged lifestyles of state officials:

> And the funny thing is, the minister of meat and dairy production does in fact exist, and he looks great. And interestingly enough the meat and dairy industry also exists . . . and the production rate is five times higher than it was in 1940 . . . with an expanded assortment and convenient packaging. . . . To see this, however, you have to be on the inside, with them. It's in there, apparently, that they produce it and, apparently, where they consume it, too.

The narratorial and authorial points of view are virtually indistinguishable; the familiar distinctive language of Zhvanetsky's *skaz* remains, yet the satirical referent is not the narrator himself but, rather, the situation and personalities referred to in the third person. The text approaches the subjective, journalistic form of nonfiction known in Russian letters as *publitsistika*.

Other leitmotivs of Zhvanetsky's early solo work include drinking, as seen in "Ranniaia ptashka" (Early Bird, 1971), "Posle vcherashnego" (After Last Night, 1974), and "Esli b ia brosil pit'" (If I Quit Drinking, 1975); Jewish life in Odessa, as conveyed in "Moi dvor v Odesse" (My Neighborhood in Odessa, 1970) and "Kak shutili v Odesse" (How They Play Jokes in Odessa, 1969); shortages and food lines, which he describes in "Ia zhdu" (I'm Waiting, 1968) and "Ia za nim" (I'm After Him, 1975); gender relations, seen in "Nashim zhenshchinam" (To Our Women, 1973); and, again, only a semi-ironic appreciation for the value of hardship and struggle in the physical and social development of *Homo sovieticus*, which he addresses in "Voennaia kost'" (Military Mettle, 1971).

In "Ikh den'" and similar pieces Zhvanetsky stayed on the peripheries of an unspoken taboo by referring to specific official institutions, implying a causative link between the party or the state and the everyday hassles and human weaknesses that were acceptable topics of post-Stalinist Soviet satire. In "Sobranie na likerovodochnom zavode" (Meeting at a Vodka Factory, performed in 1971) a factory board conducts a meeting in bureaucrat-speak, pausing with increasing frequency to fill their glasses from the carafes on the table and growing more inebriated as the discussion turns, ironically, to the problem of alcoholism. Zhvanetsky touches on the theme of corruption and theft of state property in "Chto okhraniaesh', tovarishch?" (What Are You Guarding, Comrade?, performed in 1969), which plays on an official slogan—"Everyone guard the people's property!"—in paradoxically giving career advice: "you want to read good books? Become an editor; you can read them first and not let anyone else see them! Become a forest ranger,

you'll have firewood! Guard a pharmacy, you'll have cotton balls! Sit and guard snakes, you'll have venom!"

Although by the mid 1970s Zhvanetsky was too popular for the state to prevent him from performing entirely—he even appeared occasionally on television—he was not able to give concerts in the large variety theaters, appearing instead in universities, factories, and professional clubs. He also played military and scientific research institutes that were "so secret they had no addresses" (from Suzanne Charle's *New York Times* article of 8 June 1994). Zhvanetsky even performed once via two-way radio for cosmonauts in space, a telling fact indicating that the state viewed him as a "luxury item" for the exclusive consumption of the elite on the "inside."

As Andrei Georgievich Bitov points out in his introduction to Zhvanetsky's perestroika collection *God za dva* (A Year Seems Like Two, 1989; revised, 1991), Zhvanetsky's place in the stagnation-era culture resembled that of his contemporary, the bard-poet Vladimir Semenovich Vysotsky, whose voice could similarly be heard emanating from thousands of tape recorders in homemade copies (a phenomenon known as *magnitizdat*, "self-made recordings," the audio counterpart to samizdat, or self-published literature). Like Vysotsky, Zhvanetsky eventually became so popular that the state could not risk silencing him entirely, so for years he occupied a place on the boundary between official and unofficial culture. Zhvanetsky's reputation as the leading source of bons mots in the nation was so widespread that Brezhnev himself once asked the satirist to compose him a toast for an official dinner (the result: "vodka in small doses is harmless in any quantity").

Zhvanetsky became a member of the Soviet Writers' Union in 1978, a year after the publication of *Vremia bol'shikh peremeshchenii* (A Time of Great Travels, 1977), the first of two slim volumes of his work to be published openly before perestroika. Subtitled *Repertuar dlia estradnogo kontserta* (A Repertoire for a Variety Stage Concert), the collection favors Zhvanetsky's more theatrical, comedic pieces, including several that had become well-known from Raikin's performances of them. Zhvanetsky's second book was *Vstrechi na ulitsakh* (Street Encounters, 1980), which somewhat overlaps in content with *Vremia bol'shikh peremeshchenii* but also has certain celebrated stories left out of the first, an omission testifying perhaps to Zhvanetsky's growing renown.

Despite his sparse publishing history and his reputation for public readings, Zhvanetsky was an active participant in the literary culture of the 1970s and 1980s. That culture, as Bitov points out in his introduction to *God za dva*, was necessarily reliant on oral forms of communication: "the written word gave way to the oral word when time stood still." The oral emphasis of intellectual

михаил

ЖВАНЕЦКИЙ

4

собрание
произведений
●
девяностые

Front cover for Devianostye *(The 1990s), volume four of
Zhvanetsky's* Sobranie proizvedenii *(Collection of
Works), an extensive edition published in 2001
(Reed College Library)*

culture during the Brezhnev period was responsible for
the enormous popularity of the *anekdot* (joke), a genre
related to Zhvanetsky's miniatures in tone and thematics.
Both genres were part of what Boris Briker and Anatolii
Vishevsky call in their article "Iumor v populiarnoi
kul'ture sovetskogo intelligenta 60-x–70-x godov"
(Humor in the Popular Culture of the Soviet Intellectual,
1960s–1970s), published in 1989 in *Wiener Slawistischer
Almanach* (Vienna Slavic Almanac), the "popular humor of
the intelligentsia," a phenomenon that "existed on the
boundary of fiction, stage comedy, and journalism."

In 1981 Zhvanetsky moved to Moscow, where he
worked for two years at the popular journal *Studencheskii
meridian* (Student Meridian). He continued to perform,
but even his ever-growing fame and reputation could not
prevent (and indeed, were a likely cause of) occasional
reprimands from above. A 1982 reading at the Central
House of the Actor in Moscow, for instance, prompted an
"invitation" to speak with a representative of the Soviet
Writers' Union, who subsequently filed this report:

Many of the miniatures read . . . contained tendentious
and at times mean-spirited . . . comments about certain

aspects of Soviet life. . . . M. Zhvanetsky was called
before the Secretariat of the Writers' Union of the
U.S.S.R., where he was made aware of the principal
objections regarding his reading. He was warned of the
unacceptability of irresponsible public speaking. M. Zhvanetsky admitted that the objections were fair and stated
that it would not happen again.

While Zhvanetsky himself never suffered more
than such a reprimand for his satirical performances, he
later recalled that the authorities sometimes punished
those who gave him public forums: "they would arrest
the manager of the hall. I'd perform, the next day he'd
lose his job. There are five such people on my conscience." In addition to the restrictions on where he could
perform and publish, Zhvanetsky was *nevyezdnoi*, that is,
not permitted to travel outside the country.

Zhvanetsky never tempered his satirical attacks in
response to the complaints and restrictions from above,
and continued to treat the same sociopolitical issues in his
stories—for example, the bureaucracy as a force immune
to logic, as seen in "Kak? Vam nichego ne govorili?"
(What? Nobody told you?, performed in 1982); the
unbridgeable gap between life represented in media and
real life, portrayed in "Klub kinoputeshestvii" (The
Travel-by-Television Club, performed in 1977); and the
genuine value of human relations, commiseration, and
camaraderie under such conditions.

Although *Vremia bol'shikh peremeshchenii* and *Vstrechi
na ulitsakh* were the only volumes of Zhvanetsky's writing
to be published openly under the conditions of Soviet
censorship, he was more "prolific" in the world of underground publishing, although he never self-published anything. In 1984 a fan named Aleksandr Sysoev (who also
anthologized works by Vysotsky and another legendary
author and songwriter, Bulat Shalvovich Okudzhava)
issued a three-volume samizdat edition of Zhvanetsky's
collected works. The collection grew to fourteen volumes
by the time samizdat editions had become unnecessary, as
a result of the cultural reforms initiated by Mikhail Sergeevich Gorbachev in 1986.

With the onset of Gorbachev's liberal cultural policies Zhvanetsky was able for the first time to perform in
the largest theaters of the country, appear regularly in the
mass media, and publish freely. In 1988 he became the
artistic director of the Moscow Miniatures Theater. He
began to play to sell-out crowds in huge concert venues
rather than run-down student theaters or factory assembly halls. Zhvanetsky was hailed as a hero during perestroika for having had the courage to express sentiments
that were silently shared by millions at the time, when
stating such ideas publicly—much less making a career of
it—was far from safe. Throughout the Gorbachev period
his monologues provided running commentary and satirical analysis of the sea changes under way in Soviet society.

In "Rabotaem nepreryvno, prokhodia tsiklicheskie etapy" (We Work Without Rest, Passing Through Cyclical Stages, performed in 1987), for example, he treats perestroika (restructuring) as merely the next phase of an endless cycle of destruction and reconstruction in Russo-Soviet history. His support of Gorbachev's reforms was unequivocal, however, as illustrated by the long monologue "Pis'mo ottsu" (Letter to My Father, 1991), which he wrote during the August 1991 coup attempt by a group of hard-line, old-guard Communists.

Zhvanetsky's first post-censorship collection, *God za dva,* embraces two hundred stories, more than twice the number in *Vremia bol'shikh peremeshchenii* and *Vstrechi na ulitsakh,* his two Brezhnev-era collections, combined. Not accustomed to publishing most of what he wrote, and having written "oral prose" for his entire career, Zhvanetsky expressed discomfort in suddenly seeing his work in published form. In the introduction to his collection *Moia Odessa* (My Odessa, 1993) he admits: "I write strangely, of course. I hear myself when I write. It would be better if I could read all this to you aloud. But one has to publish. To me, a book is like canned vegetables that were once fresh."

The new openness was so sudden and unfamiliar to Zhvanetsky that he wrote about it explicitly in his monologues. In "Eto bylo by nemyslimo dazhe dva goda nazad" (This Would Have Been Unthinkable Even Two Years Ago, 1987), for example, he begins:

> So, I'm standing in front of a German TV camera and nobody objects. . . . People tell me now that I had a bad life back then. But I didn't, not at all. I didn't know it was possible to live otherwise. I figured that, since my works weren't being published, that was how it should be. . . . I just read my stuff aloud. And people recorded it, copied it, somebody wrote it down and printed it in special hand-made books. Now I've crawled out into the sunlight for the first time, and I'm afraid all over again. Afraid that sunlight might not be good for me.

But in the same monologue he writes, "if my work becomes dated, that means I've won, for it will mean that life has gotten better."

In the absence of censorship and bureaucratic state socialism Zhvanetsky and his audience no longer had a common secret about which to laugh and commiserate. In the era of glasnost and free speech he was no longer counted upon to articulate the unspoken sentiments of the population; they could now do that for themselves. Unlike many of his fellow writers and performers, however, Zhvanetsky has enjoyed a successful post-censorship, post-Soviet career. A chief reason for his sustained popularity is the sheer magnitude of his celebrity; Bitov does not exaggerate when he places Zhvanetsky alongside the legendary Vysotsky as an emblem of an entire cultural epoch. Another factor is the strong current of lyricism in his

work, distinguishing it from "pure" satire, which is heavily reliant on its targets. The earnest affirmations and optimism of his miniatures are as central to his authorial persona as his ironic critiques of various pernicious influences in the lives of common people. His *skaz*-narrator's lyricism is particularly apparent in his periodic "self-portraits," each titled according to the current year, in which Zhvanetsky mixes light, self-reflexive irony directed at the aging satirist with ironic hints at the sociopolitical atmosphere and more serious, philosophical sentiments. In "Avtoportret-96" (Self-Portrait '96, 1996), for instance, he lists seventeen numbered observations, referring to himself in the third person as if describing his image in a mirror. He moves from his physical appearance ("Four. This gut arrives first wherever he goes. It misbehaves and bothers. Although it does serve as a shelf for someone's hands.") to his career ("Eight. The audience demands something funny. Nine. Why doesn't anyone wish to be sad? What about Gor'ky's *Mother?* What about *Anna Karenina?*") and concludes with a poignant, comprehensive auto-metaphor: "Seventeen. He's like a parrot in a cage covered with a blanket. They lift the blanket and suddenly there's bright light and a thousand eyes and he talks and talks. . . . Then they cover the cage again and it's quiet, dark, and nobody can tell who it is inside the cage."

Zhvanetsky has continued to be a visible participant in the cultural life of both Russia and Ukraine. He has edited the satirical magazine *Magazin* (Store) since 1992. He has also been a vocal and visible champion of democratic forces in Russian politics and supported President Boris Nikolaevich Yeltsin, who awarded Zhvanetsky the Order of People's Friendship in 1994. That same year, Zhvanetsky played a sold-out Carnegie Hall in New York during a tour celebrating his sixtieth birthday. He is the general secretary of a tongue-in-cheek party of his own, the Humor Party, and the president of the Worldwide Club of Odessites. He has also served as a member of the Consultative Council of the Russian Ministry of Culture and Tourism. In 1998 the television station Nezavisimoe televidenie (NTV, Independent Television) produced and videotaped four large concerts by Zhvanetsky and broadcast them as a sixteen-part series titled *Ves' Zhvanetsky* (The Complete Zhvanetsky). In 2001 the most extensive anthology to date of his works, *Sobranie proizvedenii,* was published in four volumes.

In September 2000 Zhvanetsky sparked a minor controversy when he published an article, titled "Pishushchemu i pokazyvaiushchemu" (translated as "To: Writers and Anchors"), in *Moskovskie novosti* (Moscow News), in which he attacked the liberal journalists at the television station NTV for their pessimistic, sensationalistically violent and obscene broadcasts. Zhvanetsky explicitly defends President Vladimir Putin, whose administration was about to acquire a de facto controlling interest in the station, the last such nationwide independent media outlet. Although many were puzzled at Zhvanetsky's seeming betrayal of the liberal democratic ideals he had championed for so many years, the article is in fact consistent with his disdain for self-serving elites and his defense of, and implicit faith in, the average citizen; he commends Putin specifically for having paid long-overdue pensions and salaries and proves that the populace did not share the journalists' mistrust of Putin by pointing out that there was no wave of Putin jokes.

Although Mikhail Mikhailovich Zhvanetsky's brand of satire was inspired and nurtured by the environment of the so-called era of stagnation with its chronic shortages, witless bureaucrats, and Aesopian language, he remains one of the most beloved cultural figures in the former Soviet Union as well as among the large Russian-speaking populations of Israel and the United States, in part because of the continuing nostalgia in Russia for Soviet popular culture of the 1960s, 1970s, and 1980s. Zhvanetsky's formidable cultural legacy is apparent in the Russian language itself; many phrases from his works have become proverbs, quoted at opportune moments in conversation, journalism, and even political speeches.

Interviews:

G. Pletinsky, "V Tashkente, kak v Odesse," *Pravda Vostoka,* 25 November 1990;

Alla Bossart, "Piat'desiat deviat' po vertikali," *Stolitsa,* no. 21 (1993): 50–53;

Suzanne Charle, "For Emigré Russians, Belly Laughs from Home," *New York Times,* 8 June 1994, p. C1;

Natal'ia Loginova, "Interv'iu, kotorogo ne bylo," *Ogonek,* no. 13 (1997): 49;

Aleksei Smirnov, "Zhvanetsky na nobelevskoi stsene," *Novye izvestiia,* 2 February 2000, pp. 1, 6;

Natal'ia Gracheva, "Esli by ne zhena Raikina, ia do sikh por sidel by na kuche uglia," *Komsomol'skaia Pravda,* 19 February 2000, pp. 8–9;

Valentina Serikova, "Polnyi Zhvanetsky," *Ogonek,* nos. 17–18 (2001): 46–50.

References:

Celestine Bohlen, "In the New Russia, Comedy Lacks Bite," *New York Times,* 24 January 1999, II: 24;

Boris Briker and Anatolii Vishevsky, "Iumor v populiarnoi kul'ture sovetskogo intelligenta 60-x–70-x godov," *Wiener Slawistischer Almanach,* no. 24 (1989): 147–170;

V. Frolov, *Muza plamennoi satiry: Ocherki sovetskoi komediografii (1918–1986)* (Moscow: Sovetskii pisatel', 1988), pp. 357–363;

Dina Goder, "Zhvanetsky. No segodnia: S 11 sentiabria na kanale NTV nachalsia pokaz novogo seriala

'Ves' Zhvanetsky,'" *Itogi,* no. 36 (15 September 1998): 58–59;

Lee Hockstader, "Dry Times for Comedians in Post-Communist Russia," *Washington Post,* 14 June 1996, p. A35;

E. Iampol'skaia, "Novyi Zhvanetsky," *Novye izvestiia,* 25 May 2000, p. 7;

Iurii Karabchievsky, "Novaia literatura–eto literatura otsutstviia," *Vremia i my,* no. 124 (1994): 262–271;

Vasilii Litvinov, "Zhvanetsky kak paradigma: Popytka sformulirovat'," *Literaturnaia gazeta,* 30 April 1997, p. 16;

Natal'ia Loginova, "Moi Zhvanetsky," *Magazin,* 26 (1997);

The Mikhail Zhvanetsky Page <http://www.jvanetsky.ru/> [accessed 17 July 2003];

Alexander Nechayev, "Soviet-Banned Best Satirist Awarded by Yeltsin," *ITAR-TASS,* 2 March 1994;

Vladimir Ivanovich Novikov, "O meste Zoshchenko v russkoi literature: Predshestvenniki i posledovateli ot Daniila Zatochnika do Mikhaila Zhvanetskogo," *Literaturnoe obozrenie,* no. 1 (1995): 25–27;

Arkadii Isaakovich Raikin, *Vospominaniia* (Moscow: ACT, 1998);

Joel Schecter, *The Congress of Clowns and Other Russian Circus Acts* (San Francisco: Kropotkin Club of San Francisco, 1998);

Schechter, "Durov's Pig, Nikulin's Dog, Zhvanetsky's Frog," *Theater,* 23, no. 3 (Summer 1992): 47–60;

Ioakim Sharoev, "Mikhail Mikhailovich," in his *Mnogolikaia estrada: Za kulisami kremlevskikh kontsertov* (Moscow: Vagrius, 1995), pp. 281–292;

V. Shauro, "O tvorcheskom vechere pisatelia-satirika M. Zhvanetskogo v Tsentral'nom Dome aktera im. Iablochkinoi," in "Dokumenty svidetel'stvuiut . . .: Iz fondov Tsentra khraneniia sovremennoi dokumentatsii (TsKhSD)," edited by Z. Vodop'ianova and others, *Voprosy literatury,* no. 5 (1994): 260–284, 283–284;

Efim Shifrin, "Mikhal Mikhalych," in his *Teatr imeni menia: Kniga o Efime Shifrine i ego neobyknovennykh prikliucheniiakh v mire estrady* (Moscow: Konets veka, 1994), pp. 67–74;

Elizaveta Uvarova, *Arkadii Raikin* (Moscow: Iskusstvo, 1992), pp. 199–209;

Anatoly Vishevsky, *Soviet Literary Culture in the 1970s: The Politics of Irony* (Gainesville: University Press of Florida, 1993);

Iuliia Zhenevskaia, "Mikhail Zhvanetsky kak zerkalo nashei evoliutsii," *Slovo,* 28 November 1997 <http://www.vista.Odessa.ua/Odessa/media/word/263/sn543.htm>.

Books for Further Reading

Adelman, Deborah. *The "Children of Perestroika" Come of Age: Young People of Moscow Talk about Life in the New Russia.* Armonk, N.Y.: M. E. Sharpe, 1994.

Ageev, Aleksandr. *Gazeta, glianets, internet.* Moscow: Novoe literaturnoe obozrenie, 2001.

Aizenberg, Mikhail Natanovich. *Vzgliad na svobodnogo khudozhnika.* Moscow: Gendalf, 1997.

Aksenov, Vasily Popovich, Viktor Vladimirovich Erofeev, Andrei Georgievich Bitov, Evgenii Anatol'evich Popov, and Fazil Abdulovich Iskander, eds. *Metropol'. Literary almanac.* New York: Norton, 1982.

Andrle, Vladimir. *A Social History of Twentieth-Century Russia.* New York: Chapman & Hall, 1994.

Appignanesi, Lisa, and Martin Walker, eds. *Novostroika=New Structures.* London: Institute of Contemporary Arts, 1989.

Arkhangel'sky, Aleksandr Nikolaevich, ed. *U paradnogo pod'ezda: Literaturnye i kul'turnye situatsii perioda glasnosti, 1987–1990.* Moscow: Sovetskii pisatel', 1991.

Ashby, Stephen M., and Kent Johnson, eds. *Third Wave: The New Russian Poetry.* Ann Arbor: University of Michigan Press, 1992.

Balina, Marina, Nancy Condee, and Evgeny Dobrenko. *Endquote: Sots-Art and Soviet Grand Style.* Evanston, Ill.: Northwestern University Press, 2000.

Barker, Adele Marie, ed. *Consuming Russia: Popular Culture, Sex, and Society since Gorbachev.* Durham, N.C. & London: Duke University Press, 1999.

Belaia, Galina Andreevna. *Literatura v zerkale kritiki: Sovremennye problemy.* Moscow: Sovetskii pisatel', 1986.

Berg, Mikhail. *Literaturokratiia: problema prisvoeniia i pererapredeleniia vlasti v literature.* Moscow: Novoe literaturnoe obozrenie, 2000.

Berry, Ellen, and Anesa Miller-Pogacar, eds. *Re-Entering the Sign: Articulating New Russian Culture.* Ann Arbor: University of Michigan Press, 1995.

Bogdnova, Ol'ga. *Sovremennyi literaturnyi protsess (K voprosu o postmodernizme v russkoi literature 70-90-kh godov XX veka).* St. Petersburg: St. Petersburg University Press, 2001.

Brown, Deming. *The Last Years of Soviet Russian Literature: Prose Fiction, 1975–1991.* Cambridge & New York: Cambridge University Press, 1993.

Brun'ko, V. A., ed. *Pisateli Rossii: Avtobiografy sovremennikov.* Moscow: Glasnost', 1998.

Clowes, Edith. *Russian Experimental Fiction: Resisting Ideology after Utopia.* Princeton: Princeton University Press, 1993.

Condee, ed. *Soviet Hieroglyphics: Visual Culture in Late Twentieth-Century Russia.* Bloomington: Indiana University Press, 1995.

Cornwell, Neil. *Reference Guide to Russian Literature.* Chicago & London: Fitzroy Dearborn, 1998.

Dubin, Boris. *Slovo-pis'mo-literatura: ocherki po sotsiologii sovremennoi kul'tury.* Moscow: Novoe literaturnoe obozrenie, 2001.

Dunlop, John B. *The Rise of Russia and the Fall of the Soviet Empire.* Princeton: Princeton University Press, 1993.

Epshtein, Aleksandr Aleksandrovich Genis, and Slobodanka Vladiv-Glover. *Russian Postmodernism: New Perspectives on Post-Soviet Culture.* New York & Oxford: Berghahn, 1999.

Epshtein, Mikhail Naumovich. *After the Future: The Paradoxes of Postmodernism and Contemporary Russian Culture.* Amherst: University of Massachusetts Press, 1995.

Epshtein. *Postmodern v Rossii: Literatura i teoriia.* Moscow: LIA Elinina, 2000.

Erofeev, Viktor Vladimirovich, and Andrew Reynolds, eds. *The Penguin Book of New Russian Writing: Russia's Fleurs du mal.* New York: Penguin, 1995.

Eshelman, Raoul. *Early Soviet Postmodernism.* Frankfurt & New York: Peter Lang, 1997.

Fisher-Ruge, Lois. *Survival in Russia: Chaos and Hope in Everyday Life.* Boulder, Colo.: Westview Press, 1993.

Genis. *Ivan Petrovich umer: Stat'i i rassledovaniia.* Moscow: Novoe literaturnoe obozrenie, 1999.

Glad, John. *Conversations in Exile: Russian Writers Abroad.* Durham, N.C.: Duke University Press, 1993.

Glinsky, Dmitri, and Peter Reddaway. *The Tragedy of Russia's Reforms: Market Bolshevism against Democracy.* Washington, D.C.: United States Institute of Peace, 2001.

Glintershchik, R. *Ocherki noveishei russkoi literatury: Postmodernizm.* Vilnius, 1996.

Gorbachev, Mikhail Sergeevich. *Memoirs.* New York: Doubleday, 1996.

Goscilo, Helena. *Dehexing Sex: Russian Womanhood During and After Glasnost'.* Ann Arbor: University of Michigan Press, 1996.

Goscilo, ed. *Balancing Acts: Contemporary Stories by Russian Women.* Bloomington: Indiana University Press, 1989.

Goscilo, ed. *Fruits of Her Plume: Essays on Contemporary Russian Woman's Culture.* Armonk, N.Y.: M. E. Sharpe, 1993.

Goscilo, ed. *Lives in Transit: A Collection of Recent Russian Women's Writing.* Dana Point, Cal.: Ardis, 1995.

Goscilo and Byron Lindsey, eds. *Glasnost': An Anthology of Russian Literature Under Gorbachev.* Ann Arbor, Mich.: Ardis, 1990.

Goscilo and Lindsey, eds. *The Wild Beach and Other Stories.* Ann Arbor, Mich.: Ardis, 1993.

Green, Barbara B. *The Dynamics of Russian Politics: A Short History.* Westport, Conn.: Greenwood Press, 1994.

Groys, Boris. *Utopiia i obmen: Stil' Stalin, O novom, Stat'i.* Moscow: Znak, 1993.

Gustafson, Thane. *Capitalism Russian-Style*. Cambridge & New York: Cambridge University Press, 1999.

Haavio-Mannila, Elina, and Anna Rotkirch, eds. *Women's Voices in Russia Today*. Aldershot, U.K.: Dartmouth, 1996.

Handelman, Stephen. *Comrade Criminal: Russia's New Mafiya*. New Haven: Yale University Press, 1995.

Hayward, Max, and Albert C. Todd, eds., with Daniel Wessbort. *20th Century Russian Poetry: Silver and Steel,* selected by Yevgeny Yevtushenko. New York: Doubleday, 1993.

High, John, and others, eds. *Crossing Centuries: The New Generation in Russian Poetry*. Jersey City, N.J.: Talisman House, 2000.

Hosking, Geoffrey A. *Russia and the Russians*. Cambridge, Mass.: Harvard University Press, 2001.

Ionov, E., and S. Kolov, eds. *Pisateli Moskvy: biobibliograficheskii spravochnik*. Moscow. Moskovskii rabochii, 1987.

Ivanov, Boris, and Boris Roginsky, eds. *Istoriia leningradskoi nepodtsenzurnoi literatury: 1950–1980-e gody: sbornik statei*. St. Petersburg: DEAN, 2000.

Ivanova, Natal'ia. *Tochka zreniia*. Moscow: Sovetskii pisatel', 1988.

Kagal, Ayesha, and Natasha Perova, eds. *Present Imperfect: Stories by Russian Women*. Boulder, Colo.: Westview Press, 1996.

Kates, J., ed. *In the Grip of Strange Thoughts: Russian Poetry in a New Era*. Brookline, Mass.: Zephyr, 1999.

Kazack, Wolfgang. *Dictionary of Russian Literature since 1917,* translated by Rebecca Atack. New York: Columbia University Press, 1988.

Kulakov, Vladislav. *Poeziia kak fakt*. Moscow: Novoe literaturnoe obozrenie, 1999.

Kulle, Viktor, ed. *The Hungry Russian Winter. The Collection of Modern Russian Poetry in English Translations*. Moscow: N-Press, 1991.

Kuritsyn, Viacheslav. *Russkii literaturnyi postmodernizm*. Moscow: OGI, 2000.

Lahusen, Thomas, and Gene Kuperman, eds. *Late Soviet Culture: From Perestroika to Novostroika*. Durham, N.C.: Duke University Press, 1993.

Laird, Sally. *Voices of Russian Literature: Interviews with Ten Contemporary Writers*. New York & Oxford: Oxford University Press, 1999.

Lapidus, Gail W. *The New Russia: Troubled Transformation*. Boulder, Colo.: Westview Press, 1995.

Latynina, Alla. *Za otkrytym shlagbaumom: Literaturnaia situatsiia kontsa 80-kh*. Moscow: Sovetskii pisatel', 1991.

Ledkovsky, Marina, Charlotte Rosenthal, and Mary Zirin, eds. *Dictionary of Russian Women Writers*. London & Westport, Conn.: Greenwood Press, 1994.

Leiderman, Naum, and Mark Lipovetsky. *Sovremennaia russkaia literatura,* 3 volumes. Moscow: URSS, 2001.

Lempert, David H. *Daily Life in a Crumbling Empire*. Boulder, Colo.: East European Monographs / New York : Distributed by Columbia University Press, 1996.

Lewin, Moshe. *Russia-USSR-Russia: The Drive and Drift of a Superstate.* New York: Norton, 1995.

Lipovetsky. *Russian Postmodernist Fiction: Dialogue with Chaos,* edited by Eliot Borenstein. Armonk, N.Y.: M.E. Sharpe, 1999.

Litherland, S. J., and Peter Mortimer, eds. *The Poetry of Perestroika.* London: Iron Press, 1991.

Magnusson, Marta-Lisa, ed. *The Louisiana Conference on Literature and Perestroika, 2–4 March 1988.* Humlebaek, Denmark: Louisiana Museum of Modern Art, 1988.

Marsh, Rosalinda. *History and Literature in Contemporary Russia.* London: Macmillan in association with St. Anthony College, Oxford, 1995.

McDaniel, Tim. *The Agony of the Russian Idea.* Princeton: Princeton University Press, 1996.

Nefagina, Galina. *Russkaia proza vtoroi poloviny 80-kh-nachala 90-kh godov XX veka.* Minsk: Ekonompress, 1998.

Nemzer, Andrei. *Literaturnoe segodnia: O russkoi proze: 90-e.* Moscow: Novoe literaturnoe obozrenie, 1998.

Nemzer. *Zamechatel'noe desiatiletie russkoi literatury.* Moscow: Zakharov, 2003.

Nikolaev, Petr Alekseevich, ed. *Russkie pisateli 20 veka. Biograficheskii slovar'.* Moscow: Bol'shaia Rossiiskaia Entsiklopediia, 2000.

Novikov, Vladimir. *Zaskok: Esse, parodii, razmyshleniia kritika.* Moscow: Knizhnyi sad, 1997.

O'Donnell, Neil F., and Vladimir Shlapentokh. *The Last Years of the Soviet Empire: Snapshots from 1985–1991.* Westport, Conn.: Praeger, 1993.

Perova, Natasha, and Arch Tait, eds. *Booker Winners and Others.* Moscow: Glas, 1995.

Perova and Tait, eds. *Captives and Latest Booker Winners.* Moscow: Glas, 1996.

Peterson, Nadya. *Subversive Imaginations: Fantastic Prose and the End of Soviet Literature, 1970s–1990s.* Boulder, Colo.: Westview Press, 1997.

Piirainen, Timo. *Towards a New Social Order in Russia: Transforming Structures and Everyday Life.* Aldershot, U.K. & Brookfield, Vt.: Dartmouth, 1997.

Porter, Robert. *Four Contemporary Russian Writers.* New York & Oxford: Berg, 1989.

Porter. *Russia's Alternative Prose.* Oxford: Berg, 1994.

Putin, Vladimir, Natalia Gevorkian, and Natalia Timakova. *First Person: An Astonishingly Frank Self-Portrait by Russia's President Vladimir Putin.* New York: Public Affairs, 2001.

Randolph, Eleanor. *Waking the Tempests: Ordinary Life in the New Russia.* New York: Simon & Schuster, 1996.

Rodnianskaia, Irina. *Literaturnoe semiletie: 1987–1994.* Moscow: Knizhnyi sad, 1995.

Roll, Serafima. *Contextualizing Transition: Interviews with Contemporary Writers and Critics.* Middlebury Studies in Russian Language and Literature, volume 16, edited by Thomas R. Beyer Jr. New York: Peter Lang, 1998.

Ryan, Karen L., and Barry P. Scherr, eds. *Twentieth-Century Russian Literature: Selected Papers from the Fifth Congress of Central and East European Studies*. Basingstoke, U.K.: Macmillan, 2000; New York: St. Martin's Press, 2000.

Ryan-Hayes, Karen L. *Contemporary Russian Satire: A Genre Study*. Cambridge & New York: Cambridge University Press, 1995.

Savitsky, Stanislav. *Andergraund: Istoriia i mify leningradskoi neofitsial'noi literatury*. Moscow: Novoe literaturnoe obozrenie, 2002.

Schneidman, Norman N. *Russian Literature, 1988–1994: The End of an Era*. Buffalo & Toronto: University of Toronto Press, 1995.

Schneidman. *Soviet Literature in the 1980s: Decade of Transition*. London & Toronto: University of Toronto Press, 1989.

Shlapentokh. *A Normal Totalitarian Society: How the Soviet Union Functioned and How It Collapsed*. Armonk, N.Y.: M. E. Sharpe, 2001.

Simmons, Cynthia. *Their Fathers' Voice: Vassily Aksyonov, Vendikt Erofeev, Eduard Limonov, and Sasha Sokolov*. New York: Peter Lang, 1993.

Skoropanova, Irina. *Russkaia postmodernistskaia literatura*. Moscow: Flinta/Nauka, 1999.

Smith, Gerald, ed. *Contemporary Russian Poetry*. Bloomington: Indiana University Press, 1993.

Smith, Kathleen E. *Mythmaking in the New Russia: Politics and Memory during the Yeltsin Era*. Ithaca, N.Y.: Cornell University Press, 2002.

Tomei, Christine D. *Russian Women Writers,* 2 volumes. New York: Garland, 1999.

Vail', Petr L'vovich, and Aleksandr Aleksandrovich Genis. *Sovremennaia russkai proza*. Ann Arbor, Mich.: Hermitage, 1978.

Yeltsin, Boris, and Catherine Fitzpatrick. *Midnight Diaries*. New York: Public Affairs, 2000.

Zubova, Liudmila. *Sovremennaia russkaia poeziia v kontekste istorii iazyka*. Moscow: Novoe literaturnoe obozrenie, 2000.

Contributors

Marina Adamovitch . . . . *Kontinent (Paris-Moscow)*

Dmitrii Bak . . . . *Russian University for the Humanities (Moscow)*

Anindita Banerjee . . . . *University of Oregon*

Evgenii Bershtein. . . . . *Reed College*

Birgit Beumers . . . . *University of Bristol*

Eliot Borenstein . . . . *New York University*

Anna Brodsky . . . . *Washington and Lee University*

Valentina G. Brougher . . . . *Georgetown University*

Evgeny Dobrenko . . . . *University of Nottingham*

Thomas Epstein . . . . *Boston College*

Alyssa Dinega Gillespie . . . . *University of Notre Dame*

Helena Goscilo . . . . *University of Pittsburgh*

Seth Graham . . . . *University of Pittsburgh*

Marina Kanevskaya. . . . . *University of Montana*

Konstantine Klioutchkine . . . . *Pomona College*

Nina Kolesnikoff . . . . *McMaster University*

Konstantin V. Kustanovich . . . . *Vanderbilt University*

Byron Lindsey . . . . *University of New Mexico*

Mark Lipovetsky . . . . *University of Colorado at Boulder*

Maria Litovskaia . . . . *Ural State University*

Gerald McCausland . . . . *University of Pittsburgh*

Andrei Nemzer . . . . *Academy of Russian Contemporary Literature (Moscow)*

Nadya L. Peterson. . . . . *Hunter College*

Robert Porter . . . . *University of Glasgow*

Alexander Prokhorov . . . . *College of William & Mary*

Elena Prokhorova . . . . *George Washington University*

Larissa Rudova . . . . *Pomona College*

Greta N. Slobin . . . . *University of California, Santa Cruz*

Alexandra Smith . . . . *University of Canterbury, New Zealand*

Tatiana Spektor . . . . *Holy Trinity Seminary*

Ivan Tolstoi . . . . *Radio Free Europe/Radio Liberty*

Jekaterina Young . . . . *University of Manchester*

Cumulative Index

Dictionary of Literary Biography, Volumes 1-285
Dictionary of Literary Biography Yearbook, 1980-2002
Dictionary of Literary Biography Documentary Series, Volumes 1-19
Concise Dictionary of American Literary Biography, Volumes 1-7
Concise Dictionary of British Literary Biography, Volumes 1-8
Concise Dictionary of World Literary Biography, Volumes 1-4

Cumulative Index

DLB before number: *Dictionary of Literary Biography,* Volumes 1-285
Y before number: *Dictionary of Literary Biography Yearbook,* 1980-2002
DS before number: *Dictionary of Literary Biography Documentary Series,* Volumes 1-19
CDALB before number: *Concise Dictionary of American Literary Biography,* Volumes 1-7
CDBLB before number: *Concise Dictionary of British Literary Biography,* Volumes 1-8
CDWLB before number: *Concise Dictionary of World Literary Biography,* Volumes 1-4

A

Aakjær, Jeppe 1866-1930 . . . . .DLB-214

Abbey, Edward 1927-1989 . . . . DLB-256, 275

Abbey, Edwin Austin 1852-1911 . . . . . . .DLB-188

Abbey, Maj. J. R. 1894-1969 . . . . .DLB-201

Abbey Press DLB-49

The Abbey Theatre and Irish Drama,
1900-1945 . . . . .DLB-10

Abbot, Willis J. 1863-1934. . . . . .DLB-29

Abbott, Edwin A. 1838-1926 . . . . .DLB-178

Abbott, Jacob 1803-1879 . . . . .DLB-1, 42, 243

Abbott, Lee K. 1947- DLB-130

Abbott, Lyman 1835-1922. . . . . .DLB-79

Abbott, Robert S. 1868-1940 . . . . .DLB-29, 91

Abe Kōbō 1924-1993 . . . . .DLB-182

Abelard, Peter circa 1079-1142? DLB-115, 208

Abelard-Schuman. DLB-46

Abell, Arunah S. 1806-1888. . . . . .DLB-43

Abell, Kjeld 1901-1961. . . . . .DLB-214

Abercrombie, Lascelles 1881-1938. . . . . . .DLB-19

The Friends of the Dymock
Poets Y-00

Aberdeen University Press Limited DLB-106

Abish, Walter 1931- DLB-130, 227

Ablesimov, Aleksandr Onisimovich
1742-1783. . . . . .DLB-150

Abraham à Sancta Clara 1644-1709 . . . . .DLB-168

Abrahams, Peter
1919- DLB-117, 225; CDWLB-3

Abrams, M. H. 1912- DLB-67

Abramson, Jesse 1904-1979 . . . . .DLB-241

Abrogans circa 790-800 . . . . .DLB-148

Abschatz, Hans Aßmann von 1646-1699. .DLB-168

Abse, Dannie 1923- DLB-27, 245

Abutsu-ni 1221-1283 . . . . .DLB-203

Academy Chicago Publishers DLB-46

Accius circa 170 B.C.-circa 80 B.C. DLB-211

Accrocca, Elio Filippo 1923-1996. . . . . . .DLB-128

Ace Books DLB-46

Achebe, Chinua 1930- DLB-117; CDWLB-3

Achtenberg, Herbert 1938- DLB-124

Ackerman, Diane 1948- DLB-120

Ackroyd, Peter 1949- DLB-155, 231

Acorn, Milton 1923-1986. . . . . .DLB-53

Acosta, Oscar Zeta 1935?-1974? DLB-82

Acosta Torres, José 1925- DLB-209

Actors Theatre of Louisville DLB-7

Adair, Gilbert 1944- DLB-194

Adair, James 1709?-1783?. DLB-30

Adam, Graeme Mercer 1839-1912 . . . . . .DLB-99

Adam, Robert Borthwick, II
1863-1940 . . . . .DLB-187

Adame, Leonard 1947- DLB-82

Adameşteanu, Gabriel 1942- DLB-232

Adamic, Louis 1898-1951 . . . . .DLB-9

Adams, Abigail 1744-1818 . . . . .DLB-183, 200

Adams, Alice 1926-1999 . . . . DLB-234; Y-86

Adams, Bertha Leith (Mrs. Leith Adams,
Mrs. R. S. de Courcy Laffan)
1837?-1912 .DLB-240

Adams, Brooks 1848-1927 . . . . .DLB-47

Adams, Charles Francis, Jr. 1835-1915 . . . .DLB-47

Adams, Douglas 1952-2001 . . . . . . DLB-261; Y-83

Adams, Franklin P. 1881-1960. . . . . .DLB-29

Adams, Hannah 1755-1832 . . . . .DLB-200

Adams, Henry 1838-1918 . . . . . . DLB-12, 47, 189

Adams, Herbert Baxter 1850-1901 . . . . . .DLB-47

Adams, James Truslow
1878-1949 . . . . DLB-17; DS-17

Adams, John 1735-1826 . . . . .DLB-31, 183

Adams, John Quincy 1767-1848. . . . . . . .DLB-37

Adams, Léonie 1899-1988 . . . . .DLB-48

Adams, Levi 1802-1832. . . . . .DLB-99

Adams, Richard 1920- DLB-261

Adams, Samuel 1722-1803 . . . . .DLB-31, 43

Adams, Sarah Fuller Flower
1805-1848 . . . . .DLB-199

Adams, Thomas 1582/1583-1652 . . . . . . .DLB-151

Adams, William Taylor 1822-1897 . . . . . .DLB-42

J. S. and C. Adams [publishing house] DLB-49

Adamson, Harold 1906-1980. . . . . .DLB-265

Adamson, Sir John 1867-1950 . . . . .DLB-98

Adcock, Arthur St. John 1864-1930 . . . . . .DLB-135

Adcock, Betty 1938- DLB-105

"Certain Gifts" DLB-105

Tribute to James Dickey Y-97

Adcock, Fleur 1934- DLB-40

Addison, Joseph 1672-1719 . . .DLB-101; CDBLB-2

Ade, George 1866-1944. . . . . .DLB-11, 25

Adeler, Max (see Clark, Charles Heber)

Adlard, Mark 1932- DLB-261

Adler, Richard 1921- DLB-265

Adonias Filho 1915-1990. . . . . .DLB-145

Adorno, Theodor W. 1903-1969. . . . . . .DLB-242

Adoum, Jorge Enrique 1926- DLB-283

Advance Publishing Company DLB-49

Ady, Endre 1877-1919 . . . . . . DLB-215; CDWLB-4

AE 1867-1935 . . . . .DLB-19; CDBLB-5

Ælfric circa 955-circa 1010. . . . . .DLB-146

Aeschines circa 390 B.C.-circa 320 B.C. DLB-176

Aeschylus 525-524 B.C.-456-455 B.C.
. . . . DLB-176; CDWLB-1

Aesthetic Papers. .DLB-1

Aesthetics
Eighteenth-Century Aesthetic
Theories DLB-31

African Literature
Letter from Khartoum Y-90

African American
Afro-American Literary Critics:
An Introduction DLB-33

The Black Aesthetic: Background DS-8

The Black Arts Movement,
by Larry Neal. DLB-38

Black Theaters and Theater Organizations
in America, 1961-1982:
A Research List DLB-38

Black Theatre: A Forum [excerpts] DLB-38

Callaloo [journal]. Y-87

Community and Commentators:
Black Theatre and Its Critics DLB-38

The Emergence of Black
Women Writers DS-8

The Hatch-Billops Collection DLB-76

A Look at the Contemporary Black
Theatre Movement. DLB-38

The Moorland-Spingarn Research
Center. DLB-76

"The Negro as a Writer," by
G. M. McClellan DLB-50

"Negro Poets and Their Poetry," by
Wallace Thurman DLB-50

Olaudah Equiano and Unfinished Journeys:
The Slave-Narrative Tradition and
Twentieth-Century Continuities, by
Paul Edwards and Pauline T.
Wangman DLB-117

PHYLON (Fourth Quarter, 1950),
The Negro in Literature:
The Current Scene DLB-76

The Schomburg Center for Research
in Black Culture DLB-76

Three Documents [poets], by John
Edward Bruce DLB-50

After Dinner Opera Company Y-92

Agassiz, Elizabeth Cary 1822-1907 . . . . . . DLB-189

Agassiz, Louis 1807-1873 . . . . DLB-1, 235

Agee, James
1909-1955 . . . . DLB-2, 26, 152; CDALB-1

The Agee Legacy: A Conference at
the University of Tennessee
at Knoxville Y-89

Aguilera Malta, Demetrio 1909-1981 . . . . DLB-145

Ahlin, Lars 1915-1997 . . . . DLB-257

Ai 1947- DLB-120

Aichinger, Ilse 1921- DLB-85

Aickman, Robert 1914-1981 . . . . DLB-261

Aidoo, Ama Ata 1942- DLB-117; CDWLB-3

Aiken, Conrad
1889-1973 . . . . DLB-9, 45, 102; CDALB-5

Aiken, Joan 1924- DLB-161

Aikin, Lucy 1781-1864 . . . . DLB-144, 163

Ainsworth, William Harrison
1805-1882 . . . . DLB-21

Aistis, Jonas 1904-1973 . . . . . DLB-220; CDWLB-4

Aitken, George A. 1860-1917 . . . . DLB-149

Robert Aitken [publishing house] DLB-49

Akenside, Mark 1721-1770 . . . . DLB-109

Akins, Zoë 1886-1958 . . . . DLB-26

Aksakov, Ivan Sergeevich 1823-1826 . . . . DLB-277

Aksakov, Sergei Timofeevich
1791-1859 . . . . DLB-198

Akunin, Boris (Grigorii Shalvovich
Chkhartishvili) 1956- DLB-285

Akutagawa Ryūnsuke 1892-1927 . . . . DLB-180

Alabaster, William 1568-1640 . . . . DLB-132

Alain de Lille circa 1116-1202/1203 . . . . . DLB-208

Alain-Fournier 1886-1914 . . . . DLB-65

Alanus de Insulis (see Alain de Lille)

Alarcón, Francisco X. 1954- DLB-122

Alarcón, Justo S. 1930- DLB-209

Alba, Nanina 1915-1968 . . . . DLB-41

Albee, Edward 1928- . . . DLB-7, 266; CDALB-1

Albert, Octavia 1853-ca. 1889 . . . . DLB-221

Albert the Great circa 1200-1280 . . . . DLB-115

Alberti, Rafael 1902-1999 . . . . DLB-108

Albertinus, Aegidius circa 1560-1620 . . . . DLB-164

Alcaeus born circa 620 B.C. DLB-176

Alcott, Amos Bronson
1799-1888 . . . . DLB-1, 223; DS-5

Alcott, Louisa May 1832-1888
. . . DLB-1, 42, 79, 223, 239; DS-14; CDALB-3

Alcott, William Andrus 1798-1859 . . . . DLB-1, 243

Alcuin circa 732-804 . . . . DLB-148

Alden, Henry Mills 1836-1919 . . . . DLB-79

Alden, Isabella 1841-1930 . . . . DLB-42

John B. Alden [publishing house] DLB-49

Alden, Beardsley, and Company DLB-49

Aldington, Richard
1892-1962 . . . . .DLB-20, 36, 100, 149

Aldis, Dorothy 1896-1966 . . . . DLB-22

Aldis, H. G. 1863-1919 . . . . DLB-184

Aldiss, Brian W. 1925- DLB-14, 261, 271

Aldrich, Thomas Bailey
1836-1907 . . . . DLB-42, 71, 74, 79

Alegría, Ciro 1909-1967 . . . . DLB-113

Alegría, Claribel 1924- DLB-145, 283

Aleixandre, Vicente 1898-1984 . . . . DLB-108

Aleksandravičius, Jonas (see Aistis, Jonas)

Aleksandrov, Aleksandr Andreevich
(see Durova, Nadezhda Andreevna)

Alekseeva, Marina Anatol'evna
(see Marinina, Aleksandra)

Aleramo, Sibilla (Rena Pierangeli Faccio)
1876-1960 . . . . DLB-114, 264

Aleshkovsky, Petr Markovich 1957- . . . DLB-285

Alexander, Cecil Frances 1818-1895 . . . . . DLB-199

Alexander, Charles 1868-1923 . . . . DLB-91

Charles Wesley Alexander
[publishing house] DLB-49

Alexander, James 1691-1756 . . . . DLB-24

Alexander, Lloyd 1924- DLB-52

Alexander, Sir William, Earl of Stirling
1577?-1640 . . . . DLB-121

Alexie, Sherman 1966- DLB-175, 206, 278

Alexis, Willibald 1798-1871 . . . . DLB-133

Alfred, King 849-899 . . . . DLB-146

Alger, Horatio, Jr. 1832-1899 . . . . DLB-42

Algonquin Books of Chapel Hill DLB-46

Algren, Nelson
1909-1981 . . . . . . DLB-9; Y-81, 82; CDALB-1

Nelson Algren: An International
Symposium Y-00

Allan, Andrew 1907-1974 . . . . DLB-88

Allan, Ted 1916-1995 . . . . DLB-68

Allbeury, Ted 1917- DLB-87

Alldritt, Keith 1935- DLB-14

Allen, Dick 1939- DLB-282

Allen, Ethan 1738-1789 . . . . DLB-31

Allen, Frederick Lewis 1890-1954 . . . . . . DLB-137

Allen, Gay Wilson 1903-1995 . . . . .DLB-103; Y-95

Allen, George 1808-1876 . . . . DLB-59

Allen, Grant 1848-1899 . . . . DLB-70, 92, 178

Allen, Henry W. 1912-1991 . . . . Y-85

Allen, Hervey 1889-1949 . . . . DLB-9, 45

Allen, James 1739-1808 . . . . DLB-31

Allen, James Lane 1849-1925 . . . . DLB-71

Allen, Jay Presson 1922- DLB-26

John Allen and Company DLB-49

Allen, Paula Gunn 1939- DLB-175

Allen, Samuel W. 1917- DLB-41

Allen, Woody 1935- DLB-44

George Allen [publishing house] DLB-106

George Allen and Unwin Limited DLB-112

Allende, Isabel 1942- DLB-145; CDWLB-3

Alline, Henry 1748-1784 . . . . DLB-99

Allingham, Margery 1904-1966 . . . . DLB-77

The Margery Allingham Society Y-98

Allingham, William 1824-1889 . . . . DLB-35

W. L. Allison [publishing house] DLB-49

The *Alliterative Morte Arthure and the Stanzaic
Morte Arthur* circa 1350-1400 . . . . . DLB-146

Allott, Kenneth 1912-1973 . . . . DLB-20

Allston, Washington 1779-1843 . . . . . . DLB-1, 235

John Almon [publishing house] DLB-154

Alonzo, Dámaso 1898-1990 . . . . DLB-108

Alsop, George 1636-post 1673 . . . . DLB-24

Alsop, Richard 1761-1815 . . . . DLB-37

Henry Altemus and Company DLB-49

Altenberg, Peter 1885-1919 . . . . DLB-81

Althusser, Louis 1918-1990 . . . . DLB-242

Altolaguirre, Manuel 1905-1959 . . . . DLB-108

Aluko, T. M. 1918- DLB-117

Alurista 1947- DLB-82

Alvarez, A. 1929- DLB-14, 40

Alvarez, Julia 1950- DLB-282

Alvaro, Corrado 1895-1956 . . . . DLB-264

Alver, Betti 1906-1989 . . . . . DLB-220; CDWLB-4

Amadi, Elechi 1934- DLB-117

Amado, Jorge 1912-2001 . . . . DLB-113

Ambler, Eric 1909-1998 . . . . DLB-77

The Library of America DLB-46

The Library of America: An Assessment
After Two Decades Y-02

America: or, A Poem on the Settlement
of the British Colonies, by Timothy
Dwight DLB-37

American Bible Society
Department of Library, Archives, and
Institutional Research Y-97

American Conservatory Theatre DLB-7

American Culture
American Proletarian Culture:
The Twenties and Thirties DS-11

Studies in American Jewish Literature Y-02

The American Library in Paris Y-93

American Literature
The Literary Scene and Situation and . . .
(Who Besides Oprah) Really Runs
American Literature? Y-99

Who Owns American Literature, by
Henry Taylor Y-94

Who Runs American Literature? Y-94

American News Company DLB-49

A Century of Poetry, a Lifetime of Collecting:
J. M. Edelstein's Collection of Twentieth-
Century American Poetry Y-02

The American Poets' Corner: The First
Three Years (1983-1986). Y-86

American Publishing Company DLB-49

American Spectator
[Editorial] Rationale From the Initial
Issue of the American Spectator
(November 1932). DLB-137

American Stationers' Company DLB-49

The American Studies Association
of Norway Y-00

American Sunday-School Union DLB-49

American Temperance Union DLB-49

American Tract Society DLB-49

The American Trust for the British Library . . Y-96

American Writers Congress
The American Writers Congress
(9-12 October 1981) Y-81

The American Writers Congress: A Report
on Continuing Business Y-81

Ames, Fisher 1758-1808 . . . . .DLB-37

Ames, Mary Clemmer 1831-1884 . . . . .DLB-23

Ames, William 1576-1633 . . . . .DLB-281

Amiel, Henri-Frédéric 1821-1881 . . . . .DLB-217

Amini, Johari M. 1935- DLB-41

Amis, Kingsley 1922-1995
. . . . . DLB-15, 27, 100, 139, Y-96; CDBLB-7

Amis, Martin 1949- DLB-14, 194

Ammianus Marcellinus
circa A.D. 330-A.D. 395 . . . . .DLB-211

Ammons, A. R. 1926-2001 . . . . .DLB-5, 165

Amory, Thomas 1691?-1788 . . . . .DLB-39

Anania, Michael 1939- DLB-193

Anaya, Rudolfo A. 1937- DLB-82, 206, 278

Ancrene Riwle circa 1200-1225 . . . . .DLB-146

Andersch, Alfred 1914-1980 . . . . .DLB-69

Andersen, Benny 1929- DLB-214

Andersen, Alexander 1775-1870 . . . . .DLB-188

Anderson, David 1929- DLB-241

Anderson, Frederick Irving 1877-1947 . . . .DLB-202

Anderson, Margaret 1886-1973 . . . . .DLB-4, 91

Anderson, Maxwell 1888-1959 . . . . DLB-7, 228

Anderson, Patrick 1915-1979 . . . . .DLB-68

Anderson, Paul Y. 1893-1938 . . . . .DLB-29

Anderson, Poul 1926-2001 . . . . .DLB-8

Tribute to Isaac Asimov Y-92

Anderson, Robert 1750-1830 . . . . .DLB-142

Anderson, Robert 1917- DLB-7

Anderson, Sherwood
1876-1941 . . . . .DLB-4, 9, 86; DS-1; CDALB-4

Andreae, Johann Valentin 1586-1654 . . . .DLB-164

Andreas Capellanus
flourished circa 1185 . . . . .DLB-208

Andreas-Salomé, Lou 1861-1937 . . . . .DLB-66

Andres, Stefan 1906-1970. . . . . .DLB-69

Andreu, Blanca 1959- DLB-134

Andrewes, Lancelot 1555-1626 . . . . . DLB-151, 172

Andrews, Charles M. 1863-1943 . . . . .DLB-17

Andrews, Miles Peter ?-1814 . . . . .DLB-89

Andrews, Stephen Pearl 1812-1886 . . . . .DLB-250

Andrian, Leopold von 1875-1951 . . . . . . .DLB-81

Andrić, Ivo 1892-1975 . . . . . DLB-147; CDWLB-4

Andrieux, Louis (see Aragon, Louis)

Andrus, Silas, and Son DLB-49

Andrzejewski, Jerzy 1909-1983 . . . . .DLB-215

Angell, James Burrill 1829-1916 . . . . .DLB-64

Angell, Roger 1920- DLB-171, 185

Angelou, Maya 1928- DLB-38; CDALB-7

Tribute to Julian Mayfield. Y-84

Anger, Jane flourished 1589. . . . . .DLB-136

Angers, Félicité (see Conan, Laure)

The Anglo-Saxon Chronicle circa 890-1154 . . .DLB-146

Angus and Robertson (UK) Limited DLB-112

Anhalt, Edward 1914-2000 . . . . .DLB-26

Annenkov, Pavel Vasil'evich
1813?-1887 .DLB-277

Henry F. Anners [publishing house] DLB-49

Annolied between 1077 and 1081. . . . . . . .DLB-148

Anscombe, G. E. M. 1919-2001. . . . . .DLB-262

Anselm of Canterbury 1033-1109 . . . . . . .DLB-115

Anstey, F. 1856-1934 . . . . DLB-141, 178

Anthologizing New Formalism DLB-282

Anthony, Michael 1932- DLB-125

Anthony, Piers 1934- DLB-8

Anthony, Susanna 1726-1791. . . . . .DLB-200

Antin, David 1932- DLB-169

Antin, Mary 1881-1949 . . . . DLB-221; Y-84

Anton Ulrich, Duke of Brunswick-Lüneburg
1633-1714 . . . . .DLB-168

Antschel, Paul (see Celan, Paul)

Anyidoho, Kofi 1947- DLB-157

Anzaldúa, Gloria 1942- DLB-122

Anzengruber, Ludwig 1839-1889 . . . . . . .DLB-129

Apess, William 1798-1839 . . . . DLB-175, 243

Apodaca, Rudy S. 1939- DLB-82

Apollinaire, Guillaume 1880-1918 . . . . . . .DLB-258

Apollonius Rhodius third century B.C. DLB-176

Apple, Max 1941- DLB-130

D. Appleton and Company DLB-49

Appleton-Century-Crofts. DLB-46

Applewhite, James 1935- DLB-105

Tribute to James Dickey Y-97

Apple-wood Books. DLB-46

April, Jean-Pierre 1948- DLB-251

Apukhtin, Aleksei Nikolaevich
1840-1893 . . . . .DLB-277

Apuleius circa A.D. 125-post A.D. 164
. . . . .DLB-211; CDWLB-1

Aquin, Hubert 1929-1977 . . . . .DLB-53

Aquinas, Thomas 1224/1225-1274. . . . . . .DLB-115

Aragon, Louis 1897-1982 . . . . .DLB-72, 258

Aralica, Ivan 1930- DLB-181

Aratus of Soli
circa 315 B.C.-circa 239 B.C. DLB-176

Arbasino, Alberto 1930- DLB-196

Arbor House Publishing Company DLB-46

Arbuthnot, John 1667-1735 . . . . .DLB-101

Arcadia House. .DLB-46

Arce, Julio G. (see Ulica, Jorge)

Archer, William 1856-1924 . . . . .DLB-10

Archilochhus
mid seventh century B.C.E. DLB-176

The Archpoet circa 1130?-? DLB-148

Archpriest Avvakum (Petrovich)
1620?-1682 .DLB-150

Arden, John 1930- DLB-13, 245

Arden of Faversham DLB-62

Ardis Publishers. Y-89

Ardizzone, Edward 1900-1979 . . . . .DLB-160

Arellano, Juan Estevan 1947- DLB-122

The Arena Publishing Company DLB-49

Arena Stage DLB-7

Arenas, Reinaldo 1943-1990 . . . . .DLB-145

Arendt, Hannah 1906-1975 . . . . .DLB-242

Arensberg, Ann 1937- Y-82

Arghezi, Tudor 1880-1967. . . DLB-220; CDWLB-4

Arguedas, José María 1911-1969 . . . . . . .DLB-113

Argueta, Manlio 1936- DLB-145

Arias, Ron 1941- DLB-82

Arishima Takeo 1878-1923 . . . . .DLB-180

Aristophanes circa 446 B.C.-circa 386 B.C.
. . . . DLB-176; CDWLB-1

Aristotle 384 B.C.-322 B.C.
. . . . DLB-176; CDWLB-1

Ariyoshi Sawako 1931-1984 . . . . .DLB-182

Arland, Marcel 1899-1986. . . . . .DLB-72

Arlen, Michael 1895-1956 . . . . DLB-36, 77, 162

Armah, Ayi Kwei 1939- . . . DLB-117; CDWLB-3

Armantrout, Rae 1947- DLB-193

Der arme Hartmann ?-after 1150 . . . . . . .DLB-148

Armed Services Editions DLB-46

Armitage, G. E. (Robert Edric) 1956- . .DLB-267

Armstrong, Martin Donisthorpe
1882-1974 . . . . .DLB-197

Armstrong, Richard 1903- DLB-160

Armstrong, Terence Ian Fytton (see Gawsworth, John)

Arnauld, Antoine 1612-1694 . . . . .DLB-268

Arndt, Ernst Moritz 1769-1860 . . . . .DLB-90

Arnim, Achim von 1781-1831 . . . . .DLB-90

Arnim, Bettina von 1785-1859 . . . . .DLB-90

Arnim, Elizabeth von (Countess Mary Annette
Beauchamp Russell) 1866-1941 . . . . .DLB-197

Arno Press DLB-46

Arnold, Edwin 1832-1904 . . . . .DLB-35

Arnold, Edwin L. 1857-1935 . . . . .DLB-178

Arnold, Matthew
1822-1888 . . . . .DLB-32, 57; CDBLB-4

Preface to *Poems* (1853) DLB-32

Arnold, Thomas 1795-1842 . . . . .DLB-55

Edward Arnold [publishing house] DLB-112

Arnott, Peter 1962- DLB-233

Arnow, Harriette Simpson 1908-1986 . . . . . DLB-6

Arp, Bill (see Smith, Charles Henry)

Arpino, Giovanni 1927-1987 . . . . .DLB-177

Arreola, Juan José 1918-2001 . . . . DLB-113

Arrian circa 89-circa 155 . . . . .DLB-176

J. W. Arrowsmith [publishing house] DLB-106

Art

John Dos Passos: Artist Y-99

The First Post-Impressionist
Exhibition DS-5

The Omega Workshops DS-10

The Second Post-Impressionist
Exhibition DS-5

Artaud, Antonin 1896-1948 . . . . DLB-258

Artel, Jorge 1909-1994 . . . . DLB-283

Arthur, Timothy Shay
1809-1885 . . . . .DLB-3, 42, 79, 250; DS-13

Artmann, H. C. 1921-2000 . . . . DLB-85

Arvin, Newton 1900-1963 . . . . DLB-103

Asch, Nathan 1902-1964 . . . . DLB-4, 28

Nathan Asch Remembers Ford Madox
Ford, Sam Roth, and Hart Crane Y-02

Ascham, Roger 1515/1516-1568 . . . . DLB-236

Ash, John 1948- DLB-40

Ashbery, John 1927- DLB-5, 165; Y-81

Ashbridge, Elizabeth 1713-1755 . . . . DLB-200

Ashburnham, Bertram Lord
1797-1878 . . . . DLB-184

Ashendene Press DLB-112

Asher, Sandy 1942- Y-83

Ashton, Winifred (see Dane, Clemence)

Asimov, Isaac 1920-1992 . . . . DLB-8; Y-92

Tribute to John Ciardi Y-86

Askew, Anne circa 1521-1546 . . . . DLB-136

Aspazija 1865-1943 . . . . DLB-220; CDWLB-4

Asselin, Olivar 1874-1937 . . . . DLB-92

The Association of American Publishers Y-99

The Association for Documentary Editing Y-00

The Association for the Study of
Literature and Environment (ASLE) Y-99

Astell, Mary 1666-1731 . . . . DLB-252

Astley, William (see Warung, Price)

Asturias, Miguel Angel
1899-1974 . . . . DLB-113; CDWLB-3

Atava, S. (see Terpigorev, Sergei Nikolaevich)

Atheneum Publishers DLB-46

Atherton, Gertrude 1857-1948 . . . . .DLB-9, 78, 186

Athlone Press DLB-112

Atkins, Josiah circa 1755-1781 . . . . DLB-31

Atkins, Russell 1926- DLB-41

Atkinson, Kate 1951- DLB-267

Atkinson, Louisa 1834-1872 . . . . DLB-230

The Atlantic Monthly Press DLB-46

Attaway, William 1911-1986 . . . . DLB-76

Atwood, Margaret 1939- DLB-53, 251

Aubert, Alvin 1930- DLB-41

Aubert de Gaspé, Phillipe-Ignace-François
1814-1841 . . . . DLB-99

Aubert de Gaspé, Phillipe-Joseph
1786-1871 . . . . DLB-99

Aubin, Napoléon 1812-1890 . . . . DLB-99

Aubin, Penelope
1685-circa 1731 . . . . DLB-39

Preface to The Life of Charlotta
du Pont (1723) DLB-39

Aubrey-Fletcher, Henry Lancelot (see Wade, Henry)

Auchincloss, Louis 1917- DLB-2, 244; Y-80

Auden, W. H. 1907-1973 . . DLB-10, 20; CDBLB-6

Audio Art in America: A Personal Memoir . . . Y-85

Audubon, John James 1785-1851 . . . . DLB-248

Audubon, John Woodhouse
1812-1862 . . . . DLB-183

Auerbach, Berthold 1812-1882 . . . . DLB-133

Auernheimer, Raoul 1876-1948 . . . . DLB-81

Augier, Emile 1820-1889 . . . . DLB-192

Augustine 354-430 . . . . DLB-115

Aulnoy, Marie-Catherine Le Jumel
de Barneville, comtesse d'
1650/1651-1705 . . . . .DLB-268

Aulus Gellius
circa A.D. 125-circa A.D. 180? DLB-211

Austen, Jane 1775-1817 . . . . . . DLB-116; CDBLB-3

Auster, Paul 1947- DLB-227

Austin, Alfred 1835-1913 . . . . DLB-35

Austin, J. L. 1911-1960 . . . . DLB-262

Austin, Jane Goodwin 1831-1894 . . . . . . DLB-202

Austin, John 1790-1859 . . . . DLB-262

Austin, Mary Hunter
1868-1934 . . . . DLB-9, 78, 206, 221, 275

Austin, William 1778-1841 . . . . DLB-74

Australie (Emily Manning)
1845-1890 . . . . DLB-230

Authors and Newspapers Association DLB-46

Authors' Publishing Company DLB-49

Avallone, Michael 1924-1999 . . . . Y-99

Tribute to John D. MacDonald Y-86

Tribute to Kenneth Millar Y-83

Tribute to Raymond Chandler Y-88

Avalon Books DLB-46

Avancini, Nicolaus 1611-1686 . . . . DLB-164

Avendaño, Fausto 1941- DLB-82

Averroës 1126-1198 . . . . DLB-115

Avery, Gillian 1926- DLB-161

Avicenna 980-1037 . . . . DLB-115

Ávila Jiménez, Antonio 1898-1965 . . . . . DLB-283

Avison, Margaret 1918-1987 . . . . DLB-53

Avon Books DLB-46

Avyžius, Jonas 1922-1999 . . . . DLB-220

Awdry, Wilbert Vere 1911-1997 . . . . DLB-160

Awoonor, Kofi 1935- DLB-117

Ayckbourn, Alan 1939- DLB-13, 245

Ayer, A. J. 1910-1989 . . . . DLB-262

Aymé, Marcel 1902-1967 . . . . DLB-72

Aytoun, Sir Robert 1570-1638 . . . . DLB-121

Aytoun, William Edmondstoune
1813-1865 . . . . DLB-32, 159

B

B.V. (see Thomson, James)

Babbitt, Irving 1865-1933 . . . . DLB-63

Babbitt, Natalie 1932- DLB-52

John Babcock [publishing house] DLB-49

Babel, Isaak Emmanuilovich 1894-1940. . .DLB-272

Babits, Mihály 1883-1941 . . . .DLB-215; CDWLB-4

Babrius circa 150-200 . . . . .DLB-176

Babson, Marian 1929- DLB-276

Baca, Jimmy Santiago 1952- DLB-122

Bacchelli, Riccardo 1891-1985 . . . . DLB-264

Bache, Benjamin Franklin 1769-1798 . . . . . DLB-43

Bacheller, Irving 1859-1950 . . . . DLB-202

Bachmann, Ingeborg 1926-1973 . . . . DLB-85

Bačinskaitė-Bučienė, Salomėja (see Nėris, Salomėja)

Bacon, Delia 1811-1859 . . . . DLB-1, 243

Bacon, Francis
1561-1626 . . . . DLB-151, 236, 252; CDBLB-1

Bacon, Sir Nicholas circa 1510-1579 . . . . . DLB-132

Bacon, Roger circa 1214/1220-1292 . . . . . DLB-115

Bacon, Thomas circa 1700-1768 . . . . DLB-31

Bacovia, George
1881-1957 . . . . DLB-220; CDWLB-4

Richard G. Badger and Company DLB-49

Bagaduce Music Lending Library Y-00

Bage, Robert 1728-1801 . . . . DLB-39

Bagehot, Walter 1826-1877 . . . . DLB-55

Bagley, Desmond 1923-1983 . . . . DLB-87

Bagley, Sarah G. 1806-1848? DLB-239

Bagnold, Enid 1889-1981 . . .DLB-13, 160, 191, 245

Bagryana, Elisaveta
1893-1991 . . . . .DLB-147; CDWLB-4

Bahr, Hermann 1863-1934 . . . . DLB-81, 118

Bailey, Abigail Abbot 1746-1815 . . . . DLB-200

Bailey, Alfred Goldsworthy 1905- DLB-68

Bailey, H. C. 1878-1961 . . . . DLB-77

Bailey, Jacob 1731-1808 . . . . DLB-99

Bailey, Paul 1937- DLB-14, 271

Bailey, Philip James 1816-1902 . . . . DLB-32

Francis Bailey [publishing house] DLB-49

Baillargeon, Pierre 1916-1967 . . . . DLB-88

Baillie, Hugh 1890-1966 . . . . DLB-29

Baillie, Joanna 1762-1851 . . . . DLB-93

Bailyn, Bernard 1922- DLB-17

Bain, Alexander
English Composition and Rhetoric (1866)
[excerpt] DLB-57

Bainbridge, Beryl 1933- DLB-14, 231

Baird, Irene 1901-1981 . . . . DLB-68

Baker, Augustine 1575-1641 . . . . DLB-151

Baker, Carlos 1909-1987 . . . . DLB-103

Baker, David 1954- DLB-120

Baker, George Pierce 1866-1935 . . . . . . .DLB-266

Baker, Herschel C. 1914-1990 . . . . .DLB-111

Baker, Houston A., Jr. 1943- DLB-67

Baker, Howard
Tribute to Caroline Gordon Y-81

Tribute to Katherine Anne Porter Y-80

Baker, Nicholson 1957- DLB-227; Y-00

Review of Nicholson Baker's *Double Fold:
Libraries and the Assault on Paper* Y-00

Baker, Samuel White 1821-1893 . . . . . . .DLB-166

Baker, Thomas 1656-1740 . . . . .DLB-213

Walter H. Baker Company
("Baker's Plays") DLB-49

The Baker and Taylor Company DLB-49

Bakhtin, Mikhail Mikhailovich
1895-1975 .DLB-242

Bakunin, Mikhail Aleksandrovich
1814-1876 .DLB-277

Balaban, John 1943- DLB-120

Bald, Wambly 1902- DLB-4

Balde, Jacob 1604-1668 . . . . .DLB-164

Balderston, John 1889-1954 . . . . .DLB-26

Baldwin, James 1924-1987
. . . . . .DLB-2, 7, 33, 249, 278; Y-87; CDALB-1

Baldwin, Joseph Glover
1815-1864 . . . . .DLB-3, 11, 248

Baldwin, Louisa (Mrs. Alfred Baldwin)
1845-1925 .DLB-240

Baldwin, William circa 1515-1563 . . . . . .DLB-132

Richard and Anne Baldwin
[publishing house] DLB-170

Bale, John 1495-1563 . . . . .DLB-132

Balestrini, Nanni 1935- DLB-128, 196

Balfour, Sir Andrew 1630-1694 . . . . .DLB-213

Balfour, Arthur James 1848-1930 . . . . . . .DLB-190

Balfour, Sir James 1600-1657 . . . . .DLB-213

Ballantine Books DLB-46

Ballantyne, R. M. 1825-1894 . . . . .DLB-163

Ballard, J. G. 1930- DLB-14, 207, 261

Ballard, Martha Moore 1735-1812 . . . . . . .DLB-200

Ballerini, Luigi 1940- DLB-128

Ballou, Maturin Murray (Lieutenant Murray)
1820-1895 . . . . .DLB-79, 189

Robert O. Ballou [publishing house] DLB-46

Balzac, Guez de 1597?-1654 . . . . .DLB-268

Balzac, Honoré de 1799-1855 . . . . .DLB-119

Bambara, Toni Cade
1939-1995 . . . . .DLB-38, 218; CDALB-7

Bamford, Samuel 1788-1872 . . . . .DLB-190

A. L. Bancroft and Company DLB-49

Bancroft, George 1800-1891 . . .DLB-1, 30, 59, 243

Bancroft, Hubert Howe 1832-1918 . . . DLB-47, 140

Bandelier, Adolph F. 1840-1914 . . . . .DLB-186

Bangs, John Kendrick 1862-1922 . . . . .DLB-11, 79

Banim, John 1798-1842 . . . . . . .DLB-116, 158, 159

Banim, Michael 1796-1874 . . . . .DLB-158, 159

Banks, Iain (M.) 1954- DLB-194, 261

Banks, John circa 1653-1706 . . . . .DLB-80

Banks, Russell 1940- DLB-130, 278

Bannerman, Helen 1862-1946 . . . . .DLB-141

Bantam Books DLB-46

Banti, Anna 1895-1985 . . . . .DLB-177

Banville, John 1945- DLB-14, 271

Banville, Théodore de 1823-1891 . . . . . . .DLB-217

Baraka, Amiri
1934- DLB-5, 7, 16, 38; DS-8; CDALB-1

Barańczak, Stanisław 1946- DLB-232

Baratynsky, Evgenii Abramovich
1800-1844 .DLB-205

Barba-Jacob, Porfirio 1883-1942 . . . . .DLB-283

Barbauld, Anna Laetitia
1743-1825 . . . . DLB-107, 109, 142, 158

Barbeau, Marius 1883-1969 . . . . .DLB-92

Barber, John Warner 1798-1885 . . . . .DLB-30

Bàrberi Squarotti, Giorgio 1929- DLB-128

Barbey d'Aurevilly, Jules-Amédée
1808-1889 .DLB-119

Barbier, Auguste 1805-1882 . . . . .DLB-217

Barbilian, Dan (see Barbu, Ion)

Barbour, John circa 1316-1395 . . . . .DLB-146

Barbour, Ralph Henry 1870-1944 . . . . . . .DLB-22

Barbu, Ion 1895-1961 . . . . . .DLB-220; CDWLB-4

Barbusse, Henri 1873-1935 . . . . .DLB-65

Barclay, Alexander circa 1475-1552 . . . . . .DLB-132

E. E. Barclay and Company DLB-49

C. W. Bardeen [publishing house] DLB-49

Barham, Richard Harris 1788-1845 . . . . . .DLB-159

Barich, Bill 1943- DLB-185

Baring, Maurice 1874-1945 . . . . .DLB-34

Baring-Gould, Sabine 1834-1924 . . . .DLB-156, 190

Barker, A. L. 1918- DLB-14, 139

Barker, Clive 1952- DLB-261

Barker, Dudley (see Black, Lionel)

Barker, George 1913-1991 . . . . .DLB-20

Barker, Harley Granville 1877-1946 . . . . . .DLB-10

Barker, Howard 1946- DLB-13, 233

Barker, James Nelson 1784-1858 . . . . .DLB-37

Barker, Jane 1652-1727 . . . . .DLB-39, 131

Barker, Lady Mary Anne 1831-1911 . . . . .DLB-166

Barker, Pat 1943- DLB-271

Barker, William circa 1520-after 1576 . . . .DLB-132

Arthur Barker Limited DLB-112

Barkov, Ivan Semenovich 1732-1768 . . . . .DLB-150

Barks, Coleman 1937- DLB-5

Barlach, Ernst 1870-1938 . . . . .DLB-56, 118

Barlow, Joel 1754-1812 . . . . .DLB-37

The Prospect of Peace (1778) DLB-37

Barnard, John 1681-1770 . . . . .DLB-24

Barnard, Marjorie (M. Barnard Eldershaw)
1897-1987 .DLB-260

Barnard, Robert 1936- DLB-276

Barne, Kitty (Mary Catherine Barne)
1883-1957 .DLB-160

Barnes, Barnabe 1571-1609 . . . . .DLB-132

Barnes, Djuna 1892-1982 . . . .DLB-4, 9, 45; DS-15

Barnes, Jim 1933- DLB-175

Barnes, Julian 1946- DLB-194; Y-93

Notes for a Checklist of Publications Y-01

Barnes, Margaret Ayer 1886-1967 . . . . .DLB-9

Barnes, Peter 1931- DLB-13, 233

Barnes, William 1801-1886 . . . . .DLB-32

A. S. Barnes and Company DLB-49

Barnes and Noble Books DLB-46

Barnet, Miguel 1940- DLB-145

Barney, Natalie 1876-1972 . . . . .DLB-4; DS-15

Barnfield, Richard 1574-1627 . . . . .DLB-172

Richard W. Baron [publishing house] DLB-46

Barr, Amelia Edith Huddleston
1831-1919 . . . . .DLB-202, 221

Barr, Robert 1850-1912 . . . . .DLB-70, 92

Barral, Carlos 1928-1989 . . . . .DLB-134

Barrax, Gerald William 1933- DLB-41, 120

Barrès, Maurice 1862-1923 . . . . .DLB-123

Barrett, Eaton Stannard 1786-1820 . . . . . .DLB-116

Barrie, J. M.
1860-1937 . . . . . .DLB-10, 141, 156; CDBLB-5

Barrie and Jenkins DLB-112

Barrio, Raymond 1921- DLB-82

Barrios, Gregg 1945- DLB-122

Barry, Philip 1896-1949 . . . . .DLB-7, 228

Barry, Robertine (see Françoise)

Barry, Sebastian 1955- DLB-245

Barse and Hopkins DLB-46

Barstow, Stan 1928- DLB-14, 139, 207

Tribute to John Braine Y-86

Barth, John 1930- DLB-2, 227

Barthelme, Donald
1931-1989 . . . . DLB-2, 234; Y-80, 89

Barthelme, Frederick 1943- DLB-244; Y-85

Bartholomew, Frank 1898-1985 . . . . .DLB-127

Bartlett, John 1820-1905 . . . . .DLB-1, 235

Bartol, Cyrus Augustus 1813-1900 . . . .DLB-1, 235

Barton, Bernard 1784-1849 . . . . .DLB-96

Barton, John ca. 1610-1675 . . . . .DLB-236

Barton, Thomas Pennant 1803-1869 . . . . . .DLB-140

Bartram, John 1699-1777 . . . . .DLB-31

Bartram, William 1739-1823 . . . . .DLB-37

Barykova, Anna Pavlovna 1839-1893 . . . .DLB-277

Basic Books .DLB-46

Basille, Theodore (see Becon, Thomas)

Bass, Rick 1958- DLB-212, 275

Bass, T. J. 1932- Y-81

Bassani, Giorgio 1916-2000 . . . . . . .DLB-128, 177

Basse, William circa 1583-1653 . . . . .DLB-121

Bassett, John Spencer 1867-1928 . . . . .DLB-17

Bassler, Thomas Joseph (see Bass, T. J.)

Bate, Walter Jackson 1918-1999 . . . . .DLB-67, 103

Bateman, Stephen circa 1510-1584 . . . . . .DLB-136

Christopher Bateman [publishing house] . . DLB-170

Bates, H. E. 1905-1974 . . . . DLB-162, 191

Bates, Katharine Lee 1859-1929 . . . . DLB-71

Batiushkov, Konstantin Nikolaevich
1787-1855 . . . . DLB-205

B. T. Batsford [publishing house] DLB-106

Battiscombe, Georgina 1905- DLB-155

The Battle of Maldon circa 1000 . . . . DLB-146

Baudelaire, Charles 1821-1867 . . . . DLB-217

Bauer, Bruno 1809-1882 . . . . DLB-133

Bauer, Wolfgang 1941- DLB-124

Baum, L. Frank 1856-1919 . . . . DLB-22

Baum, Vicki 1888-1960 . . . . DLB-85

Baumbach, Jonathan 1933- Y-80

Bausch, Richard 1945- DLB-130

    Tribute to James Dickey Y-97

    Tribute to Peter Taylor Y-94

Bausch, Robert 1945- DLB-218

Bawden, Nina 1925- DLB-14, 161, 207

Bax, Clifford 1886-1962 . . . . DLB-10, 100

Baxter, Charles 1947- DLB-130

Bayer, Eleanor (see Perry, Eleanor)

Bayer, Konrad 1932-1964 . . . . DLB-85

Bayle, Pierre 1647-1706 . . . . DLB-268

Bayley, Barrington J. 1937- DLB-261

Baynes, Pauline 1922- DLB-160

Baynton, Barbara 1857-1929 . . . . DLB-230

Bazin, Hervé (Jean Pierre Marie Hervé-Bazin)
1911-1996 . . . . DLB-83

The BBC Four Samuel Johnson Prize
for Non-fiction Y-02

Beach, Sylvia 1887-1962 . . . . DLB-4; DS-15

Beacon Press DLB-49

Beadle and Adams DLB-49

Beagle, Peter S. 1939- Y-80

Beal, M. F. 1937- Y-81

Beale, Howard K. 1899-1959 . . . . DLB-17

Beard, Charles A. 1874-1948 . . . . DLB-17

Beat Generation (Beats)
    As I See It, by Carolyn Cassady DLB-16

    A Beat Chronology: The First Twenty-five
      Years, 1944-1969 . . . . DLB-16

    The Commercialization of the Image
      of Revolt, by Kenneth Rexroth . . . DLB-16

    Four Essays on the Beat Generation . . DLB-16

    in New York City DLB-237

    in the West DLB-237

    Outlaw Days DLB-16

    Periodicals of DLB-16

Beattie, Ann 1947- DLB-218, 278; Y-82

Beattie, James 1735-1803 . . . . DLB-109

Beatty, Chester 1875-1968 . . . . DLB-201

Beauchemin, Nérée 1850-1931 . . . . DLB-92

Beauchemin, Yves 1941- DLB-60

Beaugrand, Honoré 1848-1906 . . . . DLB-99

Beaulieu, Victor-Lévy 1945- DLB-53

Beaumont, Francis
    circa 1584-1616 . . . . DLB-58; CDBLB-1

Beaumont, Sir John 1583?-1627 . . . . DLB-121

Beaumont, Joseph 1616-1699 . . . . DLB-126

Beauvoir, Simone de 1908-1986 . . . . . DLB-72; Y-86

    Personal Tribute to Simone de Beauvoir . . . Y-86

Becher, Ulrich 1910-1990 . . . . DLB-69

Becker, Carl 1873-1945 . . . . DLB-17

Becker, Jurek 1937-1997 . . . . DLB-75

Becker, Jurgen 1932- DLB-75

Beckett, Samuel 1906-1989
    . . . . DLB-13, 15, 233; Y-90; CDBLB-7

Beckford, William 1760-1844 . . . . . . DLB-39, 213

Beckham, Barry 1944- DLB-33

Bećković, Matija 1939- DLB-181

Becon, Thomas circa 1512-1567 . . . . DLB-136

Becque, Henry 1837-1899 . . . . DLB-192

Beddoes, Thomas 1760-1808 . . . . DLB-158

Beddoes, Thomas Lovell 1803-1849 . . . . . DLB-96

Bede circa 673-735 . . . . DLB-146

Bedford-Jones, H. 1887-1949 . . . . DLB-251

Bedregal, Yolanda 1913-1999 . . . . DLB-283

Beebe, William 1877-1962 . . . . DLB-275

Beecher, Catharine Esther
    1800-1878 . . . . DLB-1, 243

Beecher, Henry Ward
    1813-1887 . . . . DLB-3, 43, 250

Beer, George L. 1872-1920 . . . . DLB-47

Beer, Johann 1655-1700 . . . . DLB-168

Beer, Patricia 1919-1999 . . . . DLB-40

Beerbohm, Max 1872-1956 . . . . DLB-34, 100

Beer-Hofmann, Richard 1866-1945 . . . . . DLB-81

Beers, Henry A. 1847-1926 . . . . DLB-71

S. O. Beeton [publishing house] DLB-106

Bégon, Elisabeth 1696-1755 . . . . DLB-99

Behan, Brendan
    1923-1964 . . . . DLB-13, 233; CDBLB-7

Behn, Aphra 1640?-1689 . . . . DLB-39, 80, 131

Behn, Harry 1898-1973 . . . . DLB-61

Behrman, S. N. 1893-1973 . . . . DLB-7, 44

Beklemishev, Iurii Solomonvich
    (see Krymov, Iurii Solomonovich)

Belaney, Archibald Stansfeld (see Grey Owl)

Belasco, David 1853-1931 . . . . DLB-7

Clarke Belford and Company DLB-49

Belgian Luxembourg American Studies
    Association Y-01

Belinsky, Vissarion Grigor'evich
    1811-1848 . . . . DLB-198

Belitt, Ben 1911- DLB-5

Belknap, Jeremy 1744-1798 . . . . DLB-30, 37

Bell, Adrian 1901-1980 . . . . DLB-191

Bell, Clive 1881-1964 . . . . DS-10

Bell, Daniel 1919- DLB-246

Bell, Gertrude Margaret Lowthian
    1868-1926 . . . . DLB-174

Bell, James Madison 1826-1902 . . . . DLB-50

Bell, Madison Smart 1957- DLB-218, 278

    Tribute to Andrew Nelson Lytle Y-95

    Tribute to Peter Taylor Y-94

Bell, Marvin 1937- DLB-5

Bell, Millicent 1919- DLB-111

Bell, Quentin 1910-1996 . . . . DLB-155

Bell, Vanessa 1879-1961 . . . . DS-10

George Bell and Sons DLB-106

Robert Bell [publishing house] DLB-49

Bellamy, Edward 1850-1898 . . . . DLB-12

Bellamy, Joseph 1719-1790 . . . . DLB-31

John Bellamy [publishing house] DLB-170

La Belle Assemblée 1806-1837 . . . . DLB-110

Bellezza, Dario 1944-1996 . . . . DLB-128

Belloc, Hilaire 1870-1953 . . . . DLB-19, 100, 141, 174

Belloc, Madame (see Parkes, Bessie Rayner)

Bellonci, Maria 1902-1986 . . . . DLB-196

Bellow, Saul
    1915- . . . DLB-2, 28; Y-82; DS-3; CDALB-1

    Tribute to Isaac Bashevis Singer Y-91

Belmont Productions DLB-46

Bels, Alberts 1938- DLB-232

Belševica, Vizma 1931- . . . DLB-232; CDWLB-4

Bemelmans, Ludwig 1898-1962 . . . . DLB-22

Bemis, Samuel Flagg 1891-1973 . . . . DLB-17

William Bemrose [publishing house] DLB-106

Ben no Naishi 1228?-1271? DLB-203

Benchley, Robert 1889-1945 . . . . DLB-11

Bencúr, Matej (see Kukučin, Martin)

Benedetti, Mario 1920- DLB-113

Benedict, Pinckney 1964- DLB-244

Benedict, Ruth 1887-1948 . . . . DLB-246

Benedictus, David 1938- DLB-14

Benedikt, Michael 1935- DLB-5

Benediktov, Vladimir Grigor'evich
    1807-1873 . . . . DLB-205

Benét, Stephen Vincent
    1898-1943 . . . . DLB-4, 48, 102, 249

    Stephen Vincent Benét Centenary Y-97

Benét, William Rose 1886-1950 . . . . DLB-45

Benford, Gregory 1941- Y-82

Benjamin, Park 1809-1864 . . . . . DLB-3, 59, 73, 250

Benjamin, Peter (see Cunningham, Peter)

Benjamin, S. G. W. 1837-1914 . . . . DLB-189

Benjamin, Walter 1892-1940 . . . . DLB-242

Benlowes, Edward 1602-1676 . . . . DLB-126

Benn, Gottfried 1886-1956 . . . . DLB-56

Benn Brothers Limited DLB-106

Bennett, Arnold
    1867-1931 . . . . DLB-10, 34, 98, 135; CDBLB-5

    The Arnold Bennett Society Y-98

Bennett, Charles 1899-1995 . . . . DLB-44

Bennett, Emerson 1822-1905 . . . . DLB-202

Bennett, Gwendolyn 1902-1981 . . . . DLB-51

Bennett, Hal 1930- DLB-33

Bennett, James Gordon 1795-1872 . . . . .DLB-43

Bennett, James Gordon, Jr. 1841-1918. . . . .DLB-23

Bennett, John 1865-1956 . . . . .DLB-42

Bennett, Louise 1919- DLB-117; CDWLB-3

Benni, Stefano 1947- DLB-196

Benoit, Jacques 1941- DLB-60

Benson, A. C. 1862-1925. . . . . .DLB-98

Benson, E. F. 1867-1940. . . . . .DLB-135, 153

    The E. F. Benson Society Y-98

    The Tilling Society Y-98

Benson, Jackson J. 1930- DLB-111

Benson, Robert Hugh 1871-1914. . . . . . .DLB-153

Benson, Stella 1892-1933 . . . . .DLB-36, 162

Bent, James Theodore 1852-1897 . . . . . . .DLB-174

Bent, Mabel Virginia Anna ?-?. DLB-174

Bentham, Jeremy 1748-1832 . . DLB-107, 158, 252

Bentley, E. C. 1875-1956 . . . . .DLB-70

Bentley, Phyllis 1894-1977 . . . . .DLB-191

Bentley, Richard 1662-1742 . . . . .DLB-252

Richard Bentley [publishing house] DLB-106

Benton, Robert 1932- DLB-44

Benziger Brothers. DLB-49

Beowulf circa 900-1000 or 790-825
. . . . DLB-146; CDBLB-1

Berent, Wacław 1873-1940 . . . . .DLB-215

Beresford, Anne 1929- DLB-40

Beresford, John Davys
1873-1947 . . . . DLB-162, 178, 197

    "Experiment in the Novel" (1929)
    [excerpt] DLB-36

Beresford-Howe, Constance 1922- DLB-88

R. G. Berford Company DLB-49

Berg, Stephen 1934- DLB-5

Bergengruen, Werner 1892-1964. . . . . . . .DLB-56

Berger, John 1926- DLB-14, 207

Berger, Meyer 1898-1959 . . . . .DLB-29

Berger, Thomas 1924- DLB-2; Y-80

    A Statement by Thomas Berger Y-80

Bergman, Hjalmar 1883-1931 . . . . .DLB-259

Bergman, Ingmar 1918- DLB-257

Berkeley, Anthony 1893-1971 . . . . .DLB-77

Berkeley, George 1685-1753 . . . . DLB-31, 101, 252

The Berkley Publishing Corporation. DLB-46

Berlin, Irving 1888-1989 . . . . .DLB-265

Berlin, Lucia 1936- DLB-130

Berman, Marshall 1940- DLB-246

Bernal, Vicente J. 1888-1915 . . . . .DLB-82

Bernanos, Georges 1888-1948 . . . . .DLB-72

Bernard, Catherine 1663?-1712. . . . . .DLB-268

Bernard, Harry 1898-1979 . . . . .DLB-92

Bernard, John 1756-1828 . . . . .DLB-37

Bernard of Chartres circa 1060-1124? DLB-115

Bernard of Clairvaux 1090-1153 . . . . .DLB-208

Bernard, Richard 1568-1641/1642. . . . . . .DLB-281

Bernard Silvestris
    flourished circa 1130-1160 . . . . .DLB-208

Bernari, Carlo 1909-1992 . . . . .DLB-177

Bernhard, Thomas
1931-1989 . . . . DLB-85, 124; CDWLB-2

Berniéres, Louis de 1954- DLB-271

Bernstein, Charles 1950- DLB-169

Berriault, Gina 1926-1999 . . . . .DLB-130

Berrigan, Daniel 1921- DLB-5

Berrigan, Ted 1934-1983 . . . . .DLB-5, 169

Berry, Wendell 1934- DLB-5, 6, 234, 275

Berryman, John 1914-1972 . . . .DLB-48; CDALB-1

Bersianik, Louky 1930- DLB-60

Thomas Berthelet [publishing house]. DLB-170

Berto, Giuseppe 1914-1978 . . . . .DLB-177

Bertocci, Peter Anthony 1910-1989 . . . . . .DLB-279

Bertolucci, Attilio 1911-2000 . . . . .DLB-128

Berton, Pierre 1920- DLB-68

Bertrand, Louis "Aloysius" 1807-1841 . . . .DLB-217

Besant, Sir Walter 1836-1901 . . . . . .DLB-135, 190

Bessette, Gerard 1920- DLB-53

Bessie, Alvah 1904-1985 . . . . .DLB-26

Bester, Alfred 1913-1987 . . . . .DLB-8

Besterman, Theodore 1904-1976 . . . . .DLB-201

Beston, Henry (Henry Beston Sheahan)
1888-1968 .DLB-275

Best-Seller Lists
    An Assessment Y-84

    What's Really Wrong With
    Bestseller Lists Y-84

Bestuzhev, Aleksandr Aleksandrovich
(Marlinsky) 1797-1837 . . . . .DLB-198

Bestuzhev, Nikolai Aleksandrovich
1791-1855 .DLB-198

Betham-Edwards, Matilda Barbara
(see Edwards, Matilda Barbara Betham-)

Betjeman, John
1906-1984 . . . . .DLB-20; Y-84; CDBLB-7

Betocchi, Carlo 1899-1986. . . . . .DLB-128

Bettarini, Mariella 1942- DLB-128

Betts, Doris 1932- DLB-218; Y-82

Beveridge, Albert J. 1862-1927. . . . . .DLB-17

Beverley, Robert circa 1673-1722. . . . . .DLB-24, 30

Bevilacqua, Alberto 1934- DLB-196

Bevington, Louisa Sarah 1845-1895 . . . . .DLB-199

Beyle, Marie-Henri (see Stendhal)

Białoszewski, Miron 1922-1983 . . . . .DLB-232

Bianco, Margery Williams 1881-1944 . . . .DLB-160

Bibaud, Adèle 1854-1941. . . . . .DLB-92

Bibaud, Michel 1782-1857 . . . . .DLB-99

Bibliography
    Bibliographical and Textual Scholarship
    Since World War II Y-89

    Center for Bibliographical Studies and
    Research at the University of
    California, Riverside. Y-91

    The Great Bibliographers Series Y-93

    Primary Bibliography: A Retrospective . . Y-95

Bichsel, Peter 1935- DLB-75

Bickerstaff, Isaac John 1733-circa 1808 . . . .DLB-89

Drexel Biddle [publishing house]. DLB-49

Bidermann, Jacob
1577 or 1578-1639 . . . . .DLB-164

Bidwell, Walter Hilliard 1798-1881 . . . . . . .DLB-79

Bienek, Horst 1930-1990 . . . . .DLB-75

Bierbaum, Otto Julius 1865-1910. . . . . . . .DLB-66

Bierce, Ambrose 1842-1914?
    . . . . . . DLB-11, 12, 23, 71, 74, 186; CDALB-3

Bigelow, William F. 1879-1966 . . . . .DLB-91

Biggle, Lloyd, Jr. 1923- DLB-8

Bigiaretti, Libero 1905-1993 . . . . .DLB-177

Bigland, Eileen 1898-1970 . . . . .DLB-195

Biglow, Hosea (see Lowell, James Russell)

Bigongiari, Piero 1914-1997. . . . . .DLB-128

Bilenchi, Romano 1909-1989. . . . . .DLB-264

Billinger, Richard 1890-1965 . . . . .DLB-124

Billings, Hammatt 1818-1874. . . . . .DLB-188

Billings, John Shaw 1898-1975. . . . . .DLB-137

Billings, Josh (see Shaw, Henry Wheeler)

Binding, Rudolf G. 1867-1938 . . . . .DLB-66

Bingay, Malcolm 1884-1953 . . . . .DLB-241

Bingham, Caleb 1757-1817 . . . . .DLB-42

Bingham, George Barry 1906-1988 . . . . . .DLB-127

Bingham, Sallie 1937- DLB-234

William Bingley [publishing house] DLB-154

Binyon, Laurence 1869-1943. . . . . .DLB-19

Biographia Brittanica. DLB-142

Biography
    Biographical Documents Y-84, 85

    A Celebration of Literary Biography Y-98

    Conference on Modern Biography Y-85

    The Cult of Biography
    Excerpts from the Second Folio Debate:
    "Biographies are generally a disease of
    English Literature" Y-86

    New Approaches to Biography: Challenges
    from Critical Theory, USC Conference
    on Literary Studies, 1990 . . . . Y-90

    "The New Biography," by Virginia Woolf,
    New York Herald Tribune,
    30 October 1927 . . . . .DLB-149

    "The Practice of Biography," in *The English
    Sense of Humour and Other Essays*, by
    Harold Nicolson. DLB-149

    "Principles of Biography," in *Elizabethan
    and Other Essays*, by Sidney Lee . . .DLB-149

    Remarks at the Opening of "The Biographical
    Part of Literature" Exhibition, by
    William R. Cagle Y-98

    Survey of Literary Biographies Y-00

    A Transit of Poets and Others: American
    Biography in 1982 . . . . Y-82

    The Year in Literary
    Biography. Y-83–01

Biography, The Practice of:
    An Interview with B. L. Reid Y-83

    An Interview with David Herbert Donald. . .Y-87

    An Interview with Humphrey Carpenter . Y-84

An Interview with Joan Mellen Y-94

An Interview with John Caldwell Guilds . . Y-92

An Interview with William Manchester . . . Y-85

John Bioren [publishing house] DLB-49

Bioy Casares, Adolfo 1914-1999 . . . . DLB-113

Bird, Isabella Lucy 1831-1904 . . . . DLB-166

Bird, Robert Montgomery 1806-1854 . . . DLB-202

Bird, William 1888-1963 . . . . DLB-4; DS-15

The Cost of the *Cantos*: William Bird
to Ezra Pound Y-01

Birken, Sigmund von 1626-1681 . . . . DLB-164

Birney, Earle 1904-1995 . . . . DLB-88

Birrell, Augustine 1850-1933 . . . . DLB-98

Bisher, Furman 1918- DLB-171

Bishop, Elizabeth
1911-1979 . . . . DLB-5, 169; CDALB-6

The Elizabeth Bishop Society Y-01

Bishop, John Peale 1892-1944 . . . . . DLB-4, 9, 45

Bismarck, Otto von 1815-1898 . . . . DLB-129

Bisset, Robert 1759-1805 . . . . DLB-142

Bissett, Bill 1939- DLB-53

Bitzius, Albert (see Gotthelf, Jeremias)

Bjørnvig, Thorkild 1918- DLB-214

Black, David (D. M.) 1941- DLB-40

Black, Gavin (Oswald Morris Wynd)
1913-1998. . . . . .DLB-276

Black, Lionel (Dudley Barker)
1910-1980. . . . . .DLB-276

Black, Winifred 1863-1936. . . . . DLB-25

Walter J. Black [publishing house] DLB-46

Blackamore, Arthur 1679-? DLB-24, 39

Blackburn, Alexander L. 1929- Y-85

Blackburn, John 1923-1993 . . . . DLB-261

Blackburn, Paul 1926-1971 . . . . .DLB-16; Y-81

Blackburn, Thomas 1916-1977. . . . . DLB-27

Blacker, Terence 1948- DLB-271

Blackmore, R. D. 1825-1900 . . . . DLB-18

Blackmore, Sir Richard 1654-1729 . . . . . . DLB-131

Blackmur, R. P. 1904-1965. . . . . DLB-63

Basil Blackwell, Publisher DLB-106

Blackwood, Algernon Henry
1869-1951 . . . . .DLB-153, 156, 178

Blackwood, Caroline 1931-1996. . . . DLB-14, 207

William Blackwood and Sons, Ltd. DLB-154

Blackwood's Edinburgh Magazine
1817-1980. . . . . DLB-110

Blades, William 1824-1890. . . . . DLB-184

Blaga, Lucian 1895-1961 . . . . DLB-220

Blagden, Isabella 1817?-1873 . . . . DLB-199

Blair, Eric Arthur (see Orwell, George)

Blair, Francis Preston 1791-1876. . . . . DLB-43

Blair, Hugh
Lectures on Rhetoric and Belles Lettres (1783),
[excerpts] DLB-31

Blair, James circa 1655-1743 . . . . DLB-24

Blair, John Durburrow 1759-1823 . . . . . . DLB-37

Blais, Marie-Claire 1939- DLB-53

Blaise, Clark 1940- DLB-53

Blake, George 1893-1961 . . . . DLB-191

Blake, Lillie Devereux 1833-1913. . . DLB-202, 221

Blake, Nicholas (C. Day Lewis)
1904-1972. . . . . DLB-77

Blake, William
1757-1827 . . . . . . DLB-93, 154, 163; CDBLB-3

The Blakiston Company DLB-49

Blanchard, Stephen 1950- DLB-267

Blanchot, Maurice 1907-2003 . . . . DLB-72

Blanckenburg, Christian Friedrich von
1744-1796 . . . . DLB-94

Blandiana, Ana 1942- DLB-232; CDWLB-4

Blanshard, Brand 1892-1987 . . . . .DLB-279

Blaser, Robin 1925- DLB-165

Blaumanis, Rudolfs 1863-1908. . . . . DLB-220

Bleasdale, Alan 1946- DLB-245

Bledsoe, Albert Taylor
1809-1877. . . . . .DLB-3, 79, 248

Bleecker, Ann Eliza 1752-1783 . . . . DLB-200

Blelock and Company DLB-49

Blennerhassett, Margaret Agnew
1773-1842 . . . . DLB-99

Geoffrey Bles [publishing house] DLB-112

Blessington, Marguerite, Countess of
1789-1849. . . . . DLB-166

Blew, Mary Clearman 1939- DLB-256

The Blickling Homilies circa 971 . . . . DLB-146

Blind, Mathilde 1841-1896 . . . . DLB-199

Blish, James 1921-1975 . . . . DLB-8

E. Bliss and E. White
[publishing house] DLB-49

Bliven, Bruce 1889-1977 . . . . DLB-137

Blixen, Karen 1885-1962 . . . . DLB-214

Bloch, Robert 1917-1994. . . . . DLB-44

Tribute to John D. MacDonald Y-86

Block, Lawrence 1938- DLB-226

Block, Rudolph (see Lessing, Bruno)

Blondal, Patricia 1926-1959 . . . . DLB-88

Bloom, Harold 1930- DLB-67

Bloomer, Amelia 1818-1894 . . . . DLB-79

Bloomfield, Robert 1766-1823 . . . . DLB-93

Bloomsbury Group. DS-10

The *Dreadnought* Hoax DS-10

Blotner, Joseph 1923- DLB-111

Blount, Thomas 1618?-1679. . . . . DLB-236

Bloy, Léon 1846-1917. . . . . DLB-123

Blume, Judy 1938- DLB-52

Tribute to Theodor Seuss Geisel Y-91

Blunck, Hans Friedrich 1888-1961 . . . . . . DLB-66

Blunden, Edmund 1896-1974 . . . .DLB-20, 100, 155

Blundeville, Thomas 1522?-1606 . . . . DLB-236

Blunt, Lady Anne Isabella Noel
1837-1917 . . . . .DLB-174

Blunt, Wilfrid Scawen 1840-1922. . . . .DLB-19, 174

Bly, Nellie (see Cochrane, Elizabeth)

Bly, Robert 1926- DLB-5

Blyton, Enid 1897-1968 . . . . DLB-160

Boaden, James 1762-1839. . . . . DLB-89

Boas, Frederick S. 1862-1957 . . . . DLB-149

The Bobbs-Merrill Company DLB-46

The Bobbs-Merrill Archive at the
Lilly Library, Indiana University Y-90

Boborykin, Petr Dmitrievich 1836-1921. . DLB-238

Bobrov, Semen Sergeevich 1763?-1810. . . DLB-150

Bobrowski, Johannes 1917-1965. . . . . DLB-75

Bodenheim, Maxwell 1892-1954 . . . . . . DLB-9, 45

Bodenstedt, Friedrich von 1819-1892. . . . DLB-129

Bodini, Vittorio 1914-1970 . . . . DLB-128

Bodkin, M. McDonnell 1850-1933. . . . . . DLB-70

Bodley, Sir Thomas 1545-1613 . . . . DLB-213

Bodley Head. DLB-112

Bodmer, Johann Jakob 1698-1783 . . . . . . DLB-97

Bodmershof, Imma von 1895-1982 . . . . . . DLB-85

Bodsworth, Fred 1918- DLB-68

Boehm, Sydney 1908- DLB-44

Boer, Charles 1939- DLB-5

Boethius circa 480-circa 524 . . . . DLB-115

Boethius of Dacia circa 1240-? DLB-115

Bogan, Louise 1897-1970 . . . . DLB-45, 169

Bogarde, Dirk 1921-1999 . . . . DLB-14

Bogdanovich, Ippolit Fedorovich
circa 1743-1803 . . . . DLB-150

David Bogue [publishing house]. DLB-106

Böhme, Jakob 1575-1624 . . . . DLB-164

H. G. Bohn [publishing house]. DLB-106

Bohse, August 1661-1742 . . . . DLB-168

Boie, Heinrich Christian 1744-1806 . . . . . . DLB-94

Boileau-Despréaux, Nicolas 1636-1711 . . . .DLB-268

Bok, Edward W. 1863-1930. . . . . . DLB-91; DS-16

Boland, Eavan 1944- DLB-40

Boldrewood, Rolf (Thomas Alexander Browne)
1826?-1915. DLB-230

Bolingbroke, Henry St. John, Viscount
1678-1751 . . . . DLB-101

Böll, Heinrich
1917-1985 . . . . .DLB-69; Y-85; CDWLB-2

Bolling, Robert 1738-1775. . . . . DLB-31

Bolotov, Andrei Timofeevich
1738-1833. . . . . DLB-150

Bolt, Carol 1941- DLB-60

Bolt, Robert 1924-1995 . . . . DLB-13, 233

Bolton, Herbert E. 1870-1953. . . . . .DLB-17

Bonaventura. DLB-90

Bonaventure circa 1217-1274 . . . . DLB-115

Bonaviri, Giuseppe 1924- DLB-177

Bond, Edward 1934- DLB-13

Bond, Michael 1926- DLB-161

Albert and Charles Boni
[publishing house] DLB-46

Boni and Liveright DLB-46

Bonnefoy, Yves 1923- DLB-258

Bonner, Marita 1899-1971 . . . . DLB-228

Bonner, Paul Hyde 1893-1968 . . . . DS-17

Bonner, Sherwood (see McDowell, Katharine Sherwood Bonner)

Robert Bonner's Sons DLB-49

Bonnin, Gertrude Simmons (see Zitkala-Ša)

Bonsanti, Alessandro 1904-1984 . . . . DLB-177

Bontempelli, Massimo 1878-1960 . . . . DLB-264

Bontemps, Arna 1902-1973 . . . . DLB-48, 51

The Book Buyer (1867-1880, 1884-1918, 1935-1938 . . . . DS-13

The Book League of America DLB-46

Book Reviewing
    The American Book Review: A Sketch. . . Y-92

    Book Reviewing and the
        Literary Scene. Y-96, 97

    Book Reviewing in America Y-87–94

    Book Reviewing in America and the
        Literary Scene. Y-95

    Book Reviewing in Texas Y-94

    Book Reviews in Glossy Magazines Y-95

    Do They or Don't They?
        Writers Reading Book Reviews Y-01

    The Most Powerful Book Review
        in America [*New York Times
        Book Review*]. Y-82

    Some Surprises and Universal Truths. . . . Y-92

    The Year in Book Reviewing and the
        Literary Situation Y-98

Book Supply Company DLB-49

The Book Trade History Group Y-93

The Booker Prize. Y-96–98

    Address by Anthony Thwaite,
        Chairman of the Booker Prize Judges
        Comments from Former Booker
        Prize Winners Y-86

Boorde, Andrew circa 1490-1549 . . . . DLB-136

Boorstin, Daniel J. 1914- DLB-17

    Tribute to Archibald MacLeish. Y-82

    Tribute to Charles Scribner Jr. Y-95

Booth, Franklin 1874-1948. . . . . DLB-188

Booth, Mary L. 1831-1889 . . . . DLB-79

Booth, Philip 1925- Y-82

Booth, Wayne C. 1921- DLB-67

Booth, William 1829-1912. . . . . DLB-190

Borchardt, Rudolf 1877-1945 . . . . DLB-66

Borchert, Wolfgang 1921-1947 . . . . . . DLB-69, 124

Borel, Pétrus 1809-1859. . . . . DLB-119

Borges, Jorge Luis
    1899-1986 . . . DLB-113, 283; Y-86; CDWLB-3

    The Poetry of Jorge Luis Borges Y-86

    A Personal Tribute Y-86

Borgese, Giuseppe Antonio 1882-1952 . . . DLB-264

Börne, Ludwig 1786-1837 . . . . DLB-90

Bornstein, Miriam 1950- DLB-209

Borowski, Tadeusz
    1922-1951 . . . . DLB-215; CDWLB-4

Borrow, George 1803-1881 . . . . . . DLB-21, 55, 166

Bosanquet, Bernard 1848-1923 . . . . DLB-262

Bosch, Juan 1909-2001 . . . . DLB-145

Bosco, Henri 1888-1976. . . . . DLB-72

Bosco, Monique 1927- DLB-53

Bosman, Herman Charles 1905-1951 . . . . DLB-225

Bossuet, Jacques-Bénigne 1627-1704 . . . . . DLB-268

Bostic, Joe 1908-1988. . . . . DLB-241

Boston, Lucy M. 1892-1990 . . . . DLB-161

Boston Quarterly Review. DLB-1

Boston University
    Editorial Institute at Boston University. . . Y-00

    Special Collections at Boston University. . Y-99

Boswell, James
    1740-1795 . . . . DLB-104, 142; CDBLB-2

Boswell, Robert 1953- DLB-234

Bosworth, David Y-82

    Excerpt from "Excerpts from a Report
        of the Commission," in *The Death
        of Descartes* Y-82

Bote, Hermann circa 1460-circa 1520. . . . DLB-179

Botev, Khristo 1847-1876. . . . . DLB-147

Botkin, Vasilii Petrovich 1811-1869 . . . . . DLB-277

Botta, Anne C. Lynch 1815-1891 . . . . DLB-3, 250

Botto, Ján (see Krasko, Ivan)

Bottome, Phyllis 1882-1963. . . . . DLB-197

Bottomley, Gordon 1874-1948. . . . . DLB-10

Bottoms, David 1949- DLB-120; Y-83

    Tribute to James Dickey Y-97

Bottrall, Ronald 1906- DLB-20

Bouchardy, Joseph 1810-1870 . . . . DLB-192

Boucher, Anthony 1911-1968 . . . . DLB-8

Boucher, Jonathan 1738-1804 . . . . DLB-31

Boucher de Boucherville, Georges
    1814-1894 . . . . DLB-99

Boudreau, Daniel (see Coste, Donat)

Bouhours, Dominique 1628-1702 . . . . DLB-268

Bourassa, Napoléon 1827-1916 . . . . DLB-99

Bourget, Paul 1852-1935 . . . . DLB-123

Bourinot, John George 1837-1902 . . . . DLB-99

Bourjaily, Vance 1922- DLB-2, 143

Bourne, Edward Gaylord 1860-1908. . . . . . DLB-47

Bourne, Randolph 1886-1918 . . . . DLB-63

Bousoño, Carlos 1923- DLB-108

Bousquet, Joë 1897-1950 . . . . DLB-72

Bova, Ben 1932- Y-81

Bovard, Oliver K. 1872-1945. . . . . DLB-25

Bove, Emmanuel 1898-1945 . . . . DLB-72

Bowen, Elizabeth
    1899-1973 . . . . DLB-15, 162; CDBLB-7

Bowen, Francis 1811-1890. . . . . . . DLB-1, 59, 235

Bowen, John 1924- DLB-13

Bowen, Marjorie 1886-1952 . . . . DLB-153

Bowen-Merrill Company. DLB-49

Bowering, George 1935- DLB-53

Bowers, Bathsheba 1671-1718 . . . . DLB-200

Bowers, Claude G. 1878-1958 . . . . DLB-17

Bowers, Edgar 1924-2000 . . . . DLB-5

Bowers, Fredson Thayer
    1905-1991 . . . . DLB-140; Y-91

    The Editorial Style of Fredson Bowers . . . Y-91

    Fredson Bowers and
        Studies in Bibliography. Y-91

    Fredson Bowers and the Cambridge
        Beaumont and Fletcher. Y-91

    Fredson Bowers as Critic of Renaissance
        Dramatic Literature Y-91

    Fredson Bowers as Music Critic Y-91

    Fredson Bowers, Master Teacher Y-91

    An Interview [on Nabokov] Y-80

    Working with Fredson Bowers Y-91

Bowles, Paul 1910-1999 . . . . . . DLB-5, 6, 218; Y-99

Bowles, Samuel, III 1826-1878 . . . . DLB-43

Bowles, William Lisle 1762-1850. . . . . DLB-93

Bowman, Louise Morey 1882-1944. . . . . . . DLB-68

Bowne, Borden Parker 1847-1919 . . . . DLB-270

Boyd, James 1888-1944 . . . . DLB-9; DS-16

Boyd, John 1919- DLB-8

Boyd, Martin 1893-1972 . . . . DLB-260

Boyd, Thomas 1898-1935 . . . . DLB-9; DS-16

Boyd, William 1952- DLB-231

Boye, Karin 1900-1941 . . . . DLB-259

Boyesen, Hjalmar Hjorth
    1848-1895 . . . . DLB-12, 71; DS-13

Boylan, Clare 1948- DLB-267

Boyle, Kay 1902-1992   DLB-4, 9, 48, 86; DS-15;
    . . . . Y-93

Boyle, Roger, Earl of Orrery 1621-1679 . . . DLB-80

Boyle, T. Coraghessan
    1948- DLB-218, 278; Y-86

Božić, Mirko 1919- DLB-181

Brackenbury, Alison 1953- DLB-40

Brackenridge, Hugh Henry
    1748-1816 . . . . DLB-11, 37

    The Rising Glory of America DLB-37

Brackett, Charles 1892-1969 . . . . DLB-26

Brackett, Leigh 1915-1978 . . . . DLB-8, 26

John Bradburn [publishing house] DLB-49

Bradbury, Malcolm 1932-2000 . . . . . . DLB-14, 207

Bradbury, Ray 1920- DLB-2, 8; CDALB-6

Bradbury and Evans DLB-106

Braddon, Mary Elizabeth
    1835-1915 . . . . DLB-18, 70, 156

Bradford, Andrew 1686-1742 . . . . DLB-43, 73

Bradford, Gamaliel 1863-1932. . . . . DLB-17

Bradford, John 1749-1830 . . . . DLB-43

Bradford, Roark 1896-1948 . . . . DLB-86

Bradford, William 1590-1657 . . . . DLB-24, 30

Bradford, William, III 1719-1791. . . . . . DLB-43, 73

Bradlaugh, Charles 1833-1891 . . . . DLB-57

Bradley, David 1950- DLB-33

Bradley, F. H. 1846-1924. . . . . DLB-262

Bradley, Katherine Harris (see Field, Michael)

Bradley, Marion Zimmer 1930-1999 . . . . . . DLB-8

Bradley, William Aspenwall 1878-1939 . . . . DLB-4

Ira Bradley and Company DLB-49

J. W. Bradley and Company DLB-49

Bradshaw, Henry 1831-1886 . . . . DLB-184

Bradstreet, Anne
1612 or 1613-1672 . . . . DLB-24; CDALB-2

Bradūnas, Kazys 1917- DLB-220

Bradwardine, Thomas circa 1295-1349 . . DLB-115

Brady, Frank 1924-1986. . . . . DLB-111

Frederic A. Brady [publishing house] DLB-49

Bragg, Melvyn 1939- DLB-14, 271

Charles H. Brainard [publishing house] . . . DLB-49

Braine, John 1922-1986 . DLB-15; Y-86; CDBLB-7

Braithwait, Richard 1588-1673 . . . . DLB-151

Braithwaite, William Stanley
1878-1962. . . . . DLB-50, 54

Bräker, Ulrich 1735-1798 . . . . DLB-94

Bramah, Ernest 1868-1942. . . . . DLB-70

Branagan, Thomas 1774-1843 . . . . DLB-37

Brancati, Vitaliano 1907-1954. . . . . DLB-264

Branch, William Blackwell 1927- DLB-76

Brand, Christianna 1907-1988 . . . . .DLB-276

Brand, Max (see Faust, Frederick Schiller)

Branden Press. DLB-46

Branner, H.C. 1903-1966. . . . . DLB-214

Brant, Sebastian 1457-1521 . . . . .DLB-179

Brassey, Lady Annie (Allnutt)
1839-1887. . . . . DLB-166

Brathwaite, Edward Kamau
1930- DLB-125; CDWLB-3

Brault, Jacques 1933- DLB-53

Braun, Matt 1932- DLB-212

Braun, Volker 1939- DLB-75, 124

Brautigan, Richard
1935-1984 . . . . . . .DLB-2, 5, 206; Y-80, 84

Braxton, Joanne M. 1950- DLB-41

Bray, Anne Eliza 1790-1883 . . . . DLB-116

Bray, Thomas 1656-1730 . . . . DLB-24

Brazdžionis, Bernardas 1907- DLB-220

George Braziller [publishing house] DLB-46

The Bread Loaf Writers' Conference 1983 . . . Y-84

Breasted, James Henry 1865-1935 . . . . DLB-47

Brecht, Bertolt
1898-1956 . . . . DLB-56, 124; CDWLB-2

Bredel, Willi 1901-1964 . . . . DLB-56

Bregendahl, Marie 1867-1940. . . . . DLB-214

Breitinger, Johann Jakob 1701-1776 . . . . . DLB-97

Bremser, Bonnie 1939- DLB-16

Bremser, Ray 1934-1998 . . . . DLB-16

Brennan, Christopher 1870-1932 . . . . DLB-230

Brentano, Bernard von 1901-1964 . . . . . . .DLB-56

Brentano, Clemens 1778-1842 . . . . DLB-90

Brentano's. DLB-49

Brenton, Howard 1942- DLB-13

Breslin, Jimmy 1929-1996. . . . . DLB-185

Breton, André 1896-1966 . . . . DLB-65, 258

Breton, Nicholas circa 1555-circa 1626. . . DLB-136

The Breton Lays
1300-early fifteenth century DLB-146

Brett, Simon 1945- DLB-276

Brewer, Luther A. 1858-1933. . . . . DLB-187

Brewer, Warren and Putnam DLB-46

Brewster, Elizabeth 1922- DLB-60

Breytenbach, Breyten 1939- DLB-225

Bridge, Ann (Lady Mary Dolling Sanders
O'Malley) 1889-1974 . . . . DLB-191

Bridge, Horatio 1806-1893. . . . . DLB-183

Bridgers, Sue Ellen 1942- DLB-52

Bridges, Robert
1844-1930 . . . . DLB-19, 98; CDBLB-5

The Bridgewater Library DLB-213

Bridie, James 1888-1951 . . . . DLB-10

Brieux, Eugene 1858-1932 . . . . DLB-192

Brigadere, Anna
1861-1933 . . . . DLB-220; CDWLB-4

Briggs, Charles Frederick 1804-1877 . . DLB-3, 250

Brighouse, Harold 1882-1958. . . . . DLB-10

Bright, Mary Chavelita Dunne (see Egerton, George)

Brightman, Edgar Sheffield 1884-1953. . . .DLB-270

B. J. Brimmer Company. DLB-46

Brines, Francisco 1932- DLB-134

Brink, André 1935- DLB-225

Brinley, George, Jr. 1817-1875 . . . . DLB-140

Brinnin, John Malcolm 1916-1998 . . . . . . DLB-48

Brisbane, Albert 1809-1890 . . . . DLB-3, 250

Brisbane, Arthur 1864-1936. . . . . DLB-25

British Academy. DLB-112

The British Critic 1793-1843 . . . . DLB-110

British Library
The American Trust for the
British Library. Y-96

The British Library and the Regular
Readers' Group. Y-91

Building the New British Library
at St Pancras Y-94

British Literary Prizes. DLB-207; Y-98

British Literature

The "Angry Young Men" DLB-15

Author-Printers, 1476-1599 . . . . DLB-167

The Comic Tradition Continued. DLB-15

Documents on Sixteenth-Century
Literature. DLB-167, 172

Eikon Basilike 1649 . . . . DLB-151

Letter from London. Y-96

A Mirror for Magistrates DLB-167

"Modern English Prose" (1876),
by George Saintsbury DLB-57

Sex, Class, Politics, and Religion [in the
British Novel, 1930-1959] DLB-15

Victorians on Rhetoric and Prose
Style. DLB-57

The Year in British Fiction. Y-99–01

"You've Never Had It So Good," Gusted
by "Winds of Change": British
Fiction in the 1950s, 1960s,
and After DLB-14

British Literature, Old and Middle English
Anglo-Norman Literature in the
Development of Middle English
Literature. DLB-146

The Alliterative Morte Arthure and the
Stanzaic Morte Arthur
circa 1350-1400 . . . . DLB-146

Ancrene Riwle circa 1200-1225 . . . . DLB-146

The Anglo-Saxon Chronicle circa
890-1154 . . . . DLB-146

The Battle of Maldon circa 1000 . . . . . . DLB-146

Beowulf circa 900-1000 or
790-825 . . . . DLB-146; CDBLB-1

The Blickling Homilies circa 971 . . . . DLB-146

The Breton Lays
1300-early fifteenth century. DLB-146

The Castle of Perserverance
circa 1400-1425 . . . . DLB-146

The Celtic Background to Medieval
English Literature DLB-146

The Chester Plays circa 1505-1532;
revisions until 1575 . . . . DLB-146

Cursor Mundi circa 1300 . . . . DLB-146

The English Language: 410
to 1500 . . . . DLB-146

The Germanic Epic and Old English
Heroic Poetry: Widsith, Waldere,
and The Fight at Finnsburg. DLB-146

Judith circa 930 . . . . DLB-146

The Matter of England 1240-1400. . . DLB-146

The Matter of Rome early twelfth to
late fifteenth centuries DLB-146

Middle English Literature:
An Introduction. DLB-146

The Middle English Lyric DLB-146

Morality Plays: Mankind circa 1450-1500
and Everyman circa 1500 . . . . DLB-146

N-Town Plays circa 1468 to early
sixteenth century. DLB-146

Old English Literature:
An Introduction. DLB-146

Old English Riddles
eighth to tenth centuries DLB-146

The Owl and the Nightingale
circa 1189-1199 . . . . DLB-146

The Paston Letters 1422-1509 . . . . DLB-146

The Seafarer circa 970 . . . . DLB-146

The South English Legendary circa
thirteenth to fifteenth centuries . . . DLB-146

The British Review and London Critical
Journal 1811-1825 . . . . DLB-110

Brito, Aristeo 1942- DLB-122

Brittain, Vera 1893-1970. . . . . DLB-191

Brizeux, Auguste 1803-1858. . . . . .DLB-217

Broadway Publishing Company. DLB-46

Broch, Hermann
1886-1951 . . . . .DLB-85, 124; CDWLB-2

Brochu, André 1942- DLB-53

Brock, Edwin 1927-1997. . . . . DLB-40

Brockes, Barthold Heinrich 1680-1747. . . DLB-168

Brod, Max 1884-1968. . . . . .DLB-81

Brodber, Erna 1940- DLB-157

Brodhead, John R. 1814-1873 . . . . DLB-30

Brodkey, Harold 1930-1996 . . . . DLB-130

Brodsky, Joseph (Iosif Aleksandrovich
    Brodsky) 1940-1996 . . . . DLB-285; Y-87

    Nobel Lecture 1987 . . . . Y-87

Brodsky, Michael 1948- DLB-244

Broeg, Bob 1918- DLB-171

Brøgger, Suzanne 1944- DLB-214

Brome, Richard circa 1590-1652 . . . . DLB-58

Brome, Vincent 1910- DLB-155

Bromfield, Louis 1896-1956 . . . . DLB-4, 9, 86

Bromige, David 1933- DLB-193

Broner, E. M. 1930- DLB-28

    Tribute to Bernard Malamud Y-86

Bronk, William 1918-1999 . . . . DLB-165

Bronnen, Arnolt 1895-1959 . . . . DLB-124

Brontë, Anne 1820-1849 . . . . DLB-21, 199

Brontë, Charlotte
    1816-1855 . . . . . . DLB-21, 159, 199; CDBLB-4

Brontë, Emily
    1818-1848 . . . . . . DLB-21, 32, 199; CDBLB-4

The Brontë Society Y-98

Brook, Stephen 1947- DLB-204

Brook Farm 1841-1847 . . . . DLB-1; 223; DS-5

Brooke, Frances 1724-1789 . . . . DLB-39, 99

Brooke, Henry 1703?-1783 . . . . DLB-39

Brooke, L. Leslie 1862-1940 . . . . DLB-141

Brooke, Margaret, Ranee of Sarawak
    1849-1936 . . . . DLB-174

Brooke, Rupert
    1887-1915 . . . . DLB-19, 216; CDBLB-6

    The Friends of the Dymock Poets Y-00

Brooker, Bertram 1888-1955 . . . . DLB-88

Brooke-Rose, Christine 1923- DLB-14, 231

Brookner, Anita 1928- DLB-194; Y-87

Brooks, Charles Timothy 1813-1883 . . . DLB-1, 243

Brooks, Cleanth 1906-1994 . . . . DLB-63; Y-94

    Tribute to Katherine Anne Porter Y-80

    Tribute to Walker Percy Y-90

Brooks, Gwendolyn
    1917-2000 . . . . DLB-5, 76, 165; CDALB-1

    Tribute to Julian Mayfield Y-84

Brooks, Jeremy 1926- DLB-14

Brooks, Mel 1926- DLB-26

Brooks, Noah 1830-1903 . . . . DLB-42; DS-13

Brooks, Richard 1912-1992 . . . . DLB-44

Brooks, Van Wyck 1886-1963 . . . DLB-45, 63, 103

Brophy, Brigid 1929-1995 . . . . . . DLB-14, 70, 271

Brophy, John 1899-1965 . . . . DLB-191

Brossard, Chandler 1922-1993 . . . . DLB-16

Brossard, Nicole 1943- DLB-53

Broster, Dorothy Kathleen 1877-1950 . . . . DLB-160

Brother Antoninus (see Everson, William)

Brotherton, Lord 1856-1930 . . . . DLB-184

Brougham, John 1810-1880 . . . . DLB-11

Brougham and Vaux, Henry Peter
    Brougham, Baron 1778-1868 . . . . DLB-110, 158

Broughton, James 1913-1999 . . . . DLB-5

Broughton, Rhoda 1840-1920 . . . . DLB-18

Broun, Heywood 1888-1939 . . . . DLB-29, 171

Brown, Alice 1856-1948 . . . . DLB-78

Brown, Bob 1886-1959 . . . . DLB-4, 45; DS-15

Brown, Cecil 1943- DLB-33

Brown, Charles Brockden
    1771-1810 . . . . DLB-37, 59, 73; CDALB-2

Brown, Christy 1932-1981 . . . . DLB-14

Brown, Dee 1908-2002 . . . . Y-80

Brown, Frank London 1927-1962 . . . . DLB-76

Brown, Fredric 1906-1972 . . . . DLB-8

Brown, George Mackay
    1921-1996 . . . . DLB-14, 27, 139, 271

Brown, Harry 1917-1986 . . . . DLB-26

Brown, Larry 1951- DLB-234

Brown, Lew 1893-1958 . . . . DLB-265

Brown, Marcia 1918- DLB-61

Brown, Margaret Wise 1910-1952 . . . . DLB-22

Brown, Morna Doris (see Ferrars, Elizabeth)

Brown, Oliver Madox 1855-1874 . . . . DLB-21

Brown, Sterling 1901-1989 . . . . . . DLB-48, 51, 63

Brown, T. E. 1830-1897 . . . . DLB-35

Brown, Thomas Alexander (see Boldrewood, Rolf)

Brown, Warren 1894-1978 . . . . DLB-241

Brown, William Hill 1765-1793 . . . . DLB-37

Brown, William Wells
    1815-1884 . . . . DLB-3, 50, 183, 248

Brown University
    The Festival of Vanguard Narrative Y-93

Browne, Charles Farrar 1834-1867 . . . . . . DLB-11

Browne, Frances 1816-1879 . . . . DLB-199

Browne, Francis Fisher 1843-1913 . . . . DLB-79

Browne, Howard 1908-1999 . . . . DLB-226

Browne, J. Ross 1821-1875 . . . . DLB-202

Browne, Michael Dennis 1940- DLB-40

Browne, Sir Thomas 1605-1682 . . . . DLB-151

Browne, William, of Tavistock
    1590-1645 . . . . DLB-121

Browne, Wynyard 1911-1964 . . . . . . DLB-13, 233

Browne and Nolan DLB-106

Brownell, W. C. 1851-1928 . . . . DLB-71

Browning, Elizabeth Barrett
    1806-1861 . . . . DLB-32, 199; CDBLB-4

Browning, Robert
    1812-1889 . . . . DLB-32, 163; CDBLB-4

    Essay on Chatterron DLB-32

    Introductory Essay: *Letters of Percy
    Bysshe Shelley* (1852) DLB-32

    "The Novel in [Robert Browning's]
    'The Ring and the Book'" (1912),
    by Henry James DLB-32

Brownjohn, Allan 1931- DLB-40

    Tribute to John Betjeman Y-84

Brownson, Orestes Augustus
    1803-1876 . . . . DLB-1, 59, 73, 243; DS-5

Bruccoli, Matthew J. 1931- DLB-103

    Joseph [Heller] and George [V. Higgins] . . Y-99

    Response [to Busch on Fitzgerald] Y-96

    Tribute to Albert Erskine Y-93

    Tribute to Charles E. Feinberg Y-88

    Working with Fredson Bowers Y-91

Bruce, Charles 1906-1971 . . . . DLB-68

Bruce, John Edward 1856-1924

    Three Documents [African American
    poets] DLB-50

Bruce, Leo 1903-1979 . . . . DLB-77

Bruce, Mary Grant 1878-1958 . . . . DLB-230

Bruce, Philip Alexander 1856-1933 . . . . . . DLB-47

Bruce-Novoa, Juan 1944- DLB-82

Bruckman, Clyde 1894-1955 . . . . DLB-26

Bruckner, Ferdinand 1891-1958 . . . . DLB-118

Brundage, John Herbert (see Herbert, John)

Brunner, John 1934-1995 . . . . DLB-261

    Tribute to Theodore Sturgeon Y-85

Brutus, Dennis
    1924- DLB-117, 225; CDWLB-3

Bryan, C. D. B. 1936- DLB-185

Bryant, Arthur 1899-1985 . . . . DLB-149

Bryant, William Cullen 1794-1878
    . . . . DLB-3, 43, 59, 189, 250; CDALB-2

Bryce, James 1838-1922 . . . . DLB-166, 190

Bryce Echenique, Alfredo
    1939- DLB-145; CDWLB-3

Bryden, Bill 1942- DLB-233

Brydges, Sir Samuel Egerton
    1762-1837 . . . . DLB-107, 142

Bryskett, Lodowick 1546?-1612 . . . . DLB-167

Buchan, John 1875-1940 . . . . DLB-34, 70, 156

Buchanan, George 1506-1582 . . . . DLB-132

Buchanan, Robert 1841-1901 . . . . DLB-18, 35

    "The Fleshly School of Poetry and
    Other Phenomena of the Day"
    (1872) DLB-35

    "The Fleshly School of Poetry:
    Mr. D. G. Rossetti" (1871),
    by Thomas Maitland DLB-35

Buchler, Justus 1914-1991 . . . . DLB-279

Buchman, Sidney 1902-1975 . . . . DLB-26

Buchner, Augustus 1591-1661 . . . . DLB-164

Büchner, Georg 1813-1837 . . DLB-133; CDWLB-2

Bucholtz, Andreas Heinrich 1607-1671 . . . DLB-168

Buck, Pearl S. 1892-1973 . . . DLB-9, 102; CDALB-7

Bucke, Charles 1781-1846 . . . . DLB-110

Bucke, Richard Maurice 1837-1902 . . . . . . DLB-99

Buckingham, Edwin 1810-1833 . . . . DLB-73

Buckingham, Joseph Tinker 1779-1861 . . . . DLB-73

Buckler, Ernest 1908-1984 . . . . DLB-68

Buckley, William F., Jr. 1925- . . . DLB-137; Y-80

    Publisher's Statement From the
    Initial Issue of *National Review*
    (19 November 1955) DLB-137

Buckminster, Joseph Stevens
    1784-1812 . . . . DLB-37

Buckner, Robert 1906- DLB-26

Budd, Thomas ?-1698 . . . . DLB-24

Budrys, A. J. 1931- DLB-8

Buechner, Frederick 1926- Y-80

Buell, John 1927- DLB-53

Bufalino, Gesualdo 1920-1996 . . . . DLB-196

Job Buffum [publishing house]. DLB-49

Bugnet, Georges 1879-1981 . . . . DLB-92

Buies, Arthur 1840-1901. . . . . DLB-99

Bukowski, Charles 1920-1994 . . . DLB-5, 130, 169

Bulatović, Miodrag
1930-1991 . . . . DLB-181; CDWLB-4

Bulgakov, Mikhail Afanas'evich
1891-1940 . . . . DLB-272

Bulgarin, Faddei Venediktovich
1789-1859. . . . . DLB-198

Bulger, Bozeman 1877-1932 . . . . .DLB-171

Bullein, William
between 1520 and 1530-1576. . . . . . . DLB-167

Bullins, Ed 1935- DLB-7, 38, 249

Bulwer, John 1606-1656 . . . . DLB-236

Bulwer-Lytton, Edward (also Edward
Bulwer) 1803-1873. . . . . DLB-21

"On Art in Fiction "(1838). DLB-21

Bumpus, Jerry 1937- Y-81

Bunce and Brother DLB-49

Bunner, H. C. 1855-1896 . . . . .DLB-78, 79

Bunting, Basil 1900-1985 . . . . DLB-20

Buntline, Ned (Edward Zane Carroll
Judson) 1821-1886. . . . . DLB-186

Bunyan, John 1628-1688 . . . . . DLB-39; CDBLB-2

The Author's Apology for
His Book DLB-39

Burch, Robert 1925- DLB-52

Burciaga, José Antonio 1940- DLB-82

Burdekin, Katharine (Murray Constantine)
1896-1963 . . . . DLB-255

Bürger, Gottfried August 1747-1794 . . . . . DLB-94

Burgess, Anthony (John Anthony Burgess Wilson)
1917-1993 . . . . . DLB-14, 194, 261; CDBLB-8

The Anthony Burgess Archive at
the Harry Ransom Humanities
Research Center Y-98

Anthony Burgess's *99 Novels:*
An Opinion Poll Y-84

Burgess, Gelett 1866-1951 . . . . DLB-11

Burgess, John W. 1844-1931 . . . . DLB-47

Burgess, Thornton W. 1874-1965 . . . . DLB-22

Burgess, Stringer and Company DLB-49

Burick, Si 1909-1986. . . . . .DLB-171

Burk, John Daly circa 1772-1808 . . . . DLB-37

Burk, Ronnie 1955- DLB-209

Burke, Edmund 1729?-1797 . . . . DLB-104, 252

Burke, James Lee 1936- DLB-226

Burke, Johnny 1908-1964 . . . . DLB-265

Burke, Kenneth 1897-1993 . . . . DLB-45, 63

Burke, Thomas 1886-1945 . . . . DLB-197

Burley, Dan 1907-1962 . . . . DLB-241

Burley, W. J. 1914- DLB-276

Burlingame, Edward Livermore
1848-1922 . . . . DLB-79

Burman, Carina 1960- DLB-257

Burnet, Gilbert 1643-1715. . . . . DLB-101

Burnett, Frances Hodgson
1849-1924 . . . . .DLB-42, 141; DS-13, 14

Burnett, W. R. 1899-1982 . . . . DLB-9, 226

Burnett, Whit 1899-1973 . . . . DLB-137

Burney, Fanny 1752-1840 . . . . DLB-39

Dedication, *The Wanderer* (1814) DLB-39

Preface to *Evelina* (1778) DLB-39

Burns, Alan 1929- DLB-14, 194

Burns, John Horne 1916-1953 . . . . Y-85

Burns, Robert 1759-1796 . . . . DLB-109; CDBLB-3

Burns and Oates DLB-106

Burnshaw, Stanley 1906- DLB-48; Y-97

James Dickey and Stanley Burnshaw
Correspondence Y-02

Review of Stanley Burnshaw: The
Collected Poems and Selected
Prose Y-02

Tribute to Robert Penn Warren Y-89

Burr, C. Chauncey 1815?-1883 . . . . DLB-79

Burr, Esther Edwards 1732-1758 . . . . DLB-200

Burroughs, Edgar Rice 1875-1950 . . . . DLB-8

The Burroughs Bibliophiles Y-98

Burroughs, John 1837-1921 . . . . .DLB-64, 275

Burroughs, Margaret T. G. 1917- DLB-41

Burroughs, William S., Jr. 1947-1981 . . . . . DLB-16

Burroughs, William Seward 1914-1997
. . . . DLB-2, 8, 16, 152, 237; Y-81, 97

Burroway, Janet 1936- DLB-6

Burt, Maxwell Struthers
1882-1954 . . . . DLB-86; DS-16

A. L. Burt and Company DLB-49

Burton, Hester 1913- DLB-161

Burton, Isabel Arundell 1831-1896. . . . . . DLB-166

Burton, Miles (see Rhode, John)

Burton, Richard Francis
1821-1890 . . . . DLB-55, 166, 184

Burton, Robert 1577-1640. . . . . DLB-151

Burton, Virginia Lee 1909-1968. . . . . DLB-22

Burton, William Evans 1804-1860 . . . . . . DLB-73

Burwell, Adam Hood 1790-1849 . . . . DLB-99

Bury, Lady Charlotte 1775-1861 . . . . DLB-116

Busch, Frederick 1941- DLB-6, 218

Excerpts from Frederick Busch's USC
Remarks [on F. Scott Fitzgerald] Y-96

Tribute to James Laughlin Y-97

Tribute to Raymond Carver Y-88

Busch, Niven 1903-1991. . . . . DLB-44

Bushnell, Horace 1802-1876. . . . . .DS-13

Business & Literature
The Claims of Business and Literature:
An Undergraduate Essay by
Maxwell Perkins Y-01

Bussières, Arthur de 1877-1913. . . . . DLB-92

Butler, Charles circa 1560-1647 . . . . DLB-236

Butler, Guy 1918- DLB-225

Butler, Joseph 1692-1752 . . . . DLB-252

Butler, Josephine Elizabeth
1828-1906 . . . . DLB-190

Butler, Juan 1942-1981. . . . . DLB-53

Butler, Judith 1956- DLB-246

Butler, Octavia E. 1947- DLB-33

Butler, Pierce 1884-1953. . . . . .DLB-187

Butler, Robert Olen 1945- DLB-173

Butler, Samuel 1613-1680. . . . . . . .DLB-101, 126

Butler, Samuel
1835-1902 . . . . . . .DLB-18, 57, 174; CDBLB-5

Butler, William Francis 1838-1910. . . . . . DLB-166

E. H. Butler and Company DLB-49

Butor, Michel 1926- DLB-83

Nathaniel Butter [publishing house] DLB-170

Butterworth, Hezekiah 1839-1905 . . . . . . DLB-42

Buttitta, Ignazio 1899-1997. . . . . DLB-114

Butts, Mary 1890-1937. . . . . DLB-240

Buzzati, Dino 1906-1972. . . . . .DLB-177

Byars, Betsy 1928- DLB-52

Byatt, A. S. 1936- DLB-14, 194

Byles, Mather 1707-1788 . . . . DLB-24

Henry Bynneman [publishing house] DLB-170

Bynner, Witter 1881-1968 . . . . DLB-54

Byrd, William circa 1543-1623. . . . . .DLB-172

Byrd, William, II 1674-1744 . . . . DLB-24, 140

Byrne, John Keyes (see Leonard, Hugh)

Byron, George Gordon, Lord
1788-1824. . . . . DLB-96, 110; CDBLB-3

The Byron Society of America. Y-00

Byron, Robert 1905-1941. . . . . DLB-195

C

Caballero Bonald, José Manuel
1926- DLB-108

Cabañero, Eladio 1930- DLB-134

Cabell, James Branch 1879-1958 . . . . . . .DLB-9, 78

Cabeza de Baca, Manuel 1853-1915. . . . . DLB-122

Cabeza de Baca Gilbert, Fabiola
1898- DLB-122

Cable, George Washington
1844-1925 . . . . .DLB-12, 74; DS-13

Cable, Mildred 1878-1952 . . . . DLB-195

Cabral, Manuel del 1907-1999 . . . . DLB-283

Cabrera, Lydia 1900-1991 . . . . DLB-145

Cabrera Infante, Guillermo
1929- DLB-113; CDWLB-3

Cadell [publishing house] DLB-154

Cady, Edwin H. 1917- DLB-103

Caedmon flourished 658-680 . . . . DLB-146

Caedmon School circa 660-899 . . . . DLB-146

Caesar, Irving 1895-1996 . . . . DLB-265

Cafés, Brasseries, and Bistros DS-15

Cage, John 1912-1992 . . . . DLB-193

Cahan, Abraham 1860-1951 . . . . DLB-9, 25, 28

Cahn, Sammy 1913-1993. . . . . DLB-265

Cain, George 1943- DLB-33

Cain, James M. 1892-1977 . . . . DLB-226

Caird, Edward 1835-1908 . . . . DLB-262

Caird, Mona 1854-1932. . . . . DLB-197

Čaks, Aleksandrs
1901-1950 . . . . DLB-220; CDWLB-4

Caldecott, Randolph 1846-1886 . . . . DLB-163

John Calder Limited
[Publishing house] DLB-112

Calderón de la Barca, Fanny
1804-1882 . . . . DLB-183

Caldwell, Ben 1937- DLB-38

Caldwell, Erskine 1903-1987 . . . . DLB-9, 86

H. M. Caldwell Company DLB-49

Caldwell, Taylor 1900-1985 . . . . DS-17

Calhoun, John C. 1782-1850 . . . . DLB-3, 248

Călinescu, George 1899-1965 . . . . DLB-220

Calisher, Hortense 1911- DLB-2, 218

Calkins, Mary Whiton 1863-1930 . . . . DLB-270

Callaghan, Mary Rose 1944- DLB-207

Callaghan, Morley 1903-1990 . . . . . DLB-68; DS-15

Callahan, S. Alice 1868-1894 . . . . DLB-175, 221

Callaloo [journal]. Y-87

Callimachus circa 305 B.C.-240 B.C. DLB-176

Calmer, Edgar 1907- DLB-4

Calverley, C. S. 1831-1884 . . . . DLB-35

Calvert, George Henry
1803-1889 . . . . DLB-1, 64, 248

Calvino, Italo 1923-1985 . . . . DLB-196

Cambridge, Ada 1844-1926. . . . . DLB-230

Cambridge Press DLB-49

Cambridge Songs (Carmina Cantabrigensia)
circa 1050 . . . . DLB-148

Cambridge University
Cambridge and the Apostles DS-5

Cambridge University Press DLB-170

Camden, William 1551-1623. . . . . DLB-172

Camden House: An Interview with
James Hardin. Y-92

Cameron, Eleanor 1912-2000 . . . . DLB-52

Cameron, George Frederick
1854-1885 . . . . DLB-99

Cameron, Lucy Lyttelton 1781-1858 . . . . . DLB-163

Cameron, Peter 1959- DLB-234

Cameron, William Bleasdell 1862-1951 . . . DLB-99

Camm, John 1718-1778 . . . . DLB-31

Camon, Ferdinando 1935- DLB-196

Camp, Walter 1859-1925 . . . . DLB-241

Campana, Dino 1885-1932 . . . . DLB-114

Campbell, Bebe Moore 1950- DLB-227

Campbell, David 1915-1979. . . . . DLB-260

Campbell, Gabrielle Margaret Vere
(see Shearing, Joseph, and Bowen, Marjorie)

Campbell, James Dykes 1838-1895 . . . . . . DLB-144

Campbell, James Edwin 1867-1896 . . . . . . DLB-50

Campbell, John 1653-1728. . . . . DLB-43

Campbell, John W., Jr. 1910-1971 . . . . DLB-8

Campbell, Ramsey 1946- DLB-261

Campbell, Roy 1901-1957 . . . . DLB-20, 225

Campbell, Thomas 1777-1844 . . . . DLB-93, 144

Campbell, William Edward (see March, William)

Campbell, William Wilfred 1858-1918 . . . . DLB-92

Campion, Edmund 1539-1581 . . . . DLB-167

Campion, Thomas
1567-1620 . . . . DLB-58, 172; CDBLB-1

Campo, Rafael 1964- DLB-282

Campton, David 1924- DLB-245

Camus, Albert 1913-1960 . . . . DLB-72

Camus, Jean-Pierre 1584-1652. . . . . DLB-268

The Canadian Publishers' Records Database . Y-96

Canby, Henry Seidel 1878-1961 . . . . DLB-91

Candelaria, Cordelia 1943- DLB-82

Candelaria, Nash 1928- DLB-82

Canetti, Elias
1905-1994 . . . . DLB-85, 124; CDWLB-2

Canham, Erwin Dain 1904-1982. . . . . DLB-127

Canitz, Friedrich Rudolph Ludwig von
1654-1699 . . . . DLB-168

Cankar, Ivan 1876-1918. . . . . DLB-147; CDWLB-4

Cannan, Gilbert 1884-1955 . . . . DLB-10, 197

Cannan, Joanna 1896-1961 . . . . DLB-191

Cannell, Kathleen 1891-1974. . . . . DLB-4

Cannell, Skipwith 1887-1957 . . . . DLB-45

Canning, George 1770-1827. . . . . DLB-158

Cannon, Jimmy 1910-1973 . . . . DLB-171

Cano, Daniel 1947- DLB-209

Old Dogs / New Tricks? New
Technologies, the Canon, and the
Structure of the Profession Y-02

Cantú, Norma Elia 1947- DLB-209

Cantwell, Robert 1908-1978 . . . . DLB-9

Jonathan Cape and Harrison Smith
[publishing house] DLB-46

Jonathan Cape Limited DLB-112

Čapek, Karel 1890-1938 . . . . DLB-215; CDWLB-4

Capen, Joseph 1658-1725. . . . . DLB-24

Capes, Bernard 1854-1918. . . . . DLB-156

Capote, Truman 1924-1984
. . . . . . DLB-2, 185, 227; Y-80, 84; CDALB-1

Capps, Benjamin 1922- DLB-256

Caproni, Giorgio 1912-1990 . . . . DLB-128

Caragiale, Mateiu Ioan 1885-1936. . . . . . . DLB-220

Cardarelli, Vincenzo 1887-1959. . . . . DLB-114

Cárdenas, Reyes 1948- DLB-122

Cardinal, Marie 1929-2001 . . . . DLB-83

Carew, Jan 1920- DLB-157

Carew, Thomas 1594 or 1595-1640. . . . . DLB-126

Carey, Henry circa 1687-1689-1743. . . . . . DLB-84

Carey, Mathew 1760-1839. . . . . DLB-37, 73

M. Carey and Company DLB-49

Carey and Hart DLB-49

Carell, Lodowick 1602-1675. . . . . DLB-58

Carleton, William 1794-1869. . . . . DLB-159

G. W. Carleton [publishing house] DLB-49

Carlile, Richard 1790-1843 . . . . DLB-110, 158

Carlson, Ron 1947- DLB-244

Carlyle, Jane Welsh 1801-1866 . . . . DLB-55

Carlyle, Thomas
1795-1881 . . . . DLB-55, 144; CDBLB-3

"The Hero as Man of Letters:
Johnson, Rousseau, Burns"
(1841) [excerpt]. DLB-57

The Hero as Poet. Dante; Shakspeare
(1841). DLB-32

Carman, Bliss 1861-1929. . . . . DLB-92

Carmina Burana circa 1230 . . . . DLB-138

Carnap, Rudolf 1891-1970. . . . . DLB-270

Carnero, Guillermo 1947- DLB-108

Cărossa, Hans 1878-1956 . . . . DLB-66

Carpenter, Humphrey
1946- DLB-155; Y-84, 99

Carpenter, Stephen Cullen ?-1820? DLB-73

Carpentier, Alejo
1904-1980 . . . . DLB-113; CDWLB-3

Carr, Emily (1871-1945) DLB-68

Carr, Marina 1964- DLB-245

Carr, Virginia Spencer 1929- DLB-111; Y-00

Carrera Andrade, Jorge 1903-1978 . . . . . . DLB-283

Carrier, Roch 1937- DLB-53

Carrillo, Adolfo 1855-1926 . . . . DLB-122

Carroll, Gladys Hasty 1904- DLB-9

Carroll, John 1735-1815. . . . . DLB-37

Carroll, John 1809-1884 . . . . DLB-99

Carroll, Lewis
1832-1898 . . . . . . DLB-18, 163, 178; CDBLB-4

The Lewis Carroll Centenary. Y-98

The Lewis Carroll Society
of North America Y-00

Carroll, Paul 1927- DLB-16

Carroll, Paul Vincent 1900-1968. . . . . DLB-10

Carroll and Graf Publishers DLB-46

Carruth, Hayden 1921- DLB-5, 165

Tribute to James Dickey Y-97

Tribute to Raymond Carver. Y-88

Carryl, Charles E. 1841-1920 . . . . DLB-42

Carson, Anne 1950- DLB-193

Carson, Rachel 1907-1964 . . . . DLB-275

Carswell, Catherine 1879-1946 . . . . DLB-36

Cărtărescu, Mircea 1956- DLB-232

Carter, Angela 1940-1992 . . . . . . DLB-14, 207, 261

Carter, Elizabeth 1717-1806 . . . . DLB-109

Carter, Henry (see Leslie, Frank)

Carter, Hodding, Jr. 1907-1972 . . . . DLB-127

Carter, Jared 1939- DLB-282

Carter, John 1905-1975 . . . . DLB-201

Carter, Landon 1710-1778 . . . . DLB-31

Carter, Lin 1930-1988 . . . . Y-81

Carter, Martin 1927-1997. . . . DLB-117; CDWLB-3

Carter, Robert, and Brothers DLB-49

Carter and Hendee DLB-49

Cartwright, Jim 1958- DLB-245

Cartwright, John 1740-1824 . . . . DLB-158

Cartwright, William circa 1611-1643 . . . . DLB-126

Caruthers, William Alexander
    1802-1846 . . . . DLB-3, 248

Carver, Jonathan 1710-1780 . . . . DLB-31

Carver, Raymond 1938-1988 . . . DLB-130; Y-83,88

    First Strauss "Livings" Awarded to Cynthia
        Ozick and Raymond Carver
        An Interview with Raymond Carver. . Y-83

Carvic, Heron 1917?-1980 . . . . .DLB-276

Cary, Alice 1820-1871. . . . . DLB-202

Cary, Joyce 1888-1957 . . . DLB-15, 100; CDBLB-6

Cary, Patrick 1623?-1657 . . . . DLB-131

Casal, Julián del 1863-1893 . . . . DLB-283

Case, John 1540-1600. . . . . DLB-281

Casey, Gavin 1907-1964 . . . . DLB-260

Casey, Juanita 1925- DLB-14

Casey, Michael 1947- DLB-5

Cassady, Carolyn 1923- DLB-16

    "As I See It" DLB-16

Cassady, Neal 1926-1968 . . . . DLB-16, 237

Cassell and Company. DLB-106

Cassell Publishing Company DLB-49

Cassill, R. V. 1919- DLB-6, 218; Y-02

    Tribute to James Dickey Y-97

Cassity, Turner 1929- DLB-105; Y-02

Cassius Dio circa 155/164-post 229 . . . . . .DLB-176

Cassola, Carlo 1917-1987 . . . . .DLB-177

Castellano, Olivia 1944- DLB-122

Castellanos, Rosario
    1925-1974. . . . . DLB-113; CDWLB-3

Castillo, Ana 1953- DLB-122, 227

Castillo, Rafael C. 1950- DLB-209

The Castle of Perseverance circa 1400-1425 . DLB-146

Castlemon, Harry (see Fosdick, Charles Austin)

Čašule, Kole 1921- DLB-181

Caswall, Edward 1814-1878 . . . . DLB-32

Catacalos, Rosemary 1944- DLB-122

Cather, Willa 1873-1947
    . . . . DLB-9, 54, 78, 256; DS-1; CDALB-3

    The Willa Cather Pioneer Memorial
        and Education Foundation Y-00

Catherine II (Ekaterina Alekseevna), "The Great,"
    Empress of Russia 1729-1796 . . . . DLB-150

Catherwood, Mary Hartwell 1847-1902 . . . DLB-78

Catledge, Turner 1901-1983 . . . . DLB-127

Catlin, George 1796-1872 . . . . DLB-186, 189

Cato the Elder 234 B.C.-149 B.C. DLB-211

Cattafi, Bartolo 1922-1979 . . . . DLB-128

Catton, Bruce 1899-1978 . . . . DLB-17

Catullus circa 84 B.C.-54 B.C.
    . . . . DLB-211; CDWLB-1

Causley, Charles 1917- DLB-27

Caute, David 1936- DLB-14, 231

Cavendish, Duchess of Newcastle,
    Margaret Lucas
    1623?-1673. . . . . DLB-131, 252, 281

Cawein, Madison 1865-1914 . . . . DLB-54

William Caxton [publishing house] DLB-170

The Caxton Printers, Limited DLB-46

Caylor, O. P. 1849-1897. . . . . DLB-241

Cayrol, Jean 1911- DLB-83

Cecil, Lord David 1902-1986 . . . . DLB-155

Cela, Camilo José 1916-2002 . . . . Y-89

    Nobel Lecture 1989 . . . . Y-89

Celan, Paul 1920-1970 . . . . . . DLB-69; CDWLB-2

Celati, Gianni 1937- DLB-196

Celaya, Gabriel 1911-1991 . . . . DLB-108

Céline, Louis-Ferdinand 1894-1961 . . . . . . DLB-72

Celtis, Conrad 1459-1508. . . . . .DLB-179

Cendrars, Blaise 1887-1961. . . . . DLB-258

The Steinbeck Centennial. Y-02

Censorship
    The Island Trees Case: A Symposium on
        School Library Censorship Y-82

Center for Bibliographical Studies and
    Research at the University of
    California, Riverside Y-91

Center for Book Research Y-84

The Center for the Book in the Library
    of Congress Y-93

    A New Voice: The Center for the
        Book's First Five Years Y-83

Centlivre, Susanna 1669?-1723. . . . . DLB-84

The Centre for Writing, Publishing and
    Printing History at the University
    of Reading Y-00

The Century Company DLB-49

A Century of Poetry, a Lifetime of Collecting:
    J. M. Edelstein's Collection of
    Twentieth-Century American Poetry Y-02

Cernuda, Luis 1902-1963. . . . . DLB-134

Cerruto, Oscar 1912-1981 . . . . DLB-283

Cervantes, Lorna Dee 1954- DLB-82

de Céspedes, Alba 1911-1997 . . . . DLB-264

Ch., T. (see Marchenko, Anastasiia Iakovlevna)

Chaadaev, Petr Iakovlevich
    1794-1856. . . . . DLB-198

Chabon, Michael 1963- DLB-278

Chacel, Rosa 1898-1994. . . . . DLB-134

Chacón, Eusebio 1869-1948. . . . . DLB-82

Chacón, Felipe Maximiliano 1873-? DLB-82

Chadwick, Henry 1824-1908 . . . . DLB-241

Chadwyck-Healey's Full-Text Literary Databases:
    Editing Commercial Databases of
    Primary Literary Texts Y-95

Challans, Eileen Mary (see Renault, Mary)

Chalmers, George 1742-1825 . . . . DLB-30

Chaloner, Sir Thomas 1520-1565 . . . . . . DLB-167

Chamberlain, Samuel S. 1851-1916 . . . . . . DLB-25

Chamberland, Paul 1939- DLB-60

Chamberlin, William Henry 1897-1969 . . . DLB-29

Chambers, Charles Haddon 1860-1921 . . . DLB-10

Chambers, María Cristina (see Mena, María Cristina)

Chambers, Robert W. 1865-1933 . . . . . . DLB-202

W. and R. Chambers
    [publishing house] DLB-106

Chamisso, Adelbert von 1781-1838 . . . . . . DLB-90

Champfleury 1821-1889. . . . . DLB-119

Chandler, Harry 1864-1944. . . . . DLB-29

Chandler, Norman 1899-1973 . . . . .DLB-127

Chandler, Otis 1927- DLB-127

Chandler, Raymond
    1888-1959 . . . DLB-226, 253; DS-6; CDALB-5

    Raymond Chandler Centenary Y-88

Channing, Edward 1856-1931 . . . . .DLB-17

Channing, Edward Tyrrell
    1790-1856. . . . . DLB-1, 59, 235

Channing, William Ellery
    1780-1842. . . . . DLB-1, 59, 235

Channing, William Ellery, II
    1817-1901. . . . . DLB-1, 223

Channing, William Henry
    1810-1884 . . . . DLB-1, 59, 243

Chapelain, Jean 1595-1674. . . . . .DLB-268

Chaplin, Charlie 1889-1977 . . . . DLB-44

Chapman, George
    1559 or 1560-1634. . . . . DLB-62, 121

Chapman, Olive Murray 1892-1977. . . . . DLB-195

Chapman, R. W. 1881-1960 . . . . DLB-201

Chapman, William 1850-1917 . . . . DLB-99

John Chapman [publishing house] DLB-106

Chapman and Hall [publishing house] . . . DLB-106

Chappell, Fred 1936- DLB-6, 105

    "A Detail in a Poem" DLB-105

    Tribute to Peter Taylor Y-94

Chappell, William 1582-1649. . . . . DLB-236

Char, René 1907-1988 . . . . DLB-258

Charbonneau, Jean 1875-1960 . . . . DLB-92

Charbonneau, Robert 1911-1967 . . . . DLB-68

Charles, Gerda 1914- DLB-14

William Charles [publishing house] DLB-49

Charles d'Orléans 1394-1465. . . . . DLB-208

Charley (see Mann, Charles)

Charteris, Leslie 1907-1993. . . . . DLB-77

Chartier, Alain circa 1385-1430 . . . . DLB-208

Charyn, Jerome 1937- Y-83

Chase, Borden 1900-1971. . . . . DLB-26

Chase, Edna Woolman 1877-1957 . . . . DLB-91

Chase, James Hadley (René Raymond)
    1906-1985 .DLB-276

Chase, Mary Coyle 1907-1981 . . . . DLB-228

Chase-Riboud, Barbara 1936- DLB-33

Chateaubriand, François-René de
    1768-1848. . . . . DLB-119

Chatterton, Thomas 1752-1770. . . . . DLB-109

    Essay on Chatterton (1842), by
        Robert Browning. DLB-32

Chatto and Windus DLB-106

Chatwin, Bruce 1940-1989. . . . . . . DLB-194, 204

Chaucer, Geoffrey
1340?-1400 . . . . DLB-146; CDBLB-1

New Chaucer Society Y-00

Chaudhuri, Amit 1962- DLB-267

Chauncy, Charles 1705-1787 . . . . .DLB-24

Chauveau, Pierre-Joseph-Olivier
1820-1890 . . . . .DLB-99

Chávez, Denise 1948- DLB-122

Chávez, Fray Angélico 1910-1996 . . . . . . .DLB-82

Chayefsky, Paddy 1923-1981 . . . . DLB-7, 44; Y-81

Cheesman, Evelyn 1881-1969 . . . . .DLB-195

Cheever, Ezekiel 1615-1708 . . . . .DLB-24

Cheever, George Barrell 1807-1890 . . . . . .DLB-59

Cheever, John 1912-1982
. . . . DLB-2, 102, 227; Y-80, 82; CDALB-1

Cheever, Susan 1943- Y-82

Cheke, Sir John 1514-1557 . . . . .DLB-132

Chekhov, Anton Pavlovich 1860-1904 . . .DLB-277

Chelsea House DLB-46

Chênedollé, Charles de 1769-1833 . . . . . .DLB-217

Cheney, Brainard
Tribute to Caroline Gordon Y-81

Cheney, Ednah Dow 1824-1904 . . . . .DLB-1, 223

Cheney, Harriet Vaughan 1796-1889 . . . . .DLB-99

Chénier, Marie-Joseph 1764-1811 . . . . . . .DLB-192

Chernyshevsky, Nikolai Gavrilovich
1828-1889 . . . . .DLB-238

Cherry, Kelly 1940 . . . . Y-83

Cherryh, C. J. 1942- Y-80

Chesebro', Caroline 1825-1873 . . . . .DLB-202

Chesney, Sir George Tomkyns
1830-1895 . . . . .DLB-190

Chesnut, Mary Boykin 1823-1886 . . . . . . .DLB-239

Chesnutt, Charles Waddell
1858-1932 . . . . DLB-12, 50, 78

Chesson, Mrs. Nora (see Hopper, Nora)

Chester, Alfred 1928-1971 . . . . .DLB-130

Chester, George Randolph 1869-1924 . . . .DLB-78

The Chester Plays circa 1505-1532;
revisions until 1575 . . . . .DLB-146

Chesterfield, Philip Dormer Stanhope,
Fourth Earl of 1694-1773 . . . . .DLB-104

Chesterton, G. K. 1874-1936
. . DLB-10, 19, 34, 70, 98, 149, 178; CDBLB-6

"The Ethics of Elfland" (1908) DLB-178

Chettle, Henry circa 1560-circa 1607 . . . . .DLB-136

Cheuse, Alan 1940- DLB-244

Chew, Ada Nield 1870-1945 . . . . .DLB-135

Cheyney, Edward P. 1861-1947 . . . . .DLB-47

Chiara, Piero 1913-1986 . . . . .DLB-177

Chicanos
Chicano History DLB-82

Chicano Language DLB-82

Chincano Literature: A Bibliography .DLB-209

A Contemporary Flourescence of Chicano
Literature Y-84

Literatura Chicanesca: The View From
Without DLB-82

Child, Francis James 1825-1896. . . .DLB-1, 64, 235

Child, Lydia Maria 1802-1880 . . . .DLB-1, 74, 243

Child, Philip 1898-1978 . . . . .DLB-68

Childers, Erskine 1870-1922 . . . . .DLB-70

Children's Literature
Afterword: Propaganda, Namby-Pamby,
and Some Books of Distinction. . . .DLB-52

Children's Book Awards and Prizes . . .DLB-61

Children's Book Illustration in the
Twentieth Century DLB-61

Children's Illustrators, 1800-1880 . . . .DLB-163

The Harry Potter Phenomenon Y-99

Pony Stories, Omnibus
Essay on .DLB-160

The Reality of One Woman's Dream:
The de Grummond Children's
Literature Collection. Y-99

School Stories, 1914-1960 . . . . .DLB-160

The Year in Children's
Books Y-92–96, 98–01

The Year in Children's Literature. Y-97

Childress, Alice 1916-1994 . . . . DLB-7, 38, 249

Childs, George W. 1829-1894. . . . . .DLB-23

Chilton Book Company DLB-46

Chin, Frank 1940- DLB-206

Chinweizu 1943- DLB-157

Chitham, Edward 1932- DLB-155

Chittenden, Hiram Martin 1858-1917 . . . .DLB-47

Chivers, Thomas Holley 1809-1858 . . .DLB-3, 248

Chkhartishvili, Grigorii Shalvovich
(see Akunin, Boris)

Cholmondeley, Mary 1859-1925. . . . . . . .DLB-197

Chomsky, Noam 1928- DLB-246

Chopin, Kate 1850-1904 . . .DLB-12, 78; CDALB-3

Chopin, René 1885-1953. . . . . .DLB-92

Choquette, Adrienne 1915-1973 . . . . .DLB-68

Choquette, Robert 1905-1991 . . . . .DLB-68

Choyce, Lesley 1951- DLB-251

Chrétien de Troyes
circa 1140-circa 1190 . . . . .DLB-208

Christensen, Inger 1935- DLB-214

The Christian Examiner DLB-1

The Christian Publishing Company DLB-49

Christie, Agatha
1890-1976 . . . . DLB-13, 77, 245; CDBLB-6

Christine de Pizan circa 1365-circa 1431 . .DLB-208

Christopher, John (Sam Youd) 1922- . . .DLB-255

Christus und die Samariterin circa 950 . . . . .DLB-148

Christy, Howard Chandler 1873-1952 . . .DLB-188

Chulkov, Mikhail Dmitrievich
1743?-1792 . . . . .DLB-150

Church, Benjamin 1734-1778 . . . . .DLB-31

Church, Francis Pharcellus 1839-1906 . . . .DLB-79

Church, Peggy Pond 1903-1986 . . . . .DLB-212

Church, Richard 1893-1972. . . . . .DLB-191

Church, William Conant 1836-1917 . . . . . .DLB-79

Churchill, Caryl 1938- DLB-13

Churchill, Charles 1731-1764. . . . . .DLB-109

Churchill, Winston 1871-1947 . . . . .DLB-202

Churchill, Sir Winston
1874-1965 . . . . . . .DLB-100; DS-16; CDBLB-5

Churchyard, Thomas 1520?-1604. . . . . . .DLB-132

E. Churton and Company. DLB-106

Chute, Marchette 1909-1994 . . . . .DLB-103

Ciardi, John 1916-1986 . . . . .DLB-5; Y-86

Cibber, Colley 1671-1757. . . . . .DLB-84

Cicero 106 B.C.-43 B.C. DLB-211, CDWLB-1

Cima, Annalisa 1941- DLB-128

Čingo, Živko 1935-1987 . . . . .DLB-181

Cioran, E. M. 1911-1995. . . . . .DLB-220

Čipkus, Alfonsas (see Nyka-Niliūnas, Alfonsas)

Cirese, Eugenio 1884-1955 . . . . .DLB-114

Cīrulis, Jānis (see Bels, Alberts)

Cisneros, Sandra 1954- DLB-122, 152

City Lights Books DLB-46

Civil War (1861–1865)
Battles and Leaders of the Civil War . .DLB-47

Official Records of the Rebellion DLB-47

Recording the Civil War. DLB-47

Cixous, Hélène 1937- DLB-83, 242

Clampitt, Amy 1920-1994 . . . . .DLB-105

Tribute to Alfred A. Knopf. Y-84

Clancy, Tom 1947- DLB-227

Clapper, Raymond 1892-1944. . . . . .DLB-29

Clare, John 1793-1864 . . . . .DLB-55, 96

Clarendon, Edward Hyde, Earl of
1609-1674 . . . . .DLB-101

Clark, Alfred Alexander Gordon (see Hare, Cyril)

Clark, Ann Nolan 1896- DLB-52

Clark, C. E. Frazer, Jr. 1925-2001 . . DLB-187; Y-01

C. E. Frazer Clark Jr. and
Hawthorne Bibliography DLB-269

The Publications of C. E. Frazer
Clark Jr. .DLB-269

Clark, Catherine Anthony 1892-1977 . . . . .DLB-68

Clark, Charles Heber 1841-1915. . . . . .DLB-11

Clark, Davis Wasgatt 1812-1871 . . . . .DLB-79

Clark, Douglas 1919-1993 . . . . .DLB-276

Clark, Eleanor 1913- DLB-6

Clark, J. P. 1935- DLB-117; CDWLB-3

Clark, Lewis Gaylord
1808-1873 . . . . DLB-3, 64, 73, 250

Clark, Walter Van Tilburg
1909-1971 . . . . .DLB-9, 206

Clark, William 1770-1838 . . . . .DLB-183, 186

Clark, William Andrews, Jr. 1877-1934 . . .DLB-187

C. M. Clark Publishing Company. DLB-46

Clarke, Sir Arthur C. 1917- DLB-261

Tribute to Theodore Sturgeon Y-85

Clarke, Austin 1896-1974 . . . . .DLB-10, 20

Clarke, Austin C. 1934- DLB-53, 125

Clarke, Gillian 1937- DLB-40

Clarke, James Freeman
1810-1888 . . . . .DLB-1, 59, 235; DS-5

Clarke, John circa 1596-1658. . . . . .DLB-281

Clarke, Lindsay 1939- DLB-231

Clarke, Marcus 1846-1881 . . . . DLB-230

Clarke, Pauline 1921- DLB-161

Clarke, Rebecca Sophia 1833-1906 . . . . . . DLB-42

Clarke, Samuel 1675-1729 . . . . DLB-252

Robert Clarke and Company DLB-49

Clarkson, Thomas 1760-1846 . . . . DLB-158

Claudel, Paul 1868-1955 . . . . DLB-192, 258

Claudius, Matthias 1740-1815 . . . . DLB-97

Clausen, Andy 1943- DLB-16

Clawson, John L. 1865-1933 . . . . DLB-187

Claxton, Remsen and Haffelfinger DLB-49

Clay, Cassius Marcellus 1810-1903 . . . . . . DLB-43

Clayton, Richard (seed Haggard, William)

Cleage, Pearl 1948- DLB-228

Cleary, Beverly 1916- DLB-52

Cleary, Kate McPhelim 1863-1905 . . . . . . DLB-221

Cleaver, Bill 1920-1981 . . . . DLB-52

Cleaver, Vera 1919-1992 . . . . DLB-52

Cleeve, Brian 1921- DLB-276

Cleland, John 1710-1789 . . . . DLB-39

Clemens, Samuel Langhorne (Mark Twain)
1835-1910 . . . . DLB-11, 12, 23, 64, 74,
186, 189; CDALB-3

    Comments From Authors and Scholars on
    their First Reading of *Huck Finn* Y-85

    Huck at 100: How Old Is
    Huckleberry Finn? Y-85

    Mark Twain on Perpetual Copyright Y-92

    A New Edition of *Huck Finn* Y-85

Clement, Hal 1922- DLB-8

Clemo, Jack 1916- DLB-27

Clephane, Elizabeth Cecilia 1830-1869 . . . DLB-199

Cleveland, John 1613-1658 . . . . DLB-126

Cliff, Michelle 1946- DLB-157; CDWLB-3

Clifford, Lady Anne 1590-1676 . . . . DLB-151

Clifford, James L. 1901-1978 . . . . DLB-103

Clifford, Lucy 1853?-1929 . . . . . DLB-135, 141, 197

Clift, Charmian 1923-1969 . . . . DLB-260

Clifton, Lucille 1936- DLB-5, 41

Clines, Francis X. 1938- DLB-185

Clive, Caroline (V) 1801-1873 . . . . DLB-199

Edward J. Clode [publishing house] DLB-46

Clough, Arthur Hugh 1819-1861 . . . . DLB-32

Cloutier, Cécile 1930- DLB-60

Clouts, Sidney 1926-1982 . . . . DLB-225

Clutton-Brock, Arthur 1868-1924 . . . . DLB-98

Coates, Robert M.
1897-1973 . . . . DLB-4, 9, 102; DS-15

Coatsworth, Elizabeth 1893-1986 . . . . DLB-22

Cobb, Charles E., Jr. 1943- DLB-41

Cobb, Frank I. 1869-1923 . . . . DLB-25

Cobb, Irvin S. 1876-1944 . . . . DLB-11, 25, 86

Cobbe, Frances Power 1822-1904 . . . . . . DLB-190

Cobbett, William 1763-1835 . . . . DLB-43, 107, 158

Cobbledick, Gordon 1898-1969 . . . . DLB-171

Cochran, Thomas C. 1902- DLB-17

Cochrane, Elizabeth 1867-1922 . . . . DLB-25, 189

Cockerell, Sir Sydney 1867-1962 . . . . DLB-201

Cockerill, John A. 1845-1896 . . . . DLB-23

Cocteau, Jean 1889-1963 . . . . DLB-65, 258

Coderre, Emile (see Jean Narrache)

Cody, Liza 1944- DLB-276

Coe, Jonathan 1961- DLB-231

Coetzee, J. M. 1940- DLB-225

Coffee, Lenore J. 1900?-1984 . . . . DLB-44

Coffin, Robert P. Tristram 1892-1955 . . . . DLB-45

Coghill, Mrs. Harry (see Walker, Anna Louisa)

Cogswell, Fred 1917- DLB-60

Cogswell, Mason Fitch 1761-1830 . . . . DLB-37

Cohan, George M. 1878-1942 . . . . DLB-249

Cohen, Arthur A. 1928-1986 . . . . DLB-28

Cohen, Leonard 1934- DLB-53

Cohen, Matt 1942- DLB-53

Cohen, Morris Raphael 1880-1947 . . . . . . DLB-270

Colbeck, Norman 1903-1987 . . . . DLB-201

Colden, Cadwallader 1688-1776 . . . DLB-24, 30, 270

Colden, Jane 1724-1766 . . . . DLB-200

Cole, Barry 1936- DLB-14

Cole, George Watson 1850-1939 . . . . DLB-140

Colegate, Isabel 1931- DLB-14, 231

Coleman, Emily Holmes 1899-1974 . . . . . . DLB-4

Coleman, Wanda 1946- DLB-130

Coleridge, Hartley 1796-1849 . . . . DLB-96

Coleridge, Mary 1861-1907 . . . . DLB-19, 98

Coleridge, Samuel Taylor
1772-1834 . . . . DLB-93, 107; CDBLB-3

Coleridge, Sara 1802-1852 . . . . DLB-199

Colet, John 1467-1519 . . . . DLB-132

Colette 1873-1954 . . . . DLB-65

Colette, Sidonie Gabrielle (see Colette)

Colinas, Antonio 1946- DLB-134

Coll, Joseph Clement 1881-1921 . . . . DLB-188

A Century of Poetry, a Lifetime of Collecting:
    J. M. Edelstein's Collection of
    Twentieth-Century American Poetry Y-02

Collier, John 1901-1980 . . . . DLB-77, 255

Collier, John Payne 1789-1883 . . . . DLB-184

Collier, Mary 1690-1762 . . . . DLB-95

Collier, Robert J. 1876-1918 . . . . DLB-91

P. F. Collier [publishing house] DLB-49

Collin and Small DLB-49

Collingwood, R. G. 1889-1943 . . . . DLB-262

Collingwood, W. G. 1854-1932 . . . . DLB-149

Collins, An floruit circa 1653 . . . . DLB-131

Collins, Anthony 1676-1729 . . . . DLB-252

Collins, Merle 1950- DLB-157

Collins, Michael 1964- DLB-267

    Tribute to John D. MacDonald Y-86

    Tribute to Kenneth Millar Y-83

    Why I Write Mysteries: Night and Day . . Y-85

Collins, Mortimer 1827-1876 . . . . DLB-21, 35

Collins, Tom (see Furphy, Joseph)

Collins, Wilkie
1824-1889 . . . . . . DLB-18, 70, 159; CDBLB-4

    "The Unknown Public" (1858)
    [excerpt] DLB-57

    The Wilkie Collins Society Y-98

Collins, William 1721-1759 . . . . DLB-109

Isaac Collins [publishing house] DLB-49

William Collins, Sons and Company DLB-154

Collis, Maurice 1889-1973 . . . . DLB-195

Collyer, Mary 1716?-1763? DLB-39

Colman, Benjamin 1673-1747 . . . . DLB-24

Colman, George, the Elder 1732-1794 . . . . DLB-89

Colman, George, the Younger
1762-1836 . . . . DLB-89

S. Colman [publishing house] DLB-49

Colombo, John Robert 1936- DLB-53

Colquhoun, Patrick 1745-1820 . . . . DLB-158

Colter, Cyrus 1910-2002 . . . . DLB-33

Colum, Padraic 1881-1972 . . . . DLB-19

The Columbia History of the American Novel
    A Symposium on Y-92

Columella fl. first century A.D. DLB-211

Colvin, Sir Sidney 1845-1927 . . . . DLB-149

Colwin, Laurie 1944-1992 . . . . DLB-218; Y-80

Comden, Betty 1915- DLB-44, 265

Comi, Girolamo 1890-1968 . . . . DLB-114

Comisso, Giovanni 1895-1969 . . . . DLB-264

Commager, Henry Steele 1902-1998 . . . . . DLB-17

Commynes, Philippe de
circa 1447-1511 . . . . DLB-208

Compton, D. G. 1930- DLB-261

Compton-Burnett, Ivy 1884?-1969 . . . . . . DLB-36

Conan, Laure (Félicité Angers)
1845-1924 . . . . DLB-99

Concord, Massachusetts
    Concord History and Life DLB-223

    Concord: Literary History
    of a Town DLB-223

    The Old Manse, by Hawthorne DLB-223

    The Thoreauvian Pilgrimage: The
    Structure of an American Cult . . DLB-223

Conde, Carmen 1901-1996 . . . . DLB-108

Congreve, William
1670-1729 . . . . DLB-39, 84; CDBLB-2

    Preface to *Incognita* (1692) DLB-39

W. B. Conkey Company DLB-49

Conn, Stewart 1936- DLB-233

Connell, Evan S., Jr. 1924- DLB-2; Y-81

Connelly, Marc 1890-1980 . . . . DLB-7; Y-80

Connolly, Cyril 1903-1974 . . . . DLB-98

Connolly, James B. 1868-1957 . . . . DLB-78

Connor, Ralph (Charles William Gordon)
1860-1937 . . . . DLB-92

Connor, Tony 1930- DLB-40

Conquest, Robert 1917- DLB-27

Conrad, Joseph
1857-1924 . . . . DLB-10, 34, 98, 156; CDBLB-5

John Conrad and Company DLB-49

Conroy, Jack 1899-1990 . . . . Y-81

A Tribute [to Nelson Algren] Y-81

Conroy, Pat 1945- DLB-6

Considine, Bob 1906-1975 . . . . DLB-241

Consolo, Vincenzo 1933- DLB-196

Constable, Henry 1562-1613 . . . . DLB-136

Archibald Constable and Company DLB-154

Constable and Company Limited DLB-112

Constant, Benjamin 1767-1830 . . . . DLB-119

Constant de Rebecque, Henri-Benjamin de
(see Constant, Benjamin)

Constantine, David 1944- DLB-40

Constantine, Murray (see Burdekin, Katharine)

Constantin-Weyer, Maurice 1881-1964 . . . . DLB-92

Contempo (magazine)
Contempo Caravan:
Kites in a Windstorm Y-85

The Continental Publishing Company DLB-49

A Conversation between William Riggan
and Janette Turner Hospital Y-02

Conversations with Editors Y-95

Conway, Anne 1631-1679 . . . . DLB-252

Conway, Moncure Daniel
1832-1907 . . . . DLB-1, 223

Cook, Ebenezer circa 1667-circa 1732 . . . . . DLB-24

Cook, Edward Tyas 1857-1919 . . . . DLB-149

Cook, Eliza 1818-1889 . . . . DLB-199

Cook, George Cram 1873-1924 . . . . DLB-266

Cook, Michael 1933-1994 . . . . DLB-53

David C. Cook Publishing Company DLB-49

Cooke, George Willis 1848-1923 . . . . DLB-71

Cooke, John Esten 1830-1886 . . . . DLB-3, 248

Cooke, Philip Pendleton
1816-1850 . . . . DLB-3, 59, 248

Cooke, Rose Terry 1827-1892 . . . . DLB-12, 74

Increase Cooke and Company DLB-49

Cook-Lynn, Elizabeth 1930- DLB-175

Coolbrith, Ina 1841-1928 . . . . DLB-54, 186

Cooley, Peter 1940- DLB-105

"Into the Mirror" DLB-105

Coolidge, Clark 1939- DLB-193

Coolidge, Susan (see Woolsey, Sarah Chauncy)

George Coolidge [publishing house] DLB-49

Cooper, Anna Julia 1858-1964 . . . . DLB-221

Cooper, Edith Emma 1862-1913 . . . . DLB-240

Cooper, Giles 1918-1966 . . . . DLB-13

Cooper, J. California 19??- DLB-212

Cooper, James Fenimore
1789-1851 . . . . DLB-3, 183, 250; CDALB-2

The Bicentennial of James Fenimore Cooper:
An International Celebration Y-89

The James Fenimore Cooper Society Y-01

Cooper, Kent 1880-1965 . . . . DLB-29

Cooper, Susan 1935- DLB-161, 261

Cooper, Susan Fenimore 1813-1894 . . . . . DLB-239

William Cooper [publishing house] DLB-170

J. Coote [publishing house] DLB-154

Coover, Robert 1932- DLB-2, 227; Y-81

Tribute to Donald Barthelme Y-89

Tribute to Theodor Seuss Geisel Y-91

Copeland and Day DLB-49

Ćopić, Branko 1915-1984 . . . . DLB-181

Copland, Robert 1470?-1548 . . . . DLB-136

Coppard, A. E. 1878-1957 . . . . DLB-162

Coppée, François 1842-1908 . . . . DLB-217

Coppel, Alfred 1921- Y-83

Tribute to Jessamyn West Y-84

Coppola, Francis Ford 1939- DLB-44

Copway, George (Kah-ge-ga-gah-bowh)
1818-1869 . . . . DLB-175, 183

Copyright
The Development of the Author's
Copyright in Britain DLB-154

The Digital Millennium Copyright Act:
Expanding Copyright Protection in
Cyberspace and Beyond Y-98

Editorial: The Extension of Copyright . . . Y-02

Mark Twain on Perpetual Copyright Y-92

Public Domain and the Violation
of Texts Y-97

The Question of American Copyright
in the Nineteenth Century
Preface, by George Haven Putnam
The Evolution of Copyright, by
Brander Matthews
Summary of Copyright Legislation in
the United States, by R. R. Bowker
Analysis of the Provisions of the
Copyright Law of 1891, by
George Haven Putnam
The Contest for International Copyright,
by George Haven Putnam
Cheap Books and Good Books,
by Brander Matthews DLB-49

Writers and Their Copyright Holders:
the WATCH Project Y-94

Corazzini, Sergio 1886-1907 . . . . DLB-114

Corbett, Richard 1582-1635 . . . . DLB-121

Corbière, Tristan 1845-1875 . . . . DLB-217

Corcoran, Barbara 1911- DLB-52

Cordelli, Franco 1943- DLB-196

Corelli, Marie 1855-1924 . . . . DLB-34, 156

Corle, Edwin 1906-1956 . . . . Y-85

Corman, Cid 1924- DLB-5, 193

Cormier, Robert 1925-2000 . . . . DLB-52; CDALB-6

Tribute to Theodor Seuss Geisel Y-91

Corn, Alfred 1943- DLB-120, 282; Y-80

Corneille, Pierre 1606-1684 . . . . DLB-268

Cornford, Frances 1886-1960 . . . . DLB-240

Cornish, Sam 1935- DLB-41

Cornish, William circa 1465-circa 1524 . . . DLB-132

Cornwall, Barry (see Procter, Bryan Waller)

Cornwallis, Sir William, the Younger
circa 1579-1614 . . . . DLB-151

Cornwell, David John Moore (see le Carré, John)

Corpi, Lucha 1945- DLB-82

Corrington, John William 1932-1988 . . DLB-6, 244

Corriveau, Monique 1927-1976 . . . . DLB-251

Corrothers, James D. 1869-1917 . . . . DLB-50

Corso, Gregory 1930-2001 . . . . DLB-5, 16, 237

Cortázar, Julio 1914-1984 . . . DLB-113; CDWLB-3

Cortéz, Carlos 1923- DLB-209

Cortez, Jayne 1936- DLB-41

Corvinus, Gottlieb Siegmund
1677-1746 . . . . DLB-168

Corvo, Baron (see Rolfe, Frederick William)

Cory, Annie Sophie (see Cross, Victoria)

Cory, Desmond (Shaun Lloyd McCarthy)
1928- DLB-276

Cory, William Johnson 1823-1892 . . . . . . DLB-35

Coryate, Thomas 1577?-1617 . . . . . . DLB-151, 172

Ćosić, Dobrica 1921- DLB-181; CDWLB-4

Cosin, John 1595-1672 . . . . DLB-151, 213

Cosmopolitan Book Corporation DLB-46

Costain, Thomas B. 1885-1965 . . . . DLB-9

Coste, Donat (Daniel Boudreau)
1912-1957 . . . . DLB-88

Costello, Louisa Stuart 1799-1870 . . . . . . DLB-166

Cota-Cárdenas, Margarita 1941- DLB-122

Côté, Denis 1954- DLB-251

Cotten, Bruce 1873-1954 . . . . DLB-187

Cotter, Joseph Seamon, Jr. 1895-1919 . . . . DLB-50

Cotter, Joseph Seamon, Sr. 1861-1949 . . . . DLB-50

Joseph Cottle [publishing house] DLB-154

Cotton, Charles 1630-1687 . . . . DLB-131

Cotton, John 1584-1652 . . . . DLB-24

Cotton, Sir Robert Bruce 1571-1631 . . . . . DLB-213

Coulter, John 1888-1980 . . . . DLB-68

Cournos, John 1881-1966 . . . . DLB-54

Courteline, Georges 1858-1929 . . . . DLB-192

Cousins, Margaret 1905-1996 . . . . DLB-137

Cousins, Norman 1915-1990 . . . . DLB-137

Couvreur, Jessie (see Tasma)

Coventry, Francis 1725-1754 . . . . DLB-39

Dedication, The History of Pompey
the Little (1751) DLB-39

Coverdale, Miles 1487 or 1488-1569 . . . . . DLB-167

N. Coverly [publishing house] DLB-49

Covici-Friede DLB-46

Cowan, Peter 1914-2002 . . . . DLB-260

Coward, Noel
1899-1973 . . . . DLB-10, 245; CDBLB-6

Coward, McCann and Geoghegan DLB-46

Cowles, Gardner 1861-1946 . . . . DLB-29

Cowles, Gardner "Mike", Jr.
1903-1985 . . . . DLB-127, 137

Cowley, Abraham 1618-1667 . . . . . . DLB-131, 151

Cowley, Hannah 1743-1809 . . . . DLB-89

Cowley, Malcolm
1898-1989 . . . . DLB-4, 48; DS-15; Y-81, 89

Cowper, Richard (John Middleton Murry Jr.)
1926-2002 . . . . DLB-261

Cowper, William 1731-1800 . . . . DLB-104, 109

Cox, A. B. (see Berkeley, Anthony)

Cox, James McMahon 1903-1974 . . . . . . DLB-127

Cox, James Middleton 1870-1957 . . . . . . DLB-127

Cox, Leonard circa 1495-circa 1550 . . . . . DLB-281

Cox, Palmer 1840-1924 . . . . DLB-42

Coxe, Louis 1918-1993 . . . . DLB-5

Coxe, Tench 1755-1824 . . . . DLB-37

Cozzens, Frederick S. 1818-1869 . . . . DLB-202

Cozzens, James Gould
1903-1978 . . . . . DLB-9; Y-84; DS-2; CDALB-1

Cozzens's *Michael Scarlett* Y-97

Ernest Hemingway's Reaction to
James Gould Cozzens Y-98

James Gould Cozzens–A View
from Afar Y-97

James Gould Cozzens: How to
Read Him Y-97

James Gould Cozzens Symposium and
Exhibition at the University of
South Carolina, Columbia Y-00

Mens Rea (or Something) Y-97

Novels for Grown-Ups Y-97

Crabbe, George 1754-1832 . . . . DLB-93

Crace, Jim 1946- DLB-231

Crackanthorpe, Hubert 1870-1896 . . . . . . DLB-135

Craddock, Charles Egbert (see Murfree, Mary N.)

Cradock, Thomas 1718-1770 . . . . DLB-31

Craig, Daniel H. 1811-1895 . . . . DLB-43

Craik, Dinah Maria 1826-1887 . . . . . DLB-35, 163

Cramer, Richard Ben 1950- DLB-185

Cranch, Christopher Pearse
1813-1892 . . . . DLB-1, 42, 243; DS-5

Crane, Hart 1899-1932 . . . . . DLB-4, 48; CDALB-4

Nathan Asch Remembers Ford Madox
Ford, Sam Roth, and Hart Crane Y-02

Crane, R. S. 1886-1967 . . . . DLB-63

Crane, Stephen
1871-1900 . . . . DLB-12, 54, 78; CDALB-3

Stephen Crane: A Revaluation, Virginia
Tech Conference, 1989 . . . . Y-89

The Stephen Crane Society Y-98, 01

Crane, Walter 1845-1915 . . . . DLB-163

Cranmer, Thomas 1489-1556 . . . . . DLB-132, 213

Crapsey, Adelaide 1878-1914 . . . . DLB-54

Crashaw, Richard 1612/1613-1649 . . . . . DLB-126

Craven, Avery 1885-1980 . . . . DLB-17

Crawford, Charles 1752-circa 1815 . . . . . . DLB-31

Crawford, F. Marion 1854-1909 . . . . DLB-71

Crawford, Isabel Valancy 1850-1887 . . . . DLB-92

Crawley, Alan 1887-1975 . . . . DLB-68

Crayon, Geoffrey (see Irving, Washington)

Crayon, Porte (see Strother, David Hunter)

Creamer, Robert W. 1922- DLB-171

Creasey, John 1908-1973 . . . . DLB-77

Creative Age Press DLB-46

Creative Nonfiction Y-02

William Creech [publishing house] DLB-154

Thomas Creede [publishing house] DLB-170

Creel, George 1876-1953 . . . . DLB-25

Creeley, Robert 1926- DLB-5, 16, 169; DS-17

Creelman, James 1859-1915 . . . . DLB-23

Cregan, David 1931- DLB-13

Creighton, Donald 1902-1979 . . . . DLB-88

Crémazie, Octave 1827-1879 . . . . DLB-99

Crémer, Victoriano 1909?- DLB-108

Crescas, Hasdai circa 1340-1412? DLB-115

Crespo, Angel 1926-1995 . . . . DLB-134

Cresset Press DLB-112

Cresswell, Helen 1934- DLB-161

Crèvecoeur, Michel Guillaume Jean de
1735-1813 . . . . DLB-37

Crewe, Candida 1964- DLB-207

Crews, Harry 1935- DLB-6, 143, 185

Crichton, Michael 1942- Y-81

Crispin, Edmund (Robert Bruce Montgomery)
1921-1978 . . . . DLB-87

Cristofer, Michael 1946- DLB-7

Criticism

Afro-American Literary Critics:
An Introduction DLB-33

The Consolidation of Opinion: Critical
Responses to the Modernists DLB-36

"Criticism in Relation to Novels"
(1863), by G. H. Lewes DLB-21

The Limits of Pluralism DLB-67

Modern Critical Terms, Schools, and
Movements DLB-67

"Panic Among the Philistines":
A Postscript, An Interview
with Bryan Griffin Y-81

The Recovery of Literature: Criticism
in the 1990s: A Symposium Y-91

The Stealthy School of Criticism (1871),
by Dante Gabriel Rossetti DLB-35

Crnjanski, Miloš
1893-1977 . . . . .DLB-147; CDWLB-4

Crocker, Hannah Mather 1752-1829 . . . . DLB-200

Crockett, David (Davy)
1786-1836 . . . . .DLB-3, 11, 183, 248

Croft-Cooke, Rupert (see Bruce, Leo)

Crofts, Freeman Wills 1879-1957 . . . . DLB-77

Croker, John Wilson 1780-1857 . . . . DLB-110

Croly, George 1780-1860 . . . . DLB-159

Croly, Herbert 1869-1930 . . . . DLB-91

Croly, Jane Cunningham 1829-1901 . . . . . DLB-23

Crompton, Richmal 1890-1969 . . . . DLB-160

Cronin, A. J. 1896-1981 . . . . DLB-191

Cros, Charles 1842-1888 . . . . DLB-217

Crosby, Caresse
1892-1970 . . . . DLB-4, 15, 48; DS-15

Crosby, Harry 1898-1929 . . DLB-4, 15, 48; DS-15

Crosland, Camilla Toulmin (Mrs. Newton
Crosland) 1812-1895 . . . . DLB-240

Cross, Gillian 1945- DLB-161

Cross, Victoria 1868-1952 . . . . .DLB-135, 197

Crossley-Holland, Kevin 1941- DLB-40, 161

Crothers, Rachel 1870-1958 . . . . .DLB-7, 266

Thomas Y. Crowell Company DLB-49

Crowley, John 1942- Y-82

Crowley, Mart 1935- DLB-7, 266

Crown Publishers DLB-46

Crowne, John 1641-1712 . . . . DLB-80

Crowninshield, Edward Augustus
1817-1859 . . . . DLB-140

Crowninshield, Frank 1872-1947? DLB-91

Croy, Homer 1883-1965 . . . . DLB-4

Crumley, James 1939- DLB-226; Y-84

Cruse, Mary Anne 1825?-1910 . . . . DLB-239

Cruz, Migdalia 1958- DLB-249

Cruz, Victor Hernández 1949- DLB-41

Csokor, Franz Theodor 1885-1969 . . . . . . DLB-81

Csoóri, Sándor 1930- DLB-232; CDWLB-4

Cuala Press DLB-112

Cudworth, Ralph 1617-1688 . . . . DLB-252

Cugoano, Quobna Ottabah 1797?- Y-02

Cullen, Countee
1903-1946 . . . . DLB-4, 48, 51; CDALB-4

Culler, Jonathan D. 1944- DLB-67, 246

Cullinan, Elizabeth 1933- DLB-234

Culverwel, Nathaniel 1619?-1651?. DLB-252

Cumberland, Richard 1732-1811 . . . . DLB-89

Cummings, Constance Gordon
1837-1924 . . . . .DLB-174

Cummings, E. E.
1894-1962 . . . . DLB-4, 48; CDALB-5

The E. E. Cummings Society Y-01

Cummings, Ray 1887-1957 . . . . DLB-8

Cummings and Hilliard DLB-49

Cummins, Maria Susanna 1827-1866 . . . . . DLB-42

Cumpián, Carlos 1953- DLB-209

Cunard, Nancy 1896-1965 . . . . DLB-240

Joseph Cundall [publishing house] DLB-106

Cuney, Waring 1906-1976 . . . . DLB-51

Cuney-Hare, Maude 1874-1936 . . . . DLB-52

Cunningham, Allan 1784-1842 . . . . .DLB-116, 144

Cunningham, J. V. 1911-1985 . . . . DLB-5

Cunningham, Peter (Peter Lauder, Peter
Benjamin) 1947- DLB-267

Peter F. Cunningham
[publishing house] DLB-49

Cunquiero, Alvaro 1911-1981 . . . . DLB-134

Cuomo, George 1929- Y-80

Cupples, Upham and Company. DLB-49

Cupples and Leon DLB-46

Cuppy, Will 1884-1949 . . . . DLB-11

Curiel, Barbara Brinson 1956- DLB-209

Edmund Curll [publishing house] DLB-154

Currie, James 1756-1805 . . . . DLB-142

Currie, Mary Montgomerie Lamb Singleton,
Lady Currie (see Fane, Violet)

Cursor Mundi circa 1300 . . . . DLB-146

Curti, Merle E. 1897-1996 . . . . .DLB-17

Curtis, Anthony 1926- DLB-155

Curtis, Cyrus H. K. 1850-1933 . . . . .DLB-91

Curtis, George William
1824-1892 . . . . .DLB-1, 43, 223

Curzon, Robert 1810-1873 . . . . .DLB-166

Curzon, Sarah Anne 1833-1898 . . . . .DLB-99

Cusack, Dymphna 1902-1981 . . . . .DLB-260

Cushing, Eliza Lanesford 1794-1886 . . . . . .DLB-99

Cushing, Harvey 1869-1939 . . . . .DLB-187

Custance, Olive (Lady Alfred Douglas)
1874-1944 .DLB-240

Cynewulf circa 770-840 . . . . .DLB-146

Cyrano de Bergerac, Savinien de
1619-1655 .DLB-268

Czepko, Daniel 1605-1660 . . . . .DLB-164

Czerniawski, Adam 1934- DLB-232

D

Dabit, Eugène 1898-1936 . . . . .DLB-65

Daborne, Robert circa 1580-1628 . . . . . . .DLB-58

Dąbrowska, Maria
1889-1965 . . . . .DLB-215; CDWLB-4

Dacey, Philip 1939- DLB-105

"Eyes Across Centuries:
Contemporary Poetry and 'That
Vision Thing,'" DLB-105

Dach, Simon 1605-1659 . . . . .DLB-164

Dagerman, Stig 1923-1954 . . . . .DLB-259

Daggett, Rollin M. 1831-1901 . . . . .DLB-79

D'Aguiar, Fred 1960- DLB-157

Dahl, Roald 1916-1990 . . . . .DLB-139, 255

Tribute to Alfred A. Knopf Y-84

Dahlberg, Edward 1900-1977 . . . . .DLB-48

Dahn, Felix 1834-1912 . . . . .DLB-129

Dal', Vladimir Ivanovich (Kazak Vladimir
Lugansky) 1801-1872 . . . . .DLB-198

Dale, Peter 1938- DLB-40

Daley, Arthur 1904-1974 . . . . .DLB-171

Dall, Caroline Healey 1822-1912 . . . . .DLB-1, 235

Dallas, E. S. 1828-1879 . . . . .DLB-55

The Gay Science [excerpt](1866) DLB-21

The Dallas Theater Center DLB-7

D'Alton, Louis 1900-1951 . . . . .DLB-10

Dalton, Roque 1935-1975 . . . . .DLB-283

Daly, Carroll John 1889-1958 . . . . .DLB-226

Daly, T. A. 1871-1948 . . . . .DLB-11

Damon, S. Foster 1893-1971 . . . . .DLB-45

William S. Damrell [publishing house] DLB-49

Dana, Charles A. 1819-1897 . . . . . .DLB-3, 23, 250

Dana, Richard Henry, Jr.
1815-1882 . . . . .DLB-1, 183, 235

Dandridge, Ray Garfield DLB-51

Dane, Clemence 1887-1965 . . . . .DLB-10, 197

Danforth, John 1660-1730 . . . . .DLB-24

Danforth, Samuel, I 1626-1674 . . . . .DLB-24

Danforth, Samuel, II 1666-1727 . . . . .DLB-24

Daniel, John M. 1825-1865 . . . . .DLB-43

Daniel, Samuel 1562 or 1563-1619 . . . . . . .DLB-62

Daniel Press DLB-106

Daniells, Roy 1902-1979 . . . . .DLB-68

Daniels, Jim 1956- DLB-120

Daniels, Jonathan 1902-1981 . . . . .DLB-127

Daniels, Josephus 1862-1948 . . . . .DLB-29

Daniels, Sarah 1957- DLB-245

Danilevsky, Grigorii Petrovich
1829-1890 .DLB-238

Dannay, Frederic 1905-1982 . . . . .DLB-137

Danner, Margaret Esse 1915- DLB-41

John Danter [publishing house] DLB-170

Dantin, Louis (Eugene Seers) 1865-1945 . . .DLB-92

Danto, Arthur C. 1924- DLB-279

Danzig, Allison 1898-1987 . . . . .DLB-171

D'Arcy, Ella circa 1857-1937 . . . . .DLB-135

Dark, Eleanor 1901-1985 . . . . .DLB-260

Darke, Nick 1948- DLB-233

Darley, Felix Octavious Carr 1822-1888 . .DLB-188

Darley, George 1795-1846 . . . . .DLB-96

Darmesteter, Madame James
(see Robinson, A. Mary F.)

Darwin, Charles 1809-1882 . . . . .DLB-57, 166

Darwin, Erasmus 1731-1802 . . . . .DLB-93

Daryush, Elizabeth 1887-1977 . . . . .DLB-20

Dashkova, Ekaterina Romanovna
(née Vorontsova) 1743-1810 . . . . .DLB-150

Dashwood, Edmée Elizabeth Monica de la Pasture
(see Delafield, E. M.)

Daudet, Alphonse 1840-1897 . . . . .DLB-123

d'Aulaire, Edgar Parin 1898- DLB-22

d'Aulaire, Ingri 1904- DLB-22

Davenant, Sir William 1606-1668 . . . .DLB-58, 126

Davenport, Guy 1927- DLB-130

Tribute to John Gardner Y-82

Davenport, Marcia 1903-1996 . . . . .DS-17

Davenport, Robert ?-? DLB-58

Daves, Delmer 1904-1977 . . . . .DLB-26

Davey, Frank 1940- DLB-53

Davidson, Avram 1923-1993 . . . . .DLB-8

Davidson, Donald 1893-1968 . . . . .DLB-45

Davidson, Donald 1917- DLB-279

Davidson, John 1857-1909 . . . . .DLB-19

Davidson, Lionel 1922- DLB-14, 276

Davidson, Robyn 1950- DLB-204

Davidson, Sara 1943- DLB-185

Davie, Donald 1922- DLB-27

Davie, Elspeth 1919-1995 . . . . .DLB-139

Davies, Sir John 1569-1626 . . . . .DLB-172

Davies, John, of Hereford 1565?-1618 . . . .DLB-121

Davies, Rhys 1901-1978 . . . . .DLB-139, 191

Davies, Robertson 1913-1995 . . . . .DLB-68

Davies, Samuel 1723-1761 . . . . .DLB-31

Davies, Thomas 1712?-1785 . . . . . . .DLB-142, 154

Davies, W. H. 1871-1940 . . . . .DLB-19, 174

Peter Davies Limited DLB-112

Davin, Nicholas Flood 1840?-1901 . . . . . .DLB-99

Daviot, Gordon 1896?-1952 . . . . .DLB-10
(see also Tey, Josephine)

Davis, Arthur Hoey (see Rudd, Steele)

Davis, Charles A. (Major J. Downing)
1795-1867 .DLB-11

Davis, Clyde Brion 1894-1962 . . . . .DLB-9

Davis, Dick 1945- DLB-40, 282

Davis, Frank Marshall 1905-1987 . . . . .DLB-51

Davis, H. L. 1894-1960 . . . . .DLB-9, 206

Davis, John 1774-1854 . . . . .DLB-37

Davis, Lydia 1947- DLB-130

Davis, Margaret Thomson 1926- DLB-14

Davis, Ossie 1917- DLB-7, 38, 249

Davis, Owen 1874-1956 . . . . .DLB-249

Davis, Paxton 1925-1994 . . . . Y-89

Davis, Rebecca Harding 1831-1910 . . .DLB-74, 239

Davis, Richard Harding 1864-1916
. . . . .DLB-12, 23, 78, 79, 189; DS-13

Davis, Samuel Cole 1764-1809 . . . . .DLB-37

Davis, Samuel Post 1850-1918 . . . . .DLB-202

Davison, Frank Dalby 1893-1970 . . . . . . .DLB-260

Davison, Peter 1928- DLB-5

Davydov, Denis Vasil'evich 1784-1839 . . .DLB-205

Davys, Mary 1674-1732 . . . . .DLB-39

Preface to *The Works of Mrs. Davys*
(1725) DLB-39

DAW Books DLB-46

Dawson, Ernest 1882-1947 . . . . . . .DLB-140; Y-02

Dawson, Fielding 1930- DLB-130

Dawson, Sarah Morgan 1842-1909 . . . . . .DLB-239

Dawson, William 1704-1752 . . . . .DLB-31

Day, Angel flourished 1583-1599 . . .DLB-167, 236

Day, Benjamin Henry 1810-1889 . . . . . . .DLB-43

Day, Clarence 1874-1935 . . . . .DLB-11

Day, Dorothy 1897-1980 . . . . .DLB-29

Day, Frank Parker 1881-1950 . . . . .DLB-92

Day, John circa 1574-circa 1640 . . . . .DLB-62

Day, Thomas 1748-1789 . . . . .DLB-39

John Day [publishing house] DLB-170

The John Day Company DLB-46

Mahlon Day [publishing house] DLB-49

Day Lewis, C. (see Blake, Nicholas)

Dazai Osamu 1909-1948 . . . . .DLB-182

Deacon, William Arthur 1890-1977 . . . . . .DLB-68

Deal, Borden 1922-1985 . . . . .DLB-6

de Angeli, Marguerite 1889-1987 . . . . . . .DLB-22

De Angelis, Milo 1951- DLB-128

De Bow, J. D. B. 1820-1867 . . . . . . .DLB-3, 79, 248

de Bruyn, Günter 1926- DLB-75

de Camp, L. Sprague 1907-2000 . . . . .DLB-8

De Carlo, Andrea 1952- DLB-196

De Casas, Celso A. 1944- DLB-209

Dechert, Robert 1895-1975 . . . . DLB-187

Dedications, Inscriptions, and
Annotations Y-01–02

Dee, John 1527-1608 or 1609 . . . . . . DLB-136, 213

Deeping, George Warwick 1877-1950 . . . DLB-153

Defoe, Daniel
1660-1731 . . . . DLB-39, 95, 101; CDBLB-2

    Preface to *Colonel Jack* (1722) DLB-39

    Preface to *The Farther Adventures of
    Robinson Crusoe* (1719) DLB-39

    Preface to *Moll Flanders* (1722) DLB-39

    Preface to *Robinson Crusoe* (1719) DLB-39

    Preface to *Roxana* (1724) DLB-39

de Fontaine, Felix Gregory 1834-1896 . . . . DLB-43

De Forest, John William 1826-1906 . . DLB-12, 189

DeFrees, Madeline 1919- DLB-105

    "The Poet's Kaleidoscope: The
    Element of Surprise in the
    Making of the Poem" DLB-105

DeGolyer, Everette Lee 1886-1956 . . . . . . DLB-187

de Graff, Robert 1895-1981 . . . . Y-81

de Graft, Joe 1924-1978 . . . . DLB-117

De Heinrico circa 980? DLB-148

Deighton, Len 1929- DLB-87; CDBLB-8

DeJong, Meindert 1906-1991 . . . . DLB-52

Dekker, Thomas
circa 1572-1632 . . . . . DLB-62, 172; CDBLB-1

Delacorte, George T., Jr. 1894-1991 . . . . . DLB-91

Delafield, E. M. 1890-1943 . . . . DLB-34

Delahaye, Guy (Guillaume Lahaise)
1888-1969 . . . . DLB-92

de la Mare, Walter 1873-1956
. . . . DLB-19, 153, 162, 255; CDBLB-6

Deland, Margaret 1857-1945 . . . . DLB-78

Delaney, Shelagh 1939- DLB-13; CDBLB-8

Delano, Amasa 1763-1823 . . . . DLB-183

Delany, Martin Robinson 1812-1885 . . . . . DLB-50

Delany, Samuel R. 1942- DLB-8, 33

de la Roche, Mazo 1879-1961 . . . . DLB-68

Delavigne, Jean François Casimir
1793-1843 . . . . DLB-192

Delbanco, Nicholas 1942- DLB-6, 234

Delblanc, Sven 1931-1992 . . . . DLB-257

Del Castillo, Ramón 1949- DLB-209

Deledda, Grazia 1871-1936 . . . . DLB-264

De León, Nephtal 1945- DLB-82

Delfini, Antonio 1907-1963 . . . . DLB-264

Delgado, Abelardo Barrientos 1931- DLB-82

Del Giudice, Daniele 1949- DLB-196

De Libero, Libero 1906-1981 . . . . DLB-114

DeLillo, Don 1936- DLB-6, 173

de Lint, Charles 1951- DLB-251

de Lisser H. G. 1878-1944 . . . . DLB-117

Dell, Floyd 1887-1969 . . . . DLB-9

Dell Publishing Company DLB-46

delle Grazie, Marie Eugene 1864-1931 . . . . DLB-81

Deloney, Thomas died 1600 . . . . DLB-167

Deloria, Ella C. 1889-1971 . . . . DLB-175

Deloria, Vine, Jr. 1933- DLB-175

del Rey, Lester 1915-1993 . . . . DLB-8

Del Vecchio, John M. 1947- DS-9

Del'vig, Anton Antonovich 1798-1831 . . . DLB-205

de Man, Paul 1919-1983 . . . . DLB-67

DeMarinis, Rick 1934- DLB-218

Demby, William 1922- DLB-33

De Mille, James 1833-1880 . . . . DLB-99, 251

de Mille, William 1878-1955 . . . . DLB-266

Deming, Philander 1829-1915 . . . . DLB-74

Deml, Jakub 1878-1961 . . . . DLB-215

Demorest, William Jennings 1822-1895 . . . DLB-79

De Morgan, William 1839-1917 . . . . DLB-153

Demosthenes 384 B.C.-322 B.C. DLB-176

Henry Denham [publishing house] DLB-170

Denham, Sir John 1615-1669 . . . . . . DLB-58, 126

Denison, Merrill 1893-1975 . . . . DLB-92

T. S. Denison and Company DLB-49

Dennery, Adolphe Philippe 1811-1899 . . . DLB-192

Dennie, Joseph 1768-1812 . . . . . DLB-37, 43, 59, 73

Dennis, C. J. 1876-1938 . . . . DLB-260

Dennis, John 1658-1734 . . . . DLB-101

Dennis, Nigel 1912-1989 . . . . DLB-13, 15, 233

Denslow, W. W. 1856-1915 . . . . DLB-188

Dent, J. M., and Sons DLB-112

Dent, Tom 1932-1998 . . . . DLB-38

Denton, Daniel circa 1626-1703 . . . . DLB-24

DePaola, Tomie 1934- DLB-61

De Quille, Dan 1829-1898 . . . . DLB-186

De Quincey, Thomas
1785-1859 . . . . DLB-110, 144; CDBLB-3

    "Rhetoric" (1828; revised, 1859)
    [excerpt] DLB-57

    "Style" (1840; revised, 1859)
    [excerpt] DLB-57

Derby, George Horatio 1823-1861 . . . . . . DLB-11

J. C. Derby and Company DLB-49

Derby and Miller DLB-49

De Ricci, Seymour 1881-1942 . . . . DLB-201

Derleth, August 1909-1971 . . . . DLB-9; DS-17

Derrida, Jacques 1930- DLB-242

The Derrydale Press DLB-46

Derzhavin, Gavriil Romanovich
1743-1816 . . . . DLB-150

Desai, Anita 1937- DLB-271

Desaulniers, Gonzalve 1863-1934 . . . . . . DLB-92

Desbordes-Valmore, Marceline
1786-1859 . . . . DLB-217

Descartes, René 1596-1650 . . . . DLB-268

Deschamps, Emile 1791-1871 . . . . DLB-217

Deschamps, Eustache 1340?-1404 . . . . . . DLB-208

Desbiens, Jean-Paul 1927- DLB-53

des Forêts, Louis-Rene 1918-2001 . . . . . . DLB-83

Desiato, Luca 1941- DLB-196

Desjardins, Marie-Catherine
(see Villedieu, Madame de)

Desnica, Vladan 1905-1967 . . . . DLB-181

Desnos, Robert 1900-1945 . . . . DLB-258

DesRochers, Alfred 1901-1978 . . . . DLB-68

Desrosiers, Léo-Paul 1896-1967 . . . . DLB-68

Dessaulles, Louis-Antoine 1819-1895 . . . . DLB-99

Dessì, Giuseppe 1909-1977 . . . . DLB-177

Destouches, Louis-Ferdinand
(see Céline, Louis-Ferdinand)

DeSylva, Buddy 1895-1950 . . . . DLB-265

De Tabley, Lord 1835-1895 . . . . DLB-35

Deutsch, Babette 1895-1982 . . . . DLB-45

Deutsch, Niklaus Manuel (see Manuel, Niklaus)

André Deutsch Limited DLB-112

Devanny, Jean 1894-1962 . . . . DLB-260

Deveaux, Alexis 1948- DLB-38

De Vere, Aubrey 1814-1902 . . . . DLB-35

Devereux, second Earl of Essex, Robert
1565-1601 . . . . DLB-136

The Devin-Adair Company DLB-46

De Vinne, Theodore Low 1828-1914 . . . . DLB-187

Devlin, Anne 1951- DLB-245

DeVoto, Bernard 1897-1955 . . . . DLB-9, 256

De Vries, Peter 1910-1993 . . . . DLB-6; Y-82

    Tribute to Albert Erskine Y-93

Dewart, Edward Hartley 1828-1903 . . . . . DLB-99

Dewdney, Christopher 1951- DLB-60

Dewdney, Selwyn 1909-1979 . . . . DLB-68

Dewey, John 1859-1952 . . . . DLB-246, 270

Dewey, Orville 1794-1882 . . . . DLB-243

Dewey, Thomas B. 1915-1981 . . . . DLB-226

DeWitt, Robert M., Publisher DLB-49

DeWolfe, Fiske and Company DLB-49

Dexter, Colin 1930- DLB-87

de Young, M. H. 1849-1925 . . . . DLB-25

Dhlomo, H. I. E. 1903-1956 . . . . DLB-157, 225

Dhuoda circa 803-after 843 . . . . DLB-148

The Dial 1840-1844 . . . . DLB-223

The Dial Press DLB-46

Diamond, I. A. L. 1920-1988 . . . . DLB-26

Dibble, L. Grace 1902-1998 . . . . DLB-204

Dibdin, Thomas Frognall 1776-1847 . . . . DLB-184

Di Cicco, Pier Giorgio 1949- DLB-60

Dick, Philip K. 1928-1982 . . . . DLB-8

Dick and Fitzgerald DLB-49

Dickens, Charles 1812-1870 . . . DLB-21, 55, 70, 159,
166; DS-5; CDBLB-4

Dickey, James 1923-1997 . . . . DLB-5, 193;
Y-82, 93, 96, 97; DS-7, 19; CDALB-6

    James Dickey and Stanley Burnshaw
    Correspondence Y-02

    James Dickey at Seventy–A Tribute Y-93

    James Dickey, American Poet Y-96

    The James Dickey Society Y-99

The Life of James Dickey: A Lecture to
the Friends of the Emory Libraries,
by Henry Hart Y-98

Tribute to Archibald MacLeish. Y-82

Tribute to Malcolm Cowley Y-89

Tribute to Truman Capote. Y-84

Tributes [to Dickey] Y-97

Dickey, William 1928-1994 . . . . .DLB-5

Dickinson, Emily
1830-1886 . . . . .DLB-1, 243; CDALB-3

Dickinson, John 1732-1808 . . . . .DLB-31

Dickinson, Jonathan 1688-1747 . . . . .DLB-24

Dickinson, Patric 1914- DLB-27

Dickinson, Peter 1927- DLB-87, 161, 276

John Dicks [publishing house] DLB-106

Dickson, Gordon R. 1923-2001 . . . . .DLB-8

*Dictionary of Literary Biography
Annual Awards for Dictionary of
Literary Biography Editors and
Contributors*. Y-98–02

*Dictionary of Literary Biography
Yearbook* Awards Y-92–93, 97–02

The Dictionary of National Biography. DLB-144

Didion, Joan 1934-
  . . . . . . DLB-2, 173, 185; Y-81, 86; CDALB-6

Di Donato, Pietro 1911- DLB-9

Die Fürstliche Bibliothek Corvey. Y-96

Diego, Gerardo 1896-1987. . . . . .DLB-134

Dietz, Howard 1896-1983 . . . . .DLB-265

Digby, Everard 1550?-1605 . . . . .DLB-281

Digges, Thomas circa 1546-1595 . . . . . . .DLB-136

The Digital Millennium Copyright Act:
Expanding Copyright Protection in
Cyberspace and Beyond Y-98

Diktonius, Elmer 1896-1961 . . . . .DLB-259

Dillard, Annie 1945- DLB-275, 278; Y-80

Dillard, R. H. W. 1937- DLB-5, 244

Charles T. Dillingham Company DLB-49

G. W. Dillingham Company DLB-49

Edward and Charles Dilly
[publishing house] DLB-154

Dilthey, Wilhelm 1833-1911 . . . . .DLB-129

Dimitrova, Blaga 1922-   . . .DLB-181; CDWLB-4

Dimov, Dimitr 1909-1966 . . . . .DLB-181

Dimsdale, Thomas J. 1831?-1866 . . . . .DLB-186

Dinescu, Mircea 1950- DLB-232

Dinesen, Isak (see Blixen, Karen)

Dingelstedt, Franz von 1814-1881 . . . . . . .DLB-133

Dintenfass, Mark 1941- Y-84

Diogenes, Jr. (see Brougham, John)

Diogenes Laertius circa 200 . . . . .DLB-176

DiPrima, Diane 1934- DLB-5, 16

Disch, Thomas M. 1940- DLB-8, 282

Diski, Jenny 1947- DLB-271

Disney, Walt 1901-1966 . . . . .DLB-22

Disraeli, Benjamin 1804-1881 . . . . . . .DLB-21, 55

D'Israeli, Isaac 1766-1848 . . . . .DLB-107

DLB Award for Distinguished
Literary Criticism Y-02

Ditlevsen, Tove 1917-1976 . . . . .DLB-214

Ditzen, Rudolf (see Fallada, Hans)

Dix, Dorothea Lynde 1802-1887 . . . . . .DLB-1, 235

Dix, Dorothy (see Gilmer, Elizabeth Meriwether)

Dix, Edwards and Company DLB-49

Dix, Gertrude circa 1874-? DLB-197

Dixie, Florence Douglas 1857-1905 . . . . . .DLB-174

Dixon, Ella Hepworth
1855 or 1857-1932 . . . . .DLB-197

Dixon, Paige (see Corcoran, Barbara)

Dixon, Richard Watson 1833-1900 . . . . . .DLB-19

Dixon, Stephen 1936- DLB-130

DLB Award for Distinguished
Literary Criticism Y-02

Dmitriev, Andrei Viktorovich 1956-   . . .DLB-285

Dmitriev, Ivan Ivanovich 1760-1837 . . . . .DLB-150

Dobell, Bertram 1842-1914 . . . . .DLB-184

Dobell, Sydney 1824-1874 . . . . .DLB-32

Dobie, J. Frank 1888-1964 . . . . .DLB-212

Dobles Yzaguirre, Julieta 1943- DLB-283

Döblin, Alfred 1878-1957 . . . . . .DLB-66; CDWLB-2

Dobroliubov, Nikolai Aleksandrovich
1836-1861 . . . . .DLB-277

Dobson, Austin 1840-1921 . . . . .DLB-35, 144

Dobson, Rosemary 1920- DLB-260

Doctorow, E. L.
1931- DLB-2, 28, 173; Y-80; CDALB-6

Dodd, Susan M. 1946- DLB-244

Dodd, William E. 1869-1940 . . . . .DLB-17

Anne Dodd [publishing house] DLB-154

Dodd, Mead and Company. DLB-49

Doderer, Heimito von 1896-1966 . . . . .DLB-85

B. W. Dodge and Company DLB-46

Dodge, Mary Abigail 1833-1896 . . . . .DLB-221

Dodge, Mary Mapes
1831?-1905 . . . . DLB-42, 79; DS-13

Dodge Publishing Company DLB-49

Dodgson, Charles Lutwidge (see Carroll, Lewis)

Dodsley, Robert 1703-1764 . . . . .DLB-95

R. Dodsley [publishing house] DLB-154

Dodson, Owen 1914-1983 . . . . .DLB-76

Dodwell, Christina 1951- DLB-204

Doesticks, Q. K. Philander, P. B.
(see Thomson, Mortimer)

Doheny, Carrie Estelle 1875-1958 . . . . . . .DLB-140

Doherty, John 1798?-1854 . . . . .DLB-190

Doig, Ivan 1939- DLB-206

Doinaş, Ştefan Augustin 1922- DLB-232

Domínguez, Sylvia Maida 1935- DLB-122

Donaghy, Michael 1954- DLB-282

Patrick Donahoe [publishing house] DLB-49

Donald, David H. 1920- DLB-17; Y-87

Donaldson, Scott 1928- DLB-111

Doni, Rodolfo 1919- DLB-177

Donleavy, J. P. 1926- DLB-6, 173

Donnadieu, Marguerite (see Duras, Marguerite)

Donne, John
1572-1631 . . . . .DLB-121, 151; CDBLB-1

Donnelly, Ignatius 1831-1901 . . . . .DLB-12

R. R. Donnelley and Sons Company. DLB-49

Donoghue, Emma 1969- DLB-267

Donohue and Henneberry. DLB-49

Donoso, José 1924-1996 . . . . DLB-113; CDWLB-3

M. Doolady [publishing house] DLB-49

Dooley, Ebon (see Ebon)

Doolittle, Hilda 1886-1961 . . . . .DLB-4, 45; DS-15

Doplicher, Fabio 1938- DLB-128

Dor, Milo 1923- DLB-85

George H. Doran Company DLB-46

Dorgelès, Roland 1886-1973 . . . . .DLB-65

Dorn, Edward 1929-1999 . . . . .DLB-5

Dorr, Rheta Childe 1866-1948 . . . . .DLB-25

Dorris, Michael 1945-1997 . . . . .DLB-175

Dorset and Middlesex, Charles Sackville,
Lord Buckhurst, Earl of 1643-1706 . . . .DLB-131

Dorsey, Candas Jane 1952- DLB-251

Dorst, Tankred 1925- DLB-75, 124

Dos Passos, John 1896-1970
. . . . .DLB-4, 9; DS-1, 15; CDALB-5

John Dos Passos: A Centennial
Commemoration Y-96

John Dos Passos: Artist. Y-99

John Dos Passos Newsletter Y-00

U.S.A. (Documentary). DLB-274

Dostoevsky, Fyodor 1821-1881 . . . . .DLB-238

Doubleday and Company DLB-49

Dougall, Lily 1858-1923 . . . . .DLB-92

Doughty, Charles M.
1843-1926 . . . . .DLB-19, 57, 174

Douglas, Lady Alfred (see Custance, Olive)

Douglas, Gavin 1476-1522 . . . . .DLB-132

Douglas, Keith 1920-1944 . . . . .DLB-27

Douglas, Norman 1868-1952. . . . . . .DLB-34, 195

Douglass, Frederick 1817-1895
. . . . DLB-1, 43, 50, 79, 243; CDALB-2

Frederick Douglass Creative Arts Center   Y-01

Douglass, William circa 1691-1752 . . . . . . .DLB-24

Dourado, Autran 1926- DLB-145

Dove, Arthur G. 1880-1946. . . . . .DLB-188

Dove, Rita 1952- DLB-120; CDALB-7

Dover Publications DLB-46

Doves Press DLB-112

Dovlatov, Sergei Donatovich 1941-1990 . .DLB-285

Dowden, Edward 1843-1913 . . . . .DLB-35, 149

Dowell, Coleman 1925-1985 . . . . .DLB-130

Dowland, John 1563-1626 . . . . .DLB-172

Downes, Gwladys 1915- DLB-88

Downing, J., Major (see Davis, Charles A.)

Downing, Major Jack (see Smith, Seba)

Dowriche, Anne before 1560-after 1613 . .DLB-172

Dowson, Ernest 1867-1900 . . . . DLB-19, 135

William Doxey [publishing house] DLB-49

Doyle, Sir Arthur Conan
  1859-1930 . . . DLB-18, 70, 156, 178; CDBLB-5

  The Priory Scholars of New York Y-99

Doyle, Kirby 1932- DLB-16

Doyle, Roddy 1958- DLB-194

Drabble, Margaret
  1939- DLB-14, 155, 231; CDBLB-8

  Tribute to Graham Greene Y-91

Drach, Albert 1902-1995 . . . . DLB-85

Dragojević, Danijel 1934- DLB-181

Drake, Samuel Gardner 1798-1875 . . . . . . DLB-187

Drama (See Theater)

The Dramatic Publishing Company DLB-49

Dramatists Play Service DLB-46

Drant, Thomas early 1540s?-1578 . . . . . . DLB-167

Draper, John W. 1811-1882 . . . . DLB-30

Draper, Lyman C. 1815-1891 . . . . DLB-30

Drayton, Michael 1563-1631 . . . . DLB-121

Dreiser, Theodore 1871-1945
  . . . . DLB-9, 12, 102, 137; DS-1; CDALB-3

  The International Theodore Dreiser
    Society Y-01

  Notes from the Underground
    of *Sister Carrie* Y-01

Dresser, Davis 1904-1977 . . . . DLB-226

Drew, Elizabeth A.
  "A Note on Technique" [excerpt]
    (1926) DLB-36

Drewitz, Ingeborg 1923-1986 . . . . DLB-75

Drieu La Rochelle, Pierre 1893-1945 . . . . . DLB-72

Drinker, Elizabeth 1735-1807 . . . . DLB-200

Drinkwater, John 1882-1937 . . . . . DLB-10, 19, 149

  The Friends of the Dymock Poets Y-00

Droste-Hülshoff, Annette von
  1797-1848 . . . . DLB-133; CDWLB-2

The Drue Heinz Literature Prize
  Excerpt from "Excerpts from a Report
  of the Commission," in David
  Bosworth's *The Death of Descartes*
  An Interview with David Bosworth Y-82

Drummond, William, of Hawthornden
  1585-1649 . . . . DLB-121, 213

Drummond, William Henry 1854-1907 . . . DLB-92

Druzhinin, Aleksandr Vasil'evich
  1824-1864 . . . . DLB-238

Dryden, Charles 1860?-1931 . . . . DLB-171

Dryden, John
  1631-1700 . . . . . . DLB-80, 101, 131; CDBLB-2

Držić, Marin
  circa 1508-1567 . . . . DLB-147; CDWLB-4

Duane, William 1760-1835 . . . . DLB-43

Dubé, Marcel 1930- DLB-53

Dubé, Rodolphe (see Hertel, François)

Dubie, Norman 1945- DLB-120

Dubin, Al 1891-1945 . . . . DLB-265

Dubois, Silvia 1788 or 1789?-1889 . . . . . . DLB-239

Du Bois, W. E. B.
  1868-1963 . . . . DLB-47, 50, 91, 246; CDALB-3

Du Bois, William Pène 1916-1993 . . . . . . DLB-61

Dubrovina, Ekaterina Oskarovna
  1846-1913 . . . . DLB-238

Dubus, Andre 1936-1999 . . . . DLB-130

  Tribute to Michael M. Rea Y-97

Ducange, Victor 1783-1833 . . . . DLB-192

Du Chaillu, Paul Belloni 1831?-1903 . . . . DLB-189

Ducharme, Réjean 1941- DLB-60

Dučić, Jovan 1871-1943 . . . . . DLB-147; CDWLB-4

Duck, Stephen 1705?-1756 . . . . DLB-95

Gerald Duckworth and Company
  Limited DLB-112

Duclaux, Madame Mary (see Robinson, A. Mary F.)

Dudek, Louis 1918-2001 . . . . DLB-88

Dudley-Smith, Trevor (see Hall, Adam)

Duell, Sloan and Pearce DLB-46

Duerer, Albrecht 1471-1528 . . . . DLB-179

Duff Gordon, Lucie 1821-1869 . . . . DLB-166

Dufferin, Helen Lady, Countess of Gifford
  1807-1867 . . . . DLB-199

Duffield and Green DLB-46

Duffy, Maureen 1933- DLB-14

Dufief, Nicholas Gouin 1776-1834 . . . . . . DLB-187

Dugan, Alan 1923- DLB-5

Dugard, William 1606-1662 . . . . DLB-170, 281

William Dugard [publishing house] DLB-170

Dugas, Marcel 1883-1947 . . . . DLB-92

William Dugdale [publishing house] DLB-106

Duhamel, Georges 1884-1966 . . . . DLB-65

Dujardin, Edouard 1861-1949 . . . . DLB-123

Dukes, Ashley 1885-1959 . . . . DLB-10

Dumas, Alexandre *fils* 1824-1895 . . . . . . DLB-192

Dumas, Alexandre *père* 1802-1870 . . . . . DLB-119, 192

Dumas, Henry 1934-1968 . . . . DLB-41

du Maurier, Daphne 1907-1989 . . . . DLB-191

Du Maurier, George 1834-1896 . . . . . DLB-153, 178

Dummett, Michael 1925- DLB-262

Dunbar, Paul Laurence
  1872-1906 . . . . DLB-50, 54, 78; CDALB-3

  Introduction to *Lyrics of Lowly Life* (1896),
    by William Dean Howells DLB-50

Dunbar, William
  circa 1460-circa 1522 . . . . DLB-132, 146

Duncan, Dave 1933- DLB-251

Duncan, David James 1952- DLB-256

Duncan, Norman 1871-1916 . . . . DLB-92

Duncan, Quince 1940- DLB-145

Duncan, Robert 1919-1988 . . . . . . DLB-5, 16, 193

Duncan, Ronald 1914-1982 . . . . DLB-13

Duncan, Sara Jeannette 1861-1922 . . . . . . DLB-92

Dunigan, Edward, and Brother DLB-49

Dunlap, John 1747-1812 . . . . DLB-43

Dunlap, William 1766-1839 . . . . DLB-30, 37, 59

Dunlop, William "Tiger" 1792-1848 . . . . . DLB-99

Dunmore, Helen 1952- DLB-267

Dunn, Douglas 1942- DLB-40

Dunn, Harvey Thomas 1884-1952 . . . . . DLB-188

Dunn, Stephen 1939- DLB-105

  "The Good, The Not So Good" DLB-105

Dunne, Finley Peter 1867-1936 . . . . . . DLB-11, 23

Dunne, John Gregory 1932- Y-80

Dunne, Philip 1908-1992 . . . . DLB-26

Dunning, Ralph Cheever 1878-1930 . . . . . . DLB-4

Dunning, William A. 1857-1922 . . . . DLB-17

Duns Scotus, John circa 1266-1308 . . . . . DLB-115

Dunsany, Lord (Edward John Moreton
  Drax Plunkett, Baron Dunsany)
  1878-1957 . . . . DLB-10, 77, 153, 156, 255

Dunton, W. Herbert 1878-1936 . . . . DLB-188

John Dunton [publishing house] DLB-170

Dupin, Amantine-Aurore-Lucile (see Sand, George)

Dupuy, Eliza Ann 1814-1880 . . . . DLB-248

Durack, Mary 1913-1994 . . . . DLB-260

Durand, Lucile (see Bersianik, Louky)

Duranti, Francesca 1935- DLB-196

Duranty, Walter 1884-1957 . . . . DLB-29

Duras, Marguerite (Marguerite Donnadieu)
  1914-1996 . . . . DLB-83

Durfey, Thomas 1653-1723 . . . . DLB-80

Durova, Nadezhda Andreevna
  (Aleksandr Andreevich Aleksandrov)
  1783-1866 . . . . DLB-198

Durrell, Lawrence 1912-1990
  . . . . DLB-15, 27, 204; Y-90; CDBLB-7

William Durrell [publishing house] DLB-49

Dürrenmatt, Friedrich
  1921-1990 . . . . DLB-69, 124; CDWLB-2

Duston, Hannah 1657-1737 . . . . DLB-200

Dutt, Toru 1856-1877 . . . . DLB-240

E. P. Dutton and Company DLB-49

Duvoisin, Roger 1904-1980 . . . . DLB-61

Duyckinck, Evert Augustus
  1816-1878 . . . . DLB-3, 64, 250

Duyckinck, George L.
  1823-1863 . . . . DLB-3, 250

Duyckinck and Company DLB-49

Dwight, John Sullivan 1813-1893 . . . . . DLB-1, 235

Dwight, Timothy 1752-1817 . . . . DLB-37

  America: or, A Poem on the Settlement
    of the British Colonies, by
    Timothy Dwight DLB-37

Dybek, Stuart 1942- DLB-130

  Tribute to Michael M. Rea Y-97

Dyer, Charles 1928- DLB-13

Dyer, Sir Edward 1543-1607 . . . . DLB-136

Dyer, George 1755-1841 . . . . DLB-93

Dyer, John 1699-1757 . . . . DLB-95

Dyk, Viktor 1877-1931 . . . . DLB-215

Dylan, Bob 1941- DLB-16

E

Eager, Edward 1911-1964 . . . . DLB-22

Eagleton, Terry 1943- DLB-242

Eames, Wilberforce 1855-1937 . . . . DLB-140

Earle, Alice Morse 1853-1911 . . . . DLB-221

Earle, John 1600 or 1601-1665 . . . . DLB-151

James H. Earle and Company DLB-49

East Europe
Independence and Destruction,
1918-1941 . . . . DLB-220

Social Theory and Ethnography:
Languageand Ethnicity in
Western versus Eastern Man DLB-220

Eastlake, William 1917-1997 . . . . DLB-6, 206

Eastman, Carol ?- DLB-44

Eastman, Charles A. (Ohiyesa)
1858-1939 . . . . DLB-175

Eastman, Max 1883-1969 . . . . DLB-91

Eaton, Daniel Isaac 1753-1814 . . . . DLB-158

Eaton, Edith Maude 1865-1914 . . . . DLB-221

Eaton, Winnifred 1875-1954 . . . . DLB-221

Eberhart, Richard 1904- DLB-48; CDALB-1

Tribute to Robert Penn Warren Y-89

Ebner, Jeannie 1918- DLB-85

Ebner-Eschenbach, Marie von
1830-1916 . . . . DLB-81

Ebon 1942- DLB-41

E-Books' Second Act in Libraries. Y-02

Ecbasis Captivi circa 1045 . . . . DLB-148

Ecco Press DLB-46

Eckhart, Meister circa 1260-circa 1328 . . . DLB-115

The Eclectic Review 1805-1868 . . . . DLB-110

Eco, Umberto 1932- DLB-196, 242

Eddison, E. R. 1882-1945 . . . . DLB-255

Edel, Leon 1907-1997 . . . . DLB-103

Edelfeldt, Inger 1956- DLB-257

A Century of Poetry, a Lifetime of Collecting:
J. M. Edelstein's Collection of Twentieth-
Century American Poetry Y-02

Edes, Benjamin 1732-1803 . . . . DLB-43

Edgar, David 1948- DLB-13, 233

Viewpoint: Politics and
Performance DLB-13

Edgerton, Clyde 1944- DLB-278

Edgeworth, Maria
1768-1849 . . . . DLB-116, 159, 163

The Edinburgh Review 1802-1929 . . . . DLB-110

Edinburgh University Press DLB-112

Editing
Conversations with Editors Y-95

Editorial Statements DLB-137

The Editorial Style of Fredson Bowers . . . Y-91

Editorial: The Extension of Copyright . . . Y-02

We See the Editor at Work Y-97

Whose *Ulysses?* The Function of Editing . . Y-97

The Editor Publishing Company DLB-49

Editorial Institute at Boston University Y-00

Edmonds, Helen Woods Ferguson
(see Kavan, Anna)

Edmonds, Randolph 1900-1983 . . . . DLB-51

Edmonds, Walter D. 1903-1998 . . . . DLB-9

Edric, Robert (see Armitage, G. E.)

Edschmid, Kasimir 1890-1966 . . . . DLB-56

Edson, Margaret 1961- DLB-266

Edson, Russell 1935- DLB-244

Edwards, Amelia Anne Blandford
1831-1892 . . . . DLB-174

Edwards, Dic 1953- DLB-245

Edwards, Edward 1812-1886 . . . . DLB-184

Edwards, Jonathan 1703-1758 . . . . . . DLB-24, 270

Edwards, Jonathan, Jr. 1745-1801 . . . . DLB-37

Edwards, Junius 1929- DLB-33

Edwards, Matilda Barbara Betham
1836-1919 . . . . DLB-174

Edwards, Richard 1524-1566 . . . . DLB-62

Edwards, Sarah Pierpont 1710-1758 . . . . . . DLB-200

James Edwards [publishing house] DLB-154

Effinger, George Alec 1947- DLB-8

Egerton, George 1859-1945 . . . . DLB-135

Eggleston, Edward 1837-1902 . . . . DLB-12

Eggleston, Wilfred 1901-1986 . . . . DLB-92

Eglītis, Anšlavs 1906-1993 . . . . DLB-220

Ehrenreich, Barbara 1941- DLB-246

Ehrenstein, Albert 1886-1950 . . . . DLB-81

Ehrhart, W. D. 1948- DS-9

Ehrlich, Gretel 1946- DLB-212, 275

Eich, Günter 1907-1972 . . . . DLB-69, 124

Eichendorff, Joseph Freiherr von
1788-1857 . . . . DLB-90

Eifukumon'in 1271-1342 . . . . DLB-203

Eigner, Larry 1926-1996 . . . . DLB-5, 193

Eikon Basilike 1649 . . . . DLB-151

Eilhart von Oberge
circa 1140-circa 1195 . . . . DLB-148

Einhard circa 770-840 . . . . DLB-148

Eiseley, Loren 1907-1977 . . . . DLB-275, DS-17

Eisenberg, Deborah 1945- DLB-244

Eisenreich, Herbert 1925-1986 . . . . DLB-85

Eisner, Kurt 1867-1919 . . . . DLB-66

Ekelöf, Gunnar 1907-1968 . . . . DLB-259

Eklund, Gordon 1945- Y-83

Ekman, Kerstin 1933- DLB-257

Ekwensi, Cyprian 1921- . . . DLB-117; CDWLB-3

Elaw, Zilpha circa 1790-? DLB-239

George Eld [publishing house] DLB-170

Elder, Lonne, III 1931- DLB-7, 38, 44

Paul Elder and Company DLB-49

Eldershaw, Flora (M. Barnard Eldershaw)
1897-1956 . . . . DLB-260

Eldershaw, M. Barnard (seeBarnard, Marjorie and
Eldershaw, Flora)

The Electronic Text Center and the Electronic
Archive of Early American Fiction at the
University of Virginia Library Y-98

Eliade, Mircea 1907-1986 . . . . DLB-220; CDWLB-4

Elie, Robert 1915-1973 . . . . DLB-88

Elin Pelin 1877-1949 . . . . DLB-147; CDWLB-4

Eliot, George
1819-1880 . . . . DLB-21, 35, 55; CDBLB-4

The George Eliot Fellowship. Y-99

Eliot, John 1604-1690 . . . . DLB-24

Eliot, T. S. 1888-1965
. . . . DLB-7, 10, 45, 63, 245; CDALB-5

T. S. Eliot Centennial: The Return
of the Old Possum Y-88

The T. S. Eliot Society: Celebration and
Scholarship, 1980-1999 . . . . Y-99

Eliot's Court Press DLB-170

Elizabeth I 1533-1603 . . . . DLB-136

Elizabeth von Nassau-Saarbrücken
after 1393-1456 . . . . DLB-179

Elizondo, Salvador 1932- DLB-145

Elizondo, Sergio 1930- DLB-82

Elkin, Stanley
1930-1995 . . . . DLB-2, 28, 218, 278; Y-80

Elles, Dora Amy (see Wentworth, Patricia)

Ellet, Elizabeth F. 1818?-1877 . . . . DLB-30

Elliot, Ebenezer 1781-1849 . . . . DLB-96, 190

Elliot, Frances Minto (Dickinson)
1820-1898 . . . . DLB-166

Elliott, Charlotte 1789-1871 . . . . DLB-199

Elliott, George 1923- DLB-68

Elliott, George P. 1918-1980 . . . . DLB-244

Elliott, Janice 1931-1995 . . . . DLB-14

Elliott, Sarah Barnwell 1848-1928 . . . . . . DLB-221

Elliott, Thomes and Talbot DLB-49

Elliott, William, III 1788-1863 . . . . . . DLB-3, 248

Ellis, Alice Thomas (Anna Margaret Haycraft)
1932- DLB-194

Ellis, Edward S. 1840-1916 . . . . DLB-42

Ellis, George E.
"The New Controversy Concerning
Miracles DS-5

Ellis, Havelock 1859-1939 . . . . DLB-190

Frederick Staridge Ellis
[publishing house] DLB-106

The George H. Ellis Company DLB-49

Ellison, Harlan 1934- DLB-8

Tribute to Isaac Asimov Y-92

Ellison, Ralph
1914-1994 . . . DLB-2, 76, 227; Y-94; CDALB-1

Ellmann, Richard 1918-1987 . . . . . DLB-103; Y-87

Ellroy, James 1948- DLB-226; Y-91

Tribute to John D. MacDonald Y-86

Tribute to Raymond Chandler Y-88

Eluard, Paul 1895-1952 . . . . DLB-258

Elyot, Thomas 1490?-1546 . . . . DLB-136

Emanuel, James Andrew 1921- DLB-41

Emecheta, Buchi 1944- . . . DLB-117; CDWLB-3

Emerson, Ralph Waldo
1803-1882 . . . . . . DLB-1, 59, 73, 183, 223, 270;
DS-5; CDALB-2

Ralph Waldo Emerson in 1982 . . . . Y-82

The Ralph Waldo Emerson Society Y-99

Emerson, William 1769-1811 . . . . DLB-37

Emerson, William R. 1923-1997 . . . . Y-97

Emin, Fedor Aleksandrovich
circa 1735-1770 . . . . DLB-150

Emmanuel, Pierre 1916-1984 . . . . DLB-258

Empedocles fifth century B.C. DLB-176

Empson, William 1906-1984 . . . . DLB-20

Enchi Fumiko 1905-1986 . . . . DLB-182

Ende, Michael 1929-1995 . . . . DLB-75

Endō Shūsaku 1923-1996 . . . . DLB-182

Engel, Marian 1933-1985 . . . . DLB-53

Engel'gardt, Sof'ia Vladimirovna
1828-1894 . . . . .DLB-277

Engels, Friedrich 1820-1895 . . . . DLB-129

Engle, Paul 1908- DLB-48

    Tribute to Robert Penn Warren Y-89

English, Thomas Dunn 1819-1902 . . . . . . DLB-202

Ennius 239 B.C.-169 B.C. DLB-211

Enquist, Per Olov 1934- DLB-257

Enright, Anne 1962- DLB-267

Enright, D. J. 1920- DLB-27

Enright, Elizabeth 1909-1968 . . . . DLB-22

Epictetus circa 55-circa 125-130 . . . . .DLB-176

Epicurus 342/341 B.C.-271/270 B.C. DLB-176

Epps, Bernard 1936- DLB-53

Epshtein, Mikhail Naumovich 1950- . . DLB-285

Epstein, Julius 1909-2000 . . . . DLB-26

Epstein, Philip 1909-1952 . . . . DLB-26

Editors, Conversations with Y-95

Equiano, Olaudah
circa 1745-1797 . . . . . . .DLB-37, 50; CDWLB-3

Olaudah Equiano and Unfinished
Journeys: The Slave-Narrative
Tradition and Twentieth-Century
Continuities DLB-117

Eragny Press DLB-112

Erasmus, Desiderius 1467-1536 . . . . DLB-136

Erba, Luciano 1922- DLB-128

Erdman, Nikolai Robertovich
1900-1970 . . . . .DLB-272

Erdrich, Louise
1954- DLB-152, 175, 206; CDALB-7

Erenburg, Il'ia Grigor'evich 1891-1967 . . DLB-272

Erichsen-Brown, Gwethalyn Graham
(see Graham, Gwethalyn)

Eriugena, John Scottus circa 810-877 . . . . DLB-115

Ernst, Paul 1866-1933 . . . . DLB-66, 118

Erofeev, Venedikt Vasil'evich
1938-1990 . . . . DLB-285

Erofeev, Viktor Vladimirovich 1947- . . DLB-285

Ershov, Petr Pavlovich 1815-1869 . . . . . . DLB-205

Erskine, Albert 1911-1993 . . . . .Y-93

    At Home with Albert Erskine Y-00

Erskine, John 1879-1951 . . . . DLB-9, 102

Erskine, Mrs. Steuart ?-1948 . . . . DLB-195

Ertel', Aleksandr Ivanovich 1855-1908. . . DLB-238

Ervine, St. John Greer 1883-1971 . . . . DLB-10

Eschenburg, Johann Joachim 1743-1820 . . . DLB-97

Escoto, Julio 1944- DLB-145

Esdaile, Arundell 1880-1956 . . . . DLB-201

Eshleman, Clayton 1935- DLB-5

Espaillat, Rhina P. 1932- DLB-282

Espriu, Salvador 1913-1985 . . . . DLB-134

Ess Ess Publishing Company DLB-49

Essex House Press DLB-112

Esson, Louis 1878-1943 . . . . DLB-260

Essop, Ahmed 1931- DLB-225

Esterházy, Péter 1950- DLB-232; CDWLB-4

Estes, Eleanor 1906-1988 . . . . DLB-22

Estes and Lauriat DLB-49

Estleman, Loren D. 1952- DLB-226

Eszterhas, Joe 1944- DLB-185

Etherege, George 1636-circa 1692 . . . . DLB-80

Ethridge, Mark, Sr. 1896-1981 . . . . DLB-127

Ets, Marie Hall 1893-1984 . . . . DLB-22

Etter, David 1928- DLB-105

Ettner, Johann Christoph 1654-1724 . . . . DLB-168

Eudora Welty Remembered in
Two Exhibits Y-02

Eugene Gant's Projected Works Y-01

Eupolemius flourished circa 1095 . . . . DLB-148

Euripides circa 484 B.C.-407/406 B.C.
. . . . .DLB-176; CDWLB-1

Evans, Augusta Jane 1835-1909 . . . . DLB-239

Evans, Caradoc 1878-1945 . . . . DLB-162

Evans, Charles 1850-1935 . . . . DLB-187

Evans, Donald 1884-1921 . . . . DLB-54

Evans, George Henry 1805-1856 . . . . DLB-43

Evans, Hubert 1892-1986 . . . . DLB-92

Evans, Mari 1923- DLB-41

Evans, Mary Ann (see Eliot, George)

Evans, Nathaniel 1742-1767 . . . . DLB-31

Evans, Sebastian 1830-1909 . . . . DLB-35

Evans, Ray 1915- DLB-265

M. Evans and Company DLB-46

Evaristi, Marcella 1953- DLB-233

Everett, Alexander Hill 1790-1847 . . . . . . DLB-59

Everett, Edward 1794-1865 . . . . . . DLB-1, 59, 235

Everson, R. G. 1903- DLB-88

Everson, William 1912-1994 . . . . . DLB-5, 16, 212

Ewart, Gavin 1916-1995 . . . . DLB-40

Ewing, Juliana Horatia 1841-1885 . . . DLB-21, 163

The Examiner 1808-1881 . . . . DLB-110

Exley, Frederick 1929-1992 . . . . . . .DLB-143; Y-81

Editorial: The Extension of Copyright Y-02

von Eyb, Albrecht 1420-1475 . . . . .DLB-179

Eyre and Spottiswoode DLB-106

Ezera, Regīna 1930- DLB-232

Ezzo ?-after 1065 . . . . DLB-148

F

Faber, Frederick William 1814-1863 . . . . . DLB-32

Faber and Faber Limited DLB-112

Faccio, Rena (see Aleramo, Sibilla)

Facsimiles
    The Uses of Facsimile: A Symposium Y-90

Fadeev, Aleksandr Aleksandrovich
1901-1956 . . . . .DLB-272

Fagundo, Ana María 1938- DLB-134

Fainzil'berg, Il'ia Arnol'dovich
(see Il'f, Il'ia and Petrov, Evgenii)

Fair, Ronald L. 1932- DLB-33

Fairfax, Beatrice (see Manning, Marie)

Fairlie, Gerard 1899-1983 . . . . DLB-77

Fallada, Hans 1893-1947 . . . . DLB-56

Fancher, Betsy 1928- Y-83

Fane, Violet 1843-1905 . . . . DLB-35

Fanfrolico Press DLB-112

Fanning, Katherine 1927- DLB-127

Fanshawe, Sir Richard 1608-1666 . . . . . . DLB-126

Fantasy Press Publishers DLB-46

Fante, John 1909-1983 . . . . .DLB-130; Y-83

Al-Farabi circa 870-950 . . . . DLB-115

Farabough, Laura 1949- DLB-228

Farah, Nuruddin 1945- DLB-125; CDWLB-3

Farber, Norma 1909-1984 . . . . DLB-61

Fargue, Léon-Paul 1876-1947 . . . . DLB-258

Farigoule, Louis (see Romains, Jules)

Farjeon, Eleanor 1881-1965 . . . . DLB-160

Farley, Harriet 1812-1907 . . . . DLB-239

Farley, Walter 1920-1989 . . . . DLB-22

Farmborough, Florence 1887-1978 . . . . . . DLB-204

Farmer, Penelope 1939- DLB-161

Farmer, Philip José 1918- DLB-8

Farnaby, Thomas 1575?-1647 . . . . DLB-236

Farningham, Marianne (see Hearn, Mary Anne)

Farquhar, George circa 1677-1707 . . . . DLB-84

Farquharson, Martha (see Finley, Martha)

Farrar, Frederic William 1831-1903 . . . . DLB-163

Farrar, Straus and Giroux DLB-46

Farrar and Rinehart DLB-46

Farrell, J. G. 1935-1979 . . . . .DLB-14, 271

Farrell, James T. 1904-1979 . . DLB-4, 9, 86; DS-2

Fast, Howard 1914- DLB-9

Faulkner, William 1897-1962
. . . .DLB-9, 11, 44, 102; DS-2; Y-86; CDALB-5

Faulkner and Yoknapatawpha
Conference, Oxford, Mississippi Y-97

Faulkner Centennial Addresses Y-97

"Faulkner 100—Celebrating the Work,"
University of South Carolina,
Columbia Y-97

Impressions of William Faulkner Y-97

William Faulkner and the People-to-People
Program Y-86

William Faulkner Centenary
Celebrations Y-97

The William Faulkner Society Y-99

George Faulkner [publishing house] DLB-154

Faulks, Sebastian 1953- DLB-207

Fauset, Jessie Redmon 1882-1961 . . . . DLB-51

Faust, Frederick Schiller (Max Brand)
1892-1944 . . . . DLB-256

Faust, Irvin
  1924- DLB-2, 28, 218, 278; Y-80, 00

  I Wake Up Screaming [Response to
    Ken Auletta] Y-97

  Tribute to Bernard Malamud Y-86

  Tribute to Isaac Bashevis Singer Y-91

  Tribute to Meyer Levin Y-81

Fawcett, Edgar 1847-1904 ....DLB-202

Fawcett, Millicent Garrett 1847-1929 .....DLB-190

Fawcett Books DLB-46

Fay, Theodore Sedgwick 1807-1898 .....DLB-202

Fearing, Kenneth 1902-1961 ....DLB-9

Federal Writers' Project DLB-46

Federman, Raymond 1928- Y-80

Fedin, Konstantin Aleksandrovich
  1892-1977 ....DLB-272

Fedorov, Innokentii Vasil'evich
  (see Omulevsky, Innokentii Vasil'evich)

Feiffer, Jules 1929- DLB-7, 44

Feinberg, Charles E. 1899-1988.... DLB-187; Y-88

Feind, Barthold 1678-1721 ....DLB-168

Feinstein, Elaine 1930- DLB-14, 40

Feirstein, Frederick 1940- DLB-282

Feiss, Paul Louis 1875-1952 ....DLB-187

Feldman, Irving 1928- DLB-169

Felipe, Léon 1884-1968 ....DLB-108

Fell, Frederick, Publishers DLB-46

Fellowship of Southern Writers Y-98

Felltham, Owen 1602?-1668 ....DLB-126, 151

Felman, Shoshana 1942- DLB-246

Fels, Ludwig 1946- DLB-75

Felton, Cornelius Conway
  1807-1862 ....DLB-1, 235

Mothe-Fénelon, François de Salignac de la
  1651-1715 ....DLB-268

Fenn, Harry 1837-1911 ....DLB-188

Fennario, David 1947- DLB-60

Fenner, Dudley 1558?-1587? DLB-236

Fenno, Jenny 1765?-1803 ....DLB-200

Fenno, John 1751-1798 ....DLB-43

R. F. Fenno and Company...............DLB-49

Fenoglio, Beppe 1922-1963 ....DLB-177

Fenton, Geoffrey 1539?-1608..........DLB-136

Fenton, James 1949- DLB-40

The Hemingway/Fenton
  Correspondence Y-02

Ferber, Edna 1885-1968.......DLB-9, 28, 86, 266

Ferdinand, Vallery, III (see Salaam, Kalamu ya)

Ferguson, Sir Samuel 1810-1886 ....DLB-32

Ferguson, William Scott 1875-1954 ......DLB-47

Fergusson, Robert 1750-1774 ....DLB-109

Ferland, Albert 1872-1943 ....DLB-92

Ferlinghetti, Lawrence
  1919- DLB-5, 16; CDALB-1

  Tribute to Kenneth Rexroth Y-82

Fermor, Patrick Leigh 1915- DLB-204

Fern, Fanny (see Parton, Sara Payson Willis)

Ferrars, Elizabeth (Morna Doris Brown)
  1907-1995 ....DLB-87

Ferré, Rosario 1942- DLB-145

E. Ferret and Company DLB-49

Ferrier, Susan 1782-1854 ....DLB-116

Ferril, Thomas Hornsby 1896-1988 .....DLB-206

Ferrini, Vincent 1913- DLB-48

Ferron, Jacques 1921-1985............DLB-60

Ferron, Madeleine 1922- DLB-53

Ferrucci, Franco 1936- DLB-196

Fet, Afanasii Afanas'evich
  1820?-1892 ....DLB-277

Fetridge and Company DLB-49

Feuchtersleben, Ernst Freiherr von
  1806-1849 ....DLB-133

Feuchtwanger, Lion 1884-1958 ....DLB-66

Feuerbach, Ludwig 1804-1872..........DLB-133

Feuillet, Octave 1821-1890............DLB-192

Feydeau, Georges 1862-1921...........DLB-192

Fichte, Johann Gottlieb 1762-1814 ......DLB-90

Ficke, Arthur Davison 1883-1945 ....DLB-54

Fiction
  American Fiction and the 1930s DLB-9

  Fiction Best-Sellers, 1910-1945 ....DLB-9

  The Year in Fiction Y-84, 86, 89, 94–99

  The Year in Fiction: A Biased View Y-83

  The Year in U.S. Fiction Y-00, 01

  The Year's Work in Fiction: A Survey ... Y-82

Fiedler, Leslie A. 1917- DLB-28, 67

  Tribute to Bernard Malamud Y-86

  Tribute to James Dickey Y-97

Field, Barron 1789-1846..............DLB-230

Field, Edward 1924- DLB-105

Field, Eugene 1850-1895 .. DLB-23, 42, 140; DS-13

Field, John 1545?-1588 ....DLB-167

Field, Joseph M. 1810-1856 ....DLB-248

Field, Marshall, III 1893-1956.........DLB-127

Field, Marshall, IV 1916-1965 ....DLB-127

Field, Marshall, V 1941- DLB-127

Field, Michael (Katherine Harris Bradley)
  1846-1914 ....DLB-240

  "The Poetry File" DLB-105

Field, Nathan 1587-1619 or 1620........DLB-58

Field, Rachel 1894-1942..............DLB-9, 22

Fielding, Helen 1958- DLB-231

Fielding, Henry
  1707-1754......DLB-39, 84, 101; CDBLB-2

  "Defense of Amelia" (1752)..........DLB-39

  The History of the Adventures of Joseph Andrews
    [excerpt] (1742) DLB-39

  Letter to [Samuel] Richardson on Clarissa
    (1748) DLB-39

  Preface to Joseph Andrews (1742) DLB-39

  Preface to Sarah Fielding's Familiar
    Letters (1747) [excerpt]..........DLB-39

  Preface to Sarah Fielding's The
    Adventures of David Simple (1744) ...DLB-39

  Review of Clarissa (1748) DLB-39

  Tom Jones (1749) [excerpt] DLB-39

Fielding, Sarah 1710-1768............DLB-39

  Preface to The Cry (1754) DLB-39

Fields, Annie Adams 1834-1915 ....DLB-221

Fields, Dorothy 1905-1974............DLB-265

Fields, James T. 1817-1881..........DLB-1, 235

Fields, Julia 1938- DLB-41

Fields, Osgood and Company DLB-49

Fields, W. C. 1880-1946 ....DLB-44

Fierstein, Harvey 1954- DLB-266

Figes, Eva 1932- DLB-14, 271

Figuera, Angela 1902-1984 ....DLB-108

Filmer, Sir Robert 1586-1653...........DLB-151

Filson, John circa 1753-1788............DLB-37

Finch, Anne, Countess of Winchilsea
  1661-1720 ....DLB-95

Finch, Annie 1956-.................DLB-282

Finch, Robert 1900- DLB-88

Findley, Timothy 1930-2002...........DLB-53

Finlay, Ian Hamilton 1925- DLB-40

Finley, Martha 1828-1909 ....DLB-42

Finn, Elizabeth Anne (McCaul)
  1825-1921 ....DLB-166

Finnegan, Seamus 1949- DLB-245

Finney, Jack 1911-1995 ....DLB-8

Finney, Walter Braden (see Finney, Jack)

Firbank, Ronald 1886-1926............DLB-36

Firmin, Giles 1615-1697...............DLB-24

First Edition Library/Collectors'
  Reprints, Inc....................... Y-91

Fischart, Johann
  1546 or 1547-1590 or 1591........ DLB-179

Fischer, Karoline Auguste Fernandine
  1764-1842 ....DLB-94

Fischer, Tibor 1959- DLB-231

Fish, Stanley 1938- DLB-67

Fishacre, Richard 1205-1248 ....DLB-115

Fisher, Clay (see Allen, Henry W.)

Fisher, Dorothy Canfield 1879-1958 ...DLB-9, 102

Fisher, Leonard Everett 1924- DLB-61

Fisher, Roy 1930- DLB-40

Fisher, Rudolph 1897-1934 ....DLB-51, 102

Fisher, Steve 1913-1980 ....DLB-226

Fisher, Sydney George 1856-1927 ....DLB-47

Fisher, Vardis 1895-1968............DLB-9, 206

Fiske, John 1608-1677 ....DLB-24

Fiske, John 1842-1901 .... DLB-47, 64

Fitch, Thomas circa 1700-1774..........DLB-31

Fitch, William Clyde 1865-1909 ....DLB-7

FitzGerald, Edward 1809-1883 ....DLB-32

Fitzgerald, F. Scott 1896-1940
  ....DLB-4, 9, 86; Y-81, 92;
                           DS-1, 15, 16; CDALB-4

  F. Scott Fitzgerald: A Descriptive
    Bibliography, Supplement (2001) Y-01

F. Scott Fitzgerald Centenary
Celebrations Y-96

F. Scott Fitzgerald Inducted into the
American Poets' Corner at St. John
the Divine; Ezra Pound Banned Y-99

"F. Scott Fitzgerald: St. Paul's Native Son
and Distinguished American Writer":
University of Minnesota Conference,
29-31 October 1982 . . . . Y-82

First International F. Scott Fitzgerald
Conference Y-92

The Great Gatsby (Documentary DLB-219

Tender Is the Night (Documentary) . . . DLB-273

Fitzgerald, Penelope 1916- DLB-14, 194

Fitzgerald, Robert 1910-1985 . . . . Y-80

FitzGerald, Robert D. 1902-1987 . . . . . . DLB-260

Fitzgerald, Thomas 1819-1891 . . . . DLB-23

Fitzgerald, Zelda Sayre 1900-1948 . . . . Y-84

Fitzhugh, Louise 1928-1974 . . . . DLB-52

Fitzhugh, William circa 1651-1701 . . . . . . DLB-24

Flagg, James Montgomery 1877-1960 . . . . DLB-188

Flanagan, Thomas 1923-2002. . . . . Y-80

Flanner, Hildegarde 1899-1987. . . . . DLB-48

Flanner, Janet 1892-1978. . . . . DLB-4; DS-15

Flannery, Peter 1951- DLB-233

Flaubert, Gustave 1821-1880 . . . . DLB-119

Flavin, Martin 1883-1967 . . . . DLB-9

Fleck, Konrad (flourished circa 1220) . . . DLB-138

Flecker, James Elroy 1884-1915 . . . . . . DLB-10, 19

Fleeson, Doris 1901-1970 . . . . DLB-29

Fleißer, Marieluise 1901-1974 . . . . . . DLB-56, 124

Fleischer, Nat 1887-1972 . . . . DLB-241

Fleming, Abraham 1552?-1607 . . . . DLB-236

Fleming, Ian 1908-1964 . . DLB-87, 201; CDBLB-7

Fleming, Joan 1908-1980 . . . . .DLB-276

Fleming, May Agnes 1840-1880 . . . . DLB-99

Fleming, Paul 1609-1640 . . . . DLB-164

Fleming, Peter 1907-1971 . . . . DLB-195

Fletcher, Giles, the Elder 1546-1611 . . . . DLB-136

Fletcher, Giles, the Younger
1585 or 1586-1623 . . . . DLB-121

Fletcher, J. S. 1863-1935 . . . . DLB-70

Fletcher, John 1579-1625. . . . . DLB-58

Fletcher, John Gould 1886-1950. . . . . . DLB-4, 45

Fletcher, Phineas 1582-1650 . . . . DLB-121

Flieg, Helmut (see Heym, Stefan)

Flint, F. S. 1885-1960 . . . . DLB-19

Flint, Timothy 1780-1840 . . . . DLB-73, 186

Flores-Williams, Jason 1969- DLB-209

Florio, John 1553?-1625 . . . . .DLB-172

Fludd, Robert 1574-1637. . . . . DLB-281

Fo, Dario 1926- Y-97

Nobel Lecture 1997: Contra Jogulatores
Obloquentes Y-97

Foden, Giles 1967- DLB-267

Fofanov, Konstantin Mikhailovich
1862-1911. . . . . .DLB-277

Foix, J. V. 1893-1987 . . . . DLB-134

Foley, Martha 1897-1977 . . . . DLB-137

Folger, Henry Clay 1857-1930 . . . . DLB-140

Folio Society DLB-112

Follain, Jean 1903-1971 . . . . DLB-258

Follen, Charles 1796-1840. . . . . DLB-235

Follen, Eliza Lee (Cabot) 1787-1860 . . . DLB-1, 235

Follett, Ken 1949- DLB-87; Y-81

Follett Publishing Company DLB-46

John West Folsom [publishing house]. DLB-49

Folz, Hans
between 1435 and 1440-1513. . . . . . . .DLB-179

Fontane, Theodor
1819-1898 . . . . DLB-129; CDWLB-2

Fontenelle, Bernard Le Bovier de
1657-1757. . . . . .DLB-268

Fontes, Montserrat 1940- DLB-209

Fonvisin, Denis Ivanovich
1744 or 1745-1792 . . . . DLB-150

Foote, Horton 1916- DLB-26, 266

Foote, Mary Hallock
1847-1938. . . . . .DLB-186, 188, 202, 221

Foote, Samuel 1721-1777. . . . . DLB-89

Foote, Shelby 1916- DLB-2, 17

Forbes, Calvin 1945- DLB-41

Forbes, Ester 1891-1967 . . . . DLB-22

Forbes, Rosita 1893?-1967 . . . . DLB-195

Forbes and Company DLB-49

Force, Peter 1790-1868 . . . . DLB-30

Forché, Carolyn 1950- DLB-5, 193

Ford, Charles Henri 1913-2002 . . . . . . DLB-4, 48

Ford, Corey 1902-1969. . . . . DLB-11

Ford, Ford Madox
1873-1939. . . . . . . DLB-34, 98, 162; CDBLB-6

Nathan Asch Remembers Ford Madox
Ford, Sam Roth, and Hart Crane Y-02

J. B. Ford and Company. DLB-49

Ford, Jesse Hill 1928-1996 . . . . DLB-6

Ford, John 1586-? DLB-58; CDBLB-1

Ford, R. A. D. 1915- DLB-88

Ford, Richard 1944- DLB-227

Ford, Worthington C. 1858-1941. . . . . DLB-47

Fords, Howard, and Hulbert DLB-49

Foreman, Carl 1914-1984. . . . . DLB-26

Forester, C. S. 1899-1966 . . . . DLB-191

The C. S. Forester Society Y-00

Forester, Frank (see Herbert, Henry William)

Anthologizing New Formalism DLB-282

The Little Magazines of the
New Formalism DLB-282

The New Narrative Poetry. DLB-282

Presses of the New Formalism and
the New Narrative DLB-282

The Prosody of the New Formalism. DLB-282

Younger Women Poets of the
New Formalism DLB-282

Forman, Harry Buxton 1842-1917 . . . . . . DLB-184

Fornés, María Irene 1930- DLB-7

Forrest, Leon 1937-1997 . . . . DLB-33

Forsh, Ol'ga Dmitrievna 1873-1961 . . . . .DLB-272

Forster, E. M.
1879-1970 . . . . . . DLB-34, 98, 162, 178, 195;
DS-10; CDBLB-6

"Fantasy," from *Aspects of the Novel*
(1927) DLB-178

Forster, Georg 1754-1794 . . . . DLB-94

Forster, John 1812-1876 . . . . DLB-144

Forster, Margaret 1938- DLB-155, 271

Forsyth, Frederick 1938- DLB-87

Forsyth, William
"Literary Style" (1857) [excerpt] DLB-57

Forten, Charlotte L. 1837-1914. . . . . DLB-50, 239

Pages from Her Diary DLB-50

Fortini, Franco 1917-1994 . . . . DLB-128

Fortune, Mary ca. 1833-ca. 1910 . . . . . . DLB-230

Fortune, T. Thomas 1856-1928 . . . . DLB-23

Fosdick, Charles Austin 1842-1915 . . . . . DLB-42

Foster, Genevieve 1893-1979 . . . . DLB-61

Foster, Hannah Webster 1758-1840 . . .DLB-37, 200

Foster, John 1648-1681 . . . . DLB-24

Foster, Michael 1904-1956 . . . . DLB-9

Foster, Myles Birket 1825-1899 . . . . DLB-184

Foucault, Michel 1926-1984 . . . . DLB-242

Robert and Andrew Foulis
[publishing house] DLB-154

Fouqué, Caroline de la Motte 1774-1831 . . DLB-90

Fouqué, Friedrich de la Motte
1777-1843 . . . . DLB-90

Four Seas Company DLB-46

Four Winds Press. DLB-46

Fournier, Henri Alban (see Alain-Fournier)

Fowler, Christopher 1953- DLB-267

Fowler and Wells Company. DLB-49

Fowles, John
1926- DLB-14, 139, 207; CDBLB-8

Fox, John 1939- DLB-245

Fox, John, Jr. 1862 or 1863-1919 . . . DLB-9; DS-13

Fox, Paula 1923- DLB-52

Fox, Richard Kyle 1846-1922. . . . . DLB-79

Fox, William Price 1926- DLB-2; Y-81

Remembering Joe Heller Y-99

Richard K. Fox [publishing house] DLB-49

Foxe, John 1517-1587 . . . . DLB-132

Fraenkel, Michael 1896-1957 . . . . DLB-4

France, Anatole 1844-1924 . . . . DLB-123

France, Richard 1938- DLB-7

Francis, Convers 1795-1863 . . . . DLB-1, 235

Francis, Dick 1920- DLB-87; CDBLB-8

Francis, Sir Frank 1901-1988 . . . . DLB-201

Francis, Jeffrey, Lord 1773-1850. . . . . . . .DLB-107

C. S. Francis [publishing house] DLB-49

Franck, Sebastian 1499-1542 . . . . .DLB-179

Francke, Kuno 1855-1930 . . . . DLB-71

Françoise (Robertine Barry) 1863-1910 . . . . DLB-92

François, Louise von 1817-1893 . . . . DLB-129

Frank, Bruno 1887-1945 . . . . DLB-118

Frank, Leonhard 1882-1961 . . . . DLB-56, 118

Frank, Melvin 1913-1988 . . . . DLB-26

Frank, Waldo 1889-1967 . . . . DLB-9, 63

Franken, Rose 1895?-1988 . . . . . . DLB-228, Y-84

Franklin, Benjamin
1706-1790 . . . . . DLB-24, 43, 73, 183; CDALB-2

Franklin, James 1697-1735 . . . . DLB-43

Franklin, John 1786-1847 . . . . DLB-99

Franklin, Miles 1879-1954 . . . . DLB-230

Franklin Library DLB-46

Frantz, Ralph Jules 1902-1979 . . . . DLB-4

Franzos, Karl Emil 1848-1904 . . . . DLB-129

Fraser, Antonia 1932- DLB-276

Fraser, G. S. 1915-1980 . . . . DLB-27

Fraser, Kathleen 1935- DLB-169

Frattini, Alberto 1922- DLB-128

Frau Ava ?-1127 . . . . DLB-148

Fraunce, Abraham 1558?-1592 or 1593 . . . DLB-236

Frayn, Michael 1933- DLB-13, 14, 194, 245

Fréchette, Louis-Honoré 1839-1908 . . . . . . DLB-99

Frederic, Harold 1856-1898 . . . . DLB-12, 23; DS-13

Freed, Arthur 1894-1973 . . . . DLB-265

Freeling, Nicolas 1927- DLB-87

Tribute to Georges Simenon Y-89

Freeman, Douglas Southall
1886-1953 . . . . DLB-17; DS-17

Freeman, Judith 1946- DLB-256

Freeman, Legh Richmond 1842-1915 . . . . DLB-23

Freeman, Mary E. Wilkins
1852-1930 . . . . DLB-12, 78, 221

Freeman, R. Austin 1862-1943 . . . . DLB-70

Freidank circa 1170-circa 1233 . . . . DLB-138

Freiligrath, Ferdinand 1810-1876 . . . . DLB-133

Fremlin, Celia 1914- DLB-276

Frémont, Jessie Benton 1834-1902 . . . . . . DLB-183

Frémont, John Charles 1813-1890 . . . DLB-183, 186

French, Alice 1850-1934 . . . . DLB-74; DS-13

French, David 1939- DLB-53

French, Evangeline 1869-1960 . . . . DLB-195

French, Francesca 1871-1960 . . . . DLB-195

James French [publishing house] DLB-49

Samuel French [publishing house] DLB-49

Samuel French, Limited DLB-106

French Literature
Epic and Beast Epic DLB-208

French Arthurian Literature DLB-208

Lyric Poetry DLB-268

Other Poets DLB-217

Poetry in Nineteenth-Century France:
Cultural Background and Critical
Commentary DLB-217

Roman de la Rose: Guillaume de Lorris
1200 to 1205-circa 1230, Jean de
Meun 1235/1240-circa 1305 . . . . . DLB-208

Saints' Lives DLB-208

Troubadours, *Trobairitz*, and
Trouvères DLB-208

French Theater
Medieval French Drama DLB-208

Parisian Theater, Fall 1984: Toward
a New Baroque Y-85

Freneau, Philip 1752-1832 . . . . DLB-37, 43

The Rising Glory of America DLB-37

Freni, Melo 1934- DLB-128

Freshfield, Douglas W. 1845-1934 . . . . . . DLB-174

Freytag, Gustav 1816-1895 . . . . DLB-129

Fridegård, Jan 1897-1968 . . . . DLB-259

Fried, Erich 1921-1988 . . . . DLB-85

Friedan, Betty 1921- DLB-246

Friedman, Bruce Jay 1930- DLB-2, 28, 244

Friedrich von Hausen circa 1171-1190 . . . . DLB-138

Friel, Brian 1929- DLB-13

Friend, Krebs 1895?-1967? DLB-4

Fries, Fritz Rudolf 1935- DLB-75

Frisch, Max
1911-1991 . . . . DLB-69, 124; CDWLB-2

Frischlin, Nicodemus 1547-1590 . . . . DLB-179

Frischmuth, Barbara 1941- DLB-85

Fritz, Jean 1915- DLB-52

Froissart, Jean circa 1337-circa 1404 . . . . . DLB-208

Fromentin, Eugene 1820-1876 . . . . DLB-123

Frontinus circa A.D. 35-A.D. 103/104 . . . . DLB-211

Frost, A. B. 1851-1928 . . . . DLB-188; DS-13

Frost, Robert
1874-1963 . . . . DLB-54; DS-7; CDALB-4

The Friends of the Dymock Poets Y-00

Frostenson, Katarina 1953- DLB-257

Frothingham, Octavius Brooks
1822-1895 . . . . DLB-1, 243

Froude, James Anthony
1818-1894 . . . . DLB-18, 57, 144

Fruitlands 1843-1844 . . . . DLB-1, 223; DS-5

Fry, Christopher 1907- DLB-13

Tribute to John Betjeman Y-84

Fry, Roger 1866-1934 . . . . DS-10

Fry, Stephen 1957- DLB-207

Frye, Northrop 1912-1991 . . . . . . DLB-67, 68, 246

Fuchs, Daniel 1909-1993 . . . . . DLB-9, 26, 28; Y-93

Tribute to Isaac Bashevis Singer Y-91

Fuentes, Carlos 1928- DLB-113; CDWLB-3

Fuertes, Gloria 1918-1998 . . . . DLB-108

Fugard, Athol 1932- DLB-225

The Fugitives and the Agrarians:
The First Exhibition Y-85

Fujiwara no Shunzei 1114-1204 . . . . DLB-203

Fujiwara no Tameaki 1230s?-1290s? DLB-203

Fujiwara no Tameie 1198-1275 . . . . DLB-203

Fujiwara no Teika 1162-1241 . . . . DLB-203

Fulbecke, William 1560-1603? DLB-172

Fuller, Charles 1939- DLB-38, 266

Fuller, Henry Blake 1857-1929 . . . . DLB-12

Fuller, John 1937- DLB-40

Fuller, Margaret (see Fuller, Sarah)

Fuller, Roy 1912-1991 . . . . DLB-15, 20

Tribute to Christopher Isherwood Y-86

Fuller, Samuel 1912-1997 . . . . DLB-26

Fuller, Sarah 1810-1850 . . . . . . DLB-1, 59, 73,
183, 223, 239; DS-5; CDALB-2

Fuller, Thomas 1608-1661 . . . . DLB-151

Fullerton, Hugh 1873-1945 . . . . DLB-171

Fullwood, William flourished 1568 . . . . . . DLB-236

Fulton, Alice 1952- DLB-193

Fulton, Len 1934- Y-86

Fulton, Robin 1937- DLB-40

Furbank, P. N. 1920- DLB-155

Furetière, Antoine 1619-1688 . . . . DLB-268

Furman, Laura 1945- Y-86

Furmanov, Dmitrii Andreevich
1891-1926 . . . . DLB-272

Furness, Horace Howard 1833-1912 . . . . . DLB-64

Furness, William Henry 1802-1896 . . . . DLB-1, 235

Furnivall, Frederick James 1825-1910 . . . . DLB-184

Furphy, Joseph (Tom Collins)
1843-1912 . . . . DLB-230

Furthman, Jules 1888-1966 . . . . DLB-26

Shakespeare and Montaigne: A
Symposium by Jules Furthman Y-02

Furui Yoshikichi 1937- DLB-182

Fushimi, Emperor 1265-1317 . . . . DLB-203

Futabatei Shimei (Hasegawa Tatsunosuke)
1864-1909 . . . . DLB-180

Fyleman, Rose 1877-1957 . . . . DLB-160

G

Gadallah, Leslie 1939- DLB-251

Gadda, Carlo Emilio 1893-1973 . . . . DLB-177

Gaddis, William 1922-1998 . . . . DLB-2, 278

William Gaddis: A Tribute Y-99

Gág, Wanda 1893-1946 . . . . DLB-22

Gagarin, Ivan Sergeevich 1814-1882 . . . . . DLB-198

Gagnon, Madeleine 1938- DLB-60

Gaiman, Neil 1960- DLB-261

Gaine, Hugh 1726-1807 . . . . DLB-43

Hugh Gaine [publishing house] DLB-49

Gaines, Ernest J.
1933- DLB-2, 33, 152; Y-80; CDALB-6

Gaiser, Gerd 1908-1976 . . . . DLB-69

Gaitskill, Mary 1954- DLB-244

Galarza, Ernesto 1905-1984 . . . . DLB-122

Galaxy Science Fiction Novels DLB-46

Galbraith, Robert (or Caubraith)
circa 1483-1544 . . . . DLB-281

Gale, Zona 1874-1938 . . . . DLB-9, 228, 78

Galen of Pergamon 129-after 210 . . . . DLB-176

Gales, Winifred Marshall 1761-1839 . . . . . DLB-200

Gall, Louise von 1815-1855 . . . . DLB-133

Gallagher, Tess 1943- DLB-120, 212, 244

Gallagher, Wes 1911- DLB-127

Gallagher, William Davis 1808-1894 ..... DLB-73

Gallant, Mavis 1922- DLB-53

Gallegos, María Magdalena 1935- DLB-209

Gallico, Paul 1897-1976............DLB-9, 171

Gallop, Jane 1952- DLB-246

Galloway, Grace Growden 1727-1782.... DLB-200

Gallup, Donald 1913-2000 .... DLB-187

Galsworthy, John 1867-1933
..... DLB-10, 34, 98, 162; DS-16; CDBLB-5

Galt, John 1779-1839......... DLB-99, 116, 159

Galton, Sir Francis 1822-1911......... DLB-166

Galvin, Brendan 1938- DLB-5

Gambit DLB-46

Gamboa, Reymundo 1948- DLB-122

Gammer Gurton's Needle.............. DLB-62

Gan, Elena Andreevna (Zeneida R-va)
1814-1842..................... DLB-198

Gandlevsky, Sergei Markovich 1952- .. DLB-285

Gannett, Frank E. 1876-1957 .... DLB-29

Gao Xingjian 1940- Y-00

Nobel Lecture 2000: "The Case for
Literature".................... Y-00

Gaos, Vicente 1919-1980 .... DLB-134

García, Andrew 1854?-1943.......... DLB-209

García, Lionel G. 1935- DLB-82

García, Richard 1941- DLB-209

García Márquez, Gabriel
1928- DLB-113; Y-82; CDWLB-3

The Magical World of Macondo....... Y-82

Nobel Lecture 1982: The Solitude of
Latin America Y-82

A Tribute to Gabriel García Márquez Y-82

García Marruz, Fina 1923- DLB-283

García-Camarillo, Cecilio 1943- DLB-209

Gardam, Jane 1928- DLB-14, 161, 231

Gardell, Jonas 1963- DLB-257

Garden, Alexander circa 1685-1756 ...... DLB-31

Gardiner, John Rolfe 1936- DLB-244

Gardiner, Margaret Power Farmer
(see Blessington, Marguerite, Countess of)

Gardner, John
1933-1982 .... DLB-2; Y-82; CDALB-7

Garfield, Leon 1921-1996............ DLB-161

Garis, Howard R. 1873-1962 .... DLB-22

Garland, Hamlin 1860-1940...DLB-12, 71, 78, 186

The Hamlin Garland Society.......... Y-01

Garneau, François-Xavier 1809-1866..... DLB-99

Garneau, Hector de Saint-Denys
1912-1943..................... DLB-88

Garneau, Michel 1939- DLB-53

Garner, Alan 1934- DLB-161, 261

Garner, Hugh 1913-1979 .... DLB-68

Garnett, David 1892-1981 .... DLB-34

Garnett, Eve 1900-1991 .... DLB-160

Garnett, Richard 1835-1906 .... DLB-184

Garrard, Lewis H. 1829-1887......... DLB-186

Garraty, John A. 1920- DLB-17

Garrett, George
1929- DLB-2, 5, 130, 152; Y-83

Literary Prizes Y-00

My Summer Reading Orgy: Reading
for Fun and Games: One Reader's
Report on the Summer of 2001...... Y-01

A Summing Up at Century's End Y-99

Tribute to James Dickey Y-97

Tribute to Michael M. Rea Y-97

Tribute to Paxton Davis Y-94

Tribute to Peter Taylor Y-94

Tribute to William Goyen............ Y-83

A Writer Talking: A Collage........... Y-00

Garrett, John Work 1872-1942........ DLB-187

Garrick, David 1717-1779 .... DLB-84, 213

Garrison, William Lloyd
1805-1879....... DLB-1, 43, 235; CDALB-2

Garro, Elena 1920-1998 .... DLB-145

Garshin, Vsevolod Mikhailovich
1855-1888 ....DLB-277

Garth, Samuel 1661-1719 .... DLB-95

Garve, Andrew 1908-2001............. DLB-87

Gary, Romain 1914-1980 .... DLB-83

Gascoigne, George 1539?-1577........ DLB-136

Gascoyne, David 1916-2001 .... DLB-20

Gash, Jonathan (John Grant) 1933- DLB-276

Gaskell, Elizabeth Cleghorn
1810-1865 ..... DLB-21, 144, 159; CDBLB-4

The Gaskell Society Y-98

Gaskell, Jane 1941- DLB-261

Gaspey, Thomas 1788-1871 .... DLB-116

Gass, William H. 1924- DLB-2, 227

Gates, Doris 1901-1987 .... DLB-22

Gates, Henry Louis, Jr. 1950- DLB-67

Gates, Lewis E. 1860-1924............. DLB-71

Gatto, Alfonso 1909-1976............. DLB-114

Gault, William Campbell 1910-1995 .... DLB-226

Tribute to Kenneth Millar Y-83

Gaunt, Mary 1861-1942..........DLB-174, 230

Gautier, Théophile 1811-1872 .... DLB-119

Gauvreau, Claude 1925-1971 .... DLB-88

The *Gawain*-Poet
flourished circa 1350-1400 .... DLB-146

Gawsworth, John (Terence Ian Fytton
Armstrong) 1912-1970 .... DLB-255

Gay, Ebenezer 1696-1787 .... DLB-24

Gay, John 1685-1732 .... DLB-84, 95

Gayarré, Charles E. A. 1805-1895 ...... DLB-30

Charles Gaylord [publishing house]...... DLB-49

Gaylord, Edward King 1873-1974 ...... DLB-127

Gaylord, Edward Lewis 1919- DLB-127

Gébler, Carlo 1954- DLB-271

Geda, Sigitas 1943- DLB-232

Geddes, Gary 1940- DLB-60

Geddes, Virgil 1897- DLB-4

Gedeon (Georgii Andreevich Krinovsky)
circa 1730-1763.................. DLB-150

Gee, Maggie 1948- DLB-207

Gee, Shirley 1932- DLB-245

Geibel, Emanuel 1815-1884 .... DLB-129

Geiogamah, Hanay 1945- DLB-175

Geis, Bernard, Associates DLB-46

Geisel, Theodor Seuss 1904-1991 ...DLB-61; Y-91

Gelb, Arthur 1924- DLB-103

Gelb, Barbara 1926- DLB-103

Gelber, Jack 1932- DLB-7, 228

Gélinas, Gratien 1909-1999 .... DLB-88

Gellert, Christian Füerchtegott
1715-1769 .... DLB-97

Gellhorn, Martha 1908-1998 .... Y-82, 98

Gems, Pam 1925- DLB-13

Genet, Jean 1910-1986 ....DLB-72; Y-86

Genette, Gérard 1930- DLB-242

Genevoix, Maurice 1890-1980 .... DLB-65

Genis, Aleksandr Aleksandrovich
1953- DLB-285

Genovese, Eugene D. 1930- DLB-17

Gent, Peter 1942- Y-82

Geoffrey of Monmouth
circa 1100-1155 .... DLB-146

George, Henry 1839-1897 .... DLB-23

George, Jean Craighead 1919- DLB-52

George, W. L. 1882-1926..............DLB-197

George III, King of Great Britain
and Ireland 1738-1820 .... DLB-213

Georgslied 896?..................... DLB-148

Gerber, Merrill Joan 1938- DLB-218

Gerhardie, William 1895-1977 .... DLB-36

Gerhardt, Paul 1607-1676............. DLB-164

Gérin, Winifred 1901-1981 .... DLB-155

Gérin-Lajoie, Antoine 1824-1882 .... DLB-99

German Literature
A Call to Letters and an Invitation
to the Electric Chair DLB-75

The Conversion of an Unpolitical
Man...................... DLB-66

The German Radio Play DLB-124

The German Transformation from the
Baroque to the Enlightenment.... DLB-97

Germanophilism DLB-66

A Letter from a New Germany Y-90

The Making of a People........... DLB-66

The Novel of Impressionism DLB-66

Pattern and Paradigm: History as
Design................... DLB-75

Premisses DLB-66

The 'Twenties and Berlin DLB-66

Wolfram von Eschenbach's *Parzival*:
Prologue and Book 3.... DLB-138

Writers and Politics: 1871-1918...... DLB-66

German Literature, Middle Ages
Abrogans circa 790-800 .... DLB-148

Annolied between 1077 and 1081..... DLB-148

The Arthurian Tradition and
Its European Context DLB-138

Cambridge Songs (Carmina Cantabrigensia)
circa 1050 . . . . .DLB-148

Christus und die Samariterin circa 950 . . .DLB-148

De Heinrico circa 980? DLB-148

Ecbasis Captivi circa 1045 . . . . .DLB-148

Georgslied 896? DLB-148

German Literature and Culture from
Charlemagne to the Early Courtly
Period DLB-148; CDWLB-2

The Germanic Epic and Old English
Heroic Poetry: *Widsith, Waldere,*
and *The Fight at Finnsburg* DLB-146

Graf Rudolf between circa
1170 and circa 1185 . . . . .DLB-148

Heliand circa 850 . . . . .DLB-148

Das Hildesbrandslied
circa 820 . . . . .DLB-148; CDWLB-2

Kaiserchronik circa 1147 . . . . .DLB-148

The Legends of the Saints and a
Medieval Christian
Worldview DLB-148

Ludus de Antichristo circa 1160 . . . . . . .DLB-148

Ludwigslied 881 or 882 . . . . .DLB-148

Muspilli circa 790-circa 850 . . . . .DLB-148

Old German Genesis and *Old German
Exodus* circa 1050-circa 1130 . . . . .DLB-148

Old High German Charms
and Blessings DLB-148; CDWLB-2

The *Old High German Isidor*
circa 790-800 . . . . .DLB-148

Petruslied circa 854? DLB-148

Physiologus circa 1070-circa 1150 . . . . . .DLB-148

Ruodlieb circa 1050-1075 . . . . .DLB-148

"*Spielmannsepen*" (circa 1152
circa 1500) DLB-148

The Strasbourg Oaths 842 . . . . .DLB-148

Tatian circa 830 . . . . .DLB-148

Waltharius circa 825 . . . . .DLB-148

Wessobrunner Gebet circa 787-815 . . . . . .DLB-148

German Theater
German Drama 800-1280 . . . . .DLB-138

German Drama from Naturalism
to Fascism: 1889-1933 . . . . .DLB-118

Gernsback, Hugo 1884-1967 . . . . .DLB-8, 137

Gerould, Katharine Fullerton
1879-1944 . . . . .DLB-78

Samuel Gerrish [publishing house] DLB-49

Gerrold, David 1944- DLB-8

Gershwin, Ira 1896-1983 . . . . .DLB-265

The Ira Gershwin Centenary Y-96

Gerson, Jean 1363-1429 . . . . .DLB-208

Gersonides 1288-1344 . . . . .DLB-115

Gerstäcker, Friedrich 1816-1872 . . . . .DLB-129

Gertsen, Aleksandr Ivanovich
(see Herzen, Alexander)

Gerstenberg, Heinrich Wilhelm von
1737-1823 . . . . .DLB-97

Gervinus, Georg Gottfried
1805-1871 . . . . .DLB-133

Gery, John 1953- DLB-282

Geßner, Solomon 1730-1788 . . . . .DLB-97

Geston, Mark S. 1946- DLB-8

Al-Ghazali 1058-1111 . . . . .DLB-115

Gibbings, Robert 1889-1958 . . . . .DLB-195

Gibbon, Edward 1737-1794 . . . . .DLB-104

Gibbon, John Murray 1875-1952 . . . . .DLB-92

Gibbon, Lewis Grassic (see Mitchell, James Leslie)

Gibbons, Floyd 1887-1939 . . . . .DLB-25

Gibbons, Reginald 1947- DLB-120

Gibbons, William ?-? DLB-73

Gibson, Charles Dana
1867-1944 . . . . .DLB-188; DS-13

Gibson, Graeme 1934- DLB-53

Gibson, Margaret 1944- DLB-120

Gibson, Margaret Dunlop 1843-1920 . . . .DLB-174

Gibson, Wilfrid 1878-1962 . . . . .DLB-19

The Friends of the Dymock Poets Y-00

Gibson, William 1914- DLB-7

Gibson, William 1948- DLB-251

Gide, André 1869-1951 . . . . .DLB-65

Giguère, Diane 1937- DLB-53

Giguère, Roland 1929- DLB-60

Gil de Biedma, Jaime 1929-1990 . . . . . . .DLB-108

Gil-Albert, Juan 1906-1994 . . . . .DLB-134

Gilbert, Anthony 1899-1973 . . . . .DLB-77

Gilbert, Sir Humphrey 1537-1583 . . . . . . .DLB-136

Gilbert, Michael 1912- DLB-87

Gilbert, Sandra M. 1936- DLB-120, 246

Gilchrist, Alexander 1828-1861 . . . . .DLB-144

Gilchrist, Ellen 1935- DLB-130

Gilder, Jeannette L. 1849-1916 . . . . .DLB-79

Gilder, Richard Watson 1844-1909 . . . .DLB-64, 79

Gildersleeve, Basil 1831-1924 . . . . .DLB-71

Giles, Henry 1809-1882 . . . . .DLB-64

Giles of Rome circa 1243-1316 . . . . .DLB-115

Gilfillan, George 1813-1878 . . . . .DLB-144

Gill, Eric 1882-1940 . . . . .DLB-98

Gill, Sarah Prince 1728-1771 . . . . .DLB-200

William F. Gill Company DLB-49

Gillespie, A. Lincoln, Jr. 1895-1950 . . . . . . .DLB-4

Gillespie, Haven 1883-1975 . . . . .DLB-265

Gilliam, Florence ?-? DLB-4

Gilliatt, Penelope 1932-1993 . . . . .DLB-14

Gillott, Jacky 1939-1980 . . . . .DLB-14

Gilman, Caroline H. 1794-1888 . . . . . . .DLB-3, 73

Gilman, Charlotte Perkins 1860-1935 . . . .DLB-221

The Charlotte Perkins Gilman Society . . . Y-99

W. and J. Gilman [publishing house] DLB-49

Gilmer, Elizabeth Meriwether
1861-1951 . . . . .DLB-29

Gilmer, Francis Walker 1790-1826 . . . . . . .DLB-37

Gilmore, Mary 1865-1962 . . . . .DLB-260

Gilroy, Frank D. 1925- DLB-7

Gimferrer, Pere (Pedro) 1945- DLB-134

Gingrich, Arnold 1903-1976 . . . . .DLB-137

Prospectus From the Initial Issue of
Esquire (Autumn 1933) DLB-137

"With the Editorial Ken," Prospectus
From the Initial Issue of *Ken*
(7 April 1938) DLB-137

Ginsberg, Allen
1926-1997 . . . .DLB-5, 16, 169, 237; CDALB-1

Ginzburg, Natalia 1916-1991 . . . . .DLB-177

Ginzkey, Franz Karl 1871-1963 . . . . .DLB-81

Gioia, Dana 1950- DLB-120, 282

Giono, Jean 1895-1970 . . . . .DLB-72

Giotti, Virgilio 1885-1957 . . . . .DLB-114

Giovanni, Nikki 1943- DLB-5, 41; CDALB-7

Gipson, Lawrence Henry 1880-1971 . . . . . .DLB-17

Girard, Rodolphe 1879-1956 . . . . .DLB-92

Giraudoux, Jean 1882-1944 . . . . .DLB-65

Girondo, Oliverio 1891-1967 . . . . .DLB-283

Gissing, George 1857-1903 . . . . .DLB-18, 135, 184

The Place of Realism in Fiction (1895) .DLB-18

Giudici, Giovanni 1924- DLB-128

Giuliani, Alfredo 1924- DLB-128

Glackens, William J. 1870-1938 . . . . .DLB-188

Gladkov, Fedor Vasil'evich 1883-1958 . . .DLB-272

Gladstone, William Ewart
1809-1898 . . . . DLB-57, 184

Glaeser, Ernst 1902-1963 . . . . .DLB-69

Glancy, Diane 1941- DLB-175

Glanvill, Joseph 1636-1680 . . . . .DLB-252

Glanville, Brian 1931- DLB-15, 139

Glapthorne, Henry 1610-1643? DLB-58

Glasgow, Ellen 1873-1945 . . . . .DLB-9, 12

The Ellen Glasgow Society Y-01

Glasier, Katharine Bruce 1867-1950 . . . . . .DLB-190

Glaspell, Susan 1876-1948 . . . . . .DLB-7, 9, 78, 228

Glass, Montague 1877-1934 . . . . .DLB-11

Glassco, John 1909-1981 . . . . .DLB-68

Glauser, Friedrich 1896-1938 . . . . .DLB-56

F. Gleason's Publishing Hall DLB-49

Gleim, Johann Wilhelm Ludwig
1719-1803 . . . . .DLB-97

Glendinning, Victoria 1937- DLB-155

Glidden, Frederick Dilley (Luke Short)
1908-1975 . . . . .DLB-256

Glinka, Fedor Nikolaevich 1786-1880 . . . .DLB-205

Glover, Keith 1966- DLB-249

Glover, Richard 1712-1785 . . . . .DLB-95

Glück, Louise 1943- DLB-5

Glyn, Elinor 1864-1943 . . . . .DLB-153

Gnedich, Nikolai Ivanovich 1784-1833 . . .DLB-205

Gobineau, Joseph-Arthur de 1816-1882 . . .DLB-123

Godber, John 1956- DLB-233

Godbout, Jacques 1933- DLB-53

Goddard, Morrill 1865-1937 . . . . .DLB-25

Goddard, William 1740-1817 . . . . .DLB-43

Godden, Rumer 1907-1998 . . . . .DLB-161

Godey, Louis A. 1804-1878 . . . . DLB-73

Godey and McMichael DLB-49

Godfrey, Dave 1938- DLB-60

Godfrey, Thomas 1736-1763 . . . . DLB-31

Godine, David R., Publisher DLB-46

Godkin, E. L. 1831-1902 . . . . DLB-79

Godolphin, Sidney 1610-1643 . . . . DLB-126

Godwin, Gail 1937- DLB-6, 234

M. J. Godwin and Company DLB-154

Godwin, Mary Jane Clairmont
1766-1841 . . . . DLB-163

Godwin, Parke 1816-1904 . . . . DLB-3, 64, 250

Godwin, William 1756-1836 . . . . DLB-39, 104,
142, 158, 163, 262; CDBLB-3

Preface to *St. Leon* (1799) DLB-39

Goering, Reinhard 1887-1936 . . . . DLB-118

Goes, Albrecht 1908- DLB-69

Goethe, Johann Wolfgang von
1749-1832 . . . . DLB-94; CDWLB-2

Goetz, Curt 1888-1960 . . . . DLB-124

Goffe, Thomas circa 1592-1629 . . . . DLB-58

Goffstein, M. B. 1940- DLB-61

Gogarty, Oliver St. John 1878-1957 . . . DLB-15, 19

Gogol, Nikolai Vasil'evich 1809-1852 . . . DLB-198

Goines, Donald 1937-1974 . . . . DLB-33

Gold, Herbert 1924- DLB-2; Y-81

Tribute to William Saroyan Y-81

Gold, Michael 1893-1967 . . . . DLB-9, 28

Goldbarth, Albert 1948- DLB-120

Goldberg, Dick 1947- DLB-7

Golden Cockerel Press DLB-112

Golding, Arthur 1536-1606 . . . . DLB-136

Golding, Louis 1895-1958 . . . . DLB-195

Golding, William 1911-1993
. . . . DLB-15, 100, 255; Y-83; CDBLB-7

Nobel Lecture 1993 . . . . Y-83

The Stature of William Golding Y-83

Goldman, Emma 1869-1940 . . . . DLB-221

Goldman, William 1931- DLB-44

Goldring, Douglas 1887-1960 . . . . DLB-197

Goldsmith, Oliver 1730?-1774
. . . . DLB-39, 89, 99. 104, 109, 142; CDBLB-2

Goldsmith, Oliver 1794-1861 . . . . DLB-99

Goldsmith Publishing Company DLB-46

Goldstein, Richard 1944- DLB-185

Gollancz, Sir Israel 1864-1930 . . . . DLB-201

Victor Gollancz Limited DLB-112

Gomberville, Marin Le Roy, sieur de
1600?-1674 . . . . DLB-268

Gombrowicz, Witold
1904-1969 . . . . DLB-215; CDWLB-4

Gómez-Quiñones, Juan 1942- DLB-122

Laurence James Gomme
[publishing house] DLB-46

Goncharov, Ivan Aleksandrovich
1812-1891 . . . . DLB-238

Goncourt, Edmond de 1822-1896 . . . . . . DLB-123

Goncourt, Jules de 1830-1870 . . . . DLB-123

Gonzales, Rodolfo "Corky" 1928- DLB-122

Gonzales-Berry, Erlinda 1942- DLB-209

"Chicano Language" DLB-82

González, Angel 1925- DLB-108

Gonzalez, Genaro 1949- DLB-122

Gonzalez, Ray 1952- DLB-122

González de Mireles, Jovita
1899-1983 . . . . DLB-122

González-T., César A. 1931- DLB-82

Goodis, David 1917-1967 . . . . DLB-226

Goodison, Lorna 1947- DLB-157

Goodman, Allegra 1967- DLB-244

Goodman, Nelson 1906-1998 . . . . .DLB-279

Goodman, Paul 1911-1972 . . . . DLB-130, 246

The Goodman Theatre DLB-7

Goodrich, Frances 1891-1984 . . . . DLB-26

Goodrich, Samuel Griswold
1793-1860 . . . . .DLB-1, 42, 73, 243

S. G. Goodrich [publishing house] DLB-49

C. E. Goodspeed and Company DLB-49

Goodwin, Stephen 1943- Y-82

Googe, Barnabe 1540-1594 . . . . DLB-132

Gookin, Daniel 1612-1687 . . . . DLB-24

Goran, Lester 1928- DLB-244

Gordimer, Nadine 1923- DLB-225; Y-91

Nobel Lecture 1991 . . . . Y-91

Gordon, Adam Lindsay 1833-1870 . . . . . DLB-230

Gordon, Caroline
1895-1981 . . . . . . .DLB-4, 9, 102; DS-17; Y-81

Gordon, Charles F. (see OyamO)

Gordon, Charles William (see Connor, Ralph)

Gordon, Giles 1940- DLB-14, 139, 207

Gordon, Helen Cameron, Lady Russell
1867-1949 . . . . DLB-195

Gordon, Lyndall 1941- DLB-155

Gordon, Mack 1904-1959 . . . . DLB-265

Gordon, Mary 1949- DLB-6; Y-81

Gordone, Charles 1925-1995 . . . . DLB-7

Gore, Catherine 1800-1861 . . . . DLB-116

Gore-Booth, Eva 1870-1926 . . . . DLB-240

Gores, Joe 1931- DLB-226; Y-02

Tribute to Kenneth Millar Y-83

Tribute to Raymond Chandler Y-88

Gorey, Edward 1925-2000 . . . . DLB-61

Gorgias of Leontini
circa 485 B.C.-376 B.C. DLB-176

Görres, Joseph 1776-1848 . . . . DLB-90

Gosse, Edmund 1849-1928 . . . . . DLB-57, 144, 184

Gosson, Stephen 1554-1624 . . . . .DLB-172

The Schoole of Abuse (1579) DLB-172

Gotanda, Philip Kan 1951- DLB-266

Gotlieb, Phyllis 1926- DLB-88, 251

Go-Toba 1180-1239 . . . . DLB-203

Gottfried von Straßburg
died before 1230 . . . . . . DLB-138; CDWLB-2

Gotthelf, Jeremias 1797-1854 . . . . DLB-133

Gottschalk circa 804/808-869 . . . . DLB-148

Gottsched, Johann Christoph
1700-1766 . . . . DLB-97

Götz, Johann Nikolaus 1721-1781 . . . . DLB-97

Goudge, Elizabeth 1900-1984 . . . . DLB-191

Gough, John B. 1817-1886 . . . . DLB-243

Gould, Wallace 1882-1940 . . . . DLB-54

Govoni, Corrado 1884-1965 . . . . DLB-114

Gower, John circa 1330-1408 . . . . DLB-146

Goyen, William 1915-1983 . . . .DLB-2, 218; Y-83

Goytisolo, José Augustín 1928- DLB-134

Gozzano, Guido 1883-1916 . . . . DLB-114

Grabbe, Christian Dietrich 1801-1836 . . . DLB-133

Gracq, Julien (Louis Poirier) 1910- DLB-83

Grady, Henry W. 1850-1889 . . . . DLB-23

Graf, Oskar Maria 1894-1967 . . . . DLB-56

Graf Rudolf between circa 1170 and
circa 1185 . . . . DLB-148

Graff, Gerald 1937- DLB-246

Richard Grafton [publishing house] DLB-170

Grafton, Sue 1940- DLB-226

Graham, Frank 1893-1965 . . . . DLB-241

Graham, George Rex 1813-1894 . . . . DLB-73

Graham, Gwethalyn (Gwethalyn Graham
Erichsen-Brown) 1913-1965 . . . . DLB-88

Graham, Jorie 1951- DLB-120

Graham, Katharine 1917-2001 . . . . .DLB-127

Graham, Lorenz 1902-1989 . . . . DLB-76

Graham, Philip 1915-1963 . . . . .DLB-127

Graham, R. B. Cunninghame
1852-1936 . . . . .DLB-98, 135, 174

Graham, Shirley 1896-1977 . . . . DLB-76

Graham, Stephen 1884-1975 . . . . DLB-195

Graham, W. S. 1918-1986 . . . . DLB-20

William H. Graham [publishing house] . . . DLB-49

Graham, Winston 1910- DLB-77

Grahame, Kenneth 1859-1932 . . .DLB-34, 141, 178

Grainger, Martin Allerdale 1874-1941 . . . . DLB-92

Gramatky, Hardie 1907-1979 . . . . DLB-22

Grand, Sarah 1854-1943 . . . . .DLB-135, 197

Grandbois, Alain 1900-1975 . . . . DLB-92

Grandson, Oton de circa 1345-1397 . . . . . DLB-208

Grange, John circa 1556-? DLB-136

Granger, Thomas 1578-1627 . . . . DLB-281

Granich, Irwin (see Gold, Michael)

Granovsky, Timofei Nikolaevich
1813-1855 . . . . DLB-198

Grant, Anne MacVicar 1755-1838 . . . . . . DLB-200

Grant, Duncan 1885-1978 . . . . .DS-10

Grant, George 1918-1988 . . . . DLB-88

Grant, George Monro 1835-1902 . . . . DLB-99

Grant, Harry J. 1881-1963 . . . . DLB-29

Grant, James Edward 1905-1966 . . . . DLB-26

Grant, John (see Gash, Jonathan)

War of the Words (and Pictures): The Creation of a Graphic Novel Y-02

Grass, Günter 1927-   ...DLB-75, 124; CDWLB-2

Nobel Lecture 1999: "To Be Continued ..." Y-99

Tribute to Helen Wolff Y-94

Grasty, Charles H. 1863-1924 .... DLB-25

Grau, Shirley Ann 1929- DLB-2, 218

Graves, John 1920- Y-83

Graves, Richard 1715-1804 .... DLB-39

Graves, Robert 1895-1985 ...DLB-20, 100, 191; DS-18; Y-85; CDBLB-6

The St. John's College Robert Graves Trust Y-96

Gray, Alasdair 1934- DLB-194, 261

Gray, Asa 1810-1888 .... DLB-1, 235

Gray, David 1838-1861 .... DLB-32

Gray, Simon 1936- DLB-13

Gray, Thomas 1716-1771 .....DLB-109; CDBLB-2

Grayson, Richard 1951- DLB-234

Grayson, William J. 1788-1863 ....DLB-3, 64, 248

The Great Bibliographers Series Y-93

The Great Gatsby (Documentary) DLB-219

"The Greatness of Southern Literature": League of the South Institute for the Study of Southern Culture and History Y-02

Grech, Nikolai Ivanovich 1787-1867 .....DLB-198

Greeley, Horace 1811-1872 ...DLB-3, 43, 189, 250

Green, Adolph 1915-2002 ....DLB-44, 265

Green, Anna Katharine 1846-1935 ....DLB-202, 221

Green, Duff 1791-1875 ....DLB-43

Green, Elizabeth Shippen 1871-1954 .....DLB-188

Green, Gerald 1922- DLB-28

Green, Henry 1905-1973 .... DLB-15

Green, Jonas 1712-1767 .... DLB-31

Green, Joseph 1706-1780 .... DLB-31

Green, Julien 1900-1998 .... DLB-4, 72

Green, Paul 1894-1981 ...... DLB-7, 9, 249; Y-81

Green, T. H. 1836-1882 ....DLB-190, 262

Green, Terence M. 1947- DLB-251

T. and S. Green [publishing house] DLB-49

Green Tiger Press DLB-46

Timothy Green [publishing house] DLB-49

Greenaway, Kate 1846-1901 ....DLB-141

Greenberg: Publisher DLB-46

Greene, Asa 1789-1838 ....DLB-11

Greene, Belle da Costa 1883-1950 ......DLB-187

Greene, Graham 1904-1991 ....DLB-13, 15, 77, 100, 162, 201, 204; Y-85, 91; CDBLB-7

Tribute to Christopher Isherwood Y-86

Greene, Robert 1558-1592 ....DLB-62, 167

Greene, Robert Bernard (Bob), Jr. 1947- DLB-185

Benjamin H Greene [publishing house] DLB-49

Greenfield, George 1917-2000 .... Y-91, 00

Derek Robinson's Review of George Greenfield's *Rich Dust* Y-02

Greenhow, Robert 1800-1854 ....DLB-30

Greenlee, William B. 1872-1953 ....DLB-187

Greenough, Horatio 1805-1852 ......DLB-1, 235

Greenwell, Dora 1821-1882 ....DLB-35, 199

Greenwillow Books DLB-46

Greenwood, Grace (see Lippincott, Sara Jane Clarke)

Greenwood, Walter 1903-1974 ......DLB-10, 191

Greer, Ben 1948- DLB-6

Greflinger, Georg 1620?-1677 ....DLB-164

Greg, W. R. 1809-1881 ....DLB-55

Greg, W. W. 1875-1959 ....DLB-201

Gregg, Josiah 1806-1850 ....DLB-183, 186

Gregg Press DLB-46

Gregory, Horace 1898-1982 ....DLB-48

Gregory, Isabella Augusta Persse, Lady 1852-1932 ....DLB-10

Gregory of Rimini circa 1300-1358 ......DLB-115

Gregynog Press DLB-112

Greiff, León de 1895-1976 ....DLB-283

Greiffenberg, Catharina Regina von 1633-1694 ....DLB-168

Greig, Noël 1944- DLB-245

Grenfell, Wilfred Thomason 1865-1940 ....DLB-92

Gress, Elsa 1919-1988 ....DLB-214

Greve, Felix Paul (see Grove, Frederick Philip)

Greville, Fulke, First Lord Brooke 1554-1628 ....DLB-62, 172

Grey, Sir George, K.C.B. 1812-1898 .....DLB-184

Grey, Lady Jane 1537-1554 ....DLB-132

Grey, Zane 1872-1939 ....DLB-9, 212

Zane Grey's West Society Y-00

Grey Owl (Archibald Stansfeld Belaney) 1888-1938 ....DLB-92; DS-17

Grey Walls Press DLB-112

Griboedov, Aleksandr Sergeevich 1795?-1829 ....DLB-205

Grice, Paul 1913-1988 ....DLB-279

Grier, Eldon 1917- DLB-88

Grieve, C. M. (see MacDiarmid, Hugh)

Griffin, Bartholomew flourished 1596....DLB-172

Griffin, Bryan

"Panic Among the Philistines": A Postscript, An Interview with Bryan Griffin Y-81

Griffin, Gerald 1803-1840 ....DLB-159

The Griffin Poetry Prize Y-00

Griffith, Elizabeth 1727?-1793 ....DLB-39, 89

Preface to *The Delicate Distress* (1769) ...DLB-39

Griffith, George 1857-1906 ....DLB-178

Ralph Griffiths [publishing house] DLB-154

Griffiths, Trevor 1935- DLB-13, 245

S. C. Griggs and Company DLB-49

Griggs, Sutton Elbert 1872-1930 ....DLB-50

Grignon, Claude-Henri 1894-1976.......DLB-68

Grigor'ev, Apollon Aleksandrovich 1822-1864 ....DLB-277

Grigorovich, Dmitrii Vasil'evich 1822-1899 ....DLB-238

Grigson, Geoffrey 1905-1985 ....DLB-27

Grillparzer, Franz 1791-1872 ....DLB-133; CDWLB-2

Grimald, Nicholas circa 1519-circa 1562..............DLB-136

Grimké, Angelina Weld 1880-1958....DLB-50, 54

Grimké, Sarah Moore 1792-1873 ....DLB-239

Grimm, Hans 1875-1959 ....DLB-66

Grimm, Jacob 1785-1863 ....DLB-90

Grimm, Wilhelm 1786-1859 ....DLB-90; CDWLB-2

Grimmelshausen, Johann Jacob Christoffel von 1621 or 1622-1676 .....DLB-168; CDWLB-2

Grimshaw, Beatrice Ethel 1871-1953 .....DLB-174

Grin, Aleksandr Stepanovich 1880-1932 ....DLB-272

Grindal, Edmund 1519 or 1520-1583 ....DLB-132

Gripe, Maria (Kristina) 1923- DLB-257

Griswold, Rufus Wilmot 1815-1857 ....DLB-3, 59, 250

Grosart, Alexander Balloch 1827-1899 ...DLB-184

Grosholz, Emily 1950- DLB-282

Gross, Milt 1895-1953 ....DLB-11

Grosset and Dunlap DLB-49

Grosseteste, Robert circa 1160-1253 .....DLB-115

Grossman, Allen 1932- DLB-193

Grossman, Vasilii Semenovich 1905-1964 ....DLB-272

Grossman Publishers DLB-46

Grosvenor, Gilbert H. 1875-1966 ....DLB-91

Groth, Klaus 1819-1899 ....DLB-129

Groulx, Lionel 1878-1967 ....DLB-68

Grove, Frederick Philip (Felix Paul Greve) 1879-1948 ....DLB-92

Grove Press DLB-46

Groys, Boris Efimovich 1947- DLB-285

Grubb, Davis 1919-1980 ....DLB-6

Gruelle, Johnny 1880-1938 ....DLB-22

von Grumbach, Argula 1492-after 1563? DLB-179

Grymeston, Elizabeth before 1563-before 1604 ....DLB-136

Gryphius, Andreas 1616-1664 ....DLB-164; CDWLB-2

Gryphius, Christian 1649-1706 ....DLB-168

Guare, John 1938- DLB-7, 249

Guberman, Igor Mironovich 1936- DLB-285

Guerra, Tonino 1920- DLB-128

Guest, Barbara 1920- DLB-5, 193

Guèvremont, Germaine 1893-1968 ....DLB-68

Guglielminetti, Amalia 1881-1941 ....DLB-264

Guidacci, Margherita 1921-1992 ....DLB-128

Guillén, Jorge 1893-1984 ....DLB-108

Guillén, Nicolás 1902-1989 ....DLB-283

Guilloux, Louis 1899-1980 . . . . DLB-72

Guilpin, Everard circa 1572-after 1608? . . DLB-136

Guiney, Louise Imogen 1861-1920 . . . . . . DLB-54

Guiterman, Arthur 1871-1943 . . . . DLB-11

Günderrode, Caroline von
1780-1806 . . . . DLB-90

Gundulić, Ivan 1589-1638 . . .DLB-147; CDWLB-4

Gunesekera, Romesh 1954- DLB-267

Gunn, Bill 1934-1989 . . . . DLB-38

Gunn, James E. 1923- DLB-8

Gunn, Neil M. 1891-1973 . . . . DLB-15

Gunn, Thom 1929- DLB-27; CDBLB-8

Gunnars, Kristjana 1948- DLB-60

Günther, Johann Christian 1695-1723 . . . DLB-168

Gurik, Robert 1932- DLB-60

Gurney, A. R. 1930- DLB-266

Gurney, Ivor 1890-1937 . . . . Y-02

The Ivor Gurney Society Y-98

Gustafson, Ralph 1909-1995 . . . . DLB-88

Gustafsson, Lars 1936- DLB-257

Gütersloh, Albert Paris 1887-1973 . . . . DLB-81

Guthrie, A. B., Jr. 1901-1991 . . . . DLB-6, 212

Guthrie, Ramon 1896-1973 . . . . DLB-4

Guthrie, Thomas Anstey (see Anstey, FC)

The Guthrie Theater DLB-7

Gutzkow, Karl 1811-1878 . . . . DLB-133

Guy, Ray 1939- DLB-60

Guy, Rosa 1925- DLB-33

Guyot, Arnold 1807-1884 . . . . .DS-13

Gwynn, R. S. 1948- DLB-282

Gwynne, Erskine 1898-1948 . . . . DLB-4

Gyles, John 1680-1755 . . . . DLB-99

Gyllensten, Lars 1921- DLB-257

Gysin, Brion 1916-1986 . . . . DLB-16

H

H.D. (see Doolittle, Hilda)

Habermas, Jürgen 1929- DLB-242

Habington, William 1605-1654 . . . . DLB-126

Hacker, Marilyn 1942- DLB-120, 282

Hackett, Albert 1900-1995 . . . . DLB-26

Hacks, Peter 1928- DLB-124

Hadas, Rachel 1948- DLB-120, 282

Hadden, Briton 1898-1929 . . . . DLB-91

Hagedorn, Friedrich von 1708-1754 . . . . . DLB-168

Hagelstange, Rudolf 1912-1984 . . . . DLB-69

Haggard, H. Rider
1856-1925 . . . . DLB-70, 156, 174, 178

Haggard, William (Richard Clayton)
1907-1993 . . . . .DLB-276; Y-93

Hagy, Alyson 1960- DLB-244

Hahn-Hahn, Ida Gräfin von 1805-1880 . . DLB-133

Haig-Brown, Roderick 1908-1976 . . . . DLB-88

Haight, Gordon S. 1901-1985 . . . . DLB-103

Hailey, Arthur 1920- DLB-88; Y-82

Haines, John 1924- DLB-5, 212

Hake, Edward flourished 1566-1604 . . . . DLB-136

Hake, Thomas Gordon 1809-1895 . . . . . . DLB-32

Hakluyt, Richard 1552?-1616 . . . . DLB-136

Halas, František 1901-1949 . . . . DLB-215

Halbe, Max 1865-1944 . . . . DLB-118

Halberstam, David 1934- DLB-241

Haldane, Charlotte 1894-1969 . . . . DLB-191

Haldane, J. B. S. 1892-1964 . . . . DLB-160

Haldeman, Joe 1943- DLB-8

Haldeman-Julius Company DLB-46

Hale, E. J., and Son DLB-49

Hale, Edward Everett
1822-1909 . . . . .DLB-1, 42, 74, 235

Hale, Janet Campbell 1946- DLB-175

Hale, Kathleen 1898-2000 . . . . DLB-160

Hale, Leo Thomas (see Ebon)

Hale, Lucretia Peabody 1820-1900 . . . . . . DLB-42

Hale, Nancy
1908-1988 . . . . .DLB-86; DS-17; Y-80, 88

Hale, Sarah Josepha (Buell)
1788-1879 . . . . .DLB-1, 42, 73, 243

Hale, Susan 1833-1910 . . . . DLB-221

Hales, John 1584-1656 . . . . DLB-151

Halévy, Ludovic 1834-1908 . . . . DLB-192

Haley, Alex 1921-1992 . . . . DLB-38; CDALB-7

Haliburton, Thomas Chandler
1796-1865 . . . . DLB-11, 99

Hall, Adam (Trevor Dudley-Smith)
1920-1995 . . . . .DLB-276

Hall, Anna Maria 1800-1881 . . . . DLB-159

Hall, Donald 1928- DLB-5

Hall, Edward 1497-1547 . . . . DLB-132

Hall, Halsey 1898-1977 . . . . DLB-241

Hall, James 1793-1868 . . . . .DLB-73, 74

Hall, Joseph 1574-1656 . . . . DLB-121, 151

Hall, Radclyffe 1880-1943 . . . . DLB-191

Hall, Sarah Ewing 1761-1830 . . . . DLB-200

Hall, Stuart 1932- DLB-242

Samuel Hall [publishing house] DLB-49

Hallam, Arthur Henry 1811-1833 . . . . . . DLB-32

On Some of the Characteristics of
Modern Poetry and On the
Lyrical Poems of Alfred
Tennyson (1831) DLB-32

Halleck, Fitz-Greene 1790-1867 . . . . . . DLB-3, 250

Haller, Albrecht von 1708-1777 . . . . DLB-168

Halliday, Brett (see Dresser, Davis)

Halliwell-Phillipps, James Orchard
1820-1889 . . . . DLB-184

Hallmann, Johann Christian
1640-1704 or 1716? DLB-168

Hallmark Editions DLB-46

Halper, Albert 1904-1984 . . . . DLB-9

Halperin, John William 1941- DLB-111

Halstead, Murat 1829-1908 . . . . DLB-23

Hamann, Johann Georg 1730-1788 . . . . DLB-97

Hamburger, Michael 1924- DLB-27

Hamilton, Alexander 1712-1756 . . . . . . DLB-31

Hamilton, Alexander 1755?-1804 . . . . . . DLB-37

Hamilton, Cicely 1872-1952 . . . . .DLB-10, 197

Hamilton, Edmond 1904-1977 . . . . DLB-8

Hamilton, Elizabeth 1758-1816 . . . . .DLB-116, 158

Hamilton, Gail (see Corcoran, Barbara)

Hamilton, Gail (see Dodge, Mary Abigail)

Hamish Hamilton Limited DLB-112

Hamilton, Hugo 1953- DLB-267

Hamilton, Ian 1938-2001 . . . . DLB-40, 155

Hamilton, Janet 1795-1873 . . . . DLB-199

Hamilton, Mary Agnes 1884-1962 . . . . . .DLB-197

Hamilton, Patrick 1904-1962 . . . . .DLB-10, 191

Hamilton, Virginia 1936-2002 . . .DLB-33, 52; Y-01

Hamilton, Sir William 1788-1856 . . . . . . DLB-262

Hamilton-Paterson, James 1941- DLB-267

Hammerstein, Oscar, 2nd 1895-1960 . . . . DLB-265

Hammett, Dashiell
1894-1961 . . . DLB-226, 280; DS-6; CDALB-5

An Appeal in *TAC* Y-91

The Glass Key and Other Dashiell
Hammett Mysteries Y-96

Knopf to Hammett: The Editoral
Correspondence Y-00

Hammon, Jupiter 1711-died between
1790 and 1806 . . . . DLB-31, 50

Hammond, John ?-1663 . . . . DLB-24

Hamner, Earl 1923- DLB-6

Hampson, John 1901-1955 . . . . DLB-191

Hampton, Christopher 1946- DLB-13

Handel-Mazzetti, Enrica von 1871-1955 . . . DLB-81

Handke, Peter 1942- DLB-85, 124

Handlin, Oscar 1915- DLB-17

Hankin, St. John 1869-1909 . . . . DLB-10

Hanley, Clifford 1922- DLB-14

Hanley, James 1901-1985 . . . . DLB-191

Hannah, Barry 1942- DLB-6, 234

Hannay, James 1827-1873 . . . . DLB-21

Hano, Arnold 1922- DLB-241

Hansberry, Lorraine
1930-1965 . . . . .DLB-7, 38; CDALB-1

Hansen, Martin A. 1909-1955 . . . . DLB-214

Hansen, Thorkild 1927-1989 . . . . DLB-214

Hanson, Elizabeth 1684-1737 . . . . DLB-200

Hapgood, Norman 1868-1937 . . . . DLB-91

Happel, Eberhard Werner 1647-1690 . . . . DLB-168

Harbach, Otto 1873-1963 . . . . DLB-265

The Harbinger 1845-1849 . . . . DLB-1, 223

Harburg, E. Y. "Yip" 1896-1981 . . . . DLB-265

Harcourt Brace Jovanovich DLB-46

Hardenberg, Friedrich von (see Novalis)

Harding, Walter 1917- DLB-111

Hardwick, Elizabeth 1916- DLB-6

Hardy, Alexandre 1572?-1632 . . . . .DLB-268

Hardy, Frank 1917-1994 . . . . DLB-260

Hardy, Thomas
1840-1928 . . . . . . .DLB-18, 19, 135; CDBLB-5

"Candour in English Fiction" (1890). . .DLB-18

Hare, Cyril 1900-1958. . . . . .DLB-77

Hare, David 1947- DLB-13

Hare, R. M. 1919-2002 . . . . .DLB-262

Hargrove, Marion 1919- DLB-11

Häring, Georg Wilhelm Heinrich
(see Alexis, Willibald)

Harington, Donald 1935- DLB-152

Harington, Sir John 1560-1612 . . . . .DLB-136

Harjo, Joy 1951- DLB-120, 175

Harkness, Margaret (John Law)
1854-1923 .DLB-197

Harley, Edward, second Earl of Oxford
1689-1741 . . . . .DLB-213

Harley, Robert, first Earl of Oxford
1661-1724 . . . . .DLB-213

Harlow, Robert 1923- DLB-60

Harman, Thomas flourished 1566-1573 . .DLB-136

Harness, Charles L. 1915- DLB-8

Harnett, Cynthia 1893-1981 . . . . .DLB-161

Harnick, Sheldon 1924- DLB-265

Tribute to Ira Gershwin Y-96

Tribute to Lorenz Hart Y-95

Harper, Edith Alice Mary (see Wickham, Anna)

Harper, Fletcher 1806-1877 . . . . .DLB-79

Harper, Frances Ellen Watkins
1825-1911 . . . . .DLB-50, 221

Harper, Michael S. 1938- DLB-41

Harper and Brothers DLB-49

Harpur, Charles 1813-1868. . . . . .DLB-230

Harraden, Beatrice 1864-1943 . . . . .DLB-153

George G. Harrap and Company
Limited DLB-112

Harriot, Thomas 1560-1621 . . . . .DLB-136

Harris, Alexander 1805-1874. . . . . .DLB-230

Harris, Benjamin ?-circa 1720 . . . . .DLB-42, 43

Harris, Christie 1907-2002. . . . . .DLB-88

Harris, Errol E. 1908- DLB-279

Harris, Frank 1856-1931 . . . . DLB-156, 197

Harris, George Washington
1814-1869 . . . . .DLB-3, 11, 248

Harris, Joanne 1964- DLB-271

Harris, Joel Chandler
1848-1908 . . . . DLB-11, 23, 42, 78, 91

The Joel Chandler Harris Association. . . . Y-99

Harris, Mark 1922- DLB-2; Y-80

Tribute to Frederick A. Pottle Y-87

Harris, William Torrey 1835-1909 . . . . . .DLB-270

Harris, Wilson 1921- DLB-117; CDWLB-3

Harrison, Mrs. Burton
(see Harrison, Constance Cary)

Harrison, Charles Yale 1898-1954. . . . . . .DLB-68

Harrison, Constance Cary 1843-1920. . . .DLB-221

Harrison, Frederic 1831-1923 . . . . DLB-57, 190

"On Style in English Prose" (1898). . . .DLB-57

Harrison, Harry 1925- DLB-8

James P. Harrison Company DLB-49

Harrison, Jim 1937- Y-82

Harrison, M. John 1945- DLB-261

Harrison, Mary St. Leger Kingsley
(see Malet, Lucas)

Harrison, Paul Carter 1936- DLB-38

Harrison, Susan Frances 1859-1935. . . . . .DLB-99

Harrison, Tony 1937- DLB-40, 245

Harrison, William 1535-1593 . . . . .DLB-136

Harrison, William 1933- DLB-234

Harrisse, Henry 1829-1910 . . . . .DLB-47

The Harry Ransom Humanities Research Center
at the University of Texas at Austin Y-00

Harryman, Carla 1952- DLB-193

Harsdörffer, Georg Philipp 1607-1658. . . .DLB-164

Harsent, David 1942- DLB-40

Hart, Albert Bushnell 1854-1943 . . . . .DLB-17

Hart, Anne 1768-1834 . . . . .DLB-200

Hart, Elizabeth 1771-1833 . . . . .DLB-200

Hart, Julia Catherine 1796-1867. . . . . .DLB-99

Hart, Lorenz 1895-1943. . . . . .DLB-265

Larry Hart: Still an Influence Y-95

Lorenz Hart: An American Lyricist Y-95

The Lorenz Hart Centenary Y-95

Hart, Moss 1904-1961 . . . . DLB-7, 266

Hart, Oliver 1723-1795 . . . . .DLB-31

Rupert Hart-Davis Limited DLB-112

Harte, Bret 1836-1902
. . . . DLB-12, 64, 74, 79, 186; CDALB-3

Harte, Edward Holmead 1922- DLB-127

Harte, Houston Harriman 1927- DLB-127

Hartlaub, Felix 1913-1945 . . . . .DLB-56

Hartlebon, Otto Erich 1864-1905 . . . . . . .DLB-118

Hartley, David 1705-1757 . . . . .DLB-252

Hartley, L. P. 1895-1972 . . . . .DLB-15, 139

Hartley, Marsden 1877-1943 . . . . .DLB-54

Hartling, Peter 1933- DLB-75

Hartman, Geoffrey H. 1929- DLB-67

Hartmann, Sadakichi 1867-1944 . . . . . . .DLB-54

Hartmann von Aue
circa 1160-circa 1205. . . . DLB-138; CDWLB-2

Hartshorne, Charles 1897-2000 . . . . DLB-270

Harvey, Gabriel 1550?-1631 . . . DLB-167, 213, 281

Harvey, Jack (see Rankin, Ian)

Harvey, Jean-Charles 1891-1967 . . . . .DLB-88

Harvill Press Limited. DLB-112

Harwood, Lee 1939- DLB-40

Harwood, Ronald 1934- DLB-13

Hašek, Jaroslav 1883-1923. . . DLB-215; CDWLB-4

Haskins, Charles Homer 1870-1937 . . . . . .DLB-47

Haslam, Gerald 1937- DLB-212

Hass, Robert 1941- DLB-105, 206

Hasselstrom, Linda M. 1943- DLB-256

Hastings, Michael 1938- DLB-233

Hatar, Győző 1914- DLB-215

The Hatch-Billops Collection DLB-76

Hathaway, William 1944- DLB-120

Hauff, Wilhelm 1802-1827 . . . . .DLB-90

Haugwitz, August Adolph von
1647-1706. .DLB-168

Hauptmann, Carl 1858-1921. . . . . . . DLB-66, 118

Hauptmann, Gerhart
1862-1946 . . . . DLB-66, 118; CDWLB-2

Hauser, Marianne 1910- Y-83

Havel, Václav 1936- DLB-232; CDWLB-4

Haven, Alice B. Neal 1827-1863 . . . . . . .DLB-250

Havergal, Frances Ridley 1836-1879 . . . .DLB-199

Hawes, Stephen 1475?-before 1529 . . . . . .DLB-132

Hawker, Robert Stephen 1803-1875 . . . . .DLB-32

Hawkes, John
1925-1998 . . . . .DLB-2, 7, 227; Y-80, Y-98

John Hawkes: A Tribute. Y-98

Tribute to Donald Barthelme Y-89

Hawkesworth, John 1720-1773 . . . . .DLB-142

Hawkins, Sir Anthony Hope (see Hope, Anthony)

Hawkins, Sir John 1719-1789 . . . . . . .DLB-104, 142

Hawkins, Walter Everette 1883-? DLB-50

Hawthorne, Nathaniel 1804-1864
. . .DLB-1, 74, 183, 223, 269; DS-5; CDALB-2

The Nathaniel Hawthorne Society Y-00

The Old Manse. DLB-223

Hawthorne, Sophia Peabody
1809-1871 . . . . .DLB-183, 239

Hay, John 1835-1905. . . . . DLB-12, 47, 189

Hay, John 1915- DLB-275

Hayashi Fumiko 1903-1951. . . . . .DLB-180

Haycox, Ernest 1899-1950 . . . . .DLB-206

Haycraft, Anna Margaret (see Ellis, Alice Thomas)

Hayden, Robert
1913-1980 . . . . .DLB-5, 76; CDALB-1

Haydon, Benjamin Robert 1786-1846 . . .DLB-110

Hayes, John Michael 1919- DLB-26

Hayley, William 1745-1820 . . . . .DLB-93, 142

Haym, Rudolf 1821-1901 . . . . .DLB-129

Hayman, Robert 1575-1629. . . . . .DLB-99

Hayman, Ronald 1932- DLB-155

Hayne, Paul Hamilton
1830-1886 . . . . DLB-3, 64, 79, 248

Hays, Mary 1760-1843 . . . . .DLB-142, 158

Hayward, John 1905-1965. . . . . .DLB-201

Haywood, Eliza 1693?-1756 . . . . .DLB-39

Dedication of *Lasselia* [excerpt]
(1723) DLB-39

Preface to *The Disguis'd Prince*
[excerpt] (1723) DLB-39

The Tea-Table [excerpt] DLB-39

Willis P. Hazard [publishing house]. DLB-49

Hazlitt, William 1778-1830 . . . . DLB-110, 158

Hazzard, Shirley 1931- Y-82

Head, Bessie
1937-1986 . . . . DLB-117, 225; CDWLB-3

Headley, Joel T. 1813-1897 . . DLB-30, 183; DS-13

Heaney, Seamus 1939- . . DLB-40; Y-95; CDBLB-8

    Nobel Lecture 1994: Crediting Poetry. . . . Y-95

Heard, Nathan C. 1936- DLB-33

Hearn, Lafcadio 1850-1904 . . . . . .DLB-12, 78, 189

Hearn, Mary Anne (Marianne Farningham,
    Eva Hope) 1834-1909 . . . . DLB-240

Hearne, John 1926- DLB-117

Hearne, Samuel 1745-1792 . . . . DLB-99

Hearne, Thomas 1678?-1735 . . . . DLB-213

Hearst, William Randolph 1863-1951 . . . . DLB-25

Hearst, William Randolph, Jr.
    1908-1993 . . . . DLB-127

Heartman, Charles Frederick 1883-1953 . DLB-187

Heath, Catherine 1924- DLB-14

Heath, James Ewell 1792-1862 . . . . DLB-248

Heath, Roy A. K. 1926- DLB-117

Heath-Stubbs, John 1918- DLB-27

Heavysege, Charles 1816-1876. . . . . DLB-99

Hebbel, Friedrich
    1813-1863. . . . . DLB-129; CDWLB-2

Hebel, Johann Peter 1760-1826. . . . . DLB-90

Heber, Richard 1774-1833 . . . . DLB-184

Hébert, Anne 1916-2000. . . . . DLB-68

Hébert, Jacques 1923- DLB-53

Hecht, Anthony 1923- DLB-5, 169

Hecht, Ben 1894-1964 . . . .DLB-7, 9, 25, 26, 28, 86

Hecker, Isaac Thomas 1819-1888 . . . . DLB-1, 243

Hedge, Frederic Henry
    1805-1890 . . . . DLB-1, 59, 243; DS-5

Hefner, Hugh M. 1926- DLB-137

Hegel, Georg Wilhelm Friedrich
    1770-1831. DLB-90

Heide, Robert 1939- DLB-249

Heidish, Marcy 1947- Y-82

Heißenbüttel, Helmut 1921-1996 . . . . DLB-75

Heike monogatari DLB-203

Hein, Christoph 1944- . . . DLB-124; CDWLB-2

Hein, Piet 1905-1996 . . . . DLB-214

Heine, Heinrich 1797-1856 . . . DLB-90; CDWLB-2

Heinemann, Larry 1944- DS-9

William Heinemann Limited DLB-112

Heinesen, William 1900-1991. . . . . DLB-214

Heinlein, Robert A. 1907-1988 . . . . DLB-8

Heinrich, Willi 1920- DLB-75

Heinrich Julius of Brunswick 1564-1613 . DLB-164

Heinrich von dem Türlîn
    flourished circa 1230 . . . . DLB-138

Heinrich von Melk
    flourished after 1160 . . . . DLB-148

Heinrich von Veldeke
    circa 1145-circa 1190 . . . . DLB-138

Heinse, Wilhelm 1746-1803 . . . . DLB-94

Heinz, W. C. 1915- DLB-171

Heiskell, John 1872-1972. . . . . DLB-127

Hejinian, Lyn 1941- DLB-165

Heliand circa 850 . . . . DLB-148

Heller, Joseph
    1923-1999 . . . . . .DLB-2, 28, 227; Y-80, 99, 02

    Excerpts from Joseph Heller's
      USC Address, "The Literature
      of Despair" Y-96

    Remembering Joe Heller, by William
      Price Fox Y-99

    A Tribute to Joseph Heller. Y-99

Heller, Michael 1937- DLB-165

Hellman, Lillian 1906-1984 . . . . .DLB-7, 228; Y-84

Hellwig, Johann 1609-1674. . . . . DLB-164

Helprin, Mark 1947- Y-85; CDALB-7

Helwig, David 1938- DLB-60

Hemans, Felicia 1793-1835 . . . . DLB-96

Hemenway, Abby Maria 1828-1890 . . . . DLB-243

Hemingway, Ernest 1899-1961
    . . . . .DLB-4, 9, 102, 210; Y-81, 87, 99;
                 DS-1, 15, 16; CDALB-4

    A Centennial Celebration Y-99

    Come to Papa Y-99

    The Ernest Hemingway Collection at
      the John F. Kennedy Library. Y-99

    Ernest Hemingway Declines to
      Introduce *War and Peace*. Y-01

    Ernest Hemingway's Reaction to
      James Gould Cozzens Y-98

    Ernest Hemingway's Toronto Journalism
      Revisited: With Three Previously
      Unrecorded Stories Y-92

    Falsifying Hemingway Y-96

    Hemingway Centenary Celebration
      at the JFK Library. Y-99

    The Hemingway/Fenton
      Correspondence Y-02

    Hemingway in the JFK Y-99

    The Hemingway Letters Project
      Finds an Editor Y-02

    Hemingway Salesmen's Dummies Y-00

    Hemingway: Twenty-Five Years Later . . . Y-85

    A Literary Archaeologist Digs On:
      A Brief Interview with Michael
      Reynolds Y-99

    Not Immediately Discernible . . . but
      Eventually Quite Clear: The *First
      Light* and *Final Years* of
      Hemingway's Centenary. Y-99

    Packaging Papa: *The Garden of Eden* Y-86

    Second International Hemingway
      Colloquium: Cuba Y-98

Hémon, Louis 1880-1913. . . . . DLB-92

Hempel, Amy 1951- DLB-218

Hempel, Carl G. 1905-1997 . . . . .DLB-279

Hemphill, Paul 1936- Y-87

Hénault, Gilles 1920-1996 . . . . DLB-88

Henchman, Daniel 1689-1761 . . . . DLB-24

Henderson, Alice Corbin 1881-1949 . . . . DLB-54

Henderson, Archibald 1877-1963 . . . . . . DLB-103

Henderson, David 1942- DLB-41

Henderson, George Wylie 1904-1965 . . . . DLB-51

Henderson, Zenna 1917-1983. . . . . DLB-8

Henighan, Tom 1934- DLB-251

Henisch, Peter 1943- DLB-85

Henley, Beth 1952- Y-86

Henley, William Ernest 1849-1903 . . . . . . DLB-19

Henniker, Florence 1855-1923 . . . . DLB-135

Henning, Rachel 1826-1914 . . . . DLB-230

Henningsen, Agnes 1868-1962. . . . . DLB-214

Henry, Alexander 1739-1824 . . . . DLB-99

Henry, Buck 1930- DLB-26

Henry, Marguerite 1902-1997 . . . . DLB-22

Henry, O. (see Porter, William Sydney)

Henry, Robert Selph 1889-1970 . . . . .DLB-17

Henry, Will (see Allen, Henry W.)

Henry VIII of England 1491-1547. . . . . . DLB-132

Henry of Ghent circa 1217-1229 - 1293 . . DLB-115

Henryson, Robert
    1420s or 1430s-circa 1505 . . . . DLB-146

Henschke, Alfred (see Klabund)

Hensher, Philip 1965- DLB-267

Hensley, Sophie Almon 1866-1946 . . . . . . DLB-99

Henson, Lance 1944- DLB-175

Henty, G. A. 1832-1902. . . . . DLB-18, 141

    The Henty Society. Y-98

Hentz, Caroline Lee 1800-1856 . . . . . . DLB-3, 248

Heraclitus
    flourished circa 500 B.C. DLB-176

Herbert, Agnes circa 1880-1960. . . . . . . .DLB-174

Herbert, Alan Patrick 1890-1971 . . . . .DLB-10, 191

Herbert, Edward, Lord, of Cherbury
    1582-1648 . . . . .DLB-121, 151, 252

Herbert, Frank 1920-1986 . . . . . DLB-8; CDALB-7

Herbert, George 1593-1633 . . DLB-126; CDBLB-1

Herbert, Henry William 1807-1858 . . . . DLB-3, 73

Herbert, John 1926- DLB-53

Herbert, Mary Sidney, Countess of Pembroke
    (see Sidney, Mary)

Herbert, Xavier 1901-1984 . . . . DLB-260

Herbert, Zbigniew
    1924-1998 . . . . DLB-232; CDWLB-4

Herbst, Josephine 1892-1969 . . . . DLB-9

Herburger, Gunter 1932- DLB-75, 124

Hercules, Frank E. M. 1917-1996. . . . . . . DLB-33

Herder, Johann Gottfried 1744-1803 . . . . . DLB-97

B. Herder Book Company DLB-49

Heredia, José-María de 1842-1905 . . . . . . .DLB-217

Herford, Charles Harold 1853-1931 . . . . DLB-149

Hergesheimer, Joseph 1880-1954 . . . . . DLB-9, 102

Heritage Press. DLB-46

Hermann the Lame 1013-1054. . . . . DLB-148

Hermes, Johann Timotheu 1738-1821 . . . . DLB-97

Hermlin, Stephan 1915-1997 . . . . DLB-69

Hernández, Alfonso C. 1938- DLB-122

Hernández, Inés 1947- DLB-122

Hernández, Miguel 1910-1942 . . . . DLB-134

Hernton, Calvin C. 1932- DLB-38

Herodotus circa 484 B.C.-circa 420 B.C.
    . . . . .DLB-176; CDWLB-1

Heron, Robert 1764-1807. . . . . .DLB-142

Herr, Michael 1940- DLB-185

Herrera, Juan Felipe 1948- DLB-122

E. R. Herrick and Company DLB-49

Herrick, Robert 1591-1674 . . . . .DLB-126

Herrick, Robert 1868-1938 . . . . . . .DLB-9, 12, 78

Herrick, William 1915- Y-83

Herrmann, John 1900-1959 . . . . .DLB-4

Hersey, John
   1914-1993 . . . . . . DLB-6, 185, 278; CDALB-7

Hertel, François 1905-1985 . . . . .DLB-68

Hervé-Bazin, Jean Pierre Marie (see Bazin, Hervé)

Hervey, John, Lord 1696-1743 . . . . .DLB-101

Herwig, Georg 1817-1875. . . . . .DLB-133

Herzen, Alexander (Aleksandr Ivanovich
   Gersten) 1812-1870 . . . . .DLB-277

Herzog, Emile Salomon Wilhelm
   (see Maurois, André)

Hesiod eighth century B.C. DLB-176

Hesse, Hermann 1877-1962 . . .DLB-66; CDWLB-2

Hessus, Eobanus 1488-1540 . . . . .DLB-179

Heureka! (see Kertész, Imre and Nobel Prize
   in Literature: 2002) Y-02

Hewat, Alexander circa 1743-circa 1824 . . .DLB-30

Hewitt, John 1907-1987 . . . . .DLB-27

Hewlett, Maurice 1861-1923 . . . . . . .DLB-34, 156

Heyen, William 1940- DLB-5

Heyer, Georgette 1902-1974 . . . . DLB-77, 191

Heym, Stefan 1913-2001 . . . . .DLB-69

Heyse, Paul 1830-1914 . . . . .DLB-129

Heytesbury, William
   circa 1310-1372 or 1373. . . . . .DLB-115

Heyward, Dorothy 1890-1961. . . . . . . DLB-7, 249

Heyward, DuBose 1885-1940 . . . DLB-7, 9, 45, 249

Heywood, John 1497?-1580?. DLB-136

Heywood, Thomas 1573 or 1574-1641 . . . .DLB-62

Hibbs, Ben 1901-1975 . . . . .DLB-137

   "The Saturday Evening Post reaffirms
   a policy," Ben Hibb's Statement
   in *The Saturday Evening Post*
   (16 May 1942) DLB-137

Hichens, Robert S. 1864-1950 . . . . .DLB-153

Hickey, Emily 1845-1924 . . . . .DLB-199

Hickman, William Albert 1877-1957 . . . . .DLB-92

Hicks, Granville 1901-1982. . . . . .DLB-246

Hidalgo, José Luis 1919-1947. . . . . .DLB-108

Hiebert, Paul 1892-1987 . . . . .DLB-68

Hieng, Andrej 1925- DLB-181

Hierro, José 1922-2002 . . . . .DLB-108

Higgins, Aidan 1927- DLB-14

Higgins, Colin 1941-1988 . . . . .DLB-26

Higgins, George V.
   1939-1999 . . . . .DLB-2; Y-81, 98–99

   Afterword [in response to Cozzen's
   Mens Rea (or Something)] Y-97

   At End of Day: The Last George V.
   Higgins Novel. Y-99

The Books of George V. Higgins:
   A Checklist of Editions
   and Printings Y-00

George V. Higgins in Class. Y-02

Tribute to Alfred A. Knopf. Y-84

Tributes to George V. Higgins Y-99

"What You Lose on the Swings You Make
   Up on the Merry-Go-Round". . . Y-99

Higginson, Thomas Wentworth
   1823-1911 . . . . .DLB-1, 64, 243

Highwater, Jamake 1942?- DLB-52; Y-85

Hijuelos, Oscar 1951- DLB-145

Hildegard von Bingen 1098-1179. . . . . . .DLB-148

Das Hildesbrandslied
   circa 820 . . . . DLB-148; CDWLB-2

Hildesheimer, Wolfgang 1916-1991 . .DLB-69, 124

Hildreth, Richard 1807-1865 . . .DLB-1, 30, 59, 235

Hill, Aaron 1685-1750 . . . . .DLB-84

Hill, Geoffrey 1932- DLB-40; CDBLB-8

George M. Hill Company DLB-49

Hill, "Sir" John 1714?-1775. . . . . .DLB-39

Lawrence Hill and Company, Publishers . .DLB-46

Hill, Leslie 1880-1960 . . . . .DLB-51

Hill, Reginald 1936- DLB-276

Hill, Susan 1942- DLB-14, 139

Hill, Walter 1942- DLB-44

Hill and Wang. .DLB-46

Hillberry, Conrad 1928- DLB-120

Hillerman, Tony 1925- DLB-206

Hilliard, Gray and Company. DLB-49

Hills, Lee 1906-2000 . . . . .DLB-127

Hillyer, Robert 1895-1961. . . . . .DLB-54

Hilton, James 1900-1954 . . . . DLB-34, 77

Hilton, Walter died 1396. . . . . .DLB-146

Hilton and Company. DLB-49

Himes, Chester 1909-1984 . . . DLB-2, 76, 143, 226

Joseph Hindmarsh [publishing house] DLB-170

Hine, Daryl 1936- DLB-60

Hingley, Ronald 1920- DLB-155

Hinojosa-Smith, Rolando 1929- DLB-82

Hinton, S. E. 1948- CDALB-7

Hippel, Theodor Gottlieb von
   1741-1796 .DLB-97

Hippocrates of Cos flourished circa
   425 B.C. DLB-176; CDWLB-1

Hirabayashi Taiko 1905-1972 . . . . .DLB-180

Hirsch, E. D., Jr. 1928- DLB-67

Hirsch, Edward 1950- DLB-120

Hoagland, Edward 1932- DLB-6

Hoagland, Everett H., III 1942- DLB-41

Hoban, Russell 1925- DLB-52; Y-90

Hobbes, Thomas 1588-1679 . . .DLB-151, 252, 281

Hobby, Oveta 1905-1995 . . . . .DLB-127

Hobby, William 1878-1964 . . . . .DLB-127

Hobsbaum, Philip 1932- DLB-40

Hobson, Laura Z. 1900- DLB-28

Hobson, Sarah 1947- DLB-204

Hoby, Thomas 1530-1566. . . . . .DLB-132

Hoccleve, Thomas
   circa 1368-circa 1437. . . . . .DLB-146

Hochhuth, Rolf 1931- DLB-124

Hochman, Sandra 1936- DLB-5

Hocken, Thomas Morland 1836-1910. . . .DLB-184

Hocking, William Ernest 1873-1966 . . . . .DLB-270

Hodder and Stoughton, Limited DLB-106

Hodgins, Jack 1938- DLB-60

Hodgman, Helen 1945- DLB-14

Hodgskin, Thomas 1787-1869 . . . . .DLB-158

Hodgson, Ralph 1871-1962 . . . . .DLB-19

Hodgson, William Hope
   1877-1918 . . . . DLB-70, 153, 156, 178

Hoe, Robert, III 1839-1909. . . . . .DLB-187

Hoeg, Peter 1957- DLB-214

Hoffenstein, Samuel 1890-1947 . . . . .DLB-11

Hoffman, Charles Fenno 1806-1884 . . .DLB-3, 250

Hoffman, Daniel 1923- DLB-5

   Tribute to Robert Graves Y-85

Hoffmann, E. T. A.
   1776-1822 . . . . .DLB-90; CDWLB-2

Hoffman, Frank B. 1888-1958. . . . . .DLB-188

Hoffman, William 1925- DLB-234

   Tribute to Paxton Davis Y-94

Hoffmanswaldau, Christian Hoffman von
   1616-1679 .DLB-168

Hofmann, Michael 1957- DLB-40

Hofmannsthal, Hugo von
   1874-1929 . . . . DLB-81, 118; CDWLB-2

Hofstadter, Richard 1916-1970 . . . . . . DLB-17, 246

Hogan, Desmond 1950- DLB-14

Hogan, Linda 1947- DLB-175

Hogan and Thompson DLB-49

Hogarth Press DLB-112; DS-10

Hogg, James 1770-1835 . . . . .DLB-93, 116, 159

Hohberg, Wolfgang Helmhard Freiherr von
   1612-1688 .DLB-168

von Hohenheim, Philippus Aureolus
   Theophrastus Bombastus (see Paracelsus)

Hohl, Ludwig 1904-1980. . . . . .DLB-56

Højholt, Per 1928- DLB-214

Holan, Vladimir 1905-1980. . . . . .DLB-215

Holbrook, David 1923- DLB-14, 40

Holcroft, Thomas 1745-1809. . . . .DLB-39, 89, 158

   Preface to *Alwyn* (1780) DLB-39

Holden, Jonathan 1941- DLB-105

   "Contemporary Verse Story-telling" . . .DLB-105

Holden, Molly 1927-1981 . . . . .DLB-40

Hölderlin, Friedrich
   1770-1843 . . . . .DLB-90; CDWLB-2

Holdstock, Robert 1948- DLB-261

Holiday House .DLB-46

Holinshed, Raphael died 1580. . . . . .DLB-167

Holland, J. G. 1819-1881 . . . . DS-13

Holland, Norman N. 1927- DLB-67

Hollander, John 1929- DLB-5

Holley, Marietta 1836-1926 . . . . DLB-11

Hollinghurst, Alan 1954- DLB-207

Hollingsworth, Margaret 1940- DLB-60

Hollo, Anselm 1934- DLB-40

Holloway, Emory 1885-1977 . . . . DLB-103

Holloway, John 1920- DLB-27

Holloway House Publishing Company . . . DLB-46

Holme, Constance 1880-1955 . . . . DLB-34

Holmes, Abraham S. 1821?-1908 . . . . DLB-99

Holmes, John Clellon 1926-1988 . . . . DLB-16, 237

"Four Essays on the Beat
Generation" DLB-16

Holmes, Mary Jane 1825-1907 . . . . . DLB-202, 221

Holmes, Oliver Wendell
1809-1894 . . . . . . DLB-1, 189, 235; CDALB-2

Holmes, Richard 1945- DLB-155

Holmes, Thomas James 1874-1959 . . . . . . DLB-187

Holroyd, Michael 1935- DLB-155; Y-99

Holst, Hermann E. von 1841-1904 . . . . . . DLB-47

Holt, John 1721-1784 . . . . DLB-43

Henry Holt and Company DLB-49, 284

Holt, Rinehart and Winston DLB-46

Holtby, Winifred 1898-1935 . . . . DLB-191

Holthusen, Hans Egon 1913-1997 . . . . . . DLB-69

Hölty, Ludwig Christoph Heinrich
1748-1776 . . . . DLB-94

Holub, Miroslav
1923-1998 . . . . DLB-232; CDWLB-4

Holz, Arno 1863-1929 . . . . DLB-118

Home, Henry, Lord Kames
(see Kames, Henry Home, Lord)

Home, John 1722-1808 . . . . DLB-84

Home, William Douglas 1912- DLB-13

Home Publishing Company DLB-49

Homer circa eighth-seventh centuries B.C.
. . . . DLB-176; CDWLB-1

Homer, Winslow 1836-1910 . . . . DLB-188

Homes, Geoffrey (see Mainwaring, Daniel)

Honan, Park 1928- DLB-111

Hone, William 1780-1842 . . . . DLB-110, 158

Hongo, Garrett Kaoru 1951- DLB-120

Honig, Edwin 1919- DLB-5

Hood, Hugh 1928-2000 . . . . DLB-53

Hood, Mary 1946- DLB-234

Hood, Thomas 1799-1845 . . . . DLB-96

Hook, Sidney 1902-1989 . . . . DLB-279

Hook, Theodore 1788-1841 . . . . DLB-116

Hooker, Jeremy 1941- DLB-40

Hooker, Richard 1554-1600 . . . . DLB-132

Hooker, Thomas 1586-1647 . . . . DLB-24

hooks, bell 1952- DLB-246

Hooper, Johnson Jones
1815-1862 . . . . DLB-3, 11, 248

Hope, Anthony 1863-1933 . . . . DLB-153, 156

Hope, Christopher 1944- DLB-225

Hope, Eva (see Hearn, Mary Anne)

Hope, Laurence (Adela Florence
Cory Nicolson) 1865-1904 . . . . DLB-240

Hopkins, Ellice 1836-1904 . . . . DLB-190

Hopkins, Gerard Manley
1844-1889 . . . . DLB-35, 57; CDBLB-5

Hopkins, John ?-1570 . . . . DLB-132

Hopkins, John H., and Son DLB-46

Hopkins, Lemuel 1750-1801 . . . . DLB-37

Hopkins, Pauline Elizabeth 1859-1930 . . . . DLB-50

Hopkins, Samuel 1721-1803 . . . . DLB-31

Hopkinson, Francis 1737-1791 . . . . DLB-31

Hopkinson, Nalo 1960- DLB-251

Hopper, Nora (Mrs. Nora Chesson)
1871-1906 . . . . DLB-240

Hoppin, Augustus 1828-1896 . . . . DLB-188

Hora, Josef 1891-1945 . . . . . DLB-215; CDWLB-4

Horace 65 B.C.-8 B.C. DLB-211; CDWLB-1

Horgan, Paul 1903-1995 . . . . . . DLB-102, 212; Y-85

Tribute to Alfred A. Knopf Y-84

Horizon Press DLB-46

Hornby, C. H. St. John 1867-1946 . . . . . . DLB-201

Hornby, Nick 1957- DLB-207

Horne, Frank 1899-1974 . . . . DLB-51

Horne, Richard Henry (Hengist)
1802 or 1803-1884 . . . . DLB-32

Horne, Thomas 1608-1654 . . . . DLB-281

Horney, Karen 1885-1952 . . . . DLB-246

Hornung, E. W. 1866-1921 . . . . DLB-70

Horovitz, Israel 1939- DLB-7

Horton, George Moses 1797?-1883? DLB-50

George Moses Horton Society Y-99

Horváth, Ödön von 1901-1938 . . . . . DLB-85, 124

Horwood, Harold 1923- DLB-60

E. and E. Hosford [publishing house] DLB-49

Hoskens, Jane Fenn 1693-1770? DLB-200

Hoskyns, John circa 1566-1638 . . . . DLB-121, 281

Hosokawa Yūsai 1535-1610 . . . . DLB-203

Hospers, John 1918- DLB-279

Hostovský, Egon 1908-1973 . . . . DLB-215

Hotchkiss and Company DLB-49

Hough, Emerson 1857-1923 . . . . DLB-9, 212

Houghton, Stanley 1881-1913 . . . . DLB-10

Houghton Mifflin Company DLB-49

Hours at Home DS-13

Household, Geoffrey 1900-1988 . . . . DLB-87

Housman, A. E. 1859-1936 . . . DLB-19; CDBLB-5

Housman, Laurence 1865-1959 . . . . DLB-10

Houston, Pam 1962- DLB-244

Houwald, Ernst von 1778-1845 . . . . DLB-90

Hovey, Richard 1864-1900 . . . . DLB-54

Howard, Donald R. 1927-1987 . . . . DLB-111

Howard, Maureen 1930- Y-83

Howard, Richard 1929- DLB-5

Howard, Roy W. 1883-1964 . . . . DLB-29

Howard, Sidney 1891-1939 . . . . DLB-7, 26, 249

Howard, Thomas, second Earl of Arundel
1585-1646 . . . . DLB-213

Howe, E. W. 1853-1937 . . . . DLB-12, 25

Howe, Henry 1816-1893 . . . . DLB-30

Howe, Irving 1920-1993 . . . . DLB-67

Howe, Joseph 1804-1873 . . . . DLB-99

Howe, Julia Ward 1819-1910 . . . . DLB-1, 189, 235

Howe, Percival Presland 1886-1944 . . . . . DLB-149

Howe, Susan 1937- DLB-120

Howell, Clark, Sr. 1863-1936 . . . . DLB-25

Howell, Evan P. 1839-1905 . . . . DLB-23

Howell, James 1594?-1666 . . . . DLB-151

Howell, Soskin and Company DLB-46

Howell, Warren Richardson
1912-1984 . . . . DLB-140

Howells, William Dean 1837-1920
. . . . DLB-12, 64, 74, 79, 189; CDALB-3

Introduction to Paul Laurence
Dunbar's *Lyrics of Lowly Life*
(1896) DLB-50

The William Dean Howells Society Y-01

Howitt, Mary 1799-1888 . . . . DLB-110, 199

Howitt, William 1792-1879 . . . . DLB-110

Hoyem, Andrew 1935- DLB-5

Hoyers, Anna Ovena 1584-1655 . . . . DLB-164

Hoyle, Fred 1915-2001 . . . . DLB-261

Hoyos, Angela de 1940- DLB-82

Henry Hoyt [publishing house] DLB-49

Hoyt, Palmer 1897-1979 . . . . DLB-127

Hrabal, Bohumil 1914-1997 . . . . DLB-232

Hrabanus Maurus 776?-856 . . . . DLB-148

Hronský, Josef Cíger 1896-1960 . . . . DLB-215

Hrotsvit of Gandersheim
circa 935-circa 1000 . . . . DLB-148

Hubbard, Elbert 1856-1915 . . . . DLB-91

Hubbard, Kin 1868-1930 . . . . DLB-11

Hubbard, William circa 1621-1704 . . . . . . DLB-24

Huber, Therese 1764-1829 . . . . DLB-90

Huch, Friedrich 1873-1913 . . . . DLB-66

Huch, Ricarda 1864-1947 . . . . DLB-66

Huddle, David 1942- DLB-130

Hudgins, Andrew 1951- DLB-120, 282

Hudson, Henry Norman 1814-1886 . . . . . DLB-64

Hudson, Stephen 1868?-1944 . . . . DLB-197

Hudson, W. H. 1841-1922 . . . . . DLB-98, 153, 174

Hudson and Goodwin DLB-49

Huebsch, B. W., oral history Y-99

B. W. Huebsch [publishing house] DLB-46

Hueffer, Oliver Madox 1876-1931 . . . . . . DLB-197

Huet, Pierre Daniel
Preface to *The History of Romances*
(1715) DLB-39

Hugh of St. Victor circa 1096-1141 . . . . . DLB-208

Hughes, David 1930- DLB-14

Hughes, Dusty 1947- DLB-233

Hughes, Hatcher 1881-1945 . . . . DLB-249

Hughes, John 1677-1720. . . . . .DLB-84

Hughes, Langston 1902-1967 . . . . . . .DLB-4, 7, 48, 51, 86, 228; ; DS-15; CDALB-5

Hughes, Richard 1900-1976. . . . . . . .DLB-15, 161

Hughes, Ted 1930-1998 . . . . .DLB-40, 161

Hughes, Thomas 1822-1896 . . . . .DLB-18, 163

Hugo, Richard 1923-1982 . . . . .DLB-5, 206

Hugo, Victor 1802-1885 . . . . . . DLB-119, 192, 217

Hugo Awards and Nebula Awards DLB-8

Huidobro, Vicente 1893-1948 . . . . .DLB-283

Hull, Richard 1896-1973 . . . . .DLB-77

Hulme, T. E. 1883-1917 . . . . .DLB-19

Hulton, Anne ?-1779? DLB-200

Humboldt, Alexander von 1769-1859 . . . . .DLB-90

Humboldt, Wilhelm von 1767-1835. . . . . . .DLB-90

Hume, David 1711-1776. . . . . .DLB-104, 252

Hume, Fergus 1859-1932. . . . . .DLB-70

Hume, Sophia 1702-1774 . . . . .DLB-200

Hume-Rothery, Mary Catherine 1824-1885 .DLB-240

Humishuma (see Mourning Dove)

Hummer, T. R. 1950- DLB-120

Humor
American Humor: A Historical Survey. DLB-11

American Humor Studies Association. . . . Y-99

The Comic Tradition Continued [in the British Novel]. DLB-15

Humorous Book Illustration DLB-11

International Society for Humor Studies. . Y-99

Newspaper Syndication of American Humor DLB-11

Selected Humorous Magazines (1820-1950). DLB-11

Humphrey, Duke of Gloucester 1391-1447 .DLB-213

Humphrey, William 1924-1997 . . . . DLB-6, 212, 234, 278

Humphreys, David 1752-1818. . . . . .DLB-37

Humphreys, Emyr 1919- DLB-15

Bruce Humphries [publishing house] DLB-46

Huncke, Herbert 1915-1996 . . . . .DLB-16

Huneker, James Gibbons 1857-1921 . . . . . .DLB-71

Hunold, Christian Friedrich 1681-1721 . . .DLB-168

Hunt, Irene 1907- DLB-52

Hunt, Leigh 1784-1859 . . . . DLB-96, 110, 144

Hunt, Violet 1862-1942. . . . . DLB-162, 197

Hunt, William Gibbes 1791-1833 . . . . .DLB-73

Hunter, Evan 1926- Y-82

Tribute to John D. MacDonald. Y-86

Hunter, Jim 1939-. DLB-14

Hunter, Kristin 1931- DLB-33

Tribute to Julian Mayfield. Y-84

Hunter, Mollie 1922- DLB-161

Hunter, N. C. 1908-1971 . . . . .DLB-10

Hunter-Duvar, John 1821-1899 . . . . .DLB-99

Huntington, Henry E. 1850-1927 . . . . . . .DLB-140

The Henry E. Huntington Library Y-92

Huntington, Susan Mansfield 1791-1823 . .DLB-200

Hurd and Houghton DLB-49

Hurst, Fannie 1889-1968 . . . . .DLB-86

Hurst and Blackett. DLB-106

Hurst and Company DLB-49

Hurston, Zora Neale 1901?-1960 . . . . .DLB-51, 86; CDALB-7

Husson, Jules-François-Félix (see Champfleury)

Huston, John 1906-1987 . . . . .DLB-26

Hutcheson, Francis 1694-1746 . . . . . .DLB-31, 252

Hutchinson, Ron 1947- DLB-245

Hutchinson, R. C. 1907-1975. . . . . .DLB-191

Hutchinson, Thomas 1711-1780 . . . . . .DLB-30, 31

Hutchinson and Company (Publishers) Limited DLB-112

Huth, Angela 1938- DLB-271

Hutton, Richard Holt 1826-1897. . . . . . . .DLB-57

von Hutten, Ulrich 1488-1523. . . . . .DLB-179

Huxley, Aldous 1894-1963 . . . . . .DLB-36, 100, 162, 195, 255; CDBLB-6

Huxley, Elspeth Josceline 1907-1997 . . . . DLB-77, 204

Huxley, T. H. 1825-1895 . . . . .DLB-57

Huyghue, Douglas Smith 1816-1891 . . . . . .DLB-99

Huysmans, Joris-Karl 1848-1907 . . . . .DLB-123

Hwang, David Henry 1957- DLB-212, 228

Hyde, Donald 1909-1966. . . . . .DLB-187

Hyde, Mary 1912- DLB-187

Hyman, Trina Schart 1939- DLB-61

I

Iavorsky, Stefan 1658-1722 . . . . .DLB-150

Iazykov, Nikolai Mikhailovich 1803-1846 .DLB-205

Ibáñez, Armando P. 1949- DLB-209

Ibn Bajja circa 1077-1138 . . . . .DLB-115

Ibn Gabirol, Solomon circa 1021-circa 1058. . . . . .DLB-115

Ibuse Masuji 1898-1993. . . . . .DLB-180

Ichijō Kanera (see Ichijō Kaneyoshi)

Ichijō Kaneyoshi (Ichijō Kanera) 1402-1481 .DLB-203

Iffland, August Wilhelm 1759-1814 . . . . . .DLB-94

Ignatieff, Michael 1947- DLB-267

Ignatow, David 1914-1997. . . . . .DLB-5

Ike, Chukwuemeka 1931- DLB-157

Ikkyū Sōjun 1394-1481 . . . . .DLB-203

Iles, Francis (see Berkeley, Anthony)

Il'f, Il'ia (Il'ia Arnol'dovich Fainzil'berg) 1897-1937 .DLB-272

Illich, Ivan 1926-2002 . . . . .DLB-242

Illustration
Children's Book Illustration in the Twentieth Century. DLB-61

Children's Illustrators, 1800-1880. . . .DLB-163

Early American Book Illustration DLB-49

The Iconography of Science-Fiction Art DLB-8

The Illustration of Early German Literary Manuscripts, circa 1150-circa 1300. . . . . .DLB-148

Minor Illustrators, 1880-1914 . . . . . .DLB-141

Illyés, Gyula 1902-1983. . . . . DLB-215; CDWLB-4

Imbs, Bravig 1904-1946. . . . . .DLB-4; DS-15

Imbuga, Francis D. 1947- DLB-157

Immermann, Karl 1796-1840. . . . . .DLB-133

Inchbald, Elizabeth 1753-1821 . . . . . . .DLB-39, 89

Indiana University Press Y-02

Ingamells, Rex 1913-1955 . . . . .DLB-260

Inge, William 1913-1973 . . . DLB-7, 249; CDALB-1

Ingelow, Jean 1820-1897 . . . . .DLB-35, 163

Ingersoll, Ralph 1900-1985 . . . . .DLB-127

The Ingersoll Prizes. Y-84

Ingoldsby, Thomas (see Barham, Richard Harris)

Ingraham, Joseph Holt 1809-1860 . . . . .DLB-3, 248

Inman, John 1805-1850 . . . . .DLB-73

Innerhofer, Franz 1944- DLB-85

Innes, Michael (J. I. M. Stewart) 1906-1994 . . . . .DLB-276

Innis, Harold Adams 1894-1952 . . . . .DLB-88

Innis, Mary Quayle 1899-1972 . . . . .DLB-88

Inō Sōgi 1421-1502 . . . . .DLB-203

Inoue Yasushi 1907-1991 . . . . .DLB-182

"The Greatness of Southern Literature": League of the South Institute for the Study of Southern Culture and History Y-02

International Publishers Company DLB-46

Internet (publishing and commerce) Author Websites. Y-97

The Book Trade and the Internet. Y-00

E-Books Turn the Corner. Y-98

The E-Researcher: Possibilities and Pitfalls Y-00

Interviews on E-publishing Y-00

John Updike on the Internet. Y-97

LitCheck Website Y-01

Virtual Books and Enemies of Books Y-00

Interviews
Adoff, Arnold Y-01

Aldridge, John W.. . . . . Y-91

Anastas, Benjamin. Y-98

Baker, Nicholson. Y-00

Bank, Melissa Y-98

Bass, T. J.. . . . . Y-80

Bernstein, Harriet Y-82

Betts, Doris Y-82

Bosworth, David. Y-82

Bottoms, David. Y-83

Bowers, Fredson Y-80

Burnshaw, Stanley Y-97

Carpenter, Humphrey Y-84, 99

Carr, Virginia Spencer Y-00

Carver, Raymond Y-83
Cherry, Kelly Y-83
Conroy, Jack Y-81
Coppel, Alfred Y-83
Cowley, Malcolm. Y-81
Davis, Paxton. Y-89
Devito, Carlo Y-94
De Vries, Peter. Y-82
Dickey, James. Y-82
Donald, David Herbert Y-87
Editors, Conversations with. Y-95
Ellroy, James Y-91
Fancher, Betsy Y-83
Faust, Irvin. Y-00
Fulton, Len. Y-86
Furst, Alan Y-01
Garrett, George Y-83
Gelfman, Jane. Y-93
Goldwater, Walter. Y-93
Gores, Joe. Y-02
Greenfield, George. Y-91
Griffin, Bryan. Y-81
Groom, Winston Y-01
Guilds, John Caldwell Y-92
Hamilton, Virginia. Y-01
Hardin, James Y-92
Harris, Mark Y-80
Harrison, Jim Y-82
Hazzard, Shirley. Y-82
Herrick, William Y-01
Higgins, George V. Y-98
Hoban, Russell. Y-90
Holroyd, Michael. Y-99
Horowitz, Glen Y-90
Iggulden, John Y-01
Jakes, John Y-83
Jenkinson, Edward B.. . . . . Y-82
Jenks, Tom. Y-86
Kaplan, Justin. Y-86
King, Florence Y-85
Klopfer, Donald S. Y-97
Krug, Judith Y-82
Lamm, Donald. Y-95
Laughlin, James Y-96
Lawrence, Starling Y-95
Lindsay, Jack Y-84
Mailer, Norman. Y-97
Manchester, William Y-85
Max, D. T.. . . . . Y-94
McCormack, Thomas Y-98
McNamara, Katherine Y-97
Mellen, Joan Y-94
Menaker, Daniel Y-97
Mooneyham, Lamarr. Y-82

Murray, Les Y-01
Nosworth, David Y-82
O'Connor, Patrick Y-84, 99
Ozick, Cynthia. Y-83
Penner, Jonathan Y-83
Pennington, Lee Y-82
Penzler, Otto Y-96
Plimpton, George Y-99
Potok, Chaim. Y-84
Powell, Padgett. Y-01
Prescott, Peter S. Y-86
Rabe, David. Y-91
Rechy, John Y-82
Reid, B. L. Y-83
Reynolds, Michael Y-95, 99
Robinson, Derek Y-02
Rollyson, Carl Y-97
Rosset, Barney Y-02
Schlafly, Phyllis Y-82
Schroeder, Patricia Y-99
Schulberg, Budd. Y-81, 01
Scribner, Charles, III Y-94
Sipper, Ralph Y-94
Smith, Cork Y-95
Staley, Thomas F.. . . . . Y-00
Styron, William Y-80
Talese, Nan Y-94
Thornton, John Y-94
Toth, Susan Allen Y-86
Tyler, Anne Y-82
Vaughan, Samuel. Y-97
Von Ogtrop, Kristin. Y-92
Wallenstein, Barry Y-92
Weintraub, Stanley Y-82
Williams, J. Chamberlain. Y-84
Into the Past: William Jovanovich's
    Reflections in Publishing Y-02
The National Library of Ireland's
    New James Joyce Manuscripts Y-02
Irving, John 1942- DLB-6, 278; Y-82
Irving, Washington 1783-1859
    . . . . DLB-3, 11, 30, 59, 73, 74,
                183, 186, 250; CDALB-2
Irwin, Grace 1907- DLB-68
Irwin, Will 1873-1948. . . . . DLB-25
Isaksson, Ulla 1916-2000 . . . . DLB-257
Iser, Wolfgang 1926- DLB-242
Isherwood, Christopher
    1904-1986 . . . . .DLB-15, 195; Y-86
The Christopher Isherwood Archive,
    The Huntington Library Y-99
Ishiguro, Kazuo
    1954- DLB-194
Ishikawa Jun 1899-1987 . . . . DLB-182
The Island Trees Case: A Symposium on
    School Library Censorship
    An Interview with Judith Krug

An Interview with Phyllis Schlafly
An Interview with Edward B. Jenkinson
An Interview with Lamarr Mooneyham
An Interview with Harriet Bernstein Y-82
Islas, Arturo
    1938-1991 . . . . DLB-122
Issit, Debbie 1966- DLB-233
Ivanišević, Drago 1907-1981. . . . . DLB-181
Ivanov, Vsevolod Viacheslavovich
    1895-1963 . . . . .DLB-272
Ivaska, Astrīde 1926- DLB-232
M. J. Ivers and Company DLB-49
Iwaniuk, Wacław 1915- DLB-215
Iwano Hōmei 1873-1920. . . . . DLB-180
Iwaszkiewicz, Jarosław 1894-1980 . . . . . . DLB-215
Iyayi, Festus 1947- DLB-157
Izumi Kyōka 1873-1939 . . . . DLB-180

J

Jackmon, Marvin E. (see Marvin X)
Jacks, L. P. 1860-1955 . . . . DLB-135
Jackson, Angela 1951- DLB-41
Jackson, Charles 1903-1968 . . . . DLB-234
Jackson, Helen Hunt
    1830-1885 . . . . DLB-42, 47, 186, 189
Jackson, Holbrook 1874-1948. . . . . DLB-98
Jackson, Laura Riding 1901-1991 . . . . DLB-48
Jackson, Shirley
    1916-1965 . . . . DLB-6, 234; CDALB-1
Jacob, Max 1876-1944 . . . . DLB-258
Jacob, Naomi 1884?-1964. . . . . DLB-191
Jacob, Piers Anthony Dillingham
    (see Anthony, Piers)
Jacob, Violet 1863-1946 . . . . DLB-240
Jacobi, Friedrich Heinrich 1743-1819 . . . . DLB-94
Jacobi, Johann Georg 1740-1841. . . . . DLB-97
George W. Jacobs and Company. DLB-49
Jacobs, Harriet 1813-1897. . . . . DLB-239
Jacobs, Joseph 1854-1916 . . . . DLB-141
Jacobs, W. W. 1863-1943. . . . . DLB-135
The W. W. Jacobs Appreciation Society . . Y-98
Jacobsen, Jørgen-Frantz 1900-1938 . . . . . . DLB-214
Jacobsen, Josephine 1908- DLB-244
Jacobson, Dan 1929- DLB-14, 207, 225
Jacobson, Howard 1942- DLB-207
Jacques de Vitry circa 1160/1170-1240 . . . DLB-208
Jæger, Frank 1926-1977. . . . . DLB-214
William Jaggard [publishing house] DLB-170
Jahier, Piero 1884-1966 . . . . DLB-114, 264
Jahnn, Hans Henny 1894-1959 . . . . . DLB-56, 124
Jaimes, Freyre, Ricardo 1866?-1933 . . . . . DLB-283
Jakes, John 1932- DLB-278; Y-83
    Tribute to John Gardner Y-82
    Tribute to John D. MacDonald Y-86
Jakobson, Roman 1896-1982 . . . . DLB-242
James, Alice 1848-1892 . . . . DLB-221
James, C. L. R. 1901-1989 . . . . DLB-125

James, George P. R. 1801-1860 . . . . .DLB-116

James, Henry 1843-1916
. . . . . DLB-12, 71, 74, 189; DS-13; CDALB-3

"The Future of the Novel" (1899) DLB-18

"The Novel in [Robert Browning's]
'The Ring and the Book'"
(1912) DLB-32

James, John circa 1633-1729. . . . . .DLB-24

James, M. R. 1862-1936. . . . . .DLB-156, 201

James, Naomi 1949- DLB-204

James, P. D. (Phyllis Dorothy James White)
1920- DLB-87, 276; DS-17; CDBLB-8

Tribute to Charles Scribner Jr. Y-95

James, Thomas 1572?-1629 . . . . .DLB-213

U. P. James [publishing house] DLB-49

James, Will 1892-1942. . . . . .DS-16

James, William 1842-1910 . . . . .DLB-270

James VI of Scotland, I of England
1566-1625 . . . . .DLB-151, 172

*Ane Schort Treatise Conteining Some Revlis
and Cautelis to Be Obseruit and
Eschewit in Scottis Poesi* (1584) DLB-172

Jameson, Anna 1794-1860 . . . . .DLB-99, 166

Jameson, Fredric 1934- DLB-67

Jameson, J. Franklin 1859-1937 . . . . .DLB-17

Jameson, Storm 1891-1986 . . . . .DLB-36

Jančar, Drago 1948- DLB-181

Janés, Clara 1940- DLB-134

Janevski, Slavko 1920- DLB-181; CDWLB-4

Jansson, Tove 1914-2001. . . . . .DLB-257

Janvier, Thomas 1849-1913. . . . . .DLB-202

Japan
"The Development of Meiji Japan". . .DLB-180

"Encounter with the West" DLB-180

Japanese Literature
Letter from Japan Y-94, 98

Medieval Travel Diaries DLB-203

Surveys: 1987-1995 . . . . .DLB-182

Jaramillo, Cleofas M. 1878-1956 . . . . .DLB-122

Jarman, Mark 1952- DLB-120, 282

Jarrell, Randall
1914-1965 . . . . .DLB-48, 52; CDALB-1

Jarrold and Sons. DLB-106

Jarry, Alfred 1873-1907 . . . . .DLB-192, 258

Jarves, James Jackson 1818-1888 . . . . . . .DLB-189

Jasmin, Claude 1930- DLB-60

Jaunsudrabiņš, Jānis 1877-1962 . . . . .DLB-220

Jay, John 1745-1829 . . . . .DLB-31

Jean de Garlande (see John of Garland)

Jefferies, Richard 1848-1887 . . . . . . .DLB-98, 141

The Richard Jefferies Society Y-98

Jeffers, Lance 1919-1985 . . . . .DLB-41

Jeffers, Robinson
1887-1962 . . . . .DLB-45, 212; CDALB-4

Jefferson, Thomas
1743-1826 . . . . .DLB-31, 183; CDALB-2

Jégé 1866-1940. . . . . .DLB-215

Jelinek, Elfriede 1946- DLB-85

Jellicoe, Ann 1927- DLB-13, 233

Jemison, Mary circa 1742-1833 . . . . .DLB-239

Jenkins, Dan 1929- DLB-241

Jenkins, Elizabeth 1905- DLB-155

Jenkins, Robin 1912- DLB-14, 271

Jenkins, William Fitzgerald (see Leinster, Murray)

Herbert Jenkins Limited DLB-112

Jennings, Elizabeth 1926- DLB-27

Jens, Walter 1923- DLB-69

Jensen, Johannes V. 1873-1950 . . . . .DLB-214

Jensen, Merrill 1905-1980 . . . . .DLB-17

Jensen, Thit 1876-1957. . . . . .DLB-214

Jephson, Robert 1736-1803 . . . . .DLB-89

Jerome, Jerome K. 1859-1927 . . . . DLB-10, 34, 135

The Jerome K. Jerome Society Y-98

Jerome, Judson 1927-1991 . . . . .DLB-105

"Reflections: After a Tornado" DLB-105

Jerrold, Douglas 1803-1857 . . . . . . .DLB-158, 159

Jersild, Per Christian 1935- DLB-257

Jesse, F. Tennyson 1888-1958 . . . . .DLB-77

Jewel, John 1522-1571 . . . . .DLB-236

John P. Jewett and Company. DLB-49

Jewett, Sarah Orne 1849-1909 . . . . DLB-12, 74, 221

The Jewish Publication Society DLB-49

Studies in American Jewish Literature Y-02

Jewitt, John Rodgers 1783-1821 . . . . .DLB-99

Jewsbury, Geraldine 1812-1880 . . . . .DLB-21

Jewsbury, Maria Jane 1800-1833 . . . . . . .DLB-199

Jhabvala, Ruth Prawer 1927- DLB-139, 194

Jiménez, Juan Ramón 1881-1958 . . . . . . .DLB-134

Jin, Ha 1956- DLB-244

Joans, Ted 1928- DLB-16, 41

Jōha 1525-1602 . . . . .DLB-203

Johannis de Garlandia (see John of Garland)

John, Errol 1924-1988 . . . . .DLB-233

John, Eugenie (see Marlitt, E.)

John of Dumbleton
circa 1310-circa 1349. . . . . .DLB-115

John of Garland (Jean de Garlande,
Johannis de Garlandia)
circa 1195-circa 1272. . . . . .DLB-208

Johns, Captain W. E. 1893-1968 . . . . .DLB-160

Johnson, Mrs. A. E. ca. 1858-1922 . . . . . .DLB-221

Johnson, Amelia (see Johnson, Mrs. A. E.)

Johnson, B. S. 1933-1973 . . . . .DLB-14, 40

Johnson, Charles 1679-1748. . . . . .DLB-84

Johnson, Charles 1948- DLB-33, 278

Johnson, Charles S. 1893-1956 . . . . . .DLB-51, 91

Johnson, Denis 1949- DLB-120

Johnson, Diane 1934- Y-80

Johnson, Dorothy M. 1905–1984 . . . . . . .DLB-206

Johnson, E. Pauline (Tekahionwake)
1861-1913 . . . . .DLB-175

Johnson, Edgar 1901-1995 . . . . .DLB-103

Johnson, Edward 1598-1672 . . . . .DLB-24

Johnson, Eyvind 1900-1976 . . . . .DLB-259

Johnson, Fenton 1888-1958 . . . . .DLB-45, 50

Johnson, Georgia Douglas
1877?-1966 . . . . .DLB-51, 249

Johnson, Gerald W. 1890-1980 . . . . .DLB-29

Johnson, Greg 1953- DLB-234

Johnson, Helene 1907-1995 . . . . .DLB-51

Jacob Johnson and Company DLB-49

Johnson, James Weldon
1871-1938 . . . . .DLB-51; CDALB-4

Johnson, John H. 1918- DLB-137

"Backstage," Statement From the
Initial Issue of *Ebony*
(November 1945. . . . . .DLB-137

Johnson, Joseph [publishing house] DLB-154

Johnson, Linton Kwesi 1952- DLB-157

Johnson, Lionel 1867-1902. . . . . .DLB-19

Johnson, Nunnally 1897-1977 . . . . .DLB-26

Johnson, Owen 1878-1952. . . . . .Y-87

Johnson, Pamela Hansford 1912-1981 . . . . .DLB-15

Johnson, Pauline 1861-1913 . . . . .DLB-92

Johnson, Ronald 1935-1998 . . . . .DLB-169

Johnson, Samuel 1696-1772 . . . . DLB-24; CDBLB-2

Johnson, Samuel
1709-1784 . . . . DLB-39, 95, 104, 142, 213

Rambler, no. 4 (1750) [excerpt] DLB-39

The BBC Four Samuel Johnson Prize
for Non-fiction. Y-02

Johnson, Samuel 1822-1882. . . . . .DLB-1, 243

Johnson, Susanna 1730-1810 . . . . .DLB-200

Johnson, Terry 1955- DLB-233

Johnson, Uwe 1934-1984. . . . . . DLB-75; CDWLB-2

Benjamin Johnson [publishing house] DLB-49

Benjamin, Jacob, and Robert Johnson
[publishing house] DLB-49

Johnston, Annie Fellows 1863-1931. . . . . . .DLB-42

Johnston, Basil H. 1929- DLB-60

Johnston, David Claypole 1798?-1865. . . . .DLB-188

Johnston, Denis 1901-1984 . . . . .DLB-10

Johnston, Ellen 1835-1873 . . . . .DLB-199

Johnston, George 1912-1970 . . . . .DLB-260

Johnston, George 1913- DLB-88

Johnston, Sir Harry 1858-1927 . . . . .DLB-174

Johnston, Jennifer 1930- DLB-14

Johnston, Mary 1870-1936. . . . . .DLB-9

Johnston, Richard Malcolm 1822-1898 . . . .DLB-74

Johnstone, Charles 1719?-1800? DLB-39

Johst, Hanns 1890-1978. . . . . .DLB-124

Jolas, Eugene 1894-1952 . . . . .DLB-4, 45

Jones, Alice C. 1853-1933 . . . . .DLB-92

Jones, Charles C., Jr. 1831-1893 . . . . .DLB-30

Jones, D. G. 1929- DLB-53

Jones, David
1895-1974 . . . . .DLB-20, 100; CDBLB-7

Jones, Diana Wynne 1934- DLB-161

Jones, Ebenezer 1820-1860 . . . . .DLB-32

Jones, Ernest 1819-1868. . . . . .DLB-32

Jones, Gayl 1949- DLB-33, 278

Jones, George 1800-1870.............. DLB-183

Jones, Glyn 1905-1995 .... DLB-15

Jones, Gwyn 1907- DLB-15, 139

Jones, Henry Arthur 1851-1929 .... DLB-10

Jones, Hugh circa 1692-1760............ DLB-24

Jones, James 1921-1977........DLB-2, 143; DS-17

    James Jones Papers in the Handy
    Writers' Colony Collection at
    the University of Illinois at
    Springfield....................Y-98

    The James Jones Society..............Y-92

Jones, Jenkin Lloyd 1911- DLB-127

Jones, John Beauchamp 1810-1866...... DLB-202

Jones, Joseph, Major
    (see Thompson, William Tappan)

Jones, LeRoi (see Baraka, Amiri)

Jones, Lewis 1897-1939................ DLB-15

Jones, Madison 1925- DLB-152

Jones, Marie 1951- DLB-233

Jones, Preston 1936-1979 .... DLB-7

Jones, Rodney 1950- DLB-120

Jones, Thom 1945- DLB-244

Jones, Sir William 1746-1794 .... DLB-109

Jones, William Alfred 1817-1900........ DLB-59

Jones's Publishing House DLB-49

Jong, Erica 1942- DLB-2, 5, 28, 152

Jonke, Gert F. 1946- DLB-85

Jonson, Ben
    1572?-1637 .... DLB-62, 121; CDBLB-1

Jordan, June 1936- DLB-38

Joseph, Jenny 1932- DLB-40

Joseph and George Y-99

Michael Joseph Limited DLB-112

Josephson, Matthew 1899-1978 .... DLB-4

Josephus, Flavius 37-100 ....DLB-176

Josephy, Alvin M., Jr.
    Tribute to Alfred A. Knopf Y-84

Josiah Allen's Wife (see Holley, Marietta)

Josipovici, Gabriel 1940- DLB-14

Josselyn, John ?-1675 .... DLB-24

Joudry, Patricia 1921-2000 .... DLB-88

Jouve, Pierre Jean 1887-1976.......... DLB-258

Jovanovich, William 1920-2001 .... Y-01

    Into the Past: William Jovanovich's
    Reflections on Publishing Y-02

    [Repsonse to Ken Auletta] Y-97

    The Temper of the West: William
    Jovanovich.....................Y-02

    Tribute to Charles Scribner Jr........... Y-95

Jovine, Francesco 1902-1950 .... DLB-264

Jovine, Giuseppe 1922- DLB-128

Joyaux, Philippe (see Sollers, Philippe)

Joyce, Adrien (see Eastman, Carol)

Joyce, James 1882-1941
    .... DLB-10, 19, 36, 162, 247; CDBLB-6

    Danis Rose and the Rendering of *Ulysses* .. Y-97

James Joyce Centenary: Dublin, 1982 .... Y-82

James Joyce Conference............... Y-85

A Joyce (Con)Text: Danis Rose and the
    Remaking of *Ulysses* Y-97

The National Library of Ireland's
    New James Joyce Manuscripts...... Y-02

The New *Ulysses* Y-84

Public Domain and the Violation of
    Texts Y-97

The Quinn Draft of James Joyce's
    Circe Manuscript................ Y-00

Stephen Joyce's Letter to the Editor of
    The Irish Times Y-97

Ulysses, Reader's Edition: First Reactions .. Y-97

We See the Editor at Work Y-97

Whose *Ulysses?* The Function of Editing .. Y-97

Jozsef, Attila 1905-1937..... DLB-215; CDWLB-4

Juarroz, Roberto 1925-1995 .... DLB-283

Orange Judd Publishing Company....... DLB-49

Judd, Sylvester 1813-1853 .... DLB-1, 243

Judith circa 930.................... DLB-146

Julian of Norwich 1342-circa 1420 ..... DLB-1146

Julius Caesar
    100 B.C.-44 B.C. DLB-211; CDWLB-1

June, Jennie (see Croly, Jane Cunningham)

Jung, Franz 1888-1963 .... DLB-118

Jünger, Ernst 1895- DLB-56; CDWLB-2

Der jüngere Titurel circa 1275 .... DLB-138

Jung-Stilling, Johann Heinrich 1740-1817.... DLB-94

Justice, Donald 1925- Y-83

Juvenal circa A.D. 60-circa A.D. 130
    .... DLB-211; CDWLB-1

The Juvenile Library
    (see M. J. Godwin and Company)

K

Kacew, Romain (see Gary, Romain)

Kafka, Franz 1883-1924 ..... DLB-81; CDWLB-2

Kahn, Gus 1886-1941................ DLB-265

Kahn, Roger 1927- DLB-171

Kaikō Takeshi 1939-1989............. DLB-182

Kaiser, Georg 1878-1945 ... DLB-124; CDWLB-2

Kaiserchronik circa 1147 .... DLB-148

Kaleb, Vjekoslav 1905- DLB-181

Kalechofsky, Roberta 1931- DLB-28

Kaler, James Otis 1848-1912......... DLB-12, 42

Kalmar, Bert 1884-1947 .... DLB-265

Kames, Henry Home, Lord
    1696-1782................... DLB-31, 104

Kamo no Chōmei (Kamo no Nagaakira)
    1153 or 1155-1216 .... DLB-203

Kamo no Nagaakira (see Kamo no Chōmei)

Kampmann, Christian 1939-1988....... DLB-214

Kandel, Lenore 1932- DLB-16

Kanin, Garson 1912-1999 .... DLB-7

    A Tribute (to Marc Connelly) Y-80

Kant, Hermann 1926- DLB-75

Kant, Immanuel 1724-1804 .... DLB-94

Kantemir, Antiokh Dmitrievich
    1708-1744.................... DLB-150

Kantor, MacKinlay 1904-1977 .... DLB-9, 102

Kanze Kōjirō Nobumitsu 1435-1516 .... DLB-203

Kanze Motokiyo (see Zeimi)

Kaplan, Fred 1937- DLB-111

Kaplan, Johanna 1942- DLB-28

Kaplan, Justin 1925- DLB-111; Y-86

Kaplinski, Jaan 1941- DLB-232

Kapnist, Vasilii Vasilevich 1758?-1823 ... DLB-150

Karadžić, Vuk Stefanović
    1787-1864.............DLB-147; CDWLB-4

Karamzin, Nikolai Mikhailovich
    1766-1826.................... DLB-150

Karinthy, Frigyes 1887-1938........... DLB-215

Karsch, Anna Louisa 1722-1791 .... DLB-97

Kasack, Hermann 1896-1966 .... DLB-69

Kasai Zenzō 1887-1927 .... DLB-180

Kaschnitz, Marie Luise 1901-1974 ...... DLB-69

Kassák, Lajos 1887-1967 .... DLB-215

Kaštelan, Jure 1919-1990 ....DLB-147

Kästner, Erich 1899-1974 .... DLB-56

Kataev, Evgenii Petrovich
    (see Il'f, Il'ia and Petrov, Evgenii)

Kataev, Valentin Petrovich 1897-1986 ....DLB-272

Katenin, Pavel Aleksandrovich
    1792-1853.................... DLB-205

Kattan, Naim 1928- DLB-53

Katz, Steve 1935- Y-83

Kauffman, Janet 1945- DLB-218; Y-86

Kauffmann, Samuel 1898-1971.........DLB-127

Kaufman, Bob 1925-1986........... DLB-16, 41

Kaufman, George S. 1889-1961 .... DLB-7

Kaufmann, Walter 1921-1980 ....DLB-279

Kavan, Anna (Helen Woods Ferguson
    Edmonds) 1901-1968............. DLB-255

Kavanagh, P. J. 1931- DLB-40

Kavanagh, Patrick 1904-1967........ DLB-15, 20

Kaverin, Veniamin Aleksandrovich
    (Veniamin Aleksandrovich Zil'ber)
    1902-1989 ....DLB-272

Kawabata Yasunari 1899-1972 .... DLB-180

Kay, Guy Gavriel 1954- DLB-251

Kaye-Smith, Sheila 1887-1956........... DLB-36

Kazin, Alfred 1915-1998............... DLB-67

Keane, John B. 1928- DLB-13

Keary, Annie 1825-1879 .... DLB-163

Keary, Eliza 1827-1918............... DLB-240

Keating, H. R. F. 1926- DLB-87

Keatley, Charlotte 1960- DLB-245

Keats, Ezra Jack 1916-1983 .... DLB-61

Keats, John 1795-1821 ... DLB-96, 110; CDBLB-3

Keble, John 1792-1866 .... DLB-32, 55

Keckley, Elizabeth 1818?-1907 .... DLB-239

Keeble, John 1944- Y-83

Keeffe, Barrie 1945- DLB-13, 245

Keeley, James 1867-1934 . . . . .DLB-25

W. B. Keen, Cooke and Company DLB-49

The Mystery of Carolyn Keene. Y-02

Keillor, Garrison 1942- Y-87

Keith, Marian (Mary Esther MacGregor)
1874?-1961 .DLB-92

Keller, Gary D. 1943- DLB-82

Keller, Gottfried
1819-1890 . . . . DLB-129; CDWLB-2

Kelley, Edith Summers 1884-1956. . . . . . . .DLB-9

Kelley, Emma Dunham ?-? DLB-221

Kelley, William Melvin 1937- DLB-33

Kellogg, Ansel Nash 1832-1886. . . . . .DLB-23

Kellogg, Steven 1941- DLB-61

Kelly, George E. 1887-1974 . . . . DLB-7, 249

Kelly, Hugh 1739-1777. . . . . .DLB-89

Kelly, Piet and Company. DLB-49

Kelly, Robert 1935- DLB-5, 130, 165

Kelman, James 1946- DLB-194

Kelmscott Press .DLB-112

Kelton, Elmer 1926- DLB-256

Kemble, E. W. 1861-1933 . . . . .DLB-188

Kemble, Fanny 1809-1893 . . . . .DLB-32

Kemelman, Harry 1908-1996 . . . . .DLB-28

Kempe, Margery circa 1373-1438 . . . . . . .DLB-146

Kempner, Friederike 1836-1904 . . . . .DLB-129

Kempowski, Walter 1929- DLB-75

Claude Kendall [publishing company]. DLB-46

Kendall, Henry 1839-1882. . . . . .DLB-230

Kendall, May 1861-1943 . . . . .DLB-240

Kendell, George 1809-1867 . . . . .DLB-43

Kenedy, P. J., and Sons DLB-49

Kenkō circa 1283-circa 1352 . . . . .DLB-203

Kennan, George 1845-1924 . . . . .DLB-189

Kennedy, A. L. 1965- DLB-271

Kennedy, Adrienne 1931- DLB-38

Kennedy, John Pendleton 1795-1870 . . .DLB-3, 248

Kennedy, Leo 1907-2000 . . . . .DLB-88

Kennedy, Margaret 1896-1967 . . . . .DLB-36

Kennedy, Patrick 1801-1873 . . . . .DLB-159

Kennedy, Richard S. 1920- DLB-111; Y-02

Kennedy, William 1928- DLB-143; Y-85

Kennedy, X. J. 1929- DLB-5

Tribute to John Ciardi Y-86

Kennelly, Brendan 1936- DLB-40

Kenner, Hugh 1923- DLB-67

Tribute to Cleanth Brooks Y-80

Mitchell Kennerley [publishing house]. DLB-46

Kenny, Maurice 1929- DLB-175

Kent, Frank R. 1877-1958 . . . . .DLB-29

Kenyon, Jane 1947-1995 . . . . .DLB-120

Kenzheev, Bakhyt Shkurullaevich
1950- DLB-285

Keough, Hugh Edmund 1864-1912. . . . . .DLB-171

Keppler and Schwartzmann. DLB-49

Ker, John, third Duke of Roxburghe
1740-1804 .DLB-213

Ker, N. R. 1908-1982. . . . . .DLB-201

Kerlan, Irvin 1912-1963. . . . . .DLB-187

Kermode, Frank 1919- DLB-242

Kern, Jerome 1885-1945 . . . . .DLB-187

Kernaghan, Eileen 1939- DLB-251

Kerner, Justinus 1786-1862 . . . . .DLB-90

Kerouac, Jack
1922-1969 . . .DLB-2, 16, 237; DS-3; CDALB-1

Auction of Jack Kerouac's
On the Road Scroll Y-01

The Jack Kerouac Revival Y-95

"Re-meeting of Old Friends":
The Jack Kerouac Conference Y-82

Statement of Correction to "The Jack
Kerouac Revival" Y-96

Kerouac, Jan 1952-1996. . . . . .DLB-16

Charles H. Kerr and Company DLB-49

Kerr, Orpheus C. (see Newell, Robert Henry)

Kersh, Gerald 1911-1968. . . . . .DLB-255

Kertész, Imre Y-02

Kesey, Ken
1935-2001 . . . . .DLB-2, 16, 206; CDALB-6

Kessel, Joseph 1898-1979 . . . . .DLB-72

Kessel, Martin 1901-1990 . . . . .DLB-56

Kesten, Hermann 1900-1996. . . . . .DLB-56

Keun, Irmgard 1905-1982 . . . . .DLB-69

Key, Ellen 1849-1926. . . . . .DLB-259

Key and Biddle .DLB-49

Keynes, Sir Geoffrey 1887-1982. . . . . . . .DLB-201

Keynes, John Maynard 1883-1946 . . . . DS-10

Keyserling, Eduard von 1855-1918. . . . . . .DLB-66

Khan, Ismith 1925-2002 . . . . .DLB-125

Kharitonov, Evgenii Vladimirovich
1941-1981 .DLB-285

Kharitonov, Mark Sergeevich 1937- DLB-285

Khaytov, Nikolay 1919- DLB-181

Khemnitser, Ivan Ivanovich
1745-1784 .DLB-150

Kheraskov, Mikhail Matveevich
1733-1807 .DLB-150

Khomiakov, Aleksei Stepanovich
1804-1860 .DLB-205

Khristov, Boris 1945- DLB-181

Khvoshchinskaia, Nadezhda Dmitrievna
1824-1889 .DLB-238

Khvostov, Dmitrii Ivanovich
1757-1835. .DLB-150

Kibirov, Timur Iur'evich (Timur
Iur'evich Zapoev) 1955- DLB-285

Kidd, Adam 1802?-1831 . . . . .DLB-99

William Kidd [publishing house]. DLB-106

Kidder, Tracy 1945- DLB-185

Kiely, Benedict 1919- DLB-15

Kieran, John 1892-1981. . . . . DLB-171

Kies, Marietta 1853-1899. . . . . .DLB-270

Kiggins and Kellogg. DLB-49

Kiley, Jed 1889-1962 . . . . .DLB-4

Kilgore, Bernard 1908-1967. . . . . .DLB-127

Kilian, Crawford 1941- DLB-251

Killens, John Oliver 1916-1987 . . . . .DLB-33

Tribute to Julian Mayfield. Y-84

Killigrew, Anne 1660-1685 . . . . .DLB-131

Killigrew, Thomas 1612-1683 . . . . .DLB-58

Kilmer, Joyce 1886-1918 . . . . .DLB-45

Kilroy, Thomas 1934- DLB-233

Kilwardby, Robert circa 1215-1279 . . . . . .DLB-115

Kilworth, Garry 1941- DLB-261

Kim, Anatolii Andreevich 1939- DLB-285

Kimball, Richard Burleigh 1816-1892 . . . .DLB-202

Kincaid, Jamaica 1949-
. . . . . . DLB-157, 227; CDALB-7; CDWLB-3

King, Charles 1844-1933 . . . . .DLB-186

King, Clarence 1842-1901 . . . . .DLB-12

King, Florence 1936- Y-85

King, Francis 1923- DLB-15, 139

King, Grace 1852-1932 . . . . DLB-12, 78

King, Harriet Hamilton 1840-1920 . . . . . .DLB-199

King, Henry 1592-1669. . . . . .DLB-126

Solomon King [publishing house] DLB-49

King, Stephen 1947- DLB-143; Y-80

King, Susan Petigru 1824-1875 . . . . .DLB-239

King, Thomas 1943- DLB-175

King, Woodie, Jr. 1937- DLB-38

Kinglake, Alexander William
1809-1891 . . . . .DLB-55, 166

Kingsbury, Donald 1929- DLB-251

Kingsley, Charles
1819-1875 . . . . DLB-21, 32, 163, 178, 190

Kingsley, Henry 1830-1876 . . . . .DLB-21, 230

Kingsley, Mary Henrietta 1862-1900. . . . . DLB-174

Kingsley, Sidney 1906-1995. . . . . .DLB-7

Kingsmill, Hugh 1889-1949. . . . . .DLB-149

Kingsolver, Barbara
1955- DLB-206; CDALB-7

Kingston, Maxine Hong
1940- DLB-173, 212; Y-80; CDALB-7

Kingston, William Henry Giles
1814-1880 .DLB-163

Kinnan, Mary Lewis 1763-1848. . . . . . . .DLB-200

Kinnell, Galway 1927- DLB-5; Y-87

Kinsella, Thomas 1928- DLB-27

Kipling, Rudyard 1865-1936
. . . . .DLB-19, 34, 141, 156; CDBLB-5

Kipphardt, Heinar 1922-1982 . . . . .DLB-124

Kirby, William 1817-1906 . . . . .DLB-99

Kircher, Athanasius 1602-1680 . . . . .DLB-164

Kireevsky, Ivan Vasil'evich 1806-1856 . . .DLB-198

Kireevsky, Petr Vasil'evich 1808-1856 . . .DLB-205

Kirk, Hans 1898-1962 . . . . .DLB-214

Kirk, John Foster 1824-1904 . . . . .DLB-79

Kirkconnell, Watson 1895-1977 . . . . .DLB-68

Kirkland, Caroline M.
1801-1864 . . . . DLB-3, 73, 74, 250; DS-13

Kirkland, Joseph 1830-1893 . . . . DLB-12

Francis Kirkman [publishing house] DLB-170

Kirkpatrick, Clayton 1915- DLB-127

Kirkup, James 1918- DLB-27

Kirouac, Conrad (see Marie-Victorin, Frère)

Kirsch, Sarah 1935- DLB-75

Kirst, Hans Hellmut 1914-1989 . . . . DLB-69

Kiš, Danilo 1935-1989 . . . . . DLB-181; CDWLB-4

Kita Morio 1927- DLB-182

Kitcat, Mabel Greenhow 1859-1922 . . . . . DLB-135

Kitchin, C. H. B. 1895-1967 . . . . DLB-77

Kittredge, William 1932- DLB-212, 244

Kiukhel'beker, Vil'gel'm Karlovich
1797-1846 . . . . DLB-205

Kizer, Carolyn 1925- DLB-5, 169

Klabund 1890-1928 . . . . DLB-66

Klaj, Johann 1616-1656 . . . . DLB-164

Klappert, Peter 1942- DLB-5

Klass, Philip (see Tenn, William)

Klein, A. M. 1909-1972 . . . . DLB-68

Kleist, Ewald von 1715-1759 . . . . DLB-97

Kleist, Heinrich von
1777-1811 . . . . DLB-90; CDWLB-2

Klíma, Ivan 1931- DLB-232; CDWLB-4

Klimentev, Andrei Platonovic
(see Platonov, Andrei Platonovich)

Klinger, Friedrich Maximilian
1752-1831 . . . . DLB-94

Kliushnikov, Viktor Petrovich
1841-1892 . . . . DLB-238

Klopfer, Donald S.
Impressions of William Faulkner Y-97

  Oral History Interview with Donald
  S. Klopfer Y-97

  Tribute to Alfred A. Knopf Y-84

Klopstock, Friedrich Gottlieb
1724-1803 . . . . DLB-97

Klopstock, Meta 1728-1758 . . . . DLB-97

Kluge, Alexander 1932- DLB-75

Kluge, P. F. 1942- Y-02

Knapp, Joseph Palmer 1864-1951 . . . . DLB-91

Knapp, Samuel Lorenzo 1783-1838 . . . . . . DLB-59

J. J. and P. Knapton [publishing house] . . DLB-154

Kniazhnin, Iakov Borisovich 1740-1791 . . DLB-150

Knickerbocker, Diedrich (see Irving, Washington)

Knigge, Adolph Franz Friedrich Ludwig,
Freiherr von 1752-1796 . . . . DLB-94

Charles Knight and Company DLB-106

Knight, Damon 1922-2002 . . . . DLB-8

Knight, Etheridge 1931-1992 . . . . DLB-41

Knight, John S. 1894-1981 . . . . DLB-29

Knight, Sarah Kemble 1666-1727 . . . . DLB-24, 200

Knight-Bruce, G. W. H. 1852-1896 . . . . . .DLB-174

Knister, Raymond 1899-1932 . . . . DLB-68

Knoblock, Edward 1874-1945 . . . . DLB-10

Knopf, Alfred A. 1892-1984 . . . . .Y-84

Knopf to Hammett: The Editoral
Correspondence Y-00

Alfred A. Knopf [publishing house] DLB-46

Knorr von Rosenroth, Christian
1636-1689 . . . . DLB-168

Knowles, John 1926- DLB-6; CDALB-6

Knox, Frank 1874-1944 . . . . DLB-29

Knox, John circa 1514-1572 . . . . DLB-132

Knox, John Armoy 1850-1906 . . . . DLB-23

Knox, Lucy 1845-1884 . . . . DLB-240

Knox, Ronald Arbuthnott 1888-1957 . . . . . DLB-77

Knox, Thomas Wallace 1835-1896 . . . . . DLB-189

Kobayashi Takiji 1903-1933 . . . . DLB-180

Kober, Arthur 1900-1975 . . . . DLB-11

Kobiakova, Aleksandra Petrovna
1823-1892 . . . . DLB-238

Kocbek, Edvard 1904-1981 . .DLB-147; CDWLB-4

Koch, Howard 1902-1995 . . . . DLB-26

Koch, Kenneth 1925-2002 . . . . DLB-5

Kōda Rohan 1867-1947 . . . . DLB-180

Koehler, Ted 1894-1973 . . . . DLB-265

Koenigsberg, Moses 1879-1945 . . . . DLB-25

Koeppen, Wolfgang 1906-1996 . . . . DLB-69

Koertge, Ronald 1940- DLB-105

Koestler, Arthur 1905-1983 . . . . . .Y-83; CDBLB-7

Kohn, John S. Van E. 1906-1976 . . . . DLB-187

Kokhanovskaia
(see Sokhanskaia, Nadezhda Stepanova)

Kokoschka, Oskar 1886-1980 . . . . DLB-124

Kolb, Annette 1870-1967 . . . . DLB-66

Kolbenheyer, Erwin Guido
1878-1962 . . . . DLB-66, 124

Kolleritsch, Alfred 1931- DLB-85

Kolodny, Annette 1941- DLB-67

Kol'tsov, Aleksei Vasil'evich 1809-1842 . . DLB-205

Komarov, Matvei circa 1730-1812 . . . . . . DLB-150

Komroff, Manuel 1890-1974 . . . . DLB-4

Komunyakaa, Yusef 1947- DLB-120

Kondoleon, Harry 1955-1994 . . . . DLB-266

Koneski, Blaže 1921-1993 . . . DLB-181; CDWLB-4

Konigsburg, E. L. 1930- DLB-52

Konparu Zenchiku 1405-1468? DLB-203

Konrád, György 1933- DLB-232; CDWLB-4

Konrad von Würzburg circa 1230-1287 . . DLB-138

Konstantinov, Aleko 1863-1897 . . . . DLB-147

Konwicki, Tadeusz 1926- DLB-232

Kooser, Ted 1939- DLB-105

Kopit, Arthur 1937- DLB-7

Kops, Bernard 1926?- DLB-13

Kornbluth, C. M. 1923-1958 . . . . DLB-8

Körner, Theodor 1791-1813 . . . . DLB-90

Kornfeld, Paul 1889-1942 . . . . DLB-118

Korolenko, Vladimir Galaktionovich
1853-1921 .DLB-277

Kosinski, Jerzy 1933-1991 . . . . .DLB-2; Y-82

Kosmač, Ciril 1910-1980 . . . . DLB-181

Kosovel, Srečko 1904-1926 . . . . .DLB-147

Kostrov, Ermil Ivanovich 1755-1796 . . . . DLB-150

Kotzebue, August von 1761-1819 . . . . DLB-94

Kotzwinkle, William 1938- DLB-173

Kovačić, Ante 1854-1889 . . . . .DLB-147

Kovalevskaia, Sof'ia Vasil'evna
1850-1891 .DLB-277

Kovič, Kajetan 1931- DLB-181

Kozlov, Ivan Ivanovich 1779-1840 . . . . . . DLB-205

Kraf, Elaine 1946- Y-81

Kramer, Jane 1938- DLB-185

Kramer, Larry 1935- DLB-249

Kramer, Mark 1944- DLB-185

Kranjčević, Silvije Strahimir 1865-1908 . . .DLB-147

Krasko, Ivan 1876-1958 . . . . DLB-215

Krasna, Norman 1909-1984 . . . . DLB-26

Kraus, Hans Peter 1907-1988 . . . . .DLB-187

Kraus, Karl 1874-1936 . . . . DLB-118

Krause, Herbert 1905-1976 . . . . DLB-256

Krauss, Ruth 1911-1993 . . . . DLB-52

Kreisel, Henry 1922-1991 . . . . DLB-88

Krestovsky V.
(see Khvoshchinskaia, Nadezhda Dmitrievna)

Krestovsky, Vsevolod Vladimirovich
1839-1895 . . . . DLB-238

Kreuder, Ernst 1903-1972 . . . . DLB-69

Krėvė-Mickevičius, Vincas 1882-1954 . . . DLB-220

Kreymborg, Alfred 1883-1966 . . . . DLB-4, 54

Krieger, Murray 1923- DLB-67

Krim, Seymour 1922-1989 . . . . DLB-16

Kripke, Saul 1940- DLB-279

Kristensen, Tom 1893-1974 . . . . DLB-214

Kristeva, Julia 1941- DLB-242

Kritzer, Hyman W. 1918-2002 . . . . Y-02

Krivulin, Viktor Borisovich 1944-2001 . . DLB-285

Krleža, Miroslav
1893-1981 . . . . .DLB-147; CDWLB-4

Krock, Arthur 1886-1974 . . . . DLB-29

Kroetsch, Robert 1927- DLB-53

Kropotkin, Petr Alekseevich 1842-1921 . .DLB-277

Kross, Jaan 1920- DLB-232

Krúdy, Gyula 1878-1933 . . . . DLB-215

Krutch, Joseph Wood
1893-1970 . . . . .DLB-63, 206, 275

Krylov, Ivan Andreevich 1769-1844 . . . . . DLB-150

Krymov, Iurii Solomonovich
(Iurii Solomonovich Beklemishev)
1908-1941 .DLB-272

Kubin, Alfred 1877-1959 . . . . DLB-81

Kubrick, Stanley 1928-1999 . . . . DLB-26

Kudrun circa 1230-1240 . . . . DLB-138

Kuffstein, Hans Ludwig von 1582-1656 . . DLB-164

Kuhlmann, Quirinus 1651-1689 . . . . DLB-168

Kuhn, Thomas S. 1922-1996 . . . . .DLB-279

Kuhnau, Johann 1660-1722 . . . . DLB-168

Kukol'nik, Nestor Vasil'evich
1809-1868 . . . . DLB-205

Kukučín, Martin
　1860-1928 . . . . .DLB-215; CDWLB-4

Kumin, Maxine 1925- DLB-5

Kuncewicz, Maria 1895-1989. . . . . .DLB-215

Kundera, Milan 1929- DLB-232; CDWLB-4

Kunene, Mazisi 1930- DLB-117

Kunikida Doppo 1869-1908 . . . . .DLB-180

Kunitz, Stanley 1905- DLB-48

Kunjufu, Johari M. (see Amini, Johari M.)

Kunnert, Gunter 1929- DLB-75

Kunze, Reiner 1933- DLB-75

Kupferberg, Tuli 1923- DLB-16

Kuraev, Mikhail Nikolaevich 1939- DLB-285

Kurahashi Yumiko 1935- DLB-182

Kureishi, Hanif 1954- DLB-194, 245

Kürnberger, Ferdinand 1821-1879 . . . . . .DLB-129

Kurz, Isolde 1853-1944 . . . . .DLB-66

Kusenberg, Kurt 1904-1983. . . . . .DLB-69

Kushchevsky, Ivan Afanas'evich
　1847-1876. . . . . .DLB-238

Kushner, Tony 1956- DLB-228

Kuttner, Henry 1915-1958. . . . . .DLB-8

Kyd, Thomas 1558-1594. . . . . .DLB-62

Kyffin, Maurice circa 1560?-1598 . . . . . .DLB-136

Kyger, Joanne 1934- DLB-16

Kyne, Peter B. 1880-1957 . . . . .DLB-78

Kyōgoku Tamekane 1254-1332. . . . . . . .DLB-203

Kyrklund, Willy 1921- DLB-257

L

L. E. L. (see Landon, Letitia Elizabeth)

Laberge, Albert 1871-1960. . . . . .DLB-68

Laberge, Marie 1950- DLB-60

Labiche, Eugène 1815-1888 . . . . .DLB-192

Labrunie, Gerard (see Nerval, Gerard de)

La Bruyère, Jean de 1645-1696 . . . . .DLB-268

La Calprenède 1609?-1663 . . . . .DLB-268

La Capria, Raffaele 1922- DLB-196

Lacombe, Patrice
　(see Trullier-Lacombe, Joseph Patrice)

Lacretelle, Jacques de 1888-1985 . . . . .DLB-65

Lacy, Ed 1911-1968. . . . . .DLB-226

Lacy, Sam 1903- DLB-171

Ladd, Joseph Brown 1764-1786 . . . . .DLB-37

La Farge, Oliver 1901-1963 . . . . .DLB-9

Lafayette, Marie-Madeleine, comtesse de
　1634-1693 .DLB-268

Laffan, Mrs. R. S. de Courcy
　(see Adams, Bertha Leith)

Lafferty, R. A. 1914-2002 . . . . .DLB-8

La Flesche, Francis 1857-1932 . . . . .DLB-175

La Fontaine, Jean de 1621-1695 . . . . .DLB-268

Laforge, Jules 1860-1887 . . . . .DLB-217

Lagerkvist, Pär 1891-1974 . . . . .DLB-259

Lagerlöf, Selma 1858-1940. . . . . .DLB-259

Lagorio, Gina 1922- DLB-196

La Guma, Alex
　1925-1985 . . . . DLB-117, 225; CDWLB-3

Lahaise, Guillaume (see Delahaye, Guy)

Lahontan, Louis-Armand de Lom d'Arce,
　Baron de 1666-1715?. DLB-99

Laing, Kojo 1946- DLB-157

Laird, Carobeth 1895-1983 . . . . Y-82

Laird and Lee DLB-49

Lake, Paul 1951- DLB-282

Lalić, Ivan V. 1931-1996 . . . . .DLB-181

Lalić, Mihailo 1914-1992 . . . . .DLB-181

Lalonde, Michèle 1937- DLB-60

Lamantia, Philip 1927- DLB-16

Lamartine, Alphonse de 1790-1869 . . . . . .DLB-217

Lamb, Lady Caroline 1785-1828 . . . . .DLB-116

Lamb, Charles
　1775-1834 . . . . . . DLB-93, 107, 163; CDBLB-3

Lamb, Mary 1764-1874 . . . . .DLB-163

Lambert, Angela 1940- DLB-271

Lambert, Betty 1933-1983 . . . . .DLB-60

Lamm, Donald
　Goodbye, Gutenberg? A Lecture at
　the New York Public Library,
　18 April 1995 . . . . Y-95

Lamming, George
　1927- DLB-125; CDWLB-3

La Mothe Le Vayer, François de
　1588-1672 .DLB-268

L'Amour, Louis 1908-1988 . . . . . . DLB-206; Y-80

Lampman, Archibald 1861-1899 . . . . .DLB-92

Lamson, Wolffe and Company DLB-49

Lancer Books. DLB-46

Lanchester, John 1962- DLB-267

Lander, Peter (see Cunningham, Peter)

Landesman, Fran 1927- DLB-16

Landesman, Jay 1919- DLB-16

Landolfi, Tommaso 1908-1979 . . . . .DLB-177

Landon, Letitia Elizabeth 1802-1838 . . . . .DLB-96

Landor, Walter Savage 1775-1864. . . .DLB-93, 107

Landry, Napoléon-P. 1884-1956 . . . . .DLB-92

Lane, Charles 1800-1870 . . . . . . .DLB-1, 223; DS-5

Lane, F. C. 1885-1984 . . . . .DLB-241

Lane, Laurence W. 1890-1967. . . . . .DLB-91

Lane, M. Travis 1934- DLB-60

Lane, Patrick 1939- DLB-53

Lane, Pinkie Gordon 1923- DLB-41

John Lane Company DLB-49

Laney, Al 1896-1988 . . . . DLB-4, 171

Lang, Andrew 1844-1912 . . . . . .DLB-98, 141, 184

Langer, Susanne K. 1895-1985 . . . . .DLB-270

Langevin, André 1927- DLB-60

Langford, David 1953- DLB-261

Langgässer, Elisabeth 1899-1950. . . . . . . .DLB-69

Langhorne, John 1735-1779 . . . . .DLB-109

Langland, William circa 1330-circa 1400. .DLB-146

Langton, Anna 1804-1893 . . . . .DLB-99

Lanham, Edwin 1904-1979 . . . . .DLB-4

Lanier, Sidney 1842-1881 . . . . . . .DLB-64; DS-13

Lanyer, Aemilia 1569-1645 . . . . .DLB-121

Lapointe, Gatien 1931-1983 . . . . .DLB-88

Lapointe, Paul-Marie 1929- DLB-88

Larcom, Lucy 1824-1893. . . . . .DLB-221, 243

Lardner, John 1912-1960. . . . . .DLB-171

Lardner, Ring 1885-1933
　. . . . . DLB-11, 25, 86, 171; DS-16; CDALB-4

　Lardner 100: Ring Lardner
　　Centennial Symposium. Y-85

Lardner, Ring, Jr. 1915-2000 . . . . . . DLB-26, Y-00

Larkin, Philip 1922-1985 . . . . .DLB-27; CDBLB-8

　The Philip Larkin Society Y-99

La Roche, Sophie von 1730-1807. . . . . . . .DLB-94

La Rochefoucauld, François duc de
　1613-1680 .DLB-268

La Rocque, Gilbert 1943-1984. . . . . .DLB-60

Laroque de Roquebrune, Robert
　(see Roquebrune, Robert de)

Larrick, Nancy 1910- DLB-61

Lars, Claudia 1899-1974 . . . . .DLB-283

Larsen, Nella 1893-1964 . . . . .DLB-51

Larson, Clinton F. 1919-1994 . . . . .DLB-256

La Sale, Antoine de
　circa 1386-1460/1467 . . . . .DLB-208

Lasch, Christopher 1932-1994. . . . . .DLB-246

Lasker-Schüler, Else 1869-1945 . . . . .DLB-66, 124

Lasnier, Rina 1915-1997 . . . . .DLB-88

Lassalle, Ferdinand 1825-1864. . . . . .DLB-129

Latham, Robert 1912-1995 . . . . .DLB-201

Lathrop, Dorothy P. 1891-1980 . . . . .DLB-22

Lathrop, George Parsons 1851-1898 . . . . . .DLB-71

Lathrop, John, Jr. 1772-1820 . . . . .DLB-37

Latimer, Hugh 1492?-1555 . . . . .DLB-136

Latimore, Jewel Christine McLawler
　(see Amini, Johari M.)

Latin Literature, The Uniqueness of DLB-211

La Tour du Pin, Patrice de 1911-1975. . . .DLB-258

Latymer, William 1498-1583. . . . . .DLB-132

Laube, Heinrich 1806-1884 . . . . .DLB-133

Laud, William 1573-1645 . . . . .DLB-213

Laughlin, James 1914-1997 . . . . . DLB-48; Y-96, 97

　A Tribute [to Henry Miller] Y-80

　Tribute to Albert Erskine Y-93

　Tribute to Kenneth Rexroth. Y-82

　Tribute to Malcolm Cowley Y-89

Laumer, Keith 1925-1993 . . . . .DLB-8

Lauremberg, Johann 1590-1658 . . . . .DLB-164

Laurence, Margaret 1926-1987 . . . . .DLB-53

Laurentius von Schnüffis 1633-1702 . . . . .DLB-168

Laurents, Arthur 1918- DLB-26

Laurie, Annie (see Black, Winifred)

Laut, Agnes Christiana 1871-1936. . . . . . .DLB-92

Lauterbach, Ann 1942- DLB-193

Lautréamont, Isidore Lucien Ducasse,
　Comte de 1846-1870 . . . . .DLB-217

Lavater, Johann Kaspar 1741-1801 . . . . DLB-97

Lavin, Mary 1912-1996 . . . . DLB-15

Law, John (see Harkness, Margaret)

Lawes, Henry 1596-1662 . . . . DLB-126

Lawless, Anthony (see MacDonald, Philip)

Lawless, Emily (The Hon. Emily Lawless)
1845-1913 . . . . DLB-240

Lawrence, D. H. 1885-1930
. . . . . DLB-10, 19, 36, 98, 162, 195; CDBLB-6

The D. H. Lawrence Society of
North America Y-00

Lawrence, David 1888-1973 . . . . DLB-29

Lawrence, Jerome 1915- DLB-228

Lawrence, Seymour 1926-1994 . . . . Y-94

Tribute to Richard Yates Y-92

Lawrence, T. E. 1888-1935 . . . . DLB-195

The T. E. Lawrence Society Y-98

Lawson, George 1598-1678 . . . . DLB-213

Lawson, Henry 1867-1922 . . . . DLB-230

Lawson, John ?-1711 . . . . DLB-24

Lawson, John Howard 1894-1977 . . . . . . DLB-228

Lawson, Louisa Albury 1848-1920 . . . . . . DLB-230

Lawson, Robert 1892-1957 . . . . DLB-22

Lawson, Victor F. 1850-1925 . . . . DLB-25

Layard, Austen Henry 1817-1894 . . . . . . DLB-166

Layton, Irving 1912- DLB-88

LaZamon flourished circa 1200 . . . . DLB-146

Lazarević, Laza K. 1851-1890 . . . . DLB-147

Lazarus, George 1904-1997 . . . . DLB-201

Lazhechnikov, Ivan Ivanovich
1792-1869 . . . . DLB-198

Lea, Henry Charles 1825-1909 . . . . DLB-47

Lea, Sydney 1942- DLB-120, 282

Lea, Tom 1907-2001 . . . . DLB-6

Leacock, John 1729-1802 . . . . DLB-31

Leacock, Stephen 1869-1944 . . . . DLB-92

Lead, Jane Ward 1623-1704 . . . . DLB-131

Leadenhall Press DLB-106

"The Greatness of Southern Literature":
League of the South Institute for the
Study of Southern Culture and History
. . . . Y-02

Leakey, Caroline Woolmer 1827-1881 . . . DLB-230

Leapor, Mary 1722-1746 . . . . DLB-109

Lear, Edward 1812-1888 . . . . . . DLB-32, 163, 166

Leary, Timothy 1920-1996 . . . . DLB-16

W. A. Leary and Company DLB-49

Léautaud, Paul 1872-1956 . . . . DLB-65

Leavis, F. R. 1895-1978 . . . . DLB-242

Leavitt, David 1961- DLB-130

Leavitt and Allen DLB-49

Le Blond, Mrs. Aubrey 1861-1934 . . . . . . DLB-174

le Carré, John (David John Moore Cornwell)
1931- DLB-87; CDBLB-8

Tribute to Graham Greene Y-91

Tribute to George Greenfield Y-00

Lécavelé, Roland (see Dorgeles, Roland)

Lechlitner, Ruth 1901- DLB-48

Leclerc, Félix 1914-1988 . . . . DLB-60

Le Clézio, J. M. G. 1940- DLB-83

Leder, Rudolf (see Hermlin, Stephan)

Lederer, Charles 1910-1976 . . . . DLB-26

Ledwidge, Francis 1887-1917 . . . . DLB-20

Lee, Dennis 1939- DLB-53

Lee, Don L. (see Madhubuti, Haki R.)

Lee, George W. 1894-1976 . . . . DLB-51

Lee, Harper 1926- DLB-6; CDALB-1

Lee, Harriet (1757-1851) DLB-39

Lee, Laurie 1914-1997 . . . . DLB-27

Lee, Leslie 1935- DLB-266

Lee, Li-Young 1957- DLB-165

Lee, Manfred B. 1905-1971 . . . . DLB-137

Lee, Nathaniel circa 1645-1692 . . . . DLB-80

Lee, Robert E. 1918-1994 . . . . DLB-228

Lee, Sir Sidney 1859-1926 . . . . DLB-149, 184

"Principles of Biography," in
Elizabethan and Other Essays DLB-149

Lee, Sophia (1750-1824) DLB-39

Lee, Tanith 1947- DLB-261

Lee, Vernon
1856-1935 . . . . DLB-57, 153, 156, 174, 178

Lee and Shepard DLB-49

Le Fanu, Joseph Sheridan
1814-1873 . . . . DLB-21, 70, 159, 178

Leffland, Ella 1931- Y-84

le Fort, Gertrud von 1876-1971 . . . . DLB-66

Le Gallienne, Richard 1866-1947 . . . . DLB-4

Legaré, Hugh Swinton
1797-1843 . . . . DLB-3, 59, 73, 248

Legaré, James Mathewes 1823-1859 . . . DLB-3, 248

Léger, Antoine-J. 1880-1950 . . . . DLB-88

Leggett, William 1801-1839 . . . . DLB-250

Le Guin, Ursula K.
1929- DLB-8, 52, 256, 275; CDALB-6

Lehman, Ernest 1920- DLB-44

Lehmann, John 1907-1989 . . . . DLB-27, 100

John Lehmann Limited DLB-112

Lehmann, Rosamond 1901-1990 . . . . DLB-15

Lehmann, Wilhelm 1882-1968 . . . . DLB-56

Leiber, Fritz 1910-1992 . . . . DLB-8

Leibniz, Gottfried Wilhelm 1646-1716 . . . DLB-168

Leicester University Press DLB-112

Leigh, Carolyn 1926-1983 . . . . DLB-265

Leigh, W. R. 1866-1955 . . . . DLB-188

Leinster, Murray 1896-1975 . . . . DLB-8

Leiser, Bill 1898-1965 . . . . DLB-241

Leisewitz, Johann Anton 1752-1806 . . . . . . DLB-94

Leitch, Maurice 1933- DLB-14

Leithauser, Brad 1943- DLB-120, 282

Leland, Charles G. 1824-1903 . . . . DLB-11

Leland, John 1503?-1552 . . . . DLB-136

Lemay, Pamphile 1837-1918 . . . . DLB-99

Lemelin, Roger 1919-1992 . . . . DLB-88

Lemercier, Louis-Jean-Népomucène
1771-1840 . . . . DLB-192

Le Moine, James MacPherson 1825-1912 . DLB-99

Lemon, Mark 1809-1870 . . . . DLB-163

Le Moyne, Jean 1913-1996 . . . . DLB-88

Lemperly, Paul 1858-1939 . . . . DLB-187

L'Engle, Madeleine 1918- DLB-52

Lennart, Isobel 1915-1971 . . . . DLB-44

Lennox, Charlotte 1729 or 1730-1804 . . . . DLB-39

Lenox, James 1800-1880 . . . . DLB-140

Lenski, Lois 1893-1974 . . . . DLB-22

Lentricchia, Frank 1940- DLB-246

Lenz, Hermann 1913-1998 . . . . DLB-69

Lenz, J. M. R. 1751-1792 . . . . DLB-94

Lenz, Siegfried 1926- DLB-75

Leonard, Elmore 1925- DLB-173, 226

Leonard, Hugh 1926- DLB-13

Leonard, William Ellery 1876-1944 . . . . . . DLB-54

Leonov, Leonid Maksimovich
1899-1994 . . . . DLB-272

Leonowens, Anna 1834-1914 . . . . . . DLB-99, 166

Leont'ev, Konstantin Nikolaevich
1831-1891 . . . . DLB-277

Leopold, Aldo 1887-1948 . . . . DLB-275

LePan, Douglas 1914-1998 . . . . DLB-88

Lepik, Kalju 1920-1999 . . . . DLB-232

Leprohon, Rosanna Eleanor 1829-1879 . . . DLB-99

Le Queux, William 1864-1927 . . . . DLB-70

Lermontov, Mikhail Iur'evich 1814-1841 . DLB-205

Lerner, Alan Jay 1918-1986 . . . . DLB-265

Lerner, Max 1902-1992 . . . . DLB-29

Lernet-Holenia, Alexander 1897-1976 . . . . . DLB-85

Le Rossignol, James 1866-1969 . . . . DLB-92

Lescarbot, Marc circa 1570-1642 . . . . DLB-99

LeSeur, William Dawson 1840-1917 . . . . . DLB-92

LeSieg, Theo. (see Geisel, Theodor Seuss)

Leskov, Nikolai Semenovich 1831-1895 . . DLB-238

Leslie, Doris before 1902-1982 . . . . DLB-191

Leslie, Eliza 1787-1858 . . . . DLB-202

Leslie, Frank (Henry Carter)
1821-1880 . . . . DLB-43, 79

Frank Leslie [publishing house] DLB-49

Leśmian, Bolesław 1878-1937 . . . . DLB-215

Lesperance, John 1835?-1891 . . . . DLB-99

Lessing, Bruno 1870-1940 . . . . DLB-28

Lessing, Doris
1919- DLB-15, 139; Y-85; CDBLB-8

Lessing, Gotthold Ephraim
1729-1781 . . . . DLB-97; CDWLB-2

The Lessing Society Y-00

Lettau, Reinhard 1929-1996 . . . . DLB-75

The Hemingway Letters Project Finds
an Editor Y-02

Lever, Charles 1806-1872 . . . . DLB-21

Lever, Ralph ca. 1527-1585 . . . . DLB-236

Leverson, Ada 1862-1933 . . . . DLB-153

Levertov, Denise
1923-1997 . . . . .DLB-5, 165; CDALB-7

Levi, Peter 1931-2000 . . . . .DLB-40

Levi, Primo 1919-1987. . . . . .DLB-177

Levien, Sonya 1888-1960. . . . . .DLB-44

Levin, Meyer 1905-1981 . . . . . . .DLB-9, 28; Y-81

Levin, Phillis 1954- DLB-282

Levine, Norman 1923- DLB-88

Levine, Philip 1928- DLB-5

Levis, Larry 1946- DLB-120

Lévi-Strauss, Claude 1908- DLB-242

Levitov, Aleksandr Ivanovich
1835?-1877 . . . . .DLB-277

Levy, Amy 1861-1889. . . . . .DLB-156, 240

Levy, Benn Wolfe 1900-1973 . . . . . .DLB-13; Y-81

Lewald, Fanny 1811-1889 . . . . .DLB-129

Lewes, George Henry 1817-1878 . . . . .DLB-55, 144

"Criticism in Relation to Novels"
(1863) DLB-21

The Principles of Success in Literature
(1865) [excerpt]. DLB-57

Lewis, Agnes Smith 1843-1926 . . . . .DLB-174

Lewis, Alfred H. 1857-1914 . . . . .DLB-25, 186

Lewis, Alun 1915-1944 . . . . .DLB-20, 162

Lewis, C. Day (see Day Lewis, C.)

Lewis, C. I. 1883-1964. . . . . .DLB-270

Lewis, C. S. 1898-1963
. . . . .DLB-15, 100, 160, 255; CDBLB-7

The New York C. S. Lewis Society. Y-99

Lewis, Charles B. 1842-1924. . . . . .DLB-11

Lewis, David 1941-2001 . . . . .DLB-279

Lewis, Henry Clay 1825-1850. . . . . . .DLB-3, 248

Lewis, Janet 1899-1999 . . . . .Y-87

Tribute to Katherine Anne Porter. Y-80

Lewis, Matthew Gregory
1775-1818 . . . . DLB-39, 158, 178

Lewis, Meriwether 1774-1809 . . . . . .DLB-183, 186

Lewis, Norman 1908- DLB-204

Lewis, R. W. B. 1917- DLB-111

Lewis, Richard circa 1700-1734 . . . . .DLB-24

Lewis, Sinclair
1885-1951 . . . . . .DLB-9, 102; DS-1; CDALB-4

Sinclair Lewis Centennial Conference. . . .Y-85

The Sinclair Lewis Society Y-99

Lewis, Wilmarth Sheldon 1895-1979. . . . .DLB-140

Lewis, Wyndham 1882-1957. . . . . .DLB-15

Time and Western Man
[excerpt] (1927) DLB-36

Lewisohn, Ludwig 1882-1955 . . .DLB-4, 9, 28, 102

Leyendecker, J. C. 1874-1951 . . . . .DLB-188

Lezama Lima, José 1910-1976 . . . . .DLB-113, 283

L'Heureux, John 1934- DLB-244

Libbey, Laura Jean 1862-1924. . . . . .DLB-221

Libedinsky, Iurii Nikolaevich
1898-1959 . . . . .DLB-272

Library History Group Y-01

E-Books' Second Act in Libraries. Y-02

The Library of America. DLB-46

The Library of America: An Assessment
After Two Decades Y-02

Licensing Act of 1737. . . . . .DLB-84

Leonard Lichfield I [publishing house] . . .DLB-170

Lichtenberg, Georg Christoph
1742-1799 . . . . .DLB-94

The Liddle Collection Y-97

Lidman, Sara 1923- DLB-257

Lieb, Fred 1888-1980. . . . . .DLB-171

Liebling, A. J. 1904-1963 . . . . .DLB-4, 171

Lieutenant Murray (see Ballou, Maturin Murray)

Lighthall, William Douw 1857-1954 . . . . .DLB-92

Lihn, Enrique 1929-1988. . . . . .DLB-283

Lilar, Françoise (see Mallet-Joris, Françoise)

Lili'uokalani, Queen 1838-1917. . . . . . . .DLB-221

Lillo, George 1691-1739. . . . . .DLB-84

Lilly, J. K., Jr. 1893-1966 . . . . .DLB-140

Lilly, Wait and Company DLB-49

Lily, William circa 1468-1522 . . . . .DLB-132

Limited Editions Club DLB-46

Limón, Graciela 1938- DLB-209

Lincoln and Edmands DLB-49

Lindesay, Ethel Forence
(see Richardson, Henry Handel)

Lindgren, Astrid 1907-2002 . . . . .DLB-257

Lindgren, Torgny 1938- DLB-257

Lindsay, Alexander William, Twenty-fifth
Earl of Crawford 1812-1880 . . . . . . .DLB-184

Lindsay, Sir David circa 1485-1555. . . . .DLB-132

Lindsay, David 1878-1945 . . . . .DLB-255

Lindsay, Jack 1900-1990 . . . . .Y-84

Lindsay, Lady (Caroline Blanche
Elizabeth Fitzroy Lindsay)
1844-1912 . . . . .DLB-199

Lindsay, Norman 1879-1969 . . . . .DLB-260

Lindsay, Vachel
1879-1931 . . . . .DLB-54; CDALB-3

Linebarger, Paul Myron Anthony
(see Smith, Cordwainer)

Link, Arthur S. 1920-1998. . . . . .DLB-17

Linn, Ed 1922-2000. . . . . .DLB-241

Linn, John Blair 1777-1804. . . . . .DLB-37

Lins, Osman 1924-1978. . . . . .DLB-145

Linton, Eliza Lynn 1822-1898 . . . . .DLB-18

Linton, William James 1812-1897 . . . . . . .DLB-32

Barnaby Bernard Lintot
[publishing house] DLB-170

Lion Books DLB-46

Lionni, Leo 1910-1999. . . . . .DLB-61

Lippard, George 1822-1854. . . . . .DLB-202

Lippincott, Sara Jane Clarke
1823-1904 . . . . .DLB-43

J. B. Lippincott Company DLB-49

Lippmann, Walter 1889-1974. . . . . .DLB-29

Lipton, Lawrence 1898-1975. . . . . .DLB-16

Liscow, Christian Ludwig 1701-1760. . . . .DLB-97

Lish, Gordon 1934- DLB-130

Tribute to Donald Barthelme Y-89

Tribute to James Dickey Y-97

Lisle, Charles-Marie-René Leconte de
1818-1894 . . . . .DLB-217

Lispector, Clarice
1925-1977 . . . . .DLB-113; CDWLB-3

LitCheck Website Y-01

Literary Awards and Honors. Y-81–02

Booker Prize Y-86, 96–98

The Drue Heinz Literature Prize Y-82

The Elmer Holmes Bobst Awards
in Arts and Letters Y-87

The Griffin Poetry Prize Y-00

Literary Prizes [British] DLB-15, 207

National Book Critics Circle
Awards Y-00–01

The National Jewish Book Awards Y-85

Nobel Prize Y-80–02

Winning an Edgar. Y-98

The Literary Chronicle and Weekly Review
1819-1828 . . . . .DLB-110

Literary Periodicals:
Callaloo. Y-87

Expatriates in Paris DS-15

New Literary Periodicals:
A Report for 1987. . . . . .Y-87

A Report for 1988. . . . . .Y-88

A Report for 1989. . . . . .Y-89

A Report for 1990. . . . . .Y-90

A Report for 1991. . . . . .Y-91

A Report for 1992. . . . . .Y-92

A Report for 1993. . . . . .Y-93

Literary Research Archives
The Anthony Burgess Archive at
the Harry Ransom Humanities
Research Center Y-98

Archives of Charles Scribner's Sons . . . DS-17

Berg Collection of English and
American Literature of the
New York Public Library Y-83

The Bobbs-Merrill Archive at the
Lilly Library, Indiana University Y-90

Die Fürstliche Bibliothek Corvey Y-96

Guide to the Archives of Publishers,
Journals, and Literary Agents in
North American Libraries Y-93

The Henry E. Huntington Library Y-92

The Humanities Research Center,
University of Texas Y-82

The John Carter Brown Library Y-85

Kent State Special Collections Y-86

The Lilly Library Y-84

The Modern Literary Manuscripts
Collection in the Special
Collections of the Washington
University Libraries Y-87

A Publisher's Archives: G. P. Putnam . . .Y-92

Special Collections at Boston
University. Y-99

The University of Virginia Libraries Y-91

The William Charvat American Fiction
   Collection at the Ohio State
   University Libraries. Y-92

Literary Societies Y-98–02

The Margery Allingham Society Y-98

The American Studies Association
   of Norway Y-00

The Arnold Bennett Society. Y-98

The Association for the Study of
   Literature and Environment
   (ASLE). Y-99

Belgian Luxembourg American Studies
   Association Y-01

The E. F. Benson Society Y-98

The Elizabeth Bishop Society. Y-01

The [Edgar Rice] Burroughs
   Bibliophiles Y-98

The Byron Society of America. Y-00

The Lewis Carroll Society
   of North America Y-00

The Willa Cather Pioneer Memorial
   and Education Foundation Y-00

New Chaucer Society. Y-00

The Wilkie Collins Society Y-98

The James Fenimore Cooper Society Y-01

The Stephen Crane Society Y-98, 01

The E. E. Cummings Society. Y-01

The James Dickey Society Y-99

John Dos Passos Newsletter. Y-00

The Priory Scholars [Sir Arthur Conan
   Doyle] of New York Y-99

The International Theodore Dreiser
   Society Y-01

The Friends of the Dymock Poets Y-00

The George Eliot Fellowship Y-99

The T. S. Eliot Society: Celebration and
   Scholarship, 1980-1999 . . . . Y-99

The Ralph Waldo Emerson Society. Y-99

The William Faulkner Society Y-99

The C. S. Forester Society Y-00

The Hamlin Garland Society. Y-01

The [Elizabeth] Gaskell Society Y-98

The Charlotte Perkins Gilman Society . . . Y-99

The Ellen Glasgow Society Y-01

Zane Grey's West Society Y-00

The Ivor Gurney Society Y-98

The Joel Chandler Harris Association Y-99

The Nathaniel Hawthorne Society. Y-00

The [George Alfred] Henty Society Y-98

George Moses Horton Society Y-99

The William Dean Howells Society. Y-01

WW2 HMSO Paperbacks Society. Y-98

American Humor Studies Association Y-99

International Society for Humor Studies . . Y-99

The W. W. Jacobs Appreciation Society . . Y-98

The Richard Jefferies Society Y-98

The Jerome K. Jerome Society Y-98

The D. H. Lawrence Society of
   North America Y-00

The T. E. Lawrence Society Y-98

The [Gotthold] Lessing Society Y-00

The New York C. S. Lewis Society Y-99

The Sinclair Lewis Society. Y-99

The Jack London Research Center Y-00

The Jack London Society. Y-99

The Cormac McCarthy Society. Y-99

The Melville Society Y-01

The Arthur Miller Society Y-01

The Milton Society of America Y-00

International Marianne Moore Society . . . Y-98

International Nabokov Society. Y-99

The Vladimir Nabokov Society Y-01

The Flannery O'Connor Society Y-99

The Wilfred Owen Association Y-98

Penguin Collectors' Society Y-98

The [E. A.] Poe Studies Association. Y-99

The Katherine Anne Porter Society Y-01

The Beatrix Potter Society Y-98

The Ezra Pound Society Y-01

The Powys Society. Y-98

Proust Society of America Y-00

The Dorothy L. Sayers Society Y-98

The Bernard Shaw Society. Y-99

The Society for the Study of
   Southern Literature Y-00

The Wallace Stevens Society Y-99

The Harriet Beecher Stowe Center Y-00

The R. S. Surtees Society Y-98

The Thoreau Society Y-99

The Tilling [E. F. Benson] Society Y-98

The Trollope Societies Y-00

H. G. Wells Society Y-98

The Western Literature Association Y-99

The William Carlos Williams Society Y-99

The Henry Williamson Society Y-98

The [Nero] Wolfe Pack Y-99

The Thomas Wolfe Society. Y-99

Worldwide Wodehouse Societies Y-98

The W. B. Yeats Society of N.Y. Y-99

The Charlotte M. Yonge Fellowship Y-98

Literary Theory
   The Year in Literary Theory Y-92–Y-93

Literature at Nurse, or Circulating Morals (1885),
   by George Moore. DLB-18

Litt, Toby 1968- DLB-267

Littell, Eliakim 1797-1870 . . . . DLB-79

Littell, Robert S. 1831-1896 . . . . DLB-79

Little, Brown and Company. DLB-49

Little Magazines and Newspapers DS-15

   Selected English-Language Little
      Magazines and Newspapers
      [France, 1920-1939] DLB-4

The Little Magazines of the
   New Formalism DLB-282

The Little Review 1914-1929. . . . . DS-15

Littlewood, Joan 1914-2002 . . . . DLB-13

Lively, Penelope 1933- DLB-14, 161, 207

Liverpool University Press. DLB-112

The Lives of the Poets (1753). DLB-142

Livesay, Dorothy 1909-1996 . . . . DLB-68

Livesay, Florence Randal 1874-1953 . . . . . DLB-92

Livings, Henry 1929-1998 . . . . DLB-13

Livingston, Anne Howe 1763-1841 . . . DLB-37, 200

Livingston, Jay 1915-2001 . . . . DLB-265

Livingston, Myra Cohn 1926-1996 . . . . . . DLB-61

Livingston, William 1723-1790. . . . . DLB-31

Livingstone, David 1813-1873 . . . . DLB-166

Livingstone, Douglas 1932-1996 . . . . DLB-225

Livy 59 B.C.-A.D. 17 . . . . . . DLB-211; CDWLB-1

Liyong, Taban lo (see Taban lo Liyong)

Lizárraga, Sylvia S. 1925- DLB-82

Llewellyn, Richard 1906-1983 . . . . DLB-15

Edward Lloyd [publishing house]. DLB-106

Lobel, Arnold 1933- DLB-61

Lochridge, Betsy Hopkins (see Fancher, Betsy)

Locke, Alain 1886-1954 . . . . DLB-51

Locke, David Ross 1833-1888 . . . . DLB-11, 23

Locke, John 1632-1704 . . . . . DLB-31, 101, 213, 252

Locke, Richard Adams 1800-1871 . . . . DLB-43

Locker-Lampson, Frederick
   1821-1895 . . . . DLB-35, 184

Lockhart, John Gibson
   1794-1854. . . . . DLB-110, 116 144

Lockridge, Ross, Jr. 1914-1948. . . . . DLB-143; Y-80

Locrine and Selimus DLB-62

Lodge, David 1935- DLB-14, 194

Lodge, George Cabot 1873-1909 . . . . . . DLB-54

Lodge, Henry Cabot 1850-1924. . . . . . . DLB-47

Lodge, Thomas 1558-1625. . . . . DLB-172

   Defence of Poetry (1579) [excerpt] . . . DLB-172

Loeb, Harold 1891-1974. . . . . DLB-4; DS-15

Loeb, William 1905-1981. . . . . DLB-127

Loesser, Frank 1910-1969. . . . . DLB-265

Lofting, Hugh 1886-1947 . . . . DLB-160

Logan, Deborah Norris 1761-1839. . . . . . DLB-200

Logan, James 1674-1751 . . . . DLB-24, 140

Logan, John 1923-1987. . . . . DLB-5

Logan, Martha Daniell 1704?-1779. . . . . . DLB-200

Logan, William 1950- DLB-120

Logau, Friedrich von 1605-1655 . . . . DLB-164

Logue, Christopher 1926- DLB-27

Lohenstein, Daniel Casper von
   1635-1683 . . . . DLB-168

Lo-Johansson, Ivar 1901-1990 . . . . DLB-259

Lokert, George (or Lockhart)
   circa 1485-1547 . . . . DLB-281

Lomonosov, Mikhail Vasil'evich
   1711-1765 . . . . DLB-150

London, Jack
1876-1916 . . . . . DLB-8, 12, 78, 212; CDALB-3

The Jack London Research Center Y-00

The Jack London Society Y-99

The London Magazine 1820-1829 . . . . DLB-110

Long, David 1948- DLB-244

Long, H., and Brother DLB-49

Long, Haniel 1888-1956 . . . . DLB-45

Long, Ray 1878-1935 . . . . DLB-137

Longfellow, Henry Wadsworth
1807-1882 . . . . DLB-1, 59, 235; CDALB-2

Longfellow, Samuel 1819-1892 . . . . DLB-1

Longford, Elizabeth 1906-2002 . . . . DLB-155

Tribute to Alfred A. Knopf Y-84

Longinus circa first century DLB-176

Longley, Michael 1939- DLB-40

T. Longman [publishing house] DLB-154

Longmans, Green and Company DLB-49

Longmore, George 1793?-1867 . . . . DLB-99

Longstreet, Augustus Baldwin
1790-1870 . . . . DLB-3, 11, 74, 248

D. Longworth [publishing house] DLB-49

Lonsdale, Frederick 1881-1954 . . . . DLB-10

Loos, Anita 1893-1981 . . . . . DLB-11, 26, 228; Y-81

Lopate, Phillip 1943- Y-80

Lopez, Barry 1945- DLB-256, 275

López, Diana (see Isabella, Ríos)

López, Josefina 1969- DLB-209

Loranger, Jean-Aubert 1896-1942 . . . . DLB-92

Lorca, Federico García 1898-1936 . . . . DLB-108

Lord, John Keast 1818-1872 . . . . DLB-99

Lorde, Audre 1934-1992 . . . . DLB-41

Lorimer, George Horace 1867-1937 . . . . . . DLB-91

A. K. Loring [publishing house] DLB-49

Loring and Mussey DLB-46

Lorris, Guillaume de (see *Roman de la Rose*)

Lossing, Benson J. 1813-1891 . . . . DLB-30

Lothar, Ernst 1890-1974 . . . . DLB-81

D. Lothrop and Company DLB-49

Lothrop, Harriet M. 1844-1924 . . . . DLB-42

Loti, Pierre 1850-1923 . . . . DLB-123

Lotichius Secundus, Petrus 1528-1560 . . . . DLB-179

Lott, Emmeline ?-? DLB-166

Louisiana State University Press Y-97

Lounsbury, Thomas R. 1838-1915 . . . . DLB-71

Louÿs, Pierre 1870-1925 . . . . DLB-123

Lovejoy, Arthur O. 1873-1962 . . . . DLB-270

Lovelace, Earl 1935- DLB-125; CDWLB-3

Lovelace, Richard 1618-1657 . . . . DLB-131

John W. Lovell Company DLB-49

Lovell, Coryell and Company DLB-49

Lover, Samuel 1797-1868 . . . . DLB-159, 190

Lovesey, Peter 1936- DLB-87

Tribute to Georges Simenon Y-89

Lovinescu, Eugen
1881-1943 . . . . DLB-220; CDWLB-4

Lovingood, Sut
(see Harris, George Washington)

Low, Samuel 1765-? DLB-37

Lowell, Amy 1874-1925 . . . . DLB-54, 140

Lowell, James Russell 1819-1891
. . . . . DLB-1, 11, 64, 79, 189, 235; CDALB-2

Lowell, Robert
1917-1977 . . . . DLB-5, 169; CDALB-7

Lowenfels, Walter 1897-1976 . . . . DLB-4

Lowndes, Marie Belloc 1868-1947 . . . . DLB-70

Lowndes, William Thomas 1798-1843 . . . DLB-184

Humphrey Lownes [publishing house] . . . DLB-170

Lowry, Lois 1937- DLB-52

Lowry, Malcolm 1909-1957 . . . . DLB-15; CDBLB-7

Lowther, Pat 1935-1975 . . . . DLB-53

Loy, Mina 1882-1966 . . . . DLB-4, 54

Loynaz, Dulce María 1902-1997 . . . . DLB-283

Lozeau, Albert 1878-1924 . . . . DLB-92

Lubbock, Percy 1879-1965 . . . . DLB-149

Lucan A.D. 39-A.D. 65 . . . . DLB-211

Lucas, E. V. 1868-1938 . . . . DLB-98, 149, 153

Fielding Lucas Jr. [publishing house] DLB-49

Luce, Clare Booth 1903-1987 . . . . DLB-228

Luce, Henry R. 1898-1967 . . . . DLB-91

John W. Luce and Company DLB-46

Lucian circa 120-180 . . . . DLB-176

Lucie-Smith, Edward 1933- DLB-40

Lucilius circa 180 B.C.-102/101 B.C. DLB-211

Lucini, Gian Pietro 1867-1914 . . . . DLB-114

Lucretius circa 94 B.C.-circa 49 B.C.
. . . . DLB-211; CDWLB-1

Luder, Peter circa 1415-1472 . . . . DLB-179

Ludlam, Charles 1943-1987 . . . . DLB-266

Ludlum, Robert 1927-2001 . . . . Y-82

Ludus de Antichristo circa 1160 . . . . DLB-148

Ludvigson, Susan 1942- DLB-120

Ludwig, Jack 1922- DLB-60

Ludwig, Otto 1813-1865 . . . . DLB-129

Ludwigslied 881 or 882 . . . . DLB-148

Luera, Yolanda 1953- DLB-122

Luft, Lya 1938- DLB-145

Lugansky, Kazak Vladimir
(see Dal', Vladimir Ivanovich)

Lugn, Kristina 1948- DLB-257

Lugones, Leopoldo 1874-1938 . . . . DLB-283

Lukács, Georg (see Lukács, György)

Lukács, György
1885-1971 . . . . DLB-215, 242; CDWLB-4

Luke, Peter 1919- DLB-13

Lummis, Charles F. 1859-1928 . . . . DLB-186

Lundkvist, Artur 1906-1991 . . . . DLB-259

Lunts, Lev Natanovich 1901-1924 . . . . . . DLB-272

F. M. Lupton Company DLB-49

Lupus of Ferrières circa 805-circa 862 . . . . DLB-148

Lurie, Alison 1926- DLB-2

Lussu, Emilio 1890-1975 . . . . DLB-264

Lustig, Arnošt 1926- DLB-232

Luther, Martin 1483-1546 . . . DLB-179; CDWLB-2

Luzi, Mario 1914- DLB-128

L'vov, Nikolai Aleksandrovich
1751-1803 . . . . DLB-150

Lyall, Gavin 1932- DLB-87

Lydgate, John circa 1370-1450 . . . . DLB-146

Lyly, John circa 1554-1606 . . . . DLB-62, 167

Lynch, Patricia 1898-1972 . . . . DLB-160

Lynch, Richard flourished 1596-1601 . . . . DLB-172

Lynd, Robert 1879-1949 . . . . DLB-98

Lyon, Matthew 1749-1822 . . . . DLB-43

Lyotard, Jean-François 1924-1998 . . . . . . DLB-242

Lyricists
Additional Lyricists: 1920-1960 . . . . . DLB-265

Lysias circa 459 B.C.-circa 380 B.C. DLB-176

Lytle, Andrew 1902-1995 . . . . DLB-6; Y-95

Tribute to Caroline Gordon Y-81

Tribute to Katherine Anne Porter Y-80

Lytton, Edward
(see Bulwer-Lytton, Edward)

Lytton, Edward Robert Bulwer
1831-1891 . . . . DLB-32

M

Maass, Joachim 1901-1972 . . . . DLB-69

Mabie, Hamilton Wright 1845-1916 . . . . . . DLB-71

Mac A'Ghobhainn, Iain (see Smith, Iain Crichton)

MacArthur, Charles 1895-1956 . . . . . DLB-7, 25, 44

Macaulay, Catherine 1731-1791 . . . . DLB-104

Macaulay, David 1945- DLB-61

Macaulay, Rose 1881-1958 . . . . DLB-36

Macaulay, Thomas Babington
1800-1859 . . . . DLB-32, 55; CDBLB-4

Macaulay Company DLB-46

MacBeth, George 1932-1992 . . . . DLB-40

Macbeth, Madge 1880-1965 . . . . DLB-92

MacCaig, Norman 1910-1996 . . . . DLB-27

MacDiarmid, Hugh
1892-1978 . . . . DLB-20; CDBLB-7

MacDonald, Cynthia 1928- DLB-105

MacDonald, George 1824-1905 . . . . DLB-18, 163, 178

MacDonald, John D. 1916-1986 . . . . . DLB-8; Y-86

MacDonald, Philip 1899?-1980 . . . . DLB-77

Macdonald, Ross (see Millar, Kenneth)

Macdonald, Sharman 1951- DLB-245

MacDonald, Wilson 1880-1967 . . . . DLB-92

Macdonald and Company (Publishers) . . . DLB-112

MacEwen, Gwendolyn 1941-1987 . . . . DLB-53, 251

Macfadden, Bernarr 1868-1955 . . . . DLB-25, 91

MacGregor, John 1825-1892 . . . . DLB-166

MacGregor, Mary Esther (see Keith, Marian)

Machado, Antonio 1875-1939 . . . . DLB-108

Machado, Manuel 1874-1947 . . . . DLB-108

Machar, Agnes Maule 1837-1927 . . . . DLB-92

Machaut, Guillaume de
circa 1300-1377 . . . . DLB-208

Machen, Arthur Llewelyn Jones
1863-1947 . . . . .DLB-36, 156, 178

MacIlmaine, Roland fl. 1574 . . . . DLB-281

MacInnes, Colin 1914-1976 . . . . DLB-14

MacInnes, Helen 1907-1985 . . . . DLB-87

Mac Intyre, Tom 1931- DLB-245

Mačiulis, Jonas (see Maironis, Jonas)

Mack, Maynard 1909- DLB-111

Mackall, Leonard L. 1879-1937 . . . . DLB-140

MacKay, Isabel Ecclestone 1875-1928 . . . . DLB-92

MacKaye, Percy 1875-1956 . . . . DLB-54

Macken, Walter 1915-1967 . . . . DLB-13

Mackenzie, Alexander 1763-1820 . . . . DLB-99

Mackenzie, Alexander Slidell
1803-1848 . . . . DLB-183

Mackenzie, Compton 1883-1972 . . . . DLB-34, 100

Mackenzie, Henry 1745-1831 . . . . DLB-39

The Lounger, no. 20 (1785) DLB-39

Mackenzie, Kenneth (Seaforth Mackenzie)
1913-1955 . . . . DLB-260

Mackenzie, William 1758-1828 . . . . DLB-187

Mackey, Nathaniel 1947- DLB-169

Mackey, Shena 1944- DLB-231

Mackey, William Wellington 1937- DLB-38

Mackintosh, Elizabeth (see Tey, Josephine)

Mackintosh, Sir James 1765-1832 . . . . DLB-158

Macklin, Charles 1699-1797 . . . . DLB-89

Maclaren, Ian (see Watson, John)

MacLaverty, Bernard 1942- DLB-267

MacLean, Alistair 1922-1987 . . . . .DLB-276

MacLean, Katherine Anne 1925- DLB-8

Maclean, Norman 1902-1990 . . . . DLB-206

MacLeish, Archibald 1892-1982
. . . . . . .DLB-4, 7, 45; Y-82; DS-15; CDALB-7

MacLennan, Hugh 1907-1990 . . . . DLB-68

MacLeod, Alistair 1936- DLB-60

Macleod, Fiona (see Sharp, William)

Macleod, Norman 1906-1985 . . . . DLB-4

Mac Low, Jackson 1922- DLB-193

Macmillan and Company DLB-106

The Macmillan Company DLB-49

Macmillan's English Men of Letters,
First Series (1878-1892) DLB-144

MacNamara, Brinsley 1890-1963 . . . . DLB-10

MacNeice, Louis 1907-1963 . . . . DLB-10, 20

Macphail, Andrew 1864-1938 . . . . DLB-92

Macpherson, James 1736-1796 . . . . DLB-109

Macpherson, Jay 1931- DLB-53

Macpherson, Jeanie 1884-1946 . . . . DLB-44

Macrae Smith Company DLB-46

MacRaye, Lucy Betty (see Webling, Lucy)

John Macrone [publishing house] DLB-106

MacShane, Frank 1927-1999 . . . . DLB-111

Macy-Masius DLB-46

Madden, David 1933- DLB-6

Madden, Sir Frederic 1801-1873 . . . . DLB-184

Maddow, Ben 1909-1992 . . . . DLB-44

Maddux, Rachel 1912-1983 . . . . . .DLB-234; Y-93

Madgett, Naomi Long 1923- DLB-76

Madhubuti, Haki R. 1942- DLB-5, 41; DS-8

Madison, James 1751-1836 . . . . DLB-37

Madsen, Svend Åge 1939- DLB-214

Maeterlinck, Maurice 1862-1949 . . . . DLB-192

Mafūz, Najīb 1911- Y-88

Nobel Lecture 1988 . . . . Y-88

The Little Magazines of the
New Formalism DLB-282

Magee, David 1905-1977 . . . . DLB-187

Maginn, William 1794-1842 . . . . . . .DLB-110, 159

Magoffin, Susan Shelby 1827-1855 . . . . . . DLB-239

Mahan, Alfred Thayer 1840-1914 . . . . DLB-47

Maheux-Forcier, Louise 1929- DLB-60

Mahin, John Lee 1902-1984 . . . . DLB-44

Mahon, Derek 1941- DLB-40

Maikov, Apollon Nikolaevich
1821-1897 .DLB-277

Maikov, Vasilii Ivanovich 1728-1778 . . . . DLB-150

Mailer, Norman 1923-
. . . . . . .DLB-2, 16, 28, 185, 278; Y-80, 83, 97;
DS-3; CDALB-6

Tribute to Isaac Bashevis Singer Y-91

Tribute to Meyer Levin Y-81

Maillart, Ella 1903-1997 . . . . DLB-195

Maillet, Adrienne 1885-1963 . . . . DLB-68

Maillet, Antonine 1929- DLB-60

Maillu, David G. 1939- DLB-157

Maimonides, Moses 1138-1204 . . . . DLB-115

Main Selections of the Book-of-the-Month
Club, 1926-1945 . . . . DLB-9

Mainwaring, Daniel 1902-1977 . . . . DLB-44

Mair, Charles 1838-1927 . . . . DLB-99

Mair, John circa 1467-1550 . . . . DLB-281

Maironis, Jonas 1862-1932 . . DLB-220; CDWLB-4

Mais, Roger 1905-1955 . . . . DLB-125; CDWLB-3

Maitland, Sara 1950- DLB-271

Major, Andre 1942- DLB-60

Major, Charles 1856-1913 . . . . DLB-202

Major, Clarence 1936- DLB-33

Major, Kevin 1949- DLB-60

Major Books DLB-46

Makanin, Vladimir Semenovich
1937- DLB-285

Makarenko, Anton Semenovich
1888-1939 .DLB-272

Makemie, Francis circa 1658-1708 . . . . . . DLB-24

The Making of Americans Contract Y-98

Maksimović, Desanka
1898-1993 . . . . .DLB-147; CDWLB-4

Malamud, Bernard 1914-1986
. . . . .DLB-2, 28, 152; Y-80, 86; CDALB-1

Bernard Malamud Archive at the
Harry Ransom Humanities
Research Center Y-00

Mălăncioiu, Ileana 1940- DLB-232

Malaparte, Curzio
(Kurt Erich Suckert) 1898-1957 . . . . . DLB-264

Malerba, Luigi 1927- DLB-196

Malet, Lucas 1852-1931 . . . . DLB-153

Mallarmé, Stéphane 1842-1898 . . . . .DLB-217

Malleson, Lucy Beatrice (see Gilbert, Anthony)

Mallet-Joris, Françoise (Françoise Lilar)
1930- DLB-83

Mallock, W. H. 1849-1923 . . . . .DLB-18, 57

"Every Man His Own Poet; or,
The Inspired Singer's Recipe
Book" (1877) DLB-35

"Le Style c'est l'homme" (1892) DLB-57

Memoirs of Life and Literature (1920),
[excerpt] DLB-57

Malone, Dumas 1892-1986 . . . . .DLB-17

Malone, Edmond 1741-1812 . . . . DLB-142

Malory, Sir Thomas
circa 1400-1410 - 1471 . . . DLB-146; CDBLB-1

Malpede, Karen 1945- DLB-249

Malraux, André 1901-1976 . . . . DLB-72

Malthus, Thomas Robert
1766-1834 . . . . .DLB-107, 158

Maltz, Albert 1908-1985 . . . . DLB-102

Malzberg, Barry N. 1939- DLB-8

Mamet, David 1947- DLB-7

Mamin, Dmitrii Narkisovich 1852-1912 . . DLB-238

Manaka, Matsemela 1956- DLB-157

Manchester University Press DLB-112

Mandel, Eli 1922-1992 . . . . DLB-53

Mandeville, Bernard 1670-1733 . . . . DLB-101

Mandeville, Sir John
mid fourteenth century DLB-146

Mandiargues, André Pieyre de
1909-1991 . . . . DLB-83

Manea, Norman 1936- DLB-232

Manfred, Frederick 1912-1994 . . . .DLB-6, 212, 227

Manfredi, Gianfranco 1948- DLB-196

Mangan, Sherry 1904-1961 . . . . DLB-4

Manganelli, Giorgio 1922-1990 . . . . DLB-196

Manilius fl. first century A.D. DLB-211

Mankiewicz, Herman 1897-1953 . . . . DLB-26

Mankiewicz, Joseph L. 1909-1993 . . . . . . DLB-44

Mankowitz, Wolf 1924-1998 . . . . DLB-15

Manley, Delarivière 1672?-1724 . . . . . DLB-39, 80

Preface to The Secret History, of Queen
Zarah, and the Zarazians (1705) DLB-39

Mann, Abby 1927- DLB-44

Mann, Charles 1929-1998 . . . . Y-98

Mann, Emily 1952- DLB-266

Mann, Heinrich 1871-1950 . . . . DLB-66, 118

Mann, Horace 1796-1859 . . . . DLB-1, 235

Mann, Klaus 1906-1949 . . . . DLB-56

Mann, Mary Peabody 1806-1887 . . . . DLB-239

Mann, Thomas 1875-1955 . . . . DLB-66; CDWLB-2

Mann, William D'Alton 1839-1920 . . . . . . DLB-137

Mannin, Ethel 1900-1984 . . . . DLB-191, 195

Manning, Emily (see Australie)

Manning, Frederic 1882-1935 . . . . DLB-260

Manning, Laurence 1899-1972 . . . . DLB-251

Manning, Marie 1873?-1945 . . . . DLB-29

Manning and Loring DLB-49

Mannyng, Robert flourished 1303-1338 . . DLB-146

Mano, D. Keith 1942- DLB-6

Manor Books DLB-46

Mansfield, Katherine 1888-1923 . . . . DLB-162

Mantel, Hilary 1952- DLB-271

Manuel, Niklaus circa 1484-1530 . . . . . . DLB-179

Manzini, Gianna 1896-1974 . . . . DLB-177

Mapanje, Jack 1944- DLB-157

Maraini, Dacia 1936- DLB-196

March, William (William Edward Campbell)
1893-1954 . . . . DLB-9, 86

Marchand, Leslie A. 1900-1999 . . . . DLB-103

Marchant, Bessie 1862-1941 . . . . DLB-160

Marchant, Tony 1959- DLB-245

Marchenko, Anastasiia Iakovlevna
1830-1880 . . . . DLB-238

Marchessault, Jovette 1938- DLB-60

Marcinkevičius, Justinas 1930- DLB-232

Marcus, Frank 1928- DLB-13

Marcuse, Herbert 1898-1979 . . . . DLB-242

Marden, Orison Swett 1850-1924 . . . . . . DLB-137

Marechera, Dambudzo 1952-1987 . . . . . . DLB-157

Marek, Richard, Books DLB-46

Mares, E. A. 1938- DLB-122

Margulies, Donald 1954- DLB-228

Mariani, Paul 1940- DLB-111

Marie de France flourished 1160-1178 . . . . DLB-208

Marie-Victorin, Frère (Conrad Kirouac)
1885-1944 . . . . DLB-92

Marin, Biagio 1891-1985 . . . . DLB-128

Marinetti, Filippo Tommaso
1876-1944 . . . . DLB-114, 264

Marinina, Aleksandra (Marina Anatol'evna
Alekseeva) 1957- DLB-285

Marinković, Ranko
1913- DLB-147; CDWLB-4

Marion, Frances 1886-1973 . . . . DLB-44

Marius, Richard C. 1933-1999 . . . . Y-85

Markevich, Boleslav Mikhailovich
1822-1884 . . . . DLB-238

Markfield, Wallace 1926-2002 . . . . DLB-2, 28

Markham, Edwin 1852-1940 . . . . DLB-54, 186

Markle, Fletcher 1921-1991 . . . . DLB-68; Y-91

Marlatt, Daphne 1942- DLB-60

Marlitt, E. 1825-1887 . . . . DLB-129

Marlowe, Christopher
1564-1593 . . . . DLB-62; CDBLB-1

Marlyn, John 1912- DLB-88

Marmion, Shakerley 1603-1639 . . . . DLB-58

Der Marner before 1230-circa 1287 . . . . . . DLB-138

Marnham, Patrick 1943- DLB-204

The *Marprelate Tracts* 1588-1589 . . . . DLB-132

Marquand, John P. 1893-1960 . . . . DLB-9, 102

Marqués, René 1919-1979 . . . . DLB-113

Marquis, Don 1878-1937 . . . . DLB-11, 25

Marriott, Anne 1913-1997 . . . . DLB-68

Marryat, Frederick 1792-1848 . . . . DLB-21, 163

Marsh, Capen, Lyon and Webb DLB-49

Marsh, George Perkins
1801-1882 . . . . DLB-1, 64, 243

Marsh, James 1794-1842 . . . . DLB-1, 59

Marsh, Narcissus 1638-1713 . . . . DLB-213

Marsh, Ngaio 1899-1982 . . . . DLB-77

Marshall, Alan 1902-1984 . . . . DLB-260

Marshall, Edison 1894-1967 . . . . DLB-102

Marshall, Edward 1932- DLB-16

Marshall, Emma 1828-1899 . . . . DLB-163

Marshall, James 1942-1992 . . . . DLB-61

Marshall, Joyce 1913- DLB-88

Marshall, Paule 1929- DLB-33, 157, 227

Marshall, Tom 1938-1993 . . . . DLB-60

Marsilius of Padua
circa 1275-circa 1342 . . . . DLB-115

Mars-Jones, Adam 1954- DLB-207

Marson, Una 1905-1965 . . . . DLB-157

Marston, John 1576-1634 . . . . DLB-58, 172

Marston, Philip Bourke 1850-1887 . . . . . . DLB-35

Martens, Kurt 1870-1945 . . . . DLB-66

Martial circa A.D. 40-circa A.D. 103
. . . . DLB-211; CDWLB-1

William S. Martien [publishing house] DLB-49

Martin, Abe (see Hubbard, Kin)

Martin, Catherine ca. 1847-1937 . . . . DLB-230

Martin, Charles 1942- DLB-120, 282

Martin, Claire 1914- DLB-60

Martin, David 1915-1997 . . . . DLB-260

Martin, Jay 1935- DLB-111

Martin, Johann (see Laurentius von Schnüffis)

Martin, Thomas 1696-1771 . . . . DLB-213

Martin, Violet Florence (see Ross, Martin)

Martin du Gard, Roger 1881-1958 . . . . . . DLB-65

Martineau, Harriet
1802-1876 . . . . DLB-21, 55, 159, 163, 166, 190

Martínez, Demetria 1960- DLB-209

Martínez, Eliud 1935- DLB-122

Martínez, Max 1943- DLB-82

Martínez, Rubén 1962- DLB-209

Martinson, Harry 1904-1978 . . . . DLB-259

Martinson, Moa 1890-1964 . . . . DLB-259

Martone, Michael 1955- DLB-218

Martyn, Edward 1859-1923 . . . . DLB-10

Marvell, Andrew
1621-1678 . . . . DLB-131; CDBLB-2

Marvin X 1944- DLB-38

Marx, Karl 1818-1883 . . . . DLB-129

Marzials, Theo 1850-1920 . . . . DLB-35

Masefield, John
1878-1967 . . . DLB-10, 19, 153, 160; CDBLB-5

Masham, Damaris Cudworth, Lady
1659-1708 . . . . DLB-252

Masino, Paola 1908-1989 . . . . DLB-264

Mason, A. E. W. 1865-1948 . . . . DLB-70

Mason, Bobbie Ann
1940- DLB-173; Y-87; CDALB-7

Mason, William 1725-1797 . . . . DLB-142

Mason Brothers DLB-49

The Massachusetts Quarterly Review
1847-1850 . . . . DLB-1

Massey, Gerald 1828-1907 . . . . DLB-32

Massey, Linton R. 1900-1974 . . . . DLB-187

Massie, Allan 1938- DLB-271

Massinger, Philip 1583-1640 . . . . DLB-58

Masson, David 1822-1907 . . . . DLB-144

Masters, Edgar Lee 1868-1950 . . DLB-54; CDALB-3

Masters, Hilary 1928- DLB-244

Mastronardi, Lucio 1930-1979 . . . . DLB-177

Matevski, Mateja 1929- . . . DLB-181; CDWLB-4

Mather, Cotton
1663-1728 . . . . DLB-24, 30, 140; CDALB-2

Mather, Increase 1639-1723 . . . . DLB-24

Mather, Richard 1596-1669 . . . . DLB-24

Matheson, Annie 1853-1924 . . . . DLB-240

Matheson, Richard 1926- DLB-8, 44

Matheus, John F. 1887- DLB-51

Mathews, Cornelius 1817?-1889 . . . DLB-3, 64, 250

Elkin Mathews [publishing house] DLB-112

Mathews, John Joseph 1894-1979 . . . . . . DLB-175

Mathias, Roland 1915- DLB-27

Mathis, June 1892-1927 . . . . DLB-44

Mathis, Sharon Bell 1937- DLB-33

Matković, Marijan 1915-1985 . . . . DLB-181

Matoš, Antun Gustav 1873-1914 . . . . DLB-147

Matsumoto Seichō 1909-1992 . . . . DLB-182

The Matter of England 1240-1400 . . . . . . DLB-146

The Matter of Rome early twelfth to late
fifteenth century DLB-146

Matthew of Vendôme
circa 1130-circa 1200 . . . . DLB-208

Matthews, Brander 1852-1929 . . DLB-71, 78; DS-13

Matthews, Jack 1925- DLB-6

Matthews, Victoria Earle 1861-1907 . . . . . DLB-221

Matthews, William 1942-1997 . . . . DLB-5

Matthiessen, F. O. 1902-1950 . . . . DLB-63

Matthiessen, Peter 1927- DLB-6, 173, 275

Maturin, Charles Robert 1780-1824 . . . . . DLB-178

Maugham, W. Somerset 1874-1965
. . . . DLB-10, 36, 77, 100, 162, 195; CDBLB-6

Maupassant, Guy de 1850-1893 . . . . DLB-123

Maupin, Armistead 1944- DLB-278

Mauriac, Claude 1914-1996 . . . . DLB-83

Mauriac, François 1885-1970 . . . . DLB-65

Maurice, Frederick Denison 1805-1872 . . . . DLB-55

Maurois, André 1885-1967 . . . . DLB-65

Maury, James 1718-1769 . . . . DLB-31

Mavor, Elizabeth 1927- DLB-14

Mavor, Osborne Henry (see Bridie, James)

Maxwell, Gavin 1914-1969 . . . . DLB-204

Maxwell, William
1908-2000 . . . . DLB-218, 278; Y-80

    Tribute to Nancy Hale Y-88

H. Maxwell [publishing house] DLB-49

John Maxwell [publishing house] DLB-106

May, Elaine 1932- DLB-44

May, Karl 1842-1912 . . . . DLB-129

May, Thomas 1595/1596-1650 . . . . DLB-58

Mayer, Bernadette 1945- DLB-165

Mayer, Mercer 1943- DLB-61

Mayer, O. B. 1818-1891 . . . . DLB-3, 248

Mayes, Herbert R. 1900-1987 . . . . DLB-137

Mayes, Wendell 1919-1992 . . . . DLB-26

Mayfield, Julian 1928-1984 . . . . DLB-33; Y-84

Mayhew, Henry 1812-1887 . . . . . DLB-18, 55, 190

Mayhew, Jonathan 1720-1766 . . . . DLB-31

Mayne, Ethel Colburn 1865-1941 . . . . . . DLB-197

Mayne, Jasper 1604-1672 . . . . DLB-126

Mayne, Seymour 1944- DLB-60

Mayor, Flora Macdonald 1872-1932 . . . . . DLB-36

Mayröcker, Friederike 1924- DLB-85

Mazrui, Ali A. 1933- DLB-125

Mažuranić, Ivan 1814-1890 . . . . DLB-147

Mazursky, Paul 1930- DLB-44

McAlmon, Robert 1896-1956 . . . DLB-4, 45; DS-15

    "A Night at Bricktop's" Y-01

McArthur, Peter 1866-1924 . . . . DLB-92

McAuley, James 1917-1976 . . . . DLB-260

Robert M. McBride and Company DLB-46

McCabe, Patrick 1955- DLB-194

McCaffrey, Anne 1926- DLB-8

McCann, Colum 1965- DLB-267

McCarthy, Cormac 1933- DLB-6, 143, 256

    The Cormac McCarthy Society Y-99

McCarthy, Mary 1912-1989 . . . . DLB-2; Y-81

McCarthy, Shaun Lloyd (see Cory, Desmond)

McCay, Winsor 1871-1934 . . . . DLB-22

McClane, Albert Jules 1922-1991 . . . . DLB-171

McClatchy, C. K. 1858-1936 . . . . DLB-25

McClellan, George Marion 1860-1934 . . . . DLB-50

    "The Negro as a Writer" DLB-50

McCloskey, Robert 1914- DLB-22

McClung, Nellie Letitia 1873-1951 . . . . . . DLB-92

McClure, James 1939- DLB-276

McClure, Joanna 1930- DLB-16

McClure, Michael 1932- DLB-16

McClure, Phillips and Company DLB-46

McClure, S. S. 1857-1949 . . . . DLB-91

A. C. McClurg and Company DLB-49

McCluskey, John A., Jr. 1944- DLB-33

McCollum, Michael A. 1946- Y-87

McConnell, William C. 1917- DLB-88

McCord, David 1897-1997 . . . . DLB-61

McCord, Louisa S. 1810-1879 . . . . DLB-248

McCorkle, Jill 1958- DLB-234; Y-87

McCorkle, Samuel Eusebius 1746-1811 . . . DLB-37

McCormick, Anne O'Hare 1880-1954 . . . . DLB-29

McCormick, Kenneth Dale 1906-1997 . . . . Y-97

McCormick, Robert R. 1880-1955 . . . . . . DLB-29

McCourt, Edward 1907-1972 . . . . DLB-88

McCoy, Horace 1897-1955 . . . . DLB-9

McCrae, Hugh 1876-1958 . . . . DLB-260

McCrae, John 1872-1918 . . . . DLB-92

McCullagh, Joseph B. 1842-1896 . . . . DLB-23

McCullers, Carson
1917-1967 . . . . . . DLB-2, 7, 173, 228; CDALB-1

McCulloch, Thomas 1776-1843 . . . . DLB-99

McDonald, Forrest 1927- DLB-17

McDonald, Walter 1934- DLB-105, DS-9

    "Getting Started: Accepting the
    Regions You Own—or Which
    Own You" DLB-105

    Tribute to James Dickey Y-97

McDougall, Colin 1917-1984 . . . . DLB-68

McDowell, Katharine Sherwood Bonner
1849-1883 . . . . DLB-202, 239

Obolensky McDowell
[publishing house] DLB-46

McEwan, Ian 1948- DLB-14, 194

McFadden, David 1940- DLB-60

McFall, Frances Elizabeth Clarke
(see Grand, Sarah)

McFarland, Ron 1942- DLB-256

McFarlane, Leslie 1902-1977 . . . . DLB-88

McFee, William 1881-1966 . . . . DLB-153

McGahern, John 1934- DLB-14, 231

McGee, Thomas D'Arcy 1825-1868 . . . . . DLB-99

McGeehan, W. O. 1879-1933 . . . . .DLB-25, 171

McGill, Ralph 1898-1969 . . . . DLB-29

McGinley, Phyllis 1905-1978 . . . . DLB-11, 48

McGinniss, Joe 1942- DLB-185

McGirt, James E. 1874-1930 . . . . DLB-50

McGlashan and Gill DLB-106

McGough, Roger 1937- DLB-40

McGrath, John 1935- DLB-233

McGrath, Patrick 1950- DLB-231

McGraw-Hill DLB-46

McGuane, Thomas 1939- DLB-2, 212; Y-80

    Tribute to Seymour Lawrence Y-94

McGuckian, Medbh 1950- DLB-40

McGuffey, William Holmes 1800-1873 . . . DLB-42

McGuinness, Frank 1953- DLB-245

McHenry, James 1785-1845 . . . . DLB-202

McIlvanney, William 1936- DLB-14, 207

McIlwraith, Jean Newton 1859-1938 . . . . . DLB-92

McIntosh, Maria Jane 1803-1878 . . . DLB-239, 248

McIntyre, James 1827-1906 . . . . DLB-99

McIntyre, O. O. 1884-1938 . . . . DLB-25

McKay, Claude 1889-1948 . . . . .DLB-4, 45, 51, 117

The David McKay Company DLB-49

McKean, William V. 1820-1903 . . . . DLB-23

McKenna, Stephen 1888-1967 . . . . .DLB-197

The McKenzie Trust Y-96

McKerrow, R. B. 1872-1940 . . . . DLB-201

McKinley, Robin 1952- DLB-52

McKnight, Reginald 1956- DLB-234

McLachlan, Alexander 1818-1896 . . . . . . DLB-99

McLaren, Floris Clark 1904-1978 . . . . DLB-68

McLaverty, Michael 1907- DLB-15

McLean, Duncan 1964- DLB-267

McLean, John R. 1848-1916 . . . . DLB-23

McLean, William L. 1852-1931 . . . . DLB-25

McLennan, William 1856-1904 . . . . DLB-92

McLoughlin Brothers DLB-49

McLuhan, Marshall 1911-1980 . . . . DLB-88

McMaster, John Bach 1852-1932 . . . . DLB-47

McMurtry, Larry 1936-
    . . . . . . .DLB-2, 143, 256; Y-80, 87; CDALB-6

McNally, Terrence 1939- DLB-7, 249

McNeil, Florence 1937- DLB-60

McNeile, Herman Cyril 1888-1937 . . . . . . DLB-77

McNickle, D'Arcy 1904-1977 . . . . . . .DLB-175, 212

McPhee, John 1931- DLB-185, 275

McPherson, James Alan 1943- DLB-38, 244

McPherson, Sandra 1943- Y-86

McTaggart, J. M. E. 1866-1925 . . . . DLB-262

McWhirter, George 1939- DLB-60

McWilliam, Candia 1955- DLB-267

McWilliams, Carey 1905-1980 . . . . .DLB-137

    "The Nation's Future," Carey
    McWilliams's Editorial Policy
    in Nation DLB-137

Mda, Zakes 1948- DLB-225

Mead, George Herbert 1863-1931 . . . . . . .DLB-270

Mead, L. T. 1844-1914 . . . . DLB-141

Mead, Matthew 1924- DLB-40

Mead, Taylor ?- DLB-16

Meany, Tom 1903-1964 . . . . .DLB-171

Mechthild von Magdeburg
circa 1207-circa 1282 . . . . DLB-138

Medill, Joseph 1823-1899 . . . . DLB-43

Medoff, Mark 1940- DLB-7

Meek, Alexander Beaufort 1814-1865 . DLB-3, 248

Meeke, Mary ?-1816? DLB-116

Mei, Lev Aleksandrovich 1822-1862 . . . . .DLB-277

Meinke, Peter 1932- DLB-5

Mejia Vallejo, Manuel 1923- DLB-113

Melanchthon, Philipp 1497-1560 . . . . . . .DLB-179

Melançon, Robert 1947- DLB-60

Mell, Max 1882-1971 . . . . DLB-81, 124

Mellow, James R. 1926-1997 . . . . .DLB-111

Mel'nikov, Pavel Ivanovich 1818-1883 . . .DLB-238

Meltzer, David 1937- DLB-16

Meltzer, Milton 1915- DLB-61

Melville, Elizabeth, Lady Culross
circa 1585-1640 . . . . .DLB-172

Melville, Herman
1819-1891 . . . . . . .DLB-3, 74, 250; CDALB-2

The Melville Society Y-01

Melville, James
(Roy Peter Martin) 1931- DLB-276

Mena, María Cristina 1893-1965 . . . .DLB-209, 221

Menander 342-341 B.C.-circa 292-291 B.C.
. . . . DLB-176; CDWLB-1

Menantes (see Hunold, Christian Friedrich)

Mencke, Johann Burckhard 1674-1732 . . .DLB-168

Mencken, H. L. 1880-1956
. . . . DLB-11, 29, 63, 137, 222; CDALB-4

"Berlin, February, 1917" Y-00

From the Initial Issue of *American Mercury*
(January 1924) DLB-137

Mencken and Nietzsche: An
Unpublished Excerpt from H. L.
Mencken's *My Life as Author and
Editor* Y-93

Mendelssohn, Moses 1729-1786 . . . . .DLB-97

Mendes, Catulle 1841-1909 . . . . .DLB-217

Méndez M., Miguel 1930- DLB-82

The Mercantile Library of New York Y-96

Mercer, Cecil William (see Yates, Dornford)

Mercer, David 1928-1980 . . . . .DLB-13

Mercer, John 1704-1768 . . . . .DLB-31

Mercer, Johnny 1909-1976 . . . . .DLB-265

Meredith, George
1828-1909 . . . . DLB-18, 35, 57, 159; CDBLB-4

Meredith, Louisa Anne 1812-1895 . .DLB-166, 230

Meredith, Owen
(see Lytton, Edward Robert Bulwer)

Meredith, William 1919- DLB-5

Meres, Francis
Palladis Tamia, Wits Treasurie (1598)
[excerpt] DLB-172

Mergerle, Johann Ulrich
(see Abraham ä Sancta Clara)

Mérimée, Prosper 1803-1870 . . . . . . .DLB-119, 192

Merivale, John Herman 1779-1844 . . . . . . .DLB-96

Meriwether, Louise 1923- DLB-33

Merlin Press DLB-112

Merriam, Eve 1916-1992 . . . . .DLB-61

The Merriam Company DLB-49

Merril, Judith 1923-1997 . . . . .DLB-251

Tribute to Theodore Sturgeon Y-85

Merrill, James 1926-1995 . . .DLB-5, 165; Y-85

Merrill and Baker DLB-49

The Mershon Company DLB-49

Merton, Thomas 1915-1968 . . . . . . .DLB-48; Y-81

Merwin, W. S. 1927- DLB-5, 169

Julian Messner [publishing house] DLB-46

Mészöly, Miklós 1921- DLB-232

J. Metcalf [publishing house] DLB-49

Metcalf, John 1938- DLB-60

The Methodist Book Concern DLB-49

Methuen and Company DLB-112

Meun, Jean de (see *Roman de la Rose*)

Mew, Charlotte 1869-1928 . . . . .DLB-19, 135

Mewshaw, Michael 1943- Y-80

Tribute to Albert Erskine Y-93

Meyer, Conrad Ferdinand 1825-1898 . . . .DLB-129

Meyer, E. Y. 1946- DLB-75

Meyer, Eugene 1875-1959 . . . . .DLB-29

Meyer, Michael 1921-2000 . . . . .DLB-155

Meyers, Jeffrey 1939- DLB-111

Meynell, Alice 1847-1922 . . . . .DLB-19, 98

Meynell, Viola 1885-1956 . . . . .DLB-153

Meyrink, Gustav 1868-1932 . . . . .DLB-81

Mézières, Philipe de circa 1327-1405 . . . . .DLB-208

Michael, Ib 1945- DLB-214

Michael, Livi 1960- DLB-267

Michaëlis, Karen 1872-1950 . . . . .DLB-214

Michaels, Leonard 1933- DLB-130

Michaux, Henri 1899-1984 . . . . .DLB-258

Micheaux, Oscar 1884-1951 . . . . .DLB-50

Michel of Northgate, Dan
circa 1265-circa 1340 . . . . .DLB-146

Micheline, Jack 1929-1998 . . . . .DLB-16

Michener, James A. 1907?-1997 . . . . .DLB-6

Micklejohn, George circa 1717-1818 . . . . . .DLB-31

Middle Hill Press DLB-106

Middleton, Christopher 1926- DLB-40

Middleton, Richard 1882-1911 . . . . .DLB-156

Middleton, Stanley 1919- DLB-14

Middleton, Thomas 1580-1627 . . . . .DLB-58

Miegel, Agnes 1879-1964 . . . . .DLB-56

Mieželaitis, Eduardas 1919-1997 . . . . . . .DLB-220

Mihailović, Dragoslav 1930- DLB-181

Mihalić, Slavko 1928- DLB-181

Mikhailov, A.
(see Sheller, Aleksandr Konstantinovich)

Mikhailov, Mikhail Larionovich
1829-1865 .DLB-238

Mikhailovsky, Nikolai Konstantinovich
1842-1904 .DLB-277

Miles, Josephine 1911-1985 . . . . .DLB-48

Miles, Susan (Ursula Wyllie Roberts)
1888-1975 .DLB-240

Miliković, Branko 1934-1961 . . . . .DLB-181

Milius, John 1944- DLB-44

Mill, James 1773-1836 . . . . DLB-107, 158, 262

Mill, John Stuart
1806-1873 . . . . . .DLB-55, 190, 262; CDBLB-4

Thoughts on Poetry and Its Varieties
(1833) DLB-32

Andrew Millar [publishing house] DLB-154

Millar, Kenneth
1915-1983 . . . . DLB-2, 226; Y-83; DS-6

Millay, Edna St. Vincent
1892-1950 . . . . .DLB-45, 249; CDALB-4

Millen, Sarah Gertrude 1888-1968 . . . . . .DLB-225

Miller, Andrew 1960- DLB-267

Miller, Arthur 1915- DLB-7, 266; CDALB-1

The Arthur Miller Society Y-01

Miller, Caroline 1903-1992 . . . . .DLB-9

Miller, Eugene Ethelbert 1950- DLB-41

Tribute to Julian Mayfield Y-84

Miller, Heather Ross 1939- DLB-120

Miller, Henry
1891-1980 . . . . .DLB-4, 9; Y-80; CDALB-5

Miller, Hugh 1802-1856 . . . . .DLB-190

Miller, J. Hillis 1928- DLB-67

Miller, Jason 1939- DLB-7

Miller, Joaquin 1839-1913 . . . . .DLB-186

Miller, May 1899-1995 . . . . .DLB-41

Miller, Paul 1906-1991 . . . . .DLB-127

Miller, Perry 1905-1963 . . . . DLB-17, 63

Miller, Sue 1943- DLB-143

Miller, Vassar 1924-1998 . . . . .DLB-105

Miller, Walter M., Jr. 1923-1996 . . . . .DLB-8

Miller, Webb 1892-1940 . . . . .DLB-29

James Miller [publishing house] DLB-49

Millett, Kate 1934- DLB-246

Millhauser, Steven 1943- DLB-2

Millican, Arthenia J. Bates 1920- DLB-38

Milligan, Alice 1866-1953 . . . . .DLB-240

Mills, Magnus 1954- DLB-267

Mills and Boon DLB-112

Milman, Henry Hart 1796-1868 . . . . .DLB-96

Milne, A. A. 1882-1956 . . . . .DLB-10, 77, 100, 160

Milner, Ron 1938- DLB-38

William Milner [publishing house] DLB-106

Milnes, Richard Monckton (Lord Houghton)
1809-1885 . . . . .DLB-32, 184

Milton, John
1608-1674 . . . . .DLB-131, 151, 281; CDBLB-2

The Milton Society of America Y-00

Miłosz, Czesław 1911- DLB-215; CDWLB-4

Minakami Tsutomu 1919- DLB-182

Minamoto no Sanetomo 1192-1219 . . . . . .DLB-203

The Minerva Press DLB-154

Minnesang circa 1150-1280 . . . . .DLB-138

The Music of *Minnesang* DLB-138

Minns, Susan 1839-1938 . . . . .DLB-140

Minton, Balch and Company DLB-46

Mirbeau, Octave 1848-1917 . . . . . . .DLB-123, 192

Mirk, John died after 1414? DLB-146

Miron, Gaston 1928-1996 . . . . .DLB-60

A Mirror for Magistrates DLB-167

Mishima Yukio 1925-1970 . . . . .DLB-182

Mistral, Gabriela 1889-1957 . . . . .DLB-283

Mitchel, Jonathan 1624-1668 . . . . .DLB-24

Mitchell, Adrian 1932- DLB-40

Mitchell, Donald Grant
  1822-1908 .... DLB-1, 243; DS-13

Mitchell, Gladys 1901-1983 .... DLB-77

Mitchell, James Leslie 1901-1935 .... DLB-15

Mitchell, John (see Slater, Patrick)

Mitchell, John Ames 1845-1918 .... DLB-79

Mitchell, Joseph 1908-1996........DLB-185; Y-96

Mitchell, Julian 1935- DLB-14

Mitchell, Ken 1940- DLB-60

Mitchell, Langdon 1862-1935........... DLB-7

Mitchell, Loften 1919- DLB-38

Mitchell, Margaret 1900-1949 .. DLB-9; CDALB-7

Mitchell, S. Weir 1829-1914........... DLB-202

Mitchell, W. J. T. 1942- DLB-246

Mitchell, W. O. 1914-1998............. DLB-88

Mitchison, Naomi Margaret (Haldane)
  1897-1999............. DLB-160, 191, 255

Mitford, Mary Russell 1787-1855 ....DLB-110, 116

Mitford, Nancy 1904-1973 .... DLB-191

Mittelholzer, Edgar
  1909-1965 ....DLB-117; CDWLB-3

Mitterer, Erika 1906- DLB-85

Mitterer, Felix 1948- DLB-124

Mitternacht, Johann Sebastian
  1613-1679.................... DLB-168

Miyamoto Yuriko 1899-1951 .... DLB-180

Mizener, Arthur 1907-1988........... DLB-103

Mo, Timothy 1950- DLB-194

Moberg, Vilhelm 1898-1973 .... DLB-259

Modern Age Books.................. DLB-46

Modern Language Association of America
  The Modern Language Association of
  America Celebrates Its Centennial ... Y-84

The Modern Library DLB-46

Modiano, Patrick 1945- DLB-83

Moffat, Yard and Company............ DLB-46

Moffet, Thomas 1553-1604 .... DLB-136

Mofolo, Thomas 1876-1948 .... DLB-225

Mohr, Nicholasa 1938- DLB-145

Moix, Ana María 1947- DLB-134

Molesworth, Louisa 1839-1921 .... DLB-135

Molière (Jean-Baptiste Poquelin)
  1622-1673..................... DLB-268

Möllhausen, Balduin 1825-1905........ DLB-129

Molnár, Ferenc 1878-1952 .. DLB-215; CDWLB-4

Molnár, Miklós (see Mészöly, Miklós)

Momaday, N. Scott
  1934- DLB-143, 175, 256; CDALB-7

Monkhouse, Allan 1858-1936.......... DLB-10

Monro, Harold 1879-1932 .... DLB-19

Monroe, Harriet 1860-1936 .... DLB-54, 91

Monsarrat, Nicholas 1910-1979 .... DLB-15

Montagu, Lady Mary Wortley
  1689-1762.................... DLB-95, 101

Montague, C. E. 1867-1928 .... DLB-197

Montague, John 1929- DLB-40

Montale, Eugenio 1896-1981 .... DLB-114

Montalvo, José 1946-1994 .... DLB-209

Monterroso, Augusto 1921-2003 .... DLB-145

Montesquiou, Robert de 1855-1921..... DLB-217

Montgomerie, Alexander
  circa 1550?-1598 .... DLB-167

Montgomery, James 1771-1854...... DLB-93, 158

Montgomery, John 1919- DLB-16

Montgomery, Lucy Maud
  1874-1942................. DLB-92; DS-14

Montgomery, Marion 1925- DLB-6

Montgomery, Robert Bruce (see Crispin, Edmund)

Montherlant, Henry de 1896-1972 ...... DLB-72

The Monthly Review 1749-1844 .... DLB-110

Montigny, Louvigny de 1876-1955....... DLB-92

Montoya, José 1932- DLB-122

Moodie, John Wedderburn Dunbar
  1797-1869 .... DLB-99

Moodie, Susanna 1803-1885 .... DLB-99

Moody, Joshua circa 1633-1697 .... DLB-24

Moody, William Vaughn 1869-1910 ....DLB-7, 54

Moorcock, Michael 1939- DLB-14, 231, 261

Moore, Alan 1953- DLB-261

Moore, Brian 1921-1999............. DLB-251

Moore, Catherine L. 1911-1987 .... DLB-8

Moore, Clement Clarke 1779-1863....... DLB-42

Moore, Dora Mavor 1888-1979 .... DLB-92

Moore, G. E. 1873-1958 .... DLB-262

Moore, George 1852-1933 .... DLB-10, 18, 57, 135

  Literature at Nurse, or Circulating Morals
    (1885) DLB-18

Moore, Lorrie 1957- DLB-234

Moore, Marianne
  1887-1972 .... DLB-45; DS-7; CDALB-5

  International Marianne Moore Society ... Y-98

Moore, Mavor 1919- DLB-88

Moore, Richard 1927- DLB-105

  "The No Self, the Little Self, and
  the Poets" DLB-105

Moore, T. Sturge 1870-1944 .... DLB-19

Moore, Thomas 1779-1852........ DLB-96, 144

Moore, Ward 1903-1978 .... DLB-8

Moore, Wilstach, Keys and Company.... DLB-49

Moorehead, Alan 1901-1983 .... DLB-204

Moorhouse, Geoffrey 1931- DLB-204

The Moorland-Spingarn Research
  Center DLB-76

Moorman, Mary C. 1905-1994 .... DLB-155

Mora, Pat 1942- DLB-209

Moraga, Cherríe 1952- DLB-82, 249

Morales, Alejandro 1944- DLB-82

Morales, Mario Roberto 1947- DLB-145

Morales, Rafael 1919- DLB-108

Morality Plays: *Mankind* circa 1450-1500
  and *Everyman* circa 1500 .... DLB-146

Morand, Paul (1888-1976) DLB-65

Morante, Elsa 1912-1985 ....DLB-177

Morata, Olympia Fulvia 1526-1555 ......DLB-179

Moravia, Alberto 1907-1990...........DLB-177

Mordaunt, Elinor 1872-1942 ....DLB-174

Mordovtsev, Daniil Lukich 1830-1905... DLB-238

More, Hannah
  1745-1833.......... DLB-107, 109, 116, 158

More, Henry 1614-1687 .... DLB-126, 252

More, Sir Thomas
  1477/1478-1535 .... DLB-136, 281

Morejón, Nancy 1944- DLB-283

Morency, Pierre 1942- DLB-60

Moreno, Dorinda 1939- DLB-122

Moretti, Marino 1885-1979.... DLB-114, 264

Morgan, Berry 1919- DLB-6

Morgan, Charles 1894-1958........DLB-34, 100

Morgan, Edmund S. 1916- DLB-17

Morgan, Edwin 1920- DLB-27

Morgan, John Pierpont 1837-1913 ...... DLB-140

Morgan, John Pierpont, Jr. 1867-1943 ... DLB-140

Morgan, Robert 1944- DLB-120

Morgan, Sydney Owenson, Lady
  1776?-1859 ....DLB-116, 158

Morgner, Irmtraud 1933-1990 .... DLB-75

Morhof, Daniel Georg 1639-1691 ...... DLB-164

Mori Ōgai 1862-1922 .... DLB-180

Móricz, Zsigmond 1879-1942.......... DLB-215

Morier, James Justinian
  1782 or 1783?-1849 .... DLB-116

Mörike, Eduard 1804-1875............ DLB-133

Morin, Paul 1889-1963.............. DLB-92

Morison, Richard 1514?-1556 .... DLB-136

Morison, Samuel Eliot 1887-1976 ....DLB-17

Morison, Stanley 1889-1967........... DLB-201

Moritz, Karl Philipp 1756-1793......... DLB-94

Moriz von Craûn circa 1220-1230 .... DLB-138

Morley, Christopher 1890-1957 .... DLB-9

Morley, John 1838-1923........DLB-57, 144, 190

Morris, George Pope 1802-1864 .... DLB-73

Morris, James Humphrey (see Morris, Jan)

Morris, Jan 1926- DLB-204

Morris, Lewis 1833-1907 .... DLB-35

Morris, Margaret 1737-1816 .... DLB-200

Morris, Richard B. 1904-1989 ....DLB-17

Morris, William 1834-1896
  ..... DLB-18, 35, 57, 156, 178, 184; CDBLB-4

Morris, Willie 1934-1999 .... Y-80

  Tribute to Irwin Shaw Y-84

  Tribute to James Dickey Y-97

Morris, Wright
  1910-1998 ....DLB-2, 206, 218; Y-81

Morrison, Arthur 1863-1945 ....DLB-70, 135, 197

Morrison, Charles Clayton 1874-1966.... DLB-91

Morrison, John 1904-1998 .... DLB-260

Morrison, Toni 1931-
  ....DLB-6, 33, 143; Y-81, 93; CDALB-6

  Nobel Lecture 1993 .... Y-93

Morrissy, Mary 1957- DLB-267

William Morrow and Company DLB-46

Morse, James Herbert 1841-1923 . . . . DLB-71

Morse, Jedidiah 1761-1826. . . . . .DLB-37

Morse, John T., Jr. 1840-1937 . . . . DLB-47

Morselli, Guido 1912-1973. . . . . DLB-177

Morte Arthure, the *Alliterative* and the
   Stanzaic circa 1350-1400 . . . . DLB-146

Mortimer, Favell Lee 1802-1878 . . . . DLB-163

Mortimer, John
   1923- DLB-13, 245, 271; CDBLB-8

Morton, Carlos 1942- DLB-122

Morton, H. V. 1892-1979 . . . . DLB-195

John P. Morton and Company DLB-49

Morton, Nathaniel 1613-1685 . . . . .DLB-24

Morton, Sarah Wentworth 1759-1846. . . . .DLB-37

Morton, Thomas circa 1579-circa 1647 . . . .DLB-24

Moscherosch, Johann Michael
   1601-1669 . . . . .DLB-164

Humphrey Moseley [publishing house] . . .DLB-170

Möser, Justus 1720-1794. . . . . .DLB-97

Mosley, Nicholas 1923- DLB-14, 207

Moss, Arthur 1889-1969 . . . . .DLB-4

Moss, Howard 1922-1987 . . . . .DLB-5

Moss, Thylias 1954- DLB-120

Motion, Andrew 1952- DLB-40

Motley, John Lothrop
   1814-1877 . . . . DLB-1, 30, 59, 235

Motley, Willard 1909-1965 . . . . DLB-76, 143

Mott, Lucretia 1793-1880. . . . . DLB-239

Benjamin Motte Jr. [publishing house]. . . .DLB-154

Motteux, Peter Anthony 1663-1718. . . . . . DLB-80

Mottram, R. H. 1883-1971. . . . . .DLB-36

Mount, Ferdinand 1939- DLB-231

Mouré, Erin 1955- DLB-60

Mourning Dove (Humishuma) between
   1882 and 1888?-1936 . . . . DLB-175, 221

Movies
   Fiction into Film, 1928-1975: A List
     of Movies Based on the Works
     of Authors in British Novelists,
     1930-1959. . . . . .DLB-15

   Movies from Books, 1920-1974. . . . . . . .DLB-9

Mowat, Farley 1921- DLB-68

A. R. Mowbray and Company,
   Limited DLB-106

Mowrer, Edgar Ansel 1892-1977 . . . . .DLB-29

Mowrer, Paul Scott 1887-1971 . . . . .DLB-29

Edward Moxon [publishing house] DLB-106

Joseph Moxon [publishing house] DLB-170

Moyes, Patricia 1923-2000. . . . . DLB-276

Mphahlele, Es'kia (Ezekiel)
   1919- DLB-125, 225; CDWLB-3

Mrożek, Sławomir 1930- . . . DLB-232; CDWLB-4

Mtshali, Oswald Mbuyiseni
   1940- DLB-125, 225

Mucedorus DLB-62

Mudford, William 1782-1848 . . . . .DLB-159

Mueller, Lisel 1924- DLB-105

Muhajir, El (see Marvin X)

Muhajir, Nazzam Al Fitnah (see Marvin X)

Mühlbach, Luise 1814-1873. . . . . .DLB-133

Muir, Edwin 1887-1959 . . . . DLB-20, 100, 191

Muir, Helen 1937- DLB-14

Muir, John 1838-1914 . . . . DLB-186, 275

Muir, Percy 1894-1979. . . . . .DLB-201

Mujū Ichien 1226-1312 . . . . .DLB-203

Mukherjee, Bharati 1940- DLB-60, 218

Mulcaster, Richard 1531 or 1532-1611 . . .DLB-167

Muldoon, Paul 1951- DLB-40

Müller, Friedrich (see Müller, Maler)

Müller, Heiner 1929-1995 . . . . .DLB-124

Müller, Maler 1749-1825 . . . . .DLB-94

Muller, Marcia 1944- DLB-226

Müller, Wilhelm 1794-1827 . . . . .DLB-90

Mumford, Lewis 1895-1990 . . . . .DLB-63

Munby, A. N. L. 1913-1974. . . . . .DLB-201

Munby, Arthur Joseph 1828-1910 . . . . . . .DLB-35

Munday, Anthony 1560-1633 . . . . . . DLB-62, 172

Mundt, Clara (see Mühlbach, Luise)

Mundt, Theodore 1808-1861 . . . . .DLB-133

Munford, Robert circa 1737-1783. . . . . . . .DLB-31

Mungoshi, Charles 1947- DLB-157

Munk, Kaj 1898-1944 . . . . .DLB-214

Munonye, John 1929- DLB-117

Munro, Alice 1931- DLB-53

George Munro [publishing house] DLB-49

Munro, H. H.
   1870-1916 . . . . .DLB-34, 162; CDBLB-5

Munro, Neil 1864-1930 . . . . .DLB-156

Norman L. Munro [publishing house]. DLB-49

Munroe, Kirk 1850-1930 . . . . .DLB-42

Munroe and Francis. DLB-49

James Munroe and Company DLB-49

Joel Munsell [publishing house] DLB-49

Munsey, Frank A. 1854-1925 . . . . .DLB-25, 91

Frank A. Munsey and Company DLB-49

Murakami Haruki 1949- DLB-182

Murav'ev, Mikhail Nikitich 1757-1807. . . .DLB-150

Murdoch, Iris 1919-1999
   . . . . DLB-14, 194, 233; CDBLB-8

Murdock, James
   From *Sketches of Modern Philosophy*. DS-5

Murdoch, Rupert 1931- DLB-127

Murfree, Mary N. 1850-1922 . . . . .DLB-12, 74

Murger, Henry 1822-1861 . . . . .DLB-119

Murger, Louis-Henri (see Murger, Henry)

Murner, Thomas 1475-1537 . . . . .DLB-179

Muro, Amado 1915-1971. . . . . .DLB-82

Murphy, Arthur 1727-1805 . . . . .DLB-89, 142

Murphy, Beatrice M. 1908-1992 . . . . .DLB-76

Murphy, Dervla 1931- DLB-204

Murphy, Emily 1868-1933 . . . . .DLB-99

Murphy, Jack 1923-1980 . . . . .DLB-241

Murphy, John H., III 1916- DLB-127

Murphy, Richard 1927-1993 . . . . .DLB-40

John Murphy and Company DLB-49

Murray, Albert L. 1916- DLB-38

Murray, Gilbert 1866-1957 . . . . .DLB-10

Murray, Jim 1919-1998 . . . . .DLB-241

John Murray [publishing house] DLB-154

Murry, John Middleton 1889-1957 . . . . . .DLB-149

   "The Break-Up of the Novel"
     (1922) DLB-36

Murry, John Middleton, Jr. (see Cowper, Richard)

Murray, Judith Sargent 1751-1820. . . . DLB-37, 200

Murray, Pauli 1910-1985. . . . . .DLB-41

Musäus, Johann Karl August 1735-1787 . . .DLB-97

Muschg, Adolf 1934- DLB-75

Musil, Robert
   1880-1942 . . . . DLB-81, 124; CDWLB-2

Muspilli circa 790-circa 850. . . . . .DLB-148

Musset, Alfred de 1810-1857 . . . . DLB-192, 217

Benjamin B. Mussey and Company DLB-49

Mutafchieva, Vera 1929- DLB-181

Mutis, Alvaro 1923- DLB-283

Mwangi, Meja 1948- DLB-125

Myers, Frederic W. H. 1843-1901 . . . . . . .DLB-190

Myers, Gustavus 1872-1942 . . . . .DLB-47

Myers, L. H. 1881-1944 . . . . .DLB-15

Myers, Walter Dean 1937- DLB-33

Myerson, Julie 1960- DLB-267

Mykolaitis-Putinas, Vincas 1893-1967. . . .DLB-220

Myles, Eileen 1949- DLB-193

Myrdal, Jan 1927- DLB-257

Mystery
   1985: The Year of the Mystery:
     A Symposium Y-85

   Comments from Other Writers Y-85

   The Second Annual New York Festival
     of Mystery Y-00

   Why I Read Mysteries Y-85

   Why I Write Mysteries: Night and Day,
     by Michael Collins Y-85

N

Na Prous Boneta circa 1296-1328 . . . . . . .DLB-208

Nabl, Franz 1883-1974. . . . . .DLB-81

Nabokov, Véra 1902-1991. . . . . Y-91

Nabokov, Vladimir 1899-1977 . . .DLB-2, 244, 278;
                    Y-80, 91; DS-3; CDALB-1

   International Nabokov Society Y-99

   An Interview [On Nabokov], by
     Fredson Bowers Y-80

   Nabokov Festival at Cornell Y-83

   The Vladimir Nabokov Archive in the
     Berg Collection of the New York
     Public Library: An Overview Y-91

   The Vladimir Nabokov Society Y-01

Nádaši, Ladislav (see Jégé)

Naden, Constance 1858-1889 . . . . .DLB-199

Nadezhdin, Nikolai Ivanovich
  1804-1856 . . . . DLB-198

Nadson, Semen Iakovlevich 1862-1887 . . .DLB-277

Naevius circa 265 B.C.-201 B.C. DLB-211

Nafis and Cornish. DLB-49

Nagai Kafū 1879-1959 . . . . DLB-180

Nagel, Ernest 1901-1985. . . . . .DLB-279

Naipaul, Shiva 1945-1985. . . . . .DLB-157; Y-85

Naipaul, V. S. 1932- DLB-125, 204, 207;
  Y-85, Y-01; CDBLB-8; CDWLB-3

  Nobel Lecture 2001: "Two Worlds" Y-01

Nakagami Kenji 1946-1992 . . . . DLB-182

Nakano-in Masatada no Musume (see Nijō, Lady)

Nałkowska, Zofia 1884-1954 . . . . DLB-215

Joseph Nancrede [publishing house] DLB-49

Naranjo, Carmen 1930- DLB-145

Narbikova, Valeriia Spartakovna
  1958- DLB-285

Narezhny, Vasilii Trofimovich
  1780-1825. DLB-198

Narrache, Jean (Emile Coderre)
  1893-1970. DLB-92

Nasby, Petroleum Vesuvius (see Locke, David Ross)

Eveleigh Nash [publishing house]. DLB-112

Nash, Ogden 1902-1971 . . . . DLB-11

Nashe, Thomas 1567-1601? DLB-167

Nason, Jerry 1910-1986 . . . . DLB-241

Nasr, Seyyed Hossein 1933- DLB-279

Nast, Condé 1873-1942 . . . . DLB-91

Nast, Thomas 1840-1902 . . . . DLB-188

Nastasijević, Momčilo 1894-1938. . . . . . . DLB-147

Nathan, George Jean 1882-1958. . . . . DLB-137

Nathan, Robert 1894-1985 . . . . DLB-9

National Book Critics Circle Awards Y-00-01

The National Jewish Book Awards. Y-85

Natsume Sōseki 1867-1916 . . . . DLB-180

Naughton, Bill 1910-1992. . . . . DLB-13

Navarro, Joe 1953- DLB-209

Naylor, Gloria 1950- DLB-173

Nazor, Vladimir 1876-1949. . . . . DLB-147

Ndebele, Njabulo 1948- DLB-157, 225

Neagoe, Peter 1881-1960 . . . . DLB-4

Neal, John 1793-1876 . . . . DLB-1, 59, 243

Neal, Joseph C. 1807-1847 . . . . DLB-11

Neal, Larry 1937-1981 . . . . DLB-38

The Neale Publishing Company DLB-49

Nebel, Frederick 1903-1967 . . . . DLB-226

F. Tennyson Neely [publishing house] DLB-49

Negoiţescu, Ion 1921-1993 . . . . DLB-220

Negri, Ada 1870-1945. . . . . DLB-114

Neihardt, John G. 1881-1973 . . . . . DLB-9, 54, 256

Neidhart von Reuental
  circa 1185-circa 1240 . . . . DLB-138

Neilson, John Shaw 1872-1942 . . . . DLB-230

Nekrasov, Nikolai Alekseevich
  1821-1877. .DLB-277

Neledinsky-Meletsky, Iurii Aleksandrovich
  1752-1828. DLB-150

Nelligan, Emile 1879-1941 . . . . DLB-92

Nelson, Alice Moore Dunbar 1875-1935 . . DLB-50

Nelson, Antonya 1961- DLB-244

Nelson, Kent 1943- DLB-234

Nelson, Richard K. 1941- DLB-275

Nelson, Thomas, and Sons [U.K.] DLB-106

Nelson, Thomas, and Sons [U.S.]. DLB-49

Nelson, William 1908-1978 . . . . DLB-103

Nelson, William Rockhill 1841-1915 . . . . . DLB-23

Nemerov, Howard 1920-1991 . . . . .DLB-5, 6; Y-83

Németh, László 1901-1975 . . . . DLB-215

Nepos circa 100 B.C.-post 27 B.C. DLB-211

Nèris, Salomėja 1904-1945 . . DLB-220; CDWLB-4

Neruda, Pablo 1904-1973 . . . . DLB-283

Nerval, Gérard de 1808-1855 . . . . DLB-217

Nesbit, E. 1858-1924 . . . . .DLB-141, 153, 178

Ness, Evaline 1911-1986. . . . . DLB-61

Nestroy, Johann 1801-1862 . . . . DLB-133

Nettleship, R. L. 1846-1892 . . . . DLB-262

Neugeboren, Jay 1938- DLB-28

Neukirch, Benjamin 1655-1729. . . . . DLB-168

Neumann, Alfred 1895-1952 . . . . DLB-56

Neumann, Ferenc (see Molnár, Ferenc)

Neumark, Georg 1621-1681 . . . . DLB-164

Neumeister, Erdmann 1671-1756 . . . . DLB-168

Nevins, Allan 1890-1971. . . . . .DLB-17; DS-17

Nevinson, Henry Woodd 1856-1941. . . . DLB-135

The New American Library DLB-46

New Directions Publishing Corporation . . DLB-46

The New Monthly Magazine 1814-1884 . . . . DLB-110

New York Times Book Review. Y-82

John Newbery [publishing house]. DLB-154

Newbolt, Henry 1862-1938 . . . . DLB-19

Newbound, Bernard Slade (see Slade, Bernard)

Newby, Eric 1919- DLB-204

Newby, P. H. 1918- DLB-15

Thomas Cautley Newby
  [publishing house] DLB-106

Newcomb, Charles King 1820-1894. . . DLB-1, 223

Newell, Peter 1862-1924. . . . . DLB-42

Newell, Robert Henry 1836-1901. . . . . . . DLB-11

Newhouse, Samuel I. 1895-1979 . . . . DLB-127

Newman, Cecil Earl 1903-1976 . . . . DLB-127

Newman, David 1937- DLB-44

Newman, Frances 1883-1928 . . . . Y-80

Newman, Francis William 1805-1897. . . . DLB-190

Newman, John Henry 1801-1890. . DLB-18, 32, 55

Mark Newman [publishing house] DLB-49

Newmarch, Rosa Harriet 1857-1940. . . . . DLB-240

George Newnes Limited. DLB-112

Newsome, Effie Lee 1885-1979. . . . . DLB-76

Newton, A. Edward 1864-1940 . . . . DLB-140

Newton, Sir Isaac 1642-1727. . . . . DLB-252

Nexø, Martin Andersen 1869-1954 . . . . . DLB-214

Nezval, Vítěslav
  1900-1958 . . . . .DLB-215; CDWLB-4

Ngugi wa Thiong'o
  1938- DLB-125; CDWLB-3

Niatum, Duane 1938- DLB-175

The Nibelungenlied and the Klage
  circa 1200. DLB-138

Nichol, B. P. 1944-1988 . . . . DLB-53

Nicholas of Cusa 1401-1464. . . . . DLB-115

Nichols, Ann 1891?-1966. . . . . DLB-249

Nichols, Beverly 1898-1983 . . . . DLB-191

Nichols, Dudley 1895-1960 . . . . DLB-26

Nichols, Grace 1950- DLB-157

Nichols, John 1940- Y-82

Nichols, Mary Sargeant (Neal) Gove
  1810-1884 . . . . DLB-1, 243

Nichols, Peter 1927- DLB-13, 245

Nichols, Roy F. 1896-1973 . . . . .DLB-17

Nichols, Ruth 1948- DLB-60

Nicholson, Edward Williams Byron
  1849-1912 . . . . DLB-184

Nicholson, Geoff 1953- DLB-271

Nicholson, Norman 1914- DLB-27

Nicholson, William 1872-1949 . . . . DLB-141

Ní Chuilleanáin, Eiléan 1942- DLB-40

Nicol, Eric 1919- DLB-68

Nicolai, Friedrich 1733-1811. . . . . DLB-97

Nicolas de Clamanges circa 1363-1437. . . DLB-208

Nicolay, John G. 1832-1901 . . . . DLB-47

Nicole, Pierre 1625-1695 . . . . DLB-268

Nicolson, Adela Florence Cory (see Hope, Laurence)

Nicolson, Harold 1886-1968 . . . . . . .DLB-100, 149

"The Practice of Biography," in
  The English Sense of Humour and
  Other Essays. DLB-149

Nicolson, Nigel 1917- DLB-155

Niebuhr, Reinhold 1892-1971. . . . . .DLB-17; DS-17

Niedecker, Lorine 1903-1970 . . . . DLB-48

Nieman, Lucius W. 1857-1935 . . . . DLB-25

Nietzsche, Friedrich
  1844-1900 . . . . .DLB-129; CDWLB-2

  Mencken and Nietzsche: An Unpublished
  Excerpt from H. L. Mencken's My Life
  as Author and Editor. Y-93

Nievo, Stanislao 1928- DLB-196

Niggli, Josefina 1910-1983 . . . . Y-80

Nightingale, Florence 1820-1910 . . . . DLB-166

Nijō, Lady (Nakano-in Masatada no Musume)
  1258-after 1306 . . . . DLB-203

Nijō Yoshimoto 1320-1388. . . . . DLB-203

Nikitin, Ivan Savvich 1824-1861 . . . . . . .DLB-277

Nikitin, Nikolai Nikolaevich 1895-1963 . . .DLB-272

Nikolev, Nikolai Petrovich 1758-1815 . . . DLB-150

Niles, Hezekiah 1777-1839 . . . . DLB-43

Nims, John Frederick 1913-1999 . . . . DLB-5

  Tribute to Nancy Hale. Y-88

Nin, Anaïs 1903-1977 . . . . DLB-2, 4, 152

Niño, Raúl 1961- DLB-209

Nissenson, Hugh 1933- DLB-28

Niven, Frederick John 1878-1944. . . . . . . .DLB-92

Niven, Larry 1938- DLB-8

Nixon, Howard M. 1909-1983 . . . . .DLB-201

Nizan, Paul 1905-1940. . . . . .DLB-72

Njegoš, Petar II Petrović
    1813-1851 . . . . .DLB-147; CDWLB-4

Nkosi, Lewis 1936- DLB-157, 225

Noah, Mordecai M. 1785-1851 . . . . .DLB-250

Noailles, Anna de 1876-1933 . . . . .DLB-258

Nobel Peace Prize
    The Nobel Prize and Literary Politics. . . . Y-88

    Elie Wiesel Y-86

Nobel Prize in Literature
    Joseph Brodsky Y-87

    Camilo José Cela. Y-89

    Dario Fo Y-97

    Gabriel García Márquez Y-82

    William Golding Y-83

    Nadine Gordimer Y-91

    Günter Grass. Y-99

    Seamus Heaney Y-95

    Imre Kertész Y-02

    Najīb Mahfūz Y-88

    Toni Morrison Y-93

    V. S. Naipaul. Y-01

    Kenzaburō Ōe Y-94

    Octavio Paz. Y-90

    José Saramago Y-98

    Jaroslav Seifert Y-84

    Claude Simon Y-85

    Wole Soyinka Y-86

    Wisława Szymborska Y-96

    Derek Walcott. Y-92

    Gao Xingjian. Y-00

Nodier, Charles 1780-1844 . . . . .DLB-119

Noël, Marie (Marie Mélanie Rouget)
    1883-1967 .DLB-258

Noel, Roden 1834-1894. . . . . .DLB-35

Nogami Yaeko 1885-1985 . . . . .DLB-180

Nogo, Rajko Petrov 1945- DLB-181

Nolan, William F. 1928- DLB-8

    Tribute to Raymond Chandler Y-88

Noland, C. F. M. 1810?-1858. . . . . .DLB-11

Noma Hiroshi 1915-1991 . . . . .DLB-182

Nonesuch Press .DLB-112

    Creative Nonfiction Y-02

Noon, Jeff 1957- DLB-267

Noonan, Robert Phillipe (see Tressell, Robert)

Noonday Press. .DLB-46

Noone, John 1936- DLB-14

Nora, Eugenio de 1923- DLB-134

Nordan, Lewis 1939- DLB-234

Nordbrandt, Henrik 1945- DLB-214

Nordhoff, Charles 1887-1947 . . . . .DLB-9

Norén, Lars 1944- DLB-257

Norfolk, Lawrence 1963- DLB-267

Norman, Charles 1904-1996 . . . . .DLB-111

Norman, Marsha 1947- DLB-266; Y-84

Norris, Charles G. 1881-1945 . . . . .DLB-9

Norris, Frank
    1870-1902 . . . . . . .DLB-12, 71, 186; CDALB-3

Norris, John 1657-1712. . . . . .DLB-252

Norris, Leslie 1921- DLB-27, 256

Norse, Harold 1916- DLB-16

Norte, Marisela 1955- DLB-209

North, Marianne 1830-1890 . . . . .DLB-174

North Point Press DLB-46

Nortje, Arthur 1942-1970. . . . . .DLB-125, 225

Norton, Alice Mary (see Norton, Andre)

Norton, Andre 1912- DLB-8, 52

Norton, Andrews 1786-1853 . . . .DLB-1, 235; DS-5

Norton, Caroline 1808-1877. . . .DLB-21, 159, 199

Norton, Charles Eliot 1827-1908 . . .DLB-1, 64, 235

Norton, John 1606-1663 . . . . .DLB-24

Norton, Mary 1903-1992. . . . . .DLB-160

Norton, Thomas 1532-1584 . . . . .DLB-62

W. W. Norton and Company DLB-46

Norwood, Robert 1874-1932 . . . . .DLB-92

Nosaka Akiyuki 1930- DLB-182

Nossack, Hans Erich 1901-1977 . . . . .DLB-69

Notker Balbulus circa 840-912. . . . . .DLB-148

Notker III of Saint Gall circa 950-1022 . . .DLB-148

Notker von Zweifalten ?-1095 . . . . .DLB-148

Nourse, Alan E. 1928- DLB-8

Novak, Slobodan 1924- DLB-181

Novak, Vjenceslav 1859-1905 . . . . .DLB-147

Novakovich, Josip 1956- DLB-244

Novalis 1772-1801 . . . . .DLB-90; CDWLB-2

Novaro, Mario 1868-1944 . . . . .DLB-114

Novás Calvo, Lino 1903-1983. . . . . .DLB-145

Novelists
    Library Journal Statements and
        Questionnaires from First Novelists . . . Y-87

Novels
    The Columbia History of the American Novel
        A Symposium on Y-92

    The Great Modern Library Scam Y-98

    The Proletarian Novel DLB-9

    Novels for Grown-Ups Y-97

    The Year in the Novel Y-87–88, Y-90–93

Novels, British
    "The Break-Up of the Novel" (1922),
        by John Middleton Murry DLB-36

    The Consolidation of Opinion: Critical
        Responses to the Modernists DLB-36

    "Criticism in Relation to Novels"
        (1863), by G. H. Lewes DLB-21

    "Experiment in the Novel" (1929)
        [excerpt], by John D. Beresford . . .DLB-36

    "The Future of the Novel" (1899), by
        Henry James. DLB-18

The Gay Science (1866), by E. S. Dallas
    [excerpt] DLB-21

A Haughty and Proud Generation
    (1922), by Ford Madox Hueffer . . .DLB-36

Literary Effects of World War II DLB-15

"Modern Novelists –Great and Small"
    (1855), by Margaret Oliphant DLB-21

The Modernists (1932),
    by Joseph Warren Beach DLB-36

A Note on Technique (1926), by
    Elizabeth A. Drew [excerpts] DLB-36

Novel-Reading: *The Works of Charles
    Dickens; The Works of W. Makepeace
    Thackeray* (1879),
    by Anthony Trollope DLB-21

Novels with a Purpose (1864), by
    Justin M'Carthy DLB-21

"On Art in Fiction" (1838),
    by Edward Bulwer DLB-21

The Present State of the English Novel
    (1892), by George Saintsbury. DLB-18

Representative Men and Women:
    A Historical Perspective on
    the British Novel, 1930-1960 . . . . .DLB-15

"The Revolt" (1937), by Mary Colum
    [excerpts] .DLB-36

"Sensation Novels" (1863), by
    H. L. Manse DLB-21

Sex, Class, Politics, and Religion [in
    the British Novel, 1930-1959]. DLB-15

Time and Western Man (1927),
    by Wyndham Lewis [excerpts]. . . .DLB-36

Noventa, Giacomo 1898-1960. . . . . .DLB-114

Novikov, Nikolai Ivanovich 1744-1818 . . .DLB-150

Novomeský, Laco 1904-1976. . . . . .DLB-215

Nowlan, Alden 1933-1983. . . . . .DLB-53

Noyes, Alfred 1880-1958. . . . . .DLB-20

Noyes, Crosby S. 1825-1908 . . . . .DLB-23

Noyes, Nicholas 1647-1717. . . . . .DLB-24

Noyes, Theodore W. 1858-1946. . . . . .DLB-29

Nozick, Robert 1938-2002. . . . . .DLB-279

N-Town Plays circa 1468 to early
    sixteenth century DLB-146

Nugent, Frank 1908-1965 . . . . .DLB-44

Nušić, Branislav 1864-1938. . DLB-147; CDWLB-4

David Nutt [publishing house]. DLB-106

Nwapa, Flora 1931-1993 . . . .DLB-125; CDWLB-3

Nye, Edgar Wilson (Bill)
    1850-1896. . . . . .DLB-11, 23, 186

Nye, Naomi Shihab 1952- DLB-120

Nye, Robert 1939- DLB-14, 271

Nyka-Niliūnas, Alfonsas 1919- DLB-220

O

Oakes, Urian circa 1631-1681 . . . . .DLB-24

Oakes Smith, Elizabeth
    1806-1893 . . . . .DLB-1, 239, 243

Oakley, Violet 1874-1961 . . . . .DLB-188

Oates, Joyce Carol 1938-
    . . . . DLB-2, 5, 130; Y-81; CDALB-6

    Tribute to Michael M. Rea Y-97

Ōba Minako 1930- DLB-182

Ober, Frederick Albion 1849-1913 . . . . . . DLB-189

Ober, William 1920-1993 . . . . Y-93

Oberholtzer, Ellis Paxson 1868-1936 . . . . . DLB-47

The Obituary as Literary Form Y-02

Obradović, Dositej 1740?-1811 . . . . DLB-147

O'Brien, Charlotte Grace 1845-1909 . . . . DLB-240

O'Brien, Edna 1932- . . . DLB-14, 231; CDBLB-8

O'Brien, Fitz-James 1828-1862 . . . . DLB-74

O'Brien, Flann (see O'Nolan, Brian)

O'Brien, Kate 1897-1974 . . . . DLB-15

O'Brien, Tim
    1946- DLB-152; Y-80; DS-9; CDALB-7

O'Casey, Sean 1880-1964 . . . . . DLB-10; CDBLB-6

Occom, Samson 1723-1792 . . . . .DLB-175

Occomy, Marita Bonner 1899-1971 . . . . . . DLB-51

Ochs, Adolph S. 1858-1935 . . . . DLB-25

Ochs-Oakes, George Washington
    1861-1931 . . . . DLB-137

O'Connor, Flannery 1925-1964
    . . . . DLB-2, 152; Y-80; DS-12; CDALB-1

    The Flannery O'Connor Society Y-99

O'Connor, Frank 1903-1966 . . . . DLB-162

O'Connor, Joseph 1963- DLB-267

Octopus Publishing Group DLB-112

Oda Sakunosuke 1913-1947 . . . . DLB-182

Odell, Jonathan 1737-1818 . . . . DLB-31, 99

O'Dell, Scott 1903-1989 . . . . DLB-52

Odets, Clifford 1906-1963 . . . . .DLB-7, 26

Odhams Press Limited DLB-112

Odio, Eunice 1922-1974 . . . . DLB-283

Odoevsky, Aleksandr Ivanovich
    1802-1839 . . . . DLB-205

Odoevsky, Vladimir Fedorovich
    1804 or 1803-1869 . . . . DLB-198

O'Donnell, Peter 1920- DLB-87

O'Donovan, Michael (see O'Connor, Frank)

O'Dowd, Bernard 1866-1953 . . . . DLB-230

Ōe, Kenzaburō 1935- DLB-182; Y-94

    Nobel Lecture 1994: Japan, the
        Ambiguous, and Myself Y-94

O'Faolain, Julia 1932- DLB-14, 231

O'Faolain, Sean 1900-1991 . . . . DLB-15, 162

Off-Loop Theatres DLB-7

Offord, Carl Ruthven 1910- DLB-76

O'Flaherty, Liam 1896-1984 . . . .DLB-36, 162; Y-84

Ogarev, Nikolai Platonovich 1813-1877 . . .DLB-277

J. S. Ogilvie and Company DLB-49

Ogilvy, Eliza 1822-1912 . . . . DLB-199

Ogot, Grace 1930- DLB-125

O'Grady, Desmond 1935- DLB-40

Ogunyemi, Wale 1939- DLB-157

O'Hagan, Howard 1902-1982 . . . . DLB-68

O'Hara, Frank 1926-1966 . . . . DLB-5, 16, 193

O'Hara, John
    1905-1970 . . . . . . DLB-9, 86; DS-2; CDALB-5

John O'Hara's Pottsville Journalism Y-88

O'Hegarty, P. S. 1879-1955 . . . . DLB-201

Ohio State University
    The William Charvat American Fiction
    Collection at the Ohio State
    University Libraries Y-92

Okara, Gabriel 1921- DLB-125; CDWLB-3

O'Keeffe, John 1747-1833 . . . . DLB-89

Nicholas Okes [publishing house] DLB-170

Okigbo, Christopher
    1930-1967 . . . . DLB-125; CDWLB-3

Okot p'Bitek 1931-1982 . . . . DLB-125; CDWLB-3

Okpewho, Isidore 1941- DLB-157

Okri, Ben 1959- DLB-157, 231

Old Dogs / New Tricks? New Technologies,
    the Canon, and the Structure of
    the Profession Y-02

Old Franklin Publishing House DLB-49

Old German Genesis and Old German Exodus
    circa 1050-circa 1130 . . . . DLB-148

The Old High German Isidor
    circa 790-800 . . . . DLB-148

Older, Fremont 1856-1935 . . . . DLB-25

Oldham, John 1653-1683 . . . . DLB-131

Oldman, C. B. 1894-1969 . . . . DLB-201

Olds, Sharon 1942- DLB-120

Olearius, Adam 1599-1671 . . . . DLB-164

O'Leary, Ellen 1831-1889 . . . . DLB-240

Olesha, Iurii Karlovich 1899-1960 . . . . . .DLB-272

Oliphant, Laurence 1829?-1888 . . . . . DLB-18, 166

Oliphant, Margaret 1828-1897 . . .DLB-18, 159, 190

    "Modern Novelists—Great and Small"
        (1855) DLB-21

Oliver, Chad 1928-1993 . . . . DLB-8

Oliver, Mary 1935- DLB-5, 193

Ollier, Claude 1922- DLB-83

Olsen, Tillie 1912/1913-
    . . . . DLB-28, 206; Y-80; CDALB-7

Olson, Charles 1910-1970 . . . . DLB-5, 16, 193

Olson, Elder 1909- DLB-48, 63

Olson, Sigurd F. 1899-1982 . . . . .DLB-275

The Omega Workshops DS-10

Omotoso, Kole 1943- DLB-125

Omulevsky, Innokentii Vasil'evich
    1836 [or 1837]-1883 . . . . DLB-238

Ondaatje, Michael 1943- DLB-60

O'Neill, Eugene 1888-1953 . . . . . DLB-7; CDALB-5

    Eugene O'Neill Memorial Theater
        Center DLB-7

    Eugene O'Neill's Letters: A Review Y-88

Onetti, Juan Carlos
    1909-1994 . . . . .DLB-113; CDWLB-3

Onions, George Oliver 1872-1961 . . . . . . DLB-153

Onofri, Arturo 1885-1928 . . . . DLB-114

O'Nolan, Brian 1911-1966 . . . . DLB-231

Opie, Amelia 1769-1853 . . . . DLB-116, 159

Opitz, Martin 1597-1639 . . . . DLB-164

Oppen, George 1908-1984 . . . . DLB-5, 165

Oppenheim, E. Phillips 1866-1946 . . . . . . DLB-70

Oppenheim, James 1882-1932 . . . . DLB-28

Oppenheimer, Joel 1930-1988 . . . . . DLB-5, 193

Optic, Oliver (see Adams, William Taylor)

Orczy, Emma, Baroness 1865-1947 . . . . . . DLB-70

Oregon Shakespeare Festival Y-00

Origo, Iris 1902-1988 . . . . DLB-155

O'Riordan, Kate 1960- DLB-267

Orlovitz, Gil 1918-1973 . . . . DLB-2, 5

Orlovsky, Peter 1933- DLB-16

Ormond, John 1923- DLB-27

Ornitz, Samuel 1890-1957 . . . . DLB-28, 44

O'Rourke, P. J. 1947- DLB-185

Orozco, Olga 1920-1999 . . . . DLB-283

Orten, Jiří 1919-1941 . . . . DLB-215

Ortese, Anna Maria 1914- DLB-177

Ortiz, Simon J. 1941- DLB-120, 175, 256

Ortnit and Wolfdietrich circa 1225-1250 . . . . DLB-138

Orton, Joe 1933-1967 . . . . DLB-13; CDBLB-8

Orwell, George (Eric Arthur Blair)
    1903-1950 . . DLB-15, 98, 195, 255; CDBLB-7

    The Orwell Year Y-84

    (Re-)Publishing Orwell Y-86

Ory, Carlos Edmundo de 1923- DLB-134

Osbey, Brenda Marie 1957- DLB-120

Osbon, B. S. 1827-1912 . . . . DLB-43

Osborn, Sarah 1714-1796 . . . . DLB-200

Osborne, John 1929-1994 . . . . . DLB-13; CDBLB-7

Osgood, Frances Sargent 1811-1850 . . . . . DLB-250

Osgood, Herbert L. 1855-1918 . . . . DLB-47

James R. Osgood and Company DLB-49

Osgood, McIlvaine and Company DLB-112

O'Shaughnessy, Arthur 1844-1881 . . . . . . DLB-35

Patrick O'Shea [publishing house] DLB-49

Osipov, Nikolai Petrovich 1751-1799 . . . . DLB-150

Oskison, John Milton 1879-1947 . . . . . . .DLB-175

Osler, Sir William 1849-1919 . . . . DLB-184

Osofisan, Femi 1946- DLB-125; CDWLB-3

Ostenso, Martha 1900-1963 . . . . DLB-92

Ostrauskas, Kostas 1926- DLB-232

Ostriker, Alicia 1937- DLB-120

Ostrovsky, Aleksandr Nikolaevich
    1823-1886 . . . . .DLB-277

Ostrovsky, Nikolai Alekseevich
    1904-1936 . . . . .DLB-272

Osundare, Niyi 1947- DLB-157; CDWLB-3

Oswald, Eleazer 1755-1795 . . . . DLB-43

Oswald von Wolkenstein
    1376 or 1377-1445 . . . . .DLB-179

Otero, Blas de 1916-1979 . . . . DLB-134

Otero, Miguel Antonio 1859-1944 . . . . . . DLB-82

Otero, Nina 1881-1965 . . . . DLB-209

Otero Silva, Miguel 1908-1985 . . . . DLB-145

Otfried von Weißenburg
    circa 800-circa 875? DLB-148

Otis, Broaders and Company DLB-49

Otis, James (see Kaler, James Otis)

Otis, James, Jr. 1725-1783 . . . . .DLB-31

Ottaway, James 1911-2000 . . . . .DLB-127

Ottendorfer, Oswald 1826-1900 . . . . .DLB-23

Ottieri, Ottiero 1924- DLB-177

Otto-Peters, Louise 1819-1895 . . . . .DLB-129

Otway, Thomas 1652-1685 . . . . .DLB-80

Ouellette, Fernand 1930- DLB-60

Ouida 1839-1908 . . . . .DLB-18, 156

Outing Publishing Company DLB-46

Overbury, Sir Thomas
circa 1581-1613 . . . . .DLB-151

The Overlook Press DLB-46

Ovid 43 B.C.-A.D. 17 . . . . . .DLB-211; CDWLB-1

Owen, Guy 1925- DLB-5

Owen, John 1564-1622 . . . . .DLB-121

John Owen [publishing house] DLB-49

Peter Owen Limited DLB-112

Owen, Robert 1771-1858 . . . . DLB-107, 158

Owen, Wilfred
1893-1918 . . . . DLB-20; DS-18; CDBLB-6

A Centenary Celebration Y-93

The Wilfred Owen Association Y-98

The Owl and the Nightingale
circa 1189-1199 . . . . .DLB-146

Owsley, Frank L. 1890-1956 . . . . .DLB-17

Oxford, Seventeenth Earl of, Edward
de Vere 1550-1604 . . . . .DLB-172

OyamO (Charles F. Gordon)
1943- DLB-266

Ozerov, Vladislav Aleksandrovich
1769-1816 .DLB-150

Ozick, Cynthia 1928- DLB-28, 152; Y-82

First Strauss "Livings" Awarded
to Cynthia Ozick and
Raymond Carver
An Interview with Cynthia Ozick Y-83

Tribute to Michael M. Rea Y-97

P

Pace, Richard 1482?-1536 . . . . .DLB-167

Pacey, Desmond 1917-1975 . . . . .DLB-88

Pack, Robert 1929- DLB-5

Padell Publishing Company DLB-46

Padgett, Ron 1942- DLB-5

Padilla, Ernesto Chávez 1944- DLB-122

L. C. Page and Company DLB-49

Page, Louise 1955- DLB-233

Page, P. K. 1916- DLB-68

Page, Thomas Nelson
1853-1922 . . . . DLB-12, 78; DS-13

Page, Walter Hines 1855-1918 . . . . . . .DLB-71, 91

Paget, Francis Edward 1806-1882 . . . . . . .DLB-163

Paget, Violet (see Lee, Vernon)

Pagliarani, Elio 1927- DLB-128

Pain, Barry 1864-1928 . . . . .DLB-135, 197

Pain, Philip ?-circa 1666 . . . . .DLB-24

Paine, Robert Treat, Jr. 1773-1811 . . . . .DLB-37

Paine, Thomas
1737-1809 . . . . .DLB-31, 43, 73, 158; CDALB-2

Painter, George D. 1914- DLB-155

Painter, William 1540?-1594 . . . . .DLB-136

Palazzeschi, Aldo 1885-1974 . . . . . . .DLB-114, 264

Palei, Marina Anatol'evna 1955- DLB-285

Paley, Grace 1922- DLB-28, 218

Paley, William 1743-1805 . . . . .DLB-252

Palfrey, John Gorham 1796-1881 . . .DLB-1, 30, 235

Palgrave, Francis Turner 1824-1897 . . . . . .DLB-35

Palmer, Joe H. 1904-1952 . . . . .DLB-171

Palmer, Michael 1943- DLB-169

Palmer, Nettie 1885-1964 . . . . .DLB-260

Palmer, Vance 1885-1959 . . . . .DLB-260

Paltock, Robert 1697-1767 . . . . .DLB-39

Paludan, Jacob 1896-1975 . . . . .DLB-214

Pan Books Limited DLB-112

Panaev, Ivan Ivanovich 1812-1862 . . . . . .DLB-198

Panaeva, Avdot'ia Iakovlevna
1820-1893 .DLB-238

Panama, Norman 1914- DLB-26

Pancake, Breece D'J 1952-1979 . . . . .DLB-130

Panduro, Leif 1923-1977 . . . . .DLB-214

Panero, Leopoldo 1909-1962 . . . . .DLB-108

Pangborn, Edgar 1909-1976 . . . . .DLB-8

Panizzi, Sir Anthony 1797-1879 . . . . .DLB-184

Panneton, Philippe (see Ringuet)

Panshin, Alexei 1940- DLB-8

Pansy (see Alden, Isabella)

Pantheon Books DLB-46

Papadat-Bengescu, Hortensia
1876-1955 .DLB-220

Papantonio, Michael 1907-1976 . . . . .DLB-187

Paperback Library DLB-46

Paperback Science Fiction DLB-8

Papini, Giovanni 1881-1956 . . . . .DLB-264

Paquet, Alfons 1881-1944 . . . . .DLB-66

Paracelsus 1493-1541 . . . . .DLB-179

Paradis, Suzanne 1936- DLB-53

Páral, Vladimír, 1932- DLB-232

Pardoe, Julia 1804-1862 . . . . .DLB-166

Paredes, Américo 1915-1999 . . . . .DLB-209

Pareja Diezcanseco, Alfredo 1908-1993 . . .DLB-145

Parents' Magazine Press DLB-46

Parfit, Derek 1942- DLB-262

Parise, Goffredo 1929-1986 . . . . .DLB-177

Parish, Mitchell 1900-1993 . . . . .DLB-265

Parizeau, Alice 1930-1990 . . . . .DLB-60

Park, Ruth 1923?- DLB-260

Parke, John 1754-1789 . . . . .DLB-31

Parker, Dan 1893-1967 . . . . .DLB-241

Parker, Dorothy 1893-1967 . . . . . .DLB-11, 45, 86

Parker, Gilbert 1860-1932 . . . . .DLB-99

Parker, James 1714-1770 . . . . .DLB-43

Parker, John [publishing house] DLB-106

Parker, Matthew 1504-1575 . . . . .DLB-213

Parker, Stewart 1941-1988 . . . . .DLB-245

Parker, Theodore 1810-1860 . . . .DLB-1, 235; DS-5

Parker, William Riley 1906-1968 . . . . . . .DLB-103

J. H. Parker [publishing house] DLB-106

Parkes, Bessie Rayner (Madame Belloc)
1829-1925 .DLB-240

Parkman, Francis
1823-1893 . . . . DLB-1, 30, 183, 186, 235

Parks, Gordon 1912- DLB-33

Parks, Tim 1954- DLB-231

Parks, William 1698-1750 . . . . .DLB-43

William Parks [publishing house] DLB-49

Parley, Peter (see Goodrich, Samuel Griswold)

Parmenides late sixth-fifth century B.C. . . .DLB-176

Parnell, Thomas 1679-1718 . . . . .DLB-95

Parnicki, Teodor 1908-1988 . . . . .DLB-215

Parr, Catherine 1513?-1548 . . . . .DLB-136

Parra, Nicanor 1914- DLB-283

Parrington, Vernon L. 1871-1929 . . . . .DLB-17, 63

Parrish, Maxfield 1870-1966 . . . . .DLB-188

Parronchi, Alessandro 1914- DLB-128

Parshchikov, Aleksei Maksimovich
(Raiderman) 1954- DLB-285

Parton, James 1822-1891 . . . . .DLB-30

Parton, Sara Payson Willis
1811-1872 . . . . DLB-43, 74, 239

S. W. Partridge and Company DLB-106

Parun, Vesna 1922- DLB-181; CDWLB-4

Pascal, Blaise 1623-1662 . . . . .DLB-268

Pasinetti, Pier Maria 1913- DLB-177

Tribute to Albert Erskine Y-93

Pasolini, Pier Paolo 1922-1975 . . . . . .DLB-128, 177

Pastan, Linda 1932- DLB-5

Paston, George (Emily Morse Symonds)
1860-1936 . . . . .DLB-149, 197

The Paston Letters 1422-1509 . . . . .DLB-146

Pastorius, Francis Daniel
1651-circa 1720 . . . . .DLB-24

Patchen, Kenneth 1911-1972 . . . . .DLB-16, 48

Pater, Walter 1839-1894 . .DLB-57, 156; CDBLB-4

Aesthetic Poetry (1873) DLB-35

"Style" (1888) [excerpt] DLB-57

Paterson, A. B. "Banjo" 1864-1941 . . . . . .DLB-230

Paterson, Katherine 1932- DLB-52

Patmore, Coventry 1823-1896 . . . . . . .DLB-35, 98

Paton, Alan 1903-1988 . . . . DLB-225; DS-17

Paton, Joseph Noel 1821-1901 . . . . .DLB-35

Paton Walsh, Jill 1937- DLB-161

Patrick, Edwin Hill ("Ted") 1901-1964 . . .DLB-137

Patrick, John 1906-1995 . . . . .DLB-7

Pattee, Fred Lewis 1863-1950 . . . . .DLB-71

Patterson, Alicia 1906-1963 . . . . .DLB-127

Patterson, Eleanor Medill 1881-1948 . . . . . .DLB-29

Patterson, Eugene 1923- DLB-127

Patterson, Joseph Medill 1879-1946 . . . . . . DLB-29

Pattillo, Henry 1726-1801 . . . . DLB-37

Paul, Elliot 1891-1958. . . . . DLB-4; DS-15

Paul, Jean (see Richter, Johann Paul Friedrich)

Paul, Kegan, Trench, Trubner and
Company Limited DLB-106

Peter Paul Book Company DLB-49

Stanley Paul and Company Limited DLB-112

Paulding, James Kirke
1778-1860 . . . . .DLB-3, 59, 74, 250

Paulin, Tom 1949- DLB-40

Pauper, Peter, Press DLB-46

Paustovsky, Konstantin Georgievich
1892-1968 . . . . DLB-272

Pavese, Cesare 1908-1950 . . . . .DLB-128, 177

Pavić, Milorad 1929- DLB-181; CDWLB-4

Pavlov, Konstantin 1933- DLB-181

Pavlov, Nikolai Filippovich 1803-1864 . . . . DLB-198

Pavlova, Karolina Karlovna 1807-1893 . . . . DLB-205

Pavlović, Miodrag
1928- DLB-181; CDWLB-4

Paxton, John 1911-1985 . . . . DLB-44

Payn, James 1830-1898. . . . . DLB-18

Payne, John 1842-1916. . . . . DLB-35

Payne, John Howard 1791-1852 . . . . DLB-37

Payson and Clarke DLB-46

Paz, Octavio 1914-1998 . . . . Y-90, 98

Nobel Lecture 1990 . . . . Y-90

Pazzi, Roberto 1946- DLB-196

Pea, Enrico 1881-1958 . . . . DLB-264

Peabody, Elizabeth Palmer
1804-1894 . . . . DLB-1, 223

Preface to *Record of a School:*
*Exemplifying the General Principles
of Spiritual Culture* DS-5

Elizabeth Palmer Peabody
[publishing house] DLB-49

Peabody, Josephine Preston 1874-1922. . . DLB-249

Peabody, Oliver William Bourn
1799-1848. . . . . DLB-59

Peace, Roger 1899-1968 . . . . DLB-127

Peacham, Henry 1578-1644? DLB-151

Peacham, Henry, the Elder
1547-1634 . . . . .DLB-172, 236

Peachtree Publishers, Limited. DLB-46

Peacock, Molly 1947- DLB-120

Peacock, Thomas Love 1785-1866 . . . DLB-96, 116

Pead, Deuel ?-1727 . . . . DLB-24

Peake, Mervyn 1911-1968 . . . . . DLB-15, 160, 255

Peale, Rembrandt 1778-1860 . . . . DLB-183

Pear Tree Press. DLB-112

Pearce, Philippa 1920- DLB-161

H. B. Pearson [publishing house] DLB-49

Pearson, Hesketh 1887-1964 . . . . DLB-149

Peattie, Donald Culross 1898-1964 . . . . . .DLB-275

Pechersky, Andrei (see Mel'nikov, Pavel Ivanovich)

Peck, George W. 1840-1916. . . . . DLB-23, 42

H. C. Peck and Theo. Bliss
[publishing house] DLB-49

Peck, Harry Thurston 1856-1914. . . . . DLB-71, 91

Peden, William 1913-1999 . . . . DLB-234

Tribute to William Goyen Y-83

Peele, George 1556-1596 . . . . DLB-62, 167

Pegler, Westbrook 1894-1969 . . . . .DLB-171

Péguy, Charles 1873-1914 . . . . DLB-258

Peirce, Charles Sanders 1839-1914. . . . . . .DLB-270

Pekić, Borislav 1930-1992 . . DLB-181; CDWLB-4

Pelevin, Viktor Olegovich 1962- DLB-285

Pellegrini and Cudahy DLB-46

Pelletier, Aimé (see Vac, Bertrand)

Pelletier, Francine 1959- DLB-251

Pemberton, Sir Max 1863-1950 . . . . DLB-70

de la Peña, Terri 1947- DLB-209

Penfield, Edward 1866-1925. . . . . DLB-188

Penguin Books [U.K.] DLB-112

Fifty Penguin Years Y-85

Penguin Collectors' Society Y-98

Penguin Books [U.S.] DLB-46

Penn, William 1644-1718 . . . . DLB-24

Penn Publishing Company. DLB-49

Penna, Sandro 1906-1977 . . . . DLB-114

Pennell, Joseph 1857-1926 . . . . DLB-188

Penner, Jonathan 1940- Y-83

Pennington, Lee 1939- Y-82

Penton, Brian 1904-1951 . . . . DLB-260

Pepper, Stephen C. 1891-1972 . . . . .DLB-270

Pepys, Samuel
1633-1703 . . . . DLB-101, 213; CDBLB-2

Percy, Thomas 1729-1811 . . . . DLB-104

Percy, Walker 1916-1990 . . . . . . .DLB-2; Y-80, 90

Tribute to Caroline Gordon Y-81

Percy, William 1575-1648. . . . . .DLB-172

Perec, Georges 1936-1982 . . . . DLB-83

Perelman, Bob 1947- DLB-193

Perelman, S. J. 1904-1979 . . . . DLB-11, 44

Perez, Raymundo "Tigre" 1946- DLB-122

Peri Rossi, Cristina 1941- DLB-145

Perkins, Eugene 1932- DLB-41

Perkins, Maxwell
The Claims of Business and Literature:
An Undergraduate Essay Y-01

Perkins, William 1558-1602 . . . . DLB-281

Perkoff, Stuart Z. 1930-1974. . . . . DLB-16

Perley, Moses Henry 1804-1862 . . . . DLB-99

Permabooks DLB-46

Perovsky, Aleksei Alekseevich
(Antonii Pogorel'sky) 1787-1836 . . . . DLB-198

Perrault, Charles 1628-1703. . . . . .DLB-268

Perri, Henry 1561-1617 . . . . DLB-236

Perrin, Alice 1867-1934. . . . . DLB-156

Perry, Anne 1938- DLB-276

Perry, Bliss 1860-1954 . . . . DLB-71

Perry, Eleanor 1915-1981 . . . . DLB-44

Perry, Henry (see Perri, Henry)

Perry, Matthew 1794-1858 . . . . DLB-183

Perry, Sampson 1747-1823 . . . . DLB-158

Perse, Saint-John 1887-1975 . . . . DLB-258

Persius A.D. 34-A.D. 62 . . . . DLB-211

Perutz, Leo 1882-1957 . . . . DLB-81

Pesetsky, Bette 1932- DLB-130

Pestalozzi, Johann Heinrich 1746-1827 . . . . DLB-94

Peter, Laurence J. 1919-1990 . . . . DLB-53

Peter of Spain circa 1205-1277 . . . . DLB-115

Peterkin, Julia 1880-1961 . . . . DLB-9

Peters, Ellis (Edith Pargeter) 1913-1995 . . .DLB-276

Peters, Lenrie 1932- DLB-117

Peters, Robert 1924- DLB-105

"Foreword to *Ludwig of Bavaria*" DLB-105

Petersham, Maud 1889-1971 . . . . DLB-22

Petersham, Miska 1888-1960 . . . . DLB-22

Peterson, Charles Jacobs 1819-1887 . . . . . . DLB-79

Peterson, Len 1917- DLB-88

Peterson, Levi S. 1933- DLB-206

Peterson, Louis 1922-1998 . . . . DLB-76

Peterson, T. B., and Brothers DLB-49

Petitclair, Pierre 1813-1860. . . . . DLB-99

Petrescu, Camil 1894-1957 . . . . DLB-220

Petronius circa A.D. 20-A.D. 66
. . . . .DLB-211; CDWLB-1

Petrov, Aleksandar 1938- DLB-181

Petrov, Evgenii (Evgenii Petrovich Kataev)
1903-1942 .DLB-272

Petrov, Gavriil 1730-1801. . . . . DLB-150

Petrov, Valeri 1920- DLB-181

Petrov, Vasilii Petrovich 1736-1799 . . . . . DLB-150

Petrović, Rastko
1898-1949 . . . . .DLB-147; CDWLB-4

Petrushevskaia, Liudmila Stefanovna
1938- DLB-285

Petruslied circa 854? DLB-148

Petry, Ann 1908-1997. . . . . DLB-76

Pettie, George circa 1548-1589 . . . . DLB-136

Peyton, K. M. 1929- DLB-161

Pfaffe Konrad flourished circa 1172 . . . . . DLB-148

Pfaffe Lamprecht flourished circa 1150 . . DLB-148

Pfeiffer, Emily 1827-1890 . . . . DLB-199

Pforzheimer, Carl H. 1879-1957 . . . . DLB-140

Phaedrus circa 18 B.C.-circa A.D. 50 . . . . DLB-211

Phaer, Thomas 1510?-1560 . . . . DLB-167

Phaidon Press Limited DLB-112

Pharr, Robert Deane 1916-1992 . . . . DLB-33

Phelps, Elizabeth Stuart 1815-1852. . . . . . DLB-202

Phelps, Elizabeth Stuart 1844-1911. . . .DLB-74, 221

Philander von der Linde
(see Mencke, Johann Burckhard)

Philby, H. St. John B. 1885-1960 . . . . DLB-195

Philip, Marlene Nourbese 1947- DLB-157

Philippe, Charles-Louis 1874-1909 . . . . . . DLB-65

Philips, John 1676-1708. . . . . DLB-95

Philips, Katherine 1632-1664 . . . . .DLB-131

Phillipps, Sir Thomas 1792-1872 . . . . . . .DLB-184

Phillips, Caryl 1958- DLB-157

Phillips, David Graham 1867-1911 . . . . .DLB-9, 12

Phillips, Jayne Anne 1952- Y-80

Tribute to Seymour Lawrence Y-94

Phillips, Robert 1938- DLB-105

"Finding, Losing, Reclaiming: A Note
on My Poems" DLB-105

Tribute to William Goyen Y-83

Phillips, Stephen 1864-1915 . . . . .DLB-10

Phillips, Ulrich B. 1877-1934 . . . . .DLB-17

Phillips, Wendell 1811-1884 . . . . .DLB-235

Phillips, Willard 1784-1873 . . . . .DLB-59

Phillips, William 1907-2002 . . . . .DLB-137

Phillips, Sampson and Company DLB-49

Phillpotts, Adelaide Eden (Adelaide Ross)
1896-1993 . . . . .DLB-191

Phillpotts, Eden 1862-1960 . . DLB-10, 70, 135, 153

Philo circa 20-15 B.C.-circa A.D. 50 . . . . . DLB-176

Philosophical Library DLB-46

Philosophy
Eighteenth-Century Philosophical
Background DLB-31

Philosophic Thought in Boston DLB-235

Translators of the Twelfth Century:
Literary Issues Raised and
Impact Created DLB-115

Elihu Phinney [publishing house] DLB-49

Phoenix, John (see Derby, George Horatio)

PHYLON (Fourth Quarter, 1950),
The Negro in Literature:
The Current Scene DLB-76

Physiologus circa 1070-circa 1150 . . . . .DLB-148

Piccolo, Lucio 1903-1969. . . . . .DLB-114

Pickard, Tom 1946- DLB-40

William Pickering [publishing house] DLB-106

Pickthall, Marjorie 1883-1922 . . . . .DLB-92

Pictorial Printing Company DLB-49

Piel, Gerard 1915- DLB-137

"An Announcement to Our Readers,"
Gerard Piel's Statement in *Scientific
American* (April 1948). DLB-137

Pielmeier, John 1949- DLB-266

Piercy, Marge 1936- DLB-120, 227

Pierro, Albino 1916-1995 . . . . .DLB-128

Pignotti, Lamberto 1926- DLB-128

Pike, Albert 1809-1891 . . . . .DLB-74

Pike, Zebulon Montgomery 1779-1813 . . .DLB-183

Pillat, Ion 1891-1945 . . . . .DLB-220

Pil'niak, Boris Andreevich (Boris Andreevich
Vogau) 1894-1938. . . . . .DLB-272

Pilon, Jean-Guy 1930- DLB-60

Pinckney, Eliza Lucas 1722-1793 . . . . . . .DLB-200

Pinckney, Josephine 1895-1957 . . . . .DLB-6

Pindar circa 518 B.C.-circa 438 B.C.
. . . . DLB-176; CDWLB-1

Pindar, Peter (see Wolcot, John)

Pineda, Cecile 1942- DLB-209

Pinero, Arthur Wing 1855-1934 . . . . .DLB-10

Piñero, Miguel 1946-1988 . . . . .DLB-266

Pinget, Robert 1919-1997 . . . . .DLB-83

Pinkney, Edward Coote 1802-1828. . . . . .DLB-248

Pinnacle Books. DLB-46

Piñon, Nélida 1935- DLB-145

Pinsky, Robert 1940- Y-82

Reappointed Poet Laureate Y-98

Pinter, Harold 1930- DLB-13; CDBLB-8

Writing for the Theatre. DLB-13

Piontek, Heinz 1925- DLB-75

Piozzi, Hester Lynch [Thrale]
1741-1821 . . . . .DLB-104, 142

Piper, H. Beam 1904-1964. . . . . .DLB-8

Piper, Watty DLB-22

Pirandello, Luigi 1867-1936 . . . . .DLB-264

Pirckheimer, Caritas 1467-1532 . . . . .DLB-179

Pirckheimer, Willibald 1470-1530 . . . . . . .DLB-179

Pisar, Samuel 1929- Y-83

Pisarev, Dmitrii Ivanovich 1840-1868 . . . .DLB-277

Pisemsky, Aleksei Feofilaktovich
1821-1881 . . . . .DLB-238

Pitkin, Timothy 1766-1847 . . . . .DLB-30

Pitter, Ruth 1897- DLB-20

Pix, Mary 1666-1709 . . . . .DLB-80

Pixérécourt, René Charles Guilbert de
1773-1844 . . . . .DLB-192

Pizarnik, Alejandra 1936-1972 . . . . .DLB-283

Plaatje, Sol T. 1876-1932 . . . . .DLB-125, 225

Plante, David 1940- Y-83

Platen, August von 1796-1835 . . . . .DLB-90

Plantinga, Alvin 1932- DLB-279

Plath, Sylvia
1932-1963 . . . . .DLB-5, 6, 152; CDALB-1

Plato circa 428 B.C.-348-347 B.C.
. . . . DLB-176; CDWLB-1

Plato, Ann 1824?-? DLB-239

Platon 1737-1812 . . . . .DLB-150

Platonov, Andrei Platonovich (Andrei
Platonovich Klimentev) 1899-1951 . . .DLB-272

Platt, Charles 1945- DLB-261

Platt and Munk Company. DLB-46

Plautus circa 254 B.C.-184 B.C.
. . . . DLB-211; CDWLB-1

Playboy Press. .DLB-46

John Playford [publishing house]. DLB-170

Der Pleier flourished circa 1250. . . . . . . .DLB-138

Pleijel, Agneta 1940- DLB-257

Plenzdorf, Ulrich 1934- DLB-75

Pleshcheev, Aleksei Nikolaevich
1825?-1893 . . . . .DLB-277

Plessen, Elizabeth 1944- DLB-75

Pletnev, Petr Aleksandrovich
1792-1865 . . . . .DLB-205

Pliekšāne, Elza Rozenberga (see Aspazija)

Pliekšāns, Jānis (see Rainis, Jānis)

Plievier, Theodor 1892-1955 . . . . .DLB-69

Plimpton, George 1927- DLB-185, 241; Y-99

Pliny the Elder A.D. 23/24-A.D. 79 . . . . . .DLB-211

Pliny the Younger
circa A.D. 61-A.D. 112 . . . . .DLB-211

Plomer, William
1903-1973 . . . . .DLB-20, 162, 191, 225

Plotinus 204-270 . . . . DLB-176; CDWLB-1

Plowright, Teresa 1952- DLB-251

Plume, Thomas 1630-1704 . . . . .DLB-213

Plumly, Stanley 1939- DLB-5, 193

Plumpp, Sterling D. 1940- DLB-41

Plunkett, James 1920- DLB-14

Plutarch
circa 46-circa 120. . . . . . . DLB-176; CDWLB-1

Plymell, Charles 1935- DLB-16

Pocket Books. .DLB-46

Poe, Edgar Allan 1809-1849
. . . . DLB-3, 59, 73, 74, 248; CDALB-2

The Poe Studies Association Y-99

Poe, James 1921-1980 . . . . .DLB-44

The Poet Laureate of the United States. Y-86

Statements from Former Consultants
in Poetry. Y-86

Poetry
Aesthetic Poetry (1873) DLB-35

A Century of Poetry, a Lifetime of
Collecting: J. M. Edelstein's
Collection of Twentieth-
Century American Poetry Y-02

"Certain Gifts," by Betty Adcock DLB-105

Contempo Caravan: Kites in a
Windstorm Y-85

"Contemporary Verse Story-telling,"
by Jonathan Holden DLB-105

"A Detail in a Poem," by Fred
Chappell DLB-105

"The English Renaissance of Art"
(1908), by Oscar Wilde DLB-35

"Every Man His Own Poet; or,
The Inspired Singer's Recipe
Book" (1877), by
H. W. Mallock DLB-35

"Eyes Across Centuries: Contemporary
Poetry and 'That Vision Thing,'"
by Philip Dacey DLB-105

A Field Guide to Recent Schools
of American Poetry Y-86

"Finding, Losing, Reclaiming:
A Note on My Poems,
by Robert Phillips" DLB-105

"The Fleshly School of Poetry and Other
Phenomena of the Day" (1872) . . .DLB-35

"The Fleshly School of Poetry:
Mr. D. G. Rossetti" (1871) DLB-35

The G. Ross Roy Scottish Poetry Collection
at the University of South Carolina . . Y-89

"Getting Started: Accepting the Regions
You Own—or Which Own You,"
by Walter McDonald DLB-105

"The Good, The Not So Good," by
Stephen Dunn. DLB-105

The Griffin Poetry Prize Y-00

The Hero as Poet. Dante; Shakspeare
  (1841), by Thomas Carlyle DLB-32

"Images and 'Images,'" by Charles
  Simic DLB-105

"Into the Mirror," by Peter Cooley . . DLB-105

"Knots into Webs: Some Autobiographical
  Sources," by Dabney Stuart DLB-105

"L'Envoi" (1882), by Oscar Wilde . . . DLB-35

"Living in Ruin," by Gerald Stern . . . DLB-105

Looking for the Golden Mountain:
  Poetry Reviewing Y-89

Lyric Poetry (French) DLB-268

"The No Self, the Little Self, and the
  Poets," by Richard Moore DLB-105

On Some of the Characteristics of Modern
  Poetry and On the Lyrical Poems of
  Alfred Tennyson (1831) DLB-32

The Pitt Poetry Series: Poetry Publishing
  Today Y-85

"The Poetry File," by Edward
  Field DLB-105

Poetry in Nineteenth-Century France:
  Cultural Background and Critical
  Commentary DLB-217

The Poetry of Jorge Luis Borges Y-86

"The Poet's Kaleidoscope: The Element
  of Surprise in the Making of the
  Poem" by Madeline DeFrees DLB-105

The Pre-Raphaelite Controversy DLB-35

"Reflections: After a Tornado,"
  by Judson Jerome DLB-105

Statements from Former Consultants
  in Poetry Y-86

Statements on the Art of Poetry DLB-54

The Study of Poetry (1880), by
  Matthew Arnold DLB-35

A Survey of Poetry Anthologies,
  1879-1960 . . . . DLB-54

Thoughts on Poetry and Its Varieties
  (1833), by John Stuart Mill DLB-32

Under the Microscope (1872), by
  A. C. Swinburne DLB-35

The Unterberg Poetry Center of the
  92nd Street Y Y-98

Victorian Poetry: Five Critical
  Views DLBV-35

Year in Poetry Y-83–92, 94–01

Year's Work in American Poetry Y-82

Poets
  The Lives of the Poets (1753) DLB-142

  Minor Poets of the Earlier
    Seventeenth Century DLB-121

  Other British Poets Who Fell
    in the Great War DLB-216

  Other Poets [French] DLB-217

  Second-Generation Minor Poets of
    the Seventeenth Century DLB-126

  Third-Generation Minor Poets of
    the Seventeenth Century DLB-131

Pogodin, Mikhail Petrovich 1800-1875 . . . DLB-198

Pogorel'sky, Antonii
  (see Perovsky, Aleksei Alekseevich)

Pohl, Frederik 1919- DLB-8

Tribute to Isaac Asimov Y-92

Tribute to Theodore Sturgeon Y-85

Poirier, Louis (see Gracq, Julien)

Poláček, Karel 1892-1945 . . . DLB-215; CDWLB-4

Polanyi, Michael 1891-1976 . . . . DLB-100

Pole, Reginald 1500-1558 . . . . DLB-132

Polevoi, Nikolai Alekseevich 1796-1846 . . DLB-198

Polezhaev, Aleksandr Ivanovich
  1804-1838 . . . . DLB-205

Poliakoff, Stephen 1952- DLB-13

Polidori, John William 1795-1821 . . . . . . DLB-116

Polite, Carlene Hatcher 1932- DLB-33

Pollard, Alfred W. 1859-1944 . . . . DLB-201

Pollard, Edward A. 1832-1872 . . . . DLB-30

Pollard, Graham 1903-1976 . . . . DLB-201

Pollard, Percival 1869-1911 . . . . DLB-71

Pollard and Moss DLB-49

Pollock, Sharon 1936- DLB-60

Polonsky, Abraham 1910-1999 . . . . DLB-26

Polonsky, Iakov Petrovich 1819-1898 . . . . DLB-277

Polotsky, Simeon 1629-1680 . . . . DLB-150

Polybius circa 200 B.C.-118 B.C. DLB-176

Pomialovsky, Nikolai Gerasimovich
  1835-1863 . . . . DLB-238

Pomilio, Mario 1921-1990 . . . . DLB-177

Ponce, Mary Helen 1938- DLB-122

Ponce-Montoya, Juanita 1949- DLB-122

Ponet, John 1516?-1556 . . . . DLB-132

Ponge, Francis 1899-1988 . . . . DLB-258; Y-02

Poniatowska, Elena
  1933- DLB-113; CDWLB-3

Ponsard, François 1814-1867 . . . . DLB-192

William Ponsonby [publishing house] DLB-170

Pontiggia, Giuseppe 1934- DLB-196

Pony Stories, Omnibus Essay on DLB-160

Poole, Ernest 1880-1950 . . . . DLB-9

Poole, Sophia 1804-1891 . . . . DLB-166

Poore, Benjamin Perley 1820-1887 . . . . . . DLB-23

Popa, Vasko 1922-1991 . . . . DLB-181; CDWLB-4

Pope, Abbie Hanscom 1858-1894 . . . . . . DLB-140

Pope, Alexander
  1688-1744 . . . . . . DLB-95, 101, 213; CDBLB-2

Popov, Aleksandr Serafimovich
  (see Serafimovich, Aleksandr Serafimovich)

Popov, Evgenii Anatol'evich 1946- DLB-285

Popov, Mikhail Ivanovich
  1742-circa 1790 . . . . DLB-150

Popović, Aleksandar 1929-1996 . . . . DLB-181

Popper, Karl 1902-1994 . . . . DLB-262

Popular Culture Association/
  American Culture Association Y-99

Popular Library DLB-46

Poquelin, Jean-Baptiste (see Molière)

Porete, Marguerite ?-1310 . . . . DLB-208

Porlock, Martin (see MacDonald, Philip)

Porpoise Press DLB-112

Porta, Antonio 1935-1989 . . . . DLB-128

Porter, Anna Maria 1780-1832 . . . . . DLB-116, 159

Porter, Cole 1891-1964 . . . . DLB-265

Porter, David 1780-1843 . . . . DLB-183

Porter, Eleanor H. 1868-1920 . . . . DLB-9

Porter, Gene Stratton (see Stratton-Porter, Gene)

Porter, Hal 1911-1984 . . . . DLB-260

Porter, Henry ?-? DLB-62

Porter, Jane 1776-1850 . . . . DLB-116, 159

Porter, Katherine Anne 1890-1980
  . . . . . . DLB-4, 9, 102; Y-80; DS-12; CDALB-7

  The Katherine Anne Porter Society Y-01

Porter, Peter 1929- DLB-40

Porter, William Sydney (O. Henry)
  1862-1910 . . . . DLB-12, 78, 79; CDALB-3

Porter, William T. 1809-1858 . . . . DLB-3, 43, 250

Porter and Coates DLB-49

Portillo Trambley, Estela 1927-1998 . . . . DLB-209

Portis, Charles 1933- DLB-6

Posey, Alexander 1873-1908 . . . . DLB-175

Postans, Marianne circa 1810-1865 . . . . . DLB-166

Postgate, Raymond 1896-1971 . . . . DLB-276

Postl, Carl (see Sealsfield, Carl)

Poston, Ted 1906-1974 . . . . DLB-51

Potekhin, Aleksei Antipovich 1829-1908 . DLB-238

Potok, Chaim 1929-2002 . . . . DLB-28, 152

  A Conversation with Chaim Potok Y-84

  Tribute to Bernard Malamud Y-86

Potter, Beatrix 1866-1943 . . . . DLB-141

  The Beatrix Potter Society Y-98

Potter, David M. 1910-1971 . . . . DLB-17

Potter, Dennis 1935-1994 . . . . DLB-233

John E. Potter and Company DLB-49

Pottle, Frederick A. 1897-1987 . . . . . DLB-103; Y-87

Poulin, Jacques 1937- DLB-60

Pound, Ezra 1885-1972
  . . . . DLB-4, 45, 63; DS-15; CDALB-4

  The Cost of the Cantos: William Bird
    to Ezra Pound Y-01

  The Ezra Pound Society Y-01

Poverman, C. E. 1944- DLB-234

Povich, Shirley 1905-1998 . . . . DLB-171

Powell, Anthony 1905-2000 . . . DLB-15; CDBLB-7

  The Anthony Powell Society: Powell and
    the First Biennial Conference Y-01

Powell, Dawn 1897-1965
  Dawn Powell, Where Have You Been
    All Our Lives? Y-97

Powell, John Wesley 1834-1902 . . . . DLB-186

Powell, Padgett 1952- DLB-234

Powers, J. F. 1917-1999 . . . . DLB-130

Powers, Jimmy 1903-1995 . . . . DLB-241

Pownall, David 1938- DLB-14

Powys, John Cowper 1872-1963 . . . . DLB-15, 255

Powys, Llewelyn 1884-1939 . . . . DLB-98

Powys, T. F. 1875-1953 . . . . DLB-36, 162

The Powys Society Y-98

Poynter, Nelson 1903-1978 . . . . .DLB-127

Prado, Pedro 1886-1952 . . . . .DLB-283

Prados, Emilio 1899-1962 . . . . .DLB-134

Praed, Mrs. Caroline (see Praed, Rosa)

Praed, Rosa (Mrs. Caroline Praed)
1851-1935 .DLB-230

Praed, Winthrop Mackworth 1802-1839. . .DLB-96

Praeger Publishers DLB-46

Praetorius, Johannes 1630-1680. . . . . . . .DLB-168

Pratolini, Vasco 1913-1991 . . . . .DLB-177

Pratt, E. J. 1882-1964. . . . . .DLB-92

Pratt, Samuel Jackson 1749-1814 . . . . . . .DLB-39

Preciado Martin, Patricia 1939- DLB-209

Préfontaine, Yves 1937- DLB-53

Prelutsky, Jack 1940- DLB-61

Prentice, George D. 1802-1870 . . . . .DLB-43

Prentice-Hall DLB-46

Prescott, Orville 1906-1996 . . . . .Y-96

Prescott, William Hickling
1796-1859 . . . . .DLB-1, 30, 59, 235

Prešeren, Francè
1800-1849 . . . . .DLB-147; CDWLB-4

Presses (See also Publishing)
Small Presses in Great Britain and
Ireland, 1960-1985 . . . . .DLB-40

Small Presses I: Jargon Society Y-84

Small Presses II: The Spirit That Moves
Us Press Y-85

Small Presses III: Pushcart Press. Y-87

Preston, Margaret Junkin
1820-1897 . . . . .DLB-239, 248

Preston, May Wilson 1873-1949 . . . . . . .DLB-188

Preston, Thomas 1537-1598. . . . . .DLB-62

Prévert, Jacques 1900-1977 . . . . .DLB-258

Price, Anthony 1928- DLB-276

Price, Reynolds 1933- DLB-2, 218, 278

Price, Richard 1723-1791 . . . . .DLB-158

Price, Richard 1949- Y-81

Prichard, Katharine Susannah
1883-1969 . . . . .DLB-260

Prideaux, John 1578-1650 . . . . .DLB-236

Priest, Christopher 1943- DLB-14, 207, 261

Priestley, J. B. 1894-1984
. . . DLB-10, 34, 77, 100, 139; Y-84; CDBLB-6

Priestley, Joseph 1733-1804 . . . . .DLB-252

Prigov, Dmitrii Aleksandrovich 1940- . .DLB-285

Prime, Benjamin Young 1733-1791 . . . . . . .DLB-31

Primrose, Diana floruit circa 1630. . . . . . .DLB-126

Prince, F. T. 1912- DLB-20

Prince, Nancy Gardner 1799-?. DLB-239

Prince, Thomas 1687-1758. . . . . . .DLB-24, 140

Pringle, Thomas 1789-1834 . . . . .DLB-225

Printz, Wolfgang Casper 1641-1717. . . . . .DLB-168

Prior, Matthew 1664-1721 . . . . .DLB-95

Prisco, Michele 1920- DLB-177

Prishvin, Mikhail Mikhailovich
1873-1954 . . . . .DLB-272

Pritchard, William H. 1932- DLB-111

Pritchett, V. S. 1900-1997 . . . . DLB-15, 139

Probyn, May 1856 or 1857-1909 . . . . . . .DLB-199

Procter, Adelaide Anne 1825-1864 . . .DLB-32, 199

Procter, Bryan Waller 1787-1874 . . . . .DLB-96, 144

Proctor, Robert 1868-1903 . . . . .DLB-184

Prokopovich, Feofan 1681?-1736. . . . . . .DLB-150

Prokosch, Frederic 1906-1989 . . . . .DLB-48

Pronzini, Bill 1943- DLB-226

Propertius circa 50 B.C.-post 16 B.C.
. . . . .DLB-211; CDWLB-1

Propper, Dan 1937- DLB-16

Prose, Francine 1947- DLB-234

Protagoras circa 490 B.C.-420 B.C. DLB-176

Proud, Robert 1728-1813. . . . . .DLB-30

Proust, Marcel 1871-1922 . . . . .DLB-65

Marcel Proust at 129 and the Proust
Society of America Y-00

Marcel Proust's *Remembrance of Things Past*:
The Rediscovered Galley Proofs Y-00

Prutkov, Koz'ma Petrovich 1803-1863 . . .DLB-277

Prynne, J. H. 1936- DLB-40

Przybyszewski, Stanislaw 1868-1927 . . . . .DLB-66

Pseudo-Dionysius the Areopagite floruit
circa 500 . . . . .DLB-115

Public Lending Right in America
PLR and the Meaning of Literary
Property Y-83

Statement by Sen. Charles
McC. Mathias, Jr. PLR. Y-83

Statements on PLR by American Writers . Y-83

Public Lending Right in the United Kingdom
The First Year in the United Kingdom . . . Y-83

Publishers [listed by individual names]
Publishers, Conversations with:
An Interview with Charles Scribner III . . .Y-94

An Interview with Donald Lamm Y-95

An Interview with James Laughlin Y-96

An Interview with Patrick O'Connor Y-84

Publishing
The Art and Mystery of Publishing:
Interviews Y-97

Book Publishing Accounting: Some Basic
Concepts Y-98

1873 Publishers' Catalogues DLB-49

The Literary Scene 2002: Publishing, Book
Reviewing, and Literary Journalism. . Y-02

Main Trends in Twentieth-Century
Book Clubs. DLB-46

Overview of U.S. Book Publishing,
1910-1945 . . . . .DLB-9

The Pitt Poetry Series: Poetry Publishing
Today Y-85

Publishing Fiction at LSU Press Y-87

The Publishing Industry in 1998:
Sturm-und-drang.com Y-98

The Publishing Industry in 1999 . . . . . . Y-99

Publishers and Agents: The Columbia
Connection. Y-87

Responses to Ken Auletta Y-97

Southern Writers Between the Wars . . .DLB-9

The State of Publishing. Y-97

Trends in Twentieth-Century
Mass Market Publishing. DLB-46

The Year in Book Publishing Y-86

Pückler-Muskau, Hermann von
1785-1871 . . . . .DLB-133

Pufendorf, Samuel von 1632-1694. . . . . .DLB-168

Pugh, Edwin William 1874-1930 . . . . . . .DLB-135

Pugin, A. Welby 1812-1852 . . . . .DLB-55

Puig, Manuel 1932-1990 . . . . DLB-113; CDWLB-3

Pulitzer, Joseph 1847-1911 . . . . .DLB-23

Pulitzer, Joseph, Jr. 1885-1955. . . . . .DLB-29

Pulitzer Prizes for the Novel, 1917-1945 . . . .DLB-9

Pulliam, Eugene 1889-1975 . . . . .DLB-127

Purcell, Deirdre 1945- DLB-267

Purchas, Samuel 1577?-1626 . . . . .DLB-151

Purdy, Al 1918-2000 . . . . .DLB-88

Purdy, James 1923- DLB-2, 218

Purdy, Ken W. 1913-1972. . . . . .DLB-137

Pusey, Edward Bouverie 1800-1882 . . . . . .DLB-55

Pushkin, Aleksandr Sergeevich
1799-1837 . . . . .DLB-205

Pushkin, Vasilii L'vovich
1766-1830 . . . . .DLB-205

Putnam, George Palmer
1814-1872 . . . . DLB-3, 79, 250, 254

G. P. Putnam [publishing house] DLB-254

G. P. Putnam's Sons [U.K.] DLB-106

G. P. Putnam's Sons [U.S.] DLB-49

A Publisher's Archives: G. P. Putnam . . . Y-92

Putnam, Hilary 1926- DLB-279

Putnam, Samuel 1892-1950. . . . . . .DLB-4; DS-15

Puttenham, George 1529?-1590 . . . . . . .DLB-281

Puzo, Mario 1920-1999 . . . . .DLB-6

Pyle, Ernie 1900-1945 . . . . .DLB-29

Pyle, Howard 1853-1911 . . . . . DLB-42, 188; DS-13

Pyle, Robert Michael 1947- DLB-275

Pym, Barbara 1913-1980 . . . . . . DLB-14, 207; Y-87

Pynchon, Thomas 1937- DLB-2, 173

Pyramid Books .DLB-46

Pyrnelle, Louise-Clarke 1850-1907 . . . . . .DLB-42

Pythagoras circa 570 B.C.-? DLB-176

Q

Quad, M. (see Lewis, Charles B.)

Quaritch, Bernard 1819-1899 . . . . .DLB-184

Quarles, Francis 1592-1644. . . . . .DLB-126

The Quarterly Review 1809-1967. . . . . .DLB-110

Quasimodo, Salvatore 1901-1968 . . . . . . .DLB-114

Queen, Ellery (see Dannay, Frederic, and
Manfred B. Lee)

Queen, Frank 1822-1882. . . . . .DLB-241

The Queen City Publishing House DLB-49

Queneau, Raymond 1903-1976 . . . . . .DLB-72, 258

Quennell, Peter 1905-1993 . . . . DLB-155, 195

Quesnel, Joseph 1746-1809 . . . . DLB-99

Quiller-Couch, Sir Arthur Thomas
1863-1944 . . . . . . DLB-135, 153, 190

Quin, Ann 1936-1973 . . . . DLB-14, 231

Quinault, Philippe 1635-1688 . . . . DLB-268

Quincy, Samuel, of Georgia ?-? DLB-31

Quincy, Samuel, of Massachusetts
1734-1789 . . . . DLB-31

Quine, W. V. 1908-2000 . . . . .DLB-279

Quinn, Anthony 1915-2001 . . . . DLB-122

Quinn, John 1870-1924 . . . . DLB-187

Quiñónez, Naomi 1951- DLB-209

Quintana, Leroy V. 1944- DLB-82

Quintana, Miguel de 1671-1748

    A Forerunner of Chicano
    Literature DLB-122

Quintilian
circa A.D. 40-circa A.D. 96 . . . . DLB-211

Quintus Curtius Rufus fl. A.D. 35 . . . . . . DLB-211

Harlin Quist Books DLB-46

Quoirez, Françoise (see Sagan, Françoise)

R

Raabe, Wilhelm 1831-1910 . . . . DLB-129

Raban, Jonathan 1942- DLB-204

Rabe, David 1940- DLB-7, 228; Y-91

Raboni, Giovanni 1932- DLB-128

Rachilde 1860-1953 . . . . DLB-123, 192

Racin, Kočo 1908-1943 . . . . DLB-147

Racine, Jean 1639-1699 . . . . DLB-268

Rackham, Arthur 1867-1939 . . . . DLB-141

Radauskas, Henrikas
1910-1970 . . . . DLB-220; CDWLB-4

Radcliffe, Ann 1764-1823 . . . . .DLB-39, 178

Raddall, Thomas 1903-1994 . . . . DLB-68

Radford, Dollie 1858-1920 . . . . DLB-240

Radichkov, Yordan 1929- DLB-181

Radiguet, Raymond 1903-1923 . . . . DLB-65

Radishchev, Aleksandr Nikolaevich
1749-1802 . . . . DLB-150

Radnóti, Miklós
1909-1944 . . . . DLB-215; CDWLB-4

Radványi, Netty Reiling (see Seghers, Anna)

Rahv, Philip 1908-1973 . . . . DLB-137

Raich, Semen Egorovich 1792-1855 . . . . . DLB-205

Raičković, Stevan 1928- DLB-181

Raiderman (see Parshchikov, Aleksei Maksimovich)

Raimund, Ferdinand Jakob 1790-1836 . . . . DLB-90

Raine, Craig 1944- DLB-40

Raine, Kathleen 1908- DLB-20

Rainis, Jānis 1865-1929 . . . . . DLB-220; CDWLB-4

Rainolde, Richard
circa 1530-1606 . . . . DLB-136, 236

Rainolds, John 1549-1607 . . . . DLB-281

Rakić, Milan 1876-1938 . . . . .DLB-147; CDWLB-4

Rakosi, Carl 1903- DLB-193

Ralegh, Sir Walter
1554?-1618 . . . . DLB-172; CDBLB-1

Raleigh, Walter
Style (1897) [excerpt] DLB-57

Ralin, Radoy 1923- DLB-181

Ralph, Julian 1853-1903 . . . . DLB-23

Ramat, Silvio 1939- DLB-128

Ramée, Marie Louise de la (see Ouida)

Ramírez, Sergío 1942- DLB-145

Ramke, Bin 1947- DLB-120

Ramler, Karl Wilhelm 1725-1798 . . . . DLB-97

Ramon Ribeyro, Julio 1929-1994 . . . . . DLB-145

Ramos, Manuel 1948- DLB-209

Ramous, Mario 1924- DLB-128

Rampersad, Arnold 1941- DLB-111

Ramsay, Allan 1684 or 1685-1758 . . . . . . DLB-95

Ramsay, David 1749-1815 . . . . DLB-30

Ramsay, Martha Laurens 1759-1811 . . . . DLB-200

Ramsey, Frank P. 1903-1930 . . . . DLB-262

Ranck, Katherine Quintana 1942- DLB-122

Rand, Avery and Company DLB-49

Rand, Ayn 1905-1982 . . . . DLB-227, 279; CDALB-7

Rand McNally and Company DLB-49

Randall, David Anton 1905-1975 . . . . DLB-140

Randall, Dudley 1914- DLB-41

Randall, Henry S. 1811-1876 . . . . DLB-30

Randall, James G. 1881-1953 . . . . DLB-17

The Randall Jarrell Symposium: A Small
Collection of Randall Jarrells Y-86

Excerpts From Papers Delivered at the
Randall Jarrel Symposium Y-86

Randall, John Herman, Jr. 1899-1980 . . . .DLB-279

Randolph, A. Philip 1889-1979 . . . . DLB-91

Anson D. F. Randolph
[publishing house] DLB-49

Randolph, Thomas 1605-1635 . . . . . . DLB-58, 126

Random House DLB-46

Rankin, Ian (Jack Harvey) 1960- DLB-267

Henry Ranlet [publishing house] DLB-49

Ransom, Harry 1908-1976 . . . . DLB-187

Ransom, John Crowe
1888-1974 . . . . DLB-45, 63; CDALB-7

Ransome, Arthur 1884-1967 . . . . DLB-160

Raphael, Frederic 1931- DLB-14

Raphaelson, Samson 1896-1983 . . . . DLB-44

Rare Book Dealers
Bertram Rota and His Bookshop Y-91

An Interview with Glenn Horowitz Y-90

An Interview with Otto Penzler Y-96

An Interview with Ralph Sipper Y-94

New York City Bookshops in the
1930s and 1940s: The Recollections
of Walter Goldwater Y-93

Rare Books
Research in the American Antiquarian
Book Trade Y-97

Two Hundred Years of Rare Books and
Literary Collections at the
University of South Carolina Y-00

Rashi circa 1040-1105 . . . . DLB-208

Raskin, Ellen 1928-1984 . . . . DLB-52

Rastell, John 1475?-1536 . . . . .DLB-136, 170

Rattigan, Terence
1911-1977 . . . . DLB-13; CDBLB-7

Raven, Simon 1927-2001 . . . . .DLB-271

Rawlings, Marjorie Kinnan 1896-1953
. . . . .DLB-9, 22, 102; DS-17; CDALB-7

Rawlinson, Richard 1690-1755 . . . . DLB-213

Rawlinson, Thomas 1681-1725 . . . . DLB-213

Rawls, John 1921-2002 . . . . .DLB-279

Raworth, Tom 1938- DLB-40

Ray, David 1932- DLB-5

Ray, Gordon Norton 1915-1986 . . . .DLB-103, 140

Ray, Henrietta Cordelia 1849-1916 . . . . . . DLB-50

Raymond, Ernest 1888-1974 . . . . DLB-191

Raymond, Henry J. 1820-1869 . . . . .DLB-43, 79

Raymond, René (see Chase, James Hadley)

Razaf, Andy 1895-1973 . . . . DLB-265

Rea, Michael 1927-1996 . . . . Y-97

Michael M. Rea and the Rea Award for
the Short Story Y-97

Reach, Angus 1821-1856 . . . . DLB-70

Read, Herbert 1893-1968 . . . . DLB-20, 149

Read, Martha Meredith DLB-200

Read, Opie 1852-1939 . . . . DLB-23

Read, Piers Paul 1941- DLB-14

Reade, Charles 1814-1884 . . . . DLB-21

Reader's Digest Condensed Books DLB-46

Readers Ulysses Symposium Y-97

Reading, Peter 1946- DLB-40

Reading Series in New York City Y-96

Reaney, James 1926- DLB-68

Rebhun, Paul 1500?-1546 . . . . .DLB-179

Rèbora, Clemente 1885-1957 . . . . DLB-114

Rebreanu, Liviu 1885-1944 . . . . DLB-220

Rechy, John 1931- DLB-122, 278; Y-82

Redding, J. Saunders 1906-1988 . . . . . .DLB-63, 76

J. S. Redfield [publishing house] DLB-49

Redgrove, Peter 1932- DLB-40

Redmon, Anne 1943- Y-86

Redmond, Eugene B. 1937- DLB-41

James Redpath [publishing house] DLB-49

Reed, Henry 1808-1854 . . . . DLB-59

Reed, Henry 1914-1986 . . . . DLB-27

Reed, Ishmael
1938- DLB-2, 5, 33, 169, 227; DS-8

Reed, Rex 1938- DLB-185

Reed, Sampson 1800-1880 . . . . DLB-1, 235

Reed, Talbot Baines 1852-1893 . . . . DLB-141

Reedy, William Marion 1862-1920 . . . . . . DLB-91

Reese, Lizette Woodworth 1856-1935 . . . . DLB-54

Reese, Thomas 1742-1796 . . . . DLB-37

Reeve, Clara 1729-1807 . . . . .DLB-39

  Preface to *The Old English Baron*
    (1778) DLB-39

  The Progress of Romance (1785)
    [excerpt] DLB-39

Reeves, James 1909-1978 . . . . .DLB-161

Reeves, John 1926- DLB-88

Reeves-Stevens, Garfield 1953- DLB-251

Henry Regnery Company DLB-46

Rehberg, Hans 1901-1963 . . . . .DLB-124

Rehfisch, Hans José 1891-1960 . . . . .DLB-124

Reich, Ebbe Kløvedal 1940- DLB-214

Reid, Alastair 1926- DLB-27

Reid, B. L. 1918-1990 . . . . .DLB-111

Reid, Christopher 1949- DLB-40

Reid, Forrest 1875-1947 . . . . .DLB-153

Reid, Helen Rogers 1882-1970. . . . . .DLB-29

Reid, James ?-? DLB-31

Reid, Mayne 1818-1883 . . . . .DLB-21, 163

Reid, Thomas 1710-1796 . . . . .DLB-31, 252

Reid, V. S. (Vic) 1913-1987 . . . . .DLB-125

Reid, Whitelaw 1837-1912 . . . . .DLB-23

Reilly and Lee Publishing Company DLB-46

Reimann, Brigitte 1933-1973 . . . . .DLB-75

Reinmar der Alte circa 1165-circa 1205 . . .DLB-138

Reinmar von Zweter
  circa 1200-circa 1250 . . . . .DLB-138

Reisch, Walter 1903-1983 . . . . .DLB-44

Reizei Family DLB-203

Religion
  A Crisis of Culture: The Changing
    Role of Religion in the
    New Republic DLB-37

Remarque, Erich Maria
  1898-1970 . . . . .DLB-56; CDWLB-2

Remington, Frederic
  1861-1909 . . . . .DLB-12, 186, 188

Renaud, Jacques 1943- DLB-60

Renault, Mary 1905-1983 . . . . .Y-83

Rendell, Ruth (Barbara Vine)
  1930- DLB-87, 276

Rensselaer, Maria van Cortlandt van
  1645-1689 . . . . .DLB-200

Repplier, Agnes 1855-1950 . . . . .DLB-221

Reshetnikov, Fedor Mikhailovich
  1841-1871 . . . . .DLB-238

Rettenbacher, Simon 1634-1706. . . . . .DLB-168

Retz, Jean-François-Paul de Gondi,
  cardinal de 1613-1679 . . . . .DLB-268

Reuchlin, Johannes 1455-1522 . . . . .DLB-179

Reuter, Christian 1665-after 1712 . . . . . . .DLB-168

Fleming H. Revell Company DLB-49

Reverdy, Pierre 1889-1960 . . . . .DLB-258

Reuter, Fritz 1810-1874 . . . . .DLB-129

Reuter, Gabriele 1859-1941 . . . . .DLB-66

Reventlow, Franziska Gräfin zu
  1871-1918 . . . . .DLB-66

Review of Reviews Office DLB-112

Rexroth, Kenneth 1905-1982
  . . . . . DLB-16, 48, 165, 212; Y-82; CDALB-1

  The Commercialization of the Image
    of Revolt .DLB-16

Rey, H. A. 1898-1977 . . . . .DLB-22

Reynal and Hitchcock DLB-46

Reynolds, G. W. M. 1814-1879 . . . . .DLB-21

Reynolds, John Hamilton 1794-1852 . . . . .DLB-96

Reynolds, Sir Joshua 1723-1792 . . . . .DLB-104

Reynolds, Mack 1917-1983 . . . . .DLB-8

Reznikoff, Charles 1894-1976 . . . . .DLB-28, 45

Rhetoric
  Continental European Rhetoricians,
    1400-1600, and Their Influence
    in Reaissance England DLB-236

  A Finding Guide to Key Works on
    Microfilm DLB-236

  Glossary of Terms and Definitions of
    Rhetoic and Logic DLB-236

Rhett, Robert Barnwell 1800-1876 . . . . . . .DLB-43

Rhode, John 1884-1964 . . . . .DLB-77

Rhodes, Eugene Manlove 1869-1934 . . . .DLB-256

Rhodes, James Ford 1848-1927 . . . . .DLB-47

Rhodes, Richard 1937- DLB-185

Rhys, Jean 1890-1979
  . . . . DLB-36, 117, 162; CDBLB-7; CDWLB-3

Ricardo, David 1772-1823 . . . . DLB-107, 158

Ricardou, Jean 1932- DLB-83

Rice, Elmer 1892-1967 . . . . .DLB-4, 7

Rice, Grantland 1880-1954 . . . . DLB-29, 171

Rich, Adrienne 1929- DLB-5, 67; CDALB-7

Richard, Mark 1955- DLB-234

Richard de Fournival
  1201-1259 or 1260 . . . . .DLB-208

Richards, David Adams 1950- DLB-53

Richards, George circa 1760-1814 . . . . . . .DLB-37

Richards, I. A. 1893-1979 . . . . .DLB-27

Richards, Laura E. 1850-1943 . . . . .DLB-42

Richards, William Carey 1818-1892 . . . . . .DLB-73

Grant Richards [publishing house] DLB-112

Richardson, Charles F. 1851-1913 . . . . . . .DLB-71

Richardson, Dorothy M. 1873-1957 . . . . . .DLB-36

  The Novels of Dorothy Richardson
    (1918), by May Sinclair DLB-36

Richardson, Henry Handel
  (Ethel Florence Lindesay Robertson)
  1870-1946 . . . . DLB-197, 230

Richardson, Jack 1935- DLB-7

Richardson, John 1796-1852 . . . . .DLB-99

Richardson, Samuel
  1689-1761 . . . . .DLB-39, 154; CDBLB-2

  Introductory Letters from the Second
    Edition of *Pamela* (1741) DLB-39

  Postscript to [the Third Edition of]
    Clarissa (1751) DLB-39

  Preface to the First Edition of
    Pamela (1740) DLB-39

  Preface to the Third Edition of
    Clarissa (1751) [excerpt] DLB-39

  Preface to Volume 1 of *Clarissa*
    (1747) DLB-39

  Preface to Volume 3 of *Clarissa*
    (1748) DLB-39

Richardson, Willis 1889-1977 . . . . .DLB-51

Riche, Barnabe 1542-1617 . . . . .DLB-136

Richepin, Jean 1849-1926 . . . . .DLB-192

Richler, Mordecai 1931-2001 . . . . .DLB-53

Richter, Conrad 1890-1968 . . . . .DLB-9, 212

Richter, Hans Werner 1908-1993 . . . . .DLB-69

Richter, Johann Paul Friedrich
  1763-1825 . . . . .DLB-94; CDWLB-2

Joseph Rickerby [publishing house] DLB-106

Rickword, Edgell 1898-1982 . . . . .DLB-20

Riddell, Charlotte 1832-1906 . . . . .DLB-156

Riddell, John (see Ford, Corey)

Ridge, John Rollin 1827-1867 . . . . .DLB-175

Ridge, Lola 1873-1941 . . . . .DLB-54

Ridge, William Pett 1859-1930 . . . . .DLB-135

Riding, Laura (see Jackson, Laura Riding)

Ridler, Anne 1912- DLB-27

Ridruego, Dionisio 1912-1975 . . . . .DLB-108

Riel, Louis 1844-1885 . . . . .DLB-99

Riemer, Johannes 1648-1714 . . . . .DLB-168

Rifbjerg, Klaus 1931- DLB-214

Riffaterre, Michael 1924- DLB-67

A Conversation between William Riggan
  and Janette Turner Hospital Y-02

Riggs, Lynn 1899-1954 . . . . .DLB-175

Riis, Jacob 1849-1914 . . . . .DLB-23

John C. Riker [publishing house] DLB-49

Riley, James 1777-1840 . . . . .DLB-183

Riley, John 1938-1978 . . . . .DLB-40

Rilke, Rainer Maria
  1875-1926 . . . . .DLB-81; CDWLB-2

Rimanelli, Giose 1926- DLB-177

Rimbaud, Jean-Nicolas-Arthur
  1854-1891 . . . . .DLB-217

Rinehart and Company DLB-46

Ringuet 1895-1960 . . . . .DLB-68

Ringwood, Gwen Pharis 1910-1984 . . . . . .DLB-88

Rinser, Luise 1911- DLB-69

Ríos, Alberto 1952- DLB-122

Ríos, Isabella 1948- DLB-82

Ripley, Arthur 1895-1961 . . . . .DLB-44

Ripley, George 1802-1880 . . . . . DLB-1, 64, 73, 235

The Rising Glory of America:
  Three Poems .DLB-37

The Rising Glory of America: Written in 1771
  (1786), by Hugh Henry Brackenridge
  and Philip Freneau DLB-37

Riskin, Robert 1897-1955 . . . . .DLB-26

Risse, Heinz 1898- DLB-69

Rist, Johann 1607-1667 . . . . .DLB-164

Ristikivi, Karl 1912-1977 . . . . .DLB-220

Ritchie, Anna Mowatt 1819-1870 . . . . .DLB-3, 250

Ritchie, Anne Thackeray 1837-1919 . . . . . .DLB-18

Ritchie, Thomas 1778-1854 . . . . DLB-43

The Ritz Paris Hemingway Award Y-85

Mario Varga Llosa's Acceptance Speech . . Y-85

Rivard, Adjutor 1868-1945 . . . . DLB-92

Rive, Richard 1931-1989 . . . . DLB-125, 225

Rivera, José 1955- DLB-249

Rivera, Marina 1942- DLB-122

Rivera, Tomás 1935-1984 . . . . DLB-82

Rivers, Conrad Kent 1933-1968 . . . . DLB-41

Riverside Press DLB-49

Rivington, James circa 1724-1802 . . . . DLB-43

Charles Rivington [publishing house] DLB-154

Rivkin, Allen 1903-1990 . . . . DLB-26

Roa Bastos, Augusto 1917- DLB-113

Robbe-Grillet, Alain 1922- DLB-83

Robbins, Tom 1936- Y-80

Roberts, Charles G. D. 1860-1943 . . . . DLB-92

Roberts, Dorothy 1906-1993 . . . . DLB-88

Roberts, Elizabeth Madox
1881-1941 . . . . DLB-9, 54, 102

Roberts, John (see Swynnerton, Thomas)

Roberts, Keith 1935-2000 . . . . DLB-261

Roberts, Kenneth 1885-1957 . . . . DLB-9

Roberts, Michèle 1949- DLB-231

Roberts, Theodore Goodridge
1877-1953 . . . . DLB-92

Roberts, Ursula Wyllie (see Miles, Susan)

Roberts, William 1767-1849 . . . . DLB-142

James Roberts [publishing house] DLB-154

Roberts Brothers DLB-49

A. M. Robertson and Company DLB-49

Robertson, Ethel Florence Lindesay
(see Richardson, Henry Handel)

Robertson, William 1721-1793 . . . . DLB-104

Robin, Leo 1895-1984 . . . . DLB-265

Robins, Elizabeth 1862-1952 . . . . DLB-197

Robinson, A. Mary F. (Madame James
Darmesteter, Madame Mary
Duclaux) 1857-1944 . . . . DLB-240

Robinson, Casey 1903-1979 . . . . DLB-44

Robinson, Derek Y-02

Robinson, Edwin Arlington
1869-1935 . . . . DLB-54; CDALB-3

Review by Derek Robinson of George
Greenfield's *Rich Dust*. Y-02

Robinson, Henry Crabb 1775-1867 . . . . . DLB-107

Robinson, James Harvey 1863-1936 . . . . . DLB-47

Robinson, Lennox 1886-1958 . . . . DLB-10

Robinson, Mabel Louise 1874-1962 . . . . . . DLB-22

Robinson, Marilynne 1943- DLB-206

Robinson, Mary 1758-1800 . . . . DLB-158

Robinson, Richard circa 1545-1607 . . . . . DLB-167

Robinson, Therese 1797-1870 . . . . . . DLB-59, 133

Robison, Mary 1949- DLB-130

Roblès, Emmanuel 1914-1995 . . . . DLB-83

Roccatagliata Ceccardi, Ceccardo
1871-1919 . . . . DLB-114

Roche, Billy 1949- DLB-233

Rochester, John Wilmot, Earl of
1647-1680 . . . . DLB-131

Rochon, Esther 1948- DLB-251

Rock, Howard 1911-1976 . . . . DLB-127

Rockwell, Norman Perceval 1894-1978 . . DLB-188

Rodgers, Carolyn M. 1945- DLB-41

Rodgers, W. R. 1909-1969 . . . . DLB-20

Rodney, Lester 1911- DLB-241

Rodríguez, Claudio 1934-1999 . . . . DLB-134

Rodríguez, Joe D. 1943- DLB-209

Rodríguez, Luis J. 1954- DLB-209

Rodriguez, Richard 1944- DLB-82, 256

Rodríguez Julia, Edgardo 1946- DLB-145

Roe, E. P. 1838-1888 . . . . DLB-202

Roethke, Theodore
1908-1963 . . . . DLB-5, 206; CDALB-1

Rogers, Jane 1952- DLB-194

Rogers, Pattiann 1940- DLB-105

Rogers, Samuel 1763-1855 . . . . DLB-93

Rogers, Will 1879-1935 . . . . DLB-11

Rohmer, Sax 1883-1959 . . . . DLB-70

Roiphe, Anne 1935- Y-80

Rojas, Arnold R. 1896-1988 . . . . DLB-82

Rolfe, Frederick William
1860-1913 . . . . DLB-34, 156

Rolland, Romain 1866-1944 . . . . DLB-65

Rolle, Richard circa 1290-1300 - 1340 . . . DLB-146

Rölvaag, O. E. 1876-1931 . . . . DLB-9, 212

Romains, Jules 1885-1972 . . . . DLB-65

A. Roman and Company DLB-49

Roman de la Rose: Guillaume de Lorris
1200/1205-circa 1230, Jean de
Meun 1235-1240-circa 1305 . . . . DLB-208

Romano, Lalla 1906-2001 . . . . DLB-177

Romano, Octavio 1923- DLB-122

Rome, Harold 1908-1993 . . . . DLB-265

Romero, Leo 1950- DLB-122

Romero, Lin 1947- DLB-122

Romero, Orlando 1945- DLB-82

Rook, Clarence 1863-1915 . . . . DLB-135

Roosevelt, Theodore
1858-1919 . . . . DLB-47, 186, 275

Root, Waverley 1903-1982 . . . . DLB-4

Root, William Pitt 1941- DLB-120

Roquebrune, Robert de 1889-1978 . . . . . . DLB-68

Rorty, Richard 1931- DLB-246, 279

Rosa, João Guimarães 1908-1967 . . . . . . DLB-113

Rosales, Luis 1910-1992 . . . . DLB-134

Roscoe, William 1753-1831 . . . . DLB-163

Rose, Reginald 1920-2002 . . . . DLB-26

Rose, Wendy 1948- DLB-175

Rosegger, Peter 1843-1918 . . . . DLB-129

Rosei, Peter 1946- DLB-85

Rosen, Norma 1925- DLB-28

Rosenbach, A. S. W. 1876-1952 . . . . DLB-140

Rosenbaum, Ron 1946- DLB-185

Rosenberg, Isaac 1890-1918 . . . . DLB-20, 216

Rosenfeld, Isaac 1918-1956 . . . . DLB-28

Rosenthal, Harold 1914-1999 . . . . DLB-241

Jimmy, Red, and Others: Harold
Rosenthal Remembers the Stars of
the Press Box Y-01

Rosenthal, M. L. 1917-1996 . . . . DLB-5

Rosenwald, Lessing J. 1891-1979 . . . . . . .DLB-187

Ross, Alexander 1591-1654 . . . . DLB-151

Ross, Harold 1892-1951 . . . . .DLB-137

Ross, Jerry 1926-1955 . . . . DLB-265

Ross, Leonard Q. (see Rosten, Leo)

Ross, Lillian 1927- DLB-185

Ross, Martin 1862-1915 . . . . DLB-135

Ross, Sinclair 1908-1996 . . . . DLB-88

Ross, W. W. E. 1894-1966 . . . . DLB-88

Rosselli, Amelia 1930-1996 . . . . DLB-128

Rossen, Robert 1908-1966 . . . . DLB-26

Rosset, Barney Y-02

Rossetti, Christina 1830-1894 . . . DLB-35, 163, 240

Rossetti, Dante Gabriel
1828-1882 . . . . DLB-35; CDBLB-4

The Stealthy School of
Criticism (1871) DLB-35

Rossner, Judith 1935- DLB-6

Rostand, Edmond 1868-1918 . . . . DLB-192

Rosten, Leo 1908-1997 . . . . DLB-11

Rostenberg, Leona 1908- DLB-140

Rostopchina, Evdokiia Petrovna
1811-1858 . . . . DLB-205

Rostovsky, Dimitrii 1651-1709 . . . . DLB-150

Rota, Bertram 1903-1966 . . . . DLB-201

Bertram Rota and His Bookshop Y-91

Roth, Gerhard 1942- DLB-85, 124

Roth, Henry 1906?-1995 . . . . DLB-28

Roth, Joseph 1894-1939 . . . . DLB-85

Roth, Philip
1933- DLB-2, 28, 173; Y-82; CDALB-6

Rothenberg, Jerome 1931- DLB-5, 193

Rothschild Family DLB-184

Rotimi, Ola 1938- DLB-125

Rotrou, Jean 1609-1650 . . . . .DLB-268

Routhier, Adolphe-Basile 1839-1920 . . . . . DLB-99

Routier, Simone 1901-1987 . . . . DLB-88

George Routledge and Sons DLB-106

Roversi, Roberto 1923- DLB-128

Rowe, Elizabeth Singer 1674-1737 . . . . DLB-39, 95

Rowe, Nicholas 1674-1718 . . . . DLB-84

Rowlands, Samuel circa 1570-1630 . . . . . . DLB-121

Rowlandson, Mary
circa 1637-circa 1711 . . . . DLB-24, 200

Rowley, William circa 1585-1626 . . . . DLB-58

Rowling, J. K.
The Harry Potter Phenomenon Y-99

Rowse, A. L. 1903-1997 . . . . DLB-155

Rowson, Susanna Haswell
circa 1762-1824 . . . . DLB-37, 200

Roy, Camille 1870-1943 . . . . .DLB-92

The G. Ross Roy Scottish Poetry Collection
at the University of South Carolina Y-89

Roy, Gabrielle 1909-1983 . . . . .DLB-68

Roy, Jules 1907-2000 . . . . .DLB-83

The Royal Court Theatre and the English
Stage Company DLB-13

The Royal Court Theatre and the New
Drama DLB-10

The Royal Shakespeare Company
at the Swan Y-88

Royall, Anne Newport 1769-1854 . . . .DLB-43, 248

Royce, Josiah 1855-1916 . . . . .DLB-270

The Roycroft Printing Shop DLB-49

Royde-Smith, Naomi 1875-1964 . . . . . . .DLB-191

Royster, Vermont 1914-1996 . . . . .DLB-127

Richard Royston [publishing house] DLB-170

Różewicz, Tadeusz 1921- DLB-232

Ruark, Gibbons 1941- DLB-120

Ruban, Vasilii Grigorevich 1742-1795 . . . .DLB-150

Rubens, Bernice 1928- DLB-14, 207

Rubina, Dina Il'inichna 1953- DLB-285

Rubinshtein, Lev Semenovich 1947- . . .DLB-285

Rudd and Carleton DLB-49

Rudd, Steele (Arthur Hoey Davis) DLB-230

Rudkin, David 1936- DLB-13

Rudnick, Paul 1957- DLB-266

Rudolf von Ems circa 1200-circa 1254 . . .DLB-138

Ruffin, Josephine St. Pierre 1842-1924 . . . .DLB-79

Ruganda, John 1941- DLB-157

Ruggles, Henry Joseph 1813-1906 . . . . . . .DLB-64

Ruiz de Burton, María Amparo
1832-1895 . . . . .DLB-209, 221

Rukeyser, Muriel 1913-1980 . . . . .DLB-48

Rule, Jane 1931- DLB-60

Rulfo, Juan 1918-1986 . . . . . .DLB-113; CDWLB-3

Rumaker, Michael 1932- DLB-16

Rumens, Carol 1944- DLB-40

Rummo, Paul-Eerik 1942- DLB-232

Runyon, Damon 1880-1946 . . . . DLB-11, 86, 171

Ruodlieb circa 1050-1075 . . . . .DLB-148

Rush, Benjamin 1746-1813 . . . . .DLB-37

Rush, Rebecca 1779-? DLB-200

Rushdie, Salman 1947- DLB-194

Rusk, Ralph L. 1888-1962 . . . . .DLB-103

Ruskin, John
1819-1900 . . . . . .DLB-55, 163, 190; CDBLB-4

Russ, Joanna 1937- DLB-8

Russell, Benjamin 1761-1845 . . . . .DLB-43

Russell, Bertrand 1872-1970 . . . . . .DLB-100, 262

Russell, Charles Edward 1860-1941 . . . . . .DLB-25

Russell, Charles M. 1864-1926 . . . . .DLB-188

Russell, Eric Frank 1905-1978 . . . . .DLB-255

Russell, Fred 1906-2003 . . . . .DLB-241

Russell, George William (see AE)

Russell, Countess Mary Annette Beauchamp
(see Arnim, Elizabeth von)

Russell, Willy 1947- DLB-233

B. B. Russell and Company DLB-49

R. H. Russell and Son DLB-49

Rutebeuf flourished 1249-1277 . . . . .DLB-208

Rutherford, Mark 1831-1913 . . . . .DLB-18

Ruxton, George Frederick 1821-1848 . . . .DLB-186

R-va, Zeneida (see Gan, Elena Andreevna)

Ryan, James 1952- DLB-267

Ryan, Michael 1946- Y-82

Ryan, Oscar 1904- DLB-68

Ryder, Jack 1871-1936 . . . . .DLB-241

Ryga, George 1932-1987 . . . . .DLB-60

Rylands, Enriqueta Augustina Tennant
1843-1908 . . . . .DLB-184

Rylands, John 1801-1888 . . . . .DLB-184

Ryle, Gilbert 1900-1976 . . . . .DLB-262

Ryleev, Kondratii Fedorovich
1795-1826 . . . . .DLB-205

Rymer, Thomas 1643?-1713 . . . . .DLB-101

Ryskind, Morrie 1895-1985 . . . . .DLB-26

Rzhevsky, Aleksei Andreevich
1737-1804 . . . . .DLB-150

S

The Saalfield Publishing Company DLB-46

Saba, Umberto 1883-1957 . . . . .DLB-114

Sábato, Ernesto 1911- DLB-145; CDWLB-3

Saberhagen, Fred 1930- DLB-8

Sabin, Joseph 1821-1881 . . . . .DLB-187

Sacer, Gottfried Wilhelm 1635-1699 . . . . .DLB-168

Sachs, Hans 1494-1576 . . . . . DLB-179; CDWLB-2

Sack, John 1930- DLB-185

Sackler, Howard 1929-1982 . . . . .DLB-7

Sackville, Lady Margaret 1881-1963 . . . . .DLB-240

Sackville, Thomas 1536-1608 . . . . .DLB-132

Sackville, Thomas 1536-1608 . . . . .DLB-62

Sackville-West, Edward 1901-1965 . . . . . .DLB-191

Sackville-West, V. 1892-1962 . . . . . . .DLB-34, 195

Sadlier, Mary Anne 1820-1903 . . . . .DLB-99

D. and J. Sadlier and Company DLB-49

Sadoff, Ira 1945- DLB-120

Sadoveanu, Mihail 1880-1961 . . . . .DLB-220

Sadur, Nina Nikolaevna 1950- DLB-285

Sáenz, Benjamin Alire 1954- DLB-209

Saenz, Jaime 1921-1986 . . . . .DLB-145, 283

Saffin, John circa 1626-1710 . . . . .DLB-24

Sagan, Françoise 1935- DLB-83

Sage, Robert 1899-1962 . . . . .DLB-4

Sagel, Jim 1947- DLB-82

Sagendorph, Robb Hansell 1900-1970 . . . .DLB-137

Sahagún, Carlos 1938- DLB-108

Sahkomaapii, Piitai (see Highwater, Jamake)

Sahl, Hans 1902-1993 . . . . .DLB-69

Said, Edward W. 1935- DLB-67

Saigyō 1118-1190 . . . . .DLB-203

Saiko, George 1892-1962 . . . . .DLB-85

Sainte-Beuve, Charles-Augustin
1804-1869 . . . . .DLB-217

Saint-Exupéry, Antoine de 1900-1944 . . . . .DLB-72

St. John, J. Allen 1872-1957 . . . . .DLB-188

St John, Madeleine 1942- DLB-267

St. Johns, Adela Rogers 1894-1988 . . . . . .DLB-29

St. Omer, Garth 1931- DLB-117

Saint Pierre, Michel de 1916-1987 . . . . . . .DLB-83

St. Dominic's Press DLB-112

The St. John's College Robert Graves Trust . . Y-96

St. Martin's Press DLB-46

St. Nicholas 1873-1881 . . . . DS-13

Saintsbury, George 1845-1933 . . . . . . DLB-57, 149

"Modern English Prose" (1876) DLB-57

The Present State of the English
Novel (1892), ...DLB-18

Saiokuken Sōchō 1448-1532 . . . . .DLB-203

Saki (see Munro, H. H.)

Salaam, Kalamu ya 1947- DLB-38

Šalamun, Tomaž 1941- . . . DLB-181; CDWLB-4

Salas, Floyd 1931- DLB-82

Sálaz-Marquez, Rubén 1935- DLB-122

Salemson, Harold J. 1910-1988 . . . . .DLB-4

Salesbury, William 1520?-1584? DLB-281

Salinas, Luis Omar 1937- DLB-82

Salinas, Pedro 1891-1951 . . . . .DLB-134

Salinger, J. D.
1919- DLB-2, 102, 173; CDALB-1

Salkey, Andrew 1928- DLB-125

Sallust circa 86 B.C.-35 B.C.
. . . . DLB-211; CDWLB-1

Salt, Waldo 1914-1987 . . . . .DLB-44

Salter, James 1925- DLB-130

Salter, Mary Jo 1954- DLB-120

Saltus, Edgar 1855-1921 . . . . .DLB-202

Saltykov, Mikhail Evgrafovich
1826-1889 . . . . .DLB-238

Salustri, Carlo Alberto (see Trilussa)

Salverson, Laura Goodman 1890-1970 . . . .DLB-92

Samain, Albert 1858-1900 . . . . .DLB-217

Sampson, Richard Henry (see Hull, Richard)

Samuels, Ernest 1903-1996 . . . . .DLB-111

Sanborn, Franklin Benjamin
1831-1917 . . . . .DLB-1, 223

Sánchez, Luis Rafael 1936- DLB-145

Sánchez, Philomeno "Phil" 1917- DLB-122

Sánchez, Ricardo 1941-1995 . . . . .DLB-82

Sánchez, Saúl 1943- DLB-209

Sanchez, Sonia 1934- DLB-41; DS-8

Sand, George 1804-1876 . . . . .DLB-119, 192

Sandburg, Carl 1878-1967 . . DLB-17, 54; CDALB-3

Sanders, Edward 1939- DLB-16, 244

Sanderson, Robert 1587-1663 . . . . DLB-281

Sandoz, Mari 1896-1966 . . . . DLB-9, 212

Sandwell, B. K. 1876-1954 . . . . DLB-92

Sandy, Stephen 1934- DLB-165

Sandys, George 1578-1644 . . . . DLB-24, 121

Sangster, Charles 1822-1893 . . . . DLB-99

Sanguineti, Edoardo 1930- DLB-128

Sanjōnishi Sanetaka 1455-1537 . . . . DLB-203

Sansay, Leonora ?-after 1823 . . . . DLB-200

Sansom, William 1912-1976 . . . . DLB-139

Santayana, George
　　1863-1952 . . . . . . DLB-54, 71, 246, 270; DS-13

Santiago, Danny 1911-1988 . . . . DLB-122

Santmyer, Helen Hooven 1895-1986 . . . . Y-84

Sanvitale, Francesca 1928- DLB-196

Sapidus, Joannes 1490-1561 . . . . DLB-179

Sapir, Edward 1884-1939 . . . . DLB-92

Sapper (see McNeile, Herman Cyril)

Sappho circa 620 B.C.-circa 550 B.C.
　　. . . . . DLB-176; CDWLB-1

Saramago, José 1922- Y-98

　　Nobel Lecture 1998: How Characters
　　　Became the Masters and the Author
　　　Their Apprentice Y-98

Sarban (John W. Wall) 1910-1989 . . . . . . DLB-255

Sardou, Victorien 1831-1908 . . . . DLB-192

Sarduy, Severo 1937-1993 . . . . DLB-113

Sargent, Pamela 1948- DLB-8

Saro-Wiwa, Ken 1941- DLB-157

Saroyan, Aram
　　Rites of Passage [on William Saroyan] Y-83

Saroyan, William
　　1908-1981 . . . . . DLB-7, 9, 86; Y-81; CDALB-7

Sarraute, Nathalie 1900-1999 . . . . DLB-83

Sarrazin, Albertine 1937-1967 . . . . DLB-83

Sarris, Greg 1952- DLB-175

Sarton, May 1912-1995 . . . . DLB-48; Y-81

Sartre, Jean-Paul 1905-1980 . . . . DLB-72

Sassoon, Siegfried
　　1886-1967 . . . . DLB-20, 191; DS-18

　　A Centenary Essay Y-86

　　Tributes from Vivien F. Clarke and
　　　Michael Thorpe Y-86

Sata Ineko 1904- DLB-180

Saturday Review Press DLB-46

Saunders, James 1925- DLB-13

Saunders, John Monk 1897-1940 . . . . DLB-26

Saunders, Margaret Marshall
　　1861-1947 . . . . DLB-92

Saunders and Otley DLB-106

Saussure, Ferdinand de 1857-1913 . . . . . . DLB-242

Savage, James 1784-1873 . . . . DLB-30

Savage, Marmion W. 1803?-1872 . . . . DLB-21

Savage, Richard 1697?-1743 . . . . DLB-95

Savard, Félix-Antoine 1896-1982 . . . . DLB-68

Savery, Henry 1791-1842 . . . . DLB-230

Saville, (Leonard) Malcolm 1901-1982 . . . DLB-160

Savinio, Alberto 1891-1952 . . . . DLB-264

Sawyer, Robert J. 1960- DLB-251

Sawyer, Ruth 1880-1970 . . . . DLB-22

Sayers, Dorothy L.
　　1893-1957 . . . . . DLB-10, 36, 77, 100; CDBLB-6

　　The Dorothy L. Sayers Society Y-98

Sayle, Charles Edward 1864-1924 . . . . . . DLB-184

Sayles, John Thomas 1950- DLB-44

Sbarbaro, Camillo 1888-1967 . . . . DLB-114

Scalapino, Leslie 1947- DLB-193

Scannell, Vernon 1922- DLB-27

Scarry, Richard 1919-1994 . . . . DLB-61

Schaefer, Jack 1907-1991 . . . . DLB-212

Schaeffer, Albrecht 1885-1950 . . . . DLB-66

Schaeffer, Susan Fromberg 1941- DLB-28

Schaff, Philip 1819-1893 . . . . DS-13

Schaper, Edzard 1908-1984 . . . . DLB-69

Scharf, J. Thomas 1843-1898 . . . . DLB-47

Schede, Paul Melissus 1539-1602 . . . . DLB-179

Scheffel, Joseph Viktor von 1826-1886 . . . DLB-129

Scheffler, Johann 1624-1677 . . . . DLB-164

Schelling, Friedrich Wilhelm Joseph von
　　1775-1854 . . . . DLB-90

Scherer, Wilhelm 1841-1886 . . . . DLB-129

Scherfig, Hans 1905-1979 . . . . DLB-214

Schickele, René 1883-1940 . . . . DLB-66

Schiff, Dorothy 1903-1989 . . . . DLB-127

Schiller, Friedrich
　　1759-1805 . . . . DLB-94; CDWLB-2

Schirmer, David 1623-1687 . . . . DLB-164

Schlaf, Johannes 1862-1941 . . . . DLB-118

Schlegel, August Wilhelm 1767-1845 . . . . . DLB-94

Schlegel, Dorothea 1763-1839 . . . . DLB-90

Schlegel, Friedrich 1772-1829 . . . . DLB-90

Schleiermacher, Friedrich 1768-1834 . . . . . DLB-90

Schlesinger, Arthur M., Jr. 1917- DLB-17

Schlumberger, Jean 1877-1968 . . . . DLB-65

Schmid, Eduard Hermann Wilhelm
　　(see Edschmid, Kasimir)

Schmidt, Arno 1914-1979 . . . . DLB-69

Schmidt, Johann Kaspar (see Stirner, Max)

Schmidt, Michael 1947- DLB-40

Schmidtbonn, Wilhelm August
　　1876-1952 . . . . DLB-118

Schmitz, Aron Hector (see Svevo, Italo)

Schmitz, James H. 1911-1981 . . . . DLB-8

Schnabel, Johann Gottfried 1692-1760 . . . DLB-168

Schnackenberg, Gjertrud 1953- DLB-120

Schnitzler, Arthur
　　1862-1931 . . . . DLB-81, 118; CDWLB-2

Schnurre, Wolfdietrich 1920-1989 . . . . . . DLB-69

Schocken Books DLB-46

Scholartis Press DLB-112

Scholderer, Victor 1880-1971 . . . . DLB-201

The Schomburg Center for Research
　　in Black Culture DLB-76

Schönbeck, Virgilio (see Giotti, Virgilio)

Schönherr, Karl 1867-1943 . . . . DLB-118

Schoolcraft, Jane Johnston 1800-1841 . . . . DLB-175

School Stories, 1914-1960 . . . . DLB-160

Schopenhauer, Arthur 1788-1860 . . . . DLB-90

Schopenhauer, Johanna 1766-1838 . . . . . . DLB-90

Schorer, Mark 1908-1977 . . . . DLB-103

Schottelius, Justus Georg 1612-1676 . . . . . DLB-164

Schouler, James 1839-1920 . . . . DLB-47

Schoultz, Solveig von 1907-1996 . . . . DLB-259

Schrader, Paul 1946- DLB-44

Schreiner, Olive
　　1855-1920 . . . . DLB-18, 156, 190, 225

Schroeder, Andreas 1946- DLB-53

Schubart, Christian Friedrich Daniel
　　1739-1791 . . . . DLB-97

Schubert, Gotthilf Heinrich 1780-1860 . . . DLB-90

Schücking, Levin 1814-1883 . . . . DLB-133

Schulberg, Budd 1914- DLB-6, 26, 28; Y-81

　　Excerpts from USC Presentation
　　　[on F. Scott Fitzgerald] Y-96

F. J. Schulte and Company DLB-49

Schulz, Bruno 1892-1942 . . . . DLB-215; CDWLB-4

Schulze, Hans (see Praetorius, Johannes)

Schupp, Johann Balthasar 1610-1661 . . . . DLB-164

Schurz, Carl 1829-1906 . . . . DLB-23

Schuyler, George S. 1895-1977 . . . . DLB-29, 51

Schuyler, James 1923-1991 . . . . DLB-5, 169

Schwartz, Delmore 1913-1966 . . . . DLB-28, 48

Schwartz, Jonathan 1938- Y-82

Schwartz, Lynne Sharon 1939- DLB-218

Schwarz, Sibylle 1621-1638 . . . . DLB-164

Schwerner, Armand 1927-1999 . . . . DLB-165

Schwob, Marcel 1867-1905 . . . . DLB-123

Sciascia, Leonardo 1921-1989 . . . . DLB-177

Science Fiction and Fantasy
　　Documents in British Fantasy and
　　　Science Fiction DLB-178

　　Hugo Awards and Nebula Awards DLB-8

　　The Iconography of Science-Fiction
　　　Art DLB-8

　　The New Wave DLB-8

　　Paperback Science Fiction DLB-8

　　Science Fantasy DLB-8

　　Science-Fiction Fandom and
　　　Conventions DLB-8

　　Science-Fiction Fanzines: The Time
　　　Binders DLB-8

　　Science-Fiction Films DLB-8

　　Science Fiction Writers of America
　　　and the Nebula Award DLB-8

　　Selected Science-Fiction Magazines and
　　　Anthologies DLB-8

　　A World Chronology of Important Science
　　　Fiction Works (1818-1979) DLB-8

　　The Year in Science Fiction
　　　and Fantasy Y-00, 01

Scot, Reginald circa 1538-1599 . . . . DLB-136

Scotellaro, Rocco 1923-1953 . . . . .DLB-128

Scott, Alicia Anne (Lady John Scott)
1810-1900 . . . . .DLB-240

Scott, Catharine Amy Dawson
1865-1934 .DLB-240

Scott, Dennis 1939-1991 . . . . .DLB-125

Scott, Dixon 1881-1915 . . . . .DLB-98

Scott, Duncan Campbell 1862-1947. . . . . . .DLB-92

Scott, Evelyn 1893-1963 . . . . .DLB-9, 48

Scott, F. R. 1899-1985 . . . . .DLB-88

Scott, Frederick George 1861-1944 . . . . . . .DLB-92

Scott, Geoffrey 1884-1929 . . . . .DLB-149

Scott, Harvey W. 1838-1910 . . . . .DLB-23

Scott, Lady Jane (see Scott, Alicia Anne)

Scott, Paul 1920-1978. . . . . .DLB-14, 207

Scott, Sarah 1723-1795 . . . . .DLB-39

Scott, Tom 1918- .DLB-27

Scott, Sir Walter 1771-1832
. . . . . DLB-93, 107, 116, 144, 159; CDBLB-3

Scott, William Bell 1811-1890 . . . . .DLB-32

Walter Scott Publishing Company
Limited DLB-112

William R. Scott [publishing house]. DLB-46

Scott-Heron, Gil 1949- DLB-41

Scribe, Eugene 1791-1861 . . . . .DLB-192

Scribner, Arthur Hawley 1859-1932 . . . DS-13, 16

Scribner, Charles 1854-1930 . . . . DS-13, 16

Scribner, Charles, Jr. 1921-1995 . . . . Y-95

Reminiscences DS-17

Charles Scribner's Sons DLB-49; DS-13, 16, 17

Archives of Charles Scribner's Sons DS-17

Scribner's Magazine DS-13

Scribner's Monthly DS-13

Scripps, E. W. 1854-1926 . . . . .DLB-25

Scudder, Horace Elisha 1838-1902 . . . . DLB-42, 71

Scudder, Vida Dutton 1861-1954 . . . . .DLB-71

Scudéry, Madeleine de 1607-1701 . . . . .DLB-268

Scupham, Peter 1933- DLB-40

Seabrook, William 1886-1945 . . . . .DLB-4

Seabury, Samuel 1729-1796 . . . . .DLB-31

Seacole, Mary Jane Grant 1805-1881. . . . .DLB-166

The Seafarer circa 970 . . . . .DLB-146

Sealsfield, Charles (Carl Postl)
1793-1864 . . . . .DLB-133, 186

Searle, John R. 1932- DLB-279

Sears, Edward I. 1819?-1876 . . . . .DLB-79

Sears Publishing Company DLB-46

Seaton, George 1911-1979 . . . . .DLB-44

Seaton, William Winston 1785-1866 . . . . . .DLB-43

Martin Secker [publishing house]. DLB-112

Martin Secker, and Warburg Limited DLB-112

Sedgwick, Arthur George 1844-1915. . . . . .DLB-64

Sedgwick, Catharine Maria
1789-1867 . . . . DLB-1, 74, 183, 239, 243

Sedgwick, Ellery 1872-1960 . . . . .DLB-91

Sedgwick, Eve Kosofsky 1950- DLB-246

Sedley, Sir Charles 1639-1701 . . . . .DLB-131

Seeberg, Peter 1925-1999. . . . . .DLB-214

Seeger, Alan 1888-1916 . . . . .DLB-45

Seers, Eugene (see Dantin, Louis)

Segal, Erich 1937- Y-86

Šegedin, Petar 1909- DLB-181

Seghers, Anna 1900-1983 . . . . DLB-69; CDWLB-2

Seid, Ruth (see Sinclair, Jo)

Seidel, Frederick Lewis 1936- Y-84

Seidel, Ina 1885-1974 . . . . .DLB-56

Seifert, Jaroslav
1901-1986 . . . . . . DLB-215; Y-84; CDWLB-4

Jaroslav Seifert Through the Eyes of
the English-Speaking Reader Y-84

Three Poems by Jaroslav Seifert Y-84

Seifullina, Lidiia Nikolaevna 1889-1954 . . DLB-272

Seigenthaler, John 1927- DLB-127

Seizin Press DLB-112

Séjour, Victor 1817-1874 . . . . .DLB-50

Séjour Marcou et Ferrand, Juan Victor
(see Séjour, Victor)

Sekowski, Jósef-Julian, Baron Brambeus
(see Senkovsky, Osip Ivanovich)

Selby, Bettina 1934- DLB-204

Selby, Hubert, Jr. 1928- DLB-2, 227

Selden, George 1929-1989 . . . . .DLB-52

Selden, John 1584-1654 . . . . .DLB-213

Selenić, Slobodan 1933-1995 . . . . .DLB-181

Self, Edwin F. 1920- DLB-137

Self, Will 1961- DLB-207

Seligman, Edwin R. A. 1861-1939. . . . . . .DLB-47

Selimović, Meša
1910-1982 . . . . .DLB-181; CDWLB-4

Sellars, Wilfrid 1912-1989 . . . . .DLB-279

Sellings, Arthur (Arthur Gordon Ley)
1911-1968 .DLB-261

Selous, Frederick Courteney 1851-1917 . . DLB-174

Seltzer, Chester E. (see Muro, Amado)

Thomas Seltzer [publishing house] DLB-46

Selvon, Sam 1923-1994 . . . . . DLB-125; CDWLB-3

Semmes, Raphael 1809-1877 . . . . .DLB-189

Senancour, Etienne de 1770-1846 . . . . . . .DLB-119

Sendak, Maurice 1928- DLB-61

Seneca the Elder
circa 54 B.C.-circa A.D. 40 . . . . .DLB-211

Seneca the Younger
circa 1 B.C.-A.D. 65 . . . . DLB-211; CDWLB-1

Senécal, Eva 1905- DLB-92

Sengstacke, John 1912-1997 . . . . .DLB-127

Senior, Olive 1941- DLB-157

Senkovsky, Osip Ivanovich
(Józef-Julian Sekowski, Baron Brambeus)
1800-1858 .DLB-198

Šenoa, August 1838-1881 . . . DLB-147; CDWLB-4

Sepamla, Sipho 1932- DLB-157, 225

Serafimovich, Aleksandr Serafimovich
(Aleksandr Serafimovich Popov)
1863-1949 .DLB-272

Serao, Matilde 1856-1927 . . . . .DLB-264

Seredy, Kate 1899-1975 . . . . .DLB-22

Sereni, Vittorio 1913-1983. . . . . .DLB-128

William Seres [publishing house]. DLB-170

Sergeev-Tsensky, Sergei Nikolaevich (Sergei
Nikolaevich Sergeev) 1875-1958 . . . .DLB-272

Serling, Rod 1924-1975 . . . . .DLB-26

Sernine, Daniel 1955- DLB-251

Serote, Mongane Wally 1944- DLB-125, 225

Serraillier, Ian 1912-1994. . . . . .DLB-161

Serrano, Nina 1934- DLB-122

Service, Robert 1874-1958 . . . . .DLB-92

Sessler, Charles 1854-1935 . . . . .DLB-187

Seth, Vikram 1952- DLB-120, 271

Seton, Elizabeth Ann 1774-1821. . . . . . . .DLB-200

Seton, Ernest Thompson
1860-1942 . . . . .DLB-92; DS-13

Seton, John circa 1509-1567. . . . . .DLB-281

Setouchi Harumi 1922- DLB-182

Settle, Mary Lee 1918- DLB-6

Seume, Johann Gottfried 1763-1810 . . . . .DLB-94

Seuse, Heinrich 1295?-1366. . . . . DLB-179

Seuss, Dr. (see Geisel, Theodor Seuss)

Severin, Timothy 1940- DLB-204

Sévigné, Marie de Rabutin Chantal,
Madame de 1626-1696. . . . . .DLB-268

Sewall, Joseph 1688-1769 . . . . .DLB-24

Sewall, Richard B. 1908- DLB-111

Sewall, Samuel 1652-1730 . . . . .DLB-24

Sewell, Anna 1820-1878. . . . . .DLB-163

Sexton, Anne 1928-1974 . . .DLB-5, 169; CDALB-1

Seymour-Smith, Martin 1928-1998 . . . . . .DLB-155

Sgorlon, Carlo 1930- DLB-196

Shaara, Michael 1929-1988 . . . . Y-83

Shabel'skaia, Aleksandra Stanislavovna
1845-1921 .DLB-238

Shadwell, Thomas 1641?-1692 . . . . .DLB-80

Shaffer, Anthony 1926- DLB-13

Shaffer, Peter 1926- DLB-13, 233; CDBLB-8

Shaftesbury, Anthony Ashley Cooper,
Third Earl of 1671-1713 . . . . .DLB-101

Shaginian, Marietta Sergeevna
1888-1982 .DLB-272

Shairp, Mordaunt 1887-1939 . . . . .DLB-10

Shakespeare, Nicholas 1957- DLB-231

Shakespeare, William
1564-1616 . . . . . .DLB-62, 172, 263; CDBLB-1

The New Variorum Shakespeare Y-85

Shakespeare and Montaigne: A Symposium
by Jules Furthman Y-02

$6,166,000 for a *Book!* Observations on
*The Shakespeare First Folio: The History
of the Book* Y-01

Taylor-Made Shakespeare? Or Is
"Shall I Die?" the Long-Lost Text
of Bottom's Dream? Y-85

The Shakespeare Globe Trust Y-93

Shakespeare Head Press DLB-112

Shakhova, Elisaveta Nikitichna
1822-1899 ....DLB-277

Shakhovskoi, Aleksandr Aleksandrovich
1777-1846 .... DLB-150

Shange, Ntozake 1948- DLB-38, 249

Shapiro, Karl 1913-2000.............. DLB-48

Sharon Publications DLB-46

Sharov, Vladimir Aleksandrovich
1952- DLB-285

Sharp, Margery 1905-1991........... DLB-161

Sharp, William 1855-1905 .... DLB-156

Sharpe, Tom 1928- DLB-14, 231

Shaw, Albert 1857-1947 .... DLB-91

Shaw, George Bernard
1856-1950 ....DLB-10, 57, 190, CDBLB-6

The Bernard Shaw Society............ Y-99

"Stage Censorship: The Rejected
Statement" (1911) [excerpts]..... DLB-10

Shaw, Henry Wheeler 1818-1885....... DLB-11

Shaw, Irwin
1913-1984. ..... DLB-6, 102; Y-84; CDALB-1

Shaw, Joseph T. 1874-1952............ DLB-137

"As I Was Saying," Joseph T. Shaw's
Editorial Rationale in *Black Mask*
(January 1927) DLB-137

Shaw, Mary 1854-1929............... DLB-228

Shaw, Robert 1927-1978 .... DLB-13, 14

Shaw, Robert B. 1947- DLB-120

Shawn, Wallace 1943- DLB-266

Shawn, William 1907-1992............ DLB-137

Frank Shay [publishing house] DLB-46

Shchedrin, N. (see Saltykov, Mikhail Evgrafovich)

Shcherbakova, Galina Nikolaevna
1932- DLB-285

Shcherbina, Nikolai Fedorovich
1821-1869 ....DLB-277

Shea, John Gilmary 1824-1892......... DLB-30

Sheaffer, Louis 1912-1993 .... DLB-103

Sheahan, Henry Beston (see Beston, Henry)

Shearing, Joseph 1886-1952 .... DLB-70

Shebbeare, John 1709-1788 .... DLB-39

Sheckley, Robert 1928- DLB-8

Shedd, William G. T. 1820-1894 .... DLB-64

Sheed, Wilfrid 1930- DLB-6

Sheed and Ward [U.S.]................ DLB-46

Sheed and Ward Limited [U.K.]........ DLB-112

Sheldon, Alice B. (see Tiptree, James, Jr.)

Sheldon, Edward 1886-1946............. DLB-7

Sheldon and Company................ DLB-49

Sheller, Aleksandr Konstantinovich
1838-1900. .... DLB-238

Shelley, Mary Wollstonecraft 1797-1851
.........DLB-110, 116, 159, 178; CDBLB-3

Preface to *Frankenstein; or, The
Modern Prometheus* (1818) DLB-178

Shelley, Percy Bysshe
1792-1822. ..... DLB-96, 110, 158; CDBLB-3

Shelnutt, Eve 1941- DLB-130

Shenshin (see Fet, Afanasii Afanas'evich)

Shenstone, William 1714-1763 .... DLB-95

Shepard, Clark and Brown............ DLB-49

Shepard, Ernest Howard 1879-1976 ..... DLB-160

Shepard, Sam 1943- DLB-7, 212

Shepard, Thomas I, 1604 or 1605-1649... DLB-24

Shepard, Thomas, II, 1635-1677 .... DLB-24

Shepherd, Luke flourished 1547-1554.... DLB-136

Sherburne, Edward 1616-1702 .... DLB-131

Sheridan, Frances 1724-1766......... DLB-39, 84

Sheridan, Richard Brinsley
1751-1816.............DLB-89; CDBLB-2

Sherman, Francis 1871-1926............ DLB-92

Sherman, Martin 1938- DLB-228

Sherriff, R. C. 1896-1975 ....DLB-10, 191, 233

Sherrod, Blackie 1919- DLB-241

Sherry, Norman 1935- DLB-155

Tribute to Graham Greene Y-91

Sherry, Richard 1506-1551 or 1555..... DLB-236

Sherwood, Mary Martha 1775-1851..... DLB-163

Sherwood, Robert E. 1896-1955....DLB-7, 26, 249

Shevyrev, Stepan Petrovich 1806-1864 .. DLB-205

Shiel, M. P. 1865-1947 .... DLB-153

Shiels, George 1886-1949............ DLB-10

Shiga Naoya 1883-1971 .... DLB-180

Shiina Rinzō 1911-1973 .... DLB-182

Shikishi Naishinnō 1153?-1201........ DLB-203

Shillaber, Benjamin Penhallow
1814-1890 .... DLB-1, 11, 235

Shimao Toshio 1917-1986 .... DLB-182

Shimazaki Tōson 1872-1943 .... DLB-180

Shimose, Pedro 1940- DLB-283

Shine, Ted 1931- DLB-38

Shinkei 1406-1475................. DLB-203

Ship, Reuben 1915-1975 .... DLB-88

Shirer, William L. 1904-1993........... DLB-4

Shirinsky-Shikhmatov, Sergii Aleksandrovich
1783-1837..................... DLB-150

Shirley, James 1596-1666 .... DLB-58

Shishkov, Aleksandr Semenovich
1753-1841..................... DLB-150

Shockley, Ann Allen 1927- DLB-33

Sholokhov, Mikhail Aleksandrovich
1905-1984 ....DLB-272

Shōno Junzō 1921- DLB-182

Shore, Arabella 1820?-1901 .... DLB-199

Shore, Louisa 1824-1895 .... DLB-199

Short, Luke (see Glidden, Frederick Dilley)

Peter Short [publishing house] DLB-170

Shorter, Dora Sigerson 1866-1918 ...... DLB-240

Shorthouse, Joseph Henry 1834-1903 .... DLB-18

Short Stories
Michael M. Rea and the Rea Award
for the Short Story.............. Y-97

The Year in Short Stories............. Y-87

The Year in the Short Story...... Y-88, 90–93

Shōtetsu 1381-1459 .... DLB-203

Showalter, Elaine 1941- DLB-67

Shulevitz, Uri 1935- DLB-61

Shulman, Max 1919-1988........... DLB-11

Shute, Henry A. 1856-1943 .... DLB-9

Shute, Nevil (Nevil Shute Norway)
1899-1960 .... DLB-255

Shuttle, Penelope 1947- DLB-14, 40

Shvarts, Evgenii L'vovich 1896-1958.....DLB-272

Sibbes, Richard 1577-1635 .... DLB-151

Sibiriak, D. (see Mamin, Dmitrii Narkisovich)

Siddal, Elizabeth Eleanor 1829-1862 .... DLB-199

Sidgwick, Ethel 1877-1970.............DLB-197

Sidgwick, Henry 1838-1900 .... DLB-262

Sidgwick and Jackson Limited DLB-112

Sidney, Margaret (see Lothrop, Harriet M.)

Sidney, Mary 1561-1621 .... DLB-167

Sidney, Sir Philip 1554-1586. . DLB-167; CDBLB-1

An Apologie for Poetrie (the Olney edition,
1595, of *Defence of Poesie*) DLB-167

Sidney's Press DLB-49

Sierra, Rubén 1946- DLB-122

Sierra Club Books DLB-49

Siger of Brabant circa 1240-circa 1284 ... DLB-115

Sigourney, Lydia Huntley
1791-1865.......DLB-1, 42, 73, 183, 239, 243

Silkin, Jon 1930-1997 .... DLB-27

Silko, Leslie Marmon
1948- DLB-143, 175, 256, 275

Silliman, Benjamin 1779-1864.......... DLB-183

Silliman, Ron 1946- DLB-169

Silliphant, Stirling 1918-1996 .... DLB-26

Sillitoe, Alan 1928- DLB-14, 139; CDBLB-8

Tribute to J. B. Priestly Y-84

Silman, Roberta 1934- DLB-28

Silone, Ignazio (Secondino Tranquilli)
1900-1978..................... DLB-264

Silva, Beverly 1930- DLB-122

Silva, José Asunció 1865-1896 .... DLB-283

Silverberg, Robert 1935- DLB-8

Silverman, Kaja 1947- DLB-246

Silverman, Kenneth 1936- DLB-111

Simak, Clifford D. 1904-1988............. DLB-8

Simcoe, Elizabeth 1762-1850............ DLB-99

Simcox, Edith Jemima 1844-1901....... DLB-190

Simcox, George Augustus 1841-1905..... DLB-35

Sime, Jessie Georgina 1868-1958 .... DLB-92

Simenon, Georges 1903-1989......DLB-72; Y-89

Simic, Charles 1938- DLB-105

"Images and 'Images'"............ DLB-105

Simionescu, Mircea Horia 1928- DLB-232

Simmel, Johannes Mario 1924- DLB-69

Valentine Simmes [publishing house].....DLB-170

Simmons, Ernest J. 1903-1972 .... DLB-103

Simmons, Herbert Alfred 1930- DLB-33

Simmons, James 1933- DLB-40

Simms, William Gilmore
   1806-1870 . . . . DLB-3, 30, 59, 73, 248

Simms and M'Intyre DLB-106

Simon, Claude 1913- DLB-83; Y-85

   Nobel Lecture Y-85

Simon, Neil 1927- DLB-7, 266

Simon and Schuster DLB-46

Simons, Katherine Drayton Mayrant
   1890-1969 . . . . Y-83

Simović, Ljubomir 1935- DLB-181

Simpkin and Marshall
   [publishing house] DLB-154

Simpson, Helen 1897-1940. . . . . .DLB-77

Simpson, Louis 1923- DLB-5

Simpson, N. F. 1919- DLB-13

Sims, George 1923- DLB-87; Y-99

Sims, George Robert 1847-1922. . .DLB-35, 70, 135

Sinán, Rogelio 1904-1994 . . . . .DLB-145

Sinclair, Andrew 1935- DLB-14

Sinclair, Bertrand William 1881-1972 . . . . .DLB-92

Sinclair, Catherine 1800-1864 . . . . .DLB-163

Sinclair, Jo 1913-1995 . . . . .DLB-28

Sinclair, Lister 1921- DLB-88

Sinclair, May 1863-1946 . . . . .DLB-36, 135

   The Novels of Dorothy Richardson
      (1918) DLB-36

Sinclair, Upton 1878-1968 . . . . .DLB-9; CDALB-5

Upton Sinclair [publishing house] DLB-46

Singer, Isaac Bashevis 1904-1991
   . . . . DLB-6, 28, 52, 278; Y-91; CDALB-1

Singer, Mark 1950- DLB-185

Singmaster, Elsie 1879-1958. . . . . .DLB-9

Sinisgalli, Leonardo 1908-1981 . . . . .DLB-114

Siodmak, Curt 1902-2000 . . . . .DLB-44

Sîrbu, Ion D. 1919-1989. . . . . .DLB-232

Siringo, Charles A. 1855-1928. . . . . .DLB-186

Sissman, L. E. 1928-1976 . . . . .DLB-5

Sisson, C. H. 1914- DLB-27

Sitwell, Edith 1887-1964. . . . . . DLB-20; CDBLB-7

Sitwell, Osbert 1892-1969 . . . . DLB-100, 195

Skácel, Jan 1922-1989 . . . . .DLB-232

Skalbe, Kārlis 1879-1945 . . . . .DLB-220

Skármeta, Antonio
   1940- DLB-145; CDWLB-3

Skavronsky, A. (see Danilevsky, Grigorii Petrovich)

Skeat, Walter W. 1835-1912 . . . . .DLB-184

William Skeffington [publishing house] . . .DLB-106

Skelton, John 1463-1529 . . . . .DLB-136

Skelton, Robin 1925-1997 . . . . DLB-27, 53

Škėma, Antanas 1910-1961 . . . . .DLB-220

Skinner, Constance Lindsay
   1877-1939 . . . . .DLB-92

Skinner, John Stuart 1788-1851 . . . . .DLB-73

Skipsey, Joseph 1832-1903. . . . . .DLB-35

Skou-Hansen, Tage 1925- DLB-214

Škvorecký, Josef 1924- DLB-232; CDWLB-4

Slade, Bernard 1930- DLB-53

Slamnig, Ivan 1930- DLB-181

Slančeková, Božena (see Timrava)

Slataper, Scipio 1888-1915 . . . . .DLB-264

Slater, Patrick 1880-1951 . . . . .DLB-68

Slaveykov, Pencho 1866-1912 . . . . .DLB-147

Slaviček, Milivoj 1929- DLB-181

Slavitt, David 1935- DLB-5, 6

Sleigh, Burrows Willcocks Arthur
   1821-1869 . . . . .DLB-99

Sleptsov, Vasilii Alekseevich 1836-1878. . .DLB-277

Slesinger, Tess 1905-1945 . . . . .DLB-102

Slessor, Kenneth 1901-1971 . . . . .DLB-260

Slick, Sam (see Haliburton, Thomas Chandler)

Sloan, John 1871-1951 . . . . .DLB-188

Sloane, William, Associates DLB-46

Slonimsky, Mikhail Leonidovich
   1897-1972. . . . . .DLB-272

Sluchevsky, Konstantin Konstantinovich
   1837-1904 . . . . .DLB-277

Small, Maynard and Company DLB-49

Smart, Christopher 1722-1771 . . . . .DLB-109

Smart, David A. 1892-1957 . . . . .DLB-137

Smart, Elizabeth 1913-1986 . . . . .DLB-88

Smart, J. J. C. 1920- DLB-262

Smedley, Menella Bute 1820?-1877 . . . . . .DLB-199

William Smellie [publishing house] DLB-154

Smiles, Samuel 1812-1904 . . . . .DLB-55

Smiley, Jane 1949- DLB-227, 234

Smith, A. J. M. 1902-1980 . . . . .DLB-88

Smith, Adam 1723-1790 . . . . DLB-104, 252

Smith, Adam (George Jerome Waldo
   Goodman) 1930- DLB-185

Smith, Alexander 1829-1867 . . . . .DLB-32, 55

   "On the Writing of Essays" (1862) DLB-57

Smith, Amanda 1837-1915 . . . . .DLB-221

Smith, Betty 1896-1972 . . . . Y-82

Smith, Carol Sturm 1938- Y-81

Smith, Charles Henry 1826-1903 . . . . .DLB-11

Smith, Charlotte 1749-1806 . . . . .DLB-39, 109

Smith, Chet 1899-1973. . . . . .DLB-171

Smith, Cordwainer 1913-1966 . . . . .DLB-8

Smith, Dave 1942- DLB-5

   Tribute to James Dickey Y-97

   Tribute to John Gardner Y-82

Smith, Dodie 1896- DLB-10

Smith, Doris Buchanan 1934- DLB-52

Smith, E. E. 1890-1965 . . . . .DLB-8

Smith, Elihu Hubbard 1771-1798. . . . . . . .DLB-37

Smith, Elizabeth Oakes (Prince)
   (see Oakes Smith, Elizabeth)

Smith, Eunice 1757-1823 . . . . .DLB-200

Smith, F. Hopkinson 1838-1915 . . . . DS-13

Smith, George D. 1870-1920 . . . . .DLB-140

Smith, George O. 1911-1981 . . . . .DLB-8

Smith, Goldwin 1823-1910 . . . . .DLB-99

Smith, H. Allen 1907-1976 . . . . .DLB-11, 29

Smith, Harry B. 1860-1936 . . . . .DLB-187

Smith, Hazel Brannon 1914-1994 . . . . . . .DLB-127

Smith, Henry circa 1560-circa 1591. . . . . .DLB-136

Smith, Horatio (Horace)
   1779-1849 . . . . .DLB-96, 116

Smith, Iain Crichton 1928-1998. . . . . .DLB-40, 139

Smith, J. Allen 1860-1924 . . . . .DLB-47

Smith, James 1775-1839 . . . . .DLB-96

Smith, Jessie Willcox 1863-1935 . . . . .DLB-188

Smith, John 1580-1631 . . . . .DLB-24, 30

Smith, John 1618-1652. . . . . .DLB-252

Smith, Josiah 1704-1781 . . . . .DLB-24

Smith, Ken 1938- DLB-40

Smith, Lee 1944- DLB-143; Y-83

Smith, Logan Pearsall 1865-1946 . . . . .DLB-98

Smith, Margaret Bayard 1778-1844 . . . . .DLB-248

Smith, Mark 1935- Y-82

Smith, Michael 1698-circa 1771 . . . . .DLB-31

Smith, Pauline 1882-1959 . . . . .DLB-225

Smith, Red 1905-1982 . . . . DLB-29, 171

Smith, Roswell 1829-1892 . . . . .DLB-79

Smith, Samuel Harrison 1772-1845 . . . . . . .DLB-43

Smith, Samuel Stanhope 1751-1819 . . . . . . .DLB-37

Smith, Sarah (see Stretton, Hesba)

Smith, Sarah Pogson 1774-1870 . . . . .DLB-200

Smith, Seba 1792-1868. . . . . .DLB-1, 11, 243

Smith, Stevie 1902-1971 . . . . .DLB-20

Smith, Sydney 1771-1845. . . . . .DLB-107

Smith, Sydney Goodsir 1915-1975. . . . . . . .DLB-27

Smith, Sir Thomas 1513-1577 . . . . .DLB-132

Smith, Wendell 1914-1972. . . . . .DLB-171

Smith, William flourished 1595-1597 . . . .DLB-136

Smith, William 1727-1803 . . . . .DLB-31

   A General Idea of the College of Mirania
      (1753) [excerpts] DLB-31

Smith, William 1728-1793 . . . . .DLB-30

Smith, William Gardner 1927-1974 . . . . . . .DLB-76

Smith, William Henry 1808-1872 . . . . . . .DLB-159

Smith, William Jay 1918- DLB-5

Smith, Elder and Company DLB-154

Harrison Smith and Robert Haas
   [publishing house] DLB-46

J. Stilman Smith and Company DLB-49

W. B. Smith and Company DLB-49

W. H. Smith and Son DLB-106

Leonard Smithers [publishing house] DLB-112

Smollett, Tobias
   1721-1771. . . . . .DLB-39, 104; CDBLB-2

   Dedication to *Ferdinand Count Fathom*
      (1753) DLB-39

   Preface to *Ferdinand Count Fathom*
      (1753) DLB-39

   Preface to *Roderick Random* (1748) DLB-39

Smythe, Francis Sydney 1900-1949 . . . . . .DLB-195

Snelling, William Joseph 1804-1848 . . . . .DLB-202

Snellings, Rolland (see Touré, Askia Muhammad)

Snodgrass, W. D. 1926- DLB-5

Snow, C. P.
1905-1980 .... DLB-15, 77; DS-17; CDBLB-7

Snyder, Gary
1930- DLB-5, 16, 165, 212, 237, 275

Sobiloff, Hy 1912-1970 .... DLB-48

The Society for Textual Scholarship and
TEXT Y-87

The Society for the History of Authorship,
Reading and Publishing Y-92

Söderberg, Hjalmar 1869-1941 .... DLB-259

Södergran, Edith 1892-1923 .... DLB-259

Soffici, Ardengo 1879-1964 .... DLB-114, 264

Sofola, 'Zulu 1938- DLB-157

Sokhanskaia, Nadezhda Stepanovna
(Kokhanovskaia) 1823?-1884 .... DLB-277

Sokolov, Sasha (Aleksandr Vsevolodovich
Sokolov) 1943- DLB-285

Solano, Solita 1888-1975 .... DLB-4

Soldati, Mario 1906-1999 .... DLB-177

Soledad (see Zamudio, Adela)

Šoljan, Antun 1932-1993 .... DLB-181

Sollers, Philippe (Philippe Joyaux)
1936- DLB-83

Sollogub, Vladimir Aleksandrovich
1813-1882 .... DLB-198

Sollors, Werner 1943- DBL-246

Solmi, Sergio 1899-1981 .... DLB-114

Solomon, Carl 1928- DLB-16

Solway, David 1941- DLB-53

Solzhenitsyn, Aleksandr I. 1918-
Solzhenitsyn and America Y-85

Some Basic Notes on Three Modern Genres:
Interview, Blurb, and Obituary Y-02

Somerville, Edith Œnone 1858-1949 .... DLB-135

Somov, Orest Mikhailovich 1793-1833 ... DLB-198

Sønderby, Knud 1909-1966 .... DLB-214

Song, Cathy 1955- DLB-169

Sonnevi, Göran 1939- DLB-257

Sono Ayako 1931- DLB-182

Sontag, Susan 1933- DLB-2, 67

Sophocles 497/496 B.C.-406/405 B.C.
.... DLB-176; CDWLB-1

Šopov, Aco 1923-1982 .... DLB-181

Sorel, Charles ca.1600-1674 .... DLB-268

Sørensen, Villy 1929- DLB-214

Sorensen, Virginia 1912-1991 .... DLB-206

Sorge, Reinhard Johannes 1892-1916 .... DLB-118

Sorokin, Vladimir Georgievich
1955- DLB-285

Sorrentino, Gilbert 1929- DLB-5, 173; Y-80

Sotheby, James 1682-1742 .... DLB-213

Sotheby, John 1740-1807 .... DLB-213

Sotheby, Samuel 1771-1842 .... DLB-213

Sotheby, Samuel Leigh 1805-1861 ...... DLB-213

Sotheby, William 1757-1833 .... DLB-93, 213

Soto, Gary 1952- DLB-82

Soueif, Ahdaf 1950- DLB-267

Souster, Raymond 1921- DLB-88

The *South English Legendary* circa
thirteenth-fifteenth centuries DLB-146

Southerland, Ellease 1943- DLB-33

Southern, Terry 1924-1995 .... DLB-2

Southern Illinois University Press Y-95

Southern Literature
Fellowship of Southern Writers Y-98

The Fugitives and the Agrarians:
The First Exhibition Y-85

"The Greatness of Southern Literature":
League of the South Institute for the
Study of Southern Culture and
History Y-02

The Society for the Study of
Southern Literature Y-00

Southern Writers Between the Wars ... DLB-9

Southerne, Thomas 1659-1746 .... DLB-80

Southey, Caroline Anne Bowles
1786-1854 .... DLB-116

Southey, Robert 1774-1843 ..... DLB-93, 107, 142

Southwell, Robert 1561?-1595 .... DLB-167

Southworth, E. D. E. N. 1819-1899 .... DLB-239

Sowande, Bode 1948- DLB-157

Tace Sowle [publishing house] DLB-170

Soyfer, Jura 1912-1939 .... DLB-124

Soyinka, Wole
1934- DLB-125; Y-86, Y-87; CDWLB-3

Nobel Lecture 1986: This Past Must
Address Its Present Y-86

Spacks, Barry 1931- DLB-105

Spalding, Frances 1950- DLB-155

Spark, Muriel 1918- ... DLB-15, 139; CDBLB-7

Michael Sparke [publishing house] DLB-170

Sparks, Jared 1789-1866 .... DLB-1, 30, 235

Sparshott, Francis 1926- DLB-60

Späth, Gerold 1939- DLB-75

Spatola, Adriano 1941-1988 .... DLB-128

Spaziani, Maria Luisa 1924- DLB-128

Specimens of Foreign Standard Literature
1838-1842 .... DLB-1

The Spectator 1828- DLB-110

Spedding, James 1808-1881 .... DLB-144

Spee von Langenfeld, Friedrich
1591-1635 .... DLB-164

Speght, Rachel 1597-after 1630 .... DLB-126

Speke, John Hanning 1827-1864 .... DLB-166

Spellman, A. B. 1935- DLB-41

Spence, Catherine Helen 1825-1910 ..... DLB-230

Spence, Thomas 1750-1814 .... DLB-158

Spencer, Anne 1882-1975 .... DLB-51, 54

Spencer, Charles, third Earl of Sunderland
1674-1722 .... DLB-213

Spencer, Elizabeth 1921- DLB-6, 218

Spencer, George John, Second Earl Spencer
1758-1834 .... DLB-184

Spencer, Herbert 1820-1903 .... DLB-57, 262

"The Philosophy of Style" (1852) DLB-57

Spencer, Scott 1945- Y-86

Spender, J. A. 1862-1942 .... DLB-98

Spender, Stephen 1909-1995 .. DLB-20; CDBLB-7

Spener, Philipp Jakob 1635-1705 .... DLB-164

Spenser, Edmund
circa 1552-1599 .... DLB-167; CDBLB-1

Envoy from *The Shepheardes Calender* . DLB-167

"The Generall Argument of the
Whole Booke," from
The Shepheardes Calender DLB-167

"A Letter of the Authors Expounding
His Whole Intention in the Course
of this Worke: Which for that It
Giueth Great Light to the Reader,
for the Better Vnderstanding
Is Hereunto Annexed,"
from *The Faerie Qveene* (1590) DLB-167

"To His Booke," from
The Shepheardes Calender (1579) ... DLB-167

"To the Most Excellent and Learned
Both Orator and Poete, Mayster
Gabriell Haruey, His Verie Special
and Singular Good Frend E. K.
Commendeth the Good Lyking of
This His Labour, and the Patronage
of the New Poete," from
The Shepheardes Calender DLB-167

Sperr, Martin 1944- DLB-124

Spewack, Bella Cowen 1899-1990 ...... DLB-266

Spewack, Samuel 1899-1971 .... DLB-266

Spicer, Jack 1925-1965 .... DLB-5, 16, 193

Spielberg, Peter 1929- Y-81

Spielhagen, Friedrich 1829-1911 .... DLB-129

"Spielmannsepen" (circa 1152-circa 1500) .. DLB-148

Spier, Peter 1927- DLB-61

Spillane, Mickey 1918- DLB-226

Spink, J. G. Taylor 1888-1962 .... DLB-241

Spinrad, Norman 1940- DLB-8

Tribute to Isaac Asimov Y-92

Spires, Elizabeth 1952- DLB-120

Spitteler, Carl 1845-1924 .... DLB-129

Spivak, Lawrence E. 1900- DLB-137

Spofford, Harriet Prescott
1835-1921 .... DLB-74, 221

Sports
Jimmy, Red, and Others: Harold
Rosenthal Remembers the Stars
of the Press Box Y-01

The Literature of Boxing in England
through Arthur Conan Doyle Y-01

Notable Twentieth-Century Books
about Sports DLB-241

Sprigge, Timothy L. S. 1932- DLB-262

Spring, Howard 1889-1965 .... DLB-191

Squibob (see Derby, George Horatio)

Squier, E. G. 1821-1888 .... DLB-189

Stableford, Brian 1948- DLB-261

Stacpoole, H. de Vere 1863-1951 ...... DLB-153

Staël, Germaine de 1766-1817 ...... DLB-119, 192

Staël-Holstein, Anne-Louise Germaine de
(see Staël, Germaine de)

Stafford, Jean 1915-1979 .... DLB-2, 173

Stafford, William 1914-1993 . . . . .DLB-5, 206

Stallings, Laurence 1894-1968 . . . . .DLB-7, 44

Stallworthy, Jon 1935- DLB-40

Stampp, Kenneth M. 1912- DLB-17

Stănescu, Nichita 1933-1983 . . . . .DLB-232

Stanev, Emiliyan 1907-1979 . . . . .DLB-181

Stanford, Ann 1916- DLB-5

Stangerup, Henrik 1937-1998. . . . . .DLB-214

Stanihurst, Richard 1547-1618 . . . . .DLB-281

Stanitsky, N. (see Panaeva, Avdot'ia Iakovlevna)

Stankevich, Nikolai Vladimirovich
1813-1840 .DLB-198

Stanković, Borisav ("Bora")
1876-1927 . . . . .DLB-147; CDWLB-4

Stanley, Henry M. 1841-1904 . . . .DLB-189; DS-13

Stanley, Thomas 1625-1678. . . . . .DLB-131

Stannard, Martin 1947- DLB-155

William Stansby [publishing house]. DLB-170

Stanton, Elizabeth Cady 1815-1902. . . . . .DLB-79

Stanton, Frank L. 1857-1927 . . . . .DLB-25

Stanton, Maura 1946- DLB-120

Stapledon, Olaf 1886-1950. . . . . .DLB-15, 255

Star Spangled Banner Office DLB-49

Stark, Freya 1893-1993 . . . . .DLB-195

Starkey, Thomas circa 1499-1538 . . . . . . .DLB-132

Starkie, Walter 1894-1976 . . . . .DLB-195

Starkweather, David 1935- DLB-7

Starrett, Vincent 1886-1974 . . . . .DLB-187

Stationers' Company of London, The DLB-170

Statius circa A.D. 45-A.D. 96. . . . . .DLB-211

Stead, Christina 1902-1983 . . . . .DLB-260

Stead, Robert J. C. 1880-1959 . . . . .DLB-92

Steadman, Mark 1930- DLB-6

Stearns, Harold E. 1891-1943 . . . . . .DLB-4; DS-15

Stebnitsky, M. (see Leskov, Nikolai Semenovich)

Stedman, Edmund Clarence 1833-1908 . . .DLB-64

Steegmuller, Francis 1906-1994 . . . . .DLB-111

Steel, Flora Annie 1847-1929 . . . . . . .DLB-153, 156

Steele, Max 1922- Y-80

Steele, Richard
1672-1729 . . . . .DLB-84, 101; CDBLB-2

Steele, Timothy 1948- DLB-120

Steele, Wilbur Daniel 1886-1970 . . . . .DLB-86

Wallace Markfield's "Steeplechase" Y-02

Steere, Richard circa 1643-1721. . . . . .DLB-24

Stefanovski, Goran 1952- DLB-181

Stegner, Wallace
1909-1993 . . . . DLB-9, 206, 275; Y-93

Stehr, Hermann 1864-1940 . . . . .DLB-66

Steig, William 1907- DLB-61

Stein, Gertrude 1874-1946
. . . . . . .DLB-4, 54, 86, 228; DS-15; CDALB-4

Stein, Leo 1872-1947 . . . . .DLB-4

Stein and Day Publishers. DLB-46

Steinbeck, John 1902-1968
. . . . DLB-7, 9, 212, 275; DS-2; CDALB-5

John Steinbeck Research Center,
San Jose State University Y-85

The Steinbeck Centennial Y-02

Steinem, Gloria 1934- DLB-246

Steiner, George 1929- DLB-67

Steinhoewel, Heinrich 1411/1412-1479 . . .DLB-179

Steloff, Ida Frances 1887-1989 . . . . .DLB-187

Stendhal 1783-1842 . . . . .DLB-119

Stephen, Leslie 1832-1904 . . . . . DLB-57, 144, 190

Stephen Family (Bloomsbury Group) DS-10

Stephens, A. G. 1865-1933 . . . . .DLB-230

Stephens, Alexander H. 1812-1883 . . . . . . .DLB-47

Stephens, Alice Barber 1858-1932 . . . . . . .DLB-188

Stephens, Ann 1810-1886 . . . . . . .DLB-3, 73, 250

Stephens, Charles Asbury 1844?-1931 . . . .DLB-42

Stephens, James 1882?-1950 . . . .DLB-19, 153, 162

Stephens, John Lloyd 1805-1852. . . .DLB-183, 250

Stephens, Michael 1946- DLB-234

Stephensen, P. R. 1901-1965 . . . . .DLB-260

Sterling, George 1869-1926 . . . . .DLB-54

Sterling, James 1701-1763. . . . . .DLB-24

Sterling, John 1806-1844 . . . . .DLB-116

Stern, Gerald 1925- DLB-105

"Living in Ruin" DLB-105

Stern, Gladys B. 1890-1973 . . . . .DLB-197

Stern, Madeleine B. 1912- DLB-111, 140

Stern, Richard 1928- DLB-218; Y-87

Stern, Stewart 1922- DLB-26

Sterne, Laurence 1713-1768 . . . DLB-39; CDBLB-2

Sternheim, Carl 1878-1942 . . . . .DLB-56, 118

Sternhold, Thomas ?-1549. . . . . .DLB-132

Steuart, David 1747-1824 . . . . .DLB-213

Stevens, Henry 1819-1886. . . . . .DLB-140

Stevens, Wallace 1879-1955. . . .DLB-54; CDALB-5

The Wallace Stevens Society Y-99

Stevenson, Anne 1933- DLB-40

Stevenson, D. E. 1892-1973 . . . . .DLB-191

Stevenson, Lionel 1902-1973 . . . . .DLB-155

Stevenson, Robert Louis
1850-1894 . . . . . . DLB-18, 57, 141, 156, 174;
DS-13; CDBLB-5

"On Style in Literature:
Its Technical Elements" (1885) . . .DLB-57

Stewart, Donald Ogden
1894-1980 . . . . .DLB-4, 11, 26; DS-15

Stewart, Douglas 1913-1985 . . . . .DLB-260

Stewart, Dugald 1753-1828 . . . . .DLB-31

Stewart, George, Jr. 1848-1906 . . . . .DLB-99

Stewart, George R. 1895-1980 . . . . .DLB-8

Stewart, Harold 1916-1995 . . . . .DLB-260

Stewart, J. I. M. (see Innes, Michael)

Stewart, Maria W. 1803?-1879 . . . . .DLB-239

Stewart, Randall 1896-1964. . . . . .DLB-103

Stewart, Sean 1965- DLB-251

Stewart and Kidd Company DLB-46

Stickney, Trumbull 1874-1904 . . . . .DLB-54

Stieler, Caspar 1632-1707. . . . . .DLB-164

Stifter, Adalbert
1805-1868 . . . . .DLB-133; CDWLB-2

Stiles, Ezra 1727-1795 . . . . .DLB-31

Still, James 1906-2001 . . . . DLB-9; Y-01

Stirling, S. M. 1953- DLB-251

Stirner, Max 1806-1856. . . . . .DLB-129

Stith, William 1707-1755. . . . . .DLB-31

Stivens, Dal 1911-1997 . . . . .DLB-260

Elliot Stock [publishing house]. DLB-106

Stockton, Annis Boudinot 1736-1801. . . . .DLB-200

Stockton, Frank R. 1834-1902 . . DLB-42, 74; DS-13

Stockton, J. Roy 1892-1972 . . . . .DLB-241

Ashbel Stoddard [publishing house] DLB-49

Stoddard, Charles Warren 1843-1909. . . .DLB-186

Stoddard, Elizabeth 1823-1902 . . . . .DLB-202

Stoddard, Richard Henry
1825-1903 . . . . .DLB-3, 64, 250; DS-13

Stoddard, Solomon 1643-1729. . . . . .DLB-24

Stoker, Bram
1847-1912 . . . . . . .DLB-36, 70, 178; CDBLB-5

On Writing *Dracula,* from the
Introduction to *Dracula* (1897) . . .DLB-178

Frederick A. Stokes Company. DLB-49

Stokes, Thomas L. 1898-1958 . . . . .DLB-29

Stokesbury, Leon 1945- DLB-120

Stolberg, Christian Graf zu 1748-1821. . . . .DLB-94

Stolberg, Friedrich Leopold Graf zu
1750-1819 .DLB-94

Stone, Lucy 1818-1893 . . . . DLB-79, 239

Stone, Melville 1848-1929 . . . . .DLB-25

Stone, Robert 1937- DLB-152

Stone, Ruth 1915- DLB-105

Stone, Samuel 1602-1663. . . . . .DLB-24

Stone, William Leete 1792-1844 . . . . .DLB-202

Herbert S. Stone and Company. DLB-49

Stone and Kimball DLB-49

Stoppard, Tom
1937- DLB-13, 233; Y-85; CDBLB-8

Playwrights and Professors DLB-13

Storey, Anthony 1928- DLB-14

Storey, David 1933- DLB-13, 14, 207, 245

Storm, Theodor
1817-1888 . . . . .DLB-129; CDWLB-2

Storni, Alfonsina 1892-1938 . . . . .DLB-283

Story, Thomas circa 1670-1742 . . . . .DLB-31

Story, William Wetmore 1819-1895 . . .DLB-1, 235

Storytelling: A Contemporary Renaissance. . . Y-84

Stoughton, William 1631-1701 . . . . .DLB-24

Stow, John 1525-1605 . . . . .DLB-132

Stow, Randolph 1935- DLB-260

Stowe, Harriet Beecher 1811-1896 . . . . .DLB-1,12,
42, 74, 189, 239, 243; CDALB-3

The Harriet Beecher Stowe Center. Y-00

Stowe, Leland 1899-1994. . . . . .DLB-29

Stoyanov, Dimitr Ivanov (see Elin Pelin)

Strabo 64/63 B.C.-circa A.D. 25 . . . . . .DLB-176

Strachey, Lytton 1880-1932 ..... DLB-149; DS-10

    Preface to *Eminent Victorians*........ DLB-149

William Strahan [publishing house] DLB-154

Strahan and Company DLB-106

Strand, Mark 1934- DLB-5

The Strasbourg Oaths 842 .... DLB-148

Stratemeyer, Edward 1862-1930 .... DLB-42

Strati, Saverio 1924- DLB-177

Stratton and Barnard DLB-49

Stratton-Porter, Gene
1863-1924 .... DLB-221; DS-14

Straub, Peter 1943- Y-84

Strauß, Botho 1944- DLB-124

Strauß, David Friedrich 1808-1874..... DLB-133

The Strawberry Hill Press DLB-154

Strawson, P. F. 1919- DLB-262

Streatfeild, Noel 1895-1986........ DLB-160

Street, Cecil John Charles (see Rhode, John)

Street, G. S. 1867-1936 .... DLB-135

Street and Smith DLB-49

Streeter, Edward 1891-1976 .... DLB-11

Streeter, Thomas Winthrop 1883-1965 .. DLB-140

Stretton, Hesba 1832-1911 .... DLB-163, 190

Stribling, T. S. 1881-1965.............. DLB-9

Der Stricker circa 1190-circa 1250 ..... DLB-138

Strickland, Samuel 1804-1867.......... DLB-99

Strindberg, August 1849-1912 .... DLB-259

Stringer, Arthur 1874-1950............ DLB-92

Stringer and Townsend DLB-49

Strittmatter, Erwin 1912-1994 .... DLB-69

Strniša, Gregor 1930-1987 .... DLB-181

Strode, William 1630-1645........... DLB-126

Strong, L. A. G. 1896-1958.......... DLB-191

Strother, David Hunter (Porte Crayon)
1816-1888................... DLB-3, 248

Strouse, Jean 1945- DLB-111

Stuart, Dabney 1937- DLB-105

    "Knots into Webs: Some
    Autobiographical Sources" DLB-105

Stuart, Jesse 1906-1984......DLB-9, 48, 102; Y-84

Lyle Stuart [publishing house] DLB-46

Stuart, Ruth McEnery 1849?-1917 ..... DLB-202

Stubbs, Harry Clement (see Clement, Hal)

Stubenberg, Johann Wilhelm von
1619-1663................... DLB-164

Studebaker, William V. 1947- DLB-256

Studies in American Jewish Literature Y-02

Studio DLB-112

Stump, Al 1916-1995 .... DLB-241

Sturgeon, Theodore 1918-1985 ..... DLB-8; Y-85

Sturges, Preston 1898-1959 .... DLB-26

Styron, William
1925- DLB-2, 143; Y-80; CDALB-6

    Tribute to James Dickey Y-97

Suárez, Mario 1925- DLB-82

Such, Peter 1939- DLB-60

Suckling, Sir John 1609-1641? DLB-58, 126

Suckow, Ruth 1892-1960 .... DLB-9, 102

Sudermann, Hermann 1857-1928...... DLB-118

Sue, Eugène 1804-1857............... DLB-119

Sue, Marie-Joseph (see Sue, Eugène)

Suetonius circa A.D. 69-post A.D. 122... DLB-211

Suggs, Simon (see Hooper, Johnson Jones)

Sui Sin Far (see Eaton, Edith Maude)

Suits, Gustav 1883-1956.... DLB-220; CDWLB-4

Sukenick, Ronald 1932- DLB-173; Y-81

    An Author's Response Y-82

Sukhovo-Kobylin, Aleksandr Vasil'evich
1817-1903.......................DLB-277

Suknaski, Andrew 1942- DLB-53

Sullivan, Alan 1868-1947 .... DLB-92

Sullivan, C. Gardner 1886-1965........ DLB-26

Sullivan, Frank 1892-1976 .... DLB-11

Sulte, Benjamin 1841-1923 .... DLB-99

Sulzberger, Arthur Hays 1891-1968..... DLB-127

Sulzberger, Arthur Ochs 1926- DLB-127

Sulzer, Johann Georg 1720-1779 .... DLB-97

Sumarokov, Aleksandr Petrovich
1717-1777 .... DLB-150

Summers, Hollis 1916- DLB-6

Sumner, Charles 1811-1874 .... DLB-235

Sumner, William Graham 1840-1910.... DLB-270

Henry A. Sumner [publishing house] DLB-49

Sundman, Per Olof 1922-1992 .... DLB-257

Supervielle, Jules 1884-1960........... DLB-258

Surtees, Robert Smith 1803-1864 .... DLB-21

    The R. S. Surtees Society Y-98

Sutcliffe, Matthew 1550?-1629 .... DLB-281

Sutcliffe, William 1971- DLB-271

Sutherland, Efua Theodora 1924-1996 ...DLB-117

Sutherland, John 1919-1956 .... DLB-68

Sutro, Alfred 1863-1933 .... DLB-10

Svendsen, Hanne Marie 1933- DLB-214

Svevo, Italo (Ettore Schmitz)
1861-1928 .... DLB-264

Swados, Harvey 1920-1972 .... DLB-2

Swain, Charles 1801-1874............. DLB-32

Swallow Press...................... DLB-46

Swan Sonnenschein Limited.......... DLB-106

Swanberg, W. A. 1907-1992.......... DLB-103

Swedish Literature
    The Literature of the Modern
    Breakthrough DLB-259

Swenson, May 1919-1989.............. DLB-5

Swerling, Jo 1897- DLB-44

Swift, Graham 1949- DLB-194

Swift, Jonathan
1667-1745 ...... DLB-39, 95, 101; CDBLB-2

Swinburne, A. C.
1837-1909 .... DLB-35, 57; CDBLB-4

    Under the Microscope (1872) DLB-35

Swineshead, Richard floruit circa 1350 .. DLB-115

Swinnerton, Frank 1884-1982 .... DLB-34

Swisshelm, Jane Grey 1815-1884 .... DLB-43

Swope, Herbert Bayard 1882-1958 ..... DLB-25

Swords, James ?-1844................. DLB-73

Swords, Thomas 1763-1843 .... DLB-73

T. and J. Swords and Company DLB-49

Swynnerton, Thomas (John Roberts)
circa 1500-1554 .... DLB-281

Sykes, Ella C. ?-1939 ....DLB-174

Sylvester, Josuah 1562 or 1563-1618 .... DLB-121

Symonds, Emily Morse (see Paston, George)

Symonds, John Addington
1840-1893 ....DLB-57, 144

    "Personal Style" (1890) DLB-57

Symons, A. J. A. 1900-1941 .... DLB-149

Symons, Arthur 1865-1945 ...... DLB-19, 57, 149

Symons, Julian 1912-1994 ..... DLB-87, 155; Y-92

    Julian Symons at Eighty.............. Y-92

Symons, Scott 1933- DLB-53

Synge, John Millington
1871-1909.......... DLB-10, 19; CDBLB-5

    Synge Summer School: J. M. Synge
    and the Irish Theater, Rathdrum,
    County Wiclow, Ireland Y-93

Syrett, Netta 1865-1943 ....DLB-135, 197

Szabó, Lőrinc 1900-1957 .... DLB-215

Szabó, Magda 1917- DLB-215

Szymborska, Wisława
1923- DLB-232, Y-96; CDWLB-4

    Nobel Lecture 1996:
    The Poet and the World........... Y-96

T

Taban lo Liyong 1939?- DLB-125

Tabori, George 1914- DLB-245

Tabucchi, Antonio 1943- DLB-196

Taché, Joseph-Charles 1820-1894 .... DLB-99

Tachihara Masaaki 1926-1980 .... DLB-182

Tacitus circa A.D. 55-circa A.D. 117
..................DLB-211; CDWLB-1

Tadijanović, Dragutin 1905- DLB-181

Tafdrup, Pia 1952- DLB-214

Tafolla, Carmen 1951- DLB-82

Taggard, Genevieve 1894-1948 .... DLB-45

Taggart, John 1942- DLB-193

Tagger, Theodor (see Bruckner, Ferdinand)

Taiheiki late fourteenth century DLB-203

Tait, J. Selwin, and Sons............... DLB-49

Tait's Edinburgh Magazine 1832-1861 ..... DLB-110

The Takarazaka Revue Company Y-91

Talander (see Bohse, August)

Talese, Gay 1932- DLB-185

    Tribute to Irwin Shaw Y-84

Talev, Dimitr 1898-1966 .... DLB-181

Taliaferro, H. E. 1811-1875 .... DLB-202

Tallent, Elizabeth 1954- DLB-130

TallMountain, Mary 1918-1994 .... DLB-193

Talvj 1797-1870 . . . . DLB-59, 133

Tamási, Áron 1897-1966 . . . . DLB-215

Tammsaare, A. H.
1878-1940 . . . . DLB-220; CDWLB-4

Tan, Amy 1952- DLB-173; CDALB-7

Tandori, Dezső 1938- DLB-232

Tanner, Thomas 1673/1674-1735 . . . . DLB-213

Tanizaki Jun'ichirō 1886-1965. . . . . .DLB-180

Tapahonso, Luci 1953- DLB-175

The Mark Taper Forum DLB-7

Taradash, Daniel 1913- DLB-44

Tarasov-Rodionov, Aleksandr Ignat'evich
1885-1938 . . . . .DLB-272

Tarbell, Ida M. 1857-1944 . . . . DLB-47

Tardivel, Jules-Paul 1851-1905 . . . . DLB-99

Targan, Barry 1932- DLB-130

Tribute to John Gardner Y-82

Tarkington, Booth 1869-1946 . . . . DLB-9, 102

Tashlin, Frank 1913-1972 . . . . DLB-44

Tasma (Jessie Couvreur) 1848-1897 . . . . .DLB-230

Tate, Allen 1899-1979 . . . . . . DLB-4, 45, 63; DS-17

Tate, James 1943- DLB-5, 169

Tate, Nahum circa 1652-1715 . . . . .DLB-80

Tatian circa 830 .DLB-148

Taufer, Veno 1933- DLB-181

Tauler, Johannes circa 1300-1361 . . . . . . .DLB-179

Tavčar, Ivan 1851-1923 . . . . .DLB-147

Taverner, Richard ca. 1505-1575 . . . . .DLB-236

Taylor, Ann 1782-1866 . . . . DLB-163

Taylor, Bayard 1825-1878 . . . . . . .DLB-3, 189, 250

Taylor, Bert Leston 1866-1921 . . . . .DLB-25

Taylor, Charles H. 1846-1921 . . . . .DLB-25

Taylor, Edward circa 1642-1729 . . . . .DLB-24

Taylor, Elizabeth 1912-1975 . . . . .DLB-139

Taylor, Sir Henry 1800-1886. . . . . .DLB-32

Taylor, Henry 1942- DLB-5

Who Owns American Literature. Y-94

Taylor, Jane 1783-1824 . . . . .DLB-163

Taylor, Jeremy circa 1613-1667 . . . . .DLB-151

Taylor, John 1577 or 1578 - 1653 . . . . . . .DLB-121

Taylor, Mildred D. 1943- DLB-52

Taylor, Peter 1917-1994 . . . DLB-218, 278; Y-81, 94

Taylor, Susie King 1848-1912 . . . . .DLB-221

Taylor, William Howland 1901-1966 . . . .DLB-241

William Taylor and Company DLB-49

Teale, Edwin Way 1899-1980 . . . . .DLB-275

Teasdale, Sara 1884-1933 . . . . .DLB-45

Teillier, Jorge 1935-1996 . . . . .DLB-283

Telles, Lygia Fagundes 1924- DLB-113

The Temper of the West: William Jovanovich . . . Y-02

Temple, Sir William 1555?-1627 . . . . .DLB-281

Temple, Sir William 1628-1699 . . . . .DLB-101

Temple, William F. 1914-1989 . . . . .DLB-255

Temrizov, A. (see Marchenko, Anastasia Iakovlevna)

Tench, Watkin ca. 1758-1833 . . . . .DLB-230

Tender Is the Night (Documentary) DLB-273

Tenn, William 1919- DLB-8

Tennant, Emma 1937- DLB-14

Tenney, Tabitha Gilman 1762-1837 . . DLB-37, 200

Tennyson, Alfred 1809-1892. . DLB-32; CDBLB-4

On Some of the Characteristics of
Modern Poetry and On the Lyrical
Poems of Alfred Tennyson
(1831) DLB-32

Tennyson, Frederick 1807-1898. . . . . .DLB-32

Tenorio, Arthur 1924- DLB-209

Tepl, Johannes von
circa 1350-1414/1415 . . . . .DLB-179

Tepliakov, Viktor Grigor'evich
1804-1842 . . . . .DLB-205

Terence circa 184 B.C.-159 B.C. or after
. . . . .DLB-211; CDWLB-1

Terhune, Albert Payson 1872-1942 . . . . . . .DLB-9

Terhune, Mary Virginia 1830-1922 . . . . DS-13

Terpigorev, Sergei Nikolaevich (S. Atava)
1841-1895 . . . . .DLB-277

Terry, Megan 1932- DLB-7, 249

Terson, Peter 1932- DLB-13

Tesich, Steve 1943-1996 . . . . Y-83

Tessa, Delio 1886-1939 . . . . .DLB-114

Testori, Giovanni 1923-1993. . . . . . . DLB-128, 177

Texas
The Year in Texas Literature Y-98

Tey, Josephine 1896?-1952 . . . . .DLB-77

Thacher, James 1754-1844. . . . . .DLB-37

Thacher, John Boyd 1847-1909 . . . . .DLB-187

Thackeray, William Makepeace
1811-1863 . . .DLB-21, 55, 159, 163; CDBLB-4

Thames and Hudson Limited DLB-112

Thanet, Octave (see French, Alice)

Thaxter, Celia Laighton 1835-1894. . . . .DLB-239

Thayer, Caroline Matilda Warren
1785-1844 . . . . .DLB-200

Thayer, Douglas H. 1929- DLB-256

Theater
Black Theatre: A Forum [excerpts] DLB-38

Community and Commentators:
Black Theatre and Its Critics DLB-38

German Drama from Naturalism
to Fascism: 1889-1933 . . . . .DLB-118

A Look at the Contemporary Black
Theatre Movement. DLB-38

The Lord Chamberlain's Office and
Stage Censorship in England DLB-10

New Forces at Work in the American
Theatre: 1915-1925 . . . . .DLB-7

Off Broadway and Off-Off Broadway . .DLB-7

Oregon Shakespeare Festival. Y-00

Plays, Playwrights, and Playgoers. DLB-84

Playwrights on the Theater. DLB-80

Playwrights and Professors DLB-13

Producing *Dear Bunny, Dear Volodya:
The Friendship and the Feud* Y-97

Viewpoint: Politics and Performance,
by David Edgar DLB-13

Writing for the Theatre,
by Harold Pinter. DLB-13

The Year in Drama. Y-82–85, 87–98

The Year in U.S. Drama. Y-00

Theater, English and Irish
Anti-Theatrical Tracts DLB-263

The Chester Plays circa 1505-1532;
revisions until 1575. . . . . .DLB-146

Dangerous Years: London Theater,
1939-1945. . . . . .DLB-10

A Defense of Actors DLB-263

The Development of Lighting in the
Staging of Drama, 1900-1945 . . . .DLB-10

Education DLB-263

The End of English Stage Censorship,
1945-1968. . . . . .DLB-13

Epigrams and Satires. DLB-263

Eyewitnesses and Historians DLB-263

Fringe and Alternative Theater in
Great Britain. DLB-13

The Great War and the Theater,
1914-1918 [Great Britain] DLB-10

Licensing Act of 1737 . . . . .DLB-84

Morality Plays: *Mankind* circa 1450-1500
and *Everyman* circa 1500 . . . . .DLB-146

The New Variorum Shakespeare Y-85

N-Town Plays circa 1468 to early
sixteenth century. DLB-146

Politics and the Theater DLB-263

Practical Matters DLB-263

Prologues, Epilogues, Epistles to
Readers, and Excerpts from
Plays. DLB-263

The Publication of English
Renaissance Plays. DLB-62

Regulations for the Theater DLB-263

Sources for the Study of Tudor and
Stuart Drama DLB-62

Stage Censorship: "The Rejected
Statement" (1911), by Bernard
Shaw [excerpts]. DLB-10

Synge Summer School: J. M. Synge and
the Irish Theater, Rathdrum,
County Wicklow, Ireland. Y-93

The Theater in Shakespeare's Time . . .DLB-62

The Theatre Guild DLB-7

The Townely Plays fifteenth and
sixteenth centuries DLB-146

The Year in British Drama Y-99–01

The Year in Drama: London Y-90

The Year in London Theatre Y-92

A Yorkshire Tragedy. DLB-58

Theaters
The Abbey Theatre and Irish Drama,
1900-1945. . . . . .DLB-10

Actors Theatre of Louisville DLB-7

American Conservatory Theatre DLB-7

Arena Stage. DLB-7

Black Theaters and Theater
Organizations in America,
1961-1982: A Research List DLB-38

The Dallas Theater Center. DLB-7

Eugene O'Neill Memorial Theater Center DLB-7

The Goodman Theatre DLB-7

The Guthrie Theater DLB-7

The Mark Taper Forum DLB-7

The National Theatre and the Royal Shakespeare Company: The National Companies DLB-13

Off-Loop Theatres DLB-7

The Royal Court Theatre and the English Stage Company DLB-13

The Royal Court Theatre and the New Drama DLB-10

The Takarazaka Revue Company Y-91

Thegan and the Astronomer flourished circa 850 . . . . DLB-148

Thelwall, John 1764-1834 . . . . DLB-93, 158

Theocritus circa 300 B.C.-260 B.C. DLB-176

Theodorescu, Ion N. (see Arghezi, Tudor)

Theodulf circa 760-circa 821 . . . . DLB-148

Theophrastus circa 371 B.C.-287 B.C. . . . DLB-176

Thériault, Yves 1915-1983 . . . . DLB-88

Thério, Adrien 1925- DLB-53

Theroux, Paul 1941- DLB-2, 218; CDALB-7

Thesiger, Wilfred 1910- DLB-204

They All Came to Paris DS-15

Thibaudeau, Colleen 1925- DLB-88

Thielen, Benedict 1903-1965 . . . . DLB-102

Thiong'o Ngugi wa (see Ngugi wa Thiong'o)

This Quarter 1925-1927, 1929-1932 . . . . DS-15

Thoma, Ludwig 1867-1921 . . . . DLB-66

Thoma, Richard 1902- DLB-4

Thomas, Audrey 1935- DLB-60

Thomas, D. M. 1935- DLB-40, 207; CDBLB-8

The Plagiarism Controversy Y-82

Thomas, Dylan 1914-1953 . . . . . . DLB-13, 20, 139; CDBLB-7

The Dylan Thomas Celebration Y-99

Thomas, Edward 1878-1917 . . . . DLB-19, 98, 156, 216

The Friends of the Dymock Poets Y-00

Thomas, Frederick William 1806-1866 . . DLB-202

Thomas, Gwyn 1913-1981 . . . . DLB-15, 245

Thomas, Isaiah 1750-1831 . . . . . . DLB-43, 73, 187

Thomas, Johann 1624-1679 . . . . DLB-168

Thomas, John 1900-1932 . . . . DLB-4

Thomas, Joyce Carol 1938- DLB-33

Thomas, Lewis 1913-1993 . . . . DLB-275

Thomas, Lorenzo 1944- DLB-41

Thomas, R. S. 1915-2000 . . . . . DLB-27; CDBLB-8

Isaiah Thomas [publishing house] DLB-49

Thomasîn von Zerclære circa 1186-circa 1259 . . . . DLB-138

Thomason, George 1602?-1666 . . . . DLB-213

Thomasius, Christian 1655-1728 . . . . DLB-168

Thompson, Daniel Pierce 1795-1868 . . . . DLB-202

Thompson, David 1770-1857 . . . . DLB-99

Thompson, Dorothy 1893-1961 . . . . DLB-29

Thompson, E. P. 1924-1993 . . . . DLB-242

Thompson, Flora 1876-1947 . . . . DLB-240

Thompson, Francis 1859-1907 . . . . DLB-19; CDBLB-5

Thompson, George Selden (see Selden, George)

Thompson, Henry Yates 1838-1928 . . . . DLB-184

Thompson, Hunter S. 1939- . . . DLB-185

Thompson, Jim 1906-1977 . . . . DLB-226

Thompson, John 1938-1976 . . . . DLB-60

Thompson, John R. 1823-1873 . . . DLB-3, 73, 248

Thompson, Lawrance 1906-1973 . . . . DLB-103

Thompson, Maurice 1844-1901 . . . . . . DLB-71, 74

Thompson, Ruth Plumly 1891-1976 . . . . . DLB-22

Thompson, Thomas Phillips 1843-1933 . . . DLB-99

Thompson, William 1775-1833 . . . . DLB-158

Thompson, William Tappan 1812-1882 . . . . DLB-3, 11, 248

Thomson, Cockburn "Modern Style" (1857) [excerpt] DLB-57

Thomson, Edward William 1849-1924 . . . DLB-92

Thomson, James 1700-1748 . . . . DLB-95

Thomson, James 1834-1882 . . . . DLB-35

Thomson, Joseph 1858-1895 . . . . DLB-174

Thomson, Mortimer 1831-1875 . . . . DLB-11

Thomson, Rupert 1955- DLB-267

Thon, Melanie Rae 1957- DLB-244

Thoreau, Henry David 1817-1862 . . . . . . DLB-1, 183, 223, 270; DS-5; CDALB-2

The Thoreau Society Y-99

The Thoreauvian Pilgrimage: The Structure of an American Cult . . DLB-223

Thorne, William 1568?-1630 . . . . DLB-281

Thornton, John F. [Repsonse to Ken Auletta] Y-97

Thorpe, Adam 1956- DLB-231

Thorpe, Thomas Bangs 1815-1878 . . . . DLB-3, 11, 248

Thorup, Kirsten 1942- DLB-214

Thrale, Hester Lynch (see Piozzi, Hester Lynch [Thrale])

Thubron, Colin 1939- DLB-204, 231

Thucydides circa 455 B.C.-circa 395 B.C. DLB-176

Thulstrup, Thure de 1848-1930 . . . . DLB-188

Thümmel, Moritz August von 1738-1817 . . . . DLB-97

Thurber, James 1894-1961 . . . . DLB-4, 11, 22, 102; CDALB-5

Thurman, Wallace 1902-1934 . . . . DLB-51

"Negro Poets and Their Poetry" DLB-50

Thwaite, Anthony 1930- DLB-40

The Booker Prize, Address Y-86

Thwaites, Reuben Gold 1853-1913 . . . . . DLB-47

Tibullus circa 54 B.C.-circa 19 B.C. DLB-211

Ticknor, George 1791-1871 . . DLB-1, 59, 140, 235

Ticknor and Fields DLB-49

Ticknor and Fields (revived) DLB-46

Tieck, Ludwig 1773-1853 . . . . DLB-90; CDWLB-2

Tietjens, Eunice 1884-1944 . . . . DLB-54

Tikkanen, Märta 1935- DLB-257

Tilghman, Christopher circa 1948 . . . . . . DLB-244

Tilney, Edmund circa 1536-1610 . . . . DLB-136

Charles Tilt [publishing house] DLB-106

J. E. Tilton and Company DLB-49

Time-Life Books DLB-46

Times Books DLB-46

Timothy, Peter circa 1725-1782 . . . . DLB-43

Timrava 1867-1951 . . . . DLB-215

Timrod, Henry 1828-1867 . . . . DLB-3, 248

Tindal, Henrietta 1818?-1879 . . . . DLB-199

Tinker, Chauncey Brewster 1876-1963 . . DLB-140

Tinsley Brothers DLB-106

Tiptree, James, Jr. 1915-1987 . . . . DLB-8

Tišma, Aleksandar 1924- DLB-181

Titus, Edward William 1870-1952 . . . . DLB-4; DS-15

Tiutchev, Fedor Ivanovich 1803-1873 . . . DLB-205

Tlali, Miriam 1933- DLB-157, 225

Todd, Barbara Euphan 1890-1976 . . . . . . DLB-160

Todorov, Tzvetan 1939- DLB-242

Tofte, Robert 1561 or 1562-1619 or 1620 . . . . DLB-172

Tóibín, Colm 1955- DLB-271

Toklas, Alice B. 1877-1967 . . . . DLB-4; DS-15

Tokuda Shūsei 1872-1943 . . . . DLB-180

Toland, John 1670-1722 . . . . DLB-252

Tolkien, J. R. R. 1892-1973 . . . . . . DLB-15, 160, 255; CDBLB-6

Toller, Ernst 1893-1939 . . . . DLB-124

Tollet, Elizabeth 1694-1754 . . . . DLB-95

Tolson, Melvin B. 1898-1966 . . . . DLB-48, 76

Tolstaya, Tatyana 1951- DLB-285

Tolstoy, Aleksei Konstantinovich 1817-1875 . . . . DLB-238

Tolstoy, Aleksei Nikolaevich 1883-1945 . . DLB-272

Tolstoy, Leo 1828-1910 . . . . DLB-238

Tomalin, Claire 1933- DLB-155

Tomasi di Lampedusa, Giuseppe 1896-1957 . . . . DLB-177

Tomlinson, Charles 1927- DLB-40

Tomlinson, H. M. 1873-1958 . . . DLB-36, 100, 195

Abel Tompkins [publishing house] DLB-49

Tompson, Benjamin 1642-1714 . . . . DLB-24

Tomson, Graham R. (see Watson, Rosamund Marriott)

Ton'a 1289-1372 . . . . DLB-203

Tondelli, Pier Vittorio 1955-1991 . . . . . . DLB-196

Tonks, Rosemary 1932- DLB-14, 207

Tonna, Charlotte Elizabeth 1790-1846 . . . DLB-163

Jacob Tonson the Elder [publishing house] DLB-170

Toole, John Kennedy 1937-1969 . . . . Y-81

Toomer, Jean 1894-1967 . . .DLB-45, 51; CDALB-4

Tor Books DLB-46

Torberg, Friedrich 1908-1979 . . . . .DLB-85

Torrence, Ridgely 1874-1950. . . . . . .DLB-54, 249

Torres-Metzger, Joseph V. 1933- DLB-122

Toth, Susan Allen 1940- Y-86

Richard Tottell [publishing house]. DLB-170

"The Printer to the Reader,"
(1557) DLB-167

Tough-Guy Literature DLB-9

Touré, Askia Muhammad 1938- DLB-41

Tourgée, Albion W. 1838-1905. . . . . .DLB-79

Tournemir, Elizaveta Sailhas de (see Tur, Evgeniia)

Tourneur, Cyril circa 1580-1626. . . . . . . .DLB-58

Tournier, Michel 1924- DLB-83

Frank Tousey [publishing house]. DLB-49

Tower Publications DLB-46

Towne, Benjamin circa 1740-1793 . . . . . . .DLB-43

Towne, Robert 1936- DLB-44

The Townely Plays fifteenth and sixteenth
centuries DLB-146

Townsend, Sue 1946- DLB-271

Townshend, Aurelian
by 1583-circa 1651 . . . . .DLB-121

Toy, Barbara 1908-2001 . . . . .DLB-204

Tozzi, Federigo 1883-1920. . . . . .DLB-264

Tracy, Honor 1913-1989. . . . . .DLB-15

Traherne, Thomas 1637?-1674 . . . . .DLB-131

Traill, Catharine Parr 1802-1899. . . . . . . .DLB-99

Train, Arthur 1875-1945 . . . . .DLB-86; DS-16

Tranquilli, Secondino (see Silone, Ignazio)

The Transatlantic Publishing Company . . .DLB-49

The Transatlantic Review 1924-1925 . . . . DS-15

The Transcendental Club
1836-1840 . . . . DLB-1; DLB-223

Transcendentalism. DLB-1; DLB-223; DS-5

"A Response from America," by
John A. Heraud DS-5

Publications and Social Movements DLB-1

The Rise of Transcendentalism,
1815-1860. DS-5

Transcendentalists, American DS-5

"What Is Transcendentalism? By a
Thinking Man," by James
Kinnard Jr. DS-5

transition 1927-1938 . . . . DS-15

Tranströmer, Tomas 1931- DLB-257

Travel Writing
American Travel Writing, 1776-1864
(checklist) DLB-183

British Travel Writing, 1940-1997
(checklist) DLB-204

(1876-1909. .DLB-174

(1837-1875 .DLB-166

(1910-1939. .DLB-195

Traven, B. 1882?/1890?-1969? DLB-9, 56

Travers, Ben 1886-1980 . . . . .DLB-10, 233

Travers, P. L. (Pamela Lyndon)
1899-1996 .DLB-160

Trediakovsky, Vasilii Kirillovich
1703-1769 .DLB-150

Treece, Henry 1911-1966 . . . . .DLB-160

Treitel, Jonathan 1959- DLB-267

Trejo, Ernesto 1950-1991 . . . . .DLB-122

Trelawny, Edward John
1792-1881 . . . . DLB-110, 116, 144

Tremain, Rose 1943- DLB-14, 271

Tremblay, Michel 1942- DLB-60

Trent, William P. 1862-1939. . . . . DLB-47, 71

Trescot, William Henry 1822-1898. . . . . . .DLB-30

Tressell, Robert (Robert Phillipe Noonan)
1870-1911 .DLB-197

Trevelyan, Sir George Otto
1838-1928 .DLB-144

Trevisa, John circa 1342-circa 1402. . . . . .DLB-146

Trevor, William 1928- DLB-14, 139

Trierer Floyris circa 1170-1180 . . . . .DLB-138

Trillin, Calvin 1935- DLB-185

Trilling, Lionel 1905-1975 . . . . .DLB-28, 63

Trilussa 1871-1950. . . . . .DLB-114

Trimmer, Sarah 1741-1810 . . . . .DLB-158

Triolet, Elsa 1896-1970 . . . . .DLB-72

Tripp, John 1927- DLB-40

Trocchi, Alexander 1925-1984 . . . . .DLB-15

Troisi, Dante 1920-1989 . . . . .DLB-196

Trollope, Anthony
1815-1882 . . . . DLB-21, 57, 159; CDBLB-4

Novel-Reading: *The Works of Charles
Dickens; The Works of W. Makepeace
Thackeray* (1879) DLB-21

The Trollope Societies Y-00

Trollope, Frances 1779-1863 . . . . .DLB-21, 166

Trollope, Joanna 1943- DLB-207

Troop, Elizabeth 1931- DLB-14

Trotter, Catharine 1679-1749. . . . . . .DLB-84, 252

Trotti, Lamar 1898-1952. . . . . .DLB-44

Trottier, Pierre 1925- DLB-60

Trotzig, Birgitta 1929- DLB-257

Troupe, Quincy Thomas, Jr. 1943- DLB-41

John F. Trow and Company DLB-49

Trowbridge, John Townsend 1827-1916 . .DLB-202

Trudel, Jean-Louis 1967- DLB-251

Truillier-Lacombe, Joseph-Patrice
1807-1863 .DLB-99

Trumbo, Dalton 1905-1976. . . . . .DLB-26

Trumbull, Benjamin 1735-1820 . . . . .DLB-30

Trumbull, John 1750-1831 . . . . .DLB-31

Trumbull, John 1756-1843. . . . . .DLB-183

Truth, Sojourner 1797?-1883 . . . . .DLB-239

Tscherning, Andreas 1611-1659 . . . . .DLB-164

Tsubouchi Shōyō 1859-1935 . . . . .DLB-180

Tuchman, Barbara W.
Tribute to Alfred A. Knopf. Y-84

Tucholsky, Kurt 1890-1935. . . . . .DLB-56

Tucker, Charlotte Maria
1821-1893 . . . . .DLB-163, 190

Tucker, George 1775-1861. . . . . . .DLB-3, 30, 248

Tucker, James 1808?-1866?. DLB-230

Tucker, Nathaniel Beverley
1784-1851 . . . . .DLB-3, 248

Tucker, St. George 1752-1827 . . . . .DLB-37

Tuckerman, Frederick Goddard
1821-1873 .DLB-243

Tuckerman, Henry Theodore 1813-1871 . .DLB-64

Tumas, Juozas (see Vaizgantas)

Tunis, John R. 1889-1975 . . . . DLB-22, 171

Tunstall, Cuthbert 1474-1559 . . . . .DLB-132

Tunström, Göran 1937-2000 . . . . .DLB-257

Tuohy, Frank 1925- DLB-14, 139

Tupper, Martin F. 1810-1889 . . . . .DLB-32

Tur, Evgeniia 1815-1892 . . . . .DLB-238

Turbyfill, Mark 1896-1991 . . . . .DLB-45

Turco, Lewis 1934- Y-84

Tribute to John Ciardi Y-86

Turgenev, Aleksandr Ivanovich
1784-1845 .DLB-198

Turgenev, Ivan Sergeevich 1818-1883. . . .DLB-238

Turnbull, Alexander H. 1868-1918. . . . . .DLB-184

Turnbull, Andrew 1921-1970 . . . . .DLB-103

Turnbull, Gael 1928- DLB-40

Turner, Arlin 1909-1980 . . . . .DLB-103

Turner, Charles (Tennyson) 1808-1879 . . .DLB-32

Turner, Ethel 1872-1958 . . . . .DLB-230

Turner, Frederick 1943- DLB-40

Turner, Frederick Jackson
1861-1932 . . . . DLB-17, 186

A Conversation between William Riggan
and Janette Turner Hospital Y-02

Turner, Joseph Addison 1826-1868. . . . . .DLB-79

Turpin, Waters Edward 1910-1968. . . . . .DLB-51

Turrini, Peter 1944- DLB-124

Tutuola, Amos 1920-1997 . . .DLB-125; CDWLB-3

Twain, Mark (see Clemens, Samuel Langhorne)

Tweedie, Ethel Brilliana circa 1860-1940 . DLB-174

A Century of Poetry, a Lifetime of
Collecting: J. M. Edelstein's
Collection of Twentieth-
Century American Poetry. YB-02

Twombly, Wells 1935-1977. . . . . .DLB-241

Twysden, Sir Roger 1597-1672 . . . . .DLB-213

Tyler, Anne
1941- DLB-6, 143; Y-82; CDALB-7

Tyler, Mary Palmer 1775-1866 . . . . .DLB-200

Tyler, Moses Coit 1835-1900 . . . . . . .DLB-47, 64

Tyler, Royall 1757-1826. . . . . .DLB-37

Tylor, Edward Burnett 1832-1917. . . . . . .DLB-57

Tynan, Katharine 1861-1931. . . . . . .DLB-153, 240

Tyndale, William circa 1494-1536 . . . . . .DLB-132

U

Uchida, Yoshika 1921-1992. . . . . .CDALB-7

Udall, Nicholas 1504-1556 . . . . DLB-62

Ugrêsić, Dubravka 1949- DLB-181

Uhland, Ludwig 1787-1862 . . . . DLB-90

Uhse, Bodo 1904-1963 . . . . DLB-69

Ujević, Augustin ("Tin")
1891-1955 . . . . DLB-147

Ulenhart, Niclas flourished circa 1600 . . . DLB-164

Ulibarrí, Sabine R. 1919- DLB-82

Ulica, Jorge 1870-1926 . . . . DLB-82

Ulitskaya, Liudmila Evgen'evna
1943- DLB-285

Ulivi, Ferruccio 1912- DLB-196

Ulizio, B. George 1889-1969 . . . . DLB-140

Ulrich von Liechtenstein
circa 1200-circa 1275 . . . . DLB-138

Ulrich von Zatzikhoven
before 1194-after 1214 . . . . DLB-138

Unaipon, David 1872-1967 . . . . DLB-230

Unamuno, Miguel de 1864-1936 . . . . DLB-108

Under, Marie 1883-1980 . . . DLB-220; CDWLB-4

Underhill, Evelyn 1875-1941 . . . . DLB-240

Ungaretti, Giuseppe 1888-1970 . . . . DLB-114

Unger, Friederike Helene 1741-1813 . . . . . DLB-94

United States Book Company DLB-49

Universal Publishing and Distributing
Corporation DLB-46

University of Colorado
Special Collections at the University of
Colorado at Boulder Y-98

Indiana University Press Y-02

The University of Iowa
Writers' Workshop Golden Jubilee Y-86

University of Missouri Press Y-01

University of South Carolina
The G. Ross Roy Scottish
Poetry Collection Y-89

Two Hundred Years of Rare Books and
Literary Collections at the
University of South Carolina Y-00

The University of South Carolina Press Y-94

University of Virginia
The Book Arts Press at the University
of Virginia Y-96

The Electronic Text Center and the
Electronic Archive of Early American
Fiction at the University of Virginia
Library Y-98

University of Virginia Libraries Y-91

University of Wales Press DLB-112

University Press of Florida Y-00

University Press of Kansas Y-98

University Press of Mississippi Y-99

Uno Chiyo 1897-1996 . . . . DLB-180

Unruh, Fritz von 1885-1970 . . . . DLB-56, 118

Unsworth, Barry 1930- DLB-194

Unt, Mati 1944- DLB-232

The Unterberg Poetry Center of the
92nd Street Y Y-98

T. Fisher Unwin [publishing house] DLB-106

Upchurch, Boyd B. (see Boyd, John)

Updike, John 1932- DLB-2, 5, 143, 218, 227;
Y-80, 82; DS-3; CDALB-6

John Updike on the Internet Y-97

Tribute to Alfred A. Knopf Y-84

Tribute to John Ciardi Y-86

Upīts, Andrejs 1877-1970 . . . . DLB-220

Upton, Bertha 1849-1912 . . . . DLB-141

Upton, Charles 1948- DLB-16

Upton, Florence K. 1873-1922 . . . . DLB-141

Upward, Allen 1863-1926 . . . . DLB-36

Urban, Milo 1904-1982 . . . . DLB-215

Ureña de Henríquez, Salomé
1850-1897 . . . . DLB-283

Urfé, Honoré d' 1567-1625 . . . . DLB-268

Urista, Alberto Baltazar (see Alurista)

Urquhart, Fred 1912-1995 . . . . DLB-139

Urrea, Luis Alberto 1955- DLB-209

Urzidil, Johannes 1896-1970 . . . . DLB-85

U.S.A. (Documentary) DLB-274

Usk, Thomas died 1388 . . . . DLB-146

Uslar Pietri, Arturo 1906-2001 . . . . DLB-113

Uspensky, Gleb Ivanovich 1843-1902 . . . . DLB-277

Ussher, James 1581-1656 . . . . DLB-213

Ustinov, Peter 1921- DLB-13

Uttley, Alison 1884-1976 . . . . DLB-160

Uz, Johann Peter 1720-1796 . . . . DLB-97

V

Vadianus, Joachim 1484-1551 . . . . DLB-179

Vac, Bertrand (Aimé Pelletier) 1914- . . . DLB-88

Vācietis, Ojārs 1933-1983 . . . . DLB-232

Vaculík, Ludvík 1926- DLB-232

Vaičiulaitis, Antanas 1906-1992 . . . . DLB-220

Vaičiūnaite, Judita 1937- DLB-232

Vail, Laurence 1891-1968 . . . . DLB-4

Vail, Petr L'vovich 1949- DLB-285

Vailland, Roger 1907-1965 . . . . DLB-83

Vaižgantas 1869-1933 . . . . DLB-220

Vajda, Ernest 1887-1954 . . . . DLB-44

Valdés, Gina 1943- DLB-122

Valdez, Luis Miguel 1940- DLB-122

Valduga, Patrizia 1953- DLB-128

Vale Press DLB-112

Valente, José Angel 1929-2000 . . . . DLB-108

Valenzuela, Luisa 1938- . . . DLB-113; CDWLB-3

Valeri, Diego 1887-1976 . . . . DLB-128

Valerius Flaccus fl. circa A.D. 92 . . . . . . DLB-211

Valerius Maximus fl. circa A.D. 31 . . . . . DLB-211

Valéry, Paul 1871-1945 . . . . DLB-258

Valesio, Paolo 1939- DLB-196

Valgardson, W. D. 1939- DLB-60

Valle, Víctor Manuel 1950- DLB-122

Valle-Inclán, Ramón del 1866-1936 . . . . . DLB-134

Vallejo, Armando 1949- DLB-122

Vallès, Jules 1832-1885 . . . . DLB-123

Vallette, Marguerite Eymery (see Rachilde)

Valverde, José María 1926-1996 . . . . . . DLB-108

Van Allsburg, Chris 1949- DLB-61

Van Anda, Carr 1864-1945 . . . . DLB-25

Vanbrugh, Sir John 1664-1726 . . . . DLB-80

Vance, Jack 1916?- DLB-8

Vančura, Vladislav
1891-1942 . . . . DLB-215; CDWLB-4

van der Post, Laurens 1906-1996 . . . . . . DLB-204

Van Dine, S. S. (see Wright, Williard Huntington)

Van Doren, Mark 1894-1972 . . . . DLB-45

van Druten, John 1901-1957 . . . . DLB-10

Van Duyn, Mona 1921- DLB-5

Tribute to James Dickey Y-97

Van Dyke, Henry 1852-1933 . . . . . DLB-71; DS-13

Van Dyke, Henry 1928- DLB-33

Van Dyke, John C. 1856-1932 . . . . DLB-186

Vane, Sutton 1888-1963 . . . . DLB-10

Vanguard Press DLB-46

van Gulik, Robert Hans 1910-1967 . . . . DS-17

van Itallie, Jean-Claude 1936- DLB-7

Van Loan, Charles E. 1876-1919 . . . . DLB-171

Vann, Robert L. 1879-1940 . . . . DLB-29

Van Rensselaer, Mariana Griswold
1851-1934 . . . . DLB-47

Van Rensselaer, Mrs. Schuyler
(see Van Rensselaer, Mariana Griswold)

Van Vechten, Carl 1880-1964 . . . . . . DLB-4, 9, 51

van Vogt, A. E. 1912-2000 . . . . DLB-8, 251

Vargas Llosa, Mario
1936- DLB-145; CDWLB-3

Acceptance Speech for the Ritz Paris
Hemingway Award Y-85

Varley, John 1947- Y-81

Varnhagen von Ense, Karl August
1785-1858 . . . . DLB-90

Varnhagen von Ense, Rahel
1771-1833 . . . . DLB-90

Varro 116 B.C.-27 B.C. DLB-211

Vasilenko, Svetlana Vladimirovna
1956- DLB-285

Vasiliu, George (see Bacovia, George)

Vásquez, Richard 1928- DLB-209

Vásquez Montalbán, Manuel 1939- . . . DLB-134

Vassa, Gustavus (see Equiano, Olaudah)

Vassalli, Sebastiano 1941- DLB-128, 196

Vaugelas, Claude Favre de 1585-1650 . . . . DLB-268

Vaughan, Henry 1621-1695 . . . . DLB-131

Vaughan, Thomas 1621-1666 . . . . DLB-131

Vaughn, Robert 1592?-1667 . . . . DLB-213

Vaux, Thomas, Lord 1509-1556 . . . . DLB-132

Vazov, Ivan 1850-1921 . . . . . DLB-147; CDWLB-4

Véa, Alfredo, Jr. 1950- DLB-209

Veblen, Thorstein 1857-1929 . . . . DLB-246

Vega, Janine Pommy 1942- DLB-16

Veiller, Anthony 1903-1965 . . . . DLB-44

Velásquez-Trevino, Gloria 1949- DLB-122

Veley, Margaret 1843-1887 . . . . DLB-199

Velleius Paterculus
circa 20 B.C.-circa A.D. 30 . . . . DLB-211

Veloz Maggiolo, Marcio 1936- DLB-145

Vel'tman, Aleksandr Fomich
1800-1870 . . . . DLB-198

Venegas, Daniel ?-? DLB-82

Venevitinov, Dmitrii Vladimirovich
1805-1827 . . . . DLB-205

Vergil, Polydore circa 1470-1555 . . . . DLB-132

Veríssimo, Erico 1905-1975 . . . . DLB-145

Verlaine, Paul 1844-1896. . . . . DLB-217

Verne, Jules 1828-1905 . . . . DLB-123

Verplanck, Gulian C. 1786-1870 . . . . DLB-59

Very, Jones 1813-1880. . . . . DLB-1, 243; DS-5

Vian, Boris 1920-1959. . . . . DLB-72

Viazemsky, Petr Andreevich
1792-1878. . . . . DLB-205

Vicars, Thomas 1591-1638 . . . . DLB-236

Vickers, Roy 1888?-1965. . . . . DLB-77

Vickery, Sukey 1779-1821 . . . . DLB-200

Victoria 1819-1901 . . . . DLB-55

Victoria Press. DLB-106

Vidal, Gore 1925- DLB-6, 152; CDALB-7

Vidal, Mary Theresa 1815-1873 . . . . DLB-230

Vidmer, Richards 1898-1978 . . . . DLB-241

Viebig, Clara 1860-1952 . . . . DLB-66

Viereck, George Sylvester 1884-1962 . . . . . DLB-54

Viereck, Peter 1916- DLB-5

Vietnam War (ended 1975)
Resources for the Study of Vietnam War
Literature DLB-9

Viets, Roger 1738-1811 . . . . DLB-99

Vigil-Piñon, Evangelina 1949- DLB-122

Vigneault, Gilles 1928- DLB-60

Vigny, Alfred de
1797-1863. . . . . DLB-119, 192, 217

Vigolo, Giorgio 1894-1983 . . . . DLB-114

The Viking Press DLB-46

Vilde, Eduard 1865-1933. . . . . DLB-220

Vilinskaia, Mariia Aleksandrovna
(see Vovchok, Marko)

Villanueva, Alma Luz 1944- DLB-122

Villanueva, Tino 1941- DLB-82

Villard, Henry 1835-1900 . . . . DLB-23

Villard, Oswald Garrison 1872-1949 . . . DLB-25, 91

Villarreal, Edit 1944- DLB-209

Villarreal, José Antonio 1924- DLB-82

Villaseñor, Victor 1940- DLB-209

Villedieu, Madame de (Marie-Catherine
Desjardins) 1640?-1683. . . . . DLB-268

Villegas de Magnón, Leonor
1876-1955 . . . . DLB-122

Villehardouin, Geoffroi de
circa 1150-1215 . . . . DLB-208

Villemaire, Yolande 1949- DLB-60

Villena, Luis Antonio de 1951- DLB-134

Villiers, George, Second Duke
of Buckingham 1628-1687. . . . . DLB-80

Villiers de l'Isle-Adam, Jean-Marie
Mathias Philippe-Auguste,
Comte de 1838-1889. . . . . DLB-123, 192

Villon, François 1431-circa 1463? DLB-208

Vine Press DLB-112

Viorst, Judith ?- DLB-52

Vipont, Elfrida (Elfrida Vipont Foulds,
Charles Vipont) 1902-1992. . . . . DLB-160

Viramontes, Helena María 1954- DLB-122

Virgil 70 B.C.-19 B.C. DLB-211; CDWLB-1

Vischer, Friedrich Theodor 1807-1887 . . . DLB-133

Vitier, Cintio 1921- DLB-283

Vitruvius circa 85 B.C.-circa 15 B.C. DLB-211

Vitry, Philippe de 1291-1361 . . . . DLB-208

Vittorini, Elio 1908-1966 . . . . DLB-264

Vivanco, Luis Felipe 1907-1975 . . . . DLB-108

Vivian, E. Charles (Charles Henry Cannell,
Charles Henry Vivian, Jack Mann,
Barry Lynd) 1882-1947. . . . . DLB-255

Viviani, Cesare 1947- DLB-128

Vivien, Renée 1877-1909 . . . . DLB-217

Vizenor, Gerald 1934- DLB-175, 227

Vizetelly and Company DLB-106

Voaden, Herman 1903-1991 . . . . DLB-88

Voß, Johann Heinrich 1751-1826 . . . . DLB-90

Vogau, Boris Andreevich
(see Pil'niak, Boris Andreevich)

Voigt, Ellen Bryant 1943- DLB-120

Vojnović, Ivo 1857-1929 . . . . DLB-147; CDWLB-4

Volkoff, Vladimir 1932- DLB-83

P. F. Volland Company DLB-46

Vollbehr, Otto H. F.
1872?-1945 or 1946. . . . . DLB-187

Vologdin (see Zasodimsky, Pavel Vladimirovich)

Volponi, Paolo 1924-1994 . . . . DLB-177

Vonarburg, Élisabeth 1947- DLB-251

von der Grün, Max 1926- DLB-75

Vonnegut, Kurt 1922-
. . . . . . DLB-2, 8, 152; Y-80; DS-3; CDALB-6

Tribute to Isaac Asimov Y-92

Tribute to Richard Brautigan Y-84

Voranc, Prežihov 1893-1950 . . . . DLB-147

Voronsky, Aleksandr Konstantinovich
1884-1937 . . . . DLB-272

Vovchok, Marko 1833-1907 . . . . DLB-238

Voynich, E. L. 1864-1960 . . . . DLB-197

Vroman, Mary Elizabeth circa 1924-1967 . . DLB-33

W

Wace, Robert ("Maistre")
circa 1100-circa 1175 . . . . DLB-146

Wackenroder, Wilhelm Heinrich
1773-1798. . . . . DLB-90

Wackernagel, Wilhelm 1806-1869 . . . . . DLB-133

Waddell, Helen 1889-1965 . . . . DLB-240

Waddington, Miriam 1917- DLB-68

Wade, Henry 1887-1969 . . . . DLB-77

Wagenknecht, Edward 1900- DLB-103

Wägner, Elin 1882-1949 . . . . DLB-259

Wagner, Heinrich Leopold 1747-1779 . . . . DLB-94

Wagner, Henry R. 1862-1957 . . . . DLB-140

Wagner, Richard 1813-1883 . . . . DLB-129

Wagoner, David 1926- DLB-5, 256

Wah, Fred 1939- DLB-60

Waiblinger, Wilhelm 1804-1830 . . . . DLB-90

Wain, John
1925-1994 . . . DLB-15, 27, 139, 155; CDBLB-8

Tribute to J. B. Priestly Y-84

Wainwright, Jeffrey 1944- DLB-40

Waite, Peirce and Company DLB-49

Wakeman, Stephen H. 1859-1924. . . . . . . DLB-187

Wakoski, Diane 1937- DLB-5

Walahfrid Strabo circa 808-849. . . . . DLB-148

Henry Z. Walck [publishing house]. DLB-46

Walcott, Derek
1930- DLB-117; Y-81, 92; CDWLB-3

Nobel Lecture 1992: The Antilles:
Fragments of Epic Memory Y-92

Robert Waldegrave [publishing house] . . . DLB-170

Waldis, Burkhard circa 1490-1556? DLB-178

Waldman, Anne 1945- DLB-16

Waldrop, Rosmarie 1935- DLB-169

Walker, Alice 1900-1982 . . . . DLB-201

Walker, Alice
1944- DLB-6, 33, 143; CDALB-6

Walker, Annie Louisa (Mrs. Harry Coghill)
circa 1836-1907 . . . . DLB-240

Walker, George F. 1947- DLB-60

Walker, John Brisben 1847-1931 . . . . DLB-79

Walker, Joseph A. 1935- DLB-38

Walker, Margaret 1915-1998. . . . . . . DLB-76, 152

Walker, Obadiah 1616-1699 . . . . DLB-281

Walker, Ted 1934- DLB-40

Walker, Evans and Cogswell Company . . . DLB-49

Wall, John F. (see Sarban)

Wallace, Alfred Russel 1823-1913 . . . . DLB-190

Wallace, Dewitt 1889-1981 . . . . DLB-137

Wallace, Edgar 1875-1932 . . . . DLB-70

Wallace, Lew 1827-1905 . . . . DLB-202

Wallace, Lila Acheson 1889-1984 . . . . DLB-137

"A Word of Thanks," From the Initial
Issue of *Reader's Digest*
(February 1922) DLB-137

Wallace, Naomi 1960- DLB-249

Wallace Markfield's "Steeplechase" Y-02

Wallant, Edward Lewis
1926-1962 . . . . DLB-2, 28, 143

Waller, Edmund 1606-1687. . . . . DLB-126

Walpole, Horace 1717-1797 . . . . . DLB-39, 104, 213

Preface to the First Edition of
The Castle of Otranto (1764) DLB-39, 178

Preface to the Second Edition of
The Castle of Otranto (1765) DLB-39, 178

Walpole, Hugh 1884-1941 . . . . DLB-34

Walrond, Eric 1898-1966 . . . . DLB-51

Walser, Martin 1927- DLB-75, 124

Walser, Robert 1878-1956 . . . . DLB-66

Walsh, Ernest 1895-1926 . . . . DLB-4, 45

Walsh, Robert 1784-1859 . . . . DLB-59

Walters, Henry 1848-1931 . . . . DLB-140

Waltharius circa 825 . . . . DLB-148

Walther von der Vogelweide
circa 1170-circa 1230 . . . . DLB-138

Walton, Izaak
1593-1683 . . . . DLB-151, 213; CDBLB-1

Wambaugh, Joseph 1937- DLB-6; Y-83

Wand, Alfred Rudolph 1828-1891 . . . . . . DLB-188

Waniek, Marilyn Nelson 1946- DLB-120

Wanley, Humphrey 1672-1726 . . . . DLB-213

War of the Words (and Pictures):
The Creation of a Graphic Novel Y-02

Warburton, William 1698-1779 . . . . DLB-104

Ward, Aileen 1919- DLB-111

Ward, Artemus (see Browne, Charles Farrar)

Ward, Arthur Henry Sarsfield (see Rohmer, Sax)

Ward, Douglas Turner 1930- DLB-7, 38

Ward, Mrs. Humphry 1851-1920 . . . . DLB-18

Ward, James 1843-1925 . . . . DLB-262

Ward, Lynd 1905-1985 . . . . DLB-22

Ward, Lock and Company DLB-106

Ward, Nathaniel circa 1578-1652 . . . . DLB-24

Ward, Theodore 1902-1983 . . . . DLB-76

Wardle, Ralph 1909-1988 . . . . DLB-103

Ware, Henry, Jr. 1794-1843 . . . . DLB-235

Ware, William 1797-1852 . . . . DLB-1, 235

Warfield, Catherine Ann 1816-1877 . . . . . . DLB-248

Waring, Anna Letitia 1823-1910 . . . . DLB-240

Frederick Warne and Company [U.K.] DLB-106

Frederick Warne and Company [U.S.] DLB-49

Warner, Anne 1869-1913 . . . . DLB-202

Warner, Charles Dudley 1829-1900 . . . . . . DLB-64

Warner, Marina 1946- DLB-194

Warner, Rex 1905-1986 . . . . DLB-15

Warner, Susan 1819-1885 . . . DLB-3, 42, 239, 250

Warner, Sylvia Townsend
1893-1978 . . . . DLB-34, 139

Warner, William 1558-1609 . . . . .DLB-172

Warner Books DLB-46

Warr, Bertram 1917-1943 . . . . DLB-88

Warren, John Byrne Leicester (see De Tabley, Lord)

Warren, Lella 1899-1982 . . . . .Y-83

Warren, Mercy Otis 1728-1814 . . . . . DLB-31, 200

Warren, Robert Penn 1905-1989
. . . . DLB-2, 48, 152; Y-80, 89; CDALB-6

Tribute to Katherine Anne Porter Y-80

Warren, Samuel 1807-1877 . . . . DLB-190

Die Wartburgkrieg circa 1230-circa 1280 . . . DLB-138

Warton, Joseph 1722-1800 . . . . DLB-104, 109

Warton, Thomas 1728-1790 . . . . DLB-104, 109

Warung, Price (William Astley)
1855-1911 . . . . DLB-230

Washington, George 1732-1799 . . . . DLB-31

Washington, Ned 1901-1976 . . . . DLB-265

Wassermann, Jakob 1873-1934 . . . . DLB-66

Wasserstein, Wendy 1950- DLB-228

Wasson, David Atwood 1823-1887 . . . DLB-1, 223

Watanna, Onoto (see Eaton, Winnifred)

Waterhouse, Keith 1929- DLB-13, 15

Waterman, Andrew 1940- DLB-40

Waters, Frank 1902-1995 . . . . .DLB-212; Y-86

Waters, Michael 1949- DLB-120

Watkins, Tobias 1780-1855 . . . . DLB-73

Watkins, Vernon 1906-1967 . . . . DLB-20

Watmough, David 1926- DLB-53

Watson, Colin 1920-1983 . . . . .DLB-276

Watson, Ian 1943- DLB-261

Watson, James Wreford (see Wreford, James)

Watson, John 1850-1907 . . . . DLB-156

Watson, Rosamund Marriott
(Graham R. Tomson) 1860-1911 . . . . DLB-240

Watson, Sheila 1909-1998 . . . . DLB-60

Watson, Thomas 1545?-1592 . . . . DLB-132

Watson, Wilfred 1911- DLB-60

W. J. Watt and Company DLB-46

Watten, Barrett 1948- DLB-193

Watterson, Henry 1840-1921 . . . . DLB-25

Watts, Alan 1915-1973 . . . . DLB-16

Watts, Isaac 1674-1748 . . . . DLB-95

Franklin Watts [publishing house] DLB-46

Waugh, Alec 1898-1981 . . . . DLB-191

Waugh, Auberon 1939-2000 . . .DLB-14, 194; Y-00

Waugh, Evelyn
1903-1966 . . . . . DLB-15, 162, 195; CDBLB-6

Way and Williams DLB-49

Wayman, Tom 1945- DLB-53

Weatherly, Tom 1942- DLB-41

Weaver, Gordon 1937- DLB-130

Weaver, Robert 1921- DLB-88

Webb, Beatrice 1858-1943 . . . . DLB-190

Webb, Francis 1925-1973 . . . . DLB-260

Webb, Frank J. ?-? DLB-50

Webb, James Watson 1802-1884 . . . . DLB-43

Webb, Mary 1881-1927 . . . . DLB-34

Webb, Phyllis 1927- DLB-53

Webb, Sidney 1859-1947 . . . . DLB-190

Webb, Walter Prescott 1888-1963 . . . . DLB-17

Webbe, William ?-1591 . . . . DLB-132

Webber, Charles Wilkins 1819-1856? . . . DLB-202

Webling, Lucy (Lucy Betty MacRaye)
1877-1952 . . . . DLB-240

Webling, Peggy (Arthur Weston)
1871-1949 . . . . DLB-240

Webster, Augusta 1837-1894 . . . . DLB-35, 240

Webster, John
1579 or 1580-1634? DLB-58; CDBLB-1

The Melbourne Manuscript Y-86

Webster, Noah
1758-1843 . . . . DLB-1, 37, 42, 43, 73, 243

Webster, Paul Francis 1907-1984 . . . . . . DLB-265

Charles L. Webster and Company DLB-49

Weckherlin, Georg Rodolf 1584-1653 . . . DLB-164

Wedekind, Frank
1864-1918 . . . . .DLB-118; CDWLB-2

Weeks, Edward Augustus, Jr. 1898-1989 . .DLB-137

Weeks, Stephen B. 1865-1918 . . . . .DLB-187

Weems, Mason Locke 1759-1825 . . .DLB-30, 37, 42

Weerth, Georg 1822-1856 . . . . DLB-129

Weidenfeld and Nicolson DLB-112

Weidman, Jerome 1913-1998 . . . . DLB-28

Weigl, Bruce 1949- DLB-120

Weinbaum, Stanley Grauman 1902-1935 . . DLB-8

Weiner, Andrew 1949- DLB-251

Weintraub, Stanley 1929- DLB-111; Y82

Weise, Christian 1642-1708 . . . . DLB-168

Weisenborn, Gunther 1902-1969 . . . . DLB-69, 124

Weiss, John 1818-1879 . . . . DLB-1, 243

Weiss, Paul 1901-2002 . . . . .DLB-279

Weiss, Peter 1916-1982 . . . . DLB-69, 124

Weiss, Theodore 1916- DLB-5

Weiß, Ernst 1882-1940 . . . . DLB-81

Weiße, Christian Felix 1726-1804 . . . . DLB-97

Weitling, Wilhelm 1808-1871 . . . . DLB-129

Welch, James 1940- DLB-175, 256

Welch, Lew 1926-1971? DLB-16

Weldon, Fay 1931- DLB-14, 194; CDBLB-8

Wellek, René 1903-1995 . . . . DLB-63

Wells, Carolyn 1862-1942 . . . . DLB-11

Wells, Charles Jeremiah
circa 1800-1879 . . . . DLB-32

Wells, Gabriel 1862-1946 . . . . DLB-140

Wells, H. G.
1866-1946 . . .DLB-34, 70, 156, 178; CDBLB-6

H. G. Wells Society Y-98

Preface to The Scientific Romances of
H. G. Wells (1933) DLB-178

Wells, Helena 1758?-1824 . . . . DLB-200

Wells, Robert 1947- DLB-40

Wells-Barnett, Ida B. 1862-1931 . . . . . DLB-23, 221

Welsh, Irvine 1958- DLB-271

Welty, Eudora 1909-2001 . . . . . . DLB-2, 102, 143;
Y-87, 01; DS-12; CDALB-1

Eudora Welty: Eye of the Storyteller Y-87

Eudora Welty Newsletter Y-99

Eudora Welty's Funeral Y-01

Eudora Welty's Ninetieth Birthday Y-99

Eudora Welty Remembered in
Two Exhibits Y-02

Wendell, Barrett 1855-1921 . . . . DLB-71

Wentworth, Patricia 1878-1961 . . . . DLB-77

Wentworth, William Charles 1790-1872 . DLB-230

Werder, Diederich von dem 1584-1657 . . DLB-164

Werfel, Franz 1890-1945 . . . . .DLB-81, 124

Werner, Zacharias 1768-1823 . . . . .DLB-94

The Werner Company DLB-49

Wersba, Barbara 1932- DLB-52

Wescott, Glenway
1901-1987 . . . . .DLB-4, 9, 102; DS-15

Wesker, Arnold 1932- DLB-13; CDBLB-8

Wesley, Charles 1707-1788. . . . . .DLB-95

Wesley, John 1703-1791. . . . . .DLB-104

Wesley, Mary 1912-2002. . . . . .DLB-231

Wesley, Richard 1945- DLB-38

A. Wessels and Company DLB-46

Wessobrunner Gebet circa 787-815 . . . . .DLB-148

West, Anthony 1914-1988. . . . . .DLB-15

    Tribute to Liam O'Flaherty. Y-84

West, Cheryl L. 1957- DLB-266

West, Cornel 1953- DLB-246

West, Dorothy 1907-1998 . . . . .DLB-76

West, Jessamyn 1902-1984 . . . . .DLB-6; Y-84

West, Mae 1892-1980 . . . . .DLB-44

West, Michelle Sagara 1963- DLB-251

West, Nathanael
1903-1940 . . . . .DLB-4, 9, 28; CDALB-5

West, Paul 1930- DLB-14

West, Rebecca 1892-1983 . . . . .DLB-36; Y-83

West, Richard 1941- DLB-185

West and Johnson DLB-49

Westcott, Edward Noyes 1846-1898 . . . . .DLB-202

The Western Literature Association Y-99

The Western Messenger
1835-1841 . . . . DLB-1; DLB-223

Western Publishing Company. DLB-46

Western Writers of America Y-99

The Westminster Review 1824-1914 . . . . . . .DLB-110

Weston, Arthur (see Webling, Peggy)

Weston, Elizabeth Jane circa 1582-1612 . .DLB-172

Wetherald, Agnes Ethelwyn 1857-1940 . . . .DLB-99

Wetherell, Elizabeth (see Warner, Susan)

Wetherell, W. D. 1948- DLB-234

Wetzel, Friedrich Gottlob 1779-1819 . . . . .DLB-90

Weyman, Stanley J. 1855-1928 . . . . .DLB-141, 156

Wezel, Johann Karl 1747-1819 . . . . .DLB-94

Whalen, Philip 1923-2002 . . . . .DLB-16

Whalley, George 1915-1983 . . . . .DLB-88

Wharton, Edith 1862-1937
. . . . . DLB-4, 9, 12, 78, 189; DS-13; CDALB-3

Wharton, William 1920s?- Y-80

Whately, Mary Louisa 1824-1889 . . . . . . .DLB-166

Whately, Richard 1787-1863 . . . . .DLB-190

  Elements of Rhetoric (1828;
    revised, 1846) [excerpt]. DLB-57

Wheatley, Dennis 1897-1977 . . . . DLB-77, 255

Wheatley, Phillis
circa 1754-1784 . . . . . . .DLB-31, 50; CDALB-2

Wheeler, Anna Doyle 1785-1848? DLB-158

Wheeler, Charles Stearns 1816-1843 . . .DLB-1, 223

Wheeler, Monroe 1900-1988. . . . . .DLB-4

Wheelock, John Hall 1886-1978 . . . . .DLB-45

  From John Hall Wheelock's
    Oral Memoir Y-01

Wheelwright, J. B. 1897-1940 . . . . .DLB-45

Wheelwright, John circa 1592-1679 . . . . . .DLB-24

Whetstone, George 1550-1587 . . . . .DLB-136

Whetstone, Colonel Pete (see Noland, C. F. M.)

Whewell, William 1794-1866. . . . . .DLB-262

Whichcote, Benjamin 1609?-1683 . . . . . . .DLB-252

Whicher, Stephen E. 1915-1961 . . . . . . .DLB-111

Whipple, Edwin Percy 1819-1886 . . . . . .DLB-1, 64

Whitaker, Alexander 1585-1617 . . . . .DLB-24

Whitaker, Daniel K. 1801-1881. . . . . .DLB-73

Whitcher, Frances Miriam
1812-1852 . . . . .DLB-11, 202

White, Andrew 1579-1656. . . . . .DLB-24

White, Andrew Dickson 1832-1918 . . . . . .DLB-47

White, E. B. 1899-1985 . . . .DLB-11, 22; CDALB-7

White, Edgar B. 1947- DLB-38

White, Edmund 1940- DLB-227

White, Ethel Lina 1887-1944 . . . . .DLB-77

White, Hayden V. 1928- DLB-246

White, Henry Kirke 1785-1806 . . . . .DLB-96

White, Horace 1834-1916 . . . . .DLB-23

White, James 1928-1999 . . . . .DLB-261

White, Patrick 1912-1990 . . . . .DLB-260

White, Phyllis Dorothy James (see James, P. D.)

White, Richard Grant 1821-1885 . . . . .DLB-64

White, T. H. 1906-1964 . . . . .DLB-160, 255

White, Walter 1893-1955 . . . . .DLB-51

William White and Company DLB-49

White, William Allen 1868-1944 . . . . . .DLB-9, 25

White, William Anthony Parker
(see Boucher, Anthony)

White, William Hale (see Rutherford, Mark)

Whitechurch, Victor L. 1868-1933 . . . . . .DLB-70

Whitehead, Alfred North
1861-1947 . . . . .DLB-100, 262

Whitehead, James 1936- Y-81

Whitehead, William 1715-1785 . . . . .DLB-84, 109

Whitfield, James Monroe 1822-1871 . . . . .DLB-50

Whitfield, Raoul 1898-1945. . . . . .DLB-226

Whitgift, John circa 1533-1604 . . . . .DLB-132

Whiting, John 1917-1963 . . . . .DLB-13

Whiting, Samuel 1597-1679 . . . . .DLB-24

Whitlock, Brand 1869-1934. . . . . .DLB-12

Whitman, Albery Allson 1851-1901 . . . . . .DLB-50

Whitman, Alden 1913-1990. . . . . Y-91

Whitman, Sarah Helen (Power)
1803-1878 . . . . .DLB-1, 243

Whitman, Walt
1819-1892 . . . .DLB-3, 64, 224, 250; CDALB-2

Albert Whitman and Company. DLB-46

Whitman Publishing Company. DLB-46

Whitney, Geoffrey 1548 or 1552?-1601 . .DLB-136

Whitney, Isabella flourished 1566-1573. . .DLB-136

Whitney, John Hay 1904-1982 . . . . .DLB-127

Whittemore, Reed 1919-1995 . . . . .DLB-5

Whittier, John Greenleaf
1807-1892 . . . . .DLB-1, 243; CDALB-2

Whittlesey House DLB-46

Wickham, Anna (Edith Alice Mary Harper)
1884-1947 .DLB-240

Wickram, Georg circa 1505-circa 1561 . . .DLB-179

Wicomb, Zoë 1948- DLB-225

Wideman, John Edgar 1941- DLB-33, 143

Widener, Harry Elkins 1885-1912 . . . . . .DLB-140

Wiebe, Rudy 1934- DLB-60

Wiechert, Ernst 1887-1950. . . . . .DLB-56

Wied, Martina 1882-1957 . . . . .DLB-85

Wiehe, Evelyn May Clowes (see Mordaunt, Elinor)

Wieland, Christoph Martin 1733-1813 . . . .DLB-97

Wienbarg, Ludolf 1802-1872. . . . . .DLB-133

Wieners, John 1934- DLB-16

Wier, Ester 1910- DLB-52

Wiesel, Elie
1928- DLB-83; Y-86, 87; CDALB-7

  Nobel Lecture 1986: Hope, Despair and
    Memory Y-86

Wiggin, Kate Douglas 1856-1923 . . . . . . .DLB-42

Wigglesworth, Michael 1631-1705. . . . . . .DLB-24

Wilberforce, William 1759-1833 . . . . . . .DLB-158

Wilbrandt, Adolf 1837-1911 . . . . .DLB-129

Wilbur, Richard 1921-   . . .DLB-5, 169; CDALB-7

  Tribute to Robert Penn Warren Y-89

Wild, Peter 1940- DLB-5

Wilde, Lady Jane Francesca Elgee
1821?-1896 . . . . .DLB-199

Wilde, Oscar 1854-1900 . . . . . .DLB-10, 19, 34, 57,
141, 156, 190; CDBLB-5

  "The Critic as Artist" (1891). DLB-57

  "The Decay of Lying" (1889) DLB-18

  "The English Renaissance of
    Art" (1908) DLB-35

  "L'Envoi" (1882). DLB-35

  Oscar Wilde Conference at Hofstra
    University. Y-00

Wilde, Richard Henry 1789-1847 . . . . . .DLB-3, 59

W. A. Wilde Company DLB-49

Wilder, Billy 1906- DLB-26

Wilder, Laura Ingalls 1867-1957 . . . . .DLB-22, 256

Wilder, Thornton
1897-1975. . . . . . . .DLB-4, 7, 9, 228; CDALB-7

  Thornton Wilder Centenary at Yale. Y-97

Wildgans, Anton 1881-1932 . . . . .DLB-118

Wiley, Bell Irvin 1906-1980. . . . . .DLB-17

John Wiley and Sons DLB-49

Wilhelm, Kate 1928- DLB-8

Wilkes, Charles 1798-1877. . . . . .DLB-183

Wilkes, George 1817-1885 . . . . .DLB-79

Wilkins, John 1614-1672 . . . . .DLB-236

Wilkinson, Anne 1910-1961 . . . . .DLB-88

Wilkinson, Eliza Yonge
1757-circa 1813 . . . . DLB-200

Wilkinson, Sylvia 1940- Y-86

Wilkinson, William Cleaver 1833-1920 . . . DLB-71

Willard, Barbara 1909-1994 . . . . DLB-161

Willard, Emma 1787-1870 . . . . DLB-239

Willard, Frances E. 1839-1898 . . . . DLB-221

Willard, Nancy 1936- DLB-5, 52

Willard, Samuel 1640-1707 . . . . DLB-24

L. Willard [publishing house] DLB-49

Willeford, Charles 1919-1988 . . . . DLB-226

William of Auvergne 1190-1249 . . . . DLB-115

William of Conches
circa 1090-circa 1154 . . . . DLB-115

William of Ockham circa 1285-1347 . . . . DLB-115

William of Sherwood
1200/1205-1266/1271 . . . . DLB-115

The William Charvat American Fiction
Collection at the Ohio State
University Libraries Y-92

Williams, Ben Ames 1889-1953 . . . . DLB-102

Williams, C. K. 1936- DLB-5

Williams, Chancellor 1905-1992 . . . . DLB-76

Williams, Charles 1886-1945 . . .DLB-100, 153, 255

Williams, Denis 1923-1998 . . . . DLB-117

Williams, Emlyn 1905-1987 . . . . .DLB-10, 77

Williams, Garth 1912-1996 . . . . DLB-22

Williams, George Washington
1849-1891 . . . . DLB-47

Williams, Heathcote 1941- DLB-13

Williams, Helen Maria 1761-1827 . . . . . . DLB-158

Williams, Hugo 1942- DLB-40

Williams, Isaac 1802-1865 . . . . DLB-32

Williams, Joan 1928- DLB-6

Williams, Joe 1889-1972 . . . . DLB-241

Williams, John A. 1925- DLB-2, 33

Williams, John E. 1922-1994 . . . . DLB-6

Williams, Jonathan 1929- DLB-5

Williams, Miller 1930- DLB-105

Williams, Nigel 1948- DLB-231

Williams, Raymond
1921-1988 . . . . DLB-14, 231, 242

Williams, Roger circa 1603-1683 . . . . DLB-24

Williams, Rowland 1817-1870 . . . . DLB-184

Williams, Samm-Art 1946- DLB-38

Williams, Sherley Anne 1944-1999 . . . . . DLB-41

Williams, T. Harry 1909-1979 . . . . DLB-17

Williams, Tennessee
1911-1983 . . . . . DLB-7; Y-83; DS-4; CDALB-1

Williams, Terry Tempest 1955- . . .DLB-206, 275

Williams, Ursula Moray 1911- DLB-160

Williams, Valentine 1883-1946 . . . . DLB-77

Williams, William Appleman 1921- DLB-17

Williams, William Carlos
1883-1963 . . . . . DLB-4, 16, 54, 86; CDALB-4

The William Carlos Williams Society Y-99

Williams, Wirt 1921- DLB-6

A. Williams and Company DLB-49

Williams Brothers DLB-49

Williamson, Henry 1895-1977 . . . . DLB-191

The Henry Williamson Society Y-98

Williamson, Jack 1908- DLB-8

Willingham, Calder Baynard, Jr.
1922-1995 . . . . DLB-2, 44

Williram of Ebersberg circa 1020-1085 . . DLB-148

Willis, John circa 1572-1625 . . . . DLB-281

Willis, Nathaniel Parker 1806-1867
. . . . .DLB-3, 59, 73, 74, 183, 250; DS-13

Willkomm, Ernst 1810-1886 . . . . DLB-133

Wills, Garry 1934- DLB-246

Tribute to Kenneth Dale McCormick Y-97

Willson, Meredith 1902-1984 . . . . DLB-265

Willumsen, Dorrit 1940- DLB-214

Wilmer, Clive 1945- DLB-40

Wilson, A. N. 1950- DLB-14, 155, 194

Wilson, Angus 1913-1991 . . . . . .DLB-15, 139, 155

Wilson, Arthur 1595-1652 . . . . DLB-58

Wilson, August 1945- DLB-228

Wilson, Augusta Jane Evans 1835-1909 . . . DLB-42

Wilson, Colin 1931- DLB-14, 194

Tribute to J. B. Priestly Y-84

Wilson, Edmund 1895-1972 . . . . DLB-63

Wilson, Ethel 1888-1980 . . . . DLB-68

Wilson, F. P. 1889-1963 . . . . DLB-201

Wilson, Harriet E.
1827/1828?-1863? DLB-50, 239, 243

Wilson, Harry Leon 1867-1939 . . . . DLB-9

Wilson, John 1588-1667 . . . . DLB-24

Wilson, John 1785-1854 . . . . DLB-110

Wilson, John Anthony Burgess
(see Burgess, Anthony)

Wilson, John Dover 1881-1969 . . . . DLB-201

Wilson, Lanford 1937- DLB-7

Wilson, Margaret 1882-1973 . . . . DLB-9

Wilson, Michael 1914-1978 . . . . DLB-44

Wilson, Mona 1872-1954 . . . . DLB-149

Wilson, Robert Charles 1953- DLB-251

Wilson, Robert McLiam 1964- DLB-267

Wilson, Robley 1930- DLB-218

Wilson, Romer 1891-1930 . . . . DLB-191

Wilson, Thomas 1524-1581 . . . . . . DLB-132, 236

Wilson, Woodrow 1856-1924 . . . . DLB-47

Effingham Wilson [publishing house] DLB-154

Wimpfeling, Jakob 1450-1528 . . . . .DLB-179

Wimsatt, William K., Jr. 1907-1975 . . . . . DLB-63

Winchell, Walter 1897-1972 . . . . DLB-29

J. Winchester [publishing house] DLB-49

Winckelmann, Johann Joachim
1717-1768 . . . . DLB-97

Winckler, Paul 1630-1686 . . . . DLB-164

Wind, Herbert Warren 1916- DLB-171

John Windet [publishing house] DLB-170

Windham, Donald 1920- DLB-6

Wing, Donald Goddard 1904-1972 . . . . . .DLB-187

Wing, John M. 1844-1917 . . . . .DLB-187

Allan Wingate [publishing house] DLB-112

Winnemucca, Sarah 1844-1921 . . . . .DLB-175

Winnifrith, Tom 1938- DLB-155

Winsloe, Christa 1888-1944 . . . . DLB-124

Winslow, Anna Green 1759-1780 . . . . DLB-200

Winsor, Justin 1831-1897 . . . . DLB-47

John C. Winston Company DLB-49

Winters, Yvor 1900-1968 . . . . DLB-48

Winterson, Jeanette 1959- DLB-207, 261

Winthrop, John 1588-1649 . . . . DLB-24, 30

Winthrop, John, Jr. 1606-1676 . . . . DLB-24

Winthrop, Margaret Tyndal 1591-1647 . . DLB-200

Winthrop, Theodore 1828-1861 . . . . DLB-202

Wirt, William 1772-1834 . . . . DLB-37

Wise, John 1652-1725 . . . . DLB-24

Wise, Thomas James 1859-1937 . . . . DLB-184

Wiseman, Adele 1928-1992 . . . . DLB-88

Wishart and Company DLB-112

Wisner, George 1812-1849 . . . . DLB-43

Wister, Owen 1860-1938 . . . . .DLB-9, 78, 186

Wister, Sarah 1761-1804 . . . . DLB-200

Wither, George 1588-1667 . . . . DLB-121

Witherspoon, John 1723-1794 . . . . DLB-31

The Works of the Rev. John Witherspoon
(1800-1801) [excerpts] DLB-31

Withrow, William Henry 1839-1908 . . . . . DLB-99

Witkacy (see Witkiewicz, Stanisław Ignacy)

Witkiewicz, Stanisław Ignacy
1885-1939 . . . . .DLB-215; CDWLB-4

Wittenwiler, Heinrich before 1387-
circa 1414? .DLB-179

Wittgenstein, Ludwig 1889-1951 . . . . DLB-262

Wittig, Monique 1935- DLB-83

Wodehouse, P. G.
1881-1975 . . . . DLB-34, 162; CDBLB-6

Worldwide Wodehouse Societies Y-98

Wohmann, Gabriele 1932- DLB-75

Woiwode, Larry 1941- DLB-6

Tribute to John Gardner Y-82

Wolcot, John 1738-1819 . . . . DLB-109

Wolcott, Roger 1679-1767 . . . . DLB-24

Wolf, Christa 1929- DLB-75; CDWLB-2

Wolf, Friedrich 1888-1953 . . . . DLB-124

Wolfe, Gene 1931- DLB-8

Wolfe, Thomas 1900-1938 . . . . . DLB-9, 102, 229;
Y-85; DS-2, DS-16; CDALB-5

"All the Faults of Youth and Inexperience":
A Reader's Report on
Thomas Wolfe's *O Lost* Y-01

Emendations for *Look Homeward, Angel*. . . . Y-00

Eugene Gant's Projected Works Y-01

Fire at the Old Kentucky Home
[Thomas Wolfe Memorial] Y-98

Thomas Wolfe Centennial
Celebration in Asheville Y-00

The Thomas Wolfe Collection at
the University of North Carolina
at Chapel Hill Y-97

The Thomas Wolfe Society Y-97, 99

Wolfe, Tom 1931- DLB-152, 185

John Wolfe [publishing house] DLB-170

Reyner (Reginald) Wolfe
[publishing house] DLB-170

Wolfenstein, Martha 1869-1906 . . . . DLB-221

Wolff, David (see Maddow, Ben)

Wolff, Helen 1906-1994 . . . . Y-94

Wolff, Tobias 1945- DLB-130

    Tribute to Michael M. Rea Y-97

    Tribute to Raymond Carver Y-88

Wolfram von Eschenbach
circa 1170-after 1220 . . . . DLB-138; CDWLB-2

    Wolfram von Eschenbach's *Parzival:*
    Prologue and Book 3 . . . . DLB-138

Wolker, Jiří 1900-1924 . . . . DLB-215

Wollstonecraft, Mary 1759-1797
. . . . DLB-39, 104, 158, 252; CDBLB-3

Women
    Women's Work, Women's Sphere:
    Selected Comments from Women
    Writers DLB-200

Wondratschek, Wolf 1943- DLB-75

Wong, Elizabeth 1958- DLB-266

Wood, Anthony à 1632-1695 . . . . DLB-213

Wood, Benjamin 1820-1900 . . . . DLB-23

Wood, Charles 1932-1980 . . . . DLB-13

    The Charles Wood Affair:
    A Playwright Revived Y-83

Wood, Mrs. Henry 1814-1887 . . . . DLB-18

Wood, Joanna E. 1867-1927 . . . . DLB-92

Wood, Sally Sayward Barrell Keating
1759-1855 . . . . DLB-200

Wood, William ?-? DLB-24

Samuel Wood [publishing house] DLB-49

Woodberry, George Edward
1855-1930 . . . . DLB-71, 103

Woodbridge, Benjamin 1622-1684 . . . . . . DLB-24

Woodbridge, Frederick J. E. 1867-1940 . . . DLB-270

Woodcock, George 1912-1995 . . . . DLB-88

Woodhull, Victoria C. 1838-1927 . . . . DLB-79

Woodmason, Charles circa 1720-? DLB-31

Woodress, James Leslie, Jr. 1916- DLB-111

Woods, Margaret L. 1855-1945 . . . . DLB-240

Woodson, Carter G. 1875-1950 . . . . DLB-17

Woodward, C. Vann 1908-1999 . . . . DLB-17

Woodward, Stanley 1895-1965 . . . . DLB-171

Woodworth, Samuel 1785-1842 . . . . DLB-250

Wooler, Thomas 1785 or 1786-1853 . . . . . DLB-158

Woolf, David (see Maddow, Ben)

Woolf, Douglas 1922-1992 . . . . DLB-244

Woolf, Leonard 1880-1969 . . . . . . DLB-100; DS-10

Woolf, Virginia 1882-1941
. . . . DLB-36, 100, 162; DS-10; CDBLB-6

    "The New Biography," *New York Herald
    Tribune,* 30 October 1927 . . . . DLB-149

Woollcott, Alexander 1887-1943 . . . . DLB-29

Woolman, John 1720-1772 . . . . DLB-31

Woolner, Thomas 1825-1892 . . . . DLB-35

Woolrich, Cornell 1903-1968 . . . . DLB-226

Woolsey, Sarah Chauncy 1835-1905 . . . . . DLB-42

Woolson, Constance Fenimore
1840-1894 . . . . DLB-12, 74, 189, 221

Worcester, Joseph Emerson
1784-1865 . . . . DLB-1, 235

Wynkyn de Worde [publishing house] . . . DLB-170

Wordsworth, Christopher 1807-1885 . . . . DLB-166

Wordsworth, Dorothy 1771-1855 . . . . DLB-107

Wordsworth, Elizabeth 1840-1932 . . . . DLB-98

Wordsworth, William
1770-1850 . . . . DLB-93, 107; CDBLB-3

Workman, Fanny Bullock 1859-1925 . . . . DLB-189

World Literatue Today: A Journal for the
New Millennium Y-01

World Publishing Company DLB-46

World War I (1914-1918) DS-18

    The Great War Exhibit and Symposium
    at the University of South Carolina . . Y-97

    The Liddle Collection and First World
    War Research Y-97

    Other British Poets Who Fell
    in the Great War DLB-216

    The Seventy-Fifth Anniversary of
    the Armistice: The Wilfred Owen
    Centenary and the Great War Exhibit
    at the University of Virginia Y-93

World War II (1939–1945)
    Literary Effects of World War II DLB-15

    World War II Writers Symposium
    at the University of South Carolina,
    12–14 April 1995 . . . . Y-95

    WW2 HMSO Paperbacks Society Y-98

R. Worthington and Company DLB-49

Wotton, Sir Henry 1568-1639 . . . . DLB-121

Wouk, Herman 1915- Y-82; CDALB-7

    Tribute to James Dickey Y-97

Wreford, James 1915- DLB-88

Wren, Sir Christopher 1632-1723 . . . . DLB-213

Wren, Percival Christopher 1885-1941 . . . DLB-153

Wrenn, John Henry 1841-1911 . . . . DLB-140

Wright, C. D. 1949- DLB-120

Wright, Charles 1935- DLB-165; Y-82

Wright, Charles Stevenson 1932- DLB-33

Wright, Chauncey 1830-1875 . . . . DLB-270

Wright, Frances 1795-1852 . . . . DLB-73

Wright, Harold Bell 1872-1944 . . . . DLB-9

Wright, James 1927-1980 . . . . DLB-5, 169; CDALB-7

Wright, Jay 1935- DLB-41

Wright, Judith 1915-2000 . . . . DLB-260

Wright, Louis B. 1899-1984 . . . . DLB-17

Wright, Richard
1908-1960 . . . . . DLB-76, 102; DS-2; CDALB-5

Wright, Richard B. 1937- DLB-53

Wright, S. Fowler 1874-1965 . . . . DLB-255

Wright, Sarah Elizabeth 1928- DLB-33

Wright, T. H.
    "Style" (1877) [excerpt] DLB-57

Wright, Willard Huntington
("S. S. Van Dine") 1888-1939 . . . . DS-16

Wrigley, Robert 1951- DLB-256

Writers' Forum Y-85

Writing
    A Writing Life Y-02

    On Learning to Write Y-88

    The Profession of Authorship:
    Scribblers for Bread Y-89

    A Writer Talking: A Collage Y-00

Wroth, Lawrence C. 1884-1970 . . . . DLB-187

Wroth, Lady Mary 1587-1653 . . . . DLB-121

Wurlitzer, Rudolph 1937- DLB-173

Wyatt, Sir Thomas circa 1503-1542 . . . . . DLB-132

Wycherley, William
1641-1715 . . . . DLB-80; CDBLB-2

Wyclif, John
circa 1335-31 December 1384 . . . . . . DLB-146

Wyeth, N. C. 1882-1945 . . . . DLB-188; DS-16

Wyle, Niklas von circa 1415-1479 . . . . . . DLB-179

Wylie, Elinor 1885-1928 . . . . DLB-9, 45

Wylie, Philip 1902-1971 . . . . DLB-9

Wyllie, John Cook 1908-1968 . . . . DLB-140

Wyman, Lillie Buffum Chace
1847-1929 . . . . DLB-202

Wymark, Olwen 1934- DLB-233

Wynd, Oswald Morris (see Black, Gavin)

Wyndham, John (John Wyndham Parkes
Lucas Beynon Harris) 1903-1969 . . . . DLB-255

Wynne-Tyson, Esmé 1898-1972 . . . . DLB-191

X

Xenophon circa 430 B.C.-circa 356 B.C. . . . DLB-176

Y

Yasuoka Shōtarō 1920- DLB-182

Yates, Dornford 1885-1960 . . . . DLB-77, 153

Yates, J. Michael 1938- DLB-60

Yates, Richard 1926-1992 . . . DLB-2, 234; Y-81, 92

Yau, John 1950- DLB-234

Yavorov, Peyo 1878-1914 . . . . DLB-147

Yearsley, Ann 1753-1806 . . . . DLB-109

Yeats, William Butler
1865-1939 . . . . DLB-10, 19, 98, 156; CDBLB-5

    The W. B. Yeats Society of N.Y. Y-99

Yellen, Jack 1892-1991 . . . . DLB-265

Yep, Laurence 1948- DLB-52

Yerby, Frank 1916-1991 . . . . DLB-76

Yezierska, Anzia
1880-1970 . . . . DLB-28, 221

Yolen, Jane 1939- DLB-52

Yonge, Charlotte Mary
1823-1901 . . . . DLB-18, 163

    The Charlotte M. Yonge Fellowship Y-98

The York Cycle circa 1376-circa 1569 . . . . DLB-146

A Yorkshire Tragedy DLB-58

Thomas Yoseloff [publishing house] DLB-46

Youd, Sam (see Christopher, John)

Young, A. S. "Doc" 1919-1996 . . . . DLB-241

Young, Al 1939- DLB-33

Young, Arthur 1741-1820 . . . . DLB-158

Young, Dick 1917 or 1918 - 1987 . . . . . . .DLB-171

Young, Edward 1683-1765 . . . . DLB-95

Young, Frank A. "Fay" 1884-1957 . . . . . . DLB-241

Young, Francis Brett 1884-1954 . . . . DLB-191

Young, Gavin 1928- DLB-204

Young, Stark 1881-1963 . . . . . . DLB-9, 102; DS-16

Young, Waldeman 1880-1938 . . . . DLB-26

William Young [publishing house] DLB-49

Young Bear, Ray A. 1950- DLB-175

Yourcenar, Marguerite 1903-1987 . . .DLB-72; Y-88

Yovkov, Yordan 1880-1937 . .DLB-147; CDWLB-4

Z

Zachariä, Friedrich Wilhelm 1726-1777 . . . DLB-97

Zagajewski, Adam 1945- DLB-232

Zagoskin, Mikhail Nikolaevich
    1789-1852 . . . . DLB-198

Zajc, Dane 1929- DLB-181

Zālīte, Māra 1952- DLB-232

Zamiatin, Evgenii Ivanovich
    1884-1937 . . . . DLB-272

Zamora, Bernice 1938- DLB-82

Zamudio, Adela (Soledad) 1854-1928 . . . DLB-283

Zand, Herbert 1923-1970 . . . . DLB-85

Zangwill, Israel 1864-1926 . . . . . .DLB-10, 135, 197

Zanzotto, Andrea 1921- DLB-128

Zapata Olivella, Manuel 1920- DLB-113

Zapoev, Timur Iur'evich
    (see Kibirov, Timur Iur'evich)

Zasodimsky, Pavel Vladimirovich
    1843-1912 . . . . DLB-238

Zebra Books DLB-46

Zebrowski, George 1945- DLB-8

Zech, Paul 1881-1946 . . . . DLB-56

Zeidner, Lisa 1955- DLB-120

Zeidonis, Imants 1933- DLB-232

Zeimi (Kanze Motokiyo) 1363-1443 . . . . . DLB-203

Zelazny, Roger 1937-1995 . . . . DLB-8

Zenger, John Peter 1697-1746 . . . . DLB-24, 43

Zepheria DLB-172

Zesen, Philipp von 1619-1689 . . . . DLB-164

Zhadovskaia, Iuliia Valerianovna
    1824-1883 . . . . .DLB-277

Zhukova, Mar'ia Semenovna
    1805-1855 . . . . .DLB-277

Zhukovsky, Vasilii Andreevich
    1783-1852 . . . . DLB-205

Zhvanetsky, Mikhail Mikhailovich
    1934- DLB-285

G. B. Zieber and Company DLB-49

Ziedonis, Imants 1933- CDWLB-4

Zieroth, Dale 1946- DLB-60

Zigler und Kliphausen, Heinrich
    Anshelm von 1663-1697 . . . . DLB-168

Zil'ber, Veniamin Aleksandrovich
    (see Kaverin, Veniamin Aleksandrovich)

Zimmer, Paul 1934- DLB-5

Zinberg, Len (see Lacy, Ed)

Zincgref, Julius Wilhelm 1591-1635 . . . . . DLB-164

Zindel, Paul 1936- DLB-7, 52; CDALB-7

Zinnes, Harriet 1919- DLB-193

Zinzendorf, Nikolaus Ludwig von
    1700-1760 . . . . DLB-168

Zitkala-Ša 1876-1938 . . . . .DLB-175

Zīverts, Mārtiņš 1903-1990 . . . . DLB-220

Zlatovratsky, Nikolai Nikolaevich
    1845-1911 . . . . DLB-238

Zola, Emile 1840-1902 . . . . DLB-123

Zolla, Elémire 1926- DLB-196

Zolotow, Charlotte 1915- DLB-52

Zoshchenko, Mikhail Mikhailovich
    1895-1958 . . . . .DLB-272

Zschokke, Heinrich 1771-1848 . . . . DLB-94

Zubly, John Joachim 1724-1781 . . . . DLB-31

Zu-Bolton, Ahmos, II 1936- DLB-41

Zuckmayer, Carl 1896-1977 . . . . DLB-56, 124

Zukofsky, Louis 1904-1978 . . . . DLB-5, 165

Zupan, Vitomil 1914-1987 . . . . DLB-181

Župančič, Oton 1878-1949 . . .DLB-147; CDWLB-4

zur Mühlen, Hermynia 1883-1951 . . . . DLB-56

Zweig, Arnold 1887-1968 . . . . DLB-66

Zweig, Stefan 1881-1942 . . . . DLB-81, 118

Zwinger, Ann 1925- DLB-275

Zwingli, Huldrych 1484-1531 . . . . DLB-338

ISBN 0-7876-6822-2

90000

9 780787 668228

SPLENDOURS OF SOUTHERN AFRICA

Splendours
of Southern
Africa

GERALD S. CUBITT

Mr. Brown
With our very Best Wishes
Janet & Gerald

CAPE TOWN
C. STRUIK (PTY) LTD
1972

January 1974

© C. Struik (Pty.) Ltd.
Africana Specialist and Publisher

ISBN 0 86977 017 9

English text written by Gerald S. Cubitt
Edited by Ursula Kingwell
Afrikaans translation by Madeleine van Biljon
Title suggested by Greta den Hartog and George Francois Laurence
Dustjacket design by James Giles
Monochrome Bromide Prints produced by Gale Daniels, Johannesburg

Lithographical positives by Hirt & Carter (Pty.) Ltd.
Text printed letterpress, illustrations printed offset
Paper: Focus Matt Art 135 gsm
Bound in Scholco Bookcloth
Printed and bound by Gothic Printing Company Limited,
Printpak Building, Dacres Ave., Epping, Cape

For Janet,
and to the memory of her brother David

The Publishers wish to acknowledge the financial assistance received from the undermentioned with the production of this book:
Van Reekum Papier-Gepacy (S.A.) (Pty) Ltd
South African Tourist Corporation

INTRODUCTION

Africa is many things to many people; to some it is a rising colossus, where the once neat and tidy colonial entities have burgeoned into a host of new, self-conscious nations, each in its own way striving to cope with problems of internal development, but at the same time confronting the rest of the world with a loud voice and a powerful vote that cannot be ignored.

To others Africa represents simply a vast economic potential, a continent still relatively underpopulated and underdeveloped, and yet rich in the minerals and natural resources that are demanded by modern industrial technology.

In some, however, the concept of Africa arouses a deep nostalgia, an awareness of and appreciation for the wide open spaces – the great plains, mountains, deserts, forests and lakes. Much has changed, and is still changing, as the inevitable result of man's technological conquest over nature. Cities, towns and highways have mushroomed forth out of the dust and deserts; but the continent is huge, and with just a little effort, it is possible to leave behind city life and enter the wilds of Africa, where man may move in harmony with nature.

This book is about Southern Africa. It comprises a selection of photographs that, I hope, capture at least some of the atmosphere of natural Africa. Intentionally, there are no pictures of city life, industry or other signs of the modern world.

Moreover, to do full justice to the title chosen, many volumes would have to be filled instead of just one, and there are consequently and inevitably many gaps. The photographs are of subjects which have particularly appealed to me as a photographer.

For many people visiting Southern Africa, Cape Town is the port of arrival. When Sir Francis Drake first caught sight of the Cape in 1580 he referred to it as "the fairest we saw in the whole circumference of the earth".

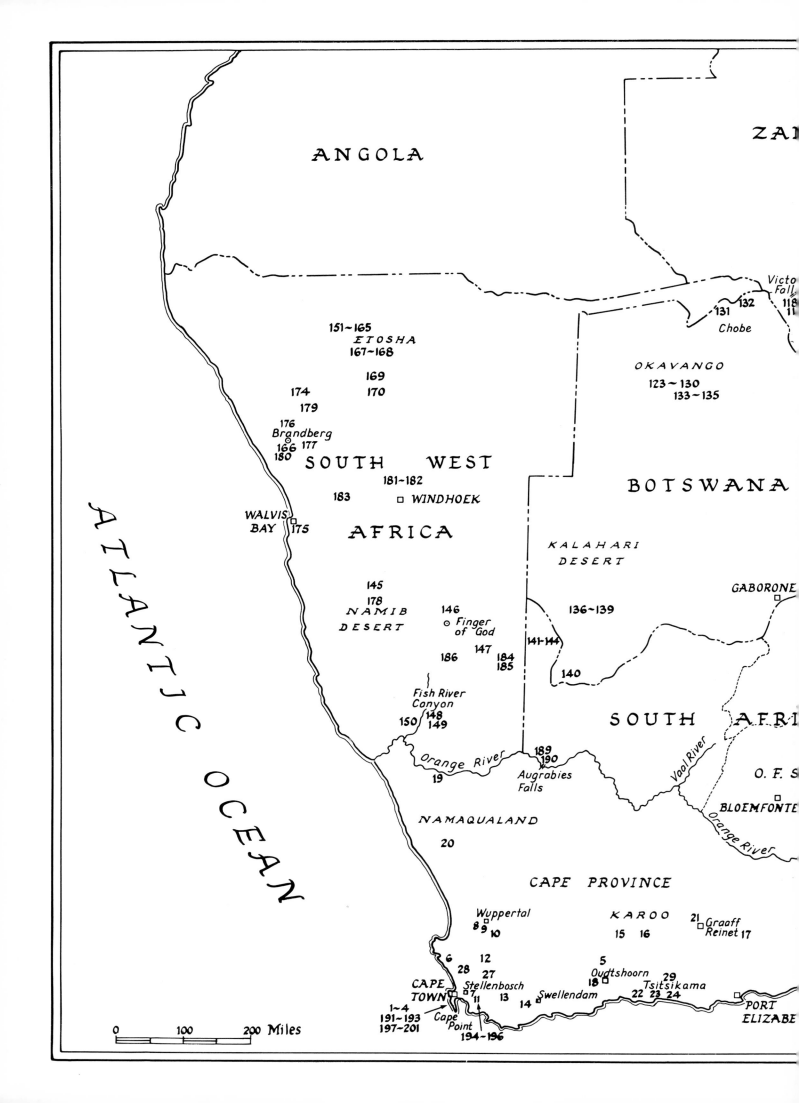

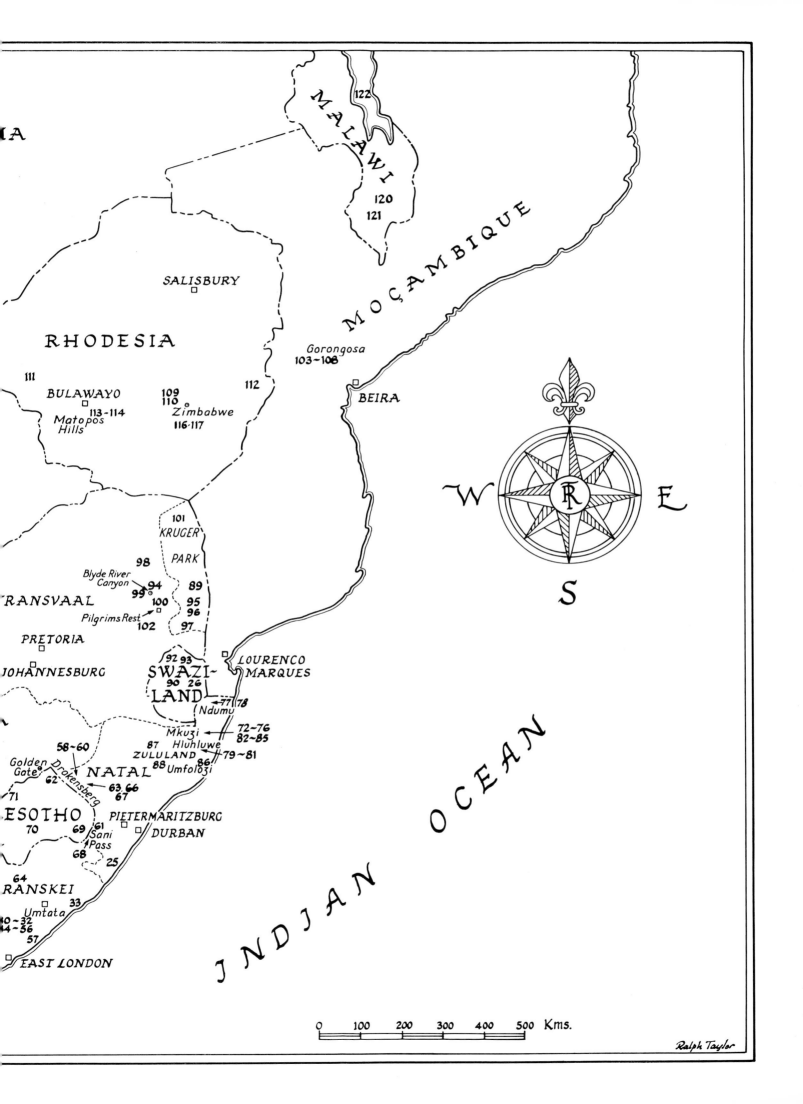

Dominated by the majestic Table Mountain that rises above Cape Town, the Peninsula stretches a rocky spine some 50 kilometres southwards to Cape Point. A magnificent marine drive along the western flank of the Peninsula takes in most of the scenic beauty that is characteristic of the south-western Cape.

The Cape mountains were formed by a buckling or crumpling of the earth's crust, which gave rise to a series of vertical and near vertical formations. With their steep crenellations and sparsely vegetated slopes, these mountains provide a rugged contrast to the fertile green valleys at their foot. The natural vegetation of the region consists of varieties of low, hardy shrubs and indigenous proteas which are able to survive the hot, dry summers and wet winters.

Over 20 000 species of flowering plants flourish in the Cape, and in springtime, in September, the countryside is transformed into a kaleidoscope of colour. The greatest concentration of wild flowers occur around Springbok in Namaqualand, about 500 kilometres north of Cape Town. For most of the year the semi-desert land is arid and bleak, but when the flowers burst into bloom, it is as though a collection of exotic and beautiful Persian carpets had been spread out on a bare floor.

Both the indigenous fauna and flora of the Cape have suffered from the advent of the early settlers. The animals that survive are mainly the smaller species of antelope such as grysbok, rhebok, mountain reedbuck and duiker, as well as baboon and hyrax that take advantage of the low-growing and often dense bush which provides a measure of camouflage and protection. Leopards still live in the remote reaches of the mountains, but they are rarely seen and their numbers are dwindling.

To get some idea of the natural forests that once covered a wide area, one must travel east to Knysna, on the Garden Route. In the Tsitsikama Forest are superb specimens of yellowwood and stinkwood, as well as many other indigenous trees. This forest is also the last refuge for the small herd of Knysna elephants. Were it not for the dense and often impenetrable tangle of vegetation, these few survivors would have been hunted down decades ago.

Inland, to the north and north-east of the Cape mountains, lies the Karroo. In the Hottentot language, this word means "an arid desert", and it is an apt description. Rainfall is low, and provides scant moisture for the stunted bush that is prolific throughout. It is a monotonous landscape, usually brown and dry, mostly flat, with occasional solitary flat-topped hills that are remnants of ancient volcanic pipes.

In the harsh glare and heat of midday, the Karroo is a place to traverse as quickly as possible, but in the early morning soon after dawn, and especially towards dusk in the evening, the colours of the veld are warm and beautiful. The softer light brings out the delicate tints of the bush, contrasting with the vivid pink and purple hues reflected from the hills.

Few areas in Africa have been so completely devastated as a result of man's activities, as has the Karroo. The original vegetation included many varieties of grasses and bush, which provided food for large nomadic herds of antelope. Over the last hundred years, widespread over-grazing by sheep, and the elimination of almost all wild life, have resulted in the predominance of shrub with a low nutritional value.

The destruction of wild life in the Karroo was an incalculable loss. The English traveller George Thompson, in his book *Adventures in Southern Africa*, published in 1827, wrote of the Karroo as it was in his time, as follows:

"As we proceeded along the plains gently declining from the Sneeuwberg we discovered thousands of antelope, quaghas and gnoos. . . . Hundreds of them were now playing round us, and ever and anon a troop of these fantastic animals would join a herd of quaghas, and all sound off helter-skelter across the plains, throwing up clouds of dust from the arid ground, which is here quite a karroo. . . .

The numbers and variety of game formed, indeed, the only feature of animation and interest throughout this desolate region. . . .

In an hour we remounted and proceeded on our course, over extensive plains, sprinkled with numerous herds of game – quaghas, elands, gnoos, koodos, hartebeest, gemsboks, and smaller antelopes, the movements of which helped to relieve our lonely journey. . . .

Travelling through the Karroo . . . I passed through prodigious flocks of springboks, spread over the plains as far as the eye could reach. The number it is impossible to estimate with any nicety but I suppose I saw at least 100,000 in the course of fifty miles. They were migrating from the great desert towards the Colony."

The Mountain Zebra National Park near Cradock today harbours the remnants of the wild life that once flourished in the Karroo. The unfortunate quagga, however, fought a losing battle and the last known specimen died at Berlin Zoo in 1875.

One has only to glance at the place-names on a modern map of the Karroo, to find haunting reminders of the animals that once roamed across the plains: Leeuberg, Elandskloof, Buffels River, Hartbeesvleiberg, Gemsbokkop, Kwaggaskop, to name but a few.

The greater part of Southern Africa consists of an elevated plateau which varies in altitude between 600 and 2 000 metres, and is rimmed by mountain ranges which form the Great Escarpment. The plateau slopes gradually from east to west, and includes both the Karroo and the Kalahari desert.

The highest and most dramatic section of the Escarpment culminates in the Drakensberg around Lesotho. These mountains divide the Natal grasslands from the Highveld of the southern Transvaal and the Orange Free State.

When looking up at the Sani Pass, or towards the summits of Champagne Castle, Cathedral Peak, Mont-aux-Sources and other towering landmarks of the Drakensberg, one may imagine that these are the first of a series of mountain ranges. Yet, on reaching the top of the spectacular Sani Pass, at 2 750 metres, instead of seeing further rising peaks and valleys, one is confronted by the high, treeless Lesotho Plateau.

In the east the Escarpment is for the most part very steep, forming a rain trap for the Transkei and the coastal lowlands, while in the west the gradient is less pronounced. The Orange River, rising in the Maluti Mountains, gathers much of the rain that falls near the crest of the Escarpment and then flows westwards on its 2 000-kilometre journey to the Atlantic coast.

The Highveld of the Orange Free State and the Transvaal lies to the west of the Drakensberg and varies in altitude from 1 200 to 1 800 metres. This area is rather flat and featureless and has few distinctive natural landmarks. Like the Karroo, it also was once thickly populated with wild animals. The few that remain today are protected in small reserves and on private farms.

Soil erosion is a scourge in the Transkei and the grasslands of Natal, and in places the land is deeply scarred. Over-grazing and deforestation have exacerbated the problem, and in many areas the poor quality of the soil has severely restricted agricultural potential.

North of Durban, in the coastal regions of Natal, there are four wonderful game reserves: Umfolozi, Hluhluwe, Mkuze and Ndumu. These are mere remnants of the formerly huge game trails of Zululand, but in spite of their small size, they are Edens of wild life for the enthusiast. White and black rhino, buffalo, wildebeest, zebra, nyala, kudu, and impala are abundant, and the bird life is rich and varied. Each reserve has its own character and appeal and is quite distinct from the other. Mkuze is particularly worth while; here, from the two game hides at the Bube and Msinga waterholes, the animals may be seen at close range as they come down to drink.

Ndumu has a special charm because of its beautiful setting. Situated in the northernmost part of Natal and bordered by the Usutu River, this reserve consists of forests, lakes and bush. Fringed by graceful yellow-barked fever trees, the lakes are a paradise for pelicans, flamingoes, storks, herons and many other water-birds, as well as for crocodiles.

A continuation of the Drakensberg range in Swaziland and the north-eastern Transvaal separates the Highveld plains from the dense bush country of the Lowveld. The Limpopo with its tributaries, the only other major river system in South Africa besides the Orange, drains much of central and northern Transvaal, before flowing into the Indian Ocean north of Lourenço Marques.

In the north-eastern Lowveld of the Transvaal lies the famous Kruger National Park, a superb ecological entity which provides sanctuary for thousands of wild animals.

Although this was formerly well-known hunting country, the animals were for years protected by the prevalence of malaria and sleeping sickness, which acted as deterrents to the settlement of man. The terrain is mainly flat, bordered on one side by the Drakensberg, and on the other by the Lebombo Mountains. The region is crossed by rivers, notably the Sabie and the Olifants, the latter of which joins the mainstream of the Limpopo in the east. These rivers offer marvellous opportunities for game-viewing. In the dry winter months, from May to October, the need for water drives many animals out of the thick bush to the banks of the rivers, where they can be seen more easily.

Elephant, giraffe, buffalo, zebra, wildebeest, waterbuck, tsessebe, eland, kudu, sable and roan antelope and impala are among the species that browse or graze in an unspoilt environment. Both species of rhinoceros have been re-introduced and their numbers are increasing. Lions, leopards, cheetahs, hyenas, jackals and wild dogs roam freely, following their predatory instinct. Baboons and vervet monkeys, ever inquisitive and curious, are plentiful throughout the park.

North of the Limpopo River, Rhodesia provides a contrasting landscape, ranging from the mountain peaks of the eastern highlands, culminating in Inyangani (2 521 metres), to the low-lying plateau that embraces the basins of the Zambezi, Limpopo, Sabi and Lundi Rivers. Much of the country lies at an altitude of 900–1 500 metres and comprises grasslands and mopane woods, broken by granite koppies. In the Matopos National Park near Bulawayo, some of the most striking of these koppies can be seen: huge boulders balanced precariously one upon the other as though by a giant's hand. They are a favourite haunt of leopards, as well as of their prey: hyrax and baboons.

In the heart of Rhodesia lies the mysterious ruined city of Zimbabwe. The origins of the strange acropolis, temples and other stone buildings remain almost as obscure today as when first discovered, in 1868. The atmosphere is brooding and haunted, especially at dawn, when the blackness of night gives way to the first rays of the morning sun, and the cold, grey ruins pose their unanswered challenge to another day.

The mighty Zambezi River rises in Angola, travels south and then east, gathering on its way the waters of countless rivers and streams. At the Victoria Falls the "Great River", nearly 2 kilometres wide at this point, pours into a deep, narrow gorge. The impact of the cascading waters is so great that a cloud of spray rises hundreds of metres into the air. Viewing the falls from the lush tropical forest that borders the precipice, one is drenched by the spray as if by rain. David Livingstone has described his first impressions of the falls on the 21st November, 1855, thus: ". . . after twenty minutes sail from Kulai, we came in sight, for the first time, of the columns of vapour appropriately called 'smoke', rising at a distance of five miles, exactly as when large tracts of grass are burned in Africa. Five columns now rose, and bending in the direction of the wind, they seemed placed against a low ridge covered with trees. The tops of the columns at this distance appeared to mingle with the clouds. They were white below, and higher up, they became dark so as to simulate smoke very closely.

"The whole scene was extremely beautiful. The banks and the islands dotted over the river are adorned with silvan vegetation of great variety of colour and form. These trees have each their own physiognomy. There, towering over all, stands the great burly baobab each of whose enormous arms would form the trunk of a large tree; besides, the groups of feathery shaped leaves depicted in the sky lend beauty to the scene. No one can imagine the beauty from anything in England. The Falls are bounded on three sides by ridges, three or four hundred feet high, which are covered with forest, with red soil, appearing through the trees.''

From the Victoria Falls the Zambezi flows into the Kariba Dam, the largest man-made lake in the world, 280 kilometres long and 65 kilometres wide. The river then continues east, entering Moçambique for the final stretch before reaching the sea north of Beira.

Gorongoza National Park, a short distance north-west of Beira, is one of the finest game parks in Africa. It is a gem. As a result of many months of patient research by Ken Tinley, a leading South African ecologist, the boundaries of this park will soon be extended to form an ecological unit that will accommodate the migratory movements of its animals.

The coastal grasslands of Gorongoza, with its scattered doum, borassus and ivory palms, conjures up visions of a prehistoric landscape, out of which dinosaurs and other long-extinct creatures could emerge.

Rising in the western highlands of Angola, the Okavango River crosses the Caprivi Strip and flows into north-western Botswana, where it is split into myriads of channels and small streams that comprise the Okavango Swamps. The maze of crystal-clear waterways and verdant marsh divides thousands of small islands from one another. This pristine corner of Africa, still to a great extent unexplored, is a paradise for wild life. Near Chief's Island, I have watched a herd of about 300 lechwe move through the marsh at speed, the sound of their hooves reminding me of an express train thundering through a railway station. Hippo, buffalo, tsessebe, impala, waterbuck, sitatunga and kudu are some of the larger animals that flourish on these swamp islands. There are also lions, leopards, cheetahs and other predators. The lagoons and rivers are inhabited by crocodiles, as well as tiger-fish, bream and barbel. Bird life is both varied and interesting: pelicans, storks, ibis, herons, geese, ducks and lily-trotters are but a few of the species that abound. The distinctive cry of the fish-eagle is frequently heard.

The vegetation of the swamps varies from lush grass and papyrus to thick forest. The trees that flourish on the islands are superb; tropical palms compete in profusion with huge wild fig, "sausage" and motsodi trees. The ubiquitous termite hills are towers of greyish brown in a sea of green.

Tsetse flies and malarial mosquitoes have helped preserve the swamps from the intrusion of man; except for a few scattered pockets of River Bushmen, the vast swamps remain uninhabited. Because of the lack of distinctive landmarks it is almost impossible to walk for any distance without becoming hopelessly lost.

Despite an annual rate of evaporation that exceeds 2 metres, some of the delta waters re-converge in the south. In years of high rainfall the surplus waters reach Lake Ngami via the Nghabe River, and Lake Xau via the Botlele River. The future of the Okavango Swamps depends largely upon the policy to be adopted by the new Orapa Diamond Mine which will require about 11 megalitres of water daily. It is a complex and controversial issue, and one hopes that it will somehow be resolved without long-term detriment to the unique ecology of the swamps.

Concentrations of wild animals are also found in the Moremi Reserve bordering the Okavango Swamps, in the Chobe National Park in northern Botswana, and in the vicinity of the great Makarikari Pan between Francistown and Maun. The Makarikari Pan is a flat mud desert, devoid of vegetation and usually dry. In 1972, however, there were exceptionally good rains and the Pan was covered with a steel-grey sheet of water. The area is well known for its vast migratory herds of wildebeest, zebra and springbok, which rival those of the Serengeti plains in Tanzania.

West of the Transvaal, the Southern African plateau slopes gradually into the Kalahari basin. The Kalahari is only a semi-desert, since some form of vegetation covers almost the entire area. Rainfall is very low, rarely exceeding 12 centimetres a year, but when it does rain, moisture is absorbed by plants which in turn provide nourishment for the nomadic animals of the desert.

Gemsbok, springbok, kudu, wildebeest and hartebeest traverse vast tracts of desert each year, moving from one pasture to the next. The Kalahari Bushmen likewise live a nomadic life. Their specialized metabolism, the result of centuries of acclimatization and adjustment to their harsh environment, enables them to survive a life of appalling hardship.

Most of the Kalahari lies in Botswana and is virtually inaccessible, but the Kalahari Gemsbok National Park, in the south-east corner, in South Africa, consists of typical desert terrain: dry riverbeds, lined with hardy acacias, and dunes scattered with shrub, thorn-trees and tsamma melons. Temperatures vary enormously, especially in winter when the days are warm but the nights bitterly cold. During the summer months it is uncomfortably hot.

Besides the larger animals, I found the ground squirrels and sociable weaver birds in this beautiful national park particularly interesting. The squirrels, attractive little creatures, gregarious and always curious, pop in and out of their holes, scampering along the ground in search of food, every now and then standing up on their hind legs to look about.

The name of the sociable weaver birds defines their chief activity: the building of their enormous communal nests. These are lined and woven with grass and small twigs and look like miniature haystacks into which holes have been driven. They usually last for many years and provide a refuge for other birds besides the weavers. Sometimes the weight becomes too great for the tree to bear and the nest tumbles to the ground, perhaps taking with it a torn-off branch or even uprooting the tree itself.

South West Africa covers a huge area. It is a land of great beauty and vivid colour.

The Namib Desert, stretching for 1 600 kilometres along the coast and with a width of 60 – 160 kilometres, is one of the oldest deserts in the world, and one of the least explored. Its ferocious climate and huge, forbidding sand dunes are effective barriers against man's intrusion, and with the exception of diamonds, the Namib has as yet yielded few of its secrets. The annual rainfall rarely exceeds 10 centimetres and hence the vegetation that exists is scant and seasonal. Along the west coast the cold Benguela current causes mist, but not rain.

The Namib gives way in the east to the escarpment and the plateau which is mountainous, and fertile in places. Most of this highland of South West Africa consists of open grassland interspersed with low bush. Water is scarce and valuable. Wild animals are encouraged and protected on many of the farms, especially browsing antelopes, which help prevent the bush from overwhelming the heavily grazed pastures upon which depend large herds of sheep and cattle.

In the south, the Great Fish River snakes its winding way through a fissure over 300 metres deep in the rocky crust.

The Fish River Canyon is surpassed in grandeur only by the Grand Canyon in Arizona. From the edge of the steep walls, a magnificent panorama is revealed. My first sight of the canyon was at dawn, when the rising sun tinted the walls a soft, alluring pink. Later, as the day progressed, the colours hardened to a deep yellow and finally became a uniform greyish brown, contrasting with the green, stagnant waters of the river far below.

The famous Etosha Pan in the north is one of the finest game parks in Africa. The Pan itself, like the Makarikari, is flat and devoid of vegetation, but the surrounding grasslands and bush are a haven for many species of animals and birds. It is wild, hot, and very dusty; this is the real Africa where nature reigns supreme, and where man is but a passing guest.

1   A peaceful sunset at the Cape Peninsula. Bartholomew Diaz, the
    Portuguese navigator, was the first European to round the Cape, in 1488.
    A treacherous coast with strong currents and a rocky, jagged shoreline,
    the Peninsula was first known as the "Cape of Storms". King John of
    Portugal, however, soon appreciated the significance of the Cape
    for opening up the sea route to India and renamed it the "Cape of Good
    Hope".

2   One of the world's most famous landmarks and a welcome sight to
    generations of sailors: Table Mountain, rising to a height of 1 086 metres,
    stands majestically facing a great bay. First climbed in 1503 by Antonia
    da Saldanha, the mountain provided a rich source of timber as well
    as water for the early European settlers. Cape Town, founded by
    Jan van Riebeeck in 1652, lies within the shadow of the dramatic
    mountain cliffs.

3   Lion's Head seen from the scattered boulders of Oudekraal along
    Victoria Drive. A prominent peak flanking Table Mountain, it was for
    many years used as a position from which signals were given to passing
    ships, and a flagpole stood at the highest point. The signalman lived at
    Kloof Nek and used a ladder to make his daily ascent to the summit.

4   Black-backed Gulls (*Larus dominicanus*), are common sight along the south and west coasts of Southern Africa. Notorious scavengers, these gulls are a scourge to sea-bird colonies, where they will swoop down to seize either egg or chick. One of their favourite foods is a sand-mussel known as Donax, which they find in shallow waters. In order to break the mussels open, the gulls drop the shells from a height to splinter on the rocks.

5   A Cape Coloured family cottage in the foothills of the Swartberg Mountains.

6   Grey Herons (*Ardea cinerea*) and little Egrets (*Egretta garzetta*), at rest in the early hours of the day on a jetty along the south-western coast.

7   Rising above autumnal vineyards in the Helshoogte Pass, the majestic Wemmershoek Mountain holds court between a fringe of wispy clouds.

8   Linked by only one road to the outside world, the Coloured village of Wupperthal shelters in a verdant, fertile valley surrounded by the rust-coloured mountains of the Cedarberg range. The hamlet owes its origin to a Rhenish Mission founded at the site in 1830.

9   The thatched, white-washed cottages at Wupperthal are laid out in neat rows against the hillside on the bank of the Tra-Tra River. Peaches, grapes, figs, Rooibos tea and tobacco are among the crops grown in the valley, while above the cottages, are pens for donkeys, pigs, sheep, goats and a multitude of chickens.

5

6

8

9

10　Wupperthal is a peaceful place, with an atmosphere somehow reminiscent of the nineteenth century. The village has retained its unique charm and character, partly as a result of its relative inaccessibility and isolation and partly because the small community wishes to accept from the modern world only essentials while rejecting many of its materialistic values.

11　The rich colours of autumn highlight the beauty of the Jonkershoek Valley near Stellenbosch. The "Twins" (1 494 metres), the highest and most dramatic peaks of the surrounding mountain range, stand like lofty sentinels guarding the secrets of the Eerste River with its cascading waterfalls and thick forests of oak and pine.

12　In the remoter parts of the Cape mountains a Coloured family travelling by donkey-cart blends in harmony with the uncluttered landscape; a poignant reminder of an age when travel was a leisurely business.

13　Thick Protea bushes and the rounded slopes of the Riviersonderend Mountains near Villiersdorp catch the last soft rays of the sun.

14   Good rains and a full river: The Breë River winds its way through fertile plains beneath the Langeberg Mountains near Swellendam.

15   It is dry and hot in the Karroo. An endless expanse of hostile, barren soil, dotted with clumps of Renosterbos, lies beneath the blue canopy of the sky. In the glare of the day it is a bleak landscape, but as evening approaches the setting sun suffuses the scene with glowing colour.

16   Although hardly any surface water exists in the Karroo and rainfall is scant, the windpumps introduced in 1885 tap resources of water deep below the ground. This makes sheep-ranching a practical proposition. Often the immediate vicinity of a waterpump is like an oasis where green grass and trees flourish. It is in such surroundings that one may see the beautiful walnut tree (*Juglans nigra*) with blossoms of bright, dazzling yellow.

17   From the Kranskop heights in the Mountain Zebra National Park near Cradock, a superb view unfolds of the Bankberg Mountains. In the early hours of a wintry morning, a thick mist clings to the valley floor, and the mountain ridges rise above it like islands in a sea of white.

18   The Little Karroo, a 100-kilometre-wide plain, lies between the Outeniqua and Swartberg Mountains. Perennial mountain streams and a dry climate provide conditions ideal for large-scale ostrich farming. This commenced in the 1860's and for years fortunes fluctuated according to the whims of fashion. Today prices are good, and some 25 000 birds thrive on fields of lucerne in the many large farms of the area.

17

18

22

23

19   The muddy waters of the Orange River reflect the sky in the glare of
      midday. The Orange flows 2 000 kilometres from the high Lesotho
      plateau to the Atlantic coast at Alexander Bay. Together with its main
      tributaries, the Vaal and the Caledon, it forms the most important river
      system in South Africa. To the Bushmen and Hottentots it was known
      simply as "The Great River". The present name was bestowed by
      the explorer Captain Gordon in 1779, in honour of the Prince of Orange.

20   Springtime in Namaqualand — the semi-desert landscape, dry and
      barren for ten months each year, suddenly comes alive in a profusion of
      orange *Ursinia*.

21   The Valley of Desolation near Graaff-Reinet: the spectacular result of
      natural erosion. Jagged teeth of crumbling red sandstone stand out
      from the main massif in a weird jumble of shape and size. From the
      mountain summit, at 1 405 metres, these strange rocks provide a
      dramatic contrast to the distant Karroo Plain.

22   From the summit of the Spitskop, north of Knysna, the Tsitsikama
      Forest covers the mountain slopes with a dark blanket of vegetation.

23   Indigenous trees in the foreground, Australian Eucalyptus behind and
      Monterey Pines in the distance: a cross-section of the Tsitsikama Forest.
      Only 1 per cent of South Africa is covered with forest and the greater
      part lies between George and Humansdorp. For many years the great
      indigenous trees were cut down at random; ancient hardwood was
      especially prized for ship building and for railway sleepers. Serious control
      began in 1886 and denuded areas were planted with exotics, but
      effective action came too late to restore the Tsitsikama to its original
      grandeur.

24   In the deep gorge cut by the Groot River near Plettenberg Bay, lush tropical vegetation thrives in the humid climate. Wild Banana trees (*Strelitzia alba*) flourish in these surroundings.

25   A wild Hibiscus (*H. tiliaceus*) displays a wondrous crown of yellow petals. This is a small shrub that occurs along the coasts of southern Natal and the Transkei. There are some 40 different species of Hibiscus in Southern Africa and all have brilliantly coloured flowers.

26   *Androcymbium striatum*, a wild liliaceous plant found only in the Eastern Transvaal and in Swaziland. The name *Androcymbium* literally means "a boat-full of stamens" and refers to the prominent stamens, each of which is held by a large, white, boat-shaped bract. About 30 other species of *Androcymbium* occur throughout Southern Africa.

27   "Pin Cushion" Proteas (*Leucospermum cordifolium*) adorn the Cape mountain slopes.

28   Wild *Ursinia* in the fields near Darling.

29   A huge Outeniqua Yellowwood tree (*Podocarpus falcatus*), its branches hung with silvery lichen (*Usnea*), in the green depths of the Groot River Valley. The steep cliffs of the gorge act as a barrier to the rays of the sun and cast strong shadows along the valley floor. It is a world of mysterious twilight, pierced at intervals by shafts of sunlight.

30   A Xhosa hut has one entrance and one tiny window. Inside, there is a place in the middle for a fire to provide warmth and a means for cooking. When the weather is fine, a fire is kindled outside and the three-legged iron cooking-pot is placed over the embers. On one side of each hut there is usually a small stock pen, fenced in for protection against marauders and predators.

25 ▲   ▼ 27   26 ▲   ▼ 28

30

31

31 A group of African huts in Pondoland surround a central enclosure that is used as a stock pen. These round huts consist of a framework of wooden poles, with wattle branches woven between. Both exterior and interior surfaces are plastered with mud. The roofs are lined with wattle brush and thatched with grass.

32 The Xhosa are a sociable people and there is always a lively chatter in and around the kraals.

33 The Umzimvubu River flows between two thickly forested ridges, known as the "Gates of St. John", before it reaches the sea near Port St. Johns on the Wild Coast.

34 A Xhosa mother, with baby wrapped securely on her back, puffs away contentedly at her pipe.

35 A coy little girl steals a glance at the intruder.

36 Xhosa girls can carry enormous loads on their heads. Sometimes, as in this case, a helping hand is needed to position the pile of wattle wood on the head of the carrier, but once in place it is carried, often for many miles, with a superb balance. This wood is used in the construction of the simple huts, and is woven around a circular framework of stakes.

37 Rounding up cattle on horseback; a common sight in the Transkei where it is the responsibility of the men to see to the welfare of livestock while their women in the kraals attend to domestic chores.

38 By wearing a rough skirt fixed above the bosom and the traditional folded turban on her head, this Xhosa woman reveals that she is married.

36

39 A Xhosa woman with painted face displays her arms brightly decorated
with bead bracelets. These are fitted tightly, one next to the other.
If with age she puts on weight, they could cause great discomfort; for
once in place, it is the custom that they should never be removed.

40 Homeward bound from the day's pasture. The Xhosa are a pastoral
people, whose wealth is measured in terms of livestock; hence their
animals are tended with lavish care.

41 A young Xhosa maiden in the warm evening sunlight. Only when she
is married will tribal custom compel her to cover her bare bosom
with a garment, to signify her new status in life.

42   In the years before initiation into manhood by the Ukwalusa circumcision ceremony, young Xhosa boys live a carefree, happy life. One of the few responsibilities is to tend the family's livestock—an important task in a rural community.

43   Laden donkeys on the road to Port St. Johns carry provisions from a nearby trading store to a distant kraal.

44   Known to the local Africans as "Esikhaleni" (Place of the Sound), the "Hole in the Wall" is a prominent feature of the Wild Coast. A massive island cliff rising precipitously above the turbulent surf, it is named for the great gash that pierces its flank, allowing the ocean swell to pound through the cavern with a mighty roar.

45   A bastion of reddish rock, known to the Pondo as "Mlengani" (Hanging One), and to Europeans as "Execution Rock", dominates the valley of the Umgazi River (Place of Blood) — so named for the savage tribal battles that occurred here in former years).

44

45

49

50

46 A mischievous group of African children in the Transkei near
    Ngcwanguba. Two of them carry long "knopkieries", a favourite but
    dangerous weapon in the hands of older boys.

47 Three little Xhosa boys with their mother. The Xhosa usually have
    large families and each new addition is warmly welcomed. Family ties are
    strong and meaningful from the start and remain so for life.

48 Destruction of the natural forest and the fierce action of sun, wind and
    water have caused extensive erosion and rendered large areas of the
    Transkei useless for cultivation. Deep crevices in the earth mark
    the paths of tempestuous seasonal streams.

49 A sweeping Transkeian landscape of green grassland dotted with kraals.
    In the distance, a mountain ridge terminates the level plain.

50 Sweets for a little girl—the joy of giving is matched by the evident
    joy of receiving—along the road to Coffee Bay.

51 A Xhosa woman with her traditional long-stemmed pipe.

52 Xhosa women usually carry their possessions on their heads. Even an umbrella can be wedged into the bundle. The weight hardly impedes movement, and the constant attention to balance helps to develop the erect carriage and graceful walk possessed by these women.

53 Donkey-cart on the highway.

54 Among the Xhosa the man's role within his family is paramount; he is the master. The husband, comfortably mounted on horseback, with his wife striding in front on foot, graphically illustrates this custom.

53

54

58

59

55 In the Transkeian plains trees are few and far between. Wood is a necessity, however, both as a building material and as fuel, and sometimes it has to be collected from far afield. This is a task for the women of the tribe who walk many miles, balancing on their heads huge bundles of sticks bound with cord.

56 A picture typical of the rural life in Pondoland: a small field of maize and a number of African huts protectively surrounding the communal stock pen. Maize, meat and milk are the staple foods, and life revolves around their bounty.

57 A Xhosa woman, her face painted with white clay, rests beneath a shady Eucalyptus near the Great Kei River.

58 Seen from the summit of Cathedral Peak (3 005 metres), the Drakensberg Mountains appear as a high plateau, with jagged cliffs falling away steeply to the rolling foothills far below.

59 Beneath a 1 200-metre mantle of basaltic lava the Drakensberg Mountains consist of richly coloured layers of sandstone. The many caves in these softer strata were once a haven for mountain Bushmen, and their rock paintings are vivid records of their chief pursuits.

60   From the valley of the Mlambonja River a great mountain ridge,
     culminating in Cathedral Peak, reaches towards the sky. The lofty Bell
     (2 922-metres), standing apart from the other peaks, is easily recognizable
     by its distinctive shape.

61   Evening shadows descend upon a peaceful mountain landscape at the
     foot of the Sani Pass.

62   The splendour of the mighty Ampitheatre at awakening day. Sunlight
     highlights the ripples of the Tugela River which flows at ease after
     a tortuous, cascading journey from the heights of Mont-aux-Sources,
     the "Mountain of Springs".

63   The summits of Cathkin Peak and Champagne Castle shimmer
     in the midday sun.

64   A shepherd drives his flock along a dusty mountain road in the
     Barkly Pass and passing motorists must surrender their right of way.

65   A lonely path in the Drakensberg foothills.

60

61

63

64

68

69

66 A fertile valley in the Drakensberg area with the towering summits of the Bell and Cathedral Peak obscured by a veil of cloud.

67 Bearing remarkable resemblance to the map of Southern Africa, a cleft in the mountain ridge near Cathedral Peak, frames a section of the Drakensberg, including the summits of Cathkin Peak and Champagne Castle.

68 Precipitous cliffs rising above the Sani Pass form the edge of the high Lesotho Plateau.

69 The bleak and cold Lesotho Plateau, at 2 750 metres, seems an anticlimax after the hair-raising twists and turns of the Sani Pass. Except for coarse, hardy grass this plain is devoid of vegetation, and stone is used as the building material in the local African kraals.

70 Basuto boys in a sandstone cave that once served as studio to a Bushman artist. Brightly coloured blankets are draped across the shoulders in traditional fashion. Though decorative, they also serve as a protection against the biting cold that grips the Lesotho highlands for much of the year.

71 An African homestead near Teyateyaneng. The circular wall is plastered with a thick layer of brown clay to help trap the warmth within, while the overlapping, conical roof is reinforced with layers of finely plaited grass.

72 A Woolly-necked Stork (*Dissoura episcopus*), a skilled fisherman with razor-sharp, pointed beak, holds aloft a frog it has just speared. A migratory bird, this stork is often found in the vicinity of waterholes in which abound its favourite food: small fish, frogs and insects. — At Mkuze in Zululand.

73 During the winter, when water is scarce, herds of Impala (*Aepyceros melampus*) file down to the Msinga Waterhole in the Mkuze Reserve. Constantly on the alert for danger, the graceful creatures bend down to quench their thirst.

74 A Nyala bull (*Tragelaphus angasii*) at the Msinga Waterhole in the Mkuze Reserve. This elegant, gregarious antelope has a limited distribution in Southern Africa, but is fairly common in the game reserves of Zululand, where it thrives in thick bush country, rarely far from water.

75 The horny armour-plating of a log-like Crocodile (*Crocodylus niloticus*) protrudes above the muddy waters of a Mkuze waterhole. As if in an hypnotic trance, the watchful reptile awaits an unsuspecting prey.

70

71

72

73

76 A Hammerhead (*Scopus umbretta*), showing off the profile that explains his name. The brown crest, of the same colour as the feathers of the body, can be neither raised nor lowered at will. This curious bird is fairly common throughout Southern Africa, and is usually found in pairs, in the vicinity of water; wading through the shallows, the Hammerhead searches for small frogs and fish.

77 One of the most beautiful game Reserves in Southern Africa, Ndumu is situated in north-eastern Natal, near the border of Mozambique. Primeval indigenous forest, thick bushland and graceful fever trees surround a series of reed-fringed lakes fed by the seasonal overflow of the Pongola and Usutu Rivers.

78 One way to face the world is to turn your back on it, but if you do, it is best not to leave a reflection in the water, even if you are Big Game.

79　After the Elephant, the White or square-lipped Rhinoceros (*Ceratotherium simum*) is the world's largest land mammal. Named "white" from the Afrikaans word "wyd", meaning wide, this massive beast stands nearly 2 metres high and weighs more than 2 721 kilograms. Whereas the smaller "black" cousin browses habitually on low bush, the "white" species is essentially a grazer, consuming vast quantities of grass during the twilight hours and at night. Once prolific throughout much of Southern Africa, both hunter and poacher have sadly reduced their numbers. The White Rhino is today mainly confined to the game reserves of Zululand, although successful efforts have been made to reintroduce them to several sanctuaries elsewhere.

80　Burchell's Zebra (*Equus burchelli*) are the most numerous members of this genus. Sociable animals, they are, however, highly strung and contagiously nervous. At the slightest disturbance, the zebra throws back his head with a shrill neigh and charges off into the bush. Only when completely reassured will he return to drink in peace.

81　At a waterhole in Hluhluwe, a group of female Kudu (*Tragelaphus strepsisceros*) timidly approach for a drink. In days gone by, due to the high quality of their meat, these attractive antelopes were mercilessly shot, in many areas to a point of extermination. Today, more sense fortunately prevails, and their distribution is once again widespread.

82　A Nyala cow at Mkuze steps daintily across a sunny glade. The female bears little resemblance to the handsome bull; she is much smaller, has no horns and her coat is a soft reddish brown, lined with vertical white stripes.

83　Mirrored in the glassy water of the Msinga Waterhole at Mkuze, two Impala, oblivious of possible danger, enjoy a long, cool drink.

81

82

84 The ecstasies of a mud bath: a Warthog (*Phacochoerus aethiopicus*) revels
in the mire. Not exactly favoured with good looks these wild pigs make up
for this shortcoming with an abundance of character. As they are
shortsighted creatures, it is often possible to approach downwind quite
close to a family group before the "paterfamilias" detects something amiss.
With a snort he sets off at a trot with family in tow behind, all with tails
erect like miniature flagpoles. A warthog's courage has to be seen to be
believed. Recklessly, and with total disregard for consequences, the plucky
pig will charge the source of danger whether large or small, often
with surprising results.

85 A gathering of Blue Wildebeest (*Connochaetes taurinus*) in the shallow
reaches of the Msinga Waterhole. Somewhat ungainly in appearance,
these shaggy animals can move with remarkable energy. If they are
surprised at the waterhole, all hell breaks loose. Snorting with indignation
they beat a noisy retreat, churning the water with their hooves,
before stampeding to the safety of the bush.

86 White Rhino mother and calf, at Umfolozi. Rudely disturbed from
the pleasures of a roll in the mud, they strike a tank-like pose with horns
upraised and sniff the threatened air.

87 Hadeda Ibis (*Bostrychia hagedash*) perched on the branches of a
dead tree. Relatively inconspicuous while at rest, when in flight they
announce their whereabouts with a piercing cry: "ha-de-dah, ha-ha".

88　Traditional beehive huts merge with more modern dwellings
　　in a Zululand landscape.

89　A young Vervet Monkey (*Cercopithecus aethiops*) in the Kruger Park.
　　These neatly marked primates are common in many parts of Southern
　　Africa, especially in heavily wooded areas. They usually travel in orderly
　　troops that can sometimes number up to 50 members. They search the
　　woodland pastures for birds' eggs and nestlings, fruit, nuts and seeds,
　　supplementing their diet with an occasional raid on a farmer's field
　　of maize.

90　An inquisitive grey Meerkat (*Suricata suricatta*). These endearing little
　　animals, common throughout the Southern African veld, live
　　in holes burrowed in the earth. During the early morning and late
　　evening they can often be seen scampering along the ground, hunting
　　for insects or small edible succulents. Every now and then they stop,
　　sit bolt upright on their haunches, and peer about with a keen,
　　searching eye.

91　A Chameleon (*Chamaeleo dilepsis*) patiently awaits a tasty insect. Though
　　slow-moving and non-poisonous, this curious reptile is an expert
　　marksman; with split-second timing and lightning speed it unleashes its
　　long, coiled, sticky tongue at an unsuspecting prey. When alarmed, the
　　Chameleon puffs up its throat menacingly and emits an angry hiss.

92　A Sibaca dance near Piggs Peak in the Swazi mountains. Teams of
　　dancers compete with each other for the prize of a fatted calf. With
　　flamboyant gyrations and a fast rhythmic tempo, the participants
　　elicit an excited response from the spectators.

91

92

93 Dressed in gowns of brightly patterned calico and wearing the traditional hairpiece, two Swazi women brave the gloom of a rainy day.

94 A panoramic vista of outstanding grandeur: the Blyde River Canyon in the north-eastern Transvaal. The distant river snakes along a tortuous passage 760 metres below the massive cliffs of the "Three Rondavels".

95 With regal nonchalance a Serval (*Felis serval*) reclines in the warmth of the evening sun. This elegant cat has a powerful, streamlined body and is an adept nocturnal hunter.

96 From a grassy hillock in the Kruger Park, a magnificent bull Waterbuck (*Kobus ellipsiprymnus*) surveys the thorny veld. These antelopes usually graze in herds near water-courses and flood plains where the grass is lush. If danger threatens they make for the water.

97 An Elephant (*Loxodonta africana*), ambles down a well-worn track in the Kruger Park. As far back as 1884 President Kruger advocated the establishment of game sanctuaries in the Northern Transvaal, where wild life would be able to recover from the depredations of hunting, but only in 1898 was the Sabie Game Reserve established. After the Anglo-Boer War in 1902, the Reserve was re-proclaimed by Lord Milner, and Colonel James Stevenson Hamilton was appointed as first Game Warden, a post he held with great distinction until his retirement in 1946. The Borders of the Reserve were subsequently increased by the inclusion of private land between the Sabie and Letaba Rivers. Finally, in 1926, a National Parks Board was appointed and the Reserve was proclaimed as the Kruger National Park.

98 A view from the heights of the Wolkberg (Cloud Mountain) near Tzaneen.

99 The waters of the Treurrivier, just before its confluence with the Blyde River, hurtle down in a froth of dazzling white foam.

100 Bourke's Potholes, a curious sculpture moulded by the Blyde River.

101 A Ground Hornbill (*Bucorvus leadbeateri*) in the Northern Transvaal Lowveld, flutters long eyelashes and peers down its broad beak as if to ask "What's next"? Small groups of these birds spend most of the day searching for insects, reptiles and rodents. At night they roost in trees.

102 In the mountains above Pilgrim's Rest the air is crisp and cool after summer rains.

103 In the Gorongoza National Park a herd of Hippopotamus (*Hippopotamus amphibius*) wallow in a shallow lake. Every few moments a huge head emerges above the floating mass, to emit a grunt and open its mouth in a gaping yawn.

104 At Gorongoza, beneath the fan-like fronds of the tall Borassus Palms, a young elephant makes his way across the Savanna, pausing here and there to uproot a tasty shoot.

105 The King of Beasts (*Panthero leo*) rests from the fierce heat of day beneath a shady palm.

106 A tiny Steenbuck (*Raphicerus campestris*) peers from a sea of high grass.

107 With a backdrop of lowering storm-clouds, the tropical vegetation of Gorongoza is illuminated by the last rays of the setting sun.

108 Sunset at Gorongoza.

109 Colourful earthenware jars line the roadside in neat rows, watched over by three little salesmen. Near Lundi in Rhodesia.

110 The Lundi River, so named from a corruption of the African name "Runde", meaning "a river liable to great floods", is here spanned by a low-level bridge. In summer a heavy downpour will suddenly transform the placid river into a wide, muddy torrent.

105

106

109

110

13

14

111 A lonely African hut in the arid bushveld of eastern Rhodesia. This is a hard, stony land, plagued by drought for most of the year, where the raising of crops is a constant struggle.

112 An African kraal in the hills south of Umtali.

113 The Matopos: a weird landscape of isolated boulders and crenellated koppies. Erosion has gradually worn away the mantle of softer rock to expose bizarre formations of hard plutonic granite.

114 Sable Antelope (*Hippotragus niger*) in the Matopos National Park. The Sable's distinctive features are its huge scimitar-shaped horns, white facial markings and a shiny black coat with tufted mane.

115   Portrait of a Chacma Baboon (*Papio ursinus*). These intelligent
       primates, common in hill country throughout Southern Africa, travel
       in troops under the leadership of one or more dominant males. They feed,
       during the daytime, upon wild fruits and berries, roots, insects,
       scorpions, and small mammals. Occasionally they raid a farmer's crop
       of maize or wheat. In the Cape Peninsula a local troop has even
       taken to fishing for mussels from the rocky beaches. Baboons are very
       protective towards their females and young. In the event of danger, the
       adult males will often fight a desperate rearguard action to enable others
       to escape to safety.

116   The mysterious ruined city of Zimbabwe, near Fort Victoria. For long
       a source of endless speculation and controversy, it is now generally
       accepted that the mass of stone buildings are walled settlements built for
       defence purposes by successive generations of the African Karanga
       Rozvi tribal group. None of the buildings appear to have been roofed
       and it is likely that the familiar type of African hut made from
       mud and thatch sheltered within the stone enclosures. Nearly one million
       chippings were used in the construction of the "Temple", a massive
       circular construction that probably housed the palace of the Great Chief.
       The strange conical tower within was perhaps symbolic of his
       authority and status.

117   The "Acropolis" at Zimbabwe: a huge granite koppie that forms a
       perfect natural fortress. Stone chippings were used to build a series of walls
       and platforms around existing boulders.

20

21

118 A cloud of spray obscures the mighty Zambezi River as it plunges into the gorge far below with a thunderous roar.

119 The Victoria Falls: one of the natural wonders of the world. Along a front more than 1 km wide, an endless sheet of water pours over the precipice, at the rate of 550 megalitres per minute.

120 The Shiré River in southern Malawi, in full flood after heavy summer rains.

121 From a clearing in the Malawi bush, an African child stares wistfully at a passing car.

122 Seen from a rocky tree-lined cove, the serene waters of Lake Malawi glisten in the morning sun. This great lake extends for 580 kilometres along the eastern flank of Malawi, and marks the southernmost arm of the Great Rift Valley.

123 The Okavango Swamps in north-western Botswana — a huge expanse of untamed Africa. The great Okavango River, emerging from the Angola highlands, is split into a maze of countless streams, forming a vast inland delta. Reeds and papyrus thickets hem the waters, and during the seasonal floods, small forested islands provide the only landmarks in the marshy wilderness.

124 A "Lily Trotter" (*Actophilornis africanus*) in the Okavango Swamps steps lightly across the floating reeds in search of insects and choice lily seeds.

125 A massive termite hill on Chief's Island bears silent witness to the industry of countless tiny workers.

126 Striding out with long, powerful legs, an Ostrich foursome (*Struthio camelus*) makes speed across the Nxai Pan.

127 A flock of Ostriches competing in an African Derby.

123

124

126

127

128   From their lofty perch in a wild fig tree, a pair of majestic Fish-eagles (*Haliaetus vocifer*) keep a watchful eye on the surrounding swamps. These birds, which feed on fish and small mammals, usually hunt in mated pairs, swooping with lightning speed to seize their prey with strong, curved talons. From time to time, their wild and piercing cry — "kue kue kuekuekue" — shatters the brooding silence of the lonely swamps.

129   Seen from the air, the vast unfettered swamps of the Okavango delta stretch from one horizon to the other. Here and there, tall Borassus Palms (*Hyhaene ventricosa*) show as glints of silver in an ocean of green.

130   A Lilac-breasted Roller (*Coracias caudata*), at rest on a thornbush in northern Botswana. The name "Roller" is derived from the rollicking, noisy aerobatics that the male bird engages in while courting.

131   A small group of Puku (*Kobus vardoni*) in the marshy flood-plains of the Chobe River.

132   Buffalo (*Syncerus caffer*) graze peacefully near the banks of the Chobe River. These sturdy beasts converge on the grass-covered flood-plains in the early morning and late afternoons. During the heat of the day they usually rest in the shade of dense bush.

133 A Batawana family group near the Boro River. The Mokoro, a dugout craft hewn from a single log of wood, is pulled up on the bank.

134 Musical interlude at Txatxaba camp on the Boro River in the heart of the Okavango Swamps. The finger instrument is known as the "Selikani", while the string accompaniment is a "Tsworoworo".

135 As the sun sinks low in the sky, the waters of the Thamalekane River, at the edge of the Okavango delta, are transformed into molten gold.

136 In the Kalahari Desert, a Bushman, clad in a loin-cloth and with bow in hand, surveys an expanse of orange dunes. The enlarged posterior, a condition known as steatopygia, is a natural endowment which offsets the effects of prolonged famine. These remarkable people once roamed over large areas of Southern Africa, but the southward migration of Bantu tribes and the expansion of the Cape Colony forced the Bushmen into the inhospitable wastes of the Kalahari, where life is a constant struggle for survival.

137 The Bushmen of the Kalahari are great story-tellers. Old traditions and stories of the past are handed down to each successive generation by the elders of the tribe, who are held in high esteem.

138 A Bushman shelter is a temporary dwelling which provides shade from the heat of day and warmth from the bitter cold of night. Signs of increasing contact with the outside world are previously unknown items such as cloth and a metal bucket.

37

38

42

43

139 With bonneted infant clinging to her back, a woman of mixed descent visits a Bushman shelter. In the background, small skins, strips of meat, and tobacco leaves are hung out to dry.

140 A single Kokerboom (*Aloe dichotoma*) in a wide expanse of treeless desert.

141 In the Kalahari Gemsbok National Park, tufts of coarse grass and scattered Camel-thorn trees thrive in a harsh environment. Against the background of a dry riverbed and rising sand dunes, a Gemsbok (*Oryx gazella*) is well camouflaged. Because of the great scarcity of water, these animals seek nourishment from wild cucumbers, Tsamma melons and certain bulbs that store water within their husks.

142 A group of Springbok (*Antidorcas marsupialis*) in the stony veld of the Kalahari. These gregarious antelopes are well adjusted to desert life and can travel for great distances without need of water. The name derives from the curious jumping motion that is a characteristic: with head down and body arched they jump up to 3 metres into the air in a series of stiff-legged leaps.

143 A herd of Wildebeest kick up the soft sand with their hooves as they move in slow formation towards a cluster of shady Acacia trees. Blue Wildebeest, like the Gemsbok and Springbok, have adapted themselves well to the parched, semi-desert condition of the Kalahari.

144 A Ground Squirrel (*Xerus inauris*) poses for his portrait. These attractive little creatures live in colonies of deep burrows. When they emerge for food they scurry along the ground in search of seeds and small bulbs, stopping every now and then to sit up erect and motionless, to make sure the coast is clear.

145 On the fringe of the great Namib Desert in South West Africa yellow dunes of shifting sand beneath an azure sky.

146 The "Mukurob", or "Finger of God", is an eroded tower of rock some 30 metres high. The head-piece of layered sandstone is joined to the main pedestal of Karroo slate by a slender neck.

147 An old man gives rein to his horses as they trot briskly along a dusty track near Koes.

148 The Great Fish River Canyon, a deep, spectacular gorge carved by the unbridled forces of nature. Some 550 metres below, the Fish River meanders towards its eventual confluence with the Orange River.

147

148

149 A diminutive Kokerboom clings precariously to a rocky ledge deep within the Fish River Canyon. Great boulders lie around in profusion to impede the progress of the weary climber. The steep walls of the canyon trap and reflect the heat of the sun, turning the valley floor into an inferno.

150 The Fish River twists and turns like a sluggish green serpent in the barren depths of the great canyon.

151 A flock of starlings in flight across the pink sky of dawn. — From Namutoni Fort in the Etosha Game Park.

152 Disturbed at the waterhole, a Giraffe (*Giraffa camelopardalis*) raises his long neck to observe the uninvited guest.

153 Large herds of Elephant roam the plains that border the vast Etosha Pan. A full-grown bull will eat up to 300 kilograms of food a day, a proportion of which, in the Etosha area, consists of bulbs, roots and tubers. These he digs out of the ground with his tusks, which sometimes splinter in the process.

154 An elegant Gemsbok strides across the Etosha plains, displaying its distinctive, symmetrical markings. When seen in complete profile, the long, tapered horns appear as one, which accounts for the fact that in former days this antelope was sometimes mistaken for the legendary unicorn.

155 A herd of Springbok in the sun-bleached Etosha grasslands.

156 Beneath the shady foliage of a thick thornbush, a Cheetah (*Acinonyx jubatus*) rests from the heat. Formerly well distributed over most of Southern Africa, their habitat today is restricted to the remote bushveld of the northern and eastern Transvaal, parts of Zululand, the Kalahari and South West Africa. In the Etosha Game Park they are fortunately still fairly numerous. The cheetah is reputed to be the fastest of all land mammals, attaining speeds of up to 90 kilometres an hour in the final sprint to achieve a kill.

157 Thorny scrub country with scattered Acacias is well suited to the Kudu. A bull with fine, lyre-shaped horns pauses for an instant before joining his cows in a dash for the thicket.

158 A Black Tree Agama (*Agama atricollis*), climbing the bark of an Acacia, suddenly stops to glance around with an inquisitive stare.

56

57

159

160

162

163

159 During the dry winter months in the Etosha Game Park, herds of Zebra congregate at waterholes to indulge themselves in the cool, refreshing water.

160 When a herd of elephant pass by, it is taken for granted by one and all that their's is the right of way.

161 Giraffe thrive in the open bushland of the Etosha Park where they browse on the leaves of the abundant Acacia trees. Palatable foliage is stripped from the upper branches of a tree by the combined use of a long flexible tongue, mobile upper lip and strong lower incisors.

162 A Zebra "mother-to-be" seems to enjoy the company of her attendants.

163 Namutoni Fort—a well-known landmark in the Etosha Game Park. Built by the Germans in 1901, it was attacked on 28th January 1904 by a force of some 500 Ovambo tribesmen. The tiny garrison of 7 men kept the besiegers at bay for a whole week before running out of ammunition. Under cover of night they succeeded in escaping and made their way to the main column of soldiers. Shortly afterwards the Fort was recaptured. Today Namutoni is a rest camp for visitors to the Park, but it still retains a romantic atmosphere reminiscent of the turbulent past.

164   The "Haunted Forest" near Okaukuejo: a copse of weird Moringa trees
      (*Moringa ovalifolia*). The contorted branches of these strange trees
      look like upturned roots grasping for nourishment. The Moringa is
      found only in South West Africa and usually grows on isolated ridges
      in mountainous areas.

165   His thirst slaked at last, a Gemsbok splashes his way through an
      Etosha waterhole to reach the opposite bank.

166   Like the aftermath of a devastating landslide, gigantic boulders
      cover the slopes of the Brandberg. These mountains rise dramatically out
      of the semi-desert plain to culminate in the Königstein peak (2 740
      metres)—the highest summit in South West Africa.

167   In the Etosha Park, wherever water is to be found, wild life abounds.

168   Daintily spreading out his forelegs, a giraffe lowers his long neck
      to reach for an evening drink.

167

168

170

171

169   The "Vingerklip", south-west of Outjo, a remarkable thumb-shaped rock, completely dwarfs the approaching figures.

170   A huge sandstone boulder keeps lone vigil over an expanse of scrub and thornbush — Some 95 kilometres south-west of Outjo.

171   Flat-topped, eroded hills are the only landmarks in the featureless plateau that stretches to the distant horizon.

172   A tall Aloe (*Aloe littoralis*), protected by a base of spiky leaves, presents a joyful spectacle with its thousand tiny blooms of vivid red.

173   A Blister Beetle (*Mylabris*) feeds upon the limp petals of a yellow desert flower (*Tribulus terrestris*) growing beside a white, egg-shaped fungus (*Podaxis pistilaris*).

174 A tall termite hill points a gaunt finger 5 metres up into the air. —
Near Welwitschia.

175 Silhouetted against the evening sky, a flight of Pelicans (*Pelecanus onocrotalus*) wings its way to a nocturnal roost; a frequent sight along the misty coast of South West Africa.

176 The "White Lady", a famous rock painting reputed to be some 3 000 years old. This masterpiece of Bushman art was discovered in 1917 in a shallow cave within the Tsisab Gorge of the remote Brandberg Mountains.

177   Water is a rare sight in the Brandberg. Only in years of exceptional rainfall do the mountain springs gush forth their precious bounty. Green tufts of grass and brightly hued wild flowers cluster beside the flowing stream, while numerous shiny tadpoles wriggle about in the quiet pools.

178   A female Welwitschia plant (*Bainesii*) sprawls upon the desert floor in an untidy tangle of green leaves. This strange plant is a primitive coniferous gymnosperm which has adapted itself to the harsh climatic conditions of the Namib Desert. The flowers are pollinated by both wind and insects. In a mature plant, the leaves can reach 10 metres in length. The age of the largest plants is estimated to be about 2 000 years.

179   The "Petrified Forest" near Welwitschia: fossilized tree trunks some 200 million years old. These blackened logs were probably uprooted elsewhere and swept to their present site by an ancient flood. Thickly encrusted with mud, they successfully withstood decomposition, and with the passage of time the wooden grain was gradually replaced by silica.

180   A Damara woman in a long dress poses in the stony veld near Uis. The origins of the Damara people are obscure and its members differ in many ways from the other Bantu groups in South West Africa. Prior to German colonization, they were enslaved by the dominant Herero and Nama tribes.

181   Wearing the traditional turban of folded cloth and a woollen shawl, a Herero woman stops in her path to flash a cheerful smile at the photographer.

182   The mode of attire introduced by Christian Missionaries of the Victorian era has continued to this day as the height of fashion. Oblivious of the heat, Herero women proudly drape themselves in full-length, long-sleeved dresses of gaily patterned material.

183   North-west of Usakos, the imposing massif known as "Spitzkoppe" (1 700 metres in height) looms eerily above the plain.

184   A Sociable Weaver Bird (*Philetairus socius*) dives from the gigantic nest, atop a dead tree, that it shares with a flock of feathered cousins. These amazing nests are not used just for breeding, but serve as permanent residences. They last for many years, each successive generation effecting repairs as well as new additions to the intricate structure.

187

188

185 Resembling a suspended haystack, a Sociable Weaver Bird's nest dwarfs a trio of residents. The birds depart and return through the communal entrance with an interminable twittering chatter.

186 The "Kokerboom Forest", a congregation of tree aloes near Keetmanshoop. In English the name means "Quiver Tree". In former days, Hottentots and Bushmen used to cut the thick stems, remove the soft core of pith, and then cover one end with a piece of leather to fashion a perfect quiver for their poison arrows. Simon van der Stel, on his journey to the Copper Mountains of Namaqualand in 1685, was the first European to record his impressions of these strange plants and their interesting usage.

187 A brightly marked Rock Agama (*Agama atra*) basks in the sun atop a smooth boulder. These insectivorous lizards have the habit, when disturbed, of bobbing their heads up and down in a most comical manner.

188 The Black-backed Jackal (*Canis mesomelas*) is common in most regions of Southern Africa. Besides feeding on small mammals and birds, it is also partial to carrion, and is thus a useful scavenger in the bush.

189 Two subsidiary waterfalls join the main stream of the Orange River as it races through a deep ravine below the Augrabies Falls. The great granite trench, carved by the furious action of the Orange, extends for 10 kilometres and has an average depth of 160 metres.

190 With a mighty roar, the great Orange River hurtles over the narrow lip of the Augrabies Falls.

191 Poised like statuettes, a group of Grey Herons greet the chilly advent of a misty morning.

192 As twilight descends upon the still waters of Rondevlei, a flock of Lesser Flamingo (*Phoenicopterus minor*) wade through the shallows, their bills skimming the surface in a methodical search for algae.

197

198

193 "Groot Constantia", one of the most beautiful and the best known of all Cape Dutch mansions. Simon van der Stel was granted the site by the Dutch East India Company in 1685, and he built the Manor House soon after his appointment as first Governor of the Cape, in 1692. Extensive alterations and additions were made by a subsequent owner, Hendrik Cloete, during the 1780's. Among these were the wide, embellished gables and lofty thatched roof that are the outstanding features of the house.

194 The "Kruithuis" or Arsenal at Stellenbosch was constructed in 1777 for the storage of gunpowder. It is a solid building with an unusual vaulted roof, designed as a precaution against the hazard of fire. On one of the stout walls, the monogram of the Dutch East India Company: "V.G.O.C.", is clearly imprinted.

195 "Schoongezicht", a gracious Cape Dutch dwelling in a superb setting. Against the backdrop of the Simonsberg Mountains, it lies surrounded by the fertile fields of Ida's Valley.
The house dates from the early 1800's, while the main gable was built in 1814 by Hendrik Cloete, similar in style to the one at Groot Constantia.

196 "Old Nektar" as it stands today was built in 1814, on a site that was originally granted by the Dutch East India Company to two freed slaves, Marquart and Jan van Ceylon.
It is well known for what is considered to be the first example in the Cape of a neo-classical gable on a small façade.
The house stands in a magnificent position, surrounded by mountains, near the head of the Jonkershoek Valley.

197 A Cape Sugarbird (*Promerops cafer*) perched in the branches of a Silvertree (*Leucadendron argentium*) on the lower slopes of Table Mountain.

198 Viewed from the flat summit of Table Mountain, Lion's Head and the timber-clad slopes of Signal Hill divide Cape Town in two.

199 The "Fairest Cape"— a view from the top of Table Mountain, looking south towards Cape Point.

200 Van Riebeeck named Hout Bay for the abundance of wood found in the locality. The rough mountainous terrain, however, proved an obstacle in transporting the timber to the Dutch Settlement in Cape Town. Today, the sheltered bay is the centre of the flourishing and prosperous fishing industry.

201 At the southernmost tip of the Peninsula, a steep cliff plunges into the restless sea: this is Cape Point. Beyond lies only the empty Atlantic Ocean.

NOTES

My wife Janet and I first came to South Africa in 1968 after four years spent in Kenya, where we were married. Well attuned to the magnetic atmosphere of the wilds of Africa after many extensive travels, we were delighted when the opportunity eventually arose for us to travel south to explore a land of wide new horizons.

Even with a lively imagination, it is always hard to picture a new country before arrival. We knew that South Africa was a land of enormous economic and agricultural potential, with fast-spreading, modern cities and flourishing industries, and we were, of course, aware of the topical problems associated with the contentious race policies. But we did not realize, at first, the amazing variety and contrast that exist for those addicted, like ourselves, to the wilder trails of Africa.

Though circumstances dictated our residence and participation in city life, we have used every opportunity to explore the natural beauty of the country.

While in South Africa we lived in Johannesburg and Cape Town, and from these two centres we started on many travels. Setting out from Johannesburg, we covered the northern and eastern Transvaal, Natal, Lesotho, Swaziland, Botswana, Rhodesia, Moçambique and Malawi, while from Cape Town we explored the Cape mountains and coast, the Karroo, the Garden Route and the Transkei in the east, as well as Namaqualand and South West Africa in the north.

Distances are vast in Africa. To someone living in Europe, a journey of 300 kilometres represents a long, frustrating day's drive through an almost endless succession of built-up areas where traffic jams are part of daily life. Flying high above Southern Africa, in a modern jet, one is struck by the great open spaces that stretch as far as the eye can see. Here and there, small dots and symmetrical patterns on the ground show evidence of man and his activities, but the main centres of population are separated one from the other by scores, and sometimes hundreds, of kilometres. When one travels by road, these impressions are confirmed, and one can often motor from one horizon to the next without seeing a human being. Three hundred kilometres in these circumstances represents about three hours of smooth driving on roads where the sight an oncoming car is almost a welcome diversion.

Our first journey out from Johannesburg was to Swaziland, a week before that country's independence. With the inexperience of the uninitiated, we relied upon a small-scale map and hopelessly misjudging the distance and condition of the road, we found ourselves at dusk driving along a rough, muddy track, made dangerous by torrential rain, towards Goedgegun. We eventually arrived late at night, very tired but wiser for the experience.

During the course of several visits to the north-eastern Transvaal, we explored the Kruger Park as well as the superb mountain country in the vicinity of Pilgrim's Rest, Graskop and Tzaneen, that in variety and splendour rivals the Cape mountains.

In order to appreciate fully the beauty of Southern Africa, we have always used our car simply as means of getting to a predetermined destination. On arrival, we have, whenever possible, taken to our feet to walk for miles in the bush and mountains. Only thus can one really learn to appreciate nature and savour the atmosphere of the wilds.

The Drakensberg has always been one of our favourite haunts. There are endless opportunities for walking and riding in these beautiful mountains. Our first visit to the Royal Natal National Park nearly landed us in trouble when, in the dark of the night, and in pouring rain, we took a wrong turning. Suddenly, on rounding a sharp corner on a steeply descending hill, the road disappeared and we were faced by the raging waters of the Tugela River in full flood. We were able to pull up just in time, but then became stuck in the mud. African rivers are deceptive and dangerous; in a matter of minutes, after heavy rain, an insignificant stream over which one can easily pass will become a treacherous torrent, sweeping away everything and everybody that obstructs its turbulent passage.

The high plateau and mountains of Lesotho have a beauty of their own, whether in the dry heat of summer or in the snows of winter. A personal friendship with King Moshoeshoe II, with whom I was at school in England, has enabled us to explore several little-known parts of this small, delightful country.

The game reserves of Zululand are my favourites in South Africa. For the wild-life enthusiast they offer superlative opportunities for the close observation of many species. On one visit to Umfolozi, we were fortunate enough to witness the amazing courage of a warthog. Two of these stocky wild pigs, with a young family in tow, were being chased through the bush by a pair of cheetahs; suddenly they whirled around to face the enemy. Not content with a mere last-ditch stand, the gallant warthogs then proceeded to charge the two cheetahs, who, with tails between their legs, made a speedy departure from the scene.

We spent two successive Christmas holidays camping at the Victoria Falls, a long day's car journey from Johannesburg. In spite of its being the rainy season in Rhodesia, December is perhaps the best time to make this trip, as the Zambezi is then in full flood, and in consequence the falls are at their most spectacular. Walking through the rain forest overlooking the great chasm, we were drenched by the soft, soaking spray – an exhilarating experience.

Blantyre, in Malawi, is only 1 760 kilometres from Johannesburg and, from a map, the journey may seem straightforward and easily accomplished in two days. This, however, is not the case. There are no problems until after Salisbury, where the tarmac ends. The main road then cuts through the western neck of Moçambique to reach the town of Tete. Here one crosses the Zambezi by ferry to rejoin the road which leads into Malawi. This is indeed a 650-kilometre "hell run" through some of the loneliest and most inhospitable bush country in Africa. The rough, dusty road is in terrible condition, deeply rutted and with bare rock protruding in places, which necessitates a snail-like pace. We made this journey in October 1970, just before the onset of the rainy season. We passed very few vehicles, saw hardly any people or dwellings, and everything seemed completely lifeless. It was, moreover, fiendishly hot.

We eventually arrived in Malawi completely exhausted and covered in dust from head to foot. That night, a bath was our idea of heaven.

On the return journey, we travelled via Tete to Gorongoza and Beira. This was another long day's ordeal on an impossible "main" road, through endless, monotonous bush, again for the most part devoid of all signs of habitation.

To reach the Okavango Swamps, a wonderful expanse of untamed Africa in northern Botswana, we flew by regular air service from Johannesburg, via Francistown, to Maun. In this small "outback" town on the edge of the great inland delta, we chartered a Cessna that flew us into the depths of the swamps to a place known as Txatxaba, where Lloyd Wilmot, son of the famous crocodile hunter, runs a delightfully casual tented safari camp. For anyone who wants to get "right away from it all", this must surely be one of the finest places to go to.

From Txatxaba I set out on two long treks through reeds and marsh to explore a number of thickly wooded islands. It was impossible to keep a sense of direction as, to my untrained eye, one island and stretch of marsh looked identical to the next. Without the company of an African guide, with his intimate knowledge of the swamps, I would have been lost within minutes. In such wild surroundings, one has to admire the courage possessed by the early explorers in Africa who set out on their travels literally "into the blue", with no idea of what might lie ahead.

We returned from Txatxaba to Maun in a small open boat powered by an outboard motor, a journey of some 130 kilometres down the Boro River, that really made us aware of the vastness and splendour of the Okavango Swamps.

At about 8 o'clock at night, some 30 kilometres from Maun, we ran out of petrol. With the use of a couple of rough branches cut by our African boatman we paddled for several miles to an island, where we made camp beneath the stars and a spreading fig-tree. A roaring fire soon warmed the chill night air, as we put up our tent and cooked a welcome meal.

Cape Town is the ideal starting-point for exploring the southern and western coasts, with many places of interest in the immediate environs of the city.

South West Africa is linked to Cape Town by an excellent road that passes through the arid hills of Namaqualand before reaching the border at Vioolsdrif. Many of the most interesting places in South West Africa lie off the beaten track, and one has to travel great distances over rough and stony roads or, even worse, over treacherous, sandy tracks, where a great deal of skill is required to prevent the car from getting bogged down.

Our travels in South West Africa were plagued with car problems. A hole developed in the petrol tank while we were crossing the Namib Desert, but we were fortunate to reach a karakul ranch, where the tank was repaired in the farm workshop. Our main tribulations, however, stemmed from the automatic gearbox. Time after time we found ourselves stuck in remote areas, with nothing to be done but wait for help.

One day, near Welwitschia, we were travelling on a reasonable road, when we were suddenly confronted by a 100-metre-wide dry riverbed. The road on the other side looked deceptively close, and we were loath to retrace our steps and waste many hours by taking a different route. We took the plunge, but ground to a halt about a third of the way across. It was a gruelling battle in the searing heat, trying to get the wheels out of the soft sand. Eventually a truck appeared on the scene, and with a few extra hands and a great deal of digging and pushing, we reached the far bank to continue our journey.

Another inconvenience and a terrible nuisance is the all-pervading, powdery dust, which penetrates every nook and cranny of the car, to the great discomfort of its occupants.

In spite of these minor hardships, however, South West Africa is a wonderful and exciting country, and very rewarding to explore.

There is really quite a story behind most of the photographs depicted in this book. Travelling in Africa does require a certain amount of endurance; it is generally hot and dusty, and there is always the hazard of the car breaking down in some remote place off the beaten track. Although this has happened to us on numerous occasions during our travels, we have rarely returned home disappointed with our safaris.

The photographic equipment I now take on my travels is the result of eight years' experience of the bush and veld of Africa. My cameras and accessories have to put up with a hard life, being bounced about not only in the car, but also in the sling-bag to which I transfer equipment when setting off on a hike.

I go to great lengths to make sure that my equipment is at all times protected from direct heat. Not only can the penetrating African sun irreparably damage film emulsions, but the heat may result in an excess of oil spilling between the camera shutter-blades, thereby causing them to stick.

For the storage of films, I use an insulated cooler-bag, and a bag of silica crystals to absorb any humidity. Cans or bags of dry ice are useful for short safaris, but the cooler-bag does suffice for longer journeys, provided it is kept out of the direct sunlight.

I always take plenty of polythene bags of various sizes, to keep out the dust. I use these not only to pack items for later use, but also to protect the camera which I keep at hand for quick action.

A blower lens brush and a packet of lens tissues are two other useful items that I carry around; the former to remove the odd specks of dust that invariably settle on the lens in spite of the polythene bag; and the latter to clean the lens, eye-piece, and view-finder, at the end of a day's photography.

A tripod is, of course, indispensable for certain types of work, but it is a bulky item to convey, and whenever possible I try and make do without it, by using low speeds and even time-exposures, with the camera balanced against a tree or other immovable object.

For colour work, I am addicted to the 6×6 cm transparency format, and use a Hasselblad with the standard 80 mm and 250 mm lenses. The former I find adequate for general use, whereas the latter is ideal for wild-life studies. I have recently acquired a 500 mm lens for specialized telephoto effects; but in this book only one picture, that of a lilac-breasted roller, was taken with this lens.

On all occasions I find it advisable to use a lens shade to cut out extraneous rays of sunlight. This is, of course, particularly important for back-lit effects, when one is pointing the camera in the direction of the sun.

To facilitate a rapid succession of photographs without the chore of changing films, I use two magazines, each of which holds a spool of 12 exposures. With the Hasselblad these are completely interchangeable.

The prismatic view-finder is an accessory I find useful, particularly when using a telephoto lens, as it magnifies clearly, and without distortion, the image on the ground-glass screen.

All the black-and-white photographs illustrated were taken with a Pentax SV camera, now about eight years old. I use the normal 55 mm lens as well as the light and handy 200 mm telephoto lens. As with the Hasselblad, the lens shade is a constant appendage when shooting.

An ultraviolet filter is usually affixed to my Pentax and provides additional protection for the lens. To bring out the drama of cloud effects, and to soften somewhat the harsh contrasts of an African landscape, I often make use of a yellow-green filter.

For colour work, I use relatively low-speed Agfa 50 S "transparency" film, which, in my opinion, brings out natural colours with a superb radiance and depth of tone. As regards black-and-white shots, I use Ilford FP4, and all the photographs in this book were taken with this film, which I have developed in Ilford ID11.

For accurate exposure readings, a Weston V Meter has been my constant companion.

When it comes to the finished photographs, much depends on the skill and judgement of the printer. For this, I am indebted to Gail Daniels, who has put in many hours of dedicated work to produce the high-quality black-and-white prints reproduced in this book.

In the belief that the beauties of Southern Africa, as described and illustrated in this book, may well have created a desire to travel amongst many of our overseas readers, we suggest that they contact any of the following offices of the South African Tourist Corporation for additional information on the tourist attractions of the Republic of South Africa: . . .

SOUTH AFRICAN TOURIST CORPORATION

SATOUR BRANCH OFFICES:

BRITAIN: 13 Regent Street, London SW1Y 4LR. Tel. 01–839–7462. Telegraphic: Satour London SW1.

GERMANY: 6 Frankfurt/Main, Alemannia-Haus, An der Hauptwache 11. Tel. 28–1505 and 28–1593. Telegraphic: Satour Frankfurt/M.

FRANCE: Rue de Richelieu 104, Paris 2e. Tel. 742–1871 and 742–1872. Telegraphic: Satourist Paris.

ITALY: Quarto Piano, Via Barberini 86, 00187 Rome. Tel. 476–778. Telegraphic: Satour Rome.

HOLLAND: Leidsestraat 64–66[11], Amsterdam C. Tel. 020–24 30 07. Telegraphic: Satour Amterdam.

UNITED STATES: Rockefeller Center, 610 Fifth Avenue, New York, N.Y. 10020. Tel. 245–3720. Telegraphic: Satourist New York.
Suite 721, 9465 Wilshire Boulevard, Beverly Hills, California 90212. Tel. 275–4111. Telegraphic: Satourist Beverly Hills California.

CANADA: Suite 1512, Proctor and Gamble Building, 2 St. Clair Avenue West, Toronto 195, Ontario. Tel. 922–5121. Telegraphic: Satourist Toronto.

AUSTRALIA: 10th Floor, Bankers and Traders' Building, 115 Pitt Street, Sydney, N.S.W. 2000. Postal Address: G.P.O. Box 4889, Sydney, N.S.W. 2001. Tel. 25–6165. Telegraphic: Tourepsa Sydney.

RHODESIA: Mercury House, Gordon Avenue, Salisbury. Postal Address: P.O. Box 1343, Salisbury. Tel. 6–1161. Telegraphic: Satour Salisbury.

HEAD OFFICE: 8th Floor, President Centre, 265/9 Pretorius Street, Pretoria. Postal Address: Private Bag X164, Pretoria. Tel. 2–5201. Telegraphic: Satourist Pretoria.